FORTUNATE THE EYES THAT SEE

Fortunate the Eyes That See

Essays in Honor of
David Noel Freedman
in Celebration of His Seventieth Birthday

edited by

Astrid B. Beck
Andrew H. Bartelt
Paul R. Raabe
Chris A. Franke

WILLIAM B. EERDMANS PUBLISHING COMPANY
GRAND RAPIDS, MICHIGAN / CAMBRIDGE, U.K.

© 1995 Wm. B. Eerdmans Publishing Co.
255 Jefferson Ave. S.E., Grand Rapids, Mich. 49503 /
P.O. Box 163, Cambridge CB3 9PU U.K.
All rights reserved
Printed in the United States of America

00 99 98 97 96 95   7 6 5 4 3 2 1

Library of Congress Cataloging-in-Publication Data

Fortunate the eyes that see : essays in honor of
David Noel Freedman in celebration of his seventieth birthday /
edited by Astrid B. Beck . . . [et al.].
p.   cm.
Includes bibliographical references.
ISBN 8028-0790-9 (pbk.)
1. Bible. O.T.—Criticism, interpretation, etc. 2. Religion.
I. Freedman, David Noel, 1922-   . II. Beck, Astrid B.
BS1171.2.F65 1995

221.6—dc20   95-17630
                                                       CIP

Contents

II. Former Prophets

III. Latter Prophets

IV. Writings

V. Hebrew Poetry

VI. Ancient Near East

VII. New Testament

VIII. Religion and Art

Preface

The publication of a second *Festschrift* dedicated to David Noel Freedman, now in celebration of his seventieth birthday, is a tribute to the continuing vitality, energy, and influence of our mentor and teacher. The title of this volume, an adaptation from John P. Meier's contribution, expresses a well-known biblical motif found in the Hebrew Bible, in the Pseudepigrapha, and in the New Testament. In this regard alone, it captures the unique importance of one whose own vision has seen the vast spectrum of biblical studies. This characteristic is borne out foremost in his contributions to the three-pronged Anchor Bible series, which now numbers seventy-four volumes and includes critical commentaries on the entire biblical corpus, the Reference Library, and the Anchor Bible Dictionary.

Throughout his career, David Noel Freedman has invited a large number of persons to share in his ecumenical vision. From its inception in 1956, the Anchor Bible series has intentionally included scholars from diverse religious backgrounds and, after William Foxwell Albright's death, Noel has continued to set the standard for an open and ecumenical approach. He has been a pioneer in fostering fair-minded, broad, and impartial scholarship, which has proven fruitful for the entire field, both in the Anchor series and in the many journals he has edited over the decades.

Reflective of this ecumenical approach, our contributors represent several generations of biblical scholars from a variety of disciplines, exemplifying the many scholars for whom he has been a model of excellence. Some of them are Noel's long-standing friends and colleagues who share with him their own distinguished and ongoing careers. We are privileged to have the two editors of the previous *Festschrift*, Carol L. Meyers and M. O'Connor, among our contributors. Roy Rappaport is his successor as Director of the Program on Studies

xi

in Religion at the University of Michigan. Hans Küng was the Program's first "Visiting Professor of Religious Thought," a lecture series begun in 1983 by Noel to promote dynamic ecumenical dialogue. His broad perspective has been a decisive influence in many arenas.

We have a number of teams in this *Festschrift:* two wife/husband teams (Gitay, Meyers), a mother/daughter team (Beck), and a student/teacher team (Kohn, Propp). Risa Levitt Kohn is the first doctoral student at the University of California, San Diego. This kind of outlook is also a key component in Noel's attitude toward pulling people together on projects, where the whole is greater than the sum of its parts. His own team projects began when he and Frank Cross wrote their dissertations at Johns Hopkins together: two dissertations both written jointly to complete their Ph.D.'s. Bill Propp was Frank Cross's student at Harvard. Thus we are now into the third generation of mentorships.

While there is a connection to the past and a celebration of the present, this collection of essays also provides an important continuation into the future that will no doubt benefit from his pioneering efforts. This *Festschrift* contains articles from a number of younger scholars, some of whom are Noel's former doctoral students. Also included are new authors in the Anchor Bible series, editors from the Anchor Bible Dictionary team, and Dahood Prize Competition winners. Their careers have been strongly influenced by Noel's wisdom, guidance, personal concern, and far-reaching vision. He has encouraged this new group of scholars by giving them important assignments, remembering that he was also "younger" when he first undertook the task of editor of the Anchor series.

As editors of this *Festschrift,* we consider ourselves fortunate to be among those whom Noel has taught to see ever more clearly. Astrid Beck has been his colleague in the Program on Studies in Religion at the University of Michigan and his co-worker on the Anchor series. Since her tenure in this capacity beginning in 1983, the two have continued work on the Anchor Bible critical commentaries (including replacement volumes), have begun the Anchor Bible Reference Library, have completed the six-volume Anchor Bible Dictionary, and are currently involved in the publication of the facsimile edition of the *Leningrad Codex.*

The other three editors know firsthand the energy with which he has served, not simply as doctoral advisor, but concomitantly as teacher, mentor, and friend. His wellspring of creative ideas, his meticulous care and attention to detail, and his gracious and generous gifts of time and concern, all seasoned with good humor, have left their imprint upon us all. Whether in the classroom or through his almost legendary editorial responses, Noel has turned his eyes, and forced his students to focus theirs, upon a close and careful reading of the text in its ancient context. From that focal point, he has expanded their vision to see, both in and through the text, what might otherwise remain unseen. Our gratitude is expressed not only by dedicating to him a piece of our own work in this volume, but also by allowing what he has modeled to continue to shape our endeavors and to be passed on through us as scholars and teachers to yet another generation.

For all of us, the task of serving as editors in honor of one who has become the archetypal editor has been daunting indeed. Unable to match him in breadth of knowledge or editorial acumen, we have taken a more modest role. In greater part, it is befitting this *Festschrift* that the articles herein are personal contributions, reflecting a broad range of style and scope, and indicative of the vast spectrum of Noel's interest and influence. Given the diversity of authorship, the contents of this *Festschrift* stand on their own merit. We are most grateful to the publisher, William B. Eerdmans, for their enthusiastic endorsement and support of this project, especially to Allen C. Myers, senior editor, who was a student of Noel's at Michigan, and, not least, to Sam Eerdmans, who has been a guiding light at every stage of difficulty. We also thank all those who graciously accepted our invitation to become a part of this celebration of Noel's seventieth birthday. We are fortunate indeed to know him, and we join his friends and colleagues in giving thanks to, and for, our teacher and friend, David Noel Freedman.

Astrid B. Beck
Andrew H. Bartelt
Paul R. Raabe
Chris A. Franke

A Personal Tribute to David Noel Freedman

PHILIP J. KING

Boston College

I am proud of my close relationship with David Noel Freedman, a person whom I esteem and whose friendship I value. I have learned much from Noel. In earlier years I knew him only professionally. But in 1969-70, when he was the annual director of the W. F. Albright Institute of Archaeological Research (AIAR) in Jerusalem, I came to known him personally.

That year, as administrative director of the archaeological expedition to Tell el-Hesi, I was responsible for getting the dig into the field for its very first season. Noel's assistance was invaluable. He was always ready to help me in accomplishing even nonscholarly tasks, such as acquiring an oversized refrigerator, buying beds and other furnishings, not to mention finding shelter for the Hesi staff and volunteers in the converted school building at Kiryat Gat. But those who resided in Kiryat Gat during that first season may not remember Noel with as much gratitude as I. Life there had its problems.

I came to know Noel even better in 1976 when I was elected president of the American Schools of Oriental Research (ASOR), and he vice-president for publications. Once we established our modus vivendi (which took a bit of time), we became fast friends, working closely together in both good days and bad. Limited finances have always plagued ASOR, making it a difficult organization to direct, and our tenure was no exception.

Noel launched an exemplary ASOR publications program. The academic members of ASOR were delighted, but the trustees, who had to pay the bills, were not always so enthusiastic. Despite the inevitable problems, those six years when I was ASOR president and Noel vice-president are now happy memories.

When visiting Boston, Noel would frequently stay with me. He was an easy guest to entertain. Soon after arrival he would regularly preempt my desk, my typewriter, and my Hebrew Bible. Thus equipped, he would settle down to edit an Anchor Bible manuscript and not emerge for several hours.

Few Americans have contributed as much to biblical scholarship as David Noel Freedman, both as author and editor. As author, his books and voluminous articles are characterized by insight, clarity, and completeness. His writings demonstrate a scholarly erudition and versatility that are enviable. He has commented on almost every book and nearly every problem in the Hebrew Bible. For generations to come, scholars and nonscholars alike will continue to profit from his countless contributions.

As editor he has no equal, so far as I am aware, in both the quality and quantity of manuscripts that have come under his careful scrutiny. His editing skills also demonstrate his broad range of knowledge. Every contributor to the Anchor Bible, for example, acknowledges in the footnotes how many insights originated with the editor. I know from personal experience how Noel edits. Shortly after an author submits a manuscript, Noel will return it along with almost as many pages of most helpful suggestions.

Editing is a selfless, oftentimes thankless, task. Some scholars think their manuscripts are letter-perfect at the moment of submission. Noel has edited the works not only of his peers but also of his juniors, whom he consistently encourages, always ready to help any serious scholar regardless of rank or status.

A striking example of Noel's generosity and thoughtfulness has stayed with me. At a particular session of an international meeting of the Society of Biblical Literature, the auditorium was poorly ventilated and the papers tediously long. Understandably, in the course of the three-hour session many in the audience slinked away. (I remained only because I was chairing the session.) Noel stayed until the end, offering suggestions on each paper as well as asking questions of the speakers. Several of the presenters that day were young scholars, who deeply appreciated the attention Noel gave them. That gesture is characteristic of his generous spirit.

Several scholarly projects are coterminous with Noel, and at the same time monumental tributes to him, especially the Anchor Bible and the *Anchor Bible Dictionary*. Both are extraordinary success stories that will survive long after the present generation of biblical scholars. Who else would have dared to undertake such herculean projects!

Finally, I am always struck by Noel's perennial enthusiasm for biblical studies. He never tires of sharing fresh insights or discussing new discoveries. At the same time, few have been so faithful in attending professional meetings, both national and international. As most of us get older, our energy and enthusiasm wane. Not so, Noel. He is as energetic today as the first day I met him. Ad multos annos!

David Noel Freedman
An Appreciation from His Colleagues

The size and scope of this volume reflect the fond respect the scholarly world accords our colleague, David Noel Freedman. No one has worked harder to explain the Hebrew Bible, to explore its substructure and take its measurements, and to defend its essential unity. Few have emitted so steady a stream of insights, major and minor, now for almost half a century. Through his editorship of the Anchor Bible and its offshoots, particularly the *Anchor Bible Dictionary*, Noel has shaped the development of virtually every branch of biblical studies. Whether accepted or challenged, his views are always addressed, and rightly so. Future generations will perceive more clearly than we today how his figure has dominated biblical research in the second half of the twentieth century.

For the past eight years David Noel Freedman has been on the faculty of the University of California, San Diego, as a member of the Judaic Studies Program and the Department of History and as tenant of the Chair in Hebrew Biblical Studies. Until two years ago, he held this appointment jointly with the University of Michigan, where he also occupied a chair as Thurnau Professor in the Program on Studies in Religion until his move to full-time status at San Diego. We, the Judaic Studies faculty of the University of California, take special delight in offering an appreciation of this rare and rich individual whom it has been our pleasure to know and our honor to call colleague. Since his return to the University of California (being a UCLA graduate himself) Noel has provided colleagues and students with a model of complete commitment, almost in-human industry, and constant geniality. Knock on his door with a question or an idea; he is always in (one listens for classical music and machine-gun typing) and eager to chat. Submit a paper for his perusal; it is promptly returned with voluminous commentary, often overnight. Our present graduate and under-graduate curricula could not function without his participation, and our own work would be impoverished.

The overall impression one forms of Noel is of a man intoxicated with his work, who unites obsession and profession, whose mature judgment tempers almost childlike enthusiasm. Each new idea or discovery is greeted with an open mind, and with astonished delight that, after two millennia, we can still learn something new from the Bible. From David Noel Freedman we have all learned much already, and we shall continue to learn more.

RICHARD ELLIOTT FRIEDMAN
DAVID GOODBLATT
THOMAS E. LEVY
WILLIAM H. C. PROPP

Toby, Ben and Noel Freedman – New York, 1930; Noel was eight years old.

David Noel Freedman and his mother, 1987.

David Noel Freedman, 1978

David Noel Freedman, 1971

P and J in Genesis 1:1–11:26: An Alternative Hypothesis

JOSEPH BLENKINSOPP

University of Notre Dame, Indiana

My intent in this paper is to propose an alternative hypothesis on the formation of one section of the Pentateuch, namely, the history of early humanity in Genesis 1–11. Briefly stated, my contention will be that the material conventionally assigned to the Yahwist (J) is a narrative expansion and explication of a reflective kind, in the manner of the later sages of Israel, of the basic Priestly (P) narrative schema. I accept with only minor modifications the division of sources as found in the standard introductions and commentaries, though the *siglum* J is retained only for convenience and continuity in the scholarly *diadochē*. I believe it can be shown that this reading of the section presents fewer problems than the alternative view, still widely accepted, that P is a later elaboration of an early J narrative. In these matters certainty is beyond our grasp; all one can aspire to is to elevate a possibility into a serious probability or, in other words, to propose a better hypothesis. If the hypothesis merits consideration, I imagine it will have some bearing on the formation of the Pentateuch as a whole, but for the moment I am concerned only with this first segment of the pentateuchal narrative.

I. Problems with the Received Opinion

A survey of scholarship over the last few decades shows that, among those who still adhere in some form or other to the "newer documentary hypothesis," there is broad agreement on the respective contributions of J and P to the narrative in Genesis 1–11.[1] Differences of opinion arise mainly with respect to the presence of an early narrative component of J, the principal candidates being Eissfeldt's Lay source (L); Fohrer's Nomadic source (N), roughly identical in content to L; Morgenstern's Kenite material (K); and Pfeiffer's Southern or Seir source (S). This last is, however, really distinct from J, which according to Pfeiffer is not attested in Genesis 1–11.[2] Allowing for these variations, the contribution of J may for convenience be set out as follows:

2:4b–3:24	The garden of Eden
4:1-26	Cain and Abel; Cainite and Sethite lines[3]
6:1-8	"Sons of God, daughters of men"; decision to destroy[4]
7:1-5	Command to enter the ark[5]
7:7-10	Execution of the command
7:12	Forty days and nights of rain
7:16b	"YHWH shut him in"
7:17b	Increase in the water level[6]
7:22-23	Destruction of life
8:2b-3a	End of rainfall; the water recedes
8:6-12	Reconnaissance by the birds[7]

1. The following is a sampling of opinion from introductions published (with one exception) in English since World War II (bracketed dates are those of the original publication that served as the basis for translation): R. H. Pfeiffer, *Introduction to the Old Testament* (2nd ed.; London: Adam & Charles Black, 1952) 142-67; A. Weiser, *Introduction to the Old Testament* (trans. D. M. Barton; 4th ed.; London: Darton, Longman, Todd, 1961 [1957]) 99-111; H. H. Rowley, *The Growth of the Old Testament* (1950; New York: Harper & Row, 1963) 16-46; H. Cazelles, *DBSup* (Paris: Letouzey & Ané, 1966) 7.770-803; O. Eissfeldt, *The Old Testament: An Introduction* (trans. P. R. Ackroyd; 3rd ed.; Oxford: Blackwell, 1966 [1964]) 194, 199-200; G. Fohrer in E. Sellin and G. Fohrer, *Introduction to the Old Testament* (trans. D. E. Green; Nashville and New York: Abingdon, 1968 [1965]) 147-61; M. Noth, *A History of Pentateuchal Traditions* (trans. B. W. Anderson; Englewood Cliffs, NJ: Prentice-Hall, 1972 [1948]) 262-63; O. Kaiser, *Introduction to the Old Testament* (trans. J. Sturdy; 2nd ed.; Minneapolis: Augsburg, 1975 [1970]) 78-91; J. A. Soggin, *Introduction to the Old Testament* (trans. J. Bowden; OTL; Philadelphia: Westminster, 1976 [1974]) 99-105.

2. Pfeiffer's S source in Genesis 1–11, parts of chaps. 14–35, 36, and 38, made its debut in "A Non-Israelite Source of the Book of Genesis," *ZAW* n.f. 7 (1930) 66-73.

3. Eissfeldt (*Introduction*, 194, 199) assigns 4:1, 17a, 18-24 to his L source and the rest to J. Fohrer (*Introduction*, 160-61) likewise credits 4:17-24 to his N source, corresponding to Pfeiffer's S source minus its supplement.

4. Eissfeldt (*Introduction*, 194), Fohrer (*Introduction*, 160-61), and Pfeiffer (*Introduction*, 160) assign 6:1-4 to L, N, and S, respectively.

5. There is some hesitancy about 7:3a; see, e.g., Noth, *Traditions*, 262; and Kaiser, *Introduction*, 86.

6. Perhaps all of this verse belongs to J since v. 17a refers to a duration of forty days; cf. 7:12; 8:6 (J).

7. Some regard the raven as an intruder; see Noth, *Traditions*, 262-63; Kaiser, *Introduction*, 86.

8:13b	Noah removes the covering of the ark
8:20-22	Noah's altar and sacrifice; a divine promise
9:18-27	Noah's sons; Noah the vintner
10:8-19	Descendants of Ham[8]
10:21	Children born to Shem
10:25-30	Descendants of Eber
11:1-9	Tower of Babel
11:28-30	Death of Haran; wives of Abram and Nahor[9]

According to the received documentary wisdom, this J narrative, including its early strand or strands, was in existence no later than about the middle of the ninth century B.C.E., therefore about three centuries earlier than the P source that incorporated it. That it must be considered a product of the heyday of the monarchy, certainly before the fall of the Northern Kingdom in the eighth century, is deduced from its "enthusiastic acceptance of agricultural life, and of national-political power and cultus,"[10] or its "delight in agriculture, cult, in national power, the state, and the kingship,"[11] or the "optimism of national and religious exaltation" with which it is suffused.[12] Other indications of an early date are its naive anthropomorphism and antique flavor in general,[13] or, along a different line, its universalistic perspective and humanism, reflective of what von Rad was wont to refer to as the Solomonic enlightenment or its dimmer afterglow in the years immediately following his death.[14] A polling of other commentators who adhere in one form or another to the documentary hypothesis will confirm that these or similar arguments have led to a date for J no later than about the mid-ninth century B.C.E.[15]

In reading through this scholarly writing one is struck by the fact that arguments for this early date are hardly ever based on Genesis 1–11. There may be good reason for this omission since, however well they may fit other sections

8. Kaiser (*Introduction*, 86) omits 10:9, Nimrod the hunter, but it is difficult to see why.

9. Uncertain; several, e.g., Fohrer and Kaiser, assign these verses to P.

10. Eissfeldt, *Introduction*, 200.

11. Fohrer, *Introduction*, 157.

12. Weiser, *Introduction*, 108.

13. Eissfeldt, *Introduction*, 194; Rowley, *Growth*, 25.

14. G. von Rad, *Old Testament Theology* (trans. D. M. G. Stalker; 2 vols.; New York: Harper & Row, 1962-65 [1957-60]) 1.48-56; in *The Problem of the Hexateuch and Other Essays* (trans. E. W. Trueman Dicken; Edinburgh and London: Oliver & Boyd, 1966 [1958]) 69, he speaks of the Yahwist as a product of "the untrammelled days of Solomon," a not very felicitous translation of "ein Hauch aus der freigeistigen Ära Salomos" (*Gesammelte Studien zum Alten Testament* [Munich: Kaiser, 1961] 76).

15. There is generally little variation in dating among documentary critics exclusive of some recent revisionists; most date J inclusive of its early component (J[1], L, N, K) ca. 950-850 B.C.E.

of the pentateuchal narrative attributed to J, they are not at all supported by a reading of these first chapters. The enthusiasm for agricultural life, nationalistic and religious optimism, idyllic pastoralism, humanism, and so on, deemed by these authors to be characteristic of J, are in fact conspicuously absent from these chapters, which speak of the curse on the soil, exile, and the vanity of human pretensions in general and in the political sphere in particular. One would imagine that this somber diagnosis of the human condition and pessimistic assessment of moral potential would fit much better a time of failure and disorientation than the heyday of the monarchy. The sense of the ineradicable human tendency to evil, expressed clearly before and after the deluge (6:5; 8:21), leaves little room for optimism. It finds its closest parallels in late prophecy, as in Jeremiah, who speaks of the desperate sickness of the human heart (Jer 17:9-10), and in some of the darker lucubrations of the later sages, as in the author of Job, who speaks of life as brief and full of trouble (Job 14:1-6).

It is also worthy of note that Genesis 1–11 contains a kind of preview or foreshadowing of the history of the nation as a whole, a history that narrates repeated failures ending in disaster which is almost but not quite terminal. It may therefore not be pure coincidence that both the early history of humanity and the national history end with the forward thrust of events stalled in Meso-potamia (Gen 11:1-9; 2 Kgs 25:27-30). The parallelism is repeated on a different scale in the first incident of the primal history (Gen 2:4b–3:24). Like Israel, the Man is placed in a propitious environment, permanency in which is contingent on obedience to a commandment. Death is threatened as punishment for violation, but what follows at both the micro- and macrolevel is not death but exile. Behind the snake with its seductive speech we detect the cults practiced by the inhabitants of the land, and the role of the Woman in Eden recalls the Deuteronomic concern about women as the occasion for adopting these cults (e.g., Deut 7:3-4; 1 Kgs 11:1-8). These structural and thematic homologies suggest that reflection on the course of the history has generated a recapitulation couched in universal, mythic terms and placed at the beginning as a foreshadow-ing of what is to follow.

Perhaps the only argument for the early date that still carries any weight is the thematic parallelism between Genesis 1–11, especially the early episodes, and the so-called Succession History in 2 Samuel 11–20 + 1 Kings 1–2.[16] The similarities have often been noted and need not concern us here.[17] But the origin of the Succession History in Solomon's court, or at any time in the early phase

---

16. I explored these common features in "Theme and Motif in the Succession History (2 Sam xi 2ff) and the Yahwist Corpus," *Volume du Congrès: Genève, 1965* (VTSup 15; Leiden: Brill, 1966) 44-57, but would not draw the same conclusions from my study now as I did then.

17. In addition to my "Theme and Motif" see W. Brueggemann, "David and His Theologian," *CBQ* 30 (1968) 156-81.

of the monarchy, cannot be considered secure. Van Seters has made out a strong case that the Succession History was not originally part of the Deuteronomistic History (DtrH), but was added to it by a postexilic author.[18] Several years earlier Whybray, while not contesting the received date, argued that it belonged to the genre of wisdom literature rather than historiography; if correct, this view removes the most important reason for assigning it to a writer of the Solomonic age.[19] Caution is therefore in order in assuming that the first segment of the J narrative and the Succession History are contemporary or near-contemporary compositions.

That the J material in Genesis 1–11 does not satisfy the criteria for identifying a source composed in the early monarchy period provides at least prima facie justification for considering a later date. Another pointer in this direction, not probative but certainly suggestive, is the absence of any allusion to this material in preexilic writings. The Eden story is nowhere mentioned in texts prior to the Neo-Babylonian period, but at that time we begin to hear of it with some frequency (Ezek 28:13; 31:9, 16, 18; 36:35; Isa 51:3; Joel 2:3). The same must be said for Noah, the first mention of whom outside Genesis is in the exilic Isaiah (Isa 54:9-10), a passage that draws a parallel between "the waters of Noah" and political disaster. That inundation occurs frequently as a metaphor for defeat and subjugation (e.g., in the Lament over Ur and in several psalms)[20] may confirm the point made earlier about the primal history as a recapitulation of the national history. The location of the Tower of Babel in Shinar points in the same direction, as we shall see shortly. Other indications of a later date will be found in a study of the vocabulary and topoi in Genesis 1–11. The thorough investigation that this study deserves cannot be pursued in detail here, but some samples will be proposed as we proceed.

II. J within the *tôlēdôt* Structure of Genesis 1–11

The most distinctive structural feature of Genesis, not found in the other four books of the Pentateuch, is the division into a series of *tôlēdôt* (generations) arranged in two pentads covering, respectively, the early history of humanity and the prehistory of Israel. The origin and function of this feature have given rise to a great deal of discussion that cannot be taken up here.[21] It must suffice

---

18. J. Van Seters, *In Search of History: Historiography in the Ancient World and the Origins of Biblical History* (New Haven and London: Yale University, 1983) 277-91.

19. R. N. Whybray, *The Succession Narrative* (London: SCM, 1968).

20. *ANET*, 455-63; Ps 124:4-5; Jonah 2:3-4 (ET 2-3).

21. I discuss the *tôlēdôt* structure in chap. 2 of *The Pentateuch: An Introduction to the First Five Books of the Bible* (Anchor Bible Reference Library; New York: Doubleday).

to note that, while it connotes primarily a genealogical structure, it does not preclude the possibility of narrative development; indeed, some of the *tôlēdôt* are almost exclusively made up of narrative. The point to be made here is that in the five *tôlēdôt* sections in Genesis 1–11, *J follows P with the exception of the last, in which there is no J.* For convenience of reference the series may be set out as follows:

I	1:1–2:4a	P
	2:4b–4:26	J
II	5:1-32	P
	6:1-8	J
III	6:9–9:19	P + J
	9:20-27	J
	9:28-29	P excipit
IV	10:1-32	P + J
	11:1-9	J
V	11:10-26	P

One cannot, of course, conclude from this arrangement that P was composed before J, for a redactor could have filled out a basic P schema with earlier material. The contribution, even the existence, of a final redactor is one of the fuzziest issues in the study of the formation of the Pentateuch. One thing does seem clear, however, though not always acknowledged:[22] the final redaction was not the work of P. Would P have omitted the distinction between clean and unclean and the concluding sacrifice in the deluge narrative and then, qua redactor, have put them back in again? Would P, acting in the same capacity, have left on the record certain allusions and incidents — especially the Golden Calf episode — that present Aaron, eponymous ancestor of the dominant priestly house, in a poor light? Hardly. We may then ask, with Job, "if it is not he, who is it?" The answer is, we do not know, but if the hypothesis presented here is correct, J would have a better claim than P.

If we take the *tôlēdôt* structure seriously as a vector of meaning in its own right, we should move beyond the important observation that in it P precedes J to inquiring how, within this structure, J relates to P. For what this structure tells us, however it came to be part of the narrative continuum, is that there is an interconnectedness within the successive blocks of material. This is what we must now try to understand. For obvious reasons we cannot engage in an exhaustive study of the first pentad in Genesis 1–11; to do so would call for a different kind of commentary on this first segment of the pentateuchal narra-

---

22. F. M. Cross (*Canaanite Myth and Hebrew Epic* [Cambridge: Harvard University, 1973] 304-5) prefers merging P and the redactor of the Tetrateuch to the less parsimonious solution of positing two P authors.

tive. It will be possible only to sketch out a preliminary account of how the J material relates to P, and to suggest that one can best explain this connection on the supposition that J is later than P.

1. *The Generations of the Heavens and the Earth (1:1–4:26)*

In this first section of the series the superscript is located, exceptionally, between the P and J material (2:4a) rather than in the initial position. This circumstance has given rise to a lengthy debate as to whether it was relocated here to make way for the solemn exordium in 1:1, or whether it should be taken to refer forward to 2:4b–3:24. The latter option has been quite popular of late,[23] but the following narrative does not deal with the heavens and the earth but only with the earth, and one bit of it in particular. Moreover, the phrase "when they were created" *(běhibbārě'ām)* refers backward rather than forward (cf. 1:1, 21, 27; 2:3). An alternative explanation would be that, while leaving the way clear for the solemn opening of the creation recitals, it also serves as a link between P and J. The contrast between "heavens and earth" (2:4a) and "earth and heavens" (2:4b), which is hardly accidental, is consistent with this function, as also the exceptional use of the designation YHWH Elohim in 2:4b–3:24, which combines the titles used in the preceding P and the subsequent J narratives.[24]

The linking of the creation recital with an account of the flowering of evil in the first human lineages suggests the possibility of reading the latter as an explication and development of the former. The point is being made, in contrast to Mesopotamian thought, that the emergence of evil is subsequent to creation and not part of the creative process itself. Evil is not, so to speak, built into the cosmic order. The first rebellion is in the human not the divine sphere, even though later reflection will, problematically, put it back into the superhuman sphere (e.g., Wis 2:24). What the J author sets out to explain, using familiar mythic topoi in the manner of the sages, is how evil could be generated in a creation declared (seven times) to be good. In this sense, therefore, one may say that the J narrative contains reflection generated by the Priestly creation recital.

The plausibility of this alternative reading is increased when one considers that the arguments for the early date of J are seriously flawed. One should also give due weight to the absence of any allusion to the Eden story in preexilic compositions and the structural and thematic parallels between this story and

23. For example, Cross, *Canaanite Myth*, 302.
24. YHWH Elohim occurs throughout Gen 2:4b–3:24 except in the conversation between the snake and the woman (3:1-5), where Elohim occurs. YHWH Elohim also occurs in Jonah 4:6, a postexilic composition that illustrates the deliberate choice of divine names to fit particular situations.

the national history prophetically interpreted.[25] The incidence in this first J section of vocabulary attested exclusively or primarily in late texts, or characteristic of the later sages (e.g., *'ārûm*, "cunning"; *lěhaśkîl*, "to confer wisdom") provides further confirmation, and even more so the use of such themes and topoi as the first man (cf. Job 15:7-8) and the tree of life (cf. Prov 13:12). Recourse to symbolic names (Adam, Havvah [Eve], Hebel [Abel]) and personification (e.g., the snake and the *robēṣ*, "demon," crouching at Cain's door) points in the same direction. Some work has been done along these lines, but a thorough study of the language, literary procedures, and themes in 2:4b–4:26 from this perspective still lies in the future.[26]

2. The Generations of Adam (5:1–6:8)

Only this superscript speaks of a generations book (5:1a), which has inevitably raised two issues: whether a *sēper tôlēdôt* once existed independently and was subsequently spliced into the Genesis narrative; and whether the series originally started at this point, as it does in 1 Chronicles 1–9. These are interesting and important issues, but it is not crucial to my argument to solve them, which is fortunate since they have been discussed inconclusively for a long time.

For my present purpose the important issue is the relation between the P linear ten-member genealogy in 5:1-32 and the J account of the spread of evil in the antediluvian world in 6:1-8. Almost without exception the latter has been read as the J prelude to the deluge. In the context of Genesis 1–11 as a whole it does, of course, serve that purpose, but in the context of the second in the *tôlēdôt* series it functions as an explication and reflective comment on the preceding genealogy. One cannot simply assume, as many do, that the P genealogy draws on the genealogical material in the preceding chapter, since it is equally possible that they represent alternative versions of traditional material. The P genealogy arranges the names, with the Seth line followed by the descendants of Kenan (= Cain), in such a way as to hint at progressive moral degeneration, and the same "message" comes across in the notice about Enoch, in the seventh position, walking with God and being taken up (5:21-24). This *aufzählende Element* (the phrase is Westermann's) is then made the object of reflection, in the manner of the sages, in the following *erzählende* passage

25. The influence of prophetic themes on Genesis 2–3 was noted by L. Alonso-Schökel, "Motivos sapienciales y de alianza en Gn 2–3," *Bib* 43 (1962) 295-316. He concluded that "se explicaria mejor el enigma literario y el silencio de otros libros aceptando una fecha posterior" (315).

26. In addition to the article of Alonso-Schökel (ibid.) see G. E. Mendenhall, "The Shady Side of Wisdom: The Date and Purpose of Genesis 3," in *A Light unto My Path: Old Testament Studies in Honor of Jacob M. Myers* (ed. H. N. Bream et al.; Philadelphia: Temple University, 1974) 319-34.

attributed to J (6:1-8). The connection is suggested strongly in the opening line, "when humanity was beginning to multiply on the surface of the ground, and daughters were born to them" (6:1), for that is what the genealogy, which also mentions daughters, records. The "message" of the genealogy is therefore restated with the help of a familiar mythic topos, the sexual union of divine and human beings. There is also the more specific point that the spread of evil leads to a further decrease in lifespan, namely, one hundred and twenty years.[27] The ensuing situation then provokes a somber and reflective meditation on the apparently ineradicable evil of the human heart (6:5-8), matched by a similar comment at the conclusion of the deluge story (8:21).

3. The Generations of Noah (6:9–9:29)

This central panel of the pentad is easily the longest. In it P and J are, for the first time, conflated, resulting in what Gunkel called "ein Meisterstück der modernen Kritik."[28] As in the other segments, J follows P both with respect to the broad narrative sequence (the J story of Noah the vintner following the deluge story itself) and within the deluge story itself where J can be read as a supplement to the basic P narrative line. This in itself, I repeat, does not oblige one to date J later than P since it is theoretically possible that an early J could have been worked into the P narrative — a position taken by Westermann in his massive commentary[29] and many others. But we have seen that we cannot simply assume the received chronological order, and the sequence in the *tôlēdôt* provides the motivation to look for an alternative explanation.

Several features of the deluge story justify a hermeneutic of suspicion with respect to the documentary *opinio communis*. In the first place, the J sections do not add up to a coherent and self-contained narrative. The ark is introduced as if already familiar to the reader (7:1); there is no command to build it or specifications as to how it is to be built (cf. 6:11-22 P). Likewise, toward the end, there is no account of Noah and company disembarking, which one could certainly expect (cf. 8:14-19 P). Moreover, the brief notice that YHWH shut Noah in (7:16b), which all allot to J, is intelligible only as a follow-up to the P paragraph immediately preceding in which Noah enters the ark (7:13-16a). Considered as part of a continuous J narrative it comes too late since the deluge of rain is already well underway (7:7, 10, 12 J). It may also be significant in this respect that *mabbûl*, the standard P word for the deluge (6:17; 7:6; 9:11, 15, 28;

---

27. A more probable meaning than a period of grace (three generations) given to humanity until the deluge; see C. Westermann, *Genesis* (trans. John J. Scullion; 3 vols.; Continental Commentary; Minneapolis: Augsburg, 1984-86) 1.376.

28. H. Gunkel, *Genesis* (6th ed.; Göttingen: Vandenhoeck & Ruprecht, 1964) 137.

29. Westermann, *Genesis*, 1.396-97.

10:1, 32; 11:10), is taken over by J and given the different connotation of a deluge of rain (*mê hammabbûl*, 7:7, 10). I detect here another example of the subtlety and sophistication of this writer since rainfall, the absence of which was a problem at the beginning of the story (2:5), is now the instrument of humanity's punishment. Here is another instance, therefore, of nature turning against those who abuse the good created order established by God.

An indication of a different kind is the use of the resumptive verse, a technique the purpose of which is to take up the thread of the narrative after an insertion. One example occurs at the beginning of this section (6:9b-10), referring back to the three sons of Noah named just before the J material in 6:1-8, and recalling at the same time another ancient worthy who walked with God (5:22 P). Further along, the phrase "on that very day" (*bĕʿeṣem hayyôm hazzeh*, 7:13a), characteristic of P, links up with the precise date for the beginning of the deluge in 7:11 after the J chronological notice in 7:12. It is generally not too difficult to detect the purposes of the J additions to the base narrative. There is the matter of chronology, a subject of long and inconclusive discussion, and the desire to describe the deluge in a way compatible with the cultural and ecological context of the J narrative up to this point — rainfall rather than a cosmic uncreation. The addition of the passage about the reconnaissance mission of the birds (8:6-12) was presumably motivated by narrative interest and the desire to find room for a familiar motif (cf. Gilgamesh 11:145-54). The same can be said of the sacrifice (Gilgamesh 11:159-61), pointedly omitted by P since according to Priestly theory sacrifice was instituted only much later at Sinai. This in its turn necessitated the distinction between clean and unclean, also omitted by P and for the same reason.

YHWH's response to the sacrifice offered on the purified earth provided occasion for reflection on a central theme, perhaps *the* central theme, of J's account of early humanity. As noted earlier, it corresponds to the comment about the evil impulse of the human will made before the deluge (8:21; cf. 6:5). In the context of Israelite religious thought, and especially in the immediate context of the sacrifice, this reflection on the *yēṣer lēb hāʾādām* is a "modern" one, not too far removed from the postbiblical doctrine of the *yēṣer hārāʿ*, "the evil impulse." It is worth noting that in the corresponding reflection of YHWH on antediluvian humanity the phrase *yēṣer maḥšĕbôt libbô*, "the impulse of the thoughts of his heart," occurs elsewhere only in Chronicles, certainly postexilic (1 Chr 28:9; 29:18).

The P conclusion to the deluge story (Gen 9:1-17) is rounded off with mention of the three sons whose descendants will populate the renewed earth (9:18-19). This summary statement is generally credited entirely to J, though it seems to me more likely that J has simply added the information that Ham was the father of Canaan (cf. 10:6, 15) to introduce the story of Noah the vintner (9:20-27). The reason for the addition of this somewhat disconcerting tale (11:1-9), which has engendered some decidedly odd interpretations, would be to explain the persistence of moral incapacity and misery in the postdeluge world, a subject on which P is silent. It is therefore structurally and thematically parallel to the sin of the first man in Eden. The occasion for the lapse is a plant in both stories. Ham (Canaan) is functionally the counterpart of the snake. Both narratives feature the clothed/naked theme, and both have a concluding curse. The oracles on Canaan, Shem, and Japheth cannot be used to establish a date in the early history (or even prehistory) of Israel, pace Gunkel, Speiser, and others,[30] since ancient ethnic names continued to be applied anachronistically to contemporary groups in the Second Temple period (e.g., Ezra 9:1, 11; Neh 9:24). The *tôlēdôt* as a whole is then rounded off with a P notice about the age and death of Noah.

4. The Generations of the Sons of Noah (10:1–11:9)

Here a similar arrangement confronts us: a basically P numerative *(aufzählende)* passage with J insertions (10:1-32) followed by a J narrative, which I will suggest was generated by it (11:1-9). The main outlines of the P schema are easily detected and call for no comment. Most documentarian commentators agree on the following J insertions: Nimrod descendant of Cush (10:8-12); Egypt (vv. 13-14); Canaan (vv. 15-19); descendants of Shem and Eber (vv. 25-30). In the most general terms, these may be read as the fruit of progress in ethnographic knowledge between the composition of the P narrative and the time of the supplements. On the one hand, the P schema serves to show how the creation command to increase and multiply (1:28), repeated after the deluge (9:1), was implemented; and in this there is perhaps a hint at the remarkable demographic expansion of the Jewish *ethnos* during the two centuries of Persian rule. On the other hand, in keeping with the drift of the story up to this point, J wishes to demonstrate that the drive for status and power continued after the deluge to exert its baleful influence.

The point is made most clearly in the short passage about Nimrod the hunter who, standing in the line of Cain who built the first city (4:17), and of the *gibbōrîm* who walked the earth in ancient times (6:4), became the first potentate and empire builder (10:8-12). The theme is further developed in the artful narrative about the city and Tower of Babel, a narrative that one may read as a commentary, somewhat in the manner of midrash, on this passage (11:1-9). The essential link is the land of Shinar in which this further example of hubris takes place (10:10; 11:2). Outside Genesis, Shinar as the name for the southern part of Mesopotamia occurs only in postexilic texts (Isa 11:11; Zech 5:11; Dan 1:2), and the plain *(biqʿâ)* in which the architects of empire settle

---

30. Ibid., 81; E. A. Speiser, *Genesis* (2nd ed.; AB 1; Garden City, NY: Doubleday, 1964) 62-63.

recalls the scene of Ezekiel's diaspora vision (Ezek 3:22-23). Far from being a naive tale embodying a primitive, anthropomorphic view of the deity, the Babel narrative is suffused with irony and ends with a satirical play on the name Babylon. It is difficult to avoid the conclusion that the author has composed a spoof or satire directed at human pretensions in the political sphere as exemplified by the Neo-Babylonian Empire. The story would then be comparable in intent if not in form to the anti-Babylonian polemic of the exilic Isaiah, also directed at both political pretensions and the cult that supported them. As late as the second century B.C.E. this empire and its greatest ruler, Nebuchadrezzar, served as prime examples of overbearing pride and tyranny (Daniel 1–4).

A careful survey of the J additions to the "Table of the Nations" would, I believe, support the chronological order I have proposed. Thus, Sidon rather than Tyre is listed as the firstborn of Canaan (10:15; Tyre is not even mentioned), which may be explained by the ascendancy of Sidon and the decline of Tyre after the debilitating thirteen-year siege of the city by Nebuchadrezzar (ca. 586-573 B.C.E.). The listing of tribes from the Arabian peninsula as "sons" of Joktan (10:26-30) could likewise reflect knowledge of Kedarite expansion in the sixth and fifth centuries B.C.E., a development amply documented in biblical and cuneiform texts. Such indications as these are by no means decisive in themselves, but they are consistent with the line of argument so far advanced.

5. The Generations of Shem (11:10-26)

This last of the series, composed entirely of summary without narrative developments, has no J additions and therefore calls for no comment. The absence of supplementary material is probably due to its final position in the first tôlēdôt series. From within this structure the link with the history of Israel's ancestors is not the call of Abraham (Gen 12:1-3) but the three sons of Terah and their descendants (Gen 11:26-27).[31]

III. Some Provisional Conclusions

The hypothesis proposed in this paper reposes, in the first place, on a critique of arguments advanced for an early dating of the J material in Genesis 1–11 together with an accumulation of positive indications of a later date. Doubts

---

31. See F. Crüsemann, "Die Eigenständigkeit der Urgeschichte Ein Beitrag zur Diskussion um den 'Jahwisten,'" in Die Botschaft und die Boten: Festschrift für Hans Walter Wolff zum 70. Geburtstag (ed. J. Jeremias and L. Perlitt; Neukirchen-Vluyn: Neukirchener Verlag, 1981) 11-29.

about the conventional early date have been in the air for some time, inspired by such characteristic features of the J source as its universalism, its use of mythic categories, its distinctive vocabulary, or its familiarity with sapiential and prophetic motifs.[32] More recently a date no earlier than the exilic period has been proposed by a number of revisionist scholars who still defend the validity of the accepted source-critical method and are not prepared to abandon the Graf-Wellhausen construct in its entirety. (Whether the construct can survive the chronological displacement of J is, however, another matter.) Perhaps the earliest of these revisionists was F. V. Winnett, whose late J was precipitated by the disaster of 587 B.C.E. and was composed as a supplement to the existing story of Israelite origins. The J material in Genesis 1–11, put together mainly on the basis of oral sources, was composed no earlier than the late sixth century B.C.E.[33] The same line of argument was pursued by his student N. E. Wagner, who also emphasized that each block of narrative material in the Pentateuch, beginning with the early history of humanity and the history of the ancestors, had its own independent history of transmission, editorial linkage being effected only in the postexilic age.[34] Another student of Winnett's, John Van Seters, has argued in a number of publications that the J source was written in response to the crisis of exile and was subsequently incorporated into the more comprehensive P work.[35] Among German scholars one of the earliest to attack the *opinio recepta* was H. H. Schmid, whose "so-called Yahwist" is subsequent and supplementary to a basic Deuteronomistic historical account of Israelite origins.[36] A somewhat similar position is taken by H. Vorländer, who makes much of the criterion of attestation or nonattestation outside the Tetrateuch, and by M. Rose, for whom J survives only as a late stratum of the Deuteronomistic work.[37] More radical is the approach of R. Rendtorff and his student E. Blum,

32. Impressed by the universalism of Genesis 1–11, J. Morgenstern ("The Mythological Background of Psalm 82," *HUCA* 14 [1939] 93-94) dated it to the early Persian period. The arguments of Alonso-Schökel ("Motivos sapienciales") and Mendenhall ("Shady Side") were restricted to Genesis 2–3.

33. F. V. Winnett, "Re-examining the Foundations," *JBL* 84 (1965) 1-19.

34. N. E. Wagner, "Abraham and David?" in *Studies on the Ancient Palestinian World Presented to Prof. F. V. Winnett* (ed. J. W. Wevers and D. B. Redford; Toronto: University of Toronto, 1972) 117-40; "Pentateuchal Criticism: No Clear Future," *CJT* 13 (1967) 225-32.

35. J. Van Seters, "Confessional Reformulation in the Exilic Period," *VT* 22 (1972) 448-59; *Abraham in History and Tradition* (New Haven and London: Yale University, 1975) 139-53; "Recent Studies on the Pentateuch: A Crisis in Method," *JAOS* 99 (1979) 663-67; "The Primeval Histories of Greece and Israel Compared," *ZAW* 100 (1988) 1-22.

36. H. H. Schmid, *Der sogenannte Jahwist: Beobachtungen und Fragen zur Pentateuchforschung* (Zurich: Theologische Verlag, 1976).

37. H. Vorländer, *Die Entstehungszeit der jehowistischen Geschichtswerkes* (Frankfurt: Europäische Hochschulschriften 23/109, 1978); M. Rose, *Deuteronomist und Jahwist: Untersuchungen zu den Berührungspunkten beiden Literaturwerke* (Zurich: Theologische Verlag, 1981); idem, "La Croissance du Corpus Historiographique de la Bible — Une Proposition," *RTP* 118 (1986) 217-36.

who deny the existence of continuous literary sources from the preexilic period and insist that the distinct blocks of narrative material in the Pentateuch were combined editorially only in the Second Temple period.[38]

One or two observations may be permitted on this recent phase of revisionist writing insofar as it bears on the thesis argued in this paper. The first is that just as the proponents for an early J rarely argued on the basis of Genesis 1–11, so most of the writers just listed concentrated on other sections of the Pentateuch, especially those which seemed to be redefinable in some way as Deuteronom(ist)ic. The second is that little attention was given to the relation between the putative J material and P. As far as I have been able to establish, no one was prepared to argue that any part of J could be later than P. Where P was mentioned, it was generally to repeat the received opinion that the P *siglum* represents an editorializing of the late J source. For example, Rose concluded that P sets out to counter the pessimistic theology of J, which is the precise opposite of the thesis that I have advanced with respect to Genesis 1–11.[39]

We may now go on to ask how, on the assumption of the chronological order suggested, the J supplementary material in the Genesis 1–11 *tôlēdôt* relates to the basic P narrative. We have seen that in some cases expansion was dictated by narrative interest (e.g., the birds, 8:6-12) or the desire to impart additional information (e.g., the Arabian tribes, 10:26-30). Some additions are explanatory, in the manner of midrash, as in the notice about YHWH shutting Noah in, which explains how the ark could have remained watertight (7:16b; cf. 6:14). The author(s) of the supplement also wished to state more explicitly, generally in narrative form, what was merely implied in the P genealogical schema, as in the reflective comment in 6:1-8 bearing on the implicit "message" of the preceding genealogy. Central to the aim of the J supplement, however, was the balancing of the optimistic and psychologically simplistic P view of human existence with a more realistic and disillusioned approach. According to J human existence, including existence *coram Deo,* is seen as fundamentally problematic. Hence the addition of the myth of deviation to P's account of creation in all its essential goodness; hence also the insistence, absent in P, that this ancient pattern of deviation reproduced itself immediately after the deluge. For J moral incapacity, the sickness of the human heart, is ineradicably part of human nature, so much so that even God has to come to terms with it, as he does after the deluge (8:21). Unlike P, the J author allows experience, including

---

38. Rolf Rendtorff, *The Problem of the Process of Transmission in the Pentateuch* (trans. J. J. Scullion; JSOTSup 89; Sheffield: JSOT, 1990) (ET of *Das überlieferungsgeschichtliche Problem des Pentateuch* [BZAW 147; Berlin: de Gruyter, 1977]); idem, *The Old Testament: An Introduction* (trans. J. Bowden; London: SCM, 1985) 131-39, 157-64 (ET of *Das Alte Testament: Eine Einführung* [Neukirchen-Vluyn: Neukirchener Verlag, 1983]); Erhard Blum, *Die Komposition der Vätergeschichte* (Neukirchen-Vluyn: Neukirchener Verlag, 1984); idem, *Studien zur Komposition des Pentateuch* (BZAW 189; Berlin: de Gruyter, 1990).

39. Rose, "Croissance," 232.

historical experience, to dictate the shape of the early history of humanity, a history that is, in effect, a diagnosis of the human condition.

It would be fitting to round off this investigation by proposing a plausible setting for the composition of the J material in Genesis 1–11, but unfortunately our limited knowledge of Jewish life in the early Second Temple period precludes anything more than an educated guess. The sense that the author is attempting to come to terms with an experience of spiritual and moral failure suggests familiarity with later prophecy, especially Jeremiah and Ezekiel, and aligns the work with certain expressions of piety from the Persian period (e.g., Ezra 9:6-15; Neh 9:6-37). I have also suggested that the author has assimilated and set out to give universal expression to the Deuteronomistic view of the national history. The Deuteronomistic identification of law observance with wisdom (Deut 4:6-7) was the point of departure for a specifically Israelite idea of practical wisdom developed in different ways by literati *(ḥăkāmîm)* during the time of the Second Commonwealth. It comes to expression in the final verse of the poem on wisdom in Job 28, often thought to have been added by a pious glossator. Its Deuteronomistic pedigree is detectable in the sage's insistence that his teaching be inscribed on the hearer's heart (Prov 3:3; 6:21; 7:3; cf. Deut 30:14; Jer 31:33). It stands opposed to other and alien forms of wisdom that hold out the promise of life enhancement but lead eventually to ruin.

If the J material in Genesis 1–11 can be read as a filling out of the P schema with the purpose of expressing the same idea in narrative forms its origins would most plausibly be sought in the lay, intellectual milieu of the province of Judah during the two centuries of Persian domination. What this proposal, if found to be acceptable, might contribute to our understanding of the formation of the Pentateuch remains to be investigated.

What They Don't Know Won't Hurt Them: Genesis 6–9

BARUCH HALPERN

Pennsylvania State University, University Park

David Noel Freedman is perhaps the most prolific editor, energetic correspondent, and effective catalyst of intellectual exchange in the history of biblical studies. A brilliant scholar whose generosity with his insights is legendary, he is also about the only figure in the field who could successfully quantify insights in such number. A particularly rare — and generous and shrewd — quality is the extent to which Noel has devoted himself with unflagging cheer to identifying and promoting the careers of young colleagues. Were someone to remake the film *It's a Wonderful Life* with James Stewart playing Noel, the resulting impoverishment of our collegium would far outstrip the bleakness of "Pottersville" without George. It is to his role of benefactor of the young as well as to his role of biblical editor that this study is dedicated.

The documentary hypothesis has been the dominant scholarly approach to the history of the Pentateuch or Hexateuch for two centuries. In its mature form, this hypothesis posits that three narrative sources, J, E, and P, have been combined with Deuteronomy to form the present Pentateuch. The first stage of this combination was the editing of the J and E sources, by R_{JE}. P was written as a bowdlerization of that combined text; Deuteronomy makes JE the basis of its historical references. Subsequently, JE was combined with P, by R_{JEP}.[1]

---

1. See generally R. E. Friedman, *Who Wrote the Bible?* (New York: Summit, 1987).

The process by which JEP was joined to the Deuteronomistic History (DtrH) is more obscure. That there are Priestly materials in the book of Joshua, including materials fulfilling enjoinders in Numbers, is indisputable (Joshua 20–22). Joshua 23–24 cite P, as well as JE, texts. Yet there are also passages in the Tetrateuch that have seemed to scholars to reflect Deuteronomistic or proto-Deuteronomistic editing.[2] In other words, P has been introduced into DtrH, yet the Deuteronomistic Historian (H[Dtr]) or one of the editors of that work (as the exilic editor, E[Dtr]x), may have laid hands on the Tetrateuch.

The study of these questions depends ultimately on what models of editing scholars bring to the text. Yet, with few exceptions,[3] techniques of editing have not been the target of detailed study. Indeed, many analysts of the sources of the Pentateuch have concluded that the editing was irrational, insensitive to contradictions and to tension arising from the combination, and even post-modern.[4] As a coeditor and an editee of David Noel Freedman, the honoree of this volume, I find such conclusions historically and morally untenable.

Historically untenable because a hypothesis that infers that the editors of the Pentateuch (and of DtrH) were mentally inferior to modern philologians lacks any basis in evidence — except the evidence of the philologian's own devising. Morally untenable because the failure of the modern analyst to arrive at a hypothesis securing the dignity of the ancient editor is not evidence of a defect in the ancient editor. To impute such a defect to the ancient is to slight his (overwhelmingly probably, his) abilities. More, it is to slight the acuity not just of the editor, nor yet of his audience, but of those elite colleagues of his who accepted his edition and valorized and propagated it. In all that company, there failed to be a single figure who embodied the intellect, the energy, and the political savvy to produce a more appealing alternative.

Under the circumstances, one should expect that the editing we *can* isolate in the biblical text is sensible editing, frequently rising to brilliance, governed by intelligible principles. Thus the editors whom we reconstruct should exhibit intellectual traits similar to those of the best editors today: not irrational, insensitive affirmers of the meaninglessness of words, but precisely individuals of the quality needed to produce the architects of an irrepressibly vital culture.

2. See, e.g., Bernard Levinson, "The Hermeneutics of Innovation: The Impact of Central-ization upon the Structure, Sequence, and Reformulation of Legal Material in Deuteronomy" (Ph.D. diss., Brandeis University, 1991), for a recent treatment with extensive bibliography.

3. J. H. Tigay, *The Gilgamesh Epic: Empirical Models for Biblical Criticism* (Philadelphia: University of Pennsylvania, 1985); R. E. Friedman, "Sacred History and Theology: The Re-daction of Torah," in *The Creation of Sacred Literature* (ed. R. E. Friedman; Los Angeles: University of California, 1981) 25-34; Baruch Halpern, *The First Historians: The Hebrew Bible and History* (San Francisco: Harper & Row, 1988) 181-204.

4. H. Hupfeld, *Die Quellen der Genesis* (Berlin: Wiegandt & Grieben, 1853) 166f.; J. A. Miles, "Radical Editing: *Redaktionsgeschichte* and the Aesthetic of Willed Confusion," in *Traditions in Transformation: Turning Points in Biblical Faith* (*Festschrift* F. M. Cross; ed. B. Halpern and J. D. Levenson; Winona Lake, IN: Eisenbrauns, 1981) 9-31.

As a first step toward illustrating this principle, the present study examines the editing of J together with P in the flood story. The question is, which choices did the editor make, and what alternatives did he reject. The first presupposition for the purposes of this analysis is that, confronted with two sources, JE and P, R$_{JEP}$ elected not to alter the internal order of either source. That is, the words of each source, though now interspersed among the words of the other, appear in the same order in the combined text as they did in the original. As it happens, this principle vindicates itself not just in the account of the flood but repeatedly, throughout the corpus of the Pentateuch, wherever JE is combined with P.

The second presupposition underlying this study is that R$_{JEP}$ did not suppress any substantial proportion of either text, and, indeed, attempted to preserve each text, interspersed with the other, intact. The operation of this principle is more or less evident in cases like that of the creation accounts, where R$_{JEP}$ juxtaposes separate intact episodes from JE and from P, without integrating them verse by verse. It is attenuated in some cases, particularly involving the introduction of direct discourse.[5] Where such suppression was unnecessary, however, R$_{JEP}$ seems to have avoided it.

$$*   *   *   *   *$$

The editor of the flood story, by a long-standing consensus, inherited two sources on the subject. For the first time in the course of the Genesis narrative, the editor determined that it was impossible to treat these sources as relating two separate events. The flood, then, had to be treated as a singleton, as a single event to which both sources (JE, P) testified equally. The sources begin as follows:

J	Chapter 6	P
1) When humankind began to multiply		
on the face of the earth, and daughters		
were born to them, 2) the sons of god		

---

5. For example, in Num 13:1ff., part of the J introduction has been lost or integrated with the P rubric in 13:1-2. The Deuteronomic retelling (1:19ff.) suggests the possibility of a J original that differed substantially from P. In that case, we should have expected the popular request for reconnaissance posited in Deuteronomy to have preceded Num 13:1. It seems more likely, therefore, that Deuteronomy here is innovating, but the matter could be better decided by a study of Deuteronomic use of tetrateuchal terminology. In Num 13:26, however, one must posit a J original running something on the lines of *wylkw 'l mšh qdšh wyšybw 'th dbr wyr'wm 't pry h'rṣ*, and a P original along the lines of *wyb'w 'l mšh w'l 'hrn w'l kl 'dt bny yśr'l 'l mdbr p'rn*. The combination conflates the versions: J italic, P roman, joint J and P in uppercase: *They went* and they came TO MOSES and to Aaron and to all the congregation of the children of Israel to the wilderness of Paran *at Qadesh and they reported and showed them the fruit of the land*. Eliminating "to Moses" from one source enables the recensionist to avoid relating the event as though it occurred twice.

saw the daughters of humankind, that they were good, and they took them as wives from all that they chose. 3) And Yhwh said, "My spirit will not abide in humankind forever, since he too is flesh, and his days will be one hundred and twenty years." 4) The Nephilim were in the land in those days, and also afterward, when the sons of god came unto the daughters of humankind they bore to them; those are the heroes that were from of aye, men of repute. 5) Yhwh saw that the evil of humankind was great in the land, and all the inclination of the thoughts of his mind were only evil all day long. 6) And Yhwh regretted that he had made humans in the land, and it pained him in his mind. 7) And Yhwh said, "I will erase the humans whom I created from on the face of the earth, from human to beast to crawling thing to the bird of the heavens, for I regret that I made them." 8) But Noah found favor in the eyes of Yhwh.

9) These are the generations of Noah. Noah was a righteous man, unblemished in his genealogy; with God Noah went about. 10) Noah begot three sons: Shem, Ham, and Japheth. 11) And the land was corrupted in the sight of God, and the land was filled with violence. 12) And God saw the land, and lo, it was corrupted, for all flesh had corrupted its way upon the land.

Immediately following this segment, in P (6:13), Yhwh announces the end of the world to Noah. It follows, on the principles enunciated at the start of this treatment, that R$_{JEP}$ could locate vv. 9-12 no later in the course of the narrative than he has done. The direct discourse introduced in v. 13 continues until v. 21. As a narrative statement, vv. 5-6 could not be introduced in any break in the direct discourse: beyond breaking the direct discourse, this would imply that Yhwh spoke to Noah before he had finished "seeing" (vv. 5, 12). Verses 7-8 or v. 8 alone could have been introduced after v. 16, had 7:1 been moved to a position before 6:18. This entailed other editorial problems, however (see below).

Within 6:1-12, several editorial alternatives beckoned, and were eschewed. Verses 9-10 could have been moved to a position before 6:1; that would entail retaining the repetition within two verses of 5:32 and 6:10, a situation R$_{JEP}$ chose to live with at 11:26-27. Even moving 6:9 alone to the start of the episode was avoided. The beginning of 6:1 was probably taken to interrupt the temporal sequence established by P in chap. 5, bringing the reader up to Noah. In short, R$_{JEP}$ analyzed 6:1-4 as action that occurred up to and in the time of Noah, not exclusively after his birth.

Why did R$_{JEP}$, however, choose to locate 6:9-10 after 6:8? Five possibilities represent a range of reasonable alternatives here: (1) 6:9-12, 5-8; (2) 6:9-10, 5-7, 11-12, 8; (3) 6:5-6, 9-12, 7-8; (4) 6:5-6, 9-11, 7, 12, 8; (5) 6:5-7, 9-10, 8, 11-12. In the first, and probably most reasonable, case, the text would introduce Noah and his sons, state that the land was, objectively, corrupted, and note the god's observation of the sorry condition of "all flesh." At that juncture, the text would note Yhwh's observation of the great evil of humanity, the regret this occasioned in him, and his resolution to wipe out all life. The section would end, "But Noah found favor in Yhwh's eyes," leading to the speech of the god to Noah.

Were the second alternative adopted, the text would introduce Noah and his sons, then relate Yhwh's observation of human evil, the regret this occasioned, and Yhwh's resolution to wipe out all life. It would state that the land was corrupt, that the god saw the corruption of "all flesh," ending, "But Noah found favor in Yhwh's eyes."

The third alternative leaves a text that relates Yhwh's observation of human iniquity and the regret this occasioned. It would introduce Noah and his sons, state that the land was corrupted, and note that the god saw the corruption of "all flesh." It would then relate Yhwh's resolution to eradicate life, ending, "But Noah found favor in Yhwh's eyes."

The fourth alternative relates Yhwh's observation of human iniquity and the regret this occasioned, introduces Noah and his sons, and states that the land was corrupted, that Yhwh resolved to end all life, and that the god observed that "all flesh" was corrupt, ending, "But Noah found favor in Yhwh's eyes."

The fifth version relates Yhwh's observation of human iniquity and the regret this occasioned, introduces Noah and his sons, notes that Noah found favor in Yhwh's eyes, and relates that the land was corrupt and that the god took note of the corruption of "all flesh."

Now, since in net content the five alternatives are identical, the decision to order the verses as they are now ordered was to an extent an aesthetic one. It merits observation, however, that the present order preserves the largest possible blocks of text from each source (6:1-8; 6:9-22). It also preserves some of the narrative strategy of each source: J begins by introducing the evil of humanity and introduces Noah *after* Yhwh has resolved to destroy the earth; P, however, first introduces Noah, and only then relates why, and in direct discourse (6:9-21), that, Yhwh will destroy the world. Placed back to back in the opposite order (P, then J;

alternative 1), the two accounts would create a frame focused on Noah (6:9-10; 6:8), with two verses about Yhwh's looking in the center (6:12, 5). That latter repetition may have troubled the redactor, whereas the central block concerning Noah (vv. 8-10) merely reduplicates the original order of P (5:32; 6:9-10) in which Noah was introduced before the *tôlĕdôt* formula was used. In a sense, then, 6:8 in the present version is used as a resumption of 5:32: everything in 6:1-7 has been narrated out of its proper chronological sequence. 6:8 brings the narrative up to the present reached at the end of chap. 5.

The next segment of narrative offers much the same sort of choices as that which went before. The sources are as follows:

J	P
	13) God said to Noah, "The end of all flesh has come before me, for the land is filled with violence from before them, and I will slaughter them with the land. 14) Make yourself an ark of gopher wood, compartmentally shall you make the ark, and pitch it inside and outside with pitch. 15) This is how you shall make it: 300 cubits is the length of the ark, 50 cubits is its width, and 30 cubits is its height. 16) You shall make a roof for the ark and finish it a cubit thick from the top, and you shall make a doorway for the ark in its side — lower, second, and third levels you shall make.
	17) "And as for me, I will bring the flood, water on the land, to destroy all flesh that has the breath of life in it from under the heavens, all that is on the land will expire. 18) I will establish my covenant with you, and you will enter the ark, you and your sons and your wife and the wives of your sons. 19) And of all that lives, of all flesh two of each you shall bring to the ark to keep them alive with you; male and female will they be. 20) Of the fowl, by its type, and of the cattle, by its type, of all that crawls on the earth by its type, two of each will come to you to be kept alive. 21) And as

7:1 Yhwh said to Noah, "Enter, you and all your house, into the ark, for you I have seen as righteous before me in this generation. 2) Of all the pure beasts, take for yourself seven and seven, a man and his wife, and of the beasts that are not pure, two, a man and his wife. 3) Also from the birds of the heavens seven and seven, male and female, to maintain seed on the face of all the earth. 4) For in another seven days, I shall rain down on the earth forty days and forty nights, and shall efface all the growth that I made from on the face of the earth." 5) And Noah did according to all that Yhwh commanded him.

7) And Noah and his sons and wife and the wives of his son entered the ark from before the waters of the flood.

10) And in seven days, the waters of the flood were on the land.

12) The rain was on the land forty days and forty nights.

for you, take with you all the food that will be eaten, and gather it unto you, and let it be food for you and them." 22) And Noah did according to all that God commanded him, so he did.

6) Noah was six hundred years old, and the flood was water on the land.

8) Of the pure beasts and of the beasts that were not pure, and of the birds and everything that crawls on the earth, 9) two by two they came to Noah to the ark, male and female, according as God had commanded Noah.

11) In the six hundredth year of Noah's life, in the second month on the seventeenth day, on this day all the fountains of the great deep were cleft and the windows of the heavens were opened.

13) In the midst of this day, Noah, and Shem and Ham and Japheth, Noah's sons, entered the ark, and Noah's wife and the three wives of his sons with them. 14) They and all the animals by their types and all the beasts by their

types and all the crawlers that crawl on
the land by their types and all the fowl
by their types, every bird, every winged
thing. 15) They came to Noah two by
two of all the flesh in which there is the
breath of life. 16) Those who came
were male and female, of all flesh they
came as Yhwh had commanded him.

16) And Yhwh closed him inside.

It would have been possible for R$_{JEP}$ to locate 6:7-8 after 6:16 (located
after 6:17, Yhwh's repeated resolution to end life on earth is intolerably repeti-
tious). In narrative voice, however, 6:8 would break the direct discourse of
6:13-21. As a result, the redactor could have moved 7:1a ("Yhwh said to Noah")
into the P speech to introduce a resumption of the direct discourse after the
break created by 6:8. But this would have entailed integrating the direct discourse of 7:1b-4 into the same speech. At the end of the combined direct
discourse, the ensuing text both in P and in J would be, "And Noah did according
to all that God/Yhwh commanded him." In other words, a strategy entailing
the movement of 7:1 into the body of the P speech in 6:13-21 would result in
a very awkward juxtaposition of 6:22 with 7:5.

By the same token, R$_{JEP}$ could have postponed inserting 6:8, "Noah found
favor in Yhwh's eyes," until just before 7:1. But the valence of that statement is
to the logic underlying Yhwh's electing Noah in the first place, an event that
takes place in 6:13. While removing it to after 6:22 would indicate that Noah
found favor in Yhwh's sight for executing Yhwh's commands, it would no longer
function, as it now does, as a reintroduction of Noah into the narrative before
the *tôlĕdôt* formula in 6:9. Moreover, the present order of the text, in this respect,
preserves the intention of the J source (6:8 explaining, in that source, why Yhwh
elected Noah).

In this respect, in 6:1–7:5, the redactor preserves insofar as possible the
thematic context of the text from each source. J's introduction of Noah and the
corruption of the world is followed by P's introduction. P's speech, then, in which
God instructs Noah to build the ark, precedes J's speech instructing Noah to enter
the ark. Whether the J text originally contained a set of instructions pertaining to
the ark is now indeterminate, though the general method of the editing — its
conservation of text — should incline one to doubt that possibility.

The command to Noah to enter the ark (J, 7:1b) could not precede, on
the rules of this exercise, 6:22, as it is only in 6:22 that the ark is in fact
constructed in P. It is again the case, however, that R allows J's complete speech
delivering instructions to Noah to finish before introducing the actual theme
of the flood's beginning. That is, 7:6 (P), which is the first indication that water
was present, could not be inserted into J's direct discourse (7:1-4) without a

means to reintroduce direct discourse (which does not follow in P). Moreover, 7:6 could not be inserted before J's speech, since it announces the start of the flood, which J, in 7:4, promises only seven days hence.

This problem nevertheless created obstacles to the combination of sources in 7:6-16. The P text announces the start of the flood (7:6) before describing Noah's entry into the ark (7:13-16). Yet the J text places Noah on board before the flood (7:7, 10). Furthermore, the J text, after Noah is on board, delays the flood for seven days (7:7, 10). This means that the earlier in the text 7:6 is placed, the more awkward the combination of the sources. At the same time, in keeping with P's presentation, in which the very day of Noah's entry into the ark is recorded (7:11, 13), the redactor chose to position the J boarding (7:7) *after* the notice of the flood's start (7:6). The fact that J claims that Noah and his family boarded "from before the waters of the flood" may have served as justification for this decision.

One of the alternatives to this strategy would have been an order such as 7:7, 10, 12, 6, 8-9, 11, 13-16, preserving the two blocks of J and P relatively intact. This yields a text that runs as follows:

> 7) Noah [et al.] entered the ark from before the waters of the flood. 10) In seven days the waters of the flood were on the land. 12) The rain was on the land forty days and forty nights. 6) Noah was six hundred years old and the flood was on the land. 8) Of the pure beasts [etc.], two by two they came to Noah to the ark. . . . 11) In the six hundredth year of Noah's life . . . all the fountains of the great deep were cleft. . . . 13) In the midst of this day, Noah [et al.] entered the ark. . . .

The problem of the double entry into the ark thus demands that R_{JEP} insert 7:6 ahead of 7:7, thus starting the flood before the boarding. Furthermore, placing 7:8-9 after 7:7 increases the space between 7:6 and 7:10. The latter text, in the framework of an already-begun flood, creates editorial difficulties — another sign of the redactor's conservatism with the inherited sources.

As the redacted text stands, however, despite these considerations, it can only be understood as achronological narrative, a genre familiar both in Mesopotamian and West Semitic literature, in particular from royal display inscriptions and related texts.[6] That is, the boarding of the ark actually occurs in 7:13. Verse 6 is a theme sentence, not a narrative: Noah was six hundred years old when the flood came. And 7:7-9 are the narrative exposition of 7:5. The sequence

---

6. See recently David Glatt, "Chronological Displacement in Biblical and Related Literatures" (Ph.D. diss., University of Pennsylvania, 1991); Baruch Halpern, "A Historiographic Commentary on Ezra 1–6: Achronological Narrative and Dual Chronology in Israelite Historiography," in *The Hebrew Bible and Its Interpreters* (ed. W. H. Propp, D. N. Freedman, and B. Halpern; Winona Lake, IN: Eisenbrauns, 1990) 81-142; also, on the Mesha stela, see K. A. D. Smelik, *Converting the Past* (Leiden: Brill, 1992) 73-83.

is: Noah did what Yhwh told him: he boarded the ark, and boarded the beasts. The notice that he was six hundred years old when the flood arrived (7:6) is out of place chronologically, just as it is in the P source alone, before 7:8-9.

Under the circumstances, the redactor may in fact be positing two boardings of the ark: the first in order to usher the animals in, and the second after seven days of making such arrangements. It is possible, too, to take a more radical view — given the boarding of the animals on the same day as Noah boarded in P (7:13-16), one could regard all of 7:7-9 as out of sequence. It is more likely, however, that the achronological element in this instance was intended by the redactor to be 7:14-16, repeating the assertion of the presence on the ark of all the specimens of the animal kingdom. In P itself, the beasts may come *to* the ark (7:8-9) before boarding it (7:14-16).[7] In the combined text, however, with Noah on the ark (7:7) to meet the animals, it seems that 7:14-16 includes the animals not in Noah's final boarding but in his and his family's presence on board. The alternative, that Noah boards the ark in 7:7 and that the animals gather outside in 7:8-9, is possible; but the implications of the phrase *bw' 'l*, almost invariably "enter unto,"[8] tell against it. Further, after 7:12, which explains that the rain lasted forty days, the notice that all boarded "in the midst of this day" — the seventeenth day of the second month (7:11) — is clearly jumping back in time. The implication is that 7:13-16 are all out of chronological sequence after 7:12 (or, conversely, that 7:12 is out of chronological sequence before 7:17).

In other respects, the redactor's latitude was severely restricted in this segment of the text. Verse 7 could conceivably have been located after 7:9 (after any smaller segment of 7:8-9 it would create grammatical awkwardness). If the redactor's rendition, with a double boarding to accommodate the animals, is correctly interpreted above, however, this alternative becomes impossible. Moreover, the double boarding is only emphasized by moving 7:7 closer to 7:13.

Verse 10a ("In seven days") could not be introduced after v. 11, since v. 11 stipulates the day on which the flood began. Verse 10b, "the waters of the flood were on the land," could again have been located in the middle of v. 11 (after "Noah's life," "on the seventeenth day," or "on this day"), or even after it. But it is difficult to see how any of these options would produce a more coherent narrative. Each of them involves further atomization of the sources. One element constricting R$_{JEP}$ was that 7:16c, "Yhwh closed him inside," came *after*, not before, 7:12 ("The rain was on the land forty days and forty nights"). This

---

7. The phrase *bw' 'l*, used in 7:9, almost invariably implies the crossing of a threshold of some sort — see n. 8. In P, however, in 7:8-9, Noah has not yet boarded the ark, so the "coming to Noah, to the ark" may well be coming into the presence of Noah and the ark, rather than boarding. The combined text, with Noah on the ark when this P segment is introduced, has a different implication.

8. See Halpern, *First Historians*, 70n.19.

meant that the idea of forty days of rain, essentially alien to the P presentation, could not on the hypotheses undergirding this discussion have been postponed until after the closing of the ark. The redactor could have postponed the notice of the forty-day downpour until after 7:16 — it would not improve matters at all to insert it inside the P block 7:13-16. But thematically it represented J's notice of the start of the flood, and thus cohered with P's 7:11. Further, as 7:14-16, and probably 7:13, were in R$_{JEP}$'s view out of chronological sequence, the placement of 7:12 before these verses is a signpost for the reader: after 7:16, this text would less effectively imply the achronological character of the verses in question.

The theme of the loading of the ark gives way to that of the raging flood with the content of 7:16 in both J (7:17) and P (7:19/7:20/7:21, 24). There is some doubt as to the actual source division in this segment, with some commentators assigning 7:17-20 as a block to J.[9] In either case, however, the description of the course of the flood follows the segment summarizing the boarding.

J	P
17) The flood was forty days on the land, and the waters increased and lifted the ark, and it rose above the land. 18) The waters prevailed and increased greatly on the land, and the ark went abroad on the face of the waters.	
	19) And the waters prevailed exceedingly on the land, and all the high mountains that are under the heavens were covered. 20) Fifteen cubits above the waters prevailed, and the mountains were covered. 21) And all flesh that moves on the land among the fowl and the cattle and the animals and all the creeping things that creep on the land expired.
22) All that had the breath of life in its nostrils,[10] of all that was on dry land, died. 23) And all the growth that was on the face of the earth was effaced, from human to cattle to crawling things to the fowl of the heavens, and they	

9. See the commentaries ad loc. and, e.g., Friedman, *Who Wrote*, 57.

10. Omit *rwḥ* with LXX. MT contains a double reading, whereas the original refers plainly to Gen 2:7.

were effaced from the earth, and Noah and those who were with him in the ark remained.

2b) And the rain was restrained from the heavens. 3) And the waters receded from on the land continuously.

6) And it was at the end of forty days that Noah opened the window of the ark which he had made.

24) And the waters prevailed on the land one hundred fifty days. 8:1) God remembered Noah and all the animals and all the cattle that were with him in the ark, and God passed a wind over the land and the waters subsided. 2) And the fountains of the deep and the windows of the heavens were stopped.

3b) And the waters abated at the end of one hundred fifty days. 4) The ark came to rest in the seventh month on the seventeenth day of the month atop the mountains of Urartu. 5) And the waters continually abated until the tenth month; in the tenth, on the first of the month, the peaks of the mountains appeared.

Were one to divide the sources such that J = 7:17-20 and P = 7:21, the redactor's choice in this segment would be very restricted. P's statement that all life was extinguished could not logically precede the description of the rising of the waters. Only when the mountains were covered (7:19-20) could all life have been ended (7:21, 22-23). On the source division presented here as well, the logic of the edition is reasonably clear. Verses 17-18 describe the waters lifting the ark, whereas vv. 19-20 describe the waters reaching the mountaintops. Thus v. 19 could not have been moved to a position before v. 17, nor, logically, before v. 18. It would have been possible to move v. 19a ("And the waters prevailed exceedingly on the land") to a position before v. 18b ("and the ark went abroad . . ."), but this would have involved immediate repetition of v. 18a. It would also have been possible to insert v. 19a ahead of v. 17, as a general introduction to this section of the episode. But the verbal sequence is: increased, prevailed and increased greatly, prevailed exceedingly, prevailed fifteen cubits above the mountains. Even if the sequence of adverbs is redactorial in some degree, and especially if it all derives from J, it progresses smartly in the present version.

Less clear, but still intelligible, is the editorial strategy in the succeeding segment. In 7:21, P relates that all flesh expired. In 7:22-23, J relates that all (animate) *life* ended. The list of animals in each case indicates that the referents are probably identical. In that instance, one would expect that the P verse (21) could have been integrated into the J sequence. But the P verse begins with a *yaqtul* verb, which is followed by a complex subject. By contrast, the J sequence begins with a subject, followed by a perfect verb. This is then resumed with a narrative *yaqtul* at the start of v. 23. It is possible that the redactor was more comfortable beginning the description of the destruction with the *yaqtul*. In addition, where the verbs *gwʿ* (v. 21) and *mwt* (v. 22) are juxtaposed by P elsewhere in pentateuchal narrative, they are found in the order in which they appear in the combined narrative here (25:8, 17; 35:29). Finally, again, R's choice is the one that preserves the integrity of a larger block of each source.

In both P and J, the narrative turns from the loss of life to the subsidence of the waters. The editor could conceivably have introduced 7:24 (P) earlier in the edition, either before 7:22 to mitigate the repetitive effect of that verse immediately after 7:21, or before 7:23, again to mitigate the repetitive effect of the sequence 7:21-23. Apparently, in the editor's mind, 7:24 cohered rather with 8:1ff., as the introduction to the winding down of the flood.

The course of 8:1-6 entailed a number of editorial choices. Plainly, R did not want to suggest that the rains stopped before God recalled Noah in v. 1 (P). Nor did he want to report that the waters receded (v. 3a, J) before the fountains of the deep and windows of the heavens were closed off (v. 2a, P). He could conceivably have inserted v. 2b (J) before 8:1b. But P portrays the wind of 8:1b as the instrument by which the active flooding was ended (i.e., v. 2a follows v. 1b rather than preceding it). Thus the best alternative to the present version was the insertion of v. 2b ahead of v. 2a: the rains stopped; the fountains and windows were stopped; and the waters receded. Yet in 7:10, 12, J had placed the waters of the flood on the land before the start of the rains. The redactor's choice at that juncture had been to deal with the fountains and windows before the rains: it is the opening of the fountains and windows that precipitates the rain, and thus here it is the closing of the fountains and windows that causes the rain to stop.

The waters had to recede (*šwb*, v. 3a) before they were so diminished (*ḥsr*, v. 3b) as to allow, first, the ark's hull to touch bottom, and then the high peaks to appear (8:4-5). Noah could have opened the ark's window at the end of forty days (8:6) at any time following the end of the rain — on the assumptions of this exercise, after 8:3a. Before 8:3b, the verse would report that as of the fortieth day after the rain stopped (as originally in J), Noah opened the window. Then at the end of one hundred fifty days, the ark will have come to rest (vv 3b-4). But the editor evidently understood the opening of the window in the context of the succeeding verses, in which Noah releases birds — that is, as a functional rather than chronologically commemorative element of the narrative. Indeed, it is again indicative of the editor's conservatism with the text that the specific date is not supplied.[11]

In the succeeding action, in both P and J, Noah sends out a bird, for which the opening of the ark's window (J, 8:6) was understood to be a preparation:

J	P
	8:7) And he dispatched the raven, and it went out, going out and returning until the waters dried up from on the land.
8:8) And he dispatched the dove from with him to see whether the waters had ebbed from on the face of the earth. 9) But the dove found no perch for the sole of her foot, and she returned to him, to the ark, for there was water on the face of all the land. And he sent forth his hand and took her, and brought her in to him into the ark. 10) And he waited again another seven days, and again dispatched the dove from the ark. 11) And the dove came to him at the time of the evening, and lo, there was an olive leaf torn off in her mouth; and Noah knew that the waters had ebbed from on the land. 12) And he waited again another seven days and he dispatched the dove, and she no longer returned to him again.	
	13a) And it was in the six hundred first year, in the first month, on the first of the month, that the waters dried up from on the land.
13b) And Noah removed the cover of the ark, and looked, and lo, the face of the earth was dry.	
	14) And in the second month, on the seventeenth day of the month, the land dried out.

Here, P's text about the raven could reasonably have been inserted after 8:8 or 8:11 as well as after 8:6 (after 8:12, the raven's reconnaissance would of

---

11. On P's assumption that the seventeenth day of the seventh month (8:4) is 150 days after (7:24; 8:3b) the seventeenth of the second month (7:11), Noah in the combined text will have opened the ark's window on the eleventh day of the eleventh month.

course be supererogatory). Apart from the fact that this interrupts the sequence (8:8-12) dealing with the dove, it also disrupts the internal chronology of the J material. As things stand, 8:10 now seems to imply retrospectively a hiatus of seven days between the dispatch of the raven and that of the dove. Indeed, one might suspect that either *ʿwd,* "again," or *'ḥrym,* "another," has been added in v. 10, under the influence of v. 12, to produce this implication. Even if so, this is a smaller editorial intervention (and not necessarily the work of R$_{JEP}$) than would be required to establish a time frame for 8:7 were it set into 8:8-12. The combined text has the implication that Noah tried, but essentially failed, to work with the raven, and then resorted to the dove, which did retrieve evidence of developments for him (8:11).

The P text in 8:13a, 14 posits a sequence in which the water drained back down into the earth, after which the soil itself dried out. Since a condition of the dove's not returning was the draining of the waters, 8:13 could conceivably have been located before 8:12b, "and she no longer returned to him again." In that position, however, the P notice would have been essentially parenthetical. Nor could 8:13 have been inserted before 8:12b, "and he sent forth the dove." In the present text, Noah presumably sends the dove out for the last time before the complete disappearance of the waters — and in the twelfth month of the year of the flood (8:6, 7, 10, 12). Moving up the chronological data of v. 13a would alter that circumstance. In other words, the editor's combination preserves the intention of the J text and the narrative function of the P text.

The redactor might have located 8:13b (J) before 8:13a (P). In that order, the P text would punctuate the J narrative: Noah saw that the face of the earth had dried; it was on such-and-such date that the waters dried from on the land. But the order of the verses now reflects the progression in P from surface water to wet soil. J's text in v. 13b focuses on the surface of the earth. So R's text relates the sequence in its "chronological" order: the surface water disappeared; then the "face of the earth," that is, the earth's surface, was dry, or seen to be dry; and, finally, the land itself dried out. The appeal of this sequence was apparently preferable to the alternative of relocating v. 13b later in the account, either after v. 14 or, where it would imply that Noah removed the ark's cover only on God's command, after v. 17. That is the latest that v. 13b could have been inserted, because in v. 18 the passengers disembark.

The editor could also have placed the removal of the ark's cover (the first part of v. 13b) before v. 13a; but without the introduction of Noah's name as the subject of the verb "and he looked" (v. 13b) after the interjection of v. 13a, v. 13a would again appear as a parenthetical rather than narrative remark. R's approach, in sum, minimizes changes to the literary character of his source texts. It may also be the case, as with the placement of v. 13b between vv. 13a and 14, that the editing reflects identification of and movement through discrete themes — the flooding, the destruction, the ebbing, Noah's checking, the drying of the land, and then disembarkation.

The final segment of combined text simply continues along the same lines:

J	P
	8:15) And God spoke to Noah, saying, 16) "Go out from the ark, you yourself and your wife and your sons and your sons' wives with you. 17) All the animals that are with you from all flesh among the fowl and among the cattle and among all the moving things that move upon the land take out with you[12] that they be fruitful and multiply on the earth." 18) And Noah went out, and his sons and his wife and his sons' wives with him. 19) All the animals, all the moving things and all the fowl, all that moves on the land according to their kinds, went out from the ark.
20) And Noah built an altar for Yhwh and took from all the pure cattle and from all the pure fowl and he offered burnt offerings on the altar. 21) And Yhwh smelled the sweet savor, and Yhwh said to himself, "No longer shall I curse the earth any more because of humans, because the inclination of humans' heart is wicked from their youth, nor shall I any longer smite all living things again as I have done. 22) Henceforth all the days of the land, seedtime and harvest, and cold and heat, and summer and winter, and day and night shall not cease."	
	9:1) And God blessed Noah and his sons, and said to them, "Be fruitful and multiply and fill the earth. . . . 7) And as for you, be fruitful and multiply and swarm in the land and dominate it."[13] 8) And God said to Noah and to his sons with him, 9) "And as for me, lo, I am erecting my covenant with you and

12. Read with LXX.
13. For MT *rbw,* read *rdw* with LXX and Gen 1:28.

with your seed after you. . . . 11) I will erect my covenant with you and all flesh will never more be cut off by the waters of the flood, and there will be no more flood to destroy the land." 12) And God said, "This is the sign of the covenant that I am making between me and you and all living souls. . . . 15) I shall remember my covenant, which is between me and you and all living souls among all flesh, and the waters will never again be a flood to destroy all flesh. 16) And the bow will be in the cloud, and I shall see it, to remember the eternal covenant between God and all living souls among all flesh that is on the land." 17) And God said to Noah, "This is the sign of the covenant that I have erected between me and all flesh that is on the land."

On the assumptions governing this exercise, 8:15 and the succeeding verses could not be advanced earlier in the narrative because they follow a P text in 8:14. Thus it was not possible for God to tell Noah to leave the ark before the stage had been reached at which the soil itself had dried up. The redactor could have moved the building of the altar (8:20a) and even the offering of sacrifices (8:20b-21/22) up before 8:15, but it was likely inconceivable to him that the altar would be built anywhere but on solid ground. Under the circumstances, it was necessary for R to describe the disembarkation (8:15-19) before describing the sacrifice.

It would also have been possible for R to move the sacrifice further down in relation to the P text. Thus, 8:20 could easily have been inserted after 9:7, and even after 9:11 or 9:17. But the redactor had three incentives to locate it where it is. First, at the formal level, 8:21-22 describe Yhwh's resolution, his speech to himself. This resolution should logically be arrived at before Yhwh articulates it to Noah. Second, at the substantive level, God renews in 9:1ff. (P) the primordial instructions to humans to be fruitful, multiply, and fill the earth (1:28). Before extending this blessing, however, Yhwh must first annul the primordial curse, imposed on the expulsion from Eden, which inhibits the soil from producing (3:17-19). In other words, the decision to make the earth fertile again is a precondition of humanity's charge to multiply and fill it. Third, and finally, R has elected not to attach 8:21b-22 to the divine promise of 9:1ff. (e.g., 8:22b after 9:11 or 9:15, thematic equivalents in the P text; 8:22 after, say, 9:16).

The decision, whatever the other reasons for it, had the effect of preserving intact the complete text of the direct discourse in J. One might add, too, that in J the sacrifice is a stimulus to Yhwh's resolution, and in the absence of such a stimulus in P (who presents the new covenant as previously planned) belongs thematically at the outset of the section.

The remainder of the text is all P.

*   *   *   *   *

Detailed study of the editing of Genesis 6–9 reveals a number of properties. Thus, although the inconsistencies in the biblical account are well known, there is nothing either arbitrary or whimsical about the editing. It is consistently governed, rather, by attention to the narrative logic created by the combination of the sources. The first concern of the editor, thus, was to put together the smoothest possible story given the imperative to preserve both narrative sources insofar as possible, or even absolutely. Nothing in the biblical text of these chapters, in fact, makes it probable, as distinct from possible, that R subtracted from either source, or added text to the combination of sources. One might consider the absence of any record of the building of the ark in J perhaps the strongest evidence of such intervention; this may even be correct. But given the remark in 7:5 that Noah did as commanded, the most suppression one might legitimately posit is of a command closely parallel to that in 6:14a.

Within this overall principle, however, other considerations also operate. For the most part, preservation of the received sources is obviously a major concern. Were it not, the inconsistencies would not register as they do — for what would be easier than to maintain the distinction between impure and pure beasts, and J's differential preservation of them on the ark?

Over and over, too, the editor attempts to preserve the original context of each source's narration. More, the editing reflects a consistent concern with a sequence of events that keeps the text of each source inside the framework of an understanding — drawn from the source — of how the drama of the flood unfolded. The thematic approach explains a great many of the decisions that R made in combining J and P.

Related, no doubt, and also evident in many cases was R's desire to keep a maximal quantity of each source intact in the editing. Indeed, this extends to things like the individual speeches of characters such as Yhwh, even when they could have been atomized to promote increased integration of the sources and thus of the story. The editor's urge was to preserve the sense of the claims of the sources as he encountered them, and yet to furnish a combined account.

In general, all this amounts to a rather conservative editorial approach. No credence, thus, should accrue to source divisions that presuppose a random or illogical or uneconomical reintegration of the sources by R_{JEP}. The presumption of care on the part of R thus implies some control on the analysis of source division. If the combination of sources is governed by intelligible principles, then the divisions of sources we should entertain are severely curtailed: any reconstructed set of sources that could be combined in a way that is materially superior to what we find in the biblical text itself is suspect; for, if we can improve significantly on the editing of the sources while operating on the same principles as — or ones very similar to — those that governed R's editing, we infer not just our own superiority to R as an editor but our superiority to his colleagues and early transmitters. Yet there is no evidence whatever that R and his colleagues were in any way inferior to ourselves; indeed, the inference itself is more of an excuse not to penetrate intended meaning than an attempt to understand the coherence of the text laid before us. This is a lesson that those who insist on the illogicality of the ancients seem to need to learn over and over again.[14]

The editor's mentality is the key to reconstructing the substance of the separate sources. It looks conservative and logical on close examination. Any other hypothesis — and there have been many — demands justification, not just in terms of "seams" and "tension," but also in terms of why the editing took the form it did. Any source division that does not include detailed analysis of the editing of the sources is essentially uncontrolled. Furthermore, any source division that implies illogical editing should be disqualified. The dignity of the "poet" is a principal concern of intelligent students of antiquity: we must presume that our ancient authors' words merited transmission, spoke to their contemporaries, and possibly even challenge the intelligence of modern readers. The dignity of the editors should be approached, and preserved, at the same level.

14. See R. G. Collingwood, *An Autobiography* (Oxford: Oxford University, 1939) 64.

Tangled Plots in Genesis

RONALD S. HENDEL

Southern Methodist University, Dallas

τί . . . μυθολογεύω
"Why should I mythologize?"

Homer, *Odyssey* 12.450[1]

The narratives of Genesis have long exerted a powerful fascination. At once they are "those old but strangely simple stories" to which Kafka referred, stories whose interpretations each generation forgets and rediscovers.[2] They are also stories whose old/new interpretations are perennially contested, whether the hermeneutical key be historical, prophetic, allegorical, mystical, or (more recently) narratological. I hope to contest some recent interpretations of Genesis, albeit indirectly, by advancing a reading that joins together some of the forms of attention that have dominated late nineteenth- and late twentieth-century biblical scholarship.[3] The hermeneutical keys of my reading will involve concepts of plots and sources as they have been developed in literary and source criticism of biblical and other texts.

That nineteenth-century "literary criticism" is now called source criticism, and that modern literary criticism is something quite different is worth

---

1. On this interesting passage, see M. Detienne, *The Creation of Mythology* (Chicago: University of Chicago, 1986) 86.

2. F. Kafka, *Sämtliche Erzählungen* (ed. P. Raabe; Frankfurt-am-Main: Fischer, 1970) 390-91: "jener alten, doch eigentlich einfältigen Geschichten."

3. Cf. R. Rendtorff's recent, somewhat ironic suggestion ("The Paradigm Is Changing: Hopes — and Fears," *Biblical Interpretation* 1 [1992] 19-20): "we should try to relate new, mainly synchronic aspects, to older, mainly diachronic insights, for what was observed in careful studies during the last two centuries was not entirely wrong."

pondering, both for what is lost when only the "old" literary criticism is done, and for other things that are lost when the "new" literary criticism is done alone, in isolation from other interests. If ours is an era "after the New Criticism," as a thoughtful book by Frank Lentricchia observes, then biblical criticism lags behind.[4] In trying to read for the plots of Genesis, with an eye toward the "old" sources — J, E, and P — I am attempting to attend to the literary and historical dimensions of the text as they imply each other. My deeper claim is that these two dimensions are not at all distinct or separable. Perhaps it is our conventional compartmentalizing of history and literature as different disciplines that burdens us with this impression.[5] I hope to show that the history of a text and its literary performance signify each other, and that, moreover, our reception of the text shows the influences of these mutual significations.

It is a pleasure to dedicate this essay to David Noel Freedman, whose pursuit of new/old knowledge has been for me a real inspiration, and whose friendship and wisdom have helped to sustain me through curious times.

I. Concepts of Plot

In the recent inquiry into the nature of narrative plots, two works stand out: Frank Kermode's *The Sense of an Ending,* and Paul Ricoeur's *Time and Narrative.*[6] Both productions have been justly influential on modern literary theory, and both, in turn, are reflections and extensions of Aristotle's theory of poetics. Aristotle defined plot (which in his technical vocabulary he called μῦθος, "myth") as "the organization of events" (ἡ τῶν πραγμάτων σύστασις).[7] One important feature of this concept of plot is that the "organization" that a poet imparts to his or her text contrasts with the lack of organization (what Aristotle

---

4. F. Lentricchia, *After the New Criticism* (Chicago: University of Chicago, 1980); note that Lentricchia dates the "death" of New Criticism to 1957! See the insightful analysis of New Criticism influences on recent biblical criticism in J. Barton, *Reading the Old Testament: Method in Biblical Study* (London: Darton, Longman and Todd; Philadelphia: Westminster, 1984) 140-79.

5. Note, however, the recent ascent of New Historicism in literary studies, a movement with which biblical scholarship has yet to engage.

6. F. Kermode, *The Sense of an Ending: Studies in the Theory of Fiction* (Oxford: Oxford University, 1967); P. Ricoeur, *Time and Narrative* (trans. K. McLaughlin et al.; 3 vols.; Chicago: University of Chicago, 1984-88). I have also learned much from P. Brooks, *Reading for the Plot: Design and Intention in Narrative* (New York: Knopf, 1984). There is little on this topic in biblical scholarship; see, e.g., L. A. Turner, *Announcements of Plot in Genesis* (JSOTSup 96; Sheffield: JSOT, 1990); cf. my review in *CR* 5 (1992) 169-71.

7. Aristotle, *Poetics* 50a15. For comment, see S. Halliwell, *The Poetics of Aristotle: Translation and Commentary* (London: Duckworth, 1987), esp. 93-110.

calls "incompleteness") in the events of a person's everyday life. A well-constructed narrative creates a model of intelligibility, a concordance of beginnings, middles, and ends, that ordinary experience lacks. Stephen Halliwell aptly characterizes Aristotle's position: "Poetry must somehow make more sense than much of the raw material of life does, and this higher intelligibility is part and parcel of what Aristotle understands by unity."[8] Hence, in one of Aristotle's famous statements, poetry is more philosophical than history, since it speaks of the universal rather than the merely contingent or successive.[9]

Kermode extends Aristotle's concept of plot by dwelling on the differences between "complete" and "incomplete" in fictions and in human experience. Taking his cue from the poetry of Wallace Stevens, he attempts the program of that "More harassing master" who

> would extemporize
> Subtler, more urgent proof that the theory
> Of poetry is the theory of life.[10]

Kermode regards plots as "images of the grand temporal consonance" that make intelligible the mutual connections of beginnings, middles, and ends. Without the aid of plots, one would experience time as mere temporal succession. Fictional plots, in essence, "humanize . . . time by giving it form."[11] They transform our sense of "life as it is" by redefining the incompleteness of ordinary events through their incorporation into an overarching intelligible form. Plots transport our vantage point from the "middle" (i.e., where we are) to the "end," and from this new perspective allow us to see things as they may truly be. In Kermode's view, fictional plots suit our needs and may even "bless us"; they are ultimately necessary for our very existence. "It is not that we are connoisseurs of chaos, but that we are surrounded by it, and equipped for coexistence with it only by our fictive powers."[12]

The concept of peripeteia, "reversal," plays an important role in Kermode's (and Aristotle's) theory. After the initial situation is set at the beginning of a narrative, some sort of reversal or change necessarily occurs, which it is the function of the rest of the story to resolve. Only by reaching this final consonance does a plot achieve a temporal concord of beginnings, middles, and ends. The nature of the peripeteia is therefore key to the function of the plot:

> peripeteia depends on our confidence of the end; it is a disconfirmation followed by a consonance; the interest of having our expectations falsified is

8. Halliwell, *Poetics of Aristotle,* 103.
9. *Poetics,* 51b6-8.
10. Kermode, *Sense,* 155.
11. Ibid., 45.
12. Ibid., 64.

obviously related to our wish to reach the discovery or recognition by an unexpected and instructive route.[13]

The fascination of a story involves how it leads ("by an unexpected and instructive route") to a concordant ending, resolving the incursion of discord and dissonance. In this way the plot is seen as a mapping of concordance over contingence, of the "as" over the "is."

Paul Ricoeur pursues a similar mode of inquiry but with a somewhat different intent. Ricoeur is more confident than Kermode that plots do indeed reconfigure our sense of reality in a more than "fictive" way. Our texts do more than console; they also have the power to transfigure and to reveal.[14] Ricoeur argues that "'seeing-as,' which sums up the power of metaphor [and of narrative plots], could be the revealer of a 'being-as,' on the deepest ontological level."[15] The plot, which is the correlate of "narrative understanding," mediates between lived experience and discourse in the manner of "reflective judgment" (following Kant's terminology) such that time and the life-world of the reader are deepened and transformed. This process of narrative understanding has the power to redescribe reality by including the discordant within the concordant, thereby making sense of peripeteia of all kinds — including all that is "fearful and pitiable" (Aristotle's phrase) such as suffering and death. For Ricoeur, "time becomes human to the extent that it is organized after the manner of a narrative."[16] This redescription of the world by means of narrative plots is a permanent one, and effects a transformation in the way one lives.

Ricoeur also makes an instructive set of distinctions in the ways a narrative figures and reconfigures the world. He analyzes the "moment of mimesis" into three dialectically interrelated phases. The first (mimesis[1]) consists of the preunderstandings of temporality, the norms and values of personal actions, and the system of cultural symbols that are implicit in the interpersonal claims of narrative discourse. The second (mimesis[2]) consists of the narrative configuration itself, the creation of "concordant dissonance" that is the literary plot. The third (mimesis[3]) consists of the reception of the narrative by the reader, which effects a reconfiguration of the life-world. Hence, for Ricoeur, the narrative function is a "process by which the textual configuration mediates between the prefiguration of the practical field and its refiguration through the reception of the work."[17] Only by attending to all three dimensions of this process does one adequately grasp the transforming function of narrative.

Ricoeur's theory of plots as modes for the redescription of reality has a close relation to Kermode's theory of plots as necessary fictions. For Kermode,

13. Ibid., 18.
14. Ricoeur, *Time*, 2.26-28, and 3.177-79.
15. Ibid., 1.xi.
16. Ibid., 1.3.
17. Ibid., 1.53; see generally pp. 52-87.

the "as" and the "is" are continuously in tension, while for Ricoeur, the act of "seeing-as" can transform the "being" of a reader's life-world. For both, as for Aristotle, the artist is above all a creator of plots, which involves a perspective beyond life in the "middle." The teller of tales is akin to a prophet,[18] who perceives the pattern and ends that are intimated in the confused or contingent events of human experience.

These reflections on the nature and functions of narrative plots provide, as we will see, an instructive field from which to consider the varieties of plots in the narratives of Genesis.

II. Autonomy and Ambiguity (J)

ותרא האשה כי טוב העץ למאכל וכי תאוה הוא לעינים ונחמד[19] להשכיל

The woman saw that the tree was good for food and that it was pleasant to the sight and desirable to make one wise. (Gen 3:6)

In approaching the J narrative I must first extend a caveat. I will not be addressing directly the scholarly debate on the existence, extent, or chronology of the tetrateuchal or pentateuchal sources, a topic that has provided much light and heat in recent years.[20] I am persuaded by linguistic, textual, and literary evidence that the "old" sources — J, E, P, and D — provide the best and most credible way to comprehend the Pentateuch, though I expect that much needs to be done to clarify and refine our understanding.[21] Having identified my point of departure on this issue, I will turn to the narrative plots of the J text.[22]

---

18. Kermode, *Sense,* 83.

19. In MT העץ[2] is probably a secondary expansion; cf. LXX and Vulgate, and discussions in the commentaries.

20. See the survey of (mostly Continental) scholarship in A. de Pury and T. Römer, "Le Pentateuque en question. Position du problème et brève histoire de la recherche," in *Le Pentateuque en question* (ed. A. de Pury; Geneva: Labor et Fides, 1989) 9-80; compare the recent marshalling of evidence by R. E. Friedman, "Torah (Pentateuch)," *ABD* 6.605-22.

21. For apt criticisms of some recent textual models, see J. Emerton, "The Origin of the Promises to the Patriarchs in the Older Sources of the Book of Genesis," *VT* 32 (1982) 14-32; idem, "An Examination of Some Attempts to Defend the Unity of the Flood Narrative in Genesis," *VT* 37 (1987) 401-20; 38 (1988) 1-21; and idem, review of *The Making of the Pentateuch: A Methodological Study,* R. N. Whybray, *VT* 39 (1989) 110-16. On the textual and compositional evidence supporting the methodology of source criticism, see J. H. Tigay, ed., *Empirical Models for Biblical Criticism* (Philadelphia: University of Pennsylvania, 1985); and E. Tov, *Textual Criticism of the Hebrew Bible* (Minneapolis: Fortress, 1992) 313-49. For the linguistic evidence bearing on J, E, and P, see M. F. Rooker, "Ezekiel and the Typology of Biblical Hebrew," *HAR* 12 (1990) 133-55 and references; also my study, "Historical Linguistics and Source Criticism" (in progress).

22. So as not to be misconstrued, I define the *siglum* "J" (and similarly "E" and "P")

The Garden of Eden story, as the first of the J narratives, provides an important entry into the concept of plot in J. The peripeteia, which is key to the organization of the plot, occurs when the Woman, enticed by the Serpent, conceives a desire for the fruit forbidden by Yahweh and eats it, joined immediately thereafter by the Man. The crucial moment of conflicted desire is presented through the Woman's subjective impressions (related in third-person narration), as if we were seeing through her eyes (Gen 3:6, above). The subjectivity of this moment is sharpened by the objective or public speech that precedes (the dialogue with the Snake in vv. 1-5),[23] and the objective action that follows (the acts of taking, eating, and giving the fruit). In this moment of subjectivity we follow an ascending chain of desire, beginning with the physical appetite, then to the visual sense, and finally to the powers of mind. This ascending scale of appetites situates the woman as a complex being, at once animal, human, and (at least potentially) divine. The last appetite is only partially satisfied, for in the next presented moment of subjectivity, we see (again in the third person, through the "opened" eyes of the couple) only objective, physical nakedness, a type of perception, with its subjective response of shame, which seems distinctively human.

The story projects peripeteia within peripeteia as a consequence of this conflicted moment of desire. The act of disobedience (a characteristic human frailty) casts the humans irrevocably into the human condition. The curses and expulsion enacted by Yahweh extend and seal this entry into the human world. Yet a residue of ambiguity remains in the story. Yahweh admits publicly that the humans have become "like one of us, knowing good and evil" (3:22), and this serves as a rationale for the expulsion of humans from Eden, so that they will not become completely "one of us." (Note the equivocal nature of the simile: "*like* one of us," as it is at best partial and incomplete.) In sum, while the humans are at end irrevocably human, the ending of the story is also conditioned on the fact that they have become "like gods" with respect to their illicitly gained knowledge. Yet this knowledge has thus far revealed only a state of subjectivity: the personal knowledge of nakedness and shame. Is this knowledge "like the gods"? Surely not, or at least not entirely so.

---

in this essay as signifying a particular body of texts. I presume, by stylistic and other criteria, that a single author is responsible for the composition of most or all of these texts (with allowance for incorporated textual material and the subsequent work of redaction), but the mind of this author is not a matter of direct concern (or of direct access) to my inquiry. With regard to some of these issues, I find attractive Brooks's position on "intentionality" in narrative (*Reading,* xi): "Plot as I conceive it is the design and intention of narrative, what shapes a story and gives it a certain direction or intent of meaning." Hence intentionality can be defined as a function of textuality, thereby bracketing or suspending (at least temporarily) the extratextual problem of the author's mind.

23. See the perceptive reading of the rhetorical turns in this scene in H. C. White, *Narration and Discourse in the Book of Genesis* (Cambridge: Cambridge University, 1991) 130-35; for some caveats see my review in *CR* 6 (1993) 187-90.

This lack of closure in the ending of this story is illustrative of the nature of plot in J. The peripeteia is caused by human desire, and the reversal thrusts the protagonists into a zone of ambiguity that is never wholly resolved by Yahweh's interventions. In the J endings Yahweh often acts (though not always, and sometimes from offstage) to effect a final resolution, though commonly the humans resolve the crisis without direct divine aid.[24] The peripeteia involves repeatedly an ambiguity in the characters or their world, a deep dissonance that is never wholly overcome. In J's plots there is a relation between the autonomy of the characters — as seen here in the Woman's and Man's autonomous choices — and the resulting, residual ambiguity. J's plots — models of "concordant dissonance" — are marked by a dissonance that is never wholly included within the consonant. The narratives of J retain a lingering sense of the unresolved, and perhaps irresolvable, condition of things.

Many of the plots in J exemplify this dialectic of autonomy and ambiguity. Without lingering overlong on J (which is a desire difficult to resist), I would mention the senses of human autonomy and lingering ambiguity in the peripeteia and denouement of the following: Cain's fratricide (4:1-16); the wife-sister story of Abram and Sarai (12:10-20); the expulsion of Hagar (chap. 16); Jacob's deceptions of Esau (25:27-34) and Isaac (chap. 27); the rape of Dinah (chap. 34); Judah and Tamar (chap. 38); and (in Exodus) Moses' murder of the Egyptian (Exod 2:11-15).[25] Moreover, only in J (in the Pentateuch) does the dialectic of autonomy and ambiguity extend to Yahweh and the divine world. Abraham and Moses in separate incidents argue with Yahweh over moral principles, and in both cases Yahweh partially relents (Gen 18:22-33; Num 14:11-20).[26] In the Primeval Cycle of J, the sons of God and even Yahweh indulge what in retrospect are seen as immoderate desires. The sons of God conceive a desire for human women (Gen 6:1-4), and Yahweh intends the destruction of all humankind (6:5-7). The former tale ends with implicit disapproval (though incongruously directed at humans), while the latter ends with Yahweh's subjective reconciliation to human evil, a crucial moment in his own moral ascent.[27] The autonomy of the divine protagonist is evident in these and other J stories, as is a lingering sense of the ambiguous — or as Harold Bloom would say, the "uncanny"[28] — nature of Yahweh. J's plots

24. Examples of the latter include Gen 9:20-27 (curse of Canaan); 25:29-34 (Jacob's pottage); 26:1, 6-11 (second wife-sister story); 27:1-45 (deception of Isaac); chap. 34 (rape of Dinah); chap. 38 (Judah and Tamar); and others.

25. For discussion of some of these stories, see my "Is the Bible a Good Book?" *BRev* 7/3 (1991) 34-37, 46-50; and *The Epic of the Patriarch: The Jacob Cycle and the Narrative Traditions of Canaan and Israel* (HSM 42; Atlanta: Scholars, 1987) 83-86, 128-29, 145-48.

26. See D. N. Freedman, "Who Asks (or Tells) God to Repent?" *BRev* 1/4 (1985) 56-59.

27. On Gen 6:1-4, see my "Of Demigods and the Deluge," *JBL* 106 (1987) 13-26; on Yahweh's curious change of heart in the J flood story, see my remarks and references in "Genesis, Book of," *ABD* 2.939.

28. H. Bloom and D. Rosenberg, *The Book of J* (New York: Grove Weidenfeld, 1990) 279-306.

(and J's Yahweh) are endlessly fascinating, perhaps because they never achieve a perfect closure. They remain open and dissonant in a productive sense, such that much can be gathered from them.

III. Divine Redescriptions (E)

גם אנכי ידעתי כי בתם לבבך עשית זאת ואחשך גם אנכי אותך מחטו לי

Indeed, I know that you did this innocently, for it was I who prevented you from sinning against me. (Gen 20:6)

The nature of plot in E has, ironically, received more attention than that in J — ironically because the existence of E is more often contested. Yet the E narratives tend to attract literary attention, including most notably Erich Auerbach's classic discussion of representation in Genesis 22, Robert Alter's treatment of the themes of knowledge and recognition in (mostly E passages in) the Joseph story, and Sean McEvenue's analysis of E's thematics and style in Genesis 20–22.[29] I hope to complement and extend these discussions by attending to the concept of plot in E.

Ricoeur's proposal that plots function to redescribe or reconfigure a life-world (mimesis[3]) can be transposed into an apt model for E's concept of plot (as mimesis[2]). The consistent nature of the peripeteia and ending in E includes a "doubled" sense of action, exerted by the human and the divine (a complementary causality), in which God's will is ultimately perceived as the prime mover of both peripeteia and ending. McEvenue notes the importance of God's role in these plots when he observes (regarding Genesis 20–22) that "in each case it is God who causes the problem, setting up the tensions which are the essential motor of the story" and that "similarly, in the conclusions God intervenes with striking directness."[30] E's God is the force behind the plot, with variations on *when* and *to whom* the divine source of the plot is revealed.

The E wife-sister story of Genesis 20, which appears to be the first complete E narrative in Genesis, exemplifies this manner of plot. In this story, the ending (the final concord that resolves the dissonance) is revealed at the beginning, so that there will be no ambiguity for the reader concerning the divine intention that impels the plot. In essence, the narrative plot *is* God's will, and this revelation at the beginning serves to set matters straight, with no remainder. This strategy of emplotment serves to circumvent some of the moral ambiguities latent in the tale, such as are manifest in the J version of the

---

29. E. Auerbach, *Mimesis: The Representation of Reality in Western Literature* (Princeton: Princeton University, 1953) 3-23; R. Alter, *The Art of Biblical Narrative* (New York: Basic, 1981) 155-77; S. E. McEvenue, "The Elohist at Work," *ZAW* 96 (1984) 315-32.

30. McEvenue, "Elohist," 318-19.

wife-sister story (Gen 12:10-20). The sequence of events to which the story refers (the *histoire,* in the terminology of French narratology) is rearranged in the actual sequence of narration (the *récit*) in order that the divine control of the peripeteia be made explicit.[31]

As a function of this revelation of the end as near the beginning as possible, Genesis 20 begins with a minimalist sketch of the initial events (vv. 1-2), lacking explanation or context. In contrast, when God appears in a dream-revelation to Abimelech (v. 3), he initiates a voluble and heated dialogue. During this exchange God reveals that he knows already what has transpired, since he has already been active in them ("it was I who prevented you from sinning against me," v. 6; see above), unbeknownst to the characters. Here the reader and the antagonist learn simultaneously that the peripeteia does not pose a definitive crisis, since matters are already in God's hand. That God reveals this already at the beginning makes the divine control of things clear. Since this revelation of the plot's denouement precludes any real tension in the narration, the story settles down to recounting in detail (primarily through Abraham's speeches) the context and explanations of the initial events of vv. 1-2. The *récit* and the *histoire* finally coincide in the last verses of the E story,[32] where God's instructions in his dream-revelation are fulfilled by the characters' actions (restoration of Sarah, rewarding of Abraham, intercession and healing of Abimelech's household), thereby bringing a definitive closure to the story.

In differing degrees, this concept of plot operates throughout the E narratives. For example, Genesis 22, the binding of Isaac, also presents the revelation of God's intention at the beginning of the narration. The reader is told (though, necessarily in this case, not the protagonist) that "God tested Abraham" (v. 1). The reader is told already at the beginning that God is in control of the plot, not only by being the source of the peripeteia (the divine command in v. 2), but also by having its resolution in mind: that it is a test and not an actual desire for human sacrifice. The Kierkegaardian dilemmas of this story are not erased by recognizing the command as, in a sense, a "fictive" element in the plot, since Abraham remains unaware of this fact until the end. In revealing God's intention at the beginning, the narration guides the reader's perceptions through some of the turmoil that the command poses. The story ends with a perfect closure, as the test is completed successfully by Abraham, and he is granted his hard-won divine approbation.

The stories where there are J and E doublets display clearly the contrast between their respective concepts of plot. Without lingering to draw out the obvious contrasts, I would mention as perspicuous examples in Genesis the

---

31. On the distinction between *histoire* and *récit* (for which there are no obvious English equivalents), see Brooks, *Reading,* 12-14 and passim.

32. Verses 14-17. Note that v. 18 is an explanatory or redactional gloss; see the commentaries.

wife-sister stories (J: 12:10-20; 26:1, 6-11; E: chap. 20); the expulsion of Hagar (J: 16:1-14; E: 21:9-21); and Jacob's acquisition of Laban's flocks (J: 30:25-43; E: 31:4-13).[33] Other contrasts between J and E stories are also instructive, such as the wholly human machinations in the J story of Jacob's deception of his father (27:1-45) and E's account of God's dream-revelation and warning to Laban (at the beginning of the story) in Rachel's deception of her father (31:19-35; cf. the dream-revelation and warning to Abimelech in 20:3-7).[34] The opening of E's plague narrative in Exodus also reveals (to the reader and to the protagonist, Moses) that God's intentions will compel the entire plot: "Now you will see what I will do to Pharaoh, for by (my) great power he will let them go, and by (my) great power he will drive them from his land" (Exod 6:1).

The most spectacular revelation in E that God's will *is* the plot, that he has included (and, in an anticipatory sense, resolved) every moment of peripeteia in his divine intent, is the moment of final revelation in the Joseph story. Genesis 45:1-8 presents a scene of multiple revelations, since Joseph exposes not only his identity to his brothers but also the meaning of the plot. In this story (unlike chaps. 20 and 22), God's will is revealed to the reader (and to the antagonists) only at the end (cf. the similar end-recognition in 32:23-33).[35] In the complicated weave of deceptions, recognitions, and true and false knowledge in this story,[36] Joseph, who by God's power is the revealer of dreams (40:8), now reveals the divine meaning of the plot:

> Now do not be distressed or reproach yourselves because you sold me here, for God sent me here ahead of you to save lives. . . . Indeed, it was not you who sent me here, but God. (45:5, 8)

Joseph, the dreamer of true dreams and the true interpreter of dreams, here interprets the plot, thereby publicly revealing God's will. The human actions, which have seemed to occur merely sequentially, are now given their intelligible, God-given meaning. Retrospectively, for both readers and characters, the sequence of events is reconfigured and redescribed as the expression of God's intentions. Behind human contingency lies a divine will, which only a Joseph — or an E — can reveal. To seal his reading of the plot, when the brothers become fearful at the death of their father, Joseph rebukes them: "Do not fear! Am I a substitute for God?" (50:9). (Note Jacob's similar rebuke to Rachel in

---

33. See McEvenue's discussion of the distinctive styles of some of these doublets: "Elohist"; and idem, "A Comparison of Narrative Styles in the Hagar Stories," *Semeia* 3 (1975) 64-80.

34. On the thematic relationships between these two stories, see Hendel, *Epic*, 94-98.

35. Note that in Gen 32:31 we (and Jacob) perceive that God was the author of the crisis *and* the hard-won blessing in this curious tale.

36. See the illuminating reading of Alter, *Art*, 155-77; also perceptive on these matters is M. Sternberg, *The Poetics of Biblical Narrative* (Bloomington: University of Indiana, 1985) 285-308.

30:2 when she demands that he provide her with a child, thereby overruling God's plot.) Joseph recognizes that the plot is in the hand of God; to change the ending would be inconceivable for a God-fearing person (note the narratological significance in E of the protagonist's "fear of God").[37] In E, humans act as they can, but are emphatically not the ones who can resolve the peripeteia.[38] E's narratives reach closure when the divine intention is fully revealed and fulfilled.

IV. Metahistorical Plots

וירא אלהים את כל אשר עשה והנה טוב מאד

God saw that everything he had made was very good. (Gen 1:31)

In P, as in E, God is the author of the plot, but the concept of plot in P is quite different from that in E. McEvenue touches on the different narratologies of E and P in a brief but astute comparison:

> Whereas the Elohist is writing a dynamic story with real interaction, the Priestly Writer has characters without personal interiorities and a history without dynamism. It is rather a set of paradigms than an unfolding drama, a static image rather than moving story.[39]

This description is perceptive, as far as it goes. I would add that the P narrative has a different sort of dynamism,[40] one that operates metahistorically, as it were, beyond the obvious temporality of events. P's plots, which seem "a set of paradigms," have their endings embedded in other beginnings and other

---

37. Attributed directly or indirectly to most of E's protagonists; see recently McEvenue, "Elohist," 320-21; J. Vermeylen, "Les premières étapes littéraires de la formation du Pentateuque," in de Pury, ed., *Le Pentateuque,* 151-54; A. W. Jenks, "Elohist," *ABD* 2.480.

38. It is interesting to compare this doubled level of action and causality in E and D. The narration of double causality has been often noted in D (see B. Halpern, *The First Historians: The Hebrew Bible and History* [San Francisco: Harper & Row, 1988] 232-35); this tendency may be one of the many shared traits of E and D. See generally M. Weinfeld, *Deuteronomy and the Deuteronomistic School* (Oxford: Clarendon, 1972) 456 (s.v. "Elohist").

39. McEvenue, "Elohist," 319; see also idem, *The Narrative Style of the Priestly Writer* (AnBib 50; Rome: Biblical Institute, 1971).

40. I should note that, with regard to the P source, I am persuaded by R. E. Friedman's arguments (modifying those of F. M. Cross) that there is a compositionally distinct P narrative *and* a Priestly (or P-oriented) redaction of JEP (hence P, or alternately Pg, and, from a later hand, R^JEP). For the arguments, see Friedman, *The Exile and Biblical Narrative: The Formation of the Deuteronomistic and Priestly Works* (HSM 22; Chico, CA: Scholars, 1981) 44-132; idem, "Torah," 617-18; see also J. Emerton, "The Priestly Writer in Genesis," *JTS* 39 (1988) 381-400.

endings in a remarkable weave of intertextuality. This intertextuality is ponder-
ous and repetitive at times, but that may be a necessary dimension of its
deliberative style. In P the concept of plot transcends and serializes time such
that each significant moment resumes a previous moment in the plot, creating
a metahistory whose ends are hidden in its beginnings.

The final moment of divine recognition in Genesis 1 provides a point of
departure for our exploration of P's concept of plot. God "sees" or "perceives"
that "everything he had made was very good" (1:31; see above). A closure —
implying moral and physical completeness — is pronounced here for the
sequence of creation ("completed" is a *Leitwort* in 2:1-2), with the closure sealed
by a last holy thing — the seventh day — which God blesses and makes holy
(2:2-3). Commentators have noted a curious hesitation in this last event, which
seems to create a gap in the pattern of creation. In 2:2-3 the seventh day is not
explicitly called the Sabbath, though the verbs וישבת (2:2) and שבת (2:3) make
this identification implicit. Some scholars have even argued that there is no
reference here to the Sabbath, since God separately institutes the Sabbath in
Exod 31:12-17.[41] This aporia in the ending of creation is, I suggest, an initial
clue to the metahistorical plot of P.

P's metaplot is organized by intertextual references, in which significant
moments are linked together in a serialized or periodized concord. In the
metahistorical plot of P the seeming closure of creation is opened up by the
next narrative beginning (the P flood story in Genesis 6–9), creating a peripeteia
that will be resolved only at Mount Sinai. The P flood story begins with a divine
recognition that pointedly reverses God's perception of creation in 1:31. In this
new moment of perception "God saw that the earth was corrupt" (6:12). The
syntax and diction make the plot reversal emphatic; both 1:31 and 6:12 share
the clause structure: . . . והנה . . . את אלהים וירא. Only Gen 1:31, 6:12, and
Exod 39:43 (all P; on the last verse see below) share this unusual syntax (with
הנה instead of כי to signal the second object of the verb of perception).[42] This
is a serious change in P: the created world, once perceived as wholly good, is
now perceived as wholly corrupt. This perception signals the larger peripeteia
in P's plot. The initially good cosmos is now recognized as having gone bad.

As a first conclusion of this peripeteia, the P flood story ends in Gen 9:1-17
with God entering into an "eternal covenant" with Noah, his descendants, and
all living creatures. God proclaims the rainbow as its perceptible "sign." This
initial conclusion begins a chain of three covenants in P.[43] As is characteristic

41. N. A. Andreasen, *The Old Testament Sabbath: A Tradition-Historical Investigation*
(SBLDS 7; Missoula, MT: SBL, 1972) 184-85, 193-94, and references.

42. On this syntax, see P. Joüon and T. Muraoka, *A Grammar of Biblical Hebrew* (Rome:
Biblical Institute, 1991) §§157d, 177i; B. K. Waltke and M. O'Connor, *An Introduction to
Biblical Hebrew Syntax* (Winona Lake, IN: Eisenbrauns, 1990) §38.8d.

43. On the following, see F. M. Cross, *Canaanite Myth and Hebrew Epic* (Cambridge:
Harvard University, 1973) 295-300; N. Lohfink, "Die Priesterschrift und die Geschichte," in

of God's presence in P, these covenants are narrated almost entirely by divine monologues. The second covenant, with Abraham in Genesis 17, echoes the diction of the Noachic covenant, and makes its extension more precise by creating a bond with a single people. The revelation of a new divine name, El Shadday, the repetition of covenant terminology, and the announcement of the "sign" of this covenant all mark this as a significant step in P's intertextual plot.

The sequence of covenants culminates in the P account of the covenant at Mount Sinai. Significantly (since this is P's climax), the intertextual markers of this third covenant are spread out across a mass of texts in Exodus. The key intertextual moments in P's covenant are related in Exod 6:2-8, 31:12-17, and 39:32–40:34. In the first of these texts God reveals to Moses his true divine name, Yahweh, and recalls and expands his covenant promises.[44] Notably, the "sign" of this covenant is not announced in this text, intimating that this covenant scene is not yet complete.

The "sign" is at last revealed in the Sabbath command of Exod 31:12-17, which is, significantly, the final command in the P divine discourse at Sinai. In this last command the twin aporia of Exodus 6 *and* Gen 2:1-2 are resolved. In this moment of closure, the themes of creation and covenant are joined together, each signaling the other as complete.[45] God commands that the Israelites observe the Sabbath as a "sign" of the Sinai covenant, and he recounts his rest on the seventh day of creation as his divine warrant (Exod 31:12-17; note the כי clause in v. 17). The Sabbath command at the end of the divine discourse at Sinai in essence completes the account of God's work of creation in Gen 1:1–2:4. Now there is a "holy" people who will share God's rest on the "holy" day (compare the diction of "making holy" in Exod 31:13 and Gen 2:3). The Sabbath command, and Israel's Sabbath performance, resumes and completes God's rest at creation and completes also the stipulations of the Sinai covenant, providing for each its definitive "sign."

The next serialized moment of completion in P's plot occurs in Exodus 39–40, with the completion and dedication of the tabernacle. This scene fulfills God's intention to dwell among the Israelites, to "tabernacle" among them as their God (note the movement of God's כבוד to the tabernacle in 40:34, and the divine intention expressed in 25:8 and 29:43-46).[46] Moreover, as several commentators have noted, the completion of the place where God's כבוד dwells

Lohfink, *Studien zum Pentateuch* (Stuttgart: Katholisches Bibelwerk, 1988) 213-53; and most recently, W. R. Garr, "The Grammar and Interpretation of Exodus 6:3," *JBL* 111 (1992) 398-408.

44. On this text, see esp. Garr, "Grammar and Interpretation."

45. Cf. J. Levenson, *Creation and the Persistence of Evil* (San Francisco: Harper & Row, 1988) 100-27.

46. Cross, *Canaanite Myth*, 298-300, 313-14. Cross (318-20) also points to another end-scene for the Sinai covenant in Lev 26, the conclusion of the Holiness Code (H), which echoes key aspects of P diction (note Lev 26:9, 11-13, 46).

on earth also signals a resumption and new conclusion to the story of creation.[47]
These last two chapters of Exodus have numerous textual allusions to the first
two chapters of Genesis. To cite only a sample of these allusions in this densely
patterned scene: when Moses sees that the tabernacle and its accoutrements
have been made (his recognition of completion), the diction and syntax revert
to that of God's perception of the cosmos in 1:31 and 6:12 and to his blessing
to humans in 1:28:

וירא משה את כל המלאכה והנה עשו אתה... ויברך אתם משה

Moses saw that they had done all the work . . . and Moses blessed them.
(Exod 39:43)

The narrative of the Israelites' completion of the tabernacle echoes God's completion of the cosmos and his divine blessing. A complementary moment of
intertextual allusion occurs at the end of this text, which states that "Moses
completed [all] the work" (ויכל משה את [כל] המלאכה),[48] at which moment
Yahweh's כבוד enters the tabernacle (Exod 40:33). This dramatic conclusion
verbally echoes God's completion of his work of creation in Gen 2:2.

The completion of the tabernacle (which in P is a proleptic model of the
temple)[49] and the crucial beginning of God's "tabernacling" among the Israelites
brings a closure to God's creation of a harmonious and "good" cosmos in which
human and divine exist together. In this refiguration of creation, Israel is
covenanted as Yahweh's people, and, reciprocally (in P's covenantal diction),
Yahweh is their God. This dense closure to P's metahistorical plot occurs geographically at Mount Sinai and in the Israelite encampment (in the figuration
of the plot: mimesis^2), and recurs (in the refiguration of the world of the reader:
mimesis^3) in time every Sabbath and in space at the Temple Mount (and its
later typological analogues: house of study, church, synagogue).[50]

The nature of the plot in P, like that in J and E, is to provide a model of
temporal concordance in which dissonance is included and resolved. In P,
however, the model of temporality is, in an important sense, meta- or transhistorical. P's intertextuality is more than a series of allusions; rather, it serves
to structure the plot above or outside the ordinary relations of time, relating a

---

47. See M. Weinfeld, "Sabbath, Temple and the Enthronement of the Lord: The Problem of the Sitz im Leben of Genesis 1:1–2:3," in *Mélanges bibliques et orientaux en l'honneur
de M. Henri Cazelles* (ed. A. Caquot and M. Delcor; AOAT 212; Neukirchen-Vluyn: Neukirchener Verlag, 1981) 501-12; J. Blenkinsopp, *Prophecy and Canon: A Contribution to the Study
of Jewish Origins* (Notre Dame: University of Notre Dame, 1977) 59-67; C. Westermann,
Genesis (trans. John J. Scullion; 3 vols.; Continental Commentary; Minneapolis: Augsburg,
1984-86) 1.170; Levenson, *Creation*, 82-86.

48. Reading כל with LXX, Samaritan Pentateuch, and Vulgate; see the commentaries.

49. See the discussions cited in n. 47.

50. On the reciprocal thematics of Sabbath and temple, see again Levenson, *Creation*,
107-27.

serialized divine consonance of creation. Notably, P's God, like the plot, transcends ordinary temporality, hardly acting in the individual stories (as McEvenue notes, P's God is always initiating, never reacting),[51] more like a cosmic author weaving together the key scenes according to his metahistorical design.

V. Conclusions: The Reception of Plots

"[the angels who] reason'd high
Of Providence, Foreknowledge, Will, and Fate,
Fixt Fate, free will, foreknowledge absolute,
And found no end, in wand'ring mazes lost."
John Milton, *Paradise Lost* 2.557-61

In brief compass I have tried to describe the concepts of plot in Genesis, and have found that the three "old" narrative sources — J, E, and P — possess quite distinctive modes of emplotment. I have characterized these differences by phrases that I trust are not overly reductive: for the J plots a dialectic of autonomy and ambiguity; for E a divine redescription of human events; and for P a metahistorical plot that encompasses the individual stories (including, in the subsequent redaction, the other narrative sources).[52] If my descriptions are apt, there are a number of implications for our understanding of Genesis, some of which we can briefly explore here.

One strong implication is that the "new" literary criticism needs to engage more complexly with the "old" literary criticism (i.e., source criticism) and vice versa. A simple dismissal, such that one ought not to bother "unscrambling the omelette" (Edmund Leach's phrase, which has been often echoed),[53] will not do, since the plots — the modes of narrative understanding and concord — are distinctively plural. Genesis is more an elaborate feast, a banquet of texts, than a single egg dish, and our readings ought to respond to this complex interplay of narrative differences.

An example of how a reading attentive to the different plots of Genesis can advance our understanding concerns the age-old argument over determinism and free will in biblical narrative. Robert Alter, in a brilliant yet oversimplifying move, suggests that the dialectic between these two forces — God's

---

51. McEvenue, "Elohist," 319.

52. For this dimension of the text, see esp. R. E. Friedman, "Sacred Literature and Theology: The Redaction of Torah," in idem, ed., *The Creation of Sacred Literature: Composition and Redaction of the Biblical Text* (Berkeley: University of California, 1981) 25-34.

53. For example, R. Alter, *The World of Biblical Literature* (New York: Basic, 1992) 69, 163.

will vs. human freedom, or stated differently, God's plan vs. the disorderliness
of historical events — creates the prime motive for the biblical conception of
human nature: "it might be possible to say that the depth with which human
nature is imagined in the Bible is a function of its being conceived as caught in
the powerful interplay of this double dialectic between design and disorder,
providence and freedom."[54] This suggestion is illuminating, yet Alter proceeds
in a simplistic manner to rank the various books of the Bible according to their
position in the spectrum between these forces. Whereas Judges, Samuel, and
Kings are on the far side of disorder, and Esther on the far side of order, Genesis
would be "somewhere toward the middle of this spectrum . . . [with the] sense
of design repeatedly counterbalanced by the awareness of man's unruly nature."[55] Such may be an acceptable global or homogenizing reading of Genesis,
but a more nuanced reading of the text, one that responds to its narratological
complexity, would perceive that Genesis occupies not the median point but the
entire spectrum between design and disorder, providence and freedom. Among
the plots of J, E, and P are exemplars of fixed fate, free will, and foreknowledge,
in varying relations. The conceptual perspective on what constitutes the meaning of events varies significantly from text to text. To perceive that the texts that
we call J, E, and P are operating according to different narratologies, portraying
different conceptual worlds, can only enhance our reception of the Genesis
narratives.

   To illustrate this point more fully I would stress that the history of reception (the genealogy of mimesis[3] in Ricoeur's scheme) is filled with examples of
the effectiveness of the different plots of Genesis (and other biblical books). To
take a classic example from the argument between determinism and free will:
in the momentous sixteenth-century dispute between Martin Luther and Erasmus, Luther consistently cited texts from P and E (especially God's hardening
of Pharaoh's heart in Exodus 7–11) to prove his contention that "free will is a
downright lie" (note the title of his peroration: "On the Bondage of the Will").[56]
In contrast, Erasmus cited texts from J (especially Adam and Eve's free acts in
Genesis 3, and God's exhortation to Cain in Gen 4:7) to prove his defense of
free will.[57] Another position in this long argument, which in Western tradition
has tended to derive from the reception of different biblical plots, is that of the
rabbinic sage, Aqiba. According to the Mishnah, Aqiba is attributed with the
saying: "All is foreseen, yet freedom of choice is given."[58] Aqiba, it seems, was a

54. Alter, *Art,* 33.
   55. Ibid., 34.
   56. *Luther and Erasmus: Free Will and Salvation* (ed. E. G. Rupp and P. S. Watson; LCC
17; London: SCM, 1969) 219-63 ("Defense of Arguments Against Free Choice"), and esp.
223-31 ("The Hardening of Pharaoh's Heart").
   57. *Luther and Erasmus: Free Will and Salvation,* 47-55 ("Scripture Passages that Support Free Choice").
   58. *m. 'Abot* 3:19.

perceptive reader of biblical plots, able to hold J, E, and P (among others) together by a hermeneutics that embraced paradox. In brief, among Luther, Erasmus, and Aqiba one finds a sampling of historic voices for the different plots and their combinations in the pentateuchal narratives. The arguments among these interpreters — and among these plots — have a history of producing new understandings and new concords, and may continue to do so.[59]

Throughout recorded time humans have made pacts against chaos, negotiating the difficult clash between "as" and "is." Our plots may console, perhaps even transfigure, but they certainly endure. As a philosopher muses, "it is like a pair of glasses on our nose through which we see whatever we look at. It never occurs to us to take them off."[60] The plots of Genesis have long informed our understandings of these necessary concordances, without which we would scarcely be human. It seems, as Ricoeur notes, that human beings are "entangled in stories,"[61] not the least significant those of the Bible. If so, it may make sense to pay attention to their tangled plots.

---

59. On the importance of argument in the (logically and historically inevitable) clash of positive values, see I. Berlin, *The Crooked Timber of Humanity* (London: Murray, 1990) 1-19 and passim. Berlin's essay has obvious relevance for a theory of biblical plots and their reception, but a discussion must await another occasion.

60. L. Wittgenstein, *Philosophical Investigations* (2nd ed.; Oxford: Blackwell, 1958) 45, §103.

61. Ricoeur, *Time*, 1.75.

Why God Rejected Cain's Offering: The Obvious Answer*

GARY A. HERION

Hartwick College, Oneonta, New York

It may seem arrogant to subtitle an article, "The Obvious Answer." Indeed, if there remain any great unanswered questions in biblical studies, surely one of them has been: "Why did God reject Cain's offering?" If the answer to this question is obvious, why have scholars during the past two millennia not seen it?

One corollary of the claim that the answer is "obvious" is that *anyone* — and therefore *everyone* — can readily see it. I do not claim to have found the answer myself; I had to be shown the answer by a first-year student at Hartwick College who had no knowledge of Hebrew or any other technical aspect of biblical scholarship. During a typical small-group discussion, another student had just asked the familiar, age-old question: "Why did God reject Cain's offering?" My answer had certainly been typical of most professional scholars: "The text really does not tell us, and scholars have offered a multitude of answers, none of which has proved very satisfactory." Thereupon yet another student — rushing in where professional biblical scholars fear to tread (that is the wont of

*It is a pleasure to offer this paper to David Noel Freedman on the occasion of his seventieth birthday. Over the past eighteen years I have benefited enormously both personally and professionally from "sitting at his feet" as a graduate student and then sitting with him "at his desk" as his associate on the Anchor Bible Dictionary Project. I wish to thank Phil Schmitz and Jack Sasson for improving this paper by commenting on earlier and longer drafts. I am sure that it would be stronger had I the space and good sense to incorporate more of their suggestions. The remaining defects are my responsibility.

After this article was submitted I came across Frank Spina's important article, "The 'Ground' for Cain's Rejection: *'adamah* in the Context of Gen 1–11" (*ZAW* 104/3 [1992] 319-32), which reinforces the conclusions presented in this article.

undergraduate Bible students!) — said, "I thought it was because Cain offered produce from the ground, which in the preceding chapter had been cursed by God." And there is the answer. It is as obvious as that — and as simple as that.

In researching the matter of Cain's offering, I was delighted to encounter a haggadic tradition that shared this understanding (see n. 10 below). This confirmed my suspicion that the solution is indeed so obvious and simple that either an American high school graduate or a medieval Jewish exegete could apprehend it. What the two seem to have in common is simply a respect for the narrative quality of the biblical text — because indeed the answer as to why God rejected Cain's offering lies right on the surface of the text in passages such as Gen 3:17; 4:3-5; 8:21.[1] All one has to do is to look *at* the text.

This perhaps also helps to explain why the answer has eluded so many of us for so many centuries. Already two thousand years ago (if not earlier) a literary reading of this story had been abandoned for an essentially homiletical reading prompted by the desire to extract a moral lesson from the story (see n. 8 below). I suspect that the enigmatic character of Gen 4:7 has "teased" Bible readers over the centuries into looking for the answer in the wrong place (i.e., *outside* the narrative). By not stating outright the problem with Cain's offering, the verse seems to have become an invitation to obtain the answer directly from deity (i.e., through some "inspired" understanding of the religious tradition, whether Jewish or Christian). Both Jewish and Christian homilists reached the similar conclusion that Cain must have had some moral flaw — some impiety in his worship — that led to the rejection of his offering.

More recently, Western scholars have favored a supposedly "historical" reading desiring to uncover the factors that influenced the ancient Israelite writer's telling of the story.[2] In the last twenty-five years scholars have developed a growing respect for the literary character of biblical narratives, but in the case of the Cain-Abel story this has still not replaced the older and more familiar ways of viewing the rejection of Cain's offering. Even scholars with demonstrated literary sensitivities have, in a sense, held the answer in their hands and have failed to recognize it for what it was. For example, one scholar argued convincingly that literarily there are many linguistic (i.e., lexical) and thematic links between the Cain-Abel narrative and the Adam-Eve narrative. In cataloguing these, this scholar juxtaposed these two sentences:

> Cain also begins with an intimate relationship with the ground: He is a "tiller of the ground" (4:2) and brings to Yahweh an offering from the "fruit of the

---

1. One wonders whether Gen 3:17 has been excluded from consideration because it is demonstrably poetic rather than prosaic. Perhaps generations have assumed that narrative plot is not advanced within poetic passages.

2. Certainly the most well-known of these is the notion that God's rejection of Cain's offering reflects an anti-agrarian bias that was prevalent in ancient Israel at the time this story was written.

ground" (4:3). Due to Adam's offense the ground will be cursed, bearing
weeds along with produce and forcing him to toil in order to eat (3:17-19).

All the lexical and thematic elements needed to answer the question of why
God rejected Cain's offering are found in these two sentences — and yet there
they lie unnoticed.

It is not that we readers have for so long ignored the significance of the
ground being cursed. It is perhaps that our attention, inspired by 3:17-19, has
focused exclusively on the effect that the curse has had upon the ground and
upon those whose livelihood has depended on the ground. For us, the curse
has become primarily an etiology for the hard work of raising crops. In viewing
the curse in this way, we have glossed over the effect that the curse had on the
character who pronounced it — God. But once we are made aware of this
dimension of a curse, we are immediately reminded that what is accursed is,
by definition, considered abhorrent to God — and so, by extension, are its fruits.

I. The Man, the Soil, and the Geography of Eden (Gen 2:4b-24)

It is often noted that while the man and the beasts and the birds are formed from
the soil (hā'ădāmâ, 2:7, 19), the woman is formed from the rib of the man
(2:21-22). What is almost always overlooked, however, is how the qualities and
characteristics (or "status") of this soil change over the course of this and following
chapters.[3] The author goes to significant — even digressive — lengths in 2:5-6 to
underscore the pristine nature of the soil from which the man is formed. The soil
is pristine (or inert) precisely because it has not yet yielded any vegetation, and it
has not yet yielded any vegetation because God has not yet caused life-giving
moisture to descend on the earth. Consequently, the narrator notes explicitly that
God must breathe life into this man created from the inert ground.

By the time God creates the beasts and the birds (2:19), however, the soil
is no longer inert. God has already caused trees to "sprout up" from the soil
(2:9). Furthermore, God has planted a garden in Eden, although it is not clear
what connection this garden may (or may not) have with the soil (see further
below). Thus, when God finally gets around to forming the beasts and the birds
from "the soil" (hā'ădāmâ), it is no longer the same pristine and inert soil from
which the man had been formed earlier. As we shall see, the quality and characteristics (or status) of the soil (hā'ădāmâ) will change at least twice more in J's
primeval history.

3. "Soil" is a Leitwort (see Alter 1981:92-95) and thus has meaning beyond the simple
geomorphological and horticultural "dirt," "ground," or "soil" with which we are all familiar.
For that reason I have preferred simply to transliterate the Hebrew (hā)'ădāmâ in many
instances.

This chapter perhaps makes one other distinction. The narrator may be deliberately drawing a categorical distinction between *hā'ădāmâ* ("the soil") and *haggān* ("the garden [of Eden]"). Such a distinction, while certainly related to the common *qualitative* contrast often made between a mundane world and a perfect Paradise, may also have a distinctive *spatial* component. But in saying this, we should avoid the common tendency of interpreting "space" in terms of the usual norms of planar geography. "Space" as construed and handled in literary worlds need not conform to the topographical requirements of "space" as encountered in the actual physical world.[4]

Just as a digression in vv. 5-6 alerts the reader to the essentially pristine nature of the soil from which the man was formed, so again a parenthetical note (*miqqedem*, v. 8) and a digression (vv. 10-14) underscore the *spatial* uniqueness of this place. The author three times refers to spatial movement from *hā'ădāmâ* to *haggān* — first, in v. 8 (note the word *šām*, "there," which emphasizes spatial contrast) and then more explicitly in v. 15, where God "takes" the man and "sets him down" in the garden. The third reference to spatial movement occurs in v. 19, where God forms the animals from *hā'ădāmâ* and then "brings" them to the man now located in *haggān* (cf. 3:23). Therefore, in this narrative *haggān* spatially may not be a subset of *hā'ădāmâ* but rather a contrasting phenomenon and place.[5] If this is the case, then technically there is no *'ădāmâ* in the "garden of Eden," and *gan-'ēden* is not rooted in "the soil."[6]

A distinction between *hā'ădāmâ* and *haggān* may help to nuance an ancillary concept that will appear in the Cain and Abel narrative: "working [or tilling] the soil." As noted above, 2:5 is part of a digression in which the author provides important qualifying remarks. At the dawn of creation "there was no man to till *hā'ădāmâ*." Later, in 2:15, God transports the man from the untilled *'ădāmâ* to *haggān*, so that he can "till it [i.e., *haggān*] and care for it." In other words, tilling *haggān* may not necessarily be equivalent to tilling *hā'ădāmâ*. Therefore, throughout Genesis 2–3 *hā'ădāmâ* may remain untilled, a situation to which the reader was alerted as early as 2:5. Only in 3:23 is the reader perhaps

4. In other words, one must distinguish between physical space (i.e., geography, which is three-dimensional) and metaphysical space (i.e., mythology, which tends to be categorical). Cf. also the narrator's use of the word *miqqedem*. This word also has temporal connotations ("former times"), unlike *mizrāḥ (haš)šemeš*, which is entirely spatial. I would therefore translate it in 2:8 and 3:24 as "ancient [or legendary] Orient." See n. 18 below.

5. As we will see in Genesis 4, yet a third phenomenon/place will be introduced: "the land of Nod, beyond [out east of] Eden" (v. 16). This is where Cain resides after he is excluded both from *hā'ădāmâ* and, of course, from *haggān*. See nn. 7 and 18 below.

6. I suggest this despite the use of verbs like *nṭ'* ("to plant") and *'bd* ("to till") in connection with "the garden." Because it is a "garden" *(gan)*, it probably has soil-like characteristics in the mind of the narrator — but it still may be categorically distinct from that which is suggested by the *Leitwort hā'ădāmâ*. I therefore see a different emphasis here than does Kikawada (1987:202), who understands 2:15 to mean that the man is to till *hā'ădāmâ* in the garden.

finally informed that *hā'ădāmâ* will begin to be tilled; but, as we shall see, by then the status of *hā'ădāmâ* will have changed yet again.

II. The Fate of the Man and the Soil (Gen 3:17-24)

As God consigns the fates of the serpent, the woman, and the man (Gen 3:14-19), we note that the status of *hā'ădāmâ* is changed yet again. Now, it is cursed by God. I should point out the obvious, however: the garden of Eden *(haggān)* seems to remain exempt from and unaffected by this curse.[7] This may reinforce the suspicion that the garden has no integral connection with *hā'ădāmâ*: it is wholly other. Indeed, the man, upon dying, will return to *hā'ădāmâ*, and — perhaps for more than one reason — this cannot take place in *haggān*. Certainly it cannot take place in *haggān* because the tree of life, with its fruit for forestalling death, is accessible to everyone present in *haggān*. But perhaps the man cannot return to *hā'ădāmâ* while in the garden because there is no *'ădāmâ* in *haggān*. Thus, the man *must* be removed from *haggān* — and coincidentally from access to the tree of life — in order for the divine consignment of his fate to be realized. It would thus appear that he cannot return to *hā'ădāmâ* as long as he remains in *haggān* in part because there is no "soil" *('ădāmâ)* in the "garden" *(haggān)*.

The verses that follow the divine consigning of fates (esp. 3:23) are therefore noteworthy. Here, at last, we have the long-delayed note that *hā'ădāmâ* will finally be tilled. From 3:18 we may anticipate what that yield will be: not only wild herbs but also thorns and thistles. Consequently, it will take great toil and sweat to tend the former and to uproot the latter. Only now that the man leaves *haggān* will *hā'ădāmâ* finally be tilled.

Also noteworthy about 3:23 is the mention that the man is returning to the soil from which he had previously been taken.

> *wayĕšallĕḥehû YHWH 'ĕlōhîm miggan-'ēden la'ōbēd 'et-hā'ădāmâ 'ăšer luqqaḥ miššām*

7. Related to this is the (geophysically logical) question of whether Eden was submerged by the waters of Noah's flood, which covered "the face of *hā'ădāmâ*" (8:8). As far as I can tell, there is no explicit tradition about Eden having escaped the flood. But the imaginative equation of the garden of Eden with Jerusalem (esp. the Temple Mount) is itself already made in the Hebrew Bible (Levenson 1985:129ff., esp. 135), and there do exist rabbinic midrashim to the effect that Jerusalem was not submerged in the flood and that the dove brought to Noah an olive branch from the Mount of Olives in Jerusalem. Another midrash asserts that this olive branch came from the garden of Eden (*Lev. Rab.* 31:10; cf. *b. Qidd.* 69a-b). Although it remains an argument from silence, given a certain mythological mind-set one could conclude that the garden of Eden indeed escaped the ravages of Noah's flood.

So YHWH God sent him [i.e., the man] forth from the garden of Eden to till the soil from which he had been taken.

This verse harks back to several earlier verses, and seems to reverberate with two different levels of meaning. On the first (and perhaps weaker) level, it may reinforce the spatial distinction between "garden" and "soil" made in 2:8 (note the spatial use of *šām*, referring now to *hā'ǎdāmâ* rather than to *gan*) and particularly the spatial distinction made in 2:15 (note the verbal forms of *lqḥ* and the infinitive construct of *'bd* in both verses). At this level of meaning, the verbs in this passage (*šlḥ min-*, as well as *lqḥ*) emphasize God's action of transporting the man from one spatial location to another: God had previously taken the man away from *hā'ǎdāmâ* (out of which he had originally been formed) and had deposited him in *haggān*. Now, after the unfortunate series of events reported in 3:1-20, God reverses the direction of the movement, taking the man from *haggān* and depositing him on *hā'ǎdāmâ* from which he had previously been transported — a geographical "return" to the original place of departure.

On the second (and perhaps stronger) level, and more immediately, this verse harks back to 3:19, where the concept of *luqqaḥ min-hā'ǎdāmâ* ("being taken from the soil") suggests God's prior action of forming the man "using dust [*'āpār*] from the soil [*hā'ǎdāmâ*]" (2:7). This reminds us that *'ǎdāmâ* and *'āpār* are not simply geographical places of departure but are more fundamentally existential states of origin, and the idea of "returning" (Heb. *šwb* in 3:19) does not mean a reversal of direction (i.e., "destination") as much as an existential reversion to the primal "stuff" from which the body was originally composed (i.e., "destiny," the decay of the corpse).

In short, in the garden the man was not only spatially removed from his place of origin but he was also existentially removed from the primal essence of his physical nature. In the garden he is removed from *hā'ǎdāmâ* and enjoys convenient and ready access to the tree of life. Exile from Eden thus entails a return to *hā'ǎdāmâ* in more than one sense.

III. Cain, Abel, and the Soil (Gen 4:1-16)

Now we turn to the crucial passage — and the important question — at hand: "Why did God reject Cain's offering?" The preceding discussion has helped to provide a literary context within which we can now hope to answer the question. In this passage the narrator further develops a motif introduced as early as 2:5 and reiterated most recently at 3:23 — "tilling the soil" (*'bd 'dmh*). Cain was a "tiller of the soil" (4:2, *'ōbēd 'ǎdāmâ*). As such, he brought to God offerings from the produce (*pěrî*) of the soil (4:3).

But what was wrong with Cain's offering? Virtually all attempts to answer this crucial question over the past two millennia have been guided by homiletic concerns that have distracted scholars from observing the basic literary elements of the narrative. In short, Cain became a model (or a foil) with which both Jewish and Christian preachers could exhort congregants to a higher level of piety and morality. This homiletic concern belabored (and distorted) two elements in 4:3-5 — the first was the depiction of Cain's anger and resentment, and the second was the specific grammar used in the text to describe the respective offerings of Cain and Abel.

Thus, one homiletic approach has been to focus primarily on *Cain's disposition and attitude* at the time he made his offering, and thereby to make him an archetype of the insincere worshiper. In other words, here Cain's offering was understood to have been rejected because his heart was not in the right place to begin with. One senses that homilists, however, in searching for evidence of Cain's impiety, have had to retroject Cain's post-offering distemper (not to mention his subsequent murder of Abel and his impertinent witticism of 4:9) into his pre-offering character and personality, even though the narrative does not support such a maneuver. One can essentially paraphrase this reasoning as follows: "God rejected Cain's offering because it was not sincerely and piously made with a contrite heart. And how does one know that Cain was not pious and contrite? Look at how he became angry, dejected, murderously jealous, and insolent toward God! Would a pious and contrite worshiper behave in this manner? Of course not."[8]

The other homiletical approach has tried to be more objective, focusing primarily on the *specific description of the offerings* brought by Cain and Abel (and, through that, to infer something about their respective dispositions and attitudes). For example, it is noted that Abel brought offerings from the choicest (*ḥălābîm*) of the firstlings (*běkōrôt*, which implies a conscientious regard for the sanctity of the offering), while Cain simply brought "from the produce" (*mippĕrî;* the preposition *min-* ["from"] suggesting to many interpreters that

8. The relative antiquity of this type of homiletic interpretation is suggested by how effortlessly it is woven into first-century references to Cain and Abel, as in Philo, Josephus, and the NT book of Hebrews (11:1-4). Cf. also the Palestinian Targums (Chilton 1982 and Bassler 1986 [esp. nn. 1, 3, 5 for bibliography]). Cain is regarded as a model of wickedness and unorthodoxy in 1 John 3:12 and Jude 11, as well as in *1 Clem.* 4:1-7, although these last Christian texts, as well as *Apoc. Abr.* 24:5, probably base their negative appraisals of Cain's character on his post-offering killing of Abel. But *Hellenistic Synagogal Prayers* 12:53-54 seems to assume that Cain's depravity existed before he presented his offering. This is a bit more explicit in the Qur'an (Sura 5:27-32), where Abel is quoted as telling Cain that "Allah accepts offerings only from the righteous" (see Stillman 1974). The notion of Cain's latent wickedness is perhaps most explicitly articulated in the Jewish haggadah that "Satan, in the guise of the serpent, approached Eve, and the fruit of their union was Cain, the ancestor of all the impious generations that were rebellious towards God and rose up against him" (cited in Ginzberg 1909-38:1.105 and 5.133-34).

Cain's selection was casual and unthinking). Or it is noted that Abel's offering was from "*his* flock" (*ṣō'nô*, the possessive suffix indicating that Abel offered something of personal value), while Cain's was simply from *hā'ădāmâ* (without the possessive suffix, implying "public goods" not of personal value to Cain). Again, the homiletical point is that a worshiper's attitude in the first place governs what he or she will chose to offer to God (and thus whether that offering will be acceptable to God).[9] In this approach, Cain's offering is deemed inferior, not because of its *generic* quality or character (i.e., the fact that it is agricultural) but because of its *specific* quality and character insofar as these have been affected by his attitude and disposition.[10]

A literary appraisal of the question draws attention to the fact that there was something *generically* wrong with Cain's offering. Whether it was a generous tithe or a miserly portion, whether it was fully ripened produce or inferior-grade leftovers, whether it was conscientiously gathered and devoutly offered or casually thrown together and uncaringly tossed on the altar — it had come from the soil (*hā'ădāmâ*), which at that time was cursed. It is one thing for mortal man to set on his own table (or in the cribs of his animals) the fruits of the damned soil; it is quite another thing, however, to set such fare on the table of the Lord.[11]

---

9. See *Gen. Rab.* 22:5: "[Cain's offering] was from the refuse. The matter may be compared to the case of a wicked sharecropper who ate from the first fruits of the figs and handed over to the king the late figs." The *Midrash ha-Gadol* (cited in Goldin 1977:32) notes that "[Abel's offering] found more favour with God, who is honoured by things that grow spontaneously and in accordance with natural laws, and not by the products forced from nature by the ingenuity of grasping man." Perhaps the most influential of those interpreters focusing on the grammar and vocabulary of the text has been Rashi, whose interpretation of the passage in question continues to have a profound impact. For example, E. A. Speiser (*Genesis* [2nd ed.; AB 1; Garden City, NY: Doubleday, 1964] 30) refers to the contrast "between the unstinted offering on the part of Abel and the minimal contribution of Cain." See Goldin 1977:n. 36 for a good review and critique of this type of explanation for why Cain's offering was rejected. I agree with J. A. Skinner (*Genesis* [2nd ed.; ICC; Edinburgh: T. & T. Clark, 1930] 104) that "it is arbitrary to suppose that [Cain's] fault lay in not selecting the best of what he had for God."

10. Fortunately, one haggadic passage (cited in Ginzberg 1909-38:1.107-8 and 5.136-37) demonstrates that at one time some Bible readers understood the problem to be the *generic* quality of Cain's offering (that it came from the cursed soil). But even here we can already notice this understanding being pushed into the background in favor of a homiletic focus on Cain's character and how his character affected the *specific* quality of his offering: "Abel selected the best of his flocks for his sacrifice, but Cain ate his (own) meal first, and after he had satisfied his (own) appetite, he offered unto God what was left over, a few grains of flax seed. *As though his offense had not been great enough in offering unto God fruit of the ground which had been cursed by God!* No wonder that his sacrifice was not received with favor!" (italics mine).

11. Given this literary appraisal, attempts to go "behind the text" and to posit some hypothetical pro-pastoral bias or anti-agrarian polemic in the mind of the author become unnecessary.

God's reaction to Cain's offering is unusual and perhaps even uncharac-
teristic. There is no expression of divine outrage at cultic indiscretion, no hint
that Cain has committed some terrible offense or transgressed some sacred
precept of cultic propriety. God simply "ignored" Cain's offering (4:5).[12] There
is no divine tirade or even a reprimand. Indeed, what finally elicits God's address
to Cain is not Cain's sacrificial faux pas but Cain's subsequent anger and dejection.[13] Even here, however, God's response is, in some respects, a gentle word
of encouragement (4:6-7). Although God's statement in v. 7 is notoriously
untranslatable,[14] the basic gist and tone seems clear enough: it is the classic
Hebrew wisdom/covenant notion that a person will receive benefits for proper
conduct and penalties for improper conduct (although here it is communicated
without the hortatory tone of the sages or the polemical tone of the prophets).

Now in the wisdom and covenant traditions "good" characteristics are
usually juxtaposed with clearly "bad" characteristics. That does not seem to be
the case in 4:7. There, the opposite of "If you do good" *('im-têṭîb)* is not "If you
do evil" *('im-tāraʿ)* but "If you do not do good" *('im lō' têṭîb)*. One may legitimately ask whether failure to do good is equivalent to actively doing evil.
Although the consequences of doing evil are clearly negative throughout the

---

12. The Hebrew expression *šāʿâ 'el-* means "to stare intently at (something)," and is
often translated "to have regard for (something)." This expression occurs in Gen 4:4, 5 and
also in Isa 17:8, where it appears in conjunction with *šāʿâ 'al* (Isa 17:7):

> In that day men will focus on [*yišʿeh 'al*] their Maker,
>   their eyes will look to the Holy One of Israel;
> they will not have regard for [*yišʿeh 'el*] their hand-built altars,
>   or look at that which their own fingers have made, the Asherim
>   and the incense stands.

13. Literally "[Cain's] face fell" *(npl)*. The expression seems to convey the sense of
being disappointed and angry at someone (cf. Jer 3:12). Gruber (1978) would prefer to
interpret this (and many other instances of anger) as a reference to "depression," and this
leads him to his somewhat stilted translation of Gen 4:7 as "Indeed, if you will make yourself
happy, you will regain your smile."

14. O. Procksch (*Genesis* [2nd ed.; KAT; Leipzig: Deichert, 1924] 47) accurately labeled
this "the most obscure verse of the chapter, indeed of Genesis." The meaning of the Hebrew
word *śĕʾēt* in 4:7 is uncertain. I follow those who view it as an abbreviated form of the idiom
nśʾ pānîm, "uplifted face," the opposite of a "fallen [*npl*] face" (see n. 13 above). This idiom
refers to a kindly disposition toward someone, which can sometimes be censured in the Bible
insofar as it is associated with biased favoritism or partiality in rendering legal judgments
(cf. Deut 10:17; Lev 19:15; Prov 18:5; also Ps 82:2; Job 13:8, 10; 32:21; 34:19). It is not clear
in Gen 4:7 whether the reference is to God being kindly disposed toward Cain, or Cain toward
God, or both (i.e., a mutually satisfying and rewarding relationship). On the one hand, *Gen.
Rab.* 22:6 is one of the earliest texts to suggest that *śĕʾēt* here refers to "forgiveness," a notion
that Rashi also embraced. On the other hand, Ibn Ezra equated it with elation (Leibowitz
1972:42-43). Thus, for example, the approximate meaning of Num 6:26 is "May the Lord
smile when he sees you." See also Deut 28:50, which refers to "a coldblooded nation that will
not be kindly disposed toward [*lōʾ-yiśśāʾ pānîm lĕ-*] the elderly nor show mercy for the young."

Bible, the consequences of Cain "not doing good" are spelled out in the MT as *lappetaḥ ḥaṭṭāʾt rōbēṣ*. Whatever else these words might mean,[15] they certainly do not seem to have the same sort of unconditional negativity that one finds elsewhere in the Hebrew Bible (or even in J's *môt tāmût*, "you will surely die"). It seems at best to be a warning that, if one does not actively do good, then the *potential* for sinfulness exists.

The same can be said for the final part of 4:7, which is also enigmatic in the Masoretic tradition: *wĕʾēleykā tĕšûqātô wĕʾattâ timšol-bô*. Whatever else it might mean,[16] this clause certainly seems to be a positive word of divine encouragement. It lacks the gloomy "finality" of the syntactically equivalent divine word consigning the fate of the woman in 3:16 ("Your desire will be for your husband, and he himself will rule over you"). It seems to be the expression of a divine hope for Cain that, unfortunately, will not be fulfilled. In the next verse (4:8), Cain in fact does not rule over "it" but instead murders Abel. Thus, one needs to remember that literarily Cain's undoing was not his cultic faux pas but, most immediately, his murder of Abel (and behind that, his anger and dejection).

What perhaps surprises one most of all is not simply the enigmatic character of the specific Hebrew words and phrases that God uses in addressing Cain (should one assume that they were not enigmatic to J and his contemporaries?), but the overall enigmatic character of the conversation in general. Why doesn't God "speak clearly" or at least authoritatively to Cain, explicitly telling him (and us) what he did wrong, and issuing a command specifying what Cain *should* do? God does this quite well throughout the rest of Scripture. I have no answer for this question, other than to speculate that the silence may have the same ambiguous texture as the well-worn admonition, "You should have known better than to do that."

Should Cain have known that *hāʾădāmâ* (and, by extension, its "fruit") was cursed? Cain was not present when the curse was issued in 3:17-19, and he could presumably protest that his parents had never informed him about it (although we readers cannot claim such ignorance). Perhaps Cain *did* know about the curse, but that as a tiller of the soil he never really had anything else to offer God but the produce that his brow-drenching toil has wrested from the damned ground.[17] If this is the case, then the seeds of Cain's eventual estrangement with God were sown not in his killing of Abel, nor even in his anger, nor even in his improper offering, but in his basic livelihood as a tiller of the

---

15. The usual "sin is lurking at the door" has become the standard largely by default.

16. "Its desire is for you; and you yourself must rule over it" is the standard translation.

17. In other words, relative to other commendable concerns (such as the desire to offer something to God), the significance of the soil being cursed may have receded in Cain's mind to the point that, for all practical purposes, he forgot this was the case. Something analogous has undoubtedly happened to generations of Bible readers: the significance of the soil being cursed has likewise receded in our minds as other commendable concerns (such as homiletic appeals to piety) have been brought to bear on the text.

(accursed) soil (4:2). As such, neither Cain nor any other tiller of the soil will ever have anything "proper" to offer God — unless, of course, God's disposition toward *hā'ǎdāmâ* changes (see below).

The consequences of Cain being cursed are spelled out in 4:12: *hā'ǎdāmâ* will no longer yield "its strength" *(kōḥāh)* to Cain. From this point on Cain clearly has no future should he remain connected with *hā'ǎdāmâ;* consequently he must become a restless wanderer. Cain realizes that his punishment means being banished from the face of "the soil" (*hā'ǎdāmâ,* which, incidentally, is not the same as *hā'āreṣ,* "the earth") and from the divine presence (4:14). The final verse in this section (v. 16) raises an interesting question: if the presence of God is not to be found "east of Eden," is *hā'ǎdāmâ* likewise absent there?[18]

IV. Noah and the Soil (Gen 5:28-29; 8:20-22; 9:20)

The Noah story further develops the theme of the cursed soil. A key statement is Lamech's "prophecy" on the occasion of the birth of Noah (5:29). That verse, divided into subunits (clauses), reads:

(a) He called his name "Noah," saying,
(b) "This one will bring us solace
(c) from our toilsome manual labor
(d) that results from the soil which YHWH cursed."

Philologically, one of the noteworthy features of this verse is the threefold repetition of the particle *min-*. The first two occurrences are in v. 5:29c, which

---

18. Note that 4:17-26 explicitly portray Cain's descendants as being engaged in non-agricultural activities. Earlier, I suggested that conceptually there may be no *'ǎdāmâ* in *haggān;* now I could push that further and say that there may be no *'ǎdāmâ* beyond (lit. "east of") *haggān* either. Again, the point to be kept in mind is that we are not dealing with physical, planar geography in these texts, but with metaphysical, mythic categories. If this mythic scheme indeed underlies these J passages (in contrast to the more familiar mythic cosmography of P underlying Genesis 1) then it appears that *hā'āreṣ* ("the earth," the nonheavenly domain created by God) would consist of three "zones": (1) *hā'ǎdāmâ* ("the soil"), which is the relatively stable zone within which all historical creatures operate; (2) *haggān* ("the garden," i.e., Eden), which is the zone of paradise (and eternal life) from which we all are currently isolated; and (3) *qidmat-'ēden* ("east of Eden"), which is the land of rootless and sorrowful wandering *(nōd)*. The theological question of whether God is absent in this third zone is moot (cf. Ps 139:7-10). Cain is probably most concerned not with this issue but with the more practical and immediately relevant question of whether *yir'at-YHWH* ("fear of God," "conscience") is absent in this zone. If no one in "the land of Nod" fears God, then Cain is truly vulnerable, unless God can provide some extraordinary sign reminding the inhabitants of this zone that they are not beyond the divine reach. I would suggest that the "mark of Cain" is just such a sign.

reads literally, "from [*min-*] our labor and from [*min-*] the toil of our hands."[19] It is the subordinate clause to the main clause expressed in v. 29b. The two *min*s in this clause seem to be part of the expression *nḥm min-* and to have a partitive sense.[20] In attaching itself to synonymous nouns ("our labor" and "the toil"), these two *min*s identify the *direct* cause of the discomfort (i.e., the discomfort immediately results from the toilsome manual labor).

The third *min* in v. 29d, however, seems not to be part of the expression *nḥm min-,* and apparently has primarily a resultative or causative (and not a partitive) sense.[21] The phrase in v. 29d explains and qualifies the subordinate clause in v. 29c; it gives the immediate reason why there is toilsome manual labor in the first place (v. 29c) and, thereby, it states the *indirect* cause of the discomfort from which people desire relief (i.e., the discomfort stems ultimately from the fact that the soil is cursed). Lamech's statement can be unpacked as follows: "Because the soil is cursed, our toilsome manual labor is unremitting; through this child Noah we will be relieved of [or delivered from] this unremitting labor." The strong implication in this statement is that, through Noah, the curse on the soil will be mitigated if not revoked. As such, Lamech's "prophetic" statement is part of a motif that J has been developing since Genesis 2, and it will, in a sense, be "fulfilled" in Genesis 8.

Earlier I noted that Cain's punishment was banishment from "the face of the soil" (4:14). In several places throughout J's account of the flood the key phrase *ʿal-pĕnê hāʾădāmâ* recurs (6:1; 7:4, 23; 8:8; cf. also 8:13b [P verse?]). Probably the most significant for our purposes is 7:23, "and [YHWH] obliterated everything that existed that was upon the face of the soil." Here the quality of the soil has apparently changed yet again. Perhaps it has reverted to the inert and pristine state that applied back in 2:4b-7. Regardless, it has undergone severe trauma that signals not only an ending but also a new beginning.

After the floodwaters recede, Noah builds an altar (8:20). This is the first description of any patriarchal cultic activity since Cain and Abel brought their respective offerings (4:3-4).[22] The narrator here (as earlier in the flood story; cf. 7:2) specifies that the sacrificial animals (no agricultural fare this time!) are

---

19. My translation ("from our toilsome manual labor") interprets this phrase to be an instance of hendiadys.

20. The root *nḥm* has an extraordinarily wide range of meanings depending on the conjugation, and this is not the place to get into a detailed discussion of the matter. In the Piel stem it seems to mean bringing consolation, comfort, or relief (to someone who is suffering) *from (min-)* some specifically named source of discomfort (see Judg 2:18; Isa 1:24; Jer 31:13).

21. On partitive *min* as representing "*origin* (e.g., of toilsome manual labor) *from* (e.g., the soil being cursed)," see GKC §119v. On causative *min* as representing "on account of, in consequence of," see GKC §119z.

22. Although it does not *describe* cultic activity per se, Gen 4:26 certainly implies that some sort of cultic activity existed.

"clean" *(ṭhr);* consequently there is no doubt that God will "have regard" for them. Indeed, in almost embarrassing detail the narrator describes how God sniffs the pleasing odor of the meat roasting on Noah's altar. Then comes the key moment (8:21) when God at least mitigates (if not revokes) the curse that he had imposed on the soil back in 3:17.[23] Just as a reason was given for imposing this curse in the first place ("because [*kî*] from it the man was taken," 3:19), so here also a reason is given for its mitigation/revocation ("because [*kî*] the inclination of the human heart has been evil from its youth," 8:21).

In a sense, what has changed? The answer seems to be: Nothing more — and nothing less — than the status of the soil *in God's eyes.* Presumably from now on someone can offer to God *mippĕrî hā'ădāmâ* ("from the produce of the soil"), and God will "take notice" (*š'h 'el;* cf. 4:4) of it. Indeed, in 8:22 God goes beyond simply modifying or lifting the curse on the soil and actually expresses a firm commitment to the agricultural cycle: the seasonal planting and harvesting of crops is now something in which even God has a stake. Furthermore, shortly after disembarking from the ark, the venerable Noah himself adopts an agrarian lifestyle, becoming a "man of the soil" (*'îš hā'ădāmâ,* but not *'ōbēd hā'ădāmâ*)[24] and planting a vineyard (9:20). But that is another story.

In short, Cain offered to God the wrong goods (produce of the soil) in the wrong era (at a time when the soil was cursed). Abel offered to God different goods in the same era as Cain, and God accepted it. Generations of subsequent Israelites would offer to God the same sort of agricultural goods that Cain had offered (Lev 2:1-16), but in a different era when the curse on the soil had been lifted. They would make such an offering confident that God would accept it.

---

23. It is not clear that *qll* in 8:21 is a virtual synonym for *'rr* ("to curse"), although it may be. If it is synonymous, then the curse would indeed hereby be revoked. Despite this, much of the character of the damned antediluvian soil (thorn, thistle, toil, and sweat) will nevertheless still persist in the postdiluvian era — as any farmer (ancient Israelite or modern Western) could attest. But in the Piel the verb *qll* often means "to denigrate or disparage something" (i.e., to consider something to be of insignificant value). Given that J elsewhere (4:4, 5) has used a verb (*š'h 'l*) that evokes an anthropomorphic image of God's subjective "tastes" or "whims," it is possible that just such an image is intended here. In essence, regardless of whether the cursed status of the soil has changed, God's esteem for it has changed: he will no longer view it with the same contempt or distaste as he had before, even if it is still cursed. If this is the case, then the curse would hereby be mitigated, but not repealed.

24. Most of the subsequent biblical references to *'bd (hā)'ădāmâ* seem to have neutral if not positive connotations (2 Sam 9:10; Isa 30:24; Jer 27:11; Zech 13:5; Prov 12:11 = 28:19). See 2 Chr 26:10, where King Uzziah is characterized as *'ōhēb 'ădāmâ* ("one who loves the soil") on account of his liberal agricultural policies.

Bibliography

Since the subject of Cain's offering has been much discussed, the secondary literature on the subject is voluminous. The discerning reader will note that my literary approach here really does not presuppose much of that literature. Although I have reviewed this literature, I hope that I will be forgiven for not interacting with it in the confines of this brief paper.

Alter, R.
1981   *The Art of Biblical Narrative.* New York: Basic.
Bassler, J.
1986   "Cain and Abel in the Palestinian Targums." *JSJ* 17:56-64.
Chilton, B.
1982   "A Comparative Study of Synoptic Development." *JBL* 101:553-62.
Ginzberg, L.
1909-38   *Legends of the Jews.* 7 vols. Philadelphia: Jewish Publication Society.
Goldin, J.
1977   "The Youngest Son or Where Does Genesis 38 Belong." *JBL* 96:27-44.
Gruber, M.
1978   "The Tragedy of Cain and Abel." *JQR* 69:89-97.
Hauser, A.
1980   "Linguistic and Thematic Links between Genesis 4:1-16 and Genesis 2–3." *JETS* 23/4:297-306.
Kikawada, I.
1987   "A Quantitative Analysis of the 'Adam and Eve,' 'Cain and Abel,' and 'Noah' Stories." Pp. 195-203 in *Perspectives on Language and Text: Essays and Poems in Honor of Francis I. Andersen's Sixtieth Birthday, July 28, 1985.* Ed. E. W. Conrad and E. G. Newing. Winona Lake, IN: Eisenbrauns.
Leibowitz, N.
1972   *Studies in Bereshit (Genesis) in the Context of Ancient and Modern Jewish Bible Commentary.* Trans. A. Newman. 4th ed. Jerusalem: World Zionist Organization.
Levenson, J.
1985   *Sinai and Zion: An Entry into the Jewish Bible.* Minneapolis: Seabury-Winston.
Stillman, N.
1974   "The Story of Cain and Abel in the Qur'an." *JSS* 19:231-39.

The Land Redeemer and the Jubilee

JACOB MILGROM

University of California, Berkeley

For Noel: editor, respondent, colleague, and dear friend: *mippî sôpĕrîm wĕlō' mippî sĕpārîm,* "(Learn) from scholars and not from books" (*Kuzari* 2:72).

I shall discuss two related texts regarding the role of the land redeemer (*gō'ēl*) in the jubilee pericope of Leviticus 25: first, the redeemer in the notorious crux of v. 33a and, then, the absence of the redeemer in laws of indebtedness (vv. 35-38) and slavery (vv. 39-43).

I begin with a postulate: The *gō'ēl* retains the land he has redeemed until the jubilee and only then returns it to the original owner. The redeemer is a kin (i.e., blood) relative *(šĕ'ēr)*, as indicated by the correspondence of *gō'ălô haqqārōb 'ēlāyw* (Lev 25:25) and *šĕ'ērô haqqārōb 'ēlāyw* (21:2). One can, therefore, assume that the indigent Israelite will first offer his land to his relative, as Hanamel did to his first cousin Jeremiah: "Buy my land . . . *kî lĕkā mišpaṭ haggĕ'ullâ liqnôt* [lit. 'for yours is the procedure of redemption by purchase']" (Jer 32:7). Note that nothing is said about the land reverting to Hanamel or his descendants in the jubilee. The land remains in possession of the kin group. As Pedersen has observed: "The centre of gravity passes from him [the original owner] to a relative; he loses in importance what the relative gains, but the family, as family, loses nothing. The property is not left to chance, but remains in the kindred with which it is familiar" (1926:1.84).

Levine (1983:100-101; 1989) argues that because the verb *qānâ,* "purchase," occurs in Jeremiah (and in a similar case in Ruth 4:4-9), but not in Leviticus 25, the redeemer in Leviticus 25 does not acquire the land but must return it immediately to the original owner. Levine is correct, but only partially. The presence or absence of *qānâ* does, indeed, indicate a difference between

66

Jeremiah and Ruth, on the one hand, and Leviticus, on the other. In my opinion, however, this difference is due to the absence of the jubilee institution in the former, which implies that the redeemer possesses the land for himself. Unless the original owner or his heirs exercise their rights of redemption and repurchase the property, it remains with the redeemer in perpetuity. In Leviticus, however, the onset of the jubilee year blocks such an acquisition. But that can hardly mean that the redeemer must return it at once. Isn't he at least entitled to get his money back? If not, what incentive does he have to redeem the field? Since the indebted owner is in no position to repay the redeemer, the only solution is that the redeemer retains and uses the field until the jubilee. In a sense, he leases, not acquires, the field just as the buyer does (Lev 25:13-16) — until he regains his costs at the jubilee. Herein, indeed, lies the innovation of Leviticus. The concern of Leviticus is to preserve individual, not kin group, inheritance. Whereas heretofore the redeemer acquired the land permanently, henceforth the land reverts to the original owner at the jubilee.

The postulate that the redeemer retains possession of the property until the jubilee is also the key, I submit, to resolving the crux of v. 33a. First, however, one must decide on the interpretation of *min* in the opening clause: *wa'ăšer yig'al min-halĕwîyim*. It can mean either "from," thus making the Levites the object, or "of," which makes the Levites the subject.

For the meaning "from" three interpretations have been suggested, each of which is subject to question: (1) The verb *gā'al* takes on the meaning "purchase" (Saadiah, Rashi, Ibn Ezra [first explanation], Ḥazzequni; cf. *b. 'Arak.* 33b) or "appropriate" (Levine). Unfortunately, neither meaning is attested anywhere. (2) Whereas v. 32 cites the case of a Levite redeeming from an Israelite, v. 33 adds the case of an Israelite redeeming from a Levite: just as an Israelite cannot possess a Levitic house forever (v. 32; i.e., Levites have permanent rights of redemption), so a Levite may not possess an Israelite house forever (i.e., the Israelites have the same redemption rights; see Bekhor Shor). This interpretation runs into the snag of v. 33b, the rationale for v. 33a, which speaks of Levitic, not Israelite, houses. (3) Whether a Levite redeems a Levite's house from an Israelite (v. 32) or even a Levite's from a Levite (v. 33a), the house must revert to the original Levite owner (*Sipra Behar* 6:6; *m. 'Arak.* 9:8; C. J. H. Wright 1990:123-24). This is the best of the three "from" solutions. But it too can be challenged. First, on what grounds would a Levite redeeming from a Levite think that his case is different from a Levite redeeming from an Israelite (v. 32)? Second, if the emphasis is on the thought process of the Levite redeemer, he should be the subject of the sentence; and that, indeed, is the case if *min* means "of," as in the interpretation below.

Three interpretations have also been proposed understanding *min* as "of": (1) Read with the Vulgate *wā'ăšer lō' yigā'ēl*, "Whatever is not redeemed (of Levite property)." This reading requires the insertion of the negative particle *lō'* and pointing *yg'l* as a passive, advocated by Shadal (second explanation), Dillmann, Bertholet, Ehrlich, Killian (1963:337), Elliger, Levine (1989:212n.34). This radical solution, for which there is no warrant in the manuscript traditions or the versions, is one of desperation. (2) Connect v. 33a to v. 32b and render "The Levites shall forever have the right of redemption; either one of the Levites shall redeem or . . . shall be released in the jubilee" (Möller). The problem is to justify rendering the two waws of wa'ăšer and wĕyāṣā' as "either . . . or." Moreover, this interpretation ignores wā'ăšer meaning "what/whoever." (3) "Whoever of the Levites redeems (should know that). . . ." This, I submit, is the preferable translation (cf. Targum Neofiti; Saalschütz 1853:150; Ginsburg [first explanation]). The Levite redeemer might think that because the house remains Levitic property, he can hold on to it forever (Ramban, Shadal [first explanation]). Or, he reasons that the Levitic house is likened to an Israelite house, which does not revert to the original owner in the jubilee (v. 30). Such reasoning is categorically rejected: the property must return to the original Levite owner in the jubilee. That is, the Levite homeowner has only sold it for its rental value until the jubilee. In effect, the Levite's city house is equivalent to the Israelite's village house (v. 31): both are subject to the law of the jubilee. Thus, the enigma of v. 33a is unraveled once the premise is granted that the gō'ēl retains the use of the redeemed land until the jubilee.

An ancillary problem is the absence of a provision for the redemption of Israelite slaves (vv. 39-43), a fact that the rabbis confirm when they declare that relatives are under no obligation to redeem their indentured kinsman (b. Qidd. 15b). Yet redemption of slaves obtained in Mesopotamia. In Sippar, during the reign of Rim-Sin, a female slave regained her freedom by paying ten shekels to her owner. As for redemption by a relative: "17 shekels of silver for the redemption of Hagaliga, his father, Zagagan has received (as a loan). (But) he had no silver, (so) he sold himself to the enum priest" (Khafajah 88, cited in Leggett 1974:63-83). Here the son borrows money to redeem his father, but being unable to repay the loan, he sells himself into bondage. The Code of Hammurapi §117 has the clause: "has sold his wife, his son or his daughter, or gives (them) into servitude." Its two verbs translate, respectively, ana kaspim nadānu and ana kiššātim nadānu, where the latter implies the power of redemption (Driver-Miles 1952-55:1.212-14). The edict of Ammiṣaduqa confirms Code of Hammurapi §117 and adds a further option: ana manzazānim ezēbu, "to leave as a pledge," where the creditor has no power of alienation (cf. Yaron 1959:158-59). Thus redemption of slaves prevails in Mesopotamia; why, then, is it missing in Israel?

The answer is this: the Israelite slave is not a slave; he is śākîr, a "hireling" (v. 40), whose work amortizes the principal — a status to which redemption does not apply. If the creditor's conditions are too harsh or the wages too low, he is free to work for someone other than his employer (wĕnimkār, "and he sells himself," v. 39). The wages he earns may even provide him a surplus with which to free himself (v. 49b). Therefore, his family has no obligation to redeem him. Furthermore, the jubilee will free him, cancel his debt, and give him back his land (v. 41). Thus, he will be able to start out afresh as a debt-free landowner who will be independent of his family.

The redemption clause is also missing in the case of the indebted Israelite (vv. 35-38), again for the same reason: the term "redemption" does not apply. Redemption is applicable only to sold land and sold (i.e., enslaved) Israelites (to a non-Israelite owner, vv. 47-52). True, the *gōʾēl* (or anyone else) may lend him money to pay off his debt. But the *gōʾēl* does not, as a consequence, come into possession of the land; his act does not constitute redemption.

Leviticus's innovation is revolutionary, especially in view of the two other slave laws in the Torah. Exodus 21:1-11 stipulates six years of servitude without any indication that this term can be shortened by redemption. Deuteronomy 15:12-18, perhaps deliberately (out of embarrassment?), omits the term "slave" in describing the six years of servitude, but the institution of slavery remains intact. Leviticus, however, effectively abolishes Israelite slavery. Whether the "owner" is an Israelite or non-Israelite, the Israelite debtor is not a slave but a hireling (vv. 40, 53). The rationale is stated twice; it forms the envelope encasing the entire slave law: "For it is to me the Israelites are slaves. They are my slaves whom I freed from the land of Egypt" (v. 55; cf. v. 42).

Bibliography

Driver, G. R., and J. C. Miles
  1952-55   *The Babylonian Laws.* 2 vols. Oxford: Clarendon.
Killian, R.
  1963   *Literarkritische und formgeschichtliche Untersuchung des Heiligkeits-gesetezes.* BBB 19. Bonn: Hanstein.
Leggett, D. A.
  1974   *The Levirate and Goel Institutions in the Old Testament.* Cherry Hill, NJ: Mack.
Levine, B. A.
  1983   "In Praise of the Israelite *Mišpāḥâ*: Legal Themes in Ruth." Pp. 95-106 in *The Quest for the Kingdom of God: Studies in Honor of George E. Mendenhall.* Ed. H. B. Huffmon et al. Winona Lake, IN: Eisenbrauns.
  1989   *Leviticus.* JPS Torah Commentary. Philadelphia: Jewish Publication Society.
Saalschütz, J. L.
  1853   *Das mosaische Recht.* 2nd ed. Berlin: Heymann.
Wright, C. J. H.
  1990   *God's People in God's Land.* Grand Rapids: Eerdmans.
Yaron, R.
  1959   "Redemption of Persons in the Ancient Near East." *Revue internationale de l'antiquite* 6: 155-76.

The Deuteronomistic School

RICHARD ELLIOTT FRIEDMAN

University of California, San Diego

The first *Festschrift* in honor of David Noel Freedman was published in 1983, before he became my colleague at the University of California, San Diego, so I missed the opportunity to express my respect for him in the traditional scholarly way. It therefore means a great deal to me to see him honored now by a second *Festschrift*. He deserves it, and I am fortunate to have my chance at last to dedicate a piece of work to him and thus to say in a formal, public way what I hope I have already conveyed to him *pānîm 'el pānîm*. Having him as my senior colleague in the modern *gan 'ēden* known as San Diego has been one of the blessings of my professional life and, for that matter, of my personal life. His extraordinary range of knowledge, his insight, his wisdom, his wit, his good nature, and his friendship have meant a great deal to me and my family. I hope that he will have many more fruitful, satisfying years here in California and that his students and colleagues will continue to reap the benefits of knowing such a man.

Every now and then a notion comes to be firmly fixed in the discourse of our field and even comes to be generally accepted without really having been proved or even systematically assembled. One of these is the matter of the Deuteronomistic school. It is a commonplace of scholarship on the Hebrew Bible to speak of this school and to identify the work of its members on numerous books of biblical narrative and prophecy. We do not know exactly who they were, what the nature of their association was, or why they were apparently so rigidly bound to using a fixed group of terms and phrases. Still, they are assumed

70

to have existed, maintaining their particular identity and looking after their particular interests through one generation after another for centuries. They are claimed to have produced major biblical works — including the Deuteronomistic History, the longest work in the Bible — and they are claimed to have acquired copies of numerous other works, from JE to Amos to portions of Jeremiah, and to have added words, phrases, and lines to them so as to make their own ideas appear to have been part of these works.

Thus the literature of the field is filled with expressions such as "the Deuteronomistic school," "the Deuteronomistic circle of tradition," "the Deuteronomistic party," "the Deuteronomistic movement," "Deuteronomistic stylistic forms," "Deuteronomistically colored passages," and "Deuteronomistically influenced traditionists." The vagueness of these terms, in the absence of clear referents in history, and in the absence of clear conceptions of the literary processes involved, is a major weakness in the entire enterprise and a serious threat to our progress in this area. As long as we biblical scholars continue to use these nonspecific, nondescriptive terms and categories, it is no wonder that literary scholars, especially comparatists, look on us as unsophisticated, and write books, both for scholars and the public, with supposedly great new discoveries — such as that J is good literature — that nonetheless pull one carpet after another out from under us. Even Harold Bloom, for all the foolishness and unoriginality of his book on J, correctly criticized biblical scholarship in general for lacking a basic sense of authors, how they work, and how their works feel.

Was there a Deuteronomistic school? What was it? Who were its members? Did they hold meetings? Did they have intervarsity competitions with the wisdom school and the J school?

Pardon my sarcasm. One of my teachers, Yohanan Muffs, once said, "I don't joke lightly." And I am being facetious precisely to draw attention to something that is becoming a scholarly idol whose feet have not yet been ascertained to be metal or clay.

It seems to me that we have made relatively little progress on the identity of this school and its writers since the essential work of Moshe Weinfeld in this area.[1] Even if one disagrees with Weinfeld's identification of the Deuteronomists as a group of scribes, in the period of Hezekiah to Josiah, especially scribes associated with wisdom, especially associated with the Shaphan family, one can respect it for being reasonable and an attempt at getting at the persons, processes, and interests involved. Similarly, Ernest Nicholson's identification of the Deuteronomists as a northern Israelite prophetic circle that came to Jerusalem following the fall of Israel deserves respect as a positive, reasonable

---

1. Moshe Weinfeld, *Deuteronomy and the Deuteronomic School* (Oxford: Clarendon, 1972). Weinfeld has continued this analysis in *Deuteronomy 1–11* (AB 5; New York: Doubleday, 1991); and "Deuteronomy," *ABD* 2.168-83.

attempt to identify these people with some specificity.[2] The most recent attempt
to identify these persons and processes, as of this writing, is an article by J. A.
Dearman, which appears to be essentially a recapitulation of Weinfeld's views.[3]

Elsewhere I have connected the Deuteronomistic works with the priesthood
that was associated with Shiloh and Anathoth and that has been identified by some
scholars as "Mushite."[4] Is this then what we are talking about when we use the term
"Deuteronomistic school"? I do not hold that view, and I do not think that it
would be correct for anyone to take this position. This priestly group is potentially
too large, and it is not what we usually mean by a literary school. It is an entire
priesthood. Indeed, I also traced the pentateuchal sourcework E to this priestly
community, and E is not Deuteronomistic in any useful sense of that term.[5]

If by "school" we mean those who actually had a hand in the writing —
and possibly those who were their close personal associates and influences in
their writing — then about whom are we talking when we speak of a Deuteronomistic school? What I mean to do is to examine the primary works that are
associated with the Deuteronomistic school, and then to try to determine how
many people over what span of time were required to produce these works.

First let us take the Deuteronomistic History, including the book of
Deuteronomy itself. Elsewhere I have detailed the evidence that this work was
produced in two editions, the first Josianic, called Dtr[1], and the second exilic,
called Dtr[2].[6] It was the convergence of evidence of numerous types that brought
me to the identification of these two editions:

> There is an inclusio constructed of ten associations betweeen Moses and
> Josiah. From the perspective of the history, developed through ten such
> associations, that which begins with Moses approaches its culmination
> at last in Josiah.
>
> Following the Josiah pericope, changes in the character of the text suggest
> a break and subsequent addition at that point. All kings are evaluated
> as good or bad relative to the criterion of their retention or destruction
> of the bāmôt. This fits with the Deuteronomistic principle of central-
> ization of worship at a single place, which is the first law of the Deuter-
> onomic law code. But the criterion stops at Josiah, and bāmôt are not

2. E. W. Nicholson, *Deuteronomy and Tradition* (Philadelphia: Fortress, 1967) 114-24.

3. J. Andrew Dearman, "My Servants the Scribes: Composition and Context in
Jeremiah 36," *JBL* 109 (1990) 403-21. Dearman includes a brief reference to an article of
Weinfeld's in a note (p. 419n.42) but does not cite Weinfeld's book. More credit is due to
Weinfeld here.

4. In *Who Wrote the Bible?* (Englewood Cliffs, NJ: Prentice-Hall, 1987) 119-30.

5. Ibid., 70-79.

6. "From Egypt to Egypt: Dtr[1] and Dtr[2]," in *Traditions in Transformation: Turning
Points in Biblical Faith: Essays Presented to Frank Moore Cross* (ed. B. Halpern and J. Levenson;
Winona Lake, IN: Eisenbrauns, 1981) 167-92.

even mentioned in the reigns of the four kings who follow him in the history. Also, each of the Judean kings is measured against the figure of their father David in the Deuteronomistic History, but this criterion ceases after the Josiah section as well. Moreover, the recurring pattern of prophecy/fulfillment in the Deuteronomistic History extends through the Josiah pericope and then ceases.

The next body of evidence of exilic, Dtr[2] additions to an earlier text is the convergence of the several types of factors that indicate such expansion in some passages. The passages that I have identified as Dtr[2] are not simply any passage that refers to exile. Rather, in each case there are convergences of multiple factors: terminology, theme, grammar, syntax, literary structure, and comparative data. Thus we can identify at least eight passages that bear multiple signs of being editorially secondary. Next, we find that all of these passages occur at structurally significant junctures in the Deuteronomistic narrative.

This collection of evidence, together with the evidence originally assembled by my teacher Frank Cross and then by Levenson, Halpern, Nelson, and Tadmor and Cogan, points to a Josianic Dtr[1] and an exilic Dtr[2] edition of the work. In *The First Historians* Halpern has done a service to the field in attempting to organize and describe the relationship between this scholarship and a number of recent works, especially by German scholars, that likewise try to identify the successive stages of the Deuteronomistic History. To this group one should add the recent work of Steven McKenzie and Iain Provan.[7]

I still hold that there are no *Deuteronomistic* works or editorial layers prior to the Josianic edition. There are *texts* in the Deuteronomistic History that were composed long before Josiah. These include such diverse texts as Priestly material in the book of Joshua,[8] at least two lengthy sources in the book of 1 Samuel,[9] the Court History of David in 2 Samuel,[10] and a history of the Judean monarchy

---

7. Frank Moore Cross, *Canaanite Myth and Hebrew Epic* (Cambridge: Harvard University, 1973) 274-89; Jon Levenson, "Who Inserted the Book of the Torah?" *HTR* 68 (1975) 203-33; Baruch Halpern, *The First Historians: The Hebrew Bible and History* (San Francisco: Harper & Row, 1988) 107-21, 207-40; Richard Nelson, *The Double Redaction of the Deuteronomistic History* (JSOTSup 18; Sheffield: JSOT, 1981); H. Tadmor and M. Cogan, *2 Kings* (AB 11; New York: Doubleday, 1988); Steven L. McKenzie, *The Chronicler's Use of the Deuteronomistic History* (HSM 33; Atlanta: Scholars, 1984); idem, *The Trouble with Kings: The Composition of the Book of Kings in the Deuteronomistic History* (VTSup 42; Leiden: Brill, 1991); Iain Provan, *Hezekiah and the Books of Kings: A Contribution to the Debate about the Composition of the Deuteronomistic History* (BZAW 172; Berlin: de Gruyter, 1988).

8. Including Josh 13:15-33; 14:1-5; 15:1-13, 20-62; 16—20; 21:1-40; 22:9-34; 24:33.

9. Samuel A = 1 Sam 9; 10:1-16a; 13—14; 17:12-58; 18:1-5, 14-15, 17-19, 30; 20—24; 31:1-7. Samuel B = 1 Sam 1—6; 7:1-2, 5-17; 8; 10:17-27; 11; 12:1-6, 16-19, 22-23; 15—16; 17:1-11, 50; 18:6-13, 16, 20-29; 19; 25—30; 31:8-13.

10. Comprising nearly all of 2 Samuel 1—21.

from Solomon to Hezekiah.[11] But one should count these among the Deuteronomist's sources, not as Deuteronomistic themselves. They reflect a variety of
ideology and terminology that is not the familiar and striking language and
point of view of the texts that we call Deuteronomistic. The Deuteronomistic
terminology flowers in the Josianic edition of the history. There, in Dtr[1], it is
unmistakable — and pervasive. It pervades the exilic edition of the Deuteronomistic History, Dtr[2], no less.

On this view of the Deuteronomistic History, how many persons were
required to produce the *Deuteronomistic* layers? The Deuteronomistic layers of
these two editions, Dtr[1] and Dtr[2], are written in a language and style that are
virtually indistinguishable from one another — in the absence of other clues.
What does that mean? How can it be?

If they are both by the same person, it is understandable, plain and simple.
Someone composed the history at the time of Josiah. When extraordinary events
subsequently rendered the history outdated, the historian made the necessary
modifications and extended the finish of the work to take the new events into
account. This would be the simplest and most likely conclusion (to anyone
except a biblical scholar) unless there is evidence against it: for example, numerous impossible contradictions, or an impossible time span. The time span is
certainly not impossible. The Dtr[1] edition of the the history had to have been
composed before Josiah's death in 609 B.C.E. The Dtr[2] edition had to have been
composed after the fall of Jerusalem in 587 B.C.E. That is a separation of
twenty-three years. Historians have been known to live that long. I see no
internal contradictions within Dtr[1] that remotely approach the order of the
contradictions between, say, J and E, let alone J and P; nor are any such contradictions visible between Dtr[1] and Dtr[2]. On the contrary, as I have discussed
in past work, the exilic Deuteronomist's task was manifestly a restricted one,
working well within the premises, perspectives, and niches of the Josianic edition, showing respect for it rather than undermining or contradicting it.[12]

This task also could conceivably have been performed by a second person,
a close acquaintance, offspring, or disciple with an exceptional mastery of the
former writer's language, though the evidence does not seem to me to push us
to hypothesize such a person. In short, the Deuteronomistic History *need* only
be by one person. It *could* reasonably be by two. A heavy burden of proof is on
anyone who claims there are more. One would have to establish not only that
there is pre-Josianic material, which is by now patent to nearly everyone, but

---

11. See Baruch Halpern, "Sacred History and Ideology: Chronicles' Thematic Structure
— Indications of an Earlier Source," in *The Creation of Sacred Literature* (ed. R. E. Friedman;
Berkeley: University of California, 1981) 35-54.

12. Friedman, "From Egypt to Egypt: Dtr[1] and Dtr[2]," 185-92; idem, *Who Wrote,*
136-44; Cross, *Canaanite Myth,* 287-89. I identify the following as Dtr[2]: Deut 4:25-31;
8:19-20; 28:36-37, 63-68; 29:21-27; 30:1-10, 15-20; 31:16-22, 28-30; 32:44; 1 Kgs 9:6-9; 2 Kgs
21:8-15; 23:26–25:26.

that clearly Deuteronomistic language and interests are integrally — and not editorially — embedded in this material.

Now let us consider the other book most associated with the Deuteronomistic works, the book of Jeremiah. The characteristic language of the Deuteronomistic History is widespread in the book of Jeremiah's prose, appearing in all but a few chapters, and it is frequently present in the poetry of Jeremiah as well. The parallels indicating some strong relationship between Jeremiah and the Deuteronomistic History have always been obvious. Thus the Talmud reports that Jeremiah wrote the books of Kings.[13] I, too, briefly toyed with the idea that Jeremiah himself might be the Deuteronomist, though it was just a suggestion of possibilities; I do not hold that view now.[14] We have been struggling to explain the relationship between Jeremiah and Dtr in modern scholarship since Mowinckel.[15] We might explain the parallels in part as owing to their common use of standard expressions of the late seventh and early sixth centuries, though this certainly cannot explain all of it, nor the comparative lack of it in other works of the period. The explanation that relates to the context of this paper is that Deuteronomistic editors (i.e., members of the Deuteronomistic "school") reworked the material in Jeremiah. To determine if this is correct, we must examine the poetic and prose layers of Jeremiah and determine whether the Deuteronomistic language appears to be native or editorially inserted.

The first step is to separate the poetry of Jeremiah from the prose, admittedly a difficult task in a number of places because of the complex character of some passages in Jeremiah that seem to walk a line between poetry and prose. Still, few if any of these difficult passages played a determinative role in the analysis related to our present purpose that I am reporting here.[16]

The next step is to identify all occurrences of characteristically Deuteronomistic terms and phrases in the poetry of Jeremiah and all occurrences in the prose. It is also necessary to determine when the Deuteronomistic language appears to be integral to the text and when it may have been an editorial

---

13. *b. B. Bat.* 15a.

14. Friedman, *Who Wrote,* 146-49.

15. S. Mowinckel, *Zur Komposition des Buches Jeremia* (Oslo: 1914); idem, *Prophecy and Tradition* (Oslo, 1946). For discussion and recent bibliography on the relationship between Jeremiah and the Deuteronomistic History see Jack R. Lundbom, "Jeremiah, Book of," *ABD* 3.706-21; and L. G. Perdue and B. W. Kovacs, eds., *A Prophet to the Nations: Essays in Jeremiah Studies* (Winona Lake, IN: Eisenbrauns, 1984).

16. My identifications of the poetic portions of Jeremiah do not differ dramatically from those of other scholars. I identify the following verses as poetry (MT): Jer 1:5, 7b; 2:2b-37; 4:3-9, 19-26, 28-31; 5:1–6:30; 8:7-23; 9:1-13, 16-25; 10:2-10, 12-25; 12:1-13; 14:2-10, 19-22; 15:21; 16:16-21; 17:1-18; 18:11-12, 18-23; 20:7-18; 22:13-18, 20-23, 28-30; 23:9-12; 25:30b-38; 30:5-25; 31:1-25, 33b-36; 45:3-4; 46:3-12, 14-28; 47:1-49:5, 7-27, 28b-33, 35-39; 50:1–51:29. Also, the following verses may be identified as poetry with less certainty: Jer 3:1-5; 4:10-18; 8:4-6; 9:14-15; 11:13-19, 22; 13:15-27; 18:13-15; 22:6-7, 10-12; 23:5-6, 13-29; 31:26-33a; 51:30-58.

addition. For example, does a Deuteronomistic phrase play a necessary part in
a poetic parallel formulation, thus indicating that it is part and parcel of its
context? Does it occur near the beginning or end of a poetic passage, where
editorial addition is more likely to occur? Does the phrase make sense as an
editorial addition; that is, does it modify the meaning of the context or serve
any ideological purpose?

I observed where each of these occurrences of Deuteronomistic terms and
phrases in Jeremiah appears in the Deuteronomistic History. The object was to
determine whether there was any meaningful relationship between these occurrences and Dtr[1], Dtr[2], or the Deuteronomistic historian's sources. There was.

The poetic portions of Jeremiah include at least forty-five occurrences of
terms or phrases that are Deuteronomistic; that is, terminology that otherwise
occurs only in the Deuteronomistic History (or by far predominantly in the
Deuteronomistic History), and especially terminology that is found in the
Deuteronomistic *layers* of the history, not just in the historian's sources. These
included such terms and phrases as:

מקטן ועד גדול
סורר ומורה
יורה ומלקוש בעתו
דגן תירוש יצהר בקר צאן
עזבוני
הלך אחרי בעל
דמן על פני השדה [אדמה]
מל לבבכם

Even limiting the cases to language that occurs only in Jeremiah and Dtr
and nowhere else in the Hebrew Bible, and further limiting these cases strictly
to occurrences of such language that are integral to their poetic contexts and
not suspect of having been added secondarily, at least a dozen appearances of
Deuteronomistic language seem to be native, not added, in the poetry of
Jeremiah. For example:

When the poet expresses the notion that the people have abandoned their
God by the term עֲזָבוּנִי in Jer 5:7, an expression that occurs only in
Jeremiah and Dtr, there is no structural or ideological reason to suspect
that a Deuteronomist slipped it into this context.

When the poet speaks of the circumcision of the foreskin of the heart (Jer
4:4; 9:24-25), a figure that occurs only in Jeremiah and Dtr, this figure,
too, appears to be native to its context and not secondary.

When the poet says (2:23):

אֵיךְ תֹאמְרִי לֹא נִטְמֵאתִי
אַחֲרֵי הַבַּעַל [הַבְּעָלִים = MT] לֹא הָלַכְתִּי

רְאִי דַרְכֵּךְ בַּגַּיְא
דְעִי מֶה עָשִׂית

— לָלֶכֶת אַחֲרֵי הַבַּעַל there are no grounds to think that the expression
which otherwise occurs only in Dtr[1] — is an editorial addition. It is
structurally part of the poetic parallel, and no particularly Deuteronomistic ideological value would have been achieved by its addition
to this context. (Other cases are Jer 2:8; 5:15, 23, 24; 9:13, 21; 12:4;
25:33; 31:11.)

Now examining all the cases of Deuteronomistic language in the poetry,
whether by the strictly limited criteria or taking all forty-five cases, one finds
the following: It is entirely language that is known from the Song of Moses
(Deuteronomy 32), from the Deuteronomic law code (Deuteronomy 12–26,
known as Dtn), or from Dtr[1] — or language from Dtr[1] that recurs in Dtr[2].
None of it is language that is known solely from Dtr[2] — with one exception,
which I shall discuss in a moment.

An examination of all the prose of the book of Jeremiah, however, produces a different picture: the characteristic language of *all* the layers of the
Deuteronomistic History is represented in the prose, utterly interwoven: the
Song of Moses, Dtn, Dtr[1], and Dtr[2]. Of some thirty chapters of prose in Jeremiah
that contain language that is characteristic of Dtr[1], all but four also contain
language that is characteristic of Dtr[2].

What does this mean? Why does Jeremiah's poetry contain the language
of Dtr[1] and older texts but not Dtr[2]? Presumably because the author of this
poetry was familiar with the text of Dtr[1] and alluded to it, but did not allude
to any of the Dtr[2] lines because they had not been added to the history yet.
This is precisely what one would expect given the relative dating of these persons
and texts. Dtr[1] is traced to the years before Josiah's death. Jeremiah's poetry is
supposed to come almost entirely from the years between Josiah's death and
the exile. Dtr[2] then comes from the time of the exile.

How else might one explain the fact that Jeremiah's poetry has Dtr[1] terms
but no Dtr[2] terms? One might say that the Dtr[2] passages are relatively few, so
there are not that many characteristically Dtr[2] terms to come up in the poetry
of Jeremiah. But the Dtr[2] terms do appear in the Jeremiah prose — frequently,
and interwoven with those of Dtr[1]. One might say that the Dtr[1] historian
worked over the poetry and the prose of Jeremiah and that later the Dtr[2]
historian worked it over again but avoided touching the poetry, only redoing
the prose. But, first of all, that is an unlikely process to imagine on the face of
it. Second, our evidence includes Deuteronomistic terms that are original and
integral in their contexts in Jeremiah, so we are not talking about anybody
"working over" or "redoing" anything here.

Moreover, I mentioned an exception. One Dtr[2] phrase does occur in

Jeremiah's poetry. The phrase is ישׁם וישׁרק and it occurs twice. But the two occurrences are in Jeremiah 49 and 50, that is, in the portion of Jeremiah's poetry that is regarded as later than the rest — presumably as exilic, or in any case later than Josiah and Dtr[1].[17] The exception proves the rule. The main body of poetry in Jeremiah has no terminology from the second edition of the Deuteronomistic History. The later poetry in Jeremiah does. The evidence of the distribution of the particular Deuteronomistic language in the prose and poetry of the book of Jeremiah therefore suggests that this language in Jeremiah was not a random use of popular terms of a Deuteronomistic school. Rather, the chain of allusions and references indicates the order in which these works were written. This evidence further supports the attribution of the poetry to Jeremiah himself (or at least to his period); and it is an extremely strong addition to the evidence that I have assembled in the past for the identification of Dtr[1] and Dtr[2].[18] It indicates that there is a particular pattern of development of this language, which we must now take into account, and which helps us to see the actual steps of the writing of these works. The order of composition is:

1. the Deuteronomic law code
2. the Song of Moses
3. Dtr[1]
4. the poetry of Jeremiah 1–45
5. (most of) the prose of Jeremiah
6. Dtr[2]
7. the poetry of Jeremiah 46–51

The first two works could have been composed in the reverse order, which does not make a difference for my present concern. The order of composition of Dtr[2] and the prose of Jeremiah might also be reversed. For now, the question I want to address is, What is the minimum number of persons that this picture *requires?* The answer: four. One writes Dtn. One writes the Song of Moses. Centuries later, one person writes the poetry of Jeremiah, some of it before the exile, some after. And one person, as I said earlier, writes Dtr[1] and Dtr[2]. That leaves the prose of Jeremiah. The number of layers in the prose has never been settled in scholarship. The point that I want to add to that discussion now is that the language that separates clearly into two stages in the Deuteronomistic History does not so easily divide in the prose of Jeremiah. Rather, the characteristic language of both Dtr[1] and Dtr[2] are thoroughly embedded in almost all the Jeremiah prose. To me the depth of similarity of language and interests between these two bodies of prose — Dtr and Jeremiah — suggests common authorship. It is far beyond the degree of similarity that we normally expect in

17. Lundbom, *ABD* 3.715.
18. See n. 12 above.

a "school" of writers. The Pythagoreans wrote extremely similarly, but they were all ascribing their work to Pythagoras — which is the opposite of what is going on in the Deuteronomistic literature, which is not presented as the work of one person. People sometimes say that all the Albrightians sound like Albright; but that is just the point: such modern schools have nothing like the depth of commonality that is found in the Deuteronomistic works. The layers of Dtr and of Jeremianic prose are close enough together in time and location, and the language of *both* stages of Dtr is so utterly merged in the prose of Jeremiah, that our starting position should be that they are by the same author. We should be drawn to propose more than one only if these corpora display intolerable contradictions. But what I said about Dtr[1] and Dtr[2] earlier applies to the Jeremianic prose and Dtr as well: There have not yet been shown contradictions of the order that persuaded us that there were multiple sources in the Torah or Joshua or Isaiah or Zechariah.

Does all of this add up to a school, then? Hardly. Dtn and the Song of Moses are early works. The poetry of Jeremiah and the prose of both Jeremiah and the Deuteronomistic History require two persons who used these early works centuries later. (The Deuteronomist may also have made additions to Dtn, which still does not change this picture of the number of hands involved in these works.) Individual authors — not a school. All are associated with the Shilonite-Anathoth priesthood — still not a school. The burden of proof and of specificity is properly on those who want to establish the existence of a school. They must establish that there is a multiplicity of authors here. Even if we do separate the author of the Deuteronomistic History from the author of the prose of Jeremiah, that would not give us a school. It would give us one more, rather unoriginal prose author. Those who would argue that there was a school probably must also establish that these authors were distributed over more than a single generation. At least that seems to be what has been meant by a Deuteronomistic school until now.

I do not mean to ignore the question of the identification of multiple layers in the prose of Jeremiah or to minimize the complexity of that territory.[19] For the purposes of relating this issue to the matter of a Deuteronomistic *school*, however, the identification of various such layers in Jeremiah scholarship need not change this picture. If we separate some of the third-person accounts — called Source B or attributed to Baruch — from Deuteronomistic passages, the non-Deuteronomistic passages are excluded from our analysis of the Deuteronomistic school in any case. Even if we distinguish between a Deuteronomistic *writer* of some sections and Deuteronomistic *editing* of other sections, that still does not bring us up to a *school*. It may not even require two separate persons.

---

19. References and a brief history of scholarship on the relationship between the prose sermons of Jeremiah and the Deuteronomistic literature can be found in Louis Stulman, *The Prose Sermons of the Book of Jeremiah* (SBLDS 83; Atlanta: Scholars, 1986).

I am not saying that a Deuteronomistic school did not exist. I am saying that no one working in this area can simply assume that such a school existed, not in the present state of the evidence.[20] What we must do, in our age of broadening literary consciousness, is to stop using "school" as a cover term for literary and social processes that we have not yet figured out. Rather we must identify specifically what authors and editors we are talking about, and then use "school" or whatever term fits.

20. McKenzie has expressed a skepticism quite similar to my own regarding the degree to which the existence of a Deuteronomistic "school" has ever been established in scholarship (*The Trouble with Kings*, 6).

All Israel's Response to Joshua: A Note on the Narrative Framework of Joshua 1*

DAVID M. HOWARD, JR.

Trinity Evangelical Divinity School, Deerfield, Illinois

This essay treats a question arising from the narrative framework of Joshua 1: How does Joshua's speech to the Transjordan tribes in 1:12-15 relate to the surrounding material? This material consists of Joshua's instructions to Israel's leaders in 1:10-11 and the response to Joshua by an unspecified group of people in 1:16-18. I deal with two related questions: (1) How did the author of Joshua 1 conceive of the relationship between Joshua's two speeches in the chapter? (2) Who are the respondents to Joshua in vv. 16-18?

The solution advanced here is recovered from the syntax of the text itself in vv. 12 and 16: a cohesion[1] in the text renders unnecessary any recourse to various traditions or sources to solve the problem. This approach brings together some trends in general linguistics, which are concerned with literary relations above the sentence level,[2] and in biblical studies, which have turned in the last two decades to synchronic literary concerns.

It is a pleasure to offer this brief study in honor of my *Doktorvater*. While

---

*I have profited in this essay from discussions with Robert Bergen, Trent Butler, Mark Hillmer, Anson Rainey, and John Sailhamer, but none should be held responsible for any deficiencies herein.

1. The term *cohesion* is used here in order to echo the title of the influential work by M. A. K. Halliday and Ruqaiya Hasan, *Cohesion in English* (London: Longman, 1976), which explores literary relations in a text above the sentence level.

2. For entrée into the field, see Walter R. Bodine, "Linguistics and Philology in the Study of Ancient Near Eastern Languages," in *"Working with No Data": Semitic and Egyptian Studies Presented to Thomas O. Lambdin* (ed. D. M. Golomb; Winona Lake, IN: Eisenbrauns, 1987) 39-54, esp. 51-54.

most of my work with Freedman was in Hebrew poetry and the Psalms, I had
one memorable seminar with him on the book of Joshua, in which a handful
of students met for an hour per week in his office and covered five or six chapters
at a time. It may be appropriate to return to this book in the present essay to
address an issue we did not discuss in that seminar.

I. The Problem

Chapter 1 of Joshua consists mainly of spoken discourse. The only narrative
portions form a framework in vv. 1, 10, 12, and 16a. Each portion is merely a brief
introduction to the discourse that follows. Verses 1, 10, and 16 all begin with the
wāw-consecutive plus prefixed verb construction *(wayyiqṭōl),*[3] which functions as
the normal mode of relating sequential actions in past-time narrative. In v. 1, the
speech introduced is YHWH's charge to Joshua; in v. 10, it is Joshua's instructions
to the officers of the people; in v. 16, it is a response to Joshua's words.

By contrast, v. 12 begins with a disjunctive construction, with three prepositional phrases intruding between the *wāw* and the (suffixed) verb. This fits
the common pattern in Hebrew, whereby nonsequential material — such as a
narrator's editorial aside, an account of concomitant or previous action, or an
action that is conceived of as part of that described in the preceding verb — is
generally introduced via a disjunctive construction of some type.[4] At least two
commentators have discussed this phenomenon in v. 12, noting the introduction of significant new material here.[5]

Some question exists, however, as to the extent of the new material or the
editorial aside here. Does the *wayyiqṭōl* construction in v. 16 hark back to the
same construction in v. 10 (i.e., to the nearest preceding *wayyiqṭōl* in the narrative framework), or does it refer back to the nearest verb of any type in the
narrative framework (i.e., the suffixed form in v. 12)? Put another way, are the
speakers/respondents in vv. 16-18 the two-and-one-half Transjordan tribes

---

3. The term "*wāw*-consecutive" is inadequate, but I use it here for convenience. Waltke
and O'Connor use the better term "*wāw*-relative" (Bruce K. Waltke and M. O'Connor, *An
Introduction to Biblical Hebrew Syntax* [Winona Lake, IN: Eisenbrauns, 1990] §29.6f and
passim). Verse 1 actually has two *wayyiqṭōls*: *wayĕhî* and *wayyōʾmar*. The first is part of the
chapter's time margin; the second is the relevant one here, in terms of the string of *wayyiqṭōl*
speech verbs introducing discourse.

4. See S. R. Driver, *A Treatise on the Use of Tenses in Hebrew* (3rd ed.; Oxford: Clarendon, 1892) 195-211; Francis I. Andersen, *The Sentence in Biblical Hebrew* (Janua Linguarum,
Series Practica 231; The Hague: Mouton, 1974) 77-91; Waltke and O'Connor, *Hebrew Syntax,*
§29.2.3. See also the works in n. 16 below.

5. Robert G. Boling and G. Ernest Wright, *Joshua* (AB 6; Garden City, NY: Doubleday,
1982) 126; Trent C. Butler, *Joshua* (WBC 7; Waco: Word, 1983) 18-19.

alone (mentioned in v. 12), or do they in some way include the representatives of all twelve tribes (mentioned in v. 10)? The issue is ambiguous because the subject of the verb in v. 16 is not directly specified; thus, it could be either the Transjordan tribes or representatives of the entire nation.

Most commentators simply assume that the words in vv. 16-18 belong to the Transjordan tribes alone.[6] If they address the issue at all, commentators usually note the close correspondence between Joshua's words in vv. 13-15 and the hortatory response in vv. 16-18, and they merely assume that the *wayyiqṭōl* of v. 16 harks back to the nearest verb in the narrative framework, in v. 12.[7]

The argument here, however, is that the respondents in vv. 16-18 are not just the two-and-one-half Transjordan tribes but rather representatives of the entire nation. The disjunctive verbal pattern at v. 12 signals the author's inclusion of both the officers of the people (v. 10) and the two-and-one-half tribes (v. 12) among the respondents, and the plural verb with unspecified subject in v. 16 brings both groups together in the response. Joshua's two speeches in the chapter are considered to be part of one event, with both groups responding to him in the end. I will support this contention on the basis of syntax, parallel constructions, and context.

II. Syntax

1. The Narrative Framework

On the syntactical level, the solution proposed here presents itself if one sees the disjunctive construction in v. 12 as a device to signal simultaneous action, which is a well-recognized feature of such disjunctions.[8] It represents a clause of the type that Andersen calls a "paragraph-level circumstantial clause."[9] This

6. Marten H. Woudstra (*The Book of Joshua* [NICOT; Grand Rapids: Eerdmans, 1981] 66n.9) mentions two who see the respondents as being the twelve tribes — A. Gelin (*Josué* [La Sainte Bible; Paris, 1955]) and J. Steinmann (*Josué* [*Connaître la Bible;* Brugges, 1960]) — but he does not give their reasoning; these works are inaccessible to me.

7. For example, Boling, *Joshua*, 126-28; Butler, *Joshua*, 18-23; J. Alberto Soggin, *Joshua* (trans. R. A. Wilson; OTL; Philadelphia: Westminster, 1972) 212; John Gray, *Joshua, Judges, Ruth* (2nd ed.; NCB; Grand Rapids: Eerdmans, 1986) 61-62; C. J. Goslinga, *Joshua, Judges, Ruth* (trans. R. Togtman; Bible Student's Commentary; Grand Rapids: Zondervan, 1986) 39-42.

8. "Wayyiqtol is also avoided if the 2nd action is **simultaneous** or represented as such" (Paul Joüon and T. Muraoka, *A Grammar of Biblical Hebrew* [Rome: Pontifical Biblical Institute, 1991] §118f; cf. also §§166d, h, on simultaneity in temporal clauses). See also Driver, *Syntax*, 195; A. B. Davidson, *Hebrew Syntax* (3rd ed.; Edinburgh: T. & T. Clark, 1901) §137; T. Muraoka, *Emphatic Words and Structures in Biblical Hebrew* (Jerusalem: Magnes; Leiden: Brill, 1985) 33-34, 36-37; Alviero Niccacci, *The Syntax of the Verb in Classical Hebrew Prose* (trans. W. G. E. Watson; JSOTSup 86; Sheffield: Sheffield Academic, 1990) 63-64.

9. Andersen, *Sentence*, 65-66.

type of clause performs the function of coordination, representing two events as simultaneous or contemporaneous.

Thus, Joshua's two speeches in the chapter — to the leaders in vv. 10-11 and to the Transjordan tribes in vv. 12-15 — are unified into one "simultaneous" event. Then, the response to Joshua in vv. 16-18, affirming him, is that of both groups already mentioned. This understanding is possible because (among other reasons) the subject of the verb in v. 16 — *wy'nw,* "and they answered" — is not directly specified, as already noted. Indeed, it is the only speech verb in the narrative framework of the chapter for which the subject is not expressed in the surface structure. This singular indeterminacy functions to reinforce the lumping of Joshua's two speeches into one event and presenting the response as all Israel's response.

One can further argue the point by noting the chiastic pattern in the words of the narrative framework that is created by the disjunctive construction in v. 12. Joshua's two speeches are introduced by narrative frames that unfold in a chiastic pattern with each other:

V. 10: *wāw* + speech verb + speaker + hearers + *lē'mōr*

V. 12: *wāw* + hearers + speech verb + speaker + *lē'mōr*

V. 10: A – B – C – D – E

V. 12: A – D' – B' – C – E

Scholars have noted the closely related nature of material bound together chiastically.[10] Andersen calls it "chiastic coordination."[11] He explains it thus: "This construction achieves the most complete integration of two clauses to represent actions of two participants as two sides of a single event. The simultaneity of the two actions is implied, and also their similarity."[12] In Joshua 1, the chiastic pattern serves precisely this function, presenting Joshua's two speeches as part of one event. The response in vv. 16-18, then, is the response of everyone who had been addressed in this one event, namely, both groups.

This analysis is confirmed by Robert Bergen, who explored the "fronting" of subject, object, or prepositional phrases in the narrative framework of the Pentateuch in the course of studying one construction (*wāw* plus subject plus "perfect" verb [WSP]) in depth.[13] Bergen states:

10. Ibid., 120-21; Muraoka, *Emphatic Words,* 36-37; Joüon-Muraoka, *Grammar,* §118f.

11. Andersen, *Sentence,* 67-68. In this section, Andersen is speaking of the sentence level (not the paragraph level), but it applies nonetheless to Joshua 1, since the narrative framework here is merely a skeleton, in which each bit of narrative harks back at the sentence level to the previous bit.

12. Andersen, *Sentence,* 67.

13. Robert D. Bergen, *Varieties and Functions of Hebrew* waw-*Plus-Subject-Plus-Perfect*

narrative-framework WSP constructions were regularly employed in Biblical Hebrew storytelling as a means of indicating actions which were chronologically simultaneous with the WI [*wāw*-consecutive plus imperfect verb] clauses which preceded them. Alternatively, WSP clauses could be used to portray actions which, while not precisely coterminous with the immediately preceding WI clauses, were conceived by the author as being part of a continuous event initiated in the WI clause.[14]

The syntax in Josh 1:12 is not "WSP," but rather *wāw* plus three prepositional phrases plus suffixed (speech) verb plus subject (as noted in §III below in more depth). But the crucial fact is the breaking of a *wayyiqṭōl* string, by whatever means, not by the subject per se. As Bergen notes, "This observation about the semantic/chronological function of WSP clauses can be demonstrated to be fully applicable to clauses initiated by a <u>waw</u>-plus-prepositional-phrase (WPrPh) such as the one found in Josh. 1:12a."[15]

2. A Note on Word Order

As is obvious, the issue at hand in the narrative framework of Josh 1:12 is bound up with the question of word order. That the verse contains an "abnormal" (i.e., disjunctive) word order is not disputed by those who address the issue. What can be disputed is the explanation for this order. One might argue that the disjunction introduced in the verse signals an emphasis on the Transjordan tribes, or performs some other function, and does not signal the simultaneity of events in two adjacent paragraphs for which I argue here.

Most grammars have addressed the question of norms and divergences from norms. In the case of word order, probably the most prominent explanation for the reversal of the normal verb-subject word order in Hebrew, or for the breaking of a *wayyiqṭōl* string, is that this serves to emphasize the subject in some way.[16]

But the notion of emphasis is frequently overapplied, misapplied, ill defined, or overly vague. As Muraoka has noted,

the term 'emphasis' is often too rashly called in, like a pinch-hitter in the baseball game, without much thought being given to precisely what is meant

---

Sentence Constructions in the Narrative Framework of the Pentateuch (Ann Arbor: University Microfilms International, 1986).

14. Bergen, private communication, November 1, 1989.

15. Ibid.

16. Driver, *Tenses*, 200-201; Davidson, *Hebrew Syntax*, §§107.1, 110; GKC, §142f; J. Wash Watts, *A Survey of Syntax in the Hebrew Old Testament* (Grand Rapids: Eerdmans, 1964) 25-26; R. J. Williams, *Hebrew Syntax: An Outline* (2nd ed.; Toronto: University of Toronto, 1976) §573; Muraoka, *Emphatic Words*, 32-33; Niccacci, *Syntax*, §48.

by the term nor, more importantly, to the question why the writer or speaker
possibly felt the need for an emphatic form or construction. The impression
is thus created that 'emphasis' is a ready panacea for Hebraists' (and Semitists')
headaches of all sorts.[17]

Muraoka's work is a sober corrective to such imprecise application of the concept of emphasis. He notes many instances of words and word order where
specific types of emphases are in view, but he also demonstrates that other
explanations are better applied in many cases, including cases of disjunctive
word order.

Such an inversion or breaking of the expected norm as we have in Josh
1:12 does not, in and of itself, and of necessity, signal emphasis (to use this
popular explanation). The same works that use the concept of emphasis to
explain such constructions almost always include other possible explanations
as well.[18] Perhaps the most common of these explanations is that such a construction may signal a circumstantial clause (which describes a variety of circumstances somehow related to the main action),[19] but this by no means
exhausts the possibilities advanced. Other possibilities include contrast, anterior
time, and creation of chiasms, to mention but three.[20]

What is relevant here is that the observation of a syntactical disjunction,
on purely formal grounds, does not yield a single, incontrovertible explanation
for its interpretation. One must further interpret it by contextual or other
considerations in order for it to be meaningful. These signal which of several
possibilities best accounts for it.

Thus, several scholars have recently attempted to account for the various
disjunctive or "abnormal" phenomena with more precision, rather than lumping them together into one convenient category labeled, for example, "emphasis." Among the most detailed treatments of this sort are those already noted
by Andersen, Muraoka, and Niccacci, to which can be added those of Richter
and Longacre.[21]

17. Muraoka, *Emphatic Words*, xi.

18. See n. 16 above.

19. Driver, *Tenses*, 195-211; Davidson, *Syntax*, §137; GKC, §142d; Williams, *Hebrew
Syntax*, §573; Muraoka, *Emphatic Words*, 33-34; Niccacci, *Syntax*, §§40, 43.

20. On contrast, see Driver, *Syntax*, 196-97; Williams, *Hebrew Syntax*, §573; Muraoka,
Emphatic Words, 33; Niccacci, *Syntax*, §42. For anterior time, see Davidson, *Hebrew Syntax*,
§39c; GKC, §142b; Williams, *Hebrew Syntax*, §573; Niccacci, *Syntax*, §40. On chiasms, see
GKC, §142fn.1; Muraoka, *Emphatic Words*, 36-37.

21. Andersen, *Sentence*; Muraoka, *Emphatic Words* (esp. 1-46, on word order); Niccacci,
Syntax; Wolfgang Richter, *Grundlagen einer althebräischen Grammatik* (3 vols.; Münchener
Universitätsschriften: Arbeiten zu Text Sprache im Alten Testament 8, 10, 13; St. Ottilien:
EOS, 1978-80), esp. vol. 3; Robert E. Longacre, *Joseph: A Story of Divine Providence: A Text
Theoretical and Textlinguistic Analysis of Genesis 37 and 39–48* (Winona Lake, IN: Eisenbrauns,
1989).

Among the numerous categories laid out by these (and other) scholars for classifying the various types of disjunctions, the explanation advanced here, that the disjunction in Josh 1:12 signals simultaneity, would best seem to satisfy conditions of syntax, parallel constructions, and context.[22]

As noted above (n. 5), only two of the major commentators on Joshua even mention the disjunction in Josh 1:12. To ignore a significant syntactical signal such as this is surely to miss something of import in the text. Even the two commentators who note the disjunction, however, have deficiencies in their analysis of it. Boling merely assumes the continuity of vv. 12-18,[23] along with most scholars, and he does not address the implications of the syntax for the two questions posed at the outset. To his credit, Butler at least classifies the circumstantial clause here,[24] but he misidentifies it as an "episode-initial cir-cumstantial clause." As detailed by Andersen (to whom Butler appeals), such a clause signals the beginning of a new episode, but it is *marginal* to what fol-lows.[25] This certainly cannot be said of the material in Josh 1:12-15.[26]

22. A recent discordant note about ways of explaining the disjunctions under con-sideration here has been sounded forcefully by Nicholas A. Bailey and Stephen H. Levinsohn, in "The Function of Preverbal Elements in Independent Clauses in the Hebrew Narrative of Genesis," *Journal of Translation and Textlinguistics* 5 (1992) 179-207. They argue that fronting of any given element to a preverbal position performs one of only two functions, that of "focusing" or of "topicalizing" that element. They use "focus" as an informal term for "highlight" or "emphasis" (179n.3). They do not define "topic" per se, but it appears in the phrase (borrowed from A. Andrews) "topic-comment articulation," where a propositional topic is introduced and a comment is made about it. Bailey and Levinsohn disagree especially vigorously with the multiple categories introduced by Andersen and Longacre.

No in-depth rebuttal can be made here except to note the following. First, Longacre has responded in some detail in the same issue of that journal ("The Analysis of Preverbal Nouns in Biblical Hebrew Narrative: Some Overriding Concerns," 208-23). Second, one should note that, as soon as Bailey and Levinsohn introduce two different explanations for preverbal fronting of elements ("topic" and "focus"), they have opened the door to the necessity of using some criteria besides the strictly formal level of syntax in making judg-ments. What they propose is not different in kind from what Andersen, Longacre, and others propose, except that the number of categories may be greater for others. In all cases, other criteria must also play a role in the interpretation.

23. Boling, *Joshua*, 126.

24. Butler, *Joshua*, 18-19.

25. Andersen, *Sentence*, 78-80.

26. Intriguingly, Butler speaks of the clause as "contemporaneous to the preceding [clause]" (p. 19), which would point toward the interpretation in this essay, but he does not pursue the implications of this point. In any case, Andersen does not speak of the "contem-poraneous" function in connection with the "episode-initial circumstantial clause" but rather with the paragraph-level circumstantial clause or the chiastic coordination mentioned above (Andersen, *Sentence*, 65-68).

III. Parallel Constructions

Additional support for the present understanding of Joshua 1 comes when one examines parallel syntactical constructions. This support depends in part on the formal characteristics of syntax, but it also depends on understanding the speech events in question. Therefore, this argument merits its own section.

I have noted above (§II.1) that the clause in Josh 1:12 does not represent the most common type of circumstantial clause, that of the *wāw* plus subject plus suffixed verb (*wāw*-S-V).[27] Rather, it consists of *wāw* plus three prepositional phrases plus suffixed verb plus subject. But the important point is not that the *wayyiqṭōl* string is broken by the subject, but that it is broken at all, by any element. As Andersen notes, "other items beside the subject can, on occasion, precede the predicator."[28] What is important is that a circumstantial clause can be "*any other kind of clause* which breaks the chain of WP (or WS) clauses."[29] This point is seconded by Joüon-Muraoka (see n. 8 above) as well, since the salient feature of such constructions is the breaking of the *wayyiqṭōl* string, by whatever means, and not the *wāw*-S-V word order per se.[30]

The closest syntactical parallels to the clause in Josh 1:12 occur in Deuteronomy 33 (the Blessing of Moses).[31] There, Moses speaks to or about each of the tribes in succession, and, in the narrative framework of that chapter, the exact syntactical construction found in Josh 1:12 also occurs. The poetic material is introduced in v. 2 with a simple *wāw*-consecutive plus prefixed (speech) verb *(wayyō'mar)*. The next narrative occurs in v. 7, which has a mixed construction, consisting of *wāw* plus pronoun plus prepositional phrase plus *wayyō'mar (wz't lyhwdh wy'mr)*. Thereafter, the pattern of *wāw* plus prepositional phrase plus suffixed (speech) verb is consistently followed through the rest of the chapter's narrative framework:

v. 8: *wllwy 'mr*
v. 12: *lbnymn 'mr*[32]
v. 13: *wlywsp 'mr*
v. 18: *wlzbwln 'mr*

---

27. This is the type cited in a large number — but not all — of the examples given in the works in n. 8.

28. Andersen, *Sentence*, 78.

29. Ibid., 77 (emphasis mine).

30. The exception to this is any negated clause of the *wĕlō'* plus suffixed or prefixed verb variety; negated circumstantial clauses must have some item besides *wĕlō'* inserted between the *wāw* and the verb (Andersen, *Sentence*, 78).

31. I am indebted to Robert Bergen for this observation, as well as most of the references in the following paragraph.

32. Strong textual evidence argues for addition of *wāw* here *(wlbnymn 'mr)*: Targum, Samaritan Pentateuch, Old Greek, Syriac, Vulgate.

v. 20: *wlgd 'mr*
v. 22: *wldn 'mr*
v. 23: *wlnptly 'mr*
v. 24: *wl'šr 'mr*

Other examples in narrative texts of the construction found in Josh 1:12 include:

Gen 1:5: *wyqr' 'lhym l'wr ywm wlḥšk qr' lylh*
Gen 1:10: *wyqr' 'lhym lybšh 'rṣ wlmqwh hmym qr' ymym*
Gen 3:14, 17: [14] *wy'mr yhwh 'lhym 'l-hnḥš* . . . [17] *wl'dm 'mr*[33]
Gen 20:15, 16: [15] *wy'mr 'bymlk* . . . [16] *wlśrh 'mr*
Exod 20:22; 24:1: [20:22] *wy'mr yhwh 'l-mšh* . . . [24:1] *w'l-mšh 'mr*[34]
Exod 24:13, 14: [13] *wy'l mšh 'l-hr h'lhym* [14] *w'l-hzqnym 'mr*
1 Sam 25:35: *wyqḥ dwd mydh 't 'šr-hby'h lw wlh 'mr*
2 Sam 19:9: *wyqm hmlk wyšb bš'r wlkl-h'm hgydw l'mr*

In each of these cases, the pattern is similar to that in Josh 1:10, 12: *wāw*-consecutive plus subject (plus intervening miscellaneous material), followed by *wāw* plus prepositional phrase plus suffixed speech verb.[35] What is notable in all cases is that each set of actions is part of one event. In almost no case are the actions actually concurrent in real time (except perhaps those in 1 Sam 25:35), but in every case the actions are presented as if they were, since they are integrally related to each other.

IV. Context

A third line of support for the argument here is contextual. In arguing that Joshua's words to the two groups were part of a single event, I do not mean to

33. YHWH's speech to Adam introduced in 3:17 is part of a string that begins in 3:14, where YHWH's speech to the serpent is introduced in the normal way: *wy'mr yhwh 'lhym 'l-hnḥš*. The sequence is continued in v. 16, with YHWH's speech to Eve. In the MT, this speech is introduced with *'l-h'šh 'mr* (with no *wāw*), but this is probably just a textual problem; in the Samaritan Pentateuch, Old Greek, Syriac, and Vulgate versions, the reading includes the article — *w'l-h'šh 'mr* — thus yielding an additional case of the pattern under discussion here.

34. The two parts of the narrative framework here are at a farther remove from each other than in the other examples, but the pattern nevertheless holds. The intervening material (Exod 20:22b–23:33) consists entirely of YHWH's words to Moses.

35. The two examples from Genesis 1 are least like the example in Joshua 1. All the others are in a true narrative framework, introducing discourse.

imply that he spoke the words in vv. 11 and 13-15 in the same *instant* to both groups. Thus, one must understand vv. 12-15 as a lengthy aside. But their precise chronological relationship to what precedes and follows is irrelevant. In the mind of the author, the two events were inextricably bound up into one, causing him to use a construction that signals concomitant action.

The actual "historical" fact was likely that Joshua spoke first to the officers and then to the Transjordan tribes. Had the author wanted, however, he could easily have expressed this via a normal *wayyiqtōl* string. Since he did not, one must ask why. The answer lies in the author's desire to present Joshua's instructions to both groups as parts of a single event, and the response to Joshua as one given by the entire nation.

One cannot deny the close correspondence between Joshua's words to the Transjordan tribes and the words of response, as well as the importance of the Transjordan tribes in the book of Joshua. Thus, the usual assumption that the respondents in vv. 16-18 are these tribes is natural enough. Many scholars have noted as well that the response echoes closely these tribes' response to Moses already in Num 32:16-27, where they committed themselves to helping their fellow Israelites and swore loyalty to what Moses had commanded (cf. also Deut 3:18-20). Furthermore, scholars have noted the importance of Joshua's comments to these tribes at the end of the book, where he commended them for their obedience and loyalty (Josh 22:1-9).

Nevertheless, one must also note that there is no *inherent* incongruity between the words of response in vv. 16-18 and Joshua's instructions to the leaders in v. 11. The words of response are general enough to represent easily the leaders' reaction to Joshua. If the close connections just noted between this response and the Transjordan tribes' texts were not apparent, one would have little question that the words in vv. 16-18 belonged to the leaders. That is, if vv. 12-15 were excised from the text, commentators would have little trouble in seeing the response of vv. 16-18 as having come from the leaders mentioned in v. 10, responding to Joshua's words in v. 11. Neither the contents of vv. 16-18 nor the syntax of the verbs in the narrative framework *demand* that the respondents be the Transjordan tribes alone.

Indeed, one can argue — from the perspective of the book's message — that this response must have come from both groups. Otherwise, we would have no record of any response to Joshua's words in v. 11, nor any affirmation of him as Israel's leader by representatives of all Israel. Seeing the words in vv. 16-18 as coming from both groups, including representatives of the entire nation, places Joshua (the man) on sound footing as Israel's leader, since he has been affirmed by all the people.

As presented in the book, Joshua is a worthy successor to Moses, Israel's great leader and lawgiver. Joshua had proved his worth earlier by being one of two spies (out of twelve) who counseled entering the land of Canaan despite seemingly prohibitive odds (Numbers 13–14). Now he was called by YHWH to function as Moses' successor (Josh 1:1-9). The book is clear that YHWH was with him, and that he enjoyed a similar stature to Moses' (1:5, 9, 16-18; 3:7; 4:14; 6:27; 10:14; 11:15, 23). He appears throughout the book speaking and acting with authority, and he is as eloquent as Moses in his farewell speeches (chaps. 22–24).

Yet, at the outset of the book, all of this is not so clear. He is merely "Moses' aide" in 1:1 *(mšrt mšh)*, whereas Moses appears here (1:1, 2, 13) and throughout (8:31, 33; 9:24; 11:12, 15; 12:6; 13:8; 14:7; 18:7; 22:2, 4, 5) in a much more exalted role, as the "servant of YHWH" *(ʿbd yhwh)*. One of the book's subthemes is to trace Joshua's rise, his growing into the job, such that, by the end of the book, he too can be called the "servant of YHWH" (24:29). Joshua rises to a stature similar to Moses' by the end: he is the undisputed leader of the people, he addresses them in hortatory addresses reminiscent of Moses' (chaps. 22–23), and he even leads them in covenant renewal (chap. 24). This rise in stature is anticipated at the beginning of the book by his affirmation as leader, not by a small portion of the nation but by representatives of the entire nation.

It would appear, then, that the close correspondences between the texts dealing with the Transjordan tribes and the response in Josh 1:16-18 have prevented scholars from considering the most likely solution: that the response represents both groups mentioned in the chapter, a solution supported contextually on the level of the chapter as well as the level of the book.

V. Conclusion

I conclude, then, that Joshua's first two speeches in the book were part of one event, and that the people's response to him was given by representatives of all Israel, not just the Transjordan tribes. Considerations of syntax, parallel constructions, and context all point in this direction. The implications of this point for an assessment of Joshua's role as Moses' worthy successor have been hinted at above, but they remain to be explored more fully.

Aaron's Calf and Jeroboam's Calves

GARY N. KNOPPERS

The Pennsylvania State University, University Park

Introduction

The descriptions of Aaron and Jeroboam's cultic innovations occupy prominent positions in the texts of Exodus and Kings. The keen attention of biblical authors to Aaron's calf and Jeroboam's calves is revealing. The Deuteronomist could have devoted greater coverage to Jeroboam's fortifications (1 Kgs 12:25) and to his military campaigns (14:19), but he privileges Jeroboam's investiture of Bethel and Dan. The establishment (12:26-33), denunciation (13:1-3, 33-34), and punishment (14:7-18) of Jeroboam's sins dominate the Deuteronomistic portrayal of Jeroboam's tenure and indeed of the entire Deuteronomistic History of the northern kingdom.

If Jeroboam's cultus is a productive historiographical and theological concern of the Deuteronomist, it was, according to modern scholars, also a substantive concern of some earlier Israelite and Judahite authors. Modern scholars typically explain the many similarities between the description of Aaron's apostasy in Exodus 32 and the description of Jeroboam's apostasy in 1 Kings 12 by seeing the former as a reflection of the latter, even though the construction of Jeroboam's calves at Bethel and Dan ostensibly occurs centuries after the construction of Aaron's calf at Sinai.[1] In this line of interpretation, literary concerns

---

1. The similarities in iconography and terminology (e.g., אלה/הנה אלהיך ישראל, אשר העלוך מארץ מצרים) are indisputable (Exod 32:4, 8; 1 Kgs 12:28). M. Aberbach and L. Smolar ("Aaron, Jeroboam, and the Golden Calves," *JBL* 86 [1967] 130-34) provide a comprehensive list of the parallels between the two accounts. More traditional scholars view Jeroboam's cult, on both historical and literary levels, as a revival of Aaron's cult. See the survey of B. Childs, *The Book of Exodus: A Critical, Theological Commentary* (OTL; Philadelphia: Westminster, 1974) 574-79.

and historical concerns merge. Assuming the basic historicity of Jeroboam's initiatives, commentators understand the present form of Exodus 32 as a thinly veiled attack on the state cult of Jeroboam. Scholars may disagree about what portions of Exodus 32 should be assigned to J, E, D, and other sources or editors, but they generally agree that this text retrojects a polemic against the legacy of Jeroboam I to the authoritative age of Moses.[2]

I would like to distinguish more clearly, however, between historical and literary issues.[3] On a historical level, the animosity felt in southern circles toward Jeroboam's cultus helps to explain why a succession of Judahite authors would impugn this cultus by having both the deity and Moses assail it as an intolerable apostasy. But, on a literary level, most scholars would agree that the Deuteronomic writers and the Deuteronomist(s) postdate the Yahwist and the Elohist.[4] Most scholars therefore believe that when the Deuteronomist composes his history, he possesses a literary account of Aaron's apostasy bequeathed to him by a succession of earlier tradents — the Yahwist, the Elohist, the Deuteronomic authors, and perhaps others.[5] From a historical vantage point, Jeroboam's calves

2. The tradition history of Exodus 32 is very complex (M. Noth, *Exodus* [trans. J. S. Bowden; OTL; Philadelphia: Westminster, 1962] 243-46; Childs, *Exodus,* 558-62; S. E. Loewenstamm, "The Making and Destruction of the Golden Calf — a Rejoinder," *Bib* 56 [1975] 333-48). A few assign the *Grundlage* or substratum of Exodus 32 to the Yahwist (e.g., Childs, *Exodus,* 558-59). Noth proposes a slightly different hypothesis, seeing the substance of Exodus 32 (vv. 1-6, 15-20, 30-35*) as an addition to the Yahwist's narrative (*Exodus,* 234-52). Those authors who assign the bulk of the narrative to J see E as making scattered contributions (e.g., vv. 21-24). But most commentators attribute the bulk of Exodus 32 to the Elohist (W. Beyerlin, *The Origins and History of the Oldest Sinaitic Traditions* [trans. S. Rudman; Oxford: Blackwell, 1965] 18-22; J. Carpenter and G. Harford, *The Composition of the Hexateuch* [London: Longmans, 1902] 332, 517; R. Clifford, "Exodus," *NJBC* 59; S. R. Driver, *An Introduction to the Literature of the Old Testament* [rev. ed.; New York: Charles Scribner's Sons, 1914] 38; O. Eissfeldt, *The Old Testament: An Introduction* (trans. P. R. Ackroyd; New York: Harper & Row, 1965) 201-2). Many scholars also see Deuteronomic editing in vv. 7-14, and some see vv. 25-29 as a later addition. Yet, as Carpenter and Harford point out, the authors of Deuteronomy 9 must have had versions of both vv. 7-14 and vv. 25-29, because they cite and rewrite them (*Composition,* 332). In any case, my concern in this essay is the version of Exodus 32 extant in the time of the Deuteronomist. Hence, I will not formally address the source criticism of Exodus 32, unless I have reason to believe that a particular verse is post-Deuteronomistic.

3. These lines are occasionally even confused. L. R. Bailey asserts, for instance, that Noth, Gray, de Vaux, et al. believe that the Exodus account is secondary to the Kings account ("The Golden Calf," *HUCA* 42 [1971] 97). While it is true that these scholars contend that Exodus 32* was written some time after the inauguration of Jeroboam's cultus, most do not believe that the Deuteronomistic version of 1 Kgs 12:26-33 postdates the Yahwistic, Elohistic, or Deuteronomic editions of Exodus 32.

4. A recent exception is J. Van Seters, *In Search of History* (New Haven: Yale University, 1983).

5. The following scholars argue for a double redaction of the Deuteronomistic History, the first Josianic and the second exilic: F. M. Cross, *Canaanite Myth and Hebrew Epic* (Cambridge: Harvard University, 1973) 274-89; R. Nelson, *The Double Redaction of the Deuter-*

may explain Aaron's calf; but, from a literary vantage point, Aaron's calf predates Jeroboam's calves. A preoccupation with how Jeroboam's state cult clarifies issues in the interpretation of Exodus 32 ironically does little, then, to clarify the portrayal of Jeroboam's cult in 1 Kings 12.[6] There are, I would argue, important disparities as well as the oft-noted similarities between Exodus 32 and 1 Kings 12. I therefore wish to explore what light both the resemblances and the differences between Aaron's and Jeroboam's actions shed on the Deuteronomist's depiction of Jeroboam's cult in 1 Kings 12. In my judgment, this comparison illumines not only the impact of Jeroboam's sins on the course of northern history, but also the Deuteronomist's view of the Solomonic temple.

Like the authors of Exodus 32, the Deuteronomist implicitly concedes the antiquity and appeal of Jeroboam's cultus, including his tauromorphic iconography. Neither Aaron nor Jeroboam is a minor or obscure figure. Moreover, if the sanctuaries at Bethel and Dan were not popular and well established, there

---

onomistic History (JSOTSup 18; Sheffield: JSOT, 1981) 29-128; R. E. Friedman, The Exile and Biblical Narrative (HSM 22; Chico, CA: Scholars, 1981) 1-43; B. Halpern, The First Historians: The Hebrew Bible and History (San Francisco: Harper & Row, 1988) 112-18; S. McKenzie, The Trouble with Kings (VTSup 42; Leiden: Brill, 1991) 122-33; and Gary N. Knoppers, Two Nations under God: The Deuteronomistic History of Solomon and the Dual Monarchies, vol. 1: The Reign of Solomon and the Rise of Jeroboam (HSM 52; Atlanta: Scholars, 1993) 1-56. Hence, when I refer to the Deuteronomist, I mean the Josianic Deuteronomist. Following Noth (The Deuteronomistic History [trans. J. Douall et al.; JSOTSup 15; Sheffield: JSOT, 1981] 12-17), D. N. Freedman ("The Deuteronomic History," IDBSup 226-27), et al., I distinguish between the Deuteronomist and the authors of the old Deuteronomic code. The Deuteronomist incorporates a version of the Deuteronomic law into his history.

6. Space does not permit me to address, at length, the composition of 1 Kgs 12:26-33. As H.-D. Hoffmann (Reform und Reformen [ATANT 66; Zurich: Theologischer Verlag, 1980] 67-68) and Van Seters ("Histories and Historians of the Ancient Near East: The Israelites," Or 50 [1981] 170-74) have argued, this passage clearly criticizes Jeroboam from a Judahite perspective. Yet I do not think that the Deuteronomist composed this passage out of whole cloth. The pericope is practically devoid of standard Deuteronomistic clichés and style. (See, e.g., the lists of Deuteronomic and Deuteronomistic phraseology in Carpenter and Harford, Composition, 399-408; and M. Weinfeld, Deuteronomy and the Deuteronomic School [Oxford: Clarendon, 1972] 320-65.) Hence, I believe that the Deuteronomist both incorporates and shapes an older tradition within his own narrative. Whatever the nature of the Deuteronomist's source, its southern Tendenz serves his purposes well. I would agree, however, with J. Trebolle ("The Text-Critical Use of the Septuagint in the Books of Kings," VII Congress of the International Organization for Septuagint and Cognate Studies [ed. Claude Cox; Atlanta: Scholars, 1989] 290) that 1 Kgs 12:32 is a later addition, inserted through repetitive resumption from ויעל על־המזבח in v. 32b to ויעל על־המזבח at the beginning of v. 33). In Two Nations under God: The Deuteronomistic History of Solomon and the Dual Monarchies, vol. 2: The Reign of Jeroboam, the Fall of Israel, and the Reign of Josiah (HSM 53; Atlanta: Scholars, 1994), I argue that much of 1 Kgs 12:33 is also a later addition, marked by repetitive resumption (from ויעל על־המזבח to ויעל על־המזבח להקטיר), to explain the origin of Jeroboam's altar. The resulting text has Jeroboam ascending (but never descending!) the altar three times, a phenomenon almost all translations (e.g., NRSV, NJPS, REB) obscure. This volume treats the critical issues of 1 Kgs 12:26-33 in substantial detail.

would be no need to privilege them with such critical coverage. Finally, by associating Jeroboam's calves at Bethel and Dan with the god(s) of Sinai, the Deuteronomist tacitly acknowledges that the struggle between Solomon and Jeroboam is an inner-Israelite controversy.[7]

Yet the Deuteronomist occludes the inner-Israelite nature of the conflict he depicts. The Deuteronomist, in my judgment, attempts to discredit Bethel, Dan, and the northern high places by presenting Jeroboam's actions as gross distortions of an established orthopraxis. In the Deuteronomistic schema, the Solomonic temple perpetuates, incorporates, and succeeds the Mosaic institutions of ark, priesthood, sacrifice, and festival (1 Kings 8). But Jeroboam's cultus revives and perpetuates Aaron's apostasy. The cult of David and Solomon is authentic and primary; the cult of Jeroboam is counterfeit and secondary. Whereas the cultic innovations of Aaron are quickly and decisively purged, the cultic innovations of Jeroboam remain. My comparative analysis will therefore involve a number of permutations — Moses and Aaron, Solomon and Jeroboam, Moses and Solomon, Aaron and Jeroboam. I will conclude by contrasting the different ramifications of Aaron and Jeroboam's actions. Inasmuch as the Deuteronomist derives royal and national fate from cultic commitments, I will argue that the very description of Jeroboam's cultus casts doubt on the long-term prospects for the northern kingdom.

I. Cult and Countercult

The cultic initiatives of both Aaron and Jeroboam follow the promulgation of divinely sanctioned institutions — covenant and law at Sinai (Exod 19:1–24:18), and temple, sacrifice, and prayer in Jerusalem (1 Kgs 6:1–9:3). The Sinaitic narrative announces and celebrates the ratification of the covenant between Israel and YHWH. This pact includes the giving of law, the people's formal commitment to this law, and the celebration of a communal meal.[8] The in-

---

7. This is explicit in Aaron's declaration: "tomorrow is a festival to YHWH" (Exod 32:5). The Deuteronomist also indirectly acknowledges the Yahwistic nature of northern religion when he depicts the troubles that attend the foreign religious practices of Assyrian-sponsored immigrants in Samaria, who "do not know the custom of the god(s) of the land" (2 Kgs 17:26). The Assyrian king has to arrange for a local priest to be reimported into Samaria. These settlers then worship YHWH as well as their own deities (2 Kgs 17:33).

8. I am assuming, along with most commentators, that Exodus 32 follows Exodus 24 in the pre-Priestly version of the Pentateuch. The Priestly redaction of the Pentateuch (Exodus 25–31, 35–40) only sharpens further, however, the contrast between the authoritative Mosaic institutions and the institutions inaugurated by Aaron. Insamuch as the ark and tabernacle are designed to symbolize or ensure divine presence among the Israelites in the post-Sinaitic period (N. Sarna, *Exploring Exodus* [New York: Schocken, 1986] 215-20), Aaron's taurine-centered cult rivals the tabernacle-centered cult ordained by God.

scription of the covenant on two stone tablets preserves it for posterity. If God's revelation at Sinai defines his relationship to Israel, the construction and adoration of the golden calf nearly terminate it. The progress of the Sinai story comes to an abrupt halt. The pact between God and Israel is formally annulled when Moses, witnessing the apostasy of Israel, shatters the covenant tablets (Exod 32:19).

Given the tremendous innovation involved in constructing the Jerusalem temple, the argument has often been made that the cultus inaugurated by David and Solomon represented as much a shift from older established institutions as that imputed to Aaron at Sinai. Indeed, there is much to be said for the view that in instituting his cultic reforms (1 Kgs 12:26-33), Jeroboam attempted to out-archaize David.[9] Jeroboam's goal was undoubtedly to reorganize and preserve a cult, not to create a new one ex nihilo. Whether the issue is iconography, location, priesthood, or festival, there is good reason to believe that Jeroboam's cultus was essentially conservative, especially when contrasted with the religious innovations of David and Solomon in Jerusalem.[10]

The Deuteronomist casts David and Solomon's actions, however, in a completely different light. In his dedication of the temple, Solomon is at pains to demonstrate the continuity between the temple and older Israelite institutions. The temple incorporates and succeeds the ark and the tent of meeting (1 Kgs 8:1-9). YHWH, in turn, manifests his approval of the Solomonic temple through a magisterial theophany (8:10-11). Solomon's prayer promotes the temple as a focal point of the people's attention in all sorts of predicaments. The Deuteronomist notes repeatedly the geographic and demographic representation of all Israelites at this national convocation (8:1, 65-66). The people's enthusiastic participation at the dedication confirms the temple's status as the center of Israel's religious life. Solomon even announces at the dedication of his shrine that YHWH has fulfilled every word he spoke to Moses (8:56). In this manner, the Deuteronomist presents Zion as the divinely authorized counterpart to Sinai. David and Solomon bring to completion what was begun at Sinai. Given that Zion complements and fulfills Sinai, it is only fitting that Solomon lead Israel in the celebration of "the festival" (8:65).

---

9. J. Wellhausen, *Prolegomena to the History of Ancient Israel* (Edinburgh: Adam and Charles Black, 1885) 283; Cross, *Canaanite Myth*, 73-74.

10. On iconography, see W. F. Albright, *Yahweh and the Gods of Canaan* (New York: Doubleday, 1968) 43, 197-98; J. Debus, *Die Sünde Jeroboams* (FRLANT 93; Göttingen: Vandenhoeck & Ruprecht, 1967) 42-47; and A. Mazar, "The 'Bull Site' — An Iron Age I Open Cult Place," *BASOR* 247 (1982) 27-41. On location, see E. Nielsen, *Shechem: A Traditio-Historical Investigation* (2nd ed.; Copenhagen: Gad, 1959) 37-294, 323-46. On Jeroboam's priesthood, see B. Halpern, "Levitic Participation in the Reform Cult of Jeroboam I," *JBL* 95 (1976) 31-42. R. de Vaux (*The Bible and the Ancient Near East* [trans. D. McHugh; Garden City, NY: Doubleday, 1971] 106-7) and S. Talmon ("Divergencies in Calendar-Reckoning in Ephraim and Judah," *VT* 8 [1958] 48-74) address the nature and timing of Jeroboam's festival.

The Deuteronomist's panegyric to the temple achieves a number of ends. First, by associating the dedication of this royal shrine with earlier pan-Israel convocations, the Deuteronomist legitimates the temple, underscoring its centrality to the history of the Israelite people. Second, by repeatedly linking Zion to Sinai, the Deuteronomist creates a scenario in which his readers will view Jeroboam's cult in much the same way readers of the Sinaitic pericope view Aaron's cult — as a countercultus that tragically distorts a divinely authorized orthopraxis. Third, by portraying the enthusiastic endorsement of the temple by all Israelites in the time of Solomon, the Deuteronomist impugns any Israelites who would depart from this divinely authorized state of affairs. Such deviation would betray the deity's imprimatur as well as all Israel's enthusiastic support for the temple in the time of Solomon. In other words, the Deuteronomist induces popular support for Zion in his own time by depicting such an unequivocal commitment by Israel in the tenth century.

II. A Cultus Misbegotten: Aaron and Jeroboam's Motivations

In view of the tremendous reception the Jerusalem temple receives in the Deuteronomistic presentation, Jeroboam's decision to (re)establish sanctuaries at Bethel and Dan requires rationalization. Like Aaron, Jeroboam reacts against an established orthopraxis. But, in this respect, the differences between Exodus 32 and 1 Kings 12 are as striking as the similarities. At Sinai the people gather against Aaron (ויקהל העם על־אהרון).[11] Aaron's decision to fashion a golden calf is therefore an improvisation, a spontaneous reaction to the people's pleas that something be done in Moses' long absence (Exod 32:1). But there is no external pressure on Jeroboam to act. Jeroboam's measures are considered and deliberate. He reflects on religious affairs in Judah and Israel and takes counsel (ויעץ) before he acts (1 Kgs 12:26-28).

According to 1 Kgs 12:26-27, Jeroboam's investiture of Bethel and Dan does not result from any deficiency or heteropraxis on the part of Solomon or the Jerusalem temple cultus. On the contrary, 1 Kgs 12:26-27 indirectly compliments the Solomonic temple. Jerusalem's allure to Israelites motivates Jeroboam to act. Granted his clear mandate, Jeroboam's innovations appear reprehensible. In a play on the root שוב ("to turn, return, restore"), the author depicts both Rehoboam and Jeroboam attempting to avoid the implications of the new status quo of the division.[12] Whereas Rehoboam tries to restore (שוב)

---

11. Exod 32:1. On the construction, see U. Cassuto, *A Commentary on the Book of Exodus* (trans. I. Abrahams; Jerusalem: Magnes, 1967) 411.
12. R. Cohn, "Literary Technique in the Jeroboam Narrative," *ZAW* 97 (1985) 23-25; A. Frisch, "Shemaiah the Prophet versus King Rehoboam: Two Opposed Interpretations of

unity to the fractured kingdom militarily and is told to return (שׁוּב) home, Jeroboam is afraid that if his people are allowed to return (שׁוּב) to Jerusalem to sacrifice, then their hearts will also return (שׁוּב) to King Rehoboam.

Jeroboam ironically establishes a cult not as an act of piety but because he doubts the durability of an arrangement in which Israel is to be politically, but not cultically, separated from Judah, an arrangement that has been repeatedly vouchsafed to him in both prophecy and history (1 Kgs 11:11-13, 29-38; 12:1-24).[13] YHWH's sanctioning the political division between Israel and Judah fails to impress Jeroboam. Jeroboam's cultus is a calculated response intended to dislodge Jerusalem from the affections of the people.

III. Deity and Iconography

Jeroboam's motivations (1 Kgs 12:26-27) clarify his actions (12:28-33). In a variety of biblical texts the trope of divine command is repeatedly employed to sanction the debut of cultic institutions. Hence, Moses' construction of the ark (Exod 25:10-22 [P]), the tent of meeting (Exod 33:7-11 [E]), and other sacred realia proceeds at divine behest and adheres to divinely ordained specifications. Similarly, the Deuteronomist repeatedly employs Nathan's oracle as divine sanction for the establishment of a temple in Jerusalem (2 Sam 7:7-16, 18-29; 1 Kgs 5:17-20; 8:15-24). Not surprisingly, the Deuteronomist devotes copious attention to Solomon's construction of and provisions for this central shrine. No such divine impetus appears anywhere in either Exodus 32 or 1 Kgs 12:26-33. Aaron and Jeroboam act according to other considerations.

In Exodus 32 Aaron and the people together share the blame.[14] Aaron makes the golden calf, builds an altar, and proclaims a feast (Exod 32:2-5). But the people offer their gold rings to Aaron, apply the Yahwistic confession to the calf (אלה אלהיך ישׂראל אשׁר העלוך מארץ מצרים), worship the calf (וישׁתחווּ־לו), offer burnt offerings and sacrifices of well-being, participate in a communal meal, and dance (Exod 32:1-8).[15] In 1 Kgs 12:28-33 Jeroboam is

---

the Schism (1 Kings XII 21-4)," *VT* 38 (1988) 466-67; Knoppers, *Two Nations under God*, vol. 2, 13-44.

13. See my "Dynastic Oracle and Secession in 1 Kings 11," *Proceedings, Great Lakes and Midwest Biblical Societies* 7 (1987) 159-72, as well as my *Two Nations under God*, 1.146-59, 186-223.

14. In Deut 9:8, 11-21 Aaron and the people are held responsible. The Deuteronomic authors even claim that were it not for Moses' mediation on Aaron's behalf, God would have destroyed Aaron. In contrast, Ps 106:19-22 blames only the people. For the interpretation of this episode in rabbinic sources, see S. E. Loewenstamm, "The Making and Destruction of the Golden Calf," *Bib* 48 (1967) 485-90; and idem, "Rejoinder," 334-38.

15. Many commentators portray the people's dancing as suggesting lewd or even

the only actor. The recurrent refrain "and he made" (ויעש), or "and he stationed" (וישם) in 12:28-33, reinforces the implication that Jeroboam is solely responsible for the realia, rites, and personnel at Bethel and Dan. Jeroboam makes (ויעש) the two golden calves, stationing (וישם) one in Bethel and the other in Dan.[16] Jeroboam establishes (ויעש) sanctuaries on the high places, appoints (ויעש) a priesthood, and creates (ויעש) a festival (12:29-32).[17] Each of Jeroboam's actions, in turn, is followed by a comment detailing the nature or effects of his initiatives.[18] Having portrayed Jeroboam's manufacture of the young bulls, the author imputes their role — the sanctuaries at Bethel and Dan are to replace Jerusalem. Following Jeroboam's positioning of the calves in Bethel and Dan, the people begin pilgrimages to both sites. The members of Jeroboam's priesthood are not of Levitic descent.[19] Jeroboam's national festival imitates the feast in Judah. Having established shrines on the high places, Jeroboam, as *summus episcopos,* ascends the Bethel altar (12:33).

That the name YHWH occurs only once in the cardinal passage describing the constitution of the northern cultus is revealing. Even then, the use of YHWH implicitly indicts Jeroboam. Rather than divine mandate, human anxiety is the motivating force behind Jeroboam's enfranchisement of Bethel and Dan. Moreover, Jeroboam's fears about his people's sacrificing at "the temple of

---

orgiastic rites. I am inclined to agree with J. Sasson ("The Worship of the Golden Calf," in *Orient and Occident: Essays Presented to Cyrus H. Gordon on the Occasion of his Sixty-Fifth Birthday* [ed. Harry A. Hoffner; AOAT 22; Kevelaer: Butzon & Bercker; Neukirchen-Vluyn: Neukirchener Verlag, 1973] 152) that the people's actions are consistent with the broad pattern of ancient Near Eastern festivals, which "consisted of a (ritual) banquet, followed by sports, miming, and antiphonal singing to honor the gods." The people's actions therefore mimic, to some degree, the earlier sequence of events in which a ritual banquet (Exod 24:1-11) is an integral part.

16. 1 Kgs 12:28-30. The MT, which reads לפני האחד עד־דן, has evidently suffered a haplography. The LXX[L] (boc₂e₂) and the Old Latin read προ προσωπου της μιας εως Δαν και προ προσωπου της αλλης εις Βαιθηλ. *BHS* and others posit a haplography by homoioteleuton, but this involves rearranging the order of the LXX[L] and the Old Latin. I would therefore suggest a more parsimonious solution: a haplography by homoioarkton (from לפני האחד עד to לפני האחד עד).

17. Reading בית במות in 1 Kgs 12:31 of the MT and the Old Latin as a composite plural (GKC, §124r). The plural of both nouns appears in the LXX and the Vulgate: בתי במות (cf. 1 Kgs 13:32; 2 Kgs 17:29, 32; 23:19).

18. Hoffmann (*Reform,* 63-70) contends that the individual items in the second half of the pericope correspond to and elaborate upon their respective counterparts in the first half. My presentation is indebted to Hoffmann's analysis; however, his formulation of this structure varies from the one I offer. See my *Two Nations under God,* vol. 2, 33-35.

19. Given the relative lack of attention devoted to the composition of the priesthood in the Deuteronomistic History, this assertion is intriguing. Cross (*Canaanite Myth,* 199) sees an older Mushite anti-Aaronide polemic underlying the account of 1 Kgs 12:26-30 and ascribes 1 Kgs 12:31ff. to the Deuteronomist. Halpern construes Jeroboam's actions as an attempt to control the Levite priesthood ("Levitic Participation," 31-42).

YHWH in Jerusalem" presupposes that the Jerusalem temple is the temple of
YHWH (1 Kgs 12:27). Hence, Jeroboam's only reference to YHWH's name
reinforces the association of YHWH with Jerusalem, not with Bethel and
Dan. The only other reference to deity (אלהים) occurs in an intriguing variation of Israel's historical confession. Jeroboam says of his golden calves:
"Here are your gods, O Israel, who brought you up from the land of Egypt!"
(ישראל אשר העלוך מארץ מצרים הנה אלהיך; 12:28).

The significance of this claim has divided commentators over the centuries. That so much controversy attends its interpretation results from at least
two factors. First, scholars have not always separated literary from historical
concerns. That is, reconstructing the origins and nature of Jeroboam's reforms
is not the same as reconstructing the portrayal of these reforms in 1 Kgs 12:26-
33. Second, Jeroboam's assertion itself is ambiguous. Are the calves divine
pedestals for YHWH, akin to the cherubim in the Jerusalem temple?[20] Or are
the calves representations of a divine attribute or deity? If the latter, with which
god(s) are Aaron's calf and Jeroboam's calves associated?[21] The text does not
say.

I would argue that the biblical authors deliberately obfuscate the origins
and nature of Aaron's and Jeroboam's religious commitments. They scorn
Jeroboam's iconography, positing as much distance between it and the iconography in Jerusalem as possible. Israel's historical confession, with three notable
exceptions (Exod 32:4, 8; 1 Kgs 12:28), always has YHWH as subject.[22] The

---

20. See Albright, *Yahweh and the Gods of Canaan*, 229; Cassuto, *Exodus*, 409; Cross,
Canaanite Myth, 74; de Vaux, *Bible and Ancient Near East*, 101-3; Y. Kaufmann, *The Religion
of Israel: From Its Beginnings to the Babylonian Exile* (trans. and abridged M. Greenberg;
Chicago: University of Chicago, 1960) 271; K. T. Obbink, "Jahwebilder," *ZAW* 47 (1929)
264-79; M. Noth, *The History of Israel* (trans. P. R. Ackroyd; 2nd ed.; London: A. & C. Black;
New York: Harper & Row, 1960) 233; M. Weippert, "Gott und Stier," *ZDPV* 77 (1961) 93;
Z. Zevit, "Deuteronomistic Historiography in 1 Kings 12–2 Kings 17 and Reinvestiture of
the Israelian Cult," *JSOT* 32 (1985) 61-62.

21. The proposals include Apis, Baal, El, Hathor, YHWH, Sin, and a deified Moses.
See the options surveyed in J. Sasson, "Bovine Symbolism in the Exodus Narrative," *VT* 18
(1968) 384-87; Bailey, "Golden Calf," 97-115; and, more recently, A. H. W. Curtis, "Some
Observations on 'Bull' Terminology in the Ugaritic Texts and the Old Testament," *OTS* 26
(1990) 17-31.

22. J. A. Montgomery and H. S. Gehman (*A Critical and Exegetical Commentary on
the Books of Kings* [ICC; Edinburgh: T. & T. Clark, 1951] 258) would emend to the singular
העלך on the grounds that Jeroboam most likely did not conceive of his actions as being
polytheistic. (Cf. the formulations of this Yahwistic confession in Neh 9:18 [singular] and
Exod 32:4 [plural]). The versions, like the MT, have the plural. אלהים is technically a plural
formation and occasionally takes a plural attributive adjective (Deut 5:23; Josh 24:19; 1 Sam
17:26, 36; Jer 10:10; 23:36; GKC, §132h) or a plural verb (Gen 20:13 [in conversation with
a non-Israelite]; 31:53; 35:7; 2 Sam 7:23). Two considerations suggest, however, that a plural
translation is warranted. First, as H. Donner ("Hier sind deiner Götter Israel!" *Wort und
Geschichte: Festschrift Karl Elliger* [ed. H. Gese and H. P. Rüger; Neukirchen-Vluyn: Neukir-

omission of a subject in 1 Kgs 12:28 is therefore hardly accidental. Historically Jeroboam may have conceived of the calves as pedestals for YHWH; but the author depicts the calves neither as pedestals nor as divine attributes. The antecedent to אלהיך is שני עגלי זהב. Moreover, the deictic particle הנה, at the beginning of v. 28b, calls attention to שני עגלי זהב.[23] Hence, the author of 12:28 has Jeroboam identifying the two golden calves with the god(s) of the exodus. The significance of this correlation should not be downplayed. It is true that the cherubim are often said to enthrone YHWH (e.g., 1 Sam 4:4; 2 Sam 6:2; 2 Kgs 19:5; Ps 80:2 [ET 1]; 99:1). Similarly, Israelite authors sometimes speak of the ark as YHWH's footstool (e.g., Ps 132:7; 1 Chr 28:2). But never does an Israelite author equate the ark or the cherubim with deity.[24]

It would seem, then, that the author of 1 Kgs 12:26-33 understands and plays on the nature and use of religious imagery. The Deuteronomist is not so steeped in Israel's aniconic tradition that he misunderstands Jeroboam's actions, regarding Jeroboam's calves as no more than "fetish-idols."[25] On the contrary, the author seems fully cognizant of the differences between iconic and aniconic worship. When Jeroboam proposes Israelite veneration for the calves that he made, the inescapable implication is that Jeroboam's cult is simultaneously idolatrous and dyotheistic, if not polytheistic. This is not misunderstanding, but invective. In the Deuteronomistic presentation, those who do not learn from history are condemned to repeat its mistakes. Aaron's calf perverts Sinaitic religion; Jeroboam's calves not only imitate but extend that perversion.

IV. The Consequences of Aaron and Jeroboam's Innovations

However heinous, the threat posed by the golden calf is quickly ended. Repeatedly describing Aaron's innovation as sinful, Moses intercedes with the deity

---

chener Verlag, 1973] 47) points out, the Yahwistic confession always employs the singular verb: עלה (e.g., Judg 6:13; 1 Sam 12:6; 2 Kgs 17:36; Jer 16:14; 23:7) or יצא (e.g., Exod 16:6; Deut 1:27; 6:12, 23; 7:8, 19; 1 Kgs 9:9; 2 Chr 7:22). Exod 32:4, 8 and 1 Kgs 12:28 are therefore exceptional. Second, the Deuteronomistic castigation of Jeroboam in 1 Kgs 14:9 states: "and you made for yourself other gods" (אלהים אחרים ותעשה־לך). The Deuteronomistic employment of אלהים אחרים clearly has a plural designation (Josh 23:16; 24:2, 16; Judg 2:12, 17, 19; 1 Kgs 11:4, 10, etc.). Hence, whatever sources the Deuteronomist may have had at his disposal, he understands אלהים as plural.

23. T. O. Lambdin, *An Introduction to Biblical Hebrew* (New York: Scribners, 1971) 168-70; B. K. Waltke and M. O'Connor, *An Introduction to Biblical Hebrew Syntax* (Winona Lake, IN: Eisenbrauns, 1990) §§16.3.5b; 40.2.1.

24. Statements by non-Israelites about Israel's sacral realia are another matter. See, for instance, the remark of the Philistines in 1 Sam 4:7 concerning the arrival of the ark: "God [אלהים] has come [בא] into the camp."

25. Contra Kaufmann, *Religion*, 270.

on the people's behalf (Exod 32:11-13). When Moses confronts Aaron, Aaron does not contest Moses' charge that a "great sin" (חטאה גדולה) has been committed (32:21). Rather, Aaron reacts defensively — blaming the people and denying that he himself made the calf (32:22-24). Moses then treats the calf as taboo. Assyrian royal inscriptions contain numerous examples of monarchs deporting religious artifacts to Assyria or, in a few cases, destroying them altogether. But these actions involve cultic symbols from conquered territories.[26] Whereas Assyrian kings deport or, in a few instances, eliminate some foreign cult symbols, Moses eliminates this Israelite cultic symbol. The parallels between Moses' destruction of the golden calf and ancient Near Eastern traditions depicting the destruction of foreign cult objects leads Begg to query: "how is it that the OT speaks of iconoclastic actions directed against objects pertaining to Israel's own cult, whereas in our extra-Biblical evidence such actions are reported only in relation to 'foreign' cult objects?"[27]

I would argue that the depiction of Exod 32:20 is deliberate. Moses treats the calf as a foreign cult symbol. He burns, obliterates, and casts the calf into the water much like Baal annihilates his archenemy Mot and much like certain Assyrian kings burn, smash, and consign to water detested foreign cult objects.[28] As if elimination were not enough, Moses seems to institute a trial by ordeal.[29] In the successive redactions of the *Grundlage* of Exodus 32 by the Elohist, the Deuteronomic writers, and perhaps others, the punishment of the people is underscored through a variety of punishments. The Levites distinguish themselves by putting three thousand people to the sword (32:25-29). Subsequently, a plague afflicts the people (32:35). Even so, Moses continues to negotiate with the deity. Despite God's pledge that he would send a messenger to go before Israel (מלאך; 33:2), Moses implores God to lead Israel himself (33:12-13, 15-16). When YHWH relents, Moses requests to see God's glory (33:17-18). This peti-

---

26. M. Cogan, *Imperialism and Religion: Assyria, Judah and Israel in the Eighth and Seventh Centuries B.C.E.* (SBLMS 19; Missoula, MT: Scholars, 1974) 24; U. Rüterswörden, "Beiträge zur Vernichtungssymbolik," *BN* 2 (1977) 16-22; H. Spiekermann, *Juda unter Assur in der Sargonidenzeit* (FRLANT 129; Göttingen: Vandenhoeck & Ruprecht, 1982) 347-54; C. Begg, "The Destruction of the Calf," in *Das Deuteronomium: Entstehung, Gestalt und Botschaft* (ed. N. Lohfink; BETL 68; Louvain: Louvain University, 1985) 225-26.

27. Begg, "Destruction," 251.

28. For Baal and Mot, see *KTU* 1.6.II.30-37; V.11-19. Loewenstamm provides an extended comparison ("Making," 481-90). For the Assyrian material, see, e.g., the letter of Sargon II rehearsing his destruction of the temple of Haldia (*AR* 2.91), Sennacherib's account of his destruction of Babylon's temples and gods (*AR* 2.152), and Ashurbanipal's crusade against the sanctuaries and deities of Elam (*AR* 2.308-9). Although Begg ("Destruction," 227) also discusses Egyptian, Sumerian, and Hittite evidence, he points out that the Assyrian parallels are closest chronologically to the date of Deuteronomy and the Deuteronomistic History.

29. Exod 32:20. Deut 9:21 speaks of Moses consigning the dust to "the wadi that comes down from the mountain." Beyerlin (*Origins,* 131) argues that the description of Deut 9:21 is consistent with the rite prescribed in Deut 21:6.

tion, too, is essentially granted (33:19-23). Moses is allowed to carve two new tablets, ascend the mountain, and witness God's revelation (34:1-7). After Moses once again implores YHWH's forgiveness, the deity consents to renew covenant and lead his people toward the promised land (34:8-29). Hence, due to Moses' personal mediation, a chastened Israel is allowed to regroup and move on.[30]

The outcome is, however, very different in Kings. Unlike the situation at Sinai, there is no swift resolution at Bethel or Dan. The sins of Jeroboam go unrequited. Like Aaron at Sinai, Jeroboam at Bethel is chastised for his actions (1 Kgs 13:1-3). But Jeroboam does not recant. Jeroboam never desists from his strategy of severing his realm from the state sanctuary established by Solomon. He responds to prophetic repudiation by redoubling his efforts to consolidate his cultus by democratizing the priesthood of the high places (13:33-34). There is no intercession, repentance, or expurgation. On the contrary, Jeroboam's tauromorphic symbols become definitive fixtures in the northern cult; even the purge of Jehu does not eradicate them (2 Kgs 10:29). No king "turns from the sin(s) of the house of Jeroboam."[31] If Aaron's calf temporarily imperils the future of Israel (Exod 32:10), Jeroboam's calves permanently imperil the future of the northern kingdom.

Conclusions

The differences between the descriptions of Aaron's calf and Jeroboam's calves elucidate why Jeroboam's establishment of a state cult constitutes a leitmotiv in Kings. The polemic against the sanctuaries at Bethel and Dan goes far beyond presenting them as competition to the Jerusalem temple. In the context of the Deuteronomist's presentation of his ascent to power, Jeroboam's establishment of a cultus is a supreme act of apostasy. Even though the northern cultus at Bethel and Dan is founded by an Israelite and serves an Israelite clientele, it perverts authentic Israelite sacral rites, incorporating a highly dangerous and long-discredited iconography.

The Deuteronomist casts aspersions on the entire course of northern history by reifying Jeroboam's cultic initiatives. The Jerusalem temple and the Josianic reforms, in turn, win vindication at the expense of Israel's demise (2 Kings 17). In depicting Jeroboam's sins, the Deuteronomist reasserts the continuing relevance of the Jerusalem temple for all Israelites in his own time. If Israel's committing a "great sin" at Sinai valorizes the authoritative cultic

---

30. Childs (*Exodus*, 560) contends that the motif of sin and forgiveness unifies the stories in Exodus 32–34.

31. 2 Kgs 3:3; 10:29, 31; 12:4; 13:2, 6; 14:4; 15:4, 18, 35; 17:22.

instititions attributed to Moses, Jeroboam's influential sin at Bethel and Dan valorizes the temple cultus Solomon established in Jerusalem.

For the Deuteronomist there could be only one central sanctuary: "the place where YHWH said he would make his name dwell," and that long hoped-for sanctuary was the temple in Jerusalem.[32] In the Deuteronomistic configuration of history, both Judah and Israel find blessing only through Zion. Given this Deuteronomistic emphasis on the adverse effects of the sanctuaries at Bethel and Dan upon Israel and the pan-Israelite domain of the Jerusalem temple, it is unlikely that 1 Kgs 12:26-33 was written at a time (i.e., the exile) when the Jerusalem temple no longer existed. Supporters of the temple could exalt the inviolability of Jerusalem in the aftermath of the Assyrian crisis (e.g., 2 Kgs 19:34; 20:6), but it would make little sense to lambaste Jeroboam's bull iconography, priesthood, sanctuaries, pilgrimage, and festival in the aftermath of Judah's humiliation in the Babylonian exile. There is every indication, then, that the Deuteronomist is waging a preexilic battle.

The unresolved episode of the golden calves renders the subsequent course of Israelite history a regression. If the golden calf valorizes the authoritative cultic institutions of Sinai through negation, the golden calves valorize the temple in Jerusalem through dialectic. That history, as the Deuteronomistic commentary on the relationship between Israel and its deity, is unkind to the northern kingdom is therefore hardly surprising. Its course testifies to the enduring value of the Jerusalem temple.[33]

---

32. Deut 12:21; 2 Sam 7:7-12; 1 Kgs 2:3; 3:6; 5:3-5; 6:1; 8; 9:3; 11:38, etc.

33. With admiration and gratitude I dedicate this essay to David Noel Freedman — not only a distinguished scholar but also an excellent editor, who has done so much to encourage younger scholars in the field.

The Transfer of Kingship: A Divine Turning

PETER MACHINIST

Harvard University

As 1 Kings 12 and its parallel in 2 Chronicles 10 narrate it, the united monarchy of David and Solomon collapsed finally in a meeting at Shechem. Forced to this important northern capital by a rebellion already underway,[1] Rehoboam, Solomon's son and successor, confronted there the angry demand of the northern tribes of Israel, now led by Jeroboam. The demand was that Rehoboam lighten the oppressive state service that Solomon had laid upon the north if he were to retain their loyalty. Rehoboam asked for three days to consider the matter, and consulted then two groups of counselors: the *zĕqēnîm*, who had served Solomon, and the *yĕlādîm*, who had grown up with Rehoboam, presumably in the court, as his mates. The *zĕqēnîm* advised compassion and acceptance of the people's demand; the *yĕlādîm* not only spoke against this but also argued for an increase in the oppressive service. With a fine sense of suspense, the narrator delays momentarily the expected report of Rehoboam's decision until he has first described the reconvening of the assembly at Shechem. Then, we are told, Rehoboam has sided with the *yĕlādîm*, the point driven home by the king's repetition, now before the assembled Israelites, of the very words that the *yĕlādîm* had used to him in their deliberation.

Rehoboam's decision comes as something of a surprise, since in the narrative of the deliberation, the weight of reason falls clearly on the *zĕqēnîm*: they are the ones, not the *yĕlādîm*, who speak explicitly about ensuring the people's loyalty. But it is the very unreasonableness of Rehoboam that is the issue, and the narrator explains why he was so — why he rejected the *zĕqēnîm* — in a parenthesis inserted immediately after Rehoboam's speech to the Shechem assembly:

---

1. On this point, see H. Tadmor, "Traditional Institutions and the Monarchy: Social and Political Tensions in the Time of David and Solomon," in *Studies in the Period of David and Solomon and Other Essays* (ed. T. Ishida; Winona Lake, IN: Eisenbrauns, 1982) 252-54.

(So) the king did not listen to the people, for it was a *sibbâ* [Kings]/*něsibbâ* [Chronicles] from Yahweh [Kings]/God [Chronicles] in order that he [Kings]/ Yahweh [Chronicles] might confirm his word, which he [Kings]/Yahweh [Chronicles] spoke through Ahiyah [Kings]/Ahiyahu [Chronicles] of Shiloh to Jeroboam son of Nebat. (1 Kgs 12:15/2 Chr 10:15)

Following this parenthesis, the narrative concludes with a description of the people's response to Rehoboam:

And when all Israel saw that the king had not listened to them, the people answered the king thus:

"We have no share in David,[2]
No inheritance in the son of Jesse.
To your tents, O Israel!
Now, take care of your (own) house, O David!"

(So) Israel went to his tents. But as for the Israelites living in the cities of Judah, Rehoboam ruled over them. (1 Kgs 12:16-17/2 Chr 10:16-17)[3]

The narrator's explanation is marked by an unusual noun, noted above as *sibbâ* in 1 Kings and *něsibbâ* in 2 Chronicles. Both are hapax legomena in the biblical text, and the question of this paper is what do they mean. The root, as almost all commentators, ancient and modern, agree,[4] is *sbb*, "to go around." Only

---

2. Here I am reading *mah* not as an interrogative but as a negative, on the basis of Arabic *mā*. See, e.g., B. K. Waltke and M. O'Connor, *An Introduction to Biblical Hebrew Syntax* (Winona Lake, IN: Eisenbrauns, 1989) 326-27 and n. 22. *Mah* as a negative allows, then, this colon to parallel the following one more closely.

3. The version in 2 Chr 10:16 has several minor variants:

2 Chr 10:16	1 Kgs 12:16
wěkol-yiśrā'ēl	*wayyar' kol-yiśrā'ēl*
lāhem	*'ălêhem*
wayyāšîbû	*wayyāšîbû*
[lacking]	*dābār*
dāwîd	*dāwīd*
'îš lě'ōhāleykā	*lě'ōhāleykā*
kol-yiśrā'ēl	*yiśrā'ēl*

4. So for the ancient versions on 1 Kgs 12:15/2 Chr 10:15, e.g., LXX: *ē metastrophē*; Vulgate: (Kgs) *aversatus eum fuerat Dominus*/(Chronicles, translating *ad sensum*) *erat enim voluntatis Dei*; Targum Jonathan (Kings), translating *ad sensum: hăwat pelugtā' min qŏdom YY;* Targum to Chronicles (R. Le Déaut and J. Robert, *Le Targum des Chroniques* [AnBib 51; Rome: Pontifical Biblical Institute, 1971] 2.105) *hăwat tûsqāpâ min qŏdom YYY.*

For medieval commentators, e.g., Meṣudat Ṣiyyon: (Kings) "the matter (concerns) the going around of the event and what causes this" (*'inyan haqqāpat haddābār wěhaggôrem lāh*).

For modern commentators, e.g., J. A. Montgomery and H. S. Gehman, *A Critical and Exegetical Commentary on the Books of Kings* (ICC; Edinburgh: T. & T. Clark, 1951) 250; M. Noth, *Könige*, vol. 1 (BKAT IX/1; Neukirchen-Vluyn: Neukirchener Verlag, 1968) 276.

John Gray, of recent scholars, tries to argue differently, that the root, presumably still *sbb*, is cognate with Arabic *ṣāba*, "to hit the mark," with which he compares the Arabic noun *muṣība*, "misfortune."[5] But in addition to the fact that the correspondence of Hebrew *samekh* with Arabic *ṣād* is nowhere attested,[6] the biblical context would seem to confirm the conventional derivation. For at least three other times in the Hebrew Bible, all as verbs, the root *sbb* clearly occurs in a sense related to the text in 1 Kings 12/2 Chronicles 10. The first is 1 Kgs 2:15, where the root in the Qal describes the turning of the kingdom of David from its expected heir, Adonijah, to his brother, Solomon: "And the kingdom turned [*wattissōb*] and became my brother's, for it was to him from Yahweh." This passage is balanced by one in the Chronicler, 1 Chr 10:13-14, where Yahweh turns — here using the Hiphil — the kingdom from Saul over to David: "And Saul died because of the transgression that he perpetrated against Yahweh, in not keeping the word of Yahweh, and also for asking a medium to make inquiry and not making inquiry by Yahweh. So he [God] killed him, and turned the kingdom over [*wayyassēb*] to David, the son of Jesse." The same "turning" from Saul to David appears yet again in 1 Chr 12:24 (ET 23), in the Hiphil: "These are the numbers of the divisions of the armed troops who joined up with David at Hebron, in the turning [*lĕhāsēb*] of the kingdom of Saul over to him according to the command [lit. mouth] of Yahweh."

Let us probe the connections among these five passages in more detail. All of them deal with succession in the united monarchy: Saul to David, David to Solomon, and finally Rehoboam to the breakup of the monarchy. It will be seen that the two passages in Kings, thus part of the Deuteronomistic History, concern David to Solomon and Rehoboam to the breakup, while of the three Chronicles passages one treats Rehoboam to the breakup as a duplicate of one of the Kings texts, and the other two, unparalleled in Kings, focus on Saul to David. The distribution here has suggested to Ackroyd that the Chronicler has taken up the Deuteronomistic phraseology and extended it backward to the beginning of the united monarchy with Saul.[7] This fits well with our general appreciation of the Chronicler's dependence on and creative use of the Deuteronomist.[8] Yet the two independent Chronicles passages are no wooden imitations of Kings, for unlike the latter they use *sbb* as a transitive active verb, in the Hiphil, with Yahweh as agent. Indeed, even the Chronicles duplicate of Kings does not use *sibbâ*, but a different nominal formation, *nĕsibbâ*.[9]

---

5. J. Gray, *I & II Kings* (2nd ed.; OTL; Philadelphia: Westminster, 1970) 306.

6. See, e.g., the comparative chart of consonants in the Semitic languages in S. Moscati et al., *An Introduction to the Comparative Grammar of the Semitic Languages: Phonology and Morphology* (Wiesbaden: Harrassowitz, 1964) 44.

7. P. R. Ackroyd, *The Chronicler in His Age* (JSOTSup 101; Sheffield: JSOT, 1991) 322.

8. This issue has been much discussed. For a recent, concise orientation, with bibliography, see G. H. Jones, *1 & 2 Chronicles* (Old Testament Guides; Sheffield: JSOT, 1993) 65-85.

9. On *nĕsibbâ* as part of the Chronicler's stylistic and grammatical changes, see Thomas Willi, *Die Chronik als Auslegung* (FRLANT 106; Göttingen: Vandenhoeck & Ruprecht, 1972) 87.

If the Chronicler is then copying and adapting Deuteronomistic phraseology, why he has not used *sbb* for the David-Solomon succession, as in Kings,
requires comment. To be sure, the Kings passage in question, 1 Kgs 2:15, is from
the end of the so-called Succession History, which is entirely missing in Chronicles, but this is no argument against the Chronicler finding another place, in his
own narration of the succession from David to Solomon, to use *sbb* if he had
wanted to. That he did not is due, I suggest, to his own view of that succession and
the incompatibility of *sbb* with his view. For what the Chronicler wanted to stress
was the smooth, inevitable, peaceful transition from David to Solomon, and so
strengthen the picture of Solomon's legitimacy. He thus has no trace of Solomon's
struggle for the throne as the Succession History narrated. But *sbb,* as we have
observed it in the five instances given above, is used for situations precisely
opposed to the one the Chronicler desired, namely, for unexpected occurrences,
breaks in the normal order of events as regulated by human social practice or
reason, which involve thus some kind of violent social disruption: Saul not
succeeded by his son, Jonathan, but by David; David not succeeded by his older
son, Adonijah, but by his younger, Solomon; and Rehoboam not easing the
burdens on Israel, but increasing them and so losing half his kingdom and more.
Clearly, then, *sbb* would have been unsuited to the Chronicler's view of how
Solomon succeeded to David's throne. Nonetheless, the Chronicler was willing to
use it for the Saul-David transferal as a way of highlighting his general thesis of
the importance of David as a new beginning for Israel.[10]

In other words, *sbb* describes a situation where divine power is displayed
and confirmed precisely as it opposes the normal order of things, and remakes
that order into a new one. It is this opposition and remaking that is the "turning,"
and while it may be given a justification in the behavior of the human protagonists concerned, it need not be.

Thus, it was the "transgression" *(ma'al)* of Saul against Yahweh — in not
keeping his command, by "inquiring" of a medium and not of Yahweh — that
for the Chronicler led to Yahweh's "turning" the kingdom from Saul to David
(1 Chr 10:13-14; 12:24 is clearly an allusion to this turning, but without mentioning the sin).[11]

By contrast, the two passages from Kings (including the Chronicles duplicate of Kings) do not explicitly identify any sin. In rejecting the advice of the
zĕqēnîm and increasing the burdens (1 Kgs 12:15/2 Chr 10:15), Rehoboam is

---

10. Of the large secondary literature on David's importance to the Chronicler, see,
e.g., Jones, *Chronicles,* 122-26; and, for the central chapter, 1 Chronicles 10, S. Japhet, *I & II
Chronicles* (OTL; Louisville: Westminster/John Knox, 1993) 221-30.

11. On *ma'al,* see J. Milgrom, *Cult and Conscience* (SJLA 18; Leiden: Brill, 1976) 16-35;
and, with specific reference to Chronicles, R. Mosis, *Untersuchungen zur Theologie des chronistischen Geschichtswerkes* (Freiburger Theologische Studien 92: Freiburg: Herder, 1973) 29-33;
H. G. M. Williamson, *1 and 2 Chronicles* (NCB; Grand Rapids: Eerdmans, 1982) 94-95; and
Japhet, *Chronicles,* 229-30.

clearly acting in a way the narrator considers wrong, and that might therefore be understood implicitly as a sin. Indeed, one might even say that Rehoboam's behavior functions as a sin, since it is made the prelude to his loss of the northern kingdom. But the narrator never labels the behavior as sinful, nor does he identify the loss as a punishment. Rather, the behavior is said to be something that God himself causes, as part of his "turning," in order to fulfill the prophecy he had given earlier to Ahijah — the prophecy of the loss of the north (1 Kgs 11:31-39). Something similar is at work in the story about the succession to Solomon instead of to Adonijah. Here, even more clearly, no sin or even unreasonable behavior on Adonijah's part is described. As Adonijah himself states, it was simply Yahweh's "turning" of the kingdom to his brother, contrary to the fact "that all Israel anticipated that I would reign" (1 Kgs 2:15). That "turning," however, is only the last stage of a process initiated at Solomon's birth, an event that was marked at that point in the story with the statement that "Yahweh loved him" (2 Sam 12:24). Thus, like the Rehoboam story, the one about Solomon/Adonijah comes to resolve an earlier affirmation, even if in Solomon-Adonijah the connection with the earlier affirmation is neither explicit nor cast formally in a prophecy-fulfillment pattern.

My analysis to this point has focused on five passages in Kings and Chronicles where the notion of a "turning" of rulership occurs. One might add yet a sixth passage, but the case is not obvious and requires particular study. The text is 2 Chr 22:7, describing the Judean king Ahaziah, who had the misfortune of being mixed up with the activities of the Omri dynasty of northern Israel, to whom he was related through his mother, Athaliah. Ahaziah visits Joram, the reigning Israelite king, as he lies mortally wounded from a battle conducted by Ahaziah and Joram against the Aramean ruler Hazael. The Chronicler then comments, in the line at issue: "And from God was a treading down/crushing [*tĕbûsat*] of Ahaziah for coming to Joram, and when he came, he went out with Jehoram to Jehu, son of Nimshi, whom Yahweh had anointed to cut off the house of Ahab." The following lines describe the outcome (vv. 8-9): "And Jehu, in the course of carrying out judgment against [lit. with] the house of Ahab, found the princes of Judah and the sons of[12] the brothers of Ahaziah, who served Ahaziah, and he slew them. And he sought out Ahaziah and they captured him, while he was hiding in Samaria. And they brought him to Jehu and they[13] killed him, and buried him."

Now the difficult word in this account is the nominal construct in v. 7, *tĕbûsat*. Joüon was the first, at least of modern commentators, to be troubled by it, because it is a hapax legomenon in the Bible, and because its apparent meaning, established on the basis of other occurrences of its root, *bws*, as "a

---

12. On the retention here of the MT reading "sons of" *(bĕnê)*, see Japhet, *Chronicles*, 822-23.

13. So the MT. As *BHS (ad* 2 Chr 22:9b) notes, the singular form of the verb, "he [= Jehu] killed him," is read by various Hebrew manuscripts and ancient versions.

trampling down," would be inappropriate in this context, unless it could be understood in the metaphorical sense of "a fall/doom" (here of Ahaziah), which Joüon judges as stretching the meaning too much.[14] Joüon opines further that the morphology is wrong: *tĕbûsâ* would be a *nomen actionis* of a Qal, yet such forms with the prefix *t-*, he argues, derive originally from the intensive (= Piel stem), from which they often pass to a derivation from the Hiphil, but not to one from the Qal. For these reasons, Joüon suggests emending *tĕbûsat* to the noun *sibbâ*, just as in 1 Kgs 12:15, with the sense that what is going on here, as in the Kings passage, is a "turning" on the part of God that leads to Ahaziah's doom. Strengthening the suggestion, as Joüon points out, are the LXX and the Peshitta, both of which translate the Hebrew noun at issue with words indicating a "turning": the LXX with *katastrophē*, or, in some other manuscripts, with *metastrophē* as is done for 1 Kgs 12:15; the Peshitta with *hapîktā*.[15] To make his sense work, however, Joüon suggests a reordering of the present syntax of the clause to: *ûmē'ĕlōhîm hāyĕtâ sibbâ lābô' 'ăḥazyāhû*, "And from God there was a turning in Ahaziah's coming [i.e., to Joram]."

Joüon's suggestion has proved persuasive to many subsequent interpreters, among which is *BHS*.[16] Most, however, like *BHS*, have opted for another form, particularly *nĕsibbâ* in conformity with 2 Chr 10:15,[17] disregarding Joüon's view that this form, as a Niphal participle, would suppose the meaning "something that turns," which for Joüon seems less appropriate to the context than *sibbâ*, which could convey the more abstract "turn(ing)." How less appropriate *nĕsibbâ* really might be is not clear; in any case, one might emend simply to *tĕsibbâ*, which would require even less change from the present *tĕbûsâ*: simply a metathesis of *b* and *s*, and the shift of *y* to *w*, which are easily confused in the square script.[18]

The question remains, however, whether the emendation in whatever form is necessary. The best argument for it is the translations of the LXX and the Peshitta, the latter probably derivative of the former. But could this be an interpretation of the translator and not presume a different Hebrew text from the present MT? Certainly, *tĕbûsâ*, while a hapax, has a root that is otherwise well attested in the Hebrew Bible, primarily as a verb, with the meaning "to trample down," but also as

---

14. P. Joüon, S.J., "Notes philologiques sur le texte hébreu de 1 et 2 Chroniques," *Bib* 13 (1932) 87-88.

15. One might also add the Targum to Chronicles, which uses here *tasqāpâ*, comparable to its *tûsqāpâ* at 2 Chr 10:15: see Le Déaut and Robert, *Targum*, 2.129.

16. *BHS ad* 2 Chr 22:7a. Among other commentators are, e.g., W. Rudolph, *Chronikbücher* (HAT 1/21; Tübingen: Mohr/Siebeck, 1955) 268; Williamson, *Chronicles*, 312; Ackroyd, *Chronicler and His Age*, 322n.1; and Japhet, *Chronicles*, 822.

17. For *nĕsibbâ*, see Rudolph, *Chronikbücher*, 268; *BHS ad* 2 Chr 22:7a (of which Rudolph was editor); Japhet, *Chronicles*, 822.

18. Ackroyd (*Chronicler and His Age*, 322) has something similar, namely, *tĕsubbâ*. Williamson (*Chronicles*, 312) is noncommittal between *tĕsubbâ* and *nĕsibbâ*.

a noun, *mĕbûsâ*, with a similar sense to *tĕbûsâ*, "trampling down."[19] Moreover, the *t-* prefix need not come only from verbal roots in the Piel or Hiphil, as Joüon supposes. Joüon himself noted in his grammar the forms *tĕšûbâ*, "return," and *tĕmûtâ*, "death," which derive from the Qal.[20] Further, the sense, once the emendation is made, is not as clear as Joüon believes. Certainly, if the syntax is not changed, as Joüon wants, the result is strange and does not comport with the other five occurrences of *sbb* for the transfer of kingship. That is, the text would read: "And from God there was a turning of Ahaziah for coming to Joram." One would expect, rather, that what "turned" was not Ahaziah but the office he held, the kingship, or else some abnormal and thus unexpected action of Ahaziah that led to his loss of kingship, as in 1 Kgs 12:15/2 Chr 10:15. Joüon's change of the syntax, as given above, does achieve this — and it is interesting that none of those who follow Joüon has addressed the problem here[21] — but the question is whether this additional emendation, beyond the change of *tĕbûsāt* to *sibbâ* (or to *tĕsibbâ*), is assuming too much. In any case, I am not sure that keeping the MT intact with *tĕbûsāt* is as unsatisfactory as Joüon and his followers have supposed. As the other occurrences of the root *bws* make clear, "treading down" can indicate a disaster or defeat (e.g., Ps 44:6 [ET 5]; 60:14 [ET 12]/108:14 [ET 13]; Isa 14:25 [cf. v. 19]; 18:2, 7; 63:6, 18), sometimes with the original and concrete image of treading someone in the mud (e.g., Zech 10:5), but often without that image and just in the more general sense of "defeat" or "ruin." The sense, then, of the present passage of 2 Chr 22:7 would be that Ahaziah's going to visit Joram was the occasion of his defeat or ruin at the hand of God, as laid out in the following two verses, and I frankly do not see that this requires any more of a metaphorical extension of meaning than would the word *tĕsibbâ*, if it were supplied by emendation here.

Therefore, 2 Chr 22:7 must remain highly problematic for *sbb* in the sense of a "turning" of rulership. But there are at least the five other biblical texts we have examined, and we must try now to clarify the broader significance of them. What are the origin and historical context of this idiom that rulership "turns" from one human holder to another? Two kinds of textual evidence can help with the answer, the first biblical, the other not.

For the biblical we must begin with certain other texts in which *sbb* occurs:

Num 36:6-7:   This is the situation that Yahweh has ordered for the daughters of Zelophehad: "They may become the wives of whomever they think best, but it must be in the clan of the tribe of their father. (In that way) the inheritance (of Zelophehad) will not

---

19. In Isa 18:2, 7; 22:5.

20. P. Joüon, *Grammaire de l'hébreu biblique* (Rome: Pontifical Biblical Institute, 1923) §88L*o*.

21. See n. 16 above. Japhet (*Chronicles*, 822) recognizes some syntactic awkwardness in the present MT text, but it is not the problem described here.

	pass through the Israelite community [lit. will not turn *(tissōb)* to the sons of Israel] from tribe to tribe, for each Israelite man will remain attached to the inheritance of the tribe of his fathers." (cf. also v. 9)
2 Sam 3:12:	And Abner sent messengers to David where he was,[22] saying: "To whom does the land belong? Make an alliance now with me, and I will give you my support to bring over [lit. make turn *(lěhāsēb)*] all Israel to you."
2 Sam 14:20:	[The woman of Tekoa tells David:] In order to change the course of affairs [lit. to turn the face of the matter *(sabbēb 'et-pěnê haddābār)*] your servant, Joab, carried out this deed.
Jer 6:12:	[God curses Jerusalem/Judah:] And their houses will be turned over [*wěnāsabbû*] to others, together with fields and women.
Hab 2:16:	You will be sated with contempt rather than glory. So drink now, and stagger.[23] The cup in Yahweh's right hand will come around [*tissōb*] against you, and shame (will come) upon your glory.

The above list is not exhaustive,[24] but it is enough to establish that the basic sense of "turning (around)" that *sbb* has in Biblical Hebrew can include the notion of a transfer, a "turning," of something from one situation or owner to another, or the change of the current, even normal, situation into its opposite. It is clearly in this context that the specific usage of a transfer of kingship is to be located. Indeed, one of the above list, 2 Sam 3:12, is rather close to our usage, although here it is Abner, not Yahweh, who claims to be the agent of change — which claim, if construed as a blasphemous challenge, may be part of what our biblical writer understands as the reason for Abner's subsequent downfall. Note in particular how Abner's statement, that he is prepared "*lěhāsēb* all Israel to you," resumes and so is to be explained by his words two verses before, that he is going "to transfer the kingdom from the house of Saul and to establish the throne of David over Israel and Judah from Dan to Beer-sheba" (*lěha'ăbîr hammamlākâ mibbêt šā'ûl ûlěhāqîm 'et-kissē' dāwīd 'al-yiśrā'ēl wě'al-yěhûdâ middān wě'ad-bě'ēr šāba'*).

The notion of "turning" as a way of expressing a change in condition is not confined to *sbb* in Biblical Hebrew. One should also consider the cognate

---

22. On the textual difficulties here, see P. K. McCarter, Jr., *II Samuel* (AB 9; Garden City, NY: Doubleday, 1984) 107 ad loc.

23. With *BHS* ad loc., emend from MT *wěhē'ārēl* to *wěhērā'ēl*, following 1QpHab, LXX, Vulgate, and Peshitta. The MT, however, has occasionally been defended, most recently by J. J. M. Roberts, *Nahum, Habakkuk, and Zephaniah* (OTL; Louisville: Westminster/John Knox, 1991) 116n.28.

24. For a more elaborate list, see F. García-López, "סבב," *TWAT* 5.730-44, esp. 732, 742.

accusative construction, *šûb šĕbî/ût*, "to execute a return," which is found in the sense of "restoring the fortunes" of someone who has been existing in an unfortunate situation like suffering or exile (e.g., Jer 29:14; 30:3; Ezek 16:53; 39:25; Job 42:10).[25] In addition, there is the root *hpk*, whether as a verb, *hāpak*, or in the nominal forms, *hăpēkâ* and *mahpēkâ*. Literally "turning over," this root occurs especially in the negative sense of "overturning" and so "destroying" a place or group (e.g., Gen 19:21, 25, 29; Jonah 3:4).[26]

Both *šûb šĕbî/ût* and *hpk* clearly have a narrower range than *sbb* and are not closely tied to our idiom of the "turning" or "transfer" of kingship. But together with the other uses of *sbb* we have examined, they establish the wider semantic context — an "(over)turning" from one situation to another — out of which our idiom must have emerged.

But establishing this wider context should not divert us from the fact that in the five biblical instances with which we began, *sbb* takes on almost the status of a technical idiom for change of rulership, reflecting what seems to be a particular view of the interaction of the divine with human politics. Is such an idiom, with the view it supposes, unique to the biblical corpus? At least two bodies of evidence suggest otherwise. The first is Mesopotamian. The critical term here is the Sumerian bala, which, as is well known, is the noun of the verbal root bal, "to turn (over, around, against)." The verb can describe the change of something into another place or state, as in "uprooting" or turning" a tree "upside down," or the change from one situation into another, as in "revolting" against a ruler.[27] The noun seems to function largely, if not exclusively, in the more restricted sense of a "turn > term of duty or office," describing a range of activities from those of laborers to the reigns of kings or even dynasties.[28] In turn, the noun was borrowed into Akkadian as *palû* — the verb was not — showing evidence of yet further semantic restriction, for as Jacobsen observes, it is applied only to a term of royal rule, whether of an individual king

25. Cf. M. H. Pope, *Job* (3rd ed.; AB 15; Garden City, NY: Doubleday, 1973) 351 *ad* 42:10. As Pope notes, following H. Ewald, *šĕbî/ût* should be derived from *šûb*, not from *šābâ*.

26. I thank Hindy Najman for making me think about *hpk* in this connection. Recall that the Peshitta uses this root, in the form *hapîkta-*, for the MT *tĕbusat* in 2 Chr 22:7.

27. See A. W. Sjöberg, ed., *The Sumerian Dictionary of the University Museum of the University of Pennsylvania*, vol. 2: B (Philadelphia: University Museum, 1984) 49-50a, s.v. bal D.

28. Ibid., 65b-71b, s.v. bala B. Cf. the compound noun, lú-bala, "man on duty," in ibid., 71b. Further discussion of bala may be found in T. Jacobsen, *Toward the Image of Tammuz and Other Essays on Mesopotamian History and Culture* (ed. W. L. Moran; Cambridge: Harvard University, 1970) 406n.66; W. W. Hallo, "A Sumerian Amphictyony," *JCS* 14 (1960) 89-93, 96; and P. Steinkeller, "The Administrative and Economic Organization of the Ur III State: The Core and the Periphery," in *The Organization of Power: Aspects of Bureaucracy in the Ancient Near East* (ed. Mc. Gibson and R. D. Biggs; Studies in Ancient Oriental Civilization 46; Chicago: Oriental Institute, 1987) 21, 27-30, which constitutes an important corrective to Hallo's view of the bala in the Ur III state.

or, in a couple of instances, of a dynasty or perhaps era.[29] In Middle and Neo-Assyrian parlance, it can, additionally, take on the even more restricted meaning of a year within the reign of a king.[30]

This brief summary of bala/*palû* makes one think of *sbb*, and that connection is deepened by a closer look at four of the occurrences of bala/*palû* as "turn/term of royal rule." The first comes from the Sumerian King List, a composition that occurs in several variants at the end of the third/beginning of the second millennium B.C.E. Bala here appears in a formula used in one group of texts of the List for indicating the change of rulership over the cities of Sumer:

(City X)^{ki}-(a) bala-bi ba(-an)-kúr
nam-lugal-bi (city Y)^{ki}-šè ba(-an)-túm
Of (city X), its turn was changed;
its kingship was brought to (city Y).[31]

The second example, approximately of the same date as the Sumerian King List, occurs in one of the Sumerian city laments, the Lamentation over the Destruction of Sumer and Ur. Here the god Enlil explains to his son, the moon god Nanna/Suen, why the latter's city, Ur, is to fall from power:

di-til-la inim pu-úḫ-ru-um-ka šu gi$_4$-gi$_4$ nu-gál
inim du$_{11}$-ga an ^{d}en-líl-lá-ka šu bal-e nu-zu

---

29. Jacobsen, *Toward the Image*, 406n.66.

30. On *palû* generally, see *AHw* 2.817, B, C; on the texts with the sense of "dynasty" or "era," see J. J. Finkelstein, "The Genealogy of the Hammurapi Dynasty," *JCS* 20 (1966) 103-7; on the Middle/Neo-Assyrian usage, see H. Tadmor, "The Campaigns of Sargon II of Assur," *JCS* 12 (1958) 22-40, esp. 26-33; and idem, "History and Ideology in the Assyrian Royal Inscriptions," in *Assyrian Royal Inscriptions: New Horizons* (ed. F. M. Fales; Orientis Antiqui Collection 17; Rome: Istituto per l'Oriente, 1981) 15-16 and n. 9. Note that in these Assyrian texts, matters become rather free, with either the singular logogram, BAL, or the plural, BAL^{meš}, each indicating, in turn, either the reign of a king or one of his regnal years.

One should also recognize another category of meaning for bala and *palû*, as concrete objects. Thus, Sumerian bala can be a "spindle" or something similar — here the sense as object is conveyed by the writing, ^{giš}bala — which is translated into Akkadian as *pilaqqu* (see Sjöberg, *Sumerian Dictionary*, 64-65, s.v. bala A). And Akkadian *palû* can refer to a staff or pole (see *AHw* 2.817a, A; 1581b, A). Whether it is the same bala/*palû* that means both "turn/term" and concrete object or whether we have here distinct, though homonymous, words is not finally certain. But it is probable that some relationship is involved. In the case of bala, the same sign is used both for "turn" and for "spindle," and the spindle, after all, is an object that allows fibers to be turned, twisted, and wound into thread. As for *palû*, the staff or pole is an object that can serve as some kind of support and unit of measure, but it also symbolizes rulership, thus corresponding to the *palû* as "term of royal rule."

31. See T. Jacobsen, *The Sumerian King List* (Assyriological Studies 11; Chicago: University of Chicago, 1939) 37 and passim; and C. Wilcke, "Zum Geschichtsbewusstsein im Alten Mesopotamien," in *Archäologie und Geschichtsbewusstsein* (ed. H. Müller-Karpe; Kolloquien zur Allgemeinen und Vergleichenden Archäologie 3; Munich: Beck, 1982) 40-41.

uri$_5$^{ki}-ma nam-lugal ḫa-ba-šúm bala da-rí la-ba-an-šúm
u$_4$ ul kalam ki gar-ra-ta zag un lu-a-šè
bala nam-lugal-la sag-bi-šè è-a a-ba-a igi im-mi-in-du$_8$-a
nam-lugal-bi bala-bi ba-gíd-e-dè šà-kúš-ù-dè
^{d}nanna-mu na-an-kúš-kúš-ù-dè uru^{ki}-zu è-bar-ra-ab
The decision of the assembly cannot be reversed.
The spoken word of An and Enlil knows no overturning.
To Ur kingship was indeed given; but a lasting turn was not given to it.
From time immemorial, since the land was established, and the people
became numerous,
Who has ever observed a turn of kingship that has dominated (forever)?
Its turn of kingship has endured long, but has now come to rest.
O my Nanna, do not tire yourself out (watching over Ur); leave your city.[32]

Our third example takes us into Akkadian and about three-quarters of a
millennium later, to the Middle Assyrian king, Tukulti-Ninurta I (1244-1207
B.C.E.).[33] One of his building inscriptions reads:

^{d}iš$_8$-tár bēltu(NIN) na-ba-at
palê(BALA^{meš}) šarrū(MAN)-ti-ia
a-bi-ik-tu māti(KUR)-šu
liš-ku-un.
May Ishtar, mistress, the one who decrees
the turn of my kingship,
bring about
the defeat of his land.[34]

The last example is again Akkadian, and belongs to a manual of divination
based on freak births, entitled by its initial words, šumma izbu. The work has a long
history that begins, apparently, in the first half of the second millennium B.C.E., the
Old Babylonian period, and continues through the first half of the first millennium
B.C.E., the Neo-Babylonian. The following entry is represented on tablets copied for
the library of the Neo-Assyrian king, Ashurbanipal (668-627 B.C.E.):

šumma(BE) MIN [= urītu(MUNUS.ANŠE.KUR.RA)] 1
ūlid(Ù.TU)-ma ēnē(IGI^{meš})-šú la ibassū(NU GÁL^{meš})

32. P. Michalowski, The Lamentation over the Destruction of Sumer and Ur (Mesopotamian Civilizations; Winona Lake, IN: Eisenbrauns, 1989) 58-59, lines 364-70, here with
a few minor changes in translation.
33. Mesopotamian dates follow J. A. Brinkman, apud A. L. Oppenheim, Ancient Mesopotamia: Portrait of a Dead Civilization (rev. ed. by E. Reiner; Chicago: University of Chicago,
1977) 345-46.
34. A. K. Grayson, Assyrian Rulers of the Third and Second Millennia B.C. (to 1115 B.C.)
(Royal Inscriptions of Mesopotamia, Assyrian Periods 1; Toronto: University of Toronto,
1987) 245-46: no. 5, lines 120-23; cf. 238-39: no. 1, vi 9ff. for a variant.

^d*Ellil*(EN.LÍL) *palâ*(BAL) *ú-šá-an-na*
If DITTO [= a mare] gives birth to one (foal) with
no eyes, Enlil will change the turn (of rule).[35]

All four of these examples clearly connect the "turn" of rule, on the part
of a city or an individual human ruler, with the will of the gods. Whether by
their collective decision or through the particular power of one of them, they
are the ones to bestow the "turn" and to take it away, "changing" it to another
city or king in what can become a sequence of "turnings." The reasons for the
gods' actions do not have to be given. Indeed, there may no other reason than
that one's "turn" is up — a "turn," by the way, that affects not simply the human
city or king, but their divine protector, as the example from the Sumer and Ur
Lamentation suggests.[36] Thus bala/*palû* stands for the process involved, but even
more, it is reified as the result: the reign, dynasty, or year of rule. And while all
of this is laid out most fully in the two Sumerian examples from the end of the
third/beginning of the second millennium B.C.E., the two Akkadian examples
that come later — and others could be mentioned — clearly belong to the same
tradition.[37]

---

35. E. Leichty, *The Omen Series Šumma Izbu* (Texts from Cuneiform Sources 4; Locust
Valley, NY: J. J. Augustin, 1970) 183: XX 34′; cf. 34: I 35, where the verb *šanû* is in the G stem
and no divine agent is indicated. On the history of the text of *šumma izbu*, see 20-26.

36. This is made explicit in another, contemporaneous Sumerian city lamentation,
that over Ur, where its moon goddess, Ningal, confesses:

u_4-tur-bi-šè bala-mu u_4-sa$_6$-ga bala-mu i-bí-ba-ra-bí-du$_8$

During the brief period of my turn, I did not experience a favorable day of my turn.
(Line 95, quoted in Sjöberg, *Sumerian Dictionary*, 67b, 2.1, s.v. bala b; cf. lines 113-14,
quoted in ibid.)

For the viewpoint at issue, with other Mesopotamian examples, see J. S. Cooper, *The Curse
of Agade* (JHNES; Baltimore: Johns Hopkins University, 1983) 29-30.

37. One might also mention here another term for periodicity, *dāru*. It is attested so
far only in one Akkadian text — although a text extant in a number of copies — from an
Amorite ruler in Mesopotamia, Šamši-Adad I (1813-1781 B.C.E.), and for this reason and its
cognates in other, esp. West Semitic, languages, most agree that it is probably a West Semitic
loanword in this text. The pertinent lines read:

bi-tam ša iš-tu
šu-lum a-kà-de^{ki}
a-di šar-ru-ti-ia
a-di ṣa-ba-at nu-ur-ru-gi^{ki}
7 da-a-ru i-ti-qú-ma
i-na šarrāni(LUGAL^{meš})
a-li-ku-ut pa-ni-ia
šarru(LUGAL) *ma-an-na-ma*
la i-pu-šu-ma

The temple which no king among those who preceded me rebuilt from the *completion*

Now what is striking is that something of the same complex appears even later, in the first centuries of Islam. The word here is Arabic *dawla*, and it also means "turning, rotating, alternating," coming from the root *dwl*, which is known in other Semitic languages as well.[38] In Arabic the root can refer to the change or transfer of something from one situation to another, like *dūlatan* in the Qur'an, which is something constantly changing ownership.[39] But already early in Arabic literature, *dwl* was associated especially with the marking of time. Thus, again in the Qur'an, it occurs as a verb to describe alternating periods of time,[40] while in other early texts it can refer to one's "turn" at office or at gaining favor or success.[41] With the Abbasid revolution in the eighth century c.e., which toppled the existing Umayyad dynasty, *dawla* took on a new life, as a key term in the intense activity of historiographic apologetic in behalf of the new regime.[42] Now it was not just any turn of time, but the one that had specifically brought the Abbasids to power as the rulers of Islam. As al-Saffah, the first Abbasid caliph, is described as saying to some of his new subjects, "you have reached our time, and God has brought to you our *dawla*."[43] Moreover, this *dawla* was not something utterly new; it was put forward as a "turning" around

of (the dynasty of) Akkad to my kingship, to (my) capture of Nurrugu — (a period in which) 7 rotations passed. . . . (Grayson, *Assyrian Rulers*, 53: no. 2 i 14-22)

Here *dāru* is clearly a unit of time, and is translated "rotation" in conformity with the meaning of its root, *dwr;* the conventional rendering of it, following that of its Biblical Hebrew cognate, *dôr*, has been "generation." In this sense of "rotation" and in its use to mark the time between two periods of political rule, those of Akkad and of Šamši-Adad I, it is similar to bala/*palû*, and for that matter, Biblical Hebrew *sbb* and Arabic *dawla*, which I discuss below. But one must note the important difference as well: that it is just a unit of time, with no particular attachment to notions of rule or, even more, to the turning or transfer of power from one ruler to another by the divine world. If it is to be connected, therefore, to bala/*palû, sbb,* and *dawla,* it should be in a broad, loose way: as a testimony to the general notion of periodicity out of which our three terms represent a specific development.

38. I want to thank Prof. Jacob Lassner for making me aware of the term *dawla* and its possible relevance to *sbb* and bala/*palû*. The discussion that follows is based on his work and that of several others: F. Rosenthal, "Dawla," *Encyclopaedia of Islam* (new ed.; Leiden: Brill, 1965) 2.177-78; B. Lewis, *Islam in History: Ideas, Men, and Events in the Middle East* (New York: Library Press, 1973) 253-54, 329, resumed in his *The Political Language of Islam* (Chicago: University of Chicago, 1988) 35-36, 131; J. Lassner, "The 'Abbasid *Dawla*: An Essay on the Concept of Revolution in Early Islam," in *Tradition and Innovation in Late Antiquity* (ed. F. M. Clover and R. S. Humphreys; Wisconsin Studies in Classics; Madison: University of Wisconsin, 1989) 247-70.

39. Qur'an, Sura 59:7.

40. Ibid., Sura 3:134.

41. See Rosenthal, "Dawla," 177b.

42. See Lassner, "'Abbasid *Dawla*"; and, more fully, idem, *Islamic Revolution and Historical Memory: An Inquiry into the Art of 'Abbasid Apologetics* (AOS 66; New Haven: American Oriental Society, 1986).

43. al-Ṭabari, iii 30, quoted here from Rosenthal, "Dawla," 178a.

back, after the evils of the Umayyads, to the model leadership of Muhammad.[44] Besides the movement of political rule, in this instance to the Abbasids, it came to denote the result, namely, the victorious Abbasid house, which hastened the emergence of a more general sense, of *dawla* as a "dynasty" and then a "state." One additional development became apparent by the ninth and tenth centuries C.E. Here the workings of *dawla* became the subject of more explicit and elaborate inquiry, wherein it was associated with *mulk*, "kingship," to designate the political power dominant at a given time which then "turns" from dynasty to dynasty and nation to nation at fixed intervals.[45]

The *dawla* just described, though separated culturally and by a millennium and more from bala/*palû*, should nonetheless seem quite familiar. This familiarity, it is plain, also reaches to our biblical usage of *sbb*. Let us review, then, what our examination has yielded and push it a bit further. In all three traditions, the change of rule is described by words — found in both nominal and verbal forms — meaning "turning," which appear not to be empty expressions but to signify a notion of the rotation of rule from one group or individual to another, caused and supervised by the divine world. On the one hand, this divine, in the Mesopotamian sphere, can be an individual god, watching over the "turn" of his human protégé, or the assembly of gods (or one of its heads like Enlil), who preside over the "turning" process altogether and to whom, therefore, an individual deity and his favorite are subject. In biblical Israel and Islam, on the other hand, consistent with their monotheistic trajectories, divine control centers on a single deity, who watches over the "turn" of his protégé but does so with a view to the cosmos as a whole, over which he is also sovereign. As for the "turning" itself, while the biblical examples apply it to the process of movement from one ruler to the next, in the Mesopotamian and Islamic it can also be concretized as the new ruler or dynasty that results from the process. Finally, why the "turning" occurs at all is not always addressed directly in our several traditions. The Bible can ascribe it to the sin of the existing ruler. But, as we have seen, it does not always do that, in at least two cases just leaving it as a manifestation of Yahweh's will and fulfillment of an earlier prophecy. That lack of a moral reason appears also in the Mesopotamian and Islamic examples — indeed, at least in the Mesopotamian, it seems uppermost — where the "turning" can also be left simply as the expression of divine will or accounted as part of an ordained cycle, in which, it is understood, nothing remains fixed forever, but has eventually to yield precedence.

There is another point here as well, which at first sight looks paradoxical. For if, on the one hand, the "turning" can be conceived as part of an orderly process of rotation of rule, on the other, "turning" as a manifestation of the divine can be used

---

44. So Lassner, "'Abbasid *Dawla*," 258ff.; idem, *Islamic Revolution*, xii-xiii.

45. See Rosenthal, "Dawla," 178a; Lewis, *Islam in History*, 254; and Y. Marquet, "Les cycles de la souveraineté selon les épîtres des Iḫwān al-Ṣafā," *Studia Islamica* 36 (1972) 47-69. Cf. the use of *dāru* (above, n. 37) as a unit of time.

in the texts to mark a disruptive occurrence in the political order — something not normally expected by human convention. This sense of disruption we have found particularly in the biblical examples of *sbb*, even as some of them have been given an orderliness by being represented as the fulfillment of Yahweh's earlier prophecy. But the disruption is also apparent, or at least not far in the background, in the other instances: so for the *dawla* of the Abbasids, the statement of whose orderly arrival reflects what was in fact a violent break with the existing Umayyad regime; so also for a Mesopotamian example like the Sumer and Ur Lamentation, where the notion of a rotating bala cannot cover up just how destabilizing was the collapse in the imperial order long provided by the city of Ur. How, then, can one explain this paradox of order and disruption in the way the words for "turning" are used? The paradox, I would propose, is deliberate: an attempt to take what appears as disruption in a narrower, human perspective — "turning" in the sense of aberration — and to reconceptualize it as orderly change, even if not fully explicable, when seen as part of the divine plane — "turning" in the sense of process. The Abbasid case adds yet another dimension to this, in which the Abbasid *dawla* is not even disruption on the human plane, but a "return" to the purity and normalcy of the era of Muhammad after the true disruption of the Umayyads.

Thus bala/*palû, sbb*, and *dawla* appear to form a rather intricate web of language and ideas, and my last question is what this might mean historically. Can one suppose some kind of actual historical connection among them? Deciding such connections is always a delicate and uncertain matter, and in the present instance, it is complicated by at least two factors. First, in each case the specialized meaning of a divine "turning" of political rule is clearly embedded in a broader context internal to each tradition of "turning" or "transferring" from one situation to another: so for the biblical *sbb, šûb šĕbî/ût,* and *hpk,* which we have examined in most detail, but also for Sumerian bal and Arabic *dwl.* Second, the notion of a "turning" of events is not restricted to Mesopotamia, Israel, and the Islamic empire, but occurs in other cultures, where nothing compels us to assume a historical relationship to our three. In this regard, perhaps the image most easily thought of is a "revolving wheel of fortune," and a passage in the Greek historian Herodotus, which he attributes to the Lydian ruler Croesus, is a good illustration:

ekeino prōton mathe hōs kyklos tōn anthrōpēiōn esti prēgmatōn, peripheromenos de ouk ea aiei tous autous eutycheein.

understand this first of all, that human affairs operate on a wheel, which in going around does not allow them [= humans] to enjoy good fortune forever.[46]

---

46. C. Hude, *Herodoti Historiae, Libri I-IV* (Oxford: Clarendon, 1912) 1.207.24-26. For similar occurrences of *kyklos,* see LSJ, 1007a, III, s.v. *kyklos.* There is also the related *anakyklōsis,* used by Polybius to describe a "cycle" of three forms of government — kingship, aristocracy, and democracy — and their three perversions — tyranny, oligarchy, and mob rule — through which, in his judgment, human societies pass (Polybius, *The Histories* [LCL;

Internal context and occurrence in other cultures are obviously troublesome to a thesis of historical connection. They suggest, rather, that the similarities among bala/*palû, sbb,* and *dawla* be explained as separate, parallel developments, independent realizations of a notion and imagery that one could
naturally infer from human experience in many places and circumstances. Still,
the similarities among our three sets of terms are close and particular ones.
They are not, for example, a "wheel of human fortune," or a general "turning
(over)" of events, people, or property, but specifically a "turning/rotation of
political rule" from one holder to another governed by divine will. Moreover,
they come from three communities, Mesopotamian, Israelite, and Islamic, which
are all Near Eastern and otherwise show cultural contact, albeit in some instances contacts that are indirect and mediated because of the chronological
and cultural distances to be traversed.[47] Perhaps, then, it is not "either-or" in
making sense of the relationship at work here. That is, perhaps one should
understand that while bala/*palû, sbb,* and *dawla* each draw on the general human
experience of the ongoing changeableness of affairs, and while they each do so
by manipulating words for "turning," the striking convergence in the way they
do this suggests that, even if they may not be *directly* connected, they are
manifestations of a common Near Eastern tradition for how to conceive of the
vicissitudes of political rule in human history.

Cambridge; Harvard University, 1979] 3.286-93 [6.9-10]). The "wheel of fortune" appears
in later European literature as well, perhaps connected with this classical tradition; cf., e.g.,
Shakespeare's "Giddy Fortune's furious fickle wheel/That goddess blind/That stands upon
the rolling restless stone" (*King Henry V* 3.6.28).

47. An overview of the issues is given by C. E. Dubler, "Survivances de l'Ancien Orient
dans l'Islam," *Studia Islamica* 7 (1957) 47-75 (reference courtesy of Wolfhart Heinrichs). For
Israel and Mesopotamia, see, e.g., the collection of essays and bibliography in H.-P. Müller, ed.,
Babylonien und Israel (Wege der Forschung 633; Darmstadt: Wissenschaftliche Buchgesellschaft,
1991). The Hebrew biblical component in classical Islam is undeniable, from the Qur'an on; but
how and in what forms the Bible got there and specifically what roles Jews and Christians played
in this are still debated. A recent and penetrating treatment of one example, with remarks on
the wider issue, is J. Lassner, *Demonizing the Queen of Sheba* (Chicago: University of Chicago,
1993). Finally, there is the Mesopotamian legacy in Islam. This remains a tricky issue because of
the chronological and cultural distance, and it is likely that one must reckon with transmission
through various intermediaries, although the fact that Iraq, the home of ancient Mesopotamia,
became a center of classical Islam suggests that some traditions could have passed more directly,
and indeed, local knowledge of many of the ancient ruins did persist. But no systematic study
of the Mesopotamian-Islamic connection exists. Among more recent efforts to discuss parts of
it are: S. Dalley, "Gilgamesh in the Arabian Nights," *JRAS* (1991) 1-17; idem, "The Tale of
Bulūqiyā and the *Alexander Romance* in Jewish and Sufi Mystical Circles," in *Tracing the Threads.
Studies in the Vitality of Jewish Pseudepigrapha* (ed. J. C. Reeves; Atlanta: Scholars Press, 1994)
239-69; and G. Azarpay, "The Eclipse Dragon on an Arabic Frontispieceminiature. With a Note
on the Babylonian Explanation of the Lunar Eclipse, by A. D. Kilmer," *JAOS* 98 (1978) 363-74.
Note also the desultory observations by H. W. F. Saggs in *The Greatness That Was Babylon* (rev.
ed.; London: Sidgwick & Jackson, 1988) 429-30, 435-37.

Murderous Fathers, Manipulative Mothers, and Rivalrous Siblings: Rethinking the Architecture of Genesis–Kings

J. DAVID PLEINS

Santa Clara University, California

Can we posit an overall structural scheme for the Genesis to Kings narrative? Are there connections between the narrative materials of Genesis–Numbers and the narratives found in the Deuteronomistic History (DtrH)? This comparison has traditionally been off limits to biblical scholars because of the belief that the DtrH is structurally separate from the narrative material of the Pentateuch that precedes the DtrH. Noth's *Überlieferungsgeschichtliche Studien* artfully framed the notion that underlying our present Deuteronomy–Kings is a major, continuous literary and theological project.[1] But Noth's theoretical constraints — his focus on Deuteronomy and the narratives that follow — did not permit him even to raise the question of possible relationships between the rest of the Pentateuch and the DtrH. Nevertheless, canonical criticism's emphasis on the final form of the text forces us to ask, albeit in a preliminary way, if Genesis–Kings exhibits any overall structuring scheme.

In fact, long ago Freedman put forward the suggestion to read Genesis–Kings as a single unit, although at that time he had not yet refined the rhetorical tools to fully elaborate his thesis that Genesis–Kings constitutes a "Primary History" — a document that he now postulates may have more extensive

---

1. Available in English as M. Noth, *The Deuteronomistic History* (2nd ed.; JSOTSup 15; Sheffield: JSOT, 1991), and *The Chronicler's History* (JSOTSup 50; Sheffield: JSOT, 1987). In chap. 25 of the latter volume, Noth discusses only the seam that ties the Pentateuch to the DtrH, namely, the latter chapters of the book of Numbers. He does not discuss any other links between the Pentateuch and the DtrH.

sources or editorial work connecting Genesis to Samuel–Kings than is discerned through traditional pentateuchal source analysis or Noth's theories concerning the DtrH.[2] To clarify his ideas, Freedman has begun to speak of an extended Super J source underlying Genesis–Samuel and possibly present in Kings.[3]

Similarly, Gunn has offered the "prognostication" that "new readings of extensive segments of narrative" will appear in biblical studies, and he at least holds out the consideration that Genesis–Kings will be a likely target.[4] Gunn offers no suggestions for a specific direction here, but I believe that we are now in a position to rethink the structuring scheme, the overall architecture, of the Genesis–Kings material. Rhetorical criticism has made this move possible and canonical criticism has made it inevitable. In this programmatic essay I want to discuss some of the apparent underlying structural features that connect the patriarchal narratives in Genesis with the narratives in Samuel–Kings. The structural and thematic connections are striking, arguing for the view that the DtrH cannot be read apart from Genesis.[5]

I. Fathers and Sons

The first structural parallel to consider here emerges from a comparison between Genesis 22 and the Saul-Jonathan-David narratives. A careful study reveals that the account of Abraham's attempt to slay Isaac in Genesis 22 can be

---

2. See D. N. Freedman, "Pentateuch," *IDB* 3.710-27; " 'Son of Man, Can These Bones Live?': The Exile," *Int* 29/2 (1975) 171-86. See also "The Earliest Bible," *Michigan Quarterly Review* 22 (1983) 167-75. This article has been reprinted in *Backgrounds for the Bible* (ed. M. P. O'Connor and D. N. Freedman; Winona Lake, IN: Eisenbrauns, 1987) 29-37.

3. D. N. Freedman, "Dinah and Shechem, Tamar and Amnon," *Austin Seminary Bulletin* 105 (1990) 52-63, esp. 52; "The Formation of the Canon of the Old Testament: The Selection and Identification of the Torah as the Supreme Authority of the Postexilic Community," in *Religion and Law: Biblical-Judaic and Islamic Perspectives* (ed. E. B. Firmage, B. G. Weiss, and J. W. Welch; Winona Lake, IN: Eisenbrauns, 1990) 315-31.

4. D. Gunn, "New Directions in the Study of Biblical Hebrew Narrative," *JSOT* 39 (1987) 72. Gunn's writings on the Saul narrative are worth noting here: *The Fate of King Saul: An Interpretation of a Biblical Story* (JSOTSup 14; Sheffield: JSOT, 1980); and "A Man Given over to Trouble: The Story of King Saul," in *Images of Man and God: Old Testament Short Stories in Literary Focus* (ed. B. O. Long; Sheffield: Almond, 1981) 89-112.

5. The attempt to parallel DtrH material with texts in Genesis is not entirely without precedent. See W. Brueggemann, "David and His Theologian," *CBQ* 30 (1968) 156-81, where he details possible parallels between the four stories in Genesis 3–11 and the four major narratives from 2 Samuel 9–20 and 1 Kings 1–2. The study of D. Damrosch, *The Narrative Covenant: Transformation of Genre in the Growth of Biblical Narrative* (San Francisco: Harper & Row, 1987) 230-33, contains only vague hints about parallels between the Yahwist and DtrH. But his attempt to link Saul's so-called blindness with the Jacob and Esau story is unconvincing in the light of the stricter parallels discussed in the present paper.

tapped to focus our understanding of Saul's relationship both to Jonathan and to David. While the comparison must take into account that the Saul-Jonathan-David narrative is more extensive regarding these points than Genesis 22, nevertheless it turns out on closer inspection that the theme of the father as son-slayer is as pivotal to the transmission of the promise in Genesis 22 as it is to the succession of the kingship as found in the Saul-Jonathan-David narrative. Indeed, invoking Genesis 22 helps one to understand the seemingly curious portrayal of David as the "son" of Saul.[6]

I begin this comparison by considering the act of attempted son-slaying as found in these texts. One of the curiosities that really begs one to set these narratives side by side, at least in some preliminary way, is that in both Genesis 22 and the Saul narrative the father endangers the son by attempting to kill him. The deed in Genesis 22 is terribly striking in its context. In the overall development of the Abraham narrative, Genesis 22 offers an unexpected twist, for only very shortly after the report of his birth in Gen 21:1-8, the narrative in Genesis 22 throws Isaac's life into mortal danger. Indeed, the very promises of God to Abraham are pushed to the limit. Of course, we know from the start of Genesis 22 that this is a test, but this does not take away from the drama of the narrative. The act of attempted son-slaying is key in the development of the Abraham-Isaac narrative. The narrator uses the act to bring out God's demands and to demonstrate Abraham's obedience.

Genesis 22, however, is not the only place where Genesis–Kings has a father attempting to slay his son. Both Saul and Abraham deliberately attempt to kill their sons. For Saul this occurs during his ill-fated dinner conversation with Jonathan (1 Sam 20:24-34). When Saul casts his spear at his son, he is not acting out of obedience to God as Abraham was; rather, he is acting out of anger over Jonathan's close ties with David — ties that Saul legitimately feared would ensure that David and not Jonathan would become heir to the throne (20:30-31). The text is quite clear about the deliberate nature of Saul's act: he hurled his spear at Jonathan in order to cut him down (i.e., to kill him; 20:33). Saul's action is terribly ironic because this very deed drives Jonathan further into the arms of David, thereby sealing Jonathan's fate in much the same way as Abraham's act seals the fate of Isaac. At this level in both stories it is the father's actions that determine the fate of the son. Because Saul is not acting on a divine command, however, his attack on Jonathan serves only to demonstrate that he is unworthy to supply an heir to the throne. He is a son-slayer like Abraham, but with one major flaw: Saul is disobedient toward God.

The second point of comparison between Genesis 22 and the Saul-David-Jonathan narrative focuses on the more thematic notion of the securing of the heir. How do the narratives use the son-slayer motif to produce an heir to the

---

6. For a more detailed study of Genesis 22 and its relation to the Saul-Jonathan-David narrative, see my article "Son-Slayers and Their Sons," *CBQ* 54/1 (1992) 29-38.

throne? It is clear that the Aqedah event recounted in Genesis 22 plays a pivotal role toward securing the place of Isaac in the succession of the promise. Through Abraham's submission to God, Abraham shows himself to be obedient, thereby gaining for his son the favor of God (22:12, 15-18). Genesis 22 forms the decisive test of Abraham's obedience. Prior to this Abraham had been skeptical of the promise (15:1-4), Sarah was disbelieving of the prospects of giving birth in her old age (18:10-15), Sarah and Hagar had fallen into bitter conflict over Sarah's barrenness and the birth of Ishmael to Hagar (chap. 16; 21:1-21), and even Sarah's own life was endangered when Abraham passed her off as his sister to both Pharaoh and Abimelech (12:10-20; 20:1-18).[7] But none of these incidents proved fatal to the promise. At each step some provision was made to ensure that Sarah would survive and that Isaac would be born. Genesis 22 provides not only the ultimate danger to Isaac and the promise but also yields the final stamp of approval for Isaac. Abraham's obedience to the sacrificial act secures the position of Isaac.

The critical dilemma of the Saul narrative is that David is to become the next king. Is the son-slayer motif used to shape the narrative of David's rise to the throne and Jonathan's fall? Can one see connections between the Saul narrative and the securing of Isaac's place in the promise? For Jonathan, as we have already seen, the structural effect of the son-slayer motif is to cut Jonathan off from the kingship. Jonathan will not inherit the kingship as Isaac inherited the promise. But why? If both Abraham and Saul attempt to kill their sons, why is the outcome different for Abraham (Isaac succeeds him as patriarch, but Jonathan does not succeed Saul as king)? The comparison of the narratives should make clear that the measure or standard used here is whether the main character is obedient to God (Gen 22:1, 12). The narrator brings this fact out elsewhere in the Saul narrative (1 Sam 15:19-26; cf. 14:24-46), but the futility of Saul's direct confrontation with Jonathan deftly hammers the point home for the reader. After Jonathan leaves his father's presence, the reader does not retain any expectation that Jonathan will rise to the throne (20:33). A comparison between the Saul narrative and Genesis 22 helps to make clear why Jonathan would be cut off from the kingship and why Isaac would succeed. When a disobedient father attempts to slay his own son, God does not permit the son to come to power (1 Sam 20:31).

Bearing in mind that the focus of the larger Saul narrative is on David, not Jonathan, one must ask whether the son-slayer motif has been used in relation to David and his securing of a place in the line of royal succession. Does knowledge of the structural position of Genesis 22 in the Abraham-Isaac narrative help one to sort out the texts concerning Saul and David? In the initial

---

7. See D. J. A. Clines, "The Ancestor in Danger: But Not the Same Danger," in *What Does Eve Do to Help?* (JSOTSup 94; Sheffield: JSOT, 1990) 67-89; and M. E. Biddle, "The 'Endangered Ancestress' and Blessing for the Nations," *JBL* 109 (1990) 599-611.

Saul-David confrontations in the court of Saul, David has only the status of son-in-law; hence the parallel with Genesis 22 is a bit inexact (1 Sam 18:12–19:10). In the later confrontations between Saul and David that take place in the Philistine realm (1 Samuel 24; 26), however, the writer deliberately has Saul and David speak of each other as "father" and "son," respectively (24:12, 17 [ET 11, 16]; 26:21). This phrasing is rather curious unless one invokes the son-slayer motif as a literary device. On the immediate level of the narrative, when Saul is portrayed as the son-slayer in relation to David, one has the obsessive Saul who is attempting to do away with any challenger to his family's control of the throne. But on the structural level of the narrative, the son-slayer motif achieves the same result for David as it did for Isaac: David succeeds to the throne by the same act that gained a place in the promise for Isaac, through the father's attempt to take the son's life. If this reading is plausible, one has a tool for explaining Saul's attempt to kill not only Jonathan but also David. The Saul-David interchange represents an expansion of the son-slayer motif beyond the proportions of the Abraham narrative. Yet the function of the motif in both settings is strikingly similar insofar as the literary dimension of the securing of the heir is concerned.

To these structural considerations, I must add a third theme: that of the son's obedience to a father who is a son-slayer. Admittedly, this a more understated element in the Genesis 22 narrative. The son's silence clearly bothered later rabbinic exegetes, who devised dialogues between a satanic adversary and the willing Isaac, hoping through these dialogues to help clarify the rather passive posture of Isaac as found in Genesis 22.[8] But the biblical narrative portrays Isaac simply as one who willingly and even knowledgeably goes to the sacrifice. The interchange between father and son is straightforward and simple. The son readily believes his father and even carries the wood for the sacrifice (22:7-8).

---

8. The notion of Isaac's obedience is more fully developed in later tradition in two ways. One is by having a satanic adversary (Samael) appear to Isaac. This figure attempts to convince Isaac that his father has gone mad and warns Isaac to flee, all of which Isaac refuses to do (cf., e.g., *Gen. Rab.* 56:4). Second, the emphasis on obedience is brought out by having Isaac tell Abraham to bind him well so that Isaac does not flinch when the sacrifice takes place, which would render the sacrifice unacceptable (cf., e.g., *Gen. Rab.* 56:8; *Tg. Ps.-J.* 22:1, 10; 4 Macc 16:20; *Pseudo-Philo* 32.3; 40.2; reflected in the Qur'an, Sura 37:101-5, though whether Isaac or Ishmael is the victim is debated by Muslim commentators; cf., e.g., al-Ṭabari §§290-303). See further *Jub.* 17:15–18:19; *Gen. Rab.* 55:4; *Lev. Rab.* 2:10. For studies of the Aqedah in later tradition see S. Spiegel, *The Last Trial: On the Legends and Lore of the Command to Abraham to Offer Isaac as a Sacrifice: The Akedah* (trans. J. Goldin; New York: Pantheon, 1967); P. R. Davies and B. D. Chilton, "The Akedah: A Revised Tradition History," *CBQ* 40 (1978) 514-46. See also R. W. L. Moberly, "The Earliest Commentary on the Akedah," *VT* 38 (1988) 302-23, who emphasizes the factor of Abraham's obedience. For the Islamic materials see R. Firestone, *Journeys in Holy Lands: The Evolution of the Abraham-Ishmael Legends in Islamic Exegesis* (New York: SUNY, 1990).

The theme of obedience/disobedience is integral to the movement of the Jonathan-David materials. The theme of obedience/disobedience is structurally dramatized as a relationship between a father who slays his son and a son who is either disobedient, as in the case of Jonathan, or obedient, as in the case of David. The movement of the kingship into David's hands hinges on both the disobedience of Jonathan and the obedience of David. The narrator makes a point of highlighting both responses. Jonathan opposes his father at several points. Early in the narrative, Jonathan inadvertently breaks one of Saul's orders and is nearly put to death for the offense (1 Sam 14:24-35). Even though the act was accidental, the incident foreshadows the break that will occur between Jonathan and his father. Later in the narrative, Jonathan openly opposes his father's desire to attack David (19:1-17). Jonathan also openly shows love and loyalty to David, much to Saul's dismay (18:1-6; 20:16, 41-42).[9] Jonathan's disobedience is one of the factors that contributes to his own demise.

In the case of David, the notion of obedience to his "father" Saul is critical. David has two opportunities to kill Saul but makes the conscious choice not to do so (1 Sam 24:5-8, 11-14 [ET 4-7, 10-13]; 26:8-12). He remains, like Isaac, the obedient son before the son-slayer. The narrator's focus on David's obedience sets Jonathan's disobedience into sharper relief. A comparison with Isaac in Genesis 22 helps to make clear where the narrative emphasis is in this regard. In each case — Isaac, David, or Jonathan — the theme of disobedience/obedience is structurally determinative for the future of the figure. In the final analysis, the disobedient Jonathan becomes the sacrificial substitute permitting the obedient David to succeed at securing his hold on the throne (1 Sam 18:3-4; cf. Gen 22:8, 13).

When read in the light of Genesis 22, Saul's attack on Jonathan stands out as structurally central to the Saul-Jonathan-David episode.[10] The above analysis makes Saul's question to the young victor over Goliath all the more revealing (1 Sam 17:55). Saul wants to know who that boy is. By birth David is, as he says, the "son of Jesse" (17:58). But the structure of the narrative takes us to another level when it insists that by reason of kingship, David is the "son" of Saul. The son-slayer motif intervenes to make both Isaac and David secure heirs to the promise and to the kingship, respectively.

---

9. Cf. D. Jobling, "Jonathan: A Structural Study in 1 Samuel," in *The Sense of Biblical Narrative: Three Structural Analyses in the Old Testament (I Samuel 13–21, Numbers 11–12, I Kings 17–18)* (JSOTSup 7; Sheffield: JSOT, 1978) 4-25.

10. Contrast Jobling, ibid., p. 14, where he says that Saul's attempt to slay Jonathan is "without narrative logic."

II. Mothers and Sons

The Isaac-Jacob and David-Solomon narratives offer another striking set of comparisons. Like the Saul narrative, these texts take up the topic of the succession to the promise and the kingship, but do so by focusing on the deeds of the ancestral mothers. If the fathers are son-slayers, what are the mothers like? If the father's actions can decisively affect the unfolding of the promise, what do the mothers do to carry this promise forward? I focus here on Rebekah's and Bathsheba's efforts to secure blessing and kingship for their sons. I think that these narratives are structurally and thematically similar to one another, and that an understanding of one narrative contributes to a fuller understanding of the other. The main point of comparison here is that the wives appear to manipulate their aging and physically ailing husbands in order to assure the child's standing. But the role and actions of the heirs and potential heirs will also form a significant point of linkage between the narratives (see §III below).

For the structural comparison, it is significant that both narratives take place in the aging years of the sons' fathers. In the case of Isaac, the narrative hinges on the fact that Isaac's eyesight has deteriorated to the point where he must ask each son to speak just to confirm which son has entered his presence (Gen 27:1, 21-23). In the case of David, his sexual vigor has waned and he lies cold on his deathbed (1 Kgs 1:1-4). The aging condition of the fathers is an essential factor in both narratives, providing the occasion for the mothers to go to work on their husbands. What the mothers seek is to secure the succession of an unlikely or ineligible heir, namely, Jacob and Solomon.

The story of Rebekah's deception of Isaac is rather straightforward (Genesis 27). The deception is clearly marked out for the reader by the description of Jacob's costume and the food that his mother prepares — all designed to imitate Esau (27:14-16). Rebekah's words leave no doubt in the reader's mind that she knows what she is up to and that she intends in this way to secure the blessing for Jacob (27:12). Rebekah's independent and deceptive course of action is thrown into sharp relief by Jacob's protests to his mother that he is not the rightful heir and that the ruse is certainly doomed to failure (27:11-12). In this way, the narrator openly portrays the nature of the deception. The mother clearly has specific designs for her son, and it is also apparent that it is the woman who is the deceiver. Her overall intentions for her son drive her to manipulate her husband to obtain the irrevocable blessing for her son. By her actions, she has ensured the success of her favored child as the bearer of the promise (Gen 27:33).

A comparison between this tale and the story of Bathsheba and the aging David is instructive not only for one's understanding of the Bathsheba narrative but also for the overall attempt to link Genesis to Samuel–Kings. Like Rebekah, Bathsheba was forced to take decisive action to secure the throne for her son, Solomon (1 Kgs 1:11-12). In much the same way that Rebekah had to make sure that Jacob's blessing did not go to Esau, Bathsheba had to see to it that Adonijah did not succeed in establishing himself as the successor to David. In both narratives, the aging and ailing fathers become the targets of the mothers' manipulation of events on behalf of their favored sons. Both mothers are working against time, social conventions, and political structures to establish their sons' positions. Indeed, Bathsheba faces the very moment of crisis, for Adonijah has begun to claim the throne for himself even before David is dead (1 Kgs 1:5).

When read in isolation, the events in 1 Kings 1–2 are somewhat ambiguous concerning the level of Bathsheba's involvement in the manipulation of the aging David. It is clear that Bathsheba is guided heavily in her words by the prophet Nathan, and there is more than a hint of deception in the fact that Nathan comes in to confirm for David the very words that Nathan has put into Bathsheba's mouth (1:12-27). From the narrative it seems clear that David never made such a promise concerning Solomon to Bathsheba, but to what extent is Bathsheba actively involved in deceiving David? Or is this simply a ploy by Nathan to exercise influence over Solomon should he rise to power?

Unlike the Rebekah narrative, where the deception is absolutely clear, the Kings narrative leaves Bathsheba's knowledge and intent unspoken. This enigmatic portrait of Bathsheba ought not to surprise us since it is the same wordless figure who bathes before David and goes in and out of the palace for sex, sending only the unambiguous message, "I'm pregnant," and leaving David to pick up the pieces (2 Sam 11:5).[11] One cannot say to what extent Bathsheba is involved in orchestrating the adultery episode and the later manipulation of the aging David. But that she is involved, participates, and derives benefits from her actions is beyond doubt. The ambiguity surrounding Bathsheba's interior world means that the accent of the Kings narrative rests not so much on the act of manipulation but on its outcome. Bathsheba, like Rebekah, is forced to manipulate to secure the dynasty for her son. A comparative reading of these narratives, however, tends to confirm Bathsheba's complicity in the deception of David.

III. Rival Brothers

The striking connection of the aging-deception motifs in the Isaac and David narratives should not cause one to miss the equally striking connection between the fraternal rivalries that undergird the mothers' deeds: the tension between Jacob and Esau finds its counterpart in the tension between Solomon and Adonijah. The narrator does not simply focus on the mother's actions for her

11. A. Berlin, *Poetics and Interpretation of Biblical Narrative* (Sheffield: Almond, 1983) 26-27.

son; the text also takes up and treats in some detail the rivalry that exists between the favored son and the son who is the rightful heir. Since the rivalries are significant structural features of the text, it is necessary to explore this connection between Genesis and Kings in more detail.

The tensions between Jacob and Esau are made apparent from the start of the narrative, where the brothers even struggle with one another in birth (Gen 25:22-25). Here the narrator self-consciously interprets this struggle within the broader context of the national antagonisms that existed between the government of Jerusalem and the peoples of Edom (25:23). The tensions between Jacob and Esau mark the flow of the entire Jacob narrative and determine the character of the reconciliation of the brothers: Jacob's robbery of birthright and blessing from his brother is balanced by their fictive restoration in the form of gifts and brotherly reconciliation at the end of the Jacob cycle (25:27-34; 27:1-45; 32:4–33:11).[12] Together they bury their father Isaac (35:29), thus sealing their reconciliation. It is an act of bonding that finally and symbolically dissolves the common strife that began in the womb prior to their birth.

Solomon has no womb rival from Bathsheba because that potential was swallowed up in the death of David and Bathsheba's firstborn (2 Sam 12:19). The notion of womb rivalry is broadened in the Solomon narrative, however, by extending the rivalry to Solomon's half-brother, Adonijah (1 Kgs 1:6). Both sets of brothers are of necessity rivals from birth. This is the case, on the one hand, because Esau and Adonijah are the elder brothers and rightful heirs, and on the other hand, because both Jacob and Solomon are favored by God from their births. God's favor comes in the form of a word of the Lord to Rebekah, extending the promises of nationhood to the youngest son, Jacob (Gen 25:22-23). Solomon's favor is initially indicated in the name given to him by Nathan the prophet, Jedidiah, which means "beloved of Yah(weh)" (2 Sam 12:25). Solomon's preeminent status is confirmed by the message from God spoken through the prophet Nathan in 2 Sam 7:12-14, which, while not explicitly mentioning Solomon, does speak of the secure status of David's successor who builds the temple, namely, Solomon. Thus we are assured by the texts that, whatever the nature and course of the rivalries between the brothers, from birth the divinely sanctioned successors will be Jacob and Solomon. The contradictions between the birth circumstances and the divine promises give rise to the fraternal tensions that the unfolding narratives attempt to resolve or overcome.

The rivalries of the brothers make clear that the promises of God are in danger. Should Esau and Adonijah succeed in becoming bearers of the promise and the kingship respectively, the land and the dynasty would not rest on God's chosen. Ultimately, the temple of Yahweh in Jerusalem would not be built. The presence of the rivals and of their legitimate claims pose grave problems for the

12. M. Fishbane, *Text and Texture* (New York: Schocken, 1979) 40-62.

forward movement of the narrative. The mother plays an important role in altering the balance to defeat the dangers of fraternal strife. In the cases of both Rebekah and Bathsheba, the mother steps in to alter the natural course of events, so as to secure a place for her own or preferred son. This is not simply a matter of balancing the interests of the rival son. The mother steps in to make the social and political structures work to the benefit of her choice. Without the mother, the tension between the brothers would not bring success for the divinely chosen child. But without the sibling rivalry, the mother would have no need to take action.

While the chosen sons are the more passive benefactors of their mothers' manipulations on their behalf, the rivalry scheme still has a place where the favored sons are called on to act more positively to effect a reconciliation with their rival brothers. As Fishbane has shown, fraternal reconciliation is one of the driving forces of the Jacob-Esau narrative. It is not until Jacob chooses the path of reconciliation that he earns the new name Israel (Gen 32:27-29).[13] In addition, although Fishbane does not note this detail, the reconciliation of Jacob and Esau is evidenced by their ability to bury Isaac together (35:28-29). The act of joint burial effectively resolves the tension introduced in Gen 27:41-45, where Esau harbors the intent to kill Jacob once Isaac has been buried.

In a similar manner, the theme of brotherly reconciliation becomes an issue twice in the Solomon narrative. Immediately after Solomon put down Adonijah's bid for the throne, Adonijah fled in fear to the sacred altar, forcing Solomon to swear that he would not kill Adonijah (1 Kgs 1:51-53). Solomon magnanimously gives Adonijah his freedom. This reconciliation is the functional equivalent of the reconciliation between Jacob and Esau. Later, however, when Bathsheba expressly calls on Solomon to accept Adonijah's request for Abishag, Solomon refuses to accede to his mother's wishes and proceeds to have Adonijah put to death, since the request was tantamount to reasserting Adonijah's claim to the throne (2:13-25). The differences between the Jacob and Solomon narratives on this point are crucial for understanding the subsequent Joseph and Kings literary blocks. I would argue that the Jacob-Esau reconciliation serves to foreshadow the brotherly reconciliation in the Joseph narrative, whereas the strife between Solomon and Adonijah functionally anticipates the divided course of the monarchy (see §V below).

The structural effect of these rival-brother scenes is to confirm the status of the heir in the midst of conflicting claims to the succession of blessing and kingship. A comparative rhetorical analysis sharpens one's understanding of the political theology embedded in these texts: dynastic succession confirmed by God carries greater weight than any other claim to rule.

---

13. Ibid., 54.

IV. Wives, Cowives, and Pseudospouses

Does the Saul narrative have a counterpart to the Hagar-Sarah rivalry? The clear connections between the rivalries of the brothers calls one to look back into the Abraham text to see if the Saul narrative has any structural equivalent for the Sarah-Hagar spouse rivalry. This rivalry greatly affects the transition from the generation of Abraham to the generation of Isaac. At first glance, the Saul narrative appears to have no direct counterpart of a rivalry among Saul's wives that affects the transition from Saul's generation to that of his heir. Indeed, Saul's wives play no literary role in the course of the narrative. Yet, on closer inspection, the rivalry of Sarah and Hagar finds a striking structural counterpart in the vying that takes place between Michal and Jonathan for the affection and loyalty of David. Let us consider the possible connections between these rivalries.

The rivalry of Sarah and Hagar is told in a straightforward manner in Genesis 16 and 21. The rivalry grows out of the barrenness of Sarah (16:5). Her inability to have children forces her by customary marital arrangements to secure a cowife for Abraham, namely, Hagar, by whom Abraham can produce an heir (16:3). The child who is born from this union is Ishmael (16:11, 15-16). This birth creates tension between Hagar and Sarah, tension that increases after Sarah successfully gives birth to Isaac, who is the divinely favored son (21:9-11). The conflict between Hagar and Sarah grows so great that Sarah orders Hagar out of the household — a demand with which Abraham complies because he is told in a vision from God that Hagar will be taken care of and that Sarah and her son, Isaac, are the ones whom God favors (21:12-13).

On the surface, these narratives find no direct counterpart in the Saul-David narrative. Nevertheless, some of the same issues and themes arise in the stories of Jonathan and Michal's relation to David. Four specific issues emerge when one compares the Hagar-Sarah texts to the narratives that concern Jonathan-Michal: (1) childlessness, (2) alienation, (3) affection, and (4) the transition to a rightful heir. Let us look at each of these themes in turn.

One of the functions of the Michal-Jonathan rivalry structure is to produce an heir to the throne in much the same way as it is the function of the Sarah-Hagar story to produce an heir to the promise. The problematic that is faced by the Michal-Jonathan materials is that the narrative must not produce a physical heir to Michal who could challenge Solomon, still less a viable physical heir to Jonathan, and yet the text must present a successor to Saul's kingship.[14] We have already seen how this process is realized at the level of Saul as father/son-slayer. The question I have in mind here is how this process looks from the level of Michal and Jonathan. As with the Sarah-Hagar rivalry, the

14. Note that the narrator apparently considers Mephibosheth, Jonathan's son, unfit to rule because of his physical disabilities. He is not seen as a serious rival to the throne (2 Sam 4:4; 9:6-13; 21:7).

thematic narrative complex of barrenness, birth, and sonship all play a role in the Jonathan-Michal materials. We know from other indications in the narrative that David is the destined successor to the throne (1 Sam 16:11-13). Whatever happens in the course of the narrative must function structurally to bring about David's rise to the throne and, most importantly, to cut off any possibility that Saul's children or the heirs of Saul's children produce a viable claimant to the throne (cf. 2 Sam 21:8-9). The childlessness motif is one element of this trajectory, playing a significant role in the story of Michal (6:23). Even though Michal pursues David, marries him, and remains under his authority all her life, the narrative stresses that Michal remained childless. This particular union produces no Saulide heir.

The notion of alienation is a critical structuring feature in both narrative blocks. Alienation is most straightforward in the Hagar story, where Sarah is the one who calls for the physical removal of Hagar from the household, thereby cutting off Hagar from Abraham, the recipient of the promise (Gen 21:10). In the Michal-Jonathan rivalry, Michal is rebuked by David and is left childless by him, presumably having barred her from any further intimate contact with him (2 Sam 6:23). In both cases, it is the alienation of one of the spouses that is an important structural feature of the narrative, affecting the movement from one generation to the next. The alienation factor enhances and directs the childlessness motif. Michal's childlessness is further heightened by the references to her previous husband, Paltiel, from whom she is taken to be returned to David as part of David's political bargaining with Abner — an additional level of alienation (2 Sam 3:12-16). In terms of literary structure, her removal from this man marks the closure of any possibility that Saul's daughter would produce an heir to challenge David. Furthermore, her removal from both Paltiel and David's presence is functionally equivalent to Hagar's banishment. The themes of childlessness and banishment, therefore, are structurally significant for both the relationship of Abraham to Hagar-Sarah and of David to Michal-Jonathan, even if the narrative treatments differ in important details.

Affection is another element that works to structure the Jonathan-Michal narrative. Here it is the male Jonathan and his affection for David that guide the close relationship established between Jonathan and David (1 Sam 18:1, 3; 20:17; 2 Sam 1:26). It is ironic that although he is the physical heir of Saul and the rightful heir to the throne, Jonathan, by virtue of his affection for David, paves the way for David to become the successor to Saul. This is an affection that Michal was never able to gain because her marriage to David was ultimately rooted in matters of political expediency (1 Sam 18:20, 27-28). Affection is, likewise, at issue in the Hagar-Sarah story, but it is Abraham's affection for Hagar and Ishmael that nearly proves problematic for the promise (Gen 21:11-12). It is out of loyalty to God, not for reasons of affection, that Abraham agrees to send Hagar away (Gen 21:12-14).

It should now be clear that the stories of Hagar-Sarah and Michal-

Jonathan function to guide the textual transition from Abraham/Saul to an heir who has God's favor to receive the blessing and the kingship. At first glance, one may not have expected the spousal rivalry in Genesis to complement or illumine the Michal-Jonathan material. Yet, as one explores the Sarah-Hagar rivalry, one finds that the spouse-rivalry scheme not only is critical to the movement from Abraham to Isaac but also functions to structure the transition from Saul to David. A comparison of the structural similarities of the Michal-Jonathan narrative complex and the Hagar-Sarah stories reveals that the narrator has developed comparable roles for the rivals. On the one hand, one of the rivals must function as a dead end in the passing on of the blessing and kingship. In these narratives, this role is filled by Hagar and Michal. Furthermore, structurally speaking, one of the rivals must give birth to the successor to the promise and the kingship. This happens literally in the case of Sarah, who gives birth to Isaac. Since the Michal-Jonathan narrative is complicated by the presence of the male figure Jonathan, however, the birthing of David can occur only figuratively, where Jonathan passes on his armor to David — an act that later permits David to be treated as Saul's "son" (1 Sam 18:3-4).[15] Since Jonathan is a male figure, the narrator must tap Jonathan's affection to provide the kind of intimate link between Jonathan and David that is more naturally provided by the womb that obviously binds Isaac to Sarah.

V. Fathers and Their Progeny

The specific placing of the fraternal and "spousal" rivalries in the Genesis–Kings narrative is hardly accidental. What begins to emerge from this study is that not only can one compare individual stories in each narrative to one another quite fruitfully, but also the sequential structuring of the stories in Genesis finds a mirror in the sequencing of stories in Samuel–Kings. Thus the overall sequencing of narratives in the tripartite scheme of Abraham-Isaac-Jacob bears strong structural similarity to the sequencing of stories in the Saul-David-Solomon narrative. We have already seen the strong similarities between the rivalries of Jacob-Esau and Solomon-Adonijah. If one looks further into the Jacob and Solomon narratives, one finds that these materials have another important structural similarity, which comes to light when one focuses on the use of the number twelve in both the Jacob-Joseph story and the narrative of King Solomon and the division of the monarchy.

The number twelve stands out in the Jacob narrative as the demarcation of the number of Jacob's sons, and hence the tribes of Israel that descend from

15. An event whose structural significance has been stressed by Jobling, "Jonathan," 12, 22.

Jacob (Gen 35:22-26; 49:28). The Joseph narrative highlights the fate of these twelve brothers, developing a narrative concerning the deeds of the ten brothers who end up at odds with Joseph and who put Benjamin at risk. In terms of structural comparison, it is significant that the number twelve comes into play in the third figure of the Abraham-Isaac-Jacob sequence, for it is precisely at this point in the Saul-David-Solomon narrative that the number twelve appears, playing a comparable structuring and thematic role. The Solomon material uses the number twelve once to characterize Solomon's dominant relationship with his sphere of political influence, namely, the land and state of ancient Israel. The narrative emphasizes that Solomon divided the land into twelve districts (1 Kgs 4:7-20; cf. Josh 15:20-63). These districts were charged with supplying the royal house in Jerusalem with goods and services necessary to the continued operation of the state. The number twelve also crops up in the narrative of the monarchy's division, which occurs upon Solomon's death (1 Kgs 11:29-39). In this text, Rehoboam selects ten of the twelve pieces from the prophet Ahijah's torn robe as a sign that he will rule over ten of Israel's tribes (11:29-31). The image of the torn robe functions to characterize the fragmentation of the brothers/tribes in both narrative blocks (cf. Gen 37:23, 31-34; 1 Kgs 11:30). The narrative's division between Joseph's ten brothers and Joseph-Benjamin balances the division of the monarchy into ten and two that occurs at Solomon's death (cf. Gen 42:4, 36; 43:14-16, 29; 45:12-14; 1 Kgs 11:35). Significantly, both narratives emphasize Benjamin's special position of loyalty and kinship amid the division of the brothers/tribes (cf. Gen 42:4; 43:14-16, 29; 45:12-14, 22; 49:22-27; 1 Kgs 12:21-24). The split between Joseph's brothers, in no small measure due to the underlying tensions that existed between the Leah and Rachel sons or tribes, resembles the tensions at work in the Rehoboam and Jeroboam conflict.

This structural comparison is clearly more thematic and general, and therefore less certain than my previous comparisons. If these structural elements are more than coincidental, however, one may go further and suggest that the narrator of Genesis–Kings is offering, through the Joseph story and the story of Solomon and the division of the monarchy, a reflection on the two choices that confronted the narrator's society. One choice was to follow in the path of political rebellion, division, and turmoil. This is the turmoil that the narrator recounts emerged after Solomon's death as a direct result of Solomon's repressive policies toward the twelve districts (cf. 1 Kgs 12:4). God even sanctions the division through the prophet Ahijah, proving that God was unwilling to work through the rebellion to bring about a social healing of the resulting political disunity (11:29-31). The other choice Genesis–Kings presents is to follow the path of communal and national reconciliation. This is the possibility raised by the story of the reconciliation of Joseph's brothers. The story of the brothers' reconciliation acknowledges the tensions between the twelve sons/tribes but looks beyond those tensions to envision a unified society. Here God proves willing to work through the brothers' division to bring life to God's people, regardless of how the brothers initially behaved toward Joseph (Gen 45:5-9). The Genesis–Kings double-edged choice is a narrative version of the "Deuteronomic" choice of blessing or curse (Deut 11:26-28). The narrative concerning the rebellion upon Solomon's death represents choosing the curse together with the death and disaster that follow in the wake of such a choice. The Joseph story represents opting for blessing, life, hope, reconciliation, and the way of peace.

Focusing only on Noth's DtrH, one fails to find the appropriate balance to the Deuteronomist's message of sin and destruction.[16] The downward spin of the Kings narrative can only teach that discord, division, and destruction come from the twelve artificially drawn political districts of Solomon. It is the Joseph story alone that opens up the possibility that tribal and kin-based ethnic relations can be the ground for a positive social unity. From the perspective of the larger Genesis–Kings narrative, destruction is *not* the only possibility for Israel's future.

Beyond national politics, the specific question of the distribution of social wealth stands at the forefront of the narrator's philosophic crisis. Where Solomon greedily forced the districts to send their wealth and workers to the capital city, earning only rebellion for Solomon's successor (1 Kgs 4:7-20; 5:27-30; cf. 9:22-23), the Joseph narrative presents a cultural hero who does not simply store up the society's treasures but knows when and how to redistribute that wealth when the crisis demands (Gen 41:33-49, 53-57; 42:1-6; 45:7). The message is clear and specific: The hoarding of wealth by the state's rulers brings social death; the sharing of wealth among the tribes brings social harmony and national peace. The nation may have been as "numerous as the sand of the sea," eating and drinking under Solomon, but his domestic policy of greed brought rebellion (1 Kgs 4:20). Joseph gathered produce "in large quantity, as the sands of the sea," but knew when to share it so all might survive and thrive together (Gen 41:49).

VI. Conclusion

Rendtorff, among others, has argued that the Deuteronomistic editor(s)/school gave the Pentateuch its essential shape:

---

16. For attempts to derive a more positive message from the DtrH see G. von Rad, "The Deuteronomic Theology of History in I and II Kings," in *The Problem of the Hexateuch and Other Essays* (trans. E. W. Trueman Dicken; New York: McGraw-Hill, 1966) 205-21; and H. W. Wolff, "The Kerygma of the Deuteronomic Historical Work," in W. Brueggemann and H. W. Wolff, *The Vitality of Old Testament Traditions* (trans. F. C. Prussner; 2nd ed.; Atlanta: John Knox, 1982) 83-100.

The Deuteronomic-Deuteronomistic circles who had played a crucial part in shaping the subsequent books were also key figures in giving the outline of the Pentateuch its shape. In both places they have worked over earlier traditions of different kinds and given them a theological interpretation.[17]

It is possible that in the structural and thematic schemes discerned in this article, we have found the hand of the Deuteronomistic editor(s)/school at work in the framing of the Pentateuch. Apparently, this editor/school had at its disposal some form of the pentateuchal traditions, but chose to develop the Pentateuch's final shape in the light of the themes and manner of presentation of the DtrH. Of course, one can read the DtrH in isolation as a grand theological-historical project. Yet, if we read DtrH in connection with Genesis, we gain a deeper appreciation for the Deuteronomistic editor(s)/school's handling of the traditions of Israel's protofathers, protomothers, and their offspring.

17. R. Rendtorff, *The Old Testament: An Introduction* (trans. J. Bowden; Philadelphia: Fortress, 1986) 162-63. See also his *The Problem of the Process of Transmission in the Pentateuch* (JSOTSup 89; trans. J. J. Scullion; Sheffield: JSOT, 1990). Cf. H. H. Schmid, *Der sogenannte Jahwist* (Zurich: Theologischer Verlag, 1976); and R. N. Whybray, *The Making of the Pentateuch: A Methodological Study* (JSOTSup 53; Sheffield: Academic, 1987) 222-25.

Linguistic Coherence in Prophetic Discourse

FRANCIS I. ANDERSEN

Victoria, Australia

The heat of prophecy like a strong wine
Shameth his reason with exultant speech

Robert Bridges, *Prometheus the Firegiver,* ll. 434-35

I. Attitudes to Prophetic Phenomena in the Ancient World

Ecstatic states, visionary experiences, and strange speech (glossolalia) are widely attested in religions. People who have such experiences are often venerated, and their utterances received as messages from gods or spirits (Gunnel 1982; Jepsen 1934; Lindblom 1962).

In the ancient Near East the *bārû,* "seer," and other kinds of diviners were recognized, "and their generic designation, *maḫḫû,* was also used of madmen, without any clear distinction" (Albright 1968:212). Balaam is an example of such a practitioner, and the description of his receptive state in Num 24:3-4, 15-16 is classic. In the Balaam wall texts from Deir Alla the prophet sees gods in dreams (Moore 1990).

The Egyptian traveler Wen-Amun gives an eyewitness report (which may be dated 1060 B.C.E.) of the delivery of an oracle in the court of Zakar-Baʿal, king of Byblos. The Egyptian hieroglyph denoting the ecstatic state ($ḫ^3wt$ in 1:39) depicts a man having a fit (Korostovtsev 1960:123). The word has generated extensive discussion (Korostovtsev 1960:48-50; Goedicke 1975:53). Anticipating a point to be made later, I note here that the reported speech of the ecstatic consists of four terse, enigmatic lines with a suggestion of poetry:

137

> Bring up [the] god!
> Bring the messenger who is carrying him!
> Amun is the one who sent him out!
> He is the one who made him come! (*ANET*, 26)

The behavior of the prophets of Baal at Mount Carmel (1 Kgs 18:28) is in this Phoenician tradition (Cody 1979). In Greek culture likewise, such persons had recognized roles in religious institutions. In his *History* (2.55-57) Herodotus attempts a rationalistic explanation of the legend of the two black doves from Thebes. They were really foreign women, carried off as slaves, one to Dodona, where she founded the oracle.

> But I think that the Dodonaeans called the women "doves" because they were βάρβαροι, and they thought that their speech was like the twittering of birds. When they say that later on the dove spoke with a human voice, they mean that the woman, who sounded like the chattering of birds so long as she ἐβαρβάριζε, was now able to speak so they could understand her.

Herodotus probably means that the foreigner learned Greek. But does the characterization of her previous speech as "barbaric" and "birdlike" refer to the way Egyptian sounded to a Greek or to twittering of glossolalia? In the *Agamemnon* (l. 1034) Clytaemnestra describes Cassandra's speech as "that uncouth unintelligible φωνὴν βάρβαρον of swallows." Again the bird comparison.

1. Attitudes to Prophetic Speech in the Old Testament

The prophet is crazy (2 Kgs 9:11). The prophet is a fool; the man of the spirit is insane (Hos 7:9; cf. Mic 2:11). Idol-makers, idol-worshipers, and their prophets are stupid, as in the contemptuous satire of Isa 40:18-20; 44:9-20; 46. Compare the brilliant, malicious exposé in Wisdom of Solomon 13. False prophets were ridiculed also for behaving like drunks, or perhaps using liquor to attain the inspired state (Mic 2:11; cf. Durand 1982). Isaiah has a particularly disgusting account:

> These also reel with wine
>   and stagger with strong drink;
> the priest and the prophet reel with strong drink,
>   they are confused with wine,
> they stagger with strong drink;
>   they err in vision,
> they stumble in giving judgment.
>
> For all tables are full of vomit,
>   no place is without excrement. (28:7-8)

In the Hebrew Bible, some of the public behaviors of prophets, in mime or symbolic activity, were abnormal, to say the least. Utterances made in a state of profound emotional disturbance, including prophecies, are compared with the cries of birds and animals.

> Like a swallow or a crane I clamor,
> I moan like a dove. (Hezekiah in Isa 38:14)

> I will howl like the jackals,
> and I will scream like the ostriches. (Mic 1:8)

The OT several times addresses the problem of differentiating between a genuine and a false prophet, the latter being fraudulent (pretending to be a real prophet of Yhwh) or the advocate of a rival god. The same term, *nābî'*, was used for all of them (Jepsen 1934; Petersen 1981). Among the several tests that people should apply none depends on the *form* of the utterance. In the obvious cases of prophets who advocated worship of other gods, the content was enough to discredit them (Deuteronomy 13). It would seem that rival prophets in Israel used the same kind of behavior and speech as genuine ones (Crenshaw 1971; De Vries 1978; Edelkoort 1948; Jacob 1957; Osswald 1962; Overholt 1970; van Winkle 1989).

2. Detection of False Prophets in Early Christianity

The choice of the Greek word προφήτης for Hebrew *nābî'* supplied a standard term that passed into other languages. This term is positive and has favorable connotations (Ellis 1970; Reiling 1971). It highlights the social role of the prophet as spokesperson, proclaiming rather than predicting. The only place in the NT where this term is used of a pagan is Titus 1:12: ἴδιος αὐτῶν προφήτης, "one of their [Cretans'] own prophets," where one might have expected "poet" or "philosopher." The choice of term could be tongue in cheek, since the point is satirical and contains a famous logical conundrum.

In the LXX the term μάντις renders *qsm* in five (Josh 13:22; 1 Sam 6:2; Jer 29:8; Mic 3:7; Zech 10:2) of its twenty occurrences (most of the others are translated as the participle). The *mantis* was a practitioner of the mantic arts (divination — using various techniques), all forbidden in Israel (Orlinsky 1965). *Mantis* is not used in the NT. The matching verb, to act as a μάντις (μαντεύομαι), occurs in the NT only at Acts 16:16. This prophet had four disqualifications: she was a woman, a slave, a pagan, a demoniac.

Mantis occurs in *Hermas* (*Man.* 11:2). The Lightfoot-Harmer edition reads μάγος. The variant is due to a gap in the Athos manuscript at this point (Lake 1907: pl. VIII). Only μα?[ ]ρχονται can be read with certainty, the partly preserved letter being ν or γ. The Latin *diuinum* (Whittaker 1967:40) indicates that μάντις is the more likely restoration. Reiling (1973:34) reviews the textual problem. *Mandate* 11 is a lengthy discussion of the difference between a true and a false prophet. The doubtful-minded consult the pseudoprophet as a fortune-teller (μάγος). The Shepherd explains that, while sometimes the *magos* simply says what the inquirer wishes to hear, sometimes "the devil fills him with his own spirit" to corrupt the righteous. Several diagnostics are suggested. Reiling (1973:67) finds four tests. His first — doctrine — seems anachronistic; Hermas does not seem to be greatly concerned for credal orthodoxy. Hermas's mentor exposes the modus operandi of the fraudulent prophets. The true Spirit speaking from God does not have to be consulted but speaks "from itself." The Shepherd supplies Hermas with some character tests. The true prophet is meek or gentle (πραΰς), tranquil (ἡσύχιος), humble (ταπεινόφρων), as well as virtuous. Nothing about these qualifications applies uniquely or distinctively to the prophetic office or function; indeed, they are general requirements of all Christians, going back to the character of Jesus (Matt 11:29). These qualities are the fruit of the Spirit (Gal 5:22-23), enjoined in the standard early Christian parenesis (Eph 4:2; 1 Pet 3:4; *Barn.* 19:4; Ign. *Eph.* 10:2). By contrast, the false prophet is "impudent and shameless and talkative." The tests are psychological and moral, not intellectual and aesthetic. Here one can see an important shift. Unlike the living, vigorous, and passionate God of the OT, the perfection of deity is now perceived as complete serenity, and this is also a qualification for any holy soul in which the Spirit would dwell. The point was already made in *Mandate* 5, where the Holy Spirit was twice characterized as τρυφερόν (Harmer translated it "delicate"; perhaps the idea is "sensitive," even "fastidious"). Hence the Spirit cannot reside in a person who has bitterness, anger, or spite; the Spirit dwells with gentleness and tranquillity.

This quality of serenity is scarcely manifested in the character of Ignatius of Antioch, who documented to the Philadelphians a charismatic incident that occurred while he was visiting them. In his letter to the Philadelphians he reminds them that, when he was in their midst, he uttered a message that made its mark in the situation; and he indignantly repudiates the suggestion that he knew about the situation ahead of time.

> I cried out. . . .
> I spoke with a loud voice,
> with God's own voice . . .
> I did not know [it] from human flesh,
> but the Spirit preached,
> saying thus:
> Apart from the bishop do nothing;
> your flesh as a shrine of God guard;
> the unity love;

the divisions flee;
imitators be of Jesus Christ,
as he also [was] of his Father.

The utterance itself is remarkable for its tautness, combined with poetic form (six lines, in rhyming pairs), which Weinel (1899:86) imitates in German:

χωρὶς τοῦ ἐπισκόπου μηδὲν ποιεῖτε	Ohne den Bischof in keinem Ding verfahret;
τὴν σάρκα ὑμῶν ὡς ναὸν Θεοῦ τηρεῖτε	Euer Fleisch als einen Tempel Gottes wahret!
τὴν ἕνωσιν ἀγαπᾶτε	Die Einigkeit liebt;
τοὺς μερισμοὺς φεύγετε	Die Spaltungen flieht!
μιμηταὶ γίνεσθε Ἰησοῦ Χριστοῦ	Werdet ähnlich Jesu, dem Christ;
ὡς καὶ αὐτὸς τοῦ πατρὸς αὐτοῦ	Wie er es selbst seinem Vater ist!

There is nothing unusual about the ideas, which are characteristic of Ignatius. The ruggedness of the poetry reflects the spontaneous utterance of an ecstatic, hardly to be distinguished from poetic inspiration, but not regular enough to be identified as a deliberate composition, let alone part of Ignatius's stock-in-trade. I shall return to the phenomenology of this case below.

The attitude of the *Didache* to prophets in the church is less suspicious than that of *Hermas* (Audet 1958:447-53). It says that "any prophet speaking ἐν πνεύματι [language like that used in Acts 20:22; 21:4; cf. 21:11] should not be tested or investigated" (11:7). The way to tell a false prophet is if he stays for three days or asks for money (the latter criterion is also mentioned in *Hermas*). In his detailed and exemplary study of *Mandate* 11 Reiling (1973) has no occasion to discuss the compositional quality or rational coherence of prophetic speech as an index of its divine origin. The truth and *power* of the utterance is what matters, not its beauty. But then none of these early authors sees literature as an end product of prophetic communication.

A resurgence of charismatic prophecy among the Montanists (late 2nd century C.E.) brought on a reaction in which these enthusiasts were condemned as no better than a pagan *mantis* (O'Malley 1967). In his Homily on 1 Cor 12:2, John Chrysostom gives a detailed contrastive analysis in terms of personal character, not by assessment of the utterances as such:

Τοῦτο γὰρ μάντεως ἴδιον τὸ ἐξεστηκέναι, τὸ ἀνάγκην ὑπομένειν, τὸ ὠθεῖσθαι, τὸ ἕλκεσθαι, τὸ σύρεσθαι, ὥσπερ μαινόμενον. Ὁ δὲ προφήτης οὐχ οὕτως, ἀλλὰ μετὰ διανοίας νηφούσης καὶ σωφρονούσης καταστάσεως, καὶ εἰδὼς ἃ φθέγγεται, φησίν ἅπαντα. ὥστε καὶ πρὸ τῆς ἐκβάσεως κἀντεῦθεν γνώριζε τὸν μάντιν καὶ τὸν προφήτην.

For this is the characteristic property of a *mantis,* to be out of his mind, to endure anguish [constraint], to rush violently, to be wrenched about and to be swept along like a maniac [*hōsper mainomenon*]. The prophet, however, is not like that, but says everything with sober thought and prudent demeanor, and knowing what he is proclaiming. So, both before the event [or outcome] and just from these features you can recognize [the difference between] the *mantis* and the *prophētēs.*

Likewise Jerome, in his introduction to Isaiah; here the emphasis is more firmly placed on the sanity of the true prophet and the rationality of his discourse.

Neque vero, ut Montanus cum insanis feminis somniat, prophetae in ecstasisunt locuti, ut nescirent, quod loquerentur, et, cum alios erudirent, ipsi ignorarent quid dicerent.

Nor indeed, as Montanus dreams in company with mad women, have prophets spoken in ecstasy, so that they could have been ignorant of what they were speaking; and, when they were instructing others, might themselves be ignorant of what they were saying.

The fathers distanced themselves from the "maniacal excitement" of pagan as well as Christian prophets like Montanus, "and describe the inspiration of the Hebrew prophets as distinguished by the opposite peculiarities of calmness, self-possession, and active intelligence" (Alexander 1846:6). The doctrine of prophetic inspiration was finally synthesized by Augustine, who distinguished three levels of apprehension of divine truth: corporeal vision, spiritual vision, and intellectual vision (the highest) (*De Genesi ad litteram,* VI-XII, 11, 22). Here we see the legacy of Neoplatonism (Ayers 1979). Aquinas's position is essentially the same (*Summa theologiae* 2a.2ae.171-74). This line of thought comes to strong expression in Maimonides (Reines 1979). In his theory of prophecy, prophetic insight is purely intellectual, prophetic inspiration is wholly natural. In prophetic composition the intellect drives the imagination and in its most perfect form dominates the imagination completely. The imagery in which the prophecy is clothed is deceptive, if taken as literal truth. But it is useful for the religious control of the ignorant masses, who cannot cope with anything but fantasy. The elite know better; they attain to the philosophical and scientific truth hidden in the *māšāl* ("proverb, parable, allegory"). Moses was the best prophet by far because he did not write poetry! Indeed, he was not at all like the others, since he did not use his imagination at all, but received revelation in a purely intellectual mode (Reines 1979:lxiii-lxiv). In this tradition quite extravagant claims could be made for the intellectual superiority of biblical prophets, with contempt for the achievements even of Greece. The sanity of Israel's prophets contrasted with the lunacy of others; the rationality of their beliefs with the absurdities of paganism; the clarity and coherence of their messages with the unintelligible mumbo jumbo of heathen oracles. Tertullian's invective is always quoted:

> What indeed has Athens to do with Jerusalem? What concord is there between the Academy and the Church? What between heretics and Christians? Our instructions come from "the porch of Solomon," who had himself taught that "the Lord should be sought in simplicity of heart." Away with all attempts to produce a mottled Christianity of Stoic, Platonic, and dialectic composition! We want no curious disputation after possessing Christ Jesus! no inquisition after enjoying the Gospel! With our faith, we desire no further belief. For this is our palmary faith, that there is nothing which we ought to believe besides. (*The Prescription against Heresies*, 7)

II. Modern Evaluations of Prophetic Character and Consciousness

Continued criticism of the biblical prophets as psychologically unbalanced, intellectually deficient, or artistically inferior has been countered by contrary assertions. A typical pronouncement:

> der gewöhnliche Zustand der Propheten bei der Begeisterung war der des Wachens, und hier ist eine charakterische Eigenschaft derselben die Besonnenheit und Klarheit des Bewusstseins in Bezug auf die sie umgebende Aussenwelt, wodurch allein auch die Propheten in Stande waren, selbst den Inhalt der empfangenen Offenbarungen dem Volke auf eine verständliche Weise vorzutragen. (Bleek 1893:253)

Mowinckel (1934-35) makes some strong statements about the use of rational tests by the prophets to discern the authentic word of the Lord: "he knows this from the *clear, intelligible, moral and religious content of the word*" (p. 287); "the prophets are religious and moral *personalities who weigh and judge rationally*" (p. 289).

Similar points were reiterated by C. A. Briggs in his book on *Messianic Prophecy* (1886). He emphasized the intellectual and moral superiority of the Hebrew prophets.

> Hebrew prophecy is through the enlightenment of the mind of the prophet, the stimulation of his moral nature, the constraining of his will, under the most sublime motives, the assurance of his soul that he is in possession of divine truth, and that he is commissioned to declare it. (p. 14)

Literary critics in particular have given biblical authors a bad time, complaining that their compositions fell far short of the standards found in classical authors. Christian apologists had two opposite ways of refuting these charges. One kind of reply admitted the vulgarity of biblical writings, but found in this a virtue, a wonderful expression of the divine συγκατάβασις, "considerateness," coming down to the level of the ordinary person, a thought that enchanted Chrysostom and Luther. An opposite response rejected the negative assessment, insisting on the literary superiority of biblical works. In its extreme form this counterattack maintained that the Greek tradition had borrowed from the older and better Hebrew.

> Or if I would delight my private hours
> With Music or with Poem, where so soon
> As in our native Language can I find
> That solace? All our Law and Story strewd
> With Hymns, our Psalms with artful terms inscrib'd,
> Our Hebrew Songs and Harps in *Babylon,*
> That pleased so well our Victors ear, declare
> That rather Greece from us these Arts deriv'd;
> Ill imitated, while they loudest sing
> The vices of thir Deities, and thir own
> In Fable, Hymn, or Song, so personating
> Thir Gods ridicullous, and themselves past shame.
> Remove thir swelling Epithets thick laid
> As varnish on a Harlots cheek, the rest
> Thin sown with aught of profit or delight,
> Will far be found unworthy to compare
> With *Sions* songs, to all true tastes excelling,
> Where God is prais'd aright, and Godlike men,
> The Holiest of Holies, and his Saints.
>
> *Paradise Regained,* book IV

Calvin had it both ways:

> Three Evangelists recite their history in a low and mean style. Many proud men are disgusted with that simplicity, because they attend not to the principal points of doctrine; whence it were easy to infer, that they treat of heavenly mysteries which are above human capacity. . . . But John, thundering from his sublimity, more powerfully than any thunderbolt, levels to the dust the obstinacy of those whom he does not compel to the obedience of faith. (*Inst.* 1.11)

In response to the devaluation of biblical literature, especially poetry, by literary critics of the classical period, a new kind of defense was mounted. Here the work of Lowth, followed by that of Herder (1782-83; Koepke 1982; cf. the chapter on Herder in Barth 1959), was just as revolutionary for finding aesthetic, if somewhat sentimental, enjoyment in Hebrew poesie as for its technical break-through in the discovery of "parallelism" as the organizing principle of Hebrew prosody (Baker 1973; Kugel 1981; Watson 1984). It was admitted that the Bible did not meet classical standards, but nevertheless it was excellent in its own way. Comparison with the classics was not appropriate. The untidiness of its style could be seen as liveliness; the extravagance of its imagery could be esteemed as a fruit of the oriental imagination. These complements were rather halfhearted, however. Lowth's and Herder's enthusiasm for the exotic charm of Hebrew poetry was still in the medieval tradition; its enjoyable qualities were the sugarcoating on the bitter pill of truth. This shift in perception has had enormous consequences right up to the present. Even so, modern criticism has been governed more by rationalistic criteria than by romanticist judgments (Housman 1933; Newman 1890; Prickett 1976, 1986; Willey 1955). Evaluations of prophets as good or bad continued to be made in terms of normalcy and rationality and by the literary quality of their oracles.

1. The Test of Rationality

The OT does not know of a distinction that became standard later on — the false prophets were deranged, their speech incoherent. (If explanation is needed, the theory of demon possession could be developed [Michaelsen 1989]. *Hermas* cannot make up his mind whether false prophets were "empty," or controlled by demons.) By way of contrast, the authentic prophets were self-composed and clearheaded; and their speech was lucid, logical. Albright (1961) has em-phasized, and with positive appreciation, the enormous importance of the early, charismatic phase in the development of Israelite prophecy, and this has enabled us to read the book of Amos in a new light, recognizing how close he still is to those wild men, Elijah and Elisha (Orlinsky [1965] finds too great a contrast and too clean a break between the "seer" and the classical prophet). Even so, from time to time scholars try their hand at psychoanalyzing biblical prophets (Allwohn 1926; Funk 1987) but without the benefit of clinical examination (Cassdem 1973).

In his book on *The Visionary Mode* Lieb (1991) traces the inexhaustible power of the biblical visions, and especially Ezekiel's "chariot," to recreate and enlarge themselves. In his chapter on "The Poetics of Vision" (pp. 306-50), largely on Dante, Lieb concentrates on motif and imagery, as "authors reconsti-tute the structures of vision to accord with their own habits of seeing" (p. 306). In view of the concluding comment of the present essay, one needs to acknowl-edge the combination of intellectual clarity with superb verbal artistry that enables Dante, in his turn, to *communicate* the vision. Yet, because he was (only!)

a poet and a layman, professional theologians do not take him seriously as a great thinker, let alone a revealer.

It is an anachronism to impose on biblical texts and other reports of visions the criteria we now apply to writings intended to be scientific or didactic — clear and distinct ideas, logically ordered. The classic essay of Albright on the history of thinking (Albright 1964:62-100) maintained that the OT did not contain a single example of consciously formalized thinking, whether the Aristotelian logic of classes and syllogisms or the Stoic logic of propositions and inference. A scholastic tradition still persists that truth (and hence revelation) must be propositional, and that the Bible, being true, is free of contradictions. Numerous concessions have to be made as soon as exegesis is needed, and a marvelous sophistry can fit the recalcitrant text to the rationalistic calculus. This approach has prevented scholars from appreciating the abundant use in the Bible of riddle, paradox, even absurdity. A recent publication has searched for humor in the OT (Radday and Brenner 1990). I believe that I am the one who recognized the use of the (quite illogical) figure of pseudosorites. O'Connor (1987a, 1987b, 1987c) has enlarged the inventory. To insist that biblical authors were always logical, and to use logic to interpret their writings, leads to grotesque results.

It is also in the domain of literary composition that the high claims for biblical authors — they were masters of Hebrew composition and never made grammatical mistakes — are not easy to square with the text we actually have. What are we to make of passages in the Bible that are defective in literary form and contain grammatical solecisms? Again there have been two opposite responses. A tradition generally regarded as "conservative" uses all its ingenuity to demonstrate that there is nothing wrong with the inerrant text, or at worst it has only a few little blemishes that do not impair its message at all, or so little that it does not make any difference. A "liberal" approach is less inhibited in recognizing that the texts we now have are often a mess. The explanation is that the text has suffered badly in transmission. Both are agreed that it must have been all right to start with. Instead of performing miracles of exegesis to torture an unintelligible text into making sense (the "conservative" policy), the "liberal" scholars are more likely to set about repairing the damage they think the text has sustained. Using their knowledge of the rules of composition (the structure of pieces established by form criticism [Westermann 1967] or the patterns of verse [Bruno 1957]) and of Hebrew grammar, some scholars have confidently "restored" what they claim is the original composition.

A notorious case is Paul Haupt's attempt to grapple with the difficulties he found in the book of Micah. "The first three chapters of the Book of Micah, in which only 32.5 lines are genuine, are more corrupt than any other Old Testament text I ever studied" (1910a:95). He goes on to defend his work: "Some Hebraists may be inclined to say that I have practically rewritten the Book of Micah . . . but the excision of later additions and excrescences is not tantamount to rewriting a book. The restoration of an old master merely restores the pristine beauty. . . . The restoration of the original connection and the elimination of subsequent additions is not a radical destruction of the original, but a conservation" (1910a:95). How did he do this? By tidying up irregularities in the verse forms and correcting supposed grammatical errors. The presupposition of such research is that the prophet knew the rules of poetry and of grammar, and obeyed them perfectly. Any irregularities now present must have been introduced by careless scribes, and it is our (sacred) duty to undo their bad work.

III. Accepting the Text as It Is

There are so many places in the Hebrew Bible where modern readers have judged the text corrupt, and the matching attempts to heal the text have been so diverse, arbitrary, and unconvincing, that one wonders if the fault lies in us modern readers, not in ancient authors or scribes. Imposing our standards of correctness in either grammar or literary form, we might have obliterated precious evidence of deviant linguistic usage or of deliberate literary artifice. We should recognize that genuine utterances of living speakers rarely attain to the required standards of textbook grammar. Literature is artificial. Raymond Chandler is a more truthful reporter of conversation than Jane Austen. I have met only two persons in my life who could make extempore speeches without grammatical errors. This leads one to ask whether part of the honesty and authenticity of biblical authors lies in giving an exact transcript of real speech, even though it might be incoherent or ungrammatical. An example may occur in Prov 23:35, the words of a drunk, not likely to be elegant. The English is more coherent than the Hebrew!

הִכּוּנִי	*hikkûnî*	they struck me
בַל־חָלִיתִי	*bal-ḥālîtî*	I was not hurt
הֲלָמוּנִי	*hălāmûnî*	they beat me
בַל־יָדָעְתִּי	*bal-yāda'tî*	I didn't know
מָתַי אָקִיץ	*mātay 'āqîṣ*	When will I wake up?
אוֹסִיף	*'ôsîp*	I'll do again
אֲבַקְשֶׁנּוּ עוֹד	*'ăbaqěšennû 'ôd*	I'll seek it again!

The notorious difficulties of the book of Job have been largely blamed on a corrupt text; but it is more likely, in my opinion, that much of the incoherence is due to the artistic representation of the turbulent outbursts and hysterical cries of rage and grief. This was already appreciated by Calvin. In his sermon on Job 1:20 he says, "Like a man whose heart is being squeezed [*qui a le coeur serré*], he does not express all the words, but he speaks half, as we see that those who are extremely sad do not express all their words." Lowth had a similar insight into the grammatical disorder in Job's outburst. He compared an ode of Horace, with this comment:

> But anger and vexation dissipated the order of his ideas, and destroyed the construction of this sentence. But should some officious Grammarian take in hand the passage (for this is a very diligent race of beings, and sometimes more than sufficiently exact and scrupulous), and attempt to restore it to its primitive purity and perfection, the whole grace and excellence of that beautiful exordium would be immediately annihilated, all the impetuosity and ardour would in a moment be extinguished. (Lecture 14, pp. 318-19)

In Micah 1 the prophet (or perhaps it is the Lord) says:

I will yell like the jackals,
and I will shriek like the ostriches!

Why is it then so surprising that what follows is not a neat and orderly poem, but something more like wild and broken sobs? In a famous paper, Elliger (1934) tried to explain why the lamentation in vv. 10-16 did not follow the rule for a song of grief, the *qînâ* meter — 3:2 (Gerstenberger 1962; Janzen 1972). Individual lines are hard to identify, but most of them seem to have only two beats. Elliger came to the conclusion that the poem must have originally followed the 3:2 pattern; words must be missing. He suggested that a strip had been torn down the side of the manuscript, removing one word from each line. He then proceeded to restore these missing words as best he could. In *BHS* (edited, incidentally, by Elliger himself!) the footnote appears against Mic 1:10-16 *omnia mutilata sunt.* Much of the material in the apparatus of *BHS* represents Elliger's suggested emendations. Many innocent students (and many scholars who should know better) pick up these footnotes as if they were part of the textual evidence, and adopt them instead of the MT. (For other attempts to solve this problem see Allen 1976; Budde 1917-18; Graham 1930-31; Schwantes 1964; van der Woude 1971.)

As a result of our joint work in preparation for the Anchor Bible *Micah*, David Noel Freedman and I came up with the crazy idea that this crazy text was exactly that. It is an effective rendition of the sobs and screams of a person who has lost all self-control in paroxysms of rage and grief (Freedman 1982). The similar observation of Ewald, that the textual difficulties of Micah 1 are caused by the prophet's agitation due to excessive grief (Yee 1987:2), seems to have been forgotten. We are inclined to think that this is not the only place in Scripture where this has been done. What we are less sure of is whether this mourning cry is a realistic documentation of a spontaneous outburst or whether it is a brilliantly successful imitation of such utterance, deliberately composed. We expect that other unintelligible passages in the OT might turn out to be designed to create this same kind of effect.

Block (1988) studied the linguistic confusion in Ezekiel's account of his inaugural vision. He found many parallels in other reports of biblical theophanies. He accepted these features not only as authentic but also as evidence that "the emotion accompanying the theophany was present also at the time of recording. This would suggest that the prophet put his experience to writing almost immediately after he had had his inaugural vision" (Block 1988:437).

Other literature of the ancient Near East contains passages that describe the terror inspired in humans by manifestation of the "splendor" of a deity. The Bible, as well as Canaanite literature, has conventional descriptions of the "fright syndrome" (Hillers 1965) induced by a theophany. The effect can be quite sensational, but the description of symptoms is usually restricted to the rattling of vertebrae and other bones (knees knocking together), sweating, hair of the scalp rising, or swooning. The victim might be robbed of speech or incapable of anything more than stuttering or spluttering. In discussing such scenes, Foster (1977) drew attention to the disjointed speech in the Agushaya Hymn, which contains four unrecognizable words in as many lines, more like babble than normal speech. Scholars could do nothing with them; they were considered to be corruptions; efforts were made to recover the correct original text by emendation. Foster accepted the text as authentic and intended; the gibberish was "intentional distortion by the poet designed to convey Ninshubur's great agitation" (Foster 1977:83).

I have already had occasion to comment on the reversal of the attitude of the Christian community to ecstatic behavior and utterance as a manifestation of the Spirit; and already in *Hermas* serenity, tranquillity, docility serve to distinguish the real prophet from the impostor. The latter is μωρός (*Mand.* 11:11) and garrulous (πολύλαος); but it is not clear whether his talkativeness betrays his self-important style of speaking at any time or more specifically his behavior when speaking from the empty evil spirit that drives him. If the latter is the case, then the true Christian prophet not only has a gentle demeanor, congruent with the delicate Spirit of God within him; his speech "in Spirit" will likewise be calm and controlled. But *Hermas* does not remark explicitly on the (orthodox) content, the (rational) coherence, or the (artistic) beauty of Spirit-given prophecy in the early church. As already pointed out above, we possibly have a specimen of such utterance, given a generation earlier than *Hermas* by a person who exhibited the vehemence, the turbulence, of an old-time biblical prophet — Ignatius of Antioch. His words have the same broken, jerky style as we find in Isaiah 1:

Wash ye,
make you clean,
put away the evil of your doings from before mine eyes,
cease to do evil,
learn to do well,
seek judgement,
relieve the oppressed,

judge the fatherless,
plead for the widow. (vv. 16-17)

Doubtless many other examples of this kind of thing, successful artistic representation of the incoherent speech of deeply disturbed persons, can be found in literature, drama, opera. In the case of biblical prophecy, direct encounter with the living God (or rather as direct as a fragile human could endure without being consumed by that devouring Fire) produces a mix of terror and delight, too high, too deep, for words. The visionary component also lies beyond the power of human utterance. I conclude with two more examples.

Elizabeth Drew (1959:43) says of the famous passage in Hamlet that begins "That it should come to this!": "no single line is entirely regular, and the almost strangling fury and disgust come out in the broken, uneven rhythms and gasps of angry pain and nausea." John D. Sinclair wrote these words as his final comment on the final canto of the *Divine Comedy*:

> The whole account might seem to suffer from an incoherence which is emphasized by the repeated exclamations in the course of it that only a little can be recalled and that that little cannot be told except in the broken utterances of an infant, were it not that that very incoherence and these exclamations so demonstrate the conditions of such a visionary experience that it becomes for us no mere poetic invention but a true report. (Sinclair 1961:492)

References

Albright, William Foxwell

1957   *From the Stone Age to Christianity: Monotheism and the Historical Process.* 2nd ed. Garden City, NY: Doubleday Anchor Books.

1961   *Samuel and the Beginnings of the Prophetic Movement.* Goldenson Lecture for 1961. Cincinnati: Hebrew Union College.

1964   *History, Archaeology, and Christian Humanism.* New York: McGraw-Hill.

1968   *Yahweh and the Gods of Canaan: A Historical Analysis of Two Contrasting Faiths.* Garden City, NY: Doubleday.

Alexander, Joseph Addison

1846-47   *The Prophecies of Isaiah: A Commentary, with the Text, on the Book of Isaiah.* 2 vols. New York and London: Wiley & Putnam.

Allen, Leslie C.

1976   *The Books of Joel, Obadiah, Jonah and Micah.* NICOT. Grand Rapids: Eerdmans.

Allwohn, A.

1926   *Die Ehe des Propheten Hosea in psychoanalytischer Beleuchtung.* BZAW 44. Giessen: Töpelmann.

Andersen, F. I., and David Noel Freedman

1980   *Hosea: A New Translation with Introduction and Commentary.* AB 24. Garden City, NY: Doubleday.

Audet, Jean-Paul

1958   *La Didachè: Instructions des Apôtres.* Paris: Gabalda.

Ayers, R. H.

1979   *Language, Logic, and Reason in the Church Fathers: A Study of Tertullian, Augustine, and Aquinas.* Altertumswissenschaftliche Texte und Studien 6. Hildesheim: Olms.

Baker, A.

1973   "Parallelism: England's Contribution." *CBQ* 35:429-40.

Barth, Karl

1959   *Protestant Thought: From Rousseau to Ritschl.* Trans. B. Cozens et al. London: SCM.

Bleek, Friedrich.

1893   *Einleitung in das Alte Testament.* 6th ed. overseen by J. Wellhausen. Berlin: Reimer.

Block, Daniel I.

1988   "Text and Emotion: A Study in the 'Corruptions' in Ezekiel's Inaugural Vision (Ezekiel 1:4-28)." *CBQ* 50:418-42.

Briggs, Charles A.

1886   *Messianic Prophecy.* New York: Charles Scribner's Sons.

Bruno, D. Arvid

1957   *Das Buch der Zwölf: Eine rhythmische und textkritische Untersuchung.* Stockholm: Almqvist and Wiksell.

Budde, Karl

1917-18   "Das Rätsel von Micha 1." *ZAW* 37:77-108.

Cassdem, Ned

1973   "Ezekiel's Psychotic Personality: Reservations on the Use of the Couch for Biblical Personalities." Pp. 59-70 in *The Word in the World: Essays in Honor of Frederick L. Moriarty, S.J.* Ed. R. J. Clifford and G. W. MacRae. Cambridge: Weston College.

Chadwick, N. K.

1942   *Poetry and Prophecy.* Cambridge: Cambridge University.

Cody, Aelred

1979   "The Phoenician Ecstatic in Wenamûn: A Professional Oracular Medium." *JEA* 65:99-106.

Conrad, Edgar W., and Edward G. Newing, eds.

1987   *Perspectives on Language and Text: Essays and Poems in Honor of*

Francis I. Andersen's Sixtieth Birthday, July 28, 1985. Winona Lake, IN: Eisenbrauns.

Crenshaw, James L.
1971   *Prophetic Conflict: Its Effect upon Israelite Religion.* BZAW 124. Berlin: de Gruyter.

De Vries, Simon J.
1978   *Prophet against Prophet: The Role of the Micaiah Narrative (1 Kings 22) in the Development of the Early Prophetic Tradition.* Grand Rapids: Eerdmans.

Drew, Elizabeth
1959   *Poetry: A Modern Guide to Its Understanding and Enjoyment.* Laurel Poetry Series. New York: Dell.

Durand, Jean M.
1982   "In vino veritas." *RA* 76:43-50.

Edelkoort, Albertus Hendrick
1948   "Prophet and Prophet." *OTS* 5:179-89.

Elliger, Karl
1934   "Die Heimat des Propheten Micha." *ZDPV* 57:81-152.

Ellis, E. Earle
1970   "The Role of the Christian Prophets in Acts." Pp. 55-67 in *Apostolic History and the Gospel: Biblical and Historical Essays Presented to F. F. Bruce on His Sixtieth Birthday.* Ed. W. W. Gasque and R. P. Martin. Exeter: Paternoster; Grand Rapids: Eerdmans.

Follis, Elaine R., ed.
1987   *Directions in Hebrew Poetry.* JSOTSup 40. Sheffield: JSOT.

Foster, Benjamin R.
1977   "Ea and Saltu." Pp. 79-84 in *Essays on the Ancient Near East in Memory of Jacob Joel Finkelstein.* Ed. Maria de Jong Ellis. Memoirs of the Connecticut Academy of Arts and Sciences 19. Hamden, Conn.: Archon, 1977.

Freedman, David Noel
1972   "Pottery, Poetry, and Prophecy: An Essay on Biblical Poetry." *JBL* 91:5-26. Reprinted in Freedman 1980:1-22.
1980   *Pottery, Poetry and Prophecy: Studies in Early Hebrew Poetry.* Winona Lake, IN: Eisenbrauns.
1982   "Discourse on Prophetic Discourse." Pp. 141-58 in *The Quest for the Kingdom of God: Studies in Honor of George E. Mendenhall.* Ed. H. B. Huffmon, F. A. Spina, and A. R. W. Green. Winona Lake, IN: Eisenbrauns.

Funk, J. J.
1987   "Spiritual Development and Spiritual Pathology, Pt. 2: Person to Person." *Journal of Psychology and Judaism* 11:15-29.

Gerstenberger, Erhard
    1962   "The Woe-Oracles of the Prophets." *JBL* 81:249-63.

Goedicke, Hans
    1975   *The Report of Wenamun.* Baltimore and London: Johns Hopkins University.

Graham, William Creighton
    1930-31   "Some Suggestions Toward the Interpretation of Micah 1:10-16." *AJSL* 27:237-58.

Gunnel, André
    1982   "Ecstatic Prophecy in the Old Testament." Pp. 187-200 in Holm 1982.

Haupt, Paul
    1910a   "Micah's Capucinade." *JBL* 29:85-112.
    1910b   "Critical Notes on Micah." *AJSL* 26:201-52.
    1911   "The Book of Micah." *AJSL* 27:1-63.
    1919   *The Book of Micah.* Reprinted from *AJSL* 26 (1910) 201-52 and 27 (1911) 1-63. Chicago: University of Chicago.

Herder, J. G.
    1782-83   *The Spirit of Hebrew Poetry.* Trans. James March. Burlington: Edward Smith, 1833. Reprinted, Naperville: Aleph, 1971.

Hillers, Delbert R.
    1965   "A Convention in Hebrew Literature: the Reaction to Bad News." *ZAW* 77:86-90.

Holm, Nils G., ed.
    1982   *Religious Ecstasy.* Symposium held in August 1981 at Åbo Finland. Scripta Instituti Donneriani Aboensis 11. Stockholm: Almqvist & Wiksell International.

Housman, Alfred Edward
    1933   *The Name and Nature of Poetry.* Cambridge: Cambridge University.

Huffmon, Hubert B., Frank A. Spina, and Alberto R. W. Green, eds.
    1983   *The Quest for the Kingdom of God: Studies in Honor of George E. Mendenhall.* Winona Lake, IN: Eisenbrauns.

Jacob, Éduard
    1957   "Quelques remarques sur les faux prophètes." *Theologie en Zielzorg* 13:479-86.

Janzen, Waldemar
    1972   *Mourning Cry and Woe Oracle.* BZAW 125. Berlin: de Gruyter.

Jepsen, Alfred
    1934   *Nabi: Soziologische Studien zur alttestamentlichen Literatur und Religionsgeschichte.* Munich: Beck.

Koepke, Wulf, ed.
    1982   *Johann Gottfried Herder: Innovator Through the Ages.* Bonn: Bouvier Verlag Herbert Grundmann.

Korostovtsev, M. A.
   1960   *The Voyage of Wen-Amun to Byblos. Egyptian Hieratic Papyrus No.
               120, Puskin Museum of Fine Art, Moscow.* Monuments of Literature
               of the Peoples of the East-Texts, Large Series IV. Moscow: Publishing
               House of Eastern Literature. (In Russian)

Lake, Kirsopp
   1907   *Facsimiles of the Athos Fragments of the Shepherd of Hermas.* Oxford:
               Clarendon.

Lieb, Michael
   1991   *The Visionary Mode: Biblical Prophecy, Hermeneutics, and Cultural
               Change.* Ithaca and London: Cornell University.

Lightfoot, J. B., and J. R. Harmer
   1891   *The Apostolic Fathers.* London: Macmillan. Reprinted, Grand Rapids:
               Baker, 1984.

Lindblom, Johannes
   1962   *Prophecy in Ancient Israel.* Philadelphia: Fortress.

Lowth, Robert
   1753   *Lectures on the Sacred Poetry of the Hebrews.* Trans. G. Gregory. Lon-
               don: J. Johnson, 1787. (This translation from the Latin of *De Sacra
               Poesi Hebraeorum* [1st ed. 1753, 2nd ed. 1763] [lectures given in
               1741] adds a selection of the notes by John David Michaelis [added
               to the Göttingen edition], the translator, and others; the American
               edition of 1829 adds further notes by Calvin Stowe.) Reprinted, New
               York: Garland, 1971.

Meyers, Carol L., and M. O'Connor, eds.
   1983   *The Word of the Lord Shall Go Forth: Essays in Honor of David Noel
               Freedman in Celebration of his Sixtieth Birthday.* Winona Lake, IN:
               Eisenbrauns.

Michaelson, Peter
   1989   "Ecstasy and Possession in Ancient Israel. A Review of Some Recent
               Contributions." *Scandinavian Journal of the Old Testament* 2:28-54.

Moore, Michael S.
   1990a   *The Balaam Traditions: Their Character and Development.* SBLDS
               113. Atlanta: Scholars.

   1990b   "Another Look at Balaam." *RB* 97:359-78.

Mowinckel, Sigmund
   1934-35   "Ecstatic Experience and Rational Elaborations in Old Testament
               Prophecy." *AcOr* 13:264-91.

Newman, John Henry
   1890   "Poetry, with Reference to Aristotle's Poetics." Pp. 1-26 in *Essays,
               Critical and Historical.* 10th ed. 2 vols. London: Longmans, Green.

O'Connor, Michael Patrick

1987a   "The Pseudosorites in Hebrew Verse." Pp. 239-53 in Conrad and Newing 1987.

1987b   "The Pseudosorites: A Type of Paradox in Hebrew Verse." Pp. 161-72 in Follis 1987.

1987c   "Irish Bull and Pseudosorites: Two Types of Paradox in English." *Ars Semeiotica* 10:271-85.

O'Malley, T. P.

1967   *Tertullian and the Bible: Language Imagery Exegesis.* Latinitas Christianorum Primaeva: Studia ad Sermonem Latinum Christianum Pertinentia 21. Utrecht: Dekker & ven de Vegt.

Orlinsky, Harry M.

1965   "The Seer in Ancient Israel." *OrAnt* 4:153-74. (Parts of this paper were used in *The World History of the Jewish People.* Ed. B. Mazar. Vol. 3, chap. 12, and reprinted as "The Seer-Priest and the Prophet in Ancient Israel." Pp. 39-63 in Orlinsky 1974.)

1974   *Essays in Biblical Culture and Bible Translation.* New York: KTAV.

Osswald, E.

1962   *Falsche Prophetie im Alten Testament.* Tübingen: Mohr.

Overholt, Thomas W.

1970   *The Threat of Falsehood: A Study in the Theology of the Book of Jeremiah.* SBT 2/16. London: SCM; Naperville, IL: Allenson.

1989   *Channels of Prophecy: The Social Dynamics of Prophetic Activity.* Minneapolis: Fortress.

1990   "Prophecy in History: the Social Reality of Intermediation." *JSOT* 48:3-29.

Parker, S. B.

1978   "Possession Trance and Prophecy in Pre-Exilic Israel." *VT* 28:271-85.

Petersen, David L.

1981   *The Roles of Israel's Prophets.* JSOTSup 17. Sheffield: University of Sheffield.

Prickett, Stephen

1976   *Romanticism and Religion: The Tradition of Coleridge and Wordsworth in the Victorian Church.* Cambridge: Cambridge University.

1986   *Words and the Word: Language, Poetics, and Biblical Interpretation.* Cambridge: Cambridge University.

Radday, Yehuda T., and Athalya Brenner, eds.

1990   *On Humour and the Comic in the Hebrew Bible.* Bible and Literature Series 23. Sheffield: Almond.

Reiling, J.

1971   "The Use of ΨΕΥΔΟΠΡΟΦΗΤΗΣ in the Septuagint, Philo, and Josephus." *NovT* 13:147-56.

1973   *Hermas and Christian Prophecy: A Study of the Eleventh Mandate.*
            NovTSup 37. Leiden: Brill.

Reines, Alvin Jay

1979   *Maimonides and Abrabanel on Prophecy.* Cincinnati: Hebrew Union
            College.

Robeck, Cecil M., Jr.

1992   *Prophecy in Carthage: Perpetua, Tertullian, and Cyprian.* Cleveland:
            Pilgrim.

Robinson, Theodore H.

1921   "The Ecstatic Element in Old Testament Prophecy." *The Expositor,*
            8th series, 21:217-38.

Schwantes, S. J.

1964   "Critical Notes on Micah 1:10-16." *VT* 14:454-61.

Shaw, Charles S.

1987   "Micah 1:10-16 Reconsidered." *JBL* 106:223-29.

Sinclair, John D.

1961   *Dante's Paradiso.* New York: Oxford University.

Van Winkle, D. W.

1989   "1 Kings XIII: True and False Prophecy." *VT* 29:31-43.

Watson, Wilfred G. E.

1984   *Classical Hebrew Poetry: A Guide to its Techniques.* JSOTSup 26.
            Sheffield: JSOT.

Weinel, Heinrich

1899   *Die Wirkungen des Geistes und der Geister im nachapostolischen Zei-
            talter bis auf Irenäus.* Freiburg: Mohr/Siebeck.

Westermann, Claus

1967   *Basic Forms of Prophetic Speech.* Trans. Hugh C. White. Philadelphia:
            Westminster.

Whittaker, Molly

1967   *Die Apostolischen Väter.* Vol. 1: *Der Hirt des Hermas.* Berlin: Aka-
            demie.

Willey, Basil.

1955   *Nineteenth Century Studies: Coleridge to Matthew Arnold.* London:
            Chatto and Windus.

Wilson, R.

1979   "Prophecy and Ecstasy: A Reexamination." *JBL* 98:321-37.

1980   *Prophecy and Society in Ancient Israel.* Philadelphia: Fortress.

Woude, A. S. van der

1971   "Micah I 10-16." Pp. 347-53 in *Hommages à André Dupont-Sommer,*
            Ed. N. Avigad et al. Paris: Adrien-Maisonneuve.

Yee, Gale A.

1987   *Composition and Tradition in the Book of Hosea: A Redaction Critical
            Investigation.* SBLDS 102. Atlanta: Scholars.

Isaiah 5 and 9: In- or Interdependence?

ANDREW H. BARTELT

Concordia Seminary, St. Louis, Missouri

I. Introduction

Several studies in the past few years have approached the vexing problem of the relationship of Isa 5:8ff. and Isa 9:7 (ET 8)–10:4 with fresh insight, not unrelated to renewed interest in methodological issues regarding the larger questions of the overall composition of the book of Isaiah, in whole and in parts.[1] The basic data regarding these two passages are well known: a series of six "woes" in 5:8-24, followed in v. 25 by the same refrain found four times in 9:7–10:4, and an additional "woe" oracle in 10:1-4. But how, or even whether, these pieces are related is by no means clear.

My concern here is not to summarize or criticize these recent articles, although I generally agree with the approach of L'Heureux, Sheppard, and Anderson in seeking a redactional plan to the present shape of the text.[2] All of

---

1. For fresh insights, see esp. the articles by Anderson (1988), Brown (1990), L'Heureux (1984), and Sheppard (1985), as well as the earlier influential article by Ackroyd (1978). On methodological issues, in addition to the major works of Barth (1977), Lack (1973), and Vermeylen (1977), I note, among an increasing literature, the monographs by Conrad (1991), Gitay (1991), Seitz (1991), Sweeney (1988), and Wiklander (1984), and the commentaries of Watts (1985, 1987). While the approaches range widely, the intent of providing a rationale, whether it be redaction-critical or "rhetorical," for the final form of the text appears to lie at the heart of recent methodology. One notes also the recent development from a session (1989) to a consultation (1990-91) to a seminar (1992-) within the SBL Annual Meeting dealing with "The Formation of the Book of Isaiah."

2. Both L'Heureux and Sheppard (with variations) suggest a double *inclusio around* the "Emmanuel booklet" in 6:1–9:6 (ET 7). I agree with Sheppard (against L'Heureux) that the material in 10:5 forms a new unit and does not belong to this section. Appropriately in a *Festschrift* to B. Childs, Anderson seeks a thematic and structural plan to the text as it now

157

these represent a step beyond previous work, which had explained the current state of the text as due either to some error of transmission that begged to be rectified, each scholar in his or her own way, or to deliberate editorial decision made somewhere along the redactional trail, probably when the so-called *Denkschrift* or "Isaianic Memoirs" in chaps. 6–8 were inserted.[3]

As research continues to break new ground toward understanding the redactional process and seeking a rationale for the placement, rather than the displacement, of textual building blocks, new questions concerning structural connections — and the method of determining them — have been raised.[4] In the face of various claims toward finding structural cohesion, a somewhat more objective criterion for determining structural connections would seem to be of help. In this regard, David Noel Freedman has helped lead the way by suggesting that length — which can be measured in various ways but most accurately by syllables — is useful as a factor in determining poetic structure and in appreciating a sense of artistic balance between literary units, both small and large.[5]

Using the two poetic pieces of Isa 5:8-25 and 9:7–10:4 as a test case, I have explored the role that length might play as an indicator of relationships both within and between specific passages. This research, first done under the aegis of Professor Freedman as doctoral supervisor and now also dedicated to him in this

---

stands, and he suggests that the "Memoir" section was intentionally inserted *into* the material now separated as 5:1-30 and 9:7ff.

3. On errors of transmission, see, e.g., the commentaries of Gray (1912), Duhm (1922), Eichrodt (1960), Kaiser (1972), and Wildberger (1991). On the insertion of the *Denkschrift*, see H. Barth (1977), Vermeylen (1977), and the commentaries of Clements (1980) and Kaiser (1983). I recognize the importance of both the form-critical and the redaction-critical approaches and note their significant contributions in understanding both the preliterary and the literary history of the text. My concern here, however, is an attempt to understand the text in its final form, to which much recent attention has turned.

4. Many of the methodological issues, already modeled in his commentary on Isaiah 40–66 (1956), were discussed in the watershed essay by J. Muilenburg (1969), e.g., a concern for determining literary boundaries and connections by means of structural markers and stylistic devices.

5. In his studies on Hebrew poetry and metrics, Freedman has come to be identified with syllable counting, but one should note that "he is open to virtually any approach to Hebrew meter" (so T. Longman III 1982). I note Freedman's own comments: "how to count . . . is almost immaterial. . . . I steer a middle course between counting words, which will work but may be a little too crude, and counting morae, which may be more precise but seems overly fussy and produces more detailed information than is necessary or desirable. But so long as a system is applied consistently, it should work reasonably well and tell us what we want to know — namely, how long a line, a stanza, or a poem is." Or, more simply put, "I have opted for syllables because there are a lot of them, and hence a disagreement about a few of them will not make much difference" (Freedman 1987:20). While Freedman's work has focused on Hebrew poetry, it is worth noting that he has begun to apply his principles not only to prose sections but also to large blocks of prose, if not to the entire Hebrew canon, where he has simply counted words. See Freedman 1991, 1992.

volume, suggests that recent studies have not yet gone far enough toward understanding the structuring of these chapters as two carefully crafted poems, which, on the one hand, reflect individually a structural plan *independent* of the other, and yet, on the other hand, appear to be deliberately linked and interrelated so that both poems must be understood as *interdependent* with each other.

I shall first analyze each of the two poems to demonstrate their structural integrity and independence. Then I shall deal with the interdependence of the two poems and the question of their function and meaning within their literary context. My data comprise a detailed, line-by-line analysis of each poem, including syllable and stress counts and commentary on individual verse structure, all of which I cannot review in detail here[6] but which do support the methodological conclusion that the factor of length is a component of poetic structure.

II. Isaiah 5:8-25 as an Independent Poem

First, borders need to be defended, and I recognize that it is by no means clear that this unit concludes after v. 25.[7] But it is precisely toward solving this sort of difficulty that this method seeks to contribute, and I believe that the evidence presented supports the assertion that the poem both includes and concludes with v. 25.

In considering Isa 5:8-25, I make the following observations:

1. The first "woe"[8] (v. 8) is followed (in vv. 9-10) by a direct quotation of YHWH's words to the prophet, apparently overheard in the divine council. The second "woe" (vv. 11-12) is longer than the first (two quatrains vs. one).

2. Following the second "woe" are two "therefore" verses (vv. 13-14), each introduced by לכן.[9]

---

6. For a fuller investigation of these passages and their placement within the overall structure of Isaiah 2–12, see Bartelt 1991.

7. Commentaries disagree over the boundaries of the literary units. Duhm, Kaiser, Wildberger, and Hayes and Irvine deal with vv. 25-30 as a unit, as do the studies of Barth, Sheppard, Sweeney, and Brown. Lack suggests a major break in the structure of Isaiah 1–39 between 5:24 and 5:25. Gray divides v. 25 itself into v. 25a-c (transitional) and vv. 25d-29, which belong with 9:7ff. The commentaries of Clements, Watts, and Oswalt divide between v. 25 and v. 26, as does the study of Anderson.

8. It is not my purpose here to deal with the form-critical questions concerning the form and function of "woe" oracles, esp. regarding their preliterary history, as I am concerned with the final form of the text. See, inter alia, Gerstenberger 1962; Hillers 1983; and Janzen 1972.

9. Admitting that "for two consecutive sayings to begin with 'therefore' is quite striking," Anderson defends their *Sitz im Text* (as opposed to an original *Sitz im Leben*) as "not necessarily inelegant stylistically." He proposes that they served the rhetorical function of expansion and emphasis. See Anderson 1988:234-35.

3. Verses 15-17 form a unit introduced by a refrain found previously in the book, in 2:9, 11, 17.[10]

4. Verses 18-23 contain four more "woes" (##3-6), and the length of this section is roughly equivalent to the length of the first two "woes" in vv. 8-12 (item 1):

vv. 8-12:	132 syllables,[11]	55 stresses,	and 63 words
vv. 18-23:	139 syllables,	58 stresses,	and 58 words

The initial "woe" in vv. 18-19 includes a direct quotation of the people's words against YHWH's counsel, similar to the quotation of YHWH's words after the first "woe" in v. 8.

"Woes" ##4-5 grow increasingly shorter and therefore would have been spoken/read in more rapid succession. The sixth "woe" (v. 22) is really only a single bicolon, as is the fifth (v. 21). But instead of a final or seventh "woe," an additional bicolon is added (v. 23), the content of which echoes the very first "woe" in v. 8.[12]

5. This series of four "woes" in vv. 18-23 is followed by a verse introduced by לכן (v. 24). This single לכן verse is roughly equivalent in length to the double "therefore" in vv. 13-14 (item 2):

vv. 13-14:	59 syllables,	23 stresses,	and 25 words
v. 24:	53 syllables,	22 stresses,	and 25 words

6. Verse 25 adds a second "therefore" to that of v. 24, but it uses the idiom על־כן, which is the only "therefore" word used in the poem in 9:7ff. (at 9:16 [ET 17]). Conversely, the refrain that gives structure to the poem in chap. 9 appears in this same v. 25 of chap. 5. Thus, as vv. 15-17 echoed a refrain found earlier in the book (item 3), v. 25 forms a link to later material. Furthermore, the length of v. 25 is roughly equivalent to that of vv. 15-17:

vv. 15-17:	59 syllables,	21 stresses,	and 22 words
v. 25:	54 syllables,	21 stresses,	and 25 words

These observations suggest a parallel structure based on a three-part sequence of formal and thematic features to be found both in vv. 8-17 (items

---

10. While not repeating an entire refrain word for word, the verses are clearly related. I believe that vv. 9, 11, and 17 in chap. 2 serve the function of a refrain in giving structure to the poetic unit in 2:5-22.

11. My method of counting syllables is that of Freedman, as described in Anderson and Freedman (1980:77) and Freedman (1986:411). My method of counting stresses is essentially that of the Ley-Sievers-Budde system. For history and description, see D. Stuart 1976:1ff.

12. The expectation of a seventh woe is such that at least some commentators (Gray, Duhm, Hayes and Irvine) have proposed that a הוי has fallen out of the text at v. 23.

1-3) and in vv. 18-25 (items 4-6): the use of הוי (items 1 and 4); the impending result introduced by לכן (items 2 and 5); and a concluding unit which contains a refrain to be found elsewhere in the larger context (items 3 and 6), the first echoing what is found previously (2:9, 11, 17), the second anticipating words yet to come (9:11, 16, 20; 10:4). Thus the whole of 5:8-25 divides into two parallel halves or "panels,"[13] vv. 8-17 and vv. 18-25, with a similar sequence in both form and content between the corresponding stanzas of each part:

Panel I:	Stanza 1:	vv. 8-10	Woe #1 and quotation
		vv. 11-12	Woe #2
	Stanza 2:	vv. 13-14	Double לכן
	Stanza 3:	vv. 15-17	Refrain found in chap. 2
Panel II:	Stanza 1:	vv. 18-19	Woe #3 and quotation
		vv. 20-23	Woes ##4-6 and "false" seventh
	Stanza 2:	v. 24	Single לכן
	Stanza 3:	v. 25	Refrain (plus על־כן) found in 9:7ff.

Turning to the criterion of length, I have already observed that the length of parallel stanzas is roughly equivalent, and I note a correspondence between the stanzas of each panel as well as between stanzas 2 and 3 within each panel:

I.	Stanza 1:	132 syllables,	55 stresses,	63 words
	Stanza 2:	59 syllables,	23 stresses,	25 words
	Stanza 3:	59 syllables,	21 stresses,	22 words
II.	Stanza 1:	139 syllables,	58 stresses,	58 words
	Stanza 2:	53 syllables,	22 stresses,	25 words
	Stanza 3:	54 syllables,	21 stresses,	25 words

Although stanza 1 of panel II is slightly longer than stanza 1 of panel I, stanzas 2-3 of panel II are slightly shorter than stanzas 2-3 of panel I. Thus an overall sense of balance is formed, and the closest equivalency in length between the two halves is found not simply by comparing the parts but by comparing the total length of each panel.

| vv. 8-17: | 250 syllables, | 99 stresses, | 110 words |
| vv. 18-25: | 246 syllables, | 101 stresses, | 108 words |

In addition to the balance in length, additional features of careful internal structure give further indication of the unity of the whole. For example, the use

---

13. I recognize that such terminology is quite arbitrary, including that of "stanza," "strophe," and even "verse" and "line" (all of which could benefit from some collegial regularization!). For my purposes, any terms that indicate a hierarchy of subsections will do.

of a divine name occurs four times in each half. In 5:8-17, the name "YHWH Sebaoth" occurs in the first "woe" (v. 9a) and "YHWH" in the second "woe" (v. 12b). The "therefore" sections have no divine names, but the final stanza has two: "YHWH Sebaoth" in v. 16a and "the Holy God" in v. 16b. In the first stanza of the second panel, v. 19b echoes the name used in the final stanza of the first panel: "the Holy One of Israel." There are no other names used in the "woe" stanzas of the second half, but the "therefore" (לכן) stanza has two: "YHWH Sebaoth" in v. 24cα and "the Holy One of Israel" in v. 24cβ. Finally, v. 25, which is, in effect, an additional "therefore" section (using על־כן), although it is, in fact, a concluding refrain, has "YHWH" in v. 25a. To summarize:

Panel I (vv. 8-17)	Panel II (vv. 18-25)
Stanza 1: יהוה צבאות (v. 9a)	Stanza 1: קדוש ישראל (v. 19b)
יהוה (v. 12b)	
Stanza 2: [ ]	Stanza 2: יהוה צבאות (v. 24cα)
	קדוש ישראל (v. 24cβ)
Stanza 3: יהוה צבאות (v. 16a)	Stanza 3: יהוה (v. 25a)
האל הקדוש (v. 16b)	

Having already observed parallels in content, sequence, and length between the corresponding stanzas of each panel, one discovers that the divine names are grouped accordingly. Considering both first stanzas together, one finds three different names in the "woe" sections: "YHWH Sebaoth," "YHWH," "the Holy One of Israel." The two second stanzas (which have לכן) have two different names (none in vv. 13-14, two in v. 24): "YHWH Sebaoth" and "the Holy One of Israel." Combining the two third stanzas, both of which contain a refrain, one finds: "YHWH Sebaoth," "the Holy God," and "YHWH." Thus each grouping of two parallel stanzas contains one use of "YHWH Sebaoth" and one use of "holy." The first and last grouping have one additional "YHWH":

Stanzas 1:	יהוה צבאות	(v. 9a)
	יהוה	(v. 12b)
	קדוש ישראל	(v. 19b)
Stanzas 2:	יהוה צבאות	(v. 24cα)
	קדוש ישראל	(v. 24cβ)
Stanzas 3:	יהוה צבאות	(v. 16α)
	האל הקדוש	(v. 16β)
	יהוה	(v. 25a)

Furthermore, one finds several instances of wordplay between and among the parts. The verb עשׂה and its cognate noun מַעֲשֶׂה link v. 10 at the end of the first "woe" with v. 12bβ at the end of the second "woe." The noun occurs again in the first strophe of the second series of "woes," v. 19a, and thus forms not only an internal link between the two "woes" in the first panel but also a link between the "woes" in the first and the second panels.

The verbal root אכל appears in the last line of vv. 8-17, and one wonders if this is an allusion also to the voracious appetite of Sheol in v. 14 as response to the insatiable quest for field and harvest discussed in vv. 8-10: those who devour will be devoured. But just as the verb indicates a turning of the "table" in panel I, its reappearance in the "therefore" section in panel II (v. 24a) makes the same point: the harvest will be consumed, but not by the intended consumer.

It is likely that the use of the participle אמרים in v. 19a and v. 20a in reference to what the people "say" is contrasted by the assertion that "they refuse the אמרת קדושׁ־ישׂראל" in v. 24cβ. Finally, I note the echo of v. 8bβ (בקרב הארץ), within the first stanza, in v. 25bβ (בקרב חוצות), within the last stanza. Not only will they be "alone *in the midst of* the earth," but they are also now described as abandoned like corpses left as refuse "*in the midst of* the streets."

To summarize, there is a structural pattern in Isa 5:8-25, divided into two halves or "panels" of three stanzas each, based on a parallel sequence of both formal and thematic features and affirmed by correspondences in length that indicate an overall sense of unity to the composition. I have further noted a number of internal rhetorical features, such as wordplay and repetition, that attest to the integrity of the pericope as a unit, including and concluding with v. 25, which contains the same refrain found in Isa 9:7ff. Since the refrain serves as a conclusion to each stanza in 9:7ff., it is likely that its use in 5:25 forms a conclusion here as well. The borders seem well defended, and I propose that 5:8-25 should be understood in its present state as a unified, independent poem, with a carefully crafted and cohesive structure.

III. Isaiah 9:7 (ET 8)–10:4 as an Independent Poem

The boundaries of this section are much less disputed. Although commentators may disagree as to the contents and order of a reconstructed original composition and its relationship to the material in 5:8ff.,[14] the unit is clearly ordered by the fourfold use of the refrain already found in 5:25. Again, my conclusions

---

14. For example, Clements places 10:1-4 immediately before 5:8ff. and discusses it at that point, although he suggests that the present dislocation has been deliberate. Likewise Kaiser, in his first edition, removes 10:1-4 for discussion with chap. 5, although he places it after 5:24 (so also Wildberger). In his second edition, however, Kaiser deals with 9:7–10:4 as a whole unit in its present position, as does Watts. Duhm would attach 5:25-30 as the conclusion to 9:7–10:4, but he discusses the latter material as one piece. Likewise Gray adds 5:25/26-30 to follow 10:4 and speaks of a poem of five strophes, for which he reconstructs several lines to produce fourteen lines in each. R. Lack deals with 10:1-4 as a separate unit, but only because of its links to chap. 5.

are based on data that cannot be completely reviewed here, but I make the following observations:

1. The four refrains appear at the conclusion of what appear to be four stanzas: vv. 7-11, 12-16, 17-20, and 10:1-4.

2. Verse 12 seems to begin the second stanza, yet the use of העם forms an inclusio with the first stanza, linking to v. 8. Further, v. 12 has clear vocabulary links to the refrain itself, which, in turn, gives structure to the whole poem. Indeed, one could well understand the theme of v. 12 as the theme for the entire poem, expressed by the words לא שב. Because the people *have not returned/repented,* YHWH's hand *has not returned/turned away.*

Moreover, v. 12 also echoes the vocabulary heard previously in 5:25, not only in the words of the refrain but also in the use of המכהו, a link to the ויכהו in 5:25. It would seem, therefore, that v. 12 is an independent subunit of 9:7–10:4, and that it forms an interlude between the first and second stanza of this poem.

3. If one lays aside 9:12 for the moment as an independent unit, the four stanzas are roughly equivalent in length:

9:7-11:	119 syllables,	44 stresses,	50 words
9:13-16:	119 syllables,	44 stresses,	55 words
9:17-20:	122 syllables,	49 stresses,	58 words
10:1-4:	115 syllables,	44 stresses,	49 words

4. Subdividing these stanzas into strophes, one finds further correspondences in length between stanzas and strophes. Stanza 1 has two strophes of unequal length: vv. 7-9 (64 syllables) and vv. 10-11a (41 syllables), followed by the refrain. Stanza 2 has strophes of similar length: vv. 13-15 (62 syllables) and v. 16ab (43 syllables). Thus within these first two stanzas, the "A" strophes correspond to one another in length (64/62), as do the "B" strophes (41/43). Stanzas 3 and 4, however, consist of two strophes of relatively equal length. The structure follows a clear outline:

Stanza 1: (9:7-11)

Strophe A:	vv. 7-9:	64 syllables,	24 stresses,	24 words
Strophe B:	vv. 10-11a:	41 syllables,	14 stresses,	18 words
Refrain:	v. 11b:	14 syllables,	6 stresses,	8 words

Stanza 2: (9:13-16)

Strophe A:	vv. 13-15:	62 syllables,	24 stresses,	26 words
Strophe B:	v. 16ab:	43 syllables,	14 stresses,	21 words
Refrain:	v. 16c:	14 syllables,	6 stresses,	8 words

Stanza 3: (9:17-20)

Strophe A:	vv. 17-18a:	50 syllables,	21 stresses,	22 words

| Strophe B: | vv. 18b-20a: | 58 syllables, | 20 stresses, | 28 words |
| Refrain: | v. 20b: | 14 syllables, | 6 stresses, | 8 words |

Stanza 4: (10:1-4)

Strophe A:	vv. 1-2:	51 syllables,	20 stresses,	20 words
Strophe B:	vv. 3-4a:	50 syllables,	18 stresses,	21 words
Refrain:	v. 4b:	14 syllables,	6 stresses,	8 words

One conclusion to draw from these observations is that the four stanzas of this poem form a linear, two-part structure: stanzas 1-2, and stanzas 3-4. Indeed, if one combines the two stanzas in each part, the correspondence in length is striking:

| stanzas 1 + 2: | 238 syllables, | 88 stresses, | 105 words |
| stanzas 3 + 4: | 237 syllables, | 93 stresses, | 107 words |

But we have yet to take into account v. 12, which has been set aside as an interlude. It is interesting — and perhaps noteworthy — that the Masoretic divisions marked by *setumah* and supported by the Qumran scroll 1QIs[a] divide 9:7–10:4 into three sections, dividing after v. 12 and then again after the third refrain in v. 20. The length of this tripartite structure would be:

Part I (9:7-12):	140 syllables,	50 stresses,	60 words
Part II (9:13-20):	241 syllables,	91 stresses,	113 words
Part III (10:1-4):	115 syllables,	44 stresses,	49 words

This structure suggests a chiastic arrangement, and if one adds together parts I and III, one gets the following totals:

| Parts I + III: | 255 syllables, | 94 stresses, | 109 words |
| Part II: | 241 syllables, | 91 stresses, | 113 words |

The correspondence is not so close as the previous division into four stanzas, but that analysis conveniently ignored v. 12. It would be tempting, therefore, to assume that the addition of v. 12 has interrupted a precise structure of four stanzas, and that this is a clear example of a later addition. But one can find numerous examples of complex and well-worked combinations of both chiastic and linear structures in individual bicola, verses, and strophes (e.g., v. 17, vv. 18b-19b). If both techniques were available to be used in a complementary way at these smaller levels, it is likely that they could be used in combination at a larger level as well, and that an entire poem could utilize both a linear and a chiastic structure together. If this is true, then 9:7–10:4 offers an example of an intentionally worked structure that both includes and cuts across the more obvious divisions marked by the refrains.

This tripartite structure also forms a helpful backdrop to the positioning of the six divine names in this poem. If one first considers stanzas 1 and 2 apart from v. 12, one finds the use of divine names once in each strophe of these two stanzas, and in reverse order: "Adonay" (v. 7 [so MT, but cf. 1QIsᵃ]) . . . "YHWH" (v. 10) in stanza 1, but "YHWH" (v. 13) . . . "Adonay" (v. 16) in stanza 2. Thus "Adonay" forms an *inclusio* from the first strophe of stanza 1 to the second strophe of stanza 2.

But if one considers the tripartite structure that includes v. 12 with vv. 7-11, one finds three different names in part I (one "Adonay," one "YHWH," and one "YHWH Sebaoth"), the same three names in part II (one "YHWH," one "Adonay," and one "YHWH Sebaoth"), and none in part III. Thus three different names occur in parts I + III, and the same three names occur in part II:

Part I: (9:7-12) אדני (v. 7)   Part II: (9:13-20) יהוה (v. 13)
                 יהוה (v. 10)   אדני (v. 16)
            יהוה צבאות (v. 12)   יהוה צבאות (v. 18)
+ Part III (10:1-4)

In sum, as with 5:8-25, one finds a careful and complex structural scheme also behind the poem in 9:7–10:4, suggesting a unified integrity also to this poem as a whole. Since the structural outlines of each poem are completely different, however, both poems are to be understood as *independent,* self-contained, and well-constructed units.

IV. Isaiah 5:8-25 and 9:7–10:4 as Interdependent Poems

Nevertheless, I have already noted links between the two poems, which suggest a sense of *interdependence:* specifically the presence of the refrain from the second poem in v. 25 of the first, and an apparent seventh "woe" in 10:1 of the second poem, as if a piece of each poem had been placed in the other.

Although this apparent exchange has been explained as accidental transposition or as the result of haphazard — or even intentional — redactional activity, the careful construction of each individual poem, which has already been observed, indicates a much more deliberate plan, as recent studies have also suggested. While it is likely, I believe, that these pieces have been intentionally exchanged as an interlocking mechanism to bind the two poems together, the two pieces cannot have been switched simply in a quid pro quo fashion, since they cannot be switched back without destroying the internal structure of each poem, which is dependent on the present position of each part. Thus whatever the nature of the interrelationship, it should be traced to a clear if complex plan that has in mind the overall composition of *both* poems, taken together, all of which reveals a sense of interdependence far beyond what has previously been proposed.

This hypothesis of a careful construction of both poems taken together is supported by other features that transcend the structure of either poem and demonstrate this deliberate interdependence between them. First, I have already noted how the refrain from the second poem appears as a *conclusion* to the first poem. Indeed, this is evidence, I have argued, that the first poem ends with 5:25. Assuming that 10:1-4 contains the missing seventh and final "woe" from the first poem, one finds this connection between the two poems in the *concluding* stanza of the second poem.

Others have suggested that 10:1 is not the seventh "woe" at all.[15] Indeed, the expected place for it would seem to be 5:23, where a pattern similar to that used to introduce the other "woes" appears, but without the use of הוי. But to generate a lost "woe" in 5:23 is, at best, a reconstruction based on text-critical principles (though without any manuscript evidence), and, at worst, a re-creation ex nihilo. In the light of the other evidence that suggests an interrelationship between the two poems, it is not only more logical but also much simpler to find, within the texts themselves, a seventh "woe," ready-made, in 10:1.

Second, the sequence of the "woes" is significant. In his second edition, Kaiser, who agrees that the seventh "woe" occurs in 10:1, suggests a "circular composition" to the entire series, noting that "the first, fourth, and seventh 'woes' are concerned with transgressors of the law; the second and sixth with drunkards; and the third and fifth with frivolity which is forgetful of God" (Kaiser 1983:79). I have come independently to a similar conclusion, but I would propose that the chiastic arrangement is much more detailed than Kaiser's analysis and that it assumes — and reveals — an intentional connection between the two poems.

For example, only the first and the seventh "woes" (5:8 and 10:1) are followed by second plural verb forms (in 5:8 and 10:3). Further, the subjects of these first and last "woes" are not simply "transgressors of the law," as Kaiser summarized, but rather more specifically those who represent the social sins of monied injustice ("joining house to house" and "decreeing decrees of evil . . . to twist the needy from the justice due them").

Further, the third and fifth "woes" (5:18-19 and 5:21) deal not so much with frivolity as with the confusion of human insight and wisdom over against the "counsel of the Holy One of Israel." Finally, the fourth or middle "woe" (5:20) is itself a carefully worked chiasm involving three bicola, all of which begin with the plural participle (no other "woe" has three participles), followed by chiastic contrast: evil:good :: good:evil . . . darkness:light :: light:darkness . . . bitter:sweet :: sweet:bitter, all of which summarize the complete inversion of

---

15. See n. 12 above.

the basic issue of right and wrong.[16] Thus the full series, concluded in 10:1-4, presents the following pattern:

> Woe #1: social sins: economic oppression (5:8)
>   Woe #2: alcohol abuse (5:11)
>   Woe #3: affront to YHWH's counsel (5:18)
>   Woe #4: confusion of good and evil (5:20, triple chiasm)
>   Woe #5: affront to true wisdom (5:21)
>   Woe #6: alcohol abuse (5:22)
> Woe #7: social sins: economic oppression (10:1 [not 5:23])

To return to the issue of 5:23, where some have attempted to recover a lost seventh "woe," one must observe that the content of that verse, dealing with the perversion of justice, would also fit the expected theme of the last "woe." Assuming that the chiasm was apparent and that the final item should match the first, one might well have expected v. 23 to be the seventh "woe." Indeed, the shortening of the verses, especially at "woes" #5 and #6, would result in the quickening of the pace through vv. 21-22, and the pronouncement of the sixth "woe" would likely have generated the anticipation of the seventh and final "woe" *immediately* after v. 22.

But although the content of v. 23 would fit the final "woe," the absence — the suspension — of the actual word הוי would create doubt in the mind of the hearer/reader whether the sequence was, in fact, complete. That the actual occurrence of the final "woe" does not come until 10:1 would have the effect of holding the hearer/reader in suspense until the announcement of the final "woe" at the end of the entire composition. If so, the message of the first poem seems to be clearly linked to that of the second. Thus the present position of the actual seventh "woe" in 10:1 is not the result of unintentional or even intentional dismembering and displacement of an original unity to be restored. Its placement is better explained as the conscious binding of the message of 5:8-25 with that of 9:7–10:4.

A third structural feature that can be found only by considering both poems in relation to each other is the placement of the divine names. I have already noted the use of eight divine names in the first poem and of six in the second. The eighth divine name in the first poem occurs in 5:25, which is the section that most directly links with the second poem. Conversely, the one stanza in 9:7–10:4 that lacks any divine name (10:1-4) is the one that links directly to the other poem. Thus there are exactly seven divine names in the "woe" material and seven divine names in the refrained stanzas, even though they are unevenly divided between the two poems.

---

16. Cf. the location of Amos 5:14-15, dealing with "good and evil" and "evil and good," as central both to the structure and the message of that book. See Andersen and Freedman 1989:506.

I have shown above that the order and placement of the specific names is integrated into each individual poem, so that one cannot simply regroup the names without affecting the structure of each poem, independent of the other. If one considers the interdependence of the two poems, however, one finds a total of exactly fourteen divine names.

Fourth, there is considerable interplay of other vocabulary and themes. For example, I have already noted that the use of עַל־כֵּן in 5:25, in contrast to לָכֵן used elsewhere in the first poem, corresponds to the עַל־כֵּן of 9:16, the single use of a word for "therefore" in the second poem. I have also observed the use of the verbal root נכה and the wordplay on the root שׁוּב as links between 9:12, a verse that catches one's attention as thematic in the second poem, and 5:25, the verse in the first poem that contains the refrain from the second poem. This connection between 9:12 and 5:25 helps explain the location of 9:12 as an "interlude" immediately following the first stanza of the second poem. As the words of the refrain in 9:11 — not heard since 5:25 — would bring to mind the first poem, so the wordplay in 9:12 would reinforce this connection and assure the hearer/reader early in the second poem that the first poem is, indeed, to be recalled.

In addition to these features already discussed, one might note the somewhat awkward poetic line that appears in 5:9a. Following the initial quatrain of the first poem, this fifth colon is a single line, and it uses elliptical syntax to introduce a direct quotation: what YHWH says, presumably in the divine council, which is overheard by the prophet and shared with the people. In parallel fashion, a somewhat awkward line (9:8b) follows the initial quatrain of the second poem. This fifth colon also stands out as a monocolon, and it uses an elliptical style to introduce a direct quotation: what the people say in pride and arrogance in response to the "word" of Adonay.

As a further example of interplay between the two poems, I would call attention to the unusual grammatical construction found in the first poem at 5:19a, where two jussive verbs are juxtaposed asyndetically: יְמַהֵר יָחִישָׁה מַעֲשֵׂהוּ = "let him hasten, let him hurry his work." The sentence might better be rendered as a hendiadys, producing the English redundancy, "let him quickly hurry his work."

The use of the two verbal roots מהר and חוּשׁ in a somewhat peculiar expression might have stood out in and of themselves, but interest is drawn back to them in the final stanza of the second poem. In 10:2b the reversed order of the common word pair "orphan . . . widow" to "widows . . . orphans"[17] calls attention to a verse in which one also finds the verbal root שׁלל matched by the use of the verbal root בזז.

---

17. I count twenty-six occurrences of the pair in the Hebrew Scriptures. Twenty-one use the order "orphan . . . widow"; five use the reverse. Of the four pairings in Isaiah 1–39, three are in the order "orphan . . . widow" (1:17; 1:23; 9:16). Only 10:2 has the order reversed.

Remembering that this verse occurs in the stanza that has the most direct link from the second poem back to the first, one returns to the awkward verbs in 5:19 and recognizes the combination of four vocables: מהר plus הוּשׁ in 5:19a, שׁלל plus בזז in 10:2b. When the first and second element of each pair is regrouped, they come together as מהר שׁלל חשׁ בז, an echo of the symbolic name of Isaiah's second son, mentioned in 8:3 as one of the children who play a significant role within the *Denkschrift*.[18] If this is true, one has a link not only between the two poems in chaps. 5 and 9 but also between the two poems together and the intervening material. This would suggest that these two poems are, indeed, intentionally placed around the chapters in between them, which would have to be read or heard — and therefore considered — before coming to the second poem.

Finally, I have already noted how the simple factor of length has served as a guide to structural analysis in these two poems, taken independently. In the light of the apparent interdependence of the poems as carefully worked units, one must ask whether they correspond also in length.

The answer is clear. When one compares the total length of the first poem with that of the second, one notes the following:

5:8-25:	496 syllables,	200 stresses,	218 words
9:7–10:4:	496 syllables,	185 stresses,	222 words

As measured by syllable counts, the two poems are exactly the same length.

This striking correspondence in length, as measured most accurately by syllables and affirmed to a lesser degree also by stress and word counts, serves to confirm the two hypotheses of this study. First, each poem is a self-contained unit in its present form, since to tamper with the construction of either individual poem would destroy this equivalency in length. Second, the exact correspondence in length between the two poems indicates that each is clearly constructed with the other in mind.

V. Conclusion

In sum, in several instances poetic and rhetorical features have indicated a carefully worked bond between the two poems in Isa 5:8-25 and Isa 9:7–10:4, the most striking of which is that they are exactly the same length.

While I have tried to show that each piece is, on its own, a carefully crafted

---

18. While this paper is limited to the two poems under discussion in Isaiah 5 and 9, it is worth noting the wordplay on Isaiah's other son שׁאר ישׁוב in 10:21-22 and the implications for the larger structure of Isaiah 2–12. See Bartelt 1991.

independent unity, the two poems so clearly complement each other that I conclude that each has been composed with specific reference to the other, and that they should be understood in the light of this *interdependence:* the first by means of anticipating, the second by means of bringing a sense of conclusion to the other.

Since the content of the first poem is addressed to the wickedness of Judah and the substance of the second has as its focus the situation in Jacob/Israel, it is logical to suggest that one should also understand the actions and fate of both North and South not simply as *independent* but also as *interdependent.*

Further, I suggest that the deliberate interrelationship of these two poems should also be considered with a view to the larger literary context, including the intervening material around which they are carefully structured and placed. If the suspension of the seventh "woe," for example, would have held the attention of the hearer/reader until the end of the second poem, the positioning of the poems around the intervening chapters would necessitate consideration of the *Denkschrift* material as well, which deals with the threat to both Ahaz and Judah posed by the Syro-Ephraimite coalition and with the word of Isaiah concerning a quiet confidence in the promise to the house of David.

That the combined theme of the two poems focuses on the interrelationship of the sins of both Israel and Judah under the impending judgment of their God served as a striking reminder, not only that the fate of both North and South were linked, but also that the faith and the future of both the king and the people in Judah were bound to the God of *all* Israel, whose promise to the Davidic line was threatened by the internecine warfare of the Syro-Ephraimite conflict. The hand of Yahweh was still outstretched, as his people pondered whether the announcement of a final "woe" would, in fact, come. Thus the content of these two *interrelated* poems forms a fitting commentary on the theological crisis reported in the intervening chapters. The analysis here presented has sought to serve the understanding not only of the message of the poems but also of their role in the interpretation of the larger context.

Finally, this method has taken seriously the simple factor of length, as measured most accurately by syllable counting, though supported also by the counting of stresses and even words, all of which generally show correspondence, balance, and symmetry at larger levels even to a greater extent than found at the smaller levels of bicola, verse, and strophe.[19] It is a fitting tribute to David Noel Freedman, who has sought greater understanding of the Hebrew Scriptures by counting and considering the length of literary components, from colon to canon, to conclude that literary analysis is well served to take into consideration the effect of length in marking especially balance and binding between and among even larger literary units.

19. Cf. the similar findings of P. Raabe 1989:309: "Symmetry in length is evident among the larger units of a psalm, but it is located on the stanza level rather than the strophe level."

References

Ackroyd, P.

1978 "Isaiah I–XII: Presentation of a Prophet." Pp. 16-48 in *Congress Volume: Göttingen, 1977*. VTSup 29. Leiden: Brill.

Andersen, F. I., and D. N. Freedman

1980 *Hosea*. AB 24. Garden City, NY: Doubleday.

1989 *Amos*. AB 26. Garden City, NY: Doubleday.

Anderson, B.

1988 " 'God with Us' — In Judgment and in Mercy: The Editorial Structure of Isaiah 5–10 (11)." Pp. 230-45 in *Canon, Theology, and Old Testament Interpretation: Essays in Honor of Brevard S. Childs*. Ed. G. Tucker, D. Petersen, and R. Wilson. Philadelphia: Fortress.

Bartelt, A.

1991 "Style and Structure in Prophetic Rhetoric: Isaiah 2–12." Ph.D. diss. Ann Arbor: University of Michigan. Forthcoming in revised form in University of California, San Diego, Biblical and Judaic Studies. Winona Lake, IN: Eisenbrauns.

Barth, H.

1977 *Die Jesaja-Worte in der Josiazeit*. WMANT 48. Neukirchen-Vluyn: Neukirchener Verlag.

Brown, W.

1990 "The So-Called Refrain in Isaiah 5:25-30 and 9:7–10:4." *CBQ* 52:432-43.

Clements, R.

1980 *Isaiah 1–39*. NCB. Grand Rapids: Eerdmans.

Conrad, E. W.

1991 *Reading Isaiah*. OBT. Minneapolis: Fortress.

Duhm, B.

1922 *Das Buch Jesaja*. HKAT. Göttingen: Vandenhoeck & Ruprecht.

Eichrodt, W.

1960 *Der Heilige in Israel: Jesaja 1–12*. BAT. Stuttgart: Calwer.

Freedman, D. N.

1986 "Acrostic Poems in the Hebrew Bible: Alphabetic and Otherwise." *CBQ* 48:408-31.

1987 "Another Look at Biblical Hebrew Poetry." Pp. 11-28 in *Directions in Hebrew Poetry*. Ed. E. R. Follis. JSOTSup 40. Sheffield: JSOT.

1991 *The Unity of the Hebrew Bible*. Ann Arbor: University of Michigan.

1992 "The Symmetry of the Hebrew Bible." *ST* 46:83-108.

Gerstenberger, E.

1962 "The Woe-Oracles of the Prophets." *JBL* 81:249-63.

Gitay, Y.

1991 *Isaiah and His Audience*. Assen: Van Gorcum.

Gray, G. B.
1912   *A Critical and Exegetical Commentary on the Book of Isaiah I–XXVI.*
            ICC. Edinburgh: T. & T. Clark.

Hayes, J., and S. Irvine
1987   *Isaiah the Eighth-Century Prophet: His Times and His Preaching.*
            Nashville: Abingdon.

Hillers, D.
1983   "*Hoy* and *Hoy*-Oracles: A Neglected Syntactic Aspect." Pp. 185-88 in
            *The Word of the Lord Shall Go Forth: Essays in Honor of David Noel
            Freedman in Celebration of His Sixtieth Birthday.* Ed. C. Meyers and
            M. O'Connor. Winona Lake, IN: Eisenbrauns.

Janzen, W.
1972   *Mourning Cry and Woe Oracle.* BZAW 125. Berlin: de Gruyter.

Kaiser, O.
1972   *Isaiah 1–12.* Trans. R. A. Wilson. OTL. Philadelphia: Westminster.
            (Original: *Der Prophet Jesaja.* ATD. Göttingen: Vandenhoeck & Ru-
            precht.)

1983   *Isaiah 1–12.* Trans. J. Bowden. OTL. Philadelphia: Westminster.
            (Original: *Der Prophet Jesaja.* 2nd ed. ATD. Göttingen: Vandenhoeck
            & Ruprecht.)

Lack, R.
1973   *La Symbolique du Livre d'Isaie.* AnBib 59. Rome: Biblical Institute.

L'Heureux, C.
1984   "The Redactional History of Isaiah 5.1–10.4." Pp. 99-119 in *In the
            Shelter of Elyon: Essays on Ancient Palestinian Life and Literature in
            Honor of G. W. Ahlström.* Ed. W. Boyd Barrick and John R. Spencer.
            JSOTSup 31. Sheffield: JSOT.

Longman, T. III
1982   "A Critique of Two Recent Metrical Systems." *Bib* 63:230-54.

Muilenburg, J.
1956   "The Book of Isaiah, Chapters 40–66." In *IB.* Vol. 5. New York:
            Abingdon.

1969   "Form Criticism and Beyond." *JBL* 88:1-18.

Oswalt, J.
1986   *The Book of Isaiah, Chapters 1–39.* NICOT. Grand Rapids: Eerdmans.

Raabe, P.
1990   *Psalm Structures: A Study of Psalms with Refrains.* JSOTSup 104.
            Sheffield: JSOT.

Seitz, C. R.
1991   *Zion's Final Destiny.* Minneapolis: Augsburg Fortress.

Sheppard, G.
1985   "The Anti-Assyrian Redaction and the Canonical Context of Isaiah
            1–39." *JBL* 104:193-216.

Stuart, D.
1976   *Studies in Early Hebrew Meter.* HSM 13. Missoula, MT: Scholars.
Sweeney, M.
1988   *Isaiah 1–4 and the Post-Exilic Understanding of the Isaianic Tradition.*
            BZAW 171. Berlin and New York: de Gruyter.
Vermeylen, J.
1977   *Du prophète Isaïe à l'apocalyptique.* Paris: Gabalda.
Watts, J.
1985   *Isaiah 1–33.* WBC. Waco: Word.
1987   *Isaiah 34–66.* WBC. Waco: Word.
Wiklander, B.
1984   *Prophecy as Literature: A Text-Linguistic and Rhetorical Approach to
            Isaiah 2–4.* Uppsala: Gleerup.
Wildberger, H.
1991   *Isaiah 1–12.* Trans. T. Trapp. Continental Commentary. Min-
            neapolis: Fortress. (Original: *Jesaja 1–12.* BKAT. Neukirchen-Vluyn:
            Neukirchener Verlag, 1965.)

Zephaniah's Oracle against the Nations and an Israelite Cultural Myth

ADELE BERLIN

University of Maryland, College Park

It is a pleasure to dedicate this paper to David Noel Freedman, who invited me to write a commentary on Zephaniah for the Anchor Bible series. This study is a small token of appreciation for the enormous effort that he has devoted to editing my work and the work of so many others.

Zephaniah's oracle against the nations, as 2:5-15[1] is usually called, is examined in the recent literature mainly from two vantage points. Form critics consider it as an example of the form or *Gattung* labeled "oracles against the nations" found in the prophetic literature; and historians mine it for a nugget of international history. Both of these approaches are legitimate and valuable; indeed, exegesis cannot proceed without them. Yet neither fully comes to terms with some peculiarities of terminology nor with the specific rhetorical impact of the pericope. While I cannot solve all of the problems in this passage, I will try to account, in a literary rather than a historical manner, for the selection of some nations and the omission of others, and for the use of several unusual terms in reference to the nations.

One has every reason to believe that behind this prophecy lay a contemporary geopolitical reality, for only then would it be meaningful in an immediate sense to Zephaniah's audience. Accepting the dating of the book to the early

---

1. Most form critics begin the pericope at 2:4. I follow the Masoretic tradition of beginning it at 2:5.

part of Josiah's reign, before his reforms (i.e., 640-622 B.C.E.), we know the general parameters of that reality — the decline of the Assyrian Empire. The details of this period are elusive because both biblical and extrabiblical sources for international history are scarce. The Mesopotamian sources have a gap from 639 (the last Assyrian document) to 626 (the beginning of the Babylonian Chronicle). While the Bible is not totally silent about the reign of Josiah, it says nothing concerning international events except to give notice that the king was killed in an encounter with the Egyptians.[2] So, while historians have pieced together a picture of the decline of Assyria, the growing influence of Egypt, the rise of Babylonia, and the activities of the smaller kingdoms, they are not in agreement on many details. The most important of them for this discussion are: When exactly did Assyria lose its hold on western Asia, especially Judah and its immediate neighbors? Did Egypt gain control of the Mediterranean coast by force or by a peaceful takeover condoned by Assyria? When did Egypt and Assyria become allies?

Zephaniah's oracle against the nations speaks against Philistia, Moab, and Ammon — all vassals of Assyria — and against Assyria itself. It does not mention Egypt, surely an important power; nor does it include Babylonia, which was perhaps not yet significant in Judean eyes. Likewise, it ignores Edom, another Assyrian vassal in close proximity to Ammon and Moab. Moreover, the "Cushites" are a puzzle. Thus, while Zephaniah's oracle fits the overall historical picture as we know it, it offers a highly selective view of the world, as a rhetorical piece is apt to do. The precise thrust of this oracle is not clear, but several hypotheses have been offered.

D. Christensen (1984) has argued that this oracle provides support for Josiah's program of political expansion, and that the particular nations listed are those whose territory Josiah wished to reclaim for Judah following his annexation of the northern provinces. Philistia to the west and Moab and Ammon to the east were the obstacles to Judah's territorial expansion in these directions. The taunts of Moab and Ammon in Zephaniah's oracle, according to Christensen, reflect the regained strength of these kingdoms (ca. 650-640), and their downfall suggests their weakening by Arab incursions and Josiah's expansion (ca. 628). "Cushites," in Christensen's view, alludes to the campaigns of Esarhaddon and Ashurbanipal against the Ethiopian dynasty (Dynasty XXV) in control of Egypt, which fell in 663. He interprets 2:12 as meaning that the Assyrians cannot take credit for their victory in Egypt, for it was God's doing. Likewise, the Assyrians themselves will be defeated when God so chooses. Assyr-

---

2. Na'aman (1991:41) observes that, contrary to the reality in which Judah was sub-jugated to Assyria for the first part of Josiah's reign and subordinate to Egypt during the latter part, the book of Kings describes Judah as free of Assyria after Sennacherib and not subject to Egypt until after Josiah's death. One of the purposes of this selective retelling of history was, according to Na'aman, to mask the fact that Josiah, the hero of the Deuteronomic History, was for most of his life not an independent ruler like David and Solomon.

ia was the major power in the area of Judah, and was in nominal control of the territories that Josiah wished to reclaim, although its control weakened noticeably from 627 until its demise in 612.

Although the scenario constructed by Christensen is perhaps plausible, his argument has too many flaws to make it convincing. First, there is no consensus on how much territory in the north Josiah was able to control;[3] moreover, it is strange, if this speech is advocating expansion, that it mentions nothing of gains in Samaria. Furthermore, there is no other convincing evidence that Josiah ever made a bid for lands in Philistia or Transjordan. Finally, the oracles against the nations of other prophets are not interpreted as advocating territorial expansion, and there is no good reason that this one should be.

As for Christensen's explanation of "Cushites," it seems odd to refer to an incident that occurred in 663, some thirty to forty years before this prophecy. Would this piece of "ancient history" that did not directly involve Judah really have been relevant to Zephaniah's audience?[4]

It seems better to interpret this prophecy, as R. Haak (1992) does, as a generally anti-Assyrian speech without reference to territorial expansion.[5] Assyria is the culmination of the speech, and Moab, Ammon, and the kingdoms that made up Philistia were all loyal vassals of Assyria. Zephaniah is speaking out against the great overlord Assyria and its vassals immediately adjacent to Judah. The most logical date for such a speech is, as Haak has suggested, after Assyria had begun to lose its grip and the threat of retaliation against such insurgency would have been minimal, and before Egypt became a strong presence. Haak dates it to 640-633; others would date it a few years later.[6] Whatever its precise date, the speech would help to revive and support Judean nationalism and stir up anti-Assyrian sentiment. Nationalism often has a "land" aspect, but it does not necessarily involve expansion. It is more a matter of promoting a sense of autonomy and national superiority.

One may thus adequately account for the historical background and the purpose of the speech, but a number of unexplained points remain: Who were the Cushites? Why were Egypt and Edom not mentioned? Why is the term "Canaan" used in reference to the Philistines? Why are Moab and Ammon compared to Sodom and Gomorrah? Who are the "islands of the nations"? The answers to these questions form a pattern that suggests that in addition to the historical considerations that influenced the formation of this pericope, there are traditional-cultural considerations. For meaningfulness does not reside in historical or political reality alone. Political events must be interpreted, must be seen as part of a larger picture, must be integrated into the ongoing story of

3. See Na'aman 1991 with previous literature.
4. But see n. 10 below for Ben Zvi's explanation.
5. I thank Prof. Haak for making his unpublished paper available to me.
6. Haak dates the Assyrian-Egyptian alliance to 633, and Zephaniah's oracle would have had to predate this event.

the nation. Zephaniah, I believe, does this by shaping this prophecy around an older mythopoetic theme. That theme has been preserved in literary form in Genesis 10, and it is Genesis 10, I will argue, that serves as the conceptual undergirding, and to a large extent the literary model, for Zeph 2:5-15. Zephaniah has taken the conventional genre *(Gattung)* of "prophecy against the nations," has tailored it to his own geopolitical reality, and has evoked an older traditional conception of the relationship among the nations of the world.

1. *Why is Philistia called "Canaan"?* (2:5). Canaan is the designation for the area in Palestine-Syria under Egyptian control during the fourteenth-thirteenth centuries B.C.E., and for the land promised to the Israelites in the Bible. Genesis 10:19 describes its western and eastern borders: "The Canaanite territory extended from Sidon in the direction of Gerar, as far as Gaza, and in the direction of Sodom, Gomorrah, Admah, and Zeboiim, as far as Lasha"; as does Num 13:29: "Canaanites dwell by the sea and along the Jordan." Canaan is the broader designation of which Philistia forms a part — cf. Josh 13:2-3: "all the districts of the Philistines and all the Geshurites . . . are accounted Canaanite."

But, although "Canaan" can be used to refer to Philistia, the term "Canaan" occurs rarely after the book of Judges. By and large it is used in accounts of the presettlement and settlement periods, in Genesis–Judges, and a few times in later literature when referring to this period. In Isa 23:11 and 2 Sam 24:7 it refers to Phoenicia, in 1 Kgs 9:16 to the inhabitants of Gezer, and in several other verses it means "merchants" (cf. Zeph 1:11). It is an archaic term and is never used during the monarchic period to refer to contemporary Philistines. Why, then, has Zephaniah used it here? Because, I suggest, Zephaniah wants his audience to make an association with something other than current cartography. Specifically, he wants to recall Gen 10:19 and the view that Philistia is part of Canaan.

2. *Moab shall be like Sodom, and the Ammonites like Gomorrah* (2:9). There are several good justifications for this simile. Sodom and Gomorrah represent catastrophic destruction (cf. Deut 29:22; Jer 49:18; 50:40), and Moab and Ammon are closely associated with Sodom and Gomorrah, not only because of geographic proximity but because Moab and Ammon came into existence, according to Gen 19:37-38, immediately following and as a result of the destruction of Sodom. In a sense, this equates Moab and Ammon with Sodom. These associations are sufficient, but yet another association, again with Gen 10:19, mentions Sodom and Gomorrah in connection with the eastern border of Canaan. Now Moab and Ammon were never part of Canaan, and they are not listed in Genesis 10; but the use of Sodom and Gomorrah both in Zeph 2:9 and in Gen 10:19, and the fact that Moab and Ammon are in some sense equated with Sodom, draw these countries into the orbit of Canaan. Moab and Ammon, apparently important enough on the contemporary scene, are made into a form of "eastern Canaanites."

3. *islands of the nations* (2:11). This is often viewed as a general designation for far-flung peoples (cf. Isa 42:10 and passim). But the precise expression "islands of the nations" occurs only here and in Gen 10:5, where it is an offshoot of the descendants of Japheth, the nations of Anatolia and the Aegean.[7] I understand the term to refer to the descendants of Japheth, with perhaps, if one seeks a more specific historical correlation, a nod to the Medes, Cimmerians, and Scythians (cf. Madai, Gomer, and Ashkenaz in Gen 10:2-3).[8] Thus the picture is not one of universal acknowledgment of the Lord but acknowledgment by the islands of the nations when they witness the Lord's judgment against Moab and Ammon.

4. *Cushites* (2:12). The use of the term is unexpected and the verse is terse and abrupt, with different syntax from the surrounding verses. There are five possible interpretations of "Cushites," none of them completely satisfying.

a. "Egypt." Most scholars translate *kûšîm* as "Ethiopians" and equate them with Egypt, as the two lands are geographically adjacent and sometimes occur in parallelisms. One should note, however, that while Cush occurs together with Egypt, it never stands in place of Egypt. Some scholars get around this point by explaining that "Cushites" refers to the Ethiopian pharaohs who had ruled Egypt before Psammetichus I. Others see here a reference to Ethiopians who served in the Egyptian army and who are mentioned in connection with the battle at Carchemish in 605 (Jer 46:8-9). All are bothered by the omission of Egypt — a major world power whose name would be expected in this list. But one wonders why the prophet did not simply come out and say "Egyptians" if that is what he meant. He was not reluctant to mention the other nations by name.

b. "Ethiopia" or "Nubia." I. J. Ball (1988:141) accepts the identification with Ethiopia proper (as opposed to Ethiopia as a substitute for Egypt). He suggests that the reference is to distant, exotic lands to the south that, like the islands of the nations (which he takes in the general sense of "all the lands of the nations"), will feel the power of the Lord.[9] Like others, Ball likes the geographic symmetry (west = Philistia, east = Moab and Ammon, south = Ethiopia, north = Assyria) that this interpretation provides.

c. "Midian," or "tribes to the south of Judah." Haak notes that "Cush" or "Cushan" may refer to Midian or another tribe in the area south of Judah (cf. Hab 3:7; Num 12:1; and perhaps 2 Chr 21:16; and see I. Eph'al 1982:78). This would mean that 2:12 is an afterthought tacked on to the fate of Moab and

---

7. See Oded 1986, esp. p. 29.

8. These peoples caused problems for the Assyrians in the north, along with the Medes. But the notion that a Scythian invasion reached Judah and prompted Zephaniah to deliver his warning against Assyria is not widely held today. See Na'aman 1991:36-37.

9. Ball raises the possibility that "Cushites" may refer to the Kassites, an interpretation that he applies to Zeph 3:10.

Ammon, mentioning another people in the general area. But Midian is not usually listed among the enemies of Judah at this time; it is rather Edom that one expects. Yet Edom is absent, and it stretches credulity to find in "Cushites" a reference to Edom.

d. "Tribes of the Arabian peninsula." Genesis 10:7 lists the "sons" of Cush, a reference to places located in northern (or perhaps southern) Arabia (see Eph'al 1982:227-29). But this seems the least relevant to Zephaniah.

e. "Mesopotamia," or, more specifically, "Assyria." The same Cush of Gen 10:7 is also the father of Nimrod, the builder of Assyria. I prefer this interpretation because in Zeph 3:10 there is an even stronger possibility that "Cush" refers to Mesopotamia, and because the order of some terms here — "Cushites" following "the islands of the nations" and then followed by "Asshur" and "Nineveh" — reinforces my feeling that this text alludes to Gen 10:5-11, where the same terms occur (along with some others) in the same order. Genesis 10:5 has "the islands of the nations." Then Gen 10:6 moves to the sons of Ham, the first of which is Cush. According to E. A. Speiser (1964:66), Cush is used to designate two widely separate lands: Ethiopia and the land of the Kassites (Akkadian *kuššu*; Greek *Kossaios*). Speiser interprets Gen 10:6 as the former; but 10:8, in which the genealogy of Cush culminates in the birth of Nimrod, who gave rise to the kingdoms of Mesopotamia whence came Asshur and Nineveh, refers to the latter. I assume that Zephaniah, not having read Speiser, did not distinguish the two meanings of "Cush." For him the brother of Egypt, Put, and Canaan, and the father of Nimrod were one and the same. In any case, all are descendants of Ham. In the context of Zeph 2:13-15, "Cushites," therefore, signifies not the military-political complex of Egypt but the descendants of the forebear of the Assyrian Empire.

5. *The absence of Egypt and Edom.*[10] Egypt was a major world power and Judah's neighbor, so it is strange, if Zephaniah intended a comprehensive view of the world, that Egypt is not mentioned here. Indeed, to most scholars its absence is unthinkable, and that is why they find it in the term "Cushites." But there is no reason that Zephaniah had to include every important nation. If he intended his words as an anti-Assyrian polemic, as seems the case, then there

---

10. Others have remarked on their omission. Ben Zvi's explanation (1991:298-306) is an interesting one, consistent with the postmonarchal dating that he assigns to the book. Since, according to Ben Zvi, the postmonarchal community saw Zephaniah's prophecy as having been fulfilled, they could include only nations that had indeed been destroyed. Philistia had been taken by Egypt and then by Babylonia, Moab and Ammon and Assyria by Babylonia. Cush had already been crushed in 664. But Egypt and Edom were not conquered by Babylonia, and so they would not have been included (even if they had appeared in an earlier version of this prophecy). This is a reasonable explanation if one accepts a late date for Zephaniah (which most scholars do not). My question is: What about the mention of Egypt and Edom in other prophecies of the late monarchy (Jeremiah 46; 49:7-22; Obadiah; Ezekiel 35)? Were not these read by the postmonarchal community in the same way? Why were Egypt and Edom not edited out of these?

is little need for Egypt, especially early in Josiah's reign, before Egypt gained control of Assyria's vassals in Philistia.[11] At this time an anti-Assyrian policy would not necessitate an anti-Egyptian policy (Haak) since Egypt's interest in Judah would have been minimal. Or perhaps, as H. Cazelles (1964) has suggested, Zephaniah may have been part of a pro-Egyptian party that had existed in Judah at various times in the late monarchy, from the times of Hezekiah to Zedekiah.[12]

As for Edom, which is often condemned along with Moab and Ammon (cf. Isa 11:14; Jer 9:25; 25:21; 49:7ff.; Amos 1:11), several observations explain its omission. (See Bartlett 1989 for the details of some of these.) Edom is most harshly viewed in the exilic and postexilic period (i.e., after the time of Zephaniah), and Deuteronomy, which seems to have influenced Zephaniah, treats Edom more gently than Moab and Ammon. From the historical point of view, Edom seems to have been somewhat less strongly attached to Assyria (it being further away) and was a growing presence in the Negev during the seventh and sixth centuries B.C.E. Judah and Edom had a commercial relationship, and the exact border between the two is unclear. But the most compelling reason for its omission in Zephaniah's oracle is that the Bible views Edom (= Esau) as a "brother" of Jacob. Edom is genealogically too close to Israel to be considered a son of Ham; and Zephaniah's prophecy is about the sons of Ham.

*   *   *   *   *

As I understand it, Zephaniah has presented a selective view of the world encompassing Assyria and its vassals bordering on Judah, and has envisioned these in terms of the Table of Nations. To do this the prophet had to choose from Genesis 10 the countries that were important to him — Philistia and Assyria — and omit others. He also had to add some that were not in Genesis 10, Moab and Ammon, which he made part of Canaan by playing on the connection with Sodom and Gomorrah. His prophecy is thus a prophecy against Canaan (Philistia, Moab, and Ammon) and Cush (Assyria). Both Canaan and Cush are sons of Ham.

Why did Zephaniah single out the descendants of Ham? What or whom do they represent in Genesis 10 and what is their relationship to the descendants of Shem? According to the analysis of B. Oded (1986), which I find compelling, the Table of Nations is ordered according to a sociocultural principle. The sons of Shem represent the nomadic or seminomadic peoples, often shepherds; the sons of Ham represent the urban, sedentary peoples, those residing in towns

---

11. Historians disagree whether Egypt fought to gain holdings from Assyria (the siege of Ashdod), or whether there was a peaceful takeover by Egypt when Assyria lost control. See Na'aman 1991 and Haak 1992.

12. Note, however, that Cazelles interprets "Cushites" as referring to Egypt.

or cities; and the sons of Japheth represent, by and large, the maritime peoples, residents of Anatolia and the Aegean, and also faraway nations, beyond the horizon of Shem and Ham. Oded goes on to discuss the natural antagonism between nomads and sedentary populations that anthropologists have studied and that is expressed in the antipathy between Ham and Shem (and Japheth) in Gen 9:25-27.

The imagery in Zephaniah correlates nicely with Oded's interpretation of Genesis 10. Notice, first, how Zephaniah stresses the urban character of Philistia and Nineveh, in contrast to the grazing lands and animal dens that they will become. The Philistine cities will be depleted of their residents and occupied by Judean shepherds. Nineveh, a city par excellence, will be home to flocks and wildlife. Even Moab and Ammon are compared to *cities* that were destroyed. It would be difficult to picture this area as lush grazing land, so this element is absent; but, as with the Philistines, Zephaniah has included the element of the subservience of Ham to Shem in that Israel will possess Moab and Ammon (cf. Jer 49:2).

One might demur that Zephaniah's images of destruction are quite ordinary. Certainly the prophet calls on convention in his portrayal of the destruction of these nations: abandonment and desolation, places unfit for human settlement, mocked by passersby. But when one compares Zephaniah's imagery with the imagery in other prophecies against the nations, one notices that the others minimize the pastoral element and include more images of violent destruction. Nahum pictures the violent ravaging of Nineveh, and the breakdown of its society and culture. In Amos the Lord will send down fire to devour the foreign enemies. Jeremiah, even in his extended descriptions of attack, destruction, exile, shame, and emptiness, does not mention the coming of other people's flocks into a destroyed land.

In Zephaniah's prophecy against the nations, images of war and violence are strikingly absent, especially in contrast to his images of the destruction of Judah. He stresses, rather, the aftermath of the destructive act — the reverting of these urban places to their preurbanized state. In this sense, chap. 2 is a sequel to chap. 1 in which the creation of the world is undone. But in a more specific sense, I find that, in a manner tailored to his needs, Zephaniah is calling on the perception of the world that informs Genesis 10. The "we" and "they" of this chapter are Shem and Ham. When "we, the shepherds" will triumph over "them, the city dwellers," their cities will fall and their land will become pastures for sheep. Zephaniah has taken the current geopolitical situation and couched it in the traditional enmity of Shem for Ham — that is, Israel for the Canaanites. Judah's immediate neighbors can easily be seen as "Canaanites." Assyria, too far removed to be part of Canaan and never in the realm of possessible land, is Canaan's brother, Cush.

Where is Japheth in this picture? The nations of Japheth were not of major political importance at this time, and so they are largely omitted from this scenario. But a hint of Japheth occurs in v. 11, in "the islands of the nations" (which occurs only here and in Gen 10:5). The islands of the nations are the descendants of the sons of Japheth. Among the sons of Japheth in Gen 10:2 are Gomer, identified with the Cimmerians, and Madai, the Medes; and one of the sons of Gomer is Ashkenaz, identified with the Scythians. Perhaps Zephaniah is making a veiled reference to these groups, and others like them, who figure in Assyrian history, sometimes as friends and sometimes as foes, beginning in the time of Esarhaddon. It is not clear if the Scythians actually penetrated as far as Judah, but they certainly wrought havoc in parts of the Assyrian Empire. According to Zeph 2:11, the islands of the nations will acknowledge and worship the Lord. They will not be destroyed like Philistia, the Transjordanian nations, and Assyria, probably because they are not perceived as enemies. They are simply "the distant islands that have not heard my name and not seen my glory" (Isa 66:19); but now they will come to know the power of God.

Zephaniah's prophecy against the nations, like other prophecies of this type, portrays a world in which Judah's current enemies will disappear (cf. chap. 3). In Zephaniah's case, the message becomes more compelling because the current political reality is set within the framework of an accepted myth. The contemporary political situation is made to look like a realization of the tradition of Gen 9:26-28: Canaan will become subservient to his brothers, and Japheth will reside in the tents of Shem.

Bibliography

Ball, I. J.
1988   *Zephaniah: A Rhetorical Study.* Berkeley: BIBAL.
Bartlett, J. R.
1989   *Edom and the Edomites.* JSOTSup 77. Sheffield: JSOT.
Ben Zvi, E.
1991   *A Historical-Critical Study of the Book of Zephaniah.* BZAW 198. Berlin and New York: de Gruyter.
Berlin, A.
1994   *Zephaniah.* AB. New York: Doubleday.
Cazelles, H.
1964   "Sophonie, Jeremie et les Scythes en Palestine." *RB* 74:24-44.
Christensen, D.
1984   "Zephaniah 2:4-15: A Theological Basis for Josiah's Program of Political Expansion." *CBQ* 46:669-82.
Eph'al, I.
1982   *The Ancient Arabs.* Jerusalem: Magnes; Leiden: Brill.

Haak, R.
    1992   "Zephaniah's Oracle against the Nations." Paper read at the Chicago Society of Biblical Research, 2 February, 1992.

Na'aman, N.
    1991   "The Kingdom of Judah under Josiah." *Tel Aviv* 18:3-71.

Oded, B.
    1986   "The Table of Nations (Genesis 10) — A Socio-cultural Approach." *ZAW* 98:14-31.

Speiser, E. A.
    1964   *Genesis.* 2nd ed. AB 1. Garden City, NY: Doubleday.

Who Knows What YHWH Will Do?
The Character of God in the Book of Joel

JAMES L. CRENSHAW

Duke University, Durham, North Carolina

The prophetic appeal for repentance in Joel 2:12-14 introduces a concept of deity incompatible with what has gone before. Nothing to this point supports the traditional attribution, which Joel may have derived from Exod 34:6 or any one of its many formulations,[1] that YHWH is "merciful and compassionate, patient and abundantly loyal." Such a confession flies in the face of reported facts: first, a devastating invasion by locusts[2] that consumed the vegetation and

---

1. The longer form of this confessional statement, Exod 34:6-7, probably belongs together despite arguments to the contrary by J. Scharbert, "Formgeschichte und Exegese von Ex 34,6f. und seiner Parallelen," *Bib* 38 (1957) 130-50. Its unity is defended by R. C. Dentan, "The Literary Affinities of Exodus XXXIV 6f," *VT* 13 (1963) 34-41. Chastened Israelites had little inclination during prayer and praise to remind the deity of the negative attributes recorded in v. 7, hence later divine predications invariably concentrate on YHWH's compassionate nature, on which see P. Trible, *God and the Rhetoric of Sexuality* (OBT; Philadelphia: Fortress, 1978) 1-5; L. Schmidt, *"De Deo": Studien zur Literarkritik und Theologie des Buches Jona, des Gesprächs zwischen Abraham und Jahve in Gen. 18, 22ff. und von Hi 1* (BZAW 143; Berlin and New York: de Gruyter, 1976) 90-96; G. Vanoni, *Das Buch Jona* (St. Ottilien: Eos, 1978) 139-41; D. N. Freedman, "God Compassionate and Gracious," *Western Watch* 6 (1955) 6-24; T. B. Dozeman, "Inner-Biblical Interpretation of Yahweh's Gracious and Compassionate Character," *JBL* (1989) 207-23; and above all, M. Fishbane, *Biblical Interpretation in Ancient Israel* (Oxford: Clarendon, 1985) 335-50 for a more nuanced view.

2. Considerable light has been shed on locust infestation in ancient Israel by J. A. Thompson, "Joel's Locusts in the Light of Near Eastern Parallels," *JNES* 14 (1955) 52-55; and R. Simkins, *Yahweh's Activity in History and Nature in the Book of Joel* (Ancient Near Eastern Texts and Studies 10; Lewiston et al.: Mellen, 1991). Popular fascination with this insect is beautifully illustrated by A. Taylor, "A Riddle for a Locust," in *Semitic and Oriental Studies:*

threatened the survival of people and animals; second, the ominous nearness of the day of YHWH.[3] Both threats directed against the Judean populace originated in its own deity, whose fury freely poured itself out. How then dare the prophet appeal to the very one bent on punishing his possession? What if Judah, like Job, is innocent of any wrongdoing? I propose to entertain the possibility that modern scholars have joined the ranks of Job's friends in being too quick to associate calamity with guilt in the book of Joel.[4] The ambiguity lies instead in the divine character as perceived by persons who attributed all events to divine causation.[5]

A Volume Presented to William Popper (ed. W. J. Fischel; University of California Publications in Semitic Philology 11; Berkeley: University of California, 1951) 429-32.

3. J. Bourke ("Le jour de Yahwe dans Joël," *RB* 66 [1959] 5-31, 191-212) concludes his exhaustive examination of the day of YHWH by isolating three principal themes in Joel (the day of YHWH combined with an army from afar, destruction and restoration of fertility, and an eschatological era) and three lines of tradition (the day of YHWH, the Deuteronomic school, and exilic and postexilic eschatology). In quite a different vein, F. E. Deist ("Parallels and Reinterpretation in the Book of Joel: A Theology of the Yom Yahweh," in *Text and Context: Old Testament and Semitic Studies for F. C. Fensham* [ed. W. Claassen; JSOTSup 48; Sheffield: JSOT, 1988] 63-79) understands the locusts and drought as purely literary metaphors for the horrors inaugurated by the day of YHWH. Deist thinks the book of Joel has three or four interpretations of the day (anti-Canaanite [?], theophanic and judgmental, eschatological, and apocalyptic). Y. Hoffmann ("The Day of the Lord as a Concept and a Term in the Prophetic Literature," *ZAW* 93 [1981] 37-50) limits the expression to an eschatological sense (cf. K.-D. Schunck, "Strukturlinien in der Entwicklung der Vorstellung vom 'Tag Jahwes,'" *VT* 14 [1964] 319-30), thus rejecting the wide basis for analysis adopted by G. von Rad, "The Origin of the Concept of the Day of Yahweh," *JSS* 4 (1959) 97-108; M. Weiss, "The Origin of the Day of Yahweh, Reconsidered," *HUCA* 37 (1966) 29-72; and A. J. Everson, "The Days of Yahweh," *JBL* 93 (1974) 329-37.

4. D. W. Cotter's remark about Eliphaz's initial speech also applies to Bildad and Zophar ("There is, in fact, no word of sympathy in the whole poem. What there is is a succession of sixteen verbal punches, sixteen 'your's' as Eliphaz relentlessly separates himself from the sufferer"; *A Study of Job 4–5 in the Light of Contemporary Literary Theory* [SBLDS 124; Atlanta: Scholars, 1992] 239). The possibility that Job may be the object of parody or satire has been advanced by B. Zuckerman (*Job the Silent* [New York: Oxford University, 1991]) and K. J. Dell (*The Book of Job as Sceptical Literature* [BZAW 197; Berlin and New York: de Gruyter, 1991]), whose history of interpretation of Job complements that by N. N. Glatzer ("The Book of Job and its Interpreters," in *Biblical Motifs* [ed. A. Altmann; P. W. Lown Institute of Advanced Judaic Studies, Studies and Texts 3; Cambridge: Harvard University, 1966] 197-220).

5. The exclusive emphasis on YHWH's control of historical events has receded in more recent studies, beginning with B. Albrektson, *History and the Gods* (ConBOT 1; Lund: Gleerup, 1967) and chronicled in R. Gnuse, *Heilsgeschichte as a Model for Biblical Theology* (College Theological Society Studies in Religion 4 [Lanham, New York, and London: University Press of America, 1989]). T. N. D. Mettinger (*In Search of God* [Philadelphia: Fortress, 1988] 175-200) brings this research into the realm of sapiential studies, on which see L. Boström, *The God of the Sages* (ConBOT 29; Stockholm: Almqvist & Wiksell International, 1990), and J. L. Crenshaw, "The Concept of God in Old Testament Wisdom," 3-18 in *In Search of Wisdom: Essays in Memory of John G. Gammie* (ed. L. G. Perdue, B. B. Scott, and W. J. Wiseman [Louisville, KY: Westminster/John Knox, 1993]).

The text of Joel's appeal for immediate turning is unproblematic.

But even now — a divine oracle — return to me with your whole mind, with fasting, weeping, and mourning. Rend your inner disposition and not just your clothes, then return to YHWH your God; for merciful and compassionate is he, patient and abundantly loyal, repenting about punishment. Perhaps he will turn and relent, leaving a blessing in his wake, a cereal offering and libation for YHWH your God (Joel 2:12-14).

The adversative *wĕgam ʿattâ*[6] acknowledges the lateness of the hour and radical boldness, like its use in Job 16:19a (*gam ʿattâ hinnēh baššāmayim ʿēdî*, "look, even now my witness is in heaven").[7] In each instance multiple signs pointed to the opposite conclusion; Judeans were buffeted by want and awesome portents of more to come, and Job bore the brunt of unsubstantiated charges of misconduct.[8] Whereas the poet has Job shift the point of view heavenward by means of the particle *hinnēh*,[9] Joel calls on a prophetic oracular formula, *nĕʾum-YHWH*, for this purpose.[10] The appeal to turn toward YHWH thus receives the highest possible legitimation,[11] one originating in the deity who for the moment is bent on destruction.

The unique occurrence of this expression in Joel indicates that the prophet

---

6. See E. Sellin, *Das Zwölfprophetenbuch* (KAT 12/1; Leipzig: A. Deichertsche . . . D. Werner Schoff, 1929); H. W. Wolff, *Joel and Amos* (trans. W. Janzen et al.; Hermeneia; Philadelphia: Fortress, 1977) 48; and H. A. Brongers, "Bemerken zum Gebrauch des adverbialen *wᵉʿattāh* im Alten Testament," *VT* 15 (1965) 289-99.

7. Despite the difficulty presented by this extraordinary statement and laid out clearly by E. M. Good, *In Turns of Tempest* (Stanford: Stanford University, 1990) 248-50, one can make reasonable sense of it as a figure parallel to the Advocate, one who will "stir God to perform his *opus proprium*" (N. Habel, *The Book of Job* [OTL; Philadelphia: Westminster, 1985] 275). This view avoids the common interpretation of a schizophrenic deity and the alternative understanding of the witness as a rival tutelary deity. In this unknown witness Job hopes to find a mediator who will vouch for him in Eloah's presence.

8. With the addition of *biśpātāyw* ("with his lips") to the narrator's denial that Job had sinned (2:10; cf. 1:22), the floodgates open wide for accusing him of rash thoughts "in the heart," as ancient interpreters quickly recognized. J. T. Wilcox (*The Bitterness of Job* [Ann Arbor: University of Michigan, 1989]) continues that tradition, now in a philosophical vein. In his view, Job cursed God by means of moral bitterness, being both ignorant and weak, and was reminded of nature's grandeur devoid of morality. This profoundly skeptical reading of the biblical book is marred by special pleading about weakened authorial powers whenever a text presents difficulty for Wilcox's thesis, a weakness not afflicting a similar denial of justice in the world by M. Tsevat, "The Meaning of the Book of Job," *HUCA* 37 (1966) 73-106.

9. J. Fokkelman (*Narrative Art in Genesis* [Assen and Amsterdam: Van Gorcum, 1975] 50-51) recognizes that *hinnēh* often marks a shift in narrative point of view from third-person omniscience to that of the person involved in the story.

10. See F. Baumgärtel, "Die Formel neʾum Jahwe," *ZAW* 73 (1961) 277-90; and D. Vetter, "neʾum Ausspruch," *THAT* 2.2-3.

11. Unless an omniscient narrator is viewed as having the last word in any written text.

did not wish to weaken its impact through indiscriminate use, unlike the prophets Haggai and Zechariah, who peppered their speech with *nĕ'um-YHWH* [*ṣĕbā'ôt*] and *kōh 'āmar YHWH ṣĕbā'ôt*.[12] In this respect Joel resembles Hosea, who found little use[13] for oracular formulae that mark prophetic utterance generally, except for the book of Habakkuk, where its literary form excluded such expressions.[14] The only other kindred feature in Joel is *kî YHWH dibbēr* in 4:8b, where the suggestion of divine authority reinforces an implausible promise that Judeans who were once sold into slavery will return to their native land and that their captors will assume the role of slaves in an unaccustomed environment. The suggestion that *wĕgam 'attâ nĕ'um-YHWH* is a nominative sentence with an implicit predicate adjective ("but even now YHWH's word is valid")[15] does not take sufficiently into account the *waw* copulative on the verb *šûb*.[16]

This verb does not necessarily imply present guilt, although it frequently appears in contexts emphasizing habitual transgression as in Amos's liturgy of wasted opportunity using the refrain *wĕlō'-šabtem 'āday nĕ'um-YHWH* ("Still you did not return to me, says YHWH").[17] Deutero-Isaiah invites a pardoned nation to turn to its redeemer (*māḥîtî kā'āb pešā'eykā wĕke'ānān ḥaṭṭō'teykā šûbâ 'ēlay kî gĕ'altîkā*, "I have obliterated your transgressions like a cloud and your sins like mist; turn unto me, for I have redeemed you," 44:22). The slate has been wiped clean and YHWH initiates a new relationship, for the guilt has been assuaged by excessive suffering, according to an earlier comment (40:2). In times of trouble, whether deserved or undeserved, turning to YHWH was the appropriate response inasmuch as he alone could remove the adversity. Joel's invitation therefore does not necessarily impute guilt to the unfortunate victims of circumstance. Perhaps the prophet's silence on this issue registers his own

12. On these prophets see C. L. and E. M. Meyers, *Haggai, Zechariah 1–8* (AB 25B; Garden City, NY: Doubleday, 1987); and D. L. Petersen, *Haggai and Zechariah 1–8* (OTL; Philadelphia: Westminster, 1984).

13. Two of the three occurrences of *nĕ'um-YHWH* (2:16, 21) are in a section often denied to Hosea on other grounds: the reversal of the prophet's judgment on the nation, Israel. The other one is in 11:11, also a text indicating a date after YHWH's people had been driven into foreign lands.

14. Dialogue between a prophet and the deity, on the one hand, and hymnic praise, on the other hand.

15. See Wolff, *Joel and Amos*, 48; W. Rudolph, *Joel-Amos-Obadja-Jona* (KAT 13/2; Gütersloh: Mohn, 1971) 50.

16. See W. S. Prinsloo, *The Theology of the Book of Joel* (BZAW 163; Berlin and New York: de Gruyter, 1985) 50.

17. See J. L. Crenshaw, "A Liturgy of Wasted Opportunity: Am. 4:6-12; Isa 9:7–10:4," *Semitics* 1 (1971) 27-37. Lexical analysis of the verb *šûb* has been provided by W. L. Holladay, *The Root šûbh in the Old Testament* (Leiden: Brill, 1958), and a survey of research appears in J. M. Bracke, "*šûb šebût*: A Reappraisal," *ZAW* 97 (1985) 233-44. H. W. Wolff ("Das Theme 'Umkehr' in der alttestamentliche Prophetie," *ZTK* 49 [1951] 129-48) treats the general concept of returning, as does T. M. Raitt ("The Prophetic Summons to Repentance," *ZAW* 83 [1971] 30-49).

inability to pinpoint any culpability on the part of the Judeans commensurate with their misery.

Hoping to fill the void left by Joel's silence, modern critics have been less hesitant than he. The charges against his contemporaries range from syncretistic worship[18] to hubris,[19] from emphasis on external ritual[20] to abdication of leadership,[21] from breach of covenant[22] to unwillingness to become identified with an impotent deity.[23] Naturally, any evidence supporting a particular version of Judah's guilt is deduced from what Joel says — or refrains from saying. The arguments from silence run something like this: (1) Joel's formulation of the invitation, "return to me," implies that the people were currently following after another deity; (2) the internalization of sorrow suggested by "rend your hearts" indicates pride that has not brought on genuine remorse; (3) the same expression in juxtaposition with ritualistic acts belies confidence in the efficacy of external behavior; (4) the necessity of commanding priests to mourn and intercede points to a failed leadership; (5) the calamity that has struck the covenant community demonstrates guilt, for the ancient treaty promised prosperity for faithfulness and adversity for breaking the conditions laid down at its ratification; and (6) mockery of the Judeans by foreigners issued in shame, which may even have driven YHWH's inheritance to another deity. Such unsubstantiated charges testify to the power exercised by a calculating morality and obscure the ambiguity of human existence that gave rise to a perceived ambiguity within the divine character.

18. G. W. Ahlström (*Joel and the Temple Cult of Jerusalem* [VTSup 21; Leiden: Brill, 1971] 26) argues from Joel's use of the stronger preposition ʿāday rather than ʾēlay that the people have turned to worshiping other gods.

19. Wolff (*Joel and Amos*, 48-53) locates the fault in the people's reliance on the fact that they were YHWH's inheritance, which seemed in their minds to guarantee divine favor. In Wolff's view, the issue is one of God's freedom, which Joel zealously guards.

20. See G. Wanke, "Prophecy and Psalms in the Persian Period," in *The Cambridge History of Judaism* (ed. W. D. Davies and L. Finkelstein; Cambridge: Cambridge University, 1984) 177. Wanke writes that "the only suggestion of a criticism of the people of Jerusalem may be contained in 2:12f, where too intensive an orientation toward external ritual can dimly be perceived as a cause for lament."

21. P. L. Redditt ("The Book of Joel and Peripheral Prophecy," *CBQ* 48 [1986] 225-40) claims that Joel's accusations against cultic leaders eventually pushed him and his followers to the periphery of society, thus limiting his effectiveness appreciably. The category of peripheral, as opposed to central, prophecy informs R. R. Wilson's study of biblical prophecy, *Prophecy and Society in Ancient Israel* (Philadelphia: Fortress, 1980).

22. See L. C. Allen, *The Books of Joel, Obadiah, Jonah and Micah* (NICOT; Grand Rapids: Eerdmans, 1976) 77-84. Although he observes that the covenant people have "evidently strayed from their Shepherd, turning to their own way," Allen also writes that "it is evidently left to the people and priests to search their own hearts and habits for evidence of the sin that God's reaction proved to be there" (78-79). In Allen's view, Joel's interpretation of the locust plague presupposes serious sin, but he fails to use the normal place in the rhetoric of v. 12 to mention the people's sin.

23. Simkins, *Yahweh's Activity*, 181-90.

The invitation attributed to YHWH displays no hint of displeasure with public ritual. To be sure, a resolute mind must precede the external manifestations of a more traditional kind. Affinities with Deuteronomy enable Joel to bring together the cognitive and affective dimensions of existence. According to Deut 4:30-31 dire circumstances will cause YHWH's people to return to him who is *rahûm*,[24] and 30:2 reports that Israel will return with all its mind and being *(wěšabtā 'ad-YHWH 'ĕlōheykā . . . běkol-lěbābkā ûběkol-napšekā)*. The compassion promised in 30:3 *(wěrihămekā)* by the same one enforcing the threats associated with the covenant resembles Joel's guarded optimism.

The triple manifestation of wholehearted remorse occurs elsewhere only in Esth 4:3 *(wěṣôm ûběkî ûmispēd,* "fasting, weeping, and mourning"), although Joel's fourfold use of the preposition *bě* contrasts markedly with the language there. The emphasis on external ritual proves that Joel values visible expressions of an inner state.[25] Various texts from the postexilic period attest to uncertainty about the status of fasting, for example, whether over worthy causes like the fall of Jerusalem and the murder of Gedaliah (Zech 7:3, 5)[26] or at the expense of good deeds (Isa 58:3-9). Both texts underline the self-interest of persons resorting to fasting and urge altruistic actions as something YHWH approves. The story about David's prayer for his sick child shows that the combination of fasting and tears, even when arising from genuine remorse, did not always result in the desired response (2 Sam 12:15b-23),[27] although it sometimes did (cf. 2 Chr 30:9b, *kî-hannûn wěrahûm YHWH 'ĕlōhêkem wělō'-yāsîr pānîm mikkem 'im-tāšûbû 'ēlāyw,* "for YHWH your God is gracious and compassionate

24. H. J. Stoebe, "*rhm* pi. sich erbarmen," *THAT* 2.762-68.

25. The inner attitude is matched by word and deed, the heart and tongue being motivated by turning to YHWH. According to T. Collins, "The Physiology of Tears in the Old Testament," *CBQ* 33 (1971) 18-38, 185-97, *bkh* ("weeping") comes from the mouth and voice, whereas *dm'* ("shedding tears") originates in the eyes (see also V. Hamp, "*bāka,*" *TDOT* 2.116-20, esp. 117). The verb *bākâ* is therefore often connected with the voice, *qōl*. Although YHWH may become angry *(k's)* and grieve *('ṣb),* he is never described as weeping. Hamp has observed that "collective penitent weeping is typically biblical, and is just as foreign to Greek texts of lamentation as is the weeping of imploring and hoping in prayer" (119).

26. The prophet uses four different verbs for weeping and fasting, *bkh* and *nzr* in 7:3, *ṣwm* and *spd* in 7:5. The combination of second person plural and infinitive absolute in 7:5 *(ṣamtem wěsāpôd)* stresses interrelatedness and intensity, providing an absolute contrast with v. 6 (Meyers, *Haggai and Zechariah 1–8,* 388).

27. Nor did such unconventional behavior by a monarch bring about a change in custom. G. A. Anderson (*A Time to Mourn, A Time to Dance* [University Park, PA: Pennsylvania State University, 1991] 2) emphasizes the performative elements of such epiphenomena as constitutive rather than ornamental. Accordingly, he understands expressions of grief and joy as creators of emotion instead of the other way around, the grief producing signs of sorrow. In this regard he follows C. Geertz, who views religion as a powerful symbolic system that produces corresponding moods and motivations. In short, religions shape reality (5-9). On this reading, when David's penitential rite failed to produce the desired result, he naturally brought it to an end and resumed ordinary activities, particularly sexual joy (83-84).

and will not look away from you if you turn to him").[28] A rare comment in Mal 3:6a attributes constancy to YHWH (*kî 'ănî YHWH lō' šānîtî*, "for I YHWH have not changed"), at the same time that the next verse promises reciprocal turning (*šûbû 'ēlay wĕ'āšûbâ 'ălêkem*, "return to me and I will turn to you").

The change in speakers apparent from third person address of the deity in v. 13 seems to be a feature of a prophetic tendency to merge the identities of a messenger and the one commissioning the spokesperson.[29] The *waw* links the divine imperative and its human exposition. Joel's adoption of symbolic language (*wĕqir'û lĕbabkem*, "and rend your heart") follows ancient precedent recorded in Deut 10:16 and Jer 4:4 for circumcising the foreskin of the heart.[30] In the light of the threefold expression of distress mentioned in YHWH's oracle, Joel's additional remark, *wĕ'al-bigdêkem*, should be rendered, "and not just your garments." The shift from *'ad* to *'el* (*'āday* in v. 12, *'el-YHWH 'ĕlohêkem* in v. 13) also marks a shift in person from first to third and prepares the way for a doxological attribution.

The search for the source of this confessional statement has led to Exod 34:6,[31] although Joel's version differs appreciably from the full expression of YHWH's nature in vv. 6-7. Indeed, the sequence *ḥannûn wĕraḥum* accords with that in Exod 33:19, but not the verbal form.[32] Moreover, Joel mentions neither

---

28. The story in 2 Kgs 20:1-11 interprets a reprieve in Hezekiah's illness as YHWH's favorable response to a tearful king who was able to call to divine memory a life characterized by faithfulness (*zĕkār-nā' 'ēt 'ăšer hithallaktî lĕpāneykā be'ĕmet ûbĕlēbāb šālēm*, "remember that I have walked before you faithfully and with an undivided mind"). The shift from the verb *bkh* in v. 3 to *dm'* in v. 5 may focus attention on the total act of grief (*wayyēbĕkĕ ḥizqîyāhû bĕkî gādôl . . . rā'îtî 'et-dim'ātekā*, "Hezekiah wept mightily. . . . I have seen your tears").

29. A similar ambiguity marks the text in Exod 34:6, which can be translated as a proclamation by YHWH or by Moses. The Masoretic accentuation favors Moses as speaker: *wayya'ăbōr YHWH 'al-pānāyw wayyiqrā' YHWH YHWH 'ēl raḥûm wĕḥannûn* ("YHWH passed by him and he called out, 'YHWH, YHWH, a compassionate and gracious God"). One can ignore the conjunctive accent linking the two instances of the divine name and the disjunctive accent on the verb *qr'*, yielding "YHWH passed by him and YHWH called out, 'YHWH, a compassionate and gracious God.'" The shorter version in Num 14:17-18 attributes the proclamation to the deity. On the divided views of modern scholars over the translation of Exod 34:6 see B. S. Childs, *The Book of Exodus* (OTL; Philadelphia: Westminster, 1974) 603-4.

30. The larger context of this metaphor for inner transformation includes YHWH's invitation for the people to turn away from inappropriate conduct (*'im-tāšûb yiśrā'ēl nĕ'um YHWH 'ēlay tāšûb*, "If you want to return, Israel, return to me," Jer 4:1a).

31. Dozeman ("Inner-Biblical Interpretation") argues that both Joel and Jonah offer conscious commentary on the implications of the covenant formulary, with completely opposite emphases. Whereas Joel concerns himself with showing how the divine attributes furnish a basis for belief in the eventual elevation of Judeans at the expense of the nations, the book of Jonah includes the worst foreign nation, Assyria, as an object of YHWH's gracious pity.

32. Joel has *kî-ḥannûn wĕraḥûm hû'*, but first person speech characterizes Exod 33:19 (*wĕḥannōtî 'et-'ăšer 'āḥōn wĕriḥamtî 'et-'ăšer 'ăraḥēm*, "I shall be gracious toward whom I wish to favor and I shall have compassion on whom I desire to be compassionate").

wě'emet nor a single attribute from v. 7. Even the four attributes in common appear in entirely different syntax,[33] and a novel element concludes Joel's statement: *wěniham 'al-hārā'â* ("and repents of evil"). For this expression in connection with the other four attributes from Joel 2:13 one must look to Jonah 4:2, the only difference being the direct address *'attâ-'ēl* ("you, God"). This affinity between the two texts becomes all the more striking when one compares the next verse in Joel, *mî yôdēa' yāšûb wěniham* with Jonah 3:9, which is exactly the same except for the addition of *hā'ělōhîm*.[34]

Does Joel cite these texts from Exodus and Jonah? Some remarkable correspondences between the text of Joel and the covenant formulary in Exodus 32–34 cannot be denied: the words *běrākâ* (32:29), *nôrā'* (34:10), the reference to mockery (32:12), and the acknowledgment that YHWH changed his mind about evil (32:14).[35] Decisive differences in the context and function of these affinities suggest caution, for the blessing results from priestly slaughter of idolatrous Israelites and the mockery has God as object rather than Judeans as in Joel 2:17. Although Joel may indeed draw on the memory of the traditional account of the exodus for language about the locust plague and its unprecedented nature, that is quite different from saying that he consciously reinterprets Scripture.

That a few expressions in the book of Joel can be identified elsewhere in the canon does not make him a compiler of anthologies.[36] No single text that he shares in common with another prophet can be shown to derive from a written source, for they belong to the religious vocabulary of ancient Israel and

33. *YHWH YHWH 'ēl raḥûm wěḥannûn 'erek 'appayim wěrab-ḥesed we'ěmet* (Exod 34:6) and *kî-ḥannûn wěraḥûm hû' 'erek 'appayim wěrab-ḥesed* (Joel 2:13bβ).

34. J. Magonet (*Form and Meaning: Studies in Literary Techniques in the Book of Jonah* [Bible and Literature; Sheffield: Almond, 1983] 77) writes that "the coincidence of two such phrases, so clearly interrelated in each case, in such similar contexts (last opportunity for repentance before destruction comes), without some sort of mutual interrelationship is unlikely." He attributes priority to Jonah, who earlier had combined Exod 32:12 and 34:6. J. Sasson (*Jonah* [AB 24B; New York: Doubleday, 1990] 280-83) improves on Vanoni's chart of every formulation of the divine attributes; in doing so Sasson makes many astute observations about distinctive features and traits held in common among several of the seventeen texts he studies, for which he has twelve different columns.

35. Dozeman ("Inner-Biblical Interpretation," 221-23) overlooks the expression *běrākâ* while concentrating on the vocabulary for awesome deeds and the idea of mockery.

36. S. Bergler (*Joel als Schriftinterpret* [Beiträge zur Erforschung des Alten Testaments und des antiken Judentums 16; Frankfurt-am-Main et al.: Peter Lang, 1988]) gives an exhaustive analysis of linguistic affinities between Joel and the rest of the Hebrew Bible. I cannot accept Bergler's assumptions about literary dependence, given the limited evidence and difficulty of establishing priority. Dozeman ("Inner-Biblical Interpretation," 207-9) thinks of Joel as a person who gathers allusions from a canon of sorts and arranges them into an anthology. The difficulty of demonstrating this hypothesis explains scholars' cool response to A. Robert's earlier efforts to apply such an approach to the Bible ("Littéraires, Genres," *DBSup* 5.405-21).

Judah. Even when Joel uses an expression that occurs in another prophetic book, he often gives it a peculiar stamp, even turning on its head the old tradition about beating one's swords into plowtips and spears into pruning hooks (4:10 [ET 3:10]). One need not assume that the prophet sat down and pored over written texts of his predecessors, gleaning useful citations and priding himself on the astute manner in which he couched inner-biblical allusions. In my judgment the bookish direction of much contemporary research[37] conceals a fundamental assumption that ancient Israelites had ready access to written Scripture. That is, in my judgment, highly unlikely.[38] Instead, much religious teaching was transmitted orally, and this spoken word is the probable source of Joel's language that occasionally coincides with something another prophet or psalmist also happened to say. The average person today who says "I have a dream" has never read Martin Luther King, Jr.'s speech, for that statement has become part of normal discourse in the same way quotations from Shakespeare have entered our daily conversation.

The addition of "psalmist" in the sentence above draws attention to religious language that probably informed the thinking of many leaders. Not surprisingly, the ancient doxology came to expression in various combinations within the Psalter and in similar confessional prayer (e.g., Pss 86:15; 103:8; 111:4; 112:4; 145:8; Neh 9:17, 31).[39] Occasionally, additional attributes found their way into the confession, particularly *ṣaddîq* (Ps 112:4),[40] perhaps an acknowledgment that divine mercy was balanced by justice as in Exod 34:6-7. The sole instance of a vindictive application of an attribute from the confession, *'erek 'appayim*, occurs in Nah 1:3 with Nineveh as the unfortunate object of divine zeal, although Jonah uses a longer formulation to accuse YHWH of injustice. The struggle between those who emphasized divine compassion and

37. Fishbane's *Biblical Interpretation in Ancient Israel* demonstrates the immense possibilities inherent to such an approach, but I am left with the suspicion that word choice in ancient Israel was often less dictated by intimate knowledge of written texts than by the accidents of religious language during a given era or geographical location. Can one really imagine such scribal activity occurring in preexilic or even exilic times? The real value of Fishbane's synthesis of texts is the brilliant demonstration of the vitality of religious tradition and richness of the ancient imagination.

38. I have described the ancient intellectual endeavor in an essay entitled "The Contemplative Life," scheduled to appear in a two-volume work on *Civilizations of the Ancient Near East*, ed. J. M. Sasson, to be published by Scribners.

39. Fishbane (*Biblical Interpretation*, 349-50) extends the psalmic petitionary use of the attribute formulary to Mic 7:18-20. Fishbane calls it "an expression of gratitude which concludes a larger liturgical structure of lament, confession, and assurance of divine grace." The only similarities between this prophetic text and the other attributions discussed above are the name *'ēl*, the nouns *ḥesed* and *'ĕmet*, and the verb *rḥm*.

40. This adjective frequently conveys a forensic assessment of innocence on all charges. In Jer 12:1 the prophet concedes YHWH's innocence as a general principle before calling it into question in his special case (Jer 12:1a, *ṣaddîq 'attâ YHWH kî 'ārîb 'ēleykā*, "You are innocent, YHWH, when I bring an accusation against you").

others who stressed YHWH's justice has left its trail in the Bible, demonstrating both the tenacity of tradition and the versatility of its transmitters.[41]

Perhaps that controversy explains Joel's rhetorical question in the wake of a confession of YHWH's readiness to shower kindness on those who turn to him. Divine freedom must also be affirmed. Hence the open-ended question, in itself an assertion: "Who knows whether he will turn and relent, leaving a blessing behind, cereal offering and libation for YHWH your God?" In short, no one knows how the deity will react, as the few uses of *mî yôdēaʿ* in the Bible demonstrate (2 Sam 12:22; Joel 2:14; Jonah 3:9; Ps 90:11; Qoh 2:19; 3:21; 8:1; Esth 4:14).[42] Joel's use of the adverb *ʾaḥărāyw* echoes his earlier reference to scarred fields left behind by locusts (2:3) and provides an effective contrast between YHWH's previous conduct and that following the people's turning.

The threefold use of the verb *šûb* in these three verses, spoken once by YHWH and twice by the prophet, each with a different referent, is matched by two uses of the verb *niḥam*, both with reference to YHWH. Their essential meaning in 2:14 may be clarified by Exod 32:12: *šûb mēḥărôn ʾappekā wĕhinnāḥem ʿal-hārāʿâ lĕʿammekā* ("turn from your intense fury and repent concerning the harm [planned] for your people"). The result of such turning will be prosperity,[43] here signified *pars pro toto* by cereal offering and libation, a well-being that also benefits YHWH, as the awkward *laYHWH ʾĕlōhêkem* concedes.

This interrelationship between the well-being of the people and their deity energizes the language of a shorter version of the old confession, Num 14:18. Here Moses persuades YHWH to forgive his people lest Egyptians conclude that he lacked power to bring them safely into the land of promise.[44] As further incentive Moses reminds YHWH of his own self-description: *YHWH ʾerek ʾappayim wĕrab-ḥesed nōśēʾ ʿāwōn wāpāšaʿ wĕnaqqēh lōʾ yĕnaqqeh pōqēd ʿāwōn*

---

41. The inevitable tension between justice and mercy, works and faith, law and gospel, human initiative and divine grace has invigorated Judeo-Christian theological discourse for over three millennia. Religious thinkers have emphasized one or other of the concepts, depending on the circumstances at the moment. A chastened people has sensed the need for the scales to tilt in favor of YHWH's mercy, and a proud, complacent religious community has generally evoked sterner descriptions of God from its spiritual leaders.

42. I have examined these texts in "The Expression *mî yôdēaʿ* in the Hebrew Bible," *VT* 36 (1986) 274-88.

43. Note the binary categories here, *hārāʿâ* in Joel 2:13 and *bĕrākâ* in the next verse. The macrostructure of the first two chapters exemplifies such binary thinking, for the restoration in Joel 2:18-27 matches in detail the things adversely affected by the invasion of locusts and accompanying drought.

44. Simkins (*Yahweh's Activity*, 184-90) emphasizes the Mediterranean concepts of honor and shame as crucial to understanding the impact of mockery in the book of Joel. The taunt "Where is their God?" (2:17) brought dishonor to Judeans and their deity, who alone could remove their shame forever (2:26-27) and restore their former honorable status. See also M. A. Klopfenstein, *Scham und Schande nach dem Alten Testament* (ATANT 62; Zurich: Theologischer Verlag, 1972).

'ābôt 'al-bānîm 'al-šilleĕšîm wĕ'al-ribbē'îm ("YHWH patient and abundantly loyal, forgiving iniquity and sin, but by no means clearing the guilty, visiting the iniquity of parents on children to the third and fourth generation"). The last verse in the book of Joel may echo this language of revenge against offenders: *wĕniqqêtî dāmām lō'-niqqêtî* ("I will by no means clear the guilty of their blood that I have not avenged").[45]

Like most of the Hebrew Bible, Joel's normal discourse about the deity focuses on the realm of actions.[46] Locusts are dispatched against the Judean countryside by YHWH, who uses them to wreak havoc like invincible soldiers. This invasion is the harbinger of an army that will inaugurate the dreaded day of YHWH amid heavenly portents and awesome signs. That accomplished, this same YHWH promises an outpouring of divine vitality on all Judeans, disposing them to conduct themselves as prophets with total disregard for customary distinctions based on age, gender, or social status.[47] Then YHWH will move to settle the score with traditional enemies of Judeans and to sit in judgment on all nations before acting to secure his sacred precincts and taking up residence in Zion. The motive for the abrupt change in YHWH's treatment of his inheritance and land is said to be zeal and pity.

In describing YHWH's actions Joel often uses traditional motifs grounded in ancient theophanies,[48] the day of YHWH,[49] the enemy from the north,[50] the sacred mountain,[51] the outpouring of the spirit,[52] the formula of acknowledg-

---

45. The text of this difficult verse probably comments on *dām-nāqî'* of v. 19. The Greek, Syriac, and Targumic renderings of the initial verb attest to a form of the verb *nqm*, "to avenge." The Greek translation of the second verb, *kai on mē athōōsō* ("and I will not leave unpunished") has an imperfect verb rather than the perfect tense in Hebrew (*lō'-niqqêtî*, "I have not declared innocent"). A. S. Kapelrud (*Joel Studies* [Uppsala: A. B. Lundequistska, 1948] 175) sees *lō'* as an ancient "*la* asservative."

46. Schmidt (*"De Deo"*) concentrates on exceptions to this statement, specifically Abraham's dialogue with YHWH about the necessity of exemplifying justice to all peoples, the prologue in Job, and the characterization of YHWH in Jonah. Schmidt's outdated source criticism detracts from an important insight, which many theologians have ignored because of a bias toward divine actions.

47. The language of this account echoes the three fundamental types of prophetic mediation: oracle, dream, and vision.

48. See J. Jeremias, *Theophanie* (WMANT 10; Neukirchen-Vluyn: Neukirchener Verlag, 1965) and T. Hiebert, "Theophany," *ABD* 6.505-11.

49. L. Černy, *The Day of Yahweh and Some Relevant Problems* (Prague: Nákladem Filosofické Fakulty University Karlovy, 1948).

50. B. S. Childs, "The Enemy from the North and the Chaos Tradition," *JBL* 78 (1959) 187-98.

51. See J. D. Levenson, *Sinai and Zion: An Entry into the Jewish Bible* (Minneapolis, Chicago, and New York: Winston, 1985); and R. J. Clifford, *The Cosmic Mountain in Canaan and the Old Testament* (HSM 4; Cambridge: Harvard University, 1972).

52. See A. Kerrigan, "The 'sensus plenior' of Joel III,1-5 in Act II,14-36," in *Sacra Pagina* (ed. J. Coppens; BETL 13; Gembloux: Duculot, 1959] 295-313; and R. Albertz and C. Westermann, "*Rûaḥ* Geist," *THAT* 2.726-53.

ment of YHWH,[53] and the nations' mocking of YHWH's people.[54] Moreover, the prophet attributes to YHWH the control of rain[55] and thus nature's productivity. In his view, this mastery of history and nature entitled YHWH to the claim of uniqueness.[56] Therein lay the problem with which Joel, like so many others in ancient Israel, struggled mightily. Experience failed to confirm traditional belief. Faced with discontinuity between confessional statements about divine compassion and the circumstances confronting Judeans in his day, Joel strove valiantly to hold together competing views of YHWH's nature. Honesty compelled him, nevertheless, to remain silent when he saw no evidence that his compatriots deserved their sorry lot. At the same time, he boldly placed his trust in YHWH's heralded compassion, which he believed would surely rectify current events. The unknown author of the satirical treatment of the prophet Jonah used the same statement about YHWH's compassionate nature to condemn the deity for unprincipled conduct in sparing repentant foreigners.[57] It thus follows that even by excising the old confession's emphasis on justice as a counterbalance to mercy, the resulting statement remains sufficiently ambiguous to evoke both a particularistic and a universalistic reading.[58] Historical events inevitably complicated faith for religious thinkers who believed in divine power and goodness. Justice and mercy make strange bedfellows, which explains the tradition's readiness to separate them. Who knows whether Joel's dream — or Jonah's — accorded with reality?

53. W. Zimmerli, *I Am Yahweh* (trans. D. W. Stott; ed. W. Brueggemann; Atlanta: John Knox, 1982).

54. The verb *mšl* has two different meanings, (1) to rule over and (2) to be like. The former sense would imply that Judeans deplore their subject status, whereas the second suggests that the enemies have turned the miserable circumstances of YHWH's people into a byword. The latter nuance seems the more probable one in context, although *mšl b* normally means "to rule over" and the versions translate it this way (LXX *katarxai,* Vulgate *dominentur*). Wolff (*Joel and Amos,* 52) argues for the usual meaning, "to rule over," but Simkins (*Yahweh's Activity,* 173-74) suggests that both senses may be intended, with "byword" as primary. Rudolph (*Joel-Amos-Obadja-Jona,* 53n.17) observes that "consensus of the versions is no guarantee of accuracy," for the context, especially YHWH's answer in 2:19, requires the meaning "taunt, mockery, byword." Marti (*Das Dodekapropheton* [KHCAT 13; Tübingen: Mohr/Siebeck, 1904] 130) appeals to Ezek 18:3 for translating *mšl b* as "mock" and to Jer 24:9 where *lěḥerpâ ûlěmāšāl* are juxtaposed as in Joel 2:17.

55. On the meaning of 2:23, see G. W. Ahlström, "*Hāmmōreh liṣdāqāh* in Joel II 23," *Congress Volume: Rome, 1968* (VTSup 17; Leiden: Brill, 1969) 25-36; idem, *Joel and the Temple Cult.* K. S. Nash ("The Palestinian Agricultural Year and the Book of Joel" [Ph.D. diss., Catholic University of America, 1989]) emphasizes changing weather patterns and a severe sirocco as the cause for dismay in the book of Joel, and O. Loretz (*Regenritual und Jahwetag im Joelbuch* [Ugaritisch-biblische Literatur 4; Altenberge: CIS, 1986]) sees the primary problem of the book as drought, to combat which the people undertake a ritual for producing rain.

56. See C. J. Labuschagne, *The Incomparability of Yahweh in the Old Testament* (Pretoria Oriental Series 5; Leiden: Brill, 1966).

57. Both Jeremiah and Ezekiel take up a popular proverb, accusing YHWH of acting without principle in transgenerational imputation of punishment for guilt, the essential point of Exod 34:7b (cf. Jer 31:26; Ezekiel 18).

58. See Dozeman, "Inner-Biblical Interpretation," 221-23.

Jonah: The Prophecy of Antirhetoric

YEHOSHUA GITAY

University of Cape Town, South Africa

As a prophetic book Jonah is unique. Jonah is a prophet who receives his call in the tradition of the classical prophets, and accordingly, the book starts in the conventional form of the prophetic commission: "The word of the Lord came to . . ." (Jonah 1:1).[1] But the book of Jonah is presented as a novella, dressed in prosaic narrative (with a poem inserted) in the literary form of the early prophets, or the prophetic indirect report (such as Amos 7:10-17 and Isa 8:1-4). Yet, the account of Jonah is not a prophetic episode that is included in the historiographical books (such as the Elijah cycle); rather, Jonah is a book in itself: one of the Twelve Prophets. Nevertheless, Jonah's prophetic activity is irregular. Unlike the classical prophets, who desire to appeal to their audience through the richness of their rhetorical utterances, Jonah's prophecy to Nineveh (3:4) is limited to only five words, thereby revealing a desire to avoid a rhetorical speech that seeks to affect the audience's behavior. It is this specific antirhetorical tendency that lies behind the particular form of the book. The purpose of this essay is to discuss the meaning of Jonah's unusual prophecy in the context of the book. My argument is that the book is designed as a narrative in order to project a particular tension that is developed between Jonah's performance and the message of the book. Hence, I argue, the employment of the narrative form of the book is functional and intentional (rather than a mere reflection of a specific prophetic genre).[2]

The clue to the enigma of the book of Jonah lies in its introduction. The

---

1. See also Joel 1:1; Mic 1:1; Zeph 1:1. Thus the Targum (on Jonah 1:1) considers him a prophet. Also consult B. S. Childs, *Introduction to the Old Testament as Scripture* (Philadelphia: Fortress, 1979) 422.
2. Consult A. Rofe, *The Prophetic Stories* (Jerusalem: Magnes, 1988).

preface is important, since it might and should in fact lead one to the essence of the story:

> The sole purpose of the Exordium is to prepare our audience in such a way that they will be disposed to lend a ready ear to the rest of our speech.[3]

As Aristotle points out:

> [The Exordium, the expository prologue] provides a sample of the subject, in order that the hearers may know beforehand what it is about, and that the mind may not be kept in suspense, for that which is undefined leads astray; so then he who puts the beginning into the hearer's hand enables him, if he holds fast to it, to follow the story.[4]

One needs to look closely at the introduction of Jonah in order to reveal the clue of the narrative. The complexity of the book of Jonah lies already in the choice of the name of its prophet. The issue arises because the book of Kings (2 Kgs 14:25-27) presents a prophet who bears the same name as the prophet of the book of Jonah: Jonah son of Amittai.[5] Even though the account in Kings is shorter than the book of Jonah, the introduction in Kings provides more biographical information than does the entire book of Jonah. The introduction to the book of Jonah lacks one specific detail: Jonah's location, which is mentioned in the account in Kings (Gath-hepher). True, missing entities of literary and artistic works might be a matter of accident but they should also be the object of inquiry. The following quotation demonstrates the problem:

> If one is looking at a pediment, and we noticed that one warrior had no spear, we should not think of asking where he had dropped it, or whether he had forgotten it; we should at once ask ourselves, why the sculptor had represented him spearless.[6]

The unknown might be meaningful. Studies in the nature of introductions of the literatures of antiquity discover that the phenomenon of missing information regarding the introduction of a new character is indeed characteristic of this literature:

> Unlike the typical novel, whose characters are created by the author for that specific work . . . the *Iliad* and *Odyssey* are stocked largely with characters

---

3. See Quintilian, *Institutio Oratorica* 4.1.

4. See Aristotle, *Rhetoric* 3.14.6.

5. A phenomenon that caused a number of critics to link the two Jonahs. Nevertheless, the book of Jonah is a later composition that relates in a particular way to the Jonah of Kings but is not associated with him. See the discussion below.

6. See H. D. F. Kitto, *Poesis: Structure and Thought* (Berkeley: University of California, 1966) 14-15.

already familiar to the original audience. Among the advantages gained by using traditional figures is the narrator's freedom from the obligation to explain who each person is.[7]

Thus, for instance, *Iliad* 1.7 stands as a sufficient introduction to the two characters: "Arteides, king of men and godlike Achilleus." The simple mention of their names touches on a longer chain of facts and attributes.[8] So also Jonah of the book appears to be an already known prophetic figure who does not necessitate a detailed introduction. Therefore something specific regarding the Jonah of Kings caused the narrator of the book of Jonah to associate his prophet with the earlier Jonah.

The preface of the book of Jonah maintains a fascinating event: God sends him over to Nineveh, and the assigned prophet literally escapes.[9] Other prophets refused to accept the mission (see Jer 1:5-6 and Exodus 3–4), yet they did not escape; they argued with God but were persuaded to deliver the divine message while they fully identified themselves as God's devoted messengers. Jonah's escape is therefore exceptional.

The deliberate attempt of the author of the book of Jonah to relate his prophet to the Jonah of Kings sheds fresh light on the meaning of the escape. Who is the Jonah of Kings? What is his reputation? What is he known for? He was a prophet who received an unusual mission, even contradictory in its nature: to deliver a message of good news to a king who was sharply condemned (by the same author of Kings) for his evil deeds (2 Kgs 14:24), and who was harshly attacked by the prophet of the time (see Amos 7:10-17). Obviously, Jonah's mission to King Jeroboam of Israel (2 Kgs 14:25-27) contradicts the Deuteronomistic concept of the doctrine of retribution that dominates the books of Kings. Hence, the historiographer adds an explanation:

> For the Lord saw that the distress of Israel was very bitter;[10] there was no one left, bond or free,[11] and no one to help Israel. But the Lord had not said that he would blot out the name of Israel from out of heaven, so he saved them by the hand of Jeroboam son of Joash. (2 Kgs 14:26-27)

7. See S. Richardson, *The Homeric Narrator* (Nashville: Vanderbilt University, 1990) 37.

8. Ibid., 36-37.

9. Over the generations critics and theologians have read the Jonah situation and his refusal to prophesy over Nineveh as a reflection of Israel's desire for revenge versus God's concern for the repentance of the Gentiles that determines his will. For an illuminating review of Jonah's scholarship as a chapter in the history of ideas, consult E. Bickerman, *Four Strange Books of the Bible* (New York: Schocken, 1967) 3-49.

10. Derived from Heb. *mrr.*

11. Cf. 2 Kgs 9:8, and see Deut 32:36 and the parallel: "impotency, inability to act." Consult M. Cogan and H. Tadmor, *2 Kings* (AB 11; New York: Doubleday, 1988) 161, 107.

Thus, it was not the divine act of trial but an act of mercy. Consequently, when Jonah is sent to Nineveh (note that the divine message was not conveyed explicitly),[12] Jonah might wonder whether he is being ordered to follow the steps of the Jonah of Kings and to deliver the message of the absurd to the wicked Nineveh (1:2). Therefore, Jonah escapes. This escape is not a total surprise for the learned audience who is already familiar with the nature of the mission of Jonah of Kings. Hence, E. Bickerman's statement, "This sermonizing theme is transformed into an exciting tale by holding back the solution and keeping the reader in suspense,"[13] is not exactly accurate.

Jonah's escape is a message in itself; a message that refers to the objective of his mission, that is, Nineveh. Assyria's capital, Nineveh is not just "another" nation involved in the history of Israel. Note the harsh prophetic utterances against Assyria, the enemy that destroyed North Israel in 722 B.C.E. and invaded Judah toward the end of that century, in Nahum, Isaiah, and Zephaniah:

> A jealous and avenging God is the Lord,
> the Lord is avenging and wrathful. (Nah 1:2)

> Nineveh is like a pool whose waters[14] run away. (Nah 2:9 [ET 2:8])

> See, I am against you, says the Lord of hosts. (Nah 2:14 [ET 2:13]; 3:5)

> Nineveh is devastated [šddh]; who will bemoan her? (Nah 3:7b)

> When the Lord has finished all his work on mount Zion and on Jerusalem,
> I[15] will punish the arrogant boasting of the king of Assyria and his haughty pride. (Isa 10:12)

> And he [God] will stretch out his hand against the north and destroy Assyria;
> ... and he will make Nineveh a desolation,
> a dry waste like the desert. (Zeph 2:13)

The prophets announce Nineveh's judgment; God will destroy Assyria as a consequence of its extremely cruel behavior toward Judah and Israel. Assyria (destroyed in 612 B.C.E.) continues apparently to symbolize the wickedness of the foreign oppressor that is to be severely punished by God. Consequently, Jonah's announcement of the overthrow of Nineveh (3:4) is indeed expected.

---

12. Cf. Kimhi on 1:2. Also see J. D. Magonet, *Form and Meaning: Studies in Literary Techniques in the Book of Jonah* (Bern: Herbert Lang; Frankfurt-am-Main: Peter Lang, 1976) 25-26.

13. See Bickerman, *Strange Books*, 4.

14. Following the LXX.

15. The translation follows the MT and not the third person of the LXX as the NRSV reads.

But because Jonah might suspect that his mission to Nineveh should be a duplicate of his predecessor's mission to Jeroboam of Israel, he escapes. When his first attempt to avoid his mission fails, he still does not give up. He employs his rhetorical skill as an antirhetorical means in order to fail in his mission and thus to determine Nineveh's fateful destiny.

Jonah's announcement is peculiar: he makes no real speech; he makes no attempt to appeal, to outline the addressees' deeds or to explain the verdict (as occurs in other prophetic speeches whose examples are presented above).[16] There is therefore a clear contrast between Jonah's long appeal on behalf of his own life (the prayer of 2:3-10 [ET 2-9], which is integrated thematically by the narrator)[17] and the evident laconic and unappealing call of Jonah to the Ninevites.

Let us look at Jonah's oracle in 3:4. He proclaims the overthrow of Nineveh within a period of forty days. This is not an unusual formula of announcing God's judgment. For instance, the announcement regarding the flood is that the judgment will take place within a period of seven days (Gen 7:4). Isaiah speaks about the destruction of the northern states within a particular period of time (Isa 7:8)[18] and again regarding the demise of Kedar (21:16). Nevertheless, Jonah's announcement is irregular; each of the announcements above contains a verb that denotes total destruction. Thus Gen 7:4 has the verb *mḥyty* ("wipe out," "destroy"; cf. Gen 6:7), Isa 7:8 contains *yḥt* (niphal of *ḥtt*, "be dashed to pieces"; cf. 51:6), and Isa 21:16 reads *klh* ("destruction"; cf. 1 Sam 20:33). But Jonah's announcement does not employ the expected definite verb of destruction. He uses instead the verb *nhpkt* (from the root *hpk*) that denotes "change, . . . upside down." The utilization of the verb *hpk* in the Hebrew Bible refers also to a situation that indicates a change in personality. Thus, for instance, upon meeting a band of prophets Saul will "be turned into a different person,"

---

16. Consult Y. Gitay, *Prophecy and Persuasion* (Bonn: Linguistica Biblica, 1981); *Isaiah and His Audience* (Assen: Van Gorcum, 1991); "Amos's Art of Speech," *CBQ* 42 (1980) 293-309.

17. The question of the poem's relationship to the narrative must be clarified. There is a tendency to associate it with a later edition of the book. The perfect verbs used in the poem have raised scholars' curiosity, suggesting already to early commentators such as Josephus that the psalm was spoken by Jonah after being spewed onto the shore. The LXX changed the verbs into the imperfect in order to fit the prayer to Jonah's desperate condition. But the incongruity between the psalm and its context indicates to Bickerman that the narrator must have used a psalm already circulating under the name of Jonah: "For the narrator as for his hero, and for religious men, of every faith, it was unthinkable that a person could fail to pray in mortal danger, and be saved without supplication" (*Strange Books,* 12). Indeed, more recent literary analyses of the poem and its relationship to its surrounding narrative reveal a literary and thematic integrity. Consult J. S. Ackerman, "Jonah," in the *Literary Guide to the Bible* (ed. R. Alter and F. Kermode; Cambridge: Harvard University, 1987) 234-43.

18. For this verse and its interpretation, see Gitay, *Isaiah*, 128-45.

wnhpkt (see, e.g., 1 Sam 10:5-6).[19] Nevertheless, a philological survey of the possible uses of a particular word may differ from a study of this same word in a given context. Ibn Ezra (on the verse) is right in his rejection of Rashi's dualistic reading of *hpk:* destruction or repentance. In this context *hpk* does not mean repentance,[20] since Jonah reacts so nervously to God's forgiveness of the Ninevites: "But this was very displeasing to Jonah, and he became angry" (4:1).

Indeed, *hpk* is the verb utilized for describing the manner in which God destroys the wicked cities of Sodom and Gomorrah (see Gen 19:21, 25). It is, therefore, the linguistic coin that alludes to this punishment in the collective memory of Israel's sacred traditions (see Deut 29:22; Amos 4:11; Lam 4:6). One should also pay attention to Haggai's language. He employs the verb *hpk* (paralleled by *šmd*): "and I *overthrew* [in *perfectum propheticum*] the throne of kingdoms . . . and I *overthrew* the chariots and their riders" (2:22). D. L. Petersen has rightly observed that *hpk* in Haggai is already a linguistic coin that functions as an oracle against a foreign nation or a city rather than referring explicitly to Sodom and Gomorrah.[21] Nonetheless, *hpk* as a verb in itself — as it is used in Jonah 3:4 — denotes just the manner of destruction. For example, when God informs Abraham regarding his intention to destroy the wicked cities, the verb that he uses in order to express this decision is not *hpk* but *šht* ("destroy"; see Gen 18:28, 31, 32; 19:13, 14). In the case of the announcement of the flood (Gen 7:4), the proclamation includes the means: *mmtyr* ([God] "send rain") and then the consequence: *mhyty* ("wiped out," "destroyed" in the *perfectum confidentiae*). A severe rhetorical problem is emerging. Jonah does not say explicitly that Nineveh will be destroyed; he states the manner but he unconventionally does not recite the consequences.

What does Jonah actually say? Jonah employs a graphic word, using it theatrically as a verb in the Niphal participle *(nhpkt)*, and announces it in itself and without further elaboration: in forty days the city is "turning upside down!" "Forty days more, and Nineveh shall be overthrown" (3:4). The use of the Niphal, which is a passive form, requires clarification. The meaning of the Niphal is related to the meaning of the Qal, which is its active equivalent.[22] Interestingly enough, the announcement of the flood in Gen 7:4 employs the Qal: "For in seven days I will send rain." Hence, God is the "actor" or the "agent."

19. Also see Hos 11:8 and Jer 2:21. That is, Jonah announces to the Ninevites that they are going to change themselves, to repent; this interpretation is considered already by the ancient rabbis (see *b. Sanh.* 89b). Also see Rashi on the verse. This reading was echoed recently by J. M. Sasson, *Jonah* (AB 24B; New York: Doubleday, 1990) 234-35.

20. Also see H. W. Wolff, *Obadiah and Jonah* (trans. M. Kohl; Continental Commentary; Minneapolis: Augsburg, 1986) 149.

21. See D. L. Petersen, *Haggai and Zechariah 1–8* (OTL; Philadelphia: Westminster, 1984) 98-106.

22. For the meaning of the Niphal and the terminology utilized here see B. K. Waltke and M. O'Connor, *An Introduction to Biblical Hebrew Syntax* (Winona Lake, IN: Eisenbrauns, 1990) §23.1.

In Jonah, however, the announcement lacks the "actor." That is, Jonah could have quoted God utilizing the Qal and stressing the agency: "Forty days more, I *will* overthrow Nineveh"; instead, he has preferred to hide God's role via the use of the passive Niphal. Further, he also omits the traditional formula of God's announcement ("Thus said God"). This form of Jonah's announcement carries important implications regarding Jonah's address to the Ninevites.

Here is an intentional attempt to conceal God's role regarding Nineveh, employing instead a colorful word: the city will turn upside down! It is a bombastic and even ridiculing announcement (while it is just by itself and without the explicit stress on the performer). That is, Jonah expresses vis-à-vis the designation of his call the implied desire that his addressees, the people of Nineveh, will dismiss his announcement as nonsense. Thus, his mission to warn the Ninevites ("forty days more") will fail; they will continue in their wickedness and God will consequently destroy them. Therefore, the immediate and sincere reaction of the Ninevites who truly repent is a total disappointment for Jonah.

Jonah's brief and cryptic oracle and the Ninevites' ultimate and constructive response call attention to the question of the book's message. In order to respond meaningfully to this question, we need to reconstruct the political-theological context of Jonah's prophecy against Nineveh. As a rule, a literary work is not composed in a cultural-contextual vacuum. Its interpretation depends therefore on the appropriate reconstruction of the political-cultural or theological conditions that gave birth to the work.[23] Thus D. LaCapra argues: "Context becomes the key explanatory variable. The notion of context may even serve as a way to get around texts."[24] Notice that the interest is not in the hard historical facts. The point is not to consider Jonah as a historical figure or archaeological document. Rather, the objective is to reveal the context of the book: its cultural-political and theological matrix.

The first question concerns the period of the book's composition. It is basically agreed — relying mainly on philological considerations — that the book of Jonah was composed no earlier than the exilic period.[25] The question of Jonah's wish for revenge concerning Nineveh has to be considered now in the light of the book's contextual and theological circumstances. Starting with the early Babylonian exile of 597 B.C.E., the prophetic literature echoes the emergence of specific messianic movements, which rejected the exile and were motivated by particular political and apocalyptic expectations that called for rebellions against the foreign-empirical rulers (see Jer 28:3, 11; 29:8-9, 21-32). Those messianic expectations for restoring the political independence of Judah

23. Recent treatments meriting mention are Wolff's *Jonah* (see esp. 85-88), and Rofe's *Stories* (esp. 170). The cultural context and the contextual interpretation are their points of departure regarding their search for the message of the book.

24. See D. LaCapra, *History and Criticism* (Ithaca: Cornell University, 1985) 19.

25. See the summary of the evidence in Sasson, *Jonah*, 20-28. Also see Wolff's forceful arguments in *Jonah*, 76-78; and Rofe's in *Stories*, 152-59.

had to be inspired by the prophecies of the earlier prophets, who called — as noted above — for God's revenge against the foreign oppressor: Assyria at their time and understood now to refer to Babylon. Jeremiah struggles against those calls for rebelling against Babylon. He condemns Hananiah son of Azzur who declares: "Thus says the Lord of hosts . . . I have broken the yoke of the king of Babylon" (28:2). He rebukes the prophecies of the leaders of this movement, Ahab son of Kolaiah and Zedekiah son of Maaseiah, and regards them as liars (29:21-23). Jeremiah's rejection of the preaching of what he considers inauthentic prophecies is the background for his famous letter to the exiles:

> Build houses and live in them; plant gardens and eat what they produce . . . but seek the welfare of the city where I have sent you into exile, and pray to the Lord on its behalf. (29:5-7)[26]

Jeremiah depicts the exile in realistic terms. He does not glorify the *golah* but rather calls for normalization. He thus rejects "the short breath" of those who denied life in exile.[27]

Later on, the prophet Haggai, during the time of the Persian emperor Darius (see Hag 1:1), encourages the Judeans who returned to Jerusalem from the Babylonian exile to rush to restore the temple. He delivers a prophecy addressed to Zerubbabel son of Shealtiel, governor of Judah and a descendant of the house of David (cf. 1 Chr 3:19), that expresses a new apocalyptical era: the overthrow of thrones and kingdoms, that is, the overthrow of the Persian Empire, the current rulers of Judah, and a new universal role for Zerubbabel (Hag 2:21-23). Zerubbabel is urged to "build the temple and the kingdom of blessedness would arrive."[28]

The prophecies of Jeremiah as well as the later theological reservations regarding the new role of the restored temple expressed in Isa 66:1, for instance ("Thus says the Lord: Heaven is my throne and the earth is my footstool; what is the house that you would build for me?"), reflect a severe tension with the messianic and eschatological movement. Jonah personally desires the overthrow of the foreign kingdom as God's revenge and consequently its apocalyptic implications (cf., e.g., Psalm 110). Jonah's oracle mirrors his personal desire. But attention should be given to the Ninevites' response: they "believed God" (3:5). Jonah addressed these people without mentioning God and concealing his role, yet they "believe God." The term "believe" invites further elaboration.

---

26. For further elaboration on Jeremiah 27–29, consult C. R. Seitz, *Theology in Conflict* (BZAW 176; Berlin: de Gruyter, 1989) 205-14.

27. Consult Y. Kaufmann, *History of the Religion of Israel* (Jerusalem: Bialik; Tel-Aviv: Dvir, 1960) 3.461 (Hebrew).

28. See P. D. Hanson, *The Dawn of Apocalyptic* (Philadelphia: Fortress, 1979) 245. Also consult C. L. Meyers and E. M. Meyers, *Haggai and Zechariah 1–8* (AB 25B; Garden City, NY: Doubleday, 1987) 66-67.

This term occurs in at least two other situations that ordinarily invite the opposite reaction: Gen 15:6 and Isa 7:9. Abraham, old and childless, was asked to believe in a promise considered to be absurd in terms of human nature and reason: "Look toward heaven and count the stars . . . so shall your descendants be" (Gen 15:5-6). But Abraham believed and God "reckoned it to him as righteousness" (v. 6). The other case revolves around a conflict between the prophet Isaiah and King Ahaz. Jerusalem is under siege, and the king and his house are in panic; yet Isaiah bids him to avoid any political-military act, to calm down, and to believe (Isa 7:1-9). In this case the king followed his human instincts and reasoning rather than the transcendental belief.[29] The Ninevites, however, show their greatness in believing God in spite of the problematic prophetic call. Indeed, their belief in God is the core of the book. As a matter of fact, the Ninevites are not the first — in the course of the book — to respond constructively to God. During the storm in the sea, both Jonah and the sailors recognized God's physical dominion over nature and consequently his control over their fate. Their recognition is conveyed via the linguistic-religious term of submission: the *fear* of God (1:4-10). Notice, however, that the narrative employs the same word both for the instinct of human fear (because of the dangerous storm) and the fear of God:

> and such a mighty storm came upon the sea that the ship threatened to break up. Then the sailors were *afraid*. (1:4-5)

> "I am a Hebrew," he replied. "I *fear* [*yr*ʾ] the Lord, the God of heaven, who made the sea and dry land." (1:9)

But the language of the Ninevites regarding their attitude toward God differs: they believe (3:5) — they do not fear. J. Pedersen's definition of *heʾĕmîn* is worth quoting:

> To make a man true, *heʾĕmîn*, means the same as to rely on him. It implies confidence. . . . The weaker members of the covenant help to uphold the stronger by their confidence. They *make* him true, i.e. firm, sure and strong.[30]

The Ninevites' belief in God reflects their confidence and true trust rather than the demonic fear of the sailors and even Jonah. Their complete repentance is fully accepted.

Therefore a deep gap exists between the prophet Jonah who tries again and again either to avoid his mission to Nineveh or to deliver a message in a form that aims to miss the audience, on the one hand, and the Ninevites' full

---

29. Consult Gitay, *Isaiah,* 128-45.

30. See J. Pedersen, *Israel: Its Life and Culture* (4 vols. reprinted in 2; London: Oxford University, 1963-64) 1-2.347.

belief in God, on the other hand. The book seeks to rationalize theologically Jeremiah's claim for coexistence in the exile, his call for normalization. The most sincere repentance of the Ninevites proclaims that the revenge is not urgent and the hated enemy of the past might be changeable ethically and religiously as well. That is, new theological conditions stronger than the prophet himself have emerged. The people of Judah and those who live abroad in exile must take this development into account.

In conclusion, I have argued that the book of Jonah is a response to current theological debates that have taken place since the early Babylonian exile in order to shape the religious-political policy toward the foreign ruler. These debates have significant applications regarding both the exilic community and the community in Judah. The issue is how to relate to hated enemies who wounded Israel almost mortally given that a number of prophets and psalmists (see also Psalm 137) called for divine revenge. The dilemma for the exilic period and the period of restoration that is dominated politically by the Persian Empire is how to interpret this desire of revenge that carries with it severe messianic expectations. This is also the major concern of the book, mirrored in the conflict between Jonah the prophet and the narrator. The aim of the book is to pave the way for cooperation with the foreign rulers and the normalization of life under the theological frame of God's dominion and universal care.

Finally, I return to my question at the beginning: the literary designation of the book as a prosaic narrative. The major theme of the book is the dramatic tension between the villain Jonah and the message of the book. In order to sharpen this tension, the narrative concentrates on Jonah and his actions. One sees the person Jonah in his wrestling:

> In order to feel concern for someone in a certain situation or to be moved by someone's plight, one has to believe that he is, or is more or less likely to be, in some parlous situation or desperate plight, and so, a fortiori, that there is such a person . . . our being moved in certain ways by works of art.[31]

One must see and feel the person in order to be moved and react. The prosaic narrative enables and provides these feelings. The issue has been presented vis-à-vis the events, depicting vividly the prophet's activities and deeds in front of us. This could be forcefully achieved through a specific literary medium, that of narrative.

---

31. See C. Redford, "How Can We Be Moved by the Fate of Anna Karenina," cited in R. M. J. Dammann, "Emotions and Fiction," *British Journal of Aesthetics* 32 (1992) 13.

The Future Fortunes of the House of David: The Evidence of Second Zechariah

CAROL L. MEYERS AND ERIC M. MEYERS

Duke University, Durham, North Carolina

The beginning of the postexilic period marks the transition for ancient Israel to existence as a community lacking the nation-state status it had enjoyed for the nearly half millennium of monarchic rule. For the southern kingdom of Judah, that rule had been dominated by the house of David. The Davidic lineage thus figures prominently in preexilic and exilic Judean prophecies depicting destruction and then restoration: the projected restoration involves the reestablishment of Davidic rule (see Jer 23:5 and 33:15) so that the eternal covenant of Nathan's oracle (2 Sam 7:13) is sustained.

It is no wonder, then, that Davidic rule is an issue in biblical sources dealing with existing leadership in the postexilic province of Yehud (Judah) and also in sources depicting the leadership of a future age. In our work on two of the early postexilic prophets, Haggai and First Zechariah,[1] we examined a number of texts involving possible remnants or expectations of royal Davidic rule. Even well into the postexilic period, which is when we assign the compilation of Second Zechariah in our commentary on that prophetic work,[2] the house of David appears as a prominent theme, although by then the actual presence of Davidides in Jerusalem leadership circles had apparently ended. Because David Noel Freedman's expert editing, professional support, and steadfast friendship contributed immeasurably to our ability to complete two Anchor Bible volumes on late biblical prophets, our observations here on the role of

---

1. C. L. Meyers and E. M. Meyers, *Haggai, Zechariah 1–8* (AB 25B; Garden City, NY: Doubleday, 1987).

2. C. L. Meyers and E. M. Meyers, *Zechariah 9–14* (AB 25C; New York: Doubleday, 1993).

the house of David in those prophets, notably Second Zechariah, are offered to him in deep gratitude.

I

The decline and disappearance of Davidic leadership in the early Second Temple period is documented in both scriptural and archaeological materials. Although lacking the office or title of king, a Davidide was part of the provincial administration of Yehud in the restoration era. The political role of descendants of the royal family of Judah in the postexilic community probably began with the unsuccessful first return from Babylonia to Palestine in the reign of Cyrus the Great, after his edict of 538 B.C.E.; the Persian-appointed governor, Sheshbazzar, was presumably a Davidide (Ezra 1:8; 5:14-16).[3] Some two decades later, the Davidic scion Zerubbabel appears as governor in the newly established sub-province of Yehud (see Hag 1:1).[4] He also is mentioned in the list of governors uncovered in Jerusalem and deciphered and published by Avigad.[5] According to this list, the daughter of Zerubbabel, Shelomith (1 Chr 3:19), is called 'āmâ, or coregent, of Elnathan, Zerubbabel's successor; the two apparently ruled jointly at the beginning of the fifth century.[6] Although in a reduced, nonroyal form, Davidic leadership thus may be documented for approximately thirty years (ca. 520-490 B.C.E.) at the outset of the Second Temple period.

In this brief period of Davidic participation in community rule, the place of Zerubbabel is noteworthy. Zerubbabel was presumably the grandson of the exiled King Jehoiachin, designated in Hag 1:1 as son of Shealtiel, who was the elder brother or uncle of Sheshbazzar. His appointment by the royal court of Persia to serve jointly with the high priest Joshua, son of Jehozadak, was apparently intended to promote a viable and enduring relationship between the Achaemenid court and the remnant of Judean leadership. This relationship was undoubtedly based on disparate goals, but ones that each party held deeply. Many Judeans wanted to return to their ancestral homeland and to reestablish their temple-based community identity. The Persians allowed them to follow their own religious practices and to have a limited political autonomy. Such freedoms stemmed from a policy meant to instill loyalty and to assure the Persians of safe trade routes in regions of critical geopolitical importance.

This understanding of Persian policy stands apart from the commonly

3. Meyers and Meyers, *Haggai, Zechariah 1–8*, xxxi-xl.
4. Ibid., 9-17.
5. N. Avigad, *Bullae and Seals from a Post-exilic Judean Archive* (Qedem 4; Jerusalem: Hebrew University Institute of Archaeology, 1976).
6. Ibid., 30ff.; and E. M. Meyers, "The Shelomith Seal and Aspects of the Judean Restoration: Some Additional Reconsiderations," *ErIsr* 17 (1985) 33-38.

held theory that Persian tolerance encouraged visions of rebellion and independence[7] at a time when the remnants of Judah were dispersed in many lands and places, and when so few chose to return either in 538 or 522 B.C.E. When a remnant did return and embark on the temple rebuilding project, the renewed community was a relatively small one[8] — one that would hardly have turned to outright rebellion. Still, numerous scholars have posited a scenario of rebellion on the basis of Haggai's heightened eschatology and military language in 2:20-23, especially in v. 21, which names Zerubbabel, and also because of First Zechariah's muted eschatology and absence of specific reference to Zerubbabel where Davidic language is employed (Zech 3:8; 6:12-14). That is, many suppose that Zerubbabel's name is omitted in such passages because he was ousted in a Persian overthrow of a putative rebellion. Where Zerubbabel's name is in fact mentioned (4:6b-10a), however, the future role of the Davidide is clearly transformed; he is depicted as a peacemaker: "Not by might and not by power, but with my spirit" (4:6).[9]

It was this accommodationist spirit, which recognized fully the location of world power with the Persians, that was to last for much of the Second Temple period. This response to the loss of Judean autonomy and to the changed world order was the essence of the early restoration community organization, one that paired civil and religious administration. This arrangement, leaving Davidic participation aside, lasted nearly seventy years until world events of the 460s tore it apart.[10] Those events were the Greco-Persian wars, which in turn led to satrapal revolts in Egypt, Babylonia, and possibly in Yehud. In any event the Persians sought to tighten their control over their Levantine holdings in the

7. The basis for such a theory is twofold: first, the language and heightened eschatology of Hag 2:20-23 apparently refer to the historical uncertainty surrounding Darius's accession to the throne (ca. 522-521 B.C.E.); second, Zerubbabel, who figures so explicitly in Haggai, appears only insignificantly at Zech 4:6-10, where the tone is quite different and the eschatology muted, and appears to be expunged from Zech 6:9-15 as a royal figure. According to such a view, Zerubbabel's disappearance from the scene could hardly have been accidental. While there is no doubt that the appointment of the direct descendant of King Jehoiachin would have raised great hopes and expectations, it is quite another matter to suggest that it occasioned thoughts of rebellion. See the discussion of the relevant texts in our commentary on *Haggai, Zechariah 1–8*.

8. See C. E. Carter, "A Social and Demographic Study of Post-Exilic Judah" (Ph.D. diss.; Duke University, 1991), and C. Meyers and E. Meyers, "Demography and Diatribes: Yehud's Population and the Prophecy of Second Zechariah," in *Scripture and Other Artifacts: Essays on the Bible and Archaeology in Honor of Philip J. King* (ed. M. D. Coogan, J. C. Exum, and L. E. Stager; Knoxville: Westminster/John Knox, 1994) 268-85.

9. E. M. Meyers, "Messianism in First and Second Zechariah and the End of Biblical Prophecy," in Dwight Young Festschrift (Winona Lake, IN: Eisenbrauns, forthcoming).

10. E. M. Meyers, "The Persian Period and the Judean Restoration: From Zerubbabel to Nehemiah," in *Ancient Israelite Religion: Essays in Honor of Frank Moore Cross* (ed. P. D. Miller, P. D. Hanson, and S. D. McBride; Philadelphia: Fortress, 1987) 509-21.

450s B.C.E.[11] Their efforts to consolidate power included the construction of a series of distinctive fortresses on both sides of the Jordan River, on the coastal plain, and throughout the hill country of Palestine. Manned by imperial garrisons, these fortresses were apparently charged with maintaining control of the empire in local affairs and preventing local populations from aligning themselves with the Greek forces that threatened Persia.

It is our contention that even though chaps. 9–14 do not explicitly mention Persia itself, Second Zechariah was compiled during this tumultuous period. Nonetheless, the overwhelming metahistorical focus of this prophetic work,[12] along with the extensive use of the language of divine power (esp. in the so-called Divine Warrior passages in chaps. 9, 10, 12, and 14) rather than human might, all reflect the collapse of any hope for political independence. Israel's dreams of a restored and independent kingdom thus were transferred increasingly to the eschatological realm. One must see the indirect references to the house of David (e.g., 9:9 and 10:4), as well as the direct ones (e.g., 12:7 and 13:1), as part of a transhistorical future hope and not in relation to the expectations of imminent historical realization. We shall examine each of these passages in turn in order to substantiate our claim that they depict eschatological yearnings.

II

1. Zechariah 9:9

The first reference in Second Zechariah to the future monarch occurs in 9:9. While it is couched in Davidic, royal language, the nonmilitary tone of this verse is similar to several passages of First Zechariah (3:8; 4:6-10; 6:11-12) where royal language is also used, especially in the so-called Zerubbabel Insertion of 4:6-10. At 6:11, leaving the plural "crowns" intact and at 6:14 reading the singular "crown" or hāʿăṭeret, the royal figure or Davidic scion functions as a symbol of the future.[13] In general the pragmatism of First Zechariah assumes it to be in the best interests of the restoration community to support the Achaemenid-sponsored theocracy of Yehud. Cooperation with the imperial power was deemed the only viable way to reestablish returnees in the Holy Land. Clearly, the Persians could not allow a monarchy to exist in Yehud when the satrapal organization was being imposed throughout the empire. This system, however, presupposed local rule through

11. K. Hoglund, *Achaemenid Imperial Administration in Syria-Palestine and the Missions of Ezra-Nehemiah* (SBLDS 125; Atlanta: Scholars, 1992).

12. C. Meyers, "Foreign Places, Future World: Toponyms in the Eschatology of Zechariah 9," *ErIsr* 24 (1993) 164-72.

13. Meyers and Meyers, *Haggai, Zechariah 1–8*, 362-64, 366ff.

rulers (governors and satraps) who supported their own indigenous cultures yet were loyal to Persia. Thus First Zechariah uses the language of royalty but omits the power imagery that would normally accompany the notion of political autonomy or a sovereign state.

In 9:9, and also in v. 10, the same construct obtains. With respect to the rest of Second Zechariah, which explicitly embraces the language of power and utilizes direct mention of the "house of David," whether this anomaly has anything to do with the fact that chap. 9 has a particularly complex redaction history — some parts of the text may be preexilic — is difficult to say. Nonetheless, the ideological similarity of 9:9-10 to 3:8, 4:6b-10a, and 6:12 is striking. In any event, the subdued militarism of the Zechariah 9 passage about a future king may reflect the political realities that impacted on the "end" of prophecy and also represents the desire of the compiler of Second Zechariah to bring his eschatological prophecies into closer alignment with the restoration-era perspectives of First Zechariah.

Having said all this, we still must note that 9:9 partakes of a more general Near Eastern typology, which views the accession of a new ruler as the inaugural event in a new era characterized by peace and well-being.[14] This new period is often depicted as having been secured through the military victories of the ascendant king, whose success in battle has succeeded in subduing opposition and in establishing political and social stability. A case in point is Ashurbanipal's declaration of worldwide peace following his installation as king:

> At the proclamation of my honored name, the four regions of the world were glad and rejoiced. . . . The hurled weapons of the enemy sank to the ground. The well-organized enemy broke their battle line. Their sharp lances came to a stop, they brought their drawn bows to rest. . . . In city and in homes, a man took nothing from his neighbor by force. . . . No deed of violence was committed. The lands were quiet. The four regions of the world were in perfect order, like the finest oil.[15]

The accession of the royal figure in Zech 9:9 and the ensuing peace are linked to the concept of the cessation of war following the destruction of Israel's enemies. The language of the next verse, about the termination of horse-and-chariot combat and of bow-and-arrow assaults, completes the imagery of the end of the violent confrontation that will accompany the future king and the associated peace. Moreover, in involving personified Zion as celebrant to the heralded event of kingship restored, the language of the preceding verse builds

---

14. B. Ollenburger, *Zion, the City of the Great King* (JSOTSup 41; Sheffield: JSOT, 1987) 143.

15. *AR* 2.380-81, text no. 987. For a more extensive discussion of Zech 9:9-10, see Meyers and Meyers, *Zechariah 9–14,* ad loc.; the NOTES section provides exegetical detail and the COMMENT section offers interpretation.

on the role of Zion in Yahweh's defeat of chaos. Psalm 76 is instructive in this regard. There, Yahweh establishes his abode "in Zion" (v. 2), having broken "the flashing arrows, the shield, the sword, and the weapons of war" (v. 3) while also stunning the "horse and rider" (v. 6).

The depiction of a royal figure in 9:9 thus is more than a mere calling forth of a familiar theme. It also provides a perspective that lies at the very core of the message of Second Zechariah. For the author of the original Hebrew oracle, the processional aspect was deeply imbedded in Near Eastern royal traditions attending moments of great significance. One such moment was almost certainly the accession of the new ruler and the expectation of political stability that accompanied such an event.[16] Because of the eschatological setting of Zech 9:9, however, it is obvious that the momentous occasion is projected into the future. The figure described is none other than a king, in biblical terms most surely a Davidic descendant. But the tone of this passage is both triumphal and pacific, standing in marked contrast to the general tone of violence in 9:1-8 and 11-16, and yet complementary to the message of those passages framing vv. 9-10. God will actively, and even violently, restore Israel's land and people; but the polity, once established under restored royal rule, will be one of peace.

Although 9:9-10 seems to stand out from its surrounding context in chap. 9 in tone and content, it actually complements the themes of its context, just as it is compatible with key sections of First Zechariah, especially 3:8; 4:6ff.; and 6:12. The rest of this essay attempts to show how such a future vision relates similarly to other portions of Second Zechariah, especially the difficult passages of 10:3-4; 12:7, 8, 10, 12; and 13:1.

2. Zechariah 10:3-4

Zechariah 10:3-4, especially v. 4, is striking in the imagery used in indirect reference to the Davidic house in the future age:

> [3]My anger has flared against the shepherds,
>   And I will attend to the he-goats.
> For Yahweh of hosts has attended to his flock,
>   the house of Judah, and will make them like
>   his mighty horse in battle.
> [4]From them will come the cornerstone,
>   from them the tent peg,
>   from them the bow of war,
>   from them every overseer — together.

---

16. Note that the NT has appropriated the processional aspect of v. 9 to depict Jesus' triumphant return to Jerusalem. See Matt 21:5-9 and John 12:14-15, where the peace-loving Messiah is riding on a donkey.

God's attention to Judah coincides in v. 3 with the introduction of military imagery, which echoes the language of chap. 9 and dominates the rest of this chapter. While the representation of God's people as sheep does not disappear — it surfaces again in v. 10 and is the dominant metaphor of chap. 11 — the vocabulary of power is expressed by the action against "shepherds" (i.e., rulers). Yahweh's anger is aroused (10:3a) against the "shepherds" and also the "he-goats," these two terms apparently representing two tiers of human leadership.

The suggestion that "shepherds" here refers specifically to the Davidic governor and his officials in the late sixth century is intriguing.[17] But since the subsequent course of action does not involve dealing with those leaders, the validity of invoking such an image seems less compelling. Furthermore, the immediately preceding critique of false prophetic leaders among the exiles may be continued in this verse. In any case, the prophet's language in v. 3 involves a clever shift. Being angry at the leaders, God deals with ("attends to") a cadre of them, presumably putting them away. But then, God "attends to" another group, the Judeans, who are not lost sheep. They are God's flock; and so God can and will use them to carry out the restoration of the lost Israelites (northerners), who have no effective leadership. The word translated "attend to" is used in two different ways, indicating a negative treatment of leaders of the dispersed northerners and then a positive treatment of exiled Judeans, from which will come true and effective leadership to help rescue "the people of Ephraim" (vv. 7ff.).

Because the issue Yahweh faces here in the eschatological restoration of all the people to Zion is a departure from earlier crises in the biblical period, the military imagery functions somewhat differently in Zechariah 10 than elsewhere in the Bible. Recent scholarship is virtually of a single voice in calling attention to the Divine Warrior language of this chapter. Such language, which derives from Canaanite mythology, occurs in the hymnic celebration of Yahweh's power, as expressed in such archaic poems as Exodus 15 and Judges 5, and in later prophetic echoes, such as Habakkuk 3 and Isaiah 42 and 63. We hesitate, however, to label Zechariah 10 as a Divine Warrior passage because its use of military imagery departs in significant ways from the classic Hebraic use of Divine Warrior themes.

For one thing, in Zechariah 10 the military language is attached to the Judeans rather than to Yahweh. It is Judah that will become "like a mighty horse in battle" (v. 3) or "heroes in battle" (v. 5); it is from Judah that the "bow of war" (v. 4) will come forth; and it is from Judah that the royal leadership that will execute God's victory plan will emerge. In other words, Yahweh's people,

---

17. This suggestion has been made most forcefully by P. D. Hanson, *The Dawn of Apocalyptic* (Philadelphia: Fortress, 1975) 329-31. We discuss Hanson's approach to Second Zechariah in *Zechariah 9–14*, in both the introduction and in the commentary at various points. While we have disagreed with many of his ideas, we have also learned from his insightful work.

specifically the Judeans, are empowered in this vision of the future. Even in Zechariah 9, Yahweh is the one to use weapons and sound the battle horn (v. 14), or to encamp against the enemy (v. 8). But Zechariah 10 represents a shift. Perhaps the partial restoration of the Judeans to Yehud has given the prophet cause to envision them as having an instrumental role, as God's agents, in the ultimate and total restoration of the future age. Only in v. 11 does Yahweh engage directly in aggressive activity.

Let us expand on these ideas by exploring in some depth the first two terms of v. 4 that are used to symbolize aspects of the royal leadership that will one day stem from the house of Judah. The first of these terms is "cornerstone" (pinnâ). Its primary and most frequently attested meaning is "corner," normally an architectural designation (e.g., Exod 27:2; 38:2; 1 Kgs 7:30, 34; Ezek 43:20; 45:19; 2 Chr 28:24). At times this word refers specifically to the wall of Jerusalem (2 Kgs 14:13; 2 Chr 25:23; 26:15). Most significantly it can designate a "cornerstone" (Jer 51:26; Job 38:6; Ps 118:22; Isa 28:16), which is evocative of "the premier stone" of Zech 4:7 (hā'eben hārō'šâ), that is, the foundation stone that was laid just before the rebuilding of the temple of Zerubbabel.[18]

All those architectural meanings lie behind its metaphoric usage in this verse. "Cornerstone" can signify an officer or chief insofar as a leader is the essential support for the group being led, in much the same way that the corner or wall is the foundation of a building's superstructure and thus of that building's ability to stand. In Judg 20:2, the term pinnâ denotes all the "chiefs of the people" who assembled at Mizpah; and in 1 Sam 14:38 it is a term for the "leaders" of the people who came to address the king. In Isa 19:13, it is used with irony in reference to foreign leaders, who as "cornerstones" led the people of Egypt astray.

The occurrence of pinnâ in Psalm 118, a song of thanksgiving and deliverance, seems particularly relevant to this Zechariah passage. Mason contends that, in Ps 118:22, pinnâ provides a wordplay on "stone" — the stone the builders reject is the cornerstone, that is, the chief leader or king (rō'š pinnâ)![19] He also argues that Ps 118:19-21 bear some similarity to Zech 9:9, especially in the use of "righteous" and "salvation." In addition, he notes that the "cornerstone" of Ps 118:22 and Zech 10:4 is identified by later Christian and Jewish tradition as "Messiah." Because of all these links and in view of the fact that the next item ("tent peg") in this series also has an association with royal leadership by virtue of the way it is used in Isa 22:23ff., the selection of the somewhat

---

18. Meyers and Meyers, *Haggai, Zechariah 1–8*, 246-48.

19. See R. A. Mason's most complete treatment in his still unpublished dissertation, "The Use of Earlier Biblical Materials in Zechariah 9–14: A Study in Inner Biblical Exegesis" (University of London, 1973). His discussion of pinnâ is on pp. 114-15. Many of Mason's valuable insights and ideas can be found in *The Books of Haggai, Zechariah, and Malachi* (Cambridge Commentary on the New English Bible; Cambridge: Cambridge University, 1977).

unusual term *pinnâ* ("cornerstone") as the first item becomes comprehensible. Its figurative meaning, representing a chief or leader — probably the royal leader, an eschatological Davidide — is appropriate not only to the immediate context of this verse, where "house of Judah" (10:3) is the source of the cornerstone/leader (king?), but also to the expectation of a future royal ruler that appears in 9:9 and at several points in First Zechariah. Judah is to provide the cornerstone. Those who will carry out God's redemptive acts will thus emerge from Judah; and the first of these will be the leader, the "cornerstone" or foundation upon which the success of the enterprise will rest.

3. Zechariah 12:7-12

The "house of David" appears four times in Zech 12:7-12. The enigmatic reference in v. 10 to a stabbing incident has often been understood to refer to the slaying of an actual Davidide holding the governor's office or other leadership position in the fifth century. Such an identification, however, is based on eschatological language and meager or nonexistent historical data and thus should be regarded as highly speculative. Although the idea of the stabbing of a Davidic governor under Persian rule seems remote, the graphic specificity of the language here may have its origins in the assassination of Gedaliah (2 Kgs 25:25), an event that apparently had a powerful affect on the postexilic community. The fast of the seventh month, mentioned in Zech 7:5, is probably the Fast of Gedaliah, commemorating his untimely death.

The disappearance of a royal figure from a position of leadership may just as easily, and perhaps more logically, be comprehended as the result of an astute move on the part of Persian authorities to have local rule securely fixed in the hands of nonroyal individuals. Such persons would not symbolize so directly as a Davidide the lost independence of the province and thus would not represent the hope of regaining independence as a dynastic state. The existence of a dynastic figure as governor, at the outset of Persian rule, was clearly efficacious in securing compliance and cooperation. Yet, as the decades wore on, the presence of a Davidide having only limited, and nonroyal, power in Yehud may have become too bitter a pill to swallow, particularly as other forms of community life resumed stability and as traditional sources focusing on the rule of Davidides gained authoritative status.

However it may have come about, the result was that, about a decade into the fifth century, governors with a connection to the house of David were a thing of the past. The appointment of Nehemiah as governor in 445 B.C.E., as documented in the book of Nehemiah, shows a very different Persian strategy in appointing a governor or *pehâ*. Nehemiah was a functionary in the Persian court and as such would have been a loyal imperial subject when sent to be an official in his ancestral homeland. Although his immediate predecessors did not leave an extant record, the Nehemiah strategy may have already been in operation. That is, the termination of Davidides as governors is comprehensible as a way for the Persians to appoint governors whose loyalty to Persia could be better assured.

The cessation of participation by the house of David in the internal administration of Yehud took place sometime at the beginning of the fifth century, at a time just prior to which one may tentatively assign Second Zechariah or its compilation. Thus, just as the intensification in Zechariah 9–14 of eschatological depiction of Judean independence and even universal dominance represents a situation opposite to the political reality of the first half of the fifth century, so too would its emphasis on the house of David arise from a historical situation in which just the opposite condition — the de-emphasis of Davidic potential — obtained.

One must recognize that the eschatological picture of Second Zechariah does not involve the projection of a future that will simply be a restoration of past conditions. The prophet is certainly influenced strongly by his reading of the past as he sets forth in vivid language a vision of the future. Yet that future is never a straightforward replication of historical circumstances. The past is held sacred but is not uniformly idealized; its shortcomings are altogether too apparent in the traditional sources, prophetic and Deuteronomic, which apparently informed the prophet's understanding of the centuries of monarchic rule in Israel. Thus the prophet's portrayal of the future involves significant departures from what had existed in Israel's past.

Israel's relationships with other peoples are dramatically altered in Second Zechariah's eschatological scenario. Not only is there a return to autonomy, but there is also a clear sense of Israel becoming central in all the world. This is not worked out explicitly in Zechariah 12, except in terms of Judah's God-given ability to establish and maintain independence despite onslaughts from without. But it is clearly present elsewhere in Second Zechariah (e.g., 9:2, 10; 10:11; 14:8-9, 16), just as it is a resounding theme in the oracles at the end of First Zechariah (8:20-23).

A revisionist perspective on the internal dynamics of the restored monarchy is an important if not central message of the attention to the house of David and the Jerusalem leadership in 12:7-11 and also vv. 12-14, although expression of these changes is more subtly conveyed than are the alterations in the view of Israel's status in the world. Perhaps because the idea of a Davidic monarchy was so firmly entrenched and absolutely accepted in Israelite belief, with Yahweh's promise in 2 Sam 7:8-16 of eternal Davidic rule apparently never questioned, any future view of the restored dynasty that included significant change might be construed as critical of the sacred idea of kingship as the divinely ordained mode of political organization.

Nonetheless, Second Zechariah offers a vision of renewed ascendancy of the "house of David" and "rulers of Jerusalem" with two significant differences.

The first of these is the apparent lessening of the wide powers that the royal bureaucracy had exercised in the preexilic period. While the inviolability of Davidic rule was never questioned, Deuteronomic and prophetic literature is often highly critical of actions taken by the crown; and many kings are portrayed as little better than oriental despots. Thus a critique of the exercise of royal powers was already firmly part of prophetic expression among Second Zechariah's predecessors.

In addition, the years of exile and then partially restored national existence — at least a century of community life without royal leadership and subject to the rule of an imperial power — meant inevitably a reordering of leadership modes. Indeed, changes in leadership patterns on the part of peoples deprived of their previous autonomy and self-determination is a critical survival mechanism for dominated groups.[20] There are clear indications, such as in the altered terminology present in biblical sources for various community officials, that internal self-governance, as opposed to the externally validated rule of the Persian-appointed governor and other officials, underwent structural shifts to accommodate the exigencies of external imperial control. Many of these shifts were no doubt made in the exiled communities, those physically removed to Mesopotamia where discontinuities were even greater than for those not uprooted from ancestral holdings, and then brought back by returning exiles and eventually aligned with adjustments made by those who had remained in Yehud.

Whatever the exact forms of such restructuring may have been, one can surely characterize it as a decentralizing and, in a sense, a democratizing process, since it represented among other things a response to the absence of the strong central royal figure of a monarchy. To some extent priestly rule and ecclesiastical hierarchies expanded to fill the gap left by the absence of a king and royal bureaucracy. But at the same time, and especially among exiles without access to the temple, grassroots forms of leadership and community organization helped sustain the identity and group life of a people removed from the defining parameters of a nation-state. On the basis of careful examination of postexilic sources, some would even suggest the formation of a self-consciously communitarian structure.[21]

These critical and transformative shifts in group structure and leadership are surely reflected in the dramatic statement of 12:7 that the "tents of Judah" (i.e., the people themselves) will be the first whom Yahweh will rescue, for they are no less important than are the traditional splendors of the royal bureaucracy.

20. D. L. Smith, *The Religion of the Landless: The Social Context of the Babylonian Exile* (Bloomington, IN: Meyer-Stone, 1989) 73-74, 77, 78, 80.

21. J. P. Weinberg, "Das *bēit 'ābōt* im 6-4 Jh. V.U.Z.," *VT* 23 (1973) 400-414; "Die Agrarverhältnisse in der Bürger-Tempel Gemeinde der Achämenidenzeit," *Acta Antiqua* 22 (1974) 473-86.

Such a reordering of the expected priorities of dynastic restoration reflects an accommodation to the decentralizing and democratizing adaptations that probably occurred in the many decades following the Babylonian conquest of Judah.

The second difference in internal matters in the prophet's vision of restored Davidic rule is depicted in startling and, at least to twentieth-century readers, enigmatic language. The language of 12:10, especially "they have stabbed," may refer to an act of violence on the part of the royal bureaucracy. Although it perhaps appropriates language derived from accounts of the slaying of Gedaliah, it may involve the historic tension between the monarchy and prophetic figures. Those tensions involved two sets of relationships — between ("true") prophets of Yahweh and other ("false") prophetic figures, who were frequently heeded while "true" prophets were ignored or even were in risk of their lives. The rivalry and tension between true and false prophets are undoubtedly of great concern to Second Zechariah. But that concern is not simply a matter of which prophetic group will hold the attention and gain the credence of the general populace. Rather, it involves what in many ways is a more fundamental issue: whether those in power, the national leaders, will adhere to God's word as communicated by the eloquent but often unwelcome voices of true prophecy.

Within the space of only one verse (Zech 12:10), though elaborated upon in the next verse and in the Catalogue of Mourners of vv. 12-13, the prophet envisions sweeping changes in historic royal attitudes to prophetic figures. Only God's intervention, as it does for Judah's political ascendancy, can bring about this fundamental change in the attitudes of leadership to the bearers of God's word. Verse 10 sets forth four distinct features of the new mode.

First, the Jerusalem leadership will undergo a striking change of disposition. In their very character as human beings, the king and leaders will show "favor" *(ḥēn)*, that is, react positively, presumably to those to whom they had previously not been so disposed.

Second, they will not only have changed their attitude to such others, but they will also ask them for forgiveness. This attitude of "supplication" makes sense only if there are past misdeeds about which they are showing remorse.

Third, they will look to God for ultimate forgiveness concerning whatever violence they have perpetrated in the past. Persons who have received bodily harm and probably death at the hands of the royal establishment are not present to be the objects of pleas for forgiveness. Only Yahweh can respond to this new "spirit" that will come upon the house of David and its officials.

Finally, and perhaps most important in terms of the attention given to this feature of change in the quality of royal leadership, is the idea of the utter remorse of those who had acted wrongly. The admission of guilt and the accompanying great dismay find expression in the metaphors of mourning that appear at the end of v. 10, in v. 11, and in the concluding section of chap. 12, vv. 12-14. Not one, not two, but three striking comparisons are offered to characterize the completeness and the intensity of the mourning that the ruling elite will experience. The efficaciousness of this outpouring of grief is assumed in this chapter but is then specified by the concept of purification in the opening verse of the next chapter (13:1).

All these extraordinary features of the royal bureaucracy signal a radical change in the restored house of David accompanying the strong sense of continuity with the past, according to Second Zechariah's future vision. In the oracular statements in 12:2-6 concerning national renewal amidst hostile nations, the language of Judah's restored power vividly depicts the full restoration of Zion. Then, in vv. 7-11, equally compelling language asserts the new role of the Davidides. The very intensity of the images in both cases bespeaks both the difficulty, given conditions in the prophet's own world, in imagining that such a future might be realized, and also the unswerving expectation that it will come to pass because Yahweh has the will and the power, as the creator of the cosmos, to bring it about.

Thus, unlike the idealistic picture of restoration in First Zechariah's eschatological visions, as well as that in Jeremiah (e.g., 23:5-6) and Ezekiel (34:23-24), Second Zechariah's depiction of the future Davidic rule is tempered by a diminution of royal powers from what they were understood to have been in preexilic reality and by signs of democratization in the power structure. Such dramatic developments are reinforced by the striking idea that the restored monarchy will not neglect the reasons for its demise — it will recall its sinful ways and have remorse for the misdeeds it has perpetrated. Furthermore, it will mourn profoundly for its reprehensible past (12:10-11 and the Catalogue of Mourners in 12:12-14).

4. Zechariah 13:1

The final explicit reference to the "house of David" in Second Zechariah occurs in 13:1. This verse functions as a bridge between similar materials in the preceding chapter where "house of David" and "leaders of Jerusalem," both of which appear in 13:1, occur in tandem three times. As we have already noted, these terms denote the royal bureaucracy that held power in Jerusalem from the time of David until the destruction by the Babylonians in 587/586 B.C.E.

At the end of Zechariah 12 the depiction of the eschatological renewal of the royal bureaucracy sets the stage for the things portrayed in 13:1. This description provides the completion of a sequence by outlining the final action that will be necessary to make the royal bureaucracy fit to reclaim power. The ruling elite experienced defeat, they admitted guilt, they have mourned for what they have done, and now they are ritually and symbolically cleansed. The corruption that led to the downfall of Judah is identified as idolatrous and immoral behavior — covenant disobedience — in Hebrew prophecy. Such behavior creates a state of impurity in interlocking moral and ritual spheres, so that the ritual cleansing implied by the waters ("fountain") to be opened in Jerusalem achieves the goal of ridding the future rulers of the impurity caused by all their sins.

The idea of a "fountain" being opened by Yahweh to such ends draws on imagery of Jerusalem as the sacred center of the universe, where the living waters are part of the quasi-mythic character of Zion's everlasting sanctity. This imagery contributes to the eschatological thrust of the oracle and implies that the cleansing wrought by the cosmic waters will be an ongoing feature of the future age, so that Israel's leadership will never again be impure.

III

It is significant, to say the least, that the glorious conclusion to the canonical book of Zechariah in chap. 14 has no direct or indirect reference to the Davidic line. The chapter is laced with Divine Warrior language, especially in vv. 1-5 and 12-15, but it is Yahweh as king who emerges as the dominant trope of the final section, vv. 16-21. The focus on God's kingship is evident in the twice-repeated (in vv. 16-17) title "King Yahweh of hosts," a unique and evocative designation. It is also expressed in the repetitive language about the nation going up to Jerusalem to bow down to Yahweh. The very term "go up" occurs five times (some of these in the negative) in vv. 16-17, and "bow down" is found twice. Both expressions contribute to the sense of the nations acknowledging Yahweh's sovereignty.

In a sense the appearance of the royal metaphor for God at the end of Second Zechariah is a development of the Divine Warrior imagery found in this chapter as well as in previous ones. Because one of the main roles of a human monarch was to establish and/or sustain an army, and often to command it, the power aspects of military language in effect depend on royal authority. In other words, one can consider the warrior imagery a submetaphor of monarchic imagery.[22] In some psalms, for example, the two metaphors are explicitly interwoven (see Psalms 29 and 47). Thus it is natural and perhaps even necessary that the powerful military image should give way here to the more general and inclusive image, Yahweh's role as king.

The royal metaphor, drawn from the human political arena, is surely among the most prominent examples of the projection of human attributes onto Yahweh. As such, it plays a central role in Israel's attempt to express the nature of its incomparable God through the vehicle of language drawn from

---

22. See M. Brettler, "Images of YHWH the Warrior in Psalms," in *Women, War, and Metaphor* (ed. C. Camp and C. Fontaine; Semeia 61; Atlanta: Scholars, 1993) 135-65.

human experience. Yet, just as the Divine Warrior trope exhibits new dimensions in chap. 14, so too does the royal metaphor operate in an altered way. The universality of God's future dominion on the one hand, and the pervasive sanctity of the world so ruled on the other, constitute a dramatically extended use of the concept of Yahweh as king.

Some scholars question whether this metaphor of Yahweh as king contradicts the royal language of 9:10, where the horse (and chariot) are removed from Israel (Ephraim and Jerusalem), but where the restored human king reigns in peace "from sea to sea, from the river to the ends of the earth." Certainly the eschatological vision of chap. 14 focuses on Yahweh's universal sovereignty, not on that of a restored Davidide. But the difference between the two chapters may be one of emphasis rather than contradiction. The removal of horse and chariot from the people is one way to express the apolitical nature of the Israelite rule at the end time. But even the elevated role of Israel and its king in those days should not supersede that of the divine king Yahweh, whose sovereignty is supreme and who is called King by the other nations.

The universality of God's future rule is made explicit in Zechariah 14 in the depiction of all the nations coming to Jerusalem, to the temple precincts, for a cultic event: the celebration of the Feast of Booths (Sukkoth). The inclusiveness of such a portrayal is extraordinary for a postexilic text. The sixth-century conquest of Judah and the subsequent exile of many Judeans only intensified the age-old problem of boundaries between God's people and other social or political groups. Israel historically, but often unsuccessfully, strove to maintain separation between its own cultural patterns and beliefs and those of its neighbors (see Deut 7:1-6). Its own cultic documents stress the ideal of Israelite holiness, in emulation of divine sanctity, and in contrast with the detested practices of other nations (e.g., Lev 18:3-5; 20:23-24, 26). Thus the vision of all peoples making an annual Sukkoth pilgrimage to Jerusalem to worship Yahweh involves a diminishing of boundaries between Israel and those perceived as other.

IV

Second Zechariah provides a unique window into the postexilic period. Still, the highly eschatological materials, frequently laced with indirect reference to or explicit mention of the "house of David" or "the leaders of Jerusalem," do not allow for easy assessment of historical allusions or specificity. Indeed, the elliptical and figurative nature of the text is such that several ways of viewing a given text may often be possible. Nevertheless, the events that have given rise to these utterances, however vague they may be in some respects, are quite clear in broad outline.

To recapitulate: At the outset of the Judean restoration a Davidic governor was appointed to rule Yehud jointly with a high priest, effectively reversing the older pattern of dominant monarchic leadership that had operated since the emergence of the nation-state. That modification of the governance pattern included Davidic participation until about 490 B.C.E., when the house of David ceased to figure in the administration of the restoration community. The increasing international turmoil during the Greco-Persian wars had its impact in Yehud. Persia's relatively loose control over the internal affairs of Yehud and international traffic was tightened, and military garrisons were stationed along strategic routes and in the major cities. In such a setting, the language of power, reflected in the metaphor of Divine Warrior, set the promise of restored autonomy for God's people into an eschatological framework. Only Yahweh could reverse the powerlessness of the people in the Persian period; thus, contrite and purified, the house of David will be restored only within the context of divine might.

The Name of "Second Isaiah":
The Forgotten Theory of Nehemiah Rabban

RISA LEVITT KOHN AND WILLIAM H. C. PROPP

University of California, San Diego

When I first began biblical studies in 1975, I little thought one day to share an office wall with the formidable, (in)famous David Noel Freedman — author of this, editor of that, president of the other thing. Since his early work in the good old Albrightian tradition, Noel has blazed astounding new paths, a farseeing Goliath with his feet planted not on the shoulders of other Anakim but on solid earth. Extreme praise of the living is rarely tasteful, even in *Festschriften;* may I nonetheless say that DNF wields the most original mind in our field's long history? More: while intellectual isolation can be the price of originality, Noel's apparent compulsion to collaborate and edit, combined with native charm and gregariousness, have made him the veritable nerve center of biblical studies. If his work often lacks precedents, many contemporary and younger scholars are not ashamed to acknowledge upon whose shoulders *they* perch to survey Israelite pottery, poetry, or prophecy. As his colleague and neighbor, I am happy to report that three-score and ten have not a whit impaired Noel's indefatigable industry, perennial inspiration, and steady good humor. May his genius be eternally fresh!   *William H. C. Propp*

When I consider the impact that David Noel Freedman has had on me personally and professionally I think back to the first time we met. I sat waiting in his office nervously wondering what I could possibly discuss with such a noted scholar. Upon his arrival it did not take long for me to relax and realize just how supportive and caring a teacher David Noel Freedman would be. Although his knowledge and wisdom often surpass that of those whom he teaches, he still learns much from his students. This, as I discovered through my contact with him, was but one of the many qualities that made him a true scholar. He has been a supportive and patient teacher whose scholarship continues to inspire me. His work and his enthusiasm serve as a model for those who humbly endeavor to follow his path. It is a great privilege for me to dedicate this article to my teacher.

Risa Levitt Kohn

In 1971 Kiriath Sepher published a small volume provocatively entitled *Yĕša'yāhû haššēnî: nĕbû'ātô, 'išîyûtô ûš(ĕ)mô (Second Isaiah: His Prophecy, His Personality, and His Name)* by Nehemiah Rabban. According to the brief introduction, the author was a founder of the Israel Society for Biblical Research. He had died a decade earlier, leaving behind, among other papers, the manuscript of a monograph on "Second Isaiah."[1] The following is a cursory evaluation, summary, and partial translation of this unjustly neglected work. It is a pleasure to dedicate our review to David Noel Freedman, our friend, teacher, and colleague. In Rabban he will find a kindred creative spirit and a precursor in his understanding of "Second Isaiah," at least in some respects.[2]

Rabban treats all of Isaiah 40–66 as the work of a single author; that is, he denies the existence of a "Third Isaiah" (pp. 26-32). Decisive for him are the numerous parallels between chaps. 40–55 and 56–66, familiar terrain for students of this question. He compares 49:8-9 with 61:1 and notes the tone of compassion in 57:15-18; 60:10, quite similar to that which pervades Isaiah 40–55 (e.g., 54:7-8). Many other themes run throughout chaps. 40–66: the polemic against idolatry and insistence that Yahweh is the sole God (57:11-13; cf. 40:12-31; 41:1–42:9; 43:9–44:5; 44:6-23; 45:20-25; chap. 48), the vision of coming salvation and Yahweh's vengeance upon the nations (59:17-18; cf. 42:13), the anticipated future prosperity of Israel (65:19-25; cf. 49:19-20), the glory of Yahweh and his people before the nations (59:19; 62:2; 66:18-19; cf. 45:6; 52:10), Israel as a beacon for the Gentiles (60:3; cf. 42:6; 49:8), the eventual vindication

---

1. Rabban also wrote a book on Jeremiah, which we have not seen.

2. For instance, Freedman's theory that the nations are the addressees of Isa 40:1 ("The Structure of Isaiah 40:1-11," in *Perspectives on Language and Text: Essays and Poems in Honor of F. I. Andersen's Sixtieth Birthday* (ed. E. W. Conrad and E. G. Newing; Winona Lake, IN: Eisenbrauns, 1987] 167-93) is anticipated by Rabban (p. 90n.112a = n. 23 below), although he assumes rather than argues the point.

(*ṣdq*) of Israel (60:21; cf. 54:14), Israel's anticipated reparations from its oppressors (chaps. 60–62; 66:20; cf. 45:24; 49:22-23; 54:3).

But Rabban is fair to the opposite view. "Third Isaiah" was postulated to explain the numerous differences between Isaiah 40–55 and 56–66,[3] and Rabban himself lists many features that distinguish chaps. 40–55 from 56–66 (p. 30). For example, the parallelistic epithet "Jacob-Israel" is absent from chaps. 56–66. "Servant of Yahweh" or "chosen one of Yahweh" as designations for Israel are replaced by "my chosen ones" and "my servants" (65:9, 15; 66:14). Isaiah 56, 63–64 are written partly in prose, whereas chaps. 40–55 are entirely poetic. The Sabbath (56:2; 58:13) and new moon (66:23) are not mentioned at all in the preceding chapters, which in general do not dwell on ritual. The tone of chastisement for idolatry, bloodshed, and corruption (57:1-13; 58:1-7; 59:1-15; 65:1-15; 66:2-4, 14-17, 24) contrasts with the spirit of compassion characterizing chaps. 40–55.

These differences are insufficient to convince Rabban, however. He both discounts the differences between the two sections and exploits them to paint a vivid portrait of a progressively embittered visionary (pp. 30-32):

> The lack of the expression "Jacob-Israel" could be coincidental. The prose style does not prove anything, since there is no reason why the prophet should always write in poetic parallelism; stylistic variations of this sort are also found in other prophets such as Jeremiah. As for the Sabbath and new moon, it is clear that both were known and sanctified since most ancient times,[4] and it is no wonder that the prophet attaches importance to them and expects the nations one day to accept them. Nor is the tone of rebuke decisive, for even in chaps. 40–55 the prophet castigates the Israelites for their sins and rebelliousness (42:24-25; 43:24; 46:8, 12; 48:1, 8), and, by contrast, one finds a tone of compassion, forgiveness, and consolation in chaps. 56–66 as well: for example, 56:8; 57:16-19; 58:8-12; 60–62. The prophet's change of stance from chapter to chapter does not at all mean a change of authors; almost all the prophets were both comforters and chasteners, and "Second Isaiah" is no exception. Nevertheless, there is an undoubted change in basic tone in chaps. 55–66, which are more fiercely zealous than the prior chapters. One gets the impression that the prophet, finding his preaching to be ineffectual, grew angry at those who refused to heed him. The stubbornness of a large, rebellious portion of the people was evidently what evoked the switch from "the Servant of Yahweh" to "the servants of Yahweh" and their opposite, "those who forsake Yahweh." "The Servant of Yahweh" is a title of the people viewed as a single unit; the prophet applied it to the entire people, despite the presence among them of sinners, as long as he was ruled by his forgiving

3. See now C. R. Seitz, "Isaiah, Book of: Third Isaiah," *ABD* 3.501-7.

4. 1 Sam 20:18; 2 Kgs 4:23; Hos 2:13; Amos 8:5; Isa 1:13-14; Jer 17:21-27; Ezek 20:12-24; 46:1-6; Lam 2:6.

nature. But when he realized that the majority of the people would not accept his teaching, he began to distinguish between the few individuals who listened to his words, "the servants of Yahweh," and the rebels, "those who forsake Yahweh," whom he attacked in his oracles of rebuke.

Rabban considers, but dismisses as unnecessary, the possibility that the author of chaps. 56–66 was merely influenced by "Second Isaiah." He thinks it more reasonable to suppose identity of authorship. This holistic approach will seem more plausible today than when Rabban wrote,[5] but he does not really eliminate the possibility that chaps. 56–66 are the work of a disciple. Rabban himself considers "Second Isaiah" a self-conscious follower of First Isaiah, so he ought not to rule out the possibility of a "Third Isaiah." This issue, fortunately, has no bearing on his identification of "Second Isaiah," since the data come from chaps. 40–55.

As for the date of the corpus, Rabban infers that all of Isaiah 40–66 was composed before the fall of Babylon, with Judah and Jerusalem still in ruins (59:9-11; 63:18; 64:9-10) and redemption yet to come (56:1; 60:4-5; 62:7; 66:8-14). Further, "Second Isaiah" preached not in Babylon but in Judah, with whose clime he appears well acquainted (65:10; 62:8).[6] The seeming mentions of the temple in 60:7 and of sacrifice in 43:23-24; 66:3 refer rather to the *site* of the temple, where, according to Jer 41:5, sacrifice was still conducted (cf. Isa 43:23-24; 66:3). Other passages referring to the temple (56:5; 60:13; 62:9; 66:20-21) are predictions of the temple still to be built; that it does not yet exist is presupposed by 66:1: "What is the house that you would build for me, and what is the place of my rest?" As for the word *hêkāl* in 66:6, it denotes the Temple Mount (cf. 65:11). Some of this argument is plainly forced, although none of it is impossible. Again, Rabban's theory about the identity of the prophet does not depend on Judean composition or exilic date.

Like many others, Rabban focuses on the Servant theme in "Second Isaiah." There are three alternative approaches: the Servant is all Israel, part of Israel, or a specific individual. Rabban recognizes that often all Israel is called Yahweh's "servant," and he develops criteria for isolating such usage (pp. 39-46). In general, when speaking of Israel the prophet does one of three things: (1) he

---

5. On the artistic (not authorial) unity of the entire book of Isaiah, see P. R. Ackroyd, "Isaiah i–xii: Presentation of a Prophet," in *Congress Volume: Göttingen, 1977* (VTSup 29; Leiden: Brill, 1978) 16-48; B. S. Childs, *Introduction to the Old Testament as Scripture* (Philadelphia: Fortress, 1979) 325-34; R. E. Clements, "The Unity of the Book of Isaiah," *Int* 36 (1982) 117-29; C. A. Evans, "On the Unity and Parallel Structure of Isaiah," *VT* 38 (1988) 129-47; M. A. Sweeney, *Isaiah 1–4 and the Post-Exilic Understanding of the Isaianic Tradition* (BZAW 171; Berlin: de Gruyter, 1988); J. Vermeylen, "L'unité du livre d'Isaie," in *The Book of Isaiah — Le livre d'Isaie* (ed. J. Vermeylen; BETL 81; Louvain: Peeters, 1989) 11-53; R. Rendtorff, "The Book of Isaiah: A Complex Unity. Synchronic and Diachronic Reading," SBLSP 1991 (ed. E. H. Lovering; Atlanta: Scholars, 1991) 8-20.

6. Cf. H. M. Barstad, "Lebte Deuterojesaja in Juda?" *NorTT* 83 (1982) 77-87.

uses the plural;[7] (2) he uses the masculine singular, with a nearby reference to the people or a plural form to indicate the subject is a collective;[8] or (3) he uses the feminine singular, speaking to or of Jerusalem/*bat ṣîyôn*.[9] These criteria allow us to determine when the Servant is Israel.

The oracles B. Duhm isolated as "Servant Songs" (42:1-4; 49:1-6; 50:4-9; 52:13–53:12) describe a masculine singular Servant without using the plural or mentioning the people (on 49:3 see below).[10] To Rabban, who rejects Duhm's view that the Servant Songs are not by "Second Isaiah,"[11] this indicates that the Servant cannot be Israel. There are further reasons to distinguish between the Servant Israel and the Servant of the Songs. Israel is a sinner (48:8), whereas the Servant is guiltless (53:9), a judge (42:1-4), and an atoning victim (53:5) *for* Israel. The Servant is childless, whereas the nation has children. In 49:5-6 God speaks to the Servant *about* Israel; the Servant is to restore Israel (49:8-13). He is to be the *běrît 'am*, "covenant of (the) people," that is, the mediator of the covenant between Yahweh and Israel (p. 59). That the Servant's tribulations at the hands of his enemies atone for their sins proves, to Rabban, that he is an individual and that his enemies are Israelites. If all Israel were the Servant, Rabban argues, then it would be paradoxical that Israel's oppression, which is the very sin of the nations, should atone for that sin. Of course, the persecution of an individual Servant would also be sin, but not the chief sin of all Israel.

As for the theory that the Servant is a nucleus of the faithful,[12] Rabban dismisses this as a "bizarre, contrived conjecture" (p. 51), a misguided attempt to identify the national Servant, Jacob-Israel, with the protagonist of the Servant

---

7. 40:21; 41:17, 20; 42:16, 18, 22-24; 43:6, 12, 14-15, 18-19, 21; 44:8; 45:11, 25; 46:8-9, 12; 47:4; 48:1-2, 6, 14, 16, 20, 21; 49:9-12; 50:1; 51:1-2, 4, 6, 11, 12; 52:3, 10, 11-12; 54:17; 55:1-3, 6, 8-12; 56:1; 57:3-5, 15; 58:3-4; 59:2-3, 5-12; 61:1, 7-9; 62:12; 63:7, 16-19; 64:2, 5-8, 10-11; 65:7, 8, 11-15, 18; 66:1, 5, 10, 14, 20-22.

8. 40:27-28; 41:8-16; 42:22; 43:1-8, 22-23; 44:1-3, 6, 21-24; 45:11; 48:4-17; 52:4-6; 57:14-17. The sole exception is 56:10, which nowhere makes explicit that the people is the antecedent of "his watchmen."

9. 45:14; 49:14-26; 51:12-13, 17-23; 52:1-2, 7-8; 54; 57:6-13; 60; 62:1-6, 8, 11; 66:2-6, 8.

10. B. Duhm, *Jesaia* (HKAT 3/1; Göttingen: Vandenhoeck & Ruprecht, 1914).

11. See also C. R. North, *The Suffering Servant in Deutero-Isaiah* (2nd ed.; London: Oxford University, 1956) 156-91; and T. N. D. Mettinger, *Farewell to the Servant* (Lund: Gleerup, 1983).

12. J. Skinner, *The Book of the Prophet Isaiah Chapters XL–LXVI* (London: Cambridge University, 1917); H. W. Robinson, *The Cross of the Servant* (London: SCM, 1925); O. Eissfeldt, "The Ebed-Yahwe in Isaiah xl–lv in Light of the Israelite Conceptions of the Community and the Individual, the Ideal and the Real," *ExpTim* 44 (1932-33) 261-68; J. Muilenburg, "Isaiah Chapters 40–66," *IB* 5.410; S. H. Blank, *Prophetic Faith in Isaiah* (New York: Harper & Row, 1958) chaps. 4–9; A. S. Kapelrud, "The Identity of the Suffering Servant," in *Near Eastern Studies in Honor of William Foxwell Albright* (ed. H. Goedicke; Baltimore: Johns Hopkins University, 1971) 307-14; J. H. Eaton, *Festal Drama in Deutero-Isaiah* (London: SPCK, 1979). For further bibliography see North, *Suffering Servant,* 35-39, 62, 203-4.

Songs. Since Rabban is convinced these are distinct servants, such a mediation has no point; if the Servant is described as an individual, he probably is one.

Rabban therefore opts for the individual approach. As for the identity of the Servant,[13] 42:19 provides a clue: "Who is blind but my servant, or deaf as my messenger whom I send?" Comparison with 44:26, where "servant(s)" and "messengers" connote prophets, indicates that the Servant is a prophet.[14]

Like S. Mowinckel, H. Schmidt, and others,[15] Rabban infers that the Servant is none other than "Second Isaiah" (pp. 52-59), and indeed many of the Songs have an autobiographical tone, though narrated in the third person.[16] The death of the Servant in 53:7-9, 12 would seem an obstacle, as Mowinckel later found it to be, but Rabban observes that we are not sure the Servant dies; he merely prepares for and imagines his own death (pp. 68-74).[17] This argument, then, is not enough to rule out the autobiographical approach.

The major difficulty for Rabban's thesis, and for any individual interpretation, is 49:1-13, particularly v. 3. Overall the passage fits his personal interpretation well; in the themes of election from the womb and mission of restoring Israel to Yahweh, the passage recalls the autobiographical passages of Jeremiah. The only problem is v. 3: "And he said to me, 'You are my servant, Israel, in whom I will be glorified.'"

Here Rabban must do a little tap dancing (pp. 59-64). But he is ultimately correct that "even if we regard this verse as one of the passages treating the Servant-Israel, this does not suffice to negate the arguments in favor of seeing

---

13. For bibliography on past attempts, see North, *Suffering Servant;* and C. C. Kruse, "The Servant Songs: Interpretive Trends since C. R. North," *Studia Biblica et Theologica* 8 (1978) 3-27.

14. On prophets as Yahweh's "servants," cf. Isa 20:3; Jer 7:25; Ezek 38:17; Amos 3:7; Zech 1:6; etc.

15. S. Mowinckel, *Der Knecht Jahwäs* (Giessen: Töpelmann, 1921). Mowinckel later retracted this interpretation; see his article "Die Komposition des deuterojesajanischen Buches," *ZAW* 49 (1931) 87-112, 242-60; H. Schmidt, *Gott und das Leid im Alten Testament* (Giessen: Töpelmann, 1926); W. Zimmerli and J. Jeremias, *"pais theou," TDNT* 5.654-717; G. Fohrer, *Das Buch Jesaja* (Zürcher Bibelkommentare 3; Zurich and Stuttgart: Zwingli, 1964); E. Kutsch, *Sein Leiden und Tod — unser Heil* (Biblische Studien 52; Neukirchen-Vluyn: Neukirchener Verlag, 1967); H. M. Orlinsky, "The So-called 'Servant of the Lord' and 'Suffering Servant' in Second Isaiah," in Orlinsky and N. H. Snaith, *Studies in the Second Part of the Book of Isaiah* (VTSup 14; Leiden: Brill, 1967) 1-133; A. Schoors, *I Am God Your Savior* (VTSup 24; Leiden: Brill, 1973); R. N. Whybray, *Thanksgiving for a Liberated Prophet* (JSOT-Sup 4; Sheffield: JSOT, 1978) 134-35. For further bibliography see North, *Suffering Servant,* 41, 72-85, 195-201.

16. The prophet uses the first person in 48:16; 61:1, 3, 10; 62:1-3; 63:7, and God addresses him as an individual in 42:6, 20; 49:7-8; 52:14; 58:1.

17. In 53:8, Rabban interprets *nigzar mēʾereṣ ḥayyîm* as "he was (metaphorically) condemned to die," and he emends the final colon with the Greek: **nāgaʿ lāmût,* "he came near [cf. Jer 48:32; Mic 1:9; Jonah 3:6; Ezra 3:1] to dying." Whybray (*Thanksgiving,* 106) reaches a similar conclusion.

the Servant-individual in the rest of the Servant Songs" (p. 62n.70). Rabban also observes that one manuscript lacks the word "Israel" entirely, but he resists the allure of this attractive (for his theory) reading. His own explanation appeals to the prophet's extreme identification with his people and supposes that the language is elliptical: "With the word 'Israel' the verse *compares the Servant to Israel in respect to their relationship with Yahweh*" (p. 64), an interpretation Ibn Ezra also espoused: "This means either 'one of the seed of Israel through whom I will be glorified,' or 'you are Israel inasmuch as you are in my eyes equivalent to all Israel' — the latter is correct."

As for the name of the prophet, key for Rabban is 42:18-19: "Hear, you deaf; and look, you blind, that you may see! Who is blind but my servant, or deaf as my messenger whom I send? Who is blind as *měšullām*, or blind as the servant of Yahweh?" Here Rabban is at his most persuasive (pp. 76-77):

> Although he is perceptive to the commands of God, and although he is the eyes and ears of the people, the prophet is himself blind and deaf. In this declaration there is, above all, an elimination of the distance between prophet and people. The prophet does not raise himself above his listeners. . . . This sense of identification should not surprise us, since compassion and forgiveness define, one might say, a prophet's relation to the nation; we might even see in compassion a quasi-admission to complicity in sin. Indeed, just as Isaiah sees himself as a man of unclean lips dwelling among a people of unclean lips (6:5), so our prophet several times identifies himself with the sinful people (e.g., 42:24; 59:12; 63:17; 64:4-8). This sense of identification explains the attempt to emphasize the equality between prophet and people in respect to blindness and deafness.

The impairment of the prophet is not a physical limitation, but a spiritual obtuseness relieved by his later enlightenment (42:20; 50:4, 5). But what might *měšullām* mean? Rabban answers (p. 78):

> Commentators are unanimous in regarding *měšullām* as a symbolic appellation for the Servant. We find throughout the Prophets symbolic names such as *šě'ār yāšûb*, "a remnant shall return" (7:3); *'immānû'ēl*, "God is with us" (7:14); *mahēr šālāl ḥāš baz*, "the spoil speeds, the prey hastens" (8:3); *pele' yô'ēṣ 'ēl gibbôr 'ăbî'ad śar-šālôm*, "Wonderful Counselor, Mighty God, Everlasting Father, Prince of Peace" (9:5 [ET 6]); *měšûbâ yiśrā'ēl*, "faithless Israel," *bōgēdâ yěhûdâ*, "false Judah" (Jer 3:6-12); *māgôr missābîb*, "terror on every side" (Jer 20:3); *yhwh ṣidqēnû*, "Yahweh is our righteousness" (Jer 23:6); *zādôn*, "proud one" (Jer 50:31-32); *yizrě'e(')l*, "Jezreel" (Hos 1:4); *lō' rūḥāmâ*, "not pitied" (Hos 1:6); *lō' 'ammî*, "not my people" (Hos 1:9); *'ohŏlâ*, "tent," *'ohŏlîbāmâ*, "my tent is a high place" (Ezek 23:4); *ṣemaḥ*, "branch" (Zech 6:12); *nō'am*, "grace," and *ḥōbĕlîm*, "union" (Zech 11:7). It is easy to divine the symbolic import of these names, which point to attributes or deeds

associated with particular persons or things. But, in contrast to the transparency of such epithets, the import of *mĕšullām* is not clear at all.

Rabban then goes through the various attempts to understand *mĕšullām* as a symbolic epithet, all of which he rightly rejects (pp. 78-79). Although many argue that *mĕšullām* conveys devotion or obedience to God, this is the meaning of the cognate root in Arabic, not in Hebrew. Kimḥi's appeal to the Qal *šālēm*, "perfect," does not reckon with the special meaning of the Piel/Pual. Also forced are the interpretations of *mĕšullām* as "paid for," that is, the Servant is Yahweh's property, or "the requited one." Rabban then explains the normal function of symbolic epithets (pp. 79-81):

> The essential difference . . . between the epithets listed above [Shear-yashub, etc.] and *mĕšullām* is that the former are all nouns, adjectives, or verbs that indicate particular acts or attributes. The essence of their symbolism lies in the invention of personal epithets out of words and phrases that are not themselves used as personal names. . . . I therefore conclude that a symbolic epithet must be a word *not* used as a personal name; a real name can never be used as a symbolic epithet.
>
> As it happens, *mĕšullām* is, above all, a personal name attested no fewer than twenty-four times, especially in the exilic and Persian period (2 Kgs 22:3; Ezra 8:16; 10:15, 29; Neh 3:4, 6, 30; 6:18; 8:4; 10:8, 21; 11:7, 11; 12:13, 16, 25, 33; 1 Chr 3:19; 5:13; 8:17; 9:8, 11, 12; 2 Chr 34:12;[18] the name also occurs in a feminine form, Meshullemeth, 2 Kgs 21:19). Hence, the most natural interpretation is that here Meshullam is the name of the Servant-prophet himself.

Admittedly, 42:22 begins "But this is a people robbed and plundered," arguably showing that the Servant in the previous lines is Israel. But Rabban's interpretation (p. 22) that *wĕhû'* indicates a shift of subject, is preferable, in the light of the use of Meshullam as a personal name. Indeed, there is a good chance that among the faceless community leaders named Meshullam in the Bible stands the Servant of "Second Isaiah," most likely the prophet himself.

This solution is indeed so simple that at first it seems baffling that it has been so rarely suggested.[19] But Rabban shows (pp. 81-82) that strong factors

18. Rabban neglects to observe that it is also common at Elephantine.

19. To our knowledge, Rabban's only precursor is J. L. Palache, *The 'Ebed-Jahve Enigma in Pseudo-Isaiah* (Amsterdam, 1934), a work only slightly less obscure than Rabban's own. We have not seen it, but according to the summary in North (*Suffering Servant*, 89-90) Palache regards the Songs as biographical rather than autobiographical, and he picks out a specific Meshullam — the elder son of Zerubbabel (1 Chr 3:19) — thereby dating "Second Isaiah" later than most commentators, including Rabban. Indeed, Palache does not consider Isaiah 40–55, let alone 40–66, the work of a single prophet, and so the oracles reflect a variety of historical settings. Palache's theory at least explains the messianic tones Rabban and others detect in the Servant Songs.

historically militated against its discovery — traditional assumptions of Isaianic authorship or of a messianic Servant, on the one hand, and scholarly identification of the Servant with Israel or a part thereof, on the other. Also, all the characters named Meshullam are extremely minor, so the name is unfamiliar to most readers of the Bible.

Further, Rabban demonstrates (pp. 85-87) the high probability that in 49:7 *'ebed mōšĕlîm*, "servant of rulers," is a corruption of **'abdô mĕšullām*, "his servant Meshullam."[20] The preceding, coordinate phrases *bĕzōh-nepeš* and *mĕtā'ēb gôy* constitute a minor problem in the MT, on account of their obscurity, but Rabban joins the majority of scholars and the witness of several versions (see *BHS* apparatus) in taking *bzh* and *mt'b* as passives: "the despised."[21] Rabban suggests plausibly that **mšlm* was interpreted as *mōšĕlîm* and eventually written as *mōšĕlîm*, "rulers," because of the proximity of *mĕlākîm*, "kings," and *śārîm*, "princes." This is as convincing as a conjectural emendation can be. Rabban caustically and effectively disparages Mowinckel's attempt, the inverse of his own, to dismiss the problem of Meshullam by labeling 42:19b a "gloss" and *mĕšullām* a corruption of *mōšĕlîm* in 49:7 (p. 84).[22]

How, then, did Meshullam get to be "Second Isaiah"? How was his name forgotten? From various thematic contacts, Rabban infers that Meshullam was a keen student of the works of Isaiah of Jerusalem, as well as of Jeremiah. The oft-mentioned "former things" (*rī'šōnôt, qadmōnîyôt* [42:9; 43:9, 18; 46:9; 48:3]) are old oracles, primarily Isa 13:1–14:23; 21:1-10; Jeremiah 50–51, that Meshullam took to forecast the great event of his time: the fall of Babylon (pp. 9-23). Since Meshullam names himself in 42:19; 49:7, it is unlikely that a later hand could have confused him with Isaiah. Rather, Meshullam purposely appended his oracles to those of his illustrious forerunner (pp. 23-26). Rabban ingenuously compares a reader scribbling his own thoughts in the margins of a beloved book (p. 25), although endpapers would be a better analogy.

Rabban believes, however, that Meshullam did not intend to attribute his oracles to Isaiah; rather, later readers drew this erroneous inference. Although the prophet identifies himself within his oracles, the lack of a superscription (e.g., "The words of Meshullam") allowed his name to be forgotten. But it is untrue, as Rabban claims, that the combining of the oracles of Meshullam with those of Isaiah made it impossible to take *mĕšullām* as a personal name. It would surely have been as clear to any early editor or reader as it is to Rabban that

20. *'abdî*, "my servant," would be equally possible, although Rabban does not suggest it.

21. While it is not Rabban's solution, he notes that 1QIsa[a] reads *bĕzûy*.

22. A similar approach is taken by J. Blenkinsopp, "Second Isaiah — Prophet of Universalism," *JSOT* 41 (1988) 99n.4. Palache (*'Ebed-Jahve Enigma*) also discovers the name Meshullam in 44:26 and 52:5, in addition to 49:7. To us 52:5 seems far-fetched, but perhaps 44:26 at least alludes to Meshullam: *'ăṣat mal'ākā(y)w yašlîm*, "he completes the plan of his messengers."

měšullām is a man's name. Rather, 42:19; 49:7 function in the received book of Isaiah as long-range prophecies, by Isaiah, of the prophet Meshullam, just as the "man of God" foretells the advent of Josiah in 1 Kgs 13:2-5.

Many, if not most, contemporary scholars are convinced that the Servant is Israel, but this is really no better grounded than Rabban's thesis. Rabban does not, as he appears to think, fully prove his point, but his work leaves us with two equally plausible scenarios: either the Servant is a collective described as a fictitious individual named Meshullam, or he is an actual individual who identifies himself with the nation of Israel. To many, the latter might seem slightly more believable.

To end this review, we can do no better than quote from Rabban's own conclusion, in which he paints a compelling picture of the prophet Meshullam (pp. 89-95):

> It seems that an inferiority complex played an important part in Meshullam's prophetic development. He was both a "man of pains, and acquainted with sickness" (53:3) and quite ugly — "he had no form or comeliness" (v. 2) — and his visage was marred beyond other men's, so that "many were astonished" at him and would hide their faces from him in disgust (52:14; 53:2-3). . . . He was "despised and rejected by men" (53:3), and people would attack him, mocking and abusing him, striking him, plucking his cheeks, and spitting in his face — and all this he accepted with love, without defending himself (50:6). Because of the natural fear and scorn that his disease and ugliness evoked, the people considered him "stricken, smitten by God, and afflicted" (53:4), that is, a sinner (53:12) punished by heaven for his iniquities. They laid blame on him and sought to kill him, "although he had done no violence, and there was no deceit in his mouth" (53:9). Still he acted with complete passivity, accepting his sufferings with love (53:7).
>
> In this silent humility one perceives a profound self-esteem, a quiet certainty in his final triumph born of faith in his own righteousness and authority. The prophet is imbued with a double idea, which is essentially one — that the God of the world is also the "Holy One of Israel," or, more properly, that the "Holy One of Israel" is the God of the world. Yahweh, the God of the entire earth and the sole God of truth, chose the Hebrew nation, called it by his own name, and loved it as a mother loves the fruit of her womb. He will one day cause it to rule over all the nations, who will also acknowledge Yahweh, join the people of Yahweh, and be called by his name. This concept is linked in the prophet's mind with an awareness that he is the one whom God has commissioned to accomplish all this; from thence derives his self-esteem, virtually unexampled among the prophets of Israel.
>
> No other prophet speaks so about himself and his office. God called him when he was still in his mother's womb (cf. Jer 1:5), he made his mouth "like a sharp sword" (to convey his message to the ears of the nations), he hid him "in the shadow of his hand" (to defend him from his enemies) and made him a "polished arrow" (to fulfill his mission) and called him "the Servant of

Yahweh" (49:3). God summoned him in righteousness, took him by the hand (42:6), was pleased by his righteousness (42:21), and answered and helped him (49:8). The prophet is God's chosen one, his messenger and emissary, on whom the spirit of Yahweh rests (42:1, 19; 43:10; 49:3; 61:1). God opened his ears and caused him to hear his words "morning by morning"; the prophet did not rebel against Yahweh's command, nor turn back, but received from God the "tongue of those who are taught" to "know how to sustain with a word him that is weary" (50:4-5). In this manner he was trained to be the "covenant to the people" and "light to the nations." He will return Israel to Yahweh (religious revival) and will raise the tribes of Jacob (political revival); he will revive the land from its desolation, will proclaim liberty to the captives, and reveal what is hidden in the dark; he will open the eyes that are blind, bring good tidings to the afflicted, bind up the brokenhearted, comfort those who mourn in Zion, and give them a garland instead of ashes, gladness instead of mourning (49:5-6, 8-9; 42:7; 61:1-3). For Zion's sake he will not keep silent or rest, "until her vindication goes forth as brightness, and her salvation as a burning torch" (62:1).

As "light to the nations," Meshullam addresses the Gentiles directly and proclaims to them his quality as prophet of Yahweh (49:1-2). "He will bring forth justice to the nations" (42:1), and the "coastlands (= nations) wait for his law" (42:4). As the judge of the nations, he will deal righteously, with moderation and compassion: "He will not cry or lift up his voice, or make it heard in the street; a bruised reed he will not break, and a dying wick he will not quench" (42:2-4).[23]

This moderation and righteous humility correspond to Meshullam's dumbness and passivity in relation to his oppressors. But they do not diminish his confidence that he is destined to receive great reparations for the indignities he has endured. Although at times he is inclined to despair of his personal reward for his suffering and efforts in pursuance of his mission, he eventually recovers his faith: "Yet surely my right is with Yahweh, and my recompense with my God" (49:4). His recompense is honor and greatness in the eyes of God and humanity (49:5; 49:7; 52:13-15); he is also destined to divide the spoil with the great and strong (53:12). . . .

23. Above all others, Second Isaiah deserves the title "prophet to the nations." His prophecy opens with "comfort, comfort my people" and ends with "from new moon to new moon, and from Sabbath to Sabbath, all flesh shall come to worship before me, says Yahweh." The first half of the first Servant Song (42:1-12) treats primarily the "nations" and "coast-lands" (= "nations"), although in vv. 6-7 "covenant to the people" appears alongside "light to the nations." Chapter 49 also discusses both the "covenant to the people," on the one hand, and the "light to the nations," on the other, but here the universal mission is described as the pinnacle of Second Isaiah's prophetic activity and its ultimate goal. The idea of the conversion of the nations, to which the polemic against the Gentiles and idolaters serves as a sort of introduction or preparation, runs throughout his oracles like a scarlet thread (45:14, 22-23; 51:4-5; 55:4-5; 56:3, 6-7; 59:19; 60:3, 14).

Meshullam is not only a prophet bearing the word of Yahweh but also a savior and redeemer, a judge and ruler. In these attributes there is undoubtedly a royal, messianic tone. Indeed, a certain similarity exists between the messianic king in First Isaiah . . . and the Servant.

It is clear that all this, however, is only a vision, quite different from reality. . . . But, out of his boundless love for the nation and out of a burning faith in its great future, the prophet converts his very lowliness and weakness into a source of might and greatness. Just as his own former "blindness" and "deafness" induced God to inspire him with his spirit and law and make him fit for his office, so his worth is not less for being "despised and rejected by men; a man of pains and acquainted with sickness" and possessed of an inhuman appearance. Indeed, all this is the sign of the authority that the hand of Yahweh has laid on him. Meshullam alone bears on his shoulders the sin of the entire people and atones for it.

Meshullam's function of representing the entire people recalls several other prophets (Hosea, Jeremiah, Ezekiel) who in their acts symbolized the fate of the nation. . . . The symbolism of spontaneous suffering atoning for the sins of the people is part of the overall, striking similarity between Meshullam's fate and identity and the fate and identity of the nation. Meshullam and the people are equally lowly in degree and objects of contempt;[24] both despair of seeing good fortune and of receiving their due recompense, yet both are comforted (40:27-31; 49:4) and are destined for victory and honor as reparations for their present conditions.[25] Even the epithets that describe their inner natures are similar. Both are called the servants of Yahweh, his chosen and beloved from the womb (42:1; 43:20; 44:1; 49:1; 46:3), both are created (*yṣr, 'śh, br'*) by Yahweh (42:6; 43:1; 44:21), called by name (43:1; 49:1), honored in the eyes of Yahweh (43:4; 49:5), and God holds their hands or supports and helps them (41:10, 14; 42:6; 49:8). Upon both rests the spirit of Yahweh, or his light and glory (42:1; 44:3; 59:21; 60:1-3, 19-20). Both are witnesses for Yahweh (43:10, 12). Finally, both are blind and deaf (42:18-19; 43:8). This resemblance (which doubtless contributed to the formation of the collective interpretation of the Servant) may, on the one hand, be coincidental: the fate of Meshullam among his people happens to parallel that of the Hebrew people among the nations. . . . On the other hand, it is not easy to distinguish between the personal element and the communal feeling in the soul of Meshullam, since he has dedicated all his life and soul to the ideal of the nation, and all his thoughts and hopes, apparently springing from his individual complex, are obsessed by this ideal. . . . It follows that his own self-glorification arises only out of and for the sake of the national-religious ideal. This internal association between his own person and the nation is manifest in Meshullam's consciousness that he suffers and is punished in place of the nation, that he has become, as it were, a concrete, personal symbol of the entire people. . . .

24. 41:14, 17; 42:22; 43:24; 49:7; 50:10; 51:7, 22; 53:3; 54:4; 60:14; 61:7.
25. 41:13, 17; 49:7, 23; 50:7-9; 51:8; 52–53; 54:4, 11, 14; 60:17; 61:9.

The people, with whom Meshullam identified so, did not preserve his name or memory. In contrast to the other major prophets, I have no reliable information concerning his life and personality. But if my surmise is correct, and I have succeeded in revealing his name, which tradition hid in the shadow of Isaiah and which modern scholarship despaired of recovering, I have at least begun to repay our debt to the memory of this great, "nameless" man.[26]

---

26. Propp has made a complete translation of Rabban's monograph, but does not currently intend to publish it. Rabban's style reads poorly in English, and there is much overargumentation and antiquated amateur philology. Interested colleagues without access to the original are welcome to copies.

Why Prophetic Oracles against the Nations?

PAUL R. RAABE

Concordia Seminary, St. Louis, Missouri

I. Introduction

In the corpus of the Hebrew Bible's Latter Prophets one frequently encounters oracles or prophecies against non-Israelite nations. Such an oracle consists typically of an announcement of future doom on a specific foreign nation, city, or ruler. The prophets proclaim in these texts that Yahweh, the God of Israel, will enact judgment and will (normally) use an army, such as Assyria or Babylonia, as the instrument.

What is somewhat surprising is the amount of space this type of material occupies. Although oracles against nations (abbreviated OAN) are scattered throughout the corpus of the Latter Prophets,[1] most of them have been gathered into collections: Isaiah 13–23; Jeremiah 46–51 (LXX 25–31); Ezekiel 25–32; Amos 1–2; Zeph 2:4-15; and Zech 9:1-8. One should also include Obadiah and Nahum, the former against Edom and the latter against Nineveh. These collections, including Obadiah and Nahum, comprise in terms of word counts 13.6% of the corpus of the Latter Prophets (see table 1). This, however, represents a conservative figure. If one would include all the texts that announce doom against foreign nations, such as Isaiah 34, Ezekiel 38–39, Joel 4 (ET 3), and others, then the percentage would probably increase to 15-20%.

That so much of the prophetic corpus is devoted to this type of material raises a basic question: Why oracles against foreign nations? What purpose or purposes do they serve? Since Gressmann's study (1929) the usual view has assumed that they function as proclamations of salvation for Israel. Moreover,

---

1. For a complete listing, see Stuart 1987:405-6.

Table 1: Word Counts (based on Andersen and Forbes 1983)

Book	Book Length	OAN	OAN Length	% of OAN
Isaiah	16,930	Isaiah 13–23	2,397	14.2
Jeremiah	21,868	Jeremiah 46–51	3,257	14.9
Ezekiel	18,731	Ezekiel 25–32	2,805	15
Amos	2,047	Amos 1:3–2:3	214	10.5
Obadiah	291	Obadiah	291	100
Nahum	559	Nahum	559	100
Zephaniah	767	Zeph 2:4-15	179	23.3
Zechariah	3,128	Zech 9:1-8	92	2.9
The Twelve	14,365		1,335	9.3
Total for Latter Prophets	71,894		9,794	13.6

some scholars simply dismiss them as regrettable examples of Israelite xenophobic nationalism. For example, Pfeiffer (1941:443) claims that "they reflect on the whole not the moral indignation of the great pre-exilic prophets, but rather the nationalism of the 'false prophets.'" He also calls them "outbursts of hatred for the heathen kingdoms" (443).

Much research has been conducted regarding the authenticity of the individual oracles and the origin of this type of literature,[2] but the question of purpose needs to be examined in a more intentional and systematic way. The present essay does not claim to present the final and definitive statement on the matter but has the more limited goal of clarifying the question and of suggesting some possible answers. I will limit the corpus for discussion to the collections of OAN. My basic thesis argues that the oracles against foreign nations in their present literary shape and context serve a variety of purposes, some of which concern Israel and others the nations themselves. I am happy to dedicate this essay to my *Doktorvater*, David Noel Freedman, whose friendship, counsel, and scholarship always provide inspiration.

2. Most scholars believe that at least some of the OAN derive from the prophet to whom they are ascribed, and the case is increasingly being made that more rather than less of the OAN are authentic. Andersen and Freedman (1989) and Paul (1991) argue that all of Amos 1–2 is genuine. Erlandsson (1970) argues for the authenticity of practically all of Isaiah 13–23, including the "Burden of Babylon" in Isa 13:2–14:23; for an opposing view, see Gosse 1988. Holladay (1989) concludes that the OAN in the book of Jeremiah are by and large authentic to Jeremiah, and Boadt (1986) and Greenberg (1983) maintain the genuineness of Ezekiel's OAN. For a recent survey of views regarding the origin of the OAN tradition, see Paul 1991:7-11. In general, they revolve around the Egyptian execration texts, Near Eastern treaty curses, and early war oracles.

II. Preliminary Illustration of Thesis

One can see that prophetic oracles against the nations may serve a variety of purposes by reading through Isaiah 13–23. According to the present shape of these chapters, the following purposes emerge:

13:9	to destroy sinners from the earth;
13:11	to put an end to human arrogance;
14:1-2	to cause nations to return Israelite exiles and to enable restored Israel to rule over their oppressors;
14:3	to give Israel rest from cruel bondage;
14:4-8	to give rest and peace to all the nations (and even nature) that suffer under the oppression of the king of Babylon;
14:11-17	to humble the self-deifying proud ruler;
14:20-23	to permanently eliminate the wicked;
14:25	to remove the Assyrian yoke from Israel (cf. 10:27);
14:32	to warn against anti-Assyrian alliances and to encourage reliance on Yahweh in Zion;
16:1-5	to lead Moabite refugees to seek refuge in Zion under the righteous rule of a Davidide;
16:6-14	to debase proud Moab;
17:7-8	to cause people to look to Yahweh instead of their shrines and Asherim;
17:14	to eliminate those who plunder Israel;
18:7	to provoke Cush into bringing gifts to Yahweh in Zion;
19:16-17	to cause Egypt to fear Yahweh and Judah;
19:18	to lead Egypt to swear allegiance to Yahweh;
19:19-22	to evoke from Egypt faith in and worship of Yahweh;
19:23-25	to result in the elevation of Egypt and Assyria to the status of Yahweh's people alongside Israel;[3]
20:1-6	to reveal to the cities of Philistia (and implicitly Israel?) the futility of an anti-Assyrian alliance with Egypt and Cush;
21:11-12	to reveal the prophet as the "watchman," the only one who can foresee the future concerning the nations;[4]
21:16	to bring to an end all the glory of Kedar;
23:17-18	to cause restored Tyre to dedicate its wealth to Yahweh as provisions for Zion.

3. The envisaged reconciliation and status of Egypt and Assyria present a stark contrast to the historical pattern of warring between the two with Israel as a pawn.

4. The *maśśā'* concerning Dumah is extremely enigmatic, but at least one inference seems clear. If "Dumah" — either a wordplay on "Edom" or Dûmet ej-Jendal in northern Arabia — wishes to know the future, only the prophet of Yahweh can reveal it.

The individual oracles recorded in Isaiah 13–23 stem from different occasions and reflect a complex history, but in their present literary context they reveal one overarching goal: the impending disasters intend to humble the proud and destroy the wicked so that Yahweh alone will be exalted and honored (cf. Isa 2:9-22; 25:2-3). The texts anticipate that after the impending disasters both Israel and the nations will know Yahweh and honor Zion as his dwelling place. The texts certainly indicate that Israel will benefit from all of this. Thus some of the OAN function as proclamations of salvation for Israel (14:1-3, 25; 17:14). But the OAN can also envisage benefits for the nations themselves. The fall of the king of Babylon means rest for the oppressed peoples of the earth (14:4-8); the fugitives of Moab can find refuge in Zion (16:1-5); Egypt and Assyria will gain the status of Israel as Yahweh's people (19:23-25).

The prophetic logic presupposes that at the time of the prophetic oracles the nations proudly carry on with business as usual, remaining indifferent to the Holy One of Israel. They have their own plans and goals (19:3, 11-15), their own schemes of alliances (14:32; 18:1-2; 20:1-6), their own gods and religion (16:12; 17:8; 19:1, 3; cf. 21:9). Therefore judgment and disaster are necessary in the near future, after which the world's scene will be altered. Then people *(h'dm)* will look to the Holy One of Israel (17:7-8); Egypt will know and worship Yahweh (19:18-22) together with Assyria (19:23); and nations will honor Yahweh by bringing gifts to Zion (18:7; 23:17-18).[5] The logic of these texts considers the impending woe to be preparatory for the subsequent weal that both Israel and the nations will experience.[6]

The oracles of Isaiah 13–23 reveal other purposes as well. Some texts function as admonitions against anti-Assyrian alliances (14:32; 20:1-6). The enigmatic oracle of 21:11-12 serves to legitimate the prophet as the only reliable seer of the future. The inclusion of the oracle against Jerusalem (chap. 22; cf. 17:10-11) within the series of OAN has the effect of accusing Jerusalem of behaving no differently than the *gôyīm*.

A reading of Isaiah 13–23 reveals that the OAN can serve a variety of purposes for both Israel and the nations. The same holds for the OAN found

---

5. A similar type of logic appears in Isaiah 2: only after the nations' complacent pride is eliminated (2:10-22) will the nations desire to go to Zion (2:2-4).

6. The perspective regarding the future relationship between Israel and the nations varies. According to Isa 14:1-2 resident aliens *(hgr)* will unite with Israel and Israel will possess *(htnhl)* other peoples as servants in "Yahweh's land," but according to Isa 19:24-25 Egypt and Assyria will receive the same status as Israel. Yet even in the latter text divine blessing is mediated to Egypt and Assyria through Israel as "a (source of) blessing in the midst of the earth," a statement that recalls the patriarchal promise of Gen 12:2-3 (see Mitchell 1987:30, 55). The OAN of Isaiah 13–23 never divorce the future of the nations from the future of Israel but remain in continuity with the Zion-centered theology found elsewhere in Isaiah; cf. Martin-Achard 1962; Webb 1990.

elsewhere. But before discussing the issue further, I should first clarify the nature of the question.

III. Clarifying the Question

The basic question of "why oracles against the nations?" needs to be broken down into two distinct questions: (1) What is the ultimate goal or purpose that the future *act* of divine judgment is expected to achieve? (2) What is the rhetorical purpose that the *speech* serves? In other words, one needs to distinguish between the purpose of the announced event and the purpose of the announcing oracle. The former seeks to ascertain the outcome expected to ensue from the impending disasters, whereas the latter investigates the persuasive function of the utterance itself.[7]

To address these questions one needs to keep in mind three methodological considerations. First, in the light of the complex nature of the material one should be open to the possibility that a given oracle might serve several concurrent purposes rather than only one.

Second, one should take seriously the present shape of the oracles and their present literary context. Previous research has focused on investigating their historical circumstances, identifying the origin of the OAN tradition, and differentiating between the various editorial layers of a given text. But what is needed is more research that concentrates on the final edited shape of the texts in an effort to understand the inner logic and argument of the whole.

Third, one should let the rest of the book inform the interpretation of a specific oracle. For example, one should understand the expected restoration of Egypt (Jer 46:26), Moab (48:47), Ammon (49:6), and Elam (49:39) in concert with the more generalized statement of 12:14-17. With these considerations in mind I now look at the purposes that the texts attribute to the future judgment-event.

7. Whether the future course of events actually occurred as envisaged is a different question, one to be answered on historical and theological grounds. But the interest here desires to describe the shape of the future as projected by the prophetic texts. Some scholars consider the OAN along the lines of Egyptian execration texts as quasi-magical curses intended to effect the downfall of Israel's enemies (Bentzen 1950; Fohrer 1966; Clements 1980:130). Thiselton's observations on the supposed inherent power of curses apply here (1974). In my opinion one should rather treat the OAN in the same way that one treats the oracles against Israel: as rhetorical speech designed to persuade. The OAN are not so different from oracles against Israel in terms of genre; one finds similarities in style, vocabulary, and motifs (Reimer 1992). This correspondence is further supported by the placement of oracles against Jerusalem in series of OAN (Isaiah 22; Zeph 3:1-8) and of oracles against Judah and Israel in Amos's OAN (Amos 2:4-16).

IV. The Purposes of the Impending Disasters

The following section surveys and illustrates with representative texts the sorts of goals the announced judgment expects to achieve. These goals concern both Israel and the nations.

1. Concerning Israel

a. The divine judgments coming on the dominant world power or on a nation that oppresses Israel have the aim of delivering Israel from the oppressor and giving Israel victory over the enemies. Only if the strong captor experiences defeat will the exiles return and Israel be restored. This theme occupies a prominent place in Nahum and Jeremiah 50–51; one also finds it in Isa 14:1-4, 25; 17:14; and Obad 18, 21.

b. The lands surrounding Israel will be abandoned, thus permitting the remnant of Israel to repossess the traditional territories of the promised land (Zeph 2:7, 9; Jer 49:1-2).

c. The nations hostile to Israel will undergo divine judgment so that the Israelites, following their future restoration, can have peace and security in their land (Ezek 28:24-26; 25:1-17; Jer 46:27; Zech 9:8).

d. The fall of Israel's allies will reveal to Israel the futility of trusting in anyone other than Yahweh (Ezek 29:16, 6-7; Isaiah 20; cf. Isa 10:20; Jer 22:20-22). Instead of emulating the nations' idolatry, wisdom, and self-sufficiency, Israel then will know Yahweh (Ezek 28:26; 29:16; cf. 39:21-22;[8] Zeph 3:6-7).

2. Concerning the Nations

a. The coming judgment will bring to an end the hubris of the nations. This theme reechoes throughout the corpus of OAN (Isa 13:11; 14:9-20; 23:9; Jer 48; 50:31-32; Ezek 28; 29:13-15; 31; Obad 3-4; Zeph 2:15; Zech 9:6).

b. The coming divine judgment seeks to reveal the impotence of the nations' gods and to eliminate the worship of these gods (Isa 16:12; 19:1, 3; 21:9; Jer 46:25; 48:7, 13, 35; 49:3; 50:2, 38; 51:17-18, 44, 47, 52; Ezek 30:13; Nah 1:14; Zeph 2:11; cf. Jer 10:11-16; 16:19-21).

c. The previous two goals serve an ultimate theological goal. By enacting judgment Yahweh will reveal himself to the nations as the only God worthy of worship. Instead of relying on their own gods, wisdom, wealth, military power, and

---

8. An important function of the OAN in Ezekiel 25–32 was to counteract the attraction that the ways of the nations held for Israel (Boadt 1980; 1986). On the significance of the recognition formula "they will know that I am Yahweh," see Zimmerli 1979:37-40.

political alliances, the nations will know Yahweh's power and authority. This theological goal plays a predominant role in the OAN (Isa 17:7-8; 19:16-25; Jer 51:15-19;[9] Ezek 25:5, 7, 17; 28:22; 29:6; 30:8, 19, 26; 32:15;[10] Zeph 2:11;[11] Zech 9:7).

d. After experiencing divine judgment the nations or their remnant will go to Zion in order to seek refuge (Isa 16:1-5) or in order to honor Yahweh with gifts (Isa 23:17-18; cf. Hag 2:6-9).[12]

The aforementioned goals focus on the nations who will experience for themselves the announced disasters. But the texts also reveal goals intended for the nations who will witness the downfall of other nations. The following illustrates the point.

e. The downfall of a powerful nation will reveal to other nations the futility of trusting or emulating that nation. When the Philistines witness the exile of Egypt and Cush, they will realize the impotence of their allies as a means of deliverance from Assyria (Isaiah 20). Ezekiel emphasizes that the destruction and disgrace coming upon Tyre and Egypt will be public events, designed to terrify their admirers (26:15-18; 27:28-36; 28:17-19; 30:9; 32:9-10; cf. Zech 9:5). According to Jer 51:44 the nations will no longer stream to Bel when Babylon falls. In modern parlance, Yahweh eliminates the competition.

f. The defeat of the oppressive power will bring relief and joy to the whole world (Isa 14:4-8; Jer 50:34; 51:48; Ezek 29:15; Nah 3:19).

g. According to Isaiah 18, after Yahweh defeats Assyria, Cush will abandon its plans of alliances and instead bring gifts to Yahweh in Zion (cf. Isa 45:14; Ps 68:32 [ET 31]; 2 Chr 32:23).

---

9. Jeremiah's OAN anticipate a future postjudgment restoration of Egypt (46:26), Moab (48:47), Ammon (49:6), and Elam (49:39). One should interpret these texts in the light of the more generalized statement concerning the restoration of nations in 12:14-17, which hopes that the nations after being punished and restored will swear allegiance to Yahweh instead of Baal (cf. 16:19-21).

10. On the use of the recognition formula, which appears frequently in Ezekiel's OAN, see n. 8. Joyce (1989:89-95) argues that the recognition formula with respect to the nations does not mean that the nations will acknowledge the God of Israel but functions only as a rhetorical device. That the same formula applies also to Israel, however, suggests that it holds a similar significance for both Israel and the nations. The judgment against Sidon (Ezek 28:22) associates the recognition formula with the manifestation to the nations of Yahweh's glory and holiness, i.e., his incomparable power and sovereign authority. The same purpose can be attributed to the judgments against the other nations in Ezekiel (cf. 38:23; 39:21).

11. Ben Zvi (1991:312-13) attributes to Zeph 2:11 an important function in Zephaniah's OAN section: "YHWH's purpose is not to destroy nation after nation — as the series of announcements of judgment may suggest — but to bring them to bow to YHWH." See also Zeph 3:8-9.

12. Frequently associated with the Zion tradition is the hope that the nations will go to Zion (1 Kgs 8:41-43; Pss 76:12 [ET 11]; 87; Isa 2:2-4; 25:6-8; 45:14; 56:3-8; 60; Jer 3:17; 16:19; Mic 4:1-3; 7:12; Zeph 3:10; Zech 8:20-23; 14:16-19; cf. Wildberger 1957; Martin-Achard 1962). But according to the prophetic logic this hope cannot be realized until after the nations' pride and idolatry have been removed.

3. Preliminary Conclusions

According to the texts that comprise the OAN collections, Yahweh, the God of Israel, holds universal claims and exercises universal imperium (Wright 1965). Therefore, Yahweh not only condemns his faithless people Israel but also executes wrath against all who display opposition or indifference to the divine will (cf. Nah 1:2-8).

The disasters to come in the near future, however, do not represent an end in and of themselves but serve a further purpose, that of leading into an ideal future beyond the era of punishment.[13] Thus the impending woe serves the subsequent weal. Furthermore, this ideal future, which centers in the knowledge of Yahweh, includes not only Israel but also the nations.

Yet, the texts do not foresee the same future for every nation. The prophets view the nations from different perspectives and address an array of concerns in the OAN, sometimes even within the same collection. For example, Jeremiah 50–51 view Babylon as incorrigibly oppressive and therefore destined for total annihilation, the only fate appropriate for such an oppressor. This precludes a second generation of Babylonian oppressors (50:26, 39-40; 51:39, 57, 64). But Jeremiah 46, 48, and 49 conceive of other nations as remediable and therefore expect their restoration after the punishment.

Or consider the little book of Obadiah. With two different portrayals of the future Obadiah addresses the fear that a second generation of Edomites might arise and attack Israel in much the same way that the previous generation did. So according to v. 18 Edom will have no survivors, but according to v. 21 Edom will be ruled by Zion, which implies that Edom will have survivors but that they will never again be able to harass Israel.

In some cases such shifts in perspective are obviously due to different historical situations and experiences. Yet in other cases, such as Obadiah, although the shifts in perspective appear mutually contradictory from a modern Western viewpoint that insists on uniformity and consistency, they rather reflect simply the nature of prophetic rhetoric.[14] A prophet can address a given concern in a variety of ways and can project for a given nation differing versions of the future.[15]

Moreover, the manner in which the OAN describe the nations varies. Some texts describe a nation in rather specific historical terms, whereas other texts

13. Ben Zvi (1991:325-46) stresses this point in his discussion of the meaning of the tripartite structure for the books of Isaiah, Jeremiah (LXX), Ezekiel, and Zephaniah.

14. Although some older source-critical studies argue that the book of Obadiah reflects a composite of several layers deriving from various times, no evidence convincingly weighs against the unity and authenticity of the book. For details, see my forthcoming Anchor Bible commentary.

15. Note the divergent versions of the future projected for Egypt in Isa 19:16-17, 18, 19-22, and 23-25.

portray a nation in a more generalized fashion as being typical and representative of the proud and wicked.[16] One thinks of Nineveh in Nahum for example,
or Ezekiel's oracles against Tyre and Egypt.

That at least some texts project a future beyond the judgment for a given
nation leads to the next issue (see table 2).

V. The Relationship between Woe and Weal

What is the relationship between woe and weal, between misfortune and good
fortune, with respect to the future destiny of the nations? For understanding
this relationship I would like to propose three models, which I will label the
Jonah model, the Amos model, and the Obadiah model. These models are
intended to serve heuristic purposes only. In fact, one can see in the same book
more than one model at work.

1. The Jonah Model. According to this model, the prophet announces
future judgment against a nation — expressed in an unconditional form (Jonah
3:4) — but if the targeted nation repents, then Yahweh changes his course of
action ("repents")[17] and does not execute the judgment. Jeremiah 18:7-8 generalizes the idea. This model represents a divine repentance view.

2. The Amos Model. According to this model, the coming judgment is
irrevocable and unavoidable. The refrain in Amos 1–2 indicates this:

> Thus Yahweh said:
> For three transgressions of X
> and for four,
> I will not revoke it.

After experiencing judgment, however, the nation can still have a future, a future
bound up with restored Israel and Israel's God. Amos 9:12 promises that restored Israel "will possess the remnant of Edom and of all the nations upon
whom my name has been called." Here the phrase "the remnant of Edom and
of all the nations"[18] refers to those who remain after the announced judgments

---

16. On the typicality of the nations, see Hummel 1964. The assumption of some
scholars that the more generalized descriptions must derive from later hands is, in my
opinion, unwarranted.

17. On divine repentance, see Andersen and Freedman 1989:638-79; and Fretheim
1988.

18. The phrase "the remnant of Edom" designates the Edomites who will survive the
judgment of 1:11-12. The reason why the text singles out Edom remains unclear, but one
possible answer explains the presence of "Edom" on literary grounds (Smith 1989:281-82).
The use of the name *'ĕdôm* evokes the common noun *'ādām* — "humanity" (cf. LXX of

Table 2: Texts Envisaging a Future beyond Judgment

Text	Nation	Future beyond Judgment
Isaiah 15–16	Moab	A few survivors who will find refuge in Zion
Isaiah 17:1-9	Syria and Ephraim	A small remnant; people will look to Yahweh
Isaiah 19	Egypt	Egyptians will fear Judah and worship Yahweh; Egypt and Assyria will be Yahweh's people
Isaiah 21:13-17	Arabia	A few survivors
Isaiah 23	Tyre	After seventy years Tyre will dedicate its profits to Yahweh
Jeremiah 46	Egypt	Egypt will be inhabited again
Jeremiah 48	Moab	Yahweh will restore Moab's fortunes
Jeremiah 49:1-6	Ammon	Yahweh will restore Ammon's fortunes
Jeremiah 49:34-39	Elam	Yahweh will restore Elam's fortunes
Ezekiel 29:1-16	Egypt	Egyptians will acknowledge Yahweh; after forty years Yahweh will restore Egypt's fortunes and make it a lowly kingdom
Obadiah 21	Edom	Zion will rule Edom
Zechariah 9:7	Philistia	Survivors will join Judah

of chaps. 1–2. They will be possessed by Israel after it experiences judgment and restoration.[19] This model represents a sequential view: woe will inevitably come and will then be followed, in at least some cases, by a future existence with some sort of weal in connection with Israel and Israel's God (see table 2).

3. The Obadiah Model.[20] In Obad 12-14 the prophet projects himself back to the fall of Judah/Jerusalem and with a series of eight vetitives prohibits Edom from gloating over Judah's fall (v. 12), from looting Judah's towns (v. 13), and from capturing Judah's refugees (v. 14). In the light of vv. 10-11 this series

---

Amos 9:12). The evocation prepares for the following phrase "all the nations." I take *wkl hgwym* as a second juxtaposed genitive of the *nomen regens* "remnant" (Joüon 1991:§129b).

19. The idea reminds one of texts such as Isa 14:2 and 54:3. But lest one think of only a military rule, the relative clause qualifies the nations to be incorporated as those upon whom Yahweh's name will have been called. This idiom denotes ownership (cf. 2 Sam 12:28; Isa 4:1) and connotes a privileged status. Note that elsewhere in the Hebrew Bible only Israelite entities have "Yahweh's name called upon them": Israel (Deut 28:10; Isa 63:19; Jer 14:9; Dan 9:19; 2 Chr 7:14), Jeremiah (Jer 15:16), Jerusalem (Jer 25:29; Dan 9:18, 19), temple (1 Kgs 8:43 = 2 Chr 6:33; Jer 7:10, 11, 14, 30; 32:34; 34:15), and ark (2 Sam 6:2). That the nations would be given such a status brings to mind Isa 19:25.

20. For details of the following interpretation, see my forthcoming commentary on Obadiah.

functions as an accusation against Edom because of its past actions of hostility toward Yahweh's people and therefore implicitly toward Yahweh himself. But grammatically the verbal clauses are vetitives or negative commands — "Do not gloat" or "Stop gloating."[21] Moreover, v. 15 provides the grounds for compliance by issuing a threat:[22]

> For [ky] the day of Yahweh is near
>   against all the nations.
> As you have done, it will be done to you.
> Your deeds will return upon your own head.

Both the grammatical form of the verbal clauses and their connection with the following motivational ky clause should be taken seriously. Therefore vv. 12-14 function also as a summons to Edom to stop its anti-Judah hostilities lest Edom be condemned along with the other nations on Yahweh's day of universal wrath. As v. 16 makes clear, this day of universal judgment is considered to be final — for those who drink the cup of God's wrath — beyond which no future exists "and they will be as if they had not been." The only hope given consists of seeking refuge in Zion — "but on Mount Zion there will be escape" (v. 17a).

Consequently, one can characterize the model of Obad 12-15 as follows: the prophet accuses a nation and summons it to change its ways before the inevitable arrival of the universal-eschatological day of Yahweh. One can infer that if the nation does change and seeks refuge in Zion, it too can escape the judgment.[23] This model represents an eschatological view.

Of the three models the first and the third hold open the possibility of the targeted nation avoiding the judgment, whereas the second denies such a possibility.[24] The first two models portray the judgment as historical in nature, but the third depicts it as universal-eschatological.

---

21. The construction — 'al + second person jussive — does not express a past subjunctive sense (contra RSV "you should not have gloated"). To convey that sense Hebrew would use lāmâ + perfect verb, "Why did you gloat." (I am indebted to Charles R. Krahmalkov for this observation.)

22. Some scholars follow Wellhausen in transposing v. 15a and v. 15b (Wellhausen 1963:213; Rudolph 1971:305; Allen 1976:159; Wolff 1986:37-38). Not only does no textual evidence exist for such a transposition of lines, however, but it also obscures the connection between the vetitives and the ky clause of v. 15a. The sequence — command + ky + the phrase "the day of Yahweh is near" — occurs elsewhere (Isa 13:6; Ezek 30:2-3; Joel 1:8-15; 2:1; Zeph 1:7). In this kind of sequence the ky clause functions as a motivational clause (Aejmelaeus 1986:204).

23. The generalized expression of v. 17a leaves open the identity of those who will enjoy refuge in Zion. It simply asserts that on Mount Zion there will be escape from the cup of wrath.

24. With respect to the avoidability of doom, the three models proposed here resemble Raitt's view of the relationship between repentance and doom according to the preexilic prophetic perspectives concerning Israel (Raitt 1971:47):

One can see more than one model or perspective at work within the same book. The OAN of Jeremiah generally exemplify the Amos model; the nations will experience judgment and at least some of them will then receive restoration (Jeremiah 46; 48; 49; cf. 12:14-16). But Jeremiah 18 applies the Jonah model to the nations, and 12:17 reflects the Obadiah model. Ezekiel's OAN generally follow the Amos model as well (note esp. 29:1-16). But Ezek 30:2-3 sets the judgment against Egypt in the context of the universal day of Yahweh,[25] which recalls the Obadiah model, and Ezek 29:17-20 resembles the Jonah model in that the announced judgment against Tyre did not occur (although Tyre did not "repent"). Isaiah's OAN generally correspond with the Amos model, but Isaiah 13 places the judgment in a universal-eschatological day of Yahweh framework and thus resembles the Obadiah model. In addition to typifying the third model, the book of Obadiah itself also reflects the Amos model in vv. 1-10 and v. 21. Finally, although Zephaniah's OAN follow the Amos model, the book gives the judgments a universal day of wrath context (1:2-3, 14-18; 3:8) and to that extent represents the Obadiah model. Yet, unlike Obad 12-14 none of the OAN collections contains texts that explicitly summon a non-Israelite nation to change its ways. In this respect Obadiah is unique.

The three models or perspectives affect how one understands the function of the OAN as speeches. This leads into the next topic.

VI. The Rhetorical Purposes of the Oracles

The oracles against the nations, like the oracles against Israel, represent prophetic rhetoric designed to persuade and influence the hearers. In considering an oracle's persuasive function the area of speech-act theory is helpful (Austin 1962; Leech and Thomas 1990; Thiselton 1992:272-312). By concentrating on the pragmatics of speech, on what an utterance does rather than on its content, speech-act theorists seek to determine an utterance's illocutionary force and its perlocutionary force. The former addresses the question "What is the speaker doing by saying this?" and the latter addresses the question "What is the utterance's intended effect on the hearers?"

By announcing future judgment against a given nation, city, or ruler, what act is the prophet doing? Is the prophet, for example, making a promise or giving a warning to Israelites? How are the Israelite hearers to respond — with

----

a. "The people must repent in order to avoid doom" (cf. Obadiah);
b. "Doom is proclaimed to incite repentance" (cf. Jonah);
c. "Failure to repent is made a basis for the certain approach of doom";
d. "Doom is inevitable" (cf. Amos).

25. On the day of Yahweh theme in the OAN, see Margulis 1967:43-79.

hope or with changed behavior? These types of questions are important and yet problematical. Ideally one should know the specific historical and social setting of the oracle and the precise composition of the audience. Unfortunately the texts as we now have them very rarely offer this kind of information — not explicitly, at any rate.[26] The following section, therefore, attempts merely to suggest a variety of more-or-less hypothetical possibilities by drawing inferences from the oracles' content.

Corresponding with the earlier discussion of the purposes of the judgment-event, I divide the material into two categories delineating the kinds of illocutionary and perlocutionary force that OAN might have possessed: (1) if Israelites were the hearers, and (2) if non-Israelites were the hearers, or at least were theoretically intended to be.

The latter category raises the issue of whether people of foreign nations were intended to hear, or to hear of, at least some of the Israelite prophetic oracles. A case can be made for such a possibility (see below). But even if non-Israelites never in actuality heard, or heard of, the prophetic oracles, one can still entertain the notion that the intended addressee or the "implied audience" for a given oracle was the nation itself (cf. House 1988:84-86). One can perhaps find an analogy in the practice of contemporary preachers who address government officials and proclaim ideal government policies, even though no government officials happen to be present in the audience. Such a practice is not merely a literary device, an example of apostrophe. Rather, preachers intend by such sermons to make a serious statement of how from their perspective the government should behave and of what policies it ought to follow. If interviewed, these preachers would express the hope that the government would heed their counsel and change for the better.

1. For All Hearers

Perhaps the one rhetorical purpose that applies to practically all of the OAN is the attempt to persuade the hearers, whoever they may be, that the targeted nations cannot escape Yahweh's judgment by relying on their own resources. Their gods, fortifications, armies, wisdom, wealth, and alliances will be of no avail before the impending doom. The will of Israel's God will hold sway over their future no matter how they may try to thwart it. Obadiah 1-9 well illustrates this persuasion goal. Edom's status among the nations (vv. 1-2), geographical location (vv. 3-4), wealth (vv. 5-6), allies (v. 7), wisdom (v. 8), and warriors (v. 9) — none of these can fend off the coming destruction. With a mélange of images and subgenres the other prophets as well stress the inability of the nations — even a distant nation

---

26. The two most common proposals are the cult and the royal court. On the issue, see Hayes 1964, 1968; and Margulis 1967.

such as Elam (Jer 49:34-39) — to evade the approaching encounter with Yahweh. Within this wide usage more specific rhetorical goals emerge, depending on whether Israelites or non-Israelites were the targeted hearers.

2. For Israelite Hearers

If one assumes that Israelites were the real addressees, then the following types of illocutionary and perlocutionary force suggest themselves.

a. Some oracles count as promises for oppressed and despairing Israelites, promises designed to produce in the hearers hope that Yahweh will effect their rescue and victory. Nahum's oracle against Nineveh provides a good example:

> Celebrate your festivals, O Judah,
> fulfill your vows;
> for never again will the wicked come against you,
> they are utterly cut off. (2:1 [ET 1:15])

The oracles assume a similar role in Isaiah 14; Jer 49:1-2; 50–51; Ezek 25; 28:24-26; Obad 18-21; Zeph 2:7-9; and Zech 9:8.

b. Some oracles function as warnings against foreign alliances. Therefore, they in effect urge Israel to reject such affiliations and instead to seek refuge in Yahweh and Zion. Isaiah 14:32, which concludes the oracle against Philistia, clearly makes the point:

> What will one answer the messengers of the nation?
> That Yahweh has founded Zion,
> and in her the afflicted of his people find refuge.

Note also Isaiah 18–20 and Jer 46:25-26 (cf. Isa 30:1-5; 31:1-3; Jer 37:7-8; Ezek 29:6-7, 16).[27]

c. In places the oracles against the nations seem to function as general warnings that aim to deter Israelites from desiring the nations' gods or envying and emulating their ways. Texts such as Jeremiah 10 and Ezek 20:32 reveal that this was considered a danger. Ezekiel's oracles against Tyre and Egypt appear to have such a force (Boadt 1986).

The presence of the connecting particle *ky* in Zeph 2:4, which joins vv. 4-5 with v. 3, indicates that the OAN of Zeph 2:4-15 reinforce the imperatives of 2:3 (Ball 1988:122; Sweeney 1991):

---

27. Wildberger (1978) emphasizes that the function of warning against alliances dominates many of Isaiah's OAN, and Holladay (1989:322, 333) attributes this role to Jeremiah's oracles against Egypt.

Seek Yahweh,
> all you humble of the land,
> you who do his justice.
Seek righteousness,
seek humility;
> perhaps you will be hidden on the day of Yahweh's wrath.
For [*ky*] Gaza will be abandoned,
> and Ashkelon will become a desolation;
Ashdod at noon will be driven out,
> and Ekron will be uprooted.

According to this text, only by continuing to seek Yahweh, righteousness, and humility can the righteous in Judah have any hope of surviving the impending doom. Otherwise they will experience the same disasters that will come upon the cities of Philistia and the other nations (cf. 3:6-7).

d. The OAN can function as the necessary background for the prophetic accusations of Israel. They set the stage for the indictment that the covenant people behave no better than the *gôyīm* and therefore will experience the same judgment as the *gôyīm*. Amos 1–2 provides the classic example by concluding the list of oracles against foreign nations with oracles against Judah and Israel. Note also the inclusion of an oracle against Jerusalem (Isaiah 22) within the Isaianic collection of OAN and the juxtaposition of Zephaniah's oracles against Nineveh (2:13-15) and Jerusalem (3:1-7). The prophetic practice of condemning Israel for acting like the nations presupposes prophetic oracles against the nations.[28]

3. For Non-Israelite Hearers

If one assumes that non-Israelites were the real or intended addressees, then the following types of rhetorical purpose seem plausible. They correlate with the three models proposed above.

---

28. The argument of Amos 1–2 differs from the argument of Jer 25:15-29 (which concludes Jeremiah's OAN according to the arrangement of the LXX). By culminating his OAN with oracles against Judah/Israel Amos reduces the covenant people to the level of the nations (cf. Jer 9:24-25 [ET 9:25-26]). In contrast, Jer 25:15-29, which begins the judgment with the covenant people and then extends it to the other nations, maintains a distinction in regard to status between the two groups. According to this argument, if even God's own special people must experience divine judgment, then certainly the noncovenant peoples must also: "For look! At the city upon which my name has been called I am beginning to work evil, and will you [nations] indeed go unpunished? You will not go unpunished" (Jer 25:29; cf. 49:12). Whereas Amos assumes judgment against the nations, Jeremiah 25 assumes judgment against Jerusalem and on that basis argues for the necessity of judgment against the nations.

a. According to the Jonah model, if a nation repents, then Yahweh also might repent and not bring upon the nation the announced doom. The divine speech of Jer 18:7-8 generalizes the concept: "Suddenly[29] when I speak concerning a nation and concerning a kingdom to uproot and to demolish and to destroy, but that nation concerning which I have spoken turns from its evil, I will repent of the evil that I intended to do to it." In the light of this text one can surmise that in Jeremiah's view the future remained open even for those nations included in his OAN collection.[30] Thus an oracle announcing impending doom might function as an indirect call to repentance.

b. According to the Amos model, the targeted nation will inevitably experience the announced judgment. In line with this perspective the prophet alerts the people ahead of time that Yahweh, the God of Israel, is planning to bring disaster on them. Thus when the disaster arrives, the survivors of the nation will be able to interpret the experience as judgment from Israel's God rather than in another way, such as the anger of a different god.[31] For example, the hope expressed in a text like Isa 19:16-18, according to which the surviving Egyptians will fear and honor Yahweh, logically presupposes the idea that they will know the identity of the deity who brought disaster on Egypt.

c. In Obad 12-15 the prophet employs eight vetitives both to accuse the Edomites of engaging in anti-Judah activities and to urge them to quit such activities before the day of divine wrath arrives. No other text in the OAN collections explicitly exhorts a nation to change its ways. Nevertheless, some texts accompany the announcement of impending doom with charges against a given nation for particular attitudes and actions. One can perhaps infer that in such cases, if the targeted nation was meant to hear of the oracle, the accusations might count as indirect warnings and appeals for the nation to change in the light of the announced judgment. For example, since Jer 49:1-2 condemns the Ammonites for occupying Israelite territory, the perlocutionary force for the Ammonites would presumably be that they should withdraw.

The foregoing section sets forth a range of possible kinds of rhetorical function that the oracles against the nations might have served. Obviously the prophets did not announce judgment against foreign nations simply to satisfy idle curiosity. Why did they speak the OAN and how did they hope to affect the hearers? Although such questions require some speculation, they deserve more attention than they often receive.

---

29. On the meaning of *rega'* in this context, see Holladay 1986:516.
30. On the authenticity of Jeremiah 18, see Holladay 1986:514.
31. One well-known example of such an interpretation comes from the Mesha stele, in which Mesha attributes Moab's previous experience of subjugation to the anger of Chemosh (l. 5).

4. Non-Israelite Hearers?

Andersen and Freedman (1989:232) have made an interesting comment: "The prophets, from Elisha (2 Kings 9) to Jeremiah (27:3 — which lists four of the six nations charged by Amos) delivered oracles *to*, not just *about*, other nations. Jonah was not as exceptional as he is sometimes made out to be." Did any of the prophetic OAN address non-Israelite hearers? Most commentators assume that they in actuality addressed only Israelites. Accordingly, the oracles were produced for in-house consumption, and their use of direct address to the nations with second person grammatical forms represents apostrophe. Such a view is quite plausible and may well be the case. It certainly applies to many of the OAN, such as Nahum.

But a text like Jer 18:7-8, which considers the prospect of a nation repenting, logically implies the notion of a prior hearing of the prophetic oracle by the targeted nation. Therefore, one should at least entertain the possibility that some of the OAN were also intended for non-Israelite ears. One can conceive of the communication process from Israelite prophet to non-Israelite hearers in several ways.

a. The Israelite prophet might have traveled to a neighboring country. The stories telling of journeys beyond Israelite borders by Elijah (1 Kings 17), Elisha (2 Kings 8; cf. 1 Kgs 19:15-16), and Jonah indicate that the idea of a traveling prophet was not unknown in Israel. Compare also Balaam. Nevertheless, the next two suggestions seem more plausible.

b. The Israelite prophet might have addressed non-Israelites who had journeyed to Israel. According to Jeremiah 27, Jeremiah had an audience of foreign envoys in Jerusalem. If the prophet is the speaker in Isa 18:2, then he addressed messengers from Cush, and with the words of Isa 14:32 he provided a response for the emissaries of Philistia.[32] Isaiah 21:11-12 apparently recounts an occasion when someone from Seir inquired of the prophet (cf. 2 Kings 5).

c. Reports of a prophetic oracle might have informally spread and reached non-Israelite ears, since ancient Israelite society was no more closed and isolated than any other.[33] 2 Kings 6:8-14 narrates an episode in which the king of Syria was informed by others of the activity and location of Elisha. According to Jeremiah 39, Nebuchadrezzar knew of Jeremiah, and Jeremiah 40 attributes to the Babylonian commander, Nebuzaradan, knowledge of Jeremiah's message. Isaiah 36–37/2 Kings 18–19 attributes to the Rabshakeh a familiarity with Je-

---

32. On the phenomenon of messengers in the ancient Near East, see Meier 1988; and Greene 1989.

33. For example, Machinist (1983) has demonstrated the influence of Neo-Assyrian propaganda upon Isaianic language.

rusalemite theology. Obadiah's words might have reached Edomite ears inasmuch as Edomites dwelt in southern Judah at the time.[34]

The whole issue of intended addressee needs more research. Yet, even if in the end one concludes otherwise, one should not prematurely dismiss the possibility that at least some of the oracles were intended to be heard by non-Israelites as well as Israelites.

VII. Conclusion

The announcement of future judgment against foreign nations in the name of Israel's God constituted a noteworthy part of the "job description" for Israel's prophets. According to Jer 28:8, Jeremiah opposed Hananiah by arguing that earlier prophets typically prophesied against nations: "The prophets who preceded me and you from early times — they prophesied to many lands and against great kingdoms, of war, of disaster, and of pestilence." Jeremiah understood himself to stand in continuity with this tradition, to have been called by Yahweh as a "prophet to the nations" (1:5, 10).[35] In the light of the amount of space devoted to OAN in the prophetic books, the same self-understanding seems to apply to other prophets.

I return to the initial question: Why prophetic oracles against the nations? In attempting to address the question one should not attribute to all of them a single purpose, such as promises of victory over enemies for Israel. Moreover, to understand them as expressions of xenophobic nationalism and Israelite hate-literature imposes on the material a misleading interpretive framework. The following points speak against such a view:[36]

1. The inclusion of oracles against Israel within series of oracles against the nations reveals that the latter represent hate-literature no more than the former.
2. Some of the oracles against the nations function as warnings for Israel.
3. A positive future subsequent to the impending woe is envisaged for the nations themselves, albeit a future in association with Israel.
4. One can make a case that some of the oracles were actually intended to influence the behavior of the nations.

---

34. I date Obadiah ca. 585-555. Recent archaeological work suggests a growing Edomite presence in the Negev for the seventh–early sixth century (Bartlett 1989:141-43).

35. On the significance of Jer 28:8, see Margulis 1967:382-86.

36. Hoffmann (1977) makes a similar point.

The prophetic speeches against the nations and the future disasters depicted therein have a variety of purposes that concern both Israel and the nations. Indeed, one can say that from the prophetic point of view when the God of Israel intervenes in history, the whole world ultimately benefits.

Bibliography

Aejmelaeus, A.
 1986 "Function and Interpretation of *Ky* in Biblical Hebrew." *JBL* 105:193-209.

Allen, L. C.
 1976 *The Books of Joel, Obadiah, Jonah and Micah.* NICOT. Grand Rapids: Eerdmans.

Andersen, F. I., and A. D. Forbes
 1983 "'Prose Particle' Counts of the Hebrew Bible." Pp. 165-83 in *The Word of the Lord Shall Go Forth: Essays in Honor of David Noel Freedman in Celebration of His Sixtieth Birthday.* Ed. C. L. Meyers and M. O'Connor. Winona Lake, IN: Eisenbrauns.

Andersen, F. I., and D. N. Freedman
 1989 *Amos.* AB 24A. New York: Doubleday.

Austin, J. L.
 1962 *How to Do Things with Words.* Oxford: Clarendon.

Ball, I. J., Jr.
 1988 *A Rhetorical Study of Zephaniah.* Berkeley: BIBAL.

Bartlett, J. R.
 1989 *Edom and the Edomites.* JSOTSup 77. Sheffield: JSOT.

Bentzen, A.
 1950 "The Ritual Background of Amos 1:2–2:16." *OTS* 8:85-99.

Ben Zvi, E.
 1991 *A Historical-Critical Study of the Book of Zephaniah.* BZAW 198. Berlin: de Gruyter.

Boadt, L.
 1980 *Ezekiel's Oracles Against Egypt: A Literary and Philological Study of Ezekiel 29–32.* BibOr 37. Rome: Pontifical Biblical Institute.
 1986 "Rhetorical Strategies in Ezekiel's Oracles of Judgment." Pp. 182-200 in *Ezekiel and His Book: Textual and Literary Criticism and Their Interrelation.* Ed. J. Lust. BETL 74. Louvain: Louvain University.

Christensen, D. L.
 1975 *Transformations of the War Oracle in Old Testament Prophecy: Studies in the Oracles against the Nations.* HDR 3. Missoula, MT: Scholars.

Clements, R. E.
1980   *Isaiah 1–39.* NCB. Grand Rapids: Eerdmans.

Erlandsson, S.
1970   *The Burden of Babylon: A Study of Isaiah 13:2–14:23.* ConBOT 4.
            Lund: Gleerup.

Fohrer, G.
1966   "Prophetie und Magie." *ZAW* 78:40-44.

Fretheim, T. E.
1988   "The Repentance of God: A Key to Evaluating Old Testament God-
            Talk." *HBT* 10:47-70.

Gosse, B.
1988   *Isaïe 13:1–14:23: dans la tradition littéraire du livre d'Isaïe et dans la
            tradition des oracles contre les nations.* OBO 78. Göttingen: Vanden-
            hoeck & Ruprecht.

Gottwald, N. K.
1964   *All the Kingdoms of the Earth: Israelite Prophecy and International
            Relations in the Ancient Near East.* New York: Harper & Row.

Greenberg, M.
1971   "Mankind, Israel and the Nations in Hebraic Heritage." Pp. 15-40 in
            No Man is Alien: Essays on the Unity of Mankind. Ed. J. R. Nelson.
            Leiden: Brill.
1983   *Ezekiel 1–20.* AB 22. Garden City, NY: Doubleday.

Greene, J. T.
1989   *The Role of the Messenger and Message in the Ancient Near East.* BJS
            169. Atlanta: Scholars.

Gressmann, H.
1929   *Der Messias.* FRLANT 43. Göttingen: Vandenhoeck & Ruprecht.

Hayes, J. H.
1964   "The Oracles against the Nations in the Old Testament: Their Usage
            and Theological Importance." Th.D. diss. Princeton Theological
            Seminary.
1968   "The Usage of Oracles against Foreign Nations in Ancient Israel."
            JBL 87:81-92.

Hoffmann, Y.
1977   *The Prophecies against Foreign Nations in the Bible.* Tel Aviv: HaKib-
            butz HaMeuhad. (Hebrew with English summary.)

Holladay, W. L.
1986   *Jeremiah 1.* Hermeneia. Philadelphia: Fortress.
1989   *Jeremiah 2.* Hermeneia. Minneapolis: Fortress.

House, P. R.
1988   *Zephaniah: A Prophetic Drama.* JSOTSup 69. Sheffield: Almond.

Hummel, H. D.
1964   "The Old Testament Basis of Typological Interpretation." *BR* 9:38-
            50.
Joüon, P.
1991   *A Grammar of Biblical Hebrew.* Trans. and rev. T. Muraoka. Subsidia
            biblica 14. Rome: Pontifical Biblical Institute.
Joyce, P.
1989   *Divine Initiative and Human Response in Ezekiel.* JSOTSup 51. Shef-
            field: JSOT.
Leech, G., and J. Thomas
1990   "Language, Meaning and Context: Pragmatics." Pp. 173-206 in *An
            Encyclopaedia of Language.* Ed. N. E. Collinge. New York: Routledge.
Machinist, P.
1983   "Assyria and Its Image in the First Isaiah." *JAOS* 103:719-37.
Margulis, B. B.
1967   "Studies in the Oracles against the Nations." Ph.D. diss. Brandeis
            University.
Martin-Achard, R.
1962   *A Light to the Nations.* Trans. J. P. Smith. Edinburgh: Oliver & Boyd.
            (Original 1959.)
Meier, S. A.
1988   *The Messenger in the Ancient Semitic World.* HSM 45. Atlanta:
            Scholars.
Mitchell, C. W.
1987   *The Meaning of BRK "To Bless" in the Old Testament.* SBLDS 95.
            Atlanta: Scholars.
Paul, S. M.
1991   *Amos.* Hermeneia. Minneapolis: Fortress.
Pfeiffer, R. H.
1941   *Introduction to the Old Testament.* New York: Harper & Brothers.
Raitt, T. M.
1971   "The Prophetic Summons to Repentance." *ZAW* 83:30-49.
Reimer, D. J.
1992   "Political Prophets? Another Look at the Oracles against Foreign
            Nations." Paper Presented at the Annual SBL Meeting, San Francisco,
            November 22, 1992.
Rudolph, W.
1971   *Joel-Amos-Obadja-Jona.* KAT 13/2. Gütersloh: Mohn.
Smith, G. V.
1989   *Amos: A Commentary.* Grand Rapids: Zondervan.
Stuart, D.
1987   *Hosea–Jonah.* WBC 31. Waco: Word.

Sweeney, M. A.
  1991   "A Form-Critical Reassessment of the Book of Zephaniah." *CBQ* 53:388-408.

Thiselton, A. C.
  1974   "The Supposed Power of Words in the Biblical Writings." *JTS* 25:283-99.
  1992   *New Horizons in Hermeneutics.* Grand Rapids: Zondervan.

Webb, B. G.
  1990   "Zion in Transformation: A Literary Approach to Isaiah." Pp. 65-84 in *The Bible in Three Dimensions: Essays in Celebration of Forty Years of Biblical Studies in the University of Sheffield.* Ed. D. J. A. Clines, S. E. Fowl, and S. E. Porter. JSOTSup 87. Sheffield: JSOT.

Wellhausen, J.
  1963   *Die Kleinen Propheten übersetzt und erklärt.* 4th ed. Berlin: de Gruyter. (= 3rd ed. Berlin: Reimer, 1898.)

Wildberger, H.
  1957   "Die Völkerwallfahrt zum Zion: Jes 2:1-5." *VT* 7:62-81.
  1978   *Jesaja 13–27.* BKAT 10/2. Neukirchen-Vluyn: Neukirchener Verlag.

Wolff, H. W.
  1986   *Obadiah and Jonah.* Trans. M. Kohl. Minneapolis: Augsburg. (Original 1977.)

Wright, G. E.
  1965   "The Nations in Hebrew Prophecy." *Encounter* 26:225-37.

Zimmerli, W.
  1979   *Ezekiel 1.* Trans. R. E. Clements. Hermeneia. Philadelphia: Fortress. (Original 1969.)
  1983   *Ezekiel 2.* Trans. J. D. Martin. Hermeneia. Philadelphia: Fortress. (Original 1969.)

A Literary Approach to Chronicles' Ark Narrative in 1 Chronicles 13–16[1]

TAMARA C. ESKENAZI

Hebrew Union College–Jewish Institute of Religion, Los Angeles

David Noel Freedman has decisively influenced virtually every major area of biblical studies and continues to do so with enthusiasm and élan. His contribution to scholarship on Chronicles has been particularly significant and prescient. Already in 1961, before the postexilic era gained the recognition that it since has acquired, Freedman's essay "The Purpose of the Chronicler"[2] charted new directions. More recently, his articles on "I and II Chronicles, Ezra, Nehemiah" and his compelling assessment of the formation of the Hebrew Bible further highlighted the pivotal place of Chronicles in biblical studies and Freedman's distinctive contribution to such studies.[3] With Freedman's achievements in mind I want to honor him on the occasion of his birthday by reflecting on how Chronicles interprets the transfer of the ark to Jerusalem.

The present essay is as much a test of a method as a study of text. The literary analysis of Chronicles' ark narrative aims, first of all, to shed more light on how the event is remembered and evaluated in the Chronicler's particular rendition. In addition, however, this study provides an occasion to examine the

---

1. A version of this essay has been presented in the special session of the "Chronicles, Ezra, Nehemiah Section" of SBL (Boston, 1987) and in the 10th World Congress of Jewish Studies (Jerusalem, 1989).

2. D. N. Freedman, "The Chronicler's Purpose," *CBQ* 23 (1961) 436-42; idem, with B. E. Willoughby, "I and II Chronicles, Ezra, Nehemiah," *The Books of the Bible I: The Old Testament/The Hebrew Bible* (ed. B. W. Anderson; New York: Charles Scribner's Sons, 1989) 155-71.

3. D. N. Freedman, *The Unity of the Hebrew Bible* (Ann Arbor: University of Michigan, 1991).

efficacy of applying current literary approaches to a biblical text. Utilizing the criteria for literary analysis cultivated by Buber, Alter, and Sternberg, for example, the paper highlights how the book's ideology is inscribed and can be discerned. The paper substantiates the reliability of literary tools by showing how they uncover Chronicles' ideology even apart from a comparison between Chronicles and Samuel-Kings. Alter claims that attention to literary features "leads not to a more 'imaginative' reading of biblical narrative but to a more precise one."[4] He observes that "the literary approach is actually a good deal *less* conjectural than the historical scholarship."[5] A comparison of Chronicles with Samuel-Kings enables us to test this claim. The implications of the essay thus extend beyond the analysis of Chronicles. In addition, the essay seeks to show how Chronicles' treatment of the ark narrative helps assess the intention and date of Chronicles.

In 1961, noting the chaotic state of Chronicles studies at the time, Freedman contributed toward building a consensus by seeking to identify the Chronicler's purpose.

> It seems clear therefore that the principal objective of the Chronicler was to write a history of the dynasty of David, not primarily in terms of its historical and political achievements (though these form the framework, appropriated from Samuel-Kings), but its accomplishments in the religious and specifically cultic areas. To summarize, the Chronicler establishes through his narrative of the reigns of David and Solomon the proper, legitimate pattern of institutions and their personnel for the people of God; and they are the monarchy represented by David and his house, the priesthood, by Zadok and his descendants, the city and the temple in the promised land.[6]

The following literary analysis of the ark narrative builds on Freedman's conclusions and helps nuance the role of the cult by highlighting the specific place that covenant and Levites have in Chronicles.

Fortunately, it is no longer necessary to justify the relevance of literary tools to the study of Chronicles. The unique position of Chronicles in the canon had made it an early candidate for literary evaluations. Similarities and differences between Chronicles and Samuel-Kings have compelled scholars early to contend with literary features of Chronicles in an attempt to reconcile discrepancies between the two versions of Israel's story. Even when Samuel was still venerated as unbiased history, Chronicles was already read as if its particular literary constructs express its own theological and historical preoccupations.[7]

---

4. R. Alter, *The Art of Biblical Narrative* (New York: Basic, 1981) 21.
5. Ibid.
6. Freedman, "Chronicler's Purpose," 437.
7. I invite the reader to explore the many important literary insights into Chronicles that have already been gathered together in several outstanding books and articles, such as

In recent decades, literary sensitivity to Chronicles has increased dramatically and has played a major role in interpretations of the book. Literary analysis of Chronicles has benefited from its unique position as a twice-told tale. Contrast and comparison with Samuel-Kings typically influenced all such readings of Chronicles and served to sharpen awareness of its distinctive ideology and style.

The present study approaches Chronicles differently. It begins by bracketing Samuel-Kings as much as possible and focuses exclusively on literary criteria as tools for analysis. Only after securing a reading based on recognized literary criteria will I bring into view a comparison with the parallels in Samuel-Kings. In other words, this essay illustrates a reading of the ark narrative based primarily on internal dynamics, apart from purported relation to a *Vorlage*. Such a study enables us to assess the limits and possibilities of applying literary tools to texts where we do not possess the advantage that we have in Chronicles studies and cannot, therefore, verify the validity of a reading through recourse to external means.

The essay has three parts. Part I briefly describes the literary approach and its presuppositions relevant for the present analysis. Part II illustrates the readings of the ark narrative in Chronicles that emerge from the use of this approach. Part III brings together the implications.

I. The Literary Approach

"Literary approach" is a deliberately vague term that covers sundry literary techniques, presuppositions, terminology, and levels of interpretation. As is well known, there are currently several new schools of literary criticism, unified by a concern with what Sternberg calls "discourse-oriented" inquiry.[8] In my analysis I loosely follow the general guidelines of Alter, Berlin,[9] and Sternberg, and am most impressed by the usefulness of what Sternberg and Berlin call "poetics" for a work such as Chronicles.

P. R. Ackroyd, *I & II Chronicles, Ezra, Nehemiah* (Torch Bible Commentaries; London: SCM, 1973); idem, *The Chronicler in His Age* (JSOTSup 101; Sheffield: JSOT, 1991); R. Braun, *1 Chronicles* (WBC 14; Waco: Word, 1986); R. Dillard, *2 Chronicles* (WBC 15; Waco: Word, 1987); S. Japhet, *The Ideology of the Book of Chronicles and Its Place in Biblical Thought* (Jerusalem: Mosad Bialik, 1977 [Hebrew]; ET trans. A. Barber; Frankfurt-am-Main: Peter Lang, 1989); R. Mosis, *Untersuchungen zur Theologie des chronistischen Geschichtswerkes* (Freiburger theologische Studien 92; Freiburg: Herder, 1973); T. Willi, *Die Chronik als Auslegung* (FRLANT 106; Göttingen: Vandenhoeck & Ruprecht, 1972); H. G. M. Williamson, *1 and 2 Chronicles* (NCB; Grand Rapids: Eerdmans, 1982); idem, "The Temple in Chronicles," in *Templum Amicitiae: Essays on the Second Temple Presented to Ernst Bammel* (ed. W. Horbury; JSNTSup 48; Sheffield: Sheffield Academic, 1992) 15-31.

8. M. Sternberg, *The Poetics of Biblical Narrative: Ideological Literature and the Drama of Reading* (Bloomington: Indiana University, 1985).

9. A. Berlin, *Poetics and Interpretation in Biblical Narrative* (Sheffield: Almond, 1983).

This literary approach assumes that one can best understand narrative by attention to plot, repetition, wordplay, representational proportions, parallelism, change of scene, and so on. The underlying assumption is that such literary devices constitute the basic tools a writer uses to convey meaning. Sternberg lists the following important literary components:

1. Temporal ordering, especially where the actual sequence diverges from the chronological.
2. Analogical design: parallelism, contrast, variation, recurrence, symmetry, chiasm.
3. Point of view, e.g., the teller's powers and manipulations, shifts in perspective from external to internal rendering or from narration to monologue and dialogue. . . .
4. Representational proportions: scene, summary, repetition.
5. Informational gapping and ambiguity.
6. Strategies of characterization and judgment.
7. Modes of coherence, in units ranging from a verse to a book.
8. The interplay of verbal and compositional patterns.[10]

These categories form the backbone of any discourse, though different works combine them in a variety of ways. Attention to their interplay in a particular text allows one to perceive the intention of a text. In addition, biblical narrative has some distinctive characteristics (see Alter for details).[11] Drawing on the work of Buber and Rosenzweig, Alter stresses in particular the role of *Leitwörter* in the analysis of biblical texts. Since biblical narrative is laconic, "fraught with background" (so Auerbach), repetition of key words plays a special role. "The repetition of single words or brief phrases often exhibits a frequency, a saliency, and a thematic significance quite unlike what we may be accustomed to from other narrative traditions."[12]

It is probably no longer necessary to reiterate that a literary approach does not demote the text from truth to fiction. The historical veracity of a text or of the events recounted therein is not slandered by the use of literary tools. In the case of historiographic material, such as Chronicles, a literary analysis neither proves nor disproves the historicity of Chronicles. The literary analysis rather explores what the text says by looking at how it says it.

Contemporary literary critics begin with the text in its final form, with the underlying assumption that the text is meaningfully arranged.[13] Further-

---

10. Sternberg, *Poetics of Biblical Narrative*, 39.

11. Alter's chaps. 4 (on the place of dialogue), 5 (on the techniques of repetition), and 8 (on narration and knowledge) are particularly illuminating. See also S. Bar-Efrat, *Narrative Art in the Bible* (Sheffield: Almond, 1989).

12. Alter, *Art of Biblical Narrative*, 179.

13. This assumption does not exclude the possibility that errors have crept into the

more, they posit that the "author," "editor," or "final redactor" had a measure of freedom in selecting and combining material and was not compelled to copy sources slavishly. The degree of such freedom is usually hard to assess. Chronicles itself is a unique example of such freedom since, according to the general consensus, it modifies and alters canonical Samuel-Kings. Chronicles is thus particularly congenial as an illustration of the usefulness of the literary method. It provides an opportunity for evaluating the limits and possibilities of literary interpretation of the particular text.

II. A Literary Analysis of the Ark Narrative

I will examine the story of the ark in three ways: (1) through a literary analysis of 1 Chronicles 13–16, looking at inner connections; (2) through a brief amplification on the basis of comparison with Samuel; (3) by setting the narrative in the larger context of the structure of Chronicles.

1. A Literary Analysis of 1 Chronicles 13–16

A literary analysis of Chronicles' ark narrative highlights the following themes:

1. The utmost importance of the ark in particular and the cult in general.
2. The wide-ranging participation by the people of Israel in the cult and the life of the nation.
3. The importance, beauty, and joy of the cult.
4. The unique role and significance of the Levites.

These interpretations of Chronicles are widely acknowledged. My analysis does not merely confirm the presence of these themes but demonstrates that one can discern them from a careful reading of Chronicles that is independent from the parallel in 1 Samuel. The use of literary techniques (such as those indicated by Buber, Alter, and Sternberg) suffices to draw out Chronicles' own agenda. A comparison with Samuel confirms the accuracy of the literary reading; Samuel, however, is not necessary for discerning Chronicles' intention. Chronicles' own emphases are not merely contingent on its rearrangement of Samuel-Kings but have been thoroughly woven into the internal development

---

text. It does, however, curtail the frequency with which a critic can resort to such explanations. Here is one of the places where the conversation with the text critic becomes crucial and literary conclusions can be challenged.

of the narrative itself with sufficient literary clues for the reader. The literary critic can discern them from narrative analysis alone.

In addition to discerning the themes and emphases in Chronicles that have been noted by scholars who rely on a comparison with Samuel-Kings, the present reading of the ark narrative makes four further points. First, this essay supports and develops Mosis's contention that Chronicles sustains a contrast between David's reign and Saul's by providing additional examples to buttress Mosis's thesis about the pervasive concern with Saul. Second, the essay illustrates how covenant has been reinterpreted in Chronicles. Third, the essay helps place Chronicles in the larger context of the canon in the light of Chronicles' special interest in proper modes of transfer of authority. Fourth, the essay illustrates the extent of Chronicles' concern with the ark. The pervasiveness of this attention to the ark, at the time when the ark had disappeared, sheds light on Chronicles' focus on other defunct institutions and therefore has a bearing on attempts to date the book.

A literary analysis begins by establishing the structure and boundaries of the narrative. Determining precisely where the ark narrative begins in Chronicles is not easy. Scholars demarcate the unit differently. Braun begins the unit at chap. 13; Ackroyd divides the ark narrative into part one (chap. 13), and part two (chaps. 15–16), with an interlude (chap. 14); Mosis begins with chap. 11, interpreting the anointing of David and the conquest of Jerusalem primarily as prerequisite for the ark material. Mosis explains the cursory description of the anointing and conquest as evidence that the Chronicler's main interest lies elsewhere, namely, in the ark story. Since the ark story is also directly related to Saul's story in 1 Chronicles 10 (as we shall see), it may be reasonable to begin with chap. 10. All of these divisions can be supported in the text and show the extent of Chronicles' preoccupation with the ark.

The end of the story is likewise difficult to establish. Braun includes chap. 17, with Nathan's promise to David. That segment, after all, begins with reference to the ark and is indeed prompted by concern for the ark: "Behold, I dwell in a house of cedar but the ark of the covenant of YHWH is under a tent" (17:1b). It is, however, plausible to consider chap. 17 (as Mosis and others do) as the beginning of a related yet separate unit. I suggest that 17:1–22:19 is another ark narrative that replays, on a larger scale, some of the thematic developments of chaps. 13–16, likewise beginning and ending with the ark (17:1; 22:19).[14]

The ark narrative also continues in the next unit, 1 Chr 23:1–29:30, in David's arrangements for the cult and the appointment of Solomon to build a place for the ark. In this section, David's major speech describes his life in terms of striving on behalf of the ark: "I had it in my heart to build a house of rest

14. Note that in 1 Chronicles 17–22, as in 1 Chronicles 13–16, an action on behalf of the ark is also followed by two sets of military victories culminating in a cultic consecration.

for the ark of the covenant of YHWH" (1 Chr 28:2). Indeed, one can label 1 Chronicles 10 to 2 Chronicles 10 as stations on the ark's way until it finally finds its rest in David's and Solomon's temple (planned and provided for by David and executed by Solomon).

The ark story ends only in the concluding portions of 2 Chronicles. In his last speech (the final edict by a Judean king in Chronicles), Josiah commands the Levites: "Put the holy ark in the house that Solomon the son of David, king of Israel, built; you need no longer carry it on your shoulders" (2 Chr 35:3).

Clearly, the ark story in 1 Chronicles 13–16 is tightly knitted with what precedes and what follows, compelling the recognition that although units can be demarcated, they are nevertheless the carefully constructed building blocks for a continuous narrative. Literarily, hence also theologically and historiographically (since theology and historiography can be expressed only literarily), the ark narrative constitutes a large and primary sequence in 1 Chronicles. Keeping that in mind, let us narrow the focus for a close-up view of a single segment of this large ark narrative: the transfer of the ark to Jerusalem. I limit myself to the most minimal unit of the ark narrative in 1 Chronicles, chaps. 13–16.[15]

The story of the transfer of the ark to Jerusalem follows a basic structure of narrative:

a. Objective defined: to bring the ark to Jerusalem (13:1-4)
b. Process of actualization: the transfer of the ark (13:5–15:29)
c. Objective reached: celebration of the ark's arrival in Jerusalem (16:1-43).[16]

a. Objective Defined (13:1-4)

According to the narrator, David consults with the leaders, then addresses the congregation (note the religious term for community, קהל).[17] The NRSV renders the text as follows:

> If it seems good to you, and if it is the will of the Lord our God, let us send abroad [נפרצה] to our kindred who remain in all the land of Israel, including the priests and Levites in the cities that have pasture lands, that they may come together to us. Then let us bring again [ונסבה] the ark of our God to us; for we did not turn to it [דרשנהו] in the days of Saul [שאול]. (13:2-3)

15. There are several good reasons to include 1 Chronicles 11–12 even in the smaller unit, as Mosis does. The brief description of both the anointing and the conquest of Jerusalem is one such reason. It suggests that these chapters mainly form the setting for the main events. This impression is intensified by a kind of "resumptive repetition" in 12:39 that, after conjuring up the totality of Israel with its military ranks in their full tribal affiliation, returns the reader to the anointing celebration at Hebron as an implicit setting for the next step.

16. For basic narrative structures, see S. Rimmon-Kenan, *Narrative Fiction: Contemporary Poetics* (London: Methuen, 1983) 22-28, esp. 22.

17. See, e.g., Braun, *1 Chronicles*, 174.

The agenda is thus stated in David's speech, all parts of which are thematically important for the development of the story. The speech expresses concern for communal consensus ("If it seems good to you") and for as wide a participation as possible (geographical and cultic); it articulates a deliberate contrast with Saul ("for we neglected it in the days of Saul"), and all combine to express the urgency of taking care of the ark.

Four key words in particular appear in this section and will resonate throughout this narrative as *Leitwörter*: שָׁאוּל, דרשנהו, נסבה, נפרצה. Forms of these terms recur in the rest of the narrative, binding it closer together. Wordplay and themes also connect the ark narrative directly, and by way of contrast, with Saul's defeat (10:14), making the latter a vivid backdrop to David's success.

These terms at first glance seem unsuited to the present context, which hints at their role as *Leitwörter*. נפרצה (13:2) is so unusual that Braun, for example, does not translate it, saying that its common meaning "is difficult to relate to the context here"[18] (the NRSV either assimilates it into part of "the will of [the Lord]" or "abroad," or omits altogether). BDB supposes a corruption. The verb ordinarily means "to break forth" or, as inflected here, "let us break forth" (the verb reappears in 13:11; 14:11; 15:13, where it does make sense). נסבה in 1 Chr 13:3 means literally "let us bring around." As Williamson observes, "This is a most unusual use of the verb. . . . Does the Chronicler thus intend a word-play on the theme of 'turning' already noted at 10:14?"[19] The answer to Williamson's (rhetorical?) question must be yes. The verb in this form occurs in Chronicles only in chaps. 13–16 (13:3; 14:14) and in the preceding judgment on Saul (10:14), although additional plays on the verb will recur elsewhere in the ark narrative. The connection — or contrast — to Saul is thus introduced immediately and sharply. Compare "Let us turn [נסבה] the ark of our God to us; for we neglected it in the days of Saul" (13:3) and "[Saul] did not seek guidance from YHWH. Therefore YHWH slew him and turned [ויסב] the kingdom over to David the son of Jesse" (10:14). David will do what Saul did not or, more, to the point, Israel under David will do what it did not under Saul.

With assent from the whole congregation (note the repetition of the religious term קהל), David and the community have determined their task and the process of actualization is ready to begin.

b. Process of Actualization (13:5–15:29)

The second part of a narrative typically describes a process of actualization that contains a complication. In the ark narrative, complications take the form of divine intervention. David's magnanimous steps to ensure the welfare of the ark

---

18. Ibid., 173.
19. Williamson, *1 and 2 Chronicles*, 115.

come to a halt by God's direct action. The sudden death of Uzza interrupts the sequence (and provides an occasion to ponder the complex character of God and God's interaction with humanity) and encourages David to conclude that, at least for the moment, God is not willing to be brought to Jerusalem (cf. 13:2).

David is portrayed primarily as one who is constantly solicitous for the care of the ark. Such a concern appears as an overarching theme. Only after taking steps to ensure the welfare of the ark does David turn to building houses for himself as he also prepares a place for the ark.[20] Because David is attentive to the ark, good fortune follows: he receives foreign recognition (14:2), is blessed with numerous children (who first appear here, 14:3-7), and wins victories against the Philistines twice and conclusively (14:8-17; contrast with Saul).

The inexorable connection between these events is indicated not only by the particular sequence of events but by several wordplays. The report about David's inquiry of God twice repeats the word "asked" (וישאל, 14:10, 14) and recalls Saul's name, שאול; it also reminds us of Saul's damnable request of the medium (Saul "consulted a medium," וגם לשאל באוב, 10:13). God's response, "turn" (הסב, 14:14), echoes the narrator's account of Saul's failure and the turning of the kingdom over to David: ויסב את המלוכה לדוד בן ישי, "And he turned the kingdom over to David son of Jesse" (10:14). The spread of the Philistines (יפשטו, 14:9, 13) recalls how the Philistines stripped Saul (ויבאו פלשתים לפשט, 10:8; ויפשיטהו, 10:9).

The play on the verb פרץ, a word out of place in the Chronicler's account of David's initial exhortation of the people (13:2), finds its full expression in this portion of the ark narrative. פרץ is repeated three times when God strikes Uzza (13:11) and again four times in the victory over the Philistines (14:11). One final repetition interprets all the preceding ones. Speaking to the Levites, David says: "Because you did not carry it [i.e., the ark] the first time, YHWH our God broke forth [פרץ] upon us" (15:13).

With God's support, the complication seems resolved and renewed efforts to return the ark ensue. David gathers another assembly (note again ויקהל, the religious term for gathering, 15:3) and appoints the Levites to carry the ark (15:2), claiming that the earlier calamity was caused by lack of proper decorum (presumably because non-Levites carried the ark).[21] Although only

---

20. Placing the battles with the Philistines after the initial attempts to bring the ark toward its destination allows Chronicles to link the ark more firmly to the dialogue between David and God. Twice in the battles against the Philistines David consults with God and receives direct answers. Indeed, these are the only semblance of dialogue in the ark narrative of chaps. 13–16. Chronicles implies that the proximity of the ark facilitates such communication between David and God. It is only now that the conversation between them actually begins, a conversation that continues in 17:1ff.

21. It is worth noting that the text presents David restoring what has been overlooked, i.e., a procedure in accordance with Moses' teachings (15:15); he does not initiate something new.

the Levites[22] are to bear the ark, all Israel is gathered to take part in the process (15:3). Chronicles reports in detail which priests and Levites came and reproduces David's speech to them. Like the opening exhortation in 13:2-3, to which this is a response, key terms recur. David identifies the earlier failure with the improper mode of seeking God. Once again, as noted above, the key term פרץ recurs (15:13), connecting this conclusion with the various stages of the process.

Chronicles describes the great procession and celebration with a profusion of detail that leaves readers possibly dizzy and quite likely bored. Lists of names and tasks dominate the account and overshadow all other reports. Music echoes from beginning to end. Although such lists discourage the casual reader, they invite one to consider the importance of such material in the narrative. Beyond simply recording events and personnel, such lists serve literary functions.[23] Together with details of celebration, the lists swell the representational proportions of the narrative. In terms of narrative proportions, the account of the procession, singing, and celebration receives twice the length of the preceding narratives. Wars with the Philistines, even David's anointing and the conquest of Jerusalem, pale in comparison with this luxuriously long description of the successful delivery of the ark. It is impossible for the reader to ignore the fact that in Chronicles, everything thus far has been for the sake of this day; this day, therefore, receives the most extensive descriptions. By granting so much space — or so much narrative time — to the account, Chronicles forces the reader to recognize what the Chronicler values most.

In this already elaborate description, the actual, final moments of the transfer of the ark receive the maximum attention. The narrative pace changes, indicating that we are no longer reading simply about one more event in a long chain. The camera, as it were, retains a steady focus on the process of transfer itself, lest the action be absorbed too quickly in past or future events. A grammatical shift in 15:25-29 underscores the unique importance of this final act of transfer. Verbs change from the typically perfect tense that hitherto characterized the narrative into participles, emphasizing continuous action: David and the elders are walking (ויהי . . . ההלכים, "the ones walking," 15:25); God is helping (ויהי . . . בעזר, "when [he] was helping," 15:26); David has been dressed (ודויד מכרבל, 15:27); "and all Israel were bringing up" (וכל ישראל מעלים, 15:28); "and the ark of the covenant of YHWH was coming" (ויהי ארון ברית יהוה בא, 15:29). Such grammatical

---

22. The context, however, implies a broad definition of "Levites" that encompasses the priests as well.

23. On the narrative uses of lists, see P. W. Coxon, "The 'List' Genre and Narrative Style in the Court Tales of Daniel," *JSOT* 35 (1986) 95-121; and T. C. Eskenazi, "The Structure of Ezra-Nehemiah and the Integrity of the Book," *JBL* 107 (1988) 641-56.

turns make the final movement of the ark the climactic event, the one on which the narrator lingers.

The God who had hindered (13:10-12) now helps (15:26). Rejoicing, song, the roaring sound of harps, lyres, and cymbals (15:16) combine with "horn, trumpets, and cymbals" (15:28) to fill the air — and the narrative: "And all Israel brought the ark of the covenant of YHWH with shouting, to the sound of horn, trumpets, and cymbals, and made loud music on harps and lyres" (15:28). To parallel the opening scene, there is the recurrent emphasis on the people as a whole, enthusiastically working with David.

Only a single sad note is sounded to remind one what the alternative had been and how far Israel had come under David: "And as the ark of the covenant of YHWH came to the city of David, Michal the daughter of Saul looked out of the window and saw David the king dancing and making merry; and she despised him in her heart" (15:29). Contrast with the ill-fated Saul rounds off the narrative, which began with a deliberate intent to reverse the actions of Saul (13:3). This reversal underscores the expression "David the king." For Chronicles, it seems, king, ark of the covenant of YHWH, city, and people are all linked together. When David and the people complete bringing the ark into the city, David's kingship is finally fully actualized.[24]

c. Objective Reached (16:1-43)

"And they brought the ark of God and placed it in the tent that David had prepared" (16:1). Thus begins the final episode of the transfer of the ark. All Israel succeeds in its mission under David's indefatigable supervision. The narrative confirms that "they," namely, "all Israel" and David, indeed brought the ark; the event was celebrated with sacrifices, music, singing of psalms, and cultic arrangements. The transfer finally ends when all the people and David, presumably like the ark, go home (16:43).

In describing the events of the day, 1 Chr 16:1-42 concentrates on the joyous celebration that marks success. The narrative grants its fullest attention to the accompanying music, the lengthy psalm (1 Chr 16:8-36), and the cultic roles for the Levites, given in almost tiresome detail (e.g., 16:5-6 and 37-42).

The narrative pace slows down drastically. Earlier, movements in time and space have been brisk. The Chronicler often described events in sweeping, quick strokes with narrative that rushes to the point (note the demise of Saul in 1 Chronicles 10 or the conquest of Jerusalem in 1 Chr 11:4-9).[25] Not so in chap.

---

24. See also Williamson, *1 and 2 Chronicles*, 127.

25. In the Hebrew Bible, narrative slows down most often when scenes replace summary. Dialogue often stops the action and portrays the present moment in a contemporaneous fashion. Dialogues, however, are sparse in Chronicles. See M. A. Throntveit, *When Kings Speak: Royal Speech and Royal Prayer in Chronicles* (SBLDS 93; Atlanta: Scholars, 1987) 12.

16. The amount of space devoted to the scene gives a clear clue to a locus of narrative interest.[26] The reader therefore knows that the present scene has special importance. Here, at the final stage, a single day suddenly receives several pages in a narrative sequence where three months had been compressed into seventeen verses (14:1-17). Such attention heightens the reality of success and its all-encompassing significance.

Several formal and thematic elements disclose the extraordinary nature of the day. First, Chronicles replicates the song and makes the reader a participant in the celebration. What we have is surely not summary, perhaps not even a depiction of a scene, but a reenactment. Second, the reiteration of the lists once again forces the narrative to linger. Third, perhaps most important, there is a persistent reminder of permanence and continuity.

Once the ark reaches Jerusalem, Chronicles turns its attention to things that endure: *continual* singing and seeking of God and remembering God's *eternal* covenant. Days of transition give way to permanence. David's leadership and arrangements now extend beyond the uniqueness of the event and the moment into the future. "That day" (ביום ההוא, 16:7) is now linked to an eternity. The repetition of תמיד, "always," occurs with unusual frequency: the thanksgiving psalm (16:8-37) is literally encircled by תמיד, "always" (16:6, 37, 39) even as it reiterates such permanence within (תמיד, "always," 16:11). Only here does Chronicles mention God's eternal covenant (16:15, 17).[27]

With the placing of the ark in Jerusalem, all the blessings of God come literally to the fore in an exuberant psalm. The psalm dominates the final act of the transfer of the ark. Not only does it exude unbounding joy, but the joy is set in the context of מן העולם ועד העלם, "for ever and ever" (16:36). With such continuity as backdrop, David establishes cultic offices forever (16:37, 40).

The thanksgiving psalm extols God's wonderous deeds in hyperbole that is common in poetry. The use of poetry, however, is uncommon in Chronicles (where even royal prayers appear primarily in prose and where only scattered, brief poetic expressions occur). Such "heightened speech" and triumphal celebration in song calls to mind other grand moments in Israel's history, such as the Song of the Sea (Exodus 15). Success is understood as God's enactment

---

26. For example, as M. Bal points out, space devoted to an event or details "indicates something about how the attention is patterned" (*Narratology: Introduction to the Theory of Narrative* [trans. C. van Boheenen; Toronto, Buffalo, and London: University of Toronto, 1985] 69). The rough distinction between summary and scene may be useful to elucidate the dynamics of this section (Alter, *Art of Biblical Narrative*, 63-67; Bal, *Narratology*, 68-77). There is always alternation between scene and summary: "The attention paid to the various elements gives us a picture of the vision on the fabula, which is being communicated to the reader. . . . The attention paid to each element can only be analysed *in relation* to the attention paid to all other elements" (Bal, *Narratology*, 69). Scenes most typically reflect important material.

27. The closest parallel appears in Solomon's speech, 2 Chr 6:14: שומר הברית והחסד.

of his eternal covenant, made to the patriarchs. The arrival of the ark in Jerusalem is a fulfillment of all that had been promised (16:15-22) and of global, even cosmic significance (16:29-33). No other event in Chronicles, not even the dedication of the temple, is enshrined in such broad-reaching terms and imagery.

The episode concludes with David returning to his home: "And David turned to bless his house" (ויסב דויד לברך את ביתו, 16:43). In addition to setting the stage for the next famous episode that revolves around "house" and "blessing" (1 Chronicles 17), this conclusion returns us to the beginning. The recurrence of ויסב reminds us, once again, of the end of Saul and how God turned the kingdom to David: ויסב את המלוכה לדויד בן ישי (1 Chr 10:14). Once more, Chronicles underscores the contrast between the good fortune of David, the king who cares for the ark and is, therefore, surrounded with blessings, and the ill-fated Saul, who neglected it. Thus ends the story of the transfer of the ark.

I have looked at 1 Chronicles 13–16 by tracing several literary devices that Chronicles uses to articulate its interest. I have left one important detail in the ark narrative for last. A key to literary interpretation is *Leitwort*.[28] Not surprisingly, the term "ark" is the key word in the ark narrative. It recurs 28 times in chaps. 13–16 (and only 18 additional times in the rest of Chronicles). The ark is called occasionally "ark of God" (e.g., 15:1), "ark of YHWH" (e.g., 15:3), or simply "the ark" (15:23). Textual considerations make it difficult to draw literary or theological conclusions from some of these alternations between God and YHWH.[29] One peculiarity, however, deserves our full attention and holds the key, in my estimation, to the significance of the entire ark narrative in Chronicles.

Until the Levites carry the ark, it is identified as the ark of God or ark of YHWH. Once the Levites are specifically appointed to carry the ark and actually do so, the terminology changes. Now, for the first time in Chronicles, the "ark of the *covenant*" occurs. The transformation takes place in 15:25. Not only does the term "ark of the covenant of YHWH" suddenly appear, but it also recurs with astonishing frequency: four times in the immediate four verses (15:25, 26, 28, 29). Indeed, of the twelve occurrences of the expression "ark of the covenant" in all of Chronicles, six are concentrated in our section, *after* the Levites carry the ark and bring it to Jerusalem.

What is the import of this rather dramatic transformation of the ark into the ark of the covenant? I suggest that at the surface level of the text, the Levites — not the ark itself — are perceived as the actual bearers of the covenant. Only when the two combine — when the Levites and the ark meet — does the ark

28. See, e.g., Alter, *Art of Biblical Narrative*, 92-93.
29. See Japhet on the names of God in Chronicles and on possible patterns in late Biblical Hebrew, *Ideology*, 18-42.

constitute a covenantal symbol.[30] Remaining strictly at a literary level and bracketing the complex historical issues concerning the Levites in Chronicles (issues sufficiently addressed by scholarly literature on Chronicles),[31] it is inevitable that one recognize the Levites, not the ark alone, as the vehicle of God's covenant.

It is noteworthy that Chronicles rarely mentions the covenant of God. The most frequent appearance of the term takes place in conjunction with the ark, with half of the references confined (as noted above) to the section under discussion. Two additional references to God's own covenant occur in the psalm of 16:15, 17 (hence also in this story).[32] As Japhet shows, other references to "covenant" in Chronicles refer to covenant between king and people or to unilateral commitment to God, not a covenant between Israel and God.[33] Japhet demonstrates clearly that in Chronicles, the covenant of God is not linked to a unique historical event such as Sinai (hence the striking omission of the references to the exodus). Instead, the covenant is with the people and has an eternal dimension in no way bound to a specific historical moment. 1 Chronicles 16:15-17 refers to an eternal, patriarchal covenant. What the present analysis adds to Japhet's is the conclusion that the ark narrative expresses this eternal covenant through the unique role of the Levites (cf. Deut 33:9; see also Mal 2:8: ברית הלוי, "covenant of Levi"). On the one hand, we have before us the transfer of the ark to Jerusalem. On the other, we have a "transfer" of covenant to the ark.

---

30. I have not been able to find in the secondary literature any adequate discussion of this striking shift to the ark of the covenant.

31. For a recent interpretation of the role of the Levites, see P. D. Hanson, "1 Chronicles 15–16 and the Chronicler's View of the Levites," in *Sha'arei Talmon: Studies in the Bible, Qumran, and the Ancient Near East Presented to Shemaryahu Talmon* (ed. M. Fishbane and E. Tov; Winona Lake, IN: Eisenbrauns, 1992) 69-78.

32. The only other references to God's covenant occur in 2 Chr 5:10 and 6:11 in connection with the ark, even though the ark is not described as the ark of the covenant.

33. Japhet differentiates between "secular" and "religious" covenants. One refers to a situation when both parties are human; the other has God as one of the parties (*Ideology,* 91). Chronicles has only three "religious" covenant texts: 1 Chr 15:15-18; 2 Chr 5:10; and 6:11. In all three, Chronicles follows its sources (ibid., 93). Japhet does not include references to the ark of the covenant in this particular discussion but addresses that issue separately (ibid., 88-91). Her comments concerning the ark of the covenant concentrate largely on ferreting out any underlying polemics behind the addition of the term "covenant" to the ark. She observes the affinity in terminology with Deuteronomy (ibid., 90) and concludes that in Chronicles the ark of the covenant no longer reflects a polemic but is rather a stylistic interest (ibid., 91). Japhet views the covenants with Asa (2 Chr 15:12-15), Hezekiah (29:10), Joash (33:15), and Josiah (34:29-33) either as covenants between king and people or a unilateral commitment of king and people to God. None represents a covenant between God and the people (ibid., 95-104, esp. summary on 103-4).

2. Chronicles and Samuel's Ark Narrative (2 Samuel 5–6)

Many of Chronicles' tendencies come into sharp relief when one compares Chronicles with Samuel's ark narrative. Practically every work on Chronicles incorporates a comparison with Samuel-Kings. Therefore, my remarks on the relation between these texts can be brief.

a. The emphasis in Chronicles on the importance, beauty, and joy of the ark and the cult is highlighted when one observes that Samuel's ark narrative is confined to a single chapter whereas Chronicles has three. Such proportionally greater narrative length reflects proportionally greater interest. Samuel's cultic ceremonies are brief; Chronicles dwells on details, lengthens the accounts, and lingers on material such as the thanksgiving psalm. These additions fix the reader's attention on cultic concerns.

David's care for the ark differentiates the two works. In Samuel, David first builds a house for himself (2 Sam 5:16) and determines only later to bring the ark (6:1). The ark proves less decisive for David's welfare and future. David's blessings multiply in Jerusalem before the ark narrative (5:10-25). Foreign recognition, progeny, and victory over the Philistines are therefore separate from his actions on behalf of the ark. In Chronicles, instead, the ark constitutes David's first and foremost concern. His good fortune, as we have seen, flows from the proper care for the ark.

b. The wide-ranging participation of the people in the life of the nation and the cult in Chronicles stands out when we note that in Samuel David carries primary responsiblity for all phases of the transfer of the ark. Whereas David in Chronicles begins by consulting the people (1 Chr 13:1), in Samuel he brings the ark without any such consultation (2 Sam 6:2). Chronicles shows communal involvement in all levels; Samuel lets David make the decisions. In Samuel, no other individual receives recognition aside from the unfortunate Uzza and Ahio (2 Sam 6:3), whereas Chronicles is replete with lists of named participants (e.g., 1 Chr 15:5-11). In Samuel, David brings the ark; in Chronicles, although the ark is carried by the Levites, the entire people somehow bring it to Jerusalem (1 Chr 15:28).

c. The Levites, so prominent in Chronicles, do not appear in Samuel's ark narrative, nor does the expression "ark of the covenant." The term "covenant" is the Chronicler's addition. These observations clearly confirm and help refine Chronicles' distinctive focus. The focus itself, however, can be garnered from the text even without a comparison with Samuel.

III. The Place of the Ark Narrative in Chronicles and Its Implications

I want briefly to set this episode in Chronicles in a larger context, limiting myself to broad generalizations to be substantiated elsewhere.

Chronicles is the story of Israel under kings, beginning with its first king Saul and concluding with its last. The ark, temple, and Jerusalem are at the center of the narrative along with the kings. The story presents a puzzle: Why does Chronicles devote so much attention to institutions (kingship) and objects (ark) that no longer exist in the Chronicler's time? Was Chronicles merely preserving a quickly vanishing past? Was Chronicles responding to the contemporary situation? If so, how? These familiar questions have received diverse answers, leading to diverse dating of the literature. The emphasis on kingship, for example, has been used to support an early date for Chronicles (e.g., ca. 500 B.C.E.) before the expectations of immediate restoration of monarchy proved hopeless.

The particular emphasis on the ark invites a reformulation of the answers to these questions. It helps to recall how much Chronicles is patterned after Deuteronomy. Like Deuteronomy, Chronicles retells Israel's formative events. For Deuteronomy, the Sinai event, the Torah, and Moses are paramount. The narrator, therefore, ignores events and characters that preceded. Chronicles seeks to do the same with the other paramount concerns: Jerusalem, the temple, and David. Like Deuteronomy, Chronicles thus complements and supplements. Both works reiterate the most significant elements of the received tradition as a way of summing up prior legacy and providing a bridge into the future. Both works take Israel to the brink, as it were, after having equipped it to respond afresh to God's charge. Deuteronomy ends just before Israel enters the promised land. Chronicles ends just before Israel returns to the promised land. Both works also establish guidelines for the future through proper transfer of authority and resources. As Moses was able to delegate authority (to Joshua, the elders, etc.), so too was David.[34] As Israel was able to leave Sinai itself and Moses behind and yet preserve and sustain their significance, so too can Israel leave some of its earlier milestones behind — David and the ark — yet retain what is central to tradition. Moses departed but had previously transferred authority to the Torah. David and kingship departed but they had previously transferred authority to the Jerusalem temple's cult.

The prominence of the lost ark, and the prominence of the lost monarchy, do not imply an expectation that either will be restored. Therefore one no longer need date Chronicles early. Instead, they demonstrate a recollection of traditions that have been transferred and transformed.

---

34. See H. G. M. Williamson, "The Succession of Solomon in the Books of Chronicles," *VT* 26 (1976) 351-61, esp. 351-55, for the ways narrative about Solomon's succession has been influenced by the succession of Joshua.

Continuities have been set in motion through personnel and blueprints. The efficacy of transfer is developed both in Deuteronomy and in Chronicles.[35] In this sense, Chronicles, like Deuteronomy, concerns troubled times of transitions and the struggle with perennial questions as to how communities endure in the midst of changing circumstances. It is, in the end, about transfer and transformation. The ark narrative both symbolizes such transfer and represents its actuality.

35. Note the detailed transfer of authority from David to Solomon in 1 Chronicles 28–29.

Qohelet's Autobiography

C. L. SEOW

Princeton Theological Seminary, New Jersey

It is a privilege to dedicate this essay in honor of Professor Noel Freedman, in gratitude for his scholarly contributions but also for his delightful friendship.

On the one hand, it is commonly held that Qoh 1:12–2:11 constitutes a "royal fiction" *(Königsfiktion)* or "royal parody" *(Königstravestie),* where the author speaks in the first person in the guise of Solomon.[1] The assumption is that Qohelet, as the renowned king and patron of sapiential activities, confesses his experiments with wisdom, pleasure, and toil, and reports how all these are of no lasting consequence. By calling the literary unit a "fiction" or "parody," however, commentators admit only the tension between the allusions to Solomon in this autobiographical account and the obvious late date of the composition. No strict form-critical category is intended by the nomenclature, and the account is just as readily designated "Solomonic fiction." The pretense of Solomonic kingship was prompted by the author's desire to be perceived as sage-king par excellence, who, having observed and experienced wisdom, pleasure, and toil firsthand, as it were, is able to offer advice with sufficient credibility. Thus, the passage is Qohelet-Solomon's "reflection" on the ephemerality

---

1. Some commentators isolate 1:12-18 from 2:1-11, but the thematic and lexical continuities in the larger unit are too compelling. One notes, for instance, the observations of the heart (1:13-14, 16; 2:3), conversations with the heart (1:16; 2:1-3), the place of the heart in the exploration of wisdom (1:13, 16; 2:3), and the motif of Solomon's priority over his predecessors (1:16; 2:7, 9). See further E. Bons, "Zur Gliederung und Kohärenz von Koh 1,12–2,11," *BN* 24 (1984) 73-91. In any case, the fiction of Qohelet's kingship extends at least to 2:11.

of these things.[2] Such designations of the unit merely state the obvious, however. They indicate only that the passage is a literary invention, a product of the author's imagination, and is not intended to be read literally or historically.[3]

On the other hand, those who venture to be more precise in their identification of the *Gattung* have not been able to establish any kind of consensus.[4] They suggest comparison with some Egyptian wisdom texts, variously called "royal lesson" *(Königslehre)*, "royal testament" *(Königstestament)*, or "royal confession" *(Königsbekenntnis)*.[5] Whatever the designation used, however, the analogy is almost always with "The Instruction of Merikare" or "The Instruction of Amenemhet."[6] The inconsistency in naming the *Gattung* suggests some uncertainty about the appropriate connection between Qohelet and those Egyptian texts: Is the link simply with the broad category of *Sebayit* ("Instruction"), the royal voice in wisdom, first person narratives, or specifically with the legacy of a departing king? Indeed, it appears that apart from kingship, the general sapiential setting of the passage, and the apparent old age of the king-sage, little commends the analogy.[7] Suffice it to say, attempts to describe the genre of the passage have not produced satisfactory results. Labels like "refection," "fiction," or "parody" are too general to be helpful; but more specific designations like "royal instruction," "royal testament," and "royal confession" have not been convincing for want of compelling parallels. It seems necessary, therefore, to investigate afresh the literary background of the passage.

---

2. So R. E. Murphy, *Wisdom Literature* (FOTL 13; Grand Rapids: Eerdmans, 1981) 134-36.

3. H.-P. Müller, however, proposes a social-historical origin for Qohelet's use of this fiction. See his "Neige der althebräischen 'Weisheit' zum Denken Qohäläts," *ZAW* 90 (1978), esp. 256-59; idem, "Theonome Skepsis und Lebensfreude: Zu Koh 1,12–3,15," *BZ* 30 (1986) 2.

4. Many commentators are willing only to point generally to the Egyptian *Sebayit* ("Instruction"). So R. E. Murphy, *Ecclesiastes* (WBC 23A; Dallas: Word, 1992) 12; W. Zimmerli, *Das Buch der Predigers Salomo* (ATD 16/1; Göttingen: Vandenhoeck & Ruprecht, 1962) 146-47.

5. On the "royal lesson," see K. Galling, "Koheleth-Studien," *ZAW* 50 (1932) 298. G. von Rad (*Wisdom in Israel* [trans. J. D. Martin; Nashville and New York: Abingdon, 1972] 226) regards not only this passage but the entire book as a "royal testament." For a discussion of this and related views, see O. Loretz, *Qohelet und der alte Orient* (Freiburg: Herder, 1964) 57-65. For the "royal confession," see J. L. Crenshaw, "Wisdom," in *Old Testament Form Criticism* (ed. J. H. Hayes; TUMSR 2; San Antonio: Trinity University, 1974) 256-57. Note Crenshaw's own certainty of the Egyptian origin of the genre, as well as his observation regarding scholarly consensus on the matter.

6. For translations of these texts, see M. Lichtheim, *Ancient Egyptian Wisdom Literature* (3 vols.; Berkeley: University of California, 1973-80) 1.99-107, 135-38.

7. Despite his earlier essay, Crenshaw classifies Qoh 1:12–2:26 as a "royal testament" in his commentary, *Ecclesiastes* (OTL; Philadelphia: Westminster, 1987) 29. One can only assume that he intends to subsume "royal testament" under the general rubric of "confessions" or "autobiographical narratives."

I

One may begin with a point of agreement: Qohelet has Solomon in mind in this passage. He identifies himself immediately as *mlk 'l-yśr'l byrwšlm*, "a king over Israel in Jerusalem" (1:12). The combination of "over Israel" (not "over Judah") and "in Jerusalem" makes it virtually certain that he is thinking of the united monarchy. Saul, David, and Solomon are all called "king over Israel" in the Bible, but only David and Solomon may be said to have ruled "in Jerusalem."[8] The superscription of the book, too, appears to be alluding to Solomon, as other sapiential superscriptions do (Prov 1:1; 10:1; 25:1; Cant 1:1), for the author is called "the son of David" and "a king in Jerusalem."[9] The focus on the search of the heart through wisdom (1:13) certainly calls to mind the reference to Solomon's "wise heart" in the tradition about his dream at Gibeon (1 Kgs 3:3-15; 2 Chr 1:1-13), and the universal scope of the exploration recalls his legendary sapiential activities (1 Kgs 5:9-14).[10]

The language in Qoh 1:16 echoes the legends of Solomon's prowess: the expression *whwspty ḥkmh*, "and I increased wisdom," recalls the queen of Sheba's comment to Solomon: "you have increased wisdom" (*hwspt ḥkmh*; 1 Kgs 10:7); and *gdlty*,[11] "I became great," is similar to the assessment in 1 Kgs 10:23: *wygdl hmlk šlmh mkl mlky h'rṣ l'šr wlḥkmh*, "King Solomon became greater than all the kings of the earth in wealth and wisdom." So Qohelet concludes that he "became great and surpassed all who preceded" him in Jerusalem (2:9) and states that he had not deprived himself of anything that his eyes "asked for" (*š'lw*, 2:10). One is instantly reminded of God's gift of wisdom to Solomon and how the king could "ask for" (*š'l*) anything that he desired (1 Kgs 3:5, 10, 11, 13). Solomon at Gibeon had asked only for wisdom, but he was granted also wealth, honor, and longevity, so that he would surpass all who preceded him and not be excelled by those who succeeded him (1 Kgs 3:10-14). It is evident, therefore, that Qohelet must have been aware of the tradition of Solomon's dream at Gibeon and probably more.[12]

8. 1 Sam 23:17; 2 Sam 5:2-5, 11, 17; 1 Kgs 1:34; 3:28. Others who are called "king over Israel" are from the northern kingdom (1 Kgs 14:13-14; 15:25; 16:29; 22:52; 2 Kgs 2:25), while those who ruled in the south — "in Jerusalem" — are never so identified.

9. See further D. Meade, *Pseudonymity and Canon* (WUNT 39; Tübingen: Mohr/Siebeck, 1986; reprinted Grand Rapids: Eerdmans, 1987) 55-62.

10. Other scholars have also seen the connection of this passage with Solomon's dream at Gibeon. See, most recently, D. M. Carr, *From D to Q: A Study of Early Jewish Interpretations of Solomon's Dream at Gibeon* (SBLMS 44; Atlanta: Scholars, 1991) 136-45.

11. MT has *hgdlty*, which probably reflects a dittography of *h*; hence one should read *hnh* < *>gdlty*. The dittography may have been prompted, too, by the Hiphil coming after this word, *whwspty*, and it anticipates *hgdlty* in 2:4. LXX reads *emagalynthen* here, as well as in 2:9, which has *gdlty*.

12. V. Peterca, *L'Immagine di Salomone nella Bibbia Ebraica e Greca* (Rome: Pontificia Universitas Gregoriana, 1981) 82-83.

The list of Solomon's deeds in Qoh 2:4-11 calls to mind the activities and legendary wealth of Solomon in 1 Kings 4–11 only in a general way. There is little evidence of literary dependence, although one may think of these verses in Qohelet as giving a different version of essentially the same thing in 1 Kings 4–11; both accounts are reminiscent of royal records, such as may have been in the so-called Book of the Acts of Solomon (1 Kgs 11:41).

In any case, several of the items on the list in Qoh 2:4-11 may refer to landmarks around Jerusalem that had been associated with Solomon. Thus, the vineyards (2:4) may be an allusion to Solomon's vineyards, one of which was reputed to have been in Baal-hamon (Cant 8:11). By the same token, the gardens (2:5) may refer to "the King's Garden" (Jer 39:4; 52:7; 2 Kgs 25:4; Neh 3:15) located near the Pool of Shelah (Neh 3:15) in the Kidron Valley,[13] and the pools may be an allusion to the King's Pool (Neh 2:14) and the Pool of Shelah located near "the King's Garden" (Neh 3:15). The historian Josephus, too, knew of "Solomon's Pool" between the Pool of Siloam and a spot called Ophlas.[14] Indeed, remnants of a plastered pool have recently been uncovered precisely in this vicinity, a pool that may have been identified with an earlier one at the same site attributed by tradition to Solomon.[15]

In sum, Qohelet intended for the reader to think of Solomon, the consummate wise king who had everything. The inspiration for the fiction was Solomon, and the author clearly drew on various traditions about the king's wisdom, wealth, and many accomplishments. But the material is presented in a first person narrative. It is in the form of a fictional autobiography.

Other first person narratives occur elsewhere in Israelite wisdom literature, but no other example — including the other first person accounts in Qohelet — has such a historical ring; nowhere else is our imagination so directed to the figure of the king. It will not be adequate, therefore, to lump together all first person narratives in biblical sapiential literature under the rubric of "autobiographies" or "confessions."[16] Only Qohelet's account in his Solomonic disguise deserves to be called an "autobiography," a fictional one though it is.

Moreover, while other first person narratives may be analogous to Egyptian didactic literature, the same conclusion is not assured in regard to Qohelet's account here. One can make at least as strong a case for comparison with the Akkadian fictional autobiographies.[17] The fictional, royal, and autobiographical

13. The Brook of Kidron apparently irrigated the various gardens and orchards that were regarded as royal property.

14. Josephus, *J.W.* 5.4.2 §145. Ophlas is no doubt to be identified with biblical Ophel ("Mound"), mentioned in Neh 3:26.

15. See D. Adan, "The 'Fountain of Siloam' and 'Solomon's Pool' in First-Century C.E. Jerusalem," *IEJ* 29 (1979) 92-100.

16. See Crenshaw, "Wisdom," 256-58.

17. A. K. Grayson ("Histories and Historians of the Ancient Near East: Assyria and Babylonia," *Or* n.s. 49 [1980] 187-88) cites the Cuthean Legend of Naram-Sin as the only

character of the text seems clear enough; one does not need to turn to the comparative evidence to demonstrate this fact. Nor does one have a clearer understanding of the passage once it is identified as a fictional autobiography of King Solomon. Rather, it is necessary to be more specific about the kind of autobiographies that this text imitates and the usual function of the genre, and then explain how Qohelet might have used that specific genre to make his point.

II

The autobiographical language in Qohelet is indeed typical of West Semitic and Akkadian royal inscriptions. Qohelet begins with a formulaic self-presentation that is characteristic of such texts,[18] with the first common singular independent personal pronoun + personal name, *'ny qhlt,* "I am Qohelet" (1:12).[19] In West Semitic royal inscriptions, this formula typically introduces the text:[20] *'nk klmw,* "I am Kilamuwa" (*KAI* 24.1); *'nk yhwmlk,* "I am Yehawmilk" (*KAI* 10.1); *'nk 'ztwd,* "I am Azitawadda" (*KAI* 26.I.1); *'nk pnmw,* "I am Panammu" (*KAI* 214.1); *'nh br rkb,* "I am Bir-Rakib" (*KAI* 216.1; 217.1); *'nk mš',* "I am Mesha" (*KAI* 181.1); *'nk tbnt,* "I am Tabnit" (*KAI* 13.1). Similarly, the *anāku RN* formula frequently introduces the king in the standard Akkadian royal inscriptions; thus, not surprisingly, the Akkadian fictional autobiographies also imitate this style.[21]

---

example of pseudo-autobiographies in Assyria and Babylonia, but H. Tadmor ("Autobiographical Apology in the Royal Assyrian Literature," in *History, Historiography, and Interpretation* [ed. H. Tadmor and M. Weinfeld; Jerusalem: Magnes, 1986] 36n.2) includes also the Legend of Sargon and a text written in the name of Nebuchadnezzar I. T. Longman III has thoroughly examined the genre (*Fictional Akkadian Autobiography* [Winona Lake, IN: Eisenbrauns, 1991]); he argues that the book of Ecclesiastes as a whole belongs to this category of literature. See esp. pp. 120-23.

18. Cf. M. V. Fox, *Qohelet and His Contradictions* (JSOTSup 71; Sheffield: Almond, 1989) 174.

19. It is also possible to take the independent pronoun as standing in apposition to the personal name. For this construction in the epigraphic materials, see A. Poebel, *Das Appositionell Bestimmte Pronomen der 1. Pers. Sing. in den Westsemitischen Inschriften und im Alten Testament* (Assyriological Studies 3; Chicago: University of Chicago, 1932).

20. Unless otherwise indicated, all citations of West Semitic inscriptions are taken from H. Donner and W. Röllig, *Kanaanäische und aramäische Inschriften* (3 vols.; 2nd ed.; Wiesbaden: Harrassowitz, 1968-71) — hereafter simply *KAI.*

21. For royal inscriptions, see, e.g., D. D. Luckenbill, *The Annals of Sennacherib* (OIP 2; Chicago: University of Chicago, 1924) 150 (inscription X, l. 1); R. Borger, *Die Inschriften Asarhaddons Königs von Assyrien* (AfO Beihefte 9; Graz: Weidner, 1967) 119 (K 2388, obv. 1.1); M. Streck, *Assurbanipal und die letzen assyrischen Könige bis zum Untergang Ninevehs* II (VAB 7; Leipzig: Hinrichs'sche, 1916) 2 (col. i, l. 1). Cf. also the discusssion of the "Ichform" in S. Mowinckel, "Die vorderasiatischen Königs- und Fürsteninschriften: Eine stilistische Studie," in *Eucharisterion* (*Festschrift* H. Gunkel; ed. H. Schmidt; Göttingen: Vandenhoeck &

Moreover, one should not take the reference to Qohelet's kingship *(hyyty mlk)* as an allusion to the past, but as referring to the present rule of the king; thus, "I have been king."[22] The use of the perfect in referring to one's royal qualities and activities is very much in keeping with the narrative style of the West Semitic royal inscriptions: *yšbt 'l ks' 'by,* "I have sat upon the throne of my father" *(KAI 24.9); gm yšbt 'l mšb 'by,* "I, too, have sat on the throne of my father" *(KAI 214.8); w'nk mlkty 'ḥr 'by,* "and I have reigned after my father" *(KAI 181.1-3).* There is no difference between the idiom *hyyty mlk* in Qohelet and *mlkty* or *yšbt(y) 'l ks'* in the West Semitic royal inscriptions.

At the outset, the passage refers to the king's wisdom. The intent is not to point to the achievements of the past, which the author denigrates in retrospect; it is not that Solomon "experimented" with wisdom but now realizes that it is all futile.[23] Rather, here as in other royal texts from the Levant, wisdom is held as a royal ideal.[24] The motif of royal wisdom is standard in royal propaganda. The Karatepe inscription mentions the wisdom of Azitawadda, as a mark of his legitimacy: *b'bt p'ln kl mlk bṣdqy w bḥkmty wbn'm lby,* "every king made me a father because of my justice, my wisdom, and the goodness of my heart" *(KAI 26.I.12-13).*[25] Akkadian royal inscriptions are replete with references to the king as "wise" *(eršu, emqu, itpēšu),* "intelligent" *(ḫassu),* and "knowing" *(mudû).* The king is often said to be one with comprehensive knowledge or experience, who "understands everything" *(ḫasis mimma šumšu),* who is "experienced in everything" *(mudū kal šiprī),* or the like.[26] Thus, Esarhaddon called himself "a wise (and) wily prince, who understands all things" *(rubû enqu itpēšu ḫāsis kal šiprī).*[27] Hammurapi introduced himself as "the wise, the active, who

---

Ruprecht, 1923) 297-99. For fictional autobiographies, see the examples in Longman, *Fictional Akkadian Autobiographies,* 215-28.

22. The verb *hyyty* is commonly taken to indicate a past fact and, hence, translated as "I was" (so LXX, KJV, ASV). In the same vein, a Jewish tradition took the verb to mean that Solomon was no longer king, having been deposed on account of his sins, his throne having been usurped by the evil Ashmedai (Asmodeus), king of the demons (*y. Sanh.* 20c; *b. Giṭ.* 68a-b). The Hebrew perfect, particularly of stative verbs, need not indicate past realities, however. The perfect of *hyh* may also indicate an existing state (Job 11:4; 30:29; Isa 25:4; Pss 59:17 [ET 16]; 61:4 [ET 3]; 63:8 [ET 7]; 90:1; Gen 26:28; 42:11).

23. So most commentators.

24. See L. Kalugila, *The Wise King: Studies in Royal Wisdom as Divine Revelation in the Old Testament and Its Environment* (ConBOT 15; Lund: Gleerup, 1980), esp. 12-68.

25. Although Azitawadda is never called "king" in the inscription, he was clearly the effective ruler of the Danunians — what we may call the regent (see *KAI* 26.I.10-11) — and the inscription is in the *form* of a royal stela. On the relation between Azitawadda and *'wrk mlk dnnym,* see F. Bron, *Recherches sur les inscriptions phéniciennes de Karatepe* (Hautes études Orientales 11; Paris: Librairie Droz, 1979) 159-63.

26. On the first expression, see S. Langdon, *Die Neubabylonischen Königsinschriften* (VAB 4; Leipzig: Hinrichs'sche, 1912) 252 (no. 6, col. 1, l. 3). On the second, see *CAD* M/II.166.

27. Borger, *Die Inschriften Asarhaddons,* 74 (l. 24).

has attained all wisdom" *(emqum muttabilum šu ikšudu nagab uršim)*, and Nabonidus claimed: "I am wise, I know (all), I see hidden things" *(enqēk mudâka ātamar ka[timta])*.[28] Ashurbanipal, Assyria's patron of the arts and wisdom par excellence, likewise boasted of his great learning and his venture into esoterica, the "secret of heaven and earth, the wisdom of Šamaš and Adad."[29] The inscription on the statue of Idrimi, which has been classified as a fictional autobiography, contains the king's claim of intellectual superiority over his peers: *man-umma awāte ša aḥšušu ul iḥšuš*, "nobody understood the things I understood."[30] Thus, while it is true that the reference to Qohelet's exploration through wisdom of all things under heaven recalls Solomon's patronage of wisdom, one should understand the entire passage against the backdrop of royal ideology.

Qohelet says in 1:16 that he surpassed all his predecessors, presumably other kings who had ruled before him. The phrase *kl-'šr-hyh lpny 'l-yrwšlm*, "all who were before me over Jerusalem," is repeated in slightly variant forms in 2:7, 9.[31] Interpreters, both ancient and modern, have been frequently troubled by the allusion to a plurality of kings "over Jerusalem" or "in Jerusalem."[32] It is easy to assume an anachronism here (since strictly only one Israelite king had ruled over Jerusalem before Solomon), or that Qohelet was thinking of the pre-Israelite rulers of the city. Yet, the historicity of the Jerusalemite kings before Solomon is not really at issue here. Rather, Qohelet is adopting the language and style of royal propagandistic literature.

The comparison with the predecessors is a prominent motif in West Semitic and Mesopotamian royal inscriptions, and it is usually repeated in each inscription, as it is here (1:16; 2:7, 9). This is evident, for instance, in the inscription of Kilamuwa (*KAI* 24), where the king puts forth his own accomplishments over against his predecessors, each of whom is judged to have done nothing *(bl p'l)*.[33] The propagandistic intent of the comparison is obvious, and the king concludes, "but I . . . whatever I did, *those who were before me* did not

---

28. On Hammurapi see G. R. Driver and J. C. Miles, *The Babylonian Laws* (2 vols.; Oxford: Clarendon, 1952-55) 2.10 (col. iv, ll. 7-10). For Nabonidus see S. Smith, *Babylonian Historical Texts Relating to the Capture and Downfall of Babylon* (London: Methuen, 1924) pl. 8, l. 9.

29. Streck, *Assurbanipal*, 362 (l. 3).

30. For the classification "fictional autobiography," see Longman, *Fictional Akkadian Autobiography*, 60-66. On Idrimi see S. Smith, *The Statue of Idri-mi* (London: British Institute of Archaeology in Ankara, 1949) 14 (ll. 8-9). For the writing of š for s, see E. L. Greenstein and D. Marcus, "The Akkadian Inscription of Idrimi," *JANESCU* 8 (1976) 60-62.

31. Instead of *'l yrwšlm*, over a hundred Hebrew MSS have *byrwšlm*, and the versions reflect the same; but that is the easier reading and it anticipates *byrwšlm* in 2:7, 9. MT is superior.

32. 1 Chr 29:25 is a close parallel inasmuch as it refers to Solomon's greatness over "any king over Israel before him." But the plurality of kings "over Israel" is not a problem in that case because the kings are not said to be "in Jerusalem" or "over Jerusalem."

33. For the ideological underpinnings of this text, see F. M. Fales, "Kilamuwa and the Foreign Kings: Propaganda vs. Power," *WO* 10 (1979) 6-22.

do" (*KAI* 24.I.4-5). Likewise, in the Karatepe inscription, Azitawadda wrote of the failure of kings before him *(kl hmlkm 'š kn lpny)* and highlighted what he himself had done (*KAI* 26.I.18-20). He repeatedly contrasted the situation in the kingdom in former days and in his own days. The comparison with predecessors is clearly formulaic in such royal texts.[34] The reference to the king's predecessors may be compared with the same phenomenon in Akkadian royal inscriptions, where phrases like *mamman maḥrīya*, "any before me," *mamman ina šarrāni ālikūt maḥrīya*, "any among kings who went before me," *šarrāni maḥrūt*, "former kings," *ša ellamūa*, "those before me," are standard fare.[35] Each time the comparison with the predecessors is brought up in the royal inscriptions, the point is to highlight the successes of the current ruler, the king of whom the text speaks.

Beginning in 2:4, Qohelet itemizes his achievements, using a series of verbs in the first common singular perfect: *hgdlty*, "I magnified" (v. 4); *bnyty*, "I built" (v. 4); *nṭʿty*, "I planted" (vv. 4, 5); *ʿśyty*, "I made," "I gained" (vv. 5, 6, 8); *qnyty*, "I acquired" (v. 7); *knsty*, "I accumulated" (v. 8). One may compare this style of narration with the West Semitic royal inscriptions.[36] In the Moabite Stone (*KAI* 181), for instance, the accomplishments of the king are given in the perfect: *mlkty*, "I reigned" (ll. 2-3, 28-29); *bnty*, "I built" (ll. 21, 22, 23, 26, 27, 29-30); *ʿśyty*, "I made" (ll. 23, 26); and *krty*, "I dug" (l. 25).[37] In the inscriptions of Zakkur, Panammu, Bir-Rakib, Kilamuwa, and Karatepe, too, the deeds of the ruler are indicated by verbs in the first common singular perfect.[38]

Qohelet's achievements include several types of deeds (2:4-9): building projects; planting of vineyards, gardens, and parks; digging of reservoirs for irrigation; accumulation of treasures; acquisition of slaves, as well as "male and female singers" *(šārîm wěšārôt)*. The list corresponds to what one finds in other royal texts from the ancient Near East. One naturally expects the mention of the king's wealth and various acquisitions in any royal texts, and building projects have been demonstrated to be standard in political propaganda.[39] The other items in Qohelet's list have striking parallels, particularly from Meso-

34. See A. K. Grayson, "Assyrian Royal Inscriptions: Literary Characteristics," in *Assyrian Royal Inscriptions* (Orientis Antiqui Collectio 17; ed. F. M. Fales; Rome: Instituto per L'Oriente, 1981) 44-45.

35. Cf. T. Ishida, " 'Solomon who is greater than David': Solomon's succession in 1 Kings i–ii in the light of the inscription of Kilamuwa, king of y'dy-sam'al," *Congress Volume: Salamanca, 1983* (ed. J. A. Emerton; VTSup36; Leiden: Brill, 1985) 145-53. For this motif in Assyrian propaganda, see M. Liverani, "The Ideology of the Assyrian Empire," in *Power and Propaganda* (ed. M. T. Larsen; Copenhagen: Akademisk Forlag, 1979) 308-9.

36. So B. Isaksson, *Studies in the Language of Qoheleth* (Studia Semitica Upsaliensia 10; Uppsala: Acta Universitatis Upsaliensis, 1987) 46-57.

37. Cf. also the verb *ʿśty* in l. 3 of the Kerak Fragment; see W. L. Reed and F. G. Winnett, "A Fragment of an Early Moabite Inscription from Kerak," *BASOR* 172 (1963) 1-9.

38. *KAI* 202, 214, 215, 216, 24, 26.

39. Grayson, "Histories and Historians," passim.

potamia. Several Neo-Assyrian inscriptions, as in Qohelet, mention the king's treasures and acquisition of slaves, harems, as well as "male and female singers" (*LÚ.NAR.MEŠ SAL.NAR MEŠ*).[40] Others regularly include in the listing of royal accomplishments the cultivation of trees in gardens, orchards, and parks, as well as various irrigation projects. In his various inscriptions, Sargon II wrote of his incomparable wisdom and boasted of his diverse building projects that he had accomplished when none of his predecessors did.[41] He told how he created "a pleasure garden like the Amanus," wherein he planted every kind of tree, set out orchards, and dug irrigation canals.[42] Sargon's successor, Sennacherib, spoke of his own achievements in a similar way, claiming to have surpassed all his predecessors in his building activities, the cultivations of gardens and orchards, and the irrigation of the land by means of reservoirs and canals.[43]

Although the inventory is not as full in the West Semitic inscriptions, the mention in the Moabite Stone (*KAI* 181) of a reservoir (ll. 9, 23), cisterns (ll. 24-25), and an enclosed park (l. 21)[44] is noteworthy, as are the allusions to various agricultural activities in the royal inscriptions from northern Syria.[45] None is as suggestive, however, as the Ammonite royal inscription from Tell Siran, which itemizes "the *deeds* of Amminadab, king of the Ammonites" — as Qohelet focuses on his deeds (2:4, 11) — including the creation of a vineyard *(hkrm)*, a garden *(hgnt)*, reservoirs *('šḫt)*, and possibly an enclosed park *(h'sḥr?)*.[46] One might also observe that this inscription ties the works of the king to pleasure for him (l. 6): *wygl wyśmḥ*, "may he rejoice and have pleasure." In a similar manner Qohelet concludes, "I did not restrain my heart from every pleasure [*śmḥh*], and my heart had pleasure [*śmḥ*] from all my toil" (2:10).

Imitating the style of royal inscriptions, then, Qohelet highlights his personal achievements as king. Encountering the text in the style of a royal auto-

40. See, e.g., Luckenbill, *Annals of Sennacherib*, 24 (col. i, ll. 32-33), 34 (col. iii, ll. 46-47), 52 (l. 32), 24.i.32, 34.iii.46; Streck, *Assurbanipal*, 2.122, l. 21.

41. The stock expression is *ša 350.ÁM malkī labīrūt ša ellamūa bēlūt KUR Aššur^{ki} ēpušu*, "(none) of the 350 previous kings who ruled over Assyria before me." So, e.g., D. G. Lyon, *Keilschrifttexte Sargons* (Leipzig: Hinrichs'sche, 1883) 15 (l. 43); H. Winkler, *Die Keilschrifttexte Sargons* (Leipzig: Eduard Pfeiffer, 1889) 1.90 (l. 66).

42. Winckler, *Die Keilschrifttexte Sargons*, 1.88-90; Lyon, *Keilschrifttexte Sargons*, 14, 20-27. Cf. Qoh 2:5.

43. Luckenbill, *Annals of Sennacherib*, 79-85, 94-98, 99-101, and passim in the inscriptions.

44. The text has *ḥmt hy'rn*, lit. "wall of the woods."

45. Passim in *KAI* 26, 214, 215, 216.

46. See H. O. Thompson and F. Zayadine, "The Tell Siran Inscription," *BASOR* 212 (1973) 5-11. I follow F. M. Cross ("Notes on the Ammonite Inscription from Tell Sīran," *BASOR* 212 [1973] 12) in reading *wh'sḥr* instead of *wh'tḥr*, assuming a partly damaged two-armed *samek*. The word *'sḥr* I assume to be a noun with a prothetic *'aleph*, related to the root *sḥr*, "encircle, circumambulate." The Hebrew form *sḥrh* in Ps 91:4 has been interpreted to mean "wall" (so *HALAT*, 708; NEB), a cognate of Akk. *siḫirtu* and Syr. *sāḥartā*.

biography, one may get the impression that Qohelet is presenting the deeds of the king as permanent, and hence assuring an immortality of sorts. In Syria-Palestine and Mesopotamia, royal deeds were typically inscribed on durable objects that were then prominently displayed, and in the case of those from Mesopotamia, sometimes deposited in foundations and other structural parts of a building or on rock faces.[47] They were intended to survive their heroes, and in many instances survive even the physical structures in which they were placed. Some were written on the back of stone slabs, so that they might be preserved even when the buildings turned to ruins. Others were buried or otherwise kept beyond the reaches of the people in the present — preserved for the eyes of the gods and future generations. Indeed, the inscriptions were intended to last forever, and with them the reputation of the kings in whose name they were made. As the Assyrian king Esarhaddon himself put it:

> I had documents made of silver, gold, bronze, lapis lazuli, alabaster, basalt, granite (?), *elallu*-stone, white limestome, (and) fired-clay monuments. I depicted upon them the *lumāšu*-stars corresponding to the writing of my name. The might of the great warrior, Marduk, the deeds which I had achieved, my works of my hand I wrote thereon and placed them into the foundations. I left them to eternity.[48]

The greatest threat to the survival of the inscriptions lay in the deliberate effacement or neglect of them, and against such the texts regularly included stern warnings of the dire consequences. The maintenance of the texts became the sacred responsibility of the descendants and successors. Thus, the inscriptions were to be the king's assurance of immortality.

Against that background, Qohelet's imitation of the genre is poignant in its irony. In the end the text makes the point that none of the deeds — even the royal deeds that are assiduously preserved in memorials — really matters. For human beings, even kings, there is no immortality of any sort. At first blush, the autobiography paints a picture of enormous success. But the mention of the king's deeds, and especially the superiority of his deeds to those of his predecessors, leads to a surprising conclusion, one that is quite contrary to the purpose of royal texts. The legendary acts, wealth, and wisdom of Solomon turned out not to have abiding significance after all. The genre of a royal inscription is utilized to make the point about the ephemerality of wisdom and human accomplishments. Qohelet itemizes the king's many deeds and surpluses only to show that kings are no better off than ordinary people, for "everything is *hebel* and a pursuit of wind, and there is no advantage under the sun" (2:11).

---

47. Grayson, "Histories and Historians," 151.
48. Borger, *Die Inschriften Asarhaddons,* 27-28 (episode 40, ll. 4-14).

III

The adaptation of genres for rhetorical purposes is nothing new in ancient Near Eastern literature. Examples abound in both Egypt and Mesopotamia. For the purposes of this essay, however, it suffices to consider only the compositional process in the Gilgamesh Epic.[49] This text is important here inasmuch as it evidences the adaptation of earlier works of various genres, some of which are employed within their new literary context in a manner contrary to their original intent.[50] It is especially pertinent in this context because it has many widely recognized affinities with Qohelet.[51]

The text, known in antiquity by its incipit, *ša nagba īmuru*, "He Who Saw All," begins in this way:

> [šá] nag-ba i-mu-ru lu-[še-e]-di ma-a-ti
> [šá kul-la-t]i i-du-ú ka-l[a-ma lu-šal-m]i-s[u]
> [ib-r]i-ma mit-ḫa-riš m[a-ta-ti]
> [ra]-áš ne-me-qi ša ka-la-a-mi i-[du-ú]
> [ni]-ṣir-ta i-mur-ma ka-tim-tú ip-t[u]. (Gilg. I, i.1-5)[52]

> [He who] saw all, let me [make know]n to the land,
> [Who] knew [everyth]ing, [let me tea]ch i[t] all.
> [He search]ed the l[ands?] fully.
> [He who re]ceived wisdom, who k[new] everything,
> He saw the [my]steries and disclo[sed] what is hidden.

Gilgamesh, the renowned king from long ago, claims in this late version of the epic to have seen it all and explored the universe fully. He "knew everything" and proposes to teach it all, which we know in context to be about the unattainability of immortality. Qohelet, too, learned by observation and

---

49. For a full discussion, see J. H. Tigay, *The Evolution of the Gilgamesh Epic* (Philadelphia: University of Pennsylvania, 1982).

50. See most recently B. F. Batto, *Slaying the Dragon* (Louisville: Westminster/John Knox, 1992) 17-26.

51. See Loretz, *Qohelet und der alte Orient*, esp. 116-22; J. de Savignac, "La sagesse du Qôhéléth et l'épopée de Gilgamesh," *VT* 28 (1978) 318-23; A. Shaffer, "The Mesopotamian Background of Qohelet 4:9-12," *ErIsr* 9 (1969) 246-50; idem, "New Light on the 'Three-Ply Cord,'" *ErIsr* 9 (1969) 138-39, 159-60; B. W. Jones, "From Gilgamesh to Qoheleth," in *The Bible in the Light of Cuneiform Literature: Scripture in Context* III (ed. W. W. Hallo, B. W. Jones, and G. L. Mattingly; Ancient Near Eastern Texts and Studies 8; Lewiston: Mellen, 1990) 349-79.

52. Reconstructed after R. C. Thompson, *The Epic of Gilgamesh* (Oxford: Clarendon, 1930) 11; Tigay, *Evolution of the Gilgamesh Epic*, 261; T. Jacobsen, "The Gilgamesh Epic: Romantic and Tragic and Romantic Vision," in *Lingering over Words: Studies in Ancient Near Eastern Literature in Honor of William L. Moran* (ed. T. Abusch, J. Huehnergard, and P. Steinkeller; HSS 37; Atlanta: Scholars, 1990) 246n.22.

experience: he "saw" and he "knew." The verb r'ḥ, "see," occurs 46 times in the book, with Qohelet himself or his heart as the subject no less than 26 times.[53] He also refers frequently to his own knowledge or quest for knowledge (1:17; 3:12; 7:25; 8:16-17). In any case, he set out to explore the whole universe through wisdom and "saw all that has been under the sun" (1:14). So now he sets out to teach.

Moreover, in tablet I of the Gilgamesh Epic, one learns that Gilgamesh had kept a record of his exploits: "he engraved all his toil on a document" (iḫruṣ ina narî kalu mānaḫti).[54] The attitude of Qohelet about his own efforts and achievements certainly echoes the reference to the king's deeds here as mānaḫtu, "toil," and elsewhere as marṣātu, "troubles."[55] The precise content of Gilgamesh's document (narû) is not known, however, although some scholars have surmised that the narû was the basis of, or one of the sources underlying, the narrative.[56] The immediate context suggests that the narû contained an account of Gilgamesh's accomplishments, including the building of the walls of Uruk and the temple Eanna, the opening of mountain passes, and the digging of wells.[57]

These are precisely the kinds of things that one expects in narû literature.[58] The narû may well have been an earlier document — a stela (the most common meaning of the word) or a foundation deposit of Gilgamesh,[59] the legendary king who built Uruk. Or it could have been pure literary fiction, as A. L. Oppenheim contends.[60] As is widely recognized, the prologue (tablet I) and epilogue (tablet IX) — the parts that do resemble the language and style of the narû genre — have been added to the original epic. If they reflect an actual earlier document, the narrator has adapted the content of that document for a purpose contrary to its original. If it is literary fiction, as is probably the case, it imitates the genre of which

---

53. Qoh 1:14, 16; 2:1, 3, 12, 13, 24; 3:10, 16, 18, 22; 4:1, 4, 7, 15; 5:12, 17 (ET 13, 18); 6:1; 7:15; 8:9, 10, 16, 17; 9:11, 13; 10:5, 7.

54. Gilg. I, i.8.

55. Gilg. I, i.26.

56. So H. Gressmann and A. Ungnad, *Das Gilgamesh-Epos* (FRLANT 14; Göttingen: Vandenhoeck & Ruprecht, 1911) 85. Others have argued that the narû is the legend itself, much like the Cuthean Legend of Naram-Sin. So P. Michalowski *apud* P. Machinist, "On Self-Consciousness in Mesopotamia," in *The Origins and Diversity of Axial Age Civilizations* (ed. S. N. Eisenstadt; New York: State University of New York, 1986) 194 and n. 53; and C. B. F. Walker, "The Second Tablet of *ṭupšenna pitema*, an Old Babylonian Naram-Sin Legend?" *JCS* 33 (1988) 194.

57. Gilg. I, i.8-36.

58. On the genre of *narû* literature, see H. G. Güterbock, "Die historische Tradition und ihre literarische Gestallung bei Babyloniern und Hethitern bis 1200," *ZA* 42 (1934) 19-22, 62-86; A. K. Grayson, *Babylonian Historical Literary Texts* (Toronto: University of Toronto, 1975) 7-8.

59. Cf. R. S. Ellis, *Foundation Deposits in Ancient Mesopotamia* (Yale Near Eastern Research 2; New Haven: Yale University, 1968) 145-47.

60. Oppenheim, *Ancient Mesopotamia* (Chicago: University of Chicago, 1964) 258.

it speaks, listing the accomplishments of the king and judging that the king was "surpassing kings, illustrious, and possessing stature."[61]

In either case, the form of the *narû* has been adapted to make a different point than an actual *narû* was supposed to make. Indeed, as the framing of the whole narrative suggests, the attainments of mortals are at best limited to these walls.[62] Physical structures were supposed to give their builders an immortality of sorts, and the commemoration of these projects in the inscriptions was a way to ensure that the fame of the kings outlasted them. That was the intent of the typical *narû*. But placed as they are in the epic, juxtaposed with the story of Gilgamesh's failure to attain immortality, the *narû*-like idioms point only to the limited significance of such human accomplishments. The walls of Uruk, which the reader is invited to view, mark the extent of the immortality that Gilgamesh had attained. One may expect no more.

As the story develops, one sees that it was the reality of death — the death of Enkidu — that brought home the ephemerality of human accomplishments. Gilgamesh, the illustrious and wise king, who has succeeded in all his kingly deeds, is in the final analysis just like any mortal.

That same movement from the accomplishments of the king to the stark reality of death is evident in Qohelet, who immediately proceeds to speak of the leveling effect of death (2:12-17).[63] In the face of death, no one has any advantage. In the face of life's mysteries and the whims of an arbitrary deity, the wise king is no better off than the ordinary fool. Everything is *hebel* and a pursuit of wind.

61. Gilg. I, i.27. See D. J. Wiseman, "A Gilgamesh Epic Fragment from Nimrud," *Iraq* 37 (1975) 160. Cf. also the reference to the incomparability of Gilgamesh's kingship in ll. 43-44 in Wiseman's enumeration and in the fictive letter of Gilgamesh, on which see F. R. Kraus, "Der Brief des Gilgamesh," *Anatolian Studies* 30 (1980) 109-21.

62. Oppenheim, *Ancient Mesopotamia*, 257.

63. I am indebted to my colleague, Julie Duncan, for calling this connection to my attention.

The Graded Numerical Saying in Job

ANDREW E. STEINMANN
Cleveland, Ohio

The graded numerical saying is a well-known rhetorical device found throughout the literature of the ancient Near East.[1] These sayings place a lower number in parallelism to a higher one. One example is Prov 6:16-19:

> 16 There are six things that the LORD hates,
>   even seven that are disgusting to him:
> 17   arrogant eyes,
>   a lying tongue,
>   and hands that kill innocent people,
> 18   a mind devising wicked plans,
>   feet that are quick to do wrong,
> 19   a dishonest witness spitting out lies,
>   and a person who spreads conflict among relatives.[2]

Several numerical sequences are used for the graded numerical saying (X/X + 1 [e.g., Amos 1:3]; X/10X [e.g., 1 Sam 18:7]; X/11X [Gen 4:25], etc.). The most common one in biblical literature and the only one to occur in the book of Job is the pattern X/X + 1 (Job 5:19 [6/7]; 33:14 [1/2]; 33:29 [2/3]; 40:5 [1/2]).

---

1. David Noel Freedman, "Counting Formulae in the Akkadian Epics," *JANES* 3 (1971) 65-81; Jacob Bazak, "Numerical Devices in Biblical Poetry," *VT* 38 (1988) 333-37; S. Gevirtz, "On Canaanite Rhetoric: The Evidence of the Amarna Letters from Tyre," *Or* 42 (1973) 162-77; Wolfgang M. W. Roth, *Numerical Sayings in the Old Testament: A Form-Critical Study* (VTSup 13; Leiden: Brill, 1965); idem, "The Numerical Sequence X/X+1 in the Old Testament," *VT* 12 (1962) 300-311; H.-P. Rüger, "Die gestaffelter Zahlensprüche des Alten Testaments und aram. Achikar 92," *VT* 31 (1981) 229-34.
2. All quotations from the Bible are from the *God's Word to the Nations* (preliminary translation), copyright God's Word to the Nations Bible Society, 1994.

This device is sometimes used to introduce an enumeration of items whose tally usually corresponds to the higher number in the graded saying (e.g., Prov 6:16-19; 30:11-14; 30:15b-16; 30:18-19; 30:21-23; 30:24-28; 30:29-31).[3] In other instances, however, it is merely a rhetorical device not intended to introduce an enumeration of items (e.g., Gen 4:24; 1 Sam 18:7 [= 21:11; 29:5]; Mic 6:7).[4] Considering the use and distribution of this device throughout the OT (Roth lists some 49 occurrences),[5] one can raise two important questions concerning its role in Job:

1. Is it used for enumeration, mere rhetoric, or both?
2. Are its occurrences randomly placed in the book or are the four occurrences placed in the book in a conscious literary pattern?[6]

I. The Graded Numerical Saying as an Enumerative Device

1. Job 5:17-27

The graded numerical saying first occurs in Job at 5:19. These words are part of the summary of Eliphaz's initial reply to Job. This is an important juncture in the book. Job had just completed his first complaint — that he should have never been born (chap. 3). Eliphaz and the rest of Job's friends recognize this as a challenge of God's wisdom in allowing Job to be born. Beginning with Eliphaz, they reply to Job, attempting to refute his claim.

The entire section containing the graded numerical saying reads (with the saying in italics, v. 19):

---

3. Roth claims that the tally always corresponds to the higher number. Haran claims, however, that sometimes the lower number is the one that matches the tally. Cf. Roth, *Numerical Sayings*, 6; Manahem Haran, "The Graded Numerical Sequence and the Phenomenon of 'Automatism' in Biblical Poetry," *Congress Volume: Uppsala, 1971* (VTSup 22; Leiden: Brill, 1972) 238-67, esp. 253.

4. In the case of the graded numerical saying in Amos the general scholarly consensus is that Amos does not use this device for enumeration. But the debate is ongoing whether some type of enumerative scheme lies behind his use of the device. Cf. Robert B. Chisholm, Jr., " 'For Three Sins . . . Even for Four': The Numerical Sayings in Amos," *BSac* 147 (1990) 188-97; Meir Weiss, "The Pattern of Numerical Sequence in Amos 1–2: A Re-examination," *JBL* 86 (1967) 416-23.

5. Roth, "Numerical Sequence," 301.

6. The question here concerns the extant structure of the book, not any previous editions of the book that may have existed. Many scholars believe one or more parts of the present book of Job are later additions, redactions, or the like. The question here is whether the graded numerical saying is tied to the structure of the book as we have it from the author and/or final redactor.

17 Blessed is the person whom God corrects.
        He should not despise discipline from the Almighty.
18   God injures, but he bandages.
            He beats you up, but his hands make you well.
19   *He will keep you safe from six troubles,*
            and when the seventh one comes, no harm will touch you:

20   In famine he will save you from death, and
            in war he will save you from the sword.

21   When the tongue lashes out, you will be safe,
            and you will not be afraid of destruction when it comes.

22   You will be able to laugh at destruction and starvation,
            so do not be afraid of wild animals on the earth.

23   You will have a binding agreement with the stones in the field,
            and wild animals will be at peace with you.

24   You will know peace in your tent;
            you will inspect your house and find nothing missing.

25   You will find that your children are many,
            and your descendants are like the grass of the earth.

26   You will come to your grave at a ripe old age,
            like a stack of hay in the right season.

27 We have studied all of this thoroughly! This is the way it is.
        Listen to it, and learn it for yourself.

The graded saying is introduced by two verses that speak about the blessings God grants to his people whom he corrects through suffering. The device serves as a balance to this suffering by stating that though God corrects, he also keeps humans from harm.

Many commentators have attempted to find a list of seven (or six) nouns in the verses that follow the saying. For instance, Tur-Sinai lists famine, war, an evil tongue, destruction (by God), stones, wild beasts, and bereavement (parental and conjugal).[7] This interpretation is less than convincing. While six items are easily identified by picking out nouns from vv. 20-23, one must ignore the double mention of two of them — destruction (vv. 21b, 22a) and wild animals (= beasts? vv. 22b, 23b) — that makes this a less-than-straightforward enumeration. In addition, the final item in the list, bereavement, is not a noun taken

---

7. N. H. Tur-Sinai, *The Book of Job: A New Commentary* (rev. ed.; Jerusalem: Kiryath Sepher, 1967).

from a subsequent verse. Instead, it is a summary of the content of several verses (presumably 24-25 and possibly 26). Both Gordis and Haran also list seven items.[8] But they, like Tur-Sinai, must manipulate the text in some way to make a case for seven items.[9]

Clines notes that if one is searching for an enumeration in vv. 20-23 by counting nouns, one has nine candidates to choose from (presumably: famine, war, tongue, destruction [twice], hunger, beasts, stones, wild animals). He offers two possible solutions. Both, however, are doubtful because they involve counting vv. 24-26 as one each, while selectively counting prominent nouns in vv. 20-23. In addition, by proposing two possible counting schemes, he has to admit that "the general point is in any case totally unaffected by our ability to determine seven distinct calamities."[10]

Because of the problem of attempting to find seven distinct nouns in vv. 20-23 (or 20-26) that serve as an enumeration of the ways God protects his people from harm, some commentators have argued that the graded numerical saying in v. 19 is merely a rhetorical device and is not intended to introduce an enumeration.[11] Dhorme states: "in this case . . . it would be useless to look for a description of seven calamities in the following verses. Clamet justifiably protests against the pretension of the rabbis to reach the number seven."[12]

But the problem in determining the enumeration intended by the author may not lie with the text itself. Rather, it may lie with the assumptions of those who seek to identify the seven situations in which God will allow no harm to come upon a person. Instead of looking for seven nouns, one ought to look at the following eight verses that form the end of Eliphaz's speech. One would immediately see that v. 27 is the summary of this section, marked as such by the words *hinnēh-zō't*. Between v. 19 and v. 27 are seven verses, each containing two lines. Each describes a different aspect of God's protection. He protects by providing:

1. safety from scourges that affect entire populations — famine and war (v. 20)
2. safety from verbal attack turning into physical harm (v. 21)
3. safety from scourges that affect individuals (v. 22)
4. safety away from home (v. 23)

8. Robert Gordis, *The Book of Job: Commentary, New Translation, and Special Notes* (New York: Jewish Theological Seminary of America, 1978); Haran, "Numerical Sequence," 263.

9. For a thorough discussion of the failure of Gordis's position, see David J. A. Clines, *Job 1–20* (WBC 17; Dallas: Word, 1989). Haran has to count *destruction* (vv. 21, 22) twice.

10. See Clines, *Job 1–20*, 151.

11. Commentators who have taken this position include E. Dhorme, *A Commentary on the Book of Job* (trans. Harold Knight; London: Nelson, 1967); Norman C. Habel, *The Book of Job: A Commentary* (OTL; Philadelphia: Westminster, 1985); Marvin H. Pope, *Job* (3rd ed.; AB 15; New York: Doubleday, 1973); and H. H. Rowley, *Job* (rev. ed.; NCB; Grand Rapids: Eerdmans, 1980).

12. Dhorme, *Job*, 69.

5. safety in one's home (v. 24)
6. many children (v. 25)
7. long life (v. 26)

These seven verses are a carefully crafted set. Each of the first three begins with a preposition.[13] The fourth and central verse begins with the phrase *kî-ʾim.* Each of the final three begins with a verb.

Such an enumeration by sentence rather than by a list of nouns or nominal phrases may seem strange at first, but it is not at all unknown. While the graded sayings of Prov 30:18-19 and 30:21-23 enumerate by nouns or nominal clauses, the very next graded saying, Prov 30:24-28, enumerates by sentence:

24 Four things on earth are small,
   yet they are very wise:
25   Ants are not a strong species,
      yet they store their food in summer.
26   Rock-badgers are not a mighty species,
      yet they make their home in the rocks.
27   Locusts have no king,
      yet all of them divide into swarms by instinct.
28   A lizard you can hold in your hands,
      yet it can even be found in royal palaces.

Eliphaz's speech ends with an enumeration of seven ways God protects his people. Thus, the graded saying and its accompanying enumeration serve to drive home the point of Eliphaz's discourse: God uses suffering to correct those who err, but he also protects his people from all real harm.

2. Job 33:13-30

The next two graded numerical sayings occur near the close of Elihu's first speech in Job 34. Like the previous graded saying in chap. 3, these two also occur at an important juncture in the book. Job had just completed another complaint (chaps. 29–31) — that his present state, as compared with his former way of life, makes his life not worth living, especially since he has committed no sin. The young man Elihu recognizes that this is another challenge to God's wisdom in allowing Job to suffer. He also recognizes that Job's friends, who rebuked him earlier when he challenged God, are not going to rebuke him this time. So Elihu attempts to rebuke Job.

13. *bᵉ*, vv. 20, 21 (probably to get the reader started on the correct reading of the enumeration by matching the beginning of the sequence that began in v. 19: *"from six . . . in seven . . . in famine . . . when the tongue"*), and *lᵉ*, v. 22.

Just as Eliphaz closes his opening speech with an argument that made use of the graded saying, so Elihu closes his opening speech in the same way.

13   Why do you quarrel with him
        since he doesn't answer any questions?

14   *God speaks in one way,*
        even in two ways without people noticing it:

15   In a dream, a prophetic vision at night,
          when people fall into a deep sleep,
          when they sleep on their beds,

16   He opens people's ears
          and terrifies them with warnings.

17   He warns them to turn away from doing wrong
          and to stop being proud.

18   He keeps their souls from the Pit
          and their lives from crossing the river of death.

19   In pain on their sickbeds they are disciplined
        with endless aching in their bones

20   so that their whole being hates food
          and they lose their appetite for a delicious meal.

21   Their flesh becomes so thin that it can't be seen.
          Their bones, not seen before, will be exposed.

22   Their souls approach the Pit.
          Their lives come close to those already dead.

23 If they have a Messenger for them,
     a spokesman, one in a thousand,
       to tell people what is right for them,

24   then he will have pity on them and say,
     "Free them from going down to the Pit.
       I have found a ransom."

25   Then their flesh will become softer than a child's.
     They will go back to the days of their youth.

26   They will pray to God, who will be pleased with them.
     They will see God's face and shout for joy
       as he restores their righteousness.

27   Each one sings before other people and says,
     "I sinned and did wrong instead of what was right,
       and it did me no good.

28   The Messenger has freed my soul from going to the Pit,
       and my life will see the light."

29   *Truly, God does all this two or three times with people*

30   to turn their souls away from the Pit and
       to enlighten them with the light of life.

Verse 14 indicates two ways God speaks to people to correct them. Some commentators do not recognize this verse as a numerical saying, choosing to translate "in one way, even two" as "in one way or another."[14] But those commentators who do translate it as a graded numerical saying generally agree that the modes are dreams (vv. 15-18) and sickness (vv. 19-22).[15] In both ways God keeps the erring person to whom he speaks from the destruction of the "Pit" (*šāḥat*), defined as "crossing the channel" in v. 18 and as "[the place of] those already dead" in v. 22.

Verses 29-30 are summary verses, claiming that God speaks with people "two or three times." If the pattern of the other graded numerical sayings is followed, one should expect there to be three "times" in this context that have described how God "turns a person's soul from the Pit." Commentators have justifiably argued that there are three such times in this context.[16] A close examination shows why this is so — there are three ways in which God rescues a person from going to the Pit: the first two are the two from the previous numerical saying, dreams ("He keeps his soul from the Pit," v. 18) and sickness ("His soul will come close to the Pit," v. 22); the third is the mediating messenger ("Free him from going down to the Pit," v. 24). Verses 23-26 describe how this messenger's words free the person from the destruction of the Pit. It is followed immediately by the redeemed person's response in vv. 26-28. In these verses the redeemed person recognizes that God has spoken to him and saved him from the Pit ("He redeemed my soul from going to the Pit," v. 28).

Thus, God speaks to people in three ways to correct them and keep them from the Pit. The first two are part of the ordinary human experience (dreams, sickness), summarized by the numerical saying of v. 14. The third way of speaking is through a personal being, the "Messenger." All three are summarized by the numerical saying in vv. 29-30.

---

14. See, e.g., the commentaries ad loc. by Dhorme, Habel, and Pope.

15. This is a long-recognized way of understanding this passage. For instance, see the nineteenth-century work by C. F. Keil and F. Delitzsch, *Commentary on the Old Testament* (10 vols.; reprinted Grand Rapids: Eerdmans, 1976) 4.223ff.; also Victor E. Reichert, *Job with Hebrew Text and English Translation* (Soncino Books of the Bible; London: Soncino, 1946) 172. Roth also concurs (*Numerical Sayings*, 58). Haran argues, however, that the first number (one), not the second number (two), is the intended tally for this graded saying. Therefore, he contends that the only mode mentioned is the dream (vv. 15-18). His reasons for eliminating sickness are that, in his opinion, sickness (vv. 19-22) is too far away from the graded saying of v. 14, and that "the very idea that God *speaks* to man by means of afflictions . . . seems to contain a flavor somewhat foreign to the biblical way of thought."

16. See, e.g., see Habel, *Job*, 471-72.

II. The Graded Numerical Saying and the Structure
of the Book of Job: Job 40:3-5

The final graded numerical saying in Job occurs in Job's answer to God's first speech to him:

> 3 Job answered the LORD,
> 4   "I'm so insignificant. How can I answer you?
>   I will put my hand over my mouth.
> 5   *I spoke once, but I can't answer —*
>   *twice, but not again."*

The previous graded numerical sayings are not mere rhetorical devices but also enumerative. But there appears to be no way to interpret this one as enumerative: Job does not go on to list the two times he spoke to the Lord.

In the poetic portion of the book preceding chap. 40 Job makes eleven separate speeches (3:1-26; 6:1–7:21; 9:1–10:22; 12:1–14:22; 16:1–17:16; 19:1-29; 21:1-34; 23:1–24:25; 26:1-14; 27:1–28:28; 29:1–31:40). In the context of 40:3-5, however, Job is clearly not referring to all the times he has spoken, but the times he has spoken to the Lord (vv. 3-4a). To determine if the graded saying in v. 5 is enumerative, one has to determine whether Job did, indeed, speak twice to God.

A careful reading of Job's speeches reveals the following as the only verses that one can reasonably understand as Job's challenges to God: 3:1-26; 6:12-21; 10:1-19; 13:17–14:22; 17:1-5; and 29:1–31:40. Of these only 3:1-26 and 29:1–31:40 are not contained in what are primarily challenges to other humans — his replies to his friends.

In 3:1-26, the beginning of the poetic section of the book, Job curses the day of his birth. In essence he is challenging God's wisdom in even allowing him to be born. As I have already pointed out, this challenge is immediately followed by Eliphaz's first speech with the first occurrence of the graded numerical saying in Job.

In 29:1–31:40 Job remembers his former way of life, compares it to his present state, and finally surveys a catalog of sins he did not commit. In essence he is challenging God's wisdom in allowing him to suffer. Again, this challenge is immediately followed by Elihu's first speech with the second and third occurrences of the graded numerical saying in Job.

Could these be the two times to which Job is referring in 40:5? I believe there is good reason to understand them in precisely this way if one looks at the structure of the book of Job.[17] It begins with a prose introduction (chaps.

---

17. Again, I should emphasize that I am speaking of the structure of the book of Job as we have it. While numerous scholars have proposed that some sections of the book (esp. chaps. 26–28) contain misplaced speeches of one of Job's friends or later additions to the book, I am proposing that the present form of the book has a conscious design, whatever the provenance of its constituent parts.

1–2). Then comes Job's first challenge to God (chap. 3). Following this Job's friends seek to rebuke him for his challenge to God and he replies to each of them in turn, including his final summary reply (chaps. 4–28). Then comes Job's second challenge to God (chaps. 29–31). This challenge is followed by Elihu's rebukes of Job (chaps. 32–37) and God's first reply to Job (chaps. 38–39).

This brings us to chap. 40, with Job's contention that he has spoken to God twice. If the analysis of the structure of the book to this point is correct, this is exactly what Job has done. He has twice challenged God, but will do so no more. Indeed, God speaks again, but Job does not challenge him (chaps. 40–41) — he only confesses his sin (42:1-6).

Therefore one could briefly outline the book as follows:

    I. Prose introduction (chaps. 1–2)
   II. Job's first challenge to God (chap. 3)
  III. Job's friends seek to rebuke him and he replies (chaps. 4–28)
  IV. Job's second challenge to God (chaps. 29–31)
   V. Elihu rebukes Job (chaps. 32–37)
  VI. God's first reply to Job (chaps. 38–39)
 VII. Job's first confession (40:1-5)
VIII. God's second reply to Job (40:6–41:34)
  IX. Job's second confession (42:1-6)
   X. Prose conclusion (42:7-17)

But is this the correct way to understand Job's statement and the use of the graded numerical saying in 40:5? Is there another way of corroborating this reading of Job? There is, and it is the graded numerical saying itself.

Note the strategic placement of the other occurrences of the graded numerical saying: at the end of Eliphaz's first speech (chaps. 4–5), which follows Job's first challenge to God; and at the end of Elihu's first speech (chaps. 32–33), which follows Job's second challenge to God.

Thus, the previous occurrences of the graded numerical saying serve to mark sections where humans began their replies to Job's challenge to God. Now it is no coincidence that the graded numerical saying has been used to mark these two human replies to Job as parallel to one another. Freedman has shown that they are parallel in that the first three speeches of Ehilu were intended to refute Job's replies to his friends in chaps. 4–28, while his final speech refutes Job's second challenge to God.[18]

Therefore, the final graded numerical saying serves to point the reader to the structure of the book and highlight God's wisdom as superior to human wisdom. It points the reader to the attempts first by Job's friends and later by

18. David Noel Freedman, "The Elihu Speeches in the Book of Job: A Hypothetical Episode in the Literary History of the Work," *HTR* 61 (1968) 51-59.

Elihu to refute Job through their words. Neither of these produced an admission from Job that he was wrong. It took only one speech by God, however, to bring such an admission from him, and in the final graded saying Job admits that he will no longer challenge God.

Conclusions

One can draw two conclusions from a careful analysis of the use of the graded numerical saying in Job:

1. Job never uses this figure of speech merely as a rhetorical device. The final number used in the saying always points to an enumeration of items. In the case of the graded saying in chap. 40, the enumeration is not apparent from the immediate context but is discernible from the wider context of chaps. 3–40.

2. The author or final editor of the book used the graded numerical saying as a marker to point the reader to important junctures in the structure of the book. Therefore, each graded numerical saying functions as a powerful rhetorical and enumerative device in its own immediate context in the book of Job. But together they function as signposts that point the reader to the larger concerns of the book.

Toward a History of Hebrew Prosody

FRANK MOORE CROSS

Harvard University

A history of Hebrew prosody has not been written. Yet I believe that no greater need exists in the study of Hebrew poetry: a systematic, diachronic investigation of one thousand years of poetic composition.[1] All artifacts, in style and form, evolve in the course of time. Like pots or scripts, or more closely allied, musical styles and forms, poetic devices, genres, and canons undergo change. Their evolution may be marked by rapid or slow development, abrupt, "revolutionary" emergence of new types or artifice, or slow, even archaizing periods in which change is little perceptible or obscure.[2] Typologies of various significant features of Hebrew poetry need to be traced and verified, and from the series of typologies, a reconstruction made of the history of Hebrew verse.

Such a task is not simple. Interference with the straightforward pursuit of such a program comes from several sources, some trivial if difficult to surmount, others serious, which will remain formidable obstacles. A trivial source of interference comes from the heritage of past ahistorical approaches to the analysis of biblical poetry, study based on the uncritical presumption that one can study Hebrew poetry as though it were a homogeneous, written corpus, composed in Masoretic Hebrew.[3] A serious source of interference stems from the effects of the long history of the transmission of our texts. Hebrew poetry — and prose for that matter — has been revised repeatedly in orthogra-

---

1. See already James L. Kugel, "Some Thoughts on Future Research into Biblical Style: Addenda to *The Idea of Biblical Poetry*," *JSOT* 28 (1984) 108.

2. See my comments in "Alphabets and Pots: Reflections on Typological Method in the Dating of Human Artifacts," *Maarav* 3/2 (1982) 121-36.

3. Such ahistorical presuppositions mar the study of Robert Alter, *The Art of Biblical Poetry* (New York: Basic, 1985).

phy, in grammar, and occasionally in lexicon by generations of scribes.[4] External controls, resisting such change, fixing the text, were applied beginning only in the first century C.E. with the promulgation of the Rabbinic Text.[5] Most of such revision was the result of unconscious or minor "modernizing," to be sure, but it distances us from the original poetic text. No less serious are textual corruptions that inevitably entered the text, and the establishment of the text by the arts of textual recension and emendation are thus preliminary to any analysis of poetry. The subjective elements introduced by text-critical reconstruction are an impediment to "assured" results. But the toleration of corruption is to insure fallacious analysis. Happily new textual resources, not least those illuminating the character and history of the Old Greek translation, greatly facilitate the text-critical task today. The graver problem is reconstructing the pronunciation of Hebrew over a thousand years of development. Advances can be made in this endeavor, thanks to epigraphic Hebrew texts as well as to transcriptions of Canaanite and Hebrew in other languages with full notation, notably Akkadian. But the description of the development of the Hebrew language and its pronunciation in the epochs of its evolution proceeds slowly. A newly published ostracon from Khirbet 'Uzza inscribed with a literary text now reveals the distance between formal or poetic Hebrew and the vernacular reflected in most of the preexilic corpus of Hebrew inscriptions.[6]

To put it sharply, I suspect that the Hebrew spoken by Hillel is as distant from the language of the Davidic court as is the language of General Haig from the English of Chaucer.

1. David Noel Freedman and I in our early studies of Ugaritic and ancient Hebrew poetry recognized two types of colon: a long colon, in the Ley-Sievers

---

4. One can draw on the manuscript 4QSam[b], dating to the mid-third century B.C.E., for a number of examples illustrating such revision. For instance, in 1 Sam 20:34 4QSam[b] has: *wyphz ywntn m'l hšlḥn*. The MT reads: *wyqm yhwntn m'm hšlḥn*. 4QSam[b] is to be translated "And Jonathan sprang up excitedly from the table." For 4Q *wyphz* the MT substituted *wyqm*, "and he rose up." 4Q is original, a textbook case of *lectio difficilior*. The text of MT has been modernized, the difficult, rare word replaced by the bland, innocuous *wyqm*. The Old Greek reads here *kai anepēdēsen*, "and he started up," obviously reflecting *wyphz*. Modernization is, perhaps, too neutral a term to apply. In Late Hebrew, Middle Hebrew, and Aramaic the root *phz* developed the primary meaning "be concupiscent," "lewd," "lascivious." The early meaning, "be excited," or "act in excitement," was forgotten or obsolescent. Hence the older reading was more than obscure — it was grotesque, and perhaps suppressed. Cf. Jonas C. Greenfield, "The Meaning of *phz*," in *Studies in the Bible and the Ancient Near East Presented to Samuel E. Loewenstamm, on His Seventieth Birthday* (ed. Y. Avishur and J. Blau; Jerusalem: Rubinstein, 1978) 35-40.

5. See my discussion of the fixation of the text of the Hebrew Bible, and the stabilization of the biblical canon in the forthcoming volume, *Kinship and Covenant in Ancient Israel*, chaps. 10 and 11.

6. I. Beit-Arieh, "A Literary Ostracon from Ḥorvat 'Uza," *Tel Aviv* 20 (1993) 55-65 (with an Appendix, "A Suggested Reading of the Ḥorvat 'Uza Ostracon," by Frank Moore Cross, 64-65).

system "3," and a short colon, in Ley-Sievers notation "2."[7] In terms of syllables, the long colon in Ugaritic is longer than the Hebrew long colon, the short colon in Ugaritic longer than the Hebrew short colon, but precisely corresponding to the addition or omission of inflectional endings, the final short vowels lost in South Canaanite toward 1200 B.C.E. In other words, the long and short colon reflected a continuity of verse form given the evolution of the Canaanite-Hebrew tongue.

I have never been convinced that early Canaanite meter can be defined as either quantitative or accentual. It is highly symmetrical at the level of the single bicolon or single tricolon, but the symmetry is not necessarily sustained over long intervals of verse. My conclusion has been that the ancient Canaanite and Hebrew poets were not counting syllables, at least in the fashion found in other oral, syllabic verse. I must emphasize, moreover, that the oral formulae of Ugaritic and early Hebrew verse are binary, not chronemic as in Greek epic verse. They are constructed in pairs: word, phrase, and colon pairs including paired epithets and proper nouns, complementing grammatical parallelism at every level.

It has been my practice for many years, therefore, to use a notation *l (longum)* and *b (breve)* to label respectively the long colon and the short colon, the building blocks fundamental to early Hebrew verse, a notation that leaves open the question of auditory subrhythms.[8]

In archaic verse, the standard verse forms were *l:l* and *l:l:l*, that is, a bicolon of two symmetrical long cola, and a tricolon of three symmetrical long cola. The verse patterns formed with the short colon, *b*, were different. The standard verse was *b:b::b:b* in which a bicolon, itself marked by an internal caesura, is parallel to a second bicolon, also marked by an internal caesura. In addition to the correspondence between the two bicola, however, parallelism between single cola, a *b* and a *b* in the *b:b* bicolon, is frequent. Thus the older notation 2:2 is misleading, and the alternate notation 4:4 is misleading, although both describe an aspect of the verse form. The verse structure is more complex. Also frequent is the triplet *b:b::b:b::b:b*, corresponding to the tricolon *l:l:l*.

Thus the Lament of David:

l:l:l
2 *(b:b::b:b)*
2 *(b:b::b:b)*
3 *(b:b::b:b::b:b)*

---

7. See F. M. Cross and D. N. Freedman, *Studies in Ancient Yahwistic Poetry* (SBLDS 21; Missoula, MT: Scholars, 1975) 8-9, and esp. 181-87.

8. See my discussion in "Studies in the Structure of Hebrew Verse: The Prosody of Lamentations 1:1-22," in *The Word of the Lord Shall Go Forth: Essays in Honor of David Noel Freedman in Celebration of His Sixtieth Birthday* (ed. C. L. Meyers and M. O'Connor; Winona Lake, IN: Eisenbrauns, 1983) 129-33.

l:l:l
b:b::b:b::b:b
l:l.

Exodus 15, the Song of the Sea, also consists of a sequence of couplets and triplets of short cola marked off by tricola and bicola of long cola *(l)*.[9]

This "mixed meter" as we called it, or alternation of two verse types, one simple with long bicola, one complex with short bicola pairs, is characteristic of archaic lyric poetry in the Hebrew Bible, but disappears early, the latest specimen apparently the Lament of David.

Poetry of the ninth-seventh centuries is dominantly of two verse types: *l:l(:l)*, familiar from Ugaritic epic meter as well as early Hebrew poetry, and a new verse type generally designated *Qinah* meter, although it is by no means restricted to the lament. In early analyses it was described as 3:2 meter or as 5:5 meter. In fact it is built of the fundamental building blocks, the long colon and the short colon in complex patterns. The dominant form in my notation is *l:b::l:b* in which the grammatical and semantic parallelism is chiefly between corresponding bicola. But "internal" parallelism between the mixed, long and short cola is not infrequent. While *l:b::l:b* is the most frequent verse pattern, variant patterns also occur: *l:b::b:l*, *b:l::l:b*, and *b:l::b:l*, especially in earlier poetry of this type.[10]

A sounding in Hellenistic Hebrew poetry by Arlis Ehlen, in the *hôdāyôt* of Qumran, has shown that the old "building blocks" of early Hebrew poetry have utterly disappeared.[11] While grammatical parallelism of a sort persists, symmetry of colon length does not exist, and in Ehlen's words, "'subrhythms' do not exist, neither quantitative nor stress meters."

Much more needs to be done in tracing the development step by step from archaic Canaanite and Hebrew poetry to late, Hellenistic, and Persian Hebrew poetry. When and why did symmetry break down, and the basic building blocks, the long and the short colon, disappear?

2. One aspect of the task is to observe movement from orally composed poetry in the early period to poetry composed in writing in the late period. I have no doubt that Ugaritic epic verse was composed orally to music. One should note that parallelism has its origins in oral composition. Parallelism is a technique of the traditional poet, the bard. To be sure, grammatical parallelism

---

9. See my *Canaanite Myth and Hebrew Epic* (Cambridge: Harvard University, 1973) 122n.34 (on the Lament of David and its reconstruction), and 126-44 (on the Song of the Sea).

10. See D. N. Freedman, "Acrostics and Metrics in Hebrew Poetry," in *Pottery, Poetry, and Prophecy* (Winona Lake, IN: Eisenbrauns, 1980) 51-76.

11. Arlis John Ehlen, "The Poetic Structure of a Hodayah from Qumran: An Analysis of Grammatical, Semantic and Auditory Correspondence in 1QH 3:19-36" (Ph.D. diss., Harvard University, 1970).

can survive in written imitation of traditional poetry, and obviously did in late Hebrew poetry.

In any case, I think one can show clearly that Ugaritic epic poetry was composed orally. Its formulae, binary pairs (including epithets), and its themes, type scenes, and narrative patterns have been studied by a number of scholars, including Whitaker, Hendel, Culley, Gevirtz, and myself.[12] The typical repetition of themes and type scenes using identical or near-identical formulae, a sure telltale of oral composition, is more frequent and impressive in Ugaritic epics than in classic Greek epic. Furthermore, the repertoire of formulae — and even complete verse forms — is continuous from Old Canaanite to archaic Hebrew verse, a phenomenon best explained by transmission in bardic tradition, not in writing.

I have called attention elsewhere to the telltale colophon of *CTA* 6.6.53ff.[13] The colophon names three principal persons: *sāpiru 'ilimilku*, "Elimelek the scribe"; *ṭāʿaiyu niqmadda malku 'ugarīti*, "Niqmadda, king of Ugarit, the donor"; and between the two names a third: *lamīdu 'attanu . . . rabbu kāhinīma*, "'Attanu . . . chief priest, the adept." The term *lamīd*, which I have translated "the adept," certainly applies to his function in the preparation of the tablet, and he is neither donor nor scribe. The term *lamīd* immediately reminds one of *mĕlummad šîr* of 1 Chr 25:7, "trained in song." The high priest was certainly no student, but evidently the master singer who dictated to the scribe. Another passage of interest is *CTA* 3.1.19.

> Rising he composed and sang,
> With cymbals the bard improvised,
> The sweet-voiced hero sang.[14]

12. See R. E. Whitaker, "A Formulaic Analysis of Ugaritic Poetry" (Ph.D. diss., Harvard University, 1970); R. S. Hendel, *The Epic of the Patriarch: The Jacob Cycle and the Narrative Tradition of Canaan and Israel* (HSM 39; Atlanta: Scholars, 1988); F. M. Cross, "Prose and Poetry in the Mythic and Epic Texts from Ugarit," *HTR* 67 (1974) 1-15; Robert C. Culley, *Oral Formulaic Language in the Biblical Psalms* (Toronto: University of Toronto, 1967); Stanley Gevirtz, *Patterns in the Early Poetry of Israel* (2nd ed.; Studies in Ancient Oriental Civilization 32; Chicago: University of Chicago, 1973). See also the massive volumes, *Ras Shamra Parallels* (ed. Loren R. Fisher and S. Rummel; 3 vols.; AnOr 49-51; Rome: Pontifical Biblical Institute, 1972-81), esp. vol. 3.

13. See my "Prose and Poetry," 1. See also Sam Meier, "Baal's Fight with Yam as Known in *KTU* 1.1,3-6?," *UF* 18 (1986) 241-54, which demonstrates that *CTA* 2 (at least 2.1 and 2.4) in the Baʿl cycle was composed by a bard different from the bard of the remainder of the cycle. His formulae, especially epithets, often vary from those of the other tablets, and the variance where it occurs is systematic.

14. The Ugaritic text in provisional vocalization reads:

qamu yabdī wa-yašīru
maṣillatêmi badā naʿīmu
yašīrŭ ġazru ṭābu qôli.

The term *naʿīm* (the vocalization is uncertain) cited above, and translated "bard," one who composed or improvised *(bdy)*, is of some interest. In Arabic the root is *ngm*, "sing," *nagmat*, "melody," an unusual but by no means rare equation with Ugaritic *nʿm*.[15] It reappears in 2 Sam 23:1, *nĕʿîm zĕmīrôt yiśrāʾēl*, "bard of Israel's songs." The term *nāʿîm*, perhaps to be revocalized *nôʿēm*, corresponds to Greek *aoidos*, "oral poet," "bard," "composer-singer."

In the Hebrew Bible all the hallmarks of oral composition adhere to the corpus of premonarchical poetry. As Freedman and I argued many years ago, there is a common set of formulae including entire cola distinctive of this archaic verse. In some cases obvious oral variants exist, for example, the blessing of Joseph in Gen 49:24-26 and the blessing of Joseph in Deut 33:13-16; or the blessing of Zebulun in Gen 49:13 and of Asher in Judg 5:17. One may compare the bicolon *kārāʿ šākab kaʾărî/ūkĕlābî* *mî yĕqîmennû* in Num 24:9 with Gen 49:9b: *kārāʿ rābaṣ kĕʾaryēh/ūkĕlābî* *mî yĕqîmennû*. These slightly variant bicola, used in very different contexts in the Blessing of Jacob and the Oracles of Balaam, are best explained as drawn from stock oral formulae, rather than as written borrowing. Again, both oral and written (textual) variants abound in the parallel texts 2 Samuel 22 and Psalm 18.[16]

One should remember that while alphabetic writing rapidly increased literacy in the Early Iron Age, oral forms still dominated in the transmission of literature and culture. This oral character of communication is reflected vividly even in written documents. Letters in Hebrew from the end of the ninth century from Kuntillet ʿAjrûd, and from as late as the seventh-sixth century from Transjordan and Egypt in Ammonite and Phoenician respectively, preserve similar introductory formulae: "Utterance of So-and-So. Say to So-and-So" (*ʾmr* PN *ʾmr l*-PN).[17] The presupposition of such a formula is that the letter is dictated by the sender, and that the letter is to be read aloud to the recipient. Perhaps it is also useful to remark that in 2 Kgs 3:15 a prophet, asked for an oracle, requested a minstrel in order to prophesy; and Jeremiah, surely literate, still dictated his verse to Baruch.

---

15. On Ugaritic *ʿayn* = Arabic *gayn*, see J. A. Emerton, "Some notes on the Ugaritic counterpart of the Arabic *ghain*," in *Studies in Philology in Honour of Ronald James Williams* (ed. G. E. Kadish and G. E. Freeman; Toronto: Benben, 1982) 31-50.

16. See *Studies in Ancient Yahwistic Poetry*, 125-68, esp. 163-68.

17. The formula appears at Kuntillet ʿAjrûd, in the Phoenician Letter from Saqqara (*KAI* 50), and on an ostracon from Tell Mazar. Cf. J. C. Greenfield, "Note on the Phoenician Letter from Saqqara," *Or* 53 (1984) 242-44; Khair Yassine and J. Teixidor, "Ammonite and Aramaic Inscriptions from Tell el-Mazar in Jordan," *BASOR* 264 (1986) 45-50, esp. 47. The introductory address should be translated "Utterance of Peleṭ: Say to his brother, to ʿAbdʾel. . . ." In the Saqqara letter one should read similarly, "Say to my sister *ʾršt*, utterance of your sister *bš*." At Kuntillet ʿAjrûd I read *ʾmr ʾšyw hhlk ʾmr lyhl[ ] wlywʿšh*, "Utterance of ʿAšyaw, the pilgrim: say to *Yhl[ ]* and to Yawʿaśāh. . . ." Cf. M. Weinfeld, "Kuntillet ʿAjrud Inscriptions and Their Significance," *Studi Epigrafici e Linguistici* 1 (1984) 122-30; and Mark Smith, "God Male and Female in the Old Testament: Yahweh and His "asherah,'" *TS* 48 (1987) 333-40.

The transition from oral to written poetry is difficult to fix. A priori, one would expect to perceive in this interval the breakdown of symmetry, of ancient repetitive patterns, and an increase in prose particles. One also would look for the increase in long-range artifice as opposed to couplets and triplets, and for the confusion of fixed, formulaic pairs. In fact all these developments are apparent in psalms of the Persian and Hellenistic periods. I am inclined to believe that in the archaizing, but not archaic, poetry of Second Isaiah one can discern clearly traits of written composition and the moribund state of older styles of orally composed poetry. I have described the acrostic laments of the book of Lamentations as written poetry.[18] But late preexilic prophecy needs thorough analysis before one can answer the question as to whether it is written or oral in origin. Much late prophetic material, above all much of Ezekiel, has been preserved in prose or decayed poetry by circles that transmitted the oracles. One could argue that owing to the breakdown of the chain of oral poets, disciples of the prophets who transmitted their lore preserved general memories of oracles but were unable to recreate their poetic-oral form. Of course, prophets may have on occasion used prose utterance in prophesying. But this also would point to the beginnings, at least, of the dissolution of older, rigid musical and oral-poetic canons that earlier constrained oracular utterance.

3. I am convinced also that one can trace typological changes in the formulation of parallelistic verse patterns, and in the meaning of parallelistic style in the history of Canaanite and Hebrew poetry.

Particularly evident is the popularity at Ugarit and in archaic Hebrew poetry of so-called repetitive parallelism described by H. L. Ginsberg and W. F. Albright. This patterned verse, in ideal form a tricolon, *ABC:ABD:EFG*, disintegrated into imitative but inexact forms very early in Israel, by the ninth century.[19]

One of the conventions or styles of early verse I have labeled "impressionistic," lacking a more precise designation, after the analogy of the literary style in which the use of details, visual glimpses, so to speak, attempted to evoke subjective and sensory impressions rather than to re-create objective reality. For example:

Take a lamb in your hand
A sacrifice in your right hand
A kid in your two hands.[20]

(See *CTA* 14.2.65-68; 14.3.159-61)

---

18. See above, n. 8.

19. See W. F. Albright, "The Psalm of Habakkuk," in *Studies in Old Testament Prophecy Presented to Theodore H. Robinson on His Sixty-fifth Birthday* (ed. H. H. Rowley; Edinburgh: T. and T. Clark, 1950) 1-18.

20. On the reconstruction, see my "Prose and Poetry," 7.

A literal-minded soul will conceive here a juggling act. But the poet uses a set of conventions, including numerical parallelism, to create three pictures, flashes, of sacrificial rite, technically irrational or overlapping, but poetically rich and evocative.

Again:

> My temple I have built of silver,
> My palace I have built of gold.[21]

(CTA 4.6.36-38)

The poet obviously is not singing of two buildings, one constructed of silver, one of gold. Rather he pictures a house ornamented with features of precious metal. But so to describe it is to surrender the impressionistic effect of the bicolon.

A third example:

> Pour wine in a silver bowl,
> In a bowl of gold mead.[22]

(CTA 14.2.71-72)

How should we read these lines? Are there two bowls, two alcoholic beverages, the second a grander bowl, the second beverage the more precious liquor? I think not. We are presented rather with two pictures of the rite of libation, two evocative, overlapping impressions.

I should argue that the same "impressionism" persists in early Hebrew verse. The Song of Deborah includes these two verses:

> Her hand reached for a tent peg,
> Her right hand for a workman's hammer.

> She struck Sisera; she smashed his head;
> She struck Sisera; she pierced his temple.[23]

(Judg 5:26)

The prosaic, later historian gives us an interpretation of the two verses in Judges 4. Jael took a tent peg, presumably in her left hand, a hammer in her right hand, and nailed the peg through Sisera's temple — adding in the interests of realism that Sisera was in a deep sleep at the time. Had the prose historian been even more literalistic, he would have had Jael (1) smash his head, and (2) pierce his

21. See ibid., 8, for variants of this bicolon.
22. Cf. *CTA* 15.2.11-16.
23. See Cross and Freedman, *Studies in Ancient Yahwistic Poetry*, 15, for reconstruction; my "Prose and Poetry," p. 7; and B. Halpern, "Doctrine by Misadventure: Between the Israelite Source and the Biblical Historian," in *The Poet and the Historian: Essays in Literary and Historical Biblical Criticism* (ed. R. E. Friedman; HSS 26; Chico, CA: Scholars, 1983) 46-49.

temple, but even he resolves a portion of the overlapping pictures. In fact the poet in his impressionistic style says only that she grasped a weapon appropriate to the tent dweller, and dispatched Sisera with a blow to the head. There are neither two weapons nor two blows. The poet is interested in two brush strokes of color to fashion a picture, not in a photographic image of reality.

Later in Hebrew verse, this impressionistic style, as I have called it, gives way to a more realistic style. Overlapping pictures and overlapping time sequences[24] are to some degree resolved. I can illustrate this from the use of so-called numerical parallelism.

At Ugarit one finds this extraordinary couplet:

They march, two by two they walk,
They march (three) by three, all of them.[25]

Mathematicians need not apply. This is an impressionistic picture of a massed march.

In Amos a familiar formula recurs, the first occurrence (1:3) of which reads:

'al-šĕlōšâ pišʿê dammeśeq
wĕʿal ʾarbāʿâ lōʾ ʾăšîbennû.

But the cycle of nations lists neither three nor four sins of the condemned nations. In the case of Israel seven sins are listed (by most counts), but this is neither three nor four. But compare this impressionistic disregard for mathematics with late wisdom's use of numerical parallelism.[26] Proverbs 6:16-19 sings of six, yea seven things that the Lord hates. Then seven items are carefully listed. Or, read Prov 30:18. Here three things, yea four, are too wonderful, and then

---

24. *CTA* 23 shows a number of cases of "overlapping time sequences." The most dramatic is the sequence: kissing and conception, labor and birth (ll. 49-54), kissing and conception, labor and birth (ll. 55-61). Another example is found in *CTA* 2.4. Kothar fashions two clubs and names them with magic names (2.3.11-13), and Baʿl bludgeons Yamm (2.4.13-17). Kothar fashions two clubs and names them with names (2.4.18-20), and Baʿl bludgeons Yamm (2.4.20-25), and finally Yamm is finished off. Still another curious sequence is found in *CTA* 6.2.30-35 (cf. 6.5.11-19) in which Môt is chopped with a sword, winnowed with a sieve, burnt with fire, ground in mills, and sowed in fields. Each of the actions is appropriate to the agricultural cycle with grain, but the order is not sequential — it is impressionistic.

25. *CTA* 14.2.94-95; 14.4.182-83:

'atarū tinê tinê halakū
'atarū talāta kulluhumu.

26. Some scholars have taken the numerical parallelism in Amos to point to the influence of "wisdom circles" on Amos. But numerical parallelism is used in mythic cycles, epic poetry, and prophecy. Indeed, the use of numerical parallelism in wisdom texts contrasts with the impressionistic usage in Amos, and could be used better as an argument against wisdom influence on Amos.

the four are enumerated carefully, the fourth the climax of the series: "the way of a man with a maid."

In the course of time the impressionistic use of numerical parallelism evidently gave way to a more realistic or rational correspondence between cola in a verse unit, with, at least according to my taste, a loss of poetic power.

At the moment two major views, two hermeneutics, of Hebrew parallelism are competing. One may be described as a unitary analysis of the meaning of parallelism, the other a climactic analysis. Steven Geller has written, "Nothing can be more misleading than to view the B Line [i.e., the second line of a couplet] as a mere echo or simple variation or even reinforcement of its A Line. In the couplet both lines form a unity of which each is less than half. . . . It is only at the perceived conclusion of the statement that the constraints of potential reanalysis are removed and the final meaning released."[27] Geller's is a useful instrument with which to lay bare the meaning of Ugaritic and early Hebrew poetry. The alternate hermeneutic is that of James Kugel, seconded by others, summarized in the catch phrase "A is so, and what's more B."[28] In this mode of interpretation, the second line of a couplet is taken as having emphatic character, and all parallelism described as climactic parallelism, the second (and third) line building, emphasizing, "going one better."

These two views of parallelism, both presented as applying to the entire corpus of Hebrew poetry, need to be tested in diachronic study. I am not sure that a typology will emerge; for example, Geller's unitary approach proving valid in the early period, Kugel's climactic theory proving a better instrument in late poetry.

I do find Geller's hermeneutic the better key to early poetry. Let us take as an example the refrain in the Lament of David.

> Ah, prince [lit. gazelle] of Israel <Saul>[29]
> On thy heights slain,
> How the warriors have fallen.
>
> How the warriors have fallen,
> In the midst of battle, Jonathan
> On thy heights slain.
>
> How the warriors have fallen,
> Perished the weapons of war.

27. Steven A. Geller, "The Dynamic of Parallel Verse: A Poetic Analysis of Deuteronomy 32,6-12," *HTR* 75 (1982) 35-56. See also Geller's "Theory and Method in the Study of Biblical Poetry," *JQR* 73 (1982) 65-77. Geller's standard study, *Parallelism in Early Biblical Poetry* (HSM 20; Missoula, MT: Scholars, 1979), has not received the attention it deserves.

28. James L. Kugel, *The Idea of Biblical Poetry: Parallelism and Its History* (New Haven and London: Yale University, 1981).

29. See my *Canaanite Myth and Hebrew Epic*, 122n.34, for a defense of this reconstruction of the text.

In these variations of the refrain, the order of A lines, B lines, and C lines is consciously and skillfully altered to provide variety and chiasm. Identical or similar cola may be in the A position, the B position, or the C position. Geller's system illuminates our understanding of such poetry. Kugel's system is not helpful.

By contrast, I am inclined to describe some couplets and triplets in Hebrew poetry as climactic, and these appear to fit Kugel's analysis. This is especially so in late, more realistic Hebrew poetry. More study is required before these issues can be resolved.

4. The history of the Hebrew language must also play a decisive role in the sequence dating of Hebrew poetry and in the reconstruction of its stages of development. In his study *Language of the Psalms*,[30] Avi Hurvitz has attempted to isolate lexical and syntactic elements that mark the language of postexilic psalmody. Moreover, by comparing the latest psalms of the canonical Psalter with the sectarian psalms of Qumran and other contemporary poetry, we can, I think, distinguish typologically psalmody of the Hellenistic age from psalmody of the Persian period. My initial impressions, garnered from such comparison, are that the canonical Psalter was closed at the end of the Persian period.[31]

One can also use the language utilized in Hebrew poetry to isolate stages in preexilic poetic composition — despite the interference of leveling by generations of scribes.

The oldest poetry eschews the use of "prosaic particles," *'ăšer, 'et, ha-* (the article). As well, the conjunction *wa-* introducing bicola or tricola is excessively rare. Freedman and Andersen have pursued computer-assisted analyses revealing the relative scarcity of prose particles in poetry, most dramatically in early poetry.[32] More delicate, I believe, than these statistical studies are analyses using humanistic methods, including textual criticism, but the computer studies are confirmatory and evidently more objective. In any case the historian of the Canaanite dialects can affirm that prose particles were developed in Canaanite only after the loss of inflectional endings, toward 1200 B.C.E. The prose particles did not belong to the bardic tradition of early poetic language. Little wonder therefore that Israel's earliest poems are virtually free of such, despite later

---

30. Avi Hurvitz, *byn lšwn llšwn* (Jerusalem: Bialik, 1972), to appear soon in English under the title (tentative) *Language of the Psalms*.

31. See my *Die Antikebibliothek von Qumran* (trans. K. Bannach and C. Burchard; Neukirchen-Vluyn: Neukirchener Verlag, 1967) 226-27 and n. 23.

32. See D. N. Freedman, "Prose Particles in the Poetry of the Primary History," in *Biblical and Related Studies Presented to Samuel Iwry* (ed. Ann Kort and Scott Morschhauser; Winona Lake, IN: Eisenbrauns, 1985) 49-63; and F. I. Andersen, " 'Prose Particle' Counts of the Hebrew Bible," in *The Word of the Lord Shall Go Forth: Essays in Honor of David Noel Freedman* (ed. C. L. Meyers and M. O'Connor; Winona Lake, IN: Eisenbrauns, 1983) 165-83, and the literature cited.

modernizing, and, remarkable to say, the Song of the Sea is totally free of such elements. Indeed, one can postulate that premonarchical poetry in its original form was free of prose particles. The use of the conjunction *wa-* to introduce bicola or tricola was sparing in early poetry, ubiquitous in late poetry. As Freedman and I showed in our early study of the parallel texts of 2 Samuel 22 and Psalm 18, many if not most conjunctions appearing in this early poetry were arbitrarily or unconsciously introduced in the history of scribal transmission.[33] Again it is noteworthy that the conjunction is wholly absent in the Song of the Sea as a particle introducing cola.[34]

The survival of archaic grammar in early Hebrew poetry is remarkable given the long history of textual transmission and scribal revision. Yet the use of the *yaqtul* preterite did survive in ancient Hebrew verse. David Robertson has analyzed the data.[35] Again Exodus 15, the Song of the Sea, presents verbal usage of the olden time, identical with Ugaritic and (Canaanite) Amarna usage. Other archaic elements survive sporadically in early poetry. For example, archaic pronominal suffixes are used flawlessly and systematically in the Song of the Sea, still another testimony to its early date and excellent state of preservation.[36]

To summarize: the forms and canons of Hebrew prosody must be studied diachronically if we are to solve many difficult problems in its analysis and interpretation. There is ample evidence of an evolution from highly formal, symmetrical patterns of orally composed verse, to written, parallelistic verse with little symmetry or density *(Dichtung)*. Whether meter marks early verse we cannot yet demonstrate with certitude. We can isolate regular building blocks in early verse, long and short cola, and their intricate combinations in several genres of verse. Finally, we can assert that in the late period, poetry was composed in writing, and that knowledge of the rigidly controlled, symmetrical verse forms of the archaic era was effectively lost and forgotten.

---

33. *Studies in Ancient Yahwistic Poetry*, 125-68, esp. 162-68. An exception to our generalization is the use of *wa-* to introduce a *casus pendens*.

34. I hasten to add that we have not overlooked the conjunction in Exod 15:2. The second bicolon of v. 2, a bicolon found elsewhere in Isa 12:2b and Ps 18:14 (ET 13), is evidently intrusive on several grounds. See my *Canaanite Myth and Hebrew Epic*, 127 and n. 49; and F. M. Cross and David Noel Freedman, "The Song of Miriam," *JNES* 14 (1955) 243 and nn. a-d.

35. David A. Robertson, *Linguistic Evidence in Dating Early Hebrew Poetry* (SBLDS 3; Missoula, MT: SBL, 1972). The language of Job, which in many ways resembles archaic poetry, is evidently written in a learned "hymnal-epic" dialect.

36. See Robertson, *Linguistic Evidence*; and Cross and Freedman, *Studies in Ancient Yahwistic Poetry*.

Shards, Strophes, and Stats

A. DEAN FORBES

Palo Alto, California

Albright argued that one ought to be able to date texts using the sorts of methods so successful in dating archaeological strata on the basis of the shared characteristics of their embedded shards. First he and later David Noel Freedman made forays along these lines, ordering early Hebrew poems in time. In this essay, I shall show how methods from statistical pattern recognition can be used to discover, quantitate, and display the relationships among Hebrew poems.

I. The Phases of Pattern Recognition

Fundamentally, pattern recognition deals with the classification of objects based on the similarities of their features. Three types of pattern-recognition problems are of interest in the context of biblical studies:

> Classification: Given a set of (somehow) predefined text clusters, into which cluster does a text under discussion best fit?
> Clustering: Given a collection of texts, into which subgroups do they naturally divide?
> Seriation: Given a set of texts, how are they ordered in time?[1]

---

1. For an introduction to text clustering written for the nonstatistician biblical researcher, see "A Tutorial on Method: A Guide for the Statistically Perplexed," in Freedman, Forbes, and Andersen (1992:17-35). For a more advanced discussion, see "Choice of Statistical Methods" (ibid., 93-110). For an almost no-holds-barred discussion of seriation in the complicated context of transmission-contaminated spelling, see "The Seriation of Portions" (ibid., 125-34).

Underlying these three problem types are substantial issues that one can best introduce by considering the phases involved in solving any pattern-recognition problem:

Phase 1. Choose the objects: Which text(s) do we choose to analyze?

Phase 2. Define the problem: Do we wish to classify a text, cluster a set of texts, or seriate a set of texts? It is necessary but not sufficient to provide an answer to this question. We must also specify the focus of our problem. Do we wish simply to describe some aspect of the texts or to infer deeper relationships — such as authorship, provenance, date? If our goal is purely descriptive, then we need only define the units of focus: the syllable counts found in various subunits of text, the incidence of word classes, the ordering of word classes, the incidence of semantic classes, and so on. If our goal is inference of deeper relationships, then we must demonstrate that the text features used in our analysis do, in fact, correlate strongly with the deeper variable(s) that we seek to infer.

Phase 3. Identify possibly relevant features: Given the nature of the problem, what features are likely to be germane? This is the crux of most pattern-recognition problems. It is the phase where the insights and intuitions of the researcher come heavily into play. Choose an improper set of features and the results will be at best unconvincing and at worst wrong.[2]

Phase 4. Select a "best" subset of features: Given a sufficiently extensive set of descriptive features and a set of correctly classified objects, there are rigorous methods for determining the subset of features that, in some well-defined sense, is best. The discipline here is to use the minimal set of features, since the use of too many features relative to the lengths of our texts will yield statistically unreliable results.

Phase 5. Define a suitable distance measure: In order to discern the relationships among the objects, one must define a measure of the distances between all pairs of objects. Differing sorts of features decree differing sorts of distance measures.

Phase 6. Select display methods: Having computed the distances between pairs of objects based on the selected set of features, one must next select methods of displaying the various relations. Many methods exist, and within each are multiple variants. Good statistical practice dictates that one apply several different methods to a problem to establish invariance of the results with respect to the methods chosen.

---

2. For example, Brainerd has published excellent analyses of Shakespeare's works. He showed that one set of text features allows formation of genre clusters (Brainerd 1979), while a quite different set allows reliable seriation (Brainerd 1980).

Phase 7. Apply the methods to the features: For even a small corpus, extraction of the features, reckoning of the distances, and construction of the displays are tasks most reliably handled by a computer.

Phase 8. Assess the reliability of the results: Having obtained results, one can assess their reliability by an extensive body of methods. The task of recognition is not complete until one carefully gauges reliability.

Phase 9. Iterate as necessary: The results will often warrant additional cycling through the phases.

Biblical researchers addressing (what amount to) pattern-recognition problems often touch on these phases, but rarely explicitly and almost never rigorously.[3] In this essay, I shall be content to sketch phases 1-7 for a clustering problem, omitting discussion of phases 8 and 9.[4]

II. Descriptive Clustering of Biblical Poems

Phase 1. Choose the Objects

As texts, I take the fourteen poems seriated by Freedman (1976), plus Psalm 18 and the five poems making up the book of Lamentations. Thus the corpus is as follows:

1. Testament of Jacob (Gen 49:2-27)
2. Song of Miriam (Exod 15:1b-18, 21bcd)
3. Oracles of Balaam (Num 23:7b-10, 18b-24; 24:3b-9, 15b-19)
4. Song of Moses (Deuteronomy 32)
5. Testament of Moses (Deuteronomy 33, less rubrics)
6. Song of Deborah (Judg 5:2-31ab)
7. Song of Hannah (1 Sam 2:1b-10)
8. David's Lament (2 Sam 1:19-27)
9. Royal Psalm (2 Sam 22:2-51)
10. Oracle of David (2 Sam 23:1b-7)
11. Psalm 18 (parallels Royal Psalm)
12. Psalm 29
13. Psalm 68
14. Psalm 72

3. For a critique of the literature on statistical inference in biblical studies, see Forbes 1992a. For a detailed critique of one aspect of Radday's pioneering work on the Isaiah authorship problem, see Forbes 1992b.

4. Readers interested in phase 8 should consult Forbes 1992a, 1992b.

15. Psalm 78
16. Lamentations 1
17. Lamentations 2
18. Lamentations 3
19. Lamentations 4
20. Lamentations 5

Phase 2. Define the Problem

To illustrate the potential of computer-assisted pattern recognition as applied to the study of the chosen texts, I shall examine how these Hebrew poems cluster in terms of the incidence of syntactic word classes. This is a purely descriptive investigation.

Phases 3 and 4. Define and Delimit the Word Classes

Since I have chosen to cluster the poems on the basis of the incidence of syntactic word classes, the next step is to specify the word classes. The Andersen-Forbes computerized text of the Hebrew Bible classifies each text morpheme into one of 72 syntactic classes such as perfect verb, common noun, and adverb.[5] Thus, in terms of phase 3 above, we have available 72 syntactic features. An analysis in the spirit of phase 4, however, discloses that 72 word classes is too many for the collection of poems I have chosen, the upper limit being around ten classes.[6] Now, one may either pick ten of the already defined classes or collapse the 72 classes into ten. Different choices will lead to different results. For the purposes of this essay, I take the second course, defining the following ten syntactic word classes:

1. Noun (proper and common nouns, numerals, adjectives, כֹּל)
2. Verb
3. Pronoun
4. Preposition
5. Coordinating conjunction
6. Verbal noun (participle, infinitive absolute, infinitive construct)

---

5. Hughes (1986:498-505) has written a concise description of our computerized texts.

6. The limit of ten results from application of a rule of thumb that the number of features used should be no more than one-fourth or one-fifth of the length of the shortest text (Andersen and Forbes 1986:205-7). Our shortest texts (Oracle of David and Psalm 29) have around 120 morphemes each, suggesting that we use no more than 20-30 features. Out of caution, we cut back to 10 features.

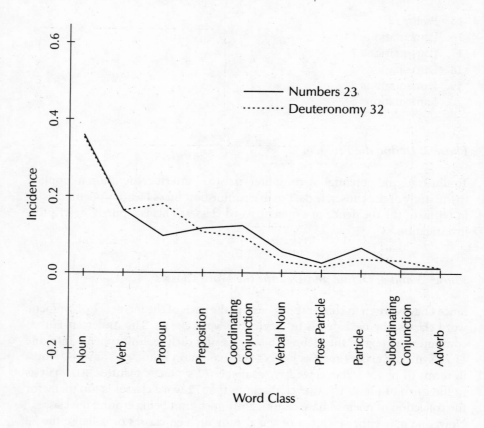

Figure 1. *Incidences of word classes in Numbers 23 and Deuteronomy 32.*

7. Prose particle (article, relative, *nota accusativi*)
8. Particle (negative quasiverbal, interrogative, גַּם)
9. Subordinating conjunction
10. Adverb

Rather than work in terms of the raw count of each word class in each poem, I choose to use the relative incidences. Therefore, for each poem, I divide the raw count for each word class by the total number of morphemes in that poem. I thereby obtain the fraction of the poem contributed by each word class. For example, I analyze Psalm 78 into 899 morphemes. Of these, thirty-eight are

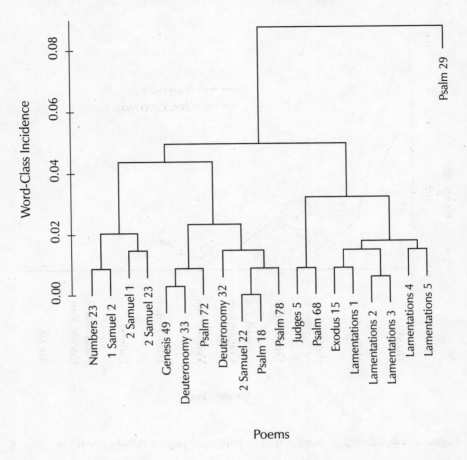

Figure 2. *Hierarchical clustering of twenty poems with respect to word-class incidence.*

prose particles. Hence, prose particles make up $^{38}/_{899} = .04227$ of Psalm 78 (4.23%). The solid line in figure 1 shows the relative incidences of the ten word classes for Numbers 23; the dotted line, for Deuteronomy 32.

Numbers 23 and Deuteronomy 32 have almost identical relative incidences of nouns, verbs, prepositions, and adverbs. Deuteronomy 32 has higher incidences of pronouns and subordinating conjunctions than Numbers 23 but fewer coordinating conjunctions, verbal nouns, prose particles, and particles.

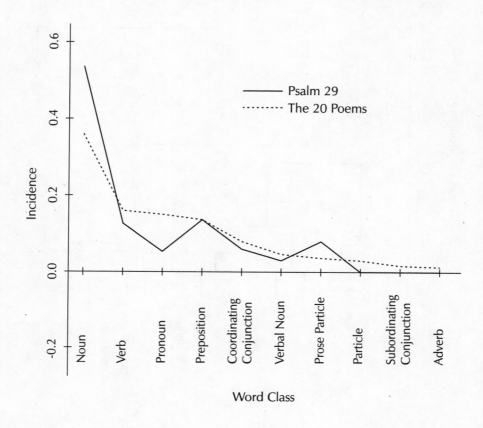

Figure 3. *Incidences of word classes in Psalm 29 and in twenty poems.*

Phase 5. Define a Distance Measure

For the purposes of determining the relations among all twenty poems, we need a number giving the distance between each pair of poems. The pattern-recognition literature abounds with candidate distances (Fukunaga 1990:441-507). The one I prefer for reckoning distances in terms of relative incidences is elegant of form and mellifluous of name: *the Bhattacharyya distance* (Jain 1976). Its definition is given in the appendix. Computation of the Bhattacharyya distances among twenty texts based on ten word classes involves 200 divisions, 1,900 multiplications, 1,890 additions, 190 square roots, and 190 logarithms. Hence, the use of a computer for the calculations is highly desirable.

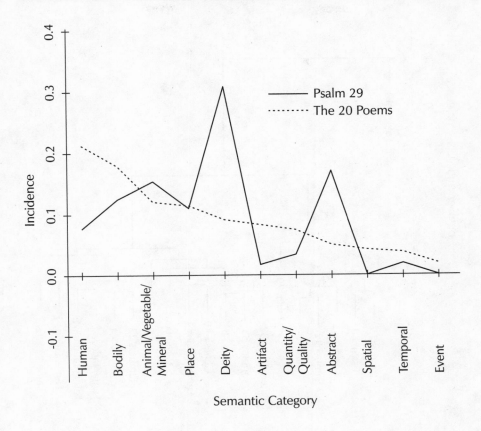

Figure 4. *Incidences of noun semantic classes in Psalm 29 and in twenty poems.*

Phase 6. Select a Display Method

Once the Bhattacharyya distances are computed, one is ready to determine and display the relations among the texts. One method of achieving this is *hierarchical clustering*.[7] The method of hierarchical clustering uses the distances to construct a tree, quite analogous to a family tree, wherein texts that are closely related appear on nearby branches and dissimilar texts terminate branches remote from one another.

---

7. Discussions of the hierarchical clustering of biblical texts may be found in Andersen and Forbes 1986:288-308; and Freedman, Forbes, and Andersen 1992:29-34.

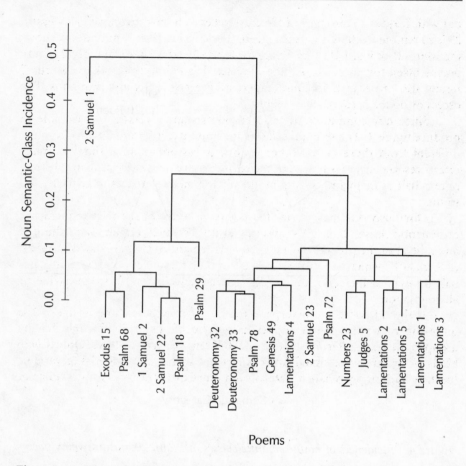

Figure 5. *Hierarchical clustering of twenty poems with respect to noun semantic-class incidence.*

Phase 7. Apply the Method to the Features

Figure 2 shows such a tree for these twenty poems. The scale to the left of the tree quantitates distances. Poems whose branches join closest to the bottom of the figure (top of the inverted tree) are closest in terms of their Bhattacharyya distance. The first two poems to join branches, being separated by a distance barely above zero, are 2 Samuel 22 and Psalm 18. This is as it should be, since 2 Samuel 22 and Psalm 18 are parallel texts. Of interest is that in terms of word-class incidence the five poems making up Lamentations cluster together, but with Exodus 15 also part of the cluster. Let us briefly investigate why Psalm 29 is so remote from its nineteen cousins. Figure 3 provides some clues. It shows the contours of word-class incidence for Psalm 29 (solid line) and for all twenty poems taken together (dotted line). We see that Psalm 29 seems to "overuse" nouns and prose particles and "underuse" the rest, especially pronouns. The excess of nouns is especially striking.

Since our computerized texts encode semantic classes, we are able to produce figure 4. The semantic classes for noun use in Psalm 29 are also quite different from those of the other poems. It has about three times as many references to deity, as is typical of the corpus, more than twice as many abstract nouns, half as many human nouns, greatly lessened references to artifacts, and so on.

Obviously one may cluster the poems in terms of the relative incidence of semantic classes. Figure 5 shows the results. Psalm 29 remains something of an oddity, but the premier isolate as regards semantic classes is David's Lament (2 Samuel 1), which has a twofold excess of both human and artifact terms, has half the typical incidence of "bodily" terms,[8] and has not a single divine or abstract noun.

It should come as no surprise that the syntax-based tree of figure 2 is quite different from the semantics-based tree of figure 5, the trees having grouped the texts in terms of two quite different kinds of features. Only if *both* kinds of feature were significantly correlated with some underlying variable (such as author, provenance, date) would one expect the trees to be similar.

III. Concluding Comments

Statistical pattern recognition has much to offer the biblical scholar engaged in classifying, grouping, and dating texts.

Two important phases of the pattern recognition process too often are absent from text analyses: principled feature selection and validation of results.

Descriptive grouping of texts is easily carried out by the computer, using appropriate distance measures, clustering algorithms, and results displays.

When one bases inferences on such analyses, it is essential to demonstrate that the features and methods used support the weight of the inferences made.

---

8. These include nouns referring to the body, its health, mental processes, and vocal productions.

Appendix: Definition of the Bhattacharyya Distance

If the relative incidences for one of a pair of texts are given by p_i ($i = 1, \ldots 10$), and those for the other text by q_i ($i = 1, \ldots 10$), then the Bhattacharyya distance between the texts, $B(p,q)$, is defined by:

$$B(p,q) = -\log \left[\sum_{i=1}^{10} \sqrt{p_i q_i} \right]$$

In words: For each word class, take the square root of the product of the relative incidence for one text times the relative incidence for the other text. Sum the results across all (ten) word classes, and then take the negative logarithm of that sum to obtain the Bhattacharyya distance between the two texts. Note that this definition yields $B(p,p) = 0$ and $B(p,q) = B(q,p)$, as should be the case for any distance measure.

References

Andersen, F. I., and A. D. Forbes

1986   *Spelling in the Hebrew Bible*. BibOr 41. Rome: Biblical Institute.

1989   "Methods and Tools for the Study of Old Testament Syntax." Pp. 61-72 in *Proceedings of the Second International Colloquium: Bible and the Computer — Methods, Tools, Results*. Paris: Champion; Geneva: Slatkine.

Brainerd, B.

1979   "Pronouns and Genre in Shakespeare's Drama." *Computers in the Humanities* 13:3-16.

1980   "The Chronology of Shakespeare's Plays: A Statistical Study." *Computers in the Humanities* 14:221-30.

Forbes, A. D.

1987   "Syntactic Sequences in the Hebrew Bible." Pp. 59-70 in *Perspectives on Language and Text: Essays and Poems in Honor of Francis Ian Andersen on His Sixtieth Birthday*. Ed. E. G. Newing and E. W. Conrad. Winona Lake, IN: Eisenbrauns.

1992a   "Statistical Research on the Bible." *ABD* 6.185-206.

1992b   "A Critique of Statistical Approaches to the Isaiah Authorship Problem." Pp. 531-45 in *Proceedings of the Third International Colloquium: Bible and the Computer — Interpretation, Hermeneutics, Expertise*. Paris: Champion; Geneva: Slatkine.

Freedman, D. N.
1976   "Divine Names and Titles in Early Hebrew Poetry." Pp. 55-107 in
            Magnalia Dei: The Mighty Acts of God: Essays on the Bible and Archae-
            ology in Memory of G. Ernest Wright. Ed. F. M. Cross et al. Garden
            City, NY: Doubleday.

Freedman, D. N., A. D. Forbes, and F. I. Andersen
1992   *Studies in Hebrew and Aramaic Orthography.* Biblical and Judaic
            Studies from the University of California, San Diego, 2. Winona
            Lake, IN: Eisenbrauns.

Fukunaga, K.
1990   *Introduction to Statistical Pattern Recognition.* 2nd ed. San Diego:
            Academic Press.

Hughes, J. J.
1986   *Bits, Bytes, & Biblical Studies.* Grand Rapids: Zondervan.

Jain, A. K.
1976   "On an estimate of the Bhattacharyya distance." *IEEE Transactions*
            on Systems, Man, and Cybernetics 6:763-66.

War and Rebel Chants in the Former Prophets

M. O'CONNOR

St. Paul Seminary School of Divinity,
University of St. Thomas, St. Paul, Minnesota

I. The Poems in the Former Prophets

The four books of the Former Prophets, Joshua, Judges, Samuel, and Kings, often known as the Deuteronomic or Deuteronomistic History, are concerned in their historical recital with the role of prophecy and the prophets in the history of Israel from the time of the settlement in the land to the moment of the exile from it. When the collection of the Former Prophets was edited during the exile, it may have had, as D. N. Freedman (1963, 1987a, 1991) has proposed, a prophetic supplement, a preliminary version of the collection of the four books of the Latter Prophets as we have them (Isaiah, Jeremiah, Ezekiel, and the Twelve). This supplement would have been as largely a poetic collection as the final version of the Latter Prophets is. In any case, the historian-redactors of the Former Prophets used a small amount of verse, the characteristic of Israelite prophecy, at least in its major phase, in their largely prose work.

One striking feature of the small body of verse in the Former Prophets is how little of it is prophetic, especially given the collection's interest in prophecy. There is one prophetic oracle in the "classical" prophetic mode, Isaiah's in 2 Kings 19. One poem earlier in the narrative's flow, Samuel's rebuke of Saul (1 Sam 15:22-23), is cast in a form similar to that of the preexilic classical prophets; the similarity is close enough that one may wonder who is quoting whom. The Last Words of David (2 Sam 23:1-7) describes revelation in terms known from Ezekiel, for example, *rûaḥ yhwh dibber bî,* "YHWH's spirit speaks through me" or, better, "YHWH speaks through me by means of the spirit," taking *rûaḥ*, which is feminine and thus cannot govern *dibber*, as an accusative of specification (2 Sam 23:2; see Waltke and O'Connor 1990:173); however, other features of the Last Words, especially the opening lines' resemblance to the Balaam Oracles (Numbers 23–24), suggest that it is archaic (see Freedman 1977:21-22; reprinted in Freedman 1980:17-18) and that Ezekiel's use of the vocabulary is archaistic. (Whether the influence in conception of prophetic role comes via the Elijah and Elisha stories is immaterial here.)

The bulk of the verse of the Former Prophets is then not directly involved in the prophetic concerns of the historian-redactors, though the unavoidable awareness of the difficulty of the verse is relevant to the difficulty of much prophetic verse. That is, if one imagines, with Freedman, that the Former Prophets collection came bundled with a proto–Latter Prophets supplement, the difficulty of Deborah's Song (Judges 5) would have served as a warning of the difficulty to come in, say, Hosea 11. The poems in the Former Prophets, from Joshua's Curse on Jericho (Josh 6:26) to Isaiah's Oracle (2 Kgs 19:21-28), are primarily not prophetic or literary; they are narrative elements in a narrative context. They comprise one among the many diverse types of material the historian-redactors used.

Let us examine this body of eighteen or so poems. I follow the distinctions between prose and verse used in modern editions and translations, with a few exceptions. In *BHS*, I exclude the lists printed with spacing. I also exclude three passages printed as verse in *BHS*: (1) Jotham's Fable (Judg 9:7-15; *BHK*, NJB, and NRSV are similar to *BHS*; the passage is treated as prose by NAB, NJPS, REB, RSV, and TEV); and (2) Nathan's Parable (2 Sam 12:1-4; *BHK* and NJB are similar to *BHS*; the passage is treated as prose by NAB, NJPS, NRSV, REB, RSV, and TEV), which are both rhythmic prose; and (3) the two sets of Philistine boasts in Judg 16:23-24 (*BHK*, NJB, NAB, NJPS, and REB are similar to *BHS*; the passage is treated as prose by NRSV, RSV, and TEV), in which the misleading feature is the use of rhyme, a phenomenon that is not here or anywhere else important to Biblical Hebrew verse. Two other passages are sometimes treated as verse: (4) Elijah's promise to the widow (1 Kgs 17:14, treated as verse by, among the authorities cited here, only NJB) and (5) Micaiah's vision (1 Kgs 22:17, treated as verse by NAB, NJB, and REB, and not by the others cited here). It may be well to say various of these passages and those listed below remain open to consideration; see further Freedman 1977:22; reprinted in Freedman 1980:18.

1. Josh 6:26: Joshua's Curse on Jericho

The poem involves only the last five words of v. 26, which comprise two poetic lines. In *BHK* and *BHS* the words are printed as prose; so also NAB and NJPS. They are printed as verse by RSV and TEV. NJB, NRSV, and REB take the poem as including four lines, beginning the poem with the curse.

2. Josh 10:12-13: Joshua's Invocation
BHK and *BHS:* 2 printed lines of verse (i.e., 2 lines of type arranged as verse, *not* 2 lines of poetry). Printed as verse by RSV, NRSV, etc.

3. Judg 5:1-31: The Song of Deborah
BHS: 50 printed lines given as verse; the end of the poem, v. 31 (cf. O'Connor 1980), is given as two printed lines of prose; *BHK* is similar. Printed as verse by RSV, NRSV (both including v. 31 in the poem), etc. Discussed in Freedman 1975; reprinted in Freedman 1980:131-66.

4a. Judg 14:14: Samson's Riddle
BHK and *BHS:* 1 printed line. Printed as verse by RSV, NRSV, etc.

4b. Judg 14:18: The Answer to Samson's Riddle
BHK and *BHS:* 1 printed line. Printed as verse by RSV, NRSV, etc.

4c. Judg 14:18: Samson's Reply
BHK and *BHS:* 1 printed line. Printed as verse by RSV, NRSV, etc. Printed as prose by REB, which takes ##4a-b and 5 as verse.

5. Judg 15:16: Samson's Boast
BHS: 2 printed lines. Printed as prose by *BHK.* Printed as verse by RSV, NRSV, etc.

6. 1 Sam 2:1-10: The Song of Hannah
BHS: 18 printed lines. *BHK* is similar. Printed as verse by RSV, NRSV, etc. Discussed in Freedman 1978; reprinted in Freedman 1980:243-61.

7. 1 Sam 15:22-23: Samuel's Rebuke of Saul
BHS: 4 printed lines. *BHK* is similar. Printed as verse by RSV, NRSV, etc. Printed as prose by TEV.

8. 1 Sam 15:33: Agag's Death Sentence
BHK: 1 printed line. *BHS:* Printed as prose. Printed as verse by NRSV, etc. Printed as prose by RSV and TEV.

9. 1 Sam 18:7 = 21:12 = 29:5: The Israelite War Chant
BHK and *BHS:* 1 printed line. Printed as verse by RSV and NRSV. Printed as prose by TEV. For Freedman's discussion, see below.

10. 1 Sam 24:14: David's Proverb
BHS: 1 printed line of three words, *mrš'ym yṣ' rš'. BHK* includes the

following words as a second poetic line. Printed as prose by RSV, NRSV, etc. Printed as verse by NAB.

11. 2 Sam 1:19-27: David's Lament for Jonathan and Saul
BHS: 16 printed lines; *BHK* is similar. Printed as verse by RSV, NRSV, etc. Discussed in Freedman 1972; reprinted in Freedman 1980:263-74.

12. 2 Sam 3:33-34: David's Lament for Abiner
BHS: 2 printed lines; *BHK* is similar. Printed as verse by RSV, NRSV, etc. Discussed in Freedman 1987b.

13. 2 Sam 20:1: Sheba's Rebel Chant
BHS: 2 printed lines; *BHK* is similar. Printed as verse by RSV, NRSV, etc. Printed as prose by TEV.

14. 2 Sam 22:2-51: The Song of David
BHS: 55 printed lines; *BHK* is similar. Printed as verse by RSV, NRSV, etc. Discussed in Cross and Freedman 1953 (cf. Cross and Freedman 1975:125-58) and Freedman 1976; reprinted in Freedman 1980:77-129.

15. 2 Sam 23:1-7: David's Last Words
BHS: 13 printed lines; *BHK* is similar. Printed as verse by RSV, NRSV, etc. Discussed in Freedman 1971; reprinted in Freedman 1980:343-45.

16. 1 Kgs 8:12-13: Solomon's Inaugural Prayer
BHS: 2 printed lines; *BHK* is similar. Printed as verse by RSV, NRSV, etc. Printed as prose by NAB.

17. 1 Kgs 12:16: Israel's Rebel Chant
BHK: 2 printed lines; *BHS:* printed as prose. Printed as verse by RSV, NRSV, etc. Printed as prose by TEV.

18. 2 Kgs 19:21-28: Isaiah's Oracle
BHS: 21 printed lines; *BHK* is similar. Printed as verse by RSV, NRSV, etc. Printed as prose by TEV.

In contrast to the poems in the Psalter, say, the poems in the Former Prophets come in two sizes: large and small; only Samuel's Rebuke might be taken as intermediate. This circumstance, like the use of the poems generally, is most often treated as a historical artifact. Part of the account suggests that the historian-redactors had on their hands some long poems associated with either events or figures in the history they were dealing with. This is plausible, though the connections are sometimes problematic — for example: Who is speaking in the Song of Deborah (see esp. Judg 5:12)? Did the Song of Hannah, like some other parts of the Hannah-Elqanah story, originally refer to Saul rather than Samuel? The insertions, as it were, of the poems, nearly all of them older than the narrative, were diverse and complex operations.

Is the insertion model also relevant to the small poems? Standard accounts allow for such a model, but not alone. How else might one understand the small poems? It has been proposed that some are remnants left behind in the reworking of an archaic Israelite epic, a work of verse that has been reworked into prose. This improbable view has largely been abandoned. The extent to which the poems belong to and derive from the smaller narrative units in which we find them is debated. The Samson poems (the group of riddle, Judg 14:14, answer [or is it another riddle?], 14:18, and reply [or yet another riddle?], 14:18; the boast in 15:16) seem to stand at an angle to the stories; other short poems seem to show a tighter fit. It is probably correct to say that more of the short poems show greater integrity with their narrative context than the long poems do.

These eighteen or so poems are generically diverse, and there are often short and long examples of the half-dozen or so types. There are two oracles, one long (2 Kgs 19:21-28) and one short (1 Sam 15:22-23), and likewise two laments, one long (2 Sam 1:19-27) and one short (2 Sam 3:33-34). Three of the prayers are long (1 Sam 2:1-10; 2 Sam 22:2-51; 2 Sam 23:1-7), and one is short (1 Kgs 8:12-13). The single proverb is a single verse line (1 Sam 24:14; on the question of the proverbs of the wise women in 2 Sam 14:14, where the proverbial utterance is not poetic, and in 2 Sam 20:18, where the proverb is obscure, see Camp 1981:18-21). Under the admittedly unsatisfactory heading of narrative recital I would group one long poem (Judg 5:1-31) and seven short poems, two associated with Joshua (Josh 6:26; 10:12-13), four with Samson (Judg 14:14; 14:18 bis; 15:16), and one with Samuel (1 Sam 15:33). One can take rebel and war chants as an allied subcategory; all the examples are short (1 Sam 18:7 = 21:12 = 29:5; 2 Sam 20:1; 1 Kgs 12:16).

One can read the overall pattern of the poems in a way that supports and enlarges on usual understandings of the Former Prophets. I offer this reading tentatively, since the genres I am working with are ad hoc. (The poems also have thematic ties one could explore: one can take Solomon's prayer as following from Joshua's invocation). The opening poems, Joshua's Curse on Jericho (Josh 6:26) and his Invocation (Josh 10:12-13), the Song of Deborah (Judg 5:1-31), and the Samson poems (Judg 14:14; 14:18 bis; 15:16), fit most closely with the aims of the collection of the Former Prophets: story and history intermingling, each narrative moderating the claims, set, and force of the others. The closing poem, Isaiah's Oracle (2 Kgs 19:21-28), looks forward to the prophetic collection to follow, which opens with the Isaiah Book; it also looks back to historical recital as an act to be contrasted with the announcement of the immediate future: 'attâ hăbê'tîhā, "Now I [YHWH] bring it [the thing spoken of long ago] out" (2 Kgs 19:25). (The first major poems are attributed to women, Deborah and Hannah, and the last to men, David and Isaiah; on the literary correlates within the book of Judges of this shift, see O'Connor 1986.) Enclosed within this frame of recital and prophecy are other uses of verse. Two are well known: prayer and lamentation; the other two are, in the large view of the Bible, less important. The lone ancient proverb quoted by David does indeed sound like and look forward to the book of Proverbs (not least in its banality): mērĕšā'îm yēṣē' reša', "From the evil, evil emerges" (1 Sam 24:14). The genre of war and rebel cries is not common in the Bible, but such "folk poetry," such street talk, plays an important role in any society's use of verse, and Israelite society was much affected by these brief compositions, as the biblical stories make clear.

II. War and Rebel Chants

The war and rebel chants play an integral role in the narratives of David's rise to kingship, the initial blows to his power, and the greatest blow to his dynasty's power. The poems are not tokens of troubles offered by the historians; they are major parts of the problem. The poems make the trouble as much as they reflect it.

The Israelite War Chant, cited three times, is associated with popular reaction, specifically among Israelite women, to the success of David and Saul in their campaign against the Philistines. David is a successful commander, Saul promotes him to head the army (1 Sam 18:5a), and the promotion is met with general approval (18:5b; or perhaps army approval — 'am is ambiguous). David is welcomed back to Israelite territory after "smiting the Philistine, and the women from all Israelite cities went out to sing and whirl [?; hammĕḥōlôt; the sense is uncertain; see Bird 1987:418-19 for another explanation] to greet Saul the king [so MT; textual witnesses differ] with tambourines [?; tuppîm], with [songs of ?] joy [śimḥâ], and with percussion [?; šāliṣîm]. And the women spoke in chorus as they rejoiced, and they said: 'Saul has smitten his companies/and David his battalions' [hikkâ šā'ûl ba'ălāpā(y)w/wĕdāwîd bĕribĕbōtayw]" (18:6-7). (On the role of women greeting returning warriors, see Trible 1986:93-116, esp. 99-101.)

The proper rendering of the number words here, 'élep, literally "thousand," and rĕbābâ, literally "myriad," is uncertain, but it seems likely that here as elsewhere in narratives of early Israel the terms are used to describe military units (see Gottwald 1979:270-84 and references). There is no delineation between the number sense and the military usage; calling a group of people an 'élep or the like involves a simple metaphorical extension. On the available evidence, Biblical Hebrew does not have two separate lexemes, and the military sense of *'élep* and similar words was linguistically transparent. However the words are rendered here (NRSV retains the traditional "thousands" and "ten thousands"), the poem is as plain as the nose on Saul's face: Saul is attributed success and David is attributed greater success, and Saul is furious about it, seeing here a sign of sedition or even revolt (1 Sam 18:8-9). The women's chant is repeated by Achish's general staff when they urge the hiring of David as a mercenary (21:12). David, acknowledging that not all publicity is good publicity, ducks out of the situation (21:13-16). He knows that fame in earlier Philistine wars may not be the best item on a résumé submitted to a Philistine ruler. The chant is quoted a third time when, in a later narrative, the other Philistine rulers insist that Achish, now David's employer, do without his services (29:5).

The poem sung by the women and repeated by the Philistines (these groups are bracketed again in David's Lament) is a simple two-line poem. (I use the description developed in O'Connor 1980.) The lines represent two of the most common syntactic types in Biblical Hebrew verse: each line forms a single clause, one with three and one with two words (here, the constituents correspond to words). The verb of the first line is gapped in the second. The subjects of the two clauses have presented no lexical problems, but the prepositional objects require further discussion. They are number words, whatever their metaphorical sense, and number words in Biblical Hebrew verse have attracted a good deal of attention.

According to various forms of what I call the Standard Description of Biblical Hebrew verse, there is a strong presumption of "synonymy" for words of the same morphological category in adjacent, syntactically matching lines, a presumption that in the case of words that are not synonymous in any obvious sense leads to various saving devices among proponents of the Standard Description. (I here use "synonymy" in its ordinary understanding; I believe that this ordinary understanding cannot be made either precise or useful in the description of verse, but I prescind from the full argument here.) One such device designed to save standard "synonymy" contends that one "synonym" "matters," the other one does not; if "father" and "mother" (to use the English words for simplicity's sake) occur in adjacent, syntactically matching ("parallel") lines, it may be that "father" "matters" to the poem and "mother" occurs only because of the demands of the verse form. (For this claim with regard to Prov 4:3, see Watson 1984:139, repeated in 1990:554, despite the apt criticisms of T. D. Andersen 1986:90-91. On the role of mothers in Israelite education, see, e.g., Camp 1981:24-25 or Crenshaw 1988.) In the case of number words, then, the first (call it "x") matters, the second (this would be "x + 1" for small numbers and usually some power of "x" or some repeating form of it for larger numbers) does not. Other saving devices involve saying that the second "synonym" "matters," the first does not; or, now one matters, now the other; or, neither really matters. The details of this set of saving devices need not be rehearsed.

Related to this strong view of "synonymy" is the Dictionary Hypothesis, the view that the words in Hebrew verse (and Ugaritic verse and perhaps other bodies of ancient Near Eastern-Semitic-language verse) are chosen from a more-or-less stock inventory of "parallel pairs." Various scholars, notably Adele Berlin (1985) and I (O'Connor 1980), have argued that both these views are wrong-headed and that they have distorted the understanding of Biblical Hebrew verse. There are no synonyms to provide a basis for the verse; rather there is a tendency in matching (i.e., syntactically or grammatically parallel) lines to use words in comparable morphological categories that are related in various ways; when words are used in matching slots, that is, they are chosen on the basis of various lexical and referential criteria that do not add up to a dictionary. The results of the many acts of choosing can be called a "dictionary," but it is our "dictionary" of verse usage, not a modern approximation of anything an ancient would have recognized.

If we apply to the war chant of 1 Samuel a strong form of the Standard Description's synonymy device and a strong form of the Dictionary Hypothesis, what do we get? Since even the strong forms of both these ideas have various shapes, it is hard to be sure, but one possibility is that we would get into a narrative pickle. The late Stanley Gevirtz in his early work on Biblical Hebrew verse (Gevirtz 1963) argues for a strongly mechanistic view of poetic composition, a view he abandoned in his later, more important work (e.g., Gevirtz 1975). Indeed, the early Gevirtz contends that the Dictionary Hypothesis of H. L. Ginsberg, Umberto M. D. Cassuto, and Moshe Held was the second major "discovery" in the history of Biblical Hebrew verse after Lowth's "discovery" of parallelism (1963:3-5). In his essay on the war chant (pp. 15-24), he contends that the two number words were inserted by rote into this poem, as in other cases where number words stand in adjacent slots (he cites most of the Biblical Hebrew cases as well as many Ugaritic and a few Akkadian cases, pp. 16-22). He further argues that there is no difference in "meaning" between the two words. A strong argument indeed, and to his credit Gevirtz does not shrink from the consequences of this view: he claims that the three narrative contexts of the war chant are wrong in supposing that the singers invidiously distinguished David and Saul, that the poem presents no "reference to superior ability on the part of David" (p. 16) and thus "contains no insult" to Saul (p. 24). Such an argument would have serious consequences for making sense of the stories.

In a review of Gevirtz's book (Freedman 1964), Freedman ponders these consequences and finds the situation in need of reassessment. The first issue is David's place in the poem: "The very fact that David was accorded equal treatment with the king in the song . . . would be sufficient to arouse the suspicions of any monarch" (p. 201). The second issue involves the number words. As Freedman notes, in nearly all cases of "numerical parallelism" the two number words in adjacent lines have comparable or related referents. Thus Amos 1–2 uses "three" and "four" again and again to refer to criminal activities, for example, ʿal-šĕlōšâ pišʿê dammέśeq/wĕʿal-ʾarbāʿâ lōʾ ʾăšîbénnû, "For three transgressions of Damascus/and for four I will not return it [the punishment there-after cited]" (Amos 1:3). "Three" and "four" here must be understood in terms of the common reference to Syrian crimes. In the 1 Samuel war chant, the number words have different referents, Saul and David; "this is the only example of standard number-parallelism . . . in which there is a significant distinction of subjects" (p. 202). The women and Philistines were, Freedman shows ele-gantly, right after all, and the chant fits the story.

The Israelite Rebel Chant occurs in two different forms and in two different circumstances, bracketing the beginning and end of maximal Davidic power. According to the first story, after the death of Absalom, the king-in-exile was prostrate with grief over his rebel son, and Joab had to force his attention back to the deteriorating political situation: some supporters came forward when the king took his seat at the Mahanaim city gate, but most did not: wĕyiśrā'ēl nās 'îš lĕ'ōholāyw, "for Israel had fled, each to his own habitation" (RSV: "every man to his own home"; 2 Sam 19:9). Negotiations concerning the restoration of the kingship ensue, with Israel, then Judah, and the king begins the march home, during which further negotiations are narrated. Ref-erences to the old division in the kingdom between the northern and southern sections appear at the beginning of this journey (19:10-16) and at its end (19:42-44). The latter passage is vague as to who is engaging, after a rebellion, in contentious talk ("The men of Judah were more stubborn in the things they said than the men of Israel," 19:44; McCarter 1984:414), though the verses are replete with apparently technical references to the conduct of the monar-chy: 'aḥênû, "our [the northerners'] kin [i.e., the southerners]," bêtô, "his [the king's] household" (v. 42); 'kl min hammélek, "to eat of/from the king" ("at the king's expense," RSV), nś' nś't, "to give a [royal] grant" (v. 43), yādôt lNN bammélek, "shares [?] of NN [tribal name?] in the king," qll NN, "to repudiate [RSV: "despise"] NN" (v. 44).

Then appears Sheba ben Bichri, a mean, shiftless, good-for-nothing rabble-rouser ('îš bĕlîyá'al), who gives the narrative a personal focus and gives the seditious talk a poetic shape (2 Sam 20:1; McCarter gives it as prose, 1984:415):

'ên-lắnû ḥéleq bĕdāwīd
wĕlō' naḥălâ-lắnû bĕben-yišay
'îš lĕ'ōholāyw yiśrā'ēl

We have no portion in David.
We have no inheritance in Ben-Jesse.
Everyone to his tents, Israel.

The threatened rebellion breaks out and is stopped by the joint action of Joab and the wise woman of Abel-Beth-Maacah (2 Samuel 20). This wise woman balances the one of Tekoa who brought about Absalom's return from disfavor and thus indirectly made possible the first of these two back-to-back rebellions (cf. Camp 1981).

The Rebel Chant is repeated forty years later, in the early days of the reign of Rehoboam, when after due consideration David's grandson refuses to grant tax relief to his subjects: *wayyélek yiśrāʾēl lĕʾōholāyw,* "and Israel went home [lit. to his tents]" (1 Kgs 12:16). Here the chant is attributed to no one rebel but rather to all Israel (12:16):

> *mâ-llánû ḥếleq bĕdāwīd*
> *wĕlōʾ-naḥălâ lánû bĕben-yišay*
> *lĕʾōholêkā yiśrāʾēl*
> *ʿattâ rĕʾê bêtĕkā dāwīd*

> We have no portion in David.
> We have no inheritance in Ben-Jesse.
> To your tents, Israel.
> Now look to your house, David.

This time the chant works: this rebellion, again separating northern Israel and southern Judah, leads to a permanent rupture.

The Rebel Chant occurs in two forms, the first of three lines and the second of four; one need not settle on one or the other shape as more original, though the disposition of the two forms is intriguing. The Chronicler preserves only the second story and thus the second form of the chant (2 Chr 10:16). The verse form requires little comment: the first two lines are made up of single clauses, and the second two have vocatives in addition to their main clauses. The third and fourth lines do not match syntactically: the third line is a nominal phrase used as an imperative, and the fourth is an ordinary verbal imperative clause. (On the syntax of nominal exclamations used to replace clauses, see Waltke and O'Connor 1990:680.)

Some differences between the two forms of the chant are noteworthy: first, the 1 Kings version seems more archaic in using the negative *mâ,* generally rare in Biblical Hebrew (pace, on this occurrence, Waltke and O'Connor 1990:326-27; Crenshaw 1988:15 accepts negative *mh* in 1 Kgs 12:16 and Cant 4:8 bis, but not in Prov 31:2 ter), in contrast to the 2 Samuel version with the more usual *ʾ ên* (the Chronicler's parallel has *mâ*); the distributive *ʾ iš* construction in the 2 Samuel text seems later than the plural in the 1 Kings form (the Chronicler has the distributive form).

If we examine the nouns used in the chant, we can continue to describe some of the poetic phenomena usually agglomerated under the heading of "parallelism." In the first two lines the terms *ḥếleq* and *naḥălâ* may represent a breakup of a stereotyped phrase, what Freedman calls a combination: a *ḥếleq* is a "portion, tract, territory" (so BDB), from *ḥlq,* "to divide"; a *naḥălâ* is a "possession" or "inheritance." The two terms occur together often, but their senses are distinct: a *ḥḗleq* is generally part of a territory or something equally tangible, while a *naḥălâ* is usually less tangible, something defined by right of title. (On the words in Deut 32:9, see O'Connor 1980:382.) The words converge in passages concerning the Levites: at base the tribe of Levi has a *naḥălâ* but no *ḥḗleq*, but the ties of this arrangement to concepts of divine service sometimes create a fusion, as in this passage: "And YHWH said to Aaron: In their land you shall not inherit [*tnḥl*] and you shall have no portion [*ḥḗleq*] in their midst; I am your *ḥḗleq* and your *naḥălâ* in the midst of the Israelites" (Num 18:20). The six passages other than the Rebel Chant where BDB glosses *naḥălâ* as "portion, share" are poetic (Second Isaiah, Psalms, Job), a circumstance suggesting that the word is best taken as meaning only "inheritance, property (possessed by right of inheritance)" and that the "poetic" use requires further study. The sense of the combination here would be "portion of inherited land," and of the lines, "We have no inherited portion in David ben Jesse," where the last phrase, the royal name, again represents a phrase distributed over matching lines.

The topic of the lines is unclear, no matter how one construes the noun phrases, the locus of the difficulty being the preposition *b*, "in, through." What does it mean to own or have inherited property "in" or "through" a person? The sense here has something to do with one of the claims in the preceding stretch of rebel talk by unnamed northern Israelites; they speak in one voice in 2 Sam 19:44: *'ḗṣer yādôt lî bammḗlek*, "I have ten hands [shares?] in the king." It is arguable that the first northern statements, at the end of 2 Samuel 19, are offered to represent the view of the kingship that prevailed in the north during the latter part of David's reign and during Solomon's; Sheba takes a more extreme view of the issues, a view not generally supported until Rehoboam's time. This does not, however, define the issues. Two possibilities for the first part of Sheba's chant present themselves: (1) "We have no apportioned land in the south," where David ben Jesse would be a synecdoche for the southern kingdom, David's real homeland; or (2) "We have no apportioned land held through the royal person of David," that is, whatever protocols applied to David's Hebron reign (2 Samuel 2) did not carry over to his all-Israel rule (2 Samuel 5). The phrases *ḥḗleq b*PN, "a portion in/through PN," and *yad b*PN, "a hand in/through PN," must be relevant to the well-known problems of royal taxation and administrations and to the conflicts of the old Yahwistic landholding system with later systems under the divided monarchy, though not in ways we understand.

The third line in the 2 Samuel form of the chant may be deceptive: it seems to use a standard idiom for going to one's home, one's permanent residence (whatever form it has; Koch 1977:120-21; Morrow 1993 ad Deut 16:7): *'îš lĕ'ōholāyw yiśrā'ēl*, "Everyone to his own tent, Israel," that is, "Let's all go home" (so roughly NEB). The going-home idiom occurs in the surrounding narrative, but the later version of the chant, with its fourth line, puts in question its appropriateness to the poem: *lĕ'ōholêkā yiśrā'ēl/'attâ rĕ'ê bêtĕkā dāwīd*, "To your tents, Israel./Now look to your house, David." The two terms for habitation contrast here, and one of them, *báyit*, is a keyword throughout the David and Solomon stories, meaning now "palace," now "temple," sometimes "dynasty," and occasionally "ancestry"; the Dynastic Oracle in 2 Samuel 7 is built up of turns on these senses. (On the house theme, see Flanagan 1988:229-32, 247-49, 266-71; *báyit* also refers, in the forms *bêt 'āb*, lit. "father's house," and the less common *bêt 'ēm*, lit. "mother's house," to family households in the literature about early Israel; see Gottwald 1979:285-92; Meyers 1991. The extent to which David was actually a temple planner is questioned by Meyers 1987.)

The location of the two forms of the Rebel Chant can perhaps now be explained: although the first chant, in 2 Samuel 20, comes after the Dynastic Oracle, it is the second chant, in 1 Kings 12, that follows on the initial working out of that oracle. With Rehoboam's accession, David's dynasty is in its third generation, the royal palace has begun to merge with the bloated and rapacious bureaucracy that surrounds it, and the temple has been completed at incalculable cost to the country. Only in the 1 Kings 12 passage, where "David" designates David's grandson, is the appalling ugliness of David's many houses evident.

Given the gruesome polyvalence of "house" here, let us assess the term *'ōhel*, "tent," and the working of the pair of terms, *báyit* and *'ōhel*. The terms are not "synonymous": the habitations of the individual members of northern Israel are nothing like any "habitation" of David. Given the special force of *báyit*, it seems unlikely that *'ōhel* is best taken in the idiomatic sense "(to go) home." Ordinarily *'ōhel* designates a movable tent dwelling, of the sort used in Israel during the wilderness wanderings, whether for people (on the military uses, with detailed references to evidence from Neo-Assyrian reliefs, see Alt 1959) or for God (the *'ōhel mô'ēd*, "tent of meeting/assembly"; see Koch 1977:122-30). Since Israel (in the sense of both the north and the whole land) was sedentarized by the eleventh and tenth centuries, it would be defensible to render the words that follow the Rebel Chant, *wayyēlek yiśrā'ēl lĕ'ōholāyw*, literally "And Israel went to its tents," as "So the Israelites went home" (1 Kgs 12:16; cf. 2 Sam 18:17; 19:8). Within the poem, however, the terms *báyit* and *'ōhel* polarize each other, and *'ōhel* stands against *báyit* as northern Israel is called to stand against the house of David. The sense of "tent" is archaizing, as if to say (as the Rechabites said much later, in Jer 35:7-10), "If having 'houses' causes this much trouble for Israel, we were better off during the wilderness wanderings. If the houses of the settlement lead to a royal 'house' and a 'house' for God and a royal dynastic 'house,' let's go back to the tents of the steppe." (On this point, cf. Stockman 1954:115, who calls the tent reference "a survival of the old desert life"; and Nelson 1987:79.)

Another struggle with the diverse associations of words for habitation can be seen in a different phase of Israelite literature, in the working out of the Deuteronomic law code: "The operative word in Deuteronomy [for residence] is *byt* not *'hl*. . . . It is everywhere assumed in the laws contained in Deuteronomy that Israelites normally live in houses" (Morrow 1993). Except apparently in the festival legislation of Deuteronomy 16, and there, too, Morrow has argued, *'ōhel* may follow the pattern of the other laws and refer not to a home but to "a temporary pilgrim residence . . . around a shrine" (1993 ad Deut 16:7), although he allows that the "range of meaning [of the verse] is commensurate both with the supposition that the worshippers are to return to their real home territory or to some temporary dwelling in the vicinity of the shrine YHWH has chosen." Even in the mundane regulations governing the pilgrim festivals various words for habitation, human and divine, collide with one another.

By way of summary of this study of the various war and rebel chants in the Former Prophets, I may review the contrasts in nouns and noun phrases in the verse. It is in the balance and contrast of nouns that a significant part of the working of Biblical Hebrew verse goes on; that balance and contrast comprise nearly all of the "parallelistic" phenomena that are not grammatical or syntactic. I have argued that one can derive gains for the reading of the poetry from considering the balance and contrast in other terms; I was set on to such arguments by my teacher, by such arguments of his as the one about the War Chant cited here.

The first distinction to draw in surveying these six lines of verse involves the structure of the verse. The use of the names "Saul" and "David" in 1 Sam 18:7 is not an aspect of the poetic structure; the lines in which the names occur are grammatically matching, and the occurrence of the names fits into that grammatical framework. Either of the names could be different and, from a structural point of view, the verse would be unchanged. Similarly in the Rebel Chant, the use of the nouns *báyit* and *'ōhel* is not structural; the lines do not match each other, and the terms, though they are semantically involved with each other, do not constitute a working element of the verse structure. A more strictly taxonomic and philological approach to Biblical Hebrew verse than mine would confine itself to observing the phenomena, but I argue that it is possible to describe them. There are nouns and noun phrases that are structurally defining of the verse; I call these tropes on the word level. The simplest word-level trope is repetition, and we have a case of repetition in the long form of the Rebel Chant, with the occurrences of "David" in the first and last of the four lines. Other word-level tropes, which are called broadly tropes of coloration, include (1) binomination, here seen in the Rebel Chant in "David" and "Ben-Jesse," two parts of a single name (thus the name "David" in its first occurrence participates in two tropes); (2) coordination, here seen in the number words, *'élep* and *rĕbābâ*, which function as a regular pair in the language; and (3) combination, perhaps seen here in the terms *ḥéleq* and *naḥălâ*, which may constitute a single phrase split across two lines. (If these words do not form a combination, then their use is not a structural element in the strict sense.) It is impossible in dealing with such short poems to demonstrate the difference between structural and nonstructural collocations of nouns, between tropes and other uses, though the difference is plain in longer poems.

This review of two small poems has, I hope, suggested some of the interest and complexity that attend careful study of Biblical Hebrew verse. One must understand these poems, like the others in the Former Prophets, in terms of the narrative, both immediate and broader, but they open away from the narrative in affording a more violently precise language for envy and oppression. These small poems are inscribed in the history of the monarchy as a result of their having inscribed themselves into the history of the monarchy.

References

Alt, Albrecht
1959   "Zelte und Hütten." In *Kleine Schriften zur Geschichte des Volkes Israel.* Ed. Martin Noth. Munich: Beck. 3.233-42.

Andersen, T. David
1986   "Problems in Analysing Hebrew Poetry." *Evangelical Australian Journal of Theology* 4:68-94.

Berlin, Adele
1985   *The Dynamics of Biblical Parallelism.* Bloomington: Indiana University.

Bird, Phyllis
1987   "The Place of Women in the Israelite Cultus." Pp. 397-419 in *Ancient Israelite Religion: Essays in Honor of Frank Moore Cross.* Ed. P. D. Miller et al. Philadelphia: Fortress.

Camp, Claudia V.
1981   "The Wise Women of 2 Samuel." *CBQ* 43:14-29.

Crenshaw, James L.
1988   "A Mother's Instruction to Her Son (Proverbs 31:1-9)." Pp. 9-22 in *Perspectives on the Hebrew Bible: Essays in Honor of Walter J. Harrelson.* Ed. James L. Crenshaw. Macon, GA: Mercer University.

Cross, Frank Moore, and D. N. Freedman
1953   "A Royal Song of Thanksgiving: II Samuel 22 = Psalm 18." *JBL* 72:15-34.

1975   *Studies in Ancient Yahwistic Poetry.* SBLDS 21. Missoula, MT: Scholars.

Flanagan, James W.
1988   *David's Social Drama: A Hologram of Israel's Early Iron Age.* JSOTSup 73. The Social World of Biblical Antiquity Series 7. Sheffield: Almond.

Freedman, David Noel

1963 "The Law and the Prophets." Pp. 250-65 in *Congress Volume: Bonn, 1962.* VTSup 9. Leiden: Brill.

1964 Review of Gevirtz 1963. *JBL* 83:201-3.

1971 "II Samuel 23:4." *JBL* 90:329-30. Reprinted in Freedman 1980:343-44.

1972 "The Refrain in David's Lament over Saul and Jonathan." Pp. 115-26 in *Ex orbe religionum: Studia Geo Widengren oblata.* Ed. C. J. Bleeker et al. Studies in the History of Religions (Supplements to *Numen*) 21. Leiden: Brill. Reprinted in Freedman 1980:263-74.

1975 "Early Israelite History in the Light of Early Israelite Poetry." Pp. 3-35 in *Unity and Diversity.* Ed. Hans Goedicke and J. J. M. Roberts. Baltimore: Johns Hopkins University. Reprinted in Freedman 1980:131-66.

1976 "Divine Names and Titles in Early Hebrew Poetry." Pp. 55-107 in *Magnalia Dei: The Mighty Acts of God: Essays on the Bible and Archaeology in Memory of G. Ernest Wright.* Ed. Frank Moore Cross et al. Garden City, NY: Doubleday. Reprinted in Freedman 1980:77-129.

1977 "Pottery, Poetry, and Prophecy: An Essay on Biblical Poetry." *JBL* 96:5-26. Reprinted in Freedman 1980:1-22.

1978 "Psalm 113 and the Song of Hannah." *ErIsr* 14:56-69. Reprinted in Freedman 1980:243-61.

1980 *Pottery, Poetry, and Prophecy: Studies in Early Hebrew Poetry.* Winona Lake, IN: Eisenbrauns.

1987a "The Earliest Bible." Pp. 5-13 in *Backgrounds for the Bible.* Ed. M. O'Connor and D. N. Freedman. Winona Lake, IN: Eisenbrauns.

1987b "On the Death of Abiner." Pp. 125-27 in *Love and Death in the Ancient Near East: Essays in Honor of Marvin H. Pope.* Ed. J. H. Marks and R. M. Good. Guilford, CT: Four Quarters.

1991 *The Unity of the Hebrew Bible.* Ann Arbor: University of Michigan.

Gevirtz, Stanley

1963 *Patterns in the Early Poetry of Israel.* Studies in Ancient Oriental Civilization 32. Chicago: University of Chicago.

1975 "Of Patriarchs and Puns: Joseph at the Fountain, Jacob at the Ford." *HUCA* 46:33-54.

Gottwald, Norman K.

1979 *The Tribes of Yahweh: A Sociology of the Religion of Liberated Israel, 1250-1050 B.C.* Maryknoll, NY: Orbis.

Koch, Klaus

1977 "'ōhel." *TDOT* 1.118-30.

McCarter, P. Kyle

1984 *II Samuel.* AB 9. Garden City, NY: Doubleday.

Meyers, Carol

1987   "David as Temple Builder." Pp. 357-76 in *Ancient Israelite Religion: Essays in Honor of Frank Moore Cross.* Ed. P. D. Miller et al. Philadelphia: Fortress.

1991   "'To Her Mother's House': Considering a Counterpart to the Israelite *Bêt-'āb.*" Pp. 39-51 in *The Bible and the Politics of Exegesis: Essays in Honor of Norman K. Gottwald on His Sixty-fifth Birthday.* Ed. David Jobling et al. Cleveland: Pilgrim.

Morrow, William S.

1993   *Coherence and Cohesion in Deuteronomy 14:1–17:13.* SBLMS. Atlanta: Scholars.

Nelson, Richard D.

1987   *First and Second Kings.* Interpretation. Atlanta: John Knox.

O'Connor, M.

1980   *Hebrew Verse Structure.* Winona Lake, IN: Eisenbrauns.

1986   "The Women in the Book of Judges." *HAR* 10:277-93.

Stockman, Ralph W.

1954   "Exposition of I Kings." *IB* 3.18-186.

Trible, Phyllis

1986   *Texts of Terror: Literary-feminist Readings of Biblical Narratives.* OBT. Philadelphia: Fortress.

Waltke, Bruce K., and M. O'Connor

1990   *An Introduction to Biblical Hebrew Syntax.* Winona Lake, IN: Eisenbrauns.

Watson, Wilfred G. E.

1984   *Classical Hebrew Poetry: A Guide to Its Techniques.* JSOTSup 26. Sheffield: JSOT.

1990   "Hebrew Poetry." Pp. 553-54 in *A Dictionary of Biblical Interpretation.* Ed. R. J. Coggins and J. L. Houlden. London: SCM; Philadelphia: Trinity Press International.

"Who Is This That Rises Like the Nile?"
Some Egyptian Texts on the Inundation
and a Prophetic Trope*

JOHN R. HUDDLESTUN

University of Michigan

I. Introduction

At last, with a good push for it, crossing hills and threading huge grasses, as well as extensive village plantations lately devastated by elephants . . . we arrived at the extreme end of the journey, the farthest point ever visited by the expedition. . . . We were well rewarded; for the "stones," [Ripon Falls] as the Waganda call the falls, was by far the most interesting sight I had seen in Africa. . . . The expedition had now performed its functions. I saw that old father Nile without any doubt rises in the Victoria N'yanza, and, as I had foretold, that lake is the great source of the holy river which cradled the first expounder of our religious belief.

Thus wrote John Hanning Speke, Captain of His Majesty's Indian Army and Fellow of the Royal Geographical Society, relating the success of his third ex-

---

*I thank John Baines for taking time away from a busy schedule in order to discuss a number of the Egyptian texts translated here and for graciously supplying copies of a handful of articles and texts unavailable to me. I am also indebted to Peter Machinist for helping me to organize more clearly my comments on the subject of methodology. Neither of the above, however, saw the manuscript prior to publication, and they should not be held accountable for its content, for which I bear sole responsibility. Robert Miller's careful reading of the final version saved me from a number of minor errors and inconsistencies in spelling.

pedition to Africa, undertaken to verify his earlier "assertion that the Victoria N'yanza . . . would eventually prove to be the source of the Nile." Speke located the river's origin on the northern shore of Lake Victoria at Jinja, the sight of the lake's only outlet and the beginning of the so-called Victoria Nile.[1] Subsequent to his discovery, Speke sent a telegram to the Royal Geographical Society proclaiming that the age-old question of the Nile's source had at last been settled — or so he thought. At 5,600 km. from the Delta outlet, Speke had not traveled quite far enough and, as we know today, was off by nearly 700 km. The river's actual origins lie within the complex of streams and rivers (in modern Rwanda and Burundi) that ultimately feed into the Kagera River, Lake Victoria's principal tributary.[2] Strictly speaking, the Nile River as a single entity begins at Khartoum with the juncture of the so-called White and Blue Niles, each of which consists up to that point of various other river systems and tributaries (excepting the Atbara, which merges north of Khartoum, midway between the Fifth and Sixth Cataracts). Nevertheless, Captain Speke should not be judged too harshly for his miscalculation; he had in fact discovered the only source, Lake Victoria, capable of matching the grandeur and majesty of the Nile itself.

The desire (often more of an obsession) of Speke and his nineteenth-

1. Speke's journal dates his discovery to July 28, 1862. For the entries quoted, see John Hanning Speke, *Journal of the Discovery of the Source of the Nile* (Edinburgh and London: William Blackwood and Sons, 1863) 1 and 466-67.

2. Two springs, one in Rwanda (west of Gikongoro) and the other in Burundi (west of Rutana), have been identified as the ultimate source of the great river. For locations, see *National Geographic Atlas of the World*, rev. 6th ed. (Washington, D.C.: National Geographic Society, 1992) 93; and further discussion in R. O. Collins, *The Waters of the Nile: Hydropolitics and the Jonglei Canal, 1900-1988* (Oxford: Clarendon, 1990) 4-9. In all fairness to Speke, he correctly named the Kagera as the "only one feeder of any importance" for Lake Victoria (*Journal*, 468), a point not mentioned by Collins.

For the course and topography of the Nile, see, e.g., W. Willocks, *The Nile in 1904* (London: E. & F. N. Spon, 1904) 11-55; H. G. Lyons, *The Physiography of the River Nile and Its Basin* (Finance Ministry, Survey Department, Egypt; Cairo: National Printing Department, 1906); W. Willcocks and J. I. Craig, *Egyptian Irrigation* (3rd ed.; 2 vols.; London: E. & F. N. Spon, 1913) 1:129-298; H. E. Hurst and P. Phillips, *The Nile Basin*, vol. 1: *General Description of the Basin, Meteorology, Topography of the White Nile Basin* (Ministry of Public Works, Egypt; Physical Department Paper no. 26; Cairo: Government Press, 1931) 68-107; H. E. Hurst, *A Short Account of the Nile Basin* (Ministry of Public Works, Egypt; Physical Department Paper no. 45; Cairo: Government Press, 1944) 1-24; idem, *The Nile Basin*, vol. 8: *The Hydrology of the Sobat and White Nile and the Topography of the Blue Nile and Atbara* (Ministry of Public Works, Egypt; Physical Department Paper no. 55; Cairo: Government Press, 1950) 97-125; D. Bonneau, *La crue du Nil: Divinité égyptienne à travers mille ans d'histoire (332 av.–641 ap. J.-C.) d'après les auteurs grecs et latins, et les documents des époques ptolémaïque, romaine et byzantine* (Études et commentaires 52; Paris: Librairie C. Klincksieck, 1964) 11-131; Collins, *Waters*, 1-26; B. B. Williams, "Nile (Geography)," *ABD* 4.1112-16; and R. Said, *The River Nile: Geology, Hydrology, and Utilization* (Oxford and New York: Pergamon, 1993).

For what little evidence we possess on the actual arrival of the inundation in ancient Egypt, see Jac. J. Janssen, "The Day the Inundation Began," *JNES* 46 (1987) 129-36.

century contemporaries to find the elusive source of the legendary river was by no means unique to their time. Ancient Greek historians in particular were most curious as to the source and course of the river.[3] Virtually every scholar or student of the ancient Near East has, at one time or another, heard or read the oft-quoted saying about the land of Egypt being the gift of the Nile.[4] Few, however, have waded through the accounts that make up the rich classical traditions on the river, its origins, and its place in ancient Egyptian society. Still fewer, if any, have considered or examined in a systemic fashion those relevant ancient Near Eastern texts outside the Greco-Roman tradition. Here one should not overlook the Hebrew Bible as a potentially important source, both for its tidbits of information relative to ancient Egypt — often given in ideologically unguarded moments — and as the primary source for one culture's "outsider" view of Egypt.

As one peruses the biblical commentaries on passages relating to the Nile and its inundation, one notes the lack of reference to Egyptian texts on the subject, excepting perhaps the so-called Hymn to the Nile, or more properly the inundation.[5] A number of these texts (e.g., those from the reigns of Smendes I and Osorkon III; see below) were initially published in the nineteenth century and have since received little, if any, mention in Egyptological literature. Excepting the texts collected by Vandier (1936) and Schenkel (1978),[6] the curious biblical scholar must ferret out the relevant materials on his or her own. In the pages that follow, I hope to remedy the situation somewhat with partial translations of selected Egyptian texts concerning the inundation. In addition, I shall comment on one biblical passage in particular relative to the king of Egypt and the Nile: Jer 46:7-8.[7] Before proceeding to the texts themselves, however, I should like first to discuss Egyptian terms signifying the inundation and the topic of comparative methodology.

---

3. For an extended discussion of the various ancient explanations for the river's source and inundation, see Bonneau, *La crue*, 135-214.

4. See A. D. Godley, trans., *Herodotus I. Books I-II* (LCL; Cambridge: Harvard University; London: William Heinemann, 1926) 281 (2.5).

5. See *ANET*, 372-73.

6. J. Vandier, *La famine dans l'Égypte ancienne* (Recherches d'archéologie, de philologie et d'histoire 7; Cairo: L'Institut français d'archéologie orientale, 1936); and W. Schenkel, *Die Bewässerungsrevolution im alten Ägypten* (Deutsches archäologisches Institut, Abteilung Kairo; Mainz am Rhein: Philipp von Zabern, 1978).

7. The following brief selection of Egyptian texts derives from research relating to my dissertation, "Images of Egypt: The Nile in the Hebrew Bible," which examines both the Egyptian evidence and those biblical passages relating to the Nile and their significance for the biblical writers' portrait and utilization of Egypt/Egyptians in biblical historiography. A number of the relevant biblical texts are discussed, albeit very briefly, in my "Nile (OT)," *ABD* 4.1108-12.

II. Hapj, the Inundation, and Methodology

The primary term denoting the inundation in Egyptian texts is ḥ'pj.[8] As one surveys the scholarly literature, one notes a variety of meanings for the word, the most common being "Nile" or "Nile god." Despite its continued usage, however, the rendering "Nile" is inaccurate. That ḥ'pj refers to the inundation, not to the river in its normal state (for which one often finds the term jtrw), was demonstrated by de Buck in 1941 with the publication of an article wherein he adduced over seventy examples in support of his thesis (some of which may be observed in the partial translations below).[9] The latter translation "Nile god" arises from a misunderstanding of the meaning and function of the many figures, depicted in relief and sculpture, intended to personify the concept of fecundity — what Baines has termed in his seminal 1985 work on the subject "fecundity figures." This iconographic form, however, is not associated exclusively with Hapj (also written Hapy). Groupings of these figures, especially in temple reliefs, vary with respect to nomenclature and function.[10] Thus, in the light of the work of de Buck and Baines, both translations, "Nile" and "Nile god" should be abandoned, despite their persistence even in more recent literature.[11]

Turning now to biblical scholarship, with respect to the Nile and Egyptian religion, one encounters little, if any, substantive treatment. Biblical scholars tend to reduce the highly complex issues of the interrelationship of deities, their aspects, manifestations, and functions, to their lowest possible level: god A is the god of X, god B is the god of Y, and so on. This is especially noticeable in

8. See A. Erman and H. Grapow, *Wörterbuch der ägyptischen Sprache* (hereafter *WbÄS*) (7 vols.; Leipzig: J. C. Hinrichs; Berlin: Akademie-Verlag, 1926-63) 3.42-43.

9. On jtrw see *WbÄS* 1.146-47. On ḥ'pj, see A. de Buck, "On the Meaning of the Name Ḥ'pj," in *Orientalia Neerlandica* (Leiden: A. W. Sijthoff, 1948) 1-22 (originally appeared in 1941 as "De naam van den Nijl bij de Egyptenaren" [not available to me]). For a brief history of the interpretation of the name, see J. Baines, *Fecundity Figures: Egyptian Personification and the Iconology of a Genre* (Warminster: Aris & Phillips; Chicago: Bolchazy-Carducci, 1985) 112-16. Compare the comments of É. Drioton, "Les origines pharaoniques du nilomètre de Rodah," *Bulletin de l'institut d'Égypte* 34 (1951-52) 294n.b; and J. Leclant, *Recherches sur les monuments Thébains de la XXVe dynastie dite Éthiopiennes* (2 vols.; Bibliothèque d'études 36; Cairo: IFAO, 1965) 1.3n.2 and 241n.4.

10. Major functions include offering bearers and central figures in the "Uniting of the Two Lands" motif (zm3-t3wj), the latter comprising the largest and most significant group. For other functions and general discussion, see Baines, *Fecundity Figures*, 208-329; for nomenclature see, e.g., lists on pp. 154-56, 162-63, 167-70, 174-79.

11. Note, more recently, the entry ḥ'pj in L. H. Lesko's *Dictionary of Late Egyptian* (5 vols.; Providence: B. C. Scribe, 1984) 2.100, which gives only "Nile" as the meaning of the term. Misconceptions about Hapj in earlier Egyptological literature naturally influenced discussions of the Nile in reference works on the Bible; for a good example, see E. Beurlier, "Nil," *DB* 4.1622-25, esp. 1624.

discussions of the plagues traditions, where the correlation of plagues and deities is, more often than not, of the highest priority.[12]

The complexity of the Egyptian evidence is well illustrated in the case of Hapj's association — both textually and pictorially — with other major deities such as Nun, Osiris, Amun(-Re), Ptah, and Thoth. While few in number, name combinations or syncretistic groupings involving the name Hapj are problematic in that his status as personification or deity is not always clear. Hapj possessed no formal temple cult as such and, despite name linkage with other gods such as Ptah and Amun, apparently was not a major deity.[13]

In some cases, the relationship between Hapj and other gods is easily explicable, as, for example, when the waters of the inundation are associated with the Primeval Waters (Nun) from which land emerged at the time of creation.[14] In others, the association is more nuanced, taking on multiple dimensions, as is the case with Amun-Re, where the majority of references derive

12. But note the restraint of Z. Zevit, who summarizes the various proposed correlations but admits that "not all of the plagues can be conveniently matched up with Egyptian gods or texts" ("Three Ways to Look at the Ten Plagues," *BARev* 6/3 [1990] 21). While his criticisms are, in my opinion, valid (esp. his comments on dating evidence), his uncritical use of Egyptian texts is problematic. Note also the more circumspect summary of J. K. Hoffmeier, "Egypt, Plagues in," *ABD* 2.374-78.

13. Following Baines, *Fecundity Figures,* 26-27, 41, and 79-80. One does, however, find evidence of festivals in honor of Hapj (see P. Barguet, "Les stèles du Nil au Gebel Silsileh," *BIFAO* 50 [1952] 8; Bonneau, *La crue,* 361-420; idem, "Les fêtes de la crue du Nil: Problèmes de lieux, de dates et d'organisation," *Revue d'égyptologie* 23 [1971] 49-65; and R. A. Caminos, "Nilopfer," *Lexikon der Ägyptologie* 4 [ed. W. Helck and E. Otto; Wiesbaden: Harrassowitz, 1982] 498-500).

I am aware of only a handful of instances where *ḥ'pj* is combined (as the second element) with other divine names (e.g., with Ptah, Sobek, or Amun). Often, the second name functions as the "distinctive modifier" (Baines, *Fecundity Figures,* 80), being equal or superior to the first, but the above examples seem to emphasize Hapj in his aspect as inundation, not deity. Thus, the linkage here is less between two deities as such and, based on examples cited below (n. 16), has rather to do with one deity's auspicious association with an event of immense importance to Egypt, i.e., the arrival and concomitant beneficial aspects of the inundation. See Baines (pages already cited) for specific examples and, for name combinations, see also B. Altenmüller, *Synkretismus in den Sargtexten* (Göttinger Orientforschungen, 4th series: Ägypten, vol. 7; Wiesbaden: Harrassowitz, 1975) 6-7; and E. Hornung, *The One and the Many: Conceptions of God in Ancient Egypt* (trans. J. Baines; Ithaca: Cornell University, 1982) 91-99.

14. See, e.g., Papyrus Anastasi I, 3.7-8 (E. F. Wente, *Letters from Ancient Egypt* [SBLWAW 1; Atlanta: Scholars, 1990] 100); the embalming ritual (J.-C. Goyon, *Rituels funéraires de l'ancienne Égypte* [Paris: Éditions du Cerf, 1972] 69-70; Leiden Papyrus I 350, V,21 (A. Gardiner, "Hymns to Amon from a Leiden Papyrus," *Zeitschrift für Ägyptische Sprache und Altertumskunde* 42 [1905] 38-39); and Hymn to Khnum (M. Lichtheim, *Ancient Egyptian Literature* [3 vols.; Berkeley: University of California, 1971-80] 3.112-13, Roman period). For Nun in fecundity figure form, see Baines, *Fecundity Figures,* 160, 194-96, 213, 311-12. Note also the discussion of the Nile and Nun in O. Kaiser, *Die mythische Bedeutung des Meeres in Ägypten, Ugarit und Israel* (BZAW 78; Berlin: Töpelmann, 1959) 27-32.

from solar hymns.[15] Here the sun god performs his beneficiary acts by means of the inundation, bringing forth Hapj from his cavern with the whole of creation in celebration.[16] As for Osiris, contrary to much of what one reads in popular handbooks (and even some more serious works), although frequently connected with the inundation, he should not be equated with the phenomenon itself but rather is revivified at Hapj's arrival. Note, for example, the following passages from the Coffin Texts (Spell 318), wherein the role of Osiris is distinct from that of Hapj:

> I [Hapj] am one who precedes the great and mighty gods, I am he who makes the going round [or cycle] of Osiris with the great flood; it has come about through me. I am Hapj in the great flood. . . . I am the transporter of Osiris by means of the flood on the day of his birth.[17]

Osiris comes via the inundation, but the two are not identical. The yearly cycle or "going round" *(pḥr)* of Osiris is made possible only with Hapj's arrival.[18] In

15. For solar hymns in general, see J. Assmann, *Ägyptische Hymnen und Gebete* (Bibliotek der alten Welt: Der alte Orient; Zurich and Munich: Artemis, 1975) 97-252; idem, *Sonnenhymnen in thebanischen Gräbern* (Theben 1; Mainz am Rhein: Philipp von Zabern, 1983); and A. Barucq and F. Daumas, *Hymnes et prières de l'Egypte ancienne* (Paris: Éditions du Cerf, 1980) 115-79.

16. Textual references associating Amun with the inundation are numerous. See generally Leclant, *Recherches*, 240-46; and J. Monnet, "Un monument de la corégence des divines adoratrices Nitocris et Ankhenesneferibré," *Revue d'égyptologie* 10 (1955) 44-45. As stated, Amun is said to bring forth Hapj from his cavern (examples in Assmann, *Sonnenhymnen,* texts 17.33-34, 206.15, 211[b].3-4). Additionally, Amun may grant the king a good inundation (e.g., Wente, *Letters,* 128; see esp. the texts of Osorkon III and Taharqa translated below). Since he is the dispenser of the inundation and renewer of life, Amun's role may overlap with that of Hapj, as, e.g., in a solar hymn from the tomb of Tjanefer at Thebes (TT Tomb 158, 19th-20th Dynasties), which reads: "You are the inundation [ḥʿpj], who makes all men live" (see K. C. Seele, *The Tomb of Tjanefer at Thebes* [OIP 86; Chicago: University of Chicago, 1959] pl. 10, l. 3; and Assmann, *Sonnenhymnen,* 203-9 [Text 156]). For Amun and Hapj in a personal name, see Baines, *Fecundity Figures,* 80. I do not discuss here the role of Assmann's so-called trinity *(Dreiheit)* — an interpretative device of which he is rather fond — consisting of šw, tзw, and ḥʿpj in this and other texts. See *Sonnenhymnen,* 206n.m and his general theme "Life-giving Elements" *(lebenspendenden Elemente)* in *Re und Amun: Die Krise des polytheistischen Weltbilds im Ägypten der 18.-20. Dynastie* (OBO 51; Freiburg: Universitätsverlag; Göttingen: Vandenhoeck & Ruprecht, 1983) 250-63.

17. For the text, see A. de Buck, *The Egyptian Coffin Texts IV. Texts of Spells 268-354* (OIP 67; Chicago: University of Chicago, 1951) 136d-e, 137a-b, and 139a (Spell 318). My translation (with modifications) and interpretation generally follow R. T. Rundle Clark, "Some Hymns to the Nile," *University of Birmingham Historical Journal* 5 (1955) 1-30 (see 15-16).

18. Note also the comments of Rundle Clark in *Myth and Symbol in Ancient Egypt* (London: Thames and Hudson, 1959) 100; as well as J. G. Griffiths, *The Origins of Osiris and his Cult* (Studies in the History of Religions 40; Leiden: Brill, 1980) 151-63. My examination of the relevant Egyptian materials extends down to, but does not include, the Ptolemaic and Roman periods, for which see Bonneau, *La crue,* 243-54.

the light of the above, the recent assertion of one biblical scholar that "the Nile was deified by the Egyptians as Hapi the Nile god, and its inundation was viewed as a manifestation of the great god Osiris" provides the reader with a rather neat and tidy explanation of the first two plagues as judgments against the gods of Egypt, but at the expense of the Egyptian evidence.[19]

Before one can confirm or deny possible Egyptian background to the Exodus narrative, one must first address such topics as context, date, access, and the limits of modern reconstruction. For example, the citation of a Pyramid Text to elucidate a particular biblical term or idea[20] requires that one take

19. See N. H. Sarna, *Exploring Exodus: The Heritage of Biblical Israel* (New York: Schocken, 1986) 79. This misconception is not unique to Sarna. I cite him as a recent example of how it is perpetuated in popular literature on the subject. In fairness to the author, he relies principally on older works (esp. those of Frankfort and even Budge), apparently unaware of the contributions to the field of Egyptian religion made by modern scholars such as Hornung, Assmann, or Baines — to name only a few. The most recent multivolume reference work dealing with the Bible and the ancient Near East, the *Anchor Bible Dictionary* (1992), correctly presents the connection between Hapj and the Nile in Hoffmeier's article "Egypt, Plagues in" (*ABD* 2.374-78).

20. For examples of this relating to Hebrew *yam sûp* of the exodus, see discussion in my "Red Sea (OT)," *ABD* 5.638. The overriding assumption here is that knowledge is acquired via texts, which need not always be the case. Because texts and textual traditions largely dominate comparative work, however, my remarks are of relevance. Other means of access are possible, whether directly from Egypt or via Levantine sources (e.g., temporary residence in Egypt, trade connections, oral tradition, observation of Egyptian monuments in Palestine, etc.). (For the latter, see the survey of S. Wimmer, "Egyptian Temples in Canaan and Sinai," in *Studies in Egyptology Presented to Miriam Lichtheim* [ed. S. Israelite-Groll; Jerusalem: Magnes, 1990] 2.1065-1106.) For example, that ancient Palestinians visited major religious centers of Egypt, whether as pilgrims or tourists, is evidenced by the many Phoenician and Aramaic graffiti (ca. fifth-third centuries B.C.E.) preserved in various parts of the Osiris temple of Seti I and Ramesses II at Abydos. Although unable to read the temple inscriptions, these visitors no doubt would have formed ideas about Egyptian religion and the king based on their observation of the reliefs. For the graffiti, see M. Lidzbarski, *Ephemeris für semitische Epigraphik* (3 vols.; Giessen: Töpelmann, 1902-15) 3.93-116 (reference courtesy of Philip Schmitz); *KAI* no. 49. Note also the so-called Abydos Papyrus (Aramaic, late fifth century B.C.E.), which documents a pilgrimage by two Sidonian brothers to the Abydos temple. See J. Teixidor, "Un nouveau papyrus araméen du règne de Darius II," *Syria* 41 (1964) 285-90; J. Naveh, "Old Aramaic Inscriptions (1960-1965)," *AION* 16 (1966) 30-31; idem, "Aramaica Dubiosa," *JNES* 27 (1968) 317-25 (doubts its authenticity); and Teixidor's reply: "On the Authenticity of the Madrid Papyrus," *JNES* 31 (1972) 340-42.

While in greater abundance than for later periods, the appeal only to New Kingdom evidence when interpreting the Exodus narratives stops well short of the period during which the texts were written and thus does not consider ways in which then current knowledge, from whatever source, undoubtedly informed the writers' or editors' presentation of matters Egyptian. See further my comments in "Red Sea," 640-41, which draw from the work of D. B. Redford ("An Egyptological Perspective on the Exodus Narrative," in *Egypt, Israel, Sinai: Archaeological and Historical Relationships in the Biblical Period* [ed. A. F. Rainey; Tel Aviv: Tel Aviv University, 1987] 144; see also his *Egypt, Canaan, and Israel in Ancient Times* [Princeton: Princeton University, 1992] 395-429).

account of the date of the text (ca. mid-third millennium B.C.E.), its context (inner hallways and chambers of a pyramid complex), and how a biblical writer might have possessed knowledge of it (access). In this case, all three factors present problems, especially the large chronological gap. The underlying assumption appears to be that whatever is found in the Pyramid Texts must somehow be common to Egyptian religion as a whole, and thus of value for comparison; no distinction is made between early or late periods. In this fashion, the whole of the ancient Near East becomes in effect a large comparative playground from which frolicking scholars may pick any text, regardless of date or genre, as a potential source of influence or at least a noteworthy parallel, with no self-imposed controls. A more logical course would be to trace, where possible, the development or evolution of similar ideas or motifs from their probable earliest attestation in the Pyramid Texts into the first millennium, thus locating them closer in time to the composition of the biblical text. Here one might, for example, examine Late Period traditions of the Book of the Dead.[21] This still leaves open the more difficult question of the ancient writers' access to and knowledge of such textual traditions, which applies in a somewhat different fashion to the modern interpreter as well.

Modern attempts to interpret the biblical account are based on what we today have been able to reconstruct of Egyptian religion and, considering quantity and availability, it is fair to say that we probably know more, but certainly not all there is to know, about the topic than did the authors or redactors of the biblical texts. For example, today's scholar has at his or her disposal hundreds of texts available in easily accessible anthologies. Drawing from these, one constructs an ideal model or type of what the religion must have looked like and then asks the biblical text to conform to it. By contrast, the Exodus account represents the authors' or redactors' own limited and at times vague understanding of Egyptian ritual and its meaning.[22] To be sure, they knew something about practices in ancient Egypt, but that knowledge did not derive from combing through anthologies or handbooks on Egyptian religion. Thus, the modern biblical scholar and/or Egyptologist must consider the disparate nature of these two bodies of evidence and keep in mind that conformity between the

---

21. For correlations between the Pyramid Texts and the Book of the Dead, see T. G. Allen, trans., *The Book of the Dead or Going Forth by Day* (Studies in Ancient Oriental Civilization 37; Chicago: University of Chicago, 1974), appendix 1. For post–New Kingdom traditions of the Book of the Dead, see M. Mosher, Jr., "Theban and Memphite Book of the Dead Traditions in the Late Period," *Journal of the American Research Center in Egypt* 29 (1992) 143-72.

22. See, e.g., R. de Vaux, *The Early History of Israel* (trans. D. Smith; Philadelphia: Westminster, 1978) 361 ("there was some knowledge, albeit clearly imperfect, of Egyptian matters"), and the conclusions of Redford (*Egypt, Canaan, and Israel*, 411-12), who suggests that those behind the plagues account might have been "Israelite aliens living among Egyptians, close enough to have limited and distorted knowledge of their customs."

two may not always be a reliable guide. At times, one may overestimate the knowledge of the biblical authors, perceiving minute distinctions or turns of irony that they themselves may not have intended or of which they were not aware. Nonetheless, particular genres within the biblical corpus point to clear Egyptian influence, even if the precise means of mediation is not always known.[23] My point here is to stress the limitations inherent to both bodies of evidence, biblical and Egyptological, when utilized for comparative purposes, and the frequent lack of methodological rigor when one approaches the biblical text from an Egyptological perspective. Precisely what the biblical authors/redactors knew and how they obtained or had access to such knowledge are questions requiring more attention in the literature.[24] Given the restricted access

---

23. I have in mind the biblical wisdom tradition and esp. the book of Proverbs (see generally G. E. Bryce, *A Legacy of Wisdom: The Egyptian Contribution to the Wisdom of Israel* [London and Cranbury, NJ: Associated University Presses, 1979]; W. McKane, *Proverbs: A New Approach* (OTL; Philadelphia: Westminster, 1970] 1-150; and the recent summary in Redford, *Egypt, Canaan, and Israel*, 389-94; for the relationship between the Teaching of Amenemope and the "Words of the Wise" in Prov 22:17–24:22, note the restrained conclusions of J. Ruffle, "The Teaching of Amenemope and its Connection with the Book of Proverbs," *TynBul* 28 [1977] 29-68). Here the case for Egyptian influence seems strongest, although it is difficult to isolate a particular period of Israel's history as decisive. Frequent appeals to the united monarchy (e.g., von Rad's "Solomonic enlightenment" with the Jerusalem court as "a centre of international wisdom-lore") and the widespread presence of "schools" in preexilic Israel as primary vehicles of mediation are not without problems. For the former, see the initial proposal in G. von Rad, "The Beginnings of Historical Writing in Ancient Israel," in *The Problem of the Hexateuch and Other Essays* (trans. E. W. Trueman Dicken; Edinburgh and London: Oliver and Boyd, 1966) 166-204 (originally published in *Archiv für Kulturgeschichte* 32 [1944] 1-42); and the critical assessment of R. N. Whybray, "Wisdom Literature in the Reigns of David and Solomon," in *Studies in the Period of David and Solomon and Other Essays* (ed. T. Ishida; Tokyo: Yamakawa-Shuppansha, 1982) 13-26. For the question of schools, see the sober evaluation of J. L. Crenshaw, "Education in Ancient Israel," *JBL* 104 (1985) 601-15.

24. I leave aside here the issues of: (1) the highly restrictive nature of literacy in Palestine and Egypt (for the latter, see J. Baines and C. J. Eyre, "Four Notes on Literacy," *Göttinger Miszellen* 61 [1983] 65-96); and (2) the potential relevance of popular or nonroyal perceptions of Egyptian religious practice and the king for biblical traditions — as opposed to the official ideology that largely informs our understanding of religion in Egypt. Many engaged in comparative work assume implicitly or at least imply that the biblical authors both had access to Egyptian texts and were capable of reading them. Possible historical or social contexts for such access, apart from those found in the biblical narrative, are, however, rarely articulated. The scant evidence relating to Egyptian texts in Palestine during the first millennium (e.g., hieratic inscriptions on bowls and ostraca) is of little, if any, value in determining the extent to which full-blown literary texts of the type often cited in comparative studies might have been available. Despite his assumption that "long before the establishment of the Hebrew kingdom, the inhabitants of Syria-Palestine must have been familiar with many of the masterpieces of Egyptian literature," R. J. Williams was unable to cite any clear evidence for such knowledge (see "'A People Come out of Egypt': An Egyptologist Looks at the Old Testament," in *Congress Volume, Edinburgh 1974* [VTSup 28; Leiden: Brill,

to religious ritual and its official interpretation in ancient Egypt itself, how much more so should one exercise caution when evaluating a text or group of texts produced outside Egypt.[25]

1975] 231-52). This is not to deny the possibility, but only to caution against uncritical appeal to Egyptian literary texts. (For first-millennium hieratic texts in Palestine, see the recent discussion and further bibliography in O. Goldwasser, "An Egyptian Scribe from Lachish and the Hieratic Tradition of the Hebrew Kingdoms," *Tel Aviv* 18 [1991] 248-53. These inscriptions are for the most part extremely fragmentary, and Goldwasser tends at times to derive more information from them than is actually there.)

To his credit, Redford has brought to the fore a number of the above-mentioned issues through his emphasis on the Egyptian Saite and Persian periods as the time during which many of the biblical narratives involving Egypt took shape (*Egypt, Canaan, and Israel*, 408-29, and note also his useful classification and survey of areas of influence, whether imagined or real, on pp. 365-94; for suggestions concerning possible avenues of access, primarily via Phoenician channels, see pp. 366, 384, and 393-94).

25. For restriction, see J. Baines, "Restricted Knowledge, Hierarchy, and Decorum: Modern Perceptions and Ancient Institutions," *Journal of the American Research Center in Egypt* 27 (1990) 1-23.

The earlier-mentioned lack of methodological rigor is very much in evidence in the work of John D. Currid, who assumes an astonishing amount of knowledge on the part of the biblical authors (see, e.g., his "Why did God Harden Pharaoh's Heart?" *BibRev* 9/6 [1993] 46-51). Currid maintains that the hardening of Pharaoh's heart in the Exodus narrative should be understood within the context of the Weighing of the Heart ceremony in ancient Egypt, apparently with Yahweh judging Pharaoh (= the deceased). At the outset he proclaims that "the [biblical] author clearly understood the Egyptian world, and especially Egyptian religion, from the inside," and thus intentionally engaged in polemic against Egyptian ideas concerning the afterlife. Space does not permit a proper critique of this thesis, although the following points are worth noting: (1) Given that he relies heavily on the Book of the Dead, Currid owes the reader an explanation as to how those responsible for the biblical account might have had access to such texts or the ideas contained therein (see also n. 20 above). Given their "inside" information, is one to assume that they lived in Egypt, and if so, when? (2) Currid ignores, or is unaware of, the vast literature produced by biblical scholarship on the subject, including the fact that others (e.g., N. Lohfink, P. Weimar, and R. R. Wilson) have traced the origins of this motif to holy war traditions (cf. Deut 2:30; Josh 11:20; Isa 63:10, 17 and discussion in R. R. Wilson, "The Hardening of Pharaoh's Heart," *CBQ* 41 [1979] 33-34). (3) Lastly, the author's repeated usage of theologically loaded terms such as "sin/sinner," "righteousness," and "perfection" to explain or represent various aspects of Egyptian religion is misleading at best. This practice does not inspire confidence in his ability to grapple with these complex religious phenomena on their own terms. (For a more detailed and judicious survey of the biblical and Egyptian evidence, see N. Shupak, "Some Idioms Connected with the Concept of 'Heart' in Egypt and the Bible," in *Pharaonic Egypt, the Bible and Christianity* [ed. S. Israelite-Groll; Jerusalem: Magnes, 1985] 202-12.)

III. Egyptian Texts

The following selected translations are arranged loosely according to content. First, two selections dealing with the inundation in general: the Hymn to Hapj and Papyrus Anastasi I. Second, three accounts, all from autobiographical texts, relating the consequences of a low inundation or series of such: Khetj I, Mentuhotpe son of Hapj, and Amenemhet from Beni Hasan. Lastly, five selections that narrate the damage and destruction resulting from an inundation that is too high: under Sebekhotpe VIII, Smendes I, Osorkon III, Taharqa, and Amasis II. Within the last-named category, one should note the role played by the king and Amun.

1. The Inundation in General

a. The Hymn to the Inundation (Ramesside period or earlier)

Of the surviving texts relating to Hapj and the inundation, this hymn is by far the most popular, in terms both of ancient attestation and modern citation. A proper treatment of the text would require a volume unto itself. Here I present one passage that appears to describe the response of the populace to the inundation.[26]

> (IId) When he [Hapj] is slow, noses stop up,[27]
> then everyone is impoverished.
> (IIe) As one reduces[28] the sacred food offerings,

---

26. For the text, translations, and discussion, see W. Helck, *Der Text des "Nilhymnus"* (Kleine ägyptische Texte; Wiesbaden: Harrassowitz, 1972); line divisions and numberings follow Helck (pp. 14-22). See also D. Meeks's lengthy review of Helck in *BibOr* 32 (1975) 18-25; *ANET,* 372-73; M. Lichtheim, "Three Philological Notes," in *Studies in Honor of John A. Wilson, September 12, 1969* (Studies in Ancient Oriental Civilization 35; Chicago: University of Chicago, 1969) 63-68; idem, *Ancient Egyptian Literature* 1.204-10; Assmann, *Hymnen,* 500-506, 640-42; idem, *Lexikon der Ägyptologie* 4.489-96; Barucq and Daumas, *Hymnes et prières,* 493-501; J. L. Foster, "Thought Couplets in Khety's 'Hymn to the Inundation,'" *JNES* 34 (1975) 1-29; idem, *Echoes of Egyptian Voices: An Anthology of Ancient Egyptian Poetry* (Oklahoma Series in Classical Culture; Norman, OK, and London: University of Oklahoma, 1992) 47-52; and esp. D. van der Plas, *L'hymne à la crue du Nil* (2 vols.; Leiden: Nederlands Instituut voor het Nabije Oosten, 1986). The important edition of van der Plas was unavailable to me at the time of writing.

27. The reference to clogged noses may refer to the stench created by a low water level (for which see W. Willcocks, *The Nile in 1904* [London: E. & F. N. Spon, 1904] 61).

28. Reading *ḫbj,* "reduce, subtract," instead of *ḫbꜣ,* "destroy, ravage." (See n. 29 below.)

countless perish among the people.[29]
(IIIa) When he plunders, the whole land suffers,[30]
both great and small wander.[31]
(IIIb) It is in accordance with his coming that people change,[32]

29. With the exception of Foster ("Thought Couplets," 17), all translations give the same general sense for these lines: reduced temple offerings and subsequent mass destruction. Yet how the former relates to the latter, if at all, is not clear. The *ḥr* preceding the second clause would seem to indicate some type of causal relationship, as would also the initial *jr* found in some texts (but not in the Golenischeff ostracon). Meeks (review, 25) begins *si l'on réduit . . .* , thus implying that a reduction in offerings results in widespread death. The same meaning is implicit in the renderings of Helck and Barucq-Daumas. Other texts on the inundation mention the doubling of offerings *(k3b.tw p3wt)* with Hapj's coming (see, e.g., Barguet, "Les stèles," 59n.3) as a means of expressing abundance; thus, their reduction here is most likely to be understood within this context. I have followed Lichtheim with "as" to convey the idea of concomitant events, each due to famine brought about by a low inundation.

30. This is Lichtheim's translation (first part only, following the Golenischeff ostracon), about which I have some reservations. The text is difficult, as the widely varying translations attest. If read as a verb, *'wn-jb*, "be rapacious, greedy" *(WbÄS 1.172)*, may well refer to the behavior of Hapj (thus Assmann, *Hymnen*), and Lichtheim ("Notes," 68) argues that the reference here is to a destructive inundation, i.e., one that is too high and thus "plunders" the land. Her subsequent reading *nšn t3 r ḏr.f* is problematic, however, particularly the verb *nšn*, "rage" *(WbÄS 1.340-41)*. The majority of texts suggest a preposition after *'wn-jb* — either *r* or *n* — followed by *mn/mnt*. This could be the prepositional phrase *r-mn-(m)*, "as far as" (A. Gardiner, *Egyptian Grammar* [3rd ed.; Oxford: Griffith Institute, 1957] 136; see Helck, *Nilhymnus,* 21-22; and Barucq-Daumas, *Hymnes,* 495), or a preposition plus the verb or noun *mn/mnt*, which generally denotes "suffering, malady" (with the bad bird determinative; see Assmann and Foster). I favor the second option, with the general sense of the text being when Hapj plunders (like a thief?), the entire land suffers. Beyond even this conjectural interpretation, one can say little with confidence. (Note that Sallier II and Anastasi VII read *mnmnt*, "cattle," which, in combination with *'wn*, may in some fashion prefigure the later idea of the inundation coming like a "cattle thief" [Egyptian *jtj k3w; WbÄS* 1.150.3]; see the text below for Taharqa sub §III.3.d and discussion in M. F. Laming Macadam, *The Temples of Kawa I: The Inscriptions* (2 vols.; London: Oxford University, 1949) 1.30; and Vandier, *La famine,* 66n.3).

31. Reading *nmj* with "winding wall" (Chester Beatty) and "walking legs" (Deir el-Medina 1051) determinatives (Helck's proposed *Urtext,* 22); see also Meeks (review, 21b). One might also read the verb as "shout, scream" (here in the sense of wail?), e.g., Lichtheim's "roar" (see *WbÄS* 2.265.17; R. O. Faulkner, *A Concise Dictionary of Middle Egyptian* [Oxford: Griffith Institute, 1981] 133; and D. Meeks, *Année lexicographie. Egypte ancienne* [Paris, 1981] 2.196).

32. *šbb rmt ḥft ḥsf.f.* Reading an emphatic *sḏm.f* with *ḥft ḥsf.f* as adverbial complement. Lichtheim ("Notes," 68) considers this statement crucial for understanding the overall purpose of these lines, i.e., to enumerate the varying responses of the populace to different types of inundations. If too low *(wsf.f)*, famine ensues, if too high *('wn-jb)*, turmoil, and if in the right abundance *(wbn.f)*, great jubilation *(m ḥ'wt . . . m ršwt)*. But this proposal hinges on her translation of two passages *(jr 'wn-jb nšn t3 r ḏr.f* and the line under discussion), both of which are problematic and subject to widely divergent interpretations. Nevertheless, the presence of *wšb*, "to respond, answer," in four texts may indicate that the general tenor of

(according to how) Khnum has made him.[33]
(IIIc) When he appears, the land is in jubilation,
then everyone rejoices;
(IIId) Every jawbone takes to laughter[34]
every tooth is bared [i.e., all are smiling].

b. Papyrus Anastasi I (the "Satrical Papyrus," late 19th Dynasty)

This lengthy letter, surviving in numerous copies and fragments,[35] contains two references to ḥʿpj (3.7-8 and 7.8–8.1), the second of which compares the writer's impartation of instruction or wisdom to the inundation:

---

this line, however problematic, involves the manner in which Hapj affects the lives of Egypt's inhabitants.

 Meeks (review, 21, 25) takes šbb rmṯ to indicate the mixing or confusing of people with respect to rank (?) under Hapj's chastisement (ḥsf.f): "les hommes (de toutes conditions?) sont confondus lorsqu'il punit." This, he believes, continues the similar idea of nondistinction between the great and small expressed in the previous lines. In addition, Meeks notes that ḥsf with the sense of "approach" is rare, and thus prefers the intransitive meaning "punish." Assmann (Hymnen, 501, 640) sees this mixing or mingling of people as their coming together, and thus renders šbb as zusammenströmen, "flow or stream together, assemble": "bei seinen Nahen aber strömen die Menschen zusammen" ("But at his approach people assemble"). This coming together contrasts with the people's wandering (wandern) in the previous line, although Assmann does not comment on this relationship (but see Helck, Nilhymnus, 22). In contrast, Foster ("Thought Couplets," 17) interprets šbb as an imperfective participle with Hapj as subject and rmṯ the object: "Who confuses mankind as to when he draws near."

 33. qd.n sw ḥnmw. As the creator of Hapj, the god Khnum fashions him as he wishes. Thus the type of inundation — and the response of the people to it in the previous line — depends on how Khnum has created Hapj in any given year. Meeks inserts a full stop after ḥsf.f, relating the sḏm.n.f with what follows: "Khnoum l'a façonné: il apparaît et la terre . . ." (review, 25).

 34. ṯzt nb.t šzp.n.s sbjt. I read ṯzt as "jawbone" (following Assmann, Hymnen, 501 [Kiefer] and Lichtheim in Ancient Egyptian Literature, 1.206).

 35. On the copies and fragments see H.-W. Fischer-Elfert, Die satirische Streitschrift des Papyrus Anastasi I: Textzusammenstellung (Kleine ägyptische Texte; Wiesbaden: Harrassowitz, 1983) 1-4; see also 51-52, 76. See further A. H. Gardiner, Egyptian Hieratic Texts. Series I: Literary Texts of the New Kingdom, Part I. The Papyrus Anastasi and the Papyrus Koller, together with the Parallel Texts (Leipzig: Hinrichs, 1911) 1*-34* (reprinted Hildesheim: 1964); ANET, 475-79; Fischer-Elfert, Die satirische Streitschrift des Papyrus Anastasi I: Übersetzung und Kommentar (Ägyptologische Abhandlungen 44; Wiesbaden: Harrassowitz, 1986) 37, 44, 68, 71; Wente, Letters, 98-110.

(7.8) I shall speak to you (of) numerous things, and pour out to you[36] choice morsels (of wisdom)[37] (8.1) just as Hapj overflows, (and) the flood-waters glisten[38] during the season of inundation when he overtakes the elevated mounds.[39]

2. Effects of Low Inundations (Famine)

a. Tomb Autobiography of Khetj I (9th Dynasty, ca. 2160-2106 B.C.E.)

As nomarch over the 13th nome of Lower Egypt, Khetj boasts of his actions on behalf of the town Asyut during an apparent period of draught due to a low inundation or perhaps a series of such. According to the text, Khetj supervised the construction of various dams and canals to insure the proper irrigation of unaffected areas.[40]

36. *ttf.j n.k.* The verb *ttf* is also used of the inundation *(ḥ'pj)* in Papyrus Leiden 348 (see A. Gardiner, *Late-Egyptian Miscellanies* (Bibliotheca Aegyptiaca 7; Brussels: Édition de la fondation Égyptologique Reine Élisabeth, 1937) 45, ll. 15-16; and R. A. Caminos, *Late-Egyptian Miscellanies* (Brown Egyptological Studies 1; London: Oxford University, 1954) 174-76.

37. My translation intentionally reflects the fact that *stp.w* also relates to food. Others (e.g., Wente, Gardiner, Wilson in *ANET,* 476a) render "choice words" or "choice things."

38. *bȝq(.tj)*, following Anastasi I and Fischer-Elfert's suggested combination of Anastasi I and variants (*Kommentar,* 68). The idea seems to be the reflection of the sun on the waters (cf. Lichtheim, *Ancient Egyptian Literature,* 3.99 [the Famine Stela]; and note also the comments of Janssen, "Inundation," 133n.46).

39. Anastasi I has *jȝd.t,* "field, meadow, pasture"; variants include *jȝ.t,* "(raised) mound, tell, kom," and *ȝ.t,* "moment." Fischer-Elfert (*Kommentar,* 68) adopts the first-mentioned reading with *Viehweiden,* but cautions that it would be difficult to defend one reading over another.

40. My translation generally follows M. Lichtheim, *Ancient Egyptian Autobiographies Chiefly of the Middle Kingdom: A Study and an Anthology* (OBO 84; Fribourg: Universitätsverlag; Göttingen: Vandenhoeck & Ruprecht, 1988) 26-29, but with some modifications. See F. Ll. Griffith, *The Inscriptions of Siut and Der Rifeh* (London, 1889 [not seen by me]); Vandier, *La famine,* 101; H. Brunner, *Die Texte aus den Gräben der Herakleopolitanzeit von Siut, mit Überstezung und Erläuterungen* (Ägyptologische Forschungen 5; Glückstadt: J. J. Augustin, 1937) 64-65; E. Edel, *Die Inschriften der Grabfronten der Siut-Gräber in Mittelägypten aus der Herakleopolitenzeit* (Abhandlungen der Rheinisch-Westfälischen Akademie der Wissenschaften 71; Opladen: Westdeutscher Verlag, 1984) 158-59. Note also the translations in *ARE* 1.188-89; W. Schenkel, *Memphis, Herakleopolis, Theben. Die epigraphischen Zeugnisse der 7.-11. Dynastie Ägyptens* (Ägyptologische Abhandlungen 12; Wiesbaden: Harrassowitz, 1965) 71-74; idem, *Bewässerungsrevolution,* 29-30.

(3) I constructed a monument with —— I dammed up(?)[41] a watercourse ten cubits (in width), excavating for it in plowland. I set up a gate[42] (4) —— . . . . I was broad with respect to the monument(s) (and) exact with respect to (5) the quay[43] —— I brought life to the town. I made the workman as one who eats northern barley. I gave out water rations in midday (6) to let the wea[ry] recover —— I constructed a sluice-way(?)[44] for this town, while Upper Egypt was in a bad way with no water in sight. (7) . . . I made the hig[h ground][45] into marshland. I made *ḥ῾pj* flow over the old mounds. (8) I let the plowlands be in[undat]ed while every neighborhood[46] thir[sted. Everyone had] *ḥ῾pj* to his heart's content. . . . (9) I am one rich in northern barley while the land is in drought; one who keeps the town alive by means of the *m῾ḏзt* measure.[47]

b. Stela of Mentuhotpe, Son of Hepj (11th Dynasty, ca. 2106-1963)

Acquired by W. Flinders Petrie in 1894, this limestone stela highlights the virtuous life and pious deeds of one Mentuhotpe, "Hereditary Prince, Nomarch, Overseer of Priests." In recounting his reign as nomarch, Mentuhotpe makes reference to his efforts on behalf of his district during a "low inundation" *(ḥ῾pj šr)*.[48]

41. *ḏbз.n(.j) jtr.w.* The precise meaning of *ḏbз* is uncertain. Schenkel opts tentatively for *blockieren* or *absperren*, which I follow here (for other options, see Schenkel, *Bewässerungsrevolution*, 30n.100). Lichtheim (*Autobiographies*, 24) suggests "layed out," with a note to Schenkel's discussion of the term.

42. Or "door" *(sbз)*. See Schenkel, *Bewässerungsrevolution*, 30n.101.

43. The intended sense of *jnk wsḥ mnw ῾qз mrt* is unclear. Note Breasted, who translates "I was liberal as to the monument" (*ARE* 1.189). For "quay," I follow Lichtheim, who reads *mrjt*, "bank, shore, quay," instead of *mr(r)t*, "street" (Lichtheim, *Autobiographies*, 29n.5).

44. ῾ plus water determinative (*WbÄS* 1.159.7). See Schenkel, *Bewässerungsrevolution*, 30n.108 for alternate readings and further discussion on pp. 33-34.

45. Reading *qз[j.t]*, on which see Schenkel, *Bewässerungsrevolution*, 60-62.

46. *gs.wj* (*WbÄS* 5.193-94). See Edel, *Inschriften*, 81, for discussion.

47. *s῾nḥ njwt m ḥз m῾ḏз.t.* For *m῾ḏз.t* as a type of measure, see D. Mueller, "A Middle Egyptian Word for 'Measure,'" *JEA* 58 (1972) 301-2; and Schenkel, *Bewässerungsrevolution*, 31n.16.

48. Text (University College, London, no. U.C. 14333) and translation in F. Ll. Griffith, "Stela of Mentuhetep son of Hepy," *Proceedings of the Society of Biblical Archaeology* 18 (1896) 195-204; Vandier, *La famine*, 113 [partial]; H. Goedicke, "A Neglected Wisdom Text," *JEA* 48 (1962) 25-35; and W. Schenkel, *Frühmittelägyptische Studien* (Bonner orientalistische Studien n.s. 13; Bonn: Orientalische Seminars der Universität Bonn, 1962) 114-15.

(8) . . . (When) a low inundation happened in the 25th year,[49] (9) I did not allow (my) nome to starve. I gave it barley and emmer from Upper Egypt and did not allow misery to overcome it before great inundations[50] returned.

c. Tomb Autobiography of Amenemhet at Beni Hasan (12th Dynasty, sub Sesostris I; Reigned ca. 1943-1898)

As an indication of his extreme benevolence in governing his nome, Amenemhet, like Khetj and Mentuhotpe, provided for his people during a time of famine due to low inundations.[51]

> There came years of famine. (20) Then I plowed all the fields of the Oryx nome to its southern and northern border, and kept alive its inhabitants, provided its supplies, and none hungered in it. . . . (21) . . . Then came high inundations,[52] rich in barley and emmer, rich in all things, and I did not exact the arrears of the field.

3. High Inundations (Destruction of Buildings, Crops, and Irrigation Works)

a. The Inundation Stela of Sebekhotpe VIII (13th Dynasty, ca. 1786-1633)

Preserved on two surviving fragments of a hard limestone stela unearthed from the foundation of the Third Pylon of the temple of Amun-Re at Karnak in the late 1950s, the following text relates the king's involvement in the inspection of flood damage to the temple of Amun, presumably at Karnak where the text was

---

49. *jw ḥpr ḥ῾pj šr r rnpt* 25. Griffith and Vandier took the preposition *r* as part of *šr* (see Vandier's arrangement of the signs). But Goedicke's photograph of the stela shows how the preposition *r* has been squeezed in between *šr* and *rnpt*, its left corner up against the slightly effaced palm branch in *rnpt*. (For *r* with reference to time, see *WbÄS* 2.387.25-26.) The name of the king to whom the year applies is not given (see Goedicke, 31, for the two options, both of which are from the 11th Dynasty).

50. Here written with plural strokes, *ḥ῾p(j).w ῾3j.w*, "great inundations." The use of *῾3j* with *ḥ῾pj*, as opposed to *ḥ῾pj šr*, suggests that the former adjective denotes a "normal," or at least not too low, inundation.

51. The translation is from Lichtheim with minor changes. See P. E. Newberry, *Beni Hasan, Part I* (Egyptian Exploration Society, Memoir 1; London: Kegan Paul, Trench, Trubner, 1893) 27 and pl. 8; *ARE* 1.253; Vandier, *La famine*, 114; and Lichtheim, *Autobiographies*, 135-39.

52. *῾ḥ῾.n ḥ῾pr.w wr.w.* Although the text uses the adjective *wr* instead of *῾3j*, the same implication (stated above) remains, i.e., that these inundations were within normal parameters. Thus, it would appear that either adjective, *῾3j* or *wr*, could denote a normal inundation — neither too low nor too high (see further sub Sebekhotpe text, §III.3.a).

discovered. The scene above the text depicts the king receiving offerings from
Hapj ($ḥ'pj$ '$3j;$ on the right in fecundity figure form) and worshiping Amun-Re.[53]

Recto (Habachi, "High Inundation," fig. 1): (2) One of these days it
[happe]ned [that His Person set out to visit the temple] (3) of Amun and
His Person discovered a great inundation (there).[54] [His Pers]on came [to
see the great inundation] (4) that was in the hall of the chapel[55] of this temple.
Then [His Person] proceeded [to wade in the water standing] (5) inside the
hall of the chapel, along with the c[ourtiers (?). . . .] (6) the[ir. . . .]

Verso (Habachi, fig. 3): (3) His Person proceeded to the hall of this temple
<in order to>[56] see the great inundation. (4) His Person came <to> the hall
of this temple, it being full of water. Then His Person (5) waded in it with
the magistrates.[57] Then the person of [this] king spoke as follows (6) [. . . text
breaks off]

53. Suggested restorations mostly follow Baines. See L. Habachi, "A High Inundation
in the Temple of Amenre at Karnak in the Thirteenth Dynasty," *Studien zur altägyptischen
Kultur* 1 (1974) 207-14; J. Baines, "The Inundation Stela of Sebekḥotpe VIII," *AcOr* 36 (1974)
39-58; idem, "The Sebekḥotpe VIII Inundation Stela: An Additional Fragment," *AcOr* 37
(1976) 11-20; W. Helck, *Historisch-biographische Texte der 2. Zwischenzeit und neue Texte der
18 Dynastie* (Kleine ägyptische Texte; Wiesbaden: Harrassowitz, 1975) 46-47 (no. 63).

54. $ḥ'pj$ wr. On both verso and recto, Sebekhotpe is given the epithet $ḥ'pj$ '$3j$ $mrjj$,
"beloved of the great inundation," and in one instance the title is followed by the divine
determinative (verso, l. 1). Elsewhere, the stela has $ḥ'pj$ wr (except in the fragmentary l. 7 of
verso, which has '$3j$ without divine determinative, but the text is broken here). Given the
divine determinative present only with '$3j$, Baines ("Inundation Stela," 41) suggests that $ḥ'pj$
wr refers to the physical inundation, while $ḥ'pj$ '$3j$ reflects its personification. This may well
be the case in this particular stela, but the oftentimes unpredictable interchange of these
adjectives in other texts (with $ḥ'pj$), as noted above, limits the applicability of such a distinction. I have as yet no logical explanation for this in these and other texts relating to the
inundation. For examples of inconsistent usage, compare de Buck's example no. 22 with nos.
3, 27, 38, 44, 45 ("Meaning of the Name $Ḥ'pj$"). See also discussion in Janssen, "Inundation,"
131. At times the two may even occur together; see, e.g., T. G. H. James, *The Ḥekanakhte
Papers and Other Early Middle Kingdom Documents* (Metropolitan Museum of Art Egyptian
Expedition 19; New York: Metropolitan Museum of Art, 1962) 28-29, n. 72; Habachi, "High
Inundation," 213; and text no. 33 from the Karnak quay (J. von Beckerath, "The Nile Level
Records at Karnak and Their Importance for the History of the Libyan Period [Dynasties
XXII and XXIII]," *Journal of the American Research Center in Egypt* 5 [1966] no. 33).

55. $ḥwt-nṯr$. See discussion in Baines, "Inundation Stela," 12-13, n. j.

56. Following Baines ("Inundation Stela," 41; and "Sebekḥotpe VIII," 13), who suggests
the omission of particular prepositions (r and $ḥr$) in the stela. Habachi's translation of $m3$
as passive with $ḥ'pj$ wr as subject (p. 210) is awkward and breaks up the expected narrative
sequence, which tends to emphasize the actions of the king (see also Baines, "Inundation
Stela," 12, who objects to the translation on other grounds).

57. Reading $qnbt$, Helck's restoration (*Texte*, 47).

b. Column from el-Dibâbîya during Smendes I (21st Dynasty, Reigned ca. 1069-1043)

This hieroglyphic inscription, partially preserved on a column fragment, was discovered by Darssey in the ruins of a quarry at el-Dibâbîya, opposite Gebelein. The column no longer survives; thus we are dependent on Darssey's 1888 publication of the text. The inscription poses many difficulties, some of which may have originated with Darssey's copy.[58]

(4) . . . Lo, His Person was sitting in the col[umned hall[59] —— said to?[60]]
(5) His Person: The canal wall(?)[61] bordering the Luxor temple,[62] the one built by king Thutmose III, has fall[en into ruin][63] —— (6) was like a great flood[64] swiftly/greatly (?) approaching . . . toward the great wall of the temple and overturned (?)[65] —— (7) [His Person responded] to them: As for this

58. B. Porter and R. L. B. Moss, *Topographical Bibliography of Ancient Egyptian Hieroglyphic Texts, Reliefs, and Paintings* (Oxford: Clarendon, 1937) 5.170 (hereafter PM). G. Daressy, "Les carrières de Gebelein et le roi Smendés," *Recueil de travaux . . . égyptiennes et assyriennes* 10 (1888) 131-38; *ARE* 4.308-9.

59. Possibly reading *w3[hj]* ?. See *WbÄS* 1.259.12-13; and Faulkner, *Concise Dictionary*, 54.

60. The space may have contained a *jw.tw* formula concerning the arrival of messengers to inform the king of an important event. See A. Spalinger, *Aspects of the Military Documents of the Ancient Egyptians* (YNER 9; New Haven and London: Yale University, 1982) 1-33, for these in military texts. Such formulae are often employed to call attention to the reaction of the king and his subsequent wisdom in handling the situation.

61. ʿ *jnt* (?). For ʿ (*WbÄS* 1.159.7) as "watercourse," see Schenkel, *Bewässerungsrevolution*, 33-34. *jnt* makes little sense to me. Perhaps one should read *jnb*, "wall" (?), or even *inr*, "stone," i.e., some type of stone construction for the passage of water (?) or to protect the temple from floodwaters (?).

62. *Ipt rsjt*, the Luxor temple complex, the earliest and southernmost portion, constructed during the reign of Amenhotpe III, for which see generally S. Aufrere, J.-C. Golvin, and J.-C. Goyon, *L'Egypte restituée: Sites et temples de haute Égypte (1650 av J.-C.–300 ap. J.C.)* (Paris: Editions Errance, 1991) 127-41; and A. P. Kozloff, B. M. Bryan, and L. M. Berman, *Egypt's Dazzling Sun: Amenhotep III and his World* (Cleveland: Cleveland Museum of Art, 1992) 82-90. It should be noted that nothing from the time of Thuthmose III survives at the site.

63. Reading *w3 r* [+ noun], "to decay, fall into ruin" (*WbÄS* 1.243ff.). One might also restore *w3[sj]*, "collapsed, decayed" (*WbÄS* 1.260-61). The text goes on to speak of a destructive flood, which I take to be the result of the decayed or fallen retaining structure, but this is uncertain. One might just as easily infer that the ruin of the wall was the result of, or at least precipitated by, a high inundation.

64. *hj(.t)* ʿ*3.t*. For *hj* see *WbÄS* 3.48-49; and Meeks, *Année*, 1.240; 2.242. One might also conceivably read *h'pj* instead of *hj(.t)*. The former does not otherwise appear in the text, at least what is preserved of it.

65. *jqh.w wr* (!) *m* [verb?] .*f r s3t* ʿ*3.t n hwt-ntr wdb.f hn*[. . . For *jqh*, see (in addition to *WbÄS* 1.138 — examples from Edfu and Dendara) Meeks, *Année*, 1.48; 2.52. The adjective *wr* is problematic, although it may be taken adverbially (see Gardiner, *Egyptian Grammar*, 156). Based on the preposition (*r*) that follows, I think some type of verbal form should be read, in parallel with *wdb.f*, which begins the next clause.

matter presented to me, not a thing (like it had occurred) during (my) reign, the like of it is unknown —— (8) . . .

c. The Flooding of the Luxor Temple under Osorkon III (23rd Dynasty, Reigned ca. 787-759)

This text, a hieratic graffito from the northwest corner of the forecourt of Amenophis III at Luxor, was discovered and first published by Darssey in 1896. Darssey found the text difficult to read due to the wall's worn and cracked surface, and it is no longer extant. As a result, we again depend on his reading of the hieratic, which most likely was not without error.[66]

(2) . . . the flood [Nun] flowed forth [covering?] this land in its entirety (3) (and) extended up to the hills as (it was) at the beginning [of creation][67] . . . this land in its power like the sea. There was no (4) man-made dyke that could withstand its might, all the people being like birds (?) in their town.[68] It ra[ged and] over[came] —— like the sky,[69] (with) (5) all the Theban temples like [Delta] marshlands. That day Amun-of-Luxor caused to appear the —— [70] of his image —— (6) which entered into the shrine of the sacred barque at the temple opening (?). Its [= Luxor's?] townspeople (were) like swimmers in the waves. . . . (13) . . . One who comes as (?) Hapj[71] (14) to flood the two lands, to cause everyone to live and flourish. . . . (32) the flood spewed forth and continued the coming of the waters. (33) Such a state of affairs was a great curse with no memory of anything like it, a side of the

---

66. PM II^2 317(98). G. Daressy, "Une inondation a Thèbes sous le règne d'Osorkon II," *Recueil de travaux . . . égyptiennes et assyriennes* 18 (1896) 181-86; idem, "Le voyage d'inspection de M. Grébaut en 1889," *Annales du Service des antiquités de l'Egypte* 26 (1926) 7n.3; *ARE* 4.369; Vandier, *La famine*, 123; J. von Beckerath, "Nile Level Records," 44-45; C. Traunecker, "Les rites de l'eau a Karnak d'apres les textes de la rampe de Taharqa," *BIFAO* 72 (1972) 199; I. E. S. Edwards, "Egypt: From the Twenty-second to the Twenty-fourth Dynasty," *CAH* III/I (2nd ed. 1982) 567; J. Assmann, *Re und Amun*, 253. I am aware of, but have not seen, A. de Buck's treatment of this text in his 1922 dissertation, *De egyptische voorstellingen betreffende den oerheuvel* (Leiden: Eduard Ijdo, 1922).

67. *zp tpj*, "the First Occasion," a reference to the creation via the emergence of land from the Primeval Waters or Nun.

68. *ḥr-nb rmṭ m ḥmwj.w ḥr njwt.f*. The sense of this passage is not clear. Vandier *(La famine)* translated *hmwj.w* (*WbÄS* 3.277) as "sandflies" *(mouches de sable)*, but the word carries a determinative indicative of some type of bird. Thus, I have rendered it as such, with no attempt to ascertain the precise meaning.

69. Following Vandier's suggested restoration of two *sḏm.n.f* forms *(nšnj.n.f* and *ḫj.n.f)* with Nun (or the flood) as subject, although this reading is by no means certain. The preserved determinative for house or temple preceding *mj* most likely indicates the destruction of buildings, probably temples.

70. Vandier reads otherwise, seeing a reference to the departure of Amun from Luxor implied by the processional elevation or appearance of his divine image.

71. The reference here appears to be to Amun-Re.

Luxor temple being swallowed up (34) by the waters. Who among the people could fathom it? (35) Hapj flows forth at your [Amun-Re's] command. . . .

d. High Inundation during the Sixth Year of Taharqa (25th Dynasty, Reigned 690-664)

Of all extant texts relating the effects of a high inundation, the one of Taharqa's sixth year from his temple at Kawa is most often cited and indeed is the fullest description we possess of such an event and its aftermath.[72]

(3) . . . This land was inundated (4) during his reign as it had been in the days of the Lord of All. (5) Miracles occurred in His Person's time during the sixth year of his reign, the like of which had not been seen since the time of the Divine Ancestors, inasmuch as his [Taharqa's] father Amun loved him. His Person (6) had been praying for an inundation[73] from his father Amun-Re, Lord of the Thrones of the Two Lands, to avert the occurrence of famine during his time. Now as for everything spoken by His Person, his father Amun-Re brings it about immediately, and when the time of the flooding (7) of Hapj arrived, he [Hapj] flooded abundantly every day and continued many days, rising at a height of one cubit per day. He penetrated the mountains of Upper Egypt and covered[74] the mounds of Lower Egypt [i.e., the turtlebacks of the Delta]. The land was like the Primeval Waters, like the inert waters.[75] There was no distinguishing (8) the

---

72. Line numbers follow the K text found in Macadam, *Temples of Kawa*, 1.24-26; see specifically 1.22-32 (Inscription V) and vol. 2, pls. 9-10. See further V. Vikentiev, *La haute crue du Nil et l'averse de l'an 6 du roi Taharqa* (Université Égyptienne, Recueil de Travaux publiés par la Faculté des Lettres 4; Cairo: L'Institut français d'archéologie orientale, 1930); Vandier, *La famine*, 124-25; J. Leclant and J. Yoyotte, "Nouveaux documents relatifs a l'an VI de Taharqa," *Kemi* 10 (1949) 28-37 and pls. I and III; idem, "Notes d'histoire et de civilisation Éthiopiennes. À propos d'un ouvrage récent," *BIFAO* 51 (1952) 1-39 (esp. 20-29); G. Posener, *De la divinité du pharaon* (Cahiers de la société asiatique 15; Paris: Imprimerie Nationale, 1960) 54-55; Leclant, *Recherches*, 244-45; Traunecker, "Les rites," 199; A. Rainey, "Taharqa and Syntax," *Tel Aviv* 3 (1976) 38-41; K. A. Kitchen, *The Third Intermediate Period in Egypt (1100-650 BC)* (2nd ed.; Warminster: Aris and Phillips, 1986) 166-70, 388-89.

73. *ḥ'pj* without a qualifying adjective. One might expect *wr* or *'3j*. Thus, one should not assume that Taharqa was asking for a high inundation. Perhaps inundations previous had been low (already implied by Vandier, *La famine*, 29; also Macadam, *Temples of Kawa*, 19) — thus producing famine according to the text — and the king was hoping for a normal flood. Or perhaps the scribe just erred with the omission of an adjective.

74. *ḥrj-tp*, "to be above," over" (*WbÄS* 3.141.12-13). The compound is attested as a verb in texts from Esna; see H. W. Fairman, "An Introduction to the Study of Ptolemaic Signs and Their Values," *BIFAO* 43 (1945) 51-138, esp. 108. But de Buck noted a Middle Kingdom example with the meaning "to rule over" (see his "The Building Inscription of the Berlin Leather Roll," in *Studia Aegyptiaca I* [AnOr 17; ed. A. M. Blackman et al.; Rome: Pontifical Biblical Institute, 1938] 49, ll. 9 and 54, n. 15). The context here requires the general meaning of "flood over" or the like.

75. Again, a reference to the time of creation (as others have recognized; see Macadam, *Temples of Kawa*, 30n.39).

emergent land[76] from the river[77] . . . [the text continues with Egypt in happy festival and the king pleased with Amun-Re's actions, etc.] (11) . . . Hapj came like a cattle thief[78] and inundated the land in its entirety. Nothing like it could be found in the records from the time of the ancestors; none stated "I (once) heard (of such a thing) from my father." He [Amun?] made the fields fertile throughout, slew the rats and snakes in it [the cultivation], drove away devouring locusts from it, and did not allow the South Wind to reap it. (13) I reaped the harvest (bringing it) into the Double Granary, its amount beyond calculation, consisting of Upper Egyptian and Lower Egyptian barley and every type of seed upon the earth.

e. A High Inundation during the Reign of Amasis (26th Dynasty, Reigned ca. 570-526)

Housed in the Cairo Museum since 1903 (Cairo #JE37494), this upper fragment of a sandstone stela was found at Mit Rahineh and first published by Darssey in 1923. The handful of preserved lines relate flood damage to the Memphis area during the king's twenty-ninth year.[79]

(2) . . . A great inundation[80] came to His Majesty; it flooded both Upper and Lower Egypt and covered the two shores. (3) One came to inform His Person (as follows): The southern revetment wall that is behind Memphis has been knocked down[81] by the floodwaters,[82] and the nor[thern?] w[all] is in danger (of collapse as well). (4) Then the king (?) res[ponded], I am the Good God [text breaks off here]

4. Discussion

A full treatment of the above texts is not possible here; however, a few general points are worthy of note, particularly with respect to the role of the king.

The texts almost invariably connect low inundations with famine, which here provides the backdrop for the subject's autobiographical self-presentation, including a recounting of his beneficent actions performed on behalf of the

76. Egyptian *m3w.t*, "new land, island"; see Schenkel, *Bewässerungsrevolution*, 62-65.
77. The use of *jtrw* here demonstrates the distinction between the inundation and the river itself.
78. Egyptian *jw.n.h'pj m jt k3.w*.
79. Suggested restorations follow Vandier, *La famine*, 125; see also p. 126. See further PM III[2] 870; Daressy, "La crue du Nil de l'an XXIX d'Amasis," *ASAE* 23 (1923) 47-48; Spalinger, *Aspects of Military Documents*, 19.
80. Egyptian *h'pj wr*.
81. *whn dnjt rsjt ntt h3 jbd-hd*. Reading a passive *sdm.f* used in past narrative.
82. Reading *jn mw.f* (with Vandier).

community.[83] Thus, calamitous low inundations in and of themselves do not necessarily possess primary textual significance, and literary descriptions of these serve principally to set in sharper relief the subject's response and subsequent normal or high floods, as one finds in the four texts here presented in §III.2a-c. The return of normal inundations becomes synonymous with well-being, abundance, and prosperity. Provincial officials even sometimes assumed epithets illustrative of their actions to avert widespread famine. For example, in his autobiography, Khetj I adds among his titles "Great Inundation."[84]

Leaving biographies, one finds that the most instructive accounts of high inundations relate to temples, the person of the king, and the granting of the latter's petition, usually to Amun, for a high inundation. That Amun hears and grants the prayer of Taharqa implies that the king pleases the god and thus partially fulfills his role as king. As with the autobiographies, the inundation itself is secondary to the overall purpose of the narrative. In nearly every case, the role and response of the king are predominant, especially with Sebekhotpe and Taharqa.

Although high inundations could be clearly destructive, accounts narrating their occurrence are often ambivalent in that they concomitantly portray the event in a positive light.[85] That is, with respect to the king and the gods, a high inundation was a very auspicious event, yet at the same time the destruction it

83. This correlation between low inundations and famine has potential implications for the traditional interpretation of Isa 19:5-10, where the drying of the Nile waters and the cessation of various industries dependent on the river have convinced many that the writer depicts the effects of a low inundation. While not denying the latter's knowledge of the Nile and its utilization in Egypt, it is, I believe, worthy of note that famine is not mentioned in these verses. An examination of the potentially relevant verbs in vv. 8-10 (principally *'bl* and *'mll*, which nearly always occur in tandem) provides, as far as I can tell, no implication of hunger or starvation. Thus, for whatever reason, the author does not mention what is, from the Egyptian point of view, the most important and indicative consequence of a low inundation, i.e., the widespread starvation of the populace. The drying up of the Nile would no doubt have crippled the entire economy and country, regardless of whether this came about via a low inundation or as the direct result of Yahweh's judgment (for the latter, see Ezek 30:12 and the drying of the Euphrates in Jer 51:36).

For iconographic evidence relative to famine in ancient Egypt, see É. Drioton, "Une représentation de la famine sur un bas-relief égyptien de la V[E] dynastie," *Bulletin de l'Institut d'Égypte* 25 (1942-43) 44-54; and J. Vercoutter, "Les 'affamés' d'Ounas et la changement climatique de la fin de l'ancien empire," in *Mélanges Gamal Eddin Mokhtar* (ed. P. Posener-Kriéger; 2 vols.; Bibliothèque d'études 97; Cairo: IFAO, 1985) 2.327-37.

84. Egyptian *ḥʿpj ʿ[ʒj]*; see Edel, *Die Inschriften*, 159, l. 44; and Lichtheim, *Autobiographies*, 27. The top portion of ʿ is preserved in Wilkinson's drawing (see Edel, *Die Inschriften*, 160).

85. Nevertheless, the destruction of temples and other buildings is prominent in almost every text relating a high inundation. Thus, its absence in the Exodus account of the first two plagues, where many have assumed an abnormally high Nile level, is, I believe, of some consequence. The most elaborate and detailed presentation of the idea that a high inundation triggered the series of plagues remains that of Greta Hort ("The Plagues of Egypt," *ZAW* 69 [1957] 84-103; 70 [1958] 48-59). See further my critical comments on Hort in "Nile (OT)," *ABD* 4.1109-10; and note also Sarna, *Exploring Exodus*, 73-77.

wrought was not so. For example, despite the apparent massive and devastating flooding during the reign of Osorkon III, graphically described in the text (leaving room for exaggeration), one reads toward the end of the inscription (l. 35) that the inundation nevertheless flows at Amun-Re's command. Elsewhere, mention is made of Hapj's causing everyone to live and flourish (l. 14), and the allusion to creation (in l. 3) is, I believe, also intended positively.

The best example of this tendency to stress only the beneficial aspects of an abnormally high, and thus largely destructive, inundation is found in the account dating to Taharqa's sixth year. According to the Nile levels at Karnak,[86] this inundation was the highest recorded, even higher than that of Osorkon III, yet the reader observes the absence of any reference to the destruction of temples or other structures, as was seen in the Osorkon text. As others have noted, an inundation of this magnitude must have produced a great deal of damage. But, lacking any hint of destruction, the text focuses on the relationship between Amun and Taharqa. Amun's love for the king insures that the latter's petition will not go unheeded, and emphasis is placed on the fact that Amun brings about the miraculous event. The high inundation results in a bumper crop, which was protected by Amun until the time of harvest. Thus, royal ideology dictates not only what the text says but what it does not say as well. Maintaining the ideologically correct position of the king vis-à-vis the gods outweighs all other considerations.

IV. Jeremiah 46:7-8

Keeping in mind the role of the king mentioned above, I turn now to the earlier mentioned passage from the book of Jeremiah. In his seminal study of the image of Assyria in First Isaiah,[87] Peter Machinist examined, among other texts, the vivid description of the Assyrian king in Isa 8:7-8. Here the march of the Neo-Assyrian monarch and his army is likened to a raging river that overflows its banks, extending to the land of Judah (the translation is that of Machinist):

> And so, look now, Yahweh is bringing upon them the waters of the River, mighty and numerous, (namely), the king of Assyria and all his glory, and he shall run over all his courses, and go over all his banks. And he will push on against Judah, overflow and sweep over, reaching even the neck. And his outspread wings will fill the breadth of your land, O Immanuel.

As Machinist has noted, the simile of the king advancing in battle like a raging flood is a familiar one in Neo-Assyrian texts and, for that matter,

---

86. For the inundation levels, see von Beckerath, "Nile Level Records," 44, 49, 53 (inscription no. 5 [Osorkon III] and nos. 34-35 [Taharqa]).

87. P. Machinist, "Assyria and Its Image in the First Isaiah," *JAOS* 103 (1983) 719-37.

occurs elsewhere in the Hebrew Bible.[88] Mesopotamian influence would seem to apply as well to Jer 46:7-8, which parallel in some respects the passage in Isaiah 8:

> Who is this that rises like the Nile, like streams whose waters surge? It is Egypt that rises like the Nile, like streams whose waters surge, that said, "I will rise, I will cover the earth, I will wipe out towns and those who dwell in them" (NJPS).

Given that the river here is the Nile, however, one might plausibly conclude that the surging waters reflect the inundation, and scholars have in fact made this connection, either directly or through citation of other biblical passages concerning the rising and falling of the Nile.[89] In a footnote mentioning this passage, Machinist observes that, while the motif appears to be Mesopotamian in origin, it is nevertheless applied to an Egyptian king, Necho II, who ironically — an intentional move on the writer's part — is defeated by Nebuchadrezzar "at the river Euphrates."[90]

88. See ibid., 726-27, for an example from the reign of Esarhaddon. See the earlier discussion and relevant examples of D. Hillers, who noted a possible connection to some prophetic passages (*Treaty-Curses and the Old Testament Prophets* [BibOr 16; Rome: Pontifical Institute, 1964] 70-71), and, prior to him, the recognition of this topos in the ancient Near East and the Bible by P. Reymond (*L'eau, sa vie, et sa signification dans l'ancien testament* [VTSup 6; Leiden: Brill, 1958] 108-9). The flood or deluge may refer to the king in battle (e.g., "the warrior among the gods, Deluge of battle") or to the weapon wielded by the king (e.g., "they [the gods] put into my hand their mighty weapons, the Deluge [weapon] for the battle"; see *CAD* A, s.v. *"abūbu,"* 79 [2c and 3b]). The idiom predates Neo-Assyrian usage, but is lacking in Neo-Babylonian texts.

Biblical examples include Jer 47:2; Dan 11:10 and 40; Exod 15:8; 2 Sam 5:20 (= 1 Chr 14:11); and Nah 1:8. While the language is similar to Jer 46:7-8, the destructive waters from the north in Jer 47:2 most likely refer to the Babylonians. This "enemy from the north" motif is esp. prominent in the book of Jeremiah (see B. S. Childs, "The Enemy from the North and the Chaos Traditions," *JBL* 78 [1959] 187-98, esp. 190-95; and W. L. Holladay, *Jeremiah* [2 vols.; Hermeneia; Minneapolis: Fortress, 1986-89] 2.336-37).

89. See, e.g., E. A. Leslie, *Jeremiah Chronologically Arranged, Translated, and Interpreted* (New York and Nashville: Abingdon, 1954) 161; Reymond, *L'eau*, 89; W. Rudolph, *Jeremia* (2nd ed.; HAT I/12; Tübingen: Mohr/Siebeck, 1958) 249; Hillers, *Treaty-Curses*, 71; S. Morenz, "Nil," *BHH* 2.1313-14; A. Weiser, *Das Buch Jeremia* (6th ed.; ATD 20-21; Göttingen: Vandenhoeck & Ruprecht, 1969) 383; J. G. Snaith, "Literary Criticism and Historical Investigation in Jeremiah Chapter XLVI," *JSS* 16 (1971) 17; J. A. Thompson, *The Book of Jeremiah* (NICOT; Grand Rapids: Eerdmans, 1980) 688-89; K. A. Kitchen, "Nile," *New Bible Dictionary* (2nd ed.; Leicester, Eng.: Inter-Varsity, 1982) 836; and Holladay, *Jeremiah*, 2.320.

90. Machinist, "Assyria," 728n.49: "To be sure, in Jeremiah 46:7-8, it is Necho, not Nebuchadnezzar, who is made to boast that he will rise like the Nile and destroy. Yet in this, the Biblical author seems to be playing not only with an Egyptian image, the Nile overflowing, but also with the Mesopotamian tradition of the king as raging flood, since he creates Necho's boastful words precisely to lampoon them in the light of the Pharaoh's actual defeat by Nebuchadnezzar 'at the river Euphrates.'"

Note, however, Holladay's differing view of vv. 7-8 in his comments on the waters

Given that Jeremiah 46 deals with Egypt, that is, the defeat of Necho (Neco) by the Babylonians, one might additionally expect to find evidence of Egyptian influence behind the portrayal of the king. Military inscriptions or reliefs would seem a good place to start. Is the king of Egypt in battle (or his army) ever compared to a raging, destructive flood (in this case the inundation, if the Jeremiah passage has been interpreted correctly)? The answer here would seem to be no. I have as yet been unable to locate any Egyptian evidence that might support the association.[91] Indeed, the contrary seems to be the case. The one recurring element in the king's relationship to the inundation is that the association is invariably a *positive* one, and this relates to my earlier remarks concerning official ideology with respect to the king of Egypt and the inundation.[92] Regardless of how brilliant or brave in the heat of battle — at least according to the official ideology

---

from the north in Jer 47:2: "the metaphor of waters from the north fits the Babylonians in 46:6-8, and there is no reason to find another identification here" (*Jeremiah*, 2.337). Earlier (p. 318) he concludes that the battle orders in 46:3-4 are addressed to the Babylonian army and thus "by implication" to the same in vv. 5-8. Holladay rejects the commonly held view that the Egyptian army is addressed due to the mention of cavalry in v. 4a (note Hebrew *sûsîm* and *pārāšîm*) and the supposed absence of such in the Egyptian military. Given this apparent lack, Holladay thus reasons that vv. 5-8 also must refer to the Babylonians (p. 318). His supporting references for this position (p. 319n.20), however, all of a secondary nature, are not persuasive. One does find evidence for the use of horse and rider in a military context (see A. R. Schulman, "Egyptian Representations of Horsemen and Riding in the New Kingdom," *JNES* 16 [1957] 263-71; and, for the 25th Dynasty, A. J. Spalinger, "Notes on the Military in Egypt during the XXVth Dynasty," *Journal of the Society for the Study of Egyptian Antiquities* 11 [1981] 35-58, esp. 47-48 and 52-58).

91. The only possible exception might be the Egyptian idiom *jtj + mj gp n mw*, which refers to the seizing of a city "like a cloudburst of water." The phrase occurs in the Instruction of King Merikare (l. 73; see J. F. Quack, *Studien zur Lehre für Merikare* [Göttinger Orient-forschungen, 4th series: Ägypten, vol. 23; Wiesbaden: Harrassowitz, 1992] 42-43, 179) and is later echoed (intentionally) in the victory stela of the Nubian king Pi(ankh)i regarding his capture of Permedjed and Memphis (see Lichtheim, *Ancient Egyptian Literature*, 3.71, 76; for the text, see N.-C. Grimal, *La stèle triomphale de Pi(ʿankh)y au Musée du Caire, JE 48862 et 47086-47089* [Études sur propogande royale Égyptienne I, MIFAO 105; Cairo: IFAO, 1981] 16*, l. 4; 32*, l. 18; 33*, l. 17; and p. 285). Granted, the king is associated with destructive waters in a military context; however, these passages in no way imply that the Nile or its inundation is involved. The phrase may be nothing more than an idiom signifying the rapidity and surprise with which an action is done (cf., e.g., our English "taken by storm"). For *gp* ("cloudburst"), see *WbÄS* 5.165-66; and W. A. Ward, "The Biconsonantal Doublet *gp/gb*, 'overflow,'" *JEA* 59 (1973) 228-31.

92. Evidence is not sparse on the king and the inundation. (See, e.g., the selections in N.-C. Grimal, *Les termes de la propoganda royale Égyptienne: De la XIXe dynastie à la conquête d'Alexandre* [Mémoires de l'Academie des Inscriptions et Belles-Lettres, n.s. 6; Paris: Imprimerie Nationale, 1986] 264-66; P. Germond, "Le roi et le retour de l'inondation," *Bulletin société d'égyptologie Genève* 1 [1979] 5-12; and discussion in Posener, *La divinité*, 54-61 and Leclant, *Recherches*, 243.) Note, e.g., the following: (1) bountiful inundations at the accession of the king (Caminos, *Miscellanies*, 324; (2) Hapj comes forth at the mention of the king's name (A. J. Peden, "The Quarrying Inscription of Ramesses V at West Silsila," *Or* 60 [1991] 336; (3) the king "makes verdant more than great Hapj" (Stela of Sehetep-ib-Re; Lichtheim, *Ancient Egyptian*

that pervades many texts — his destructive military might apparently bears no relation to an equally damaging flood due to a high inundation.

Thus, the inspiration for the writer's simile most likely derives not from Egypt but from Mesopotamia, as Machinist has maintained. At the same time, given the elements of waters, destruction, and so on, one should by no means overlook probable echoes of the so-called biblical *Chaoskampf* traditions, but one need not consider the two mutually exclusive. Other biblical passages relating to the inundation manifest this same tendency to portray the phenomenon in natural and mythological terms.[93] Jeremiah 46:7-8 is unique among biblical texts on this theme, however, in that the king is not Israelite or Mesopotamian but Egyptian. Did the writer intentionally apply Assyrian royal ideology to an Egyptian king, aware that such linkage was not itself Egyptian in origin? This seems unlikely. Perhaps he drew from, or was influenced by, already existing traditions, both Mesopotamian (via Isa 8:7-8?) and biblical (via Amos 8:8 and 9:5?).[94] Regardless of his sources or motivation, the application of Mesopotamian royal idiom to an Egyptian subject is instructive in and of itself, and one does find other examples of biblical writers portraying the king of Egypt in non-Egyptian terms.[95] If anything, these verses provide a much needed caution for those engaged in comparative studies: one should not take the content of a particular passage, in this case an oracle against Egypt, as the sole indicator of where, geographically speaking, one might search for suitable comparative material.

Literature, 1.128); (4) "the inundation is at his [the king's] service, he opens his cavern in order to give life to the Beloved Land" (scarab of Thuthmose III; see B. Jaeger, *Essai de classification et datation des scarabées Menkhéperrê* [OBO, Series archaeologica 2; Fribourg: Éditions Universitaires; Göttingen: Vandenhoeck & Ruprecht, 1982] 65). For examples of the king identified with fecundity figures, see Baines, *Fecundity Figures*, 211-12, 222-23, 238.

93. Observe, e.g., the description of the inundation in Amos 8:8 and 9:5, which clothes the bare facts of the phenomenon, i.e., the rising and falling of the Nile, in cosmic and mythological language. The resulting ambivalence is best perceived by F. I. Andersen and D. N. Freedman, who approach the imagery of these verses with the query "inundation or undulation?" (see their *Amos* [AB 24A; New York: Doubleday, 1989] 812-13). Compare also *gʾš* in Jer 46:7-8 (Hithpael and Hithpoel) with its use in Jer 5:22 (Hithpael), where one could make a case for mythological connotations (cf. Ps 104:9). Such overtones are also recognized in Jeremiah 46 by (among others) Reymond, *L'eau*, 123-24; Hillers, *Treaty-Curses*, 71; Snaith, "Literary Criticism," 18; Machinist, "Assyria," 727n.45; R. P. Carroll, *Jeremiah* (OTL; Philadelphia: Westminster, 1986) 764; and esp. H. G. May, "Some Cosmic Connotations of *mayim rabbîm*, 'Many Waters,'" *JBL* 74 (1955) 16, 19 (a seminal study frequently cited in this context).

94. One should not dismiss too hastily the possibility of inner biblical allusion given Jeremiah's apparent dependence on earlier prophetic traditions, including Amos and Isaiah (see Holladay, *Jeremiah*, 2.44-50). Holladay draws attention to these and other similarities (pp. 45, 49), noting in addition the reflection of Amos 2:14 in Jer 46:6, but he employs imprecise language with respect to the various degrees or types of borrowing.

95. See, e.g., the words attributed to the king of Egypt in Ezek 29:3, where Hebrew *tannîm* (read *tannîn*) is more at home within the context of Canaanite mythology. See my brief comments and further bibliography in "Nile (OT)," *ABD* 4.1111.

Writing and Editing

BRIAN PECKHAM

University of Toronto

In its heyday the historical-critical method was renowned for its ability to detect sources and the work of redactors. As time passed it was criticized for its excesses and omissions, for its obsession with attributing every conceivable inconcinnity to some intrusive hand, for its unscrupulous fragmentation of a perfectly good text in its search for a hypothetical original, and for its benign neglect of the secondary material and of the editorial processes that produced the books. Criticism yielded to discontent and disinterest as other methods emerged that could deal with the sources and redactions by integrating them into the final form of the text, or into the books they produced, or into the exegetical traditions to which they belonged.[1]

In the historical-critical method the editorial process, although it was not comprehended, guaranteed the historical sense of the texts. The work of the redactors was ignored but they themselves were the sigla and symbols of the amalgamation of sources and the proof that the tradition had developed over time. Their work stood out quite plainly and was marked by the literary oddities, repetitions, inconsistencies, and inconsequences in the text. The later methods that integrated these puzzles into the structure of books and the flow of the final form had to abandon the sources that they signified and the development of tradition that they hailed to save the literary and theological face of the text.[2]

---

1. Good examples of these methods include: Adele Berlin, *Poetics and Interpretation of Biblical Narrative* (Sheffield: Almond, 1983); G. A. Rendsburg, *The Redaction of Genesis* (Winona Lake, IN: Eisenbrauns, 1986); and M. Fishbane, *Biblical Interpretation in Ancient Israel* (Oxford: Clarendon, 1985).

2. Cf. R. Polzin, *Samuel and the Deuteronomist: A Literary Study of the Deuteronomistic History, Part Two: I Samuel* (New York: Harper & Row, 1989).

As this compromise of methods makes plain, the editorial process is a constant embarrassment that is integral to literary and historical tradition and that cannot be neglected without betraying one or the other. The combined methods must admit that authors composed from sources and that their editors contributed to the development of literary and historical tradition by rewriting their works under different circumstances, at a later time, and in the light of the literary and historical works that had appeared in the meantime. The contribution of the editors is clearly marked and deliberately separated from the original.[3] The original is preserved as the origin, inspiration, and norm of the later works that in turn provoked its reedition.[4] One can see composition and redaction, working together, as the substance of tradition, the reason for its complexity and depth, the origin of its literary form, and the source of its historical significance.[5]

Editing comprises annotation, commentary, and interpretation. Annotations mark the text to be considered. Commentary follows in the same place or is added at a more convenient spot and presents an alternative description, explanation, or argument that develops or conflicts with the original statement, narrative, or continuing train of thought. Interpretation is a complete rewriting of the whole original text that consists in bracketing and omitting some parts, emphasizing others, and substituting different narrative, dramatic, or logical developments to situate the original in a new or contemporary setting. Each step in the editing is marked in an obvious way. No part is isolated, but all are cross-referenced to the ongoing revision. The editing is piecemeal but envisages and embraces the whole of the original text. Annotation, commentary, and interpretation are phases in a single process, and the edited version turns out to be a completely different literary work with another structure and another interpretation of history.[6]

3. Cf. Fishbane, *Biblical Interpretation,* 39. Fishbane occasionally allows for unmarked editing, but every edited text, it seems, is marked at least by simple repetition (e.g., Gen 30:38, pp. 64-65).

4. The marking of an edited text allows the original text to be read by following and undoing the editorial procedure. It can be read, like its reedition, as a separate work and in relation to the works that preceded and followed it. Literary and historical tradition, from this perspective, is not the unknown origin or motive of the text, or the collecting of fragments from an almost forgotten past, but the relationships between original and edited works as their authors and editors created and understood them.

5. The determination to weigh literature and history, to keep composition and redaction in balance, and to deal with the whole text in all its intricacy is evident in the commentaries of D. N. Freedman and F. I. Andersen on *Hosea* (AB 24; Garden City, NY: Doubleday, 1980) and *Amos* (AB 24A; New York: Doubleday, 1989).

6. Fishbane *(Biblical Interpretation)* deals with a *traditum,* the Bible and the oral traditions that produced and sustained it, and a *traditio,* the principles of the schools of interpretation that studied the fixed and authoritative text. In this essay I am dealing with authors and the composition of texts and with individual editors who rewrote these texts for a different readership, in the light of the books they had read, and on the basis of the historical evidence that had accumulated since the original was written.

The editorial marks are repetition and reversion. Simple or literal repetition consists in taking a few words, or a key word, from the original in an opposite order, a contrasting context, or a contradictory sense.[7] It occurs at the beginning or at the end of the editorial text and is taken resumptively from the text that just precedes or proleptically from the text that follows next. Deictic repetition consists in proper nouns, the definite article, personal or demonstrative pronouns, pronominal suffixes, particles, adverbs and adverbial phrases that specify or modify subjects, objects, or verbs in the original context.[8] Reversion consists in a literarily unmotivated or grammatically irregular change of person, number, or gender combined with some repetition that, besides modifying the adjacent text, signals a connection between it and a prior or later noncontiguous context.[9] The marks are always more or less obvious, but they suppose the kind of careful attention to all the words in the text, starting at the beginning, that is assured by fervor or study and articulated by verbalization or reading aloud.

I. Simple Repetition

The earliest story of creation began: "On the day that Yahweh God made earth and heaven" (Gen 2:4b). The Priestly editor and author[10] prefixed another version by repeating the key words in an opposite order at the beginning and the end of the new version and by using deictics to emphasize the editorial change: "In the beginning God created the ['et ha-] heavens and the ['et ha-] earth" (1:1); "And the [ha-] heavens and the [ha-] earth . . . were finished" (2:1);

---

7. Cf. P. C. Beentjes, "Inverted Quotations in the Bible: A Neglected Stylistic Pattern," *Bib* 63 (1982) 506-23.

8. Fishbane (*Biblical Interpretation,* 44-55) has described the use of deictic repetition.

9. The significance of the change of person was noted by Fishbane (*Biblical Interpretation,* 47) and by W. Morrow ("The Composition of Deut 15:1-3," *HAR* 12 [1990] 115-31). Change of number is common in Deuteronomy: its significance as an editorial marker was noted by N. Lohfink (*Das Hauptgebot: Eine Untersuchung literarischer Einleitungsfragen zu Dtn 5–11* [Rome: Biblical Institute, 1963] 241), C. T. Begg ("The Literary Criticism of Deut 4,1-40: Contributions to a Continuing Discussion," *ETL* 56 [1980] 10-55, esp. 18, 22), and P. E. Dion ("Deuteronomy 13: The Suppression of Alien Religious Propaganda in Israel During the Late Monarchical Era," in *Law and Ideology in Monarchic Israel* [ed. B. Halpern and D. W. Hobson; JSOTSup 124; Sheffield: JSOT, 1991] 147-216). Change of gender was designated a "cue gloss" by K. S. Freedy ("The Glosses in Ezekiel 1–24," *VT* 20 [1970] 129-52, esp. 131-36) and was used by W. Zimmerli to describe the process of redaction in Ezekiel (*Ezekiel 1* [trans. R. E. Clements; Hermeneia; Philadelphia: Fortress, 1979] 100-110).

10. Using the standard editorial techniques, the Priestly writer affixed new material to the Yahwist text and usually enclosed it rather than intruding into it. Therefore, one can read the Priestly document in conjunction with the Yahwist text or, by skipping it, as a complete and continuous composition.

". . . which God created and *made*" (2:3bβ); "These [*'ēlleh*] are the generations of *the* [*ha-*] heavens and *the* [*ha-*] earth when they were created" (2:4a). The new edition is not trivial or isolated. For instance, the original day becomes a week, the vague past of the original becomes real time that the Priestly writer goes on to measure in days and months and years, and the creation of the world becomes the model for the tabernacle where Yahweh dwells with his people and around which they celebrate their Sabbath.[11]

Resumptive repetitions at the beginning of the editorial insertions are not always as impressive, but they are always as clear in a continuous reading of the text. When Abraham and Lot separate, Lot pitches his tent at Sodom but, before Abraham can move to Hebron, an editor interrupts the narrative to introduce Abraham's vision of the promised land; the new text (Gen 13:13-17) begins the way the preceding original ended, with a mention of Sodom (13:13aα = 13:12bβ), and with a reminder that Lot had separated from Abraham (13:14 = 13:11b). In the original version Yahweh visited Sarah as he said he would, and she conceived and bore a son to Abraham in his old age (21:1a, 2a); but in the Priestly version this is related to the prior covenant that God made with Abraham (chap. 17) by repeating that "Yahweh did for Sarah what he promised . . . at the time that God had promised her" (21:2b, 3b).[12] In the Yahwist version Jacob acquires the best of Laban's flock and, when Laban becomes wary of him, Yahweh tells Jacob to return home, where he will be with him (31:1-3); the Elohist interpreted Jacob's success as a proof of divine providence and appended this alternate version by having Jacob tell the story to his wives and begin by repeating exactly what Laban did and what Yahweh said at the end of the original (31:4-16).

This type of repetition is common throughout the historical and prophetic books. In the Yahwist version Yahweh appears to Moses and says that he has seen the affliction of his people and heard their cry and has come down to bring them out of Egypt (Exod 3:7-8); the Elohist version, manifesting its usual interest in divine providence, wants to change this to read that Moses will bring the people out of Egypt and that God will be with him and begins by repeating, in opposite order, that God has heard the cry of the people and seen their affliction (3:9-14). When the Yahwist says that Israel defeated Sihon king of the Amorites and occupied his territory as far as the Jabbok and the Ammonites (Num 21:21-24abα), an editor with a better grasp of geography and history begins again with the Ammonites and explains that Israel did not cross the border into Ammon, that Sihon was not the king of the Amorites but the

---

11. Cf. M. Weinfeld, "Sabbath, Temple and the Enthronement of the Lord — The Problem of the Sitz im Leben of Genesis 1:1–2:3," in *Mélanges bibliques et orientaux en l'honneur de M. Henri Cazelles* (ed. A. Caquot and M. Delcor; AOAT 212; Neukirchen-Vluyn: Neukirchener Verlag, 1981) 501-12.

12. Cf. C. Westermann, *Genesis* (trans. J. J. Scullion; 3 vols.; Continental Commentary; Minneapolis: Augsburg, 1984-86) 2.332.

Amorite king of Heshbon, that it was his land and not all the land of the Amorites that Israel conquered (21:24bβ-26), and that it was Sihon and not Israel who had taken cities and territory from Moab (21:27-31).[13] When a historian records that Shishak took away the treasures of the temple and the palace (1 Kgs 14:25-26aα, *wayyiqqaḥ 'et . . .*), an editor refers to the poverty of the temple in comparison with its magnificence in the time of Solomon by repeating, in the opposite word order, that Shishak took everything (1 Kgs 14:26aβb-28, *wĕ'et hakkol lāqāḥ*). When a text of Isaiah envisions all the nations flocking to Jerusalem and calls on the house of Jacob to walk in the light of the Lord (Isa 2:5) an editor, infuriated by the trouble that these foreigners caused, repeats the reference to the house of Jacob and, by changing from plural to singular, says that it was because of them that Yahweh rejected his people (Isa 2:6-22).[14] When Jeremiah complains that the people did not say "Where is Yahweh?" (Jer 2:6), his editor remarks that *the* priests [*ha*-] did not say "Where is Yahweh?" (Jer 2:8). When Amos remarks that the Philistines sold prisoners of war to Edom (Amos 1:6), his editor, repeating Amos's oracular format, makes the same remark about Tyre (Amos 1:9) to bring the list of troublesome nations up to date. When Amos refers to his audience in the plural as those who turn justice into wormwood (Amos 5:7), this editor refers to Yahweh in the singular as the one who turns dawn into darkness (Amos 5:8).

Resumptive repetition at the end of editorial remarks lets the text return to normal but also creates a literary framework that sets them apart as obvious insertions.[15] In the mythical perspective of the original story the garden of Eden was watered from below, but from a later historian's point of view it was watered by a river whose four streams made the garden the center of the known world (Gen 2:10-14); the editorial insertion ends by repeating that God put Adam in the garden (2:15bα = 2:8b) but now in order to work and take care of it (2:15). In the first version Isaac goes to Gerar to escape a famine in the land (26:1aαb), but in the second version it is only after Yahweh appears to him, reviews the story of Abraham, and transfers to him the promises to Abraham that Isaac finally settles in Gerar (26:1aβ, 2-6). In the Yahwist version Balaam, after much deliberation, sets out with the messengers from Moab (Num 22:21), but the editor who thought that he was responsible for the sin of Baal of Peor inserted

---

13. Cf. M. Noth, *Numbers* (trans. J. D. Martin; OTL; Philadelphia: Westminster, 1968) 160-66. The entire editorial text is affixed by repeating a few words from the end of the original (*kî 'az gĕbûl bĕnê 'ammôn* instead of *'ad bĕnê 'ammôn*). The historical interpretation was critical: the corrected version of the wars in Transjordan is repeated by the Deuteronomist in Deut 2:1–3:11 and the mistaken idea that Israel had invaded Ammon is corrected in Judg 11:12-28.

14. Cf. M. A. Sweeney, *Isaiah 1–4 and the Post-Exilic Understanding of the Isaianic Tradition* (BZAW 171; Berlin: de Gruyter, 1988) 139-46.

15. Cf. C. Kuhl, "Die 'Wiederaufnahme,' ein literarkritisches Prinzip?" *ZAW* 64 (1952) 1-11.

the ridiculous story of Balaam's ass (Num 22:22-35a) before once again allowing the seer to set out with the messengers from the king of Moab (Num 22:35b). In one version Joshua is commissioned as the successor of Moses to take possession of the land and is assured that Yahweh will be with him (Josh 1:1-5), but in another he is confirmed as the custodian of the law and the distributor of tribal inheritances (Josh 1:6-9a) and again, but with opposite word order, assured that Yahweh will be with him (1:9b). In one version Solomon's kingdom is established (1 Kgs 2:12b) but in the other the conspirators are killed before it is established again with the same words in the opposite order (1 Kgs 2:46b). Isaiah blamed the people for making an alliance with Egypt that would neither help nor profit them (Isa 30:1-5), and an editor shifted the blame to Egypt in an oracle that ended by repeating that the Egyptians were neither helpful nor profitable (Isa 30:6-7).[16]

Proleptic repetition at the beginning of an editorial text marks the insertion as an alternative or antecedent to the following text whose beginning it mimics. In the Elohist version Abimelech asks what Abraham was thinking about when he said that Sarah was his sister (Gen 20:10), but in the edited version Abraham is a prophet who will intercede for the king, and the original question is anticipated by another that asks Abraham, beginning with almost exactly the same words, what he thought he was doing and why he brought this great sin on Abimelech and his kingdom (Gen 20:9). The Song of the Sea begins with the words of the Song of Miriam that follows (Exod 15:1b = 15:21). The oath of the covenant in the land of Moab is sworn by those actually standing in the presence of Yahweh (Deut 29:1a, 9a), but the ceremony is interrupted to explain in advance that those standing are those who saw all that Yahweh did for Israel (Deut 29:1b-8). In the original dialogue Saul's servant suggests that they ask for directions from the man of God, and Saul replies that his servant's advice is sound (1 Sam 9:6aαb, 10); in the edited version Saul's reply is anticipated by another in which it turns out that the man of God is a venal prophet or seer (9:7-9). Before his encounter with Goliath David tells Saul that there is no reason for alarm because Yahweh who saved him from lions and bears will deliver him from the Philistine (17:37); the editor who changed the encounter into a holy war anticipated this speech with another that begins the same way and repeats the same story but also interprets the Philistine challenge as blasphemy against God (17:34-36). In summoning the Assyrians against his people Yahweh points out that the Assyrians do not understand his plan, and he quotes their words to prove the point (Isa 10:5-7, 13-14); the edited version anticipated this quotation with another that begins like it, repeats parts of it,

---

16. H. Wildberger noted the repetition (*Jesaja* [BKAT X/3; Neukirchen-Vluyn: Neukirchener Verlag, 1978] 1159), but he considered it to be redactional (i.e., the reason that a redactor linked these two texts that originated with Isaiah) rather than editorial (i.e., the mark of the editor who discretely rewrote Isaiah's text and disrupted its original continuity).

and explains the rest but that nevertheless diverges completely from it in searching out the sinful causes of the invasion (Isa 10:8-12).[17] Amos recites a lament for Israel who has fallen in battle and then quotes the words that Yahweh spoke to the house of Israel (Amos 5:1-2, 4-7); his editor was eager to exempt a remnant and anticipated the quotation with another that begins with the same prophetic formula and ends with another reference to the house of Israel (5:3).[18]

Proleptic repetition also occurs at the end of editorial insertions and smooths out the transition to the original text. In the Yahwist version Abraham and Lot set out as Yahweh directed and arrive in the land of Canaan (Gen 12:4a, 5bβ); the Priestly writer supplied all the information that the original omitted by noting that Abraham was seventy-five, that he had a wife named Sarah, that Lot was his nephew, and that his wealth, which the Yahwist seems to suggest had been acquired in Canaan (13:2), was transported from Haran by his household staff, and then ended the editorial insertion by repeating that they set out for the land of Canaan (12:4b-5abα). With a typical preference for compressed or symbolic time, the Yahwist has the people arrive in the wilderness of Sinai and camp at the mountain on the very day that Yahweh defeated the Egyptians at the Sea (Exod 19:1b, 2b; cf. 14:30-31); the Priestly version, with its usual interest in real time, explains that it was three months after they left Egypt and on a journey that had taken them from the wilderness of Zin to Rephidim (16:1; 17:1abα), and fits in the editorial correction by ending as the Yahwist did with the people arriving again and camping in the wilderness of Sinai (19:1a, 2a).[19] In the Yahwist narrative Moses is told to send spies into the land, and he does just that (Num 13:1-2aα, 17); the Priestly version adds that the spies were representatives of the tribes and ends in anticipation of the following Yahwist text by saying that Moses sent the spies and by remarking that he did exactly what he was told (13:2aβb-3); another editor added the names of the spies, beginning with the simple deictic expression "These are their names," and ending with the same expression and another proleptic reference to the fact that Moses sent the spies (13:4-16).

Literal repetition is the simplest and least obtrusive way of marking an edition. It is distinguished from the repetitions that occur in original literary works by being partial, contrary, and part of an ongoing commentary and interpretation. It is not usually disconcerting and, without attention to the

---

17. The significance of the repetition (Isa 10:8 [kî yō'mar], 13 [kî 'āmar]) and the intrusiveness of 10:9-12 are recognized, but explained differently, by H. Wildberger, *Isaiah 1–12* (trans. T. H. Trapp; Continental Commentary; Minneapolis: Fortress, 1991) 417-24.

18. Andersen and Freedman (*Amos*, 475-77) treat Amos 5:3 separately, evaluate its peculiarities, and explain its position in the text.

19. Cf. M. Noth, *Überlieferungsgeschichtliche Studien* (Stuttgart: Kohlhammer, 1948), 14, 18, nn. 32, 55. To accommodate the order of the Yahwist text (Exod 19:1b, 2b) the Priestly writer had to work backward from the date of their arrival in Sinai (19:1a) to the journey that brought them there (19:2a).

structure and development of the continuous text, is easily missed. It begins as insertion into an original composition but gradually overtakes the original and often becomes the predominant form of the text.

II. Deictic Repetition

Editions of original works begin as glosses or footnotes that are included in the text and are more or less integrated with it but that accumulate and develop into a subtext with its own ideas, interests, sources, forms, and style. The individual changes are marked, the editor's hand becomes familiar, and the edition is recognized with more and more ease as the original and its revision expand.

Deictic repetitions are often more glaring because they are marked by elements that are intrusive in the text and by sudden shifts in the logical or narrative or dramatic direction of the original. Nominal or pronominal deictic repetition is related to specific elements of the preceding, rarely the following, text and either explains the original or situates it in the edition's ongoing interpretation. Adverbial repetition usually refers in general to the preceding original context and introduces either incongruous or conflicting comments. In every instance, whether the reference to the original is specific or vague, the editorial text introduced by deictic repetition is interruptive and barely consistent with the original to which it is affixed.

Demonstrative pronouns point to specific elements of the surrounding composition. At the end of the Priestly version of creation the editorial transition to the original Yahwist story is marked by the deictic formula "These are the generations of the heavens and the earth" (Gen 2:4a) that refers to the first clause in the following original (2:4b) and also repeats its key words in the opposite order. The deictic formula "This is the book of the generations of Adam" (5:1a) marks the preface to the Priestly genealogy of the antediluvians by referring back in a general way to the Yahwist story of Adam in the garden of Eden and, by means of literal repetition, in a more particular way to the preceding Priestly account of creation (5:1b-2 = 1:26-27). In the original story, when Pharaoh's daughter took pity on the crying baby in the reed basket, the baby's sister spoke up and offered to find a wet nurse for him (Exod 2:6abα, 7aαb); the edited version, in order to identify him as one of the Hebrew children mentioned in an earlier story (2:15-21), has Pharaoh's daughter speak up first and say, demonstratively, "*This* is one of the Hebrew children" (2:6bβ), and has his sister offer to find a wet nurse "from *the* Hebrew women" (2:7aβ). The original version noted parenthetically that Jeroboam led a revolt against Solomon (1 Kgs 11:26); the edited version considered it a divinely inspired punishment for the sins of Solomon and introduced its explanation with the deictic note "Now *this* is the reason he revolted" (1 Kgs 11:27). When an Isaian describes the future Davidic king (Isa 9:1-6abα [ET 2-7abα]), another editor who is more interested in the reunification of Israel than in the restoration of the monarchy adds a redundant demonstrative remark (9:6bβ [ET 7bβ], "The jealousy of the Lord of hosts will do *this*") in order to lead into a totally tangential analysis of the ancient conflicts between Israel and Judah (9:7-20 [ET 8-21]).[20] In the original presentation by Jeremiah Yahweh complains that Israel, like an animal in heat, or a flighty young wife, has abandoned him to go after her lovers (Jer 2:23-25, 31aβb-32); his editor abandoned the metaphors and put the blame on the prophets, priests, princes, and kings (2:26-30) and then, to return to the flow of the original text, added a doubly deictic apostrophe ("You, this generation!") and a peculiar appeal to "see the words of the Lord" (2:31aα).[21] Ezekiel began his prophecy with the visions that he had at the end of his career in the thirtieth year of his exile (Ezek 1:1); but his editor, who thought of them as inaugural visions, redated them by repeating part of the original and explaining: "*That* was the fifth year of the exile of King Jehoiachin" (1:2).[22] In the original version Ezekiel relives the distress of Jerusalem under siege (4:1-3abα), but his editor remarks: "*This* is a sign to the house of Israel" (4:3bβ) to explain that Ezekiel relived the punishment of Israel and Judah (4:4-8).

Personal pronouns or pronominal suffixes, referring to the preceding or following context, introduce editorial remarks that interpret the original in a distinct or divergent sense. In the Yahwist story Jacob marries Leah and Rachel (Gen 29:16-23, 25-28); but an editor, in anticipation of the birth of the twelve tribes of Israel, adds a reference to their maids: "And Laban gave *to her* Zilpah

---

20. The remark is quoted verbatim from 2 Kgs 19:31b, where it concludes the Deuteronomist's description of the remnant that will be left in Zion. It is typical of this Isaian editor to counter every reference to the restoration of the Davidic monarchy with a reference to the restoration of the remnant of Israel; cf. Isa 2:1-5 and 4:1-6, 7:1-15 and 7:16-25, 10:15-19 and 10:20-23, 11:1-10 and 11:11-16.

21. Jeremiah's metaphor of infidelity (Jer 2:33, 35-37) was interrupted again by the same editor to include documented crimes (2:34a refers to Deut 27:25 and 2 Kgs 21:16; Jer 2:34b [and 2:26] refers to Exod 22:1), and in order to return to the original text the editor added "But for all this" *(kî 'al-kol-'ēlleh)*. These editorial markers are usually considered separately from their editorial contexts, labeled as glosses or errors, and then omitted or ignored: W. McKane (*Jeremiah* [ICC; Edinburgh: T. & T. Clark, 1986] 49-54) deletes them and considers the second to be unintelligible; W. L. Holladay (*Jeremiah 1* [Hermeneia; Philadelphia: Fortress, 1986] 55-56, 107, 110) recognizes the quotations in the second comment but rewrites both the texts; R. P. Carroll (*Jeremiah* [OTL; Philadelphia: Westminster, 1986] 137-39) includes the first in a history of prophetic discourse but thinks the second is incomprehensible.

22. Cf. Zimmerli, *Ezekiel 1*, 100-101; M. Greenberg, *Ezekiel 1–20* (AB 22; Garden City, NY: Doubleday, 1983) 41. The editing is marked by the literal repetition of "on the fifth day of the month" (1:1, 2), by the demonstrative "that was . . . ," and by changing from Ezekiel's first person reference to himself to the editor's third person singular reference to Ezekiel (1:2-3).

her maid, *to Leah* his daughter, as a maid" (29:24); and "Laban gave to Rachel his daughter, Bilhah his maid, *to her as her maid*" (29:29). The same editor, when the original narrative notes that Joseph was seventeen (37:1aα), repeats that Joseph was a boy and adds a reference to the maids' children by starting with the deictic personal pronoun "And *he . . .*" (37:1aβ). The Elohist narrates that Jethro, the father-in-law of Moses, came to the mountain with Zipporah, the wife of Moses, and *his* children (Exod 18:1-5); an editor, eager to draw the theological lesson to be learned from the exodus, inserted Jethro's confession of faith (Exod 18:6-12) by beginning the text with repetition, deictic identifications, and a change of gender ("I, your father-in-law Jethro, have come with your wife and with *her* two children"). The first version says that Yahweh was angry at all the men who had reconnoitered the land (Deut 1:35aαb, 36), and an editor uses the deictic definite article and the demonstrative pronoun to let Moses add that Yahweh was angry at "*this* evil generation" (1:35aβ) and a pronominal suffix, in a person and number that conflict with the context, to let him add that Yahweh was angry "even at *me*" (1:37).[23] When the first version says that Yahweh spoke to the people face-to-face (5:4), this editor, in order to reaffirm the mediation of Moses, uses pronominal and adverbial deictics to let Moses comment: "*I* was standing between you and Yahweh *at that time*" (5:5).[24] When the first version urges total submission to Yahweh (10:20), the second adds the deictic remark: "*He* is your praise, *he* is your God" (10:21) to begin the summary history of those who did not submit (10:22–11:7). When Nathan's oracle assures David that his offspring will succeed him (2 Sam 7:12), an editor, anticipating the succession of Solomon, adds "*He* will build a house for my name" (2 Sam 7:13). When the original says that Samaria was captured in the sixth year of Hezekiah (2 Kgs 18:10a), an editor corrected it with a deictic and repetitive synchronism: "*It* was the ninth year of Hoshea, king of Israel, that Samaria was captured" (2 Kgs 18:10b). Amos condemned those who oppressed the poor to support their extravagances in the house of their God (Amos 2:6-8); and his editor, in order to include among their crimes the silencing of the prophets, lets their God speak to them in the first person singular and begin with the emphatic personal pronoun (Amos 2:9-12). In Ezekiel's vision there were four living creatures with four faces and four wings for each "*of them*" (Ezek 1:5-6); but his editor, who was interested in making the creatures immobile representations on a wheeled vehicle, began with a pronominal suffix and an irregular change of number to add that "*their* legs *was* a straight leg" (1:7). When Ezekiel compared Israel to an ungrateful child who grew up to be an unfaithful wife who was humiliated and beaten into submission (16:1-43a), his editor retold the story to distinguish Israel from Judah and to leave some hope

23. Cf. M. Weinfeld, *Deuteronomy 1–11* (AB 5; Garden City, NY: Doubleday, 1991) 149-50.
24. Ibid., 240.

for Jerusalem (16:43b-63) and added this version by beginning with the deictic pronominal expression: "*And I*, behold, your ways I have requited" (16:43b).

An analogous means of inserting explanatory material is by including nouns and names and definite subjects or objects that identify or specify some preceding or following element that is either grammatically or narratively undefined. The Yahwist says that Abraham set out and that Lot went with him (Gen 12:4a), and the Priestly writer specifies "him" by beginning parenthetically "Now, Abraham . . ." (12:4b). Similarly, in the Elohist version when God visits Abimelech in a dream and speaks "to him" (20:3), an editor can insert reflections on innocence and guilt by beginning abruptly "And Abimelech . . ." (20:4) to redefine the grammatically indefinite person to whom God spoke. The original story of Isaac begins with a famine in the land (26:1aα), but the editor adds the definite article to specify that this indefinite famine was not "*the first* famine that occurred in the time of Abraham" (26:1aβ). When the Yahwist version says that messengers from the king of Moab went to Balaam (Num 22:7b), an editor, eager to discredit the prophet, specifies that "they" were elders of Moab and Midian who were bringing him payment for his services (Num 22:7a). In the original preface to the covenant on Horeb Moses summons Israel and recalls how Yahweh made a covenant with them (Deut 5:1aα, 2-4); the edited version recalls, on the contrary, that it was the law that was revealed on Horeb and, by interrupting the original preface with personal pronouns, deictic object markers (*'et ha-*), and adverbs summons the people to hear "*the* [*'et ha-*] statutes and *the* [*'et ha-*] commandments that *I* am speaking in your hearing *today*, and you will hear *them* [*'ōtām*] and be careful to do *them*" (5:1aβb). When the original law of centralization lists those who are to participate in the festivals (12:18aαb), the Deuteronomist uses the definite article and a proper noun to add "and *the* Levite who is in your towns" (12:18aβ). When the original dietary laws (12:4-5, 11-12) were supplemented, all of the additions were introduced by demonstrative pronouns, the object marker (*'et*), or the deictic formula "according to their kinds" (14:6-10, 13-20).[25] The covenant is sealed with those present (29:9a, 11), but the Deuteronomist specifies that those present include tribal and military leaders, family and friends, and Gibeonite slaves (29:9b-10). In the introduction to the conquest Yahweh tells Joshua and the people to cross the Jordan to the land that is being given "to them" (Josh 1:1-2); but the Deuteronomist, who changed the narrative of the conquest into a description of tribal allotments, added the nominal specification "to the sons of Israel" (1:2) to make clear that the land belonged to the twelve tribes. Similarly, when the original says that *they* arrived at the Jordan (3:1aαb), the reference is narratively unambiguous; but the editor clears up the grammatical imprecision by specifying, with both

---

25. The basis of the new edition was the complete list of clean and unclean animals in the earlier dietary laws; cf. W. L. Moran, "The Literary Connection between Lev 11,13-19 and Dt 14,12-18," *CBQ* 28 (1966) 271-77.

nominal and pronominal deictics, that "they" included Joshua and the sons of Israel (3:1aβ). The original told of David's defeat of an unnamed Philistine champion (1 Sam 17:4aα, 7b-9); but the edited version, which identified him as a giant, called him by his name Goliath and described *his* armor in lavish detail (1 Sam 17:4aβb-7a). Hosea said that Yahweh would not have mercy on the house of Israel (Hos 1:6); but his editor, by starting with the deictic object marker *('et)* and by using his words in the opposite sense, said that Yahweh would have mercy on the house of Judah (1:7). When Hosea says that the people are perishing for lack of knowledge (4:6a), the same editor blames it on the Bethel priesthood by changing the person and adding "because *you* have rejected *the* knowledge" (4:6b). Zephaniah announced the end of the world (Zeph 1:2-3aαb), but his editor was concerned to limit the destruction to evildoers in Judah and Jerusalem and pointed them out with the definite article and the object marker (Zeph 1:3aβ, 4-6). Ezekiel mimed the breaching of the walls of Jerusalem and the trek into captivity (Ezek 12:8-10a, 11b); but his editor, who understood it as the flight, capture, and blinding of Zedekiah, broke into the mime with nouns and the definite article (12:10b: "*The* prince is *the* gist of *this* . . .") and returned to the original prophecy with a pleonastic pronoun (12:11a, "Say, *I* am a sign to you").[26]

Adverbial deictics refer vaguely to the fact, time, or place of things mentioned in the preceding text but introduce opposite or extraneous times, places, or facts. When the Yahwist says that Abraham moved to the oaks of Mamre (Gen 13:18a), the editor, who is keeping track of the altars he built (cf. 12:7b, 8b; 13:4a), adds that he built an altar *there* (13:18b). When the Yahwist says that Abraham surveyed the destruction of Sodom and Gomorrah (19:28), the Elohist version begins by saying that Abraham moved on *from there* (20:1). When Ezekiel says that he was carried into exile on the wings of the wind and settled by the river Chebar where the exiles lived (Ezek 3:12a, 14b-15aα),[27] his editor introduces the theme of his prophetic responsibility by repeating "*they* were living *there*, and I settled *there*" (Ezek 3:15aβb). In the Elohist version an angel speaks to Abraham from heaven and tells him not to harm Isaac (Gen 22:11-14), but in the edited version the angel speaks *a second time* to reconfirm the promises (Gen 22:15-18). In the Yahwist story it happened "in those days" that Moses killed an Egyptian who was hitting one of his brothers (Exod 2:11-12), and an editor who was concerned about Moses' alleged crime adds that he went

---

26. After Ezekiel's explanation (Ezek 12:11b) the editor returns to Zedekiah with the deictic article and a personal pronoun that stands out by its disruption of narrative word order ("*The* prince . . . *he* . . ."; cf. Greenberg, *Ezekiel 1–20*, 213-16).

27. The intervening material (Ezek 3:12b-14a) was added through an initial nominal deictic "Blessed be the glory of Yahweh from his place" (3:12b) and a concluding resumptive repetition in the opposite order (3:13b-14a: "and a sound of a great roar and the spirit lifted me and took me . . ." = 3:12a: "And the spirit lifted me and I heard behind me the sound of a great roar").

out *"the second day"* and became involved in a similar altercation that exonerated him by proving the guilt of the initial assailant (2:13-14). Reacting against the covenantal attributes ascribed to Yahweh (34:6-7), the Elohist preempted the Yahwist version by having God speak to Moses and proclaim that his principal attribute was providential care (3:9-14); an editor, eager to reconcile the divergent texts, has God speak to Moses *again* and explain that all the names the Yahwist, Elohist, and Priestly writers ascribed to him were proper (3:15). Similarly, the Priestly writer, faced with the story of Jacob wrestling with a man and becoming Israel because he had overcome God, understood it as a vision, as the earlier encounter with the three men had been understood (cf. Genesis 17 and 18), and replaced it with a proper vision in which God appeared to Jacob *again* and changed his name to Israel (Gen 35:9-15). Hosea married a harlot to illustrate Yahweh's troubles with the land (Hos 1:2), but his editor had him get married *again* to explain the delay in the return of the exiles and the restoration of the Davidic monarchy (Hos 3:1-5).

The commonest adverbial deictics are temporal references that allow the intrusion of tangential or contradictory material that is critical to the editorial version. The story of Joseph is interrupted by the ribald history of Tamar and Judah by saying "Now it happened at that time" (Gen 38:1), and Potiphar's wife attempted to seduce Joseph "after these things . . ." (Gen 39:7). The Song of the Sea is intruded by saying *"Then* Moses sang . . ." (Exod 15:1), and the story of the spies is interrupted to talk about the courts by noting that "At that time I spoke to you" (Deut 1:9). Isaiah likened the invading Assyrians to a lioness that growls over the prey it has seized (Isa 5:29), and an editor changed the subject by repeating that it will growl "on that day" (Isa 5:30). Jeremiah described an invasion that he thought should prompt the people to repentance and tears (Jer 4:5-8); but his editor, with an inconsequential "And on that day it will happen . . . ," described the discomfiture of the princes and kings (Jer 4:9-12). Amos described the frustration of those who trample on the poor (Amos 5:10-12), and his editor introduced an impertinent commentary (Amos 5:14-15, 16-17) by adding "therefore a smart person will be silent *at that time* because *it* is an evil time" (Amos 5:13).[28] Micah said that Zion would become a ploughed field, Jerusalem a ruin, and the temple mount a wooded height (Mic 3:12), but his editor blithely added that "at some later time" the city would be restored (Mic 4:1-5).

Deictic repetitions work on the basic grammatical level of subject, object, and verb. An undefined subject or object can be specified by proper nouns, the definite article, or the object marker. A definite subject or object can be modified

---

28. Cf. Andersen and Freedman, *Amos,* 506-18. The commentary does not pertain to its immediate context: the first part (5:14-15) is a commentary on 5:4-6; the second part (5:16-17) belongs to the editorial subtext that describes the famines, plagues, and wars that accompany the day of Yahweh (4:6-13; 5:3; 6:8-10; 8:11-14; 9:1-4, 9-10).

by pronouns or pronominal suffixes that are in apposition to them or refer to them directly. Particular actions, attitudes, and states occasion references to analogous or parallel events in different times and places. Deictic repetitions are obtrusive but merely mark the beginning or end of the editor's work, and, far from revealing its substance, are artificial links between the original text and a progressively divergent editorial development.

III. Reversion

Simple repetition is lexical or morphological, literal or verbatim. Deictic repetition is grammatical and operates at the clause-level connection between subjects, objects, and verbs. Reversion, an irregular or unmotivated and truncated change in person, number, or gender, is syntactic and works at the sentence-level connection between clauses.[29]

Reversion, like repetition, is a feature of composition and redaction and cannot be appreciated without careful attention to the ongoing text. In composition it is used to mark a continuous series of quotations from a source or cross-references to earlier parts of the composition itself.[30] In redaction reversion is used in the same way to mark dependence on a source or sources in an earlier or noncontiguous context, or to mark a text that must be understood in relation to the ongoing original and edited text.

Change of person is common in poetic and dramatic texts and in narratives whose plot turns on direct discourse, but its redactional uses are distinguished by the syntactic abruptness, topical isolation, and narrative irrelevance of the passages that they mark. For instance, Passover is associated with the death of the Egyptian children by shifting abruptly from a third person singular reference to Yahweh (Exod 12:11b: "it is the Passover of the Lord") to Yahweh speaking in the first person (Exod 12:12-13). The journey from Horeb to Kadesh-barnea (Deut 1:6-8, 19-20) is delayed to allow Moses to reinstitute the lower courts (Deut 1:9-18); the passage has nothing to do with its context but retrieves and combines earlier passages from the Pentateuch and is marked by

---

29. Many instances of change in person, number, or gender (cf. G. A. Rendsburg, *Diglossia in Ancient Hebrew* [AOS 72; New Haven: American Oriental Society, 1990]) are simply isolated morphemic irregularities that are attributable to dialectal or colloquial interference in the standard or written language.

30. Reversion in Deuteronomy is like citation formulas *(kaʾăšer ṣiwwâ/nišbaʾ/ dibbēr/ʾāmar)* that refer to sources in the Pentateuch, and like the promulgation formula *(ʾăšer ʾānōkî mĕṣawwe-)* that marks cross-references to other texts in the book; cf. Fishbane, *Biblical Interpretation,* 164; D. E. Skweres, *Die Rückverweise im Buch Deuteronomium* (AnBib 79; Rome: Biblical Institute, 1979). It differs from these systems in marking not a quotation or allusion to a particular text but an interpretation of a text or combination of texts.

having Moses refer to himself in the first person although the original context referred to him in the third person and reserved the first person for Yahweh. When Moses says that he is too old to lead the conquest (31:1-2a), an editor refers to the historical reason given at the beginning of the book (cf. 1:37) by changing from the original first person address to a quotation of Yahweh's words to him in the second person (31:2b). In legislating the cities of refuge the second person singular text (19:1-3, 7-10) is interrupted by a third person singular text (19:4-6); and the change of person marks a quotation from the covenant code (19:4aβ = Exod 21:13bβ) and a recapitulation of earlier rules (Num 35:9-34; Deut 4:41-43). At the point where the song of the vineyard changes from a song about the lover in the third person to the lover speaking in the first person (Isa 5:1-2, 4-5), an editor inserted a second person plural summons to the people of Jerusalem (Isa 5:3) and, along with it, the theme of justice and due process that this editor introduced earlier and will continue to elaborate.[31] When Yahweh addresses Israel in the second person singular feminine (Jer 2:20-25), an editor interrupts to talk in the third person about a thief who is caught stealing and about the leaders of the house of Israel who worship sticks and stones (Jer 2:26).[32] In Amos's visions Yahweh speaks in the first person to him in the second person (Amos 7:7-9); but an editor, who from the start has been concerned with the attempt to silence the prophets, adds the attempt to silence Amos at Bethel (Amos 7:10-17) by referring to Amos in the third person and having him speak in the first person that Amos himself reserved for Yahweh. Micah, on the contrary, spoke to the people in the first person singular (Mic 3:1: "And I said"); but his editor added an otherwise unmarked and incongruous passage in which the subject of the first person verbs is Yahweh (Mic 2:12-13). To Ezekiel's condemnation of hilltop rituals (Ezek 20:27-28, 30-31) his editor, by going from third person narrative to second person discourse, added a reference to Micah's saying that one such hilltop shrine was the high place of the temple in Jerusalem (20:29).[33] Ezekiel concluded from his survey of the history of Israel that Yahweh would punish the innocent and the guilty (21:6-8, 11-15a); his editor was appalled and, in order to introduce a different interpretation, marked the spot with the incongruous apostrophe, "Or should we rejoice, my son, in the rod that holds all wood in contempt" (21:15b).[34]

---

31. Cf. Isa 1:16-17; 2:1-5; 3:13-15; 5:6-10, 20-24; 9:1-6 (ET 2-7); 11:1-10.

32. The editor's text (Jer 2:26-28) includes quotations from Exod 22:1; Deut 4:28b; 32:38; and Jer 3:4. The same editor also interrupted Yahweh's conversation with the land and her children (Jer 3:1-5, 19) by referring to Yahweh in the third person and by allowing the prophet to speak in the first person that Jeremiah reserved for Yahweh (Jer 3:6-18).

33. Ezek 20:29; Mic 1:5; 3:12. Change in person is reinforced by nominal, pronominal, and adverbial deictics: " 'What is *the* high place which *you* are *the ones going there*,' and *its* name is called High Place *to this day*" (cf. Greenberg, *Ezekiel 1–20*, 370-71).

34. Cf. Zimmerli, *Ezekiel 1*, 426-28. The marker alludes to earlier texts (Ezek 19:10-14; 20:32-38; 21:1-5) and urges further reading (21:16-37; 22:1-31).

Change of number is a way of editing a particular part of a continuous original composition in relationship to a cumulative editorial context. The law against becoming a creditor to the people of God (Exod 22:24a) was edited by the Deuteronomist in the light of legislation in Deuteronomy: the law was limited to becoming a creditor to a poor person by repeating the preceding context and its object marker (Exod 22:24aα), and then credit was distinguished from usury by changing from the singular of the original to the second person plural (22:24b).[35] At the end of the law code the gradual and providential occupation of the land that the original legislator described (23:27-31a) is assimilated to Deuteronomistic thinking by appending a warning against making covenants with the inhabitants of the land or worshiping their gods (23:32-33); the addition is made by repeating and contradicting some of the immediate context and by changing from the singular of the original to the plural (23:31b).[36] The legislator's description was also elaborated, by resumptive repetition, to include instructions on dealing with the idols of the indigeneous nations (23:23-26),[37] and these in turn were intruded into the Sinai covenant by changing from the original singular to an editorial plural (34:13).

In Deuteronomy laws are usually phrased in the second person singular while exhortations lapse into the second person plural, and deviations in the system are significant in the composition or redaction of the book. Moses refers to himself and the people in the first person plural (Deut 1:6; 5:2-3) to mark a paraphrase and reinterpretation of the covenant on Sinai and the journey to the land.[38] The journey from Horeb to Kadesh-barnea (1:19) was prolonged by

---

35. To the original *'im-kesep talweh 'et-'ammî* (Exod 22:24a) the editor added the restrictive *'et-he'ānî 'immāk* (22:24a) to bring it into line with the laws in Deuteronomy that deal specifically with the poor in the matter of loans and wages (Deut 22:10-15); the addition copies the original, repeating the object marker, and replacing *'ammî* with *'immāk*. The plural interpretation (Exod 22:24b: "You shall not demand interest from him") relates the law to the law in Deut 23:19-20. For a different interpretation cf. Fishbane, *Biblical Interpretation,* 174-77.

36. In the original it is God and his agents who drive out *(grš)* the people (Exod 23:20-22, 27-31a), but in the editor's text the people of Israel take control and drive them out (23:31b). The addition assimilates the original to the revised version of the Sinai covenant (34:15-17), which in turn becomes central to the final form of Deuteronomy (cf. Deuteronomy 7, 12). The addition is clearly marked and can be recognized as Deuteronomistic by its use of the archaic suffix *-mô* (Exod 23:31b).

37. The addition begins by repeating the start of the original paragraph to which it is appended (Exod 23:23 = 23:20). The list of nations that the editor includes is taken, with a change in order, from the Sinai covenant to which the present text is being assimilated (cf. 23:23 and 34:11).

38. Cf. Weinfeld, *Deuteronomy 1–11,* 237-39. The Yahwist text says that the covenant was made with Moses and with Israel (Exod 34:27), but the interpretation (Deut 5:2-3) says that it was made with the people who subsequently made Moses their representative (Deut 5:27). In the Yahwist text Moses spends forty days and nights on the mountain before Israel sets out for the land (Exod 34:28; Num 10:29-33a; 13:1-2a, 17), and the paraphrase omits Moses and says Israel spent too much time at the mountain (Deut 1:6).

a repetitive and deictic intrusion to include the years in the wilderness (1:19aα), and a further reference to these years is made by a singular insertion in a second plural context (1:31).[39] The exhortation not to worship idols includes a second plural paraphrase of the Priestly account of creation (4:16-18) that concludes with a second person singular exhortation not to worship the sun, the moon, or the stars (4:19); this suits the context and its source but it is a contrary quotation from Joseph's second dream in which his father, mother, and brothers are the sun, the moon, and the stars that worship him (Gen 37:9). According to this exhortation the result of idol-worship will be exile (Deut 4:25-28); but when the writer turns to them in exile and encourages them to repent and obey, there is a change to the second person singular to indicate quotations from the combined texts of Hosea and the Yahwist (4:29-31).[40] The original text commands the people in the singular to serve Yahweh, who is a jealous God (6:13, 15a); the Deuteronomistic editor added plural commands not to worship other gods and not to test Yahweh as they did at Massah (6:14, 15b-16).[41] The original obligation to love Yahweh is put in the second person singular (6:5-9), but it is repeated in the second person plural in the exhortation to observe the law of centralization that Moses is about to promulgate (11:18-20). The law of centralization desacralized sacrifice (12:15), but an editor disagreed and added the rituals governing the slaughter of animals for food by repeating one word of the original and turning from the singular to the plural (12:16).[42]

Change of number is an easy way of editing a text without dealing at length with its original content. Isaiah chastises those who spend whole days

---

39. The wilderness is critical for this writer as the time and place of rebellion (cf. Deut 2:14-16) and the antithesis of the occupation of the land by a law-abiding people (Joshua 5). The addition in Deut 1:31 is marked by beginning in the singular, but it ends in the second plural to smooth out the transition to the original.

40. Cf. Weinfeld, *Deuteronomy 1–11*, 217-21. Hosea said that the people would seek Yahweh and not find him (Hos 5:6); and the Deuteronomist, by relying on the original text of Deut 6:5b ("with all your heart and all your soul"), says just the opposite (Deut 4:29). Hosea said that Yahweh first hurt and then abandoned Ephraim and Judah so that, in their distress, they would return to him and seek him (Hos 5:15–6:1); and the editor refers to their distress in exile (Deut 4:30: *baṣṣar lĕkā* = Hos 5:15: *baṣṣar lāhem*, with change of person and number) and to the fact that they will seek Yahweh (Deut 4:29: *ûbiqqaštem* = Hos 5:15: *ûbiqĕšû pānāy*). The Yahwist gave prominence to mercy as Yahweh's motive for making a covenant with Israel (Exod 34:6, 10), and the writer assures the people that Yahweh is merciful and will not forget the covenant with their fathers (Deut 4:31).

41. The motive clause (Deut 6:15b = Exod 32:10-12) is in the singular like the original whose key words it repeats (Deut 6:15a = Exod 34:14b). The reference to Massah (Deut 6:16) supposes that Massah is at Horeb (Exod 17:6), where the present address takes place, and that the testing of Yahweh was to determine whether he was among his people (Exod 17:7 = Deut 6:15a).

42. This editor maintains, despite the original (Deut 12:13-15), that sacrifice is to be performed at the central sanctuary (*zbḥ*, 12:6, 11). The ritual aspects of slaughter are a constant preoccupation of this writer (12:21-25, 27).

and nights worshiping Yahweh without any idea what is happening (Isa 5:11-12); and his editor turns to the third and first person singular to let Yahweh quote Hosea and talk about the exile (Isa 5:13 = Hos 4:6a). When Amos rejects the *offerings* that the people make to Yahweh and pleads with them in the second person singular to stop the music and songs at their festivals (Amos 5:22-24), an editor reproves them in the plural and refers to the time in the wilderness when there was not a single *offering* (Amos 5:25). When Hosea describes the people in the plural hungry for wrongdoing (Hos 4:8), his editor talks in the singular about the people and the priest who misled them (4:9). When Hosea addresses the people in the second person singular to bewail their inconstancy (6:4-6), this editor refers to them and to their priests in the third person plural to recall their persistence in wrongdoing (6:7).[43] When Hosea says that the people will not remain in the land but will eat unclean food in Assyria (9:3abβ), his editor, by changing to the third person singular to quote a Deuteronomistic curse, says that they will return to Egypt (9:3bα).[44] Hosea said that Ephraim made molten images and idols (13:2aα), and his editor, referring to the curse that had been invoked on such people (Deut 27:15), turns to the singular and with a deictic flourish adds "the work of a craftsman, *all of it*" (Hos 13:2aβ).

Change of gender is usually consonant with a change in the grammatical subject, but its editorial character is emphasized by an accompanying repetition of the original. The covenant code was expanded to cover, besides theft and loss, cases concerning loans and deposits and the like (Exod 22:9-19): the editorial expansion begins with a literal but reversed repetition of elements from the preceding summary law (cf. 22:9a = 8aα), but instead of bringing their case (*dābār*, masculine) before God (22:8aβb), requires them to take an oath (*šĕbûʿāh*, feminine) before Yahweh (22:10aα).[45] When Moses objects that he is unable to bear the burden of the people all by himself, he protests that he is not the woman who conceived and bore them and cannot carry them in his bosom as the maid who nursed them (Num 11:11-12); but when he reminds the people that it was Yahweh who took care of them, he uses the image of a father carrying his son (Deut 1:31). When an editor explains that the consequences of the nonchalance that Isaiah described are famine and exile (Isa 5:13), another editor,

---

43. The change in person indicates compound quotations: there is an allusion to Adam in the garden of Eden (Hos 6:7), to the crime of the people of Jabesh-gilead (Hos 6:8; cf. Judg 21:8-12), to the irregularities at Shiloh (Hos 6:9 [the road to Shechem]; cf. Judg 21:19), and a quotation from the original text of Hosea (Hos 6:10b = 5:3b).

44. The third person singular marks a contradiction of Hosea's statement that Israel would not return to Egypt (Hos 11:5) and a nonliteral agreement with Deut 28:68 in which the Deuteronomist explicitly retracts the statement in Hosea to affirm that they will return to Egypt, in ships this time, instead of across dry land as they left.

45. The editorial change is also marked by adding to the list of animals in Exod 22:8 the general provision regarding "any animal" (22:9); cf. Fishbane, *Biblical Interpretation*, 170-74.

beginning with a literal repetition, turns from the masculine to the feminine singular to explain that its consequences are death and being devoured by Sheol (Isa 5:14). Hosea describes the people in the third person plural masculine relaxing in shady groves (Hos 4:13a), and his editor changes to second person and feminine to repudiate the women of the priestly family at Bethel who join in the relaxation (Hos 4:13b). When Zephaniah parses the word "seacoast" as feminine and says that the Philistine cities will become pastureland (Zeph 2:6), his editor says that it will be pastureland for the remnant of Israel and parses the word as masculine (Zeph 2:7). In his version Ezekiel mimes the siege of Jerusalem and measures the bread and water that he is allowed to eat (Ezek 4:10-11); but in the edited version the scene shifts to the exile, where he and Israel must eat unclean food, and the shift is marked by giving him to eat, instead of masculine bread, an unclean feminine cake (4:12-15).[46] Ezekiel saw that Jerusalem was doomed because *she* had neglected the law of God more than the nations around *her* (5:1-2, 5-6), but his editor spared a remnant (5:3-4, 7-10) by repeating his words and shifting from the feminine singular to the masculine plural (5:7-10).[47] Ezekiel heaped scorn on the prophets (13:1-16), and his editor, in an effort to separate the innocent who had to be spared from the guilty who deserved to be punished, continued with a speech to the prophetesses (13:17-23).

Conclusion

Editing was always marked and meant to be noticed. Editors maintained the distinction and integrity of the original to which they were literarily bound but, relying on other authors and texts, felt free to interpret and change it. It was critical to the editorial process that their individual comments be taken as pertaining not only to the particular text to which they were affixed but to the complete and continuous text that they were in the process of interpreting. It was also imperative that their annotations and comments be understood with reference to one another in the discrete and cumulative but complete rewriting of the original composition. Marking an editorial change preserved the original, left it in its place in the development of literary and historical traditions, and let the editorial contribution to those traditions stand out and be understood

---

46. Compare Ezekiel's *mēʾēt ʿad-ʿēt tōʾkălennû* (4:10b) and the editor's *wĕʿugat śĕʿōrîm tōʾkălennâ* (4:12a).

47. The first editorial insertion (Ezek 5:3-4), made by means of the adverbial deictic phrase "from there" (5:3, *miššām*), allows a few of those driven into exile to escape. The second insertion (5:7-10) is *marked* by the change to the second person plural masculine but it continues in the original second person singular feminine (5:8-9): it ends in the masculine plural to mark a nonliteral reference to Deut 28:53-55; cf. Greenberg, *Ezekiel 1–20*, 113-14.

in its relationship to the original and to the developing tradition that the original text had inspired.

Editors are often misunderstood and their work despised. It seems intrusive and short of the original literary mark. They may seem pedantic, mediocre, and mean. The misunderstanding generally depends on taking the token for the substance and in supposing that the mark that they made is all that they meant. The mark is meant for the reader, however, and the reader is supposed to know that any text has a beginning, from which it may be read, and an end to which the reading tends. The signs of editing are signals to read on, pay attention, and look for more. Editors generally did not set out to spoil the text they transmitted and preserved, but they regularly made it more complex, meaningful, and difficult to understand. If there is misunderstanding it is the reader who picks and chooses and shuns the task, rather than the editors who understood what they read, who may be at fault.

Mixed Marriage Metaphor in Ezekiel 16*

MARVIN H. POPE

Metaphor or transfer in human discourse has remained a problem since Aristotle long ago tried to explain it. Metaphors tend to get mixed, sometimes with amusing effect. Nowhere is the problem more acute than in theology or God-talk. Sacred scriptures, in particular those of the so-called Abrahamic religions (Judaism, Christianity, and Islam), are replete with figurative language, striking metaphor and simile, intended to be taken seriously but often difficult to evaluate or apply in strictly literal senses of the words. The following comments concerning a strange marriage are no venture into terra incognita where humans have not already set foot.

In a significant contribution to the appreciation of biblical language, M. C. A. Korpel surveyed theories of metaphor from Aristotle to the present and found no basic difference between sacred and secular usage.[1] To speak of the "arm of god," she observed, is no less accurate or inaccurate than when

---

*The mixed marriage metaphor was borrowed and adapted by Christians and has had an extended afterlife that will continue into the approaching third millennium c.e. unless the long expected New Age dawns with some sort of divine-human metaphorical marriage as envisioned by seers from Patmos, Waco, Kiev, or wherever. The editors of the latest *Festschrift* for David Noel Freedman agreed on conditional faith in my sanity to consider the unexpurgated version of this essay. Noel has edited two volumes of my contributions to the Anchor Bible and, though we often disagreed, never sought to impose his view or to exercise undue editorial influence. If Noel is offended by any notion mentioned herein, he will know how to ignore it or react creatively. Noel has added immensely to the ever growing Treasury of salvific Supererogatory Works, both by his own writings and by monumental editorial labors for others. He could well rest on his laurels, but the work is unending and it is predictable that he will not be able to desist from it. May years of life and health be added to and for him.

1. Korpel 1990. Cf. M. Pope, *UF* 22 (1990) 497-502, for a review of Korpel's study.

astronomers today talk of a "black hole." According to Korpel, with its capacity to hint at a truth that cannot be adequately described in terms of human experience, metaphor is the ideal vehicle to talk about God, whom no one has seen. Korpel selected 1,454 terms from the Ugaritic mythological poems descriptive of deities and their world and found that 49 percent of these have fairly certain counterparts in biblical references to God. This, she concluded, effectively contradicts the assertion by some "biblical theologians" (specifically G. E. Wright) that it is impossible on empirical grounds to understand how the God of Israel could have evolved out of polytheism.

Doubtless due to the venerable legacy of pious pudor in many parts of the world, sexual metaphor presents particular problems. Korpel noted that not a single biblical text mentions God's nakedness. He does not seem to have a physical backside (p. 95). Thus Hezekiah's declaration to the Lord (Isa 38:17), "you have cast all my sins behind your back," according to Korpel, "only permits a metaphorical understanding" (ibid.). True, even the Lord cannot literally throw sins. But if one says "put this behind you," it is understood that the one addressed has a backside behind which items may be put, literally or figuratively. Exodus 33:23 admittedly "appears" to oppose YHWH's face to his back(side), which part Moses was allowed to see. Korpel, however, supposed that the Yahwist thought of the deity's rear as a column of smoke! Israel's God has feet, but there is no mention of legs, buttocks, or toes (p. 116). One may reasonably assume that the feet were attached to legs. Though male, YHWH is allegedly nonsexual. Since he has no consort, he needs no sexual organs (p. 125). Yet he loves his people like an affectionate husband (p. 219n.15), and his heart is in heat for them (p. 220nn.53, 54). According to Korpel, "no sexual behaviour of God has been described in the Old Testament" (p. 246).

Similarly, T. Frymer-Kensky opines concerning the metaphysics of sexuality, "There is no sexuality in the divine sphere; God, usually envisioned as male in gender, is not phallic; God does not represent male virility, and is never imaged below the waist. The prophets use a powerful marital metaphor for the relationship between God the 'husband' and Israel the 'wife,' but the relationship is not described in erotic language. God neither models nor grants sexual potency or attraction. This absence of sex from the divine realm and of God from the sexual realm is accompanied by a separation of sexuality from the realm of the holy."[2] Both Korpel and Frymer-Kensky appear to have overstated the case with regard to YHWH's nonsexuality.

---

2. T. Frymer-Kensky 1992b. See also Frymer-Kensky 1992a:144: "The husband is God, masculine in gender, but never conceived as male in sexual terms. The wife is Israel, portrayed as a woman despite the maleness of the prophetic writers and, we assume, many of their listeners. The marriage between God and Israel is non-corporeal, never portrayed in physical or sexual terms, and the rules of this marriage do not conform to the legal norms of Israelite marriage." It is difficult to see how anyone could read Ezekiel 16 and detect no physical or sexual terms.

In prebiblical myths from the ancient Near East sexual activity is a prominent motif. Among the Ugaritic myths that are closest to the patriarchal era of the Bible in time, locale, language, and poetic structure, one poem depicts the father of the gods in the process of procreating gods.[3] The divine father's "hand" (a standard circumlocution for the male organ, as in Isa 57:8) is said to be long as the sea or the flood, the maximum hyperextension imaginable. Yet one should not suppose that the member in question is disproportionate to other parts of the divine body. The medieval Hebrew document Shi'ur Qomah ("table of stature") gives dimensions of parts of God's body in millions of parasangs, yet all parts are humanoid in proportion.[4] The divine privy member ('ēber šel 'eryâ) is mentioned but its dimensions are not divulged. The prime epithet of El/God in the Ugaritic myths is tr, "bull." The young rain god Ba'l or Hadd, before he is swallowed by Mot/Death, copulates 77 or 88 times with a heifer who bears a male child. Such grossly sexual motifs were certainly part of the religious heritage of the Canaanites and Amorites with whom the Israelites coexisted for a time. Much of such vital material has been expurgated from the Bible, but vestiges remain. Genesis 1:26 states that God created humanity in his image as male and female, reflecting the primordial presupposition that gods, like mortals, were sexual beings. Indeed, the garden of Eden story suggests that God/gods intended originally to keep the first human pair from discovering the joys of sex, as something too good to be shared with the hired help. But the wily serpent persuaded our curious mother Eve to eat the forbidden fruit and she shared it with her phlegmatic partner, with momentous consequences both bitter and sweet.

Genesis 6:1-8 is a striking sample of the sort of material that would usually have been deleted or altered by censorious scribes concerned to suppress vestiges of pagan polytheism. This episode was retained despite its objectionable features because it was an integral part of the flood story, supplying one tradition concerning the offense that provoked the deity to wipe out all but a remnant of humanity. It was the recovery of the Mesopotamian version of the flood in the eleventh tablet of the Gilgamesh Epic that sparked the Babel-Bibel controversy which exercised scholars in the late nineteenth and early twentieth centuries. Subsequent recovery of the Atrahasis Epic supplies a variant and fuller account of the flood more than twice as long as the version given in the Gilgamesh Epic. The Atrahasis Epic explains how humans were created because the working-class gods became disgruntled at the heavy demands of the executive and managerial gods and made such a fuss about it to the chief executive

3. Cf., e.g., M. Pope, *El in the Ugaritic Texts* (VTSup 2; Leiden: Brill, 1955) 35-42; idem, "Ups and Downs in El's Amours," *UF* 11 (1976) 701-8, in particular p. 705.

4. Cf. M. S. Cohen 1983:5ff., 9-10, 84-85; M. Pope, "Metastases in Canonical Shapes of the Super Song," in *Canon, Theology, and Old Testament Interpretation: Essays in Honor of Brevard S. Childs* (ed. Gene M. Tucker, David L. Peterson, and Robert R. Wilson; Philadelphia: Fortress, 1988) 312-28.

officer of the gods that it was decided to make a still lower class of workers, humans, to ease the pressure on the working gods. This stratagem was successful for a time, but other problems developed eventually. After twelve hundred years humans became so numerous and so boisterous that Enlil, chief executive of the managerial class of gods, could not sleep. So he diminished the noisemakers, first by famine, but after another twelve hundred years they were again in oversupply and were reduced by drought, and again after another twelve hundred years, by flood. After the third unsuccessful try at controlling over-breeding of humans, Enlil convened the divine council and they agreed on three new control measures: to make some women barren, to create the baby-snatching demon, and to establish three classes of priestesses or nuns, banned from childbearing.

The problem of overpopulation figured also in the biblical story about the interbreeding of the gods (sons of gods/God) with human females (Gen 6:1-4). The gods saw that some women were especially attractive and took them as wives and sired children who, in the nature of the case, were half-gods. The ability to interbreed and produce viable offspring is the practical test of specia-tion, as has long been appreciated. It was also observed long ago that selective crossbreeding of variant strains under healthy conditions usually produces superior, hardier offspring; this is called "hybrid vigor" by proponents of eugen-ics and "mongrelization" by those who favor ethnic purity or inbreeding. The offspring of the union of lusty divine males with pretty and presumably cooperative human females were naturally superior specimens. (Only male offspring are mentioned, but there is no reason to assume that semidivine females were not also born.) These became the giants or heroes of old, men of renown. They were called Nephilim, and some of their descendants reportedly still survived in Canaan when the Israelite scouts spied out the land (Num 13:33).[5] Among the outstanding features of this ancient race of half-gods, in addition to size, would be exceptional fertility and longevity. The Yahwist in Gen 6:1 mentions the increase of humans on the face of the ground in direct connection with the crossbreeding of the gods with humans. The Mesopotamian gods took genocidal measures against the repeated human population explo-sions. Nothing is said about the interbreeding with gods as a factor in these bursts of fertility. But longevity was apparently an acute problem, resulting from the mixing of gods and humans. It was then that YHWH decided to set a ceiling of 120 years on human life spans (Gen 6:3).

At this point (Gen 6:4-5) the Yahwist abruptly connects the sexual affairs of the gods with humans and the innate human proclivity (*yēṣer*) toward evil. YHWH was sorry and pained that he had made humanity and resolved to wipe them from the face of the ground along with all other living things. But Noah found favor with YHWH. In mitigation of human guilt in connection with these

---

5. Cf. Richard S. Hess, "Nephilim," *ABD* 4.1072-73.

liaisons with gods, one should consider that the gods must have initiated the activity since humans were not equal or independent partners in the affairs. How could a mortal maid resist a god and what effect would it have had she tried? Were the pretty girls at fault for their natural appeal to male instincts or for the "urge" *(tĕšûqâ)* with which their first mother had been blessed or cursed (Gen 3:16)?

The notion that gods and humans could and did mix sexually is widely attested in antiquity. The famous example in Christian literature is the impregnation of the Virgin Mary by the Most High (Luke 1:35), who "adumbrated" her. The conception of the demigod Alexander the Great was supposed to have occurred when Zeus had ado with Olympia, wife of Philip of Macedon, which event the poet Dryden depicts with exquisite delicacy:

> When he to fair Olympia pressed;
> And while he sought her snowy breast;
> Then round her slender waist he curled,
> And stamped an image of himself, a sovereign of the world.

Attention has been called recently to affinities between Gen 6:1-4 and Hesiod's explanation of the reason for the Trojan War, in contrast to the more familiar and romantic account given by Homer.[6] In a fragment of his Catalogue of Women, Hesiod relates that there was dissent among the gods about Zeus's plan to wipe out the human race as a means to destroy the mongrel half-gods who had been spawned by the gods' consorting with wretched mortals. The war with Troy was to be the means of eliminating both the half-gods and humans, thus restoring the ethnic purity of the gods by keeping them away from mortals. There is, however, no mention in Gen 6:1-4 that the demigod Nephilim were to be destroyed. They were supposed to have survived the flood and were later reported by Israelite spies to be living in the land of Canaan (Num 13:33). Elsewhere (Deut 2:11, 20) these aboriginal giants are connected with the Rephaim, the ancestor spirits, and with the extinct aboriginal giants in the promised land called variously Emim (terrors), Anaqim, and Zamzumim. R. Hendel has suggested that the function of the Nephilim in Israelite tradition is to die.[7] This idea may be supported by Ezek 32:27, which pictures the Nophelim (doubtless an error for Nephilim) as giants/warriors/heroes who live in the netherworld. My interest in the Nephilim is not to seek to solve the many problems concerning them but simply to stress their hybrid nature as produced by interbreeding of gods and humans. This is the first instance in Scripture of what may be called mixed marriage, but other examples are equally provocative.

The city Jerusalem is often personified as a female, a girl, a wife, a mother. The expressions *bat yĕrûšālayim* and *bat ṣîyyôn* were long mistranslated

---

6. Cf. R. S. Hendel 1987.
7. Ibid., 21-22.

"daughter of Jerusalem" or "daughter of Zion" before it was eventually recognized that the sense is appositive: "Miss Jerusalem" or "Miss Zion."[8] Similarly, the expression *bĕtûlat bat yĕrûšālayim/ṣîyyôn* means "Virgin Girl Jerusalem/Zion," not "virgin daughter of Jerusalem/Zion." This virgin had children, as we see in Isa 51:18 or Ps 149:2. The mother metaphor naturally implies a father, just as the term "father," whether used literally or figuratively, normally implies a mother, unless the father is viewed as androgynous and able to be both father and mother. The husband of Jerusalem, or of the nation Israel, was the God of Israel, YHWH, metaphorically speaking, of course. The marriage of the god with a bride who becomes mother of a whole nation may be seen as tantamount to the apotheosis of the bride and her children.

The idea that God/El, father of a family of seventy gods, was also somehow father of (all) humanity (*'abū 'adam*) is attested at least four times in the pre-Israelite Ugaritic mythological poems. Who the mother of humanity might be is not indicated, but there are hints in Scripture that she is (Mother) Earth from whom we come and to whom we return. In Israelite tradition the seventy children of God and of his wife Athirat were assigned to look after the (seventy) heathen nations, but the care of Israel became the (full-time) concern of the only real God, YHWH. Moreover, it was later supposed that YHWH had married Jerusalem or Israel. Some theoreticians of figurative language judge the quality of metaphor by the degree of hyperbole or "metaphoric distance." The marriage of YHWH and Jerusalem/Israel (personified) is certainly bold metaphor. Marital affairs between gods and humans have often been less than happy. When the deity initiates the affair, he or she must be held responsible. Humans who imagine they are somehow "wedded" to divinity, if they mistake metaphor for reality, may become paranoid.

The biblical locus classicus for the marriage of YHWH with Jerusalem or Israel is Ezekiel 16. This long chapter of more than threescore verses is replete with marital and sexual motifs that have offended readers and interpreters since it was composed some two and a half millennia ago. The scenario was doubtless intended to be offensive. Rabbi Eliezer ben Hyrcanus (one of the most learned and nationalistic of sages, whose zeal for Israel and hatred of heathen were unsurpassed) forbade the public reading of Ezekiel 16 as a prophetic lection or *hapṭarah* (*m. Meg.* 4:10) and strongly censured any who transgressed the ban (*b. Meg.* 25b).[9] What bothered Eliezer was not the marital metaphor but the

---

8. Cf. W. F. Stinespring, "No Daughter of Zion," *Encounter* 26 (1965) 133-41.

9. Eliezer was renowned for his learning and phenomenal memory. His teacher Yohanan ben Zakkai called him "a cemented cistern that does not lose a drop" and "a pitched vessel that preserves its wine." Yohanan opined that if all Israel's sages were in one scale of the balance and Eliezer ben Hyrcanus were in the other, he would outweigh them all. Eliezer considered such praise richly deserved. He pitted his own opinion against that of the majority of sages till they felt compelled to excommunicate him. His pride and bitterness in sick old age were also outstanding. He predicted that scholars who had not come to study with him

insult to the pedigree *(yiḥ[ḥ]ûs)* of Jerusalem/Israel in the opening declaration by the deity himself that Jerusalem's origin and birth were "of the land of the Canaanite," her father being an Amorite and her mother a Hittite (16:3, 45). This assertion contradicts the tradition that of the nations supposedly descended from Noah's sons, Shem, Ham, and Japheth, Israel's progenitor was Shem. Now it is doubly emphasized (Gen 9:18, 22) that Ham was Canaan's father. Ham also was father of Cush (Ethiopia), Miṣraim (Egypt), and Put (Libya?), North African nations with dark skin. *Kûšî* and *Kûšît* in Modern Hebrew are equivalent to "negro" and "negress." Moses' marriage to a Cushitess offended Miriam and Aaron, but YHWH rebuked them for their censure and punished Miriam (though not Aaron) with a seven-day spell of leprosy, which turned her for the time snow-white (Num 12:9-10). In support of the divine approval of Moses' dusky wife, Rashi showed by *gematria* that black is beautiful since the numerical value of the letters of "Cushitess" *(kwšyt)* equals that of the phrase "good looking" *(ypt mr'h).*[10] The classification of the Canaanites as descendants of Ham (Gen 10:6) along with the Egyptians, Ethiopians, and Libyans may have been intended to suggest that the Canaanites were dark skinned. In any case, the intent was to separate the Canaanites as alleged descendants of Ham from the offspring of Noah's favored son Shem.

Noah's curse of his grandson Canaan for the offense or dereliction of duty committed by Canaan's father Ham while Noah was dead drunk has been hard to explain.[11] The curse (Gen 9:25-27) condemned Canaan to abject enslavement to Shem and Japheth. An ulterior motive for Noah's cursing of Canaan is not far to seek. By some means not explained, the Canaanites had managed to preoccupy the territory that YHWH had supposedly reserved for the descendants of Abraham through Isaac. Noah's foresight in condemning his grandson Canaan to slavery supplies a pretext to justify the dispossession of the Canaanites from the land that they had long occupied before Abraham, Isaac, and Jacob came on the scene. Slaves have no property rights. Whatever a slave has belongs to his master (*b. Sanh.* 91a). Thus Noah's curse sets the stage for

---

would likely die unnatural deaths. Those who did study with him, he reckoned, had taken no more than a dab of a paintbrush from the palette of his learning, which was so vast that if all the seas were ink, all reeds quills, and all people scribes, they would not suffice to write all his learning (*b. Sanh.* 68a). Toward the heathen Eliezer he was even more severe. All their charity and kindness he counted as sin, because they did it only to magnify themselves (*b. B. Bat.* 10b).

10. Cf. Pope 1977:368 on black beauty in the Super Song.

11. It has been variously surmised that the offense against the comatose and naked Noah was a homosexual assault or castration; cf. Ephraim Isaac, "Ham," *ABD* 3.31-32; and Richard S. Hess, "Canaan," *ABD* 1.828. The Ugaritic Epic of Aqhat shows that care of a drunken father was an important filial duty, and Isa 51:17-18 suggests that the mother also expected a helping hand when she was drunk. There is thus no reason to suppose that Ham's crime was anything more than a failure to cover his naked father without looking at him, as his brothers managed to do when they learned of their father's predicament.

dispossession of the Canaanites and the ethnic cleansing divinely ordained in Deuteronomy 7.

The declaration by YHWH himself (Ezek 16:3) concerning Jerusalem's mixed pedigree accords with the ethnolinguistic evidence. Languages, of course, are not genetically transmitted. The child Jerusalem learned her language by listening to the Canaanites and Amorites who were around her as she grew like a weed. The "Semitic" languages do have striking affinities with Egyptian and other Hamitic and Cushitic languages of North Africa.[12] The German scholar A. L. Schlözer coined the term "Semitic" in 1781 based on the tripartite division of the postdiluvian world as descended from Noah's three sons. The use of the term "Japhethitic" for the thousands of languages of the third world outside the Hamito-Semitic divisions was short-lived for obvious reasons. The term "Semitic" was soon perverted to a pseudoracist term by the Jew-hater Wilhelm Marr in his "Zwangslose antisemitische Hefte" (1890). This misnomer is still widely used even by Semitologists who should know better. The Semitic term for "anti-Semitism" in Modern "Hebrew" (properly neo-Canaanite) is *śin'at ha-yĕhûdîm,* "hatred of Jews," translating precisely the German locution *Jüden-hass,* "Jew-hate."

Isaiah 19:16-24 predicts that eventually Judah will put the fear of the Lord on the Egyptians, and five cities of Egypt will speak the Canaanite language, "the lip of Canaan," and swear allegiance to the Lord of hosts. Assyria (present-day Iraq and Syria) will also join Egypt and Israel in blessing and being blessed by the Lord of hosts, who will say, "Blessed be Egypt my people, and Assyria the work of my hands, and Israel my heritage."[13] Of specific interest here is the expression "lip of Canaan" for the language to be spoken in some cities of Egypt. The language in question is what is now called "Hebrew," but should be more properly called "Canaanite" since in Semitology (scientific study of Semitic languages), the Northwest Semitic branch is composed of Canaanite and Aramaic. Canaanite is attested already in the early second millennium B.C.E., while Aramaic began to be differentiated from Canaanite near the end of the

---

12. See the introductory survey of the Afroasiatic Language Family by John Huehnergard in "Language," *ABD* 4.155-62. "The Semitic languages constitute one branch of a large language family now usually called Afroasiatic (or Afrasian; formerly Hamito-Semitic)." The Afroasiatic family comprises six branches: (1) Semitic, (2) Egyptian, (3) Berber, (4) Cushitic, (5) Omotic, (6) Chadic. The Semitic languages have the longest recorded history of any linguistic group, from the middle of the third millennium B.C.E. with Akkadian and Eblaite to present-day Arabic, Amharic, Modern Hebrew (basically neo-Canaanite), and several surviving Aramaic dialects. Canaanite and its congeners Amorite, Ugaritic, and Aramaic fall in the Northwest Semitic or Syro-Palestinian branch of the Semitic languages. One scholar has called the Amorites or Western Semites who moved into Mesopotamia and founded the First Dynasty of Babylon "East Canaanite" (Theo Bauer, *Die Ostkananäer* [Leipzig, 1926]).

13. While I was teaching Ugaritic at the University of Aleppo in 1980, some of the students confided to me that they listened betimes to Israeli radio and found they could understand a great deal on the basis of cognates with Arabic.

second millennium B.C.E. Ugaritic, from the fourteenth-thirteenth century
B.C.E., has some Canaanite and some Aramaic features, representing a stage
before the clear separation of the two distinct speech types. The languages of
Israel's close neighbors and despised kin, the Moabites, Ammonites, and
Edomites, are also Canaanite and mutually intelligible, as would be the various
Israelite dialects of what Semitists also call Canaanite. The later replacement of
Canaanite by Aramaic in everyday speech in the area was no great problem, as
indicated by rabbinic usage, which freely mixes and switches Canaanite and
Aramaic. It seems highly likely that the Canaanites and Amorites were closely
related genetically to the Israelites, as they were linguistically. The pre-Israelite
name of Jerusalem was *Yĕbûs*, which may be related to the West Semitic
Amorite-Canaanite term *yābēš*, "dry." There is no basis for serious doubt that
the ancient city Yebus, alias Yerushalayim, had a mixed Canaanite and Hurro-
Hittite population, so that one may trust the word of the Lord transmitted by
Ezekiel that the city's pedigree was Amorite-Canaanite-Hittite along with other
mixes. When David took the city, there is no mention of slaughter of the
inhabitants (2 Sam 5:6-9). Solomon, however, is said to have enslaved what
remained of the Amorites, Hittites, Perizzites, Hivites, and Jebusites whom the
Israelites had not been able to eradicate (1 Kgs 9:20ff.). What really happened
is openly admitted in Ps 106:34-39:

> They did not destroy the peoples,
> as YHWH commanded them,
> but they mixed with the heathen
> and learned their practices.
> They served their idols,
> which became a snare to them.
> They sacrificed their sons
> and their daughters to demons;
> they shed innocent blood,
> blood of their sons and daughters,
> whom they sacrificed to the idols of Canaan.
> Thus the land was fouled with blood.
> They were dirty in their doings,
> they whored in their dealings.

These are the kinds of deeds YHWH characterized as harlotry in Ezekiel 16.

Jerusalem's early childhood, as Ezekiel tells it, was far from ideal. Spawned
by a mongrel Amorite-Hittite pair,[14] she was thrown out in the open field with

---

14. The Targum to Ezek 16:3-14 notes that Jerusalem's birthplace and home was indeed
the land of the Canaanite, but totally ignores her Amorite kith and kin except to recall the
divine promise to destroy them. The blood in which the female infant wallows becomes the
blood of circumcision on which account the Lord takes pity and the blood of the paschal

navel cord uncut, unwashed, unsalted, unswaddled, left to writhe in her blood. But YHWH happened to pass by and pitied the infant and decided she should live. Nothing is said of any subsequent care or even feeding of the lively babe. We are told only that she continued naked when YHWH passed again — it must have been some years later — and saw that she had developed "superb ornamentation," breasts and (pubic) hair, but was still stark naked. He came back again for another look and noted that it was her time for love. So he spread his wing/skirt over her and covered her nakedness. Just what this means is not difficult to divine, unless one comes to the story with the presupposition that the deity was wholly void of sexual urge or capability, which certainly was not the ancient idea of gods or goddesses. The girl was already bare so that she could not be further exposed. "Uncovering nakedness" is a common locution for sexual congress. When a male spreads his cloak over a nude nubile maid ripe for love, one would assume that sexual intercourse is likely to occur, unless it be the case that the male has neither the equipment nor the urge, as some suppose. When Ruth, at Naomi's behest, bathed and oiled herself and went to the threshing floor where Boaz was sleeping and uncovered his "feet," that is, genitals ("foot-water" means urine and "foot-hair" pubic hair), Ruth lay at Boaz's bare "feet" till he stirred and was startled to find a woman there. Ruth identified herself and directed Boaz to spread his skirt over her, since he was a "redeemer" or kinsman of her dead husband (obligated to marry her and beget an heir for the defunct kinsman). Probably Boaz did what comes naturally. Anyhow, he invited Ruth to spend the rest of the night with him. Before daylight, after loading her mantle with barley, he sent her home. Commentators have generally assumed that nothing passed between the two but conversation, though some have noted that Ruth's stratagem of baring Boaz's "feet" and lying with him for hours was risky. The famous Catholic commentator Dom Calmet suggested that the Holy Spirit was watching over Ruth and protecting her. In any event, Ruth got what she wanted. The expression "spread one's cloak" over a female occurs in Scripture only in Ruth 3:9 with reference to a human pair and in Ezek 16:8 with respect to the God of Israel and Jerusalem personified as a nubile maid ready for love. The equivalent of the locution "spread one's skirt/cloak/wing over a girl" lives on in modern Arabic usage with patent sexual sense. S. H. Stephan relates how in 1915 near Baghdad he was unwilling witness to an incident of alfresco copulation when by the roadside he saw a man in broad daylight spread his cloak (ʿabāya-t) over a girl, a deed so repugnant as to

---

sacrifices for which he will redeem them. The baby's growth like the plants of the field evokes the righteous deeds of her fathers. Her conspicuous puberty is seen as the delivery from slavery. Instead of YHWH's union with the child bride there is the appearance to Moses in the burning bush and Israel's delivery from slavery in Egypt. The fine bridal clothing and jewelry become the finery of the priests and the ornament of the words of Torah, of the tabernacle, and the rich food provided the bride becomes the manna in the wilderness, leaving no hint of the marital metaphor.

be expressed only in the decent obscurity of Latin: "expandit amiculum suum super puellam."[15]

As YHWH testified in his own words (Ezek 16:9), "Then I passed by you and looked at you and lo your time was love time, so I spread my skirt over you and covered your nakedness and swore to you (says YHWH) and you became mine." It seems reasonable to assume that YHWH was still in his cloak when he spread it over Jerusalem to cover her previously bare "nakedness." What happened under cover is discreetly unmentioned, but the action was accompanied or followed by a covenant and oath (of marriage) and Jerusalem became his. This was the most simple and primitive mode of marriage by physical union or coition, aptly called by the rabbis *bîʾâ*, "entry." Directly after the undercover action, the oath, and the covenant, YHWH recounts that he bathed the girl with water, rinsed off her blood, and anointed her with oil (16:9). From the wording one cannot tell whether this was the first bath Jerusalem had experienced since birth. The blood in question could conceivably have been the residue of that in which she had wallowed when she was born. It seems unlikely, however, that even an orphan waif would come to puberty without having bathed. But that is hardly less odd than continuing to go about naked even after puberty. The blood YHWH himself washed off his bride could have been that of her (first) menses, which she would have experienced in the course of developing her outstanding ornamentation. Given the strong aversion to menstrual blood, it is unlikely that the deity would take under his robe a *niddah*, a menstruant. Accordingly, logic favors the conclusion that the blood in question was hymeneal. Thus YHWH deflowered the naked maid but did so responsibly and honorably, plighting troth to her with a covenant of marriage. This is stark metaphor intended to be taken seriously. This motif of YHWH's marriage with Jerusalem/Zion, representing his chosen people, pervades postexilic Scriptures. But nowhere is the event so vividly recounted as here in Ezekiel 16.

This marriage of YHWH with Jerusalem fell apart almost immediately after it was consummated, before there was a honeymoon. YHWH began by lavishing on his new bride finery, clothing, jewelry, ornaments, nose ring, earrings, gold crown, fine food, honey, and oil, so that she became queenly and renowned among nations for her beauty and splendor. She, however, immediately developed an acute seizure of nymphomania for lovers other than her husband. The catalog of her phrenetic fornication with any and all comers, and even with artificial male organs, are too much to recount. The like had never been before nor would ever be again, according to her repeatedly betrayed husband (16:16).

Modern alienists could find some rationale for Jerusalem's strong antipathy to her husband. In some contemporary societies this marriage would

---

15. S. H. Stephan, "Modern Palestinian Parallels to the Song of Songs," *JPOS* (1922) 1-80, 198-278, esp. 260.

be regarded as statutory rape. In any event Jerusalem was not happy with her husband and showed her feelings by using his lavish wedding gifts to bribe her numerous lovers. YHWH, it seems, could not imagine anything he might have done to provoke such behavior by his very young wife. In view of her pedigree, he attributed her aberration to hereditary defect of character: it ran in the family. Like mother like daughter, only more so. Jerusalem was much worse than her biological parents, than her sisters Sodom and Samaria, and her cousins, worse even than the Philistine girls (16:43-58).

As the wronged husband, YHWH was hurt but kept himself under control. Adultery was a capital crime, and it is interesting to see how the deity dealt with it when he was the cuckold. There was apparent indecision and wavering at first as to just what he might do. First he resolved to strip the wanton naked and gather all her lovers to see her shame (nothing new for them). He speaks of bringing an army against her to hack her with swords, to burn her houses, thus to sate his fury. This reflects what had already been done by Nebuchadrezzar's armies. But then (16:53-58) he speaks of restoring the fortunes of Sodom, Samaria, and Jerusalem too, so that she (Jerusalem) might be a consolation to her sisters. Finally (16:59-63) he remembers his (marriage) covenant and speaks of establishing an everlasting covenant. Since nothing is said of this being a new covenant, it refers, presumably, to the original marriage. YHWH, for his part, will remain faithful to his vows, and this, he supposes, will make the errant wife contrite and confounded, never again to open her mouth because of shame when he forgives her for all she has done.[16]

16. This story of an abandoned newborn girl who survived to be chosen as bride not of a human king but by God himself has puzzled literary analysts since H. Gunkel (1917) dealt with fairy tales in the Bible. The abandoned foundling that rises to royal estate is often a prodigy that was reluctantly given up by its poor but honest parents due to circumstances beyond their control. In the present story, however, the parents are not poor but uncaring, disreputable, morally derelict, even criminal, with no excuse for abandoning a healthy child (unless it could have been a matter of gender; female infants were regarded as expendable in many societies). The unfortunate aspect of this birth and marriage was the bride's parents, who had the bad luck to belong to pariah peoples deemed deserving of slavery or death by the very God who tells how he knowingly condescended to marry their unwanted daughter. The unwelcome information from a reliable source is the bride's Canaanite-Amorite heritage. This is what moved Eliezer ben Hyrcanus to forbid the public airing of the real but unpalatable contradiction to the falsified official version of Israel's pedigree in order to obscure her known Canaanite origins. This is why Genesis 9 twice tells the reader that Ham was the father of Canaan (vv. 18, 22), to distance Noah's favored son Shem and his descendants from the impious Ham and his alleged son Canaan deemed worthy of slavery or death. M. Greenberg (1983:301-2) observes that the motive of baseness is unexampled in exposure stories and notes that the wanton cruelty and immorality of the parents are inherited by the child who is not intended to be admired. Greenberg also comments: "The assertion that the tale is remote from Jerusalem's history loses most of its weight when it is realized that Jerusalem stands for Israel; God entered into a covenant only with the people, never with the city (vs. 8)." But since Jerusalem obviously stands for Israel, as commonly recognized, there is no difference between the histories of one and the other and the two can be easily interchanged.

This marriage metaphor[17] for the relation of Israel's God to his chosen people lived on through postexilic times and was later adopted and adapted by Christians who saw themselves as the true Israel, the faithful Bride of God's Son, the Christ, the (Passover) Lamb of God who takes away the sins of the world. In the last book of canonical Christian Scripture (Rev 21:1-4), after visions of the judgment and resurrection, the death of Death and Hell, and the second death of all whose name is not found written in the Book of Life, the old heaven and old earth, and Sea (an early enemy of Ba'l in pre-Israelite West Semitic myth) pass away. Then the visionary sees a new heaven and new earth and the holy city, New Jerusalem, descends out of heaven from God, prepared as a bride adorned for her husband (i.e., the Lamb/Christ). A loud voice from God's throne proclaims: "Behold, the dwelling of God is with humanity, and he will dwell with them, and they shall be his people." This New Jerusalem is now the Bride of God's Son, the Lamb, the Christ, as noted elsewhere by the visionary. Humanity (what is left of it) becomes God's dwelling and his people. No more exterminations are envisioned. It is noteworthy that the Greek words here used for "dwelling" *(skēnē)* and "dwell" *(skēnoō)* resemble phonetically the postbiblical Semitic term for YHWH's feminine counterpart and consort, *šĕkîna-t* (a feminine passival participial noun), connoting symbiosis with an indwelt female. In traditional Jewish gnosticism or mysticism (Qabbalah), Shekinah is, in effect, wife of the God of Israel and the two are one, as husband and wife are one. Somewhat like the Shakti (female energy) ideology of India, the Shekinah is the active female principle through whom the world is sustained.

R. Patai has elaborated this theme in his study *The Hebrew Goddess.* Only a few details need be noted here. The God of Israel and his Shekinah (Jerusalem or Israel personified) were initially very active sexually, in constant contact, face-to-face, as symbolized by the male and female cherubim above the ark of the covenant. But they became estranged and separated because of Israel's

---

17. J. Galambush (1992) has produced the most thorough and detailed study to date of the metaphor of Jerusalem as YHWH's wife in Ezekiel 16 and 23. The origins of this conception of the city as a woman and the personification of cities as goddesses married to a god are still obscure. J. Lewy (1944) argued from West Semitic and Akkadian appellations of cities (such as "The City of Assur Is Queen" or "The City of Arba'il Is Ruler") and from Assyrian personal names in which city names appear as feminine theophoric elements that major cities were regarded as goddesses married to the city's patron god. Lewy cited further Phoenician coins depicting women wearing city turrets as crowns, which suggests that the city was believed to be a goddess. Gods and goddesses, of course, married one another, and earthly kings of Mesopotamia reenacted these sacred marriages. Since married deities cohabited in conjugal bliss, Lewy (1944:441) reasoned, "it follows that, on principle, their temples lay within the towns whom [the gods] married. In other words, . . . according to an ancient West Semitic doctrine, the god who chose a town as seat of his sanctuary made that town his divine wife." Galambush deftly shows how Ezekiel and earlier biblical writers were dependent on ancient Near Eastern mixed marriage metaphor in the personification of Jerusalem as YHWH's wife.

adulteries (as detailed in Ezekiel 16). The goal of Jewish piety, in the thought of M. Buber and F. Rosenzweig, is to reunite Israel's God and his Shekinah, the chastened and purified people of Israel. This is essentially the same metaphor as the Christian visionary's view of the New Jerusalem, as purified humanity, in symbiosis with God and/or his Son on earth.

People still have difficulty in distinguishing metaphor and reality. The metaphor of God's marriage to Jerusalem/Zion still has power to stir hope, joy, sorrow, love, and hate in millions who claim some sort of kinship, real or metaphorical, with Abra(ha)m. In praying for the peace of Jerusalem, we cannot completely forget her pedigree and her marital history as related by her devoted husband in Ezekiel 16, nor her present state. Post-Holocaust theology, Jewish, Christian, and Muslim, is vexed with the same problems that beset former generations. Lesser holocausts and "ethnic cleansings" continue in various parts of the world. The numbers and identities of the victims are not the crucial issue. Murder is ever the same, since the first instance when Cain killed Abel. The insight (*m. Sanh.* 4:5) that whoever destroys a single life or saves a single life Scripture reckons as though he destroyed or saved a whole world applies to one murder as to millions. It is not only lives "from Israel" that count. That is why humanity was created from a common ancestor so that none may claim superior pedigree, and any human has as much right as another to say, "for my sake the world was created."

The fancied union of any human group, city, or nation, with any God worthy of the name, any presumed special "God-with-us" relationship not open to all on equal basis, will surely fare as badly as has YHWH's marriage with Jerusalem to date. The same applies to the Christian church's claim of marriage with God's Son, the Lamb, and to every claim to monopoly on access to salvation. The pedigree and honest history of every earthly city is essentially like that of unregenerate Jerusalem/Zion. Our alabaster cities may gleam when spotlighted to bedazzle simpletons, but behind the facades none is as yet "undimmed by human tears." I have sojourned in modern Jerusalem under British, Jordanian, and Israeli rule and in Aleppo, Damascus, New Haven, and other cities long enough to understand that there is no easy resolution to human conflicts that stem from individual and collective selfishness. One may sing "From Zion shall go forth Torah," but it will not help unless the essence of that Torah is justice for all by which alone every human society must be redeemed.

Jacob Neusner (1993) has begun a new project called The Bible of Judaism Library, which he introduces with portions of *Midrash Rabbah* on the Song of Songs under the title *Israel's Love Affair with God*. The first brief chapter is entitled "The Passionate Love Affair of God and Israel." Nowhere does the book mention YHWH's own account of the affair in Ezekiel 16. In the projected library Neusner intends to show how all Judaisms differ from all Christianities and Islams in their readings of ancient Israel's holy writings, which all three revere in addition to other scriptures or traditions: the Qur'an, the New Testament, and the corpus of oral Torah, respectively. Neusner's goal "is to open up for contemporary faith yet another route to Sinai: the one explored by the sages of Judaism who received the Torah as God's letter to each of them personally, this morning." "If this library succeeds in its mission, faithful Jews and Christians will renew for themselves a program of Bible study that brings to scripture profoundly religious concerns in place of the prevailing program of historical and philological research." Neusner acknowledges the importance of scholarship for informed exegesis, "but scholarship does not deliver scripture into our hands, and scholarship does not teach lessons of transcendence such as Torah does. . . . So let us get our perspectives in line with the facts of faith." With this projected library Neusner proposes to show how faithful Judaic sages accomplished their readings that "endowed scripture with sanctity and authority through the ages to our day." This is indeed a consummation devoutly to be wished. Reconciliation of proponents of various Judaisms, Christianities, and Islams, all claiming seminal connection (genetic and/or ideological) with Abra(ha)m seems a remote prospect. Bible study by negotiators of the ATF (Bureau of Alcohol, Tobacco, and Firearms, an unholy trinity in today's common life and death) did not prevent holocaust of the faithful followers of the Waco Branch Davidian Messiah before he could finish his commentary on the seven seals of the Apocalypse that would have clarified everything. Unfortunately both ATF and Koresh lacked patience.

The Apostle of Allah saw it as his mission to lead his people out of ignorance and idolatry to the worship of the one true God revered by Jews and Christians who read the Book but disputed its meaning. He had hoped to reconcile the "People of the Book" under the inclusive tent of Islam, submission to the one and only God. Today that tent is rent with sectarian religiopolitical strife. The symbol of Christian ecumenism is one boat in which all life on earth is contained. It is within human power to scuttle the craft or make it unfit for life of any kind. If study of any sort can help prevent this catastrophe, we should all be at it. The metaphor of a love affair of any select human group with God, or of God with them, is transcendent madness. The choice is all or none.

Bibliography

Cohen, Martin S.
> 1983   *The Shi'ur Qomah — Liturgy and Theurgy in Pre-Kabbalistic Jewish Mysticism.* Lanham, MD: University Press of America.

Frymer-Kensky, Tikva
> 1992a   *In the Wake of the Goddesses: Women, Culture, and the Biblical Transformation of Pagan Myth.* New York and Toronto: Free Press (Macmillan).
> 1992b   "Sex and Sexuality: D. The Metaphysics of Sexuality." *ABD* 5.1146.

Galambush, Julie
1992   *Jerusalem in the Book of Ezekiel: The City as Yahweh's Wife*. SBLDS
            130. Atlanta: Scholars.
Greenberg, Moshe
1983   *Ezekiel 1–20*. AB 22. Garden City, NY: Doubleday.
Hendel, Ronald S.
1987   "Of Demigods and the Deluge." *JBL* 105:13-26.
Korpel, Marjo Christine Annette
1990   *A Rift in the Clouds: Ugaritic and Hebrew Descriptions of the Divine*.
            Theologische Akademie Uitgaande van de Johannes Calvijnstichting
            te Kampen. Ugaritisch-Biblische Literatur 8. Münster: UGARIT-
            Verlag.
Lewy, Julius
1944   "The Old West Semitic Sun God Hammu." *HUCA* 18:436-44.
Neusner, Jacob
1993   *Israel's Love Affair with God: Song of Songs*. The Bible of Judaism
            Library. Valley Forge, PA: Trinity Press International.
Patai, Raphael
1967   *The Hebrew Goddess*. New York: Ktav. Cf. M. Pope, 1977:153-79, for
            highlights of Patai's portrait of the Goddess.
Pope, Marvin H.
1977   *Song of Songs*. AB 7C. Garden City, NY: Doubleday.

Prepositions with Pronominal Suffixes
in Phoenician and Punic

PHILIP C. SCHMITZ

Eastern Michigan University, Ypsilanti

Europeans never quite lost the memory of the Phoenicians as a people, nor the awareness that their language was akin to Hebrew.[1] Knowledge of the Phoenician language, however, was eclipsed from the turn of the current era[2] until

1. "En-effet, les Cananéens sont les mêmes que les Phéniciens, et la langue Hebräique dans laquelle les Livres Sacrés sont écrits, est la même que la Phénicienne," observed Richard Simon in his *Histoire critique du Vieux Testament* (1685) 83. Simon appealed in this matter to the authority of Samuel Bochart (1599-1667), whose *Geographia Sacra, seu Phaleg et Canaan* (1646) was extremely influential in the formation of comparative Semitic philology. (The copy of Bochart's *Geographia Sacra* available to me was printed in Lyon in 1707; his statements concerning the identity of Canaanites and Phoenicians appear in col. 300, ll. 38-39. The 1678 edition of Simon's *Histoire critique* is among "the rarest of books" [so Louis I. Bredvold, *The Intellectual Milieu of John Dryden* (Ann Arbor: University of Michigan, 1934; reprinted 1966) 101-2]; I have consulted the Amsterdam edition of 1685.)

Survivals from Phoenician and Punic in the language of Malta were noted at least as early as Jean Quintin's *Insulae Melitae descriptio ex commentariis rerum quotidianarum* (Lyons: Seb. Gryphium, 1536) and were cataloged by eighteenth-century grammarians (see M. Sznycer, "Antiquités et épigraphie nord-sémitiques," *Annuaire de l'Ecole pratique des Hautes Etudes, IVe section: Sciences historiques et philologiques* [hereinafter *AEHE* IV] 105 [1971-72] 145-61; on Maltese philology, p. 154).

2. According to F. Briquel-Chatonnet, "Les derniers témoignages sur la langue phénicienne en Orient," *Rivista di Studi Fenici* 19 (1991) 3-21, written texts in Phoenician had become a rarity in Western Asia by the end of the first century B.C.E., having been replaced by Greek in the Hellenistic period and perhaps by Aramaic in the Roman period (pp. 8-15). The spread of Greek in the Phoenician homelands during the Seleucid period is discussed by John D. Grainger (*Hellenistic Phoenicia* [Oxford: Clarendon, 1991] 108-9), with some examples of the continued use of Phoenician in inscriptions and, presumably, in speech. To refer as Grainger does (p. 191) to Phoenician as "an Aramaic dialect" is, however, simply to

1758, when Jean-Jacques Barthélemy announced his successful decipherment of the Phoenician alphabet.[3] Study of the language and interpretation of surviving inscriptions was slow to progress until the formative work of Gesenius in the second quarter of the nineteenth century.[4] By the third quarter of the

increase confusion. W. von Landau (*Die phönizischen Inschriften* [Der Alte Orient 3; Leipzig: J. C. Hinrichs, 1907] 6) was of the opinion that spoken Phoenician survived until the time of Constantine.

In the Western Mediterranean, particularly in North Africa in the vicinity of Carthage, Neo-Punic continued to be spoken and written perhaps as late as the Byzantine period. With the victory of the Egyptian Abdullah Ibn Saad over Gregory at Sufetula in 25-26 A.H. (647-648 C.E.) the growing cultural hegemony of Islam brought the supplanting of older languages by Arabic. On the earlier periods, see F. Millar, "Local Cultures in the Roman Empire: Libyan, Punic and Latin in Roman Africa," *JRS* 58 (1968) 126-34; W. Röllig, "Das Punische im römischen Reich," in *Die Sprachen im römischen Reich der Kaiserzeit* (ed. G. Neumann and J. Untermann; Beihefte der Bonner Jahrbücher 40; Cologne: Rheinland-Verlag, 1980) 285-99.

3. J. Barthélemy, "Réflexions sur quelques monumens [*sic*] phéniciens et sur les alphabets qui en résultent," *Mémoires de l'Académie des inscriptions et belles-lettres* 30 (1758) 405-27. The laudatory biography by Maurice Badolle (*L'Abbé Jean-Jacques Barthélemy (1716-1795) et l'hellenisme en France dans la seconde moitié du XVIIIe siècle* [Paris: Presses Universitaires du France, 1927]) documents the acclaim that this decipherment won Barthélemy (p. 70) and traces his long quarrel with John Swinton (1703-1777) over claims to priority. On Barthélemy's achievement, see M. Lidzbarski, *Handbuch der nordsemitischen Epigraphik* (2 vols.; Weimar, 1898; reprinted Hildesheim: Olms, 1962) 1.435-36; Madeleine V. David, "En marge du mémoire de l'abbé Barthélemy sur les inscriptions phéniciennes," *CRAIBL* (1961) 30-40; A. Dupont-Sommer, "Jean-Jacques Barthélemy et l'ancienne Académie des Inscriptions et Belles-Lettres," *CRAIBL* (1971) 11-13. The Phoenician inscriptions from Malta that Barthélemy deciphered have been examined anew by Sznycer ("Antiquités et épigraphie nord-sémitiques," *AEHE* IV 106 [1974] 191-208).

Abbé Barthélemy had already deciphered the Palmyrene alphabet in 1754; see Peter T. Daniels, "'Shewing of Hard Sentences and Dissolving of Doubts': The First Decipherment," *JAOS* 108 (1988) 419-36. On the fascinating history of type fonts for printing Phoenician characters, see Philippe Berger, "Notice sur les caractères phéniciens destinés à l'impression du *Corpus inscriptionum semiticarum*," *JA*, 7th series, 15 (1880) 5-34.

4. Wilhelm Gesenius, *Scriptura linguaeque Phoeniciae monumenta quotquot supersunt* (2 vols.; Leipzig, 1837). Almost entirely forgotten is Gesenius's article "Paläographie" in *Allgemeine Encyklopädie der Wissenschaften und Künste* (ed. J. S. Ersch and J. G. Gruber; Leipzig: F. U. Brockhaus, 1837), section 3, 9.287-316 and pls. 1-3. Gesenius's concern for precision, and the care he expended to establish the proper reading of even a single letter, were warmly appreciated by O. Eissfeldt, "The Beginnings of Phoenician Epigraphy according to a Letter Written by Wilhelm Gesenius in 1835," *Palestine Exploration Quarterly* 79 (1947) 68-86. The German original of Eissfeldt's address, *Von den Anfängen der Phönizischen Epigraphik* (Hallische Monographien 5; Halle: Niemeyer, 1948), is more amply documented but lacks the final section of the English version. (October 23, 1992, marked the 150th anniversary of the death of Gesenius.)

The three-volume collection by Gesenius's contemporary Franz Karl Movers (*Die Phönizier* [Bonn: E. Weber, 1841-56]) was more broadly historical and cultural in its interests. While Movers assembled numerous sundered fragments of Phoenician civilization, he made no significant independent contribution to linguistic study. The comments of W. F. Albright are judicious: "Movers has been unduly criticized in some quarters for his hazardous conjectures and especially for his wild etymologies. However, he was in these respects only a child of a nineteenth century, study of the Phoenician language had been placed on a more secure foundation, partly through discoveries of new texts,[5] and especially through the tireless exertions of Ernst Renan to collect and publish neglected artifacts and inscriptions.[6] Grammatical study of the language reached a new level in the work of Paul Schröder.[7] Further discoveries of new texts in the last quarter of the nineteenth century, and the inauguration of a *Corpus* of Phoenician and Punic inscriptions under Renan's editorship, ensured continuing scholarly attention to the language.[8]

---

generation which was so dazzled by the rapidity of philological and archaeological discovery that it followed mirages with as much confidence as it did solid horizons" ("The Role of the Canaanites in the History of Civilization," in *The Bible and the Ancient Near East: Essays in Honor of William Foxwell Albright* (ed. G. Ernest Wright; Garden City, NY: Doubleday, 1961] 329).

5. The "Marseille Tariff," still the longest extant Punic inscription, was discovered in 1844 or 1845 and published in 1846 (F. de Saulcy, "Des études phéniciennes," *Revue des Deux-Mondes* [Dec. 1846] 1064-67). The corpus of Phoenician was significantly enlarged by the discovery and publication in 1855 of an inscribed sarcophagus from the royal tombs of Sidon (C. V. A. van Dyck, *Transactions of the Albany Institute* 4 [1855] 68-72). This now famous epitaph of Eshmunazar is twenty-two lines long and almost perfectly preserved.

6. Particularly during his archaeological expedition to the Lebanon during the years 1860 and 1861, related in E. Renan, *Mission de Phénicie* (Paris, 1864). Landau called Renan's *Mission* "noch jetzt ein Quellenwerk der phönizischen Altertumskunde" (*Phönizischen Inschriften*, 7). The historical circumstances of Renan's "mission" are examined by Neil Asher Silberman, *Digging for God and Country* (New York: Knopf, 1982) 69, 74. Martin Bernal's controversial study, *Black Athena: The Afroasiatic Roots of Classical Civilization*, vol. 1: *The Fabrication of Ancient Greece 1785-1985* (New Brunswick, NJ: Rutgers University, 1987), examines the social context of European fascination with the language and history of the Phoenicians (pp. 337-99); Bernal draws attention to Renan's attitudes concerning race, and situates Renan with respect to the climate of academic anti-Semitism fashionable in his day.

7. P. Schröder, *Die Phönizische Sprache* (Halle: Waisenhaus, 1869). This grammar still richly rewards those who read it, and is at some points unsurpassed by subsequent scholarship. Schröder (b. Elsterwerda, 1844; d. Jena, 1915) took his doctorate at Halle (1867), continuing in the linguistic tradition initiated there by Gesenius, and published his Phoenician grammar two years later. For a biographical sketch, see Martin Hartmann, "Dr. Paul G. A. Schroeder," *Die Welt des Islams* 3 (1915-16) xxii. From 1869 to 1909 Schröder was in consular service in Constantinople and Beirut (retiring as Generalkonsul in Beirut). His later studies bearing on Phoenician remain uncollected: "Phönicische Miscellen," *ZDMG* 34 (1880) 675-84; "Phönicische Miscellen 4. Fünf Inschriften aus Kition," *ZDMG* 35 (1881) 423-31; "Phönicische Inschrift aus Tyrus," *ZDMG* 39 (1885) 317-21; "Berichtigung zur Phönicischen Inschrift aus Tyrus (Z.D.M.G. 39, 318)," *ZDMG* 39 (1885) 516.

8. *Corpus inscriptionum semiticarum ab Academia inscriptionum et litterarum humaniorum conditum atque digestum,* part 1 (Paris: Republicae typographeo, 1881-). Cited below as *CIS*. Volumes 1 (1881) and 2 (1890) were edited by Renan. Volume 1 (text nos. 1-437) includes 164 Phoenician texts and 273 Punic texts from Carthage; vol. 2 (text nos. 438-3251) and vol. 3 (text nos. 3252-6067) contain only Punic texts from Carthage. Volume 3 appeared in three fascicles: 1926 and 1947, edited by J.-B. Chabot; 1962, edited by Chabot and J.-G. Février. I have commented further on the *Corpus* in "Epigraphic Contributions to a History of Carthage in the Fifth Century B.C.E." (Ph.D. diss., University of Michigan; Ann Arbor: University Microfilms, 1990) 9-14.

Discoveries in the first half of the twentieth century enlarged the corpus of Phoenician and Punic still further.[9] As Semitists struggled with older and newer texts, it became clear that fundamental elements of the language(s) were not yet well understood. A particularly troublesome area of uncertainty was the morphological and orthographic representation of anaphora and reference. Pronominal suffixes on nouns, verbs, and particles present a perplexing distribution of forms: where expected from the syntax, they are not necessarily represented in the orthography; where they are represented, their form is not that anticipated by a reader of Hebrew. Apparent conflicts between orthography and morphology required resolution.

Zellig Harris wrote the first grammar of the Phoenician language in English that consistently applied the principles of modern historical linguistics.[10] Harris observed the complementary distribution of possessive suffixes of the first person singular, and their contrasting representation in the writing system: "Early Phoenician in Zenjirli [= Kilamuwa, *KAI* 24] has *'b* 'my father' in the nominative, from Sem. **'abī*, but *'by* 'of my father' in the genitive, from Sem. **'abiia*."[11] In later inscriptions, he observed, the suffix -*y* came to be written even with nouns in the nominative. In discussing suffixes of the third person singular, however, he did not apply the principle of complementarity.[12] With regard to suffixes of the third person plural, Harris attempted to explain the origin of the two forms -*m* and -*nm*, but could not explain their distribution: the two forms "are employed after verbs, nouns and particles, without any apparent reason for the alternation."[13]

It was a brief article by Frank M. Cross and David Noel Freedman that brought the beginnings of order to the grammatical description of third person singular suffixes.[14] In two and a half pages, Cross and Freedman described the complementary distribution of pronominal suffixes of the third person singular. Their contribution was to recognize that "in addition to the normal form of the 3d m.s. suffix represented by *yodh,* there was in Phoenician a form of the 3d m.s. suffix not indicated in the orthography (i.e., a pure vowel, probably -*ô* as in Hebrew)."[15] This observation permitted the following formalization: "the

---

9. For example, the ninth-century inscription of Kilamuwa from Zenjirli was unearthed in 1902 and published nine years later (F. von Luschan, *Ausgrabungen in Sendschirli,* vol. 4 [Mitteilungen aus den orientalischen Sammlungen; Berlin: W. Spemann, 1911] 374-77).

10. Z. S. Harris, *A Grammar of the Phoenician Language* (AOS 8; New Haven: American Oriental Society, 1936).

11. Ibid., 48.

12. Ibid., 48-49.

13. Ibid., 49. The historical explanation Harris offered in *Development of the Canaanite Dialects* (AOS 16; New Haven: American Oriental Society, 1939; reprinted Millwood, NY: Kraus, 1978), 77-78, correctly restricted the suffix -*nm* to bases with final long vowels.

14. Frank M. Cross, Jr., and David Noel Freedman, "The Pronominal Suffixes of the Third Person Singular in Phoenician," *JNES* 10 (1951) 228-30.

15. Ibid., 228.

[3rd masculine singular] suffix appears as *yodh* in the orthography with nouns or verbs ending in long vowels, and with singular nouns in the *genitive case;* with nouns in the *accusative case,* the suffix appears as zero in the orthography, and its presence must be determined from the context."[16]

Charles Krahmalkov described third person masculine plural pronominal suffixes in 1970.[17] He demonstrated that the two forms -*m* and -*nm* are found in complementary distribution of precisely the same sort described by Cross and Freedman for third person singular suffixes. The suffix -*m* is affixed to bases ending in a consonant; the form -*nm* affixes to bases ending in a long or short vowel.[18] Krahmalkov further established the phonetic shape of the allomorphs as [-óm] and [-nóm].

Having established the morphology of masculine pronominal suffixes, Krahmalkov went on to demonstrate the same pattern of complementarity in pronominal suffixes of the third person feminine singular.[19] Affixed to bases ending in a consonant, the form is [-ā]; affixed to vocalic bases, the form is [-yā]. With the paradigm established, Krahmalkov reexamined the prevailing interpretation of pronominal suffixes on verbs, eliminating an entire class of "phantom suffixes" and reinterpreting a number of forms.[20]

The description of pronominal suffixes of the third person resulting from Cross and Freedman's initial study and Krahmalkov's further researches is accepted in linguistically informed discussions of Phoenician morphology, but is not as widely disseminated as might be desired.[21] In the interests of furthering

16. Ibid., 229. William R. Lane ("The Phoenician Dialect of Larnax tes Lapethou," *BASOR* 194 [1969] 39-45) studied the distribution of pronominal suffixes in Byblian and Sidonian Phoenician as part of his argument that first common singular and third masculine singular suffixes link the Phoenician dialect of Larnax tēs Lapēthou with Byblos rather than (Tyre and) Sidon. He did not undertake a comprehensive description of the morphology.

17. Charles Krahmalkov, "Studies in Phoenician and Punic Grammar," *JSS* 15 (1970) 181-88.

18. Ibid., 183.

19. Charles R. Krahmalkov, "Comments on the Vocalization of the Suffix Pronoun of the Third Feminine Singular in Phoenician and Punic," *JSS* 17 (1972) 68-75.

20. The prevailing interpretation is found in J. Friedrich and W. Röllig, *Phönizisch-Punische Grammatik* (2nd ed.; AnOr 46; Rome: Pontifical Biblical Institute, 1970) §§187-90. Cf. C. Krahmalkov, "The Object Pronouns of the Third Person of Phoenician and Punic," *Rivista di Studi Fenici* 2 (1974) 39-43. On "phantom suffixes," see p. 40.

21. See, e.g., W. Randall Garr, *Dialect Geography of Syria-Palestine, 1000-586 B.C.E.* (Philadelphia: University of Pennsylvania, 1985) 101-13. More recently, J. Huehnergard, "The Development of the Third Person Suffixes in Phoenician," *Maarav* 7 (1991) 183-94. A recent example of its lack of dissemination is evident in Gary N. Knoppers, "'The God in His Temple': The Phoenician Text from Pyrgi as a Funerary Inscription," *JNES* 51 (1992) 105-20, who isolates the sequence of letters *bntw* in ll. 5-6 of the Phoenician text incised on a gold plaque excavated at ancient Pyrgi as the sentence "I built it." Knoppers understands the final letter -*w* to represent a third masculine singular suffix on a Qal perfect first common singular verb (p. 113). This analysis is highly problematic; the Qal perfect first common singular is

awareness of this important element of Phoenician and Punic grammar, the following comments are directed to a systematic description of affixational patterns observable in prepositions with pronominal suffixes.[22] Prepositions are a morphologically complex class of particles with considerable diversity of structure. The following tables recognize three categories: *simple prepositions; compound prepositions,* composed of two or more simple prepositions; and *complex prepositions,* made up of a preposition plus a noun.[23] Within these categories, prepositions are distinguished by spelling as monoconsonantal, biconsonantal, or triconsonantal.

---

not attested with a pronominal suffix in inscriptions from Byblos, but does occur in Tyrian-Sidonian Phoenician: *bnty,* "I built it" (*CIS* 1.7.4; on the phonological shape, see Garr, *Dialect Geography,* 110). Knoppers is compelled by his analysis of the verb to argue that the morphology of the inscription is Byblian (despite his earlier argument [pp. 207-8] linking the paleography of the text with the sixth- and fifth-century Sidonian series) and to gloss over the shift from third to first person. Knoppers's treatment of the Pyrgi text needs close discussion in another context; I raise it here only as an example of a continuing tendency on the part of scholars to regard the morphology of pronominal suffixation in Phoenician as unsystematic and susceptible to ad hoc interpretation.

22. The dialect of Byblos has a distinct set of pronominal suffixes that partly differentiates it from the language of Tyre and Sidon. I will note Byblian morphology where relevant, but the paradigms given above reflect the morphology of Tyrian-Sidonian Phoenician.

In later Byblian Phoenician, suffix pronouns of the third person masculine singular are found in a pattern of complementary distribution, -o (not written) following consonant bases and -*w* (vocalization unattested) following vocalic bases (see C. R. Krahmalkov, "The Byblian Phoenician Inscription of *ʾbdʾšmn:* A Critical Note on Byblian Grammar," *JSS* 38 [1993] 25-32).

23. The category "complex preposition" is adumbrated by D. G. Pardee, "The Preposition in Ugaritic (Part II)," *UF* 8 (1976) 306. For a similar analysis of Biblical Hebrew prepositions, see B. K. Waltke and M. O'Connor, *An Introduction to Biblical Hebrew Syntax* (Winona Lake, IN: Eisenbrauns, 1990) §11.1.2b.

Simple prepositions

Monoconsonantal

b- [CV-] and [C-]
+ 3ms	bn /bin(n)ō/		+3cpl	bnm[24]
+ 3fs	bn /bin(n)ā/			bm /bōm/[25]

l- [CV-] and [C-]
+ 1cs	ly /lî/, /liya/[26]		+ 1cpl	ln */lōn/[27]
+ 2ms	lk		+ 2mpl	*lkm /lōkom/[28]
+ 3ms	l /lō/		+ 3cpl	lm */lōm/
+ 3fs	l /lā/			

k- (unattested with pronominal suffixes)

24. The vocalization is uncertain. The paradigm assumes that the homographic forms -nm with either masculine or feminine antecedents are identical in vocalism and thus epicene. In *KAI* 14.9 the antecedent of the prepositional phrase bnm is a compound noun phrase consisting of one morphologically feminine noun and one morphologically masculine noun: respectively, $mmlkt$ and *'dm;* the gender agreement may be semantic rather than morphological, and thus masculine, or the result of attraction to the second noun of the phrase (for equivalent Biblical Hebrew constructions, see Waltke and O'Connor, *Biblical Hebrew Syntax,* §6.6).
Huehnergard ("Development of the Third Person Suffixes," 191) analyzes the prepositional base of the third masculine singular, third feminine singular, and third common plural forms as bVn-. In this case they would belong in the category of biconsonantal prepositions.
25. This form occurs in the Kition tariff (*KAI* 37B.7). The sentence *l'dm. 'š lqḥ mknbm,* heretofore interpreted as "To the person who took *mknbm,*" has puzzled scholars. Modern Arabic *muknib,* "(skin) callous," has not previously been proposed as an equivalent of a putative Phoenician *$mknb$ (H. Wehr, *Arabic-English Dictionary* [ed. J. M. Cowan; Ithaca, NY: Spoken Language Services, 1976] 842), but the Arabic word is of little help in making sense of the context.
I propose the following interpretation: *l'dm. 'š lqḥ mkn bm,* "To the person who received [or took] a pedestal from them." The noun *mkn,* "pedestal," is an architectural term attested in Neo-Punic (*KAI* 119.4); the Kition tariff has two references (A.13, B.5) to *'štt,* "pillars" (on the word, see J. C. L. Gibson, *Textbook of Syrian Semitic Inscriptions,* vol. 3: *Phoenician Inscriptions* [Oxford: Clarendon, 1982] 99), to which *mkn,* "pedestal," provides an appropriate complement. The prepositional phrase *bm* may involve a third common plural pronominal suffix.
26. Frank M. Cross, Jr., and David Noel Freedman (*Early Hebrew Orthography: A Study of the Epigraphic Evidence* [AOS 36; New Haven: American Oriental Society, 1952] 13) indicate a final long vowel; cf. Garr, *Dialect Geography,* 99-100.
27. See the comments of Garr, *Dialect Geography,* 104.
28. This follows Krahmalkov's analysis of Punic *syllohom* in Latin transcription as *$šlkm$,* "(which is) yours" (*Poenulus* l. 933; see C. R. Krahmalkov, "The Punic Speech of Hanno," *Or* 39 [1970] 62). The second feminine plural pronominal suffix remains unattested in Phoenician. In reconstructing the form one can assume a consonantal opposition m (masculine)/n (feminine) consistent with the morphology of all the Central and South Semitic languages; the feminine suffix would thus be written *-kn. In proposing the vocalization */ōkon/ I depend on the trenchant observation of Y. Arbeitman that "no Semitic

Biconsonantal

$'t$ [CVCC-]
+ 1cs   * $'t$ /'ittī/[29]
+ 2ms $'tk$
+ 3ms $'t$ /'ittō/[30]   + 3cpl $'tm$ (?)[31]
+ 3fs $'t$ /'ittā/[32]

mn (not attested with pronominal suffixes)

$'l$ [CVCV-]
+ 1cs $'ly$ /ʿalaya/[33]
+ 2ms $'lk$ /ʿalêkā/[34]
+ 3ms $'ly$ /ʿalayū/[35]   + 3cpl $'lnm$ /ʿalênom/[36]
+ 3fs $'ly$ /ʿalayā/

pn [CVCV-]
+ 3ms   *pny* /pānêyū/[37]
+ 3fs   **pny* /pānêyā/[38]

---

language preserves the putative original double distinction of both vocalism and consonantism between masculine and feminine. . . . the pronominal morpheme was over the long range allowed only one distinct feature: either consonantism or vocalism" ("Ugaritic Pronominals in the Light of Morphophonemic Economy," in *Semitic Studies in Honor of Wolf Leslau* [ed. Alan S. Kaye; Wiesbaden: Harrassowitz, 1991] 1.82-106; the citation is from p. 89).

29. Attested only in the Roman alphabet (*CIL* 8.23372).

30. See, e.g., *KAI* 50.5. The vocalization can be seen in the Phoenician name *Ithōbalos* (Josephus, *Ag. Ap.* 1.156), corresponding to [']*tbʾl* in Phoenician script (*KAI* 1.1). The Neo-Punic spelling $'tm$ (*KAI* 145.9) shows the allomorph /-îm/ characteristic of Punic and later dialects (Krahmalkov, "Studies," 185-88).

31. The form is a personal name (*CIS* 1.5548) and the suffix may be hypocoristic. F. Benz (*Personal Names in the Phoenician and Punic Inscriptions* [Studia Pohl 8; Rome: Biblical Institute, 1972] 281) lists the name as unexplained.

32. *KAI* 50.6. The Punic name *Itamonis* written in the Latin alphabet shows the vocalization (see F. Vattioni, "Per una ricerca dell'antroponimia fenicio-punica," *Studi Magrebini* 11 [1979] 83, with full bibliography; I have commented further on this name type in "Epigraphic Contributions," 167n.5).

33. Cross and Freedman, *Early Hebrew Orthography*, 17.

34. Ibid., 13.

35. The phonetic shape follows ibid., 17; and Garr, *Dialect Geography*, 107.

36. The form occurs in Punic (*CIS* 1.3920.4) and in the long Neo-Punic inscription from Mactar (J.-G. Février and M. Fantar, "Les nouvelles inscriptions monumentales néopuniques de Mactar," *Karthago* 12 [1963-64] 49-59, col. 3, l. 1). The Phoenician dialect of Byblos uses the form $'lhm$ (*KAI* 10.6 [bis]).

37. The form is Punic (*CIS* 1.3778.5). The Punic spelling *pʿny* (*KAI* 173.1) shows the long vowel in the first syllable.

38. Spelled with vowel letters in Neo-Punic **pnyʿ* (Trip. 35). See n. 41 below.

Triconsonantal

    'lt [CVCCV-]
    + 1cs   *'lty* /ˈaltaya/
    + 3ms   *'lty* /ˈaltayū/

    pnt (not attested with pronominal suffixes)

    tḥt [CVCCV-]
    + 1cs   *tḥtn* /taḥtēnī/[39]
                           + 3cpl   *tḥtnm* /taḥtēnom/

Compound Prepositions

Monoconsonantal + monoconsonantal

    l- + *b-* (not attested with pronominal suffixes)

Monoconsonantal + biconsonantal

    l- + *mn* (not attested with pronominal suffixes)
    l- + *pn*
    + 3ms   *lpny*[40]

Monoconsonantal + biconsonantal + monoconsonantal

    l- + *mn* + *b-* (not attested with pronominal suffixes)

Biconsonantal + biconsonantal

    't pn (not attested with pronominal suffixes)
    'l pn
    + 3fs   *'l pˁnyˁ* /ˈal pānêyā/[41]

39. Cross and Freedman, *Early Hebrew Orthography,* 18.
    40. Neo-Punic (*KAI* 126.7). The morphology of the compound follows the affixational pattern of genitive nouns with prefixed preposition.
    41. The spelling is Neo-Punic (Trip. 35).

Triconsonantal + biconsonantal

'lt pn (not attested with pronominal suffixes)

Complex prepositions

Monoconsonantal + biconsonantal noun

bd
+ 3ms   bdy /bōdêyū/[42]

The affixational pattern evident from the morphology of prepositions with pronominal suffixes is in keeping with the pattern established from other evidence. Vocalic suffixes attach directly to consonantal bases; vocalic bases receive suffixes with an initial consonant.[43] Suffixation is a function of the morphology of the preposition; variations in bases before suffixes are therefore of particular interest.[44]

Only monoconsonantal simple prepositions show variation between consonantal and vocalic bases before pronominal suffixes. A nearly complete paradigm is attested for the preposition *l-* with suffixes; the pattern of bases is instructive:

+ 1cs	[CV-]	+ 1cpl	[C-] or [CV-]
+ 2ms	[C-][45]	+ 2mpl	[CV-]
+ 2fs	[C-] (?)	+ 2fpl	[CV-] (?)
+ 3ms	[C-]	+ 3cpl	[C-]
+ 3fs	[C-]		

The monoconsonantal preposition *b-* has a slightly different pattern of bases.

42. This phrase is generally analyzed as a compound of the preposition *b-* and the noun *yd*, "hand." The spelling of the form with pronominal suffix supports this analysis, for it follows the affixational pattern of genitive nouns governed by a preposition.

43. This pattern is recognized by, e.g., Garr, *Dialect Geography*, 101-2, 105, 107, 109, 110.

44. The discussion of prepositions with pronominal suffixes in S. Segert's *Grammar of Phoenician and Punic* (Munich: Beck, 1976) §56 (pp. 160-63) pays attention to the morphological complexity of prepositions and draws attention to bases (e.g., §56.4).

45. This paradigm assumes, by analogy with Biblical Hebrew, that the connecting vowel of second person singular suffixes is to be regarded as part of the suffix rather than part of the base, while connecting vowels of second person plural suffixes are part of the base. See the discussion by T. O. Lambdin, *Introduction to Biblical Hebrew* (New York: Charles Scribner's Sons, 1971) 86-87.

Before third person singular suffixes, the base is vocalic. Before third person plural suffixes, both consonantal and vocalic bases are attested.[46]

Simple prepositions of more than one consonant keep the same base before all pronominal suffixes.[47] The preposition *'t* is the only member of this category with a consonantal base.[48]

Compound and complex prepositions are indistinguishable from other prepositional phrases with regard to suffixation. The suffix attaches to the second member of the construct and is invariably the allomorph that follows vocalic bases.

* * * * *

The brief paper of which David Noel Freedman was joint author appeared early in a distinguished career of scholarship and publication, and has been followed by nearly five hundred subsequent published items. The study of Phoenician morphology was advanced because of his contribution to it; indeed, the wide range of ancient Near Eastern and biblical studies has benefited immensely from his untiring labor and penetrating vision. To have known him as teacher, editor, and dissertation adviser is to have seen how scholarship should be done. In dedicating this study to him, I experience the anxiety of knowing that its flaws will not pass unnoticed, but also the reassurance of knowing that they will remain uncounted. Freedman could, with no offense to modesty, make the boast that a Phoenician-speaking king permitted himself with dubious warrant:

m'š . p'lt bl . p'l . hlpnyhm .
What I accomplished those who were before me did not accomplish.[49]

---

46. Note the pattern in Biblical Hebrew, where the preposition *b-* takes third masculine plural suffixes of two different types: /bāhem/ and /bām/.

47. Not included in this discussion is the particle *dl*, which, despite its clearly attested meaning "with," is manifestly not a preposition but a conjunction or adverb. See my comments in "Epigraphic Contributions," 81, 124-25.

48. Friedrich and Röllig list *ṣd'* (*KAI* 78.6) as a preposition with third masculine singular pronominal suffix (*Grammatik* §254 [p. 128]), but the word is a noun (so Röllig in *KAI,* vol. 2, 97-98) and should be vocalized /ṣiddō/, "its back."

49. It is fitting that the last word of the Phoenician sentence should be a complex preposition with an anomalous pronominal suffix. The translation represents the analysis favored by Cross and Freedman, *Early Hebrew Orthography,* 15-19, which was that of Arno Poebel (*Das appositionell bestimmte Pronomen der 1. Pers. Sing. in den westsemitischen Inschriften* [Assyriological Studies 3; Chicago: University of Chicago, 1932] 34n.4). Essentially identical interpretations include E. Lipiński, "From Karatepe to Pyrgi: Middle Phoenician Miscellanea," *Rivista di studi fenici* 2 (1974): 50; and P. Swiggers, "Commentaire philologique sur l'inscription phénicienne du roi Kilamuwa," *Rivista di Studi Fenici* 11 (1983) 138. The analysis proposed by Gibson (*Textbook* 3.36) understands the phrase as meaning "those who were before them." I am inclined to interpret the final pronominal element, *hm*, as a pronominal copy of the object phrase, which is in initial position: "(as for) what (things) that I accomplished, my predecessors did not accomplish *them.*"

The Raised Hand of God as an Oath Gesture

DAVID ROLPH SEELY

Brigham Young University, Provo, Utah

The image of the raised hand of God occurs seventeen times in the Hebrew Bible in the expression *nś' yd*. Fifteen of these occurrences are found in the context of God swearing an oath: ten times in the promise of the land (Exod 6:8; Num 14:30; Ezek 20:5 [bis], 6, 15, 28, 42; 47:14; Neh 9:15), and five times in oaths of judgment against Israel (Ezek 20:23; 44:12; Ps 106:26) and its enemies (Deut 32:40; Ezek 36:7). Translations often obscure the occurrence of this image of "raised hand" in Hebrew by usually translating simply as "swore." The other two occurrences of the raised hand of God are gestures of signaling (Isa 49:22) and deliverance (Ps 10:12). This study will look first at the occurrences of the raised hand of God as a gesture accompanying an oath, and then examine several possibilities as to its significance.

The phrase *nś' yd* occurs with human hands only five times in the Hebrew Bible and never in the case of an oath. Twice *yd* occurs in the singular representing a hostile gesture, "lifting the hand against the king" (2 Sam 18:28; 20:21); and three times in the plural *(ydym)* in contexts of blessing, prayer, and praise (Lev 9:22; Pss 28:2; 134:2; see also Hab 3:10, where the Deep "lifts its hands"). In addition, the phrase *nś' kpyw* occurs three times as a gesture of prayer, reverence, or supplication (Pss 63:5 [ET 4]; 119:48; Lam 2:19).

Genesis 14:22 has one occurrence of a human swearing an oath with the gesture of an upraised hand: Abram swears an oath, expressed with *hrym yd*. Thus the gesture of swearing an oath with an upraised hand (or forearm) is expressed with *nś'* in the case of divine oaths and with *hrym* for mortal oaths. The phrase *hrym yd* is also synonymous with *nś' yd* in the idiomatic usage "to lift one's hand against" in 1 Kgs 11:26-27. Daniel 12:7 mentions a man, or divine messenger, raising *(hrym)* both hands to heaven and then swearing an oath. It is difficult to tell whether an oath gesture or a prayer gesture is intended.

411

Although the verb *hrym* is never used as a gesture of prayer elsewhere (usually *nś' ydym*), because the gesture includes both hands raised — which is never attested in oath gestures — I assume that the intended image was one of prayer or supplication done in conjunction with an oath.

I. Linguistic Description and Context

The image of God's raised hand is expressed fourteen times in the first person, "I raised my hand" *(nśty 't-ydy; nśty ydy; 'ś' ydy)*, indicating that it is a phrase most often found in direct discourse; once in the second person, "you raised your hand" *(nś't 't-ydk);* once in the third person, "he raised his hand" *(yś' ydw);* and once in the imperative *(nś' yd).*[1] Every occurrence of *yd* as the hand of God in this phrase is singular. This is in contrast to the most common usage of *nś' yd* with mortal hands, where *yd* almost always occurs in the plural *(ydym)* — usually in a gesture of prayer. Indeed, the phrase *nś' yd* in respect to a mortal hand — with *yd* in the singular — occurs only in the idiom "to lift one's hand against" in rebellion (2 Sam 18:28; 20:21). This clearly distinguishes the divine gesture represented by *nś' yd* — involving one hand — from the more common human prayer gesture involving both hands.

Ten of the oaths are found in the context of the divine promise of the land to the fathers (Exod 6:8; Num 14:30; Ezek 20:5 [bis];[2] 20:6, 15, 28, 42; 47:14; Neh 9:15) characterized by Exod 6:8, "And I will bring you into the land which I swore [raised my hand] to give to Abraham, to Isaac, and to Jacob." These passages generally follow a formulaic pattern including mention of entrance to the land, the raising of the hand in an oath, and the promise to the fathers and the tribes of Israel. Six of the examples include some form of the verb *hby'* as an indication that the Lord "brought them" into the land (Exod 6:8; Num 14:30; Ezek 20:5, 28, 42; Neh 9:15); all ten passages contain some form of *'l-'rṣ/'dmh;* and nine of the ten include a prepositional phrase *l-* with personal pronouns or designations of "fathers" (all but Num 14:30).

It is clear that in the context of the promise of the land the phrase *nś' yd* is synonymous with the more frequent verb "to swear," *nšb',* which occurs 74 times in the Hebrew Bible denoting a divine oath — 49 in the Exodus traditions

---

1. *nśty 't-ydy:* Exod 6:8; Num 14:30; Ezek 20:28, 42; 36:7; 47:14; *nśty ydy:* Ezek 20:6, 15, 23; 44:12; *nś't 't-ydk:* Neh 9:15; *'ś'ydy:* Isa 49:22; Ezek 20:5 [bis]; *'ś' 'l-šmym yd:* Deut 32:40; *yś' ydw:* Ps 106:26; *nś' yd:* Ps 10:12.

2. The phrase *bywm* in v. 5 paired with *bywm hhw'* in v. 6 suggests that the clause in v. 5 — regarding the oath — is incomplete and resumed in v. 6. Therefore the oath represented by all three occurrences of the phrase *nś'yd* refers to the land. This reading is supported by the same construction in Ezek 24:25-26. See Moshe Greenberg, *Ezekiel 1–20* (AB 22; Garden City: NY: Doubleday, 1983) 363-64.

in the context of the promise of the land to the fathers. Also one passage in which Yahweh swears an oath mentions his right hand and arm with *nšb*ʿ instead of *nśʾ yd*: "The Lord has sworn [*nšbʿ*] by his right hand [*bymynw*] and by his mighty arm [*wbzrwʿ ʿzw*]: 'I will not again give grain to be food for your enemies'" (Isa 62:8). The usage of *nšb*ʿ may be a reference to the gesture of the raised hand. One could also interpret the context of this passage as the Lord simply swearing by his strength (as he does by his name, etc.) or perhaps by metonymy that he is swearing by himself. The verb *nšb*ʿ occurs in the context of a divine oath about the land in the books of Genesis (4 times), Exodus (4 times), Numbers (4 times), Deuteronomy (28 times), Joshua (5 times), Judges (once), Jeremiah (twice), and Micah (once).[3] These occurrences contain the same formulaic elements identified above: *hbyʾ; ʾl-ʾrṣ/ʾdmh; l-* with personal pronouns; designations of "fathers"; and description, *zbt ḥlb wdbš*.

It is significant that while the phrase *nśʾ yd* as a gesture of divine oath in regard to the land does not occur in Deuteronomy, where *nšb*ʿ is most prominent, the more common *nšb*ʿ does not occur in Ezekiel — which contains the preponderance of the occurrences of *nśʾ yd*. This is another case where Ezekiel avoids Deuteronomic language and relies on other traditions.[4] Indeed, *nśʾ yd* occurs in Deuteronomy only in the archaic poem (32:40) in regard to divine judgment, and *nšb*ʿ occurs in Ezekiel only in 16:8, where Yahweh enters into a covenant of marriage with the foundling in the wilderness.

While the wording of the phrases in Ezekiel is very similar to the tradition in Exod 6:8 and those attested with *nšb*ʿ in Deuteronomy, Ezekiel significantly changes the context. In Exodus (and everywhere else with *nšb*ʿ) the oath of the land is made (where it is specified) with the "fathers." In Ezekiel the oath is specifically made with the Israelites in Egypt. In this Ezekiel varies not only from the Deuteronomic material but from all other traditions as well.[5]

The other category of oaths expressed by *nśʾ yd* is a sworn promise of judgment against Israel (Ezek 20:23; 44:12; Ps 106:26) and its enemies (Deut 32:40; Ezek 36:7). The occurrence of the raising of the hand in an oath gesture in the archaic poetry of Deuteronomy 32 demonstrates that *nśʾ yd* is an oath gesture not exclusively connected with the promise of the land and was in fact very early associated with judgment. Elsewhere in the Bible judgment is also expressed by divine oaths using the verb *nšb*ʿ (against Israel in Num 32:10; Deut

---

3. Gen 22:16; 24:7; 26:3; 50:24; Exod 13:5, 11; 32:13; 33:1; Num 11:12; 14:16, 23; 32:11; Deut 1:8, 35; 4:31; 6:10, 18, 23; 7:8, 12, 13; 8:1, 18; 9:5, 10:11; 11:9, 21; 13:18; 19:8; 26:3, 15; 28:9, 11; 29:12; 30:20; 31:7, 20, 21, 23; 34:4; Josh 1:6; 5:6 (bis); 21:43, 44; Judg 2:1; Jer 11:5; 32:22; Mic 7:20.

4. See Walther Zimmerli, *Ezekiel 1* (trans. R. E. Clements; Hermeneia; Philadelphia: Fortress, 1979) 23, 46, for further examples.

5. Ezekiel recognizes the patriarchs in 20:5 and 33:24 and the covenant with the fathers in 20:42 but chooses to juxtapose the apostasy with the election in the wilderness. See Greenberg, *Ezekiel 1–20*, 364.

4:21; Josh 5:6; Judg 2:15; Jer 22:5; Amos 4:2; 6:8; Ps 95:11; against Assyria in Isa 14:24; Babylon in Jer 51:14; and Bozrah in Jer 49:13), further supporting the synonymity of the two expressions.

II. *nś' yd* in Comparative Semitic Perspective

The expression *nś' yd* as an oath gesture is unique to Biblical Hebrew. The linguistic equivalent of Hebrew *nś' yd* is well attested in Akkadian *qāta našû*, Aramaic *nś' yd*, as well as in Ugaritic *nš' yd*. But there is no semantic equivalent of *nś' yd* — as a gesture accompanying an oath — outside Hebrew.[6] In these other languages the phrase is almost always used with mortals and signifies gestures of worship or prayer, and is usually associated with mortals rather than deities.[7]

Discussing Akkadian idioms containing the names of the parts of the body, Oppenheim demonstrated the homonymy of many Akkadian idioms: "A semantic development, the phases of which we can rarely trace, supplied the language with fairly numerous homonymous idioms (in some cases there are as many as four homonyms) which preserve their strictly determined meaning even when appearing side by side."[8] While he did not deal specifically with the various homonymous idioms of *qāta našû*, he did identify several idioms involving hands and arms and demonstrated their respective homonyms in their contexts.[9] More recently Gruber resumed an aspect of Oppenheim's work and dealt extensively with the Hebrew, Akkadian, and Ugaritic usages of hand and arm gestures including *nś' yd*. He explains the development of two homonymous idioms expressed by *qāta našû* as follows:

> The expression *qāta/qātī našû* "lift the hand(s)" refers to a series of kinemes [body movement], the meaning of each of which is determined by the context.

---

6. The Akkadian phrase *našû ilāni*, "raising the gods," is associated with oaths, and is usually interpreted as a symbolic act of raising images in one's hand before the gods in order to witness the truthfulness of a sworn statement. In the past some have argued a relationship between Akkadian *nišu*, "oath," and the gesture of "lifting up" *(našû)*. It has recently been demonstrated that *nišu* is probably derived from *nēšu*, "life," rather than *našû*. For a discussion see Tikva Frymer-Kensky, "Suprarational Legal Procedures in Elam and Nuzi," in *Studies on the Civilization and Culture of Nuzi and the Hurrians in Honor of Ernest R. Lacheman* (ed. M. A. Morrison and D. I. Owen; Winona Lake, IN: Eisenbrauns, 1981) 115-31, esp. 120-31.

7. For a list and discussion of such occurrences see Mayer I. Gruber, *Aspects of Non-Verbal Communication in the Ancient Near East* (Studia Pohl 12; Rome: Biblical Institute, 1980) 22-89. In Akkadian "hand" occurs in this expression in both the singular and the plural, while in Aramaic and Ugaritic the phrase occurs almost always with the plural.

8. A. Leo Oppenheim, "Idiomatic Akkadian," *JAOS* 61 (1941) 251.

9. Ibid., 269-70.

Hence the homonymous idioms *qāta našû* "raise the hand to attack" and *qāta našû* "pray." These idioms did not arise from a primitive view that the hand embodies the personality. . . . These homonymous idioms have arisen from the inadequacy of words to distinguish a series of distinct culturally significant body motions all of which share in common the feature of elevating one or both hands.[10]

While these observations derive from a study of Akkadian idioms they are relevant to Hebrew idioms as well.

III. *nś' yd* as an Oath Gesture in the Biblical Text

By their different functions in their context, Gruber identifies at least four distinct homonymous idioms of *nś' yd* in Biblical Hebrew: (1) swearing an oath (the majority of occurrences described above); (2) lifting of the hand in order to confer blessings (Lev 9:22); (3) lifting the hands in a hostile gesture of rebellion (2 Sam 18:28; 20:21; Ps 10:12?); (4) a gesture of prayer, supplication (Ps 28:2), or praise (Ps 134:2).[11] Gruber's particular interest is prayer gestures, which he describes at length in Hebrew, Akkadian, and Ugaritic.

Besides the contexts themselves I have noted further distinctions between several of these categories or homonyms. For example, the category of oaths is confined to deity while the other occurrences describe human gestures, and the categories of oath and the hostile gesture involve a gesture with one hand, while the other three categories involve both hands. While the distinction between praise, blessing, and prayer could perhaps be argued, the categories of oaths and hostile gestures are clearly distinct from these. Because of the above distinctions I find the identification of different homonyms a useful way to explain the different categories.

Hebrew *nś' yd* as an idiom describing an oath gesture is statistically the most common usage in the Hebrew Bible and yet is the only usage not attested in Akkadian, Aramaic, or Ugaritic. Since there are no parallel usages of *nś' yd*

---

10. Gruber, *Aspects*, 60n.2. Gruber goes on to illustrate his point with various examples from Akkadian literature that must be interpreted according to their contexts in order to make sense. The discussion of homonyms is really not as complicated as some would make it, nor is it as enlightening. Each idiom occurs in contexts that demand obviously different interpretations, and understanding them as different idioms merely allows the interpreter to feel free to take them as the context suggests. This approach does not help to identify origins for the gestures but allows one to look for various origins rather than for one single explanation.

11. Gruber, *Aspects*, 32-33. In addition Hebrew has the idiom *nś' kpym*, attested only in the human sphere, as either supplication or praise: Pss 63:4-5 (ET 3-4); 141:2; Lam 2:19; and perhaps 3:41.

as an oath gesture in other Semitic languages, comparative material is helpful only if it can identify common ground in the development of these homonymous idioms from the gesture of an upraised hand/arm.

Gruber identifies one aspect of common ground in the category of prayer/supplication that may be relevant to divine oaths. He describes the gesture of prayer in its many Hebrew expressions as a gesture "to point to the deity's abode" and notes that "it is always followed by a phrase defining that abode."[12] Therefore many of the hand gestures of prayer are described as "raising the hand to the heavens [*'l-šmym*]" (Dan 12:7; cf. *prś kpym*, 2 Kgs 8:54); and Ps 28:2 *('l-dbyr qdšk)* and 134:2 *(qdš)* referring to the Lord's abode in the temple. This is also true in Ugaritic: Keret raises his hands "heavenward" (*UT* Krt 76: *šmm;* and 168: *šmmh = KTU* 1.14:II:23 and 1.14:IV:5), as well as in Aramaic: the hands are lifted up "toward" the gods (*w's' ydy 'l b'lšmyn*, Zakir A.11 = *KAI* 202.A.11; *ys' ydyh l'lh*, Hadad 29 [cf. *KAI* 214.29]). In relation to divine oaths the archaic example of *nś' yd* as an oath gesture in Deut 32:40 contains the qualifier *'l-šmym*. The same qualifier with both idioms perhaps gives a clue to an original common ground present in both gestures that might help to explain the homonymity.

While biblical or comparative evidence is inconclusive, one can argue for several different explanations as to the origin and significance of the raised hand as an oath gesture.

1. As suggested by biblical and comparative evidence it is most likely that the raised hand is pointed to heaven — as in Deut 32:40, *'l-šmym* — indicating that the oath is sworn in some way "by the heavens" — as the heavenly abode of God. As noted above, this is characteristic of *nś' yd(ym)* as a human prayer gesture as well.

In Gen 14:22 Abraham swears an oath while he raises his hand *(hrym yd)* "to [*'l-*] the Lord God Most High, maker of heaven and earth." This example of a similar oath gesture of a mortal suggests that the upraised hand is directed toward God, who functions either as the second party or as a witness to this solemn oath.

In the contexts of the *nś' yd* gesture of oaths a hint is given as to the indication of the raised hand. In Exod 6:8 the Lord says, "And I will bring you into the land that I swore to give to Abraham, to Isaac, and to Jacob; I will give it to you for a possession. I am the Lord." The same phrase "I am the Lord" occurs with the oath gesture in Ezek 20:5, 7. While this phrase in Exod 6:8 has

---

12. Gruber, *Aspects*, 37. He cites the Ugaritic phrase *ša ydk šmmh*, "lift your hands heavenward" (*UT* Keret 75-76). As further evidence he gives a quote from Aurelius Theodosius Macrobius (ca. 400 c.e.): "When one addresses Earth, he touches the earth with his hands, when one addresses Jupiter, he lifts his hands heavenward, when he speaks of making a vow he touches his breast with his hands." See also the symbolic act performed by Moses when he stretched one hand *(nṭh)* toward the heavens in two of the plagues in Exod 9:22, 23; 10:21, 22.

often been understood as a separate declaration, in Ezek 20:5 it is placed in direct discourse apparently as part of the promise of the land indicating the Lord as witness or guarantor of the oath. Two of the passages where *nšb'* occurs as the semantic equivalent of *nś' yd* provide evidence that this is a statement that the Lord was swearing by himself. Twice in contexts with *nšb'* the Lord designates that the oath of the land was sworn "by himself" ("by myself [*by*]," Gen 22:16; "by thine own self [*bk*]," Exod 32:13). In Deut 11:21 the designation is made "as long as the heavens are above the earth." So the text bears out the suggestion that the promise of the land to the fathers was accompanied by an oath in which the Lord swore "by himself."

While the Hebrew Bible has no evidence of an oath "by the heavens," the NT has an injunction against it (Matt 5:34; 23:22), and some texts in the Hebrew Bible designate the heavens as witnesses to oaths (Deut 4:27; 30:19; 31:28). More important is that often Yahweh swears an oath "by his life" (Deut 32:40; Ezek 17:16; Amos 6:8; Zeph 2:9), or "by himself" (Gen 22:16), or by his name (Jer 44:26). Likewise humans also swear by the life of Yahweh (Judg 8:19; 1 Sam 14:39) and by his name (Exod 20:7; Josh 23:7; Isa 48:1; Ps 16:4).

In the light of this biblical evidence, the image of God raising his hand toward heaven is most likely a hand gesture pointing to his heavenly abode wherein an oath is made "by the heavens" either as a guarantee or as a witness. Furthermore, as in other oaths, the image of the Lord pointing his hand to his heavenly home — by metonymy — may be tantamount to the Lord swearing by himself. Incidentally, this imagery implies that the Lord is not in heaven when he makes such a gesture but rather on earth among humans.

2. The passage in Isa 62:8, "The Lord has sworn [*nšb'*] by his right hand and by his mighty arm," suggests another similar explanation. The image intended here may be the same upraised hand/arm as a divine gesture above. It is possible that what is meant is that the Lord is actually swearing by his arm — either as a metaphor of his "power" or by synecdoche that he is swearing "by himself."

3. Several biblical passages suggest the image of humans "spreading their hands [*prś kpym*]" — the usual prayer gesture — indicating whether their hands are "clean." In Isa 1:15 the people spread forth their hands in prayer to the Lord, and he does not hear them because their hands are full of blood. See similar imagery in Ps 24:4, where clean hands are symbolic of righteousness. It is possible by analogy to imagine the "raised hand" in a divine oath as such a symbol showing righteousness, innocence — that the oath is made in good faith without treachery. The raised hand may in this context be an image demonstrating that the hand holds no weapons. This is supposedly the significance of shaking hands with the right hand, showing that there is no weapon in the fighting hand.

4. Many examples of other hand gestures occur in biblical pledges, assurances, and oaths. The most common is the phrase *tq' yd/kp* as a gesture of

a pledge or assurance found only in Proverbs (6:1; 11:15; 17:18; 22:25) and Job (17:3). This can be interpreted as a hand clap, as *tqʿ* elsewhere refers clearly to the gesture of hand clapping (Ps 47:2 [ET 1]; Nah 3:19). Most likely it refers to a handclasp when one individual "claps," or briefly clasps, his hand with the hand of another in a handshake. This is suggested by Job 17:3, *my hwʾ lydy ytqʿ*, "who will strike my hand [as a surety]?" This same image may be intended in the phrase *yd lyd* (Prov 11:21; 16:5).

Also the phrase *ntn yd*, "to give one's hand," is used in reference to political alliances (Ezek 17:18, Israel with Babylon; Lam 5:6, Israel with Egypt; 1 Chr 29:24, allegiance to Solomon; also perhaps in 2 Kgs 10:15) as well as when the Israelites in Ezra 10:19 agree to give up their foreign wives. This gesture could also be a handshake of some sort or could be similar to raising the hand, although the verb *ntn* has no particular sense of "raising." In addition there is the example of hand gestures in oath making in the gesture of the hand under the thigh (Gen 24:2, 9; 47:29). It is possible, especially in the light of the human gesture of oath in Gen 14:22, that the raised hand is another such gesture whose exact significance is obscure.

5. One passage suggests a hand gesture as a sign of self-curse in an oath. Job 13:14, "and I will put my throat in my hand" *(wnpšy ʾśym bkpy)*, may refer to an oath gesture.[13] In addition, two references to self-imprecations involve the hand or arm: *tškḥ ymyn*, "if I forget you, O Jerusalem, let my hand wither" (Ps 137:5); and *ktpy mškmh tpwl wʾzrʿy mqnh tšbr*, "then let my shoulder blade fall from my shoulder, and let my arm be broken from its socket" (Job 31:22). One could speculate that the gesture of a raised hand represents such a self-curse — known in oath making elsewhere. While some would argue that it would be inappropriate for God to make such a gesture, he does in fact make such a solemn act of self-deprecation in Gen 15:17 when he passes between the animal carcasses.[14]

I would reconstruct the history of the idiom *nśʾ yd* within the semantic field of oath gestures as follows. Gruber makes a distinction between the usage of expressions referring to gestures when they are meant to evoke the gesture itself, and when they have become idioms that maintain the sense of the gesture without necessarily evoking it. He defines the main meaning as "a verb or

---

13. M. H. Pope (*Job* [3rd ed.; AB 15; Garden City, NY: Doubleday, 1973] 99) suggests that this gesture is a symbolic act. "It is not clear whether the act of touching the throat symbolized strangulation or cutting the throat, but it is best understood as a symbolic act representing the jeopardy of one's life as sanction in an oath." He cites a similar expression in Akkadian: *napištam lapātum*, "to touch the throat," found in the Mari Letters in connection with treaties. See J. M. Munn-Rankin, "Diplomacy in Western Asia in the Early Second Millennium B.C.," *Iraq* 18 (1956) 68-110.

14. By passing through the parts of the sacrificed animals God "identified himself with the slaughtered animals as a guarantee of the reliability of the promise." See G. E. Mendenhall and Gary Herion, "Covenant," *ABD* 1.1190.

expression whose primary meaning refers to a gesture, posture, or facial expression used to conjure up that feature of non-verbal communication," and the secondary meaning as "a verb or expression employed idiomatically to convey an attitude, idea, or feeling."[15] One of the major theses of his work is the establishment of criteria by which one can determine in each case the primary or secondary meaning of expressions of gestures throughout the ancient Near East.

According to Gruber the main criteria in determining if an expression is meant in its primary sense are if such expressions of gestures are found juxtaposed "with *verbum dicendi,* synonymous parallelism, and juxtaposition with other words or expressions referring to specific gestures, postures, or symbolic acts."[16] He demonstrates the validity of these criteria throughout his book with numerous examples of nonverbal expressions. While Gruber does not pursue the historical implications of such a distinction for the development of idioms (secondary meaning) from original gestures, one could assume that through time expressions once understood as vivid gestures become simply idioms expressing the function of such gestures.

Perhaps the earliest attestation of *nś' yd* as a divine oath gesture in the Hebrew Bible is found in the archaic poetry in Deut 32:40:

> *ky-'ś' 'l-šmym ydy*
> *w'mrty ḥy 'nky l'lm*
> *'m-šnwty brq ḥrby*
> *wt'ḥz bymšpṭ ydy.*

> For I lift up my hand to heaven
>   and say, "As I live forever"
> if I whet the lightning of my sword,
>   and my hand takes hold on judgment.

This passage fulfills at least one of the criteria for determining primary meaning — juxtaposition with a *verbum dicendi*. The imagery of "whetting a sword" and "grasping judgment" are parallel hand gestures supporting the image of the upraised hand that would fulfill the other aspects of Gruber's criteria as well.[17] The raising of the hand in a divine oath gesture here occurs in a context of

---

15. Gruber, *Aspects,* 19.

16. Ibid., 20.

17. The "lightning" *(brq)* of the sword is an apt description of the thunderbolt that the Lord will sharpen and then will seize for the purpose of executing justice. See the numerous iconographic depictions of such imagery in A. Vanel, *L'iconographie du dieu de l'orage* (Paris: Gabalda, 1965). D. N. Freedman, in private correspondence, argues that the intended image is the "sword of justice," an example of a broken construct, like other stereotypical phrases discussed by E. Z. Melamed, "Break-Up of Stereotype Phrases as an Artistic Device in Biblical Poetry," *ScrHier* 8 (1961) 115-53.

judgment. This gesture occurs with the Lord's promise of the land as well as in the context of judgment both against Israel and against its enemies. It does not occur in the Deuteronomic material. In the human sphere the gesture of the raised hand is also known (Gen 14:22) but expressed with *hrym yd*. At the same time the Bible has at least two (if not more) homonymous idioms involving *nś' yd* in the mortal sphere: with *ydym* as a gesture of prayer, blessing, praise, and with *yd* as a hostile gesture of rebellion.

Nine of the ten occurrences of the divine oath gesture occur in formulaic contexts of the divine promise of the land that one can identify as Gruber's "secondary meaning" — without *verbum dicendi* or any parallelism that would suggest a vivid hand gesture is necessarily intended. The expression without *verbum dicendi* has the functional meaning "to swear" as it is often translated (KJV, RSV, JPS, etc.). One can interpret this as the historical development of an expression of gesture into an idiom that is still based on the image of the upraised hand but where such imagery is no longer vivid. Ezekiel 20:5 does preserve a usage of *nś' yd* with a *verbum dicendi:* "I swore to them saying [*l'mr*], I am the Lord your God," which I have shown to be similar to Exod 6:8, where the *verbum dicendi* is lacking. The raised hand as a gesture accompanying a divine oath was originally expressed in its primary meaning in order to evoke the image of the gesture itself. Later it occurs in its secondary meaning as an idiom meaning "to swear," and it became part of the formulaic expression of the promise of the land to the fathers found in the books of Exodus, Numbers, and Ezekiel.

In Deuteronomy and elsewhere the semantic equivalent *nšb'* occurs in numerous passages about the promise of the land, demonstrating the same formulaic elements known from the few occurrences of *nś' yd*. One can attribute these two distinct variations (*nś' yd* and *nšb'*) to two separate traditions or simply to poetic variation. It is possible that such variation is a historical development — that the original formula was *nś' yd*, which was gradually replaced by its less ambiguous semantic equivalent *nšb'*.[18] This is the same process that occurs in translation when the phrase *nś' yd* is rendered "he swore." Ezekiel prefers *nś' yd* while the Deuteronomic material is full of *nšb'*. This may show an archaizing tendency in Ezekiel, or simply that he prefers other traditions to Deuteronomy.

The occurrence of the phrase *nś' yd* in Neh 9:15 is most likely a deliberate archaism. This passage shows that, however infrequent, this expression is found throughout the biblical traditions, both in the earliest and latest material.

---

18. *nšb'* is semantically equivalent only to Gruber's "secondary meaning" of *nś' yd*.

IV. Summary: *nśʾ yd* as Divine Oath Gesture

The expression *nśʾ yd* occurs fifteen times with the hand of God to introduce divine oaths: ten in sworn promises of the land, and five in oaths of judgment against Israel and its enemies. The semantic equivalent of the raised hand as an oath gesture is found only in the expression *hrym yd* (Gen 14:22) used in relation to a mortal hand. The usage of *nśbʿ* in the same formulaic contexts of the promise of the land and in oaths of judgment is a semantic equivalent to the secondary meaning of *nśʾ yd* as "to swear."

Linguistic equivalents of *nśʾ yd* are Akkadian *qāta našû*, Aramaic *nśʾ yd*, and Ugaritic *nśʾ yd*, which give many parallels to *nśʾ yd* as a human gesture of prayer/supplication. No semantic equivalents to the raised hand in an oath gesture, either divine or human, occur outside Hebrew.

I have concluded that God's raised hand is most likely a gesture pointing his hand toward heaven to symbolize the swearing of the oath "by the heavens" — as the guarantee, or as a witness, or by circumlocution that God is swearing by himself, pointing to his heavenly abode. Other possibilities are that the raised hand is the metaphor of the divine "power" being sworn by, a synecdoche for, God himself, a gesture that there is no treachery in the oath, an obscure gesture of assurance of some sort, or a gesture of self-curse.

On Being "Damned Certain":
The Story of a Curse in the Sefire
Inscription and Its Interpretation

BRUCE ZUCKERMAN
University of Southern California

If there used to be one thing I felt absolutely certain about in the field of Northwest Semitic epigraphy and philology, it was this: that you could not be *absolutely* certain about anything. Now, I'm not so sure.

In particular, I used to hold an especially dubious opinion of a particular tendency among my teachers and colleagues, an attitude toward ancient Northwest Semitic texts that one might best describe as "damned certainty." That is, in the face of an overwhelming lack of clear evidence — say, for example, an imposing lacuna or a line of writing that has faded or worn away to nearly nothing — they claim absolutely to *know,* absolutely *for sure,* exactly what the text *has to read.* Thus, they proceed to fill in the blanks, not with trepidation (as I always think I tend to do), but with confidence, one might even be tempted to say with hubris.

Beyond this, I used to deem even more unconscionable a variation of this "damned certain" attitude — what one might call the "I-don't-give-a-damn!" viewpoint. I refer specifically to those cases where, in the face of clear evidence to the contrary, a given scholar simply declares with little or no hesitation, "I don't care what the text appears to read — I *know* (despite all evidence to the contrary) that it can read no other way than thus and so. If the text appears to show things otherwise, it is simply wrong! If the scribe actually wrote what he appears to have written, then he is simply wrong. I know Hebrew (or Aramaic, Phoenician, Ugaritic, or whatever) and there is *no way* the text could read anything else than what I know it has to read!"

I always used to feel that when scholars began to show such "damned certainty," it was a weakness, not a strength. They were simply letting their virtuosity in interpretation (and, I should add, that it is frequently the most talented philologists and epigraphers who succumb to "damned certainty") get the better of them. At worse this could border on foolhardiness, at best it was a quirk to be tolerated as a kind of unwelcome fellow traveler of genius.

This used to be my view . . . but now all that has changed. I no longer have complete confidence in my lack of confidence, all because of a cursed little curse that has always been a bit of a nuisance in the Sefire inscription.[1]

The curse in question occurs on line 24 of face "A" of the first Sefire stela and is sometimes known as the "killer-chickens curse." It is the last in a series of apparently stock maledictions that we can begin to follow in line 21 (the preceding several lines being too damaged for reading). This previous group[2] (with slight restoration) read, insofar as they are attested:

21   ]šʾt wʾl thry wšb[ʿ mhy]nqn ymšḥ[n šdyhn w]
22 yhynqn wʾl ʿlym yšbʿ wšbʿ ssyh yhynqn ʾl wʾl yš[bʿ wšbʿ
23 šwrh yhynqn ʿgl wʾl yšbʿ wšbʿ šʾn yhynqn ʾmr w[ʾl yš
24 bʿ . . .

21   . . .]a ewe, may she not conceive; and should seven nurses
      anoi[nt their breasts]
22 and suckle a child, may he not be satisfied; and should seven mares
      suckle a colt, may it not be satis[fied; and should seven]
23 cows suckle a calf, may it not be satisfied; and should seven ewes
      suckle a lamb, [may it not be satis-]
24 fied . . .

Finally we come to our problem imprecation, which, if we accept the reading and interpretation of A. Dupont-Sommer, the editor of the editio princeps, has to be one of the weirdest curses ever cursed. He read the text:

. . .wšbʿ bkth yhkn bšṭ lḥm wʾl yhrgn

and translated it,

1. For the most complete and up-to-date bibliography on the Sefire inscription, see J. A. Fitzmyer and S. A. Kaufman, *An Aramaic Bibliography, Part I: Old, Official, and Biblical Aramaic* (Baltimore: Johns Hopkins University, 1992) 17-19.

2. All readings are based primarily on the edition of J. A. Fitzmyer, *The Aramaic Inscriptions of Sefire* (BibOr 19; Rome: Pontifical Biblical Institute, 1967), but have been checked against new photographs of the text made by Wayne Pitard in 1989 and made available to me by him. I wish to take this opportunity to thank Prof. Pitard for his kind generosity in making all his photographs of the Sefire inscription available to me for study and for allowing me to publish the pictures utilized in this study.

Et que sept poules aillent en quête de nourriture, et qu'elles ne tuent rien![3]

J. A. Fitzmyer, who accepted this reading and interpretation — although with understandable reluctance — renders in English:

and should seven *hens* go looking for food, may they not *kill* (anything)![4]

Needless to say, this curse, so read and interpreted, borders on the non-sensical, and beyond this, the philological interpretation of the various forms has to be stretched a considerable degree in order to work things out the way Dupont-Sommer would have it. To begin with, the form *bkth*, interpreted as "hens," depends on a rather tenuous etymology. Dupont-Sommer connected it with Targumic Aramaic *'abbakā'* and Syriac *'ābbakā', bākā'*, "rooster"; cf. also Syriac *bāktā'*, "hen."[5] Moreover, the form, an ostensible determined plural, is out of place. As Fitzmyer notes, "why should it be emphatic when used with a cardinal [number] (all the other examples are absolute)?"[6] Dupont-Sommer tries to sidestep this problem by labeling the form a double feminine plural.[7] While such a thing is not unprecedented (although one would be hard pressed to come up with another case in Old Aramaic),[8] it is clearly indicative of a fairly desperate attempt to force the form *bkth* into something resembling etymological sense.

There is also a question about the form *lḥm*, understood as "food" rather than in its far more common meaning "bread," or, for that matter, the use of *hrg* for "to kill" as opposed to the expected form, *qtl*, employed frequently elsewhere in the inscription.[9] One might also expect that such an inherently transitive verb as "to kill" would have a specific grammatical object rather than

---

3. A. Dupont-Sommer (in collaboration with J. Starcky), *Les Inscriptions Araménnes de Sfiré (Stèles I et II)* (Paris: Imprimerie Nationale, 1958). For the reading, see p. 17; for the translation, p. 19; for his discussion of the passage, pp. 40-41.

4. Fitzmyer, *Sefire*, 14, 15.

5. Cf., e.g., M. Jastrow, *A Dictionary of the Targumim, the Talmud Babli and Yerushalmi, and the Midrashic Literature* (reprinted Brooklyn: Shalom, 1967) 6; G. Dalman, *Aramäisch-Neuhebräisches Handwörteruch zu Targum, Talmud und Midrasch* (Göttingen: Vandenhoeck & Ruprecht, 1938; reprinted Hildesheim: Olms, 1967) 3, defined as "starker Hahn." The form is not, however, listed in M. Sokoloff, *A Dictionary of Jewish Palestinian Aramaic* (Ramat Gan: Bar Ilan University, 1990). On Syriac *'ābakā'* and *bākā'* cf., e.g., C. Brockelmann, *Lexicon Syriacum* (Tübingen: Niemeyer, 1928; reprinted Hildesheim: Olms, 1966) 2, 73; R. Payne Smith, *A Compendious Syriac Dictionary* (Oxford: Clarendon, 1903; reprinted 1967) 2, 45. On Syriac *bāktā'* cf. Brockelmann, *Lexicon Syriacum*, 73; Payne Smith, *Syriac Dictionary*, 45.

6. Fitzmyer, *Sefire*, 43.

7. Dupont-Sommer, *Sfiré*, 40. See further Fitzmyer's comments on other proposed interpretations, *Sefire*, 43-44.

8. No such form is cited by R. Degen in his *Altaramäische Grammatik* (Wiesbaden: Steiner, 1969).

9. Cf. I.B.27; II.B.9, III.11, 18, 21. For the normative *qtl*, cf., e.g., Fitzmyer, *Sefire*, 67.

an implicit object as the context demands. To be sure, one can muster vaguely reasonable defenses to counter each of these objections, but in aggregate the result can only be most unsatisfying. There are simply too many problems in too little space.

Not surprisingly, other proposals have found their way into the scholarly literature, for example, by P. Ronzevalle, H. Bauer, J. Epstein, G. Garbini, D. Hillers, J. Gibson, E. Y. Kutscher (via J. Greenfield), A. Lemaire, and E. Puech.[10] I will not, for purposes of this study, look these over, one by one. They all have their problems.[11] In general, none of these solutions feels "right"; rather, they all have the sense of being what scholars often call "ingenious" — too clever for their own good and, in the final analysis, about as far-fetched as the killer chickens.

Out of all these efforts, perhaps one little bit of progress was made — the proposal to read *bnth,* "his daughters," in lieu of *bkth,* "chickens."[12] This at least had the ring of legitimacy in that the form made sense in and of itself. Working off this reading, some more reasonable interpretations were made. Of all these, perhaps the one suggested by A. Lemaire and J.-M. Durand was the best. They proposed translating, "et que ses sept *fille* aillent pour un morceau de pain et qu'elles ne soient pas désirées!" ("and may his seven daughters go for a bit of bread but not be content"), taking *šṭ* as "morsel" and *yhrgn* as a Huphal of *rgg,* "to desire."[13] The proposal is not without drawbacks (e.g., the transitive use of *hwk b* in the sense "to go for"); still, of all the proposals, it made the most sense and at least got rid of those offensive killer chickens.

Nonetheless, all in all, no proposal made for reading and interpreting this curse seemed to do the trick. In my mind, and, I am sure, in the minds of many scholars working in Northwest Semitic philology, the curse remained unsolved. We applied whatever solution seemed least objectionable like a band-aid and waited for something better to turn up.

Indeed, something better *did* turn up, in the form of the Tell Fakheriyeh

---

10. Cf. P. Ronzevalle, "Fragments d'inscriptions araméennes des environs d'Alep," *MUSJ* 15 (1930-31) 237-60; H. Bauer, "Ein aramäischer Staatsvertrag aus dem 8 Jh. v. Chr. Die Inschrift der Stele von Sudschin," *AfO* 8 (1932-33) 1-16, esp. 7. For the fullest survey of translations and interpretations up to 1982, cf. E. Peuch, "Les Inscriptions Arámennes I et III de Sfiré: Nouvelles Lectures," *RB* 89 (1982) 576-83.

11. Again, note the observations and criticisms of Peuch, "Inscriptions."

12. First proposed by D. Hillers, *Treaty-Curses and the Old Testament Prophets* (BibOr 16; Rome: Pontifical Biblical Institute, 1964) 71-74.

13. Cf. A. Lemaire and J.-M. Durand, *Les Inscriptions Araméenes de Sfiré et l'Assyrie de Shamshi-Ilu* (Geneva and Paris: Droz, 1984) 121. Presumably, this translation is based on context alone; at least, Lemaire and Durand do not propose any etymological justification for this interpretation of *šṭ*. This follows Hillers's original proposal (*Treaty-Curses,* 15); cf. Syriac *rg,* "to desire, covet"; Brockelmann, *Lexicon Syriacum,* 710; Payne Smith, *Syriac Dictionary,* 527.

bilingual inscription.[14] It was Stephen A. Kaufman who first noticed that there were not simply a series of curses in this latter inscription (ll. 20ff.) clearly informed by the same tradition lying behind the Sefire curses, but also that this parallel was a key that offered a brilliant solution to the problem of the "killer-chickens curse."[15] His reasoning went as follows:

> First, . . . the "sheep suckling a lamb," "oxen suckling a calf" and "women suckling a child" [curse] formulae are virtual parallels in both inscriptions. Hence there is good reason to look for further parallels to Fakheriyeh in the crux that is the remaining Sefire curse. Secondly, there is the clearly read form *lḥm* in Sefire I A:24 which matches *lḥm* in Fakheriyeh in line 22. In consideration of the common curse tradition, this should hardly be dismissed as simply a coincidence.[16]

Kaufman then proceeded to reconstruct the Sefire curse in I.A.24 using the Fakheriyeh curse in line 22 and came up with virtually a word-for-word, nearly a letter-for-letter, match. Fakheriyeh 22 reads:

wmʾh nšwn lʾpn btnwr lḥm wʾl ymlʾnh

and may a hundred women bake bread in an oven and not fill it.

He accordingly read the Sefire curse:

wšbʿ bnth yʾpn b°°ṭ lḥm wʾl ymlʾn

and may his seven daughters bake bread in an oven and not fill (it).[17]

Note that Kaufman adopted the reading *bnth*, "his daughters," in lieu of the chickens and read *yʾpn*, "let them [feminine plural] bake," for *yhkn*, "let them go," and *ymlʾn*, "let them (not) fill," for *yhrgn*, "let them (not) kill/be content." Note too that everything fits perfectly, and, more to the point, everything makes sense. Beyond this, instead of having an obscure and difficult-to-interpret curse with one grammatical objection after another, one has a clean and simple curse with a tradition — paralleled not only in the Fakheriyeh inscription but also in a curse formula in Lev 26:26, *ʾpw ʿśr nšym lḥmkm btnwr ʾḥd whšybw lḥmkm bmšql wʾkltm wlʾ tśbʿw*, "Then ten women will bake your bread in a single oven but have to dole out your bread by measure — and you will eat but not be satisfied."

---

14. For a comprehensive bibliography on this text, cf. Fitzmyer and Kaufman, *Aramaic Bibliography*, 36-37.

15. Cf. S. Kaufman, "Reflections on the Assyrian-Aramaic Bilingual from Tell Fakhariyeh," *Maarav* 3 (1982) 137-75, esp. 170-72.

16. Ibid., 170.

17. Ibid., 172.

I became peripherally involved in the development of Kaufman's approach to this curse as the editor who shepherded the relevant article to publication. In fact, I added, with his blessing, a fairly detailed letter-by-letter analysis of line 24 designed to show that what he said *had* to be there, indeed, really *was* there. This was based on careful scrutiny of the then best published photographs, those in Dupont-Sommer's original publication.[18] All in all, I found the total result produced by Kaufman immensely satisfying. It just goes to show, I thought, you *can* make real progress in Northwest Semitic philology. You can, if the right evidence becomes available, turn a patently absurd curse about predatory poultry into a perfectly correct reading that not only makes sense but simply — by the mere logic of the argument — *has to be right.*

But then . . . all this changed again, this time thanks to an encounter in Paris with my colleague André Lemaire (whose keen erudition in reference to the Sefire inscription has already been mentioned) about a year after Kaufman's article was published. In the course of conversation he made reference to Kaufman's article, and I could not help but draw his attention to the tour de force that had finally solved the "killer-chickens curse." Lemaire agreed that the solution was brilliant — truly "ingenious." But alas, he further declared, it is also wrong.

"Wrong!" I responded. "How could it be wrong? It *can't* be wrong!"

"But the readings show that it is wrong," Lemaire told me.

"And how do you know this?"

"We have a squeeze taken from the stela in the Institut d'Études Sémitiques," he replied. So off we went to the institute to see the squeeze.

The result was both good news and bad news. The good news was that the squeeze appeared to indicate that the reading at the beginning of the curse was almost certainly *bnth*, despite Dupont-Sommer's claim that the *bkth* reading was "tout à fait sûre."[19] The key indicator here was that a distinct trace could be seen of a top diagonal stroke high above the line that would represent the initial "zig" of the zigzag shape of a *nun* and that would not be at all compatible with a *kap*. It was not that a reading of *kap* was indefensible, but rather that a reading of *nun* was not only quite possible but actually preferable on purely epigraphic grounds.[20] In consideration that "his daughters" was contextually far preferable to "chickens," there was little question as to the correct reading. I took a picture of the reading as shown by the squeeze in order to document it (see fig. 1).

The bad news came with the form of the following verb, read by everyone

18. See Dupont-Sommer, *Sfiré*, pl. II.

19. Ibid., 40.

20. For a discussion of "epigraphy" as formally distinct from "philology," cf. R. Ratner and B. Zuckerman, " 'A Kid in Milk'? New Photographs of *KTU* 1,23, Line 14," *HUCA* 57 (1986) 22n.26.

Figure 1. The arrows indicate, right to left, B, N, T, and H.

before Kaufman as *yhkn*, "they [feminine plural] will go," and by Kaufman as *y'pn*, "they [feminine plural] will bake." This is the way I described the reading in Kaufman's article:

> The form in Sefire read *yhkn* is equally capable of being read *y'pn*. Indeed, the reading of a *pe* as the third letter of the form is preferable to the traditional interpretation, *kap*. If the lightly scratched marks at the top are not viewed as part of the letter, a well-formed, deeply etched *pe* is certainly the correct reading. Equally ambiguous is the second letter of the form, read as a *he* according to the earlier interpretation. Again, interpretation depends on distinguishing abrasions in the stone from the actual letter form, but the clear vertical stroke could very well be the crossing stroke of an *'alep*. . . . Traces of the two legs of an *'alep* appear also to be visible — and it is possible that the upper leg may be seen extending to the right beyond the vertical stroke as well. (This has previously been read as part of the preceding *yod*, but note that the stroke does seem to intersect the vertical of our form. Possibly, two strokes are involved here — the short lower horizontal stroke of *yod* "running into" the bottom leg of an *'alep*.)[21]

The squeeze told a different story. There was no question that the reading of the initial *yod* and final *nun* were correct. But then no one had ever disputed them. The second letter definitely looked more like a *he* than an *'alep*. But the strokes were just faded enough to raise a question in my mind. In a pinch, I thought to myself, I might just be able to defend the reading I *knew* had to be there, the reading of *'alep*. But the coup de grace was the third letter. I looked at it with incredulity; for there before my eyes was a definite *kap* in the form characteristic for Sefire — with the short hook stroke on the left and a straight looking, long diagonal, which clearly extended above the hook, on the right. No doubt about it, as Lemaire compelled me to admit, this was a *kap*, plain and simple. Only the most stubborn fool would read the entire form as anything else but *yhkn*.

At this point something in my brain snapped, or perhaps I should say, something snapped shut. I looked Lemaire in the eyes and said those fateful words: "I don't care what the squeeze shows. The squeeze is *wrong*. And, if the squeeze actually does show the readings correctly, then the scribe wrote it wrong — because I know, absolutely for certain, what the reading *has to be: y'pn*. Kaufman's solution is simply too perfect — it defies every sense I have of philology in Northwest Semitic studies to believe otherwise. I don't give a damn! No matter what you say, I will not be moved."

I must say that Lemaire gave me one of those looks when I said this — a look of dubious pity for someone who had succumbed to the vice of "damned certainty" — indeed, a look that I myself had often given so many times to

---

21. Kaufman, "Reflections," 170-71.

colleagues who had dug in their philological heels and refused to acknowledge the evidence before their eyes. In any case, I made a picture of that reading as well (see fig. 2).

I would hesitate to say that this encounter with the evidence of the Sefire squeeze was a seminal experience for me — but I will have to admit that I brooded on this whole business of the curse in Sefire I.A.24 for years. In weaker moments, I would almost succumb to the belief that the "right" reading was wrong. But I could never quite give in; rather, like Pharaoh, I would harden my heart. Some day, I thought, I'll get to Damascus and look that curse straight in the eye: then, and only then, shall we see what we shall see!

What finally happened was not too different from this. I did not get to Damascus myself, but my good friend Wayne Pitard did — and he brought along his camera too. Later on, he sent me his negatives to do prints for him, and among them were several excellent pictures of face A of stela I of the Sefire inscription — pictures that were a substantial improvement over those published by Dupont-Sommer. Needless to say, those negatives were in the darkroom and printed almost as soon as I realized what they were. Pitard has kindly allowed me to use this material for this study (see fig. 3).

So what did I see when I had blown things up sufficiently so that the readings were at long last a good deal more readable? Of course the first thing I looked for was the third letter of the verb: was it a *pe* or a *kap?* To say that the moment had its pleasure is to understate the case. There could be no doubt about it: the letter was a *pe* after all. Those traces that had made it look like a *kap* were spurious — simply light abrasions in the stone. In fact, my original description in Kaufman's article had been right on the mark. Once again, it was not that it was impossible to interpret the form as a *kap;* rather, visual inspection showed that not only was the reading of *pe* eminently defensible, it definitely was the preferred reading.

It was also very nice to see that the evidence in favor of *bnth* was stronger than ever. In the squeeze, it was difficult to see whether there might be a hook stroke coming off the curving downstroke of the second letter of this form, as would be necessary if the reading were a *kap.* But the picture showed no trace of such a stroke. *Kap* was even more difficult to defend than before — the chickens were dead; long live the baking daughters!

But just as I was about to give this story a happy ending, a cursed little problem suddenly reared its head: something completely unexpected, although, in retrospect, I had had ample forewarning from the Sefire squeeze. The problem was once more in the letters of the verb, but in the *second letter* rather than the third. This should have been an *'alep,* but it was not. As the Sefire squeeze had already indicated and Pitard's photograph now confirmed beyond any reasonable doubt, the letter was a *he.* So, as it turns out, the reading here was one that no one had predicted or even come close to proposing: *yhpn.* What was one to make of that?

Figure 2. The arrow indicates the crucial letter.

Figure 3.   *The bracket indicates the verb.*

But then I remembered that another form in the Sefire inscription showed a marked resemblance to this odd and unexpected reading. It occurs in the fifth line of face C of stela II and reads *'hbd*, which is universally interpreted as a Haphel first common plural from *'bd*, translate: "I shall destroy."[22] But the expected form should be *'h'bd* — in fact, precisely this "correct" form is found in the previous line (II.C.4). The easiest and most obvious explanation is to assume a simple scribal error has occurred in line 5 in which the scribe has inadvertently dropped the second *'alep*. Hence the reading in II.C.5 should be corrected to *'h<'>bd*.

Dupont-Sommer had suggested otherwise, however: "Si l'absences du א radical n'est pas ici purement accidentelle, cette graphie אהבד indique sans doute que ce א était devenu quiescent."[23] Moreover, this is not the only case where the orthography in the Sefire text indicates a potential quiescent *'alep*. There is also the form *byr'* in I.B.34, apparently meaning "well" but not written *b'r'* as we would expect if the *'alep* were retained and pronounced as a full consonant.

Hence the "strange" form *yhpn* may not be so strange after all; indeed, one can see it fit into this general picture rather well as a Haphel third feminine plural of *'py* with quiescent *'alep;* translate: "they will make bake." One could once again appeal to scribal error and read *yh<'>pn*. But then one would have to countenance two almost identical errors in the same text. Actually, this may not be entirely wrong. Clearly, the scribe of the Sefire inscription is intent on preserving his *'alep*s in all conditions, wherever possible. But if he slips just occasionally, perhaps this indicates that the *'alep*s he writes are not *'alep*s that he hears.

When W. R. Garr surveyed the evidence for quiescent *'alep* in early Aramaic, the only examples he could suggest came from the Sefire inscription. He noted but discounted *'hbd* and could cite only the aforementioned *byr'* as a definite "possible." On the basis of this lone example he would not sanction the probability of quiescent *'alep* in Sefire since its evidence "is counterbalanced by the otherwise consistent preservation of *aleph* in all positions."[24] But perhaps *yhpn*, not to mention *'hbd*, in the light of this latter form, tips the scales and makes the case for quiescence of syllable-closing *'alep* stronger than anyone had previously imagined.

---

22. See, e.g., Fitzmyer, *Sefire*, 91.

23. Dupont-Sommer, *Sfiré*, 120-21. H. Donner and W. Röllig argue even more forcefully for elision of the *'alep;* cf. *KAI*, vol. 2, 262-63, a position that Fitzmyer also admits is possible, though with far greater caution; cf. *Sefire*, 91. More recent scholars who assume a scribal error include Degen, *Grammatik*, 19n.76; J. C. L. Gibson, *Textbook of Syrian Semitic Inscriptions*, vol. 2: *Aramaic Inscriptions* (Oxford: Clarendon, 1975) 45; Lemaire and Durand, *Inscriptions*, 143.

24. W. R. Garr, *Dialect Geography of Syria-Palestine, 1000-586 B.C.E.* (Philadelphia: University of Pennsylvania, 1985) 49. For a defense of *'alep* as having consonantal force in the Sefire inscription, cf. Fitzmyer, *Sefire*, 147-48.

While this explanation seems plausible, it has, one must admit, a major problem. If one reads *yhpn* as a Haphel of *'py,* this would be, to my knowledge, the only case of a causative of this verb attested in Northwest Semitic. This is a serious concern; one does not like to create an otherwise unknown conjugation just to satisfy the classification of one example. Of course, one can get around this problem by proposing that a simple scribal error occurred (although note my reservations immediately above). The scribe, having just written a whole series of Haphel verbs in the previous curses, accidentally wrote this one as a causative, too. This could even be a simple visual error. The correct reading would therefore be in accordance with Kaufman's original proposal and should be corrected to *y'pn.* Another possibility is to assume that *yhpn* is an intentionally artificial form, made into a Haphel in order to conform with all the previous Haphels. Others may wish to propose different, possibly better (or at least ingenious) solutions. Perhaps the most intelligent thing to do is to admit that, while the form *yhpn* is clear, what to make of it is less than clear. Perhaps, by now, we should expect that for every step or two forward in the progress of Northwest Semitic epigraphy and philology there is going to be a step backward, or at least a step sideways.

There remain two further loose ends to consider. The reading *bšṭ* should be retained, despite my arguments to the contrary in Kaufman's article.[25] This should be understood as the equivalent of *btnwr* in the Fakheriyeh inscription and be translated "in an oven." In consideration that *swṭ* occurs in Syriac in the sense "to burn, consume," this is far from unreasonable.[26] Hence, read *bšṭ* (i.e., with the sibilant interpreted as a *śin* rather than a *šin*).

The reading of the final verb, understood by all previous to Kaufman as *yhrgn* and by Kaufman as *yml'n,* is not further clarified by Pitard's new photographs. Either reading or some other reading is quite possible on purely epigraphic grounds. In actuality, either interpretation is justifiable in context on philological grounds. If one reads *yhrgn,* then we can borrow from Lemaire and understand the curse: "and may his seven daughters make bread bake in an oven and not be content." Note that such an interpretation would hark back to the last phrase in the Leviticus curse: "you will eat but not be satisfied."[27]

---

25. Cf. Kaufman, "Reflections," 172.

26. Cf. Brockelmann, *Lexicon Syriacum,* 463; Payne Smith, *Syriac Dictionary,* 364.

27. One might argue against Lemaire's *yhrgn,* "they [feminine plural] may (not) be content," based on reference to the preceding curses in the Sefire inscription. In each such curse, the operative verb at the conclusion of the oath is *šb',* "to be satisfied." One might therefore wonder why there would be a switch in this last oath to the Huphal of *rgg* when this is essentially a synonym of *šb'.* Would not the rhetorical effect be intensified if the same verb were used throughout? In fairness, one could also argue against Kaufman's proposal to read *yml'n* that it does not take a direct pronominal object as does its parallel *yml'nh* in the Fakhariyeh inscription. Rather, the object must be assumed, "they [feminine plural] may (not) fill *(it)*." But implied direct objects have ample precedence in Northwest Semitic syntax; besides, in consideration that the reading is far from clear in the existing photographs, one could just as easily read/restore the form exactly as it is found in Fakhariyeh.

Alternatively, read the closer parallel to Fakheriyeh and Leviticus: "and may his seven daughters make bread bake in an oven, and not fill (it)." We will just have to wait for more information on this wayward verb. Perhaps someone will get back to Damascus someday and take the photograph that will decide the matter.

In conclusion, there should be a moral to this tale of a curse and the way scholars (especially this scholar) interpreted it. I suggest this: It certainly is correct to be damned certain if you know for certain you are right. But have a care that you aren't *too* damned certain! Because you may discover, after all, that you were wrong.

Of this, at least, I am absolutely certain.

Topography and Theology
in the Gospel of John

CRAIG R. KOESTER

Luther Seminary, St. Paul, Minnesota

Throughout his distinguished career as a writer and an editor, David Noel Freedman has persistently stressed the importance of the land and cultures of Palestine for the interpretation of biblical texts. Taking this emphasis as my point of departure, I find that attention to the physical context of Jesus' ministry offers a valuable perspective on the Fourth Gospel. The prologue begins with references to the transcendent Word of God, but when relating at greater length how the Word became flesh and came to his own home, the text carefully follows the contours of the land of Palestine. Comparison of the Johannine topographical notices with information from other sources has shown that the Gospel writer generally has a high level of familiarity with places he describes.[1] Although some interpreters regard the topographical notices mainly as remnants of early tradition, others have explored possible connections with the evangelist's broader theological interests.[2] Ways in which topography may help to communicate theologically with the Gospel's readers will be our focus.

At a basic level, topographical information can enhance the credibility of the author in the eyes of the readers. For example, John Chrysostom said that references to the places where events in Jesus' ministry occurred served

---

1. See, e.g., William F. Albright, "Recent Discoveries in Palestine and the Gospel of John," in *The Background of the New Testament and Its Eschatology: Studies in Honor of C. H. Dodd* (ed. W. D. Davies and D. Daube; Cambridge: Cambridge University, 1956) 153-71; Benedikt Schwank, "Ortskenntnisse im Vierten Evangelium?" *Erbe und Auftrag* 57 (1981) 427-42.

2. For a survey of approaches to Johannine topography see Charles H. Scobie, "Johannine Geography," *SR* 11 (1982) 77-84.

to validate the evangelist's message.[3] His point is that if the evangelist can be trusted in minor details he can also be trusted in weightier issues. Yet the Gospel's comments about Judea, Jacob's well, and other places suggest that remarks about specific places may do more than lend credibility to the narrative, and that topographical notices may play a larger theological role. The audience of the final form of John's Gospel was probably mixed: some readers may have been familiar with the places mentioned in the Gospel, others would have known only what the evangelist presented.[4] For topographical information to function effectively, its significance would have to be plausible to those familiar with the various sites mentioned, yet accessible to those without such information.

I. The Regions

The Gospel's treatment of regions is a useful point at which to begin, since their theological significance is well developed in the text.[5] The opening chapters of the Gospel show that positive responses to Jesus were typical of encounters in places outside Judea, and that negative or fickle responses were typical of Judea itself. The first disciples of Jesus began following him in Transjordan (1:28, 35-51), and their initial faith was confirmed by the sign Jesus performed at Cana in Galilee (2:1, 11). By way of contrast, some in Jerusalem responded skeptically to Jesus' remarks in the temple and others exhibited an unreliable form of miracle-faith (2:18-20, 23-25). The next pair of episodes contrasts the incredulity of Nicodemus, who was a Jewish leader in Jerusalem (3:1, 11-12), with the more positive response of the Samaritan woman, who brought her townspeople to a believing encounter with Jesus (4:29, 39). Similarly, the royal official in Galilee was willing to believe Jesus' word that his dying son would live (4:50, 53), but the invalid by the pool of Bethzatha in Jerusalem exhibited no faith before or after he was healed and even reported to the authorities, who persecuted Jesus for a Sabbath violation (5:15).

---

3. *Homilies on the Gospel of St. John* 16.1. Cf. Carl Bjerklund, *Tauta Egeneto: Die Präzisierungssätze im Johannesevangelium* (WUNT 40; Tübingen: Mohr/Siebeck, 1987) 149.

4. On the reading audience see R. Alan Culpepper, *Anatomy of the Fourth Gospel: A Study in Literary Design* (Philadelphia: Fortress, 1983) 224-25.

5. On the regions see esp. Jouette M. Bassler, "The Galileans: A Neglected Factor in Johannine Community Research," *CBQ* 43 (1981) 243-57. Cf. Robert T. Fortna, *The Fourth Gospel and Its Predecessor: From Narrative Source to Present Gospel* (Philadelphia: Fortress, 1988) 294-314; Wayne A. Meeks, "Breaking Away: Three New Testament Pictures of Christianity's Separation from the Jewish Communities," in *"To See Ourselves as Others See Us": Christians, Jews, "Others" in Late Antiquity* (ed. J. Neusner and E. S. Frerichs; Chico, CA: Scholars, 1985) 93-115, esp. 94-104.

In the first five chapters, the evangelist associates particular types of faith responses with regions; but beginning in chap. 6, he extends the regional identification to anyone exhibiting the faith response typical of that region. When the crowd at Capernaum in Galilee manifested the same kind of animosity that Jesus had encountered in Judea, the evangelist identified them as *Ioudaioi*, a term that could mean "Jews" in a religious and ethnic sense, and "Judeans" in a geographic sense (6:41, 52). Similarly, Nicodemus was initially identified with the dubious responses of people in Jerusalem, but when he later expressed more openness to Jesus, the authorities wondered if he might actually be from Galilee (7:51-52). Pilate was a Roman, but when interrogating Jesus he asked, "Am I a *Ioudaios?*" (18:35), a question that could be answered affirmatively because of his collaboration with the Jewish authorities during Jesus' trial and execution. People like the man born blind, Martha, and Mary, all of whom lived in the vicinity of Jerusalem and voiced traditional Jewish beliefs, are never called *Ioudaioi*. The term is not applied indiscriminately to all the inhabitants of a region but identifies those who manifest either negative or unreliable responses to Jesus (11:36-37, 45-46; 12:9, 17, 34).

The regional traits depicted in the Gospel and their extension to persons who did not necessarily live in those regions would have been congruent with what many readers knew from other sources. Historically, opposition to Jesus climaxed in Judea where he was crucified; but through their own clashes with the synagogue, Johannine Christians found that conflicts with *Ioudaioi* transcended that particular locale, while collaboration between rabbinic and Roman authorities in the period after 70 c.e. showed that opposition was not confined to one ethnic group.[6] Historically, Jesus' earliest disciples were from Galilee, and the term "Galilean" came to connote a follower of Jesus (cf. Mark 14:70). The postresurrection missionary activity of early Christians also met with some positive results among the Samaritans (cf. John 4:38-39) and among others who lived outside Judea and were not of Jewish background (7:35; 11:51-52; 12:20).

The regions in the Gospel are not significant in themselves. Rather, the negative responses associated with Judea and the positive responses associated with other places help to communicate theologically with readers by characterizing people in their relationship to Jesus. Specific sites within each region also help disclose something about the people mentioned in the story. Since I cannot treat all the places mentioned by the evangelist, I will select one from each region and consider how traits associated with that place contribute theologically to the Gospel.

---

6. John 21:19 apparently alludes to Peter's death by crucifixion, which was a Roman form of execution (cf. 18:32). On the significance of collaboration between Jewish and Roman leaders after 70 c.e. for John's Gospel, see David Rensberger, *Johannine Faith and Liberating Community* (Philadelphia: Westminster, 1988) 87-90; and my " 'The Savior of the World' (John 4:42)," *JBL* 109 (1990) 678.

II. Jacob's Well in Samaria

I turn first to Jacob's well in Samaria, since the accuracy of the topographical details in John 4 is widely accepted. The text says that when Jesus journeyed to Samaria, he halted near the town of Sychar beside Jacob's well, which was in the field he had given to his son Joseph (4:5-6). The conversation with the Samaritan woman discloses that the well is deep (4:11) and that it can be called either a "spring" (*pēgē*, 4:6) or a "well" (*phrear*, 4:11). It was located within eyesight of "this mountain," Mount Gerizim, where the Samaritans worshiped (4:20), and was near fields suitable for growing grain (4:35). Readers familiar with the area would have found the topographical details accurate. A deep ancient well called *Bir Ya'aqub* is in the vicinity of Mount Gerizim, and since it is an artesian water source rather than a cistern, it can conceivably be called a "well" or a "spring." The fertile plain that extends to the east of the well was known for its grain production in ancient times. It is uncertain whether Sychar should be identified with the village of Askar or with Shechem, but it is clear that in the first century there was a village not far from the well.[7]

The first topographical detail taken up in the chapter is Jacob's well. Although located at a particular place in Samaria, the encounter beside this well acquires a typical or representative quality through its similarities to biblical courtship scenes. The Scriptures relate how several of the woman's ancestors — including Jacob (4:4, 12) — met their future wives beside wells.[8] The pattern in these stories is that a man traveling in a foreign land meets a young woman beside a well. After water is given, the woman tells her family about the visitor, the man is invited to stay, and a betrothal is arranged. Earlier in the Gospel, Jesus assumed the role of the bridegroom by providing wine for the wedding at Cana (2:1-11), and John the Baptist identified Jesus as the bridegroom who had come to claim the bride (3:29). In John 4, Jesus was traveling through Samaria, which was foreign territory, and met one of Jacob's descendants, a woman who had come to the well at midday as Rachel had (Gen 29:7; John 4:6). These typical traits rightly suggest that the Samaritan woman, like Rachel, would be receptive to the one she met.

Comments about the water in the well, however, show that Jesus is someone "greater than Jacob" (4:12). The well Jacob provided was bound to a place and quenched thirst only for a time; Jesus promised water that would spring up within a person and issue into eternal life (4:13-14). The language recalls traditions about the water given to Israel in the time of Moses — a figure whom Samaritans

---

7. On the location see Zdravko Stefanovic, "Jacob's Well," *ABD* 3.608-9. On the grain fields see Str-B 2.431; Clemens Kopp, *The Holy Places of the Gospels* (New York: Herder, 1963) 165n.42.

8. The similarities to biblical courtship scenes have often been noted. See the summary in Paul D. Duke, *Irony in the Fourth Gospel* (Atlanta: John Knox, 1985) 101-3.

deemed greater than Jacob. On several occasions Moses had wondrously provided water for Israel in the desert, and tradition held that the water that had sprung up at different times and places actually came from a single miraculous well.[9] In addition to water, Moses had brought the people the Law, which was the "gift of God" and a source of life (cf. John 4:10, 14). Water was a common image for the Law in both Jewish and Samaritan tradition.[10] Jesus contrasted his true "living water" with the water in the well, indicating that it was of another order, something more like the revelation delivered through Moses than the water provided by Jacob. When Jesus displayed his knowledge of the woman's life, she recognized that he was indeed a prophet (4:19).

The second topographical detail is Mount Gerizim. As the scope of the conversation broadens from the woman's personal life to matters of national concern, the discussion of topography also shifts from Jacob's well to the Samaritan holy place. The woman said, "Our fathers worshiped on this mountain, and you say that in Jerusalem is the place where it is necessary to worship" (4:20). By speaking of national concerns in the first person plural, the woman acts as a spokesperson for her people. Jesus responds in the plural by saying, "You people worship what you do not know; we worship what we know, for salvation is from the Jews" (4:22). His comment recalls the common Jewish accusation that worship in Samaria had been idolatrous ever since Jacob had buried Rachel's stolen household gods there (Gen 35:4). Idolatry meant worshiping what one did not know (cf. Isa 44:9, 18; Wis 13:1-2). Such ignorance characterized those who worshiped at "this mountain," but from a Johannine perspective was also typical of "the world" generally (John 1:10).[11]

After referring to the holy mountain, the woman spoke about "the Messiah" who was expected to tell her people "all things" (4:25). The passage conveys Samaritan expectations through a Jewish expression. Samaritans in the first century apparently did not use the term "messiah," which was often associated with the heir of David, a Jewish king, but looked for the prophet like Moses foretold in Deut 18:15-18. A Moses-like figure did gain a following among the Samaritans in the mid-first century, promising to reveal on Mount Gerizim the sacred vessels used in the Mosaic tabernacle (Josephus, *Ant.* 18.4.1 §§85-88).[12]

---

9. On Moses traditions and the well see Birger Olsson, *Structure and Meaning in the Fourth Gospel: A Text-Linguistic Analysis of John 2:1-11 and 4:1-42* (ConBNT 6; Lund: Gleerup, 1974) 162-73; Germain Bienaimé, *Moïse et le don de l'eau dans la tradition juive ancienne: targum et midrash* (AnBib 98; Rome: Biblical Institute, 1984). Cf. the Samaritan *Memar Marqah* 4.4; 4.8; 5.3; 6.3.

10. See, e.g., CD 6.2-5; 3.12-17a; 19.32-35; *Memar Marqah* 2.1; 6.3; cf. Philo, *Drunkenness* 112-13; *Dreams* 2.271.

11. On this section see my "Savior of the World," 672-74.

12. See my discussion in *The Dwelling of God: The Tabernacle in the Old Testament, Intertestamental Jewish Literature, and the New Testament* (CBQMS 22; Washington, D.C.: Catholic Biblical Association, 1989) 55-58.

Jesus disclosed that he was the Messiah, and indeed told the woman "all things" about herself (John 4:25-26, 29, 39). The arrival of the Messiah rightly presaged the establishment of true worship, but contrary to Samaritan expectations it would not be bound to a location: the hour had come when people would worship God "neither on this mountain nor in Jerusalem" but "in Spirit and in truth" (4:21-24).

The third topographical element is the grainfields to the east of the well. As the woman exits, the disciples appear on the scene and encourage Jesus to eat. Jesus replies that he has food, explaining that "food" is a metaphor for doing the will of God. Then he directs their attention to the fields nearby, transforming them into a metaphor for missionary activity (4:31-38). At the ordinary agricultural level, there was a four-month interval between the sowing and harvesting of a crop; but Jesus says that the time of harvest has already come and that the sower and reaper can rejoice together, recalling biblical promises concerning God's future blessings (Lev 26:5; Amos 9:13). The harvest itself — like the water promised to the woman — would be for eternal life (John 4:36). The disciples had just returned with some food purchased in Sychar, near Joseph's field (*chōrion*, 4:5), but were participating in a missionary harvest of the fields (*chōrai*, 4:35) for which they had not labored, as a throng of villagers came to Jesus in response to the Samaritan woman's testimony (4:29-30, 38-39).

The final topographical element is Sychar. This episode began with a personal conversation between Jesus and a woman, but it expanded to deal with issues of national differences and the Christian mission, and concludes when Jesus is acclaimed "the Savior of the world" (4:42), a title that connotes world-wide dominion. Similarly, the evangelist initially located Sychar in relation to Jacob's well and Joseph's field, but suggests that Jesus was welcomed there in a manner suitable for a Greco-Roman city (*polis*, 4:5, 39). When figures like Vespasian and Titus approached a city, people would stream out to the roadsides to greet them, escort them into their town, and acclaim them "savior and benefactor." By going out to meet Jesus on the road, inviting him into their town, and hailing him as "the Savior of the world," the people of Sychar bore witness to the universal scope of his power.[13] Each topographical element in the story contributes to a disclosure of Jesus' identity and what it means to receive him.

III. The Pool of Bethzatha

I noted earlier that the evangelist initially connected Judea with unfavorable and unreliable responses to Jesus, but eventually applied the term *Ioudaioi* to

---

13. On the reception at Sychar see my "Savior of the World," 665-68.

people of other locations and backgrounds who exhibited the same kinds of responses. In a similar way, the response of the invalid in John 5:1-16 was appropriate for the place known as Bethzatha, but readers could discern in him something of more far-reaching significance. The description of Bethzatha is detailed, and despite several textual problems it is corroborated by other literary sources and archaeological excavations. The site, which was located north of the Temple Mount, included two large reservoirs with smaller bathing pools nearby.[14] The five porticoes described by the evangelist sheltered the sick.

Although located in Jerusalem, this cult of healing was not a typical Jewish institution. Invalids were resident there, sometimes for extended periods of time (5:6), seeking help for various ailments. The expectation was that when the water in the pool was mysteriously disturbed, someone who entered immediately would be healed and that latecomers would not be helped (5:7). These practices are not well attested in Jewish sources, which commonly associated healing with prayer to a God who did not reserve his favor for those best able to help themselves. Later legend ascribed the moving of the water to an angel of the Lord (5:4), but the best manuscripts do not include this verse and most translations rightly omit it.

The Bethzatha cult resembles the healing shrines of Asclepius and Serapis, which were found throughout the eastern Mediterranean. Like the pool described in John 5, these sanctuaries were normally built beside bubbling springs, where people might remain for some time seeking aid. Vitruvius Pollio, a leading builder of the Augustan age, said that "the healthiest regions and suitable springs of water therein" are chosen "for all temples and particularly for Asclepius" and other gods of healing. For when the sick "are treated with water from wholesome fountains they recover more quickly."[15] The small bathing pools discovered at Bethzatha were similar to those used at such shrines, where people hoped to be among those who were healed of blindness, foot problems, and other infirmities by means of the water.[16] The second-century votive offerings to the god Serapis that were found at Bethzatha indicate how readily the shrine could be adapted for pagan use. It is not clear that Greco-Roman deities were actually invoked at the pool prior to the destruction of Jerusalem in 70 c.e., but Antoine Duprez observed that in the time of Jesus Bethzatha was located outside the city walls and near the Antonia fortress, the largest Roman military installation in the city, making it potentially useful for the pagans stationed there.[17]

14. On the textual problems of John 5:2 and other pertinent information see James F. Strange, "Beth-zatha," *ABD* 1.700-701. The most important discussion of the site is by Antoine Duprez, *Jésus et les dieux guérisseurs, à propos de Jean V* (CahRB 12; Paris: Gabalda, 1970). See also W. D. Davies, *The Gospel and the Land: Early Christianity and Jewish Territorial Doctrine* (Berkeley: University of California, 1974) 302-13.

15. *On Architecture* 1.2.7.

16. On the power of water to cure such ailments see Aelius Aristides, *Orations* 39.6 and 15; Pausanias, *Description of Greece* 4.31.4; 5.5.11; 6.22.7; 8.19.2.

17. Duprez, *Jésus et les dieux guérisseurs,* 96-97.

The invalid was Jewish, but his perspective on healing reflected a religious attitude that was common throughout the Greco-Roman world. The man was preoccupied with the mysterious power of the water in the pool, assuming that a well-timed entry would virtually guarantee results. Jesus healed the man without using water from the pool, but when the man was later faulted for carrying his mat on the Sabbath, he tried to shift the blame to his healer (5:11). Later, his readiness to report Jesus to the authorities suggests that he perceived healing as something that magically had happened to him, requiring no further commitment on his part. The deities typically associated with Greco-Roman healing shrines did not demand exclusive allegiance from worshipers, who could move from one cult to another with relative ease. Yet this text shows that those who assumed that loyalty to Jesus was optional remained in sin and under the threat of judgment (5:14).

IV. Tiberias in Galilee

In the wake of conflicts in Jerusalem over the healing at Bethzatha, "Jesus went across the Sea of Galilee of Tiberias" (6:1). This seemingly redundant designation connects the lake not only with the region of Galilee but with the city of Tiberias, which was the major urban center on its shores. Although the evidence is complex, there are good reasons to think that the Fourth Evangelist locates the feeding of the five thousand in proximity to the city of Tiberias, as Raymond Brown has suggested. The transition from Jerusalem in chap. 5 to Galilee in chap. 6 is abrupt, but the basic movement in the narrative is from south to north, and a number of manuscripts actually say that "Jesus went across the Sea of Galilee to the region [*eis ta merē*] of Tiberias." This movement is more plausible than assuming that Jesus crossed to the eastern shore.[18]

Tiberias is mentioned a second time in the transitional scene that traces the crowd's journey from the site of the feeding to Capernaum. The day after the miracle, the crowd wanted to find Jesus but discovered that his disciples had taken the only boat. Then "boats came from Tiberias, (which was) near the place where they ate the bread after the Lord had given thanks," and took them to Capernaum (6:23-24). The word "near" (*engys*) could be taken to mean that boats from Tiberias came "near to the place" where Jesus fed the multitude;[19] but word order indicates that "near" should be taken with Tiberias, and given the use of "near" (*engys*) with place-names elsewhere in the Gospel, it is best

---

18. Brown, *The Gospel According to John* (2 vols.; AB 29-29A; Garden City, NY: Doubleday, 1966-70) 1.232, 257-58.

19. In 6:19 "near" (*engys*) describes the movement of Jesus, who was coming "near to the boat." In 6:23 it identifies Tiberias in relation to the place of the feeding.

to say that boats came from Tiberias, "which was near the place where they ate the bread."[20] Moreover, if the evangelist set the feeding in the vicinity of Tiberias, the appearance of boats from that city is not hard to explain. It is more difficult to imagine why boats from a city on the western shore would travel to an unknown spot on the eastern side, then embark for yet a third location on the northwestern shore. When the crowd went "across the sea" (6:25), one can best picture them following a common navigational route from a site near Tiberias to Capernaum. The evangelist's language is similar to that of Josephus, who said that when people traveled from Tiberias to Taricheae — a town on the western side that was closer to Tiberias than Capernaum was — they "crossed over" the sea (*Life* 59 §304). The intervening description of Jesus walking on the sea is congruent with this scenario.[21]

The crowd that followed Jesus is depicted in a distinctly Johannine way. After Jesus had fed them with bread and fish, they declared initially that he was "the prophet who is coming into the world" (6:14), identifying him as the prophet like Moses who was foretold in Deut 18:15-18. The prophet Elisha had also fed a multitude with a small amount of bread (2 Kgs 4:42-44), but Jesus' miraculous gift of bread during the Passover season (John 6:4) would have been especially appropriate for someone like Moses, in whose time Israel had eaten

20. *Engys* is used for a place called "Aenon (which is) near Salim" (3:23), and Jesus is said to have gone from the village of Bethany "to the region "(which is) near the desert" (11:54). Other occurrences of *engys* in connection with places make the connection clear by coupling it with a form of the word "to be": Bethany "was near Jerusalem" (11:18), Golgotha "was near the city" (19:20), and the tomb "was near the place" (19:42). Significantly, the original text of Codex Sinaiticus said that "boats came from Tiberias, which was [*ousēs*] near where they ate the bread" (6:23).

21. The miraculous elements in John's account of Jesus walking on the sea are remarkably muted. The disciples had rowed for three or four miles (6:19), but John does not state that they were in the middle of the lake (cf. Matt 14:24). After meeting Jesus the evangelist notes that "immediately the boat reached the land to which they were going" (John 6:21). Some insist that the boat was miraculously whisked the remaining miles across the water (e.g., Rudolph Bultmann, *The Gospel of John* [trans. G. R. Beasley-Murray et al.; Philadelphia: Westminster, 1971] 216; Ernst Haenchen, *John* [trans. Robert W. Funk; 2 vols.; Hermeneia; Philadelphia: Fortress, 1984] 1.280; Fortna, *Fourth Gospel and Its Predecessor,* 82). But it is at least as plausible to think that they had nearly reached their destination when they met Jesus. Unlike the other Gospels, John does not say that Jesus looked like a ghost, that he stilled the storm, or even that he got into the boat, only that "the disciples wanted to take him into the boat" when they reached the shore (6:21). A nonmiraculous interpretation is proposed by J. H. Bernard, *A Critical and Exegetical Commentary on the Gospel According to St. John* (ICC; 2 vols.; Edinburgh: T. &. T. Clark, 1929) 1.185; J. N. Sanders, *A Commentary on the Gospel According to St. John* (completed by B. Mastin; HNTC; New York: Harper & Row, 1969) 183; Charles H. Talbert, *Reading John: A Literary and Theological Commentary on the Fourth Gospel and the Johannine Epistles* (New York: Crossroad, 1992) 133. The obscure points are noted by Brown, *Gospel According to John,* 1.252; C. K. Barrett, *The Gospel According to St. John* (2nd ed.; Philadelphia: Westminster, 1978) 280-81. By muting the miraculous elements, the evangelist focuses attention on the theophanic character of Jesus' words, "I Am" (6:20).

manna or "bread from heaven" (cf. 6:31-32). Next, the crowd tried to seize Jesus and make him king (6:15). This reaction also is plausible within the framework of Jewish eschatological expectations. In some traditions, Moses was depicted as both prophet and king (Philo, *Moses* 2.292), and other sources said that the advent of the Messiah would be accompanied by a reappearance of manna (*2 Apoc. Bar.* 29:8). The crowd's attempt to make Jesus king implies that a ruler's authority comes from popular acclaim rather than "from above" (cf. John 18:36), and Jesus fled from them. When they sought him out the next day to demand more bread, Jesus upbraided them for simply seeking to eat their fill without regard for what his signs conveyed (6:25-34).

A crowd from Tiberias would have been well suited to play the role of people preoccupied with bread and kingship. The characteristics of people from Tiberias were probably well known to some readers. Josephus called them "a promiscuous rabble" that included magistrates and poor folk "from any and all places of origin" (*Ant.* 18.2.3 §§36-38). The city itself, which bore the name of the emperor Tiberius, had been founded about 19 C.E. by Herod Antipas, a Roman vassal. The king established it as his capital with a Hellenistic constitution, but found it difficult to get Jews to settle there since he had built it on the site of a graveyard, and contact with the dead made people unclean according to Jewish law. Therefore, to find residents for his new city, Herod freed slaves and offered free land and houses to those who would settle there.[22] Although a synagogue was eventually established, the memory of the city's origins tainted its reputation for some time, and when Tiberias became an important center of rabbinic learning, Jewish sources recounted carefully how the city had been cleansed from its defilement.[23]

By the time the Gospel was completed, many of its readers would probably not have known the history of Tiberias. Yet the Gospel enables readers to see in the crowd traits that were not limited to Tiberias but were typical of the masses in various Greco-Roman cities. Roman rulers frequently placated the populace with distributions of bread or grain. Cicero recalled that the practice was agreeable to many people, since it enabled them to get adequate food without working for it, but others opposed it since it induced idleness and drained the treasury. The satirist Juvenal mocked the citizens who dutifully accompanied the Roman consul because they had received tickets for free meals, and he ridiculed the fickleness of the crowds that were willing to voice support for any ruler who mollified them with "bread and circuses." Similarly, Dio Chrysostom chided the people of Alexandria who were reputed to be a group "to whom you need only throw plenty of bread and a ticket to the hippodrome, since they have no interest in anything else."[24]

22. On the history of Tiberias see James F. Strange, "Tiberias," *ABD* 4.547-49.
23. *y. Sheb.* 9, 38d; *Gen. Rab.* 79:6; *Eccl. Rab.* 10:8.
24. Cicero, *Pro Sestio* 48 §103; Juvenal, *Satires* 10.44-46, 73-80; Dio Chrysostom, *Dis-*

The multitude in John 6, like the masses in various Greco-Roman cities, had no interest in anything but bread, and their eagerness to make Jesus king on the basis of a food distribution would have been familiar to a broad spectrum of the Gospel's readers. The crowd's loyalty was based on eating their fill of the loaves, and Jesus repudiated it, warning against their preoccupation with the kind of food that perishes (6:27). By noting the connection of the crowd to the city of Tiberias, the evangelist helped to convey a disposition that was congruent with the origins of the place yet representative of an attitude evident among many in the Mediterranean world.

V. Bethany in Transjordan

The final site is "Bethany beyond the Jordan," where John was baptizing and Jesus' ministry began (1:28). Toward the close of his ministry, Jesus returned to Bethany, where he received word of Lazarus's illness (10:40; 11:1-3). By noting that Bethany was "beyond the Jordan," the evangelist directs attention to the eastern side of the river. Although some scholars have suggested that Bethany was actually the region of Batanaea,[25] the Gospel refers to it as "a place" (*topos*, 10:40), a term that refers consistently to particular locations like the Jerusalem sanctuary (4:20; 11:48), the shrine at Bethzatha (5:13), and other specific sites; it is not used as a regional designation.[26] The precise location of Bethany in Transjordan has not been determined, but the site that has enjoyed most consistent support is the Wadi el-Charrar, which is opposite Jericho.[27] A place in this vicinity is compatible with the movements depicted in John 1 and 11, and is especially appropriate for the conversations the evangelist locates there.[28]

courses 32.31. See also Juvenal, *Satires* 7.174 and 8.118; Fronto, *Correspondence* (ed. and trans. C. R. Haines; LCL; Cambridge: Harvard University; London: Heinemann, 1963) 2.17. Cf. E. Courtney, *A Commentary on the Satires of Juvenal* (London: Athlone, 1980) 104-5, 372, 472; E. G. Hardy, *The Satires of Juvenal* (2nd ed.; London: Macmillan, 1891) 198-99, 232; Paul Veyne, *Bread and Circuses: Historical Sociology and Political Pluralism* (London: Penguin, 1990) 99-100.

25. On Bethany as Batanaea see esp. Rainer Riesner, "Bethany Beyond the Jordan (John 1:28): Topography, Theology and History in the Fourth Gospel," *TynBul* 38 (1987) 29-63; idem, "Bethany Beyond the Jordan," *ABD* 1.703-5.

26. Other "places" include the garden where Jesus was arrested (18:2), the pavement where Pilate's judgment seat was located (19:13), and the site of Jesus' crucifixion (19:17, 20, 41). Cf. 6:10, 23; 11:30; 20:7, 25.

27. Gustav Dalman, *Sacred Sites and Ways: Studies in the Topography of the Gospels* (trans. Paul P. Levertoff; London: SPCK, 1935) 89-92; Kopp, *Holy Places of the Gospels*, 110-29; cf. Rudolph Schnackenburg, *The Gospel According to St. John* (trans. Kevin Smyth et al.; 3 vols.; New York: Herder/Seabury/Crossroad, 1968-82) 1.295-96; Riesner, "Bethany Beyond the Jordan," *ABD* 1.704.

28. A period of three days would allow Jesus to travel from a location opposite Jericho,

After arriving at Bethany, a Jewish delegation asked about three figures: the Christ, Elijah, and the prophet like Moses (1:19-21, 25). Elijah was said to have parted the Jordan near Jericho before being swept into heaven by a whirlwind and chariot of fire on the plains across the river. His successor, Elisha, received the spirit of the prophet and parted the Jordan yet again (2 Kgs 2:6-14). The return of Elijah was an element in Jewish eschatological expectations (Mal 3:22-24 [ET 4:4-6]). Earlier, Moses was said to have addressed Israel on the plains across from Jericho (Deut 1:1), promising that in the future God would raise up for them another prophet like himself (18:15-18). Afterward, his successor, Joshua, who bore the Spirit of God as Moses had (Num 11:24-25; 27:18; Deut 34:9), led the people into the land by parting the waters of the Jordan as Moses once parted the sea (Exod 14:21; Josh 3:7-17). Moses was said to have been buried near Mount Nebo, which overlooks the area, and some expectations concerning the appearance of a Mosaic deliverer were associated with the burial site.[29] The vitality of these local traditions is evident in the attempt of Theudas, a self-proclaimed prophet, to claim the mantle of Moses, Elijah, and their successors by leading a group to the Jordan River, where he promised to part the water for them. The Roman cavalry interfered with his plans.[30]

John the Baptist denied that he was the Christ, Elijah, or the prophet like Moses; it was Jesus who would fulfill God's promises to Israel. Bethany in Transjordan was a suitable place for Jesus to appear, since the Fourth Gospel's presentation of Jesus' messiahship combines Davidic hopes with expectations for an eschatological prophet. This is especially apparent in signs like the gift of bread and raising the dead, which are reminiscent of miracles performed by Moses and Elijah (Exod 16:4-8; 1 Kgs 17:17-24). At Bethany, John testified that he "saw the Spirit descend and remain" on Jesus (John 1:32-33), which was appropriate for Jesus as God's anointed one (Isa 11:2; 61:1) as well as for a figure who stood in the line of Moses and Elijah. Like these earlier figures, Jesus bore the Spirit; but unlike them he bore it permanently. The Spirit "remained" on Jesus. Jesus would eventually give the Spirit to his followers, but that did not mean he would give it away. No other prophet or messianic figure would succeed him.

---

where he met his first disciples, to Cana in Galilee (2:1). The objection that one of the days allotted for travel would have been the Sabbath (Riesner, *TynBul* 38 [1987] 45-47) relies too heavily on a possible parallel between "the third day" and Easter. In chap. 11, it would have taken a day to travel from Bethany near Jerusalem to a site across from Jericho. If Lazarus died and was buried just after the messenger departed, one can calculate a day for the messenger to reach Jesus, a delay of two more days, and one final day for Jesus to travel to Bethany near Jerusalem. In support of Batanaea, Riesner proposes that Lazarus died only after Jesus had delayed for two days, so that it took Jesus four days to reach Bethany near Jerusalem (ibid., 43-45). While this alternative in itself is plausible, it does not override evidence favoring a site nearer Jericho.

29. *Lives of the Prophets* 2.14-19. See the comments by D. R. Hare in *OTP* 2.383.

30. Josephus, *Ant.* 20.5.1 §§97-98. The incident occurred ca. 44 C.E.

The Fourth Evangelist depicts the persons in the Gospel in a manner suitable for the places in which they appear. His portrayals make use of traditions associated with particular locations, but these are developed to disclose something of more far-reaching significance. Enough information is given so that readers unfamiliar with these places can interpret the scene, yet each episode is presented so that readers who do know about particular sites will find it plausible. By developing the theological significance of places in the Gospel, the evangelist maintains an integral connection with the land in which the first generation of Jesus' disciples lived and worked, and he also helps readers of subsequent generations to know who Jesus is and what it means to encounter him.

Mark and Isaiah

JOEL MARCUS

University of Glasgow

I. The Way of the Lord

In one of the innumerable prefaces to his satire *A Tale of a Tub*, Jonathan Swift makes the following request of his reader:

> There are certain common privileges of a writer, the benefit whereof, I hope, there will be no reason to doubt; particularly, that where I am not understood, it shall be concluded, that something very useful and profound is couched underneath, and again, that whatever word or sentence is printed in a different character, shall be judged to contain something extraordinary either of wit or sublime.[1]

Now, in standard editions of the Greek NT, citations of OT passages are printed in italic or boldface type. Contrary to Swift, however, these highlighted quotations are often treated by exegetes not as "something extraordinary either of wit or sublime" but as matters of relatively little import for the great task of elucidating the NT writer's theology (or, more recently, his literary purpose). Many exegetes think that they have discharged their obligation to their readers vis-à-vis these passages if they append a few dutiful notes about the OT source and the text-type employed; at most they may draw a comparison between the NT author's usage of his text and the Qumran *pesher* method or one of Hillel's thirteen hermeneutical rules.

Recently, however, an increasing number of studies have tried to take Scripture use seriously as an expression of an author's theological purpose.

---

1. Jonathan Swift, *A Tale of a Tub and the Battle of the Books* (London: Hamish Hamilton, 1948) 343.

Scholars have seen the ubiquity of NT quotation of the OT, and the frequent obscurity of its purpose, as an invitation to conclude, in Swift's terms, "that something very useful and profound is couched underneath." In this study I hope to make a small contribution along these lines, cheered by the spirit of intrepid exploration that Noel Freedman has encouraged during my acquaintance with him.

The Gospel of Mark starts: "The beginning of the good news of Jesus Christ as written in Isaiah the prophet";[2] this introduction is then followed by a biblical citation that, in characteristic Markan fashion, conflates passages from Exodus, Malachi, and Deutero-Isaiah.[3] This odd beginning immediately alerts Mark's readers that they cannot understand his narrative of the life, death, and resurrection of Jesus without the superimposition upon it of other narratives from the sacred saga of Israel, particularly those found in the book ascribed to Isaiah.[4] Indeed, although many biblical citations occur throughout Mark's narrative,[5] Isaiah is the only OT author who is cited by name, not only here in 1:2 but also in 7:6.

Just how far-reaching are the reverberations of Isaiah within Mark? A minimalist answer to this question is common;[6] the citation of "Isaiah" in 1:2-3, for example, is usually taken merely as a preparation for vv. 4-8, which introduce John the Baptist, the messenger who goes before Jesus in the wilderness to prepare his way. Evidence that would tend to support this minimalist interpretation is not hard to find; the messenger's subordination to the one whose way he prepares has its counterpart in John's subordination of himself to the "stronger one" who comes after him, and the resounding of the "voice crying in the wilderness" has its counterpart in the proclamation of John in the wilderness.[7]

2. For this way of punctuating 1:1-2, see J. Marcus, *The Way of the Lord: Christological Exegesis in the Gospel of Mark* (Louisville: Westminster/John Knox, 1992) 17-18.

3. On the Markan technique of conflation, see H. C. Kee, "The Function of Scriptural Quotations and Allusions in Mark 11–16," in *Jesus und Paulus: Festschrift für Werner Georg Kümmel zum 70. Geburtstag* (ed. E. E. Ellis and E. Grässer; Göttingen: Vandenhoeck & Ruprecht, 1975) 181; and Marcus, *Way,* index s.v. "conflation of OT passages."

4. Of course, Mark would have regarded passages from "Deutero-Isaiah" as having come from the pen of Isaiah of Jerusalem.

5. For an overview, see the helpful little book of R. G. Bratcher, *Old Testament Quotations in the New Testament* (2nd ed.; Helps for Translators; London, New York, and Stuttgart: United Bible Societies, 1984) 12-17.

6. See, e.g., the standard commentaries of R. Pesch, *Das Markusevangelium* (2 vols.; HTKNT 2; Freiburg: Herder, 1976) 1.77-79; and J. Gnilka, *Das Evangelium nach Markus* (2 vols.; EKKNT 2; Zurich: Benziger, 1978-79) 1.44-45.

7. Although I do not agree with the minimalist position on the horizon of Mark 1:2-3, the correspondence just described at least refutes the suggestion of M. A. Tolbert (*Sowing the Gospel: Mark's World in Literary-Historical Perspective* [Philadelphia: Fortress, 1989] 239-48) that the "you" addressed in 1:2 is the reader rather than Jesus and that the messenger before the Lord's face is Jesus rather than John.

Doubts about the adequacy of this minimalist position, however, follow immediately upon recognition of its superficial cogency. Why does Mark, in the course of his Gospel, drop Isaiah's name twice, whereas he does not identify any of the other biblical authors whose sayings stud his narrative? Why does he do so for the first time here, in the very first sentence of his work? Is he only referring, in a rather artificial manner, to John's forerunner status and wilderness location when he says that the gospel is "as it has been written in Isaiah the prophet"?

One does not have to be very skilled in rhetorical analysis to divine that the present study favors an answer of no to this last question. That answer rests in large measure on the realization that the concept of "gospel" is linked with Isaiah not only by the juxtaposition of Mark 1:1 with 1:2a but also by the juxtaposition of Isa 40:3, the passage that Mark proceeds to cite in 1:3, with its immediate Isaian context. Isaiah 40:1-11 speaks of the preparation of "the way of the Lord," Yahweh's triumphal procession through the Judean wilderness as he leads his people back from their captivity in Babylon. Yahweh, the prophet announces, is about to return to Zion, magnificently displaying his sovereign power in a saving act of holy war. The climax of the passage is reached in the joyful exhortation to proclaim good news to Zion:

> Get you up to a high mountain,
> O herald of good tidings to Zion [מבשרת ציון/ὁ εὐαγγελιζόμενος Σιών];
> lift up your voice with strength,
> O herald of good tidings to Jerusalem (מבשרת ירושלם/ὁ
>   εὐαγγελιζόμενος Ἰερουσαλήμ);
> lift it up, fear not;
> say to the cities of Judah, "Here is your God!" (Isa 40:9)[8]

The Septuagint's use of the substantive participle ὁ εὐαγγελιζόμενος to translate מבשרת ("one who brings [good] news") creates a strong link with Mark 1:1-3, since the Septuagint's participle is cognate with the word Mark uses, εὐαγγέλιον ("good news" or "gospel"), in the very first verse of his Gospel to announce his theme. Indeed, as P. Stuhlmacher has shown, the term "gospel" has its most important history-of-religions background in Deutero-Isaiah, and within Deutero-Isaiah Isa 40:9 is one of the fountainhead verses for the NT concept.[9]

This connection between the gospel announced in Mark 1:1, the book of Isaiah mentioned in 1:2, and the larger context of the particular Isaian passage

---

8. The translation is NRSV, but I have chosen the reading from the margin rather than the text for the second and fourth lines. Unless otherwise stated, biblical translations are from the NRSV.

9. P. Stuhlmacher, *Die paulinische Evangelium*, vol. 1: *Vorgeschichte* (FRLANT 95; Göttingen: Vandenhoeck & Ruprecht, 1968) 109-79, 218-25. Besides Isa 40:9, Stuhlmacher singles out 41:27 and 52:7 as esp. important background for the NT εὐαγγέλιον.

cited in 1:3 suggests strongly that Mark is not simply quoting Isaiah because the OT prophet conveniently speaks of a forerunner in the wilderness. Rather, Mark has his eye on the larger flow of the Isaian story, and if so it is plausible that he knows that in his biblical prototype "the way of the Lord" is Yahweh's own way — not just the path in which he wants people to walk, but also and more essentially the way that *Yahweh himself creates* as he advances through the desert to lead his people back to the promised land after the sad interlude of the Babylonian captivity. When, later in Mark's story, "the way" (ὁδός) of Jesus up to Jerusalem becomes the controlling redactional theme of the crucial central section, 8:22–10:52 (8:27; 9:33-34; 10:17, 32, 46, 52),[10] it is furthermore plausible that Mark would wish his readers to see what is said about Jesus' ὁδός there against the backdrop of the Isaian way of the Lord that is referred to in the introductory verses, especially since these verses already parallel Jesus' ὁδός ("your way" in 1:2) with the ὁδός of the Lord (1:3).[11]

Further support for seeing the Markan theme of the "way" against an Isaian background comes from the story of Bartimaeus, the man whose blindness is healed by Jesus in a wilderness location (Jericho, on the edge of the Judean desert),[12] and who follows him "in the way" (ἐν τῇ ὁδῷ; Mark 10:46-52). This story is strongly reminiscent of several Isaian texts, since it is a peculiar Isaian feature to associate the coming of the new age with a cure for blindness (Isa 29:18; 32:3; 35:1-7; 42:16), and Isa 35:1-7 links this cure with God's way through the wilderness:

> Then the eyes of the blind shall be opened,
>   and the ears of the deaf unstopped;
> then the lame shall leap like a deer,
>   and the tongue of the speechless sing for joy.
> For waters shall break forth in the wilderness,
>   and streams in the desert . . .
> A highway shall be there,
>   and it shall be called the way of holiness. (Isa 35:5-8, NRSV altered)

The combination of the same three themes — a cure for blindness, the way, and, by implication, a wilderness location — in both Isaiah and Mark creates

---

10. Of these references to Jesus' ὁδός in the central section, the majority are redactional; see E. Best, *Following Jesus: Discipleship in the Gospel of Mark* (JSNTSup 4; Sheffield: JSOT, 1981) 15-17.

11. The parallelism between the ὁδός of Jesus and that of the Lord in 1:2-3 does not mean that Jesus *is* the κύριος for Mark, but neither can one sharply separate the two figures; in Markan Christology, where Jesus is acting, there God is seen to be at work. On the relationship between Jesus and God in Mark, see Marcus, *Way*, 37-41, 72, 90-92, 143-46.

12. On Jericho's wilderness location, see U. Mauser, *Christ in the Wilderness: The Wilderness Theme in the Second Gospel and Its Basis in the Biblical Tradition* (SBT 1/39; Naperville, Ill.: Allenson, 1963) 19.

a strong presumption that Mark is deliberately shaping the Bartimaeus tradition to reflect Isaiah, especially since his redaction has apparently highlighted both the theme of the way and the location in Jericho.[13] Incidentally, this Isaian passage speaks of the healing not only of the blind but also of the deaf and the dumb, and the latter feature is echoed in Mark 7:37, which is also probably a redactional verse.[14] But to return to the Isaian theme of God's enlightenment of the blind and its relationship to Mark's Bartimaeus story: another passage, Isa 42:16, is even closer to Mark's terminology because it speaks not only of God healing the blind but also of his *leading* them *in a way:*

> I will lead the blind
> in a way they do not know,[15]
> in paths that they have not known
> I will guide them.
> I will turn the darkness before them into light,
> the rough places into level ground. (NRSV altered)

As the Bartimaeus episode illustrates, then, Mark seems to have deliberately patterned his interlocking themes of "the way of the Lord" and the way of Jesus on Isaian motifs, and at least some of his readers would probably have seen the story of Jesus' way superimposed on an Isaian background.[16] Indeed, in a passage such as 10:32-34, which begins with the description, "And

13. The reference to the "way" in 10:52, like most of the usages of ὁδός in Mark's central section (see above, n. 10), is probably redactional, since it makes sense only within the larger Markan context of 8:27–11:1. (The usage in 10:46, however, is probably traditional, since it is an integral part of the story.) The localization of the story in Jericho has been redactionally emphasized by Mark, resulting in the awkward repetition of the city's name in 10:46; see C. Burger, *Jesus als Davidssohn: Eine traditionsgeschichtliche Untersuchung* (FRLANT 98; Göttingen: Vandenhoeck & Ruprecht, 1970) 43-45, 62-63.

14. See H. Räisänen, *The "Messianic Secret" in Mark's Gospel* (trans. C. Tuckett; Studies of the New Testament and Its World; Edinburgh: T. & T. Clark, 1990) 151-52, for a strong defense of the redactional nature of 7:36-37. Räisänen's argument for redaction in 7:37 is based mainly on vocabulary. Other data supporting this view are the words καλῶς πάντα πεποίηκεν, "he has done all things well," which burst the bounds of the tale, and the fact that the crowd, which had disappeared from the story in v. 33, suddenly and without explanation reappears in vv. 36-37. Cf. Gnilka (*Evangelium*, 1.296), who ascribes Mark 7:37 to tradition merely because it is a biblical allusion.

15. LXX καὶ ἄξω τυφλοὺς ἐν ὁδῷ ᾗ οὐκ ἔγνωσαν, phraseology that has several echoes in Mark 10:46-52.

16. Within Mark's community there was probably a range of acquaintance with the OT and alertness to scriptural allusions. Some within that community were probably (like Mark himself?) Jewish Christians, though the majority were Gentiles (see 7:3). Even some of the gentile Christians, however, may have been well versed in the OT if they came from "God-fearing" backgrounds. On the ethnic background of Mark and his community, see J. Marcus, "The Jewish War and the *Sitz im Leben* of Mark," *JBL* 111 (1992) 485-87, 495-96; on different levels of appreciation of the OT within the community, see idem, *Way*, 45-46.

they were on the way [ἐν τῇ ὁδῷ] going up to Jerusalem, and Jesus was going before them" (my trans.), *three* ways may be said to overlap: the old processional way of Israelite pilgrims up to Jerusalem, following (in preexilic times) the ark;[17] the Deutero-Isaian way of Yahweh through the Judean wilderness and into the city, with the redeemed people in tow; and Jesus' way up to that same city, followed by his disciples.

II. Looking without Seeing

This superimposition of the three ways, however, is not without an element of deeply significant irony. The festal way up to Jerusalem is always a joyful one: "I was glad when they said to me, 'Let us go up to the house of the Lord!'" (Ps 122:1, RSV). Similarly, Yahweh's way through the wilderness and into the city in Deutero-Isaiah, which fuses this festal way with Deuteronomic traditions about the entry into the land,[18] is a way of triumphant holy war on Israel's behalf against threatening gentile enemies: "See, the Lord God comes with might, and his arm rules for him" (Isa 40:10).[19] But Jesus' way up to Jerusalem is, at first glance, a way not of victory and life but of defeat and death meted out by both Israel's leaders and the Gentiles:

> He took the twelve aside again and began to tell them what was to happen to him, saying, "See, we are going up to Jerusalem, and the Son of Man will be handed over to the chief priests and the scribes, and they will condemn him to death; then they will hand him over to the Gentiles; they will mock him, and spit upon him, and flog him, and kill him." (Mark 10:32-34)

Does this difference mean that I have been wrong to posit an Isaian background for the Markan picture of Jesus' way up to Jerusalem? No, partly because the opposition that Jesus alludes to here is, throughout the Gospel, itself painted in Isaian colors, and partly because there is Isaian precedent for the idea of the suffering of God's agent as part of God's holy-war victory.

The Isaian background of the opposition to Jesus in Mark is sufficiently clear from the Gospel's second explicit citation of Isaiah, in 7:6. "Isaiah proph-

---

17. "Going up to Jerusalem" (ἀναβαίνοντες εἰς Ἱεροσόλυμα) is standard terminology for the cultic ascent to the holy city and the Temple Mount; see J. Schneider, "βαίνω, κτλ.," *TDNT* 1.519. This ascent reenacted still another "way," the entry into the land that climaxed the first exodus; see F. M. Cross, *Canaanite Myth and Hebrew Epic: Essays in the History of the Religion of Israel* (Cambridge: Harvard University, 1973) 108.

18. See Cross, *Canaanite Myth,* 108.

19. Despite the well-known universalism of some passages in Deutero-Isaiah, that book still contains many remnants of the old idea of God's holy-war victory over pagan enemies; for example, in the immediate context of Isaiah 40, see 41:1-16.

esied rightly about you hypocrites," Jesus says in 7:6, going on to cite an ex-
coriation of those who honor God with their lips but keep their hearts far from
him (Isa 29:13). This denunciation of the addressees' "hypocrisy" is not to be
understood, either in its Isaian original or in its Markan reapplication, as a
charge of deliberate dissimulation. The malady goes far deeper than that; those
addressed *cannot* distinguish between lip service and heart service, between
mere human tradition and the piercing word of God (cf. Mark 8:33), because
God himself has blinded them:

> Stupefy yourselves and be in a stupor,
>   blind yourselves and be blind!
> Be drunk, but not from wine;
>   stagger, but not from strong drink!
> For the Lord has poured out upon you a spirit of deep sleep,
> and has closed your eyes, you prophets,
>   and covered your heads, you seers. (Isa 29:9-10)

Admittedly, Mark does not cite these verses, which form the introduction to
the verse he does cite, Isa 29:13. He does, however, use another renowned Isaian
text about blinding, Isa 6:9-10, in his notorious "parable theory" passage (Mark
4:10-12). Indeed, as J. Jeremias argued in a classic study, it is probable that Mark
himself is responsible for inserting this Isaian text into his parable chapter and
giving it its present prominent position.[20]

In the resultant Markan creation, the disciples ask about the purpose of
Jesus' parabolic speech. They are told in reply that in the parables they have
been given the mystery of the kingdom of God,

> but for those outside everything comes in parables in order that [ἵνα] "look-
> ing they may look and never see, and hearing they may hear and never
> understand, lest they turn and it be forgiven to them." (Mark 4:11-12, citing
> Isa 6:9-10; my trans.)

Parables, then, have a double purpose, which presumably must be traced back
to God's will; for insiders such as the disciples they are means of revelation of
the kingdom's mystery, but for outsiders they are weapons of blinding. The
blindness of the outsiders, which at first might seem to challenge the view that
God is bringing the kingdom in through Jesus, is revealed by the ἵνα clause to
be within God's purpose. God's chosen people (or, in Mark, at least their
leaders)[21] have fallen into a trancelike state in which they are not only unwilling

---

20. J. Jeremias, *The Parables of Jesus* (trans. S. H. Hooke; 2nd ed.; New York: Scribner's,
1972) 13-14.

21. On the identity of the "outsiders" in Mark, see J. Marcus, *The Mystery of the
Kingdom of God* (SBLDS 90; Atlanta: Scholars, 1986) 93-96.

but also unable to hear the divine voice; paradoxically, however, such radical evil can only be attributed to the will of God.

III. The Coming of Sight

Yet in spite of the dark picture painted by Isaiah 6 and its quotation in Mark 4, spiritual blindness and deafness do not have the last word in either passage. After he receives the prophecy of God-induced blindness, Isaiah cannot restrain himself from asking, עד־מתי אדני, "how long, O Lord?" — thus suggesting that he, at least, hopes and believes that the people's insensitivity to the word of God will not last forever. The pronouncement of judgment that follows does little at first to encourage this hope, as it prophesies the desolation of Judah and the exile of its inhabitants, comparing the land to a mighty tree that will be cut down; subsequently even the trunk that remains will be consumed by fire. But the passage in its canonical form, in what is almost surely a gloss intended to attenuate the gloom of the original, concludes by saying that "the seed of holiness [זרע קדש] is the trunk [of the land]."[22] By this mixed metaphor the trunk is transformed from a symbol of desolation to a token of hope; if God has planted the people, if it still contains within itself the seed of holiness that reflects that origin, then even the judgment that falls upon it cannot totally extirpate it. Elsewhere in Isaiah, this hint of restoration blossoms into a full-blown reversal of the verdict announced in chap. 6, so that Isa 32:3, for example, repeats the language of 6:9-10 but uses it to speak of what will *no longer* be the case in the new era when "a king reigns in righteousness":

> Then the eyes of those who have sight will *not* be shut
> and the ears of those who have hearing *will* listen.[23]

This reversal is part of the Isaian association between the new age and a cure for blindness that has already been explored.

Like Isaiah, Mark believes that the divinely willed insensibility announced in Isaiah 6 has a time limit set to it. The ἵνα of 4:12 — "*in order that* the outsiders might neither see, nor understand, nor be forgiven" — is

---

22. The feminine possessive in מצבתה can refer only to הארץ at the end of the previous verse. On the end of Isa 6:13 as a gloss, see H. Wildberger, *Isaiah 1–12* (trans. T. H. Trapp; Continental Commentary; Minneapolis: Fortress, 1991) 275.

23. NRSV altered. Isaiah 6:10 and 32:3 use the same rare verb שעע ("shut"). Cf. B. W. Anderson (*Understanding the Old Testament* [3rd ed.; Englewood Cliffs: Prentice-Hall, 1975] 447), who asserts that God's call to the heavenly council in Isa 40:1-2 reverses the call to proclaim judgment in 6:9-13.

explicitly taken up in the repeated and probably redactional usages of ἵνα in 4:21-22:[24]

> Does the lamp come *in order that* [ἵνα] it may be put under the bushel or under the bed? Does it not come *in order that* [ἵνα] it might be put on the lampstand? For there is nothing hidden except *in order that* [ἵνα] it might be manifested, nor anything hid except *in order that* [ἵνα] it might come into manifestation. [My trans.]

As in Isaiah itself, therefore, the hiding of truth spoken of in Isaiah 6 is seen to be only a penultimate reality. A day is coming when the hiddenness will give way to revelation.

Is Mark dependent on Isaiah for the thought that the insensibility spoken of in Isa 6:9-10 will one day give way to revelation? The general idea of the coming age as a time of revelation is common in biblical and postbiblical traditions, especially in apocalyptic texts,[25] so by itself it does not necessarily point to Isaiah. Two features of Mark 4:11-12, 21-22, however, are peculiarly reminiscent of Isaiah.

First, there is the jarring juxtaposition of the ἵνα in 4:12 with those in 4:21-22 — Jesus speaks in parables *in order that* the outsiders might be blinded, but nothing is hidden except *in order that* it might come into the light. We have already seen that this juxtaposition is probably redactional, as Mark has inserted the "parable theory" passage and the sayings collected in 4:21-22 into their present contexts and introduced the ἵναs into the latter. The net effect of this redactional juxtaposition is unflinchingly to attribute both good (the revelation of truth) and evil (the hiding of truth from the "outsiders") to the divine will in linked passages that employ imagery of light and darkness.

This combination of themes recalls Isaiah, who perhaps above all other OT writers emphasizes God's uncontested sovereignty over all events and conditions. It is especially reminiscent of the famous passage in Isa 45:5-7:

> I am the Lord, and there is no other,
>> besides me there is no god . . .
> I form light and create darkness,
>> I make weal and create woe,
>> I the Lord do all these things.

Here Deutero-Isaiah uncompromisingly ascribes responsibility for evil as well as good to Yahweh in a passage that employs imagery of light and darkness. Is

---

24. On the redactional features of Mark 4:21-22, including the ἵναs, see Marcus, *Mystery,* 129-36. ἵνα is a preferred Markan conjunction, and the Q versions of these verses lack it. The ἵνα in 4:22 renders a commonsensical adage paradoxical, but the paradox is part of Mark's messianic secret motif; see the beginning of the next section.

25. See Marcus, *Mystery,* 146-47.

this similarity to Mark just a coincidence? Perhaps, but it seems more likely that Mark, who has inserted an Isaian "blinding" text into his parable chapter, then balanced it with another passage that speaks of divine enlightenment, has done so partly under the influence of Isaiah.

IV. The Suffering Servant as Holy Warrior

Besides the emphasis on divine determinism, the other feature of Mark 4:11-12, 21-22 that is reminiscent of Isaiah is the strange statement in 4:22 that nothing is hidden except in order that (ἵνα) it might be manifested. Here Mark picks up a commonsensical adage, still visible in the Q form of the saying (Luke 12:2 par. Matt 10:26), to the effect that no secret can remain hidden forever, and renders it paradoxical with his ἵνα. What sense does it make to hide a secret *in order that* it might come into the light?

In my dissertation I tried to show that this turn of phrase corresponds to the broad sweep of Mark's Gospel and particularly of his messianic secret motif: the truth of Jesus' identity is hidden from the outsiders, so that they oppose him and eventually drive him to his death; in his death, however, the new age of revelation dawns.[26] What I did not realize then was that there is a sense in which this sequence of events is already adumbrated in some Isaian texts.

The famous passage about Yahweh's Suffering Servant (Isa 52:13–53:12) includes, as in Isa 32:3, epistemological imagery reminiscent of Isa 6:9 that has been reversed to bear a positive sense:

For that which had not been told them they shall see,
and that which they had not heard they shall understand. (Isa 52:15)[27]

The link with the terminology of Isa 6:9-10 lies in the conjunction of the motifs of seeing, hearing, and understanding; now, however, in contrast to the earlier passage, people *will* understand. This reversal is coupled with the story of Yahweh's humble servant, whose status of favor before his master is disguised so thoroughly under his unprepossessing appearance that people esteem him "stricken, struck down by God, and afflicted" (Isa 53:4). The "looking without seeing" of Isaiah 6, therefore, is still lurking in the background; indeed,

---

26. Ibid., 147-51.

27. NRSV altered; because of the context, RSV "understand" is preferable to NRSV "contemplate" as a translation for התבוננו; this rendering is supported by LXX συνήσουσι. Cf. C. R. North's translation in *The Suffering Servant in Deutero-Isaiah: An Historical and Critical Study* (London: Oxford University, 1948) 121.

epistemological language abounds in Isaiah 53, and much of it emphasizes the hiddenness of the Servant.[28]

The end result of this hiddenness is that the Servant's life is taken from him "by oppression and judgment" (Isa 53:8). Yet this outrage is not the end of the story, because the Servant's death, which is salvific for the people, is followed by his exaltation (52:13), and both the death and the exaltation are mysteriously connected with revelation and understanding.[29] The hiding of truth in Isaiah 6, therefore, corresponds to the hiddenness of the Servant in 52:13–53:12; this hiddenness culminates in the Servant's death on behalf of "many"; that death, however, inaugurates a new era of revelation.

Is it just modern eisegesis to think that Mark is following this Isaian pattern? On the contrary, there is evidence throughout the Gospel for the importance to Mark of Isaiah 53 (and, to a lesser extent, of the other "Suffering Servant" passage, Isa 50:4-9). For example, I have already noted Isa 53:11 LXX, where the Servant is referred to as "the just one who serves many well"[30] who "shall bear [the people's] sins." This Isaian statement is strikingly paralleled in Mark 10:45, the only Markan passage that alludes specifically to the purpose of Jesus' death: "For the Son of Man came not to be served but to serve, and to give his life a ransom for many." The contacts between the two passages, which include the "many" language and the ideas of serving and bearing others' sins, are too numerous to be ascribed to chance.[31]

The section of Mark most strongly stamped with the image of the Suffering Servant of Isaiah is the passion narrative (chaps. 14–16).[32] Like the Suffering

28. Besides 52:15, see 53:1: "Who has believed what we have *heard?* And to whom has the arm of the Lord been *revealed?*" and 53:2, esp. in the LXX: "We *saw* [εἴδομεν] him, but he had no *form* [εἶδος] nor comeliness" (Isa 53:2; translation from L. C. L. Brenton, *The Septuagint with Apocrypha: Greek and English* [reprinted Grand Rapids: Zondervan, 1982]). The language of hiding becomes explicit in 53:3: the Servant is one from whom people hide their faces (though the LXX speaks of the *Servant* hiding his face).

29. The LXX of Isa 53:11 connects revelation with the Servant's atoning death: "The Lord also is pleased . . . to show him light and form him with understanding; to justify the just one who serves many well; and he shall bear their sins." The Servant's perception is linked with his exaltation in Isa 52:13, where the LXX takes ישכיל as a reference to his understanding: "My servant shall understand" (συνήσει ὁ παῖς μου).

30. δίκαιον εὖ δουλεύοντα πολλοῖς.

31. Cf. C. S. Mann (*Mark* [AB 27; Garden City, NY: Doubleday, 1986] 343), who points out that "the technical phrase 'for the many' . . . not only in all probability looks back to Isa 53:11 but also provides an interpretation of the suffering and death otherwise lacking in the passion predictions."

32. C. Maurer ("Knecht Gottes und Sohn Gottes im Passionsbericht des Markusevangeliums," *ZTK* 50 [1953] 1-38) has certainly overplayed his hand by finding allusions to the Isaian Suffering Servant everywhere in the Markan passion narrative, sometimes on very slim evidence (see the criticism in Marcus, *Way*, 188n.137). But it would be unwise to go to the other extreme and eliminate the Suffering Servant completely as a background for the figure of the Markan Jesus on his way to death, as, e.g., H. C. Kee does ("Function," 182-83).

Servant, the Markan Jesus is handed over to judgment (see the use of παραδι-δόναι throughout the passion narrative, beginning in 14:10-11; cf. Isa 53:6, 12 LXX), maintains silence before his accusers (Mark 14:61; 15:5; cf. Isa 53:7), endures spitting, slapping, and scourging (Mark 14:65; 15:15; cf. Isa 50:6), amazes Gentiles and their rulers by the way he undergoes his travail (Mark 15:5, 39; cf. Isa 52:15), is delivered to death while a transgressor or transgressors go free (Mark 15:6-15; cf. Isa 53:6, 12), pours out his blood for many (Mark 14:24; cf. Isa 53:12), and is subsequently raised up by God (Mark 16:1-8; cf. Isa 52:13). Many of these motifs were probably already present in the pre-Markan passion narrative,[33] but one cannot simply dismiss them for that reason.

To illustrate why not, one may consider the third Markan passion prediction, Mark 10:33-34, which contains the most concentrated collection of Suffering Servant motifs in Mark's Gospel:

handed over	Isa 53:6, 12
appears before gentile authorities	Isa 52:15
condemned to death	Isa 53:8
spat upon and scourged	Isa 50:6
killed	Isa 53:8-9
raised up	Isa 52:13

This passage, however, appears to be a Markan redactional creation. It is much fuller than the two previous passion predictions, which apparently enshrine pre-Markan tradition, and it has striking linguistic contacts, which they lack, with the passion narrative itself.[34] Mark, therefore, is not unaware of the Isaian Servant figure; that figure, indeed, is important enough to him that he has shaped the third of his passion predictions, which provide the linchpins for the central section of the Gospel, in a way that deliberately recalls the Servant.

This apparent Markan awareness of the Isaian figure of the Suffering Servant has some important theological ramifications, which can be highlighted by contrasting the view of H. C. Kee. Kee believes that the primary scriptural background for the picture of Jesus in the Markan passion narrative is not the Suffering Servant of Isaiah but the Righteous Sufferer of the Psalms, and he therefore concludes:

> There is no explicit doctrine of atonement. . . . Suffering is viewed as an inevitable, divinely ordained, and therefore necessary stage on the way to vindication of the elect and fulfillment of the divine redemptive plan [not as having atoning significance].[35]

33. See Marcus, *Way,* 189.
34. Gnilka (*Evangelium,* 2.96n.3) lists καταχρίνειν ("to condemn," 14:64), ἐμπαίζειν ("to mock," 15:20, 31), and ἐμπτύειν ("to spit on," 14:65; 15:19).
35. Kee, "Function," 182-83.

It is certainly right that the Righteous Sufferer figure of the Psalms has shaped Mark's passion narrative in important ways, but it is misleading to play this figure off against the Isaian Suffering Servant. Since the latter, as we have seen, *does* provide a substantial amount of the background for the Markan picture of Jesus, it is inadequate to say that Mark views Jesus' suffering merely as "an inevitable, divinely ordained, and therefore necessary stage on the way to vindication." Rather, Jesus' suffering has saving significance for Mark; it is the means by which the divine warrior strikes the decisive blow against his opposition.

For it would be wrong to treat the Suffering Servant figure in isolation from the larger Isaian context in which he appears.[36] The author or editor of Deutero-Isaiah did not forget the overriding theme of Yahweh's triumphal way, with its strong connections with ancient holy-war ideas, when he included the passages about the atoning death of the Servant in the corpus. Indeed, the Suffering Servant takes on some of the features that belong to the king as a holy warrior in the royal Psalms; like the king in Psalms 2 and 110, for example, he silences and triumphs over the hostile nations through the power of Yahweh (see Isa 52:15). He wins this victory, however, not by defeating the nations in battle but by establishing justice among them (Isa 42:1-4), becoming a light to them (49:6), and discomfiting them through his suffering on their behalf (52:13–53:12).[37] Within the Isaianic corpus, therefore, the Servant serves as a vital bridge between the theme of God's victorious way and that of the God-induced opposition to that way: the full violence of the opposition falls on the Servant's head, but in his salvific death the opposition is shattered and a new era of revelation dawns.

In an equally paradoxical way, the Jesus of the Markan passion narrative remains the holy warrior whose God-given power has routed God's demonic and human enemies in the earlier sections of the narrative. Indeed, the royal title "king" (βασιλεύς), which aligns Jesus unmistakably with the apocalyptic inbreaking of God's rule that he has proclaimed throughout the Gospel, is deliberately withheld from him until chap. 15, when it is repeatedly cast at him in disbelief and mockery by Roman and Jewish officials and scornful passersby (Mark 15:2, 9, 12, 18, 26, 32). In the ironical logic of Mark's passion narrative, however, these mockers unwittingly testify to the truth of the kingship of Jesus, whose sovereign authority and kingly concern for his people are revealed above all by his willing self-sacrifice on their behalf.[38]

36. See T. N. D. Mettinger (*A Farewell to the Servant Songs: A Critical Examination of an Exegetical Axiom* [Scripta Minora, Regiae Societatis Humaniorum Litterarum Lundensis; Lund: Gleerup, 1983]), who argues that the "Servant Songs" are not a foreign body in Deutero-Isaiah and that therefore they cannot be interpreted in isolation from their context.

37. See J. Gray, *The Biblical Doctrine of the Reign of God* (Edinburgh: T. & T. Clark, 1979) 180-81, 281-93.

38. See D. Juel, *Messiah and Temple: The Trial of Jesus in the Gospel of Mark* (SBLDS

Jesus, then, does not cease to be the "Stronger One" even as he hangs on the cross with his life ebbing away, his ears filled with the mockery of his opponents (15:29-32), and his spirit oppressed by the cosmic darkness that has fallen upon the whole earth (15:33-34). The cross is the climax of oppositional blindness,[39] but it is also the undoing of the opposition, the apocalyptic defeat of which is clinched by the salvific death of the Suffering Servant. The victory of light over darkness is symbolized by the tearing of the temple's inner curtain at the instant of Jesus' death, a rupture that enables the previously veiled glory of God to burst forth into the dark world; and a new age of seeing such as Isaiah had prophesied begins at the very next instant with the centurion's acclamation: "Truly this man was the Son of God!" (15:38-39, my trans.).[40]

V. The Servant and the Community of Servants

Because of the peculiar Christian dialectic of already and not yet, however, the dawn of the new age of seeing does not mean the complete disappearance of old-age blindness. The Gospel itself ends on a note of incomprehension, as the women who have received the Easter proclamation fearfully hide it and say nothing to anyone. Mark's community, therefore, knows that "looking without seeing, hearing without understanding" continues to be a factor in the post-Easter world.

This awareness comes to the fore above all in chap. 13, a section of the Gospel that has often, and rightly, been seen as a mirror of the situation the community faces. Mark himself lives in the time of "tribulation such as has never been" (13:19),[41] and the fearsome prophecies of persecution and societal disintegration in 13:9-13 apply to experiences that he and his community are presently undergoing:

31; Missoula, MT: Scholars, 1977) 47-48; and F. J. Matera, *The Kingship of Jesus: Composition and Theology in Mark 15* (SBLDS 66; Chico, CA: Scholars, 1982) passim.

39. In 15:32, Jesus' enemies use epistemological language that recalls 4:12: "Let the Messiah, the King of Israel, come down from the cross now, "*in order that we might see* [ἵνα ἴδωμεν] and believe"; cf. 15:36.

40. At least part of the background for the Markan title "Son of God," esp. as it is used in the passion narrative, is provided by Wis 2:12-20; 5:1-7; and those passages in turn are strongly influenced by the Servant Songs of Deutero-Isaiah, esp. Isaiah 53; see L. Ruppert, *Jesus als der leidende Gerechte? Der Weg Jesu im Lichte eines alt- und zwischentestamentlichen Motivs* (SB 59; Stuttgart: Katholisches Bibelwerk, 1972) 23-24; D. Lührmann, "Biographie des Gerechten als Evangelium," *WD* 14 (1977) 37-39.

41. See Marcus, "Jewish War." Daniel 12:1 speaks of "tribulation such as has never been . . . *until that day*" (ἕως τῆς ἡμέρας ἐκείνης); Mark 13:19 adopts this phrase but significantly changes it to "*until now*" (ἕως τοῦ νῦν), thus dropping a broad hint that he sees himself as living in the time of tribulation.

Beware! For they will hand you over [παραδώσουσιν] to councils, and you will be beaten in synagogues, and you will be made to stand before governors and kings for my sake, as a witness to them. . . . And when they lead you away, handing you over [παραδιδόντες], do not worry about what you are to say. . . . Brother will hand over [παραδώσει] brother to death, and a father his child, and children will rise up against their parents and put them to death. You will be hated by all on account of my name. (My trans.)

It is striking that the verb παραδιδόναι ("to hand over") is used three times in this short section to speak of the betrayal Jesus' disciples will suffer; the same verb is also applied to John the Baptist's arrest in 1:14. I have previously noted that the use of this verb throughout the passion narrative is one of the signs that Mark's picture of Jesus has been shaped by the description of the Suffering Servant of Isaiah 53, since the latter figure is handed over (παρεδόθη) to death according to Isa 53:12 LXX, and the Lord hands him over (παρέδωκεν) for his people's sins according to 53:6. The use of the same verb with reference to John the Baptist and the disciples does not seem to be a coincidence but an indication that, for Mark, John and the Christian disciples find their fates bound up with that of Jesus.[42]

This notion of participation in Jesus' fate is another Markan idea that has significant background in the Deutero-Isaian concept of the Lord's Servant. It is of the essence of the Suffering Servant figure that others are mysteriously involved in his destiny: "He was wounded for our transgressions, . . . and by his bruises we are healed" (Isa 53:5). This transference can happen because the Isaian Servant is a figure with marked collective dimensions. True, the Servant as depicted in Isa 50:4-9 and 52:13–53:12 seems to be an individual,[43] but other Deutero-Isaian passages use "my servant" as a collective term for Israel or an elect group within it.[44] In Deutero-Isaiah as a whole, therefore, the figure

42. Cf. N. Perrin and D. C. Duling (*The New Testament: An Introduction: Proclamation and Parenesis, Myth, and History* [2nd ed.; New York: Harcourt Brace Jovanovich, 1982] 110, 238) who note the pattern: first John preaches and is handed over (1:7, 14); then Jesus preaches and is handed over (1:14; 9:31; 10:33), and finally Christians preach and are handed over (3:14; 13:9-13).

43. This is a controversial statement, since some scholars, such as Mettinger (*Farewell*, 29-46), maintain that the Deutero-Isaian Servant is always a collective figure for Israel, even in the so-called Servant Songs (Isa 42:1-4; 49:1-6; 50:4-9; and 52:13–53:12). Others, however, point to the Servant Songs' concreteness of detail, the innocence of the Servant's suffering, and that he appears to have a mission to Israel as factors pointing away from an identification with Israel and toward an individual referent (see, e.g., North, *Suffering Servant*, 202-7). Even if one maintains the collective interpretation of the Servant Songs, it is easy to see how an individual interpretation might arise; it did so in rabbinic exegesis of Isaiah 53 (e.g., the Isaiah Targum) in spite of a wariness caused by Christian application of the passage to Jesus. Mark certainly interpreted the Servant Songs in this way; besides the passages already cited, see also the application of Isa 42:1 to Jesus by the divine voice in Mark 1:11.

44. This happens even in Isa 49:1-6, which is one of the four Servant Songs (see n. 43 above). This is a particularly puzzling passage, because here the Servant is both identified as Israel (v. 5) and portrayed as having a mission to Israel (v. 6).

oscillates between a collective and an individual reference, and this oscillation appears to have had great appeal to early Christians seeking to understand the intimate relationship they intuited between their own experiences of suffering and divine empowerment, on the one hand, and those of Jesus before them, on the other.[45]

It should not be surprising, therefore, that the Jesus of Mark's Gospel, whose persona is so similar to that of the Servant of Isaiah in other ways, is also, like the Servant, in some sense a collective figure. According to Mark 3:14, the Twelve are those chosen by Jesus "in order that they might be with him" (my trans.), and this description presumably applies to post-Easter disciples as well as pre-Easter ones.[46] Moreover, the three passion predictions are followed by instructions to the disciples on the necessity of following Jesus in the way of the cross (8:34-37), becoming the last of all and the servant of all (9:35), and being baptized with the baptism that Jesus is baptized with (10:38-39). The combined effect of these juxtapositions is to convey the impression that the destiny of Jesus extends beyond himself to include his followers.[47] Although this extension probably takes its scriptural point of departure not only from the Isaian Servant but also from the Righteous Sufferer of the Psalms and the Son of Man of Daniel 7, both of whom are collective figures,[48] the Servant still forms an important part of the picture. When the members of Mark's community are "handed over," therefore, they are reliving Jesus' own experience as the Suffering Servant.

Yet if the Servant's suffering and death are extended to the disciples, so are his vindication and life; for those who lose their lives find them (Mark 8:35), and disciples who sacrifice houses, lands, and family relationships for Jesus' sake and the gospel's receive them back a hundredfold — with persecutions (Mark 10:29-30). In union with the Servant, the disciples find that knowledge of the good news blossoms in the midst of death; as Jesus' own death led to the centurion's confession, so now the persecution of Christians becomes the occasion for the worldwide proclamation of the gospel (cf. 13:9-13). Taking part in that proclamation, the Markan community finds itself swept up into the triumphal march of the divine warrior, which is at the same time the suffering way of the Lord's Servant; the union of those two ways *is* the gospel for Mark.

---

45. See C. H. Dodd, *According to the Scriptures: The Sub-structure of New Testament Theology* (London: Nisbet, 1952) 118-19; J. Jeremias, "παις θεοῦ," *TDNT* 5.682-84. Later Jewish texts (the LXX, Wisdom of Solomon, and Qumran texts) transform even the Suffering Servant of Isaiah 53 into a collective figure; see Marcus, *Way,* 191-92.

46. See K. Stock, *Leben aus dem Mit-Ihm-Sein: Das Verhältnis zwischen Jesus und den Zwölf nach Markus* (AnBib 70; Rome: Biblical Institute, 1975).

47. Cf. J. Schaberg, "Daniel 7–12 and the New Testament Passion-Resurrection Predictions," *NTS* 31 (1985) 215-17.

48. See Marcus, *Way,* 169-71, 184-86.

VI. Conclusion

The last sentence brings us back to Mark 1:1-3, with its assertion that the gospel is "as it has been written in Isaiah the prophet" and its parallelism between the way of Jesus and the way of the Lord. In view of the strategic placement of this reference to Isaiah at the beginning of Mark's work, its allusion to broad Isaian themes, and the other connections between Isaiah and Mark that I have traced in this study, the conclusion seems justified that Isaian patterns have played a major role in shaping Mark's thinking.

Isaiah is, of course, not the key to everything in Mark. For example, the book of Isaiah lacks a developed demonology, while Mark's picture of Jesus as the holy warrior against Satan and the unclean spirits is a vital element in his Gospel.[49] A great gulf separates the stark Markan landscape with its screaming demons from Deutero-Isaiah's radiant vision of the exiles' return as the beginning of the general redemption. Part of that gulf is attributable to the intervening centuries of crushed Jewish national hopes, political and economic oppression, party strife, and violence; all of these afflictions have left their teethmarks in the fierce works of the apocalypticists, to which Mark is heir. Mark does share Deutero-Isaiah's confidence in the ultimate triumph of God against all opposition; he even believes that God has struck the decisive blow against the opposition through Jesus' death and resurrection. Somehow, however, in the "mystery of the kingdom" (see Mark 4:11), the blindness associated with the old aeon hangs on even after the dawning of the new age, in a way unforeseen by Isaiah.

But perhaps Mark would respond that even the unforeseen way in which Isaiah's prophecies have been fulfilled shows that the gospel is "as it has been written in Isaiah the prophet." The discontinuity of God's new action with precedent and expectation, after all, is an integral part of the Isaian message:

> Do not remember the former things,
>   or consider the things of old.
> See, I am doing a new thing;
>   now it springs forth, do you not perceive it?
>   (Isa 43:18-19, NRSV altered)

"I am doing a new thing. . . . Do you not perceive it?" This question might well serve as the caption for the powerful final scene in Mark's Gospel, in which the women flee in uncomprehending terror from the the revelation in the empty tomb and say nothing about it to anyone. If so, however, another Isaian passage might be used to express what is implicit in the mere existence of this scene in the Gospel: nothing, not even the human timorousness that

---

49. See J. M. Robinson, *The Problem of History in Mark and Other Marcan Studies* (reprinted Philadelphia: Fortress, 1982).

sometimes holds back from repeating it, can stop God's word from spreading
and accomplishing its purpose.

> For as rain and snow come down from heaven,
>   and do not return there but water the earth,
> impregnating it and making it sprout,
>   giving seed to the sower and bread to the eater;
> So will my word be that comes from my mouth:
>   It will not return to me empty
>   but do the thing I wish it to do
>   and thrive in what I send it for.

(Isa 55:10-11, my trans.)

"Happy the Eyes That See":
The Tradition, Message, and Authenticity
of Luke 10:23-24 and Parallels

JOHN P. MEIER

Catholic University of America, Washington, D.C.

I. Introduction

Those who have had the pleasure of working firsthand with Prof. David Noel Freedman have come to know a man who seems truly happy with his work. And well he might be. Looking back at all that he has accomplished and helped others to accomplish in his seventy-plus years, one might well imagine him a fitting subject of a beatitude, that biblical definition of happiness that extols an ideal way of life by extolling the individual who embodies it. Since Prof. Freedman has known the happiness of hearing and seeing the immense fruits of his scholarly labors over a full lifetime — something not all academics are granted — I think it especially fitting that in a volume honoring his achievements an essay be dedicated to an examination of a beatitude of Jesus that, in the grand tradition of the accommodated sense, can be applied to Prof. Freedman as well. As we shall see, it applies especially well to the thrust of his scholarship.

II. The Tradition and Its Message

In a stray Q tradition (Matt 13:16-17 par. Luke 10:23-24), which both Matthew and Luke secondarily joined to other blocks of material in their Gospels, Jesus uses a beatitude to felicitate those who are privileged to experience his ministry firsthand. The wording differs somewhat in Matthew and Luke, but fortunately the differences do not affect the substance of the beatitude. A likely reconstruction of the original Q form of the beatitude (using the verse enumeration of Luke 10:23-24) would run as follows:

> v. 23 Happy (are) the eyes that see what you see
>   [and the ears that hear what you hear]
>
> v. 24 For [amen] I say to you that
>   many prophets and kings longed
>
>   to see what you see and did not see [it],
>   and to hear what you hear and did not hear [it].[1]

One is immediately struck by the coherence of this beatitude with two other Q traditions that many critics also consider authentic: the Q beatitudes at the beginning of the Sermon on the Mount/Plain (Luke 6:20-23 par.) and Jesus' reply to the emissaries of John the Baptist (Matt 11:2-6 par.). As in Luke 6:20-23, Jesus uses the literary genre called "beatitude" to congratulate actual or potential disciples. Moreover, the overall structure of the beatitude in Luke 10:23-24 corresponds roughly to that of the three beatitudes of the Sermon:

1. initial cry of "happy" *(makarios),* followed by
2. a terse description of the people who are happy (definite article plus adjective or participle in the plural), followed in turn by
3. a causal or explanatory clause (*hoti,* "for," in the beatitudes of the Sermon; *gar,* "for," in Luke 10:24) that gives a reason for the eschatological happiness Jesus ascribes to his audience. The reason involves a reversal of expectations in the end time.

Unlike many beatitudes in the OT, Jesus' beatitudes in the Q form of the Sermon were addressed directly to a given audience and so are phrased in the second person plural. The same direct address to an audience and the use of the second person plural are found in Luke 10:23-24.[2]

At the same time, Luke 10:23-24 displays some important variations in the characteristic gestalt of Jesus' beatitudes. The beatitude as a whole is noticeably longer than the Q beatitudes of the Sermon, mostly because the explanatory

---

1. For detailed argumentation on the original Q form of the beatitude, see the appendix to this essay.

2. Here one must distinguish carefully between form and content. Strictly speaking, the form of the beatitude in Luke 10:23 is in the third person plural: "Happy are the eyes that see what you see." But obviously this is simply a poetic way of saying: "Happy are you who see." Hence the beatitude is effectively (in its meaning) if not formally (in its wording) in the second person plural. On this see Sato, *Q und Prophetie,* 260.

(gar) sentence is much more complex. The entire sprawling beatitude is built in an intricate fashion on the principle of parallelism: parallelism in both its large and small units, parallelism that is both synonymous and antithetical, parallelism that rests on the two primordial images of seeing and hearing. The parallelism in the smallest units of the beatitude results from the simple repetition of these two images. In the first half of the beatitude (v. 23), this parallelism is simply synonymous: "the eyes that *see* what you *see* . . . the ears that *hear* what you *hear.*" In the second half (v. 24, the explanatory *gar* clause), this pattern is repeated but also expanded by adding antithetical to synonymous parallelism: "to *see* what you *see* and [= but] did *not see* [it], and to *hear* what you *hear* and [= but] did *not hear* [it]." On a larger scale, one may see the two verses that make up the beatitude as standing in a rough sort of antithetical parallelism that contrasts two groups.[3] Verse 23 felicitates the eyes that see and the ears that hear (i.e., the happy audience of Jesus), while v. 24 contrasts these happy eyes and ears with the prophets and kings of Israel's past who did not see or hear.

What is intriguing here is that, despite all the differences between Luke 10:23-24 and the core beatitudes in the Q Sermon on the Mount/Plain, the gestalt perdures. The first half of the beatitude declares happy a particular group of people who are described in terms of some state or action of theirs (poor, hungering, mourning, seeing) that is true now, even as Jesus speaks. Why this state or action constitutes happiness even now (perhaps contrary to the judgment of outsiders) is then explained in the *hoti* or *gar* clause, which involves an eschatological reversal. Here we touch on the most significant difference between the Q beatitudes of the Sermon and the beatitude in Luke 10:23-24. In the Q beatitudes of the Sermon, the *hoti* ("for") clause prophesies the reversal of the present sad lot of Jesus' audience when the last day comes: those mourning will be comforted by God, and those hungering will be fed to the full by God at the eschatological banquet.

Luke 10:24 also expresses a kind of eschatological reversal, but one of a notably different type.[4] The antithesis now lies not between present suffering and future joy but between past frustration of desire and its present fulfillment.

---

3. Joachim Jeremias (*New Testament Theology, Part One: The Proclamation of Jesus* [trans. John Bowden; London: SCM; New York: Scribner's, 1971] 14-20) claims that the authentic sayings of Jesus show a preference for antithetical parallelism, since it is found in all four strata in the Synoptic tradition (Mark, Q, M, and L) and is more or less equally distributed among the four strata. Jeremias (p. 15n.2) lists Matt 13:16-17 par. Luke 10:23-24 as one of the 34 instances of antithetical parallelism in the Q material.

4. On this point Sato's comment (*Q und Prophetie*, 261) needs further nuance. He notes that because the experience of the time of salvation is declared to be already present, "therefore the eschatological *hoti* is lacking." But a different sort of explanatory eschatological clause is to be found in Luke 10:24, introduced by "for I say to you that. . . ." This clause, like the *hoti* clause in the Q beatitudes of the Sermon, supplies an eschatological grounding for the beatitude; but now the grounding refers to realized as opposed to future eschatology.

The great prophets and kings of Israel longed to see and hear the fulfillment of God's promise to Israel of final salvation, but they did not. Instead, contrary to any sane expectation, a bunch of ragtag Galilean peasants is hailed by Jesus as experiencing now the hoped-for salvation denied to the heroes of Israel's sacred past. This is indeed eschatological reversal, but now the reversal lies in the present moment, because the definitive object of Israel's centuries-long hopes and prophecies is present in what Jesus' audience is seeing and hearing.

The repeated emphasis on "seeing" and "hearing" echoes Jesus' reply to the emissaries sent by the Baptist. As an indirect, cryptic answer to their direct question about his identity and role, Jesus orders the emissaries to tell John what they "see" and "hear" (Matt 11:4 par. Luke 7:22). The verses that follow contain both a list of various miraculous healings performed by Jesus and the climactic point that the poor have the good news proclaimed to them (Matt 11:5 par. Luke 7:22). This, then, is what the emissaries "see" and "hear": the deeds of Jesus (esp. the miracles) and his message of good news to the poor. Most likely, this is also what is intended by the reference to what Jesus' audience sees and hears in Luke 10:23-24: the astounding deeds and joyful message of Jesus.[5] As we see in Luke 11:20 par., Jesus saw his exorcisms as proof that the kingdom of God had already come to those who experienced them, and in his preaching he dared to claim that the kingdom of God was already "in the midst" of his hearers. This is why Jesus' audience can be described as possessing an eschatological happiness that leaves Israel's prophets and kings behind in the dust. In seeing and hearing what Jesus does and says, his audience experiences to some degree, however partially, what the great figures of Israel's past could only hope for and what many pious Jews of Jesus' day still looked for at some future date: the kingdom of God, God come in power to reign definitively over his people Israel. That hoped-for future event happens now, in the ministry of Jesus.

One can grasp how remarkable this claim of eschatological salvation in the present moment must have seemed to many pious Jews of Jesus' day from two beatitudes in the pseudepigraphical *Psalms of Solomon,* written by devout Jews in Jerusalem during the first century B.C.E.[6] These two beatitudes occur, significantly, in two psalms that pray for the coming of the "Son of David," "the Lord Messiah," in "the last days," within the larger theological context of God's kingship, fully realized in the end time. *Psalms of Solomon* 17:44 presents this eschatological beatitude: "Happy [shall be] those born in those days, to see the

---

5. Granted the general nature of the beatitude in Luke 10:23-24, it would probably be a mistake to restrict what the audience *sees* to miracles alone. Other striking actions of Jesus (e.g., table fellowship with tax collectors and sinners, accepting women as disciples) may also be included.

6. Comparison with the *Psalms of Solomon* is a commonplace in the interpretation of Luke 10:23-24 par.; see, e.g., Beasley-Murray, *Jesus and the Kingdom of God,* 84-85; Grimm, "Selige Augenzeugen," 173-74.

good things of Israel, when God brings about the gathering of the [twelve] tribes." Similarly, *Ps. Sol.* 18:6 proclaims: "Happy [shall be] those born in those days, to see the good things of the Lord, which he shall accomplish for the coming generation under the rod of discipline of the Lord Messiah." The eschatological happiness that is extolled, the people who will know this happiness, and the experience of God's salvation all lie in the future.

In sum, from the comparison of the beatitude in Luke 10:23-24 with the Q beatitudes of the Sermon and the reply to the emissaries of John, and from the contrast with the *Psalms of Solomon,* one can draw four conclusions: (1) Jesus felicitates his audience for experiencing what was hoped for but never experienced by the great ones of Israel's past.[7] (2) Jesus' audience therefore lives in the time of the fulfillment of Israel's hopes and prophecies, a time that many pious Jews of Jesus' day still expected at some future date. (3) This fulfillment, which the audience is seeing and hearing right now, is contained in the miraculous deeds Jesus performs and the good news he preaches. (4) Finally, if one may draw on what Jesus says explicitly elsewhere (Luke 11:20 par.; 17:21), what the audience is now experiencing through his deeds and words is nothing less than the coming of God's kingdom — even though the beatitude does not directly mention the key phrase.[8] Reginald Fuller's attempt to water down the implication of this beatitude by claiming that the disciples "see and hear [only] the signs of the coming Kingdom, . . . not its arrival, but its dawning," hardly does justice to the amazing antithesis in the saying between the longing of all the great figures of Israel's past and the actual experience of the disciples of Jesus.[9] Was the object of the prophets' longing merely the signs of the kingdom, and not the kingdom itself — merely its dawning, and not its arrival? That does not seem to be the implication of Luke 10:23-24.

III. The Authenticity of the Beatitude

The claim of this beatitude is so amazing that one might well wonder whether it can be ascribed to the historical Jesus. The lack of multiple attestation of

---

7. See the comment of Manson, *Sayings of Jesus,* 80: "The point of the saying is that what for all former generations lay still in the future is now a present reality. What was for the best men of the past only an object of faith and hope is now matter of present experience." For a similar interpretation, see W. G. Kümmel, *Promise and Fulfilment: The Eschatological Message of Jesus* (trans. Dorothea M. Barton; SBT 1/23; London: SCM, 1957) 112-13.

8. So Gnilka, *Jesus von Nazaret,* 152.

9. See Reginald Fuller, *The Mission and Achievement of Jesus* (SBT 1/12; London: SCM, 1967) 34. Fuller's interpretation serves as a good example of a type of exegesis that avoids any kind of realized eschatology in the sayings of Jesus by regularly importing such words as "signs" and "dawning" into texts that do not contain them.

sources makes any conclusion difficult. Yet even a skeptic like Bultmann thinks that Luke 10:23-24 comes from the historical Jesus.[10] In my view, the argument from coherence is in this instance fairly strong, especially since we find more than one kind of coherence. There is first of all coherence in literary form and structure, since Luke 10:23-24 evinces more or less the same striking beatitude-form seen in Jesus' beatitudes of the Sermon on the Mount/Plain. As a survey of beatitudes in the books of the NT outside the Gospels shows, the rest of the NT does not reflect a great interest in or production of new beatitudes, especially ones that imitate the form and message exhibited in the beatitudes of Jesus.

Then, too, there is a coherence in the implied message of the presence of the kingdom in and through the ministry of Jesus. The new, happy state of things proclaimed in Luke 10:23-24, a state that demarcates sharply the time of Jesus and his disciples from Israel's sacred past, jibes perfectly with many of the sayings and actions of Jesus that many critics generally accept as authentic: Jesus' reply to the emissaries of the Baptist (Matt 11:2-6 par.); Jesus' assertion that the least in the kingdom of God is greater than John (Matt 11:11 par.; cf. the prophets and kings who long to see what the disciples see); Jesus' claim that from the time of John onward a new situation with regard to the kingdom exists (Matt 11:12-13 par. Luke 16:16); Jesus' appeal to his audience to recognize that through the exorcisms he performs the kingdom of God has come to them (Luke 11:20 par.); and Jesus' dismissal of apocalyptic calculations of a future coming of the kingdom with the assertion that the kingdom is already in their midst (Luke 17:21b).

A further aspect of coherence in Luke 10:23-24 argues in favor of the saying's authenticity as opposed to a creation by first-generation Christians. If one examines the sayings just listed — as well as sayings that refer to a future coming of the kingdom — one observes an intriguing pattern. Implicitly Jesus made himself and his ministry the pivotal means by which the kingdom would or had come, and yet one usually finds no direct reference to him in the sayings in which he announces the kingdom.[11] What personal references there may be tend to be allusive or oblique. Matthew 11:2-5 mentions miracles, but not the one who performs them. Mark 3:27 alludes to Jesus the exorcist under the hardly flattering metaphor of a robber. So too, in Luke 10:23-24, what the happy disciples see and hear is ultimately the presence of the kingdom. But it stands to reason that what they are immediately seeing and hearing are the deeds and

---

10. Bultmann, *Geschichte*, 133, 135; so also Hoffmann, *Studien*, 38, 210; Sato, *Q und Prophetie*, 261; Gnilka, *Jesus von Nazaret*, 152. Helmut Merklein (*Jesu Botschaft von der Gottesherrschaft: Eine Skizze* [SBS 111; Stuttgart: Katholisches Bibelwerk, 1983] 66) remains doubtful about the saying's authenticity, though he thinks that it correctly reflects the eschatological situation proclaimed by Jesus.

11. Even in the exceptional case of Luke 11:20, Jesus' self-reference ("If by the finger of God I cast out the demons . . .") is in the conditional clause, the main clause being reserved for the proclamation of the kingdom's arrival.

words of Jesus — though the logion does not openly affirm this. As in other sayings, Jesus is implicitly made the sole and necessary mediator of this present experience of the kingdom. Yet here as elsewhere he does not appear in the saying; his role is implied rather than expressed. The various christologies of the post-Easter church are simply absent.

A final observation points in the direction of authenticity rather than a creation by the early church. The whole rhetorical argument of Luke 10:23-24 draws its force from the unique experience of being eyewitnesses of Jesus' ministry. Those witnessing Jesus' activity are uniquely happy because, unlike all the great religious figures of Israel's past, they are directly, personally, on a firsthand basis experiencing the deeds and words of Jesus and thus the kingdom's presence: "Happy are the eyes that see what you are seeing." The happiness extolled in the beatitude is thus implicitly restricted to those who are actually seeing and hearing what Jesus says and does as he goes about healing and preaching. Such a beatitude is strikingly dissimilar to — indeed, the very opposite of — the beatitude with which the Fourth Evangelist ends his Gospel (John 20:29). After the risen Jesus comments ironically on the belief of Thomas, who demanded firsthand experience of the risen Lord before he would believe, a final beatitude praises the members of the later church who did not have or need the experience of being eyewitnesses in order to believe: "Have you [i.e., Thomas] come to believe because you have seen me? Happy [*makarioi*] are those who have not seen and [yet] believe."

Indeed, John 20:29 reflects the very reason why sayings of Jesus were created or adapted by the early church: to make the past event and teachings of Jesus of Nazareth speak to and be relevant to the very different present of the church. In a sense, Luke 10:23-24 does just the opposite by emphasizing the unique experience and happy privilege of the eyewitnesses of Jesus' public ministry — a privilege members of the later church could not have, a privilege that might even be seen to devalue the status of members of the church vis-à-vis Jesus' original audience. When one takes this point together with the converging lines of coherence and the lack of any explicit christological claim, it seems on the whole more likely that Luke 10:23-24 is a saying of the historical Jesus rather than a creation of the church. Hence, according to this logion, Jesus saw his ministry as the unique time that fulfilled Israel's hopes and prophecies, the time when the kingdom of God that was to come was in some way already present. This is reason enough for the believer to be happy.

IV. Conclusion

As a concluding reflection, I would suggest that Jesus' beatitude addressed to the eyewitnesses of his public ministry has a salutary message for both scholars and ordinary believers today. Each group, though in different ways and for different reasons, tends to emphasize updating and relevance. NT critics are intent on understanding how the sayings of Jesus were changed and new ones created to make Jesus and his message relevant to the needs of the church of the late first century. Ordinary believers today, as well as the preachers charged with bringing the gospel to them, are concerned with making Jesus' first-century proclamation of the kingdom relevant to late twentieth-century audiences. All of this naturally puts a premium on the "present moment," be it the present moment of 80 C.E. or the present moment of 2001 C.E. — so ephemeral is the present moment. Nothing wears out faster than relevance.

In such an atmosphere it is healthy to have within the canon of Jesus' words and deeds a reminder that in one sense the premium, the center of attention, must always be on the unique, not-to-be repeated past moment of the earthly Jesus. What Paul and the Epistle to the Hebrews hammer home with cries of "once and for all" (hapax, ephapax), Jesus himself hammered home in his own characteristic way with a beatitude. As Luke 10:23-24 proclaimed the importance of the pivotal event of Jesus' ministry to his own age, so it continues to do to future ages that all too readily see themselves as the center and goal of the universe. In this logion, then, believers are reminded of their being rooted in the originating events and words of Jesus' ministry. This beatitude is a standing reminder to later generations of the perpetual relevance of the past that has begotten and shaped them. I can think of no better logion to ponder as we honor a scholar so dedicated to reminding present believers of their rootedness in the sacred past of Israel, Jesus, and the church. 'ašrê!

APPENDIX: THE ORIGINAL Q FORM OF THE BEATITUDE

Although any judgment based on such a small amount of data remains debatable, it seems probable that, with the exceptions of (1) the second line that I insert into v. 23 from Matthew's version and (2) the verb "longed" (Matthew's *epethymēsan*) instead of Luke's "wished" (*ēthelēsan*), Luke represents the original Q form of the logion (similarly T. W. Manson, *The Sayings of Jesus* [reprinted Grand Rapids: Eerdmans, 1979] 80); see also Rudolf Bultmann, *Die Geschichte der synoptischen Tradition* (8th ed.; FRLANT 29; Göttingen: Vandenhoeck & Ruprecht, 1970) 114; Siegfried Schulz, *Q: Die Spruchquelle der Evangelisten* (Zurich: Theologischer Verlag, 1972) 420-21. To take the questions of redaction step-by-step:

a. Redactional contexts. The contexts supplied by the evangelists differ widely. Matthew places the beatitude within the explanation of why Jesus speaks to the crowds in parables but restricts his explanations to his disciples. Luke has Jesus deliver the beatitude in private to his disciples (the seventy-two who have returned from their mission?) right after his intimate prayer of joy and thanksgiving to the Father for having given revelation to "the little ones" (i.e., the disciples) rather than to the "wise and intelligent" (e.g., the lawyers and Pharisees). Shorn of these two redactional settings, the beatitude could have been spoken originally to any audience standing before Jesus (cf. Luke 17:21b). Yet that this audience is felicitated as a type or model of anyone who has the experience of seeing and hearing Jesus ("happy are the eyes [of anyone] that see what you see") may point to the circle of committed disciples. While the form of a beatitude does not demand such an audience, it certainly fits it perfectly.

b. Matthew's *hymōn* in 13:16 ("*your* eyes . . . *your* ears") may be a redactional addition that assimilates the Q saying to his Markan context (Matt 13:10-17 par. Mark 4:10-12). In Matt 13:10-17 the Matthean Jesus sharply distinguishes the crowds (13:2, 10), who have refused to see and hear (i.e., believe), from the disciples, who do see and hear. The latter group does so because knowledge of the mysteries of the kingdom has been given "to you [i.e., the disciples]" (13:11). Hence one can readily understand why Matthew in the beatitude would emphasize "*your* eyes" and "*your* ears" as contrasted with the eyes and ears of the crowds that do not see, hear, or understand (13:13).

c. Matthew's redactional context in 13:10-15 may also be responsible for the reading "happy your eyes *because* [*hoti*] they see" instead of Luke's "happy the eyes that see *what* [*ha*] you see." As G. R. Beasley-Murray notes (*Jesus and the Kingdom of God* [Grand Rapids: Eerdmans; Exeter: Paternoster, 1986] 358n.67, depending on C. F. Burney and Matthew Black), the difference between "because" and "what" could reflect alternate translations of the ambiguous Aramaic word *dî* (or *dě*), which can be either a causal conjunction or a relative pronoun. While possible, such a theory is not necessary to explain Matthew's editing. Matthew's "because" echoes perfectly the redactional change he has made just a few verses earlier in his Markan text. While Mark 4:12 introduces the quotation of Isa 6:9-10 with a conjunction indicating purpose (*hina*, "in order that . . . they may not see"), Matthew changes the conjunction (in 13:13) to the same causal conjunction he also uses in the beatitude in 13:16 (*hoti*, "because . . . they do not see"). The same neat redactional link between the Q beatitude and the immediate context is not apparent in Luke.

d. The second line of the beatitude in Matt 13:16 (referring to the disciples' ears that hear) is difficult to judge, since one can argue both for and against its inclusion in the Q form. Since we already suspect that Matthew is assimilating 13:16 to the larger context, the reference to ears hearing as well as eyes seeing could easily come from the two citations of Isaiah that parallel seeing and hearing four times within three verses (Matt 13:13-15). Nevertheless, a consideration arising from the very structure of the Q beatitude militates against this argument. As I argue in the text, the beatitude in Matt 13:16-17 par. has a structure built on synonymous and antithetical parallelism. The presence of "ears" in v. 16 would fit both the parallelism within the verse and the parallelism between the two verses. Luke may well have omitted the material in Matt 13:16b for stylistic reasons: he felt that the repetition of so many similar phrases and metaphors in two successive verses was clumsy and tiresome for Greek literary taste. I readily admit that neither side in the argument has a clear edge; hence I put Matt 13:16b in brackets when I add it to the end of Luke 10:23. It is not surprising that on the one hand Beasley-Murray (*Jesus and the Kingdom of God,* 84) includes Matt 13:16b in the Q saying, while on the other hand Ivan Havener (*Q: The Sayings of Jesus* [GNS 19; Wilmington, DE: Glazier, 1987] 131) omits it.

e. Matthew's "amen" at the beginning of Matt 13:17 is also difficult to judge. The Gospels give examples of Matthew adding and of Luke omitting the word in Jesus' sayings. Hence I leave the word in brackets. In any case, it simply adds further to the solemn emphasis of "I say to you." In favor of "amen" being in the Q document's version of the saying is Joseph A. Fitzmyer, *The Gospel According to Luke* (2 vols.; AB 28, 28A; Garden City, NY: Doubleday, 1981-85) 2.875; against (though not without hesitation), Schulz, *Q. Die Spruchquelle der Evangelisten,* 420 (also n. 112).

f. While scholars are divided on the issue, I think it more likely that Matthew substituted "righteous men" *(dikaioi)* for Q's "kings" *(basileis),* which Luke retained. The word field of "just, justice, justify" is important to both Matthew and Luke (while being largely absent in Mark and John), and so a decision between "kings" and "righteous men" is not easy. Still, Matthew's Gospel uses the adjective "just" *(dikaios)* more often (17 times) than any other book in the NT; moreover, *dikaios* and *dikaiosynē* represent key concepts in Matthew's overall theological vision of morality, eschatology, and salvation history. It may not be sheer coincidence that twice elsewhere in material that betrays his redactional hand Matthew presents righteous men joined to prophets (10:41; 23:29; see Manson, *Sayings of Jesus,* 80). In contrast, it is in a Q text that Matthew mentions a prophet alongside a monarch (Matt 12:41-42 par. Luke 11:31-32). In addition, "kings" goes well with "prophets" as a group of concrete, specific historical figures in Israel's past history recorded in the Scriptures. The kings appear alongside the prophets not because the former were so admirable as a group but because, along with prophets, they summarize the salvation history of Israel in its thrust forward to fulfillment; Joachim Gnilka (*Jesus von Nazaret: Botschaft und Geschichte* [HTKNT Supplement 3; Freiburg, Basel, and Vienna: Herder, 1990] 152) points in particular to King David, the supposed author of the book of Psalms. "Righteous men" were present at the time of Jesus just as they were in Israel's past; the word "kings" conjures up much better that sacred past. For a different view, see Beasley-Murray, *Jesus and the Kingdom of God,* 84. I consider farfetched the suggestion by Alan Hugh McNeile (*The Gospel According to St. Matthew* [reprinted Grand Rapids: Baker, 1980] 192) that the difference between Matthew and Luke is due to a confusion between Aramaic *yšryn* ("the upright," "the righteous") and Aramaic *śryn* ("princes," "leaders"; the Hebrew equivalent [*śār*] is translated as "king" [*basileus*] in Codex Vaticanus of 3 Kgdms 22:26); Matthew's redactional interest is a much simpler explanation. For a highly speculative tradition history that derives the phrase "many prophets and kings" from the fourth Servant Song of Yahweh in Deutero-Isaiah, see Werner Grimm, "Selige Augenzeugen, Luk. 10,23f. Alttestamentlicher Hintergrund und ursprünglicher Sinn," *TZ* 26 (1970) 172-83. Grimm tries to extract "many prophets and kings" from the reference to "many nations . . . [and] kings" in Isa 52:15. Supposedly Jesus spoke of "many nations and kings," but later Christian tradition missed the reference to Isaiah and changed the wording. All this is fanciful.

g. There is not much difference between Matthew's *epethymēsan* ("longed, desired") and Luke's *ēthelēsan* ("wished, wanted"). The one other time Matthew uses the verb *epithymeō* (5:28), it carries the pejorative sense of lusting for a woman who is not one's wife. At the same time, Matthew uses the verb *thelō* more often than any other book in the NT (42 times to Luke's 28 times in his Gospel). Hence it is unlikely that Matthew would have gone out of his way to alter a verb he employs quite often in favor of a verb he uses only once elsewhere, and there in a pejorative sense. As for Luke, he uses the word *epithymeō* in his Gospel four times in a variety of contexts (twice in a neutral or secular sense, twice in a positive religious sense), as well as once in Acts. In contrast, he uses *thelō* not only 28 times in his Gospel but also 14 times in Acts. Thus, it is not surprising that Luke substituted for the relatively rare *epithymeō* a verb he employed much more often. While none of these considerations is strictly probative, taken together they incline me to conjecture that Matthew's relatively rare and emphatic *epithymeō* is original, and Luke's common and bland *thelō* is secondary (so Schulz, *Q,* 420).

The original unity of Luke 10:23-24 is supported by the special pattern of beatitude it exhibits, which is typical of Jesus. Against the idea that v. 24 was originally a separate saying is Migaku Sato, *Q und Prophetie: Studien zur Gattungs- und Traditionsgeschichte der Quelle Q* (WUNT 2/29; Tübingen: Mohr/Siebeck, 1988) 260n.464; similarly, Paul Hoffmann, *Studien zur Theologie der Logienquelle* (NTAbh 8; Münster: Aschendorff, 1972) 210; Schulz, *Q,* 421.

Images of Transcendence and Divine Communion: The Queen Mother of the West in Chinese Pictorial Art from the Han through the Sung Dynasties

SUZANNE CAHILL

University of California, San Diego

I. Introduction

The Queen Mother of the West, Hsi Wang Mu[a], is the highest goddess in the pantheon of Taoism, the native higher religion of China. Taoists consider her the ultimate embodiment of yin, the dark female force. They believe that the Queen Mother, together with other high deities, created the universe before historical time began, and continues in the present to maintain cosmic harmony by regulating the balance of yin and yang forces. In addition, Taoists particularly associate the Queen Mother of the West with two main themes: immortality and communication between gods and humans.[1]

1. This article began as background research for a longer study of the Queen Mother of the West during the T'ang dynasty, published as *Transcendence and Divine Passion: The Queen Mother of the West in Medieval China* (Stanford: Stanford University, 1993). I am currently working on the goddess's depiction from the Yuan dynasty to the present.

Superscript letters given in the text refer to the Chinese and Japanese terms listed on pp. 514 and 515.

The Queen Mother of the West appears prominently in Chinese art from the Han (206 B.C.E.-220 C.E.) through the Sung (960-1279) dynasties. Throughout this long time, she is depicted in a variety of media in many different regions and social contexts. Artists portray her on objects used for several different purposes from burial goods to icons to decoration. During these centuries, the goddess's pictorial image achieves definition and then undergoes successive transformations corresponding to developments in the Taoist religion. Taoism in the meantime changes from a collection of local cults to the first organized schools in the Han, followed during the Six Dynasties (220-589) and T'ang (618-907) by the growth and flourishing of the great medieval traditions, including Shang-ch'ing[b] or Supreme Clear Realm Taoism, and finally by the Taoist renaissance accompanying the arising of new schools in the Sung dynasty.[2]

The people of early China used written words as well as visual images to represent the Queen Mother. Taoist religious texts help us define and interpret her basic appearance and iconography. Written materials also explain historical change and continuity in her pictorial image; through successive periods in diverse styles the image conveys her constant role as creator and maintainer of the universe, expressing the two unwavering themes of eternal life and communication between the divine and human realms. Comparison of Taoist scriptures with visual images demonstrates how the goddess's depiction in art reflects changes in

---

The most important textual source on the Queen Mother through the T'ang dynasty is a biography by the Shang ch'ing master Tu Kuang-t'ing (850-933 C.E.), entitled *Chin mu yüan chun*[q] (The Primordial Ruler, Metal Mother), in *Yung chi'eng chi hsien lu*[r] (A record of the collected transcendents of the fortified Walled City) (Taoist texts are commonly cited by reference to their number in Weng Tu-chien, *Tao tsang tzu mu yinte* [combined indexes to the authors and titles of books in two collections of Taoist literature], Peking: Harvard-Yenching Institute, 1935 [hereafter HY] 782), *Cheng t'ung tao tsang*[s], 30, 24158-24164 (hereafter *Primordial Ruler*). I have consulted studies of the Queen Mother of the West that appear in Kominami Ichiro[t], "Hsi Wang Mu and the Traditions Concerning Seventh Night," *Tōhō gakuhō*[u] 46 (1974) 33-81; June Li, "Hsi Wang Mu: A Study of Early Textual and Visual Records" (master's thesis, University of Pennsylvania, 1978); Michael Loewe, *Ways to Paradise: The Chinese Quest for Immortality* (George Allen and Unwin, London, 1979), chap. 4; Wu Hung, "Xiwangmu, the Queen Mother of the West," *Orientations* (April 1987) 24-33; idem, *The Wu Liang Shrine: The Ideology of Early Chinese Pictorial Art* (Stanford: Stanford University Press, 1989), chap. 4. I would like to thank Richard Edwards, Esther Jacobsen, Kathlyn Liscomb, Martin Powers, Audrey Spiro, and Ann Waltner for their comments.

2. On developments in Taoism during the Han dynasty, see Holmes Welch, *Taoism: The Parting of the Way* (Boston: Beacon, 1957); Max Kaltenmark, "The Ideology of the T'ai p'ing ching," in *Facets of Taoism* (ed. Holmes Welch and Anna Seidel; New Haven: Yale University, 1979) 19-52; Rolf A. Stein, "Religious Taoism and Popular Religion from the Second to the Seventh Centuries," in *Facets*, 53-82. For the history of Shang ch'ing (or Mao shan) Taoism during the Six Dynasties era, see Michel Strickmann, "The Mao shan Revelations: Taoism and the Aristocracy," *T'oung Pao* 63 (1977) 1-64. On the Sung Taoist renaissance, see Judith M. Boltz, *A Survey of Taoist Literature: Tenth to Seventeenth Centuries* (Berkeley: University of California, 1987); Suzanne Cahill, "Taoism at the Sung Court: The Heavenly

the Taoist religion. Using words and pictures, the present paper defines the image of the Queen Mother of the West, traces it from the Han through the Sung dynasties, and relates it to developments in Taoism during this long period.

II. Textual Sources

The Queen Mother's image in art corresponds to her presentation in texts; textual materials in turn illuminate her visual image. She figures in numerous texts from the Warring States (403-221 B.C.E.) and later periods, most of which are found today in the Taoist canon or *Tao tsang*c. Pictorial representations of the goddess reflect canonical descriptions and stories. Textual descriptions of the goddess's physical appearance provided the artists with verbal models to embody and contributed narrative content and iconography.

1. Descriptions

Early literary descriptions included in the Taoist canon offer two basic images of the Queen Mother of the West: one fierce and the other benign. One of the earliest mentions of the goddess reveals her fierce aspect. A passage in the "Classic of Mountains and Seas," a work of mythic geography that contains material from the Warring States period, reads: "As for the Queen Mother of the West, her appearance is like that of a human, with a leopard's tail and tiger's teeth. Moreover, she is good at whistling. In her disheveled hair, she wears a *sheng*d headdress."[3]

As described in this book, the goddess possesses a bizarre and frightening appearance, part human and part ferocious beast. Her therianthropic form accords with that of other ancient Chinese creator deities such as Fu Hsie and Nu Waf, a primal pair who are brother and sister as well as husband and wife, and who appear in art of the Han dynasty with lower bodies in the shape of entwined serpents. The Queen Mother's tiger teeth, leopard tail, and disheveled hair represent her violence and power. Skill in whistling demonstrates her control over Taoist techniques for attaining immortality and her ability to summon spirits. The special headdress, explained below, is her iconographical signature. Illustrations (now lost) originally accompanied this text, which probably served as a pattern book for Han dynasty artists.

Text Affair of 1008," *Bulletin of Sung and Yüan Studies* 16 (1980) 23-44; Michel Strickmann, "The Longest Taoist Scripture," *History of Religions* 17/3-4 (1978) 331-54.

3. "The Classic of Mountains and Seas," *Shan hai ching*v (Shanghai: Antiquarian Press, 1979) 2, 19a. For the *sheng* headdress, see fig. 3.

A text dating to the early Han dynasty, also found in the Taoist canon, the *Huai nan-tzu*g, shows the Queen Mother as an omnipotent hag, a creator deity who "breaks her loom"[4] when the Way is lost. When the goddess smashes her loom, with which she has literally woven the universe into being, the created cosmos must cease. Such early descriptions do not make her humanly attractive. She does not embody the physical or social ideal of womanhood presented in contemporary texts, but another understanding of yin as a primary creative force.

After the Han dynasty, the Shang ch'ing or Supreme Clear Realm School of Taoism, which was favored by the literati and imperial courts, redefines old deities as it incorporates them into its hierarchical pantheon. From this time on, texts in the Taoist canon begin to present the Queen Mother in a regal and powerful but also more beautiful and less menacing guise. The "Inner Transmissions Concerning the Martial Thearch of the Han Dynasty," a sixth-century account of the Queen Mother's visit to the Han dynasty emperor known as the Martial Thearch (Han Wu-tih, often called Emperor Wu of the Han, r. 140-86 B.C.E.) on the festival nights of Double Seven in 110 B.C.E., describes her:

> The Queen Mother ascended the basilica and sat facing east. She was wearing a long, unpadded robe of multicolored damask with a yellow background; its colors and patterns were fresh and bright. Her radiant propriety was clear and serene. Belted with the great cord of the numinous flying beings, at her waist she wore a sword for dividing phosphors. On top of her head was a great floriate chignon. She wore the crown of the Grand Realized Infants of the Dawn, and stepped forth on phoenix-patterned soles. To look at her, she might have been around thirty years old. Her stature was about average. Her heavenly appearance eclipsed and put in the shade all others. Her face and countenance were incomparable. Truly she was a numinous person.[5]

This description, echoed in many other texts, grants the goddess great power and presence, which she demonstrates in part by wearing the belt and crown of the Taoist deities known as numinous flying beings and Grand Realized Infants of the Dawn. But imposing and stately as she may be, she now looks like a human being.

---

4. *Huai nan-tzu* (Shanghai: Commercial Press, 1926) 6, 13a. Contrast this image and that in the *Shan hai ching* with Han ideals of womanly virtue portrayed in the *lieh nü chuan*w (Transmissions of the arrayed women) of Liu Hsiang and the *Nü Chieh*x (Admonitions for women) of Pan Chao.

5. "Inner Transmissions Concerning the Martial Thearch of the Han," *Han Wu-ti nei chuan*y (Shanghai: *T'u shu chi ch'eng*z, 1937) 2-3. For a French translation of this work, see Kristopher M. Schipper, *L'emperour wou des han dans le legende taoiste: han wou-ti nei tchouan* (Paris, 1965). Similar descriptions appear in contemporary Taoist encyclopediae such as the *Wu shang pi yao*aa (Compendium of insurpassable essentials) (HY 1130). A condensed version of the *Han Wu ti nei chuan* depiction appears in *Primordial Ruler*.

2. Narrative Content

The narrative content of pictorial representations of the Queen Mother of the West follows stories and themes present in textual sources. Here her cosmological and intermediary roles came into view.

Some works identify the goddess as the yin half of creation. Such texts tell the story of her yearly meeting on the night of Double Seven with a divine consort identified as the King Commonlord of the East (sometimes called the King Father of the East),[6] the embodiment of the ultimate yang. The annual meeting of the two deities is a divine marriage or hierogamy that renews the cosmos and keeps natural forces in motion.

Another literary tradition stresses the Queen Mother's solitary control of creation and cosmic harmony. As a single creator, she has changing or weak mates, who may also be her disciples, or she has no mate at all. She is autonomous and androgynous. Alone and complete, she "possesses the Way,"[7] lives forever, rules the sun and moon, and maintains the balance of yin and yang forces in the universe.

During the Six Dynasties period, following the rise of the elite Shang ch'ing of Supreme Clear Realm school of Taoism, which emphasized individual salvation, many texts emphasize the role of the Queen Mother of the West in bestowing immortality and fostering communication between humans and deities. Most important are two sets of royal biographies, fictional narratives of the encounters of Hsi Wang Mu with famous Chinese emperors, which include mythical, legendary, and religious material in historical guise. These become parables illustrating the Taoist adept's search for immortality, a journey on which the hero meets many obstacles and obtains the divine help of the Queen Mother.

One set of accounts centers on King Mu of the Chou dynasty[i] (r. 1001-946 B.C.E.). Stories about King Mu circulated throughout the Han dynasty and found their fullest expression in texts written at the end of the third century C.E. The best known of these narratives, "Transmissions Concerning Mu, Son of Heaven," and the Chapter of the Lieh-tzu[j] named after King Mu, tell of the meeting of the goddess and the king beside the Turquoise Pond on Mount K'un-lun[k] where the goddess resides. At this meeting, supposed to have taken place in 1017 B.C.E., the royal pair toasted each other with wine and exchanged poems. King Mu requested the Queen Mother's teachings concerning immortality, but did not stay to practice them. He returned to his imperial duties in the Middle Kingdom, where, in the end, he died.[8]

---

6. See, e.g., the "Commentary on the Classic of the Waterways," *Shui ching chu*[ab] (Harvard-Yenching Institute Sinological Index Series; Peking, 1934) 17, 1.20a.

7. *Chuang-tzu*[ac], *Szu pu ts'ung k'an*[ad], 6, 11a.

8. *Lieh-tzu*, Chung hua shu chu[ae] (Peking, 1979): "Transmissions Concerning Mu, the Son of Heaven," *Mu T'ien-tzu chuan*[af] (Shanghai: *T'u shu chi ch'eng*, 1937). The *Lieh-tzu* dates from ca. 300 C.E. The dates of the *Mu T'ien-tzu chuan* are controversial; it has been

The other group of narratives tells the life story of the emperor known posthumously as the Martial Thearch of the Han dynasty (Han Wu ti). These tales first circulated during the second half of the Han dynasty and appeared in texts shortly thereafter. The most widely read include the "Monograph on Broad Phenomena," "Old Stories of the Martial One of the Han," and the "Inner Transmissions Concerning the Martial Thearch of the Han" (cited above). All describe a meeting of the Queen Mother and the Han emperor at his palace in the capital city of Ch'ang and during the night of Double Seven, the night of transcendent feasts. She spent the night and departed at dawn. Although she gave him peaches of immortality to eat and taught him transcendent arts, the Martial Thearch, like King Mu before him, was unable to perfect himself and ultimately died.[9]

Several stories of the Queen Mother's encounters with immortals or Taoist adepts follow the same pattern as the two royal legends: the hero meets the Queen Mother, receives her secrets of immortality, and puts his new learning into practice. Unlike the imperial failures, however, the most famous among the Taoist saints, including founders of the Supreme Clear Realm school, achieve immortality and ascend to heaven in broad daylight. The instability of her mates in the various accounts reflects the goddess's own superior importance, while their presence shows the need to find a yang to match her yin. Legends of her communication with mortal men always held out to the Shang ch'ing believer the hope that he might be selected for divine instruction. When the great Shang ch'ing Taoist master Tu Kuang-t'ing[l] (850-933) wrote the definitive biography of the Queen Mother, revealing her activities and functions, he emphasized her meeting with human kings and adepts.

3. Worship

In addition to describing the Queen Mother and narrating her activities, early texts provide information about her worship. The Han dynasty saw the flowing together of many native streams of Chinese worship to form the Taoist reli-

---

assigned dates ranging from the eighth century B.C.E. to the third C.E. I accept the late third century C.E. date.

9. Chang Hua[ag], *Po wu chih*[ah] (Monograph on broad phenomena) (Shanghai: *T'u shu chi ch'eng*, 1939); *Han Wu ku shih*[ai] (Old stories of the martial one of the Han), in Lu Hsün[aj], *Hsiao shuo kou ch'en*[ak] (Fishing in the depths of old fiction), in *Lu Hsün ch'uan chi*[al] (Lu Hsün's Collected Works) (Shanghai, 1938) 8, 463; and the *Han Wu-ti nei chuan* (Inner transmissions concerning the martial thearch of the Han) (Shanghai: *T'u shu chi ch'eng*, 1937). All these works are from the Six Dynasties period. The "Monograph on Broad Phenomena," dating to the third century C.E., is the earliest, while the "Inner Transmissions Concerning the Martial Thearch of the Han," from the sixth century C.E., is the latest.

gion. Near the end of the second century, under the influence of the collapse of the Han and competition from Buddhism, two large religious organizations known as the Way of the Celestial Masters and the Way of Great Peace came together with Lao-Chuang Taoist thought of the Hundred Schools period, local nature and ancestor cults, practices for attaining immortality, and alchemical and magical traditions to create the first organized Taoist church. The church emphasized collective worship by the community and services performed by the clergy on behalf of believers. Practice centered on the great gods of the newly organized Taoist pantheon. At this time, separate regional cults to the Queen Mother as a manifestation of yin-yang cosmology and a conduit to worldly blessings and eternal life joined together, also combining with an immortality cult centered on a western paradise at the semimythical K'un-lun Mountain. The Queen Mother of the West emerged as a high deity of great power.[10]

The Queen Mother was revered by the Han peasant and aristocrat alike. Three entries in the "Book of Han" by the historian Pan Ku[m] and his colleagues refer to a soteriological popular cult that swept across northeastern China, reaching its peak of activity in 3 B.C.E. The account in the "Monograph on Strange Phenomena" best captures the hysteria of the movement:

> In the first month of the fourth year of the Establishing Peace reign period (3 B.C.E.), the population was running around in a state of alarm, each person carrying a mannikin of straw or hemp. People exchanged these emblems with one another, saying that they were carrying out an advent procession. Large numbers of persons, amounting to thousands, met in this way on the roadsides, some with disheveled hair or going barefoot. Some of them broke down the barriers of gates by night; some clambered over walls to make their way into houses; some harnessed teams of horses to carriages and rode at full gallop, setting relay stations so as to convey the tokens. They passed through twenty-six commanderies and kingdoms, until they reached the capital city.
>
> That summer the people came together in meetings in the capital city and in the commanderies and kingdoms. In village settlements, lanes, and paths across the fields, they held services and set up gaming boards for a lucky throw; and they sang and danced in worship of the Queen Mother of the West. They also passed around a written message, saying "the Mother tells the people that those who wear this talisman will not die; let those who do not believe her words look below the pivots of their gates, and there will be white hairs there to show that this is true."[11]

10. On worship of the Queen Mother from the Han through the T'ang dynasties, see Suzanne Cahill, "Beside the Turquoise Pond: The Shrine of the Queen Mother of the West in Medieval Chinese Poetry and Religious Practice," *Journal of Chinese Religions* 12 (1984) 19-32.

11. *Pan Ku*[am], *Han shu*[an] (The book of Han) (Ch'ang sha, 1900) 11, 6b; 26, 59a; 27c (A), 22a. The passage translated here is 27C (A), 22a. The Han cult is studied in Homer H.

The historians record that the Queen Mother's peasant followers worshiped her with images of hemp and straw, as well as talismans and tokens. They joined processions, rode horses, and played games of chance. They expected nothing less than immortality. Both actions and their purposes as described in the "Book of Han" become hallmarks of the goddess's cult during the Han dynasty.

The Queen Mother also had an elite following in the Han. A tale preserved in the "Springs and Autumns of Wu and Yüeh," a history book of Han date, reflects the goddess's imperial cult. We read there that as part of a strategy to conquer his neighbor, one monarch constructed an altar to the Queen Mother in his capital, where he worshiped her "as the embodiment of the ultimate yin."[12] Mirror inscriptions and texts in the Taoist canon attest to worship of the goddess by civil and military officials and their families.

During the following Six Dynasties period, the Queen Mother's peasant cult continues. In addition, her worship is incorporated into the new elite school of Taoism, known as Shang ch'ing or Supreme Clear Realm. During the fourth century, revelations to a young mystic named Yang Hsi from the great celestial deities led to the founding of the new system of Supreme Clear Realm Taoism that quickly gained favor among literati and the courts. Pulling together northern and southern strains of worship along with Buddhist influences, this school emphasized individual salvation through meditation and austerities. The Queen Mother of the West is the highest goddess of the new tradition. Supreme Clear Realm Taoists believed that she controlled the secrets of immortality, contact between men and goddesses, and entrance to heaven: all gifts she could bestow at will upon favored adepts.

The goddess appears in scriptures created to instruct Taoist adepts in techniques for nourishing the vital essence. One such technique, physiological microcosmology, rests on correspondences between the cosmos and the individual human body. In Taoist practice, this involves visualizing celestial divinities as lodged within the body and petitioning them for various benefits. An early example of this category of scripture, dating to the fifth century, is the "Central Classic of Lao-tzu from the Realm of Supreme Clarity." The Queen Mother appears here as an object of inner visualization:

> She is the primal pneuma [breath] of the grand yin. Her surname is So-of-itself, her cognomen Ruling Thought. Below, she governs the Mountain of K'un-lun with its golden city walls in nine layers, its cloudy pneuma of

---

Dubs, "An Ancient Chinese Mystery Cult," *HTR* 35/4 (1942) 221-40, as well as in Loewe, *Ways to Paradise.*

12. Chao Yeh, *Wu Yüeh ch'un ch'iu*[ao] (Springs and autumns of Wu and Yueh) (Shanghai: *T'u shu chi ch'eng*, 1937). This annals-style history, which purports to cover events of the fifth century b.c.e., dates from the first century c.e. and provides information on Han customs.

the five colors, and its mountain passes tens of myriads of feet in height. On high, she governs the Northern Dipper and Floriate Canopy, beneath the purple Chamber and Northern Chronogram [constellations].

Humans also have her: she resides in the center of a person's right eye, where her surname is Grand Yin, her name Mysterious Radiance, and her cognomen Supine Jade. A person must obtain the King Father and the Queen Mother and guard them in his two eyes. Only then will he be able to practice pacing [the void], observing and looking upward, and with acute hearing and eyesight distinguish and recognize good and evil. Then he can cause to flow down the various deities, just as a mother thinks of her child and as a child also thinks of its mother. The germinal essence and pneuma will obtain each other, and for a myriad generations he will prolong his way.

Now as for a person's two nipples, they are the germinal pneuma of the myriad divinities, where yin and yang pour down and bubble up. Below the left nipple is the sun; below the right nipple is the moon. These are the residences of the King Father and the Queen Mother. Above they rule in the center of the eye and play on top of the head. They stop beneath the nipples and lodge in the purple chambers of the Scarlet Palace. This is the pneuma of yin and yang.[13]

This scripture and others of the class emphasize the Taoist adept's capacity to prolong his own life by nourishing his vital essence. The vital essence was nurtured by perfection of religious practice. The Queen Mother still represents the creative force of yin and possesses the secrets of immortality, but now the Supreme Clear Realm of Taoist believer, whose very body incorporates her, must take charge of his own destiny. Visualizing the goddess inside himself, he can balance his own yin and yang and ascend to heaven in broad daylight. Exactitude in describing the goddess's image became critical: the adept must know what deity he is addressing in order to avoid disaster and obtain the proper blessings. As a result, Six Dynasties Taoist texts become precise and detailed in their descriptions, as the passage on the Queen Mother of the West from the "Inner Transmissions Concerning the Martial Thearch of the Han" translated above illustrates. The same descriptions are found in contemporary Taoist encyclopedias.

---

13. *Shang ch'ing lao-tzu chung ching*[ap] (The central classic of Lao-tzu from the Realm of Supreme Clarity) (HY 1160), 3b-4a. On this text, see Kristofer Schipper, "Le livre du centre de Lao-tseu," *Nachrichten der Gesellschaft für Natur und Völkerkunde Ostasiens* 125 (1979) 75-80. On Taoist ideas about the body, see Kristofer Schipper, *Le Corps Taoiste* (Paris: Rayard, 1982). On nourishing the vital spirits, see Henri Maspero, *Taoism and Chinese Religion* (trans. Frank A. Kierman, Jr.; Amherst: University of Massachusetts, 1981).

III. Historical Development of the Image of the Goddess

Representations of the Queen Mother in religious literature offer a key to understanding her pictorial image. A complete understanding, however, depends on a study of the pictures themselves. The image of the Queen Mother of the West developed over time, responding in part to changes in its function and context. This section of the article explores the historical development of that image, from the Han through the Sung Dynasties. During this long period, the image moves from funerary through devotional and meditative to decorative art.

1. The Han Dynasty (206 B.C.E.–200 C.E.)

The image of the Queen Mother of the West appears frequently in the arts of the Han dynasty, especially in the Later or Eastern Han (25-220 C.E.). The most important influence on the image of the Queen Mother during this era is the development of the Taoist religion out of earlier traditions. The earliest forms of Taoism as an organized religion date to the end of this period, when the Celestial Masters and Great Peace Ways, in competition with Buddhism and under the stress of dynastic decline, pulled together many earlier strands of Chinese worship. At the same time, numerous local cults to the Queen Mother of the West merged to create a single great goddess who governed cosmogony and immortality. Her appearance and iconography, varied at first, receive their characteristic form at this time.

Han dynasty craftsmen depicted the Queen Mother of the West in many media. The entrances, walls, and ceilings of tombs display iconographic programs featuring the goddess in painted murals (fig. 1), stone reliefs (figs. 3, 4, and 7), and stamped pottery tiles (fig. 5). Clan members commissioned stone reliefs showing the image of the goddess for their ancestral shrines (figs. 3 and 4). Tomb furnishings included such objects as painted lacquer bowls (fig. 2), carved stone screens (fig. 8), pottery bases of bronze money trees, and bronze mirrors (fig. 9), which represent the goddess. While the images appear in diverse media, they always occur in the context of burial or ancestor worship, clearly connected to the cult of the dead and the life of the world to come. During the Han one cannot separate funerary from devotional uses of her image, and one may assume that the goddess's appearance in burial art reflects her image in icons used for worship. No matter what the material, some elements of the appearance and iconography of the Queen Mother in the Han dynasty remain fundamentally consistent. The following discussion considers depictions of the goddess in several media.

Han artists painted the image of the Queen Mother on tomb ceilings. The ceiling painting in the Western Han tomb of Po Ch'ien-ch'iu, dated 86-49 B.C.E.,

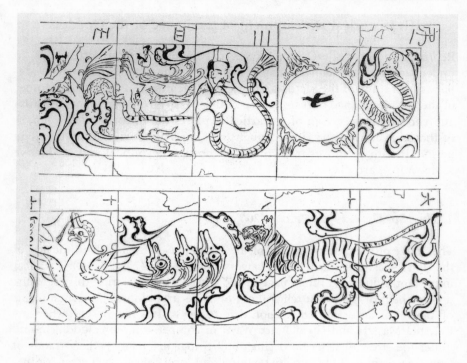

Figure 1. *Line drawing of ceiling painting from the tomb of Po Ch'ien-ch'iu at Lo yang, showing bricks 1-10, depicting the yellow serpent, sun with crow inside, Fu Hsi, tomb occupant and his wife, Queen Mother of the West (top left), white tiger, and vermillion bird (Wenwu, 1977.6).*

near Loyang may be one of the earliest depictions of the goddess (fig. 1). A figure wearing Chinese robes and a headdress sits in three-quarter view at the far left of the painting. The painting also shows the celestial and directional symbols emphasizing the goddess's role as creator and maintainer of cosmic balance. A nine-tailed fox and other mythical creatures appear, as well as two mounted attendants and an exorcist. The Queen Mother welcomes the soul of the dead Po Ch'ien-ch'iu and enrolls him as a new transcendent, performing her function of bestowing immortality and sponsoring contact between the human and divine worlds.[14]

14. See "Excavation of the Western Han Tomb of Po Ch'ien-ch'iu with Murals at Loyang," by the Archaeological Team of the City Museum, *Wenwu* 6 (1977) 3-8; and Sun Tso-yün[aq], "An Analysis of the Western Han Murals in the Western Han Tomb of Bo Qianqiu (Po Ch'ien-ch'iu)[ar]," *Wenwu* 6 (1977) 17-22, the latter translated in Suzanne Cahill, *Chinese Studies in Archaeology* 1/2 (1979) 44-79.

Figure 2. *Painted lacquer bowl excavated at Lolang, Korea, made in Szechwan in the first century* C.E., *showing the Queen Mother of the West and an attendant* (Wenwu, *1977.6*).

The Queen Mother also appears on a painted lacquer bowl, dated C.E. 69, made in Szechwan province and found in a tomb in the Han dynasty colony of Lolang in Korea (fig. 2). She wears a spotted cap as a headdress and sits facing outward on a spotted mat. The cap and mat are probably leopard skin, in view of her descriptions in such works as the "Classic of Mountains and Seas" (translated above) that associate her with leopards. Here, instead of being half cat herself, as in the early texts, the Queen Mother has become a beautiful woman dressed in the animal's fur. Her mat rests on top of a world-mountain throne. One kneeling attendant waits on her.

When Han dynasty stone carvers of the second century C.E. depicted the Queen Mother in reliefs at the Wu family ancestral shrines in Shantung province, they showed her sitting facing outward, in the highest position on the

Figure 3. *Rubbing from stone relief of second century* C.E. *on western gable of Wu Liang shrine in Shantung, showing paradise of the Queen Mother of the West (Edouard Chavannes,* Mission archéologique dans la Chine septentrionale *[Paris: Imprimerie National, 1913] vol. 2, pl. 44).*

western wall, presiding over narrative and figural scenes below (fig. 3). Stone reliefs of the second to third century C.E. from the mausolea at I-nan represent the Queen Mother wearing her characteristic headdress, winged and seated on a mountain throne with a tiger underneath. Two elixir-pounding hares flank her (fig. 4). Her consort wears the same headdress and robes; he is distinguished only by his moustache, the dragon beneath his mountain throne, and his anthropomorphic attendants.[15]

A rubbing taken from a stamped clay brick excavated in a tomb in Szechwan province illustrates important elements of the later Han dynasty image of the Queen Mother (fig. 5). A mature woman, fully human in form and wearing long robes, the goddess sits facing the viewer, legs crossed and arms folded in her lap. Among the most important features of her iconography are her *sheng* headdress, throne, animal companions, anthropomorphic attendants, and consort.

In the picture on the stamped clay brick, the Queen Mother wears a *sheng* headdress or crown, her most constant and significant attribute. The *sheng*, which resembles an axle with a wheel at either end, occurs independently in art from the Han dynasty onward (fig. 6). In her image on the clay brick, the headdress appears in abbreviated form as two ornaments on either side of the Queen Mother's chignon. The bar that joins the two elements crosses the center of the chignon. This object has received various interpretations. One plausible theory identifies it as the brake mechanism of a loom,

---

15. See Wu Hung, *The Wu Liang Shrine: The Ideology of Early Chinese Pictorial Art* (Stanford, 1989) chap. 4.

Figure 4. *Rubbings from reliefs at I-nan, Shantung, second-third century* C.E., *showing the Queen Mother of the West and her consort (Tseng Chao-yu, I nan ku hua hsiang shih mu fa chueh pao kao [Shanghai, 1956], pls. 25-26).*

Figure 5. *Rubbing of pottery tile from Szechwan, first-second century* C.E., *showing Queen Mother of the West and attendants (from the author's collection).*

connecting the goddess to the creation and maintenance of the universe through weaving its fabric.[16] The *sheng* appears in Han dynasty and later art as an auspicious symbol. People gave each other *sheng* as presents on stellar holidays. Commentators gloss the word *sheng* as related to "overcoming" and "high." I believe that, in addition to the brake wheel of a cosmic loom, the *sheng* headdress was originally a star crown. That interpretation suits the glossary definition, the stellar festivals upon which the *sheng* was exchanged as a gift, and the role of the Queen Mother as the ruler of asterisms. The *sheng* depicted in Chinese art resembles the conventional Chinese representations of constellations from star maps of the same period that show circles, often

16. This theory is explicated most fully in Kominami Ichiro, "Hsi Wang Mu and Traditions Concerning the Seventh Night (of the Seventh Month)," *Tōhō gakuhō* 46 (1974) 33-81. Loewe (*Ways to Paradise*), chap. 4, discusses the theory, summarizing Kominami's argument.

Figure 6. *Sheng headdress (drawing by Peg Cahill).*

in groups of two or three, connected by straight lines. Later Taoists explicitly describe the Queen Mother as wearing a star crown.[17]

As represented on the clay brick, the goddess's throne is a simple mat under a canopy with a dragon on the left and a tiger on the right. The dragon, symbolizing east and yang, is the goddess's counterpart and the mount of her consort. The tiger, signifying in contrast west and yin, is her familiar and alter

17. A large color photograph of a fifth-century Chinese star map appears in Edward H. Schafer, *Ancient China* (New York: Time-Life Books, 1967) 124. T'ang dynasty poets often describe the goddess's starry headdress. For example, Li Ch'i's[as] "Song of the Queen Mother" states: "On top of her head she wore the nine-starred crown." The poem is found in the anthology *Ch'üan T'ang shih*[at] (Complete T'ang poetry) (Taipei: Fu hsing Books, 1967) 750.

Figure 7. *Stone pillar relief from Shantung, first-second century* C.E., *showing Queen Mother of the West on mountain throne (Shantung Provincial Museum).*

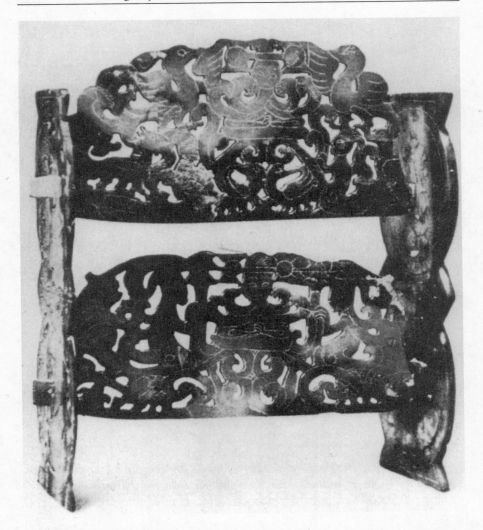

Figure 8. *Screen showing Queen Mother of the West and her consort from tomb no. 43, Ting hsien, Hopei, dated after 174* C.E. *(Wenwu, 1973.11).*

ego. The dragon represents life and energy, the tiger death and the spirit world. The dragon-and-tiger throne is a local feature of the Queen Mother's image in Szechwan province. In stone reliefs from the northeast, she sits instead on a mountain throne (fig. 7). The throne rests on a platform atop a high, sheer-sided column, which may twist like a snake. Upward-curving strips extending out from the platform on each side may represent clouds, while three tighter curls springing from either side of the goddess's torso may be her wings. Column

Figure 9.   *Eastern Han bronze mirror, second-third century* C.E., *showing
Queen Mother of the West and horse-drawn chariots
(courtesy Freer Gallery of Art, Smithsonian Institution, Washington, D.C., 37.14).*

and platform represent the world mountain, K'un-lun, an *axis mundi* or cosmic
pillar where heaven and earth meet and gods and humans can descend and
ascend. Mount K'un-lun, a perfect and complete microcosm, is the goddess's
paradise where she lives at the center of the world. A heavenly horse, property
of her consort, grazes beneath the mountain. A celestial bird, perhaps a crane,
the preferred mount of transcendents, poses halfway up. The mountain seat,
like her dragon-tiger throne, associates the goddess with Han cosmogony,
cosmic order, and the heavens.[18]

18. On the association of K'un-lun and Taoist cosmogony, see Norman Girardot,
"'Returning to the Beginning' and the Arts of Mr. Hun-t'un in the *Chuang-tzu*," *Journal of
Chinese Philosophy* 5 (1978) 21-69. On K'un-lun and paradise, see Sofukawa Hiroshi, "Kun-
lun Mountain and Paintings of Immortality," *Tōhō gakuhō* 51 (1979) 83-186.

In addition to the yin tiger and yang dragon on her throne, the goddess's animal companions on the clay brick include a nine-tailed fox, a hare holding numinous fungus (an ingredient of the elixir of immortality), a dancing toad, and a three-legged crow. Each of these appears elsewhere in connection with the Queen Mother, but it is rare to find them all together. The nine-tailed fox, a denizen of paradise, is a creature of auspicious omen. The hare inhabits the moon, where he prepares the elixir of immortality. The toad is another lunar resident. The three-legged crow represents the sun and serves as the goddess's messenger. Sometimes three blue birds replace him. Her association with the animals symbolizing yang and yin, sun and moon, life and death, reveals the goddess's control over the universe. Her simultaneous identification with the forces of both yang and yin suggests androgyny, independence, and completeness.

The Queen Mother's anthropomorphic attendants are either minor Taoist deities known as blue lads and jade girls, or human followers seeking immortality. On the clay brick from Szechwan two seated or kneeling female figures, perhaps goddesses, appear in the lower right corner, while two male figures, a deeply bowing attendant holding a jade tablet and a standing guard holding a halberd, fill the lower left corner. The Szechwan tile shows the goddess ruling alone above a hierarchy of spirits; in other situations she is accompanied by her mate, the King Commonlord of the East or King Father of the East.

The Queen Mother's pose on the clay brick, seated and facing straight out at the viewer, along with her clothing, which resembles monk's robes, may reflect the influence of the seated Buddha image imported to China from Gandhara in northwestern India, to which it bears a remarkable resemblance. Medieval Chinese may have perceived the Queen Mother and the Buddha as comparable in function and meaning, since both were depicted in funerary contexts and associated with death and hopes for an immortal afterlife in paradise. In addition, the Chinese may have noticed a similarity in form between the Gandharan Buddha and extant images of their goddess. The goddess's standard image in the Han may represent in art the beginning of the mutual influence between Taoism and Buddhism, which we know from the scriptures of both religions to have been taking place on the doctrinal level at the same time. This reciprocal relationship between Taoism and Buddhism profoundly affected both faiths as they matured together in medieval China. The effects continue to make themselves manifest in the image of the Queen Mother in the centuries that follow the Han.[19]

19. For a discussion of the image of the Queen Mother in relation to Buddhist art, see Wu Hung, "Buddhist Elements in Early Chinese Art," *Artibus Asiae* 47 (1986) 263-352. Wu Hung points out that the goddess is often juxtaposed on the money trees and in other later Han art with what appears to be the image of the Buddha. Indeed, the relationship of images of the two deities presents some interesting questions for further study.

The image of the Queen Mother near the end of the Han dynasty resembles the earliest Chinese representations of the seated Buddha that began to appear at around the same time.

Objects buried with the dead depict the goddess. A "jade" screen decorated with pierced carving (fig. 8), dated after 174 C.E., shows the Queen Mother seated frontally in the upper register and her consort, the King Father of the East, in the lower register. This object was intended to assist the soul of the tomb occupant in his journey to the next world by making present in his burial chamber the two deities he was required to greet before registering as an immortal.

Similar seated figures of the Queen Mother of the West sculpted in relief appear on the pottery stands of bronze "money trees" buried with the dead in later Han times. The goddess faces frontward, sitting sometimes on a dragon-tiger throne; often she is attended by immortals and juxtaposed with her divine consort, the King Commonlord of the East. Money trees, associated with worship of the earth god, prevalent in southwestern China during this era, may provide funds for the soul's journey to immortality and for use in paying the local gods of the soil for the burial plot. The Queen Mother's image on clay and stone bases of the money trees links her with the local cult of the earth god as well as the cult of immortality.

The Queen Mother also appears frequently on the nonreflective surface of bronze mirrors, which were manufactured in great numbers toward the end

---

It seems that images of the Buddha and the native Chinese goddess were often juxtaposed or interchanged in third-century art. Perhaps the image of the Queen Mother provided the iconographic entry point for depictions of the Buddha in China. Third-century Chinese may have perceived the two deities as comparable in function and meaning, since both were depicted in funerary contexts and related to hopes for an immortal afterlife in paradise. The medieval Chinese Buddhists may also have noted a similarity in form between the seated Buddha in the Gandharan art of northern India, which they took as their model, and the already extant native image of the Taoist goddess. If this is the case, the process of accepting Buddhism by comparing it to the major religion of Taoism that occurred on the doctrinal level had a visual manifestation in art.

The origin of the Han dynasty image of the Queen Mother is unclear, and one must admit the possibility that the Buddha image is the source of the first depiction of the goddess. Or perhaps both images derive from a Central Asian prototype. The relation between the images of the Queen Mother of the West and the Buddha is an important subject that needs further research.

The textual and doctrinal transmission of Buddhism from India across Central and Southeast Asia into China has been studied by Richard Robinson in *Early Mādhyamika in India and China* (Madison: University of Wisconsin, 1967); and Eric Zürcher, *The Buddhist Conquest of China* (Leiden: Brill, 1959). Taoism profoundly influenced the reception and understanding of Buddhist words and meanings. The same must be true of images. In turn, Taoist art — as well as doctrine — is never the same after the introduction of Buddhism to China, but develops in concert and in competition with the rival iconographic tradition. The Queen Mother's image from the Han dynasty onward develops in relation to images of Buddhist deities. The history of depictions of the Queen Mother and other Taoist deities in Chinese art needs to be studied alongside the history of Buddhist art in China. For illustrations of money trees, see *Stories from China's Past* (San Francisco: Chinese Cultural Foundation of San Francisco, 1987), pls. 59-60.

of the Han dynasty and during the centuries that followed. (The earliest extant image of the goddess on a mirror dates to 8 C.E.) These were buried with the dead to light their way to the next world. The mirrors are particularly important because they link visual image and text in a single object. Both depiction and word reveal, in condensed form, the story and functions of the goddess. She sits on a mat, facing forward, as on the tomb reliefs and tiles. Her consort, the King Father of the East, may sit opposite her. Inscriptions occasionally identify both the goddess and her mate. Male and female attendants frequently surround her. Other portions of the design may show the dragon and tiger. Accompanying inscriptions, often naming the Queen Mother and King Father, request longevity, worldly blessings, and descendants. The earliest dated mirror inscription to mention the goddess, from 105 C.E., offers a wish for "longevity like that of the King Father of the East and the Queen Mother of the West."[20] Some inscriptions describe the charmed life of the immortals. For example, a mirror showing an image of the goddess is inscribed:

> The imperial armory made this mirror; it is truly of great craftsmanship. On the surface are transcendent people who do not know old age. When thirsty they drink from the jade springs; when hungry they eat jujubes. Their longevity resembles that of metal or stone. Heaven for an extended time protects them.[21]

The goddess's image on mirrors differs from that found in other contemporary media in that horse-drawn chariots, a favorite subject occurring independently in Han dynasty art, accompany her on the mirrors (fig. 9). These vehicles and steeds allow several interpretations.

The horse itself is an emblem of transcendence in Han funerary art; one of the best-known pieces of Chinese art in the world is the small bronze flying horse unearthed in a tomb in Kansu province.[22] Han people compared some highly prized horses to dragons and believed they could fly. A single horse appears with the goddess in stone reliefs from the northeast (fig. 7). Whatever its specific reference, the horse on mirrors reinforces the goddess's connection with transcendence.

Horses and chariots juxtaposed with the Queen Mother on mirrors, in

---

20. Umehara Sueji[au], *An Illustrated Discussion of Two Dated Mirrors of the Han and Six Dynasties Period* (Tokyo, 1943) 14. On the religious significance of inscriptions on Chinese mirrors of the Han, Three Kingdoms, and Six Dynasties periods, see Suzanne Cahill, "The Word Made Bronze: Inscriptions on Medieval Chinese Bronze Mirrors," *Archives of Asian Art* 39 (1986) 62-70.

21. Han dynasty bronze mirror in the collection of MacKenzie Gordon in Washington, D.C.

22. The horse appears, for example, on the cover of Michael Sullivan's popular paperback, *The Arts of China* (Berkeley and Los Angeles: University of California, 1986).

addition to general implications of material blessings and high worldly status for the tomb occupant and his descendants, permit four related interpretations. They may represent followers of the goddess who, Han historians report, race across the countryside on horseback or in carriages to assemble in her honor.[23] Alternatively, the scene may refer to the Chou dynasty King Mu who, as we read in the "Transmissions Concerning Mu, the Son of Heaven," journeyed in his war chariots to the far west to meet the goddess and beg for immortality. Or the horse-drawn chariots may illustrate the goddess's winged transport as she descends to visit the Martial Thearch of the Han dynasty on the seventh night of the seventh month in 110 B.C.E., the story recounted in the "Inner Transmissions Concerning the Martial Thearch of the Han." Finally, such vehicles and steeds may show the Queen Mother condescending to meet a worthy adept. Han dynasty and later tomb paintings represent the goddess coming down to welcome the deceased to transcendence. Each of the interpretations suggested above, and they are by no means mutually exclusive, expresses the Queen Mother's role in assisting the tomb occupant to achieve transcendence. Our uncertainty in identifying her mate reflects a situation found also in canonical texts and in poetry, indicating the relative importance of the goddess in comparison to her male counterpart. Perhaps the faithful Taoist, imagining himself playing the masculine role in the legend, believed he could be her next student.

Images of the goddess dating to the Han dynasty appear not only in many media but in many regions of China. Stone reliefs prevail in the northeast and stamped tile bricks in Szechwan province in the southwest, while mirrors occur in large numbers in the central plain near the old capitals and in the south around the town of Shao-hsing. Important variations of iconography occur from region to region: the dragon-and-tiger throne, as mentioned above, is a special feature of the goddess's image in Szechwan, while she perches on a mountaintop in northeastern stone carvings. The shape of the goddess's characteristic *sheng* headdress varies from one place to another. These visual distinctions reflect local differences in her cult, including the way in which the people of various regions identified the goddess with local symbols of yin and yang, creation and immortality. On the whole, however, the images are remarkably consistent. They indicate that by the end of the Han dynasty the Queen Mother was not just the patron deity of an isolated local cult; on the contrary, her worship was widespread in Han dynasty China.

Worship of the goddess crossed class as well as regional boundaries. Members of the bureaucracy and aristocracy commissioned images of the Queen Mother of the West; the funerary art excavated so far testifies to her veneration

---

23. See the sketch of the relief of the Queen Mother of the West and the King Commonlord of the East from tomb no. 2 at Wang tu in Sun Tso-yün, "An Analysis of the Western Han Murals in the Luoyang Tombs of Bo Qianqiu (Po Ch'ien-ch'iu)," *Chinese Studies in Archaeology* 1/2 (1979) 62.

by officials and the great families. Han historical records (cited above) also identify the Queen Mother as the central deity of a popular cult. Her peasant followers, who carried amulets and mannikins, must have depicted the goddess in images, perhaps not unlike those they saw on mirrors and in the ancestral shrines of the elite. Unfortunately, at the present we have no objects from the Han dynasty that clearly derive from a peasant background; such images were undoubtedly executed in perishable media such as paper or wood, as they are among Chinese peasants today.

Conditions of production as well as materials influenced the form and development of the image of the goddess. All the extant Han dynasty objects picturing the Queen Mother of the West appear to have been commissioned by wealthy patrons and fashioned in workshops by anonymous craftsmen.[24] Such workshops provided mass-produced funerary art for the consumers, but they added an element of customization. A patron could select design motifs and their arrangement; the final product was then manufactured by stamping in clay or casting in metal. Although painting and stone carving provided more opportunity for individual variation, images of the goddess in all media remain remarkably consistent. The repetition of standard themes suggests a conservative tradition dependent on a few models. Pressure on the craftsman to make the image "correct" by making it identical to standard prototypes provided a force resisting change. Under such circumstances, innovation was gradual and cumulative, with old patterns surviving alongside new ones.

The Queen Mother's image already contains the essence of all the meanings it will convey for the next thousand years. Juxtaposing the image with such symbols of yang and yin as the dragon and tiger or the sun and moon expresses her role as solitary creator and maintainer of cosmic order. Scenes pairing her with a divine mate suggest a hierogamy that creates and recreates the world. In addition, Han dynasty images of the goddess already express her control over transcendence and divine communion in several ways. These include context, content, placement, and inscriptions.

First, the goddess's image appears in a funerary context, in tombs or ancestral shrines, connecting her with death and entrance into the spirit realm. In such contexts, her image was intended to provide for the needs of the dead

---

24. Most of the craftsmen who produced these images must have been illiterate. Mistakes and omissions in bronze mirror inscriptions suggest that the artisans who made them were simply executing patterns laid out by others. They perceived the graphs of the Chinese written language as elements of design, to be shifted around, altered, or omitted like any other units of their vocabulary of form. Their illiteracy takes nothing away from the skill of the craftsmen or their achievement; it simply identifies them as belonging to a different economic class from the scholar-officials and military men who commissioned the works as well as from the literati and academic artists who painted some of the later images of the Queen Mother.

in the next life and to instruct the soul on how to proceed to transcendence. The pictures often illustrate the process of attaining immortality.

Second, the narrative content of the image involves communication between the divine and human realms. Artists explicitly show the goddess descending to visit believers or waiting to receive her followers in formal audience; sometimes an artist simply presents the goddess together with her human disciples. Iconongraphic details accompanying her image include the elixir of immortality and the numinous fungus.

Third, the simple presence of her image in the tomb of a dead person provides an example of contact between deities and humans. In tombs, the goddess is almost always located at the highest point of the wall or on the ceiling, allowing her to preside over the tomb. She often sits in the west, the direction of death and the spirit realm. She may appear in scenes of paradise.

Finally, inscriptions explicitly link the goddess to the pursuit of immortality, suggesting that she was regarded as a model for seekers to emulate. In addition to the inscription of 105 c.e. quoted above that requests longevity like that of the Queen Mother, another describes her life and that of her transcendent followers:

> On its surface are transcendent beings who do not know old age. When thirsty, they drink from the jade spring; when hungry, they eat jujubes. They go back and forth to the divine mountains, collecting mushrooms and grasses [for drugs]. Their longevity is superior to that of metal or stone. The Queen Mother of the West. . . .[25]

By the end of the Han dynasty, various local traditions of art and worship have combined to produce images of the Queen Mother of the West that match in iconography the descriptions we have of her in the texts of the Taoist religion in formation. The images refer to stories connecting humans with the goddess and illustrate her religious function of helping the soul to attain immortality and enter paradise.

2. Six Dynasties and Sui (220-618 c.e.)

During the centuries that followed the Han, in the kingdoms of a divided China, the great medieval systems of Taoism arose and prospered. The most important single influence on the Queen Mother of the West was the growth of the new school of Supreme Clear Realm Taoism, which revered her as its highest female divinity. This sect, which emphasized individual practice directed toward attaining immortality, appealed to wealthy and influential patrons. She appears

25. See Umehara Sueji, "Illustrated Discussion," 14-16.

in poetry and fiction written by the literati who comprised medieval China's bureaucracy and rulers. Through her grace, worshipers seek divine contact, immortality, and posthumous celestial office. Her image in art reflects her powers.

Archaeologists have excavated somewhat fewer images of the Queen Mother from the Six Dynasties and Sui periods than from the Han. Abundant textual references in the Taoist canon and in Chinese literary and historical texts continue.[26] Historical texts provide evidence that her worship continues among the peasantry, probably taking much the same artistic form as it had during the Han. No known examples of peasant renderings of the Queen Mother survive. Images deriving from a literati or aristocratic background are more plentiful.

Most surviving images of the Queen Mother from the Six Dynasties period are found in tombs or on the walls of Buddhist cave temples. Contemporary documents suggest that icons of the goddess are now used for individual meditation and visualization as well as for worship and for funerary purposes. Images intended for personal meditative and devotional use, which may have outnumbered funerary ones during these centuries, were probably fashioned of perishable materials and used until they disintegrated. This fact, along with the turmoil of the times, may account for the decrease of identifiable Six Dynasties and Sui portrayals of the Queen Mother in comparison with the Han.

The goddess's image during this era shows many points of continuity with Han depictions. She remains important in funerary art, such as the lacquer painting on the cover of a wooden coffin excavated in 1981 in Ku Yuan county in Ning hsia province that dates to the Northern Wei dynasty (368-535 C.E.).[27] The badly damaged picture shows the Queen Mother of the West seated inside a small square pavilion similar to those depicted in two favorite subjects of Buddhist art around the same time. A similar building shelters the seated Buddha preaching the *Lotus Sutra* in stone stelae too numerous to count. The same pavilion appears in a famous design, perhaps traceable to Ku K'ai-chih[n] and repeated in wall paintings at Tun huang, which illustrate a scene from the *Vimalakirti Nirdesa Sutra*.[28] In this Mahayana Buddhist scripture, a very popular one in China, the layman Vimalakirti debates a bodhisattva. Like Vimalakirti in the paintings at Tun huang, the Queen Mother sits in profile, under a canopy. Such similarities of pose and architectural detail show the continuing rivalry,

---

26. See the sixth-century encyclopedia, *Wu shang pi yao* (The compendium of insurpassable essentials) (HY 1160), chap. 4.

27. Han K'ung-yüeh[av] and Lo Feng[aw], "The Discovery of a Northern Wei Tomb with a Lacquered Coffin in the Central Plain," in *Mei-shu Yan-jiu*[ax] 2 (1984) 3-16. See also Luo Feng, "Lacquer Painting on a Northern Wei Coffin," *Orientations* (July 1990) figs. 3 and 3a.

28. For examples of the Vimalakirti and bodhisattva murals at Tun huang, see *Tun huang Cave Temples*[ay], 2 (Sui) (Peking: Cultural Press, 1984) 68-69, 122-23, 135-36, 188-89.

exchange, and mutual influence taking place between Taoist and Buddhist art as it was in doctrine during the same period.

Instead of a standing bodhisattva, the Queen Mother's seated consort, the King Father of the East, sits opposite her on the Ning hsia coffin lid. An inscription in a cartouche to his side identifies the god; time and accidents of excavation have obliterated the goddess's label. Both wear high chignons instead of their characteristic headdresses. Their Chinese robes have led archaeologists to date the painting after the period of 475-494 C.E. when the Wei dynasty ruler Wen ti decreed that his people, who were of Turkic stock, should adopt Chinese dress. The two pavilions face each other on either side of a long serpentine pillar that represents the world mountain, K'un-lun. The sun, containing an image of the three-legged crow, and the moon, inscribed with an unidentifiable animal, appear above the deities. The representation of the Queen Mother and King Father on the coffin along with such symbols of creation and cosmic balance testify to their unchanging power to harmonize earth and heaven, yin and yang, death and eternal life, and human beings and gods.

The Queen Mother continues to dominate iconographic programs of medieval tombs. A recently excavated Taoist tomb dated to the early sixth century and located near Loyang contains designs intended to assist the soul of the departed in ascending to heaven.[29] Along the left and right side walls of the burial chamber are representations of celestial processions, including the Queen Mother of the West seated on a dais drawn along by her tiger and the King Commonlord of the East riding his dragon. The deities, approaching each other in full flight across the sky, are seen seated in three-quarters view. As in the Ning hsia coffin painting, the pairing of goddess and god echo Han associations with yin and yang cosmology, including creation through divine marriage. The deities also continue the Han theme of greeting the new soul as it journeys to heaven. Where the Han tomb of Po Ch'ien-ch'iu shows the Queen Mother alone receiving the new spirit, the Loyang tomb shows god and goddess performing this function together. Contemporary Taoist texts inform us that the spirits of the departed, on its route to the Clear Realms, must ceremonially greet both the Queen Mother and the Lord of the East.[30] While the Ning hsia coffin cover shows the divine pair receiving homage in static splendor, the Loyang reliefs show the same deities actively seeking the soul of the deceased.

A new use of the Queen Mother's image appears in Chinese Buddhist art during this period (fig. 10). Depictions of the goddess together with her consort

29. See excavation report in *Kaogu* 3 (1980) 229ff., discussed in Patricia Eichenbaum Karetzky, "A Scene of the Taoist Afterlife on a Sixth Century Sarcophagus Discovered in Loyang," *Artibus Asiae* 44/1 (1983) 5-20.

30. To salute the Queen Mother and take leave of the King Father is a formula appearing frequently in Six Dynasties and T'ang Taoist inscriptions, poetry, and canonical texts. See, e.g., *Wu shang pi yao* (The compendium of insurpassable essentials) (HY 1160), chap. 25.

Figure 10. *Tun-huang, cave 419, ceiling painting showing
Queen Mother of the West, Sui dynasty (Tun-huang wen wu yen chiu so,
Tun-huang mo kao k'u, vol. 2, pl. 84).*

flying across the heavens to worship the Buddha are found in ceiling paintings
from the Northern Wei and Sui dynasties in desert cave temples at Tun huang
along the silk route in Chinese Central Asia, and also in stone reliefs in the cave
temples at the cliffs of Lung men near Loyang. These provide evidence of the
continuing artistic exchange between Buddhism and Taoism since the Han
dynasty. While Taoist craftsman may have adapted Buddhist figures and architectural settings to represent and house native gods and goddesses, Buddhists
were appropriating Taoist imagery. The forms taken by the Queen Mother and
the King Father in the Buddhist murals at Tun huang derive from depictions
of the goddess flying down to receive the departed soul in Han and Six Dynasties
tomb art. Such images show the foreign faith absorbing elements of the native
religion and transforming these elements to suit its missionary aims. Buddhist
proselytizers could hardly put forth a more convincing visual argument for their
conquest of China: the Buddha must surely be supreme if the highest deities
of the native faith of Taoism worship him.[31]

31. For the Queen Mother and King Father at Tun huang, see *Art Treasures of Tun
huang* (New York, 1981) pls. 25 (cave 249 of N. Chou), 41 (296 of N. Chou), 44 (305 of Sui),
45 (419 of Sui). For the same design at Lung men, see *Lung men Stone Caves*[az] (Peking:

Six Dynasties bronze mirrors continue to feature the goddess in designs that originated in the later Han. Inscriptions and images similar to Han examples but dated decades and even centuries later have been excavated in both China and Japan. This is not surprising in view of the conservative nature of iconic art, in which sacred patterns are copied over and over again precisely because the efficacy of the image rests in its correctness. The same repetition appears in designs on tomb walls — change in sacred art is slow and often accidental. What we call creativity today was not considered a virtue in the production of holy icons.

Although old schemes remain, new combinations of deities and new arrangements do appear (fig. 11). The innovations reflect changes in Taoism. The Shang ch'ing school brings order and system to the apparent chaos of earlier worship. Shan ch'ing texts arrange all the deities in hierarchical order, placing the school's own gods securely at the top.[32] The Queen Mother is prominently featured in a type of mirror design labeled "deities in registers," after the arrangement of the divinities in tiers. Sometimes the tiers are further divided into compartments. The impulse toward system and hierarchy is as unmistakable in the mirror design as it is in contemporary canonical texts.

3. T'ang Dynasty (618-907 c.e.)

Curiously enough, no images of the Queen Mother dating to the following period, the T'ang dynasty, have yet been identified. Supreme Clear Realm Taoism, which held her in high esteem, continued to flourish during this time. The goddess was deeply venerated by the T'ang imperial family and the common people, and she appears in countless tales and poems. Texts on meditation and visualization in the Taoist canon describe her in minute detail. The descriptions closely match Taoist texts of the Six Dynasties. In addition to her earlier roles as teacher of male adepts, she now becomes the patron of all women in the Tao.[33] At the end of the T'ang, she is the subject of a lengthy and still definitive Taoist hagiography by the great master Tu Kuang-t'ing. We can only hope that future scholars will discover and recognize examples of her lost T'ang image, perhaps among depictions of deities previously identified as Buddhist.

Cultural Press, 1980); and "New Developments Concerning the Images in the Lung men Stone Caves," *Wenwu* 4 (1988) 21-26.

32. One of the most important and earliest of these texts is T'ao Hung-ching's[ba] *Shang ch'ing chen ling wei yeh t'u*[bb] (Chart of the ranks and functions of the realized ones and the numina from the Realm of Supreme Clarity) (HY 167), which lays out the deities and their offices in hierarchical order.

33. On the Queen Mother as a model and patron for women in Taoism, see Suzanne Cahill, "Performers and Female Taoist Adepts: Hsi Wang Mu as the Patron Deity of Women in Medieval China," *JAOS* 106/1 (1986) 155-68.

Figure 11. *Six Dynasties inscribed bronze mirror showing Queen Mother of the West to the right of the central knob (Eugene Fuller Memorial Collection, Ch. 61.16, with permission from the Seattle Art Museum, Seattle, WA).*

4. The Sung Dynasty (960-1278 C.E.)

The most powerful impact on the Queen Mother's image in the Sung dynasty came from the rise of new schools of Taoism that overshadowed the Shang ch'ing tradition. The early Sung witnessed what is often called a Taoist renaissance, with new revelations and lineages springing up. Divinities like the Queen Mother who had been worshiped by old schools began to receive less attention as emperors and people alike turned to new gods. One new sect began with revelations to the Sung emperor Chen tsung (r. 998-1023).

With the rise of new Sung schools, the Queen Mother of the West loses her power and position as first female Taoist deity. Her prestige among the imperial family, official class, and aristocracy declines. At the same time, her image changes. Where before she was forbidding and impressive, under the brush of the Sung dynasty artist she becomes familiar and pretty. Her image appears debased and trivialized on the one hand, approachable and attractive on the other. She joins the ranks of the lovely but not very formidable goddesses, such as the nymph of the Lo River, who no longer receive active worship from peasants or literati.[34]

The debasement of the Queen Mother's image also corresponds to changes in the status of women that took place in the Sung dynasty. With the advent of Neo-Confucian philosophy, which stressed the models of the dutiful daughter, obedient wife, self-sacrificing mother, and chaste widow as the only appropriate patterns for women to follow, women were more restricted to the family than ever before. Their opportunities for education and work outside the home had diminished. The great goddess, representing the yin or female side of human nature, correspondingly diminished in religion and art.[35]

Whereas earlier artists represented the Queen Mother of the West mainly in cast or carved media, she now appears in numerous paintings on silk and paper: in handscrolls and hanging scrolls, on fans and album leaves (figs. 12-14). These images of the goddess serve primarily an aesthetic rather than a funerary or iconic function. The painter seeks a decorative rather than a potent image. The media of the brush stroke and the beauty of the finished object are emphasized over the religious message of the subject.

If the image of the goddess is no longer powerful or challenging, neither is the style with which she is rendered. The artists use a figure-painting style which echoes that of the T'ang and Five Dynasties periods and which was already conservative by the Sung dynasty. Associated with academic and court painters, the traditional style is characterized by the use of heavy mineral pigments and fine line drawing. Most makers of the Queen Mother's image in Sung painting are anonymous craftsmen, in contrast to their innovative contem-

34. At the same time, in a corresponding change, the great Buddhist bodhisattva known in Chinese as Kuan yin undergoes a sexual metamorphosis. From a handsome young prince who embodies the masculine ideal of beauty, the bodhisattva whom the Chinese associate primarily with compassion is transformed into a beautiful woman. The feminization and humanization of deities in both Taoism and Buddhism reflect doctrinal and social developments within the two religions, such as the growth of salvation teachings and the increased role of lay members in the church. The changes in appearance of the deities should be studied in the light of historical change taking place within Taoism and Buddhism during the Sung dynasty.

35. Other great goddesses of early China such as the Nymph of the Lo River and the daughters of Yao are diminished even earlier. See Edward Schafer, *The Divine Woman: Dragon Ladies and Rain Maidens in T'ang Literature* (Berkeley: University of California, 1973).

The social history of women is a fascinating subject which is unfortunately outside the scope of this article. Information on the decline in status of women during the Sung dynasty and its connection to the rise of Neo-Confucianism may be found in Richard H. Van Gulik, *Sexual Life in Ancient China* (Leiden: Brill, 1961), chap. 8; Howard S. Levy, *Chinese Footbinding: The History of a Curious Erotic Custom* (New York: Bell, 1967); Theresa Kelleher, "Confucianism," in *Women in World Religions* (ed. Arvind Sharma; Albany: State University of New York, 1987) 135-60; Suzanne Cahill, "China: Han Through Sung Dynasties," in *Women's Studies Encyclopedia* (ed. Helen Tierny; forthcoming).

Figure 12. *Fan painting on silk by anonymous artist of the Sung dynasty, showing the Queen Mother of the West on a phoenix (Palace Museum, Beijing).*

poraries: the literati or *wen jen* painters who were beginning to emphasize the concept of individual creation and to sign their works.

Many Sung dynasty images of the Queen Mother illustrate her visit to the palace of the Martial Thearch of the Han dynasty. Paintings of this meeting often bear the title "Autumn in the Han Palace" and show the ritual feast of the emperor and the goddess. Our example, a fan (fig. 12), shows her ascent to heaven following her departure from the palace of the Han emperor toward dawn on the festival of Double Seven. The artist employs a relatively up-to-date style featuring ink monochrome in loose strokes and washes for the background, and more conservative detailed style with outlines and pale colors to delineate the figure. The ability of the Sung painter to evoke a mood of gentle melancholy and contemplation through the use of muted tones and areas left undefined suits the subject well.

Other paintings portray visits of various divine and human rulers to the Queen Mother's palace beside the Turquoise Pond in the western paradise of

Figure 13. *Fan from album, painted on silk by an anonymous artist of the Sung dynasty, entitled "A Transcendent Meeting Beside the Turquoise Pond" (Palace Museum, Taipei).*

Figure 14. *Hanging scroll on silk attributed to Liu Sung-nien of the Sung dynasty, entitled "Birthday Congratulations Beside the Turquoise Pond" (Palace Museum, Taipei).*

Mount K'un-lun. One album leaf (fig. 13) shows her consort, the King Commonlord of the East, attending a transcendents' gathering. A hanging scroll (fig. 14, attributed to Liu Sung-nien° but no longer accepted as an original work by that artist), entitled "An imperial visit to the Turquoise Pond of the Queen Mother of the West, amidst hollow cliffs and tortuous pines," depicts a Chinese emperor, probably King Mu of the Chou dynasty, offering the goddess birthday congratulations beside the Turquoise Pond.[36]

Liu Sung-nien (active 1195-1224), an academic painter from Chekiang province, is best known for his figures in landscape settings. His compositions often have a narrative content, showing no special preference for Taoist over Buddhist or Confucian subjects. Typical of Liu's work, even though it is almost certainly an imitation, is the hanging scroll in the Palace Museum in Taipei, which shows a strong concern for style, brushwork, and composition; it must have presented a pleasing appearance to its intended audience of literati officials, educated men who conformed to Confucian values in their careers, but may have embraced Buddhism or Taoism in their private lives.

The goddess's visit and visiting the goddess remain popular subjects of Chinese pictorial art from this time on. The magic night of Double Seven, the time of transcendent meetings, becomes the date of the goddess's birthday celebration. A single scene lifted from the story calls to the viewer's mind the whole narrative with all its attendant associations. Using the technical means at his disposal, the Sung painter evokes a mood connected with the stories. At the same time, the festivities provide an excuse for the fashioner of religious images to depict hosts of Taoist deities together, each with his or her iconographical marker. Some characters, such as the Eight Immortals and the goddess Ma Ku°, appear repeatedly. Yet many of the subsidiary figures seem to have mutable and transient identities; their characteristics are interchangeable and their individual identities insignificant. They all provide surrogates for the viewer, especially for the Taoist adept, who may imagine himself or herself present at the scene.

The iconography of the goddess also undergoes degeneration in the Sung dynasty. Her characteristic *sheng* headdress becomes a gold and jeweled crown or a phoenix-shaped tiara. The beneficent phoenix rather than the dangerous tiger is now her animal companion. Her mountain throne has disappeared. All these changes correspond to her domestication, humanization, and waning power as a deity.

Yet the goddess is still associated with transcendence and immortality, as the popularity of depictions of her visit to the royal palace of the Martial Thearch of the Han dynasty makes clear. She regularly holds or receives the peaches of immortality. The peaches had become her trademark in literature

---

36. See James Cahill, *An Index of Early Chinese Painters and Paintings* (Berkeley: University of California, 1980) 136.

from the Six Dynasties period onward, but they do not constantly accompany her image in art until the Sung dynasty. From the Sung on, the peach rather than the *sheng* headdress is the goddess's most important iconographic attribute. This strengthens her association in the viewer's mind with the gift of transcendence, which she can bestow on worthy human adepts. Despite her declining popularity among members of the imperial bureaucracy during this era, the goddess retains her link with immortality and communication between gods and humans.

IV. Conclusion

Changes in the pictorial image of the Queen Mother of the West correspond to changes in the use of that image: its function is first funerary, then meditative and devotional, and finally decorative. All these functions, once initiated, continue alongside one another. In the case of individual images of the goddess, functional lines such as the boundary between decorative and devotional art, may be indistinct. The case of the image of the Queen Mother of the West reminds us that Chinese art, no matter how beautiful it may be, cannot be divorced from its context without a serious loss of meaning. Here the context is the history of Taoism, and in particular the Queen Mother's role in that history. Transformations in her image reflect historical changes in her reputation as a divinity, which we can chronicle by examining scriptures in the Taoist canon. She changes from the powerful central deity of a popular and elite cult mirrored in the compact, impressive image prevalent in the Han dynasty, to the marginal figure reflected in the flirtatious image popular during the Sung. In time some manifestations of her image become secularized and trivialized among both the elite and the people, reflecting more concern for aesthetics than for devotion. But the goddess herself plays the same eternal role in different temporal guises. Even in its prettiest and most vapid form, the pictorial image of the goddess retains its connection with creation and order, transcendence and divine communion, throughout history.

Chinese and Japanese Terms

a. Hsi Wang Mu　西王母

b. Shang ch'ing　上青藏

c. Tao tsang　道藏

d. sheng　勝

e. Fu hsi　伏羲媧

f. Nu Wa　女媧

g. Huai nan-tzu　淮南子

h. Han Wu-ti　漢武帝

i. Chou Mu Wang　周穆王

j. Lieh-tzu　列子

k. K'un-lun　崑崙

l. Tu Kuang-t'ing　杜光庭

m. Pan Ku　班固

n. Ku K'ai-chih　顧愷之

o. Liu Sung-nien　劉松年

p. Ma Ku　麻姑

q. Chin mu yuan chün　金母元君

r. Yung ch'eng chi hsien lu　墉城集仙錄

s. Cheng t'ung tao tsang　正統道藏

t. Kominami Ichiro　小南一郎

u. Toho gakuho　東方學報

v. Shan hai ching　山海經

w. Lieh nü chuan (Liu Hsiang)　列女傳 (劉向)

x. Nü chieh (Pan Chao)　女誡 (班昭)

y. Han Wu-ti nei chuan　漢武帝內傳

z. T'u shu chi ch'eng　圖書集成

aa. Wu shang pi yao　無上必要

ab. Shui ching chu 水經注

ac. Chuang-tzu 莊子

ad. Szu pu ts'ung k'an 四部叢刊

ae. Chung hua shu chu 中華書局

af. Mu T'ien-tzu chuan 穆天子傳

ag. Chang Hua 張華

ah. Po wu chih 博物志

ai. Han Wu ku shih 漢武故事

aj. Lu Hsün 魯迅

ak. Hsiao shuo kou ch'en 小說鈎沈

al. Lu Hsün ch'uan chi 魯迅全集

am. Pan Ku 班固

an. Han shu 漢書

ao. Wu Yüeh ch'un ch'iu 吳越春秋

ap. Shang ch'ing Lao-tzu chung ching 上清老子中經

aq. Sun Tso-yün 孫作雲

ar. po Ch'ien-ch'iu 卜千秋

as. Li Chi 禮記

at. Ch'üan T'ang shih 全唐詩

au. Umehara Sueji 梅原末治

av. Han K'ung-yüeh 韓弘

aw. Lo Feng 羅辛

ax. Mei-shu Yan -jiu 美術研究

ay. Tun huang mo kao k'u 敦煌莫高窟

az. Lung men shih k'u 龍門石窟

ba. T'ao Hung-ching 陶弘景

bb. Shang ch'ing chen ling wei yeh t'u 上清眞靈位業圖

The Portrayal of Job's Wife and Her Representation in the Visual Arts

ZEFIRA GITAY

University of Cape Town, South Africa

In the book of Job, Mrs. Job appears only once. In 2:9 she advises her husband to "bless" or maybe "curse"[1] God and die. This short reference to Job's wife has resulted in contrasting ideas about the woman's role in the saga of Job and his tests by the Satan (1:9).[2]

During the events prior to her short speech, Mrs. Job did not take an active role in the various tests and ordeals that her husband endured (1:12ff.), nor was she subjected to the physical suffering experienced by Job when he was afflicted with sore boils (2:7).[3] There is a consistent attempt to eliminate Job's wife from the numerous activities in which her husband was involved, and in which she too had been involved as a passive participant or a partner in the marriage. One would have expected her to voice an opinion, or for that matter a statement, but not silence. After all, Job may have been on trial, but his wife also lost all her worldly possessions, her children died, and her husband suffered physically with sore boils.[4] What kind of woman was this mysterious figure of

---

1. For the details consult E. Dhorme, *A Commentary on the Book of Job* (trans. H. Knight; London: Nelson, 1967) 19-20.

2. Consult ibid., xviii-xix.

3. Mrs. Job is not even referred to in the background of the story in the same way as some references might allude to the existence of Sarah in the shadows of the sacrifice of Isaac. Scholars tend to suggest that the immediate death of Sarah after the return of Abraham from Mount Moriah was the result of the test of her husband. See, e.g., L. Ginzberg, *The Legends of the Jews* (trans. H. Szold et al.; 7 vols.; Philadelphia: Jewish Publication Society, 1909-38) 1.286-87.

4. See Driver and Gray's note in regard to a later verse, 19:17, where they suggest that "the loathsome features of his disease repel Job's nearest and dearest relations — his wife"

Mrs. Job? What kind of personality did she possess to enable her to cope with such trying circumstances? How did she react to her husband's total and passive acceptance of these disasters and his utter obedience to the Lord as proclaimed by him in his faithful statements in 1:21 and 2:10?

Mrs. Job is not the only woman in the biblical literature who is faced with a situation in which she is being called to stand by her husband in his trial.[5] She is not the heroine but a subordinate character in the trial. It was not necessary to involve Mrs. Job in the tests. There was no need to elaborate on her activities, because they are irrelevant to the image of Job's righteousness.[6] Nevertheless, Mrs. Job was not a mute bystander. Her relationship with her husband had to be expressed in one way or another, and the audience who was expecting a reaction from her could almost anticipate what she would say. Thus, the words that Job's wife uttered (2:9) are not her reflections on Job's situation but only draw attention to the fact that she herself has been affected by the disasters that the Satan had brought on her husband.[7]

Job's wife was the first to act, and she did it in a complex manner. She did not involve herself directly, but hinted to her husband that she was part of the altered family situation, whether he intended it to be so or whether he was only passively involved in it. She, the wife, had become an integral participant[8] in the changing events and her viewpoint has to be expressed. The one who approached Job first was not a friend or an outsider, but the person who was closest to him, the one who was an equal participant in his life, the one who shared in his wealth as well as in his misfortune — his wife.[9] More than that, if Job was unable to accept criticism from his wife, he would not have been able to stand up against any remarks expressed by his "friends" who would blame him for what had happened. Job's wife, regardless of her attitude toward her husband's situation, is therefore one additional test.[10] She might have been sympathetic, or she might have been angry at what had happened, but she would have been the one whose role it was to point out to Job that the outside world would be perplexed. Some might comfort him, but others would condemn him. Job's response would be his decision, and if he could stand up to his wife, there was no reason why he could not stand up to his friends.

(S. R. Driver and G. B. Gray, *A Critical and Exegetical Commentary on the Book of Job* [ICC; Edinburgh: T. & T. Clark, reprinted 1964] 167-68).

5. See, e.g., the stories of Sarah (Gen 12:10ff.) and Lot's wife (Gen 19:16).

6. M. Weiss, *Hassippur al Reshito shel Ieob* (Jerusalem: Jewish Agency, 1969) 76.

7. See Weiss, who suggested that Mrs. Job in expressing herself exposed her feelings and her own emotions (ibid., 76-77).

8. See Rowley's remark suggesting that Job's wife "seems to have accepted the terrible blows of the day with no more complaint than Job" (H. H. Rowley, *Job* [rev. ed.; NCB; Grand Rapids: Eerdmans, 1980] 35).

9. Weiss, *Hassippur*, 75.

10. See Rowley, *Job*, 39.

The short sentence that Mrs. Job said to her husband: "Do you still persist in your integrity? Curse [in Hebrew 'bless'] God and die" (2:9) opens the door for the audience to penetrate into the complex relationship that might have existed between Job and his wife, a relationship that might have been polarized in its nature when on the one hand the woman felt compassion for her husband in his suffering while on the other hand she felt outrage at the situation in which she too had become involved. This situation was illuminated by the LXX, which added a further speech to Job's wife (2:9) before her statement, describing the hardship of her situation and her misery as a result of the loss of her children and her husband's situation. She complained: "I am a wanderer and a servant from place to place and house to house, waiting for the setting of the sun, that I may rest from my labors and my pangs that now beset me." She was expected to feel sorry for her husband's painful aches while trying to understand him and bestowing comforting words and actions upon him. At the same time, however, she herself was suffering, not because of her own ill doing but because of her husband, and she was therefore tempted to act as a woman who had reached the limits of patience. As a result, some have perceived Mrs. Job as the devil's advocate (Augustine called her *diaboli adiutrix*),[11] while others have uplifted her to a saintly position. In the *Testament of Job*, Mrs. Job is so devoted to her husband that she is even willing to sell her hair in order to buy some bread.[12]

Thus, it is not surprising that biblical commentators over the generations have been confused about the image of Job's wife, and have presented her in varied and even contradictory characterizations. Whether she was being treated positively or negatively in her role as a companion to her husband, Mrs. Job is rarely referred to as a person in her own right. The biblical account refers to her anonymously since she is never given a proper name, emphasizing her subordinate role to her husband, similar to an itinerant domestic.[13]

It might be that the name of Job's wife was irrelevant because of the nature of the woman's role in her husband life, just as it had been a common practice in the biblical account to eliminate the names of the wives. But the situation is not quite so simple. While some married women are not named except in connection with their husbands, most female characters in the biblical material are known to us by name, as well as by their own genealogical heritage.[14]

It is therefore interesting that in the *Testament of Job* Mrs. Job is referred to not only as Job's wife but also by a proper name: Sitidos (25:1).[15] This name

11. Cited in ibid., 39.

12. See, e.g., *The Testament of Job* (ed. R. A. Kraft; SBLTT 5, Pseudepigrapha Series 4; Missoula, MT: Scholars, 1974) 23:7-13.

13. R. Gordis, *The Book of Man and God* (Chicago: University of Chicago, 1965) 93.

14. See, e.g., Rebekah, "the daughter of Bethuel son of Milcah, whom she bore to Nahor" (Gen 24:24), or Bathsheba, "daughter of Eliam" (2 Sam 11:3).

15. The Greek name "Sitidos" is a short version of the city "Ausitis," *T. Job* 25:1. Also see A. Kahana, *Haspharim Hajizonim* (Tel Aviv: Massada, 1960) 1.528.

is quite transparent and in a way is not a mere invention of the writer, or even a proper name; it derives from the geographical location associated with her husband (Job 1:1), the country of his origin: Uz. It is a common practice in the biblical narrative to create a name on the basis of one's geographical origin.[16]

Thus, if it was not a common practice to name a woman only after her husband's name, the question arises whether other episodes similar to that of the story of Job and his wife might have occurred. Moreover, if cases like this one existed, they might also shed light on our heroine, Mrs. Job.

In the story of Lot, Lot's wife, who suffered from the destruction of her home in Sodom, was asked to follow her husband and their two daughters in order to be saved from the destruction of her hometown (Gen 19:15). Lot's wife, who is faced with a situation where all her world would be turned upside down and she was going to lose all her physical possessions, does not follow her husband in blind obedience, and she does not intend to leave everything behind her without second thoughts. She turns back to look at the disaster. As a result, she is punished and turned into a pillar of salt (Gen 19:26). In this story, Lot's wife, like Job's wife, does not have a proper name. She is named after her husband. Since she acted on her own and was disobeying God's word, she is left nameless. Hence, it seems that one might be tempted to draw a comparison between these two situations of married women whose husbands obeyed God, and who were asked to accept their husband's change of status without questioning the drastic changes. Lot's wife, who did not accept this change, was killed. The text makes no references to the fate of Job's wife. If one can draw any parallel from one event to the other, however, then the situation might reflect that Job's life was restored and he had a new family (42:13), while his wife (who spoke in 2:9) died, and the new family that Job gained at the epilogue was from his second wife. This second wife was, according to the *Testament of Job,* Dinah, the daughter of Jacob (1:5).[17]

Are there any other similarities upon which one might dwell when the tales of Lot and Job are compared? In order to illuminate the matter, I would like to draw on a source of data that is rooted in a medium other than the verbal text — one that is in visual imagery. In an illustration of the story of Job in the *Jabach Altarpiece* (1503/4, Frankfurt, Stadelsches Kunstinstitut, fig. 1) the German artist Dürer (1471-1528) has illustrated Job's wife standing beside her suffering husband and pouring water over his head. Such an iconography of Mrs. Job is complex. It is not a simple pose, since the woman could have acted either out of anger or out of compassion. If Dürer intended to depict Job's wife as a compassionate woman, he might have been influenced by his patron, Fredrick the Wise. The latter had a personal motive in selecting the story of Job

---

16. See, e.g., names such as Abishag the Shunammite in 1 Kgs 1:3, who is a woman who came from the city of Shunam.

17. See, e.g., the references in Ginzberg, *Legends,* 1.396.

Figure 1.   *"Job and His Wife," by Albrecht Dürer (reproduced by permission of the Städelsches Kunstinstitut, Frankfurt am Main, Germany, owner of the painting).*

for illustration, as he was from early Christian times a protective saint against the plague.[18] If one considers the *Altarpiece*'s wings as well, and if the two musicians who appear on it are part of the entire composition, then it suggests that the composition of Job's wife was not that of a compassionate woman but rather of a contrary woman who scolds her husband, and Dürer intended to contrast the friendly spirit of the musicians with the spite of Job's wife.[19] Whatever the artist's intention, it is interesting that the background for this composition is not exclusive to the story of Job. In an earlier painting of *Lot and His Daughters* (1498), Dürer portrayed the destruction of the city of Sodom in the background, with Lot and his daughters in the foreground.

The similarity in landscapes that Dürer illustrated in the *Jabach Altarpiece* and in *Lot and His Daughters* suggests more than just coincidence. The artist chose these backgrounds for the two stories because of the similarities between these two episodes as they are portrayed in the biblical text. The wife of Lot and the wife of Job witnessed the disaster of their homes, both were called to join their husbands who had lost everything, and as a result both were uprooted from their familiar background and had to adjust to new environments. The wife of Lot is turned into a pillar of salt, but what happened to the wife of Job? Dürer introduces the comparison by using the same flaming background for both episodes. The two flaming cities and the messenger who is saved to bring the message to Job are equated with the saved wife of Lot who did not make it beyond the borders of the city. Thus, it is interesting that the artist intended to remind his audience of the close relationship between the two events, one in which the wife of Lot could not be saved because she objected to the fact that she had to obey blindly, the other in which the total faith of Job might have been reflected in his wife's behavior as well. But the artist refrains from stating an explicit viewpoint by portraying Mrs. Job as she is depicted in the story — a woman whose action one can interpret in a dual way. The composition could then be read either as a woman who mocks her husband, or as a wife who comforts her suffering husband. But whichever the case, for the artist these two events have a common bond. The audience might therefore find the clue for the anonymity of Mrs. Job in the counterpart of Mrs. Lot.

If Mrs. Job was portrayed as an enigmatic figure in the case of Dürer in fifteenth-century Germany, in eighteenth-century England Mrs. Job also did not command any identity of her own, since she appears only as a component of her husband's character in a series of illustrations on the book of Job (1825) created by William Blake (1757-1827). For Blake the artist, Mrs. Job is the "emanation" of the feminine counterpart of Job.[20] She is an integral part of her

---

18. E. Panofsky, *Albrecht Dürer* (2 vols.; 3rd ed.; Princeton: Princeton University, 1943) 1.93.

19. Ibid., 2.4.

20. K. Raine, *The Human Face of God* (London: Thames and Hudson, 1982) 78.

husband's character who follows her husband through all the events almost as though she were his shadow. Moreover, she even participates in the suffering itself (pl. 5 in Blake's illustrations, fig. 2) by sitting next to her husband at the arrival of the messenger, holding his hand. Her role is to be part of her husband's life, and thus she is included in every test that her husband undergoes. Hence, it is not surprising that when Blake turns to the next event (pl. 6, fig. 3), *And smote Job with sore Boils from the sole of his foot to the crown of his head,* he draws Mrs. Job grieving at her husband's feet. She is portrayed here as a compassionate woman who worries about her husband and tries to attend to his needs. Her portrayal as an understanding wife might reflect on the artist's own relationship with his wife, Catherine, "who so faithfully shared the tribulations, the poverty, and also the visions, of her husband."[21] For Blake, therefore, Mrs. Job plays an important role in the story. She is not an anonymous figure but is integrated into her husband's existence.

What is interesting is that these two artists, whose backgrounds differ in time and location, have succeeded in penetrating into the complex portrayal of Mrs. Job. While Mrs. Job is nameless in the biblical text, both artists did not need her name to identify her as a heroine in the story. She is a subordinate figure whose character is unavoidably included in the saga of Job. Both Dürer and Blake saw the woman as an instrumental figure who is involved in the trial of her husband. In the case of Dürer, however, Job's wife has to be punished, since her portrayal is reminiscent of the story of Lot. Hence there will be no room for her in the hero's restored life. In regard to Blake, however, the wife is an integral part of her husband's existence, and Mrs. Job takes part in her husband's new life. In pl. 19 (fig. 4), *Everyone also gave him a piece of Money,* Job is not seated alone in front of the crowd. He is accompanied by his wife, who shares the glorious restoration of his status with him. It might not be what the biblical discourse had intended to bring out, but for Blake the story could not have ended otherwise: "Job and his wife — in Blake's version his true and faithful companion in adversity — are now once again seated under their own fig-tree with a field of sturdy wheat beyond."[22]

Thus, one of the questions that Blake solved differently from the textual elaborations as in the *Testament of Job* is that Job's wife accompanies her husband not only during the disasters but also when Job's circumstances are restored. In her few words to her husband, Mrs. Job gained a position that enabled her to participate and enjoy the new situation. Hence she is rewarded together with her husband for her obedience, patience, and compassion.

In conclusion, it is interesting to note that both the biblical commentators and the visual artists had to face the same perplexing text. The commentators in both media were able to see the two different characteristic features of Mrs.

21. Ibid., 78.
22. Ibid., 250.

Figure 2. "*Then went Satan forth from the presence of the Lord,*" *an engraving by William Blake, illustration of the Book of Job: V, 1826 (gift of Miss Ellen Bullard; courtesy, Museum of Fine Arts, Boston).*

Figure 3. "And smote Job with sore Boils from the sole of his foot to the crown of his head," an engraving by William Blake, illustration of the Book of Job: VI, 1826 (gift of Miss Ellen Bullard; courtesy, Museum of Fine Arts, Boston).

Figure 4. *"Every one also gave him a piece of Money," an engraving by William Blake, illustration of the Book of Job: IXX, 1826 (gift of Miss Ellen Bullard; courtesy, Museum of Fine Arts, Boston).*

Job to which the text alludes. In the visual medium, the artists had found a way to shed light on their interpretive mode. On the one hand, Dürer compared the story of Job's wife with another biblical episode — the story of Lot; on the other hand, Blake used a live exemplum, Catherine, his own devoted wife, to illuminate the characteristic figure of Mrs. Job. Nonetheless, both the Bible and the artists are unclear as to the role that Job's wife might have played in her husband's trial. The short verse that is attributed to her words had opened the door for two opposing perceptions of her character. Even though she is only a subordinate figure in the biblical narrative, she does have an important role and her statement is expounded and elaborated. Moreover, neither the textual material nor the visual imageries intend to dismiss her existence. They both allow the portrayal of Mrs. Job as an individual in her own right, who shared with her husband the disasters of the heavenly trial.

Needlework and Sewing in Israel from Prehistoric Times to the Roman Period*

AVIGAIL SHEFFER

Hebrew University, Jerusalem

> There is a reason for everything, a time for every occupation under
> heaven . . . a time for tearing and a time for sewing.
>
> Eccl 3:1, 7

This article is concerned with examples of needlework and sewing preserved
on ancient textile remains and what one can learn from them about the way of
life, the economic and even spiritual conditions of the early inhabitants of
Palestine during its early historical periods.

Because of the generally humid climate of most of Palestine and the
consequent destruction of most of its ancient textiles, our knowledge of sewing
and needlework in the early periods is extremely scanty. In fact, remnants of
textiles have been found only in the most arid regions of the area (Judean Desert,
Dead Sea area, and Sinai; see fig. 1). Hence, many gaps exist in our knowledge
of sewing and needlework, although these gaps can sometimes be supplemented
by a study of garments worn by people depicted in ancient artwork. Although
we lack the data for an all-round picture, I shall try, from surviving textile

---

*The name Israel, which has no significance for the prehistoric period, is used here
for convenience to designate the territory known in the distant and recent past as Canaan,
Eretz-Yisrael, and Palestine.

I would like to thank Uza Zevulon for her welcome help and advice, and Ernest
Heineman for editing the English text. I want also to acknowledge here my indebtedness
to the late Amalia Tidhar and the late Ziva Amir, both of whose expertise was put at my
disposal early in this work.

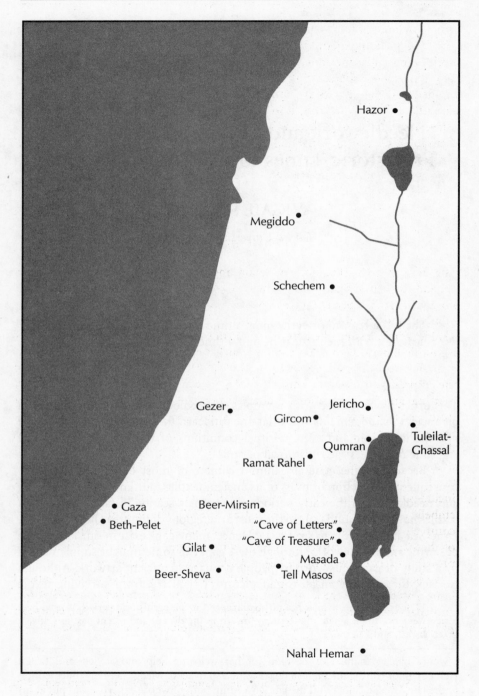

Figure 1. *Map of Eretz-Israel.*

remains and artwork, to learn something about the kinds of needles and the variety of stitches employed, along with the various kinds of sewing and needlework practiced in ancient times in Palestine.

The basic requisites for sewing are obviously some kind of material, needles, and thread. Needles suitable for sewing have to be round and very smooth, with a pointed tip at one end and an eyehole for the threads at the other. The small size of needles makes it difficult, almost impossible, to find them in an excavation, truly like finding a needle in a haystack. To be suitable for sewing, threads must be plied from at least two spun threads, since a single spun thread is not strong enough for sewing.

I. Prehistoric Period

The Bible recounts the story of Adam and Eve, who, in order to cover their nakedness, "sewed fig leaves together to make themselves loincloths" (Gen 3:7). From this it has been inferred that sewing was the first work invented by humans, and that the needle bone was the first tool used (Hallo and Simpson 1971:9).[1] In Palestine, the first use of the needle can be traced to the Prepottery Neolithic B period (ca. 7000 B.C.E.), in an assemblage of cultic objects found in a small cave in Nahal Hemar in the Judean Desert (Bar-Yosef 1985). Among the impressive objects of this assemblage were perishable items of cordage, matting, and basketry, and two unusual items of "attire." The last are plaited from bast fiber (the earliest occurrence of linen) and show evidence of sewing. One of these is a headdress in the form of a circular high-domed cap, of which the two narrow edges of the band are sewn together with a stroke stitch. The dome is in the form of a knotted net. In the center of the band that rested on the forehead is sewn a green serpentine bead (see fig. 2). The knotted net includes triangles and rhomboids made by knotted looping; some of these are embellished with sewn-on shells (Schick 1988b). The second item is a nearly complete rectangular napkin, 17 × 30 cm. in size, made by looping. The edges of the napkin are secured all around with a compact buttonhole stitch, most probably executed with the aid of a needle (Schick 1988a:34, 38).

Sewing was evidently involved in the making of these two articles. Various bone implements were found in the cave, some of which were pierced at one end (Bar-Yosef 1985). Unfortunately, none was complete so that the character of the other end is not known. These bone implements are thin and flat and

---

1. Stitching is known from a Norse site in Greenland. Among the frozen remains of a deposit from the mid-third millennium B.C.E. were remains of stitched skin clothing. Their positions in the garments were not clear. The site had many fine bone needles (Ryder 1993:4).

Figure 2. *Headdress —*
Nahal Hemar (Schick
1988: fig. 2).

could perhaps have served as needles for sewing delicate items like the headdress
and napkin mentioned above.

II. Chalcolithic Period

The earliest known textiles from Palestine are scraps of carbonized fabric
found at Teleilat Ghassul, the Chalcolithic site in the Jordan Valley (fourth
millennium B.C.E.). These items, woven apparently from plant fibers, are too
badly preserved to recognize any stitching that might have been present
(G. Crowfoot 1956:432-33).

Many textile items, which in more humid conditions would have disin-
tegrated, were at least partially preserved in the arid climate of the Judean Desert.
Fragments of textiles were recovered from the "Cave of the Treasure," in the
Judean Desert near the Dead Sea. From the Chalcolithic period a hoard of 430

objects of copper, ivory, and stone were found. Among the copper objects were numerous mace heads with socket holes, in one of which were scraps of linen fabric, which apparently served to secure the wooden shaft in the socket (Bar-Adon 1980:119).

Other fragments of wool and linen found in the cave, some with signs of stitching still apparent, were classified by the excavator into three periods: Chalcolithic, Roman (Bar-Kochba rebellion, 135 c.e.), and Intermediate. The Intermediate group could not be positively identified as either Chalcolithic or Roman. (A few of the wool fragments identified by Bar-Adon as Chalcolithic were submitted for examination to the laboratory of Dr. Ryder in England and identified by him as definitely Roman — privately communicated by T. Schick.) With regard to the textiles with stitches identified by Bar-Adon as "Chalcolithic," positive confirmation of their date has not yet been done.

We do not know if the Chalcolithic textiles from Teleilat Ghassul and from the "Cave of the Treasure" are indeed the remnants of garments. Graphic evidence from this period showing dressed figures is very rare. Luckily, one such group is preserved in a wall painting from Teleilat Ghassul (Bienkowski 1991:6, fig. 4), but the coverings or garments they wear cannot be determined.[2]

All the human figurines found at Chalcolitic sites around Beersheba are of ivory and represent naked men and women (Perrot 1959: pl. II; Perrot 1964: pl. LI; Perrot 1969: pl. XIII; Amiran and Tadmor 1980: pl. 17).

Two especially interesting clay figurines were discovered at the Chal-colithic cultic center of Gilat, in the western Negev (Alon 1976:5). One shows a naked woman seated on a stool, her right hand holding a churn on her head. The face and body are painted with red, mostly horizontal bands that apparently do not represent garments since the anatomical features of her nudity are modeled explicitly, perhaps suggesting the custom of painting the body and face for ritual purposes.

The other figure is that of a ram with a red-colored pattern painted on his back that may be interpreted as a cover made of plaited, woven, or felted material, since the ram is burdened with three vessels on his back. It has also been suggested that the cover was made of leather and that the triangles along the margins were joined to the main element by stitching (Tadmor 1986:11).

Although textile finds from the Chalcolithic period are scarce, many articles made from plant fibers dating from this period have been found: trays, baskets, mats, sieves, and so on (Aharoni 1961: pl. 7:E, F; Bar-Adon 1961: pl. 16:a, b; Bar-Adon 1980:139, 190-97). Also many pottery vessels and ossuaries have plaited mat impressions on their bases (Mallon et al. 1934:91-92, pl. 39;

2. I am grateful to Uza Zevulun for drawing my attention to this picture. An explora-tion in the Judean Desert in the winter of 1993 found a burial cave with a Chalcolithic or Early Bronze warrior with his weapon. He was covered with linen fabric and wrapped in a beautiful plaited mat. The textile has not yet been examined and its purpose is not clear (personal communication from T. Schick).

Koppel 1940: pls. 83, 84; Shapira 1964; G. Crowfoot 1938; Macdonald 1932: pl. XXXIV:10-12; Perrot 1961: pl. VII:15-17; Shipton 1939: pl. 19:19, 20; pl. 20:27, 28).

No proper needles from the Chalcolithic period have yet been found, but we know of polished bone tools pointed at one end and pierced at the other (Dothan 1959: pl. VII:10, fig. 18:40, 48; Hennessy 1969: fig. 11, 13; Perrot 1955: pl. 17a; Bar-Adon 1980:177). Also found, sometimes together with the latter, are polished bone awls (Perrot 1955: pl. 17a; Dothan 1959:10, pl. 7; Hennessy 1969: fig. 11:1-9, 14; Bar-Adon 1961: pl. 17a). Neither of these implements is suitable for sewing, but each could have been used for plaiting, matting, and wicker work.

The small amount of textiles that has survived from the Chalcolithic period, compared to the wealth of plaited items, suggests that the latest may have been used in this period also for garments and coverings along with woven cloth.

III. Canaanite Period[3]

Metal needles with a point at one end and an eyehole at the other appear in Palestine during the Middle Bronze II period (1800-1500 B.C.E.). Two types of needles are found: one pierced at one end (like today's sewing needles), and the other with an eye produced by looping over one end of the stem (see fig. 3) (Loud 1948:186, 187; 219:1-9; Petrie and Tufnell 1930: pls. XVI:10-15; XXI:110; Petrie 1934: pl. XXXIV; Petrie 1933: pl. XXIV; Lemon and Shipton 1939: pl. 84:1-14). The latter type was not suitable for sewing.

1. Canaanite Textiles and Garments

Textiles from the Middle Bronze II period in the form of poorly preserved fragments of cloth have been found so far only in Jericho (E. Crowfoot 1960, 1982).[4] Some fragments from tomb H22 had remnants of sewing threads (E. Crowfoot 1960:520). One fragment from burial M has a decoration of twined cord in which the weft threads pass alternately over and under the warps but do not penetrate them (as it would in sewing) (see fig. 4) (ibid. 1960:520,

3. The only era in the history of Israel that should properly be called "Canaanite" is the second millennium B.C.E. It was in this millennium that the city-states differed markedly from earlier or later periods in the country's history. The local inhabitants are called "Canaanites" in the Bible, and their kings are known as "kings of Canaan."
4. Textile remnants were found in the following Jericho tombs; B3, B35, G46, H6, H11, H18, H22, J1 (E. Crowfoot 1960:519; Kenyon 1965:566-74).

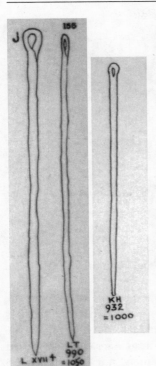

Figure 3. *Needles: (left) bronze needles with looped eyehole, (right) bronze needle with eyehole (Dothan 1959: figs. 18, 44; Petrie 1933: pl. XXIV 950, 980).*

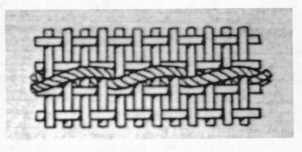

Figure 4. *"Twined embroidery line" (E. Crowfoot 1960:520, fig. 226, 2).*

fig. 226, 2). Crowfoot called this decoration "twined embroidery line," probably because she was uncertain whether it was integral to the weaving process or inserted with a needle after completion of the weaving, since both techniques achieve the same results. On a second fragment, however, the stitching was clearly done with a needle since the threads pass through the warp threads and not through the interstices of the weave (see fig. 5). The stitch is a running stitch applied along the edge of the selvage, probably serving as a draw-thread for tightening the edge of a cap (ibid. 1960:520, fig. 226, 3).

Since only small textile fragments were found at Jericho it could not be determined to what type of garments or other articles they belonged. Kenyon suggested that the deceased were buried in their garments with their caps on (Kenyon 1960:266; 1965:570ff.).[5]

In Jericho tombs, as in other tombs from this period, toggle pins (see fig. 6) were found near the skeletons. One may assume that toggle pins were used

5. Zipper (1990:52) suggested another interpretation: that the caps were actually headbands of the kind worn by the women in the Beni-Hasan caravan and that the twined embroidery is probably what remained of a pattern that embellished the band.

Figure 5. *Running stitch (E. Crowfoot 1960:520, fig. 226, 3).*

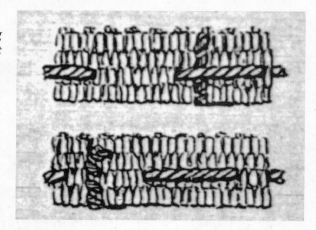

to secure items of wear, and their position near the skeletons may relate to the original form of the garments in which the dead were buried.

From 150 undisturbed tombs in Jericho, it was possible to observe the location of the toggle pins in only 35 cases. Since in most instances the pin was found near the shoulders (in 10 cases near the left shoulder and in 4 cases near the right shoulder), Kenyon (1965:567) suggested that the dead in Jericho were buried in a togalike garment. But neither the togalike garment nor other wrapped garments, like kilt or loincloth, need a toggle pin.[6] Therefore, one may suggest that most people were buried in their ordinary draped garments, which did not need a toggle pin. The latter would only be found alongside people of rank who could afford an upper garment that would need to be held in place by the pin.

In Jericho tombs J1 and P17 were found scarabs that had been attached to rings. These rings were apparently not worn on the finger but were suspended on toggle pins (Kenyon 1965:571, pls. 1, 2; fig. 174, no. 11). Also, in Beth-Pelet tomb 1021 (Starkey and Harding 1932: pl. XLII) were found three rings with attached scarabs, together with five scarabs and two toggle pins, one with a ring still attached. The other scarab had probably dropped from the toggle pin. In Beth-Pelet tomb 1018 scarab seals were found alongside toggle pins suggesting that the seals were originally attached to the toggle pins. An inlaid frieze from third-millennium Mari illustrates how the toggle pin (or 2 toggle pins) was fastened to the upper garment (see fig. 7); it also shows a cylinder seal suspended from the pin (Weiss 1985: fig. 49; Ziffer 1990:34).[7] The toggle pin apparently

6. A toggle pin is needed only when two parts from the same garment or from two different garments have to be joined. With the draped garment, the end of which is thrown over the shoulder, the toggle pin is superfluous. Kilts and loincloths were usually knotted at their ends.

7. In Mari, a cylinder seal hangs from the toggle pin, while in Palestine it may have been a scarab.

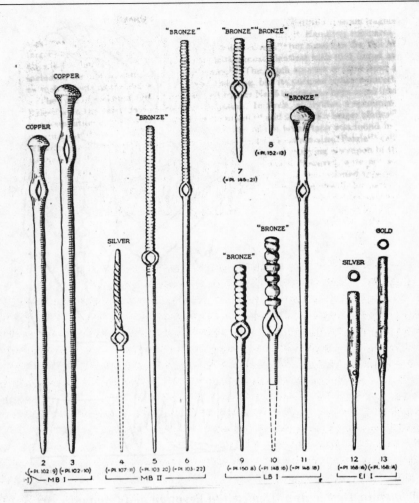

Figure 6. *Toggle pins (Kenyon 1965: fig. 174:10, 20).*

had a twofold use, securing the upper garment and holding a cylinder seal or scarab.

The seal, apparently serving as a kind of identification tag, was carried on the upper garment by persons of rank. In this connection note the biblical story of Judah and Tamar (Gen 38:14) in which Tamar asks Judah for his seal and cord as a pledge.

The needles found in the Bronze Age tombs are evidence that sewing was done, but precisely for what purpose and in connection with what kind of articles (garments, coverings, spreads, sacks, etc.) cannot be determined until more data are gathered.

Figure 7. *Toggle pin*
fastened to an upper
garment (inlaid frieze
from the third millen-
nium B.C.E., *Mari)*
(Weiss 1985:155; Zipper
1990: fig. 86).

2. Canaanite Garments as Depicted in Egyptian and Canaanite Art

Though we lack direct evidence of how Canaanite garments looked, how they
fitted the human body, and how they were made (e.g., was stitching used), we
can derive some ideas from depictions in ancient Near Eastern art. The evidence
from Egypt comes mainly from paintings, but from Canaan there survive
scarabs, ivories, stelae, plaques, and other artifacts.

Egyptian wall paintings showing Asiatics arriving in Egypt are found as
early as about 2000 B.C.E. The paintings in the tomb of Khnumhetep at Beni-
Hasan depict the arrival of a caravan of Asiatics dressed in multicolored patterned garments. Each garment is brightly colored with woven or embroidered
patterns (Newberry 1983: pls. 28, 30-31).[8]

8. The men in the caravan are dressed in kilts or draped gowns. The women have the

Figure 8. *Canaanite wearing draped garment as depicted in Egyptian paintings.*

Half a millennium later, in the period of the Egyptian New Kingdom, the style of the Canaanite garment appears to have changed, as evidenced by the wall paintings of the 18th-20th dynasties. Many of these paintings depict Canaanites coming to Egypt, either as merchants, tribute bearers, or captives, dressed in colorful garments, some of which were probably sewn. These decorated garments contrast vividly with the plain white Egyptian dress.

Two main types of male garments are depicted: (a) a draped garment (fig. 8) and (b) a long white, tightly fitted, sleeved robe (fig. 9). In some paintings the two types of garments are shown together (fig. 10). Characteristic for both types is the use of colored threads in the weaving or for ornamental sewing.

(a) The draped garment worn by the Syrians bringing tribute to Tutankhamen appears in the wall painting in the tomb of Huy (*ANEP,* nos. 52, 111) and on a ship carrying Syrians (Davies and Falkner 1947: pl. 8) (see fig. 8). The

same kind of dress, except for one who wears a tuniclike garment. These highly decorated garments were apparently not tailored or sewn but woven in one piece from colored threads and fastened at the hip or shoulder by a knot or pin.

Figure 9. *Canaanite*
wearing a sewn
garment as depicted in
Egyptian paintings
(Prichard 1951:39b).

long wrapped robe of the men is made of two-colored (red and blue) material decorated with dots. The edges of the robes are decorated with a different design. A colorful patterned garment is worn by the Syrian porter (*ANEP,* no. 56) and also by the man depicted on Tutankhamen's ceremonial stick (Desroches-Noblecourt 1963: pl. XVIII). Toward the end of this period the draped garment is more colorfully decorated, as can be observed on the Syrians walking in line in the wall paintings of Ramses III's tomb, as well as on the faience tile from his temple (*ANEP,* nos. 53, 54).

(b) The long, white, tightly fitted, sleeved robe is sewn and has colorful seams in red and blue (Davies and Davies 1933: pls. 41, 43, 4, 20) (see fig. 9). These seams are decorated with dots or bands, as seen in the painting in the

Figure 10. *Canaanites wearing sewn garments with draped skirts above
(Prichard 1951:39d).*

tomb of Rekh-mi-Re (Davis 1943: pls. XXII, XXIII). The robe was apparently
made by sewing together different rectangular-shaped pieces with colored edges
or, alternatively, colorful bands were applied along the seams.[9]

In some cases, the Canaanites wear over their close-fitting white robe a

9. Some of the Palestinian dresses are made of rectangular pieces that were sewn
together by embroidery stitches, or the rectangular pieces were sewn together and strips of
embroidery were applied along the seams afterward (Weir 1989:275).

kiltlike cloth around the lower part of the body from the waist down (*ANEP*, nos. 46, 47) (see fig. 10).

To the wealth of Egyptian evidence one can add a handful of local Canaanite works of art, such as a group of Hyksos scarabs, stelae from Tel Beit Mirsim, Megiddo, and Shechem, as well as a few plaques and late Canaanite ivories from Megiddo.

Many Hyksos scarabs portray human figures. The males are depicted either with kilts or an upper draped garment (Tufnell 1984: front page). The short kilts are probably draped, sometimes secured with a knot or a belt, and tucked in at the waist. Many kilts are hatched, perhaps to represent weaving in color (Tufnell 1984:136) or embroidery. The upper togalike garment is made up of a length of cloth wrapped around the body and thrown over the left shoulder, leaving the right arm bare. These draped garments were finished at the bottom edge with a wide selvage, or a thick coil strip of embroidery or tassel was joined on by sewing.

Several artworks from Palestine depict draped garments. Among them is the Middle Bronze stele from Tel Beit Mirsim stratum D (Albright 1928:3; 1936-37: pl. 22). From this fragmentary stele only the lower part of the figure can be seen, whose legs are encompassed by a thick coil.[10] The draped garment with thick coil is also depicted on the Megiddo statue (Loud 1948: pl. 235:23) and on the Shechem plaque (Merhav 1985:36). The thick coil that adorned the edge of the draped robe may have been an integral part of the garment produced by folding its hem. Alternatively, it may have been a separate piece of rolled fabric that was sewn onto the edge of the robe.

An interesting garment is depicted on a bronze plaque from Hazor (see fig. 11). It shows a Canaanite dignitary wearing a draped garment consisting of a length of cloth wound five times around the body (Yadin et al. 1961: pl. 339:11). The selvage of the garment is finished by some kind of thickening or embroidery. A similar garment is depicted on the gold plaque from Gezer (Seger 1976: figs. 2B, 3B), which shows the wrapped cloth covering the full length of the body, the edges of the cloth adorned by dots or perhaps by tassels.

Late Bronze Age artwork depicts another type of garment that was apparently sewn. The most detailed depictions of this new type of garment are found on the famous fragmentary ivories from Megiddo VII (Loud 1939: pls. 4, 2a, 3a). One of these ivories depicts scenes of victory and banquet (see fig. 12). The king and his companions wear long draped cloths with marked bands at their lower edge. The queen's garment is embroidered around the lower hem

---

10. Albright (1928:6; 1936-37:42-43, pl. 21A) interpreted the coil as a serpent, and he called the figure "Serpent Goddess." This interpretation has recently been challenged. It is now proposed that the figure is that of a male of rank wearing the characteristic wraparound Canaanite garment with thickened coil along the lower part (Merhav 1985:27).

Figure 11. *Bronze plaque of a nobleman from Hazor (Yadin et al. 1961: pl. 339, 1).*

Figure 12. *The king and his companions — banquet scene, ivory from Megiddo (Loud 1939: pl. 4).*

and neck.[11] The same embroidery around the neck occurs also on the robe of the king. Suspended from the queen's left hand is a stripelike length of cloth, which seems to have the same kind of decoration as on her dress. The stripe held by the lyre player standing behind the queen is, like her dress, plain and undecorated. The decorated garments of the royal couple clearly emphasize the elevated status of the latter over their attendant.

Another ivory depicts a woman holding a staff (ibid., pl. 38) (see fig. 13). She wears a long dress and a mantle above it. Both garments are adorned at the front and at the lower hem with tassels, which may have been sewn on. The neck opening is also embroidered like that of the queen, but it is round here, while that of the queen is angled.

To judge by the evidence of surviving artwork, the basic Canaanite garment was of the draped type, that is, wrapped around the body, sometimes fastened with a knot. There was no need for stitching with a needle. Over their draped garment persons of rank wore a cape or an upper garment held by a toggle pin or a coiled fabric, and here too no stitching was needed. But some Egyptian paintings depict garments that are evidently made up of rectangular pieces joined together by sewing, and decorated along their vertical seams with colored bands or colorful embroidery.

One may assume that there were also other woven articles that had to be sewn, like the caps with their still-adhering threads found in the Jericho tombs, or the above-mentioned "tailored" garments depicted in the Egyptian paintings. It is probable that sewing as well as embroidering was involved in fashioning some of the garments seen on the Megiddo ivories.

IV. A Canaanite Robe from Egypt

The only fully preserved garment that may be of Canaanite origin is an embroidered sleeved tunic found in the fourteenth-century B.C.E. tomb of Tutankhamen in Egypt (Carter 1933:124, 125). The decorative motifs it depicts are clearly foreign to Egypt. The garment has decorative bands of colored embroidery, in the form of a cross, around and below the neck opening, down the sides, and around the bottom of the tunic (G. Crowfoot and Davies 1941). The colored embroidery is mostly blue with touches of red, green, and dark brown. The decorative bands, like the tunic, are of linen. The sewing is by means of running and chain stitches. The brilliantly decorative bands are made up of separately embroidered squares, which were sewn to the tunic. Two squares of

11. Stripes along the lower edge of the dress, resembling those of the queen's dress, are still used in the traditional dress of bedouin women in the village of Tuba in northern Galilee (Amir 1984; Weir 1989:86-87).

Figure 13. *Woman holding a staff; ivory from Megiddo (Loud 1939: pl. 38).*

various designs alternate with one square of spreading palmette without stem leaves (see fig. 14). Each square has a design of a mythological scene or motif, most of them distinctly foreign to Egypt. In particular there appear winged griffins, female sphinx, galloping and biting animals, which have close connections with Mesopotamian and Syrian motifs. There are also distinctly Egyptian designs, however, like the cartouche with the name of Tutankhamen and the royal uraeus.

Figure 14.   *Embroidery from Tutankhamen, lower edge of tunic — a detail (Crowfoot and Davies 1941: pl. 20, 3-8).*

The unique Syrian-Egyptian character of the embroidery suggests that the tunics were not fashioned by Egyptian artisans but by foreign, probably Canaanite, ones. No embroidery is known in Egypt before the New Kingdom or afterward.[12] Canaan was known for its colorful threads, which were highly prized. One may speculate that Sisera's mother waited eagerly for her son to bring her colored threads as booty, since only the conqueror and his family could afford to wear brightly decorated garments with colorful threads (Judg 5:31).[13] We know that the embroidered tunic was specifically made for King Tutankhamen because his royal cartouche is included in the design of the front cross below the neck opening, the most important location from an iconographical point of view (Barber 1991:161). It could have been made by Canaanite artisans in their native land, as Thutmose III had boasted a century earlier that he brought "much clothing of the foe" after conquering Megiddo and other cities in Canaan (*ARE*

12. The fabrics thought to be embroidered with colored threads were examined by Barber (1982:442-43) and found to be woven.

13. Two families of the tribe of Issachar have names of dyes: Pua (madder) and Tola (kermes) (Num 26:20). The tribe of Issachar occupied a coastal area in northern Israel in which dyeing was a prominent industry. These names were probably given to them because they were experts in the art of dyeing (Mazar 1989).

2.188). Another possibility is that the embroidery was executed by Syrian captives in Pharaoh's workshops. In his annals Thutmose III states that cloth makers from Syria were brought as captive artisans to the temple of Amun (Riefstahl 1944:31n.77). As to the manufacture of the tunic, the Syrian character of the patterns, the Syrian captives working in Amun's temple, and the appearance of the vertical loom (Roth 1913-1978:15ff.), which is foreign to Egypt, suggest that the tunic was made by Syrian artisans.

In summary, though actual textile remnants from the Canaanite period are almost nonexistent, the evidence of Egyptian paintings and works of art shows that Canaanite garments were made up of richly colored fabrics and decorated with beautiful colored sewn-on bands.

V. The Monarchy Period

That the art of sewing was well known during the monarchy period is indicated by the many and varied metal needles that look exactly like the needles of today, found in excavations (Frits and Kempinski 1983: Tafel 103, pl. IX; Pritchard 1963: fig. 51, 7; Lemon and Shipton 1939: pl. 84:1-3, 9, 10). Needles were considered valuable and carefully kept in boxes when not in use. Ivory boxes with needles still inside them were found at Hazor (Yadin et al. 1961: pl. 343:10) and at Megiddo (Loud 1948: pl. 187:21) (see fig. 15).

The only dressed male figure known to me from Israel during the monarchial period is found on the painted sherd from Ramat-Rachel (Aharoni 1962:42-43, pl. 28, fig. 30, 1) (see fig. 16), which dates to the second half of the seventh century B.C.E. (Matthiae 1964:94). The style is probably influenced by Neo-Assyrian art. The person depicted wears a close-fitting garment over which is a red mantle held at the waist by a belt. The sleeves are short and wide. The person may be a king of Judea performing some ritual act (ibid.:92). It is impossible to tell from the painting if any stitching was used.

Although very few textiles survive from the monarchy, a wide variety of fabrics was clearly used in this period both for clothing and for other purposes.

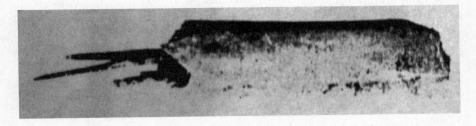

Figure 15. *Needles in a bone box from Megiddo (Loud 1948: pl. 187:21).*

Figure 16. *A dignitary seated on a throne, painted on sherd from Ramat Raḥel (Matthiae 1964:4).*

For example, there is the evidence of textile imprints on the bases of the so-called Negev ware (Sheffer 1976) and also on many metal objects (Sheffer and Tidhar 1991:23).

But the main evidence for the style, appearance, and fabric of garments comes from Assyrian artworks. The two most famous of these are the Black Obelisk (*ANEP*, nos. 351, 355) from Nimrud showing the Israelite king Omri, the son of Jehu, presenting tribute to Shalmaneser III; and the well-known relief from Nineveh showing the attack on Lachish by Sennacherib (Ussishkin 1982:86, 87). In this relief the men, women, and children are dressed in long garments, but, because of the schematic depiction, one can tell almost nothing as to their mode of manufacture and if any stitching was used.

One may glean some information, if only incidentally, from the Bible about the names of garments (Isa 3:18-26; Exodus 28; 39). But it is difficult to identify in artwork any of the garments mentioned there.[14]

14. The loincloth that was usually worn by workers depicted in Egyptian paintings and other artwork is probably the *mahălāzôt* of the Bible (Isa 3:22). The *'aderet* was apparently

Actual textile fragments from the monarchy period were found only at Kuntillet ʿAjrûd (Meshel 1978). This isolated hill in eastern Sinai, near the border with Judea, served as a caravanserai and cultic enclosure; it dates to ninth-eighth century B.C.E. Owing to the arid climate almost one hundred textile fragments were preserved (Sheffer and Tidhar 1991).

Besides inscriptions and inscribed votive offerings, the site also yielded two pithoi with paintings of people engaged in ceremonial activities. One painting (see fig. 17) shows two standing Bes figures[15] dressed in short kilts and sleeved shirts. The garments appear to be represented by dots, but Beck (1982:29, 30) disputes this assumption. There is also a seated woman, nude above the waist, playing a lyre. She wears an ankle-length skirt held at the waist by a belt tied in front with two long appendages. The skirt is represented by polka dots and may be diaphanous. On her shoulders is a shawl like the one worn by high-ranking Canaanites of the Middle Bronze-Late Bronze period (Dever 1984:23).

The procession of the worshipers depicted on the second pithos (see fig. 18) comprises five persons, all of whom appear to be dressed in garments consisting of adjoining squares and rectangles mostly, but not all enclosing dots. Assuming that the geometrical figures and dots represent the material of the garments, one may infer that two different types of cloth are depicted here. But one can extract no information concerning stitching or embroidery from the figures. The people were evidently dressed, but one can only conjecture about what kind of garments, whether draped or sewn from separate pieces. Incised lines, squares, and dots are visible on the figures, but whether these represent stitching or embroidery is not clear.

As to actual textile fragments from the site, most are woven from linen, some from wool, and just a few from mixed wool-linen threads.[16] In some fragments stray blue linen threads remain, while in others one can still see sewing stitches, mostly simple ones like running, basting, and overcasting; but there is evidence also of some rather complicated sewing techniques. All these

---

an expensive upper garment, since this is what the prophet Elijah casts on his disciple Elisha and so appoints him his successor. It was perhaps made of fur; in art it is depicted in the form of a thickened coil draped around the shoulders of persons of authority (Merhav and Orman 1979:95). The typical draped Canaanite garment should perhaps be identified with the *śimlâ*, usually an inner item of closing but sometimes a person's only garment, which served both for daytime wear and nighttime covering (Exod 22:25; Deut 22:17).

15. Bes is a collective name for a group of Egyptian deities characterized by their grotesque facial features, bandy legs, and nudity except for the loincloth skin, the tail of which is seen between the legs.

16. The mixture of linen and wool is termed *šaʿaṭnēz* in the Bible. The wearing of such mixed linen wool material is expressly forbidden to Jews (Lev 19:19; Deut 22:9-11). Nevertheless, the Bible contains descriptions of the priests' garments made of fine linen mixed with colored wool (Exod 28:39). These *šaʿaṭnēz* vestments were sacred and could be worn by the priests only.

Figure 17. *A lyre player and two Bes figures — Kuntillet ʿAjrûd (Beck 1982: fig. 5).*

stitches were used for various purposes, such as patching, securing edges, joining together, and so forth.

Two fragments present impressive demonstration of sewing skill: in one the edges of a rectangular padded fragment are reinforced by a rolled strip attached by sewing (see fig. 19) (resembling the much later item from the Cave of Wadi ed-Daliyeh; see E. Crowfoot 1974:63, fig. F). In the second fragment the border is carefully secured by insertion of the cut warp threads within the whipped rolled edge, so that the sewing threads went around the rolled edge (see fig. 20). This arrangement was evidently designed to secure the hem of a garment and may be the kind of sewing mentioned in the Bible (Exod 28:33, 39).

Another impressive example of sewing craftsmanship is provided by items consisting of two pieces of fabric joined together by strong, neat seams not previously found anywhere locally. The two pieces were first joined together with a running stitch about 1 cm. inside the edge; subsequently each edge was

Figure 18.   *A procession of 5 people — Kuntillet ʿAjrûd*
(Beck 1982: fig. 6).

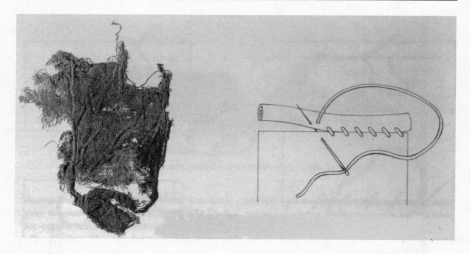

Figure 19.   *Kuntillet 'Ajrûd — a rolled strip attached by sewing (drawing and photo) (Sheffer and Tidhar 1991: fig. 19).*

folded over twice on itself and then sewn to its own fabric with a slip stitch (see fig. 21).[17] In some cases the seam was torn open, and it was then found that the selvages of the two pieces had been sewn together. In view of the special character of this type of seam, one may suggest that it was specifically designed for the kind of tunic that was made up of two identical pieces of fabric joined together by sewing.[18]

As one can observe, the stitching of these textiles was expertly and meticulously executed. One may suppose that the extreme care bestowed on this stitching was connected to its intended purpose — to enhance the beauty and splendor of the ceremonial attire worn by the priests and leading personages, and so to impress the community with the full solemnity of the cultic rite.

VI. Roman Period — Masada

When Yadin excavated Masada, where the Zealots lived during part of the revolt against the Romans, he found a large collection of textiles (Yadin 1966:154). Most of these were of high quality and of amazing brilliance of color.

17. This type of stitch was reconstructed by the late Ziva Amir.

18. A child's tunic *(kutōnet)*, made up of two identical rectangular pieces, was found by Yadin's expedition in the Cave of Letters (Yadin 1963:258, fig. 85). The find from Kuntillet 'Ajrûd suggests that the *kutōnet* was known perhaps much earlier, as early as the monarchy, and that the tunic found in the Roman-period Cave of Letters may have been similar in style to the early tunics *(kutōnet)*.

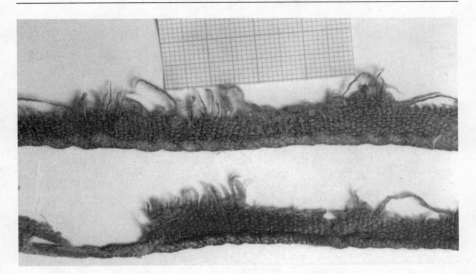

Figure 20. *Kuntillet 'Ajrûd — rolled hem (photo)*
(Sheffer and Tidhar 1991: fig. 17f).

The Masada fragments included textiles woven from linen, wool, and other threads. Especially on the wool fragments, different kinds of stitching, mending, and patching were observed. Sewing threads were generally of wool and of the same color as the material, but here and there white linen threads were also used. Moreover, sometimes the color of the sewing threads did not match the material. Some patches were well done and neatly fitted to the material, but on other patches the torn part was basted unevenly with big stitches, as if done hastily by an unskilled hand unconcerned about aesthetic effect.

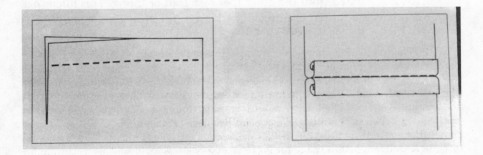

Figure 21. *Kuntillet 'Ajrûd — (left) running stitch, (right) slip stitch*
(Sheffer and Tidhar 1991: fig. 17a, d; fig. 22).

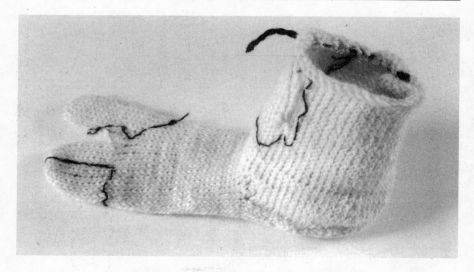

Figure 22.   *Single needle knitted sock from Egypt.*

The mending and patching of the pieces, which is mostly slovenly done, suggests that the people of Masada were indifferent to the state of their often beautiful garments. If anything was torn, it was apparently mended rather quickly with any available patch or thread. The stress in which these people lived is evidently reflected in the deplorable state of their clothing.

An unexpected item among the fragments was a child's linen sock produced by an unusual technique similar to knitting (and indeed called "single needle knitting" by Burnham [1972]).[19] It is done with a needle and a short length of thread in which a single loop is worked through a single loop. The shape of the sock suggests that it was probably worn with the typical Roman sandal, many of which were found at Masada (Yadin 1966:57). On these socks the big toe is separated from the other toes by a leather thong. This linen sock from Masada is the earliest example of its kind in the Near East (see fig. 22).

19. This technique is known from many regions of the world, and in each region under a different name. Needlework textiles were apparently known in Denmark as far back as ca. 2500 B.C.E. (letter of 8.11.90 from Lis Dokkedol and Anne Botzer). But according to Hald, who calls this technique "looped needle netting," the earliest examples of it date from the first century C.E. (1980:299). Three wool fragments from Dura Europos (256 C.E.) are described by Bellinger as knitting (Pfister and Bellinger 1954:54ff., pl. XXVI), but careful examination shows them to have been done in the looped technique with the help of a needle. In Egypt socks made by this technique from red and yellow wool threads were dated to the fourth-fifth century C.E. (Kendrick 1921:88). At the beginning of the twentieth century this technique (called here "cross-knit looping") was still employed in Nigeria to produce ceremonial garments (Collingwood 1987:23).

Figure 23. *The wrapper from Masada.*

An outstanding item was found in the lower terrace of the northern palace at Masada: an embroidered wrapper 25 × 32 cm. in size, made from a blue wool material, now badly insect-damaged and faded. A double lining, also of wool, is sewn to it with running stitches. Unfortunately when opened nothing was found inside it.

The wrapper was probably intended for some precious scroll and, therefore, in keeping with its function, was elaborately embroidered. The Mishnah (*Kelim* 28:4) states that it was customary to decorate scroll wrappers in various ways. The decorated linen scroll wrappers found at Qumran had elaborate patterns of rectangles within each other, woven in blue linen threads in a complicated technique (G. Crowfoot 1955:24, fig. 4).[20] Three different kinds of embroidered stitches were used to finish the edges of the wrapper: an overcasting stitch, which secured a string around the cut edges; a decorative stitch resembling leaf-stitch; and a chain stitch.[21]

Along the wrapper's upper short edge (see fig. 23) is a special embroidery,

20. The complicated technique used to make the rectangular pattern is probably due to the religious significance of this form. Perhaps it was intended to represent a religious building (G. Crowfoot 1955:25). The multicolored wool fabrics found in the Cave of Letters were probably used as scroll wrappers (Yadin 1963:246).

21. I am grateful to Anne Morrell and Bracha Sadovski for deciphering the embroidery stitching and to Bracha Sadovsky for her useful remarks on the wrapper.

consisting of seven double triangles, six of them large and distinct, but the seventh small and pinched in as if by force. As is well known, the number seven had magical and mystical connotations in Jewish tradition, and these seven triangles probably had talismanic significance.

The embroidery appears to have been executed by two people, one an expert embroiderer and the other someone learning the craft, perhaps a mother and daughter. One may speculate that the small even stitches were executed by the expert mother while the larger uneven stitches were done by her apprentice daughter.

VII. Summary

At Kuntillet ʿAjrûd one can see that the ceremonial function of the sumptuous garments worn by the "priests" was reflected in the careful work expended on the stitching and mending of these garments. By their splendor, they were intended to make a lasting impression on those who saw them. By contrast, the slovenly work of the mending and patching on the once-beautiful garments of the Jerusalem fugitives in the Masada fortress tells much about their despairing psychological condition at this moment of their history. Even here, however, one notes that a concern for craftsmanship and aesthetics was not entirely absent, demonstrated by the carefully wrought sock and the embroidered wrapper, the two earliest such items known from the Near East.

Finally, we see that the different elements examined in this essay on the textile history of Palestine, such as the mended and stitched garments, the various kinds of sewing and needlework, and the embroidered wrapper, are held together in an intimate web of association with the Bible and the Mishnah.

Bibliography

Aharoni, Y.
1961   "Expedition B." *IEJ* 11:11-24.

Aharoni Y., et al.
1962   *Excavations at Ramat-Rahel, Seasons 1959, 1960.* Rome: Centro die studi semitici.

Albright, W. F.
1928   "The Second Campaign at Tell Beit Mirsim (Kiriath-Sepher)." *BASOR* 31:1-11.
1936-37   "The Excavation of Tel Beit-Mirsim, Vol. II: The Bronze Age," *AASOR* 17:37, 42-43, pl. 21a.

Alon, D.
1976   "Chalcolithic Temple at Gilat." *Qadmoniot* 36/4:102-5 (Hebrew).

Amir, Z.
1984   "The Embroidered Costume of the Women of Tuba-Tradition and Modernization in a Bedouin Village." *Edot* 1:3-16.

Amiran, R., and M. Tadmor
1980   "A Female Cult Statuette from the Chalcolithic Beer-Sheva." *IEJ* 30:137-39.

Bar-Adon, P.
1961   "Expedition C." *IEJ* 11:25-35.
1980   *The Cave of the Treasure: The Finds from the Caves in Nahal Mishmar.* Jerusalem: Israel Exploration Society.

Barber, E. J. W.
1982   "New Kingdom Egyptian Textiles: Embroidery vs. Weaving." *AJA* 86:442-45.
1991   *Prehistoric Textiles.* Princeton: Princeton University Press.

Bar-Yosef, O.
1985   *A Cave in the Desert: Nahal Hemar.* Jerusalem: Israel Museum.

Beck, P.
1982   "The Drawing from Horvat Teiman (Kuntillet Ajrud)." *Tel-Aviv* 9:3-86.

Bienkowski, P., ed.
1991   *Treasures from an Ancient Land: The Art of Jordan.* Wolfeboro Falls, NH: A. Sutton.

Burnham, D. K.
1972   "Coptic Knitting: An Ancient Technique." *Textile History* 3:117-24.

Carter, H.
1963   *The Tomb of Tut-ankh-Amen.* 3 vols. Reprinted New York: Cooper Square.

Collingwood, P.
1987   *The Maker's Hand.* Colorado.

Crowfoot, E.

1960   "Textiles, Matting and Basketry." Pp. 519-26 in K. M. Kenyon, *Excavations at Jericho*, vol. 1: *The Tombs Excavated in 1952-4*. London: British Society of Archaeology in Jerusalem.

1974   "The Textiles." In P. W. Lapp and N. L. Lapp. *Discoveries in Wadi ed-Daliyeh. AASOR* 46.60-77.

1982   "Textiles, Matting and Basketry." In K. M. Kenyon, *Excavations at Jericho*. 4.546-50. London: British School of Archaeology in Jerusalem.

Crowfoot, G. M.

1938   "Mat Impressions on Pot Bases." *AAA* 25:3-11.

1955   "The Linen Textiles." Pp. 18-38 in D. P. Barthélemy and J. T. Milik. *Quman Cave I*. DJD 1. Oxford: Clarendon.

1956   "Textiles, Basketry, and Mats." In S. Singer et al., eds. *History of Technology*. 7 vols. Oxford: Clarendon. 1954-78. 1.413-15.

Crowfoot, G. M., and N. de G. Davies

1941   "The Tunic of Tutankhamun." *JEA* 27:113-30.

Davies, N. de G.

1943   *The Tomb of Rekh-mi-re'at Thebes II*. New York: Metropolitan Museum of Art.

Davies, N. de G., and N. de G. Davies

1933   *The Tomb of Menkheperrasomb, Amenmose, and Others*. London.

Davies N. de G., and R. D. Faulkner

1947   "A Syrian Trading Venture to Egypt." *JEA* 33:40-46.

Desroches-Noblecourt, C.

1963   *Life and Death of a Pharaoh Tutankhamen*. London.

Dever, W. G.

1984   "Asherah, Consort of Yahweh? New Evidence from Kuntillet Ajrud." *BASOR* 255:21-37.

Dothan, M.

1959   "Excavations at Horvat Batar (Beersheva)." *Atiqot* 2:1-42.

Engberg, R. M.

1934   *Notes on the Chalcolithic and Early Bronze Pottery of Megiddo*. Chicago.

Engberg, R. M., and P. L. O. Guy.

1938   *Megiddo Tombs*. Chicago.

Frits, V., and A. Kempinski.

1983   *Ergebnisse der Ausgrabungen auf der Hirbet El-Masos (Tel-Masos) 1972-75*. Wiesbaden.

Hald, M.

1980   *Ancient Danish Textiles from Bogs and Burials*. Denmark.

Hallo, W. W., and W. K. Simpson
1971   *The Ancient Near East: A History.* New York: Harcourt Brace Jovanovich.

Hennessy, J. B.
1969   "Preliminary Report on a First Season of Excavation at Teleilat Ghassul." *Levant* 1:1-24.

Kendrick, A. F.
1921   *Catalogue of Textiles from Burying Ground in Egypt.* London.

Kenyon, K. M.
1960   *Excavations at Jericho,* vol. 1: *The Tombs Excavated in 1952-4.* London: British School of Archaeology in Jerusalem.
1965   *Excavations at Jericho,* vol. 2. Jerusalem.

Koppel, R.
1940   *Teleilat Ghassul II.* Rome.

Lemon, R., and G. M. Shipton
1939   *Megiddo I.* Chicago.

Loud, G.
1939   *The Megiddo Ivories.* Chicago.
1948   *Megiddo II.* Chicago.

Macdonald, E.
1932   *Beth-Pelet II.* London.

Mallon A., R. Koppel, and R. Neuvill
1934   *Teleilet Ghassul I.* Rome.

Matthiae, P.
1964   "The Painted Sherd of Ramat-Rahel." In Y. Aharoni. *Excavations in Ramat-Rahel 1961-1962.* Rome.

Mazar, B.
1989   "The House of Omri." *ErIsr* 20:215-19 (Hebrew).

Merhav R., and T. Ornan
1979   "The Attire of a Canaanite Goddess." *The Israel Museum News* 15:91-97.

Merhav, R.
1985   "The Stele of the 'Serpent Goddess' from Tell Beit Mirsim and the Plaque from Schechem Reconsidered." *The Israel Museum Journal* 4:27-42.

Meshel
1978   "Kuntillet Ajrud: An Israelite Religius Center in Northern Sinai." *Expedition* 20:50-54.

Perrot, J.
1955   "The Excavations at Tell Abu Matar near Beersheba." *IEJ* 5:17-40.
1959   "Statuettes en ivoire et autres objects en ivoire et en os provenant des gisements préhistorique de la region de Beersheba." *Syria* 36:8-19.

1964   "Les Ivories de la 7 Campagne de Fouilles a Safadi, pres de Beer-
            sheva." *ErIsr* 7:92-93.
1969   "Le Venus de Beersheva." *ErIsr* 9:100-101.
Petrie, W. F., and O. Tufnell
1930   *Beth-Peleth I.* London.
Pfister, R., and L. Bellinger
1954   "The Textiles." In M. I. Rostovtzeff et al. *The Excavations at Dura
            Europus — Final Report IV.* New Haven: Yale University.
Pritchard, J. B.
1963   *The Bronze Age Cemetery at Gibeon.*
Riefstahl, E.
1944   *Patterned Textiles in Pharaonic Egypt.* Brooklyn.
Roth, H. L.
1913-1978   *Ancient Egyptian and Greek Looms.* Halifax: Edford.
Schick, T.
1988a   "Nahal Hemar Cave Cordage, Basketry & Fabrics." *Atiqot* 18:31-43.
1988b   "A Neolithic Cult Headress from Nahal Hemar Cave." *Israel Musum
            Journal* 7:25-33.
Seger, J. D.
1976   "Reflections on the Gold Hoard from Gezer." *BASOR* 221:133-40.
Shapira, Y.
1964   "Mats from the Chalcolithic Period in Azur." *Teva Veeretz* 6:423-24
            (Hebrew).
Sheffer, A.
1976   "Comparative Analysis of a 'Negev Ware' Textile Impression from
            Tel-Masos." *Tel-Aviv* 3:81-88.
Sheffer, A., and A. Tidhar
1991   "Textiles and Basketry at Kuntillet Ajrud." *Atiqot* 20:1-26.
Shipton, G. M.
1939   *Notes on the Megiddo Pottery of Strata VI-XX.* Chicago.
Starkey, J. L., and L. Harding
1932   *Beth-Pelet II: Beth Peleth Cemetery.* London.
Tadmor, M.
1986   "Naturalistic Depictions in the Gilat Sculpture Vessels." *The Israel
            Museum News* 5:8-11.
Tufnell, O.
1984   *Studies in Scarab Seals.* Warminster.
Ussishkin, D.
1982   *The Conquest of Lachish by Sennacherib.* Tel Aviv.
Weiss, H.
1985   *Ebla to Damascus.* Washington.

Yadin, Y.
  1963   *The Finds from the Bar Kochba Period in the Cave of Letters.* Jerusalem.
  1966   *Masada.* Trans. M. Pearlman. New York: Random House.
Yadin, Y., et al.
  1961   *Hazor III-IV.* Jerusalem: Israel Exploration Society.
Zipper, I.
  1990   *At the Time the Canaanites Were in the Land.* Tel Aviv.

An Examination of the Prophetic Impetus in the Celtic and Norse Mythical Traditions in Juxtaposition with the Biblical Corpus

ASTRID B. BECK

University of Michigan

> Then Yahweh put forth his hand and touched my mouth. And Yahweh said to me, "Behold, I have put my words in your mouth. . . ." The word of Yahweh was addressed to me asking, "Jeremiah, what do you see?" "I see a branch of the Watchful Tree," I answered. Then Yahweh said, "Well seen! I too watch over my word to see it fulfilled."
>
> Jer 1:9-12

The prophetic word and its conception, delivery, and interpretation have been central to human religious belief and a people's relationship to their deity. In the biblical tradition, the primary focus has been on "Scripture," the written word and its observation of sacred tradition. As Scripture is connected to ritual, so it is also imbued with sanctity. In the Celtic and Nordic traditions, the relationship of language to religion is not scriptural. Their sacred word is not written and canonized. Rather, it rests on oral tradition, and it is more variable among the different cultures. Nonetheless, the prophetic word was also considered sacred.

These diverse traditions have common themes, and it is this commonality, specifically in terms of the prophetic word, that I wish to explore in this essay, as well as some fundamental differences. I shall begin with a description of imagery in the Nordic myths and include pertinent background information.

I will continue with an examination of the interrelationship between the prophetic voice and the perception of the prophet in the Celtic and Norse cultures in comparison with the biblical tradition. I will attempt to demonstrate important features that are unique to each of these cultures, giving examples from Celtic tales and Nordic sagas that shed light on this topic. In that sense, also, I will explore prophetic traditions in the biblical account. I hope, in the end, to have demonstrated significant points of contact in these traditions, as well as differences, that are specific to each of the cultural aspects, and to have enlisted the reader in this exploration.

I

We know of the Celtic and Norse religious beliefs primarily through their myths and legends, which are supplemented by archaeological evidence. Perhaps some have assumed these tales to be pure entertainment or the simple legends of a credulous people. The power of a myth is as much visual as verbal, however, and a major part of its impact lies not in its argument or *logos* but in its imagery, its metaphor. When we encounter

> the conception of the northern Ragnarok, when the gods go down fighting against the giants and the world is engulfed by fire and covered by the advancing sea, [we] may appreciate (better) the strength and power of the Scandinavian myths and . . . the religious beliefs which inspired them.[1]

Myths combine both the events and the images of the philosophy intrinsic to them. They incorporate these through the symbolism of the ritual or cosmogony inherent in the myths: the actions and their meanings.

It is relevant, then, that one should ask whether it is possible to fit the Celtic and Norse legends into a general pattern of Indo-European religious beliefs, extending far back into prehistory, as Dumézil believed, and to examine evidence about the religious practices and the conception of a supernatural world as background to the ancient tales. For example, the beliefs and mythology associated with battle indicate that the Celts and Vikings had few illusions about the nature of battle, and that the deities to whom they appealed for protection and aid were thought to be two-faced, with double personalities, like the description of Yahweh in the Hebrew Bible. Snorri Sturluson described Odin as fair and generous to his friends and terrible to his enemies. Yahweh is described in similar terms, as in the Song of Deborah: "So let all thine enemies perish, O Yahweh: but let them that love him be as the sun when he goes forth in his might" (Judg 5:31).

---

1. Ellis Davidson 1988:1.

Moreover, battle was associated with wisdom and inspiration, and the procuring of the heads of slaughtered victims was perceived as a means of attaining supernatural wisdom and knowledge in addition to its more obvious expression of destructive ferocity. The many descriptions of severed head motifs in the literature lend evidence to their cultic importance.[2] Those with powerful skills, like the druids, were sought out to work elaborate propitiatory magic[3] and thereby seek divine intervention to bring about the desired outcome. The battle mythology of these people provides some of the finest heroic poems and sagas. The horrors of blood, carnage, hideous wounds, and tragic heroic deaths are transmuted by the emphasis on fate and the imagery of supernatural guardians, protectors, and deities. The religion of the Celts was not superficial. It shaped their conception of the supernatural world and pervaded their attitude toward life and death.

The imagery of their underworld is a reflection of their world, a place of ice and eternal cold, much as the Judeo-Christian imagination depicts the underworld as one of fire and flame, perhaps a reflection of the burning desert sands that consume the exposed traveler, although this tradition has other aspects, like Gehenna and its eternally burning fires.

II

The origin and movements of the Celts as such remain elusive. The Greeks and Romans referred to them as *Keltoi* and *Celtae, Galatai* and *Galli*. The Greek *Keltoi* goes back to as early as 500 B.C.E., and may have been a corruption of the name *Galatai. Galli* may have been a shortened form.[4]

The Germans came into prominence in Europe in the first century C.E. According to Tacitus, *Germania* was the name of one tribe that came into general use and is linked with the Latin *germanus* ("brother"). The term *teutonic* is a Latinized form of the Anglo-Saxon *theodisc,* from *theod* ("people/nation"), a term also used by the Goths to denote themselves and their language. The earlier

---

2. The head was considered to contain the *essence* of the person, and severed heads were collected for cultic purposes. References to this practice are numerous in Celtic literature. Cross and Slover (1969) illustrates this aspect in many of the stories contained in the volume. We see this motif also in *Beowulf, The Mabinogi,* and *The Táin,* to mention only three. This practice is corroborated by the Greek and Roman historians. See also Ellis Davidson 1988:71ff.

3. Ellis Davidson (1988:150) cites some fine examples, such as a druidical fire that brought about a reversal in the outcome of a major battle. The literature has many such instances.

4. Elston 1934:3-4; for theories of the relationship between Celts and Germans see Evans 1982:233ff.

form *teuta* may have meant strength and power.[5] The early Irish invaders used this form; they were supposedly a godlike race called the *Tuatha de Danaan,* the people of the god Danaan, the ancestors of the Irish people.

The Celtic peoples invaded and overran most of Europe in the fifth and sixth centuries B.C.E., much as they later overran and destroyed Rome and portions of the Roman Empire.[6] Yet in spite of the threat that they posed, the Mediterranean peoples were fascinated by the Celts. They tended to idealize them as noble barbarians, led by druids who possessed the secrets of ancient wisdom.

The other set of peoples from northern Europe were the Scandinavians or Vikings, who were of the same heritage as the northern Germans. Church chroniclers used the term "Viking" (*vikingr* in Old Norse) to refer to pirates or raiding bands who burned and pillaged, and who had no respect for sacred church properties. Etymologically, the term derives from *vik* ("bay/fjord"). What we know of their character is similar to that of the earlier Celts and Germans, but while the continental Germans and Anglo-Saxons accepted Christianity fairly early, the Vikings held steadfast in their old religion until about 1000 C.E.

III

What was the role of the prophet in the Celtic and Norse societies as it is reflected in the mythological cycle, and what was the prophetic relationship to the deities? Chiefly, the prophet-sage-druid, *fili* or *thul,* was the one who carried out various rituals to obtain supernatural knowledge and to communicate with the gods or the ancient venerated ancestors. The prophets were the repositories of ancient wisdom, which they were to use toward beneficent ends for their people, in fecundity and regeneration as well as in battle prowess and victory. In the Old Norse literature, the *thul*'s function was to discern hidden wisdom. The word is derived from the verb *thylja,* "chant" or "murmur."

What was this ancient wisdom that the prophet was to discern and communicate to the people? In the Norse *Poetic Edda,* the poem *Voluspa* describes the revelation of a prophetess or *volva.* It depicts the creation of the world from chaos, the golden age of the gods, strife, treachery, and disaster, and the final cosmic catastrophe. Only *Yggdrasil,* the World Tree, survived, and a new world arose from the sea to signify a new age and a new generation of gods. In other words, the prophet revealed their theodicy as part of their cultural heritage. The

5. Evans 1982:247-48.
6. Piggott (1968: chap. 1) presents an excellent overview of the prehistoric account of the Celts, the height of their culture, and their migrations and early conquests.

poem displays great imaginative power, and its essential message is that fate is the supreme power to which all things are subject.

In this sense, divination, or the foretelling of the destiny of persons and peoples, is the key to the world picture of the Celtic peoples. In the Irish lore, the ancient poem *The Táin* is inspired by a prophetic vision. In the Norse poem *Hávamál,* the inquiry concerns the skills needed to use the runes as a source of wisdom. Here the deity, Odin, determines the messages of the runes. Odin recites:

> I peered at the world below, I seized the runes. . . . I learned nine powerful songs . . . then I began to thrive, my wisdom grew. . . . I prospered and was fruitful. One word gained me many words, one deed gained me many deeds. The charms I know are not known by the wives of kings or by any man.

He then goes on to recite eighteen charms that describe the mysteries of the power over the forces of nature, such as,

> I know a ninth: If I should need to save my ship in a storm, I can calm the wind that whips off wavecrests and puts the sea to sleep.

or,

> I know an eleventh: If I have to lead loyal, long-loved friends into a fight, I can sing behind my shield and they will go from strength to strength — unscathed to the battle, unscathed after battle; unscathed they return home.

or even,

> I know a twelfth: If I see a hanged man swinging from a tree, with his heels above my head, I can cut and colour the runes so that he will come down and talk to me.[7]

One should notice the power of the word in all this. It is the key element to the deed, the impetus to action. It is the word that can unlock the secrets of all the elements known to humanity: it is employed by the storm god Odin to calm the storm or to create it, it is the murmuring behind the shield that protects the battle warrior, it is the word in the form of a rune that gives Odin access to the wisdom of the dead. This is the wisdom of Odin that is imparted to humanity through the seer or prophet. It is this ancient wisdom and lore that unlocks the doors of secret knowledge.[8]

---

7. Crossley-Holland 1980:16-17.

8. One source of Odin's wisdom, as it is recounted in Snorri Sturluson's *Skaldskaparmal* (Poetic diction), which was to explain various *kennings* for poetry, concerns the man Kvasir, who was fashioned from the spittle of all the gods and was steeped in wisdom. He was killed by the dwarfs Fjalar and Galar. Through cunning, Odin drank up his essence, a sort of mead

IV

Now I will examine briefly the role of the prophet and the prophetic word in the biblical corpus. In the Joseph "novella," Joseph is a sage or diviner, a precursor to the later prophet,[9] as he haughtily reports his dreams and visions about the sheaves, and the sun, moon, and eleven stars, to his brothers and father. His brothers terribly resented him (Genesis 37): "They hated him yet the more for his dreams and for his words" (v. 8). But in Egypt, when they ask for an interpreter and Joseph interprets dreams, what does he say? He maintains, "Do not interpretations belong to God?" (40:8). When Pharaoh asks Joseph to interpret his dreams, Joseph responds, "It is not in me. Yahweh shall give Pharaoh an answer of peace" (41:16). Thus, one might view Joseph in the preprophetic or patriarchal tradition,[10] the seer, visionary, and patriarch: the venerated ancestor.

The biblical corpus makes clear that the prophet is understood to be the mouthpiece of God and that the word that the prophet utters is the word of God. Abraham is the first one called a prophet, but he, as well as Moses, is regarded as in the preprophetic tradition. As the biblical history unfolds, the prophetic role expands beyond that of only God's mouthpiece. One sees this, for example, with the prophet Amos. Here, the unusual relationship between God and prophet reveals important features of the divine personality. Amos's visions in chaps. 7–9 provide an outline and a guide both for the course of Amos's ministry and for the historical development of the prophetic message. Amos represents a turning point, the first of a new breed of prophets after a gap. He accuses the leadership of Israel of silencing the prophets, a possible reference to the bands of prophets established and led by Elijah and Elisha (Amos 2:12). There are prophets, certainly, but these merit neither respect nor title. They are hirelings of the court who give prophecy a bad name. Yet they have the ear of the king, whereas Amos's message turns out to be very unpopular at court (7:10-17).

When Amos sees the terrible visions of disaster in the forms of the locust plague and the great fire (chap. 7), he flings himself into the breach as intercessor for his people. He speaks first, before God does, and says, "O Lord God, forgive, I beseech you" (vv. 2, 5). Even more remarkable, Yahweh repents and affirms

---

the dwarfs had made of him, with which he flew back to Asgard. Some of this precious mead fell outside the wall of Asgard, and was offered from time to time to a man or two in Midgard. This was called the poetaster's portion. Cf. Crossley-Holland 1980:190ff.

9. See *ABD* 5.477-95, s.v. "Prophecy (ANE)," by Herb Huffmon; "Prophecy (Preexilic Hebrew)," by John J. Schmitt; and "Prophecy (Postexilic Hebrew)," by John Barton; as well as their bibliographies.

10. One might say that the preprophetic "tradition" was perhaps altered by later redactors to become part of a "prophetic" tradition, i.e., Abraham, Moses, even Joseph, were claimed to be "prophetic" at a later date. See also Wilson 1980:150-66.

both times, "It shall not happen" (vv. 3, 6). Thus, although Amos fits the traditional role of prophet in the sense that he proclaimed condemnation and predicted doom to his people for their transgressions against the deity, his speeches also reflect successful intervention and show that Amos's message from the beginning was tempered by provisionally suspended conviction and condemnation. Divine repentance was real, even though temporary.[11]

This brings us to the central point concerning the special relationship between the prophet and the deity that is unique to the biblical corpus:[12] divine decisions can be and are influenced by the specially chosen servant or prophet. It incorporates the ideas (1) that Yahweh is gracious, compassionate, and merciful; (2) that these are essential elements of his character; and (3) that he, above all, repents of evil. One sees this influence in his promise after the flood story, without prophetic intervention, but the idea becomes even more emphatic in the relationship between the deity and the prophet. The book of Amos not only portrays a speaking God — *deus loquens* — but also a listening God — *deus audiens*. In fact, the listening God appears first, because Amos speaks first in both instances after the first two visions, and only then does God respond (7:1-16). Thus we have a God who could not only reflect, reconsider, and change his mind, but who also did so in response to human intervention and intercession.

There are other important instances in the biblical corpus in which God repented or changed his mind, and in which the prophet played a predominant role in influencing the deity. Abraham attempted to intervene or intercede for Sodom and Gomorrah, although the deity has no real change of mind in that account. It seems clear that God would find a way to save the innocent (Lot and his family) while punishing the guilty.

In the famous episode in Exod 32:10-14, Moses intercedes with God, who decided to destroy his people in the wilderness because they made and were worshiping a golden calf. The intercession is effective and Yahweh changes his mind; he reverses an earlier decision:

> And now let me alone that my anger may burn against them, and that I may destroy them. . . . And Moses placated the face of his God Yahweh. And he said, "Why, O Yahweh, should your anger be kindled against your people, whom you brought out of the Land of Egypt with great strength and a mighty forearm? . . . Turn from your hot rage and repent about the evil to your people."

Moses reminded Yahweh of the promises he had made to Abraham and to Isaac. Verse 14 says:

---

11. See D. N. Freedman's outstanding "Excursus: When God Repents" (Andersen and Freedman 1989:638-79).

12. Ibid.

And Yahweh repented concerning the evil that he thought to do to his people.

Only then did Moses turn and come down from the mount with the tablets of the law. Divine repentance occurs in response to the intercession of Moses, the prophetic figure, who actually commanded God to repent. Moses uses the imperative *hnḥm* in Exod 32:12, which also occurs in the poetic version in Ps 90:13,

> Return Yahweh —
> and repent concerning your servants!

This psalm, attributed to Moses, is consistent with the view that in the Bible, only Moses used such forceful language with God.[13]

Another case of prophetic intervention occurs in 1 Sam 15:11, 29, 35. This is the story of Saul's rejection of Yahweh and represents the interaction between deity and prophet, prophet and king. As we know from other stories (cf. 1 Sam 7:5-9), Samuel has a reputation as an effective intercessor with the deity, and in this respect he is linked with Moses.

These stories illustrate the special relationship according to the biblical account of the prophet to the deity, one that is unique to Israel in its very personal relationship with its God. The relationship is personal, as Yahweh assumes personal responsibility for the people Israel. He makes covenants with them, just as he also punishes and exiles them for their transgressions. It is for the prophet to deliver the awful message. In the latter stages of the prophetic corpus, the people and their leaders not only resist the word, they also reject the messenger, as, for example, Amos.

V

We do not have documented evidence of this kind of interaction between prophet and deity in Celtic and Norse mythology. The position of *Thul* or *Druid* was an office held in high esteem in royal halls or courts. In the Anglo-Saxon poem *Beowulf*, the man Unferth in the court of Hrothgar, king of the Scyldingas or Danes, bears the title *thyle* (ll. 1165, 1456), the equivalent of *thulr*, "sage, orator," in an Old English gloss.[14] He sits at the feet of the king, the seat of honor, and interrogates Beowulf upon his arrival at the hall. The Old English poet states, "he onband beadurune" ("he unbound the battle*rune*," l. 501), indicating that he had prior knowledge of Beowulf concerning the hero's origin and past deeds, information that others apparently did not possess. It is inter-

13. See Freedman 1985.
14. Ellis Davidson 1988:155; also Klaeber 1950:148-50 and cl-cli.

esting to note the word *rune (beadurune)* as it is used in this context by the Beowulf poet. Unferth was adviser to the king, not necesssarily clairvoyant but certainly a man of high rank and esteem; and Beowulf generously honored him by returning to him the sword Hrunting, the cherished iron, as a gift of farewell.

In the heroic Irish tale *The Táin*, which describes the epic battle among the ancient tribes of Ireland, King Conchobar is featured as the majestic king par excellence of Ulster, surpassed by none, the founder of his tribe. A variant rendition reiterates the awe in which he was held: "all the knights knew that heavy was the king's hand, and fierce his wrath if provoked"; and "that his memory never failed."[15] He is described thus in *The Táin*: "Ulster grew to worship Conchobar . . . there was no wiser being in the world. He never gave a judgement until it was ripe, for fear it might be wrong or the crops worsen."[16] When the battle was at crisis stage and Sualdam offered the three final frenzied battle challenges to the Ulstermen, the poet says, "Nobody answered. In Ulster no man spoke before Conchobar, and Conchobar wouldn't speak before the three druids. Then a druid spoke. . . ."[17]

The deference paid to the druid at court as adviser to the king and pillar in the clan is unsurpassed in these cycles. In matters of gravity, the king kept silence until the druid had spoken. Never, in any stories, is a druid killed or even gainsaid. Cúchulainn, the epic hero in *The Táin*, who slaughtered thousands of Connacht heroes single-handedly, was never said to have killed any of Medb's druids, nor Medb any of Conchobar's. Diodorus speaks of the obedience given to them in peace and war, even by those who opposed them.[18] Their most powerful sanction was that of excommunication or exile,[19] like *kārēt* in the biblical tradition.

VI

Where does the term *druid* come from and what does it mean? In the classical texts, it appears only in the plural forms, *druidai* in Greek, and *druidae* or *druides* in Latin. In Old Irish, the word is *druí*, plural *druid*. Scholars have argued much over the probable etymology of the name, and current thinking tends to concur with those ancient scholars, such as Pliny, who thought the word was related to the Greek word for oak tree, *drus*. The second syllable is regarded as a cognate with the Indo-European root **wid-*, "know." Thus, according to Pliny, a sage

15. Pilkington 1965:136, 154, respectively.
16. Kinsella 1969:4.
17. Ibid., 219.
18. MacCulloch 1911:72.
19. Piggott 1968:109.

who has knowledge of the oak, possibly great deep knowledge, is a "seer" or "sage" (since knowledge was a matter of "seeing") or a "remembrancer" with the ability to obtain prior knowledge, to see the invisible, to communicate with the supernatural, especially with the symbol of the deity, the oak or other sacred tree. Strabo also mentions *vates*, which is cognate with the Irish *f'athi*, from a root meaning "inspired" or "ecstatic," and thence a prophet or poet, or a shaman.[20] The relationship with such a tree-word and its connections with knowledge seem plausible and appropriate, since Celtic religion and sanctuaries were intricately connected with oak forests and groves, and the specific association with the oak tree is attested.

Caesar reports on the organization of the druids in his *Gallic Wars*, and he describes the annual meetings of a druid assembly in a sacred place (*in loco consecrato*). The status of the prophets or druids in Celtic society was immediately below the rank of nobility, but exceptionally they could themselves be of highest rank. In the earliest hero tales, Conchobar, the high king of Ulster, had the druid Cathbad as his father. Cathbad himself was the leader of a warrior band while young, and was later his son's druid and adviser. In the Welsh cycle, *The Mabinogi*, Math was both a druid and a king in Mab. In the same source, Arawn, king of Annwfn, had druidical powers. This seems to corroborate the classical sources, in which Caesar described the Aeduan chieftain, Diviciacus, as both soldier and statesman, but Cicero described him as druid.[21] Cicero also claimed that King Deiotaurus was the most skillful augur of his people.[22]

VII

A word about women in the prophetic role seems appropriate in this context. As in the biblical corpus, some women as well as men could have the gift of prophecy and were sought out for this gift. Tacitus insisted on the importance of these women. He described one famous druid or seeress called Veleda of the Bructeri of the Rhineland, whose name was derived from *veles* ("seer"), presumably her professional title. According to Tacitus, Veleda "enjoyed extensive authority according to the ancient Germanic custom which regards many women as endowed with prophetic powers, and, as the superstition grows, attributes divinity to them."[23] Veleda was one of the arbitrators in an agreement between the Romans and the people of Cologne. She did not meet with the Roman representatives directly, but is said to have remained in a high tower

20. Ibid., 100ff.
21. Ibid.
22. Ibid.
23. Tacitus 1937: 4.61.

while one of her male relatives carried messages back and forth, "as if he were the messenger of a god."[24] Later, a captured Roman flagship was taken up the river and presented to Veleda.[25]

In the Irish literature, women have important functions within their societies, and that prominence carries over to seeresses as well. In *The Táin*, Cúchulainn woos Emer, whom we may call a seeress, because she predicts many battles and feats of arms for his short life. Their meeting is beautifully described:

> Cúchulainn himself went to a place called the Gardens of Lug — Luglochta Logo — to woo a girl he knew there. Her name was Emer and she was the daughter of Forgall Monach, the cunning. . . . She was out on the green with her foster sisters . . . they were studying embroidery and stitching with Emer. Cúchulainn greeted the troop of girls and Emer lifted up her lovely face. She recognized Cúchulainn, and said: "May your road be blessed!" "May the apple of your eye see only good," he said. Then they spoke together in riddles.[26]

She predicts the epic battle central to the story of *The Táin:*

> "no man will travel this country," she said, "who hasn't gone sleepless from Samain, when the summer goes to its rest, until Imbolc, when the ewes are milked at spring's beginning; from Imbolc to Beltine at the summer's beginning and from Beltine to Brón Trogain, earth's sorrowing autumn."[27]

The festivals she recites are the ritual sacred feasts that mark the Celtic year. Cúchulainn's epic battle will revolve around the cycle of sacred time. Note also that Emer is the headmistress of the symbolic art of stitching, which carries implications of fate and foretelling, much as do the Greek Parcae. That they speak in riddles has druidic implications. The poet does not relate these riddles, much as the druidic riddles were kept secret and are not borne out in the literature or in the texts.

It is in the otherworld that Cúchulainn begins his serious study of "brave deeds and craft of arms" with his chief teacher, Scátach. "Scátach spoke to him of his future and his end. She chanted to him through the *imbas forasni*, the Light of Foresight."[28] Scátach is a druid, a poet, a diviner, a trainer-at-arms. Her poem is elegiac; she ends, as she began, with the words: "I salute you," but she wisely withholds from Cúluainn his final end.

At the onset of battle, Queen Medb consults Fedelm for prophecy, who is described thus,

---

24. Ibid., 65.
25. Ibid., 5.22. See also Ellis Davidson 1988:159.
26. Kinsella 1969:26-27.
27. Ibid., 27.
28. Ibid., 34.

She held a light gold weaving-rod in her hand, with gold inlay. Her eyes had triple irises. Two black horses drew her chariot, and she was armed. "What is your name?" Medb said to the girl. "I am Fedelm, and I am a woman poet of Connacht."

"Where have you come from?" Medb said.

"From learning verse and vision in Alba," the girl said.

"Have you *imbas forasni,* the Light of Foresight?" Medb said.

"Yes I have," the girl said.

"Then look for me and see what will become of my army." So the girl looked.

Medb said, "Fedelm, prophetess, how seest thou the host?"

Fedelm said in reply:

"I see it crimson, I see it red."

Fedelm continues to recite this motif, even though Medb counters:

"It doesn't matter. . . . Wrath and rage and red wounds are common when armies and large forces gather. So look once more. . . ."

And Fedelm repeats, and adds,

"I see a battle: a blond man with much blood about his belt and a hero-halo round his head. His brow is full of victories. . . . In thousands you will yield your heads. I am Fedelm. I hide nothing."[29]

The confrontation between mature queen and young prophetess is dramatic. The biblical narrative has a similar confrontation between Saul and Samuel, after Saul's battle with Agag and the Amalekites, when both God and Samuel turn their backs on Saul and he becomes a tormented king (1 Samuel 15, 16). The particular details of the confrontation between ruler and prophet are different in the sense that Queen Medb has not disobeyed the deity. Nonetheless, Medb rejects the seriousness of the prophetic word, and therein lies the key to the confrontation in both cases.

Let us briefly examine the role of women prophets in the biblical narrative. There are not many, so that their appearance is all the more remarkable. In 2 Samuel 14, after David banished his son Absalom for murder of his brother, Joab wants him restored to favor. Joab sends to the town of Tekoa for a "wise woman" and instructs her. She is clearly a professional, a female seer, who is described as wise because she has extraordinary knowledge or insight.[30]

---

29. Ibid., 60-63.

30. She is considered a female sage, and she has been characteristically grouped in the wisdom tradition. But I would maintain that she can also be properly placed in the prophetic tradition, for she clearly exhibits qualities of leadership. See Claudia V. Camp, "The Female Sage in the Biblical Wisdom Literature," in Gammie and Perdue 1990:185-203, esp. 187-88; also R. N. Whybray, "The Sage in the Israelite Royal Court," in ibid., 133-39, esp. 135.

Deborah, another woman prophet in the biblical account, is called "proph-etess" in Judges 4. She is one of the judges, clearly a military figure, and she is the one who sends for Barak to gather armies and chariots to command the attack against Sisera and the Caananites. Barak demands that she accompany him to battle. Her role is significant. She not only directs the general and forecasts the outcome of the battle, but she also tells Barak that he will not receive glory for this feat; rather the honor shall go to a woman, namely, Jael. Then, in true prophetic fashion, she celebrates and recounts the event in her heroic Song of Deborah (Judges 5).

Another prophetess, Miriam, the sister of Moses, is restricted in her role as prophet. She directs the maidens of Israel in song and dance, in recounting the dramatic battle in the Song of the Sea (Exodus 15). There is some dispute as to whether she and Aaron share in the gift of prophecy, along with Moses, and things turn out badly for her. Nonetheless, she is celebrated as a significant member of this gifted and magical family.[31]

Huldah, also, is an important woman prophet who lived in the days of Josiah the king. She predicted a peaceful death for Josiah, which turned out to be untrue, for he was killed at Megiddo (2 Kings 22). Here is a classic case of unfulfilled prophecy. She was very much respected at court, unlike Jeremiah,[32] and seems to be at the top of her field.

VIII

One of the specific functions of druids was to determine holy places and sacred landmarks. These were established for the burial of the noble dead and the enactment of the laws. We can identify a number of these sites. They dominate the landscape of mountains, glaciers, and the winding coastline in splendid fashion, much like Mount Carmel dominates the coastal plain or Mount Sinai dominates the surrounding region. They are like the seats of the gods. No violence could be committed on the hill, humans and animals were protected from injury there, and the sagas say that men should not look on the hill unwashed.

MacCulloch interprets the verb *líta* used in the sagas to mean to turn toward the sacred site in prayer and supplication.[33] When Iceland made it a

31. Phyllis Trible, lecture at the University of Michigan, November 16, 1987, as part of the Visiting Professor of Religious Thought series. See also Trible 1984, 1989. Also Wilson 1980:155.

32. Although Jeremiah did have his good days, e.g., Jer 37:3-4. See Pauline Viviano, "Hulda," *ABD* 3.321. See also Lundbom 1975, as well as idem, "Jeremiah, Book of," *ABD* 3.706-21.

33. MacCulloch 1911:310.

policy to accept Christianity as the national religion in 1000 C.E., the national assembly met at the *Althing* at the summer solstice on the sacred mount at *Thingvellir* to decide on the new laws. Much ceremony was associated with this decision. Ari Thorgilsson records the prophet/lawspeaker Thorgeirr's "inspired" pronouncement. Thorgeirr was accepted as "lawspeaker" because he was a pagan, but he was highly respected by the Christian camp. According to the account, Thorgeirr

> sequestered himself, lying under a cloak for part of a day and a night . . . he received assurances that both sides would abide by his ruling, since "if we divide the law we will also divide the peace." . . . Then it was made law that all people should become Christian and that those who here in the land were yet unbaptized should be baptized; but as concerns the exposure of infants, the old laws should stand, as should those pertaining to the eating of horse-flesh. If they wished, people might sacrifice to the old gods in private, but it would be lesser outlawry [*fjörbaugsgarthr*] if this practice were verified by witnesses. But a few years later this custom was abolished, as were the others.[34]

On the most hallowed of Celtic festivals, Samain (eve of October 31), the onset of winter and the beginning of the sanctified Celtic calendar year, the ancient Celts believed that on that night the way lay open to the otherworld and could be entered by living human beings through the sacred mounds. At the consecrated feasts held at this time, men and women partook of animals sacrificed to the gods. They ate and drank to honor the gods and to renew contact with the supernatural world.

In the Norse tradition, horses were often used for such divination. In the *Heimskringla*, Snorri Sturluson described a horse sacrifice in the saga of Hakon the Good, in which the Christian king Hakon was forced to take part against his will. His followers wanted him to sacrifice for good seasons and peace, in the tradition of his fathers. Sigurd, Jarl of Halogaland, the prophet of the king, presided and hallowed the bowls to Odin. The king made the sign of the cross over it, but Jarl interpreted that as the hammer sign to Thor for the assembly. On the second day, the king refused to partake of the horse sacrifice, but Sigurd urged him to touch the greasy handle of the cauldron with his lips. But the king put a linen cloth over it and the people were not satisfied. During the midwinter feast, again a horse was sacrificed and the king agreed to eat a little of the liver and to drink from the *minni* bowls, the bowls containing the blood of the horse, for it was important that the king consume some of the sacrificial blood, since the welfare of the land depended on this. In spite of his Christian scruples, Hakon was a popular king, the land prospered during his reign, and the poem composed at his death in 961 praised him warmly because he had dealt rever-

---

34. *Islendigabok*, chap. 7, in Byock 1988:142.

ently with holy places. He was represented by the prophet as a welcome warrior in Odin's hall.[35]

The *Ynglinga Saga* narrates that when the bodies of the followers of Odin were burned, the direction and height of the smoke were interpreted as signs of how Odin had received the dead. This is reminiscent of biblical sacrifice and the frequent expression that God smelled the sweet odor of the sacrifice, implying that it was pleasing to him. The funeral fire as a sign of the fate of the dead is borne out by Ibn Fadlan who watched and described the funeral of a Scandinavian chief on the Volga in 921. The Scandinavians told him, "Out of love of him his lord has sent his wind to take him away," as the funeral fire burned up the ship and its contents.[36] The *Beowulf* epic, for example, corroborates the sacred aspect of the funeral fire. We are told of Beowulf's funeral pyre: *"heofon rēce swealg"* ("heaven swallowed the smoke," l. 3155).

The votive offerings after battle were of great significance to the Celts, and their manner of dealing with booty is of some interest. Julius Caesar describes such offerings in his *Gallic War*:

> To Mars, when they have determined on a decisive battle, they dedicate as a rule whatever spoil they may take. After a victory they sacrifice such living things as they have taken, and all the other effects they gather into one place. In many states heaps of such objects are to be seen piled up in hallowed spots and it has not often happened that a man, in defiance of religious scruple, has dared to conceal such spoils in his house or to remove them from their place, and the most grievous punishment, with torture, is ordained for such an offence.[37]

Such a crime against the deity is interpreted as sin, for which the entire people are responsible, as also in Joshua, where Achan "took some of the devoted things; and the anger of the Lord burned against the people of Israel" (7:1). Achan's crime against God implicated all Israel. As the biblical account states, "Israel has sinned . . . they have taken some of the devoted things . . . therefore the people of Israel cannot stand before their enemies" (7:10-12). Because of this sin Israel deemed it lost the battle against Ai. The punishment was death for Achan and his household, his sons and daughters, his oxen, asses, and sheep — all that he had — in other words, *kārēt:* "All Israel stoned him with stones; they burned them with fire, and stoned them with stones" (7:25). Here we also have one of the few accounts in the biblical narrative of the burning of the dead.

---

35. *Hákonarmál;* see also Ellis Davidson 1988:55ff.
36. Smyser 1965:101.
37. Caesar 1917: 6.17.

IX

I have explored and tried to elucidate the importance of the role of the prophet in these different cultures, and their relationships with their deities. Often the primary sources stand in the way between us and the people who accepted the myths as truths. In the Celtic and Norse, more so than in the biblical corpus, the filters of imagination, fragmented manuscripts, prejudice, and contempt arising out of conflicting religious beliefs and hindsight obscure the view. Still, the body of material that remains proffers a glimpse into the inherent values held by these peoples, and the importance that they attributed to their deities. The connecting link between people and divinity was the prophet, who served as the mouthpiece for the deity. The prophet was not only the source and repository of knowledge, but also the interpreter of divine law, the propitiator for the people, and occasionally the intercessor on their behalf. In that sense, there is an affinity among these cultures in their perception of the persona who served as the connecting link between deity and human offspring. Just as prophets interpreted for the king and the people in the Celtic and Nordic cultures, so also was their influence deemed crucial for the survival and welfare of the people in the biblical tradition.

Bibliography

Andersen, F. I., and D. N. Freedman
  1989   *Amos.* AB 24A. New York: Doubleday.

Byock, Jesse L.
  1988   *Medieval Iceland.* Berkeley: University of California.

Caesar, Julius.
  1917   *De bello Gallico.* Trans. H. J. Edwards. LCL. Cambridge: Harvard University.

Chickering, Howell D., Jr., ed.
  1977   *Beowulf: A Dual Language Edition.* New York: Doubleday.

Cross, T. P., and C. H. Slover, eds.
  1969   *Ancient Irish Tales.* New York: Barnes and Noble.

Crossley-Holland, Kevin, ed.
  1980   *The Norse Myths.* New York: Random House.

de Vries, Ján
  1961   *Keltische Religion.* Stuttgart: Kohlhammer.

Dumézil, Georges.
  1959   *Les dieux des germains, essai sur la formation de la religion scandinave.* Paris: Presses universitaires de France. ET: *Gods of the Ancient Northmen.* Ed. Einar Haugen. Berkeley: University of California, 1973.

Ellis Davidson, Hilda R.
1988   *Myths and Symbols in Pagan Europe.* New York: Syracuse University.

Elston, Charles Sidney.
1934   *The Earliest Relations Between Celts and Germans.* London: Methuen.

Evans, D. E.
1982   *Celts and Germans.* Bull Board. Celtic Studies 29 (ii). Pp. 230-55.

Ford, Patrick K., trans. and ed.
1977   *The Mabinogi.* Berkeley: University of California.

Freedman, David Noel
1985   "Who Asks (or Tells) God to Repent?" *BibRev* 1/4:56-59.

Gammie, John G., and Leo G. Perdue, eds.
1990   *The Sage in Israel and the Ancient Near East.* Winona Lake, IN: Eisenbrauns.

Gelling, M.
1961   "Place-Names and Anglo-Saxon Paganism." *University of Birmingham Historical Journal* 8:7-25.

Gregory, Augusta
1905   *Gods and Fighting Men.* London: John Murray. (Tuatha De Danann)

Grimm, Jacob
1882-88   *Teutonic Mythology.* Trans. J. S. Stallbrass. 4 vols. London: G. Bell and Sons.

Jóhannesson, Jón
1974   *A History of the Old Icelandic Commonwealth.* Trans. H. Bessason. University of Manitoba Icelandic Studies 2. Winnipeg: University of Manitoba.

Kinsella, Thomas, trans.
1969   *The Táin.* Oxford: Oxford University.

Klaeber, Fr.
1950   *Beowulf and the Fight at Finnsburg.* 3rd ed. Lexington, MA: D. C. Heath.

Lundbom, Jack R.
1975   *Jeremiah: A Study in Ancient Hebrew Rhetoric.* SBLDS 18. Missoula, MT: Scholars.

MacCulloch, John A.
1911   *The Religion of the Ancient Celts.* Edinburgh: T. & T. Clark.

Nordal, S., ed.
1978   *Voluspa.* Trans. B. S. Benedikz and J. McKinnell. Durham and St. Andrew Medieval Texts 1. Durham: University of Durham.

Owen, Gale R.
1985   *Rites and Religions of the Anglo-Saxons.* Dorsett: Dorsett.

Piggott, S.
1968   *The Druids.* London: Thames and Hudson.

Pilkington, F. H. ed.
1965 "Deidre and the Sons of Uisne." Pp. 127-232 in *The Three Sorrowful Tales of Erin.* London: Bodley Head.

Powell, T. G. E.
1958 *The Celts.* London: Thames and Hudson.

Procopius
1914 *History of the Wars.* 6.15.5-6. Trans. H. B. Dewing. LCL. New York: Macmillan.

Rolleston, T. W.
1986 *Myths and Legends of the Celtic Race.* New York: Schocken.

Smyser, H. M.
1965 *Ibn Fadlan's Account of the Rus: Medieval and Linguistic Studies in Honour of Francis Peabody Magoun Jr.* Ed. G. Bessinger and R. P. Creed. London: Thames and Hudson.

Tacitus, Cornelius
1937 *Historiae.* Trans. Clifford H. Moore. LCL. Cambridge: Harvard University.

Trible, Phyllis
1984 *Texts of Terror: Literary-Feminist Readings of Biblical Narratives.* OBT. Philadelphia: Fortress.
1989 "Five Loaves and Two Fishes: Feminist Hermeneutics and Biblical Theology." *TS* 50:279-95.

Turville-Petre, E. O. G.
1964 *Myth and Religion of the North: The Religion of Ancient Scandinavia.* Westport, CT: Greenwood.

Wilson, Robert R.
1980 *Prophecy and Society in Ancient Israel.* Philadelphia: Fortress.

An Orange Peeling (A Chapter from *The Book of the State*): A Translation of S. Y. Agnon's Short Story *"Qlypt tpwḥ zhb"*

CHRIS FRANKE

The College of St. Catherine, St. Paul, Minnesota

An orange peeling was thrown in a public place, one of those peelings that you find examples of in the alleys and in the streets and around every corner. Everyone that passed by it, by the peeling, bumped into it. A fastidious person would stop and check his shoes to see whether they were dirty, then walk on; a person who wasn't fastidious would drag his feet and walk right over it. But, even if seven pairs of eyes were given to a person these wouldn't be enough to look after every peeling that might lie in the way. The peeling was lying there, and everyone who passed it bumped into it. One old man slipped and fell. He collected himself and got up. And the very thing that happened to the old man happened to a young woman. And if her bones weren't scattered about, the things from her case were scattered about: a mirror and a comb for her head, golden dust for her hair, and red powder with which to paint her lips and her nails, and oil for anointing, and cosmetics for applying, and love notes of the husband of her girlfriend, and the rest of the things she carried for the gratification of body and soul. Since this young woman was not old and was not ugly, everyone ran to help her and they picked up her scattered things. An orange peeling certainly wasn't one of those things, and it was left lying where it was.

Malcontents, the kind of people who always see themselves as objects of discrimination, saw the peeling and became jealous of it, because it just lay there comfortably and was the cause of damage, sorrow, and shame, and it didn't have a care in the world. Because their jealousy grew, so did their anger. They began to be resentful and angry about all the tranquility of the world and about the peeling. But the moderates of the country who put logic before feelings looked at it — at the peeling — with an indulgent eye and said, "It's not about the peeling that we complain, but about whom do we complain? About the one who threw the peeling! A glutton like him, filling his belly with oranges, and throwing the peelings away, and increasing the number of injured people in the country!" Others, who had no concern with any ideas except for those that had to do with politics but couldn't resist criticizing anything that related to the government, said, "It's not about the one who threw that we are complaining, but about the town council, which didn't send its workers out to sweep up the peeling. Anyway, what did he do? Eat an orange! After all, was it imported produce that he ate? He ate native-grown produce! If only there would be more like him in the country, who are content with what the country provides, and don't demand imported products bought with foreign currency. But the town council that didn't clean up the peeling — it should be reprimanded! Taxes are raised, and what does it give us? Fruit peelings it gives! Is the only task of the country to raise taxes without doing a thing?"

Someone heard what he heard and said, "On your life, if the tax collector comes, I'll lock my house against him! Surely it is better that we protect ourselves in a responsible way with our taxes, so that what happened to the old man when the peeling struck him and he slipped and fell won't happen to us."

A wife of a government worker stood up and cried out: "Oy, oy! It was on a peeling just like this that my mother-in-law broke her foot. She was minding her own business going wherever she goes when it struck her — this peeling of an orange or of a grapefruit or perhaps of a banana or the devil knows what kind of peeling it was — and she slipped and fell and broke her right (or was it her left?) foot. Seven changes of rotten bedding from all this lying down! Do you think when she got up from her affliction that it was better for me? When she was groping her way around the house and rattling her cane, I picked myself up and fled the country! Since the days of the last congress I haven't experienced the fresh air from abroad." Then, because they were reminded of the congress, they began discussing it.

The peeling continued to lie there and it became dirtier and dirtier until its outside turned dark yellow and its splendor was lost. But this peeling was lucky and it wasn't forgotten like its companions that were lying in the garbage since the days of the first congress when no one paid any attention to them.

There was a grammarian in the country who used to follow all the conversations of the common folk and correct their errors. He saw the peeling and looked for something in it that might need fixing. He grabbed whoever he grabbed and said to him: "What do you say of this peeling?" He said to him: "What is there to say? It is a peeling like all other peelings!" He said to him: "That's not what I mean! It's not about the peeling that I'm asking, but about the spelling that I am asking! All the time I'm telling people that to write "peeling" with a *yod* is an out-and-out mistake. But still, the world, as usual, keeps on writing "peeling" with a *yod*, and because of this flaw we ought to go into mourning."

Again there was a fear that because of the spelling of "peeling" people would forget the peeling. But, as we said, the peeling was lucky and it was taken up again as an item of conversation in the mouths of the people. At that point, someone passed by and whoever it was that passed by saw the peeling. He said to them, to those standing by it: "I'm astonished that no one is taking a photograph of the peeling, and that no one is publishing it in the newspapers. But first, they have to ask those kinds of people who like to form committees and they will turn to the writers to appeal in their articles to people to contribute money for the photographs so they will recognize that it was likely to be a hazard for people moving to and fro. Even people in the diaspora will not hold back from contributing. Moreover, it is necessary that the photographs be made by photographers who are specialists in order that the eyes of our relatives in the diaspora will feast on these mirrors of the land."

One of the men stood up and said: "How can you find fault in this peeling? On the contrary, it is a sign of freedom, that every one in the country can act as if it were his own property." Another man stood up and said to that man who wanted freedom in the midst of garbage: "This thing that we are doing is spoken of in the Gemara — 'don't make garbage in Jerusalem.'"

It happened that there was an old man who went around the city, begging for torn pages of the Bible. He said to him: "Have you fulfilled all the obligations of the Gemara except for this one? Leave the Gemara to whoever has fulfilled its commands! Look at those people that don't even cover their heads anymore. It is not enough that they took over the Bible. Now they are even coveting the Gemara!"

The official chronicler of the state was afraid that perhaps matters would come to the point of a serious fight. He wanted to pick up the peeling that caused the enmity and jealousy. He bent down and picked up the peeling and put it in the place he put it in. One woman saw this and said: "What about all the rest of the peelings? And what about the rest of the papers and the newspapers and other kinds of rubbish that the whole city is filled with? I ask you, mister, look — there's a peeling of an apple, and there is a peeling of a grapefruit and there is a carcass of a book, and there is a broken trap with a dead mouse in it; are these going to lie there like that until they make the air foul?"

Another man heard the conversation and said to her: "Take it easy, lady! Look here, the land is destined to be partitioned, and at this point, no one knows which part of this place will belong to whom. Maybe it will fall into the hands of the enemy. If so, what does it matter to us whether this garbage is lying around?" Because he reminded them about the partitioning of the land, they jumped on him and began to fight with him. So he cried out: "What do you want from me? Did I say anything about wanting the partition? I said nothing more than what is written in the newspaper." They went on yelling. The official chronicler of the state said to himself: "Partition or no partition, as long as we are settled here we should clear up all the garbage." He bent down and began to pick up the rubbish.

Because he began picking up the rubbish, everyone began helping with words of advice, some with good advice, some with better advice — how to pick up the peelings and where to throw them, and on and on in a similar vein. With such advice they could support an entire empire!

Not all the advice was the same. The official chronicler of the state took a peeling of an orange to throw it, and someone came and advised him to take grapefruit peelings first. He took the grapefruit, and came another and advised him to take banana. He took a banana peeling, and came another and said: "No, take some other peeling first!"

In order to satisfy all of their wishes, the official chronicler of the state began working with both hands simultaneously. But the expert advisers were in the majority while the hands of the man were in the minority. While this one was trying to do what each man wanted, the rest of the expert advisers got together and began discussing what was worthwhile to pick up first and what was worthwhile to pick up last. And in the midst of their discussion they begin to quarrel.

Now it's time for the official chronicler of the state to speak about something new, something that doesn't happen every day. As a rule, the country was used to seeing its people quarrel, and there wasn't any policeman to come and stop the quarrel, but at that very moment, suddenly, up jumped a policeman, and he was angry about the crowd that caused a quarrel in a public place. They saw that the policeman was not happy about the situation, so they drifted away. When the official chronicler of the state saw that they were drifting away, he said to himself: "Now no one will make you stop your work." Quickly, he doubled his efforts and continued picking up till the street began to be a little bit cleaner.

The policeman saw the official chronicler of the state standing alone in the street, and he called to him and said to him, "You, you caused this unruly crowd!" He brought out his notebook and wrote his name in it in order to charge him in court with causing unlawful assemblies in the street and creating scandals.

The official chronicler of the state said to him, "Permit me, sir, and I will tell you the heart of the matter, how it was. The fact is that I was passing through the street and I saw a peeling lying there in the public place, a hazard to those moving to and fro, and no one picked it up. I said to myself 'let me go and pick it up,' and once I began I was drawn into picking up the whole street."

The policeman clicked his tongue, and said: "So, you admit you were engaged in picking up the garbage?" Said the official chronicler of the state, "There's no denying it. The things I told you are truthful, sir, and I am prepared to say these things again." Said the policeman: "Do you have a license to work?" Once again he brought out his notebook and slapped on more charges because here was a case of someone passing himself off as a professional without the proper license. But the policeman, to his credit, did not take me with him since that very hour was the hour of the afternoon meal, the mealtime for everyone, and he was in a big hurry to eat. The official chronicler of the state stopped and looked at the garbage and said to himself, "Woe to the one that wants to pick up a little of the garbage in the country, and what about the fate of the country that still hasn't cleaned up its own rubbish!"

About twenty-five years ago, I sat in a classroom at San Francisco Theological Seminary, in San Anselmo, California, with about forty other students, most of them seminarians. We were waiting for the professor who was going to teach us to read the Hebrew Bible. There was an air of anticipation in the classroom — we didn't know what to expect from the professor. All we knew about Hebrew was the letters of the alphabet, the names and sounds of which we had been instructed to memorize beforehand. The professor strode into the classroom, with teaching assistants following. The assistants passed out Hebrew Bibles to each of us and then waited for the fun to begin.

The professor explained the procedure that he would follow through the next three weeks of this Hebrew class. Each of our names was written on a 3 × 5 card. He would call on the person named on the card, and ask that person to read the passage in question. After each person had been called on, the cards would be shuffled, and in a different order we would be asked to read again. This meant that it would be useless to try to count ahead to the verse or passage that would come to you. You never knew when your name would be called, so you had to pay attention to what the professor was teaching.

"Open your Bible to 1 Samuel 3, and we will begin to read," said the professor. An air of confusion now began to take over. Many of us thought, "I must be in the wrong room — this seems to be the advanced class!" We were assured that indeed this was the beginning Hebrew class, and instructed that this is the way we would learn to read Hebrew — by reading it. Memorize paradigms? Not for beginning students! We were to learn vocabulary — five hundred words by the end of the first week, to be exact. Confusion was replaced by shock, fear, disbelief. Then, when the professor called on the first student, and asked him to read from 1 Sam 3:1, the realization began to dawn that this would be no ordinary first-year language class.

The experience changed the way I thought about language and about learning and teaching language. More important, it was my first encounter with this phenomenal teacher-scholar-editor, who has become an important part of my life as a teacher and scholar.

Several years ago, when we discussed the creation of this *Festschrift,* I was once again studying Hebrew, this time Modern Hebrew at the University of Minnesota. I had planned to write an article for the *Festschrift* on the poetic structure of Isa 44:9-20. During my study of Modern Hebrew, however, the intriguing and mysterious stories of S. Y. Agnon, an Israeli author and the winner of the Nobel Prize for Literature, captured my attention. In the end, I decided to make my own translation of one of these stories and contribute it to this *Festschrift*. After all, it was Noel Freedman, my first teacher of Hebrew, who made this venture into Modern Hebrew a possibility.

I selected this particular Agnon story — *qlypt tpwḥ zhb* — because of the many elements that Noel would especially appreciate. It is a satirical piece on politics in Israel, but it can be understood and appreciated by anyone who has dealt with politics and bureaucracies at any time and in any place. This is a story about ordinary people in all their glory and folly (mostly folly), and is told with great wit. No one appreciates a good sense of humor more than Noel Freedman. Finally, this story has a character — the grammarian — who is concerned about *plene* and defective spelling. No one can appreciate this concern as much as Noel.

This story, like most of Agnon's work, can be read and interpreted on many levels. Agnon draws on the entire corpus of Hebrew literature from ancient to modern in the crafting of his stories. The title and theme of this story, an orange peeling (lit. "a golden apple peeling"), I believe plays on a line in Prov 25:11, the only place in the Bible where the phrase *tpwḥy zhb* occurs. The proverb emphasizes the value of well-spoken words, of good advice given to a receptive learner. This would heighten the irony in the story, which has an overabundance of words of advice and a dearth of deeds.

While this translation is somewhat of a departure from what is expected in a *Festschrift*, it is meant to reflect in a small way some of the many lessons I learned from my teacher, and to thank him for his generous spirit.

Jewish Christianity and Its Significance for Ecumenism Today

HANS KÜNG

Institut für ökumenische Forschung, Tübingen

translated by Astrid B. Beck*

To David Noel Freedman
my colleague and friend
in gratitude for our time together at the
University of Michigan, a time both fruitful
in scholarly accomplishments and deeply fulfilling

In his *Church History*,[1] Eusebius reports that the early Jewish-Christian community of Jerusalem left that city after the execution of James and before the outbreak of the Jewish-Roman War in the year 66 C.E., and that they settled in Pella in Transjordan. This has been disputed.[2]

---

*The German quotations in the text are also translated by Astrid B. Beck. The original German is cited below in the footnote.

1. Eusebius, *Church History (Historia Ecclesiastica)* 3.5.3a.

2. According to M. Joël (1883) and then E. Schwartz, S. G. F. Brandon, and J. Munck, and in particular, with modification, G. Luedemann, *Opposition to Paul in Jewish Christianity* (trans. M. Eugene Boring; Minneapolis: Fortress, 1989) 200-213: appendix, "The Successors of Earliest Jerusalem Christianity: An Analysis of the Pella Tradition." Most recently, the dissertation by J. Verheyden attempted to prove through the redaction-historical method that Eusebius (dependent on Epiphanius) himself sketched the Pella memorandum for reasons of (anti-Jewish) historical-theological motives: "De vlucht van den Christenen naar Pella. Onderzoek van het getuigenis van Eusebius en Epiphanius" (Brussels, 1988).

I. The End of the Early Christian Community of Jerusalem

Why, however, should an emigration be dismissed out of hand, considering that Jesus himself deliberately rejected being chosen as "king," which meant serving as leader of an anti-Roman revolt? What has been transmitted to us in the Sermon on the Mount as a whole is the opposite of an ideology of national revolt against the Roman Imperium; it is a message of nonviolence. It is in line with the orientation of the prophets Isaiah and Jeremiah, who expressly warned against war, specifically against armed resistance to considerably superior foreign powers. And now — after James, the head of the early Christian church, and others had been executed by the Jewish authorities — should they now act contrary to their religious convictions by participating in an armed political revolt against Rome?

At any rate, the most recent investigations have confirmed as credible the idea that important components at least of the early Christian community emigrated from Jerusalem to Transjordan before the Jewish revolt against the Romans, which seemed doomed to fail.[3]

> The execution of James, Jesus' brother (and other Christians?) during the interregnum through the office of the procurator in the year 62 endangered the community in Jerusalem and created great insecurity particularly among its most respected members. Fear led to the decision of the Jerusalem community, sanctioned by a divine revelation to these *dokimoi*, to turn their backs on the city and to emigrate to the neighboring territory, the Decapolis, where they (or at least most of them?) settled in Pella. Thus, possibly already in the year 62, a larger group of Christians from Jerusalem (and from other Judean towns?) left Jewish jurisdiction and reached the city of Pella, perhaps by way of Jericho and the Jordan Valley, where they (or at least most of them?) settled.[4]

---

3. In reference to the Jewish-Christian *Pseudo-Clementines* (*Recognitions* 1.37.2; 39.3) and Luke 21, and in connection with the historians E. Meyer and M. Simon, who pleaded for historicity, J. Wehnert dissected Verheyden's arguments hermeneutically, historically, and exegetically: "Die Auswanderung der Jerusalemer Christen nach Pella — historisches Faktum oder theologische Konstruktion?" *ZKG* 102 (1991) 231-55. See C. Koester, "The Origin and Significance of the Flight to Pella Tradition," *CBQ* 51 (1989) 90-106 (interaction esp. with G. Luedemann).

4. Wehnert, "Die Auswanderung," 252. "Die durch die Hinrichtung des Herrenbruders Jakobus (und anderer Christen?) während des Prokuratoreninterregnums im Jahr 62 enstandene Gefährdung und tiefe Verunsicherung der Jerusalemer Gemeinde, namentlich ihrer 'angesehenen' Mitglieder, nährte den (durch eine göttliche Offenbarung an eben jene 'dokimoi' sanktionierten) Entschluss, der Stadt den Rücken zu kehren und ins nächstgelegene Ausland, die Dekapolis, zu emigrieren. Möglicherweise noch im Jahr 62 verliess daher eine grössere Anzahl Jerusalemer (und anderer judäischer?) Christen den jüdischen Herrschaftsbereich und erreichte — womöglich auf dem Weg über Jericho und das Jordantal die zur Dekapolis gehörende Stadt Pella, wo sie sich (in ihrer Mehrheit?) niederliess."

We cannot now determine how many members of the early community remained in Jerusalem or returned there after the war. But prior to that fateful year 135 — when the Second Jewish Revolt led to the complete destruction of Jerusalem, the expulsion and dispersion of all the Jews, and the demise of the Jewish-Christian community of Jerusalem with its dominant position in early Christianity — we count no fewer than fifteen Jewish-Christian "bishops" in Jerusalem, according to Eusebius's list of bishops,[5] all of them circumcised (although presbyters [= elders] and relatives of Jesus may have been counted among them). That year, which followed the renewed Jewish uprising, brought about the complete destruction of Jerusalem, the expulsion and dispersion of all the Jews, the renaming of the city as Aelia Capitolina, and thus also the end of the Jewish-Christian community of Jerusalem and its dominant position in early Christianity. Its prestige for gentile Christians was now gone: modern church historians have termed Jewish Christianity deprecatingly as "the paleontological period" of church history. With justification?

II. The Dark History of Jewish Christianity

I admit: the history of Jewish Christianity in the first centuries belongs to the darkest chapters of church history. But why?[6] First, for a long time, the "study of the ancient world" (Altertumswissenschaft) in Europe was initially oriented exclusively toward Greco-Roman antiquity, while Christian patristics viewed Jewish Christianity uncritically as it was described in statements against heresies by the church fathers as a uniform, and specifically a uniformly heretical, entity. Second, Christian theologians, beginning with the Greek and Latin speakers of the first centuries, showed little interest in manuscripts witten in Semitic languages, including first Aramaic/Hebrew, then Syriac and Arabic, and later Ethiopic. Third, Jewish-Christian communities outside the Roman Empire were a priori suspected of being heretical since they had been in contact with Jewish baptismal and gnostic sects. Fourth, a large part of the writings from Jewish-Christian communities near the Euphrates and Tigris was lost since they were less fortunate than the people from Qumran on the Dead Sea or the Gnostics in the Egyptian Nag Hammadi, whose writings were saved from destruction by the dry desert climate.

With respect to the Jewish-Christian communities of the Near East — for which we often have only a few documents for hundreds of years of history —

---

5. Eusebius, *Church History* 4.5.1-4.

6. I received valuable suggestions from Professor James Robinson, NT scholar, leading Gnosis researcher, and director of the Institute for Christianity and Antiquity in Claremont, Calif., during his tenure as visiting scholar at our Institut für ökumenische Forschung.

we depend much more on assumption than with respect to the church of the West, where we often must sift through thousands of pages of source material for each decade. While Simon Peter is mentioned roughly 190 times in the NT, and Saul/Paul about 170 times, James is mentioned only 11 times (in the Acts of the Apostles only 3 times), which can be interpreted, according to many exegetes of our day, as a displacement of Jewish Christianity (and of the brothers of Jesus) in the gentile Christian church.

Did, then, Jewish Christianity soon turn into a heretical sect, as is likewise maintained in traditional church history, because it (persistently) remained as it had developed in its beginning? Today, at least, it is no longer contested that Jewish Christianity continued after the destruction of Jerusalem in 70 C.E., and many experts are dedicating themselves to the fascinating task of finding early traces of the many branches of Jewish Christianity.[7] There is general agreement that the so-called Synoptic Sayings Source of the first century (abbreviated Q for German *Quelle*) is of Jewish-Christian origin. Due to a fortunate set of circumstances, this Aramaic collection of the earliest sayings of Jesus was translated into Greek and integrated into the Gospels of Matthew and Luke. More writings originated from the Jewish-Christian milieu of the first century: the Gospel of Matthew (written ca. 80, possibly in Antioch), the Epistle of James, and the Gospel of John (ca. 100), the latter precisely because here the disagreement with "the Jews" is even more pointed than it is in Matthew.

After the NT writings, we have the noncanonical Jewish-Christian Gospels (reconstructed from fragments in the church fathers), such as especially the

---

7. We already have an impression of the intensive, detailed work of the most important researchers in this field in *Judéo-Christianisme* (*RSR* 60 [1972] 1-323), a *Festschrift* dedicated to J. Daniélou, whose many works include *Théologie du Judéo-Christianisme: Histoire des doctrines chrétiennes avant Nicée*, vol. 1 (Paris: Desclée, 1958); ET: *The Theology of Jewish Christianity* (trans. J. A. Baker; London: Darton, Longman, and Todd, 1964). For the history of Jewish Christianity, H.-J. Schoeps, *Theologie und Geschichte des Judenchristentums* (Tübingen, 1949), is still important. For the individual Jewish-Christian groupings as they appear in the patristic (nongnostic) sources (Cerinthians, Ebionites, Nazoreans, Symmachianites, Elkesaites), the material of A. F. J. Klijn and G. J. Reinink, *Patristic Evidence for Jewish-Christian Sects* (Leiden: Brill, 1973), offers a fairly complete picture. G. Strecker, "Judenchristentum," *TRE* 17.310-25, reconstructs the historical development in the newest arena of research; cf. also his "On the Problem of Jewish Christianity" (trans. G. Krodel), appendix 1 in W. Bauer, *Orthodoxy and Heresy in Earliest Christianity* (trans. P. Achtemeier et al.; ed. R. A. Kraft and G. Krodel; Philadelphia: Fortress, 1971) 241-85. S. Legasse ("La polemique antipaulinienne dans le judéo-christianisme hétérodoxe," *BLE* 90 [1989] 5-22, 85-100) investigates the individual Jewish-Christian documents that are oriented toward anti-Paulinism. See B. Bagatti, *Alle origini della chiesa*, vol. 1: *Le comunita giudeo-cristiane* (Rome, 1986), within the archaeological orientation (vol. 2 deals with the gentile Christian communities). See also F. Manns, *Bibliographie du judéo-christianisme* (Jerusalem, 1979), for the older literature. Presented in a didactically clever way, the materials for "conservative" as well as "liberal" Jewish Christianity are available in T. Carran, *Forgetting the Root: The Emergence of Christianity from Judaism* (New York: Paulist, 1986).

Ebionite Gospel, which may be related to the Gospel of Matthew, but which, like the oldest canonical Gospel (Mark), consciously dispenses with an infancy narrative and views Jesus' son-relationship to God as stemming from the descent of the Holy Spirit at Jesus' baptism. If we can trust the hypothesis of J. Louis Martyn, Jewish Christians appear to have carried out a mission to the Gentiles that insisted on observance of the law as late as the second century.[8] These Jewish Christians may already be seen behind the opponents of Paul in Galatia (also in Philippi). They obviously understood Jesus in the light of God's law, not, like Paul, the law in light of Christ.[9] They wanted to perceive themselves as the true children of Abraham, because they obeyed the law (circumcision, sacred feast days, purification rituals).[10] Also instructive is the Jewish-Christian text "The Ascension of Isaiah" (ca. 100-130), in which a group of prophets places the revelations into the mouth of the prophet Isaiah, thus giving expression to their faithfulness to Jesus as the Messiah.[11]

The continuous existence of Jewish Christians who based themselves on Peter or James — rather than on Paul — and who were not yet infected by Gnosis appears to be attested also in some traditions that have been incorporated into the Christian recognition-story ascribed to Clement of Rome (the *Pseudo-Clementines*). The story narrates the conversion of Clement of Rome, the companion of Peter in Palestine and Syria, and the discovery of Clement's family, believed to be dead. I refer, in particular, to the *Proclamations of Peter (Kerygmata Petrou)* and primarily to the *Ascension (Anabathmoi) of James*.[12] The background is formed by Greek-speaking Jewish Christians probably in Transjordan during the second half of the second century, who practiced baptism in the name of Jesus, although they also observed the law of Moses (and probably also circumcision). They venerated James as the leader of the community in Jerusalem and accused Paul as the one who prevented the possible conversion of the entire Jewish population to the Messiah Jesus because his mission was without the law. This Jewish-Christian community separated itself (through insistence on observance of the law) from the new gentile great church, but also from mainstream Judaism through faith in Jesus, who as a prophet like Moses was identical to the Messiah whom so many Jews had awaited.[13] Further, observant Jewish-Christian communities, which are

---

8. See J. L. Martyn, "The Law-Observant Mission to Gentiles: The Background of Galatians," *SJT* 38 (1985) 307-24.

9. See Gal 1:6-9; 3:1-2, 5; 4:17.

10. See Gal 3:6-29.

11. See A. Acerbi, *L'ascensione di Isaia: cristologiae profetismo in Siria nei primi decenni del II secolo* (2nd ed.; Milan, 1989).

12. *Pseudo-Clementine Recognitions* 1.33-71. Also H. Waitz, O. Cullmann, E. Schwartz, H.-J. Schoeps — primarily G. Strecker, *Das Judentum in den Pseudoklementinen* (Berlin, 1957; 2nd ed. 1981).

13. This interpretation was worked out by R. E. Van Voorst, *The Ascents of James:*

attested in the *Didaskalia* ("instruction"), existed in Syria, while in the Jordan Valley and at the upper course of the Euphrates we find the various followers of the book of *Elkesai,* which combines Jewish-Christian and gnostic-syncretistic elements.

Even as late as the time of Constantine's conversion, Christian synods still felt compelled to take positions against manifestly extensive Jewish-Christian customs: in Spain, the Synod of Elvira (in 305), and in Asia Minor, the Synod of Laodicea (between 343 and 381).[14] Even at the turn of the fifth century, Jerome writes about the existence of a small Jewish-Christian community, known to him as "*Nazarae*" *(Nazareni)* in Beroea (Aleppo/Syria) — evidently not yet separated from the great church — that thoroughly recognized Paul as the apostle of the Gentiles but that evidently used a Hebrew Gospel of Matthew.[15]

But even so, we still know infinitely more about the gentile Christians in the Near East — and these also were later viewed as "heretics" (Monophysites or Nestorians) from the Orthodox-Chalcedonian perspective of the majority — than we do about the Jewish Christianity that preserved the oldest perspectives of the faith and the regulations of life after the downfall of Jerusalem, and was still centered in Palestine and the surrounding regions but had followers as far away as Rome and Egypt, Mesopotamia and South Arabia. According to the sources of the church fathers, which we must read critically, we certainly need to distinguish various groupings in different regions and with differing names, even if we can reconstruct historically only with difficulty what is essentially hidden behind their names.[16] "Nazoreans" (in connection with the "Nazorean" Jesus) goes back to the Hebrew-Aramaic designation of the Christians by the Jews (to be differentiated from the "Nasaraites," a pre-Christian sect), and "Ebionites" (the "poor" before God) was the self-designation of a particular Jewish-Christian group (an "Ebion" did not exist), while "Cerinthians," "Symmachians," and "Elchasaites" were named for their "founders" (Cerinth, Symmachus, Elchasai or Elxai).

We have already described what qualifies all these groupings as "Jewish Christian," in the strict sense, in relation to the section about the Jewish context and the Christian center: Jewish Christians simply embody — to state it succinctly — that form of Christianity whose members (primarily of Jewish origin)

History and Theology of a Jewish-Christian Community (SBLDS 112; Atlanta: Scholars, 1989), esp. 163-80.

14. Synod of Elvira, canons 26, 49, 50; Synod of Laodicea, canon 16.29.

15. See Jerome, *Concerning Famous Men* 3; see also his *In Isa* 40:9-11. For comment on this, see Strecker, "Judenchristentum," 312 and 321.

16. C. Colpe (*Das Siegel der Propheten: Historische Beziehungen zwischen Judentum, Judenchristentum, Heidentum and frühem Islam* [Berlin, 1990] 166-67) emphatically points this out. [For a detailed study and further references see also R. Brown, *The Gospel According to John XIII–XXI* (AB 29A; Garden City, NY: Doubleday, 1970) 809-10. — Trans.]

have linked their faith to Jesus as the Messiah while retaining observance of Mosaic ritual law. These Jewish Christians wanted to live in the footsteps of Jesus, precisely in observance of the law. These Christians also wanted to retain the imprint of their own Jewish orientation toward life and theology, for they frequently retained contacts with the nascent great church, and meanwhile they celebrated their Sabbaths and Lord's Days side by side.

III. Heretical or Legitimate Heirs of Early Christianity?

It was the fate of these Jewish-Christian communities early on, no matter where they lived, to be ignored, disdained, and finally — because they could no longer compete with the developments of the continuously elevated and more complex Hellenistic Christology — to be branded as heretics by the gentile Christians who were educated in the classic tradition: branded first by bishops, such as Ignatius of Antioch, who had already categorically excluded any connection between Christian faith and Jewish praxis around 110, and then from 180 to 185 by Irenaeus of Lyons, who also wrote in Greek and who classified the Jewish Christians as "Ebionites" (this name occurs initially in his writings) in a totally undifferentiated manner and labeled them expressly as "heretics."[17]

By contrast, Justin Martyr, a church father who was himself a Palestinian (from Nablus), demonstrates himself as well informed about Judaism. He reported about these Jewish Christians in the mid-second century and still articulated a differentiated picture of this multifaceted Jewish Christianity (similarly also Hegesippus). He avoided the word "heresy" and differentiated precisely between, on the one hand, the majority of absolute orthodox Jewish Christians, who as Christians kept Jewish ritual laws and circumcision, but who, like Paul or the council of apostles, wanted to force as little on the Gentiles as possible; and, on the other hand, those unacceptable legalistic Jewish Christians who, in his viewpoint, wanted to impose the law on gentile Christians as necessary for salvation. According to Justin, Jewish Christians accepted Jesus as Messiah/Christ but maintained that he had been "a human being from human beings" and that he had been "chosen" to be the Messiah/Christ.[18] But was that already heretical? The East, at any rate — thus perhaps Origen and Eusebius — was less prone to reject Jewish Christianity, something familiar partly from personal perspectives. Only the heresy-specialist Epiphanius of Salamis lists numerous Jewish-Christian groups from the years 374-377 *(Panarion)* in his famed representation of eighty heretics with whom he was familiar either personally or from writings subsequently lost. Whatever reality lies hidden behind

17. Ign. *Magn.* 8-10; Irenaeus, *Against Heresies* 1.26.2; 5.1.3.
18. Justin, *Dialogue with Trypho the Jew* 48.3-4; 49.1.

the names of the individual heretics can certainly not be verified historically. Of the "Nazoreans," for example, he says only: "The Nazoreans acknowledged Jesus as the Son of God, but they otherwise lived entirely according to Jewish law."[19]

Indeed, this declaration cannot be heretical, because the first disciples of Jesus, the majority of the early community, and all those Christian missionaries known to us were Jews, or more precisely — as we heard — "Jewish Christians" (what else?). In principle, they kept the law and circumcision, advocated a Christology with a Jewish imprint offering an illuminating connection between faith in the Messiah and observance of the law, a Christology only later stamped as heretical (because it was presumably "natural" or "adoptionistic"). Jean Hadot attempts to differentiate seven types of Jewish-Christian Christology, which are not mutually exclusive. Three Christologies "from below": the royal (Jesus as "David's son"), the prophetic (as "new Moses"), and the priestly (as "high priest"); four Christologies "from above": that of the "son of man," that of the one standing above "all the angels," that of the "son of God," and that of the "word of God" — all clearly concepts based on Jewish background.[20] For, in fact, it is well known that, from the perspective of the Jewish disciples of Jesus, Christology began in all humility "from below": not with high metaphysical speculations but rather with the question "Who is he?" and "Can anything good come out of Nazareth?"[21] If we wanted to pronounce judgment on the Christians of the pre-Nicene time from the vantage point of the Council of Nicea, then not only the Jewish Christians but also almost all Greek church fathers would be judged heretics (at least, "material" heretics); for they self-evidently taught subordination of the "son" to the "father" ("subordinationism"), which was considered heretical according to the later standard of equality of rank, in the definition of a "uniformity of being" (*homōousios*) by the Council of Nicea. In the light of this finding, we can hardly avoid the following question: If we wanted simply to accept the standard of the Council of Nicea in place of the NT, who then was still orthodox in the old church of the first centuries?

In whatever light the Jewish-Christian sources are to be evaluated individually, the present state of scholarship looks more at the continuity of Jewish Christianity from its origins in primitive Christianity and less at its heretical distortions. The Jewish Christians stand as legitimate heirs of primitive Christianity, while the rest of the NT largely mirrors the view of gentile Christianity, as it was promoted by Paul and his followers.

Georg Strecker, the exegete from Göttingen, a specialist in Jewish Chris-

---

19. Epiphanius, *Panarion* 29. References also occur in Jerome and Augustine.

20. See J. Hadot, *La formation du dogme chrétien des origines à la fin du 4e siècle* (Charleroi, 1990) 5-6.

21. For the first question, see Mark 4:41; Luke 7:49; 8:25; for the second question, see John 1:46.

tianity, sets forth the actual theological meaning of Jewish Christianity in terms of the relationship of Christians and Jews:

> The universality in which Jewish Christianity appears and that from early Christian times until the present has taken concrete shapes in multitudinous ways shows Jewish Christianity as the connecting link between synagogue and church. Vis-à-vis the synagogue, it confirms that the promises of the fathers are revealed through the Christ-event, and that the will of God, which is revealed in the OT, is actualized. Vis-à-vis the church, it validates the Jewish inheritance and represents the permanent claim of Israel. Although Jewish Christianity should not be identified with a "natural" Ebionite Christology (we also find the concept of preexistence), it helps to limit the tendency toward docetism and spiritualization, found in the larger church as well as outside the church, by returning to the historical foundations of the Christian faith.[22]

Thus, we find in Jewish-Christian theology a critical corrective measure against a Christology that is vulnerable to the danger of docetism and to spiritualization.

Certainly: since Epiphanios, Jewish Christianity is stamped as "heresy" in the East now as well. In 386/387, John Chrysostom felt obliged to give eight anti-Jewish sermons in which he rails against the Christians who were drawn to synagogal worship services, and Jewish festivals and customs (including circumcision).[23] Yet after the first half of the fifth century, the traces of Jewish Christianity seem to be more and more obliterated. Syncretistic tendencies, especially with gnostic religions, became stronger. Neither Judaism nor the greater church was able to absorb them fully.

We need to refer also to the charismatic Persian Mani (Greek *Manēs*, *Manichaios*, 216-276), who, in contrast to Zarathustra, Buddha, and Christ, wanted to establish a new world religion. Dualistic and ascetic Manichaeism was a serious rival to Christianity from the Atlantic all the way to China in the third/fourth century. The discovery in our own day, however, is that, according

---

22. Strecker, "Judenchristentum," 323. "In der Universalität seines Erscheinungsbildes, das nicht nur in der frühchristlichen Zeit, sondern bis in die Gegenwart sich vielfältig konkretisiert hat, zeigt sich das Judenchristentum als Bindeglied zwischen Synagoge und Kirche. Gegenüber der Synagoge bezeugt es, dass durch das Christusgeschehen die Väterverheissungen erschlossen werden und der im Alten Testament geoffenbarte Gotteswille sich verwirklicht. Gegenüber der Kirche bringt es das jüdische Erbe zur Geltung und repräsentiert den bleibenden Anspruch Israels. So wenig Judenchristentum mit einer 'natürlichen' ebionitischen Christologie identifiziert werden darf (es findet sich auch die Vorstellung der Präexistenz), so sehr kann es durch die Rückwendung zu den historischen Grundlagen des christlichen Glaubens die grosskirchliche oder ausserkirchliche Neigung zu Doketismus und Spiritualisierung begrenzen helfen."

23. Chrysostom, "Sermons Against the Jews," *PG* 48.843-942.

to the Arabic bibliographer Ibn an-Nadim and the recently discovered Greek Mani Codex,[24] Mani belonged to the Jewish-Christian sect of Elkesaites in his youth. On the occasion of his own conference about the Codex in Cologne, the Mani specialist Alexander Böhlig stated: "He [Mani] became familiar with Jewish influences, such as observance and apocalyptic thought, through Jewish Christianity. The baptists, among whom Mani grew up, were Elkesaites. They regarded Elkesai as the founder of their law. . . . The legality of Jewish Christianity shapes the basis for the legal character of Manichaeism."[25] The Elkesaites are also the connecting link between Palestinian baptists and Jewish Christians on the one hand, and Manichaeans on the other. But there is still a much more important trail.

Another surprising effect of Jewish Christianity needs to occupy us further, precisely because of our ecumenical interests. If we can trust the corresponding research, then the Jewish-Christian communities must have had an impact in their theology — despite all the difficulties in their being branded as heretics, their amalgamation, and their extinction — that was to become significant even for world history: namely, in Arabia through the monotheistic reform movement that the Arabic prophet Muhammad illumined six hundred years after the death of Jesus and three hundred years after the Council of Nicea.

24. *The Mani-Codex of Cologne* (Inventory no. 4780) was published in 1975-81, with commentary by A. Henrichs and L. Koenen. We now have a standard edition by L. Koenen and C. Roemer: *Der Kölner Mani-Kodex; Über das Werden seines Leibes* (Kritische edition; Abhandlungen der Rheinisch-Westfälischen Akademie der Wissenschaften, Sonderreihe Papyrologica Colonensia 19; Opladen, 1988). A revised German translation that took a few new readings into account was published by the same scholars (with a preface by J. Sudbrack): *Mani; Auf der Spur einer verschollenen Religion* (Freiburg: Herder, 1993).
25. A. Böhlig, preface, in *Codex Manichaicus Coloniensis: Atti del Simposio Internazionale, 1984* (ed. L. Cirillo; Cosenza, 1986), here esp. important the contributions by J. Maier, K. Rudolph, G. Strecker, L. Cirillo, A. F. J. Klijn. "Die Täufer, unter denen Mani gross wurde, waren ja Elkesaiten. Sie sahen Elkesai als den Stifter ihres Gesetzes an. . . . Der gesetzliche Charakter des Judenchristentums bildet die Grundlage für den gesetzlichen Charakter des Manichäismus." For the Elchasaite baptists of the Cologne Codex, see A. Henrichs, *HSCP* 83 (1979) 339-76, and esp. 454ff.; R. Merkelbach, in *Manichaean Studies, Proceedings of the First International Conference on Manichaeism* (Lund Studies in African and Asian religion 1; Lund, 1988) 105-33; K. Rudolph, *Antike Baptisten* (Sitzungsbericht der Sächsischen Akademie der Wissenschaften, phil.-hist. Kl. 121.4; Berlin, 1981), esp. 13-17; L. Koenen, "From Baptism to the Gnosis of Manichaeism," in *Das römisch-byzantinische Ägypten, Akten des Symposiums, 26.-30. Sept. 1978* (Aegypt. Trev. 2; Mainz, 1983) 93-108; also in *Rediscovery of Gnosticism, Proceedings of the International Conference on Gnosticism at Yale, New Yaven, Connecticut, March 28-31, 1978*, vol. 2 (ed. B. Layton; 2 vols.; Studies in the History of Religions, Supplement to *Numen* 41; Leiden: Brill, 1981) 2.734-56; and in *Codex Manichaeus Coloniensis*, 285-332, esp. 286-91; see also A. Henrichs and L. Koenen, *ZPE* 32 (1978), index, 88 and 44 (1981), index, 205-6 s.v. "Elchasaios," "Taufsekten," und "Täufer."

IV. Jewish Christianity on the Arabian Peninsula?

Christian scholars have long discussed hidden connections between Jewish Christianity and the message in the Qur'an.[26] Already in 1926, the prominent Protestant exegete Adolf Schlatter wrote in his *Geschichte der ersten Christenheit:*

> Nevertheless, it was only in the part of Palestine west of the Jordan that the Jewish Christian Church ceased to exist; in the districts further east, in the Decapolis, in the Batanea, among the Nabateans, at the edge of the Syrian desert, and in Arabia, there were Jewish Christian communities which followed Jewish customs. They were entirely isolated from the rest of Christendom and without contacts with it. . . . The Christian now regarded the Jew as his enemy; the Greek view that the murders committed by Trajan's and Hadrian's generals were a well-deserved punishment of the wicked and contemptible Jews prevailed even in the Church. Even great Churchmen, like Origen and Eusebius, who lived and taught in Caesarea, were astonishingly ignorant about the end of Jerusalem and its Church. Similarly the Church itself knew next to nothing about the continued existence of Jewish Christianity. Because the Christian Jews would not adopt the ways and customs of the rest of Christendom, they were dismissed as heretics and kept at arm's length.

But Schlatter adds:

> None of the ecclesiastical statesmen in the imperial Church ever dreamt that the day would come when this despised Christian sect would shake the world and destroy much of the ecclesiastical organization which the Gentiles had built up. That day arrived when Mohammed took over the traditions which the Jewish Christians had so carefully preserved — their awareness of God, their eschatology with its proclamation of a day of judgement, their customs and their legends — and as "one sent by God" built a new apostolate.[27]

---

26. See H. Küng, *WR*, chap. A IV,2: "Jesus als Gottesknecht."

27. A. Schlatter, *The Church in the New Testament Period* (trans. P. P. Levertoff; London: SPCK, 1955) 311-12. The original (*Geschichte der ersten Christenheit* [Gütersloh, 1926] 367-68) reads: "Ausgestorben war die Jüdische Kirche jedoch nur in Palästina westlich vom Jordan. Christengemeinden mit der jüdischen Sitte bestanden dagegen in den östlichen Gegenden weiter, in der Dekapolis, in der Batanäa, bei den Nabatäern, am Rand der syrischen Wüste und nach Arabien hinein, völlig von der übrigen Christenheit gelöst und ohne Gemeinschaft mit ihr. . . . Der Jude war für den Christen nur noch ein Feind, und die griechische Stimmung, die über das Morden der Generäle Trajans und Hadrians als über das wohlverdiente Schicksal der boshaften und verächtlichen Juden hinwegsah, ging auch in die Kirche hinüber. Auch ihre führenden Männer, die in Cäsarea lebten und lehrten, wie Origenes und Eusebios, blieben über das Ende Jerusalems und seiner Kirche erstaunlich unwissend. Ebenso sind ihre Nachrichten über die fortbestehende jüdische Christenheit dürftig. Sie [sic] waren, weil sie sich dem in der übrigen Christenheit geltenden Gesetz nicht unterwarfen, Häretiker und

Monotheism instead of Trinity, suffering-servant Christology instead of dual-nature Christology: the thesis of the influence of Jewish Christianity on the Qur'an had earlier been discussed by Adolf von Harnack and later by Hans-Joachim Schoeps.[28] Even the researchers of today, such as Christopher Buck, are arriving at the standpoint: "In the course of time, Ebionites along with Sabian baptists appear to penetrate Arabia. This fertilization invites the hypothesis that the Qur'an echoes Ebionite prophetology."[29] Georg Strecker calls it "indisputable that Islam was open not only to Jewish and Christian influences, but also to Jewish-Christian ones, even if we are here dealing with a wide and yet unworked area of research."[30] The original Jewish-Christian paradigm should thus, in whatever form, have been able to continue within the tradition. But is there truly a connection to the Qur'an? There is certainly more than a hundred-year span between Jewish Christianity of the fourth/fifth century and the Qur'an.

We should probably not think of the primitive Christian Nazoreans as a direct potential connecting link between Jewish Christianity and the Qur'an. Rather, ever since Harnack, reference has been made to the gnostically influenced Jewish Christians such as the Elkesaites, who, according to the most recent research, may have been identical to the so-called Sabians mentioned in the Qur'an.[31] At any rate, today we can hardly dispute the existence of Jewish-

---

deshalb von ihr geschieden." But Schlatter adds, "Keiner von den Führern der Reichskirche ahnte, dass dieser von ihnen verachteten Christenheit noch einmal der Tag kommen werde, an dem sie die Welt erschüttern und einen grossen Teil des von ihnen aufgebauten Kirchentums zertrümmern werde; er kam damals, als Muhammad den von den jüdischen Christen bewahrten Besitz, ihr Gottesbewusstsein, ihre den Gerichtstag verkündende Eschatologie, ihre Sitte und ihre Legende, übernahm und als 'der von Gott Gesandte' ein neues Apostolat aufrichtete."

28. A. von Harnack, *Lehrbuch der Dogmengeschichte* (4th ed.; Tübingen, 1909; reprint Darmstadt, 1964) 2.529-38; Schoeps, op. cit. (in the collection of works by C. Clemen, T. Andrae, and H. H. Schaeder), p. 342, "Und somit ergibt sich als Paradox wahrhaft weltgeschichtlichen Ausmasses die Tatsache, dass das Judenchristentum zwar in der christlichen Kirche untergegangen ist, aber im Islam sich konserviert hat und in einigen seiner treibenden Impulse bis in unsere Tage hineinreicht."

29. C. Buck, report at the American Academy of Religion; see SBLASP, 1983 (Atlanta: Scholars) 86, A87.

30. Strecker, "Judenchristentum," 323. "nicht bestreitbar, dass der *Islam* nicht nur jüdischen und christlichen, sondern auch judenchristlichen Einwirkungen gegenüber offen stand, auch wenn es sich hierbei um ein weitgehend noch unbearbeitetes Forschungsgebiet handelt."

31. For this question, see C. Buck, "Exegetical Identification of the Sabi'un," *Muslim World* 73 (1982) 95-106; G. Quispel, "The Birth of the Child: Some Gnostic and Jewish Aspects," in Quispel and G. Scholem, *Jewish and Gnostic Man* (Eranos Lectures 3; Dallas: Spring, 1986) 3-26. For the Elkesaites as Jewish-Christian propagandists, see — according to Harnack and the early monograph of W. Brandt (1912) — two monographs that appeared almost simultaneously: L. Cirillo, *Elchesai e gli Elchasaiti. Un contributo alla storia delle*

Christian literature in the Arabic language. Not only did Ibadier von Hira and Anbar become renowned, but some of the poetic personalities also became known through the work of Julius Wellhausen.[32] We have been able to find enough references to liturgical books, to which the scholarly authority on religion, Carsten Colpe,[33] already refers, for an Arabic-language Christian liturgy that directs us to the presence of Christian communities on the Arabian Peninsula. Arabic translations seem to have existed ranging from the Psalter to the Gospels. Indeed, Colpe made the surprising discovery that the notable designation for the Prophet Muhammad as "Seal of the Prophets" can be found already in one of the earliest writings of the earliest Latin church father, in Tertullian's *Adversus Judaeos* (before 200) — naturally referring to Jesus.[34] One wonders whether the title "Seal of the Prophets" was used by the Prophet Muhammad in the dispute with Jewish Christians or Manichaeans. Colpe says,

> We do not need to go so far as to declare the Jewish tribes with which Muhammad carried on warfare in Medina as Jewish-Christian in totality. But there is no doubt that the Jewishness on the Arabian Peninsula was infused by a variant that we may specify with the compound term "Jewish-Christian." It is possible that it was this Jewish Christianity which came into use under the title "Seal of the Prophets," and it can have been used there, as basically everywhere within Jewish Christianity, in order to guarantee a specific confessional identity.[35]

We can find still further traces. Colpe himself pursues one trail on the basis of a text from the church history of the Byzantine author Sozomen, dated 439-450, which refers to Jewish Christians who traced their legitimacy from the lineage of Ishmael and his mother (Hagar), therefore to Ishmaelites or Hagarites:

---

communita giudeo-cristiane (Cosenza, 1984); and G. P. Luttikhuizen, *The Revelation of El-chasai: Investigations into the Evidence for a Mesopotamian Jewish Christian Apocalypse of the Second Century and Its Reception by Judeo-Christian Propagandists* (Tübingen: Mohr/Siebeck, 1985).

32. J. Wellhausen, *Reste arabischen Heidentums* (2nd ed.; Berlin: de Gruyter, 1927) 231-33.

33. See Colpe, *Das Siegel*, 237-38.

34. See Qur'an, Sura 33:40; Tertullian, *Adversus Judaeos* 8.12 (correct reading with C. Colpe, "Signaculum omnium prophetarum," not *prophetiarum* ["prophecies"], as E. Kroymann [in CSEL 70 and in CChr Series Latina, II/2.1361] conjectures (in contradiction to p. 1383: *prophetarum*). See Colpe, *Das Siegel*, 28-34.

35. Colpe, *Das Siegel*, 238. "Man braucht nicht soweit zu gehen, die jüdischen Stämme, mit denen sich Mohammed in Medina kriegerisch auseinandersetzte, im Ganzen für judenchristlich zu erklären. Aber daran, dass das Judentum auf der arabischen Halbinsel von einer Variante durchsetzt war, die wir im Sinne eines Additionswortes judenchristlich nennen dürfen, ist kein Zweifel. Es kann dieses Judenchristentum gewesen sein, zu dem der Titel 'Siegel der Propheten' gelangte, und er kann dort wie grundsätzlich überall im Judenchristentum benutzt worden sein, um eine bestimmte konfessionelle Identität zu gewährleisten."

Thus, an oriental Jewish-Christian "confession" comes into prominence that is older than the Nestorians and Jacobites. The latter remained extant principally among the Arabs. According to their type, they could have been Jews, from whom Muhammad received his Jewish traditions — Jews with Midrashim but without the Talmuds, simultaneously Christians who revered Jesus and Mary, but without duo- or monophysitic Christology. Such a Jewish Christianity is also conceivable on the Arabian Peninsula, above all in Medina. It might have been the carrier of biblical and exegetical traditions of the kind that we find in the Qur'an.[36]

A second trail was found by the Jewish scholars S. M. Stern and S. Pines in an Arabic manuscript by ʿAbd-al Javar (Gabbar), who was active in the tenth century in Baghdad, and also that of an earlier Muslim scholar, in which a Jewish-Christian text probably from the fifth/sixth century was reworked. This text contains an early history of a Christian community, bewails the schism of Judaism and Christianity, and criticizes the "Romanization" of Christianity. At the same time it demands the continuance of the original, not yet despoiled, tradition of the Jerusalem community as it was founded by the first disciples of Jesus who believed that he was a human being, but not divine, and who observed the Mosaic laws.[37] Here we have attested a Jewish Christianity not only for the Palestinian-Syrian realm but also for the Arabic-Babylonian realm — alive certainly into the seventh century.[38]

V. Relationship between the Jewish-Christian and the Qur'anic Image of Jesus?

Even if it must finally remain an open question as to which historically genetic relationships the Qur'an exhibits, in what intensity, and to which Christian group, this one element should not be refutable: although the contextual analogies between the Qur'anic image of Jesus and a Christology stamped with Jewish

---

36. Ibid., 169-70. "Damit tritt eine orientalisch-judenchristliche 'Konfession' hervor, die älter ist als Nestorianer und Jakobiten, und die später neben den letzteren vornehmlich unter Arabern bestehen blieb. Nach ihrem Typus könnten sie Juden gewesen sein, von denen Mohammed seine jüdischen Überlieferungen bekam — Juden mit Midraschim aber ohne Talmude, gleichzeitig Christen mit Jesus- und Marienverehrung, aber ohne dyo- oder monophysitische Christologie. Ein solches Judenchristentum ist auch auf der arabischen Halbinsel denkbar, vor allem in Medina. Es kann der Träger biblischer und bibelauslegender Traditionen von der Art gewesen sein, wie sie sich im Koran finden."

37. See S. Pines, "The Jewish Christians of the Early Centuries of Christianity According to a New Source," *Proceedings of the Israel Academy of Sciences and Humanities* 2 (1968) 237-309. Pines was also the one who alerted Colpe to the Sozomen text.

38. See also Colpe, *Das Siegel*, 171-72.

Christianity remain perplexing, the parallels are indisputable and await a historical explanation. Claus Schedl hazarded an initial attempt at a comprehensive study of the Qur'anic image of Jesus. The result is this:

> The sketch of a servant-of-God-Christology, as it is contained in fragmentary form in the Acts of the Apostles, was certainly not further developed by the Hellenistic church of the West. The designation of Jesus as servant ('bd) seems, instead, to have been the dominating christological confessional formula for the Syriac-Semitic Christianity of the East. When, therefore, Muhammad places the title servant at the center of his proclamation concerning 'Isa (= Jesus), he thereby establishes an early Christian design, cleanses it of contemporary misinterpretations, but avoids — what we might have expected from a Hellenistic-Eastern orientation — precise ontological definitions. . . . We should therefore cease to allege that Muhammad had only a rudimentary acquaintance with Christianity; certainly, in the Qur'an he does not take issue with the dogma of the councils of the Western church. The total picture, however, that we have gained through our research should demonstrate that he was well acquainted with the basic structure of the Syriac-Semitic Christology and that he developed it further independently. If a Muslim-Christian dialogue should become fruitful, then we must proceed from these basic data.[39]

Indeed, these historical connections present a surprising arena of possibilities for the dialogue between Jews and Muslims. But we must certainly reassure the Muslim partner in this dialogue beforehand: we will not reanimate old apologetics in this glimpse into history, with whose aid Christians diminished the Qur'an to Jewish or Jewish-Christian sources and demoted its composition as "heretical." Is it not a fact that Islam has often been disqualified as "Christian heresy" among Christians since the days of the last church father, John of Damascus? No, we do not question the authenticity of the Qur'anic

---

39. C. Schedl, *Muhammad und Jesus* (Freiburg, 1978) 565-66. "Den Entwurf einer Knecht-Gottes-Christologie, wie er fragmentarisch in der Apostelgeschichte erhalten ist, hat zwar die hellenistische Kirche des Westens nicht weiter ausgebaut, für die syrisch-semitische Christenheit des Ostens scheint aber die Bezeichnung Jesu als Knecht ('bd) die dominierende christologische Bekenntnisformel gewesen zu sein. Wenn daher Muhammad den Knechts-Titel in das Zentrum seiner Verkündigung über 'Isa (= Jesus) stellt, nimmt er damit einen urchristlichen Entwurf auf, reinigt ihn von zeitgenössischen Missdeutungen, vermeidet aber — was man vom hellenistisch-östlichen Denken her erwarten würde — genaue ontologische Präzisierungen. . . . Man sollte daher aufhören zu sagen, Muhammad habe nur eine mangelhafte Kenntnis des Christentums gehabt; sicher setzt er sich im Koran nicht mit den Lehrentscheidungen der Konzilien der Westkirche auseinander; das Gesamtbild, das wir aus unseren Untersuchungen gewonnen haben, dürfte aber zeigen, dass er die Grundstruktur der syrisch-semitischen Christologie sehr wohl gekannt und eigenständig weiterentwickelt hat. Soll ein muslimisch-christlicher Dialog fruchtbar werden, muss von diesen Grundgegebenheiten ausgegangen werden."

revelation when we create connections to the Christian traditions, just as we do not dilute the Christian revelation when we reconstruct all of the possible Jewish sources.[40] We are not indicating parallels and analogies in order to prove the superiority of Christianity or to dispute the authenticity of Qur'anic revelation, but rather in order to point out the Christian-Islamic relationship, which signifies an expectation and, at the same time, an opportunity for all those participating in the dialogue.

I should take a moment to make clear what the significance for such a dialogue among Jews, Christians, and Muslims would be: Christians could understand Muhammad as a "Jewish-Christian apostle" of the one true God, in Arabic garb, whose day came when he "took over the traditions which the Jewish Christians had so carefully preserved — their awareness of God, their eschatology with its proclamation of a day of judgement, their customs and their legends — and when he, as the 'one sent by God,' built a new apostolate."[41]

If the signs of the times do not deceive us, and despite all the political differences and all the ethnic and religious tensions, we stand before new theological approaches to dialogue that could allow us to see the differences among the three great monotheistic religions, which we know only too well and which are not to be denied, in a different light. Even Jewish-Christian dialogue did advance decisively, after a history of mutual anathema over the centuries, at the moment when Jews and Christians mutually took seriously the lasting and fundamentally Jewish features of the form and message of Jesus for their faiths. For the Christian-Muslim dialogue, it would be possible to make the implications of insight into the early Christian–early Islamic correlation fruitful — the earlier, the better: the Qur'anic comprehension of Jesus no longer as a Muslim heresy but rather as a Christology on Arabic soil, colored by early Christianity. These insights would be highly uncomfortable, at the very least, for all three religions — that is clearly understood. Yet if we are to come to some kind of understanding, we must answer precisely these intrusive questions.

VI. Questions for the Future

Christians can no longer appeal simply to the high Christology of Hellenistic councils and designate those as the only norm for all the "children of Abraham" in the orientation of their faith in Jesus as the one sent by God. What significance do they ascribe to the Jewishness of Jesus of Nazareth, what pride of place do they assign to him in their faith? To what extent are they prepared to take

---

40. See H. Küng, *WR*, chap. A I,2: "Muhammad — ein Prophet? Der Koran — Wort Gottes?"

41. Schlatter, *Church*, 312.

seriously the much more primary Christology of the Jewish disciples of Jesus and the early Jewish-Christian communities as it is also reflected in the Qur'an?

Jews can no longer restrict the figure of Jesus polemically or ignore him as irrelevant for the vitality of the Jewish faith. What position do we assign to Jesus also for the Jewish faith of today, if we are to take him seriously as the last great prophet of the Jewish people, with lasting Jewish traits, as indeed the Qur'an does?

Muslims can no longer content themselves with the critique of Hellenistic Christology (presumably threatening to monotheism): are they ready to comprehend the religious significance of Jesus not only from the Qur'anic perspective, but rather to reflect on it anew from the perspective of the NT, in order thus to understand the authentic figure of Jesus in a more comprehensive way and to avoid narrow and one-sided approaches?

No question: much is demanded of all three Abrahamic religions. Yet this same uncomfortable insight into the relationship of Jewish-Christian and Qur'anic Christology could prove highly fruitful. An opportunity is thus provided for all three prophetic religions — we need to be aware of this.

An opportunity for Jews: They could remain absolutely firm in their faith in the one God of their fathers, of Abraham, Isaac, and Jacob. They could still recognize the Nazarene as the great son of Israel and place him as the last of the great prophets, who, only for the sake of God and humanity, relativized the absolute validity of descent, Sabbath, and law, and who, in his message and his destiny as successor to Moses, demonstrated himself as still "more than Moses."

An opportunity for Christians: They would not need to veer from their faith in Jesus as the one Messiah or Christ of God. Yet they could proclaim their understanding of the "sonship" in a manner more comprehensive for Jews and Muslims: to the extent that the Hebrew Bible and the Jewish-Christian community cannot consider a sexual-physical, or even a metaphysical-ontological, "procreation," but can consider the "establishment" and enthronement of Jesus on the basis of his being raised from the dead through God himself as "Messiah" (king) "in power."[42]

An opportunity for Muslims: They could totally and completely hold fast to their faith in the one and only God and the impossibility of an "association" or "partnership" of an earthly being to God. Yet they could attempt to understand Jesus in a more comprehensive way from the NT, the "one sent by God," the "word," the "messiah" of God, who, according to the Qur'an, was raised to be with God.

42. See Rom 1:3-4; Acts 2:36; Phil 2:9-10; 1 Tim 3:16; 1 Pet 3:21; John 3:14.

Logos, Liturgy, and the Evolution of Humanity

ROY A. RAPPAPORT

University of Michigan

David Noel Freedman's life has been devoted to the illumination of the words of the Hebrew Bible in all their dimensions and through all their scales — from the spelling of individual words (e.g., Freedman 1984), the shaping of those words into poetry (e.g., Freedman 1986), the grand but previously unnoticed symmetries underlying the structure of *Tanakh* in its entirety (Freedman 1991), to, finally, the ordering of all those scriptural words into the Word of the Hebrew God (Freedman: in press). Nor has he confined himself to Scripture per se. He has also been concerned with how its Word has been lived in the communities it has defined and guided, particularly the community of ancient Israel.

I am an anthropologist, not a biblical scholar, more a student of ritual than of texts, one whose own field research has been among a nonliterate people living in Papua New Guinea. This essay, my tribute to my colleague and friend David Noel Freedman, is, consequently, more concerned with the expression of Word in liturgy than in Scripture. As such it does not contribute directly to his project so much as it complements it in a modest way. Among other things, the sanctity that Scriptures claim, be they Jewish, Christian, Islamic, Hindu, Buddhist, is, I believe, a product of ritual, and I will so argue later in this essay. More generally, consideration of both ritual and Scripture cannot help but provide us with a more comprehensive grasp of the relationship of words to Word, that is, language to religion, than can consideration of either ritual alone or sacred text alone.

I said "the relationship of language to religion," rather than to biblical religion or Christianity or Judaism or Buddhism or the religion of the Maring people of Papua New Guinea. As an anthropologist I recognize profound differences among religious traditions. For example, Buddhist conceptions of language and attitudes toward language are, to understate the case, radically different from those of the People of the Book. Nevertheless, in an age in which it is humanity's most pressing task to find principles of unity underlying its plurality we need to be at least as concerned with the commonalities underlying the particularities of distinct religions as we are with what distinguishes them. The ultimate concern of this essay is, therefore, with what is true of religion always and everywhere, not with that which distinguishes each religion from all others.

Always and everywhere. No society known to history or anthropology is devoid of what any reasonable person would agree is religion. Conversely, no reasonable person could plausibly argue that religion, a term at minimum denoting more or less integrated corpora of doctrines and practices informed by sacred conceptions, is present in any earthly species other than our own simply because the sacred is inconceivable in the absence of language, and language properly so-called (a matter to be discussed) is unique to humanity.

Language is that which distinguishes humanity most fundamentally from the rest of nature. It has been central to humanity's evolution, and I have already noted that conceptions that are, in part, definitive of religion are contingent upon it. Less obviously, I shall argue that the converse is also the case. As religion would be inconceivable in the absence of language, language could not have emerged in the absence of religion. The two, I believe, must have emerged together in the early stages of humanity's evolution. Thus religion is as old as language.

To claim an antiquity approaching the primordial for religion is not to confer upon it special privileges. A large number of nineteenth- and early twentieth-century thinkers, Marx and Freud being the most obvious, thought that religion's day, if it ever had one, had passed and that it would eventually wither away under the gaze of an ever more comprehensive, humane, and wide-eyed secular reason. Events of the twentieth century have shown us that the nineteenth-century's late or post-Enlightenment faith in reason was, to be kind about the matter, tragically and perhaps even touchingly naive. I will, at the end, propose that religion, even in this day of science, has a continuing part to play in human adaptation, but the road to that conclusion is a rather long one. I shall proceed from a discussion of language in human emergence to the general consequences of language for the world as a whole. I shall then take up problems set by language, emphasizing particular vices intrinsic to its virtues, and then proceed to the conception of logos. Logos will lead to the sacred and to sanctity, sanctity to ritual and to the religious foundations on which humanity stands. I will then note some of the ills to which sanctity is vulnerable, the dissolution of logos concurrent with technology's explosion, and some aspects of our current dilemmas. Evolution includes, it is well to remember, extinction as well as emergence. Finally I will speculate briefly on religion's place in human adaptation. Coherence will require me, in the course of this discussion, to rehearse some matters that will seem to some readers elementary or obvious. Please bear with me.

I

I have not said that I will deal with "hominid" or "human evolution" but with "the evolution of humanity." The difference is one of connotation. The phrase "hominid evolution," or "human evolution," would have emphasized what our species has in common with other species: that we are animals living among and dependent on other organisms, and, further, that our species emerged through processes of natural selection no different in principle from those producing limpets or lions. I assume these commonalities, but the phrase the "evolution of humanity" emphasizes the characteristic that sets our species apart from all others. Our hominid forebears became what might loosely be called "fully human" with the emergence of language. All animals communicate and even plants transmit information, but only humans, so far as we know, are possessed of languages properly so-called, systems, that is, of conception and communication composed, first, on lexicons made up of *symbols* in Peirce's (1960: 2.143ff.) sense, that is, signs related only "by law" or convention to that which they signify; and second, of *grammars,* sets of rules for combining symbols into semantically unbounded discourse.

The possession of language makes possible ways of life inconceivable to nonverbal creatures. With language, after all, communication not only can escape from the here and now to report in detail on the past and the distant. It can also order, to a degree, the future by facilitating the division of labor and by making more precise planning and coordination possible. With language one can say things like "You hunt up the valley past the three boulders, I will take the children to the swamp to collect water lily roots, and we will meet at dusk by the oak trees on the hillside where we camped last winter." The advantages the ability to transmit such messages confers upon those who possess it are patent, and in the light of them it is plausible to assume that linguistic ability, once it began to emerge, would have been selected for strongly, which is to say that the anatomical structures upon which it is based could have been elaborated and transformed comparatively quickly. Language, therefore, may well have emerged relatively rapidly. Physical anthropologists are in no agreement as to when this might have been, but the cranial expansion from the 300-600 cc. range to the 800-1200 cc. range marking or even defining the transition from the *Australopithecinae* to *Homo erectus* could indicate it. Brains, after all, are metabolically very expensive. It is plausible to assume that *Homo erectus* must have been doing something new and useful with all that extra brain, otherwise it would not have been worth pumping all that blood straight up to it.

II

Although the sort of planning and coordination just mentioned may have been exceptionally important with respect to early selection for linguistic ability, I do not wish to exaggerate its continuing significance. Other entailments of language have been at least as consequential. With language, it is obvious, discourse can escape from the here and now not only to enter the actual and distant past or to approach the foreseeable future. It can also search for such parallel worlds as those of the "might have been," the "should have been," the "never will be," the "could be," the "always will be." It can explore the realms of the desirable, the moral, the proper, the possible, the imaginary, the general, the eternal, and their negatives: the undesirable, the immoral, the impossible, the transitory.

It is important to realize that "to explore" in these instances is not simply to discover what is there. It is to *create* it. Language does not merely facilitate the communication of what is thought but expands by magnitudes what *can* be thought. This expansion in conceptual power as much as the ability to communicate to others the products of that expanded power — understandings, abstractions, evaluations — underlies the general human mode of adaptation and the specific adaptations of the many societies into which the species is ever redividing itself. As such language has been absolutely central to human evolutionary success.

I have used the term *adaptation* as well as the term *evolution. Adaptation* in my usage denotes the processes through which living systems of all sorts — organisms, populations, societies, ecosystems, perhaps even the biosphere as a whole — maintain themselves in the face of perturbations continuously impinging upon and threatening them. Bateson (1972) put the matter in informational terms, stating that adaptive systems are organized in ways that tend to preserve the truth value of particular propositions about themselves in the face of perturbations continually threatening to falsify them. In organisms these propositions are, as it were, descriptions of their structure or physiology. Among humans they may be fundamental postulates (e.g., The Lord our God, the Lord is One).

Adaptive responses, among which cybernetic processes are prominent, include both short-term reversible changes of state and long-term irreversible changes in structure. Such responses are not isolated but seem to be organized into sequences possessing particular temporal and logical characteristics (Bateson 1972; Rappaport 1971, 1977, 1979a). They seem to commence with quickly mobilized, easily reversible changes in state, then proceed through less easily reversible state changes to, in some cases, the irreversible changes not in state but in structure that are called "evolutionary." The generalization connecting reversible "functional" and irreversible evolutionary changes is sometimes known as "Romer's Rule" after the zoologist who illustrated it in a discussion of the emergence of the amphibia from the lobe-finned fish during the Devonian Period. Those creatures did not first venture onto dry land in order to take advantage of a promising set of open niches. Rather, as denizens of shallow pools during a period of intermittent dessication, they were frequently left high and dry. Under such circumstances relatively minor modifications in limb structure (bony fins into legs) and other subsystems were strongly selected for because they facilitated significantly locomotion over land *back to water*. Thus, the earliest terrestrial adaptations among the vertebrates made it possible to maintain an aquatic way of life. To put it a little differently, structural transformations in some subsystems made it possible to maintain more basic aspects of the system unchanged. This proposes that one of the fundamental questions to ask about any evolutionary change is, What does this change maintain unchanged? To translate the matter once again into informational terms, changes in the descriptions of substructures may preserve unchanged the truth value of more fundamental propositions concerning the whole system in the face of changes in conditions threatening to falsify them.

Flexibility is central to adaptation so conceived, and the adaptive flexibility of humans following from the possession of language seems to be unparalleled. It has made it possible for a single interbreeding species to enter, and even to dominate, the great variety of environments the world presents to it without spending generations transforming itself into a spectrum of new species. When social organization and rules for behavior are stipulated in conventions expressed in words rather than specified in genes inscribed on chromosomes, they can be replaced within single lifetimes.

Language and its entailment, culture — the general way of life consisting of understandings, institutions, customs, and material artifacts the existence, maintenance, and use of which are contingent upon language — must have emerged through processes of natural selection as part of the adaptive apparatus of the hominids.[1] But even such far-reaching claims as "language is the foundation of the human way of life" do not do justice to the momentousness of language, for its significance transcends the species in which it appeared. Leslie White (1949) claimed many years ago that the appearance of the symbol — by which he meant language — was not simply an evolutionary novelty enhancing the survival chances of a particular species but the most radical innovation in

---

1. I am, in general, following Leslie White's (1949) definition of culture here: "Culture is the name of a distinct order, or class, of phenomena, namely those things and events that are dependent upon the exercise of a mental ability peculiar to the human species, that we have termed symboling [i.e., the invention and use of symbols in Peirce's sense]. It is an elaborate mechanism, an organization of ways and means employed by a particular animal, man, in the struggle for existence and survival." It seems to me to be useful to define culture as phenomena contingent on the symbol (a term that White meant to be broadly construed to include syntax as well as lexicon). As will soon become apparent, I do not subscribe to the simple and, indeed, simplistic assertion constituting the second sentence of White's definition.

the evolution of evolution itself since life first appeared. Such a claim may be uncomfortably reminiscent of theological assertions of a status for humans only one step lower than the angels; but, bearing in mind the dangers of such assertions and insisting that humanity remains squarely in nature, we should recognize that White's claim is not extravagant. A quibbler could argue that the development of language was nothing more than the most radical innovation in the evolutionary process since the appearance of sex, to which it may be likened in some respects. Both, after all, are means for recombining and transmitting information, and sex laid the groundwork for a sociability that language elaborated. It can be argued, however, that linguistic transmission of information is much more rapid than sexual transmission, that it is not unidirectional, and that it is not confined to the transmission of genetic information. More epochally, the operations of language are not confined to the recombination and transmission of a previously existing form of information. With language an entirely new form of information (in the widest sense of the word) appears in the world. This new form brought with it new content, and the world as a whole, not merely the hominid species, has not been the same since.

The epochal significance of language for the world beyond the species in which it appeared did not become apparent for many millennia — perhaps hundreds of millennia — after it had emerged. But earlier effects on the lifeways of the hominids in its possession were already enormous. I have already observed that language permits thought and communication to escape from the solid actualities of here and now to discover other realms, for instance, those of the possible, the plausible, the desirable, and the valuable. This was not quite correct. It both *requires* such thought and makes it *inevitable*. Humanity is a species that lives and can only live in terms of meanings it itself must construct. These meanings and understandings not only reflect or approximate a separately existing world but participate in its very construction. The worlds in which humans live are not fully constituted by tectonic, meteorological, and organic processes. They are not only made of rocks and trees and oceans but also constructed out of symbolically conceived and performatively established cosmologies, institutions, rules, and values (Austin 1962). With language the world comes to be furnished with qualities like good and evil; abstractions like democracy and communism; values like honor, valor, and generosity; imaginary beings like demons, spirits, and gods; imagined places like heaven and hell. All of these concepts are reified, made into *res*, real things, by social actions contingent upon language. Human worlds are, therefore, inconceivably richer than the worlds inhabited by other creatures.

"Human worlds." Each society develops a unique culture, which is also to say that it constructs a unique world that includes not only a special understanding of the trees and rocks and water surrounding it but other things, many unseen, as real as those trees and animals and rocks. It is in terms of their existence, no less than in terms of the existence of physical things, that people operate in and transform ecosystems which, in all but the cases of hunters and gatherers, they have dominated since the emergence of agriculture ten thousand or so years ago. Language has ever more powerfully reached out from the species in which it emerged to reorder and subordinate the natural systems in which populations of that species participate.

III

Although it conforms to this account to say that language is central to human adaptation, such a statement is clearly inadequate or even misleading as a characterization of the relationship of language to language user. If people act, and can only act, in terms of meanings they or their ancestors have conceived, they are as much in the service of those conceptions as those conceptions are parts of their adaptations. In the course of human evolution, there is an inversion or partial inversion of the relationship of the adaptive apparatus to the adapting species. The capacity that is central to human adaptation gives birth to concepts that come to possess those who have conceived them, concepts like god, heaven, and hell. To argue that all such concepts or the actions they inform or guide enhance the survival and reproduction of the organisms who maintain them is not credible.

That the implications of these suggestions may be obvious does not make them any the less profound. First, if the metaphor of inversion (surely a simplification) is at all apt, the extent to which concepts like inclusive fitness and kin selection account for cultural phenomena is rather limited. Second, and related, whatever the case may be among other species, group selection (selection for perpetuation of traits tending to contribute positively to the survival of the groups in which they occur but negatively to the survival of the particular individuals in their possession) is not only possible among humans but of great importance in humanity's evolution. All that is needed to make group selection possible is a device that leads individuals to separate their conceptions of well-being or advantage from biological survival. Notions like god, heaven, hell, heroism, honor, shame, fatherland, and democracy encoded in procedures of enculturation representing them as factual, natural, public, sacred (and, therefore, compelling) have dominated every culture of which we possess ethnographic or historical knowledge. In more general terms, if one can characterize adaptive systems as systems that operate (consciously or unconsciously) to preserve the truth value of particular propositions about themselves in the face of perturbations tending to falsify them, then it is appropriate to propose that the favored propositions in human systems are about such conceptions as God, Honor, Freedom, and The Good. That their preservation has often required great or even ultimate sacrifice on the parts of individuals hardly needs saying.

Postulates concerning the unitary or triune nature of God are among those for whom countless individuals have sacrificed their lives, as are such mundane apothegms as "Death before dishonor" or "Better dead than Red."

A final implication: we approach here a generally unrecognized evolutionary law or rule, possibly the evolutionary equivalent of the old adage about the nonexistence of free lunches: every evolutionary advance sets new problems as it responds to and ameliorates earlier ones, and language was no exception.

We have been led from a panegyric of language to a consideration of its problems. In addition to the unprecedented possibility just mentioned of contradiction between the symbolic and genetic, two problems are intrinsic to language's very virtues. The first is this: when a sign is only conventionally related to what it signifies, as in Peirce's sense of symbol, the sign can occur in the absence of the signified and events can occur without being signaled. Thus the same conventional relationship that permits discourse to escape from the here and now also facilitates lying. Although elaborate deception and even some rudimentary lying may occur among other species, trust, trustworthiness, truth and falsehood, and deceit in its many forms become especially serious and even fundamental problems for a species whose social life is built on language. If a system of communication accommodates falsehood, how can recipients of messages be assured that the information they receive is sufficiently reliable to act on? In the absence of such assurance social life becomes disorderly. What were called during the Viet Nam years "credibility gaps" are extremely disruptive.

The second problem is more closely related to grammar than to symbol use, for grammar makes the conception of alternatives to prevailing conditions, practices, and customs virtually ineluctable. If, for instance, the lexicon and syntax are sufficient to say "Yahweh is God and Marduk is not," it is possible to imagine, say, and act on the converse, "Marduk is God and Yahweh is not." At the same time that this ability to conceive alternative orders as well as states of affairs enhances the adaptive flexibility of the species, it presents a continuing challenge to prevailing social and conceptual orders. The dark side of enhanced flexibility is increased possibility for disorder. It is of interest that Buber (1952) took lie and alternative to be the grounds of all evil. Be this as it may, if there are to be any words at all it may be necessary to establish what may be called The Word; the "True Word," to stand against the dissolving power of lying words and of many words, against falsehood and Babel.

The question we face here is close to the one posed by Hans Küng in the first paragraph of his massive *Does God Exist?*:

> And since the emergence of modern, rational man there has been an almost desperate struggle with the problem of human certainty. Where, we wonder, is there a rocklike, unshakable certainty on which all human certainty could be built? (1980:1)

I would modify Küng's question only by dropping the terms "modern" and "rational," for I have just proposed that the problem of certainty is as old as language, which is to say as old as humanity. Modern rational humanity may be faced with the breakdown of ancient means for establishing certainty but that is another matter, one to which we must return. For now we can turn to those ancient means. We will turn, that is, to logos and its establishment.

IV

I use the term *logos* to designate a category of conceptions found in many or perhaps even most societies, at least most premodern societies. Each conception is unique in particulars, and there are also variations in outline and emphasis. Nevertheless, they all bear one another a family resemblance. In some societies such conceptions are no more than implicit in myth, liturgy, cosmology, or philosophy, but in a surprising number of cases they are named. Among them are *Ma'at* of ancient Egypt, the Zoroastrian *Asha*, the Vedic *Rta*, *Tao* in China, *Wakan-Tanka* of the Lakota, *Hozho* of the Navajo, *Nomane* of the Maring people of New Guinea, *Djugaruru* of the Central Australian Walbiri people, *Yurlubidi* of the Pitjanjara of the Western Australian desert, and perhaps *Torah* in some Jewish mystical thought (Scholem 1965: chap. 2). Finally, there is the ancient Greek *Logos*, the "type species," so to speak, from which I have derived the genus name.

In the NT, *logos* is usually glossed into English as "Word." I am not following this usage; rather, I take the term in its earlier pre-Socratic sense. By Heraclitus's time the term, which may have earlier covered such meanings as "account," "list," "collection," and "narrative" (Debrunner 1967), had come to designate, among other things, "the rational relation of things to one another" (Kleinknecht 1967) and also seems to have acquired the more general sense of order or, more particularly, the divine principle underlying the world's order. I say "seems" because Heraclitus is now known only through more or less Delphic fragments preserved in the works of later writers. Aristotle referred to their author as "Heraclitus the Obscure," and some of his modern commentators, notably Heidegger (1959), are not what anyone would call paragons of clarity either. It is, nevertheless, generally agreed that "logos" in Heraclitus's work is the dynamic but enduring and even divine ordering principle organizing the world, or even the organization of the world itself. It is also agreed that Heraclitus's logos had particular, albeit still very general characteristics, some of which are widespread among the world's logoi, but I shall focus first on the Greek species in particular, not the genus generally.

First, although the notion of unity may be implicit in all concepts of order, unity is an explicit feature of the logos according to Heraclitus. One of the crucial fragments is translated by G. S. Kirk (1954) as follows: "Listening not to me but to the Logos it is wise to agree all things are one." It is ironic that the philosopher of unity is best remembered for a few dubious fragments concerning flux. Be this as it may, the logos is an eternal unified order within which ceaseless flux takes place. Its opposite is *sarma:* muddle, heap, chaos.

Second, the logos is accessible to human comprehension because the same logos that orders the universe orders human minds as parts of the universe. This makes possible not only human understanding of the cosmos, but understanding among humans as they join in common understanding of the cosmos. It follows that only one activity is genuinely wise: understanding how everything in the world is part of a unified whole. Only the divine possesses this wisdom to the full, but insofar as humans are wise their wisdom is no different from divine wisdom. It is, however, radically different from other forms of cleverness, and only through it can humans assimilate themselves to the ordered whole of which they are parts. Several comments follow.

To begin with, it is clear that comprehension of the logos is not merely intellectual. One grasps it by becoming part of it. As one modern commentator puts it, "it claims a man" (Kleinknecht 1967:81), and he goes on to say, "the particular logos of man is only part of the great general logos . . . which achieves awareness in man, so that through it God and man . . . the true man who . . . has the *orthos* logos, and thus who lives [as a follower of it], are combined into a great *kosmos*" (ibid.:85).

This modern interpretation may take Heraclitus's logos to have a mystical dimension. It certainly recognizes its social aspects. For one thing it is normative — there is a logos that is *orthos*. People *should* follow it, and those who do are bound into a community. But it is possible for humans to do other than follow it. It is, indeed, likely for them to do otherwise because, although the logos can be comprehended, it is hidden.

This broaches another of its general features. The unity that wisdom is to grasp encompasses obviously disparate and conflicting things, but one of logos's explicit qualities is harmony. In view of the strife with which the world is filled, this could not be a flabby harmony of sweetness and compromise. It is, rather, a harmony arising out of, or underlying, conflict itself. Heraclitus's harmony is a harmony of tension. He notes that many things, like the strings of bows and lyres, are necessarily the products of opposing forces, but not all such forces relate to each other as benignly as those producing harp songs. Playing on the word *bios*, which means both "bow" and "life," one of the fragments reads: "For the bow the name is life but the work is death" (Kahn 1979). Nature is maintained by the continuous violence of creatures eating each other. This violence is apparent to those participating in it, but the order or harmony of nature as a whole, at what we would now call the level of the ecosystem of which the participants are parts, is not. In transcending them it is concealed from them.

We are brought here to another of logos's qualities, *alētheia,* which, according to Heidegger (1959), denotes nonconcealment but is usually glossed "truth." It is, however, a special sort of truth, not the truth that some statements may possess by virtue of their correspondence to states of affairs but, as one modern scholar puts it, "The real state of affairs to be maintained against different statements" (Bultmann 1967:238). As such, it is closely related to *physis,* which Kirk (1954) takes to denote "the real constitution of a thing" and which is often glossed as "nature." The contraries of *alētheia,* and prominent among the enemies of logos, are *pseudos,* "deception," and *doxa,* "opinion." *Alētheia* is that which is the case regardless of opinion. It is verity and not mere veracity. I shall return to this matter later. For now it is important to emphasize that if one feature is common to all the species of logos I have named it is that they all claim what the Greeks called *alētheia,* not contingent veracity but absolute verity. Some of their names suggest as much. The root of the Nahuatl logos, *nelli,* which is translated as "true" in Molina's sixteenth-century Spanish-Nahuatl dictionary, is *nel,* which also appears in forms designating "rootedness," and Leon-Portilla (1963) proposes that perdurance or even eternal truthfulness is connoted by it. *Ma'at,* the ancient Egyptian term, is said by Wilson (1951) to encompass a wide and complex range of meanings including truth, order, justice, precision, exactitude, righteousness, and immutability. Ptah created the world in conformity to it, and even the gods are bound by it. Lakota address Wakan-Tanka as "Truth Itself" (Brown 1971).

To return to Heraclitus specifically: although logos orders the universe, the mere existence of *doxa* and *pseudos* indicates that logos is likely to be ignored and that it can be violated. It may be violated for reasons of self-concern or selfishness, and another of its enemies is *idia phronēsis,* which may be understood as "individual calculation" or the "reason of private advantage," perhaps what economists mean by "rationality." Logos is often ignored simply because, being hidden, it is unrecognized. Its unconcealment must be achieved by work of some sort, according to Heidegger (1959): the work of words in poetry, of stone in temples and statues, the work of sound in music, and, I would add, perhaps most importantly, the work of people in ritual. It is of interest that the word "liturgy" is said to derive from *laos ergon,* "work of the people."

I should make clear that there is no evidence for any connection between Heraclitus's conception of logos and the liturgical practices of his day. There are, indeed, good reasons to believe that it was entirely independent of liturgy. This independence may well have been the unrecognized ground of his main complaint about his fellow human beings. Here is an excerpt from the first fragment according to Kirk:

> Of the Logos which is as I describe it men always prove uncomprehending
> both before they have heard it and when once they have heard it. For although
> all things happen according to this Logos they are like people of no experience

even when they experience such words and deeds as I explain . . . men fail to notice what they do after they wake up just as they do when asleep. (Kirk 1954:33)

And from the second:

Although the Logos is common the many live as though they had a private understanding. (Kirk 1954:57)

It is one thing for a thinker like Heraclitus to conceive or grasp a logos. It is quite another to establish that conception as regnant in any community.

V

Heraclitus's conception is, however, virtually unique among the instances I have named in its independence of ritual. In all of the other cases cited, logos is established and sanctified in liturgy. We are brought to a consideration of the sacred and the sanctified.

Central to the bodies of discourse (composed of words and acts and objects given meaning by words) constituting logoi represented in liturgy are some sentences that I call "ultimate sacred postulates." Familiar examples include the *Shema* of the Jews: "The Lord our God, the Lord is One." Such sentences have peculiar characteristics. They usually contain no material terms and sometimes seem internally self-contradictory, or at least to contradict ordinary logic. These characteristics make them invulnerable to empirical falsification and tacitly assert ineligibility for logical falsification as well. Nor are they subject to objective verification. Nevertheless, they are taken to be unquestionable. I take this unquestionableness to be of the essence and elsewhere have defined sanctity as *"the quality of unquestionableness imputed by congregations to postulates in their nature absolutely unfalsifiable and objectively unverifiable"* (1971, 1979b). As such they may seem indistinct from axioms but there are differences. For one thing they cannot be derived as theorems from logics of higher type. Reciprocally, sentences contingent upon them are not derived from them logically but are *sanctified* by them.

This definition, be it noted, takes sanctity to be a characteristic of discourse rather than of objects of discourse. It is not, for instance, Christ that is sacred. It is the stipulation of his divinity (in discourse) that is sacred. Christ may be divine, but that is another matter. Divinity is a possible characteristic of some *objects* of discourse.

Although sanctity has its source in ultimate sacred postulates, it flows from them throughout the bodies of discourse constituting the liturgically grounded logoi at the apices of which they stand. In the course of this flow sanctity is likely to escape from the confines of religious discourse and ritual to enter into social processes generally. If, for instance, kingship is part of the logos, and if kings are crowned in the name of God in coronations, then even their mundane directives are sanctified and disobedience is more than lese majesty. It is sacrilege.

Expressions establishing the authority of chiefs and kings — expressions like "Charles the Most Pious Augustus Is Crowned by God Great and Peacekeeping Emperor" — are not alone in being sanctified. Others commonly sanctified include those ordaining rituals and specifying taboos, some myths, some classifications, cosmological axioms, commandments, testimony, and oaths. That is, sanctity escapes from ritual not only to sanctify logoi but to underwrite discourse generally.

VI

Ritual, or liturgy, is not the only conduit through which sanctity is conducted from ultimate sacred postulates to other sentences, but it is surely the most ancient, ubiquitous, and effective of all channels for reasons that should soon become apparent.

First one must ask, How do certain postulates attain their ultimately sacred, which is to say unquestionable, status? The answer, I believe, is that their representation in ritual confers ultimate sacred status upon them. Ritual, which I have not yet defined, is a means, possibly the only means, for manufacturing sanctity. I take the term to denote *the performance of more or less invariant sequences of formal acts and utterances not entirely encoded by the performers.*

A word or two about this definition. First, it specifies neither the subject of ritual nor its functions. It is formal in nature, defining ritual in terms of its most obvious features and the relations among them. Second, because it is terse it may not adequately distinguish ritual from other performance forms, such as drama. I can only note that among the important differences are those between audiences, which watch dramas on the one hand, and congregations, which participate in rituals on the other. There is also an important difference in their rhetorical force. To the extent that dramas affect the world they do so through what speech-act theorists would call "perlocutionary force" (Austin 1962; Searle 1969). In contrast, liturgy is fundamentally "illocutionary" with, in some instances, subsidiary perlocutionary effects.[2] Third, the definition also

---

2. A "perlocutionary speech act" is one that achieves its result through its effect on the mind or emotion of the hearer: it persuades, cajoles, alarms, soothes, or whatever. In contrast, an "illocutionary act" achieves its effect in its very utterance. For example, if the

does not distinguish human ritual from animal ritual. It could cover with no difficulty what ethologists mean when they speak, for example, of "the courtship rituals of Fiddler Crabs." This is deliberate. I take ritual among humans to be continuous with ritual among our preverbal forebears, and suggest that sanctity emerged when particular expressions from burgeoning language were assimilated into and subordinated to the already existent ritual form. Thus sanctity is as old as language. Indeed, given language's subversive possibilities the development of language might have been no more possible in the absence of the sacred than the emergence of the sacred would have been in the absence of language (see Rappaport 1979c).

I have argued at length elsewhere (1979b, 1979c) that ritual grounds the unquestionableness of the sacred in three ways, two of which depend on the relative invariance characteristic of the ritual form.

The first is rather convoluted, but I will not apologize because I believe this convolution to be intrinsic to the phenomenon and not simply to my account of it. Liturgical orders, or rituals, are sequences of acts and utterances and as such must be performed. If performance is discontinued they, which is also to say the logoi they represent, cease to be. We know of liturgies performed in Ur, but they are dead, for they are no longer given voice by the breath of the living. Liturgical orders are orders of acts and utterances, and they and the logoi they represent are realized (i.e., made into *res*), in all of their propriety and precision, only in instances of their performance. The relationship of the act of performance to the order performed — that it realizes it — cannot help but specify as well the relationship of the performers to that order. They *participate* in — become *parts* of — it.

To perform an invariant order encoded by someone else is necessarily to *conform* to that order. As such, authority is intrinsic to liturgical orders. But the notion of participation proposes a relationship more intimate and binding than terms like "authority" and "conformity" convey. Elsewhere (1979b) I have argued that performers in ritual are likely to be the most important receivers of the messages they themselves transmit. There is, thus, a partial fusion of transmitter and receiver in ritual. I now propose that there is a further fusion of the transmitter-receiver with the message being transmitted and received. In conforming to the order to which their performance gives life the performers become parts of it, indistinguishable from it, for the time being. For the performer to reject an order of which he or she is a part while a part of it seems to me to be self-contradictory and thus impossible. Thus by performing a liturgical order the participants accept, and indicate to themselves and others

---

formula "I name this ship *Queen Elizabeth*" is uttered by an authorized person with respect to a proper object under proper circumstances, the effect (naming the ship) is thereby achieved even if some or all of those present believe that the ship is, or should be, named *Hortense*.

that they accept, the logos encoded in that order. Acceptance constitutes a formal agreement not to question. Formal agreement not to question is one ground of unquestionableness. To put this a little differently, acceptance, signified by some sort of visible act, usually if not always a ritual act, is contractual or even covenantal. We may recall here the public act of ritual acceptance, reported in Neh 8:1-6, that reestablished the authority, and by my account the sanctity or even the sacredness, of the Torah after years of neglect, violation, and even desecration during the Babylonian exile.

> When all the people assembled themselves as one man at the plaza in front of the Water Gate, they requested Ezra the scribe to bring the book of the law of Moses which Yahweh had prescribed for Israel.
>
> So on the first day of the seventh month Ezra the priest brought the law before the congregation consisting of men and women, and of all who could listen intelligently, and he read from it in front of the plaza before the Water Gate from dawn until midday before the men and women and [the others] who could understand [it]; all the people listened attentively to the book of the law. Now Ezra the scribe stood upon a wooden podium which they had constructed for the purpose; beside him, to his right, stood Mattithiah, Shema, Anaiah, Uriah, Hilkiah, and Maaseiah; to his left stood Pedaiah, Mishael, Malchijah, Hashum, Hashbaddanah, Zechariah, and Meshullam. Then Ezra opened the book in the sight of all of the people — for he stood higher than all the people — and when he opened it all the people stood. When Ezra praised Yahweh, the great God, all the people responded, "Amen, Amen," with their hands uplifted, knelt down and worshiped Yahweh with their faces to the ground. (Myers 1965:149)

The argument that acceptance is intrinsic to participation, being on the face of it either dubious or indubitable, is itself questionable. Two elaborating remarks are required to make it acceptable. First, by "acceptance" I do not mean "belief." Belief is a private state, knowable subjectively if at all. In contrast, acceptance is a *public* act visible to both the self and others. As such it can serve as the ground, *as invisible and volatile belief cannot,* for public orders.

Second, closely related, and obvious: an act of acceptance does not guarantee that the accepter will subsequently abide by the terms of the logos accepted. Acceptance entails an *obligation* to conform to that order, but people can obviously act in violation of their obligations. The Hebrew Bible could, indeed, be read as a history of covenantal violation. The important point here, however, is that if there is no acceptance there is no obligation, and if there is no obligation no obligation can be violated. We must note here that societies must find ways to establish order that are insulated from the vagaries and violations with which ordinary behavior abounds. The representation of logos in liturgy is, I propose, the fundamental way for at least two reasons. First, in establishing obligation it establishes morality. Breach of obligation is not only always immoral but is, arguably, the essential component of all acts so regarded. Second, whereas an order could be decreed by an authority, it is generally agreed that the conditions permitting some people to issue decrees by which others are forced to abide are relatively recent, possibly not antedating the appearance of plant cultivation. Furthermore, acceptance by subjects is not an entailment of the enunciation of decrees by authorities, and compliance if coerced does not constitute acceptance. If there is no acceptance there is no obligation. Violation of a legally valid decree may always be illegal but it is not always immoral.

Whereas the first ground of unquestionableness is an effect of the performance of invariance on the social condition of the performers, the second is the significance of the self-same invariance for the text performed. Anthony F. C. Wallace (1966) observed that if ritual is a mode of communication it is, in information theoretical terms, a peculiar one. To the extent that a ritual order is invariant its unfolding in performance reduces no uncertainty. Inasmuch as information (in a technical sense) is that which reduces uncertainty, ritual is devoid of information. But to say that it is informationless is not to say that it is meaningless, for *the meaning of informationlessness,* Wallace notes, *is certainty.* The certainty of that which is invariantly encoded is the second ground of unquestionableness.

A further consequence of invariance is that to perform a liturgy is ipso facto to "follow the logos." Although there is room for private understandings of a publicly realized logos, that is, for performers to interpret it in idiosyncratic ways, the logos itself, constituted by acts and utterances performers do not invent but find encoded in the invariant liturgy, is held in common and stands beyond *doxa.*

VII

The unquestionable status of ultimately sacred postulates must, however, stand on more than formal acceptance and a trick in information theory. I have defined the sacred in a way that associates it with the discursive, or linguistic, aspect of religious phenomena. It has its source in bodies of discourse, and it ameliorates problems of language. But it is not the whole of the holy. The other aspect of the holy, the nondiscursive, affective, experiential aspect, may, following Rudolf Otto (1923), be called "the numinous." The numinous is experienced as a direct and immediate awareness of an extraordinary presence or even as participation in such a presence. Informants agree that it is deeply, even ultimately, meaningful. We must ponder what they may mean by this.

We may, in a rough-and-ready way, distinguish three "levels" of meaning. First, there is what one might call *low-order meaning,* the semantic meaning of every day. If it is not coextensive with what is meant by "information" in information theory it is close to it, for it is grounded in distinction: the meaning of "dog" is dog, which is distinct from cat, which is denoted by "cat." The paradigmatic form for the organization of low-order meaning is taxonomy. Increase in low-order meaning as a consequence of the elaboration of distinction may be one of language's fundamental contributions to the distinctiveness of human life.

Whereas distinction is the ground of low-order meaning, *middle-order meaning* is based not on distinction but on the recognition of similarities hidden beneath the differences distinguishing apparently disparate things. As taxonomy provides a paradigm for low-order meaning, so metaphor does for middle-order meaning. This middle-order meaning, be it noted, is much lower in information in the technical sense than is low-order meaning but, possibly because it is based in some degree on nondiscursive pattern recognition, it seems more affect-laden, more subjective, in sum "more meaningful," than low-order meaning. It is not surprising that the multivocalic representations (Turner 1967) of ritual are meaningful in this way.

But not only in this way, for there is also what one may call *high-order meaning*, based on neither distinction nor similarity but unification, the unification of that which is meaningful with those for whom it is meaningful. If taxonomy is the house of low-order meaning and metaphor the vehicle of middle-order meaning, then *participation, particularly in ritual,* is the way to highest-order meaning. Whereas low-order meaning seems highly objective, highest-order meaning seems absolutely subjective, for in it the distinction between that which is meaningful and those for whom it is meaningful breaks down. Yet, despite its apparently absolute subjectivity, highest-order meaning when grasped in ritual is public, and among the distinctions that may be dissolved are those dividing the separate selves joined together in following the liturgy's logos.

If participation annihilates distinction, it itself tends toward information-lessness, and we are faced with the paradoxical possibility that information is the enemy of the most meaningful of all meanings. Be this as it may, we may recall here Kleinknecht's claim that the logos is not merely comprehended intellectually but that it "claims a man." One grasps or is grasped nondiscursively by highest-order meaning by participating in — becoming part of — that which is meaningful, as in the performance of a liturgical order. *Highest-order meaning is not referential. It is a state of being.*

I take the numinous experience to be the grasp of highest-order meaning. Unlike sacred postulates, which are unfalsifiable, *numinous experiences, because immediately and directly felt, seem undeniable.* Such experiences are more usually engendered in ritual, generated by such of its "effervescent" (see Durkheim 1915) features as unison, rhythmicity, stylization, singing, and dancing, than it is by the simple reading or contemplation of Scripture. Multivocality, the simultaneous signification in a single ritual representation of multiple *significata* ranging from the physiological and affective through the social to the cosmic, is especially meaningful because it seems to bind together disparate parts of the world and to make everything an icon of everything else. Numinous experience, when it occurs, reinforces formal acceptance with deep and heartfelt belief, with a conviction that claims those convinced or, to use an evangelical term, "convicted," more profoundly than the merely moral claims of obligation or the persuasions of mere certainty. This is the third of ritual's grounds for unquestionableness.

VIII

Acceptance, certainty, belief: three grounds of unquestionableness. But the concept of unquestionableness itself may not be clear. To speak of the representation of logoi in liturgy is to speak of expressions — words, and acts, and objects given meaning by words, reinforced, possibly, by experiences interpreted and directed by words — but it may be hard for those of us born in the twentieth century to grasp how expressions, no matter what their basis, can be unquestionable — to grasp the special nature of their claim to truth.

In ordinary usage, truth is a quality that some expressions may or may not possess. They are true, we say, if they "agree with reality" or "conform to fact," to cite two dictionary definitions expressing what is called "the correspondence theory," probably the most naive theory of truth, but closest to what people other than philosophers have in mind, and some philosophers also stand by it. For instance, Aristotle asks in the *Metaphysics* (10.1051b): "When is what is called truth or falsity present? . . . It is not because we think truly that you are pale that you are pale, but because you are pale we who say this have the truth" (McKeon 1941). A modern theologian-philosopher (Smith 1956) comments that the truth exists in "two situations," first in the state of affairs whether or not it is known — the truth is that you are pale even if I am blind — and second, in the situation of knowing the state of affairs and, possibly, of speaking it — "you are pale." Another modern author puts it this way: "To discover whether what is said is true is to discover whether there is a . . . corresponding fact. Whatever is truly said has its corresponding fact" (White 1970).

In this theory, it would seem, expressions or representations can be no more than contingently true. But what of the truth of the state of affairs to which a true expression corresponds? Its truth is not contingent. It simply *is*. It possesses the "truth of things." It is in the truth of things that unquestionableness is located. This form of truth is not mere veracity, a possible property of expressions, but verity, a necessary property of the existent. This is, I believe, the form of truth that the ancient Greeks called *alētheia,* and that is claimed by logoi generally.

I am proposing, then, that ultimate sacred postulates are expressions, but inasmuch as they are taken to be unquestionable they are expressions claiming the truth of things. As such their verity cannot be discovered, proved, or confirmed through examinations of their correspondence to fact. To justify them by arguing correspondence to fact could at best show them to be only contingently true and could open them to falsification. I have argued that they are established as certain, beyond question, and undeniable not by correspondence but by their mode of expression.

This does not, however, invalidate the correspondence theory with respect to them. Recall a statement of the correspondence theory already cited and note its ambiguity: "Whatever is truly said has its corresponding fact." Liturgy, I have argued, is a mode of "truly saying." If something is "truly said" there must be a corresponding fact. The correspondence theory is, as it were, stood on its head as the fact comes into being to correspond to the "true expression." The expression, for reasons other than the correspondence, has been granted the status of verity, and verity it becomes by, so to speak, creating, through tacit illocutionary action, an object corresponding to itself. It is worth noting that the English term "God" is said to be derived from a proto-Indo-European term meaning "that which is invoked" (*American Heritage Dictionary* 1969). Be this as it may, this reflexive sleight-of-ritual, which could be understood as a performative passing itself off as a statement, can work only with proper objects, like divinities and the proper and moral logoi over which they preside.

It is also important to emphasize that such verities are not necessarily threatened by states of affairs that do not correspond to them. When a state of affairs varies from the stipulations of logos it is the state of affairs that is false. In Zoroastrian Persia, for example, rebellions against the Achaemenid emperors were said to be *druj,* a term that also meant "lie." Similar conflations of lie and violations of logos seem to have been current in ancient Egypt according to Lichtheim (1971), Vedic India according to Brown (1972), and I have a case among the Maring of New Guinea. What may be called "Vedic" or "Zoroastrian" lies, states of affairs violating the world's proper order, are the inverse of common lies.

We come, at length, to something of an answer to Hans Küng's question: "Where . . . is there a rocklike . . . certainty on which all human certainty can be built?" I say "something of an answer" because what we have found is hardly rocklike. We are faced with a remarkable spectacle. The unfalsifiable supported by the undeniable yields the unquestionable, which transforms the dubious, arbitrary, and conventional into the apparently correct, necessary, and natural. This is, I have argued so far, the foundation on which the human way of life is built, and it is laid in ritual.

Two general comments on this understanding of ritual are necessary. First, the claim that ritual is the furnace within which the images of gods are forged says nothing whatsoever about the possibility of divinity independent of its human conception. As an anthropologist I take religion to be a human, which is to say natural, phenomenon. Second, following my discussion of verity, to propose that images of the divine are human fabrications does not deny their truth. Unlike the truths underlying physical nature, which must be discovered, those underlying humanity must be constructed. One may recall here Giambattista Vico's (1710) famous dictum concerning all that is distinctively human: "The true and the made are one and the same."

A third comment needs to be made. The structure that I have proposed is intrinsic to the ritual form may have been the foundation on which the human way of life once stood, but it is doubtful that it continues to stand there. We may, at any rate, recall what I take to be an important if generally unrecognized evolutionary rule, namely, that every evolutionary advance sets new problems as it ameliorates older ones. The new problems may not become apparent immediately, or even for millennia, but in any event sanctity is no exception to this generalization. Although it may have ameliorated problems of lie and alternative intrinsic to the use of language, it has problems of its own.

IX

There are many such problems and space is limited. Because I have discussed some of them at greater length elsewhere (1971, 1977, 1979a, 1979c), I will do no more here than recognize a few of the obvious ones and say a little about some of those that are less obvious. Among the most obvious is the capacity for differing sacred truths to engender conflict and persecution between and among the separate groups whose discourse and trust is founded on them. Countless people have died over disagreements concerning the names of gods. A second is that the numinous, although deeply meaningful and often ineffably beautiful, can be put into the service of what most of us would take to be great evil. The Nuremberg rallies may well have been among the most numinous events of the century.

One should keep in mind that sanctity emerged millennia, or even hundreds of millennia, before agriculture, writing, or state organization appeared. With these developments, generally regarded as advances, and with the development of ever more powerful technology, sanctity's problems became ever more manifest.

The first problem is oppression. In simple tribal societies such discrete authorities as exist depend for their prerogatives on their sanctification. As we have seen, however, their sanctification derives from rituals in which those presumably subject to them participate. That is, in such societies subjects can deprive authorities of sanctity should they perform incompetently or oppressively, either passively by withdrawing from participation in a ritual from which (directly or indirectly) the sanctity of the authority is drawn, or actively, either by participating in rituals sanctifying alternative authorities or by participating in rites of degradation. Among pre-Christian Germans, for instance, it was not only a right but a duty to desecrate and depose kings who had, as it was said, "lost their luck," even though they were descendants of Wodin (Cheney 1971). In sum, in simple societies sanctity is an important constituent of the cybernetic processes limiting as well as underwriting authorities' prerogatives. This cybernetic process, be it noted, may well engage numinous emotions as well as sacred and sanctified conceptions. The operations of incompetent or oppressive authorities are likely to have adverse affects on their subordinates' sense of well-being. Suffering or dissatisfaction may make them unwilling to participate in rituals sanctifying what they perceive to be the source of their suffering, or leave them unable to have numinous experiences if they do participate. Thus the process of sanctification is weakened by the loss or reduction of its numinous support. At the same time, suffering makes the oppressed increasingly willing to give numinous support to rival authorities such as prophets. It is of considerable interest that such challengers are often if not always highly charismatic: they are gifted with an ability to generate numinous experiences among their followers.

In more developed societies, in which authorities have at their command organized bodies of people equipped with increasingly powerful weapons, the situation changes. The authorities can now stand on power rather than sanctity. They do not abandon their claims to sanctity, but their relationship to it is inverted. Whereas in the simpler society authority is contingent on its sanctification, in the more developed society sanctity may be degraded to the status of authority's instrument.

Ritual participation may continue, of course, in developed societies. If it is coerced, as it sometimes is, it does not constitute acceptance, but even when participation is eager it is likely to be profoundly different in orientation and consequences. The established religions of state-organized societies tend to focus on salvation in the hereafter and to become detached from the correction of the ills of here and now. Years ago de Rougemont (1944) spoke of a special form of lie, not simply transmissions of information known by the transmitter to be false, but transmissions that tamper with the very canons of truth. In honor of Satan's putative proclivity for appearing to be what he is not, he dubbed them "diabolical lies." I would include in this class sanctified expressions delivering misery and oppression while promising salvation and heaven.

This characterization is not meant to be a general indictment of religion in complex societies. Although sanctity has been degraded in the churches of some oppressive regimes, unfettered sanctity supported by spontaneous numinous experience has emerged hundreds if not thousands of times in revitalistic movements, and significant constituents of the Catholic Church in contemporary Latin America are animated by "liberation theology." What one could call "the Cybernetics of the Holy" (Rappaport 1971, 1979c) may continue to function, albeit probably less effectively than in less technologically developed and politically centralized societies. Sanctity is, however, subject to related problems of a subtler sort, some of which seem germane to current conditions.

First, what Tillich (1957) called "Idolatry" may be intrinsic to humanity's later evolution. Characteristic of or, in the view of some scholars, even definitive of this evolution is increasing differentiation of society into specialized subsystems or sectors that inevitably come to differ in power and influence. It follows that the narrowly drawn interests of the most powerful of them can come to dominate the values of society as a whole. As a consequence, these subsystems are able to usurp greater degrees of sanctity than is appropriate to their specialized and instrumental nature. For example, if America is "one nation under God" as stipulated in our ritual pledge of allegiance, a God in whom we trust as it says on our money, and if "the business of America is business" as asserted by a man ritually sworn into our highest office, then business becomes highly sanctified, and the logic of "what's good for General Motors is good for America" becomes compelling. In the terms of our earlier discussion of adaptation, highly specific propositions are raised to ultimate status, to the preservation of the truth of which the entire system becomes devoted. In theological terms this elevation of the specialized, instrumental, and mundane to the status of general, fundamental, and highly sanctified seems to be an instance of idolatry, an "absolutizing of the relative" inevitably leading to a "relativizing of the absolute." Tillich took idolatry to be an evil. Whatever the moral case may be, I take it to be maladaptive because, aside from the loss of meaningfulness intrinsic to such relativizing, to invest specialized and instrumental institutions or sectors, like business, with high degrees of sanctity makes them increasingly resistant to change. In other words, idolatry reduces adaptive flexibility and impedes orderly evolutionary transformation.

"Oversanctification," of which idolatry is a form, can also occur through mistakes of logical typing within religious traditions themselves. Conservative clergy can take minor rules to be fundamental, and accord to them inappropriately high degrees of sanctity. A case in point is the Catholic Church's stand on birth control. It seems not only to me, an outsider, but to a good many people inside the church that a degree of sanctity appropriate only for matters of faith like the doctrine of the Immaculate Conception is being accorded to a low-order rule concerning the mechanics of nonimmaculate nonconception. The results have included not only a widespread decline in Catholic devotional practice but also a general challenge by some Catholic theologians, most notably Hans Küng and Charles Curran, to papal authority itself (see esp. Küng 1971).

X

A related but less obvious ill of sanctity is a consequence of another epochal advance: writing. Writing has surely opened up new ways to explore and construct the world, but it has also made some problems for the dynamics of religious discourse.

In nonliterate societies ultimate sacred postulates are generally brief, cryptic, and low in social specificity. This remains the case even in some literate traditions. What, after all, does the sentence "The Lord our God, the Lord is one" mean? Or the Lord our God is three? Such expressions stand at the border between discursive sense and the ineffable. In adaptive and evolutionary terms this is as it should be. For one thing, their vague and cryptic qualities protect them against the possibility of falsification. More important is this: inasmuch as they are low in, or even devoid of, specific social directives, their relationship to the more specific conventions, understandings, and institutions through which social life is ordered is a matter of interpretation. Interpretations of the ultimate, although they may be sanctified, are themselves mere *doxa,* and as such open to reinterpretation without challenge to the ultimate itself. It is therefore possible to claim sanctity not only for the conventions and institutions regulating society but for changes in those conventions and institutions without threatening the ultimate sacred postulates themselves. Not only can the organization of society change while the ultimately sacred remains unchanged, but such organizations can be understood to change for the sake of preserving the ultimately sacred unchanged. There is an important lesson here. If expressions are to be granted unquestionable status, it is important that no one understand them. More generally, the very characteristics of ultimate sacred postulates that lead critics of religion to dismiss them as without sense or even nonsense — that they are unfalsifiable, that they are cryptic, that they are low in or even devoid of social and material content — are the very features that make them adaptively true.

But with writing come scriptures. Being written, they easily become absolutely invariant. They also tend to become very long and full of specifics. Fundamentalists are inclined to take whole scriptures to be ultimately sacred, which is to say not only unquestionable but immutable. Very specific accounts, understandings, and rules thereby become, as it were, set in concrete. If flexibility is central to adaptiveness, loss of adaptive capacity is a general consequence. Political and social conservatism is a likely outcome, as we know from recent history, and so may be resistance to secular scholarship, as the history of the last four hundred years tells us. Such developments, however, endanger sanctity more than they impede intellectual exploration. To put sanctity into the service of, for instance, the geocentric theory during the seventeenth century or creationism in the late twentieth has, among its likely effects, the discreditation not only of particular scriptural accounts in their confrontations with more persuasive naturalistic explanations, but of sanctity itself as a principle of certification.

XI

Many of the most gifted thinkers of the last few hundred years have struggled to escape from sanctity's constraints, and the success of their liberated efforts to discover natural law has added to sanctity's disrepute. Moderns have been inclined to celebrate the liberation of knowledge from its subordination to a clerically and scripturally defined sacred, but this liberation has had its costs. With the emergence of modern science an order of knowledge very different from Egypt's *Ma'at*, the Zoroastrian *Asha*, or Maring *Nomane* comes to prevail. Indeed, it is an inversion of the structure characteristic of logoi generally.

Ultimate knowledge in all of the logoi I have named is sacred knowledge, knowledge that, because numinously known or liturgically accepted, is unquestionable. Taken to be eternally true, ultimate sacred postulates sanctify, or certify, other sentences — axioms concerning the enduring structure of the cosmos, values grounded in those structural principles, rules for realizing them. Knowledge of mundane facts is, as it were, at the bottom of such hierarchies. Such knowledge is taken to be obvious, transient, low in or devoid of sanctity, and contingent rather than fundamental.

When, in the course of evolution, science is liberated from religion, ultimate knowledge becomes knowledge of fact. Facts, of course, are subsumed under generalizations called "theories," but theories continue to fall victim to anomalous facts. If facts are both ultimate and transient, certainty disappears. Moreover, theories are not only transient but of limited scope. Attempts to apply concepts developed in one domain to another, let us say animal ecology to human society, tend to be dismissed as "mere analogies" or even improper "reductions," and middle-order meaning shrivels. The result is a fragmentation of knowledge, and if oneness is intrinsic to the conception of logos, logos is threatened with dissolution.

Not only are facts sovereign, but there are more of them. Facts breed facts, and as knowledge of facts burgeons, the domains into which they are organized fragment into yet smaller pieces as individuals become increasingly specialized. The result is the loss of the sense of the world's wholeness.

When facts become sovereign, what is the fate of that which had been ultimate knowledge? In the realm of fact nothing is sacred except perhaps the maxim "Nothing is sacred," and knowledge that had been ultimately sacred is no longer knowledge at all. It is no more than "mere belief," belief now being reduced to the status of *doxa*. Values sanctified by the ultimately sacred are degraded to the status of tastes or preferences. They are relativized, and *idia phronēsis* in the form of economic rationality is not only given free rein but is elevated to the status of organizing principle and may even claim sanctity.

Finally, unlike logoi, which make moral and emotional claims on those who follow them, the new order of knowledge makes explicit that its claim on those operating in accordance with it is no more than intellectual. Explorers are *supposed* to become disengaged from the worlds they objectively explore. Participation in scientific acts of observing and analyzing the world in accordance with natural law is very different from participation in ritual acts constructing and maintaining the world in accordance with logos. Rituals, once ultimately meaningful acts of participation in orders the performances themselves realize, become "mere rituals," empty or even hypocritical formalisms. Under such circumstances highest-order meaning and the quest for it are dismissed as "mystical" or even stigmatized as "fanatic" or "weird." The world becomes a less meaningful place as the sacred certainty on which all human certainty is built, whether rocklike as Küng would have it, or made of words as I would have it, is threatened. Ritual as an instrument for establishing the foundations of human worlds has been seriously damaged, and it is not clear that other effective means for establishing such foundations have yet been developed.

In sum, we face a terrible contradiction. The reordering of knowledge that has liberated human exploration of physical law is, *in its nature*, inimical to the sacred and sanctified processes on which human worlds are founded and through which they are constructed. Conversely, as the epistemologies of discovery may be subversive of the sacred and sanctified understandings on which human institutions are founded, so may those understandings misconstrue the physical world and lead to actions that will cause it irreparable damage.

XII

Humanity is a species that lives, and can only live, in terms of meanings it itself must construct, only loosely constrained by its nature from fashioning self-destructive or world-destroying follies, in a world devoid of intrinsic meaning but subject to physical laws that can neither be changed nor, perhaps, ever be fully understood. Physical law and conventional meaning: the lawful and meaningful are not coextensive, and they are differently known. If physical laws and the states of affairs they constitute are to be known they must be discovered and explained. In contrast, humankind's meanings must be constructed and accepted. Laws and facts and the scientific procedures for discovering them may provide some of the materials out of which meanings are made, but they do not by themselves constitute meaning, nor can they do meaning's work of organizing human action. Conversely, although constructed meanings are often represented as discovered law, they do not constitute nature. The laws of physics, chemistry, and biology, and the states of affairs contingent on them are the case whether or not they are known. In the course of evolution, the lawful emergence of the ability to construct meaning provided humans with no exemption from physical law but did increase by magnitudes their capacity not only to conceive the world but to misunderstand it as well. Thus, as the epistemologies of discovery threaten with demystification the fabricated sacred truths on which human institutions are founded, so may meanings constructed by humans misconstrue the physical world and cause it irreparable damage.

Such meanings may be highly sanctified. Many years ago the historian Lynn White Jr. (1967) proposed that the postulation, in the first chapter of Genesis, of human mastery of the earth and all that inhabits it constitutes the ideological and even moral grounds of the current ecological crisis. Perhaps so, but such conceptions of mastery are not intrinsic to religion in general, nor are they even widespread, and more benign interpretations of Genesis are possible. What are apparently more secular conceptions seem to me to be more immediately culpable. Consider the epistemology inhering in money, the dominant mode of assigning value in contemporary, particularly capitalist, societies. Consider it especially as a means for understanding and assessing physical environments and for making decisions concerning them. Money's analytic power rests on its most peculiar and interesting property: it annihilates distinction. That is, it dissolves the distinctions between qualitatively unlike things, reducing them to mere quantitative differences by providing a common metric against which all things can be assigned values directly comparable to the values of all other things. But the world on which this metric is imposed is not as simple as the metric itself. Living systems — humans, plants, societies, ecosystems — all require a great variety of *qualitatively distinct* materials to survive. Protein and vitamin C, for example, cannot substitute for each other. You can stuff yourself with protein-rich foods, but if you do not get some vitamin C your teeth will fall out. The logic of money, however, through such analytic techniques as cost-benefit analysis, imposes a more-less logic on systems — organisms and ecosystems, most obviously — that do not operate in terms of more-less but in terms of complementarity among incommensurables. It is in the nature of such a monetary logic, a simple-minded logic of addition, subtraction, and "bottom lines," to rip the top off such complex systems as West Virginia to get at a simple substance, coal, or to endanger marine ecosystems in offshore searches for oil.

I introduced monetized epistemology as an apparently secular conception, and so it is, but when it is embedded in a capitalist economy, one in which "the business of America is business," it can and does become highly sanctified. As such, it becomes, as we have already seen, idolatrous. Evolution has armed our powers of misunderstanding with an ever increasing capacity, technological, economic, and political, to degrade or even destroy the world for increasingly narrow, trivial, or abstract reasons, and religion has sometimes sanctified the agents and forces of that degradation.

XIII

Human worlds, then, are worlds whose operations must be constructed as well as discovered by those participating in them. But a caveat should be introduced here. Although we may *distinguish, as classes,* the physically constituted from the culturally constructed, they *cannot be separated* in nature, and the world is increasingly an outcome of their interaction. The reconciliation and continuing accommodation of discovery and construction, difficult at best, becomes ever more difficult as our capacities to destroy the world increase and the certainties of our symbolic constructions crumble.

To say that problems arising from our entrapment between law and meaning become ever more acute does not mean that our situation is irremediable. Stephen Toulmin, for one, in *The Return to Cosmology* has advocated the development of what he calls a postmodern science, which, once again, would open itself up to what was called, in the seventeenth, eighteenth, and nineteenth centuries, "natural theology." According to Toulmin, a science capable of participating in this reunion would differ in several ways from modern science as Descartes defined it.

First, it would return scientists to the systems from which the Cartesian program separated them, either elevating them or exiling them to the status of detached observers. Such a detached status is no longer tenable (if it ever was) in light of Heisenberg's recognition of indeterminacy, of the growing awareness that living systems under study have subjective as well as objective characteristics, that opinion polls affect opinion, and that studies of ecological systems entail participation in those systems.

That scientific detachment is impossible leads to a second difference. Whereas a presumably detached modern science has attempted to confine itself to theory, recognition that participation in the world is inescapable must lead postmodern science to incorporate practice into itself. The distinction between "theory" and "praxis" will be blurred although not obliterated.

A third difference is implicit. If postmodern science is to be concerned with thinking and acting subjects and not merely inanimate objects or subjects treated as such, it must grant validity to subjective as well as objectively derived knowledge.

A fourth difference follows from the first three. Whereas modern science claims to be nonmoral or morally neutral, a moral dimension is intrinsic to postmodern science.

A fifth difference is yet more general. As a practical matter the specialized observations demanded by modern science have required an ever ramifying division of labor. Disciplines have therefore multiplied, knowledge has become increasingly fragmented, and the organization of the world as a whole has become no serious scholar's business. In Toulmin's view, postmodern science will, on the contrary, revive concern with cosmos, the world as an integrated and ordered whole, banished from the considerations of serious scientists since the seventeenth century when the new astronomy and the subsequent Cartesian revolution made forever untenable the cosmological model based on astronomy that had dominated thought since antiquity. That astronomy ultimately proved an inadequate ground for the conception of cosmos does not mean, however, that no good cosmological models are possible, and in Toulmin's view postmodern science will be ultimately concerned (I use Tillich's expression deliberately) with the world's unity, both with understanding the principles of that unity and with its continuing integrity. In sum, "postmodern science" is an order of epistemology *and* action in which both those who seek to discover natural law and those who seek to understand the nature of the world's constructed meanings are reunited with a world that they do not merely observe but in which they do participate for better or for worse.[3]

Whereas premodern cosmology was based on astronomy, Toulmin suggests (as have many others, using different words) that postmodern cosmology could be founded on ecology. Cosmologies built on astronomy on the one hand and ecology on the other have important differences. It may once have been plausible to believe that the stars' courses could affect us, but it has never been easy to believe that we could have any effect on them. Indeed, their imperviousness to our manipulation was part of their cosmological appeal. In contrast, the reciprocity of our relations with our environments is not only undeniable but manifestly obvious. Whereas the relationship of human lives to the movements of heavenly bodies was one of the correspondences between radically separate systems, the relationship of humans to the plants and animals and soils surrounding them is one of ceaseless interaction, and in postmodern times humans are clearly the most consequential actors in the systems they seek to understand.

Toulmin speaks of resurrecting the concept of cosmos, but I prefer the term *logos* because intrinsic to its use is a recognition that the world's order is not only constituted by tectonic, meteorological, chemical, and organic processes but, ever since the emergence of humanity, is in part constructed socially and symbolically by humans. Indeed, the notion that the world possesses a general or comprehensive order of any sort is outside the scope of modern scientific discourse, nor is the more specific concept of the ecosystem an ineluctable extrapolation from empirical procedures of discovery. It is a constructed understanding, and a con-

---

3. Toulmin's use of the term has, obviously, little in common with the rather solipsistic, narcissistic, nihilistic, and precious trend, also styled "postmodernism," that has recently become fashionable among a small circle of highly vocal intellectuals.

tested one at that (see Worster 1993: chap. 13), bearing, perhaps, as much resemblance to religious conceptions as it does to statements of modern science. Indeed, it may, as it were, mediate between them. On the one hand, as a regulative principle (Angeles 1981:225), it provides a framework within which one can rigorously formulate and investigate empirical problems. On the other hand it provides a general conception within which people can formulate their relationship to the encompassing world in which they participate, and as such it is not only a conception or understanding of the world but a guide to acting in it. As such it is part of humanity's means for maintaining a world that it is increasingly capable of disrupting, degrading, or even destroying.

I have said that the concept of the ecosystem, which Toulmin would make central to a revitalized conception of cosmos and I to that of logos, bears resemblance to or is related to religious conceptions. Its truth is not demonstrable, for one thing. As such its validity is a function of acceptance, and actions guided by it will tend to confirm it. It further proposes a conception of humanity's place in the world that has pervasive moral entailments. Ecosystemic conceptions are not explicit in the religions of the Book but they do not seem to me to be incompatible with those religions. Assertions of human domination of nature found in Genesis and elsewhere are not beyond the reach of a reinterpretation that transforms exploitation into stewardship and protection, as is implicit in the account of Noah in which even unclean animals are welcomed aboard. I earlier argued that sanctity originates in ultimate sacred postulates but flows from them to other more specific and concrete expressions and understandings, thereby underwriting their truth, correctness, legitimacy, propriety, or morality. It seems to me that ecosystemic conceptions that, in some non-Western societies themselves approach ultimately sacred status, are worthy of high sanctification by religions of the West as well. High and explicit sanctification of such conceptions and the actions flowing from them not only might contribute to the world's preservation but could contribute to the revitalization of those religions in a time of doubt and infirmity.

References

Angeles, Peter A.
1984   *Dictionary of Philosophy.* New York: Barnes and Noble.
Austin, J. H.
1962   *How to Do Things with Words.* London, Oxford, and New York: Oxford University.
Bateson, Gregory
1972   "The Role of Somatic Change in Evolution." Pp. 346-63 in *Steps to an Ecology of Mind.* Ed. G. Bateson. New York: Ballantine.

1979   *Mind and Nature: A Necessary Unity.* New York: Dutton.

Brown, Joseph Epes (recorder and editor)

1971   *The Sacred Pipe: Black Elk's Account of the Seven Rites of the Oglala Sioux.* Baltimore: Penguin (first published by University of Oklahoma, 1953).

Brown, Norman W.

1972   "Duty as Truth in Ancient India." *Proceedings of the American Philosophical Society* 116/3:252-68.

Buber, Martin

1952   *Good and Evil: Two Interpretations.* New York: Charles Scribner's Sons.

Bultmann, R.

1967   "The Greek and Hellenistic Use of *Alētheia.*" *TDNT* 1.238-41.

Cheney, William

1970   *The Cult of Kingship in Anglo-Saxon England: The Transition from Paganism to Christianity.* Manchester: Manchester University.

Debrunner, A.

1967   "*Logos.*" *TDNT* 4.69-77.

Freedman, David Noel

1984   "The Spelling of the Name 'David' in the Hebrew Bible." Pp. 89-104 in *Biblical and Other Studies in Honor of Robert Gordis* (= *HAR* 11). Ed. R. Ahroni. Columbus: University of Ohio.

1986   "Deliberate Deviation from an Established Pattern of Repetition as a Rhetorical Device." Pp. 45-52 in *Ninth Congress of Jewish Studies.* Jerusalem: Hebrew University.

1991   *The Unity of the Hebrew Bible.* Ann Arbor: University of Michigan.

In press   "The Word of God in the Hebrew Bible." In *The Concept of the Word.* Ed. J. Swearingen. Tucson: University of Arizona.

Heidegger, Martin

1959   *Introduction to Metaphysics.* Trans. Ralph Manheim. New Haven: Yale University.

Kahn, Charles H.

1979   *The Art and Thought of Heraclitus.* Cambridge: Cambridge University.

Kirk, G. S.

1954   *Heraclitus: The Cosmic Fragments.* Cambridge: Cambridge University.

Kleinknecht, H.

1967   "The Logos in the Greek and Hellenistic World." *TDNT* 4.77-91.

Küng, Hans

1980   *Does God Exist?* Trans. Edward Quinn. Garden City: Doubleday.

Leon-Portilla, Miguel

1963   *Aztec Thought and Culture: A Study of the Ancient Nahuatl Mind.* Trans. J. E. Davis. Norman: University of Oklahoma.

Lichtheim, Miriam
 1971 *Ancient Egyptian Literature.* Vol. 1. Berkeley: University of California.
Lovelock, J. E.
 1987 *Gaia: A New Look at Life on Earth.* Oxford: Oxford University.
McKeon, Richard
 1941 *The Basic Works of Aristotle.* New York: Random House.
Myers, Jacob M.
 1965 *Ezra. Nehemiah.* AB 14. Garden City, N.Y.: Doubleday.
Otto, Rudolph
 1923 *The Idea of the Holy.* Trans. John W. Harvey. London: Oxford University.
Peirce, Charles Sanders
 1960 *The Collected Papers of Charles Sanders Peirce.* Ed. Charles Hartshorne and Paul Weiss. Cambridge: Harvard University.
Rappaport, Roy A.
 1971 "The Sacred in Human Evolution." *Annual Review of Systematics* 2:23-44.
 1977 "Maladaptation in Social Systems." Pp. 49-72 in *Evolution in Social Systems.* Ed. J. Friedman and M. Rowlands. London: Duckworth.
 1979a "Adaptive Structure and Its Disorders." Pp. 145-72 in *Ecology, Meaning, and Religion.* Berkeley: North Atlantic.
 1979b "The Obvious Aspects of Ritual." Pp. 173-222 in *Ecology, Meaning, and Religion.* Berkeley: North Atlantic.
 1979c "Sanctity and Lies in Evolution." Pp. 222-46 in *Ecology, Meaning, and Religion.* Berkeley: North Atlantic.
de Rougemont, Denis
 1956 *The Devil's Snare.* Trans. Haakon Chevalier. New York: Meridian Books (Original, 1944).
Scholem, Gershom G.
 1965 *On the Kabbalah and Its Symbolism.* New York: Schocken.
Searle, J. R.
 1969 *Speech Acts.* Cambridge: Cambridge University.
Smith, Gerard
 1956 *The Truth That Frees.* Aquinas Lecture for 1956. Milwaukee: Marquette University.
Tillich, Paul
 1957 *Dynamics of Faith.* New York: Harper & Row.
Toulmin, Stephen
 1982 *The Return to Cosmology: Post-Modern Science and the Theology of Nature.* Berkeley: University of California.
Turner, Victor
 1967 *The Forest of Symbols: Aspects of Ndembu Ritual.* Ithaca: Cornell University.

Vico, Giambattista
    1988   *On the Most Ancient Wisdom of the Italians.* Trans. L. H. Palmer.
                Ithaca: Cornell University. (Original, 1710)
Wallace, Anthony F. C.
    1966   *Religion: An Anthropological View.* New York: Random House.
White, Alan
    1970   *Truth.* London and Basingstoke: Macmillan.
White, Leslie
    1949   *The Science of Culture.* New York: Farrar Strauss.
White, Lynn, Jr.
    1967   "The Historical Roots of Our Ecological Crisis." *Science* 155:1203-7.
Wilson, John
    1951   *The Culture of Ancient Egypt.* Chicago: University of Chicago.
Worster, Donald
    1993   "The Ecology of Order and Chaos." Chapter 13 in *The Wealth of
                Nations.* New York: Oxford University.

Bibliography of the Works of
David Noel Freedman, 1947-1982*

M. O'CONNOR

*Reprinted with permission from: *The Word of the Lord Shall Go Forth: Essays in Honor of David Noel Freedman in Celebration of His Sixtieth Birthday* (ed. C. L. Meyers and M. P. O'Connor; Winona Lake, IN: Eisenbrauns, 1983).

This is a reader's bibliography, not a bibliographer's, and therefore a few words of explanation may be wanted; it is one reader's bibliography, and therefore a few words of justification may be needed. The listing is complete to the end of 1981, though some pieces of devotional ephemera from the fifties may have been lost track of and some further items dated 1981 may yet appear; all items dated 1982 or marked forthcoming (f/c) refer to work completed and in press. A few works in preparation are referred to in this note. [See further the second bibliography by Kathleen Beck.] Nonprint media are not represented here.

The first three sections list Freedman's own work over the past two dozen years, and the fourth section records his editorial labors; incidental contributions to journals he has edited are listed in IV.N. The division of materials over the first three sections is not meant to be prejudicial, as I shall try to explain.

Section I. The works here constitute Freedman's scholarly contribution to Near Eastern and biblical studies. The range is evident, so it may be useful to mark out principal areas of study, proceeding from least to most important.

(1) *Qumranic studies.* The major papers are 1962a, 1968d, 1974b; relevant reviews and notes are 1949, 1957, 1959.

(2) *Orthographic studies.* The major work is the earliest, Cross and Freedman 1952; subsequent studies include Freedman 1962a, 1969b, 1969c, and Freedman and Ritterspach 1967.

(3) *Studies in the Tetragrammaton.* Two papers only, both major, Freedman 1960b and Freedman and O'Connor 1980.

(4) *Poetic studies.* (a) *Early work.* Cross and Freedman 1947, 1948, 1953a, 1955, 1972, and 1975. (b) *Studies since 1960 in nonprophetic poetry.* Work on poetic structure is chiefly represented in the fifteen papers and four notes collected in 1980a, which must be supplemented by the inaugural paper of this phase of work, 1960c, as well as by the major paper of Freedman and Franke-Hyland 1973, and the smaller pieces 1963b and 1964c; since the gathering of 1980a, other work has been done, 1980b, 1981a, 1981b, and the forthcoming papers. (c) *Studies in the eighth-century prophets.* The work underway since the early seventies with F. I. Andersen finds its first monument in Andersen and Freedman 1980; the Anchor Bible volume on Amos and Micah is in preparation. Though Freedman 1955 is superseded by *Hosea,* Freedman 1979a retains some interest.

(5) *The History of Israelite Literature.* Whether Freedman will bring to completion the work he has long projected under this title, I cannot say; some of the materials are to hand: 1963c is programmatic; 1961, 1962k, 1969d, 1973c, 1975c, 1976d, 1976e, and 1979c are basic; 1960a, 1963a, 1964b, and 1967b are tangential.

The listing of these five areas is problematic: fundamental concerns with historical study and with Israelite theology are obscured here; the constant attention to grammatical phenomena on all levels cannot be highlighted directly.

Section II. Grouped together here are materials tangential to the major enterprise of Near Eastern studies as Freedman has undertaken it. Along with Freedman's most controversial work, this section includes his least appreciated labors, those involving scholarly biography. The major realms can be listed. (1) Scholarly biography, whether obituary, appreciation, or biography and bibliography in the amplest sense. (2) Archeological reporting, chiefly on Ashdod (add to the materials here Cross and Freedman 1964, Dothan and Freedman 1967, and Freedman 1967c and 1979d, from Section I) and Tell Mardikh (add from Section I, Freedman 1979e). (3) Reflection on the scholarly study of the Bible (add from Section I, Freedman 1965) and of religion in general.

Section III. The sermons written by Freedman alone and in collaboration with his Princeton Theological Seminary classmate T. A. Gill are among the most moving pieces in the entire body of work. The work written for children and young people seems to be of little interest. The few pieces of religious-political speculation from the fifties are dated.

Section IV. The material is for the most part self-explanatory. All the categories remain open except for I and M; Freedman has handed on the editorship of the publications of the American Schools, and complexities in the estate of William Foxwell Albright make it unlikely that Freedman will continue to serve as Albright's literary executor.

Sigla and structure. In Part I.B., * indicates contributions of under one hundred words. In Part II.D., * indicates contributions written for children, young people, and their teachers. Only materials in Section I are lettered to coordinate various publications within a single year; the letter sigla span the three parts of Section I.

The material in Section I is ordered by category (books, papers, and notes; contributions to reference works; book reviews), by authorship (DNF alone; with others), by type of contribution (books; contributions to books; contributions to periodicals), then alphabetically (in case of contributions, by book or periodical rather than article title). Sections II and III follow the same pattern, *mutatis mutandis.* In Section IV, all parts are arranged by year, except for IV.H. and IV.J., which are arranged alphabetically.

There are 152 entries in Section I (A: 78 entries; B: 52 entries; C: 22 entries); 27 entries in Section II; 62 entries in Section III (E: 37 entries; F: 25 entries); and 112 entries in Section IV (G: 6 entries; H: 36 entries; I: 24 entries; J: 24 entries; L: 14 entries; N: 6 entries; and K and M, 1 entry each), a total of 353 entries, slightly fewer than the number of years Enoch lived on earth before he was assumed into heaven.

I. The Bible and the Ancient Near East

I.A. Books, papers, and notes

A1. F. M. Cross and DNF
1947

A Note on Deuteronomy 33:26. *Bulletin of the American Schools of Oriental Research* 108:6-7.

A2. [F. M. Cross and DNF]
1948

The Evolution of Early Hebrew Orthography: The Epigraphic Evidence. Johns Hopkins Dissertation [nominally submitted by DNF]. 260 pp. Revised as Cross and Freedman 1952.

A3. F. M. Cross and DNF
1948

The Blessing of Moses [Deuteronomy 33]. *Journal of Biblical Literature* 67:191-210. See Cross and Freedman 1950.

A4. DNF
1949

The "House of Absalom" in the Habakkuk Scroll [4QpHab 5:9, a literal, not symbolic term; note, e.g., 1 Macc 11:70]. *Bulletin of the American Schools of Oriental Research* 114:11-12.

A5. [F. M. Cross and DNF]
1950

Studies in Ancient Yahwistic Poetry. Johns Hopkins Dissertation [nominally submitted by F. M. Cross]. 358 pp. Various chapters published, usually in revised form, as Cross and Freedman 1948, 1953a, 1955; the whole published without revision but with a postscriptum as Cross and Freedman 1975. A small offset edition of the unrevised dissertation appeared in 1964.

A6. DNF
1951a

The Orthography of the Masoretic Text of the Pentateuch (abstract). *Journal of Biblical Literature* 70:iv.

A7.   F. M. Cross and DNF
      1951   The Pronominal Suffixes of the Third Person Singular in
                              Phoenician [notably KAI 10, 24, 26; cf. KAI 189]. *Journal
                              of Near Eastern Studies* 10:228-30.

A8.   1952   *Early Hebrew Orthography: A Study of the Epigraphic Evi-
                              dence.* American Oriental Series 36. New Haven: American
                              Oriental Society. viii + 77. See Cross and Freedman 1948.

A9.   DNF
      1953a   Notes on Genesis [grammar in 1:9, 11; 2:20; 3:17; the text
                              of 4:22; verse in 5:29; 12:1-2; 14:4, 6, 19-20]. *Zeitschrift für
                              die alttestamentliche Wissenschaft* 64:190-94.

A10. F. M. Cross and DNF
      1953a   A Royal Song of Thanksgiving: II Samuel 22 = Psalm 18.
                              Journal of Biblical Literature 72:15-34. See Cross and Freed-
                              man 1950.

A11. 1953b   Josiah's Revolt Against Assyria [esp. in 2 Chronicles 34].
                              Journal of Near Eastern Studies 12:56-58.

A12. DNF
      1954   The Book of Ezekiel. Studia Biblica 27. *Interpretation* 8:446-
                              71.

A13. 1955   PŠTY [*pištay*] in Hosea 2:7. *Journal of Biblical Literature*
                              74:275.

A14. F. M. Cross and DNF
      1955   The Song of Miriam [Exodus 15]. *Journal of Near Eastern
                              Studies* 14:237-50. See Cross and Freedman 1950.

A15. DNF
      1956   The Babylonian Chronicle. *The Biblical Archaeologist* 19:50-
                              60. Rpt. 1961 as pp. 113-27 in *The Biblical Archaeologist
                              Reader, 1,* ed. G. E. Wright and D. N. Freedman. Garden
                              City: Doubleday. (See G1 below.)

A16. 1957   The Prayer of Nabonidus [4QPrNab]. *Bulletin of the Amer-
                              ican Schools of Oriental Research* 145:31-32.

A17. 1958   Jonah 1:46 [read a form of *ḥwb*, not of *ḥšb*]. *Journal of
                              Biblical Literature* 77:161-62.

A18. 1960a   History and Eschatology: The Nature of Biblical Religion
                              and Prophetic Faith. *Interpretation* 14:143-54.

A19. 1960b   The Name of the God of Moses. *Journal of Biblical Literature*
                              79:151-56.

A20. 1960c   Archaic Forms in Early Hebrew Poetry [Judg 5:26; 2 Sam
                              22:16; Deut 33:11b; Num 23:10b; 21:17-18; 21:27b; Ps 29:1-
                              2; Exod 15:6, 9, 16]. *Zeitschrift für die alttestamentliche Wis-
                              senschaft* 72:101-7.

A21. R. M. Grant in collaboration with DNF
      1960   *The Secret Sayings of Jesus: The Gnostic Gospel of Thomas.*
                              With a translation by W. R. Schoedel. Garden City: Dou-
                              bleday [hardcover, 206 pp.; Dolphin paperback, 198 pp.]
                              and London: Collins [paperback, 192 pp.]. Trans. 1960 into
                              German as *Geheime Wörter Jesu* by S. George with a trans-
                              lation by H. Quecke and with a contribution by J. B. Bauer.
                              Frankfurt-am-Main: Heinrich Scheffler. 228 pp. Also trans.
                              1962 into Dutch as *Het Thomas Evangelie* by J. Mooy.

Utrecht: Aula Boeken. 188 pp. [Jacket design for original hardcover edition by Edward Gorey.]

A22. DNF
      1961
The Chronicler's Purpose. *Catholic Biblical Quarterly* 23:436-42.

A23. DNF and E. F. Campbell
      1961
The Chronology of Israel and the Ancient Near East. A. Old Testament Chronology [Freedman]. B. The Ancient Near East: Chronological Bibliography and Charts [Campbell]. Pp. 203-28 in *The Bible and the Ancient Near East: Essays in Honor of William Foxwell Albright*, ed. G. E. Wright. Garden City: Doubleday. Rpt. 1965 as pp. 265-87 of paperback reissue. Volume rpt. with original pagination, 1979, Winona Lake, Indiana: Eisenbrauns.

A24. DNF
      1962a
The Massoretic Text and the Qumran Scrolls: A Study in Orthography. *Textus* 2:87-102. Rpt. 1975 as pp. 196-211 in *Qumran and the History of the Biblical Text*, ed. F. M. Cross and S. Talmon. Cambridge: Harvard University Press.

A25. 1963a
On Method in Biblical Studies: The Old Testament. *Interpretation* 17:308-18.

A26. 1963b
The Original Name of Jacob [in Deut 33:28]. *Israel Exploration Journal* 13:125-26.

A27. 1963c
The Law and the Prophets. *Supplements to Vetus Testamentum* 9:250-65. Rpt. 1974 as pp. 5-20 in *The Canon and Masorah of the Hebrew Bible: An Introductory Reader*, ed. S. Z. Leiman. The Library of Biblical Studies. New York: Ktav.

A28. 1964a
A Second Mesha Inscription [cf. KAI 181:1-2]. *Bulletin of the American Schools of Oriental Research* 175:50-51.

A29. 1964b
Divine Commitment and Human Obligation: The Covenant Theme. *Interpretation* 18:419-31.

A30. F. M. Cross and DNF
      1964
The Name of Ashdod. *Bulletin of the American Schools of Oriental Research* 175:48-50.

A31. DNF
      1965
Archaeology and the Future of Biblical Studies: The Biblical Languages. Pp. 294-312 in *The Bible in Modern Scholarship: Papers Read at the One Hundredth Meeting of the Society of Biblical Literature*, ed. J. P. Hyatt. Nashville: Abingdon.

A32. 1967a
The Song of the Sea. Pp. 1-10 in *A Feeling of Celebration: A Tribute to James Muilenburg*, ed. R. Shukraft. San Anselmo, California: San Francisco Theological Seminary. Rpt. as pp. 179-86 in Freedman 1980a.

A33. 1967b
The Biblical Idea of History. *Interpretation* 21:32-49.

A34. M. Dothan and DNF
      1967
Ashdod I. The First Season of Excavations 1962. ʿAtiqot English Series VII. Jerusalem: The Department of Antiquities and Museums, [The State of] Israel. 171 pp. + 28 plates.

A35. DNF and A. Ritterspach
      1967
The Use of *Aleph* as a Vowel Letter in the Genesis Apocryphon. *Revue de Qumran* 6:293-300.

A36. DNF
1968a   The Structure of Job 3. *Biblica* 49:503-8. Rpt. as pp. 323-28 in Freedman 1980a.

A37. 1968b   Isaiah 42:13. *Catholic Biblical Quarterly* 30:225-26. Rpt. as pp. 345-46 in Freedman 1980a.

A38. 1968c   The Elihu Speeches in the Book of Job. *Harvard Theological Review* 61:51-59. Rpt. as pp. 329-37 in Freedman 1980a. Trans. 1968 into Japanese in *Kirisutokyo Ronshū* [*The Journal of Christian Studies*] #14 [In Honor of Prof. Junichi Asano]: 25-37.

A39. 1968d   The Old Testament at Qumran. *McCormick Quarterly* 21 #3 (March 1968): 299-306. Rpt. 1969 as pp. 131-41 in *New Directions in Biblical Archaeology,* ed. DNF and J. C. Greenfield. Garden City: Doubleday. (See G3 below.)

A40. 1969a   The Burning Bush [Exod 3:2-3]. *Biblica* 50:245-46.

A41. 1969b   Orthographic Peculiarities in the Book of Job. *Eretz-Israel* 9 [W. F. Albright Volume]:35-44.

A42. 1969c   The Orthography of the Arad Ostraca. *Israel Exploration Journal* 19:52-56.

A43. 1969d   The Flowering of Apocalyptic [Daniel, Qumran]. *Journal for Theology and the Church* 6 [Apocalypticism]:166-74.

A44. 1970   "Mistress Forever." A Note on Isaiah 47,7. *Biblica* 51:538.

A45. DNF and F. I. Andersen
1970   Harmon in Amos 4:3. *Bulletin of the American Schools of Oriental Research* 198:41.

A46. DNF
1971a   The Structure of Psalm 137. Pp. 187-205 in *Near Eastern Studies in Honor of William Foxwell Albright,* ed. H. Goedicke. Baltimore: Johns Hopkins University Press. Rpt. as pp. 303-21 in Freedman 1980a.

A47. 1971b   Is Justice Blind? (Is 11,3f). *Biblica* 52:536.

A48. 1971c   A Note on Judges 15:5. *Biblica* 52:535.

A49. 1971d   II Samuel 23:4. *Journal of Biblical Literature* 90:329-30. Rpt. as pp. 343-44 in Freedman 1980a.

A50. F. M. Cross and DNF
1971   An Inscribed Jar Handle from Raddana. *Bulletin of the American Schools of Oriental Research* 201:19-22.

A51. DNF
1972a   The Refrain in David's Lament over Saul and Jonathan. Pp. 115-26 in *Ex Orbe Religionum. Studia Geo Widengren Oblata. 1,* ed. C. J. Bleeker et al. Studies in the History of Religions (Supplements to *NUMEN*) 21. Leiden: Brill. Rpt. as pp. 263-74 in Freedman 1980a.

A52. 1972b   Prolegomenon. Pp. vii-lvi in George Buchanan Gray, *The Forms of Hebrew Poetry Considered with Special Reference to the Criticism and Interpretation of the Old Testament.* The Library of Biblical Studies [reprint of the original 1915 edition]. New York: Ktav. The Annotated Bibliography on Hebrew Poetry from 1915 to the Present was compiled with the help of Bonnie Kittel. Rpt. without the bibliography as pp. 23-50 in Freedman 1980a.

A53. 1972c   The Broken Construct Chain. *Biblica* 53:534-36. Rpt. as pp. 339-41 in Freedman 1980a.

A54. 1972d   Acrostics and Metrics in Hebrew Poetry. *Harvard Theological Review* 65:367-92. Rpt. as pp. 51-76 in Freedman 1980a.

A55. 1973a   God Almighty in Psalm 78,59. *Biblica* 54:268. Rpt. as p. 347 in Freedman 1980a.

A56. DNF and C. Franke-Hyland
      1973   Psalm 29: A Structural Analysis. *Harvard Theological Review* 66:237-56.

A57. DNF
      1974a   Strophe and Meter in Exodus 15. Pp. 163-203 in *A Light Unto My Path: Old Testament Studies in Honor of Jacob M. Myers*, ed. H. N. Bream, R. D. Heim, and C. A. Moore. Gettysburg Theological Studies IV. Pittsburgh: Temple University Press. Rpt. as pp. 187-227 in Freedman 1980a.

A58. 1974b   Variant Readings in the Leviticus Scroll from Qumran Cave 11 [11QpaleoLev]. *Catholic Biblical Quarterly* 36/4 [P. W Skehan Number]:525-34. For the proper *siglum* assignment see J. A. Fitzmyer, S.J. 1975. Correction. *Catholic Biblical Quarterly* 37:238. For the complete text see K. Mathews. 1980. *The Paleo-Hebrew Leviticus Scroll from Qumran*. Michigan Dissertation. The final publication will be D. N. Freedman and K. A. Matthews. *The Paleo-Hebrew Leviticus Scroll from Qumran Cave 11*. With a contribution by R. S. Hanson.

A59. 1975a   The Aaronic Benediction (Numbers 6:24-26). Pp. 35-47 in *No Famine in the Land: Studies in Honor of John L. McKenzie*, ed. J. L. Flanagan and A. W. Robinson. Missoula/Claremont: Scholars Press/The Institute for Antiquity and Christianity. Rpt. as pp. 229-42 in Freedman 1980a.

A60. 1975b   Early Israelite History in the Light of Early Israelite Poetry. Pp. 3-35 in *Unity and Diversity: Essays in the History, Literature, and Religion of the Ancient Near East*, ed. H. Goedicke and J. J. M. Roberts. Baltimore: Johns Hopkins University Press. Rpt. as pp. 131-66 in Freedman 1980a.

A61. 1975c   "Son of Man, Can These Bones Live?" — The Exile. *Interpretation* 29/2 [John Bright Number]:171-86. With the help of M. O'Connor.

A62. F. M. Cross and DNF
      1975   *Studies in Ancient Yahwistic Poetry*. Society of Biblical Literature Dissertation Series 21. Missoula: Scholars Press. viii + 191 pp. See Cross and Freedman 1950.

A63. DNF
      1976a   Divine Names and Titles in Early Hebrew Poetry. Pp. 55-107 in *Magnalia Dei: The Mighty Acts of God: Essays on the Bible and Archaeology in Memory of G. Ernest Wright*, ed. F. M. Cross, W. E. Lemke, and P. D. Miller. Garden City: Doubleday. Rpt. as pp. 77-129 in Freedman 1980a.

A64. 1976b   The Twenty-Third Psalm. Pp. 139-66 in *Michigan Oriental Studies in Honor of George G. Cameron*, ed. L. L. Orlin et al. Ann Arbor: Department of Near Eastern Studies, The University of Michigan [distributed by Eisenbrauns]. Rpt. as pp. 275-302 in Freedman 1980a.

A65. 1977
Pottery, Poetry, and Prophecy: An Essay on Biblical Poetry [The Society of Biblical Literature Presidential Address for 1976]. *Journal of Biblical Literature* 96:5-26. Rpt. 1979 as pp. 77-100 in *The Bible in its Literary Milieu: Contemporary Essays*, ed. V. L. Tollers and J. R. Maier. Grand Rapids: Eerdmans. Also rpt. as pp. 1-22 in Freedman 1980a.

A66. 1978
Psalm 113 and the Song of Hannah. *Eretz-Israel* 14 [H. L. Ginsberg Volume]:56-69. With the assistance of Clayton Libolt. Rpt. as pp. 243-61 in Freedman 1980a.

A67. 1979a
Problems of Textual Criticism in the Book of Hosea. Pp. 55-76 in *The Critical Study of Sacred Texts*, ed. W. D. O'Flaherty. Berkeley Religious Studies Series. Berkeley: Graduate Theological Union [Lancaster-Miller].

A68. 1979b
Early Israelite Poetry and Historical Reconstructions. Pp. 85-96 in *Symposia Celebrating the Seventy-Fifth Anniversary of the Founding of the American Schools of Oriental Research (1900-1975)*, ed. F. M. Cross. Zion Research Foundation Occasional Publications 1-2. Cambridge: The American Schools of Oriental Research. Rpt. as pp. 167-78 in Freedman 1980a.

A69. 1979c
The Age of David and Solomon. Pp. 101-25, 327-29 in *The World History of the Jewish People. First Series: Ancient Times. Volume 4. The Age of the Monarchies. Part I. Political History*, ed. A. Malamat. Jerusalem: Massada. With the help of M. O'Connor.

A70. 1980a
Pottery, Poetry, and Prophecy: Studies in Early Hebrew Poetry. Winona Lake, Indiana: Eisenbrauns. A reprinting, with a foreword by F. M. Cross, a preface by the author, and indexes, of DNF 1967a, 1968a, b, c, 1971a, d, 1972a, b, c, d, 1973a, 1974a, 1975a, b, 1976a, b, 1977, 1978, 1979b (15 papers and 4 notes), xiv + 376 pp.

A71. 1980b
The Poetic Structure of the Framework of Deuteronomy 33. Pp. 25-46 in *The Bible World: Essays in Honor of Cyrus H. Gordon*, ed. Gary Rendsburg et al. New York: Ktav and the Institute of Hebrew Culture Education of New York University.

A72. 1980c
Foreword. Pp. 13-15 in Millard C. Lind, *Yahweh Is a Warrior: The Theology of Warfare in Ancient Israel.* Scottdale, Pennsylvania: Herald Press.

A73. F. I. Andersen and DNF
1980
Hosea. Anchor Bible 24. Garden City: Doubleday. xviii + 701 pp.

A74. DNF
1981a
Preface. Pp. 7-8 in *Chiasmus in Antiquity*, ed. J. W. Welch. Hildesheim: Gerstenberg.

A75. 1981b
Temple [Made] Without Hands. Pp. 21-30 in *Temples and High Places in Biblical Times*, ed. A. Biran et al. Jerusalem:

		The Nelson Glueck School of Biblical Archaeology of the Hebrew Union College.
A76.	f/c	On the Death of Abiner [2 Sam 3:33-34]. Pp. 125-27 in *Love and Death in the Ancient Near East: Essays in Honor of Marvin H. Pope on the Occasion of His Sixty-fifth Birthday,* ed. J. H. Marks and R. M. Good. Guilford, Connecticut: Four Quarters Publishing.
A77.	f/c	Discourse on Prophetic Discourse [Mic 1:3]. Pp. 141-58 in *The Quest for the Kingdom of God: Studies in Honor of G. E. Mendenhall,* ed. H. B. Huffmon, F. A. Spina, and A. R. W. Green. Winona Lake, Indiana: Eisenbrauns.
A78.	f/c	Prose Particles in the Poetry of the Primary History. Pp. 45-62 in *Biblical and Related Studies Presented to Samuel Iwry,* ed. A. Kort and S. Morschauser. Winona Lake, IN: Eisenbrauns.

I.B. Contributions to Reference Works
* = under 100 words

Biblisch-Historisches Handwörterbuch, ed. B. Reicke and L. Rost. 3 vols. Göttingen: Vandenhoeck und Ruprecht, 1962[-1966].

| B1. | DNF 1962b | Ältester. Band I, Sp. 76-77. |

The Interpreter's Dictionary of the Bible, ed. G. A. Buttrick et al. Nashville and New York: Abingdon Press, 1962.

B2.	DNF *1962c	D (Deuteronomist). Vol. A-D, p. 756.
B3.	1962d	Documents. Vol. A-D, pp. 860-61.
B4.	*1962e	E (Elohist). Vol. E-J, p. 1.
B5.	*1962f	Elohist. Vol. E-J, p. 94.
B6.	*1962g	H [Holiness Code]. Vol. E-J, p. 503.
B7.	1962h	Hexateuch. Vol. E-J, pp. 597-98.
BS.	*1962i	J [Jahwist]. Vol. E-J, p. 777.
B9.	*1962j	P. Vol. K-Q, p. 617.
B10.	1962k	Pentateuch. Vol. K-Q, pp. 711-27.

Dictionary of the Bible[2], ed. J. Hastings, rev. F. C. Grant and H. H. Rowley. New York: Charles Scribner's Sons, 1963. All the entries except the one on Mari are revisions of entries in the first edition of the *Dictionary.*

B11.	DNF 1963d	Armour, Arms. Pp. 54-55.
B12.	1963e	Army. Pp. 55-56.
B13.	1963f	Calneh, Calno. P. 119.
B14.	1963g	Camel. Pp. 119-20.
B15.	1963h	Chariot. P. 131.
B16.	*1963i	Ezion-Geber. P. 285.
B17.	1963j	Hazor. P. 368.

B18.	1963k	Hebron. P. 375.
B19.	1963l	High Place, Sanctuary. Pp. 382-84.
B20.	1963m	Horse. P. 397.
B21.	1963n	Jachin and Boaz. P. 452.
B22.	1963o	Mari. P. 618
B23.	1963p	Millo. P. 660.
B24.	1963q	Mining and Metals. Pp. 660-61.
B25.	1963r	Nob. Pp. 700-701.
B26.	1963s	Plain, Cities of the. P. 776.
B27.	1963t	Sisera. P. 923.
B28.	1963u	Taanach. P. 948.

New Catholic Encyclopedia, ed. W. J. McDonald et al. New York: McGraw-Hill, 1967.

B29. DNF
      1967c   Azotus (Ashdod). Vol. I, pp. 1144-45.

Theologisches Wörterbuch zum Alten Testament, ed. G. J. Botterweck and Helmer Ringgren. Stuttgart: Kohlhammer, 1973- .

B30.	DNF and J. Lundbom 1973	*beṭen.* Band I, Sp. 616-20.
B31.	1977a	*dôr.* With a contribution by G. J. Botterweck. Band II, Sp. 181-94.
B32.	1977b	*ḥādal.* Band II, Sp. 748-55.
B33.	1977c	*ḥānan.* With a contribution by H.-J. Fabry. Band III, Lieferung 1, Sp. 23-40.
B34.	1978a	*ḥārâ.* With a contribution by G. J. Botterweck. Band III, Lieferung 2/3, Sp. 182-88.
B35.	1978b	*ḥāraṣ.* With a contribution by G. J. Botterweck. Band III, Lieferung 2/3, Sp. 230-34.
B36.	1981a	*jṣt.* Band III, Lieferung 6/7, Sp. 840-43.
B37.	1981b	*jāqad.* Band III, Lieferung 6/7, Sp. 845-49.
B38.	DNF and M. O'Connor 1980	*JHWH.* Band III, Lieferung 4/5, Sp. 533-54.
B39.	f/c	*kĕrubîm.*
B40.	f/c	*kuttōnet.*
B41.	f/c	*māgēn.*
B42.	DNF and B. E. Willoughby f/c	*mal'ak.*

Theological Dictionary of the Old Testament, ed. G. J. Botterweck and Helmer Ringgren; trans. D. E. Green, J. T. Willis, G. Bromiley. Grand Rapids: Eerdmans, 1975- .

B43.	DNF and J. Lundbom 1975	*beṭen.* Vol. II, pp. 94-99.
B44.	1978c	*dôr.* With a contribution by G. J. Botterweck. Vol. III, pp. 169-81.
B45.	1980	*ḥādal.* Vol. IV, pp. 216-21.

(further contributions to appear, as sub the German original above)

Diccionario Teologico del Antiguo Testamento, ed. G. J. Botterweck and H. Ringgren; trans. A. de la Fuente and J. L. Zubizaretta. Madrid: Ediciones Christiandad, 1978- .

B46.   DNF and J. Lundbom
          1978d   *beṭen.* Tomo I, pp. 622-27.
(further contributions to appear, as sub the German original above)

Interpreter's Dictionary of the Bible. Supplementary Volume, ed. K. A. Crim et al. Nashville: Abingdon, 1976.

B47.   DNF
          1976c   Ashdod. Pp. 71-72. With the help of M. O'Connor.
B48.   1976d   Canon of the Old Testament. Pp. 130-36. With the help of
                                               M. O'Connor.
B49.   1976e   The Deuteronomic History. Pp. 226-28. With the help of
                                               M. O'Connor.
B50.   DNF and M. O'Connor
          1976   Bastard. Pp. 92-93.

The International Standard Bible Encyclopedia, ed. G. W. Bromiley et al. Grand Rapids: Eerdmans, 1979.

B51.   DNF
          1979d   Ashdod. Vol. 1, pp. 314-16.

New Catholic Encyclopedia. Volume XVII. Supplement: Change in the Church, ed. T. C. O'Brien et al. New York: McGraw Hill, 1979.

B52.   DNF
          1979e   Ebla. P. 198.

I.C. Book Reviews

C1.   DNF
          1950   Old Testament Literature, 1949 [brief notes on 84 books].
                                               Interpretation 4:78-88.
C2.   1951b   J. Touzard. 1949. *Grámmaïre hebraïque, abrégée.* Paris:
                                               Gabalda.
                                               Journal of Biblical Literature 70:174-75.
C3.   1952   H. J. Schoeps. 1950. *Aus frühchristlicher Zeit. Reli-
                                               gionsgeschichtliche Untersuchungen.* Tübingen: Mohr.
                                               Journal of Biblical Literature 71:58-60.
C4.   1953b   E. R. Thiele. 1951. *The Mysterious Numbers of the Hebrew
                                               Kings.* Chicago: University of Chicago Press.
                                               Journal of Bible and Religion 21:122, 124.
C5.   1953c   T. W. Auer. 1951. *Die Pharaonen des Buches Exodus.* Regens-
                                               burg: F. Pustet.
                                               Journal of Biblical Literature 72:271.
C6.   1959   K. Stendahl, ed. 1957. *The Scrolls and the New Testament.*
                                               New York: Harper.
                                               Journal of Biblical Literature 78:326-34.

C7.   1960d
Z. Vilnay. 1960. *The Guide to Israel.* Cleveland: World.
Journal of Biblical Literature 79:293.

C8.   1962l
Y. Kaufmann. 1960. *The Religion of Israel . . . to the Baby-
lonian Exile.* Chicago: University of Chicago Press.
Journal of Biblical Literature 81:185-90.

C9.   1964c
S. Gevirtz. 1963. *Patterns in the Early Poetry of Israel.* Chi-
cago: University of Chicago Press.
Journal of Biblical Literature 83:201-3.

C10. 1964d
J. Gray. 1963. *I & II Kings.* Philadelphia: Westminster.
Journal of Biblical Literature 83:310-13.

C11. 1966
J. Bonsirven. 1964. *Palestinian Judaism in the Time of Jesus
Christ.* New York: Holt, Rinehart, and Winston.
Journal of Ecumenical Studies 3:554-55.

C12. 1969e
R. E. Brown, J. A. Fitzmyer, and R. E. Murphy, eds. 1968.
The Jerome Biblical Commentary. Englewood Cliffs: Pren-
tice-Hall [reviewer for the Old Testament].
Catholic Biblical Quarterly 31:405-8.

C13. 1971e
G. W. Buchanan. 1970. *The Consequence of the Covenant.*
Leiden: Brill.
Catholic Biblical Quarterly 33:554-57.

C14. 1972e
T. H. Gaster. 1969. *Myth, Legend and Custom in the Old
Testament.* New York: Harper and Row.
Journal of American Oriental Society 92:185-86.

C15. F. M. Cross and DNF
1972
Some Observations on Early Hebrew [Review of D. W.
Goodwin. 1969. *Text Restoration Methods in Contemporary
U.S.A. Biblical Scholarship.* Naples: Istituto Orientale].
Biblica 53:413-20.

C16. DNF
1973b
W. L. Holladay. 1972. *A Concise . . . Lexicon of the Old Testa-
ment . . . Koehler . . . and Baumgartner.* Grand Rapids:
Eerdmans.
Interpretation 27:102-4.

C17. 1973c
J. Sanders. 1972. *Torah and Canon.* Philadelphia: Fortress.
Journal of Biblical Literature 92:118-19.

C18. 1973d
A. A. van Ruler. 1973. *The Christian Church and the Old
Testament.* Grand Rapids: Eerdmans.
Journal of Biblical Literature 92:119-22.

C19. 1975d
J. Gutmann, ed. 1972. *No Graven Images: Studies in Art and
the Hebrew Bible.* New York: Ktav.
Journal of Ecumenical Studies 12:590-92.

C20. 1976c
W. D. Davies. 1974. *The Gospel and the Land.* Berkeley:
University of California Press.
Journal of Biblical Literature 105:503-6.

C21. 1982c
John Bright. 1981. *A History of Israel*^{3}. Philadelphia: West-
minster.
Biblical Archaeologist 45:61.

C22. 1982d
A. R. Ceresko. 1980. *Job 29–31 in the Light of Northwest
Semitic.* Biblica et Orientalia 36. Rome: [Pontifical] Biblical
Institute Press.
Journal of Biblical Literature 101.

II. Modern Intellectual History

II.D. Books, papers, and articles

D1. DNF
1951   James Anderson Kelso in Memoriam. *Bulletin of the American Schools of Oriental Research* 124:11-12.

D2. 1961   Portrait of an Archaeologist [W. F. Albright at 70]. *Presbyterian Life* 14 #4 (December 1961): 7-11.

D3. 1962   Letter from Ashdod: A Report of Excavations 1962. *Pittsburgh Perspective* 3 #4 (December 1962): 17-19, 39.

D4. 1963   The Second Season of Ancient Ashdod. *Biblical Archaeologist* 26:134-39.

D5. 1963   Modern Scripture Research and Ecumenism [chiefly Protestant-Catholic contact]. *Pittsburgh Perspective* 4 #3 (September 1963): 15-22.

D6. W. F. Albright and DNF
1963   The Continuing Revolution in Biblical Research: [A] Setting for the Anchor Bible. *Journal of Bible and Religion* 31:110-13.

D7. DNF
1964   Excavating in an Old Testament Town [Ashdod]. *Presbyterian Life* 17 #6 (March 1964): 5, 10-15, 30-32.

D8. 1965   Toward a Common Bible? Pp. 133-49 in *Scripture and Ecumenism: Protestant, Catholic, Orthodox and Jewish*, ed. L. J. Swidler. Pittsburgh: Duquesne University Press.

D9. 1966   William F. Albright. Pp. 380-86 in *Tendenzen der Theologie im 20. Jahrhundert*, ed. H. J. Schultz. Stuttgart: Kreuz-Verlag. Volume rpt., 1967.

D10. 1968   *The New World of the Old Testament* [Inaugural Lecture as Professor of Hebrew and Old Testament Literature, Delivered 7 May 1968]. San Anselmo, California: San Francisco Theological Seminary. 15 pp.

D11. 1969   Archaeology in the Promised Land — 1968. *Action/Reaction* 2 #2 (Winter 1969): 8-10.

D12. 1970   The American Schools of Oriental Research. *Qadmoniot* 3 #2: 75-76 (in Hebrew).

D13. 1972   William Foxwell Albright in Memoriam. *Bulletin of the American Schools of Oriental Research* 205:3-13. Rpt. as pp. 24-34 in Freedman, MacDonald, and Mattson 1975.

D14. 1974   James Alan Montgomery. Pp. 594-96 in *Dictionary of American Biography, Supplement 4*, ed. J. A. Garraty, and E. T. James. New York: Charles Scribner's Sons.

D15. 1975   In Memoriam G. E. Wright. *Bulletin of the American Schools of Oriental Research* 220:3.

D16. DNF and A. T. Kachel, eds.
1975   *Religion and the Academic Scene* [Essays by Krister Stendahl, Theodore A. Gill, and Robert Bellah]. Waterloo, Ontario: Council on the Study of Religion in cooperation with the

Program on Studies in Religion and the Office of Religion and Ethics of the University of Michigan. Introduction by Freedman, pp. vi-viii.

D17. DNF with the assistance of R. B. MacDonald and D. L. Mattson
      1975   *The Published Works of William Foxwell Albright: A Compre-hensive Bibliography* [preceded by seven memorial tributes]. Cambridge: The American Schools of Oriental Research.

D18. L. G. Running and DNF
      1975   *William Foxwell Albright: A Twentieth Century Genius*. New York: Two Continents Publishing Group/Morgan Press.

D19. DNF
      1977   Ebla is a Four-Letter Word. *LSA Magazine* (Ann Arbor) for Spring 1977:8-9, 17-18. Rpt. 1980, in *The Imprint of the Stanford Library Associates* (Palo Alto: Associates of the Stanford University Libraries) 6 #2 (October 1980): 20-24.

D20. 1978   The Ebla Tablets and the Abraham Tradition. Pp. 67-77 in *Reflections on Mormonism: Judaeo-Christian Parallels,* ed. T. G. Madsen. Religious Studies Monograph Series 4. Provo, Utah: Religious Studies Center, Brigham Young University.

D21. 1978   A City Beneath the Sands [Tell Mardikh]. Pp. 182-95 in *Science Year: The World Book Science Annual 1978*. Chicago: Field Enterprises Educational Corporation.

D22. 1978   The Real Story of the Ebla Tablets, Ebla and the Cities of the Plain. *Biblical Archaeologist* 41:143-64.

D23. 1979   The Tell Mardikh Excavations, the Ebla Tablets, and Their Significance for Biblical Studies. *Near East Archaeological Society Bulletin* NS #13:5-35.

D24. 1980   On Studying the Bible. P. 5 in *Recommending and Selling Biblical Reference Works* [ed. S. J. Anderson]. Grand Rapids: Eerdmans.

D25. 1981   Frank Moore Cross, Jr.: An Appreciation. Pp. 3-7 in *Traditions in Transformations: Turning Points in Biblical Faith,* ed. B. Halpern and J. Levenson. Winona Lake, Indiana: Eisenbrauns.

D26. 1981   "Epigraphic Evidence from Ebla . . .": A Correction [*in re* A. Archi; cf. Freedman 1978/D22]. *Biblica* 62:103.

D27. DNF and B. E. Willoughby
      1981   Archeology and the Bible: Volunteer and Student Programs; Archeology and the Bible: Recent Discoveries. *Your Church* (King of Prussia, Pennsylvania) 27 #1:24, 26, 30-34.

III. Popular, Devotional, and Ephemeral Works

III.E. Books and articles
* = written for children, young people or their teachers

E1.   *DNF and J. D. Smart
      1949   *God Has Spoken*. Philadelphia: Westminster.
E2.   DNF
      1950

		When Saints Were Sinners. *The Dawn* 21 #2 (March-April 1950): 2-3.
E3.	*1950	Family Life in the Old Testament. *Growing* 2 #3 (April-June 1950): 4-6.
E4.	*1950	The Birth of a Nation. *Junior-Hi Kit* #7 (September 1950): 111-14.
E5.	*1950	The Bible Tells the Truth. *Opening Doors* 2 #2 (January-March 1950): 10-11.
E6.	1951	The Key to Old Testament History. *The Dawn* 22 #3 (May-June 1951): 2-3.
E7.	1951	Israel in God's Redemption Plan. *The Dawn* 22 #4 (September-October 1951): 213.
E8.	1951	Abraham, God's Pioneer. *Westminster Teacher* 2 #1 (October-December 1951): 23-24.
E9.	DNF and D. M. Thompson *(manu secunda)*	
	1951	Pioneers for God: The Beginnings of the Hebrew Nation. *Crossroads* 2 #1 (October-December 1951): 43-59, 61.
E10.	DNF and D. M. Thompson	
	1951	The American Heritage. *Western Watch* 2 #4 (15 September 1951): 3-10.
E11.	1953	The Key to Old Testament History. *Western Watch* 4 #4 (15 October 1953): 15-19. Rpt. 1954, as The Key to the Old Testament, in *The Dawn* 25 #2 (March-April 1954): 2-3.
E12.	DNF	
	1955	A Passover Question [the hardening of Pharaoh's heart]. *The Dawn* 26 #2 (March-April 1955): 1.
E13.	1955	God Compassionate and Gracious [Inaugural Lecture as Professor of Hebrew and Old Testament Literature in Western Theological Seminary] [Exod 34:6-7]. *Western Watch* 6 #1 (1 March 1955): 6-24.
E14.	1955	Bridging the Gulf. *Western Watch* 6 #4 (15 December 1955): 9-17. Rpt. 1980 as pp. 98-105 in *The Messiahship of Jesus: What Jews and Jewish Christians Say,* ed. A. W. Kac. Chicago: Moody Press. Abridged as E17.
E15.	1956	Question and Answer [Exod 20:5-6]. *The Dawn* 27 #1 (January-February 1956): 6.
E16.	*1956	Why Should the Innocent Suffer? [Job]. *Discovery* 8 #4 July-September 1956): 3-4.
E17.	1956	Jew and Christian: Is Reconciliation Possible? *Presbyterian Life* 9 #5 (3 March 1956): 10-11, 26-27. Rpt. 1956 in *Israel's Anchorage* [Australian organ of the Jewish Evangelical Witness] 10 #3 (September-November 1956): 8-11.
E18.	1956	The Unity of the Bible. *Western Watch* 7 #4 (15 December 1956): 744. Rpt. 1980 as pp. 173-84 in *The Messiahship of Jesus: What Jews and Jewish Christians Say,* ed. A. W. Kac. Chicago: Moody Press.
E19.	DNF and T. A. Gill	
	1956	[Three Sermons on Jeremiah:] The Next Step. Who Would Valiant Be. Changed Gods. *The Pulpit* 27 #9 (September 1956): 10-12; 27 #10 (October 1956): 11-13 = 27:291-93; 27 #11 (November 1956): 16-19 = 27:328-31.

E20.	1957	What Next? [Jeremiah 4]. *The Pulpit* 28 #2 (February 1957): 22-24 = 28:70-72.

E21. DNF
      1958   The Sabbath and the Lord's Day. *Presbyterian Life* 11 #2 (January 1958): 30-31.

E22. 1959   The Dead Sea Scrolls: The Library of the Essenes. *Carnegie Magazine* 33 #2 (February 1959): 60-63, 65.

E23. 1959   The Slave of Yahweh [The Suffering Servant]. *Western Watch* 10 #1 (March 1959): 1-19.

E24. DNF and T. A. Gill
      1959   Great Expectations [on Jeremiah and Baruch]. *The Pulpit* 30 #4 (April 1959): 14-15 = 30:110-11.

E25. DNF
      1960   Question and Answer [on Esau's birthright]. *The Dawn* 31 #5 (November-December 1960): 4.

E26. 1961   *Let My People Go* [Jeremiah 34]. A Sermon Preached 12 November 1961. University Park, Pennsylvania: The Office of the University Chaplain, The Pennsylvania State University. 6 pp.

E27. 1962   When Did Christ Die? [on Qumran and the Johannine chronology of Holy Week]. *Pittsburgh Perspective* 3 #1 (March 1962): 52-57.

E28. 1964   *Naboth's Vineyard.* A Sermon Preached 26 January 1964. University Park, Pennsylvania: The Office of the University Chaplain, The Pennsylvania State University. 6 pp.

E29. 1964   The Hebrew Old Testament and the Ministry Today: An Exegetical Study of Leviticus 19:18b. *Pittsburgh Perspective* 5 #1 (March 1964): 9-14, 30.

E30. 1965   The Biblical Idea of History. A One Hundredth Anniversary Sermon Preached, at the Grosse Pointe Memorial Church, 10 October 1965. Pp. 11-16 in *The Shape of the Church and the Future.* Grosse Pointe Farms: United Presbyterian Church in the U.S.A.

E31. *1965   Amos and the Judgment of God. *Opening Doors* 17 #3 (April-June 1965): 4-6.

E32. 1966   Religious Freedom and the Old Testament. Pp. 83-94 in *Religious Liberty: An End and a Beginning. The [Vatican II] Declaration on Religious Freedom: An Ecumenical Discussion,* ed. J. C. Murray. New York: Macmillan.

E33. 1967   Another View of the Middle East Crisis. *Presbyterian Life* 20 #18 (15 September 1967): 28-29. With letters to the editor, all negative, in *Presbyterian Life* 20 #20 (15 October 1967): 6, 43.

E34. 1969   An Essay on Jewish Christianity. *Journal of Ecumenical Studies* 6 #1 (Winter 1969): 81-86.

E35. 1972   State of Religion. *The Ann Arbor News* for 21 May 1972 at section 4, p. 41, cols. 4-6.

E36. C. B. Templeton, with DNF, T. A. Gill, W. Summerscales, and T. Harpur, eds.
      1973   *Jesus: The Four Gospels . . . Combined in One Narrative and Rendered in Modern English.* New York: Simon and Schuster/Toronto: McClelland and Stewart.

E37. DNF
      1977   Afterword. Pp. 338-44 in Rudolf Augstein, *Jesus Son of Man.*
                                             Trans. H. Young. Preface by Gore Vidal. New York: Urizen.

III.F. Book reviews

F1.   DNF
      1949   R. M. Grant. 1948. *The Bible in the Church: A Short History
                                             of Interpretation.* New York: Macmillan.
                                             Monday Morning 14 #7 (14 February 1949): 15-16.
F2.   1950   J. A. Brewer. 1949. *The Book of the Twelve Prophets.* New
                                             York: Harper.
                                             Theology Today 7:128-30.
F3.   1950   Recent Literature on the Old Testament [notably
                                             Dorothy C. Wilson. 1949. *Prince of Egypt.* Philadelphia:
                                             Westminster].
                                             Western Watch 1 #1 (January 1950): 8-10.
F4.   1951   J. Paterson. 1950. *The Praises of Israel: Studies Literary and
                                             Religious in the Psalms.* New York: Charles Scribner's Sons.
                                             Theology Today 8:271-73.
F5.   1951   H. H. Rowley. 1950. *From Joseph to Joshua: Biblical Tradi-
                                             tions in the Light of Archaeology.* London: The British
                                             Academy.
                                             Westminster Bookman 10 #4 (June 1951): 12-13.
F6.   1952   G. Walter. 1952. *Caesar: A Biography.* Trans. E. Craufurd.
                                             New York: Charles Scribner's Sons.
                                             Western Watch 3 #2 (15 March 1952): 19-20.
F7.   1953   G. A. Buttrick et al., eds. 1952. *The Interpreter's Bible I*
                                             [General Articles, Genesis, Exodus]. Nashville: Abingdon-
                                             Cokesbury.
                                             Western Watch 4 #2 (15 March 1953): 20-21.
F8.   1953   J. B. Pritchard, ed. 1950. *Ancient Near Eastern Texts Relating
                                             to the Old Testament.* Princeton: Princeton University Press.
                                             Western Watch 4 #2 (15 March 1953): 21.
F9.   1955   For Antiquarians Only [Review of C. A. Muses, ed. 1954.
                                             The Septuagint Bible (The Charles Thomson Translation).
                                             Indian Hills, Colorado: Falcon's Wing Press].
                                             The Christian Century 72 #9 (2 March 1955): 272.
F10. 1955   A New Light on the Past [Review of E. Wilson. 1955. *The
                                             Scrolls from the Dead Sea.* New York: Oxford University
                                             Press].
                                             Pittsburgh Press for 23 October 1955.
F11. 1956   G. A. Buttrick et al., ed. 1956. *The Interpreter's Bible* V
                                             [Ecclesiastes, Song of Songs, Isaiah, Jeremiah]. Nashville:
                                             Abingdon.
                                             Westminster Bookman 15 #3 (September 1956): 7-9.
F12. 1958   More About Scrolls [Review of F. M. Cross. 1958. *The An-
                                             cient Library of Qumran and Modern Biblical Studies.* Gar-
                                             den City: Doubleday; and M. Burrows. 1958. *More Light on
                                             the Dead Sea Scrolls.* New York: Viking].
                                             Pittsburgh Press for 11 May 1958 at section 5, p. 8, col. 6.

F13. 1958   M. Burrows. 1955. *The Dead Sea Scrolls*. New York: Viking; and C. T. Fritsch. 1956. *The Qumran Community: Its History and Scrolls*. New York: Macmillan.
Theology Today 15:422-25.

F14. 1958   D. Baly. 1957. *The Geography of the Bible*. New York: Harper.
Westminster Bookman 17 #1 (March 1958): 1-2.

F15. 1959   A. R. Johnson. 1955. *Sacral Kingship in Ancient Israel*. Cardiff: University of Wales Press.
Theology Today 15:571-73.

F16. 1959   U. Simon. 1958. *Heaven in the Christian Tradition*. New York: Harper.
Westminster Bookman 18 #3 (September 1959): 5-7.

F17. 1960   H. H. Rowley. 1957. *The Faith of Israel: Aspects of Old Testament Thought*. Philadelphia: Westminster.
Pittsburgh Perspective 1 #1 (March 1960): 21-22.

F18. 1960   A. J. Heschel. 1955. *God in Search of Man: A Philosophy of Judaism*. New York: Farrar, Straus, and Cudahy.
Pittsburgh Perspective 1 #2 (June 1960): 22-23.

F19. 1961   R. H. Pfeiffer. 1961. *Religion in the Old Testament*. New York: Harper.
Westminster Bookman 20:4-6.

F20. 1962   I Recommend [notices on books by Bright, Eichrodt, Kaufmann, Noth, and von Rad]. *Monday Morning* 27 #11 (21 May 1962): 22.

F21. 1963   G. von Rad. 1961. *Genesis: A Commentary*. Trans. J. Marks. Philadelphia: Westminster.
Theology Today 20:114-18.

F22. 1964   W. H. Brownlee. 1964. *The Meaning of the Qumran Scrolls for the Bible*. New York: Oxford University Press.
Pittsburgh Perspective 5 #2 (June 1964): 33-34.

F23. 1964   H. H. Rowley. 1963. *From Moses to Qumran*. New York: Association Press.
Presbyterian Outlook 146 #23 (June 1964): 15.

F24. 1964   B. W. Anderson, ed. 1963. *The Old Testament and Christian Faith: A Theological Discussion*. New York: Harper and Row.
Theology Today 21:225-28.

F25. 1968   C. Westermann. 1967. *Handbook to the Old Testament*. Trans. R. H. Boyd. Minneapolis: Augsburg.
Action/Reaction 1 #3 (Spring 1968): 11.

IV. Editorial Work

IV.G. Books Outside Series

G1.   G. Ernest Wright and DNF, eds.
1961   *The Biblical Archaeologist Reader [1]*. Garden City: Doubleday (original paper edition). Volume rpt. 1961, Chicago: Quadrangle Books. Doubleday reissues after 1964 bear the title *The Biblical Archaeologist Reader, 1*. Volume also rpt. 1975, Missoula: Scholars Press. Volume also rpt. 1978,

Cambridge: American Schools of Oriental Research. Preface by DNF, pp. ix-xii.

G2.   E. F. Campbell, Jr., and DNF, eds.

1964   *The Biblical Archaeologist Reader, 2.* Garden City: Doubleday. Volume rpt. 1975, Missoula: Scholars Press. Volume also rpt. 1978, Cambridge: American Schools of Oriental Research. Preface by DNF, pp. vii-xi.

G3.   DNF and J. C. Greenfield, eds.

1969   *New Directions in Biblical Archaeology.* Garden City: Doubleday. Volume rpt. 1971 in paper. Preface by Freedman and Greenfield, pp. ix-xi.

G4.   E. F. Campbell, Jr., and DNF, eds.

1970   *The Biblical Archaeologist Reader, Volume III.* Garden City: Doubleday. Preface by Campbell and Freedman, pp. vii-viii.

G5.   [E. F. Campbell, Jr., and DNF, eds.].

1979   *Seisho kōkogaku nyūmon* [*Introduction to the Archeology of the Bible*] by G. E. Wright, B. M. Metzger, and others. Trans. Yasuo Shiono. Seisho no kenkyū [Studies on the Bible] Series 1. Tokyo: Kyobunkan. [A selection of six essays from Campbell and Freedman 1964 = *BAR* 2 and Campbell and Freedman 1970 = *BAR* 3, with a conspectus of those two volumes and Wright and Freedman 1961. The essays are: I. R. H. Smith, The Tomb of Jesus (*BAR* 3); II. G. E. Wright, Samaria (*BAR* 2); III. B. M. Metzger, Antioch-on-the-Orontes (*BAR* 2); IV. B. Kanael, Ancient Jewish Coins and their Historical Importance (*BAR* 3); V. R. B. Y. Scott, Weights and Measures of the Bible (*BAR* 3); and VI. H. O. Thompson, Science and Archaeology (*BAR* 3).]

G6.   E. F. Campbell and DNF

f/c   *The Biblical Archaeologist Reader 4.* Philadelphia: The American Schools of Oriental Research. Preface by Freedman.

IV.H. The Anchor Bible

Edited by William Foxwell Albright and DNF from 1956 until Albright's death in 1971 (during which period the first eighteen volumes were published), and since by DNF alone, and published by Doubleday and Company in Garden City, New York.

H1.   W. F. Albright and C. S. Mann
1971   *Matthew.* AB 26.

H2.   F. I. Andersen and DNF
1980   *Hosea.* AB 24.

H3.   M. Barth
1974a   *Ephesians 1–3.* AB 34.

H4.   1974b   *Ephesians 4–6.* AB 34A.

H5.   R. G. Boling
1975   *Judges.* AB 6A.

H6.   1982   *Joshua.* With an introduction by G. E. Wright. AB 6.

H7.   J. Bright
1965   *Jeremiah.* AB 21.

H8. R. E. Brown, S.S.

    1966 *The Gospel According to John (i–xii).* AB 29.

H9. 1970 *The Gospel According to John (xiii–xxi).* AB 29A.

H10. 1982 *The Epistles of John.* AB 30.

H11. G. W. Buchanan

    1972 *To the Hebrews.* AB 36.

H12. E. F. Campbell, Jr.

    1975 *Ruth.* AB 7.

H13. M. Dahood, S.J.

    1966 *Psalms I (1–50).* AB 16.

H14. 1968 *Psalms II (51–100).* AB 17.

H15. 1970 *Psalms III (101–150).* With a contribution by T. Penar. AB 17A.

H16. J. A. Fitzmyer, S.J.

    1981 *The Gospel According to Luke (I–IX).* AB 28.

H17. J. M. Ford

    1975 *Revelation.* AB 38.

H18. J. A. Goldstein

    1976 *I Maccabees.* AB 41.

H19. L. E. Hartman, C.SS.R, and A. A. Di Lella, O.F.M.

    1978 *The Book of Daniel.* AB 23.

H20. D. R. Hillers

    1972 *Lamentations.* AB 7A.

H21. P. K. McCarter, Jr.

    1980 *I Samuel.* AB 8.

H22. J. L. McKenzie

    1968 *Second Isaiah.* AB 20.

H23. C. A. Moore

    1971 *Esther.* AB 7B.

H24. 1977 *Daniel, Esther, and Jeremiah: The Additions.* AB 44.

H25. J. Munck

    1967 *The Acts of the Apostles.* With contributions by W. F. Albright and C. S. Mann. AB 31.

H26. J. M. Myers

    1965a *I Chronicles.* AB 12.

H27. 1965b *II Chronicles.* AB 13.

H28. 1965c *Ezra. Nehemiah.* AB 14.

H29. 1974 *I and II Esdras.* AB 42.

H30. W. F. Orr and J. A. Walther

    1976 *I Corinthians . . . With a Study of the Life of Paul.* AB 32.

H31. M. Pope

    1965 *Job*[1]. AB 15. *Job*[3], 1973.

H32. 1977 *Song of Songs.* AB 7C.

H33. B. Reicke

    1964 *The Epistles of James, Peter, and Jude.* AB 37.

H34. R. B. Y. Scott

    1965 *Proverbs. Ecclesiastes.* AB 18.

H35. E. A. Speiser

    1964 *Genesis.* AB 1.

H36. D. Winston

    1979 *The Wisdom of Solomon.* AB 43.

IV.I. American Schools of Oriental Research Publications

Published by the Schools in Cambridge, Massachusetts.

Annuals of ASOR (AASOR)
I1. E. M. Meyers; A. T. Kraabel; and J. E Strange
1976   *Ancient Synagogue Excavations at Khirbet Shema`, Upper Galilee, Israel 1970-1972.* AASOR 42. Published for the Schools, Durham: Duke University.
I2. DNF, ed.
1978   *Preliminary Excavation Reports: Bâb edh-Dhra`, Sardis, Meiron, Tell el-Hesi, Carthage (Punic).* AASOR 43.
I3. DNF, with the help of J. M. Lundquist, ed.
1979   *Archeological Reports from the Tabqa Dam Project — Euphrates Valley, Syria.* AASOR 44.
I4. N. L. Lapp, ed.
1981   *The Third Campaign at Tell el-Fûl: The Excavations of 1964.* AASOR 45.

Bulletin of the American Schools of Oriental Research/Supplement[al] Studies (BASOR/SS).
I5. C. T. Fritsch, ed.
1975   *Studies in the History of Caesarea Maritima.* The Joint Expedition to Caesarea Maritima I. BASOR/SS 19. Published for the Schools, Missoula: Scholars Press.
I6. C. B. Moore, ed.
1974   *Reconstructing Complex Societies: An Archaeological Colloquium . . . 1972.* BASOR/SS 20.
I7. G. M. Landes, ed.
1975   *Report on Archaeological Work at Ṣuwwānet eth-Thanīya, Tananir, and Khirhet Minḥa (Munḥata).* BASOR/SS 21. Published for the Schools, Missoula: Scholars Press.
I8. A. Ben-Tor
1978   *Cylinder Seals of Third-Millennium Palestine.* BASOR/SS 22.

Dead Sea Scrolls Committee Publications. Edited by F. M. Cross, DNF, and J. M. Sanders.
I9. J. C. Trever [et al.]
1972   *Scrolls from Qumrân Cave I: The Great Isaiah Scroll, the Order of the Community, the Pesher to Habakkuk.* Published for the Schools through the Albright Institute for Archaeological Research and by the Shrine of the Book, both in Jerusalem, and produced by William Clowes and Sons of London. (Edition with both color and black and white plates.)
I10. 1974   *Scrolls from Qumran Cave I: The Great Isaiah Scroll, the Order of the Community, the Pesher to Habakkuk.* (Edition with black and white plates only.)

Dissertation Series/ASOR (DASOR)
I11. A. R. W. Green
1975   *The Role of Human Sacrifice in the Ancient Near East.*

DASOR 1. Published for the Schools, Missoula: Scholars Press.

I12. C. L. Meyers
1976   *The Tabernacle Menorah.* DASOR 2. Published for the Schools, Missoula: Scholars Press.

I13. V. H. Matthews
1978   *Pastoral Nomadism in the Mari Kingdom (ca. 1830-1760 B.C.).* DASOR 3.

I14. B. Lewis
1980   *The Sargon Legend: A Study of the Akkadian Text and the Tale of the Hero Who Was Exposed at Birth.* DASOR 4.

Excavation Reports/ASOR (ERASOR)
I15. W. E. Rast, ed. A. E. Glock
1978   *Taanach I. Studies in Iron Age Pottery.*

I16. J. A. Blakely and L. E. Toombs, ed. K. G. O'Connell, S.J.
1980   *The Tell el-Hesi Field Manual.* The Joint Archaeological Expedition to Tell el-Hesi 1.

I17. J. A. Callaway et al.
1980   *The Early Bronze Age Citadel and Lower City at Ai (et-Tell).* Reports of the Joint Archaeological Expedition to Ai (et-Tell) 2.

Monograph Series/ASOR (MASOR)
I18. R. T. Anderson
1978   *Studies in Samaritan Manuscripts and Artifacts: The Chamberlain-Warren Collection.* MASOR 1.

I19. Z. Zevit
1980   *Matres Lectiones in Ancient Hebrew Epigraphs.* MASOR 2.

I20. J. H. Charlesworth with G. T. Zervos
1981   *The New Discoveries in St. Catherine's Monastery: A Preliminary Report on the Manuscripts.* MASOR 3. Foreword by DNF, pp. xi-xii.

Zion Research Foundation Occasional Publications
I21. F. M. Cross, ed.
1979   *Symposia Celebrating the Seventy-Fifth Anniversary of the Founding of the American Schools of Oriental Research (1900-1975).* ZRFOP 1-2 [!].

Volumes *hors serie*
I22. E. F. Campbell and R. G. Boling, eds.
1976   *Essays in Honor of George Ernest Wright* [Reprint of *Bulletin of the American Schools of Oriental Research* 220/221].

I23. M. K. Lyons, M.D.
1978   *The Care and Feeding of Dirt Archeologists.*

I24. R. S. Hanson
1980   *Tyrian Influence in the Upper Galilee.* Meiron Excavation Project #2.

IV.J. The Computer Bible Series.

Edited by J. Arthur Baird and DNF, and published by Biblical Research Associates in Wooster, Ohio.

J1. F. I. Andersen and A. D. Forbes
     1972   *A Synoptic Concordance to Hosea, Amos, Micah.* CBS 6.
J2. 1976a   *A Linguistic Concordance of Ruth and Jonah: Hebrew Vocabulary and Idiom.* CBS 9.
J3. 1976b   *Eight Minor Prophets [Hosea, Joel, Amos, Obadiah, Micah, Nahum, Habakkuk, and Zephaniah]: A Linguistic Concordance.* CBS 10.
J4. 1978a   *A Linguistic Concordance of Jeremiah: Hebrew Vocabulary and Idiom.* CBS 14.
J5. 1978b   *A Linguistic Concordance of Jeremiah: Common Names.* CBS 14A.

J6. J. A. Baird
     1971   *A Critical Concordance to the Synoptic Gospels.* CBS 1. (Revised edition of a 1969 private publication.)

J7. R. A. Martin
     1977   *Syntactical and Critical Concordance to the Greek Text of Baruch and the Epistle of Jeremiah.* CBS 12.

J8. P. M. K. Morris and E. James
     1975   *A Critical Word Book of Leviticus, Numbers, Deuteronomy.* CBS 8. Published for BRA, Missoula: Scholars Press.
J9. n.d.   *A Critical Word Book of the Pentateuch.* CBS 17.

J10. A. Q. Morton and S. Michaelson
     1971   *I, II, III John: Forward and Reverse Concordance and Index.* CBS 3.
J11. 1974   *A Critical Concordance to the Gospel of John.* CBS 5.
J12. 1976   *A Critical Concordance to the Acts of the Apostles.* CBS 7.
J13. A. Q. Morton; S. Michaelson; and J. D. Thompson
     1977   *A Critical Concordance to the Letter of Paul to the Romans.* CBS 13.
J14. 1979   *A Critical Concordance to I and II Corinthians.* CBS 19.
J15. 1980   *A Critical Concordance to the Letter of Paul to the Galatians.* CBS 21.

J16. n.d.   *A Critical Concordance to the Letter of Paul to the Ephesians.* CBS 22.

J17. n.d.   *A Critical Concordance to the Letter of Paul to the Philippians.* CBS 23.

J18. n.d.   *A Critical Concordance to the Letter of Paul to the Colossians.* CBS 24.

J19. H. V. D. Parunak
     1979   *Linguistic Density Plots in Zechariah.* CBS 20.
J20. Y. T. Radday
     1971   *An Analytical, Linguistic Concordance to the Book of Isaiah.* CBS 2.
J21. 1973   *An Analytical, Linguistic, Key-Word-in-Context Concordance to the Books of Haggai, Zechariah, and Malachi.* CBS 4.

J22. Y. T. Radday and G. M. Leb
1978   *An Analytical, Linguistic, Key-Word-in-Context Concordance to Esther, Ruth, Canticles, Ecclesiastes, and Lamentations.* CBS 16.

J23. 1979   *An Analytical, Linguistic, Key-Word-in-Context Concordance to the Book of Genesis.* CBS 18.

J24. Y. T. Radday, G. M. Leb, and L. Natziz
1977   *An Analytical, Linguistic, Key-Word-in-Context Concordance to the Book of Judges.* CBS 11.

J25. J. B. Tyson and T. R. W. Longstaff
1978   *Synoptic Abstract.* CBS 15.

IV.K. The International Concordance Library

Edited by J. Arthur Baird and DNE and published by Biblical Research Associates in Wooster, Ohio.

K1. W. E. Aufrecht and (for EDP) J. C. Hurd
1975   *A Synoptic Concordance of Aramaic Inscriptions (According to H. Donner & W. Roellig).* ICL 1. Published for BRA, Missoula: Scholars Press.

IV.L. Consulting Editorial Work

L1. J. M. Allegro
1958   *The People of the Dead Sea Scrolls.* Garden City: Doubleday.
L2. 1960   *The Treasure of the Copper Scroll.* Garden City: Doubleday.
L3. G. A. Buttrick et al., eds.
1962   *The Interpreter's Dictionary of the Bible.* 4 vols. Nashville: Abingdon.
L4. G. Cornfeld
1962   *From Daniel to Paul: Jews in Conflict with Graeco-Roman Civilization.* New York: Macmillan.
L5. 1964   *Pictorial Biblical Encyclopedia.* New York: Macmillan.
L6. Catholic Biblical Association
1970   *The New American Bible Translated from the Original Languages with Critical Use of All the Ancient Sources by Members of the Catholic Biblical Association of America. Sponsored by the Bishops' Committee of the Confraternity of Christian Doctrine.* New York and elsewhere: P. J. Kenedy and Sons and others. [See special note *ad finem.*]
L7. G. J. Botterweck and H. Ringgren, eds.
1973-   *Theologisches Wörterbuch zum Alten Testament* (Band I, 1973; Band II, 1977; Band III, in publication). Stuttgart: Kohlhammer.
L8. 1974-   *Theological Dictionary of the Old Testament* (Vol. I, 1974, revised 1977; Vol. II, 1975; Vol. III, 1978; Vol. IV, 1980). Trans. J. T. Willis, G. Bromiley, D. Green. Grand Rapids: Eerdmans.
L9. 1978-   *Diccionario Teologico del Antiguo Testamento* (Tomo 1,

1978). Trans. A. de la Fuente and J. L. Zubizaretta. Madrid: Ediciones Christiandad.

L10. Avram Kampf
     1975   *Jewish Experience in the Art of the Twentieth Century.* New York: The Jewish Museum.

L11. Benjamin Mazar, assisted by G. Cornfeld
     1975   *The Mountain of the Lord.* Garden City: Doubleday.

L12. Wendell Phillips
     1975   *An Explorer's Life of Jesus.* New York: Two Continents Publishing Group/Morgan Press.

L13. G. Cornfeld
     1976   *Archaeology of the Bible: Book by Book.* New York: Harper and Row.

L14. J. L. Gardner et al., eds.
     1981   *Reader's Digest Atlas of the Bible.* Pleasantville, New York: The Reader's Digest Association.

IV.M. Special Editorial Work

As literary executor for W. F. Albright.

M1. W. F. Albright
     1972   Neglected Factors in the Greek Intellectual Revolution. *Proceedings of the American Philosophical Society* 116:225-42.

IV.N. Journals

N1. *Western Watch*

Member, Editorial Committee, vols. 1-3 (1950-1952). Managing Editor, vols. 4-8 (1953-1957).

N2. *Journal of Biblical Literature*

Associate Editor, vols. 72-73, 1953-1954.
Editor, vols. 74-78, 1955-1959. Reports of the editor appear in the first part of each volume edited: 75 (1956) xiii; 76 (1957) xiv; 77 (1958) xvi; 78 (1959) xvii-xix; 79 (1960) xii.

N3. *Presbyterian Life*

Columnist, "We've Been Asked," 1953-1955. 6 #21 (31 October 1953) 28 [Genesis 28; Joshua 7–8]. 6 #25 (26 December 1953) 37 [the hardening of Pharaoh's heart; Isaiah's messianism]. 7 #4 (20 February 1954) 33-34 [Genesis 1; Joshua 10]. 7 #11 (29 May 1954) 30 [Conquest; cherubs]. 7 #15 (24 July 1954) 28 [Hebrew words in English; Esau's birthright]. 7 #17 (4 September 1954) 26 [manuscripts; prophets]. 7 #23 (27 November 1954) 28 [commandments; prophets; feasts]. 8 #1 (8 January 1955) 36 [resurrection; Genesis 15]. 8 #5 (5 March 1955) 35 [angels; Nazirites]. 8 #8 (16 April 1955) 37 [tithing; Baalzebub]. 8 #12 (11 June 1955) 34 [jealous God; sour grapes]. 8 #16 (6 August 1955) 37 [Gen 9:25; Daniel in Ezek 14:13].

N4. *Bulletin of the American Schools of Oriental Research*

Editor, #215 (October 1974)–#231 (October 1978).

N5. *Newsletter* [of the American Schools of Oriental Research]

Editor, 1976-1979 (runs from July-August 1976 to May 1977, numbered #1/2-10; from July 1977 to June 1978, numbered #1-8; and from August 1978 to June 1979, numbered #1-8; and from August 1979 until November 1979, #1-4 of that run) with incidental contributions: "ASOR Publication Policy," 1975 #2 (September 1975): 1-4 (before Freedman's editorship); "The Jerusalem [ASOR Anniversary] Conference," 1976 #7 (February 1976): 1-4 (before Freedman's editorship); "A Tour of the Tells," 1976 #5 (November 1976): 1-10; "Tourists on Parade," 1976 #6 (November 1976, sic): 1-9; "An Abandoned Site Near Ramallah," 1976 #7 (December 1976): 15; "A Note on ASOR Publications," 1977 #3 (November 1977): 11; and, with other members of the Publications Committee, "ASOR Publication Policy," 1979 #7 (May 1979): 1-5 (after Freedman's editorship).

N6. *Biblical Archaeologist*

Editor, Volume 39-45, 1976-1982. The Column "A Letter to the Readers" was occasionally written by DNF. 40 #1 (March 1977) 2-4 [Ebla]. 40 #2 (May 1977) 46-48 [sanctuaries and temples; Exodus 15; Psalm 78]. 40 #3 (September 1977) 94-97 [Qumran; dereliction of duty, his own; quoted by H. Shanks. 1978. Leading Scholar Calls for Prompt Publication. *BAR* 4 #1 (March 1978): 2-3]. 40 #4 (December 1977) 134: The Flood and Other Matters. 41 #1 (March 1978) 2 [magic; seals; jewelry]. 41 #2 (June 1978) 42: "The [Biblical] City and the County [Jordan Valley]." 41 #3 (September 1978) 82-83: Ancient Woman, Future [Qumran] Temple, and Current Study. 42 #1 (Winter 1979) 4 [genealogies, etc.]. 42 #2 (Spring 1979) 68 [documents, etc.]. 42 #3 (Summer 1979) 132 [the Aleppo Codex, etc.]. 43 #1 (Winter 1980) 4 [archeology, etc.]. 43 #2 (Spring 1980) 68 [Ebla; Turin Shroud, etc.]. 43 #3 (Summer 1980) 132 [Persepolis; G. G. Cameron, etc.]. 43 #4 (Fall 1980) 196 [Ebla; etc.]. 44 #1 (Winter 1981) 4 [the Adon letter; *i.m.* H. T. Frank, etc.]. 44 #2 (Spring 1981) 68 [Sodom; Ebla; Aphek, etc.]. 44 #3 (Summer 1981) 132 [Ebla; Funeral rites; etc.].

A Note on the New American Bible

Since there has been some misunderstanding concerning Freedman's role in the New American Bible, a word of explanation is in order. In the war years, the American Roman Catholic community set out to provide a new English-language Bible, translated from the original sources rather than from the Latin version associated with St. Jerome. Working with the Bishops' Committee of the Confraternity of Christian Doctrine, the members of the Catholic Biblical Association of America produced, in several volumes published through the 'fifties and 'sixties, the CCD Bible. When it came time to reissue these materials in a single volume, changes in textual study and scholarly understanding necessitated revision of the parts finished earliest. By this time, further, the American Roman Catholic church had been mandated, along with all Roman Catholics, to embrace the work of other Christians in scriptural study; the Second Vatican Council had urged that "with the approval of Church authority . . . translations be produced in cooperation with separated brothers." In undertaking the final version of the CCD Bible, now named the New American Bible, the Catholic Biblical Association rose to the conciliar occasion, and the final body of the editors and translators included, beyond fifty Roman Catholic priests and one sister, several ordained ministers of the United Presbyterian Church U.S.A. It is as a member of a committee of fifty-four people that Freedman is to be associated with the NAB.

Since it is sometimes stated in print that Freedman translated and annotated the NAB Book of Genesis, we need to be more specific. At the request of the editorial chair for the Old Testament, the late Louis F. Hartman, and of the editorial vicechair, the late P. W. Skehan, Freedman wrote an introduction to Genesis, a set of explanatory notes, and a group of textual notes, and prepared a new translation of the book — all with a distant eye on the already published CCD versions. All of Freedman's materials were submitted to the committee and revised by it; the committee of the CBA is responsible for the final NAB version.

Thanks for aid in the labor of compilation to J. Kselman and J. Jensen in Washington, D.C.; R. G. Boling and E. F. Campbell in Chicago; J. A. Baird in Wooster; and L. E. Fyfe, L. O. Gómez, D. F. Graf, Li Chi, and B. E. Willoughby in Ann Arbor.

Bibliography of the Works of David Noel Freedman, 1982-1995

KATHLEEN G. BECK

A Note on the Second Bibliography
of the Works of David Noel Freedman

We have retained, for the most part, the categories and format of the first bibliography by Michael O'Connor, but there have been major additions, particularly in category IV, Editorial Work. There, the major new thrust of Dr. Freedman's work in the Anchor Bible series has now become a three-pronged effort: H. Anchor Bible Commentaries, I. Anchor Bible Dictionary, J. Anchor Bible Reference Library. This expansion of category IV reflects the intensity of his concentration on editing. Twenty-three volumes have been added to the Anchor Bible Commentary series, including one revised volume (some replacement volumes are also in progress). The Commentary series is now more than three-fourths complete.

The *Anchor Bible Dictionary,* of which he was editor-in-chief, was completed in 1992. It entailed a major effort by nearly one thousand authors throughout the world, as well as the editorial team located in Ann Arbor.

The Anchor Bible Reference Library is David Noel Freedman's most recently conceived series. The first volume came off the press in 1988 and has since been joined by a dozen more, with many others now in progress.

The reader will also note the many contributions to *Festschriften,* especially in the later years. By contrast, new contributions to category III, Popular, Devotional, and Ephemeral Works, are almost nonexistent. This indicates a shift in direction and emphasis but no diminishment of energy, and the magnitude of his editorial contribution may have made him, as one commentator recently put it, only partially in jest, the Bible's most important redactor since Ezra the scribe.

Our thanks go to John Huddlestun, DNF's former Arthur F. Thurnau Fellow, for his aid in this compilation.

ASTRID B. BECK

I. The Bible and the Ancient Near East

I.A. Books, papers, and notes

A79.	1982	Ebla and the Old Testament. Pp. 309-35 in *Studies in the Period of David and Solomon and Other Essays,* ed. Tomoo Ishida. Tokyo: Yamakawa-Shuppansha.
A80.	1983	The Earliest Bible. Pp. 167-75 in *The Bible and its Traditions,* ed. M. P. O'Connor and DNF. Ann Arbor: University of Michigan Press (= *Michigan Quarterly Review* 22/3).
A81.	1983	Symposium on the Territorial Dimension of Judaism: Introductory Reflections, ed. W. D. Davies. *Midstream: A Monthly Jewish Review* 29/3:32-37.
A82.	1983	The Spelling of the Name "David" in the Hebrew Bible. Pp. 89-104 in *Biblical and Other Studies in Honor of Robert Gordis,* ed. R. Ahroni. Columbus: Ohio State University Press (= *Hebrew Annual Review* 11).
A83.	DNF and K. A. Mathews 1985	*The Paleo-Hebrew Leviticus Scroll. (11QpaleoLev).* American Schools of Oriental Research. xii + 97 pp. + 20 plates (distributed by Eisenbrauns, Winona Lake, Indiana).
A84.	1985	Prose Particles in the Poetry of the Primary History. Pp. 49-62 in *Biblical and Related Studies Presented to Samuel Iwry,* ed. A. Kort and S. Morschauser. Winona Lake, Indiana: Eisenbrauns.
A85.	1985	What the Ass and the Ox Know — But the Scholars Don't. *Bible Review* 1/1 (February 1985): 42-44.
A86.	1985	Who Asks (or Tells) God to Repent? *Bible Review* 1/4 (Winter 1985): 56-59.

A87. 1986   Deliberate Deviation from an Established Pattern of Repetition in Hebrew Poetry as a Rhetorical Device. Pp. 45-52 in *Ninth Congress of Jewish Studies*. Jerusalem: Hebrew University Press.

A88. 1986   Acrostic Poems in the Hebrew Bible: Alphabetic and Otherwise. *Catholic Biblical Quarterly* 48/3 (July 1986): 408-31.

A89. 1986   Early Christianity and the Scrolls: An Inquiry. Pp. 97-102 in *Jesus in History and Myth*, ed. R. J. Hoffman and G. A. Larue. Buffalo: Prometheus.

A90. 1986   Canon of the Bible. Pp. 211-16 in *Illustrated Dictionary and Concordance of the Bible*, ed. G. Wigoder, W. M. Paul, B. T. Viviano, O.P., and E. Stern. New York: Macmillan.

A91. 1987   Headings in the Books of the Eighth Century Prophets. Pp. 9-26 in *Festschrift in Honor of Leona Glidden Running*, ed. W. Shea. Berrien Springs: Andrews University Press (= *Andrews University Seminary Studies* 25).

A92. 1987   "Who is Like Thee Among the Gods?" The Religion of Early Israel. Pp. 315-35 in *Ancient Israelite Religion: Essays in Honor of Frank Moore Cross*, ed. P. D. Miller, Jr., P. D. Hanson, and S. D. McBride. Philadelphia: Fortress Press.

A93. 1987   Another Look at Hebrew Biblical Poetry. Pp. 11-28 in *Directions in Biblical Hebrew Poetry*, ed. E. R. Follis. Sheffield: Sheffield Academic Press.

A94. 1987   On the Death of Abiner. Pp. 125-27 in *Love and Death in the Ancient Near East: Essays in Honor of Marvin H. Pope*, ed. J. H. Marks and R. M. Good. Guilford, CT: Four Quarters Publishing.

A95. 1987   The Earliest Bible. Pp. 29-37 in *Backgrounds for the Bible*, ed. M. P. O'Connor and D. N. Freedman. Winona Lake, Indiana: Eisenbrauns, rpt. *Michigan Quarterly Review* 22/3 (1983) (= reprint of A.80).

A96. 1987   The Structure of Isaiah 40:1-11. Pp. 167-93 in *Perspectives on Language and Text: Essay and Poems in Honor of Francis I. Andersen on his Sixtieth Birthday*, ed. E. W. Conrad and E. G. Newing. Winona Lake, Indiana: Eisenbrauns.

A97. 1988   Yahweh of Samaria and His Asherah. *Biblical Archaeologist* 50/4 (December 1987): 241-49.

A98. 1988   Is It Possible to Understand the Book of Job? *Bible Review* 4/2 (April 1988): 26-33, 44.

A99. DNF and F. I. Andersen
1988   The Orthography of the Aramaic Portion of the Tell Fekherye Bilingual. Pp. 9-49 in *Text and Context: Old Testament and Semitic Studies for F. C. Fensham*, ed. Walter T. Claassen. JSOT Supplement Series 48. Sheffield: JSOT Press.

A100. DNF and F. I. Andersen
1989   *Amos.* AB 24A. New York: Bantam Doubleday Dell Publishing Group, Inc. xlii + 926 pp. (= H37)

A101. DNF and B. E. Willoughby
1989   I and II Chronicles, Ezra, Nehemiah. Pp. 155-71 in *The Books of the Bible*, vol. 1: *The Old Testament/The Hebrew*

Bible, ed. B. W. Anderson. New York: Charles Scribner's Sons.

A102. 1989   The Nine Commandments: The Secret Progress of Israel's Sins. *Bible Review* 5/6 (December 1989): 28-37, 42.

A103. DNF and F. I. Andersen
1989   Another Look at 4QSam b. *Revue de Qumran* 14/53 (June 1989): 7-29.

A104. F. I. Andersen and DNF
1989   Aleph as a Vowel Letter in Old Aramaic. Pp. 3-14 in *To Touch the Text: Biblical and Related Studies in Honor of Joseph A. Fitzmyer, S.J.,* ed. M. P. Horgan and P. J. Kobelski. Crossroad.

A105. DNF and F. I. Andersen
1989   The Spelling of Samaria Papyrus 1. Pp. 15-32 in *To Touch the Text: Biblical and Related Studies in Honor of Joseph A. Fitzmyer, S.J.,* ed. M. P. Horgan and P. J. Kobelski. Crossroad.

A106. 1990   The Formation of the Canon of the Old Testament: The Selection and Identification of the Torah as the Supreme Authority of the Post-Exilic Community. Pp. 315-33 in *Religion and Law: Biblical-Judaic and Islamic Perspective,* ed. E. B. Firmage, B. G. Weiss, and J. W. Welch. Winona Lake, Indiana: Eisenbrauns.

A107. 1990   Dinah and Shechem, Tamar and Amnon. Pp. 55-63 in *God's Steadfast Love: A Festschrift in Honor of Prescott Harrison Williams, Jr.* Austin: Austin Seminary Bulletin Faculty Edition, 105/2 (Spring 1990).

A108. 1990   Did God Play a Dirty Trick on Jonah at the End? *Bible Review* 6/4 (August 1990): 26-31.

A109. 1990   Confrontations in the Book of Amos. *Princeton Seminary Bulletin* n.s. 11/3 (November 1990): 240-53.

A110. 1990   The Book of Job. Pp. 33-51 in *The Hebrew Bible and Its Interpreters,* ed. W. H. Propp, B. Halpern, and D. N. Freedman. Winona Lake, Indiana: Eisenbrauns.

A111. 1990   The Biblical Canon of Prophetic Books. Pp. 151-66 in *He Came Here and Loved Us: A Festschrift in Honor of William F. Orr,* ed. R. C. Curry, T. J. Kelso, and C. S. Mave. Watsontown, PA: William F. Orr Festschrift Foundation.

A112. 1990   Jonah and the Big Fish. Pp. 199-209 in *He Came Here and Loved Us: A Festschrift in Honor of William F. Orr,* ed. R. C. Curry, T. J. Kelso, and C. S. Mave. Watsontown, PA: William F. Orr Festschrift Foundation.

A113. 1990   The Flying Scroll in Zechariah 5:1-4. Pp. 42-48 in *Studies in Near Eastern Culture and History: In Memory of Ernest T. Abdel-Massih,* ed. J. A. Bellamy. Ann Arbor: University of Michigan Center for Near Eastern and North African Studies.

A114. 1991   *The Unity of the Hebrew Bible.* Distinguished Senior Faculty Lecture Series. Ann Arbor: University of Michigan Press. vii + 125 pp. (Notes and Bibliography by John R. Huddlestun.)

A115. 1992	Patterns in Psalms 25 and 34. Pp. 125-38 in *Priests, Prophets and Scribes: A Festschrift in Honour of Joseph Blenkinsopp*, ed. E. Ulrich, J. W. Wright, R. P. Carroll, and P. R. Davies. Sheffield: Sheffield Academic Press.
A116. 1992	The Symmetry of the Hebrew Bible. *Studia Theologica: Scandinavian Journal of Theology* 46/2:83-108.
A117. DNF, F. I. Andersen, and D. Forbes	
1992	*Studies in Hebrew and Aramaic Orthography.* Winona Lake, Indiana: Eisenbrauns. xi + 328 pp.
A118. DNF and S. Mandell	
1993	*The Relationship Between Herodotus' History and The Primary History.* Atlanta: Scholars Press. xiii + 204 pp.
A119. 1993	Kingly Chronologies: Then and Later. Pp. 41*-65* in *Eretz-Israel*, vol. 24 (Avraham Malamat vol.). Jerusalem: Israel Exploration Society.
A120. 1995	Psalm 119: Part II, for a *Festschrift* in honor of Reuben Ahroni, Professor at Ohio State University.
A121. 1995	Psalm 119: Part I, for a *Festschrift* in honor of Jacob Milgrom, Professor at the University of California, Berkeley.
A122. 1995	Human Nature in the Old Testament (= Hebrew Bible). Paper to be published in the conference volume by Brigham Young University Center for Near Eastern Studies (Jerusalem).
A123. f/c	Prophecy in the Dead Sea Scrolls. Paper to be published for Florida Southern College.
A124. f/c	*Divine Commitment and Human Obligation: Selected Writings of David Noel Freedman*, ed. with an Introduction by John R. Huddlestun. 2 vols. Grand Rapids: Eerdmans.
A125. f/c	Between God and Man: Prophets in Ancient Israel (with John R. Huddlestun). Forthcoming in a *Semeia* volume devoted to prophecy.

I.B. Contributions to reference works

Theologisches Wörterbuch zum Alten Testament, ed. G. J. Botterweck, Helmer Ringgren, and H.-J. Fabry. Stuttgart: Kohlhammer, 1973- .

B39.	DNF and M. O'Connor	
	1983	*kᵉrûḇ.* Band IV, Sp. 321-34.
B40.		*kuttonæt.* Band IV, Sp. 398-401.
B41.		*māḡen*(!) Band IV, Sp. 646-59.
B42.	DNF and B. E. Willoughby	
	1984	*nāʾap.* Band V, Sp. 123-29.
B43.	1986	*nāśāʾ.* Band V, Sp. 626-42.
B44.	1986	*ʿiḇrî.* Band V, Sp. 1039-56.
B45.	1987	*ʿammûḏ.* Band VI, Sp. 204-09.
B46.	DNF and Andrew Welch	
	1993	*šāḏaḏ.* Band VII, Sp. 1072-78.

A Dictionary of Biblical Tradition in English Literature, ed. D. L. Jeffrey. Grand Rapids: Eerdmans, 1992.

B47.   1992   Joel. P. 406.

I.C. Book Reviews

C23.   1990   J. Barr. 1989. *The Variable Spellings of the Hebrew Bible.* Schweich Lectures 1986. Oxford University Press. *Journal for the Study of Judaism* 22/1:114-21.

C24.   1991   J. C. de Moor. 1990. *The Rise of Yahwism: The Roots of Israelite Monotheism.* Leuven: Leuven University Press; and M. S. Smith. 1990. *The Early History of God: Yahweh and the Other Deities in Ancient Israel.* San Francisco: Harper & Row.
Journal of Biblical Literature 110/4:693-98.

II. Modern Intellectual History

II.D. Books, papers, and articles

D28.   1981   A Letter to the Readers. *Biblical Archaeologist* 44/3 (Summer 1981): 132.

D29.   1981   Foreword. In *The New Discoveries in St. Catherine's Monastery: A Preliminary Report on the Manuscripts,* by J. H. Charlesworth. In the American Schools of Oriental Research Monograph Series, ASOR.

D30.   1982   Foreword. In *Justice and History in the Old Testament: The Evolution of Divine Retribution in the Historiographies of the Wilderness Generation,* by R. Adamiak. Cleveland: John T. Zubal, Inc.

D31.   1982   From the Editor's Desk. *Biblical Archaeologist* 45/4:195-96.

D32.   1987   Francis I. Andersen. An Appreciation. Pp. xix-xxii in *Perspectives on Language and Text: Essay and Poems in Honor of Francis I. Andersen on his Sixtieth Birthday,* ed. E. W. Conrad and E. G. Newing. Winona Lake, Indiana: Eisenbrauns.

D33.   1989   W. F. Albright as an Historian. Pp. 33-45 in *The Scholarship of William Foxwell Albright: An Appraisal,* ed. G. W. Van Beek. Harvard Semitic Studies 33. Atlanta: Scholars Press.

D34.   1990   He Never Let Me Fall. A Reminiscence. Pp. 7-15 in *He Came Here and Loved Us: A Festschrift in Honor of William F. Orr,* ed. R. C. Curry, T. J. Kelso, and C. S. Mave. Watsontown, PA: William F. Orr Festschrift Foundation.

D35.   1993   Editing the Editors: Translation and Elucidation of the Text of the Bible. Pp. 227-56 in *Palimpsest: Editorial Theory in the Humanities,* ed. G. Bornstein and R. G. Williams. Ann Arbor: University of Michigan Press.

III. Popular, Devotional, and Ephemeral Works

III.E. Books and articles

D38. 1982

Methods of Biblical Study. Pp. 23-27 in *The United Presbyterian Church Task Force on Biblical Authority and Interpretation* (Report to the 194th General Assembly). The Advisory Council on Discipleship and Worship, New York.

IV. Editorial Work

IV.G. Books Outside Series

G7. F. I. Andersen and A. D. Forbes
1986   *Spelling in the Hebrew Bible.* Rome: Biblical Institute Press.
G8. E. F. Campbell, Jr., and DNF, eds.
1982   The Biblical Archaeologist Readers, 1 and 2. Tokyo, Japan: Kyo Bun Kwan (Japanese translation of the original volumes published by Doubleday, 1970).
G9. G. Cornfeld
1982   *Archaeology of the Bible: Book by Book.* New York: Harper and Row (rpt. from 1976)
G10. E. F. Campbell and DNF, eds.
1983   *The Biblical Archaeologist Reader* 4. Sheffield: Almond Press.
G11. DNF and D. F. Graf, eds.
1983   *Palestine in Transition: The Emergence of Ancient Israel.* The Social World of Biblical Antiquity Series, gen. ed. J. W. Flanagan. Sheffield: Almond Press (in association with ASOR).
G12. M. P. O'Connor and DNF, eds.
1983   *The Bible and Its Traditions.* Ann Arbor: University of Michigan Press (= *Michigan Quarterly Review* 22/3). (= A80)
G13. M. P. O'Connor and DNF, eds.
1987   *Backgrounds for the Bible.* Winona Lake, Indiana: Eisenbrauns.
G14. W. H. Propp, B. Halpern, and DNF, eds.
1990   *The Hebrew Bible and Its Interpreters.* Winona Lake, Indiana: Eisenbrauns.

IV.H. Anchor Bible Commentaries

Edited by William Foxwell Albright and David Noel Freedman from 1956 until Albright's death in 1971 (during which period the first eighteen volumes were published), and since by DNF alone. Published by Doubleday and Company, New York, NY.

H37. F. I. Andersen and DNF; DNF also ed.
1989   *Amos.* AB 24A. xlii + 926 pp.
H38. M. Barth and H. Blanke, trans. A. B. Beck
1995   *Colossians.* AB 34B. xxi + 557 pp.

H39. A. Berlin
      1994   *Zephaniah.* AB 25A. xxi + 165 pp.
H40. M. Cogan and H. Tadmor
      1988   *II Kings.* AB 11. xxxv + 371 pp.
H41. J. A. Fitzmyer, S.J.
      1985   *The Gospel According to Luke X–XXIV.* AB 28A. xxxvi + 801
                              pp.
H42. J. A. Fitzmyer, S.J.
      1993   *Romans.* AB 33. xxxiv + 793 pp.
H43. V. P. Furnish
      1984   *II Corinthians.* AB 32A. xxii + 619 pp.
H44. J. A. Goldstein
      1983   *II Maccabees.* AB 41A. xxiii + 595 pp.
H45. M. Greenberg
      1983   *Ezekiel 1–20.* AB 22. xv + 388 pp.
H46. D. Hillers
      1992   *Lamentations.* (rev.) AB 7A. xiv + 175 pp.
H47. B. A. Levine
      1993   *Numbers 1–20.* AB 4. xvi + 528 pp.
H48. C. S. Mann
      1986   *Mark.* AB 27. xxvi + 715 pp.
H49. P. K. McCarter, Jr.
      1984   *II Samuel.* AB 9. xvii + 553 pp.
H50. C. L. Meyers and E. M. Meyers
      1987   *Haggai, Zechariah 1–8.* AB 25B. xcv + 478 pp.
H51. C. L. Meyers and E. M. Meyers
      1993   *Zechariah 9–14.* AB 25C. xxiii + 552 pp.
H52. J. Milgrom
      1991   *Leviticus 1–16.* AB 3. viii + 1163 pp.
H53. C. A. Moore
      1985   *Judith.* AB 40. xxiv + 286 pp.
H54. J. H. Neyrey
      1993   *2 Peter, Jude.* AB 37C. ix + 287 pp.
H55. J. M. Sasson
      1990   *Jonah.* AB 24B. xvi + 368 pp.
H56. P. W. Skehan and A. A. DiLella
      1987   *The Wisdom of Ben Sira.* AB 39. xxiii + 620 pp.
H57. J. D. Quinn
      1990   *The Letter to Titus.* AB 35. xlviii + 334 pp.
H58. J. D. Quinn and P. Wacker
      1995   *I & II Timothy.* AB 35A.
H60. M. Weinfeld
      1991   *Deuteronomy 1–11.* AB 5. iv + 458 pp.

IV.I. The Anchor Bible Dictionary

The *Anchor Bible Dictionary* presents the essence of critical scholarship on subjects pertaining to the Bible, and is intended as a companion reference work to the Anchor Bible Commentaries and the Anchor Bible Reference Library. Published by Doubleday in New York, NY.

I1-6.   *The Anchor Bible Dictionary,* 6 vols. (editor-in-chief)
1992   G. A. Herion, D. F. Graf, J. D. Pleins, associate editors.
                         A. B. Beck, managing editor.
                         P. C. Schmitz, assistant editor

                         Volume 1: lxxviii + 1232 pp.
                         Volume 2: xxxv + 1100 pp.
                         Volume 3: xxxii + 1135 pp.
                         Volume 4: xxxv + 1162 pp.
                         Volume 5: xxxiv + 1230 pp.
                         Volume 6: xxxv + 1176 pp.

IV.J. The Anchor Bible Reference Library

The Anchor Bible Reference Library examines the Bible in the light of the latest research and revelations in the fields of anthropology, archaeology, ecology, economics, geography, history, literature and languages, philosophy, religion, and theology. Published by Doubleday in New York, NY.

J1.   J. Blenkinsopp
        1992
                         The Pentateuch: An Introduction to the First Five Books of the Bible. x + 271 pp.

J2.   R. E. Brown, S.S.
        1994
                         The Death of the Messiah. Vol. 1: xxvii + 877 pp.; vol. 2: xix + pp. 878-1608.

J3.   R. E. Brown, S.S.
        1993
                         The Birth of the Messiah: A Commentary on the Infancy Narratives in the Gospels of Matthew & Luke. 752 pp. (new rev. ed.; 1st ed. 1977, Doubleday).

J4.   J. H. Charlesworth
        1988
                         Jesus within Judaism: New Light from Exciting Archaeological Discoveries. xvi + 265 pp.

J5.   J. H. Charlesworth
        1992
                         Jesus and the Dead Sea Scrolls. xxxvii + 370 pp.

J6.   J. J. Collins
        1995
                         The Scepter and the Star: Jewish Messianism in Light of the Dead Sea Scrolls. xiv + 270 pp.

J7.   A. Mazar
        1990
                         Archaeology of the Land of the Bible: 10,000-586 B.C.E. xxx + 572 pp.

J8.   J. P. Meier
        1991
                         A Marginal Jew: Rethinking the Historical Jesus. Vol. 1: ix + 484 pp.

J9.   J. P. Meier
      1994   *A Marginal Jew: Rethinking the Historical Jesus.* Vol. 2: xvi
                                + 1118 pp.

J10. D. Mendels
      1992   *The Rise and Fall of Jewish Nationalism: Jewish and Christian
                                Ethnicity in Ancient Palestine.* x + 450 pp.

J11. R. E. Murphy, O. Carm.
      1990   *The Tree of Life: An Exploration of Biblical Wisdom Litera-
                                ture.* xi + 194 pp.

J12. J. Neusner
      1994   *Introduction to Rabbinic Literature.* xxxi + 720 pp.

J13. B. Peckham
      1993   *History and Prophecy: The Development of Late Judean Lit-
                                erary Traditions.* xiv + 880 pp.

IV.K. American Schools of Oriental Research Publications

K2.   1981   *The New Discoveries in St. Catherine's Monastery: A Prelimi-
                                nary Report on the Manuscripts.* In the American Schools
                                of Oriental Research Monograph Series, by J. H. Charles-
                                worth. Published by the American Schools of Oriental Re-
                                search. xv + 45 pp. (DNF, ed.)

K3.   1985   The Paleo-Hebrew Leviticus Scroll. D. N. Freedman and
                                K. A. Mathews. American Schools of Oriental Research. xii
                                + 97 pp. + 20 plates. (= A83)

IV.L. Consulting Editorial Work

L15. 1984   *Family Guide to the Bible.* (Principal Consultant.) Pleas-
                                antville, NY: Reader's Digest Association, Inc.

L16. 1987   G. J. Botterweck and H. Ringgren. *Diccionario Theologico
                                del Antiguo Testamento,* Tomo I. Fasciculos 1-10. Madrid:
                                Artes Graficas Benzal.

L17. 1988   *Mysteries of the Bible: The Enduring Questions of the Scrip-
                                tures.* (Contributing Consultant and Writer.) Pleasantville,
                                NY: Reader's Digest Association, Inc.

V. *Festschriften* for DNF

1983 *The Word of the Lord Shall Go Forth: Essays in Honor of David Noel Freedman in
      Celebration of His Sixtieth Birthday,* ed. C. L. Meyers and M. P. O'Connor. Winona
      Lake, Indiana: Eisenbrauns. xviii + 742 pp.

1995 *Fortunate the Eyes That See: Essays in Honor of David Noel Freedman in Celebration
      of His Seventieth Birthday,* ed. A. Beck, A. Bartelt, P. Raabe, and C. Franke. Grand
      Rapids: Eerdmans.

Contributors

Francis I. Andersen Emeritus Professor of Studies in Religion, University of Queensland, Victoria, Australia.

Andrew H. Bartelt Associate Professor of Old Testament, Concordia Seminary, St. Louis, Missouri.

Astrid B. Beck Program Associate, Program on Studies in Religion, University of Michigan, Ann Arbor, Michigan.

Kathleen G. Beck Student, Eastern Michigan University, Ypsilanti, Michigan.

Adele Berlin Robert H. Smith Professor of Hebrew Bible, Departments of English and Jewish Studies, Associate Provost for Faculty Affairs, University of Maryland, College Park, Maryland.

Joseph Blenkinsopp John A. O'Brien Professor of Biblical Studies, University of Notre Dame, Notre Dame, Indiana.

Suzanne Cahill Adjunct Associate Professor of History, Chinese Studies, University of California at San Diego, La Jolla, California.

James L. Crenshaw Robert L. Flowers Professor of Old Testament, Duke University, Durham, North Carolina.

Frank Moore Cross Emeritus Hancock Professor of Hebrew and Other Oriental Languages, Harvard University, Cambridge, Massachusetts.

Tamara C. Eskenazi Professor of Bible, Hebrew Union College–Jewish Institute of Religion, Los Angeles, California.

A. DEAN FORBES Principal Medical Department Scientist, Hewlett-Packard Laboratories, Palo Alto, California.

CHRIS FRANKE Associate Professor of Theology, The College of St. Catherine, St. Paul, Minnesota.

RICHARD ELLIOT FRIEDMAN Katzin Professor of Jewish Civilization, Judaic Studies Program, University of California at San Diego, La Jolla, California.

YEHOSHUA GITAY Isadore and Theresa Cohen Chair of Hebrew Language and Literature, University of Cape Town, Cape Town, South Africa.

ZEFIRA GITAY Lecturer in Biblical Art, Department of Art History, University of Cape Town, Cape Town, South Africa.

BARUCH HALPERN Professor of Ancient History and Religious Studies, Chair in Jewish Studies, Pennsylvania State University, University Park, Pennsylvania.

RONALD S. HENDEL Associate Professor of Religious Studies, Southern Methodist University, Dallas, Texas.

GARY A. HERION Assistant Professor of Religious Studies, Hartwick College, Oneonta, New York.

DAVID M. HOWARD, JR. Associate Professor of Old Testament and Semitic Languages, Trinity Evangelical Divinity School, Deerfield, Illinois.

JOHN R. HUDDLESTUN Ph.D. Candidate, Department of Near Eastern Studies, University of Michigan, Ann Arbor, Michigan.

PHILIP J. KING Professor of Theology, Department of Theology, Boston College, Boston, Massachusetts.

GARY N. KNOPPERS Associate Professor of Religious Studies and Jewish Studies, Pennsylvania State University, University Park, Pennsylvania.

CRAIG R. KOESTER Associate Professor of New Testament, Luther Seminary, St. Paul, Minnesota.

RISA LEVITT KOHN Ph.D. Candidate, Judaic Studies Program, University of California at San Diego, La Jolla, California.

HANS KÜNG Director, Institut für ökumenische Forschung, Tübingen, Germany.

PETER MACHINIST Hancock Professor of Hebrew and Other Oriental Languages, Harvard University, Cambridge, Massachusetts.

JOEL MARCUS Lecturer in Biblical Studies, Department of Biblical Studies, University of Glasgow, Glasgow, Scotland.

JOHN P. MEIER   Professor of New Testament, Catholic University of America, Washington, D.C.

CAROL L. MEYERS   Associate Professor, Department of Religion, Duke University, Durham, North Carolina.

ERIC M. MEYERS   Professor, Department of Religion, Duke University, Durham, North Carolina.

JACOB MILGROM   Emeritus Professor of Hebrew and Bible, University of California, Berkeley, California.

M. O'CONNOR   Assistant Professor of Hebrew Bible, Saint Paul Seminary School of Divinity, University of St. Thomas, St. Paul, Minnesota.

BRIAN PECKHAM   Professor of Biblical and Near Eastern Studies, University of Toronto, Canada.

J. DAVID PLEINS   Associate Professor, Department of Religious Studies, Santa Clara University, Santa Clara, California.

MARVIN H. POPE   Emeritus Professor of Northwest Semitic Languages, Yale University, New Haven, Connecticut.

WILLIAM H. C. PROPP   Professor of History, Judaic Studies Program, University of California at San Diego, La Jolla, California.

PAUL R. RAABE   Associate Professor of Old Testament, Concordia Seminary, St. Louis, Missouri.

ROY A. RAPPAPORT   Director, Program on Studies in Religion, Walgreen Professor for the Study of Human Understanding, Department of Anthropology, University of Michigan, Ann Arbor, Michigan.

PHILIP C. SCHMITZ   Assistant Professor of History of Religion, Department of History and Philosophy, Eastern Michigan University, Ypsilanti, Michigan.

DAVID ROLPH SEELY   Assistant Professor of Religious Education, Department of Religious Education, Brigham Young University, Provo, Utah.

C. L. SEOW   Associate Professor of Old Testament, Princeton Theological Seminary, Princeton, New Jersey.

AVIGAIL SHEFFER   Lecturer, Hebrew University, Jerusalem, Israel.

ANDREW E. STEINMANN   Cleveland, Ohio.

BRUCE ZUCKERMAN   Associate Professor, School of Religion, University of Southern California, Los Angeles, California.